June 25-28, 2017
Troy, NY, USA

Association for Computing Machinery

Advancing Computing as a Science & Profession

WebSci'17

Proceedings of the 2017 ACM Web Science Conference

Sponsored by:

ACM SIGWEB

Supported by:

TetherlessWorld, IDEA, Innovate518, and Renssselear Institute of Technology

Association for
Computing Machinery

Advancing Computing as a Science & Profession

The Association for Computing Machinery
2 Penn Plaza, Suite 701
New York, New York 10121-0701

ISBN: 978-1-4503-4896-6 (Digital)

ISBN: 978-1-4503-5604-6 (Print)

Additional copies may be ordered prepaid from:

ACM Order Department
PO Box 30777
New York, NY 10087-0777, USA

Phone: 1-800-342-6626 (USA and Canada)
+1-212-626-0500 (Global)
Fax: +1-212-944-1318
E-mail: acmhelp@acm.org
Hours of Operation: 8:30 am – 4:30 pm ET

Printed in the USA

Web Science 2017 Program Chairs' Welcome

Welcome to Web Science! The ACM Web Science Conference 2017 is the 9th conference of the series (the 7th being sponsored by ACM-SIGWEB), and it is a unique venue where different disciplines are brought together in a creative and critical dialogue with the aim of understanding the Web. It is a very inclusive, interdisciplinary congress that welcomes participation from all fields including art, anthropology, computer and information sciences, communication, economics, humanities, informatics, law, linguistics, philosophy, political science, psychology, and sociology. In particular, this conference is a *unicum* in that it has a tradition for contributions that seek to cross traditional disciplinary boundaries.

This year we were very pleased to receive 85 long paper submissions, 42 short paper submissions, and 32 extended abstract/poster submissions, totaling 159 candidate contributions. Given the high quality of submission, it has been a hard job to decide which of the contributions to select for the conference. We are grateful for the support of the Program Committee which consisted of 12 senior members and 66 regular members, plus 50 subreviewers for the research track and 23 regular members plus 3 subreviewers for the poster track. All PC members worked hard, producing 478 reviews and 127 meta-reviews; the process generated intense discussions, with more than 220 comments, based on which we could select an interesting, varied, exciting program comprising 30 long,15 short papers and 23 extended abstracts/posters.

The final program for the main track will include sessions touching different, interesting, timely topics, as one can judge from their titles:

- Aggression, controversy, crime
- Groups and individuals, attention, opinion
- Talking, thinking and living online
- Networks: structure, identifiers, search
- Time, space, archives
- Reflecting, thinking, understanding

We thank all the authors who have contributed to Web Science, as well as the PC members and reviewers for their commitment, patience, and hard work.

We are confident that the participants will be able to appreciate the high quality of all the contributions that have been selected.

The Web Science 2017 Program Chairs
Paolo Boldi
Katharina Kinder-Kurlanda

The WebScience 2017 Poster Chair
Stefan Dietze

Table of Contents

Long Session III: Talking, Thinking, and Living Online

Long Session IV: Networks – Structure, Identifiers, Search

Short Session I

Short Session II

Long Session V: Time, Space, Archives

Long Session VI: Reflecting, Thinking, Understanding

Posters

Alphabetically by Lead Author's Last Name

WEBSCI 2017 Conference Organization

Program Chairs: Paolo Boldi *(Universita degli Studi di Milano, Italy)*
Katharina Kinder-Kurlanda *(GESIS – Leibniz Institute for the Social Sciences, Germany)*

Main Conference Chairs: Peter Fox *(Rensselaer Polytechnic Institute, USA)*
Deborah McGuinness *(Rensselaer Polytechnic Institute, USA)*
Lindsay Poirer, co-chair *(Rensselaer Polytechnic Institute, USA)*

Workshop Chairs: Matthew Weber *(Rutgers University, USA)*
Fabrizio Silvestry *(Facebook UK, UK)*

Tutorial Chair: Elena Simperl *(University of Southampton, UK)*

Poster Chair: Stefan Dietze *(L3S Research Center, Germany)*

Hackathon Chairs: Dominic DiFranzo *(Cornell University, USA)*
Xiaogang (Marshall) Ma *(University of Idaho, USA)*

Sponsorship Chair: Jason Kuruzovich *(Rensselaer Polytechnic Institute, USA)*

Proceedings Chair: Ramine Tinati *(University of Southampton, UK)*

Local Arrangements Chair: Kathleen Fontaine *(Rensselaer Polytechnic Institute, USA)*

Local Arrangements Committee: Jacqueline Carley *(Rensselaer Polytechnic Institute, USA)*
Melissa Anderson *(Rensselaer Polytechnic Institute, USA)*

Publicity Chair: Kristine Gloria *(Communications and Society Program, Aspen Institute, USA)*

Senior Program Committee: Ricardo Baeza-Yates *(Universitat Pompeu Fabra, Spain)*
Carlos Castillo *(Eurecat, Spain)*
Ciro Cattuto, *(ISI Foundation, Italy)*
Emilio Ferrara *(University of Southern California, Information Science, USA)*
Susan Halford *(University of Southampton, UK)*
Cecilia Mascolo *(University of Cambridge, UK)*
Wagner Meira Jr. *(UFMG, Brazil)*
Wolfgang Nejdl *(L3S and University of Hannover, Germany)*
Paolo Parigi *(Stanford University, USA)*
Isabella Peters *(ZBW, Germany)*
Steffen Staab *(Institut WeST, University Koblenz-Landau, Germany)*
Michael Zimmer *(UW-Milwaukee, School of Information Studies, USA)*
Paul Bernal *(University of East Anglia, UK)*

Regular Program Committee:

Javier Borge-Holthoefer *(Internet Interdisciplinary Institute (IN3-UOC), Spain)*
Elena Cabrio *(Universite Cote d'Azur, CNRS, Inria, I3S, France)*
Michele Catasta *(Stanford, USA)*
Oscar Corcho *(Universidad Politecnica de Madrid, Spain)*
Claudia D'Amato *(University of Bari, Italy)*
David De Roure *(Oxford e-Research Centre, University of Oxford, UK)*
Ying Ding *(Indiana University, USA)*
Alessandro Epasto *(Google Research)*
Catherine Faron Zucker *(Universite Nice Sophia Antipolis, France)*
Miriam Fernandez *(Knowledge Media Institute, UK)*
Aldo Gangemi *(Universite Paris 13 & CNR-ISTC, France)*
David Garcia *(ETH Zurich, Switzerland)*
Marco Genuzio *(University of Milan, Italy)*
Fabio Giglietto *(Universita' degli Studi di Urbino Carlo Bo, Italy)*
Oana Goga *(Pierre and Marie Curie University, France)*
Bruno Goncalves *(New York University, USA)*
Bernhard Haslhofer *(AIT Austrian Institute of Technology GmbH, Austria)*
Wilhelm Hasselbring *(Kiel University, Germany)*
Conor Hayes *(Insight Centre for Data Analytics, NUI Galway, Ireland)*
Andreas Hotho *(University of Würzburg, Germany)*
Leif Isaksen *(Lancaster University, UK)*
Krzysztof Janowicz *(University of California, Santa Barbara, USA)*
Lorraine Kisselburgh *(Purdue University, USA)*
Gertraud Koch *(University of Hamburg, Germany)*
Juhi Kulshrestha *(Max Planck Institute for Software Systems, Germany)*
David Laniado *(Eurecat, Spain)*
Kristina Lerman *(University of Southern California, USA)*
Elisabeth Lex *(Graz University of Technology, Austria)*
Markus Luczak-Roesch *(Victoria University of Wellington, New Zealand)*
Athanasios Mazarakis *(Kiel University / ZBW, Germany)*
Stasa Milojevic *(Indiana University, USA)*
Pascal Molli *(University of Nantes – LINA, France)*
Alexandre Monnin *(INRIA, France)*
Claudia Mueller-Birn *(Freie Universitat Berlin, Germany)*
Mirco Musolesi *(University College London, UK)*
Anastasios Noulas *(Lancaster University, UK)*
Alexandra Olteanu *(IBM Watson Research Center, USA)*
Andre Panisson *(Data Science Lab, ISI Foundation, Italy)*
Nicola Perra *(University of Greenwich, UK)*
Jürgen Pfeffer *(Technischen Universität München, Germany)*
Barbara Poblete *(University of Chile, Chile)*
Axel Polleres *(Vienna University of Economics and Business - WU Wien, Austria)*
Alessandro Provetti *(Birkbeck University of London, UK)*
Hemant Purohit *(George Mason University, USA)*

Regular Program Committee (continued):

Cornelius Puschmann *(Hans Bredow Institute, Germany)*
Luca Rossi *(IT University of Copenhagen, Denmark)*
Giancarlo Ruffo *(Universita' di Torino, Italy)*
Marianne Saam *(Centre for European Economic Research (ZEW), Germany)*
Harald Sack *(FIZ Karlsruhe, Leibniz Institute for Information Infrastructure & KIT Karlsruhe, Germany)*
Michael Saker *(Southampton Solent University, UK)*
Massimo Santini *(Universita' degli Studi di Milano, Italy)*
Nishanth Sastry *(King's College London, UK)*
Salvatore Scellato *(Google, UK)*
Patrick C. Shih *(Indiana University Bloomington, USA)*
Marcus Specht *(Open University of the Netherlands, Netherlands)*
Markus Strohmaier *(University of Koblenz-Landau, Germany)*
Lisa Sugiura *(University of Portsmouth, UK)*
Thanassis Tiropanis *(University of Southampton, UK)*
Christoph Trattner *(MODUL University Vienna, Austria)*
Ingmar Weber *(Qatar Computing Research Institute, Qatar)*
Katrin Weller *(GESIS - Leibniz Institute for the Social Sciences, Germany)*
Michele Willson *(Curtin University, Australia)*
Jane Winters *(School of Advanced Study, UK)*
Sergej Zerr *(University of Southampton, UK)*

Poster Program Committee:

Claudia Wagner *(GESIS - Leibniz Institute for the Social Sciences, Germany)*
Elisabeth Lex *(KNOW Center, Austria)*
Robert Jäschke *(Sheffield University, UK)*
Peter Holtz *(IWM, Germany)*
Miriam Fernandez *(The Open University, UK)*
Besnik Fetahu *(L3S Research Center, Germany)*
Ujwal Gadiraju *(L3S Research Center, Germany)*
Jane Winters *(Digital History, London University, UK)*
Matthew Weber *(Rutgers University, USA)*
Thanassis Tiropanis *(University of Southampton, UK)*
Niels Brügger *(Aarhus University, Denmark)*
Andreas Hotho *(University of Würzburg, Germany)*
Djellel Difallah *(University of Fribourg, Switzerland)*
Joachim Kimmerle *(IWM, Germany)*
Gianluca Demartini *(Sheffield University, UK)*
Mathieu d'Aquin *(Galway University, Ireland)*
Pavlos Fafalios *(L3S Research Center, Germany)*
Dragan Gasevic *(University of Edinburgh, UK)*
Dominik Kowald *(KNOW Center, Austria)*
Fabian Gandon *(INRIA, France)*
Bernardo Nunes *(PUC Rio, Brazil)*
Elena Demidova *(L3S Research Center, Germany)*
Konstantin Todorov *(LIRMM, France)*

Additional reviewers:

Ahmad Alrifai
Erik Aumayr
Farshad Bakhshandega Moghaddam
Yi Bu
Pasquale De Meo
Edoardo Galimberti
Mariano Gaston
Simon Gottschalk
Jose Herrera
Hugo Hromic
Francisco J. Gutierrez
Musfira Jilani
Sagar Joglekar
Janani Kalyanam
Philipp Kemkes
Christoph Kling
Florian Lautenschlager
Haiko Lietz
Dionysis Manousakas
Thomas Niebler
Vanessa Pena-Araya
Mauricio Quezada
Jan Roerden
Markus Rokicki
Silvia Ronchiadin
Anna Samoilenko
Hernan Sarmiento
Daniel Schloer
Miroslav Shaltev
Nirmal Sivaraman
Hala Skaf-Molli
Nicolas Tempelmeier
Michele Tizzoni
Pablo Torres-Tramon
To Tu Cuong
Rima Tuerker
Anthony Young
Albin Zehe

WebSci 2017 Sponsor & Supporters

Sponsor: sig web

Supporters: TetherlessWorld

IDEA Rensselaer Institute for Data Exploration and Applications

innovate 518

Rensselaer

The Ethics of doing Web Science Research

Katharina Kinder-Kurlanda
GESIS – Leibniz Institute for the Social Sciences
Cologne, Germany
katharina.kinder-kurlanda@gesis.org

Paolo Boldi
Computer Science Department
University of Milano, Italy
paolo.boldi@unimi.it

ABSTRACT

[1] The panel continues the discussion of ethics within web science from previous years. Beyond fundamental notions such as privacy and intellectual property new challenges arise continuously for researchers as new technologies, platforms, contingencies and people become involved in building the web. Examples for ethical challenges include crowdsourcing as a method, social media data sharing, and, most recently, social media reliability. In the face of 'fake news', trolling, cyberbullying and automated content the question is whom to trust: are social media more or less reliable than traditional media? who should regulate their content? using which criteria? and what is the impact on research?

ACM Reference format:

K. Kinder-Kurlanda, P. Boldi. 2017. The ethics of doing web science research. In Proceedings of the 9th International ACM Conference on Web Science, Troy, NY, USA June 25-28, 2017 (Websci'17).
DOI: http://dx.doi.org/10.1145/3091478.3098883

WebSci '17, June 25-28, 2017, Troy, NY, USA

ACM ISBN 978-1-4503-4896-6/17/06.
http://dx.doi.org/10.1145/3091478.3098883

Beyond Cyberbullying: Self-Disclosure, Harm and Social Support on ASKfm

Zahra Ashktorab
College of Information Studies
University of Maryland, College Park
parnia@umd.edu

Eben Haber
Couchbase, Inc.
Mountain View, CA
eben@habers.us

Jennifer Golbeck
College of Information Studies
University of Maryland, College Park
jgolbeck@umd.edu

Jessica Vitak
College of Information Studies
University of Maryland, College Park
jvitak@umd.edu

ABSTRACT

ASKfm is a social media platform popular among teens and young adults where users can interact anonymously or semi-anonymously. In this paper, we identify the modes of disclosure and interaction that occur on the site, and evaluate why users are motivated to post and interact on the site, despite its reputation for facilitating cyberbullying. Through topic modeling–supplemented with manual annotation–of a large dataset of ASKfm posts, we identify and classify the rich variety of discourse posted on ASKfm, including both positive and negative forms, providing insights into the why individuals continue to engage with the site. These findings are complemented by a survey of young adults (aged 18-20) ASKfm users, which provides additional insights into users' motivations and interaction patterns. We discuss how the affordances specific to platforms like ASKfm, including anonymity and visibility, might enable users to respond to cyberbullying in novel ways, engage in positive forms of self-disclosure, and gain social support on sensitive topics. We conclude with design recommendations that would highlight the positive interactions on the website and help diminish the repurcussions of the negative interactions.

CCS CONCEPTS

•Human-centered computing → Collaborative and social computing systems and tools; Social networking sites;

KEYWORDS

ASKfm; cyberbullying; self-disclosure; topic modeling

WebSci'17, June 25–28, 2017, Troy, NY, USA
© 2017 ACM. 978-1-4503-4896-6/17/06...$15.00
DOI: http://dx.doi.org/10.1145/3091478.3091499

1 INTRODUCTION

Recent years have seen a rise in the use of social media platforms that afford anonymous communication such as ASKfm and Formspring [5, 37] and mobile applications that allow anonymous sharing like YikYak and Kik [18]. While anonymous online communication has existed for decades (e.g., Usenet, anonymous chat rooms) [27], platforms like ASKfm are novel because they allow users to anonymously communicate with known recipients (i.e., semi-anonymous communication). Because anonymity has been shown to lower people's inhibitions [33], it is not surprising that these platforms have been used for cyberbullying [22, 16]. While Formspring shut down in 2015, ASKfm (which is based on Formspring's interaction model) remains quite popular among young users, suggesting that the anonymity that likely leads to problematic interactions may also enable positive outcomes for users. In this paper we examine ASKfm to better understand how users interact, as well as the impact of semi-anonymity on those interactions.We make design recommendations for semi-anonymous platforms that foster the positive interactions that lead to social support and self-disclosures. We make recommendations that would help to mitigate and diminish the repurcussions of the negative interactions on the platform.

ASKfm facilitates a variety of interactions between users with different degrees of anonymity: it allows users to follow others anonymously and to send anonymous or pseudonymous questions to specific known recipients in exchanges visible to all of the recipients' followers. ASKfm users can also non-anonymously indicate approval of an exchange (i.e., "liking" it), and give virtual "gifts." While ASKfm describes its central interactions in terms of questions (the profile post prompt is "Ask me a Question"), users' interactions are much more diverse and represent a variety of types of discourse. ASKfm should not be confused with Q&A sites that allow the posting of information-seeking questions to a broad community, soliciting answers from any member (e.g., Yahoo! Answers, Google Answers, Stack Overflow) [8] or with more general platforms like Facebook and Twitter, where interactions can include non-anonymous questions directed to an individual or broadcast to a wide audience. On ASKfm, questions are directed to a particular individual, and are often posed anonymously.

In this paper, we evaluate the following research questions:

RQ1: What kinds of interactions occur alongside cyberbullying discourse on ASKfm?
RQ2: How does anonymity on ASKfm shape users' disclosure and interaction behaviors on the platform?
RQ3: What kinds of design changes can make ASKfm a safer space?

We address these research questions through two studies. First, we analyze user data collected from ASKfm–the publicly available data for each user, including basic profile information as well as exchanges with other users within an individual's network–and conduct topic modeling on these exchanges, followed by coding of data to discover the diverse kinds of interactions and discourse that occur on ASKfm. We identified 11 types of discourse posted on ASKfm, including many positive modes that provide examples of why individuals continue to engage with the site. We extend these computational findings through a survey of young ASKfm users to further understand users' motivations for disclosure and interaction, especially when they have negative experiences on the site.

This study contributes new insights into the benefits and drawbacks of online anonymity, as well as how adolescents and young adults navigate an online space that can be fraught with negativity and harm. Based on our findings, we push the discussion of anonymous interactions [18] beyond the standard focus on negative and bullying messages to consider the range of positive and negative outcomes associated with site use. While we acknowledge the importance of minimizing user risks, our study highlights how and why these sites are useful to young people, i.e., by providing an outlet for interactions that may be perceived as stigmatizing in less anonymous environments.

2 RELATED WORK

Current research on semi-anonymous websites has largely focused on automatic detection of cyberbullying [20, 14] and specific exploration of cyberbullying practices[26]. By broadening the focus to consider all potential motivations for disclosure on these platforms, we can better explain users' motivations for engagement and continued use. In order to make recommendations on how to improve the platform, we must understand the context in which the cyberbullying occurs. Below, we provide an overview of the ASKfm platform and discuss the state of existing research on anonymous and semi-anonymous social media platforms.

2.1 ASKfm: Description of Platform

ASKfm's interaction model comprises of asking questions and reacting to those questions. When navigating to a user's profile, a box prompts you to "Ask @User" a question. The question can also be asked anonymously (by checking the "Ask anonymously" box) or non-anonymously. A user's profile displays the questions that they have chosen to answer. The question is only published to the user profile if the recipient chooses to answer the question. The "Friend" feed displays all questions answered by individuals that a ASKfm user follows. In recent years, ASKfm has received significant media coverage related to cyberbullying occurring on the site; for example, a Google Search of "ASKfm" reveals the headlines "10 Frightening facts about ASKfm all parents should know" and "ASKfm: A Guide for Parents and Teachers - Webwise". These headlines are a reflection of the reputation garnered by suicide incidents reported over the years that were thought to be the direct result of cyberbullying on the website. While this reputation persists, we know that all users are not collectively engaging in cyberbullying. Other types of interaction exist on the website, and this work aims to explore these types of interactions.

2.2 Discourse on Semi-Anonymous Social Media

Previous studies on semi-anonymous Q&A websites have focused on detecting and understanding the nature of cyberbullying behaviors[20, 16]. Research on semi-anonymous websites such as Formspring and ASKfm has primarily explored negative interactions, with a specific focus on cyberbullying because of the links between cyberbullying and teen suicide [22]. For example Kontostathis et al. [20] used data from Formspring to automatically detect cyberbullying content on the site. Hosseinmardi et al. [15] explored ASKfm by examining the occurrence of "negative" words and interactions on ASKfm and found that individuals with negative content on their profiles are less active and the least sociable. They also found that as positive words increase on a user's profile, the more active and engaging that user will be. Moore et al. [26] evaluated cyberbullying and anonymity on formspring and identified aggression in both online attacks and defense posts (i.e., posts that defend the victim); they further noted that anonymity correlated positively with attacks and negatively with defense posts.

2.3 Anonymity, Disinhibition, and Online Behavior

Kang et. al. contend that ephemerality is an intrinsic part of anonymous communication application [18]. However, semi-anonymous social web applications like ASKfm do not embrace the same ephemerality as other fully anonymous social web applications since posts are recorded on user profiles. Literature on anonymous media applications further reveals that anonymity empowers individuals to disclose personal information [18]. All three types of anonymity identified by Suler are present on semi-anonymous social media platforms: users can opt to be anonymous to others; others can opt to be anonymous to a particular user; and someone's language use and writing style may further anonymize them if it is not personally identifiable. Through an analysis of personal journal blogs, Hollenbaugh et al. demonstrate that those who share photos of themselves tend to participate more in self-disclosure, revealing more information about themselves. This study makes a distinction between discursive anonymity and visual anonymity, suggesting that users believe visual cues (such as photos) to be less identifying than discursive cues (like real names) [13].

2.4 Positive Outcomes of Anonymous Disclosures

Research has identified a number of positive outcomes associated with anonymous disclosures. Self-presentation is done through self-disclosure [29], revealing personal information about oneself which is compatible with the image a person is trying to project about themselves and is an important step for the development of close relationships [19]. Kang et. al. [18] observed that a high degree self-disclosure (sharing of private personal information) occurs in anonymous mobile communications like YikYak because users felt comfortable sharing private information about themselves without the risk of being judged by their network of friends. They found comfort in the anonymity and thus were able to disclose information about themselves. Likewise, numerous researchers have identified benefits to pseudonymous health forums, especially in cases of stigmatized or rare diseases, where individuals may find it difficult to find people to talk to in their offline settings [7]. More recent work has highlighted positive uses of the social media platform Reddit for highly sensitive topics like discussions of sexual abuse [1]; in addition to pseudonymity, the site offers additional features to further separate a poster from their permanent identity (e.g., temporary accounts; see [21]). Individuals who have experienced any form of past trauma are more likely to use Web-based services when they can do so anonymously [17]. Schoenebeck contends that websites like You Be Mom, a online social outlet for mothers that allows anonymous communication provides a safe forum for moms to "trespass social norms and expectations" [30].

In summary, the existing literature on anonymous mediated interactions provides a conflicting picture. On one hand, sites that facilitate anonymous interactions may encourage cyberbullying and other negative behaviors. On the other, there is significant potential for positive outcomes, especially in the form of social support, to be generated from semi-anonymous disclosures. While research has already established the benefits of anonymous platforms to narrowly focused communities like cancer forums, we will now explore the motivations for disclosure on more general question-asking sites. In the following sections, we describe findings from two studies, including topic modeling of data from more than 40,000 ASKfm users and survey data from 243 young adults who actively used the site.

3 STUDY I: DISCOURSE DISCOVERY ON ASKFM

In our first study, our goal was to discover the the kinds of interactions and discourse that occur alongside cyberbullying discourse on ASKfm (**RQ1**). The primary mode of interaction on ASKfm involves one user sending a question or message to another user. By default, these messages are anonymous, but with an affirmative action (unchecking the box immediately under the post) the initiator can make their identity visible. The recipient can then reply to the post publicly or privately. On ASKfm, users have public profiles, yet the act of "following" or friending another user occurs anonymously – i.e., a user is aware of the number of followers but does not know who is following them [2]. A user can infer who is following them by the exchanges they receive on their profile like questions and likes on questions. Each person's feed consists of exchanges which belong to individuals whom that person follows. Each person can express approval for other people's exchanges using a "like" mechanism, and each user has a page in which their "best" exchanges are viewable, i.e., those exchanges that received the greatest number of "likes" from user's network. The "Like" mechanism is exchanged non-anonymously. This enables a mix of anonymous and non-anonymous interactions; for example, we observed anonymous posts soliciting "likes" from the broader anonymous network. Those who like the question however, are identified.

3.1 Data Collection

Studies have demonstrated that websites that allow anonymous question-asking experience greater cyberbullying [20, 14]. We therefore began the data collection process by searching ASKfm using common terms that are *unambiguously* associated with cyberbullying. Our first step was to query ASKfm through Google for variations of the terms "go kill yourself" and "go die" [12, 22]. We used this as the starting point for our data collection for two reasons: (1) to capture discourse that occurred alongside cyberbullying and these terms are unambiguously malicious and (2) to explore how individuals who have instances of such behavior on their profiles or within their network used ASKfm to engage in other types of interactions. We pulled data for subsequent analysis by crawling users who interacted with the original Google search result users (through likes and questions) and then crawling their interactions iteratively (snowball sampling).

We acknowledge that our sampling choice is limited by the fact that the "like core" in our sample are users who used a variation of terms "go kill yourself", so the data explored in this study are likely biased toward more negative forms of interaction. However, our results show that despite the source of our sample, our snowballing was able to capture a wide variety of positive discourse types in addition to negative discourse types. Furthermore, our sampling choice was influenced by media attention directed towards ASKfm centered around the many individuals who have taken their lives because of comments instructing them to using terms like: "drink bleach", "go die", and "every1 will be happy if u died" [31]. We used these terms to capture the most extreme cases of cyberbullying and the discourse that occurs alongside these negatively valenced interactions. We break down the percentage of discourse types later in this paper and demonstrate the large presence of other discourse types despite the search query starting point.

We used Google search to find these posts, with the initial search yielding 19 public profiles. Before collecting user information, we contacted ASKfm and notified them of our study and data collection process.At the time of data collection (October 4, 2013), ASKfm's Terms of Service had no restrictions on users scraping or otherwise collecting user information. The interactions on ASKfm have remained the same between 2013 and the current version with the only changes occurring in color and aesthetic. AskFM does not have an Application Programming Interface (API). We expanded our search in a snowball fashion, collecting user information from all public profiles of those users who had liked exchanges on the "best" pages of the 19 original profiles. We repeated this method of data collection until we yielded over 8 million exchanges from over 40,000 users. We collected user profile information including username, user biography, user headline, the 100 most recent exchanges with time posted, author information if applicable, and the respective answer. Additionally, we collected the 25 "best" exchanges for each user, which also includes respective time posted,

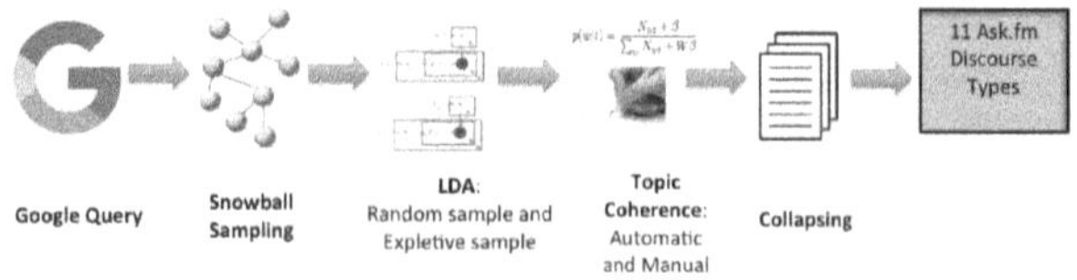

Figure 1: Methodology Pipeline: Query, LDA, Topic Coherence, and Collapsing

answer, author information (if question was non-anonymous), and likers of that particular exchange.

3.2 Topic Modeling to Discover Discourse Types

Once we collected the very large corpus of posts, our next task was to discover the different types of discourse that occurred between the users. To discover different types of discourse, we approached the data using Latent Dirichlet Allocation topic modeling (LDA). Previous researchers have found topic modeling to be an efficient way to automatically discover topics, organize, and categorize large amounts of text [6, 38]. We detail how we refine the LDA process, first by using Minmo et al.'s topic coherence algorithm followed by human annotation of topics to ensure only topics that were coherent were included in the study.

While LDA is widely used for discovering topics and analyzing text, we acknowledge it's limitations. One limitation is that a user pre-defines the number of topics K. The size of K can lead to nuanced topics that overlap semantically or more general topics. Another limitation of topic modeling is that each topic is generated in the form of the most common keywords found across documents in the topic - interpretation of the meaning left to the user [3]. We addressed both limitations by 1) repeating the analysis with a wide variety of values for K, 2) using an automated measure to select those topics with the highest topic coherence values for each value of K, and 3) using multiple human annotators to validate topic coherence, label each topic, and collapse overlapping topics. The flow from data collection to the resulting topics is summarized in Figure 3.

For this analysis, we ran LDA on two samples of data. The full dataset was not analyzed because of processing limitations and a random sample would be representative of the different types of discourse. Our first sample of data consisted of 300,000 random documents from our data set. For LDA purposes, we define documents as ASKfm exchanges comprising of a question and answer combination. Our second sample was filtered for a list of expletives to contain approximately 80,000 documents. We used an expletive sample because we wanted to ensure that we captured any hint of cyberbullying in our dataset. While cyberbullying discourse may not necessarily include expletives, previous studies have found that the existence of expletives in documents are indicative of the presence of cyberbullying [20].

LDA requires, as input, a specific number K of topics to search for, and not all topics found will be coherent. Since we did not know, a priori, the number of topics covered on ASKfm, we ran LDA asking for $K = 10$, then again with $K = 20$, then with $K = 30$, all the way to $K = 100$ topics. This produced a total of 550 topics. Our next step was to automatically calculate topic coherence for each topic. Minmo et al. [25] demonstrate that calculating topic coherence is an efficient way of evaluating a topic model. They define topic coherence is the measure of co-occurrence of the top words within a topic in a document. Highly coherent topics were found within each LDA run. We wanted the data to inform our categories, so from each LDA run, we selected the most coherent 20% topics as our initial categories for qualitative coding, giving us 110 coherent topics.

We then performed a manual evaluation for each coherent topic. Our evaluators were graduate students in Computer Science who had conducted research on social networking platforms. A total of 12 annotators were recruited to annotate the coherence for each topic and rate whether a particular topic was coherent. Each topic was evaluated by three annotators. For each topic model, we presented the words in the topic and we computed the most probable documents that would fall in that topic model group. We asked evaluators whether they thought that the documents were coherent and belonged in the same category. We also asked evaluators to "in their own words" label the topic group. These labels were later used to collapse similar topic models. Cohen's Kappa inter-rater reliability score was calculated for each pair of annotators, and the total average was 0.8125 [24]. From the topic models, we selected those categories deemed coherent by all evaluators (scored higher than 3 by all three raters on a likert score), resulting in a total of 53 coherent topics.

We then analyzed the 53 user-validated coherent categories and collapsed the categories based on similarities in the labels given by annotators. For example a topic model resulting from $K = 30$ (top words: love beautiful perfect xxx amazing gorgeous aw babe girl xx thankyou sweet lovely stay he) was judged very similar to a topic model resulting from $K = 10$ (top words:love lt xxx haha xx omg thoughts hahaha amazing funny pretty aw nice cute hahah bby aha omfg). The annotators labelled both with: "complimenting a friend", "positive sentiment" and "compliments". Given the similarity in topic labels, we combined these topics into the emergent "Compliments and Positivity Discourse" category. We combined overlapping topics manually based on similarities in labels generated by human annotators. The categories represent the most coherent discourse types from the LDA sample. Combining the topic model groups based on overlapping labels resulted in 11 distinct categories (detailed below). We acknowledge that these categories do not cover *all* types of interactions, but these represent the most common modes of interaction from our sample.

Bullying/Inflammatory/Insulting Discourse:: malicious messages aimed to threaten or insult the recipient and may include in/direct threats and expletives. Responses may reciprocate inflammatory remarks.

Question: *oi mate when you go back to school am gona f****** stab you and im gona beat the shit out of you and im gona put you in hospital*

Answer: *i never new that mate come find me you c****

Compliments and Positivity Discourse:: kindness and compliments; characterized by compliments directed at the recipient.

Question: *you are so beautiful you are the nicest girl ever you have the coolest personality*

Answer: *awe c: it did make me smile .thats super nice of you to take your time and make me feel good about myself cx and umm...can i know who you are ?*

Defense of Bullied Victim Discourse:: message to cyberbullying victim in defense of previously receiving negative comment. Posters often tell victim to disregard inflammatory remarks and are sometimes include a compliment to mitigate harm.

Question: *dont listen to people who send you hate just remember that i love you and haters are gonna hate on how pretty you are its probably some fat little c*** behind a computer screen who cant say it to your face*

Answer: *phhahahhahahaha that made me laugh :)*

Like Solicitation and Rating Discourse:: asks that whoever "likes" the discourse will receive some sort of interaction on the website through "rating", "compliments", or reciprocated "likes". In the example below, each liker is promised a certain amount of reciprocated "likes" on their profile.

Question: *Likers get 5 likes and 5 questions?*

Answer: *like if you want this x*

Listing All people you follow:: asks a user to list everyone they follow on the site (via @username). This discourse type reveals "hidden" information as the site structure prevents users from seeing their followers list unless they receive a "like" interaction or are tagged in a discourse type like this one.

Question: *list of people you follow*

Answer: *@[redacted] @[redacted] @[redacted]*

Picture/Video Request:: asks for a picture/video of the recipient; sometimes coupled with a conditional that states if a user receives more than a certain amount of likes, they are deemed "pretty."

Question: *selfie?*

Answer: *[redacted].jpg*

Preference Questions:: asks about a user's preference in movies, music, pets, jewelry, etc. Answers associated with these questions tend to be straight-forward.

Question: *do you prefer gold or silver jewelry?*

Answer: *haha gold but i only have silver jewelry*

Self-Harm Discourse:: questions inquiring about someone's opinion on self harm, whether they participate in it, and how they engage in self-harm (e.g., cutting, starvation).

Question: *what is your opinion on self harming? x*

Answer: *i think its a horrible thing. for someone or something make someone feel like they should use their skin as paper. some people right now feel unwanted or ugly or fat or like they just dont belong with the world because theyre being bullied*

Sexual Content Discourse:: exchanges that are sexual in nature. These questions often ask for sexual favors or preferences in sexual exchanges.

Question: *big boobs, small butt OR small boobs, big butt?*

Answer: *small boobs, big butt*

Things that Annoy you/you Hate:: questions about users' dislikes. Answers to these question vary from hatred of things like "spiders" or hatred of things that "guys do."

Question: *:something you hate?*

Answer: *actually hate everything. i hate guys who say they hate this girl and then they text every f****** day. i hate people who always try to start shit*

Thoughts and Opinions:: asks a user's attitudes toward the question asker or mutual acquaintances; responses are expected to be honest appraisals.

Question: *opinions on [redacted] [redacted]?*

Answer: *haseena:shes soooo funnny we always get the giggles ive know.her for agesss she always knows how to mke mea laugh we hv the weirdest memories! and yea she just amazing and i tell her*

3.2.1 Classifying Discourse Types. LDA topic models predict the probability that a given document belongs to a topic. To permit automatic categorization of exchanges on ASKfm, we built a Naive Bayes classifier to assign documents to the above 11 categories. The features for the classifier were the key words identified by each topic model. For our training set, we manually annotated a sample of 1100 documents according to our derived discourse types. The collapsing of topics for each discourse type generated key words for our feature engineering process. Since a document in each of our topic models consisted of a question-answer combination (the way discourse types are presented on ASKfm and other self-anonymous social websites), our features checked for the existence of the keywords in the question-answer combination. The performance of this classifier can be seen in Table 1. The performance of our classifer is encouraging, suggesting that is it possible to perform reasonably accurate automatic detection of different discourse categories. The performance is not suprising since the LDA topics are based on keyword frequency and a predictive model based on the same keywords should be accurate.

3.2.2 Anonymity and Discourse Types. While messages sent on ASKfm are anonymous by default, senders may choose to make a message non-anonymous. To understand whether this choice was related to the type of discourse, we measured the fraction of each

Table 1: Naive Bayes Classification Results

Discourse Type	Precision	Recall	F-Measure
Complimenting/Positivity	0.987	0.865	0.922
Bullying/Inflammatory	0.798	0.753	0.775
Picture or Video Request	0.888	0.978	0.93
Preference Question	0.989	1	0.994
Like Solicitation and Rating	0.89	0.91	0.9
Thoughts/Opinions	0.971	0.382	0.548
Defense Discourse	1	0.933	0.965
Sexual Content	0.883	0.933	0.907
List of Followers	0.953	0.91	0.931
Things that you Hate	0.944	0.955	0.95
Self Harm	0.888	0.807	0.845
None of the Above	0.53	0.865	0.658
Weighted Avg.	0.886	0.858	0.856

category for which the messages were anonymous. The results are shown in Figure 2. The majority of the exchanges were anonymous. While bullying may seem to be a natural byproduct of anonymity on ASKfm, other more positive discourse is also associated with anonymity. It is worth noting that the most anonymous categories include both healthy/fun things, such as "like" solicitation and picture requests, as well as bullying. It wasn't surprising that the positive discourse types such as *Compliments and Positivity Discourse* and *Defense Discourse* were more often less anonymous than their negative counterparts like Bullying Discourse.

3.3 Limitations

We acknowledge that our sampling choice is limited by the fact that the core of our sample are users who used a variation of terms "go kill yourself" and thus captures a facet of the ASKfm usership. Our results show that despite the core of our sample, our snowballing was able to capture a wide variety of positive discourse types in addition to negative discourse types. We discovered that despite the negativity associated with ASKfm [20], the existence of the other discourse types we discovered in this study shed light on the unique affordances the semi-anonymous social media platforms offer users who are seeking social support or self-disclosing information on the website. We acknowledge that these aren't the only discourse types that occur on the website. To unpack disclosure and interaction behaviors on askFM, we describe Study II below.

4 STUDY II: ASKFM USE MOTIVATIONS

To understand users' disclosure practices and interaction behaviors on askFM ASKfm (**RQ2**) and ways the site could be improved (**RQ3**), we conducted a survey in January 2015 of young adults (ages 18-20) who identified as active site users. In our survey, we asked participants about their personal experiences with bullying and cyberbullying, their question-asking practices, as well as demographic information and measures of personality [11] and self-esteem [28]. After receiving IRB approval, we first pre-tested the items with 50 Mechanical Turkers, then opened the HIT to include up to 250 responses. In total, we received 243 usable cases for analysis. We added our age restrictions to the Mechanical Turk

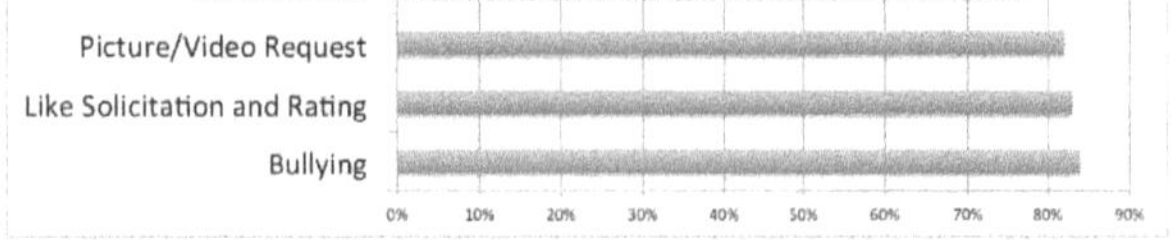

Figure 2: Percentage of Anonymous Posts for Each Mode of Discourse

HIT and participants selected a box confirming they were 18-21 years old. Though this is not foolproof, it is the most we could do given Mechanical Turk ToS restrictions.

4.1 Participant Demographics

In the full dataset, 35% of participants were female, and the average age was 19.6 (*SD*=.82). Two-thirds of participants were American, with the remaining participants representing 17 nations. The majority were enrolled in school full-time (60%) or part-time (15%) and lived at home with their family (57%). Participants reported spending just under five hours online per day (median=4.5 hours; *SD*=3 hours, 15 minutes), and said they used seven social media platforms on average (median = 6, *SD* = 3.76) from a list of 16 options.

4.2 Experiences with Bullying and Cyberbullying

Because popular media accounts have highlighted the prevalence of cyberbullying on ASKfm, we asked participants about their experiences with cyberbullying. Nearly three-quarters (73%) of participants reported that they had been bullied offline at some point, while 49.6% said they had been victims of cyberbullying. Conversely, when asked if they had ever participated in seven bullying activities (e.g., teasing, spreading rumors, name calling, threatening), 91.4% of participants said they had participated in at least one activity and 24.5% said they had engaged in all seven at some point. Females reported being victims of bullying (M=2.58, SD=1.12 vs. M=2.21, SD=1.09), $t(241)$=-2.52, p=.012, and cyberbullying (M=2.10, SD=1.20 vs. M=1.79, SD=1.02), $t(242)$=-2.15, p=.03, more often than men, but there were no gender differences in engaging in bullying activities. Females were also significantly more likely to experience verbal bullying than males (M=3.77, SD=1.02 vs. M=3.24, SD=1.03), $t(172)$=-3.35, p<.001, but no differences were reported in experiences with physical bullying.

4.3 ASKfm Interactions

The aim of our survey was to understand how ASKfm users communicated through the site, given specific affordances like anonymity and high visibility of content. We asked participants how often they interacted with strangers on the site, finding that just 7.7% of respondents reported they never interact with strangers, while more than 60% said they interact with strangers with some regularity. Given the ability to post questions anonymously on ASKfm, we asked participants if they had ever asked themselves a question anonymously, and 21% said they had. When asked about the reasons behind this practice,the most notable responses were that they did it to increase activity on their profile (71.4%), to make identity disclosures they wanted others to see (67.8%), and to cheer themselves up (54.4%). We also asked users how much they agreed with the following statement: *Posting anonymous questions on my page makes me feel better about myself*; 51.8% agreed or strongly agreed, suggesting that the simple act of posting and viewing content on their profile page–even when the content is self-written–can positively impact well-being.

We asked respondents why they think people decide to answer questions that are mean and hurtful, ultimately publishing the mean and hurtful comment to a wider audience; 54.8% said they posted the malicious comments they received because they wanted people in their network to comment on the malicious post to show support and defend them against the poster, while 52.5% said they are angry or upset and want to say that the comment is not true or they want to look like they don't care.

Finally, we asked participants if other users had ever posted malicious comments to their page. Approximately half (48.7%) said they had received negative comments about their appearance (weight, looks), 35.4% had received negative comments about their sexuality, 33.6% had received insulting comments about personal relationships, 21.4% had received "threatening comments," and 45.1% had received comments that made them feel excluded.

5 DISCUSSION

5.1 Emergent Behaviors on ASKfm

The discourse types we discovered suggest that there are other interactions and behaviors on ASKfm that occur beyond cyberbullying – interactions that are afforded by the same designs that lead to cyberbullying (anonymity for example). We found that users (1) engage in self-disclosure practices and (2) seek social support. We observe these practices across many of the discourse types we discovered.

5.1.1 Self-Disclosure on Semi-Anonymous Q&A Websites. On ASKfm, we observed very revealing acts of self-disclosure as part of *Self Harm* and *Thoughts and Opinions* discourse. *Thoughts and Opinions* discourse allows users to openly state their opinions about people mutually known by the questioner and recipient know, i.e "thoughts on Sarah?". In our survey, one highly cited reason for anonymous self-questioning was to share information that a user wanted others to see (57.1%), suggesting that anonymous self-questioning lowers the barrier to disclosing sensitive information. Self-disclosing on a semi-anonymous social media platform can be cathartic and comforting. Disclosures can occur as part of a question (usually anonymous), or in the response. What these sites offer is the opportunity to discuss something without explicitly bringing up a topic. A user might anonymously self-question, to give themselves an excuse to respond publicly, or they might ask others anonymously to recruiting those others to join in. For example, a user who anonymously posts a "suicide-list" list question can find out if anyone else in the network is experiencing the same things without identifying himself/herself.

Disclosures need not be sensitive, as we saw with *Things you Hate* and *Preference Questions. Things you hate* questions typically asked a person "What are some things that annoy you?" and a user would respond about the things that the particular person disliked. *Preference Questions* were diverse in the subject matter. They ranged from but were not limited to favorite foods, bands, mode of entertainment, and mode of communication. Questions and answers in *Things you Hate* and *Preference Questions* were innocuous invitations for users to self-disclose.

5.1.2 Social Support on Semi-Anonymous Q&A Websites. Our results demonstrate that social-support seeking behaviors are common on ASKfm. Our conceptualization of "social support" is in line with other computer-mediated communication research focused on social media and resource provision (eg, Ellison et al. found that liking behaviors were linked to bridging social capital perceptions) [9]. Support from social media can manifest through low-cost interactions (e.g., PDAs) depending on a sitefis affordances. In this section we discuss how users seek social support through: (1) self-questioning anonymously, (2) choosing to publish cyberbullying content to one's profile and (3) Like-Solicitation exchanges. The *Self-Harm Discourse* category included people seeking social support on taboo subjects like self-harm, self-injury and depression. In previous studies, users reached out for social support completely anonymously on social media platforms like YikYak or anonymous message boards [18]. On ASKfm, while a topic is brought up anonymously through the question-asking format, users can identify that they need help, or support those who need help, through a low-cost interaction of liking the post.

A common example of *Self-Harm Discourse* are Suicide List Questions, where the questioner asks any readers who have considered suicide to identify themselves publicly (by liking the post) in order to receive support. The poster and commenter(s) are working together to identify themselves by liking the question if they have ever been hurt in any of the ways specified by the answerer of the question. The answerer then promises to send *Compliments and Positivity* to the victims of these kinds of hate. A "Suicide List" can also qualify as a form of like bartering. Users who "like" the question are bartering for *Compliments and Positivity.* This kind of discourse demonstrates how users seek and receive social support on taboo topics.

A study looking at self-injurious behavior on message boards observed that these message boards provide essential social support, but also normalize such behaviors [36]. It is not surprising to discover taboo discourse like *Self-Harm Discourse* on a semi-anonymous social media platform. What is unique however is the transition from anonymous questioning to non-anonymous social support permitted by ASKfm–users can ask for help anonymously, but replies in support are shown visibly.

In our survey, 47.4% of self-questioners reported that they had asked themselves questions anonymously to respond to negative or harassing posts on their page, suggesting that some ASKfm users publish negative "questions" and respond by posting an anonymous "question" to their own pages as a form of support to imply they have a supportive network. Users may also be asking themselves questions in order to defend themselves when they experience cyberbullying or other negative comments. Sometimes requests for social support were more explicit (and less serious). *Like Solicitation* discourse involved users exchanging "likes" or "ratings". For example, an anonymous user posted, "likes for anyone who likes this post", and the recipient replied, "sure". In this exchange, the recipient would then have to return the "likes" for all the friends who "liked" that conversation.

5.2 ASKfm Specific Affordances

The discourse types we discovered along with our survey responses demonstrate that ASKfm affords at least three specific types of interactions: (1) Anonymous Self-Questioning Practices, (2) Transitioning from Anonymity to Visibility, and (3) Built-in Filtering of Content. We discuss each of these in detail below.

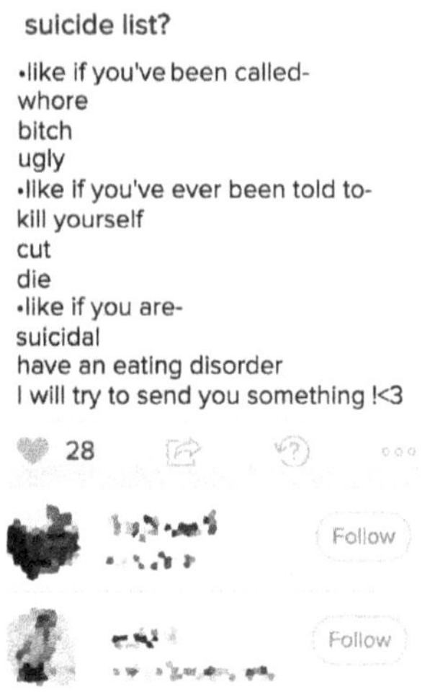

Figure 3: Example of a "Suicide List" question-answer pair on ASKfm. The question is asked anonymously. The 28 likers however are identified users. A preview of those who "liked" the question-answer pair appears at the bottom of the image. *Content has been changed to both reflect the reality of the content of these posts and to protect the identity of people involved in this post.*

5.2.1 Self-Directed Anonymous Questions. ASKfm's interaction model permits anonymous, self-directed questioning. The anonymous feature allows users to interact with themselves anonymously making it appear that they have more social support than what actually exists. This interaction is not much different than someone guilefully sending themselves flowers or gifts to their workplace anonymously to indicate to others more social approval than really exists. In our survey, 21% of the respondents said that they had asked themselves a question anonymously on their profiles, and their justifications for doing so included making identity disclosures that they wanted others to see, increasing activity on their profile, and feeling better about themselves.

While research has found that users make identified disclosures on sites like Facebook as part of their "identity work" [35], guiding self-presentation anonymously may provide users with a greater perception of control. The potential for positive effects of self-posting on perceptions of well-being is also worth further investigation; for example, researchers have found that text-based interactions have a greater positive effect on well-being than face-to-face interactions [10] while public disclosures on social media serve a self-affirming purpose by satisfying needs for self-worth [34].

5.2.2 Transition from Anonymity to Visibility. The mix of anonymous and non-anonymous interactions on ASKfm provides the ability to transition from anonymity to visibility: while "questions" can be asked either anonymously or non-anonymously, "likes" are *always* visible. Users can broach a sensitive topic anonymously, safely, and only reveal themselves through a "like" if enough of their social circle does likewise. At first glance, the use cases for such a transition might seem trivial. However, after further examination of the discourse types like *Like Solicitation, Compliments and Positivity*, and *Self Harm*, this transition can be an important strategy garnering social support. For example, research has found that people with lower self-esteem consider Facebook a good place to disclose information; however, they also post more negative posts, which receive fewer "likes." In turn, these users are less likely to obtain social resources from the site [9].

5.2.3 Built-In Filtering. ASKfm differs from other more conventional social media platforms because of it's implicit built-in filtering mechanism. When a user navigates to another user's profile to "ask a question", the "question" is not automatically published on the recipient's profile. Instead, the recipient receives the question in a private inbox and then can *choose* whether to respond to the message. If a user declines answering a bullying question, only the bully and the recipient know about the question. Our results reveal that users sometimes decide to answer questions even if they are hurtful or embarrassing, publicizing the hurtful question by answering it.

ASKfm's filtering allows users to reject cyberbullying and other malicious content and prevent it from becoming replicable, permanent and searchable. Users don't always reject such content, and it appears that the option to publish (or not) gives victims a degree of agency. We describe later how some users decide to publish content on their own terms, to gain social support after being bullied. This built-in filtering has implications for privacy as well. The built-in filtering allows users to consider content that may breach their privacy before it is published to their profiles. The question-asking format implicitly gives users the ability to filter *who* and *what* is being posted to their profiles.

5.3 Design Recommendations

The results of our study demonstrate that while cyberbullying is a reality of the ASKfm platform, users utilize ASKfm's affordances to transition from anonymity to visibility on taboo subjects or self-direct anonymous questions for various purposes. We can use our results to help inform better features to minimize negative interactions and possibly highlight positive interactions. We make following design recommendations:

(1) **Topic Model Filters** Our topic modeling results revealed the various words and terms that appear in cyberbullying posts. We found that top words associated with cyberbullying included a range of words like: "hate" "ugly" and "gay". The various ways these words can be interpreted based on their respective contexts demonstrate that the degree to which words can hurt depends on many factors including the context in which the word was used. Furthermore, our topic modeling results demonstrate that askFM users might use expletives affectionately and using only expletives as features in a filtering algorithm may lead false positives. For example, one document classified as "Compliments and Positivity" category was, "B****[redacted] u my bff", which was captured as this category correctly despite the fact that it included an expletive. Based on our results, we suggest that topic modeling be used to determine categories of discourse that users can then choose to filter. This approach to filtering is an alternative approach

to previous automated methods of filtering that might not take into consideration context.

(2) **Increasing Accountability by Identifying Followers:** While ASKfm users are aware of *how many* people are following them, they do not know *who* is following them on the platform. While social media users generally do a poor job at estimating the audience of their posts on more popular social media sites like Facebook [23], it more difficult to estimate who views one's content since users do not know who is "following" their posts. One of the discourse types that emerged in our first study was *Listing People You Follow*, precisely because people do not know who is "following" them. By making audiences visible to users, users will have a better understanding of who sees their content and they will be held more accountable for the content that they post or send to one another. Studies show that perception of audiences influence content production and self-presentation practices [4]. Social media platforms that allow visible subscriptions and unsubscriptions give some degree of feedback about quality of content to users, but since ASKfm's subscriptions are unknown to the user, it is more difficult to understand how people react to the content beyond other cues like reshares [32] and likes. Giving this minimal level of audience transparency to users would increase accountability on ASKfm.

6 CONCLUSION

In this work, we discovered interactions occur alongside cyberbullying discourse on ASKfm, offered reasons why people use ASKfm despite the site's propensity for cyberbullying, and concluded with making design changes that can make ASKfm a safer space. We approached these questions through a data-driven approach coupled with a survey of active ASKfm users. We used topic modeling, and manual coding to derive discourse types on ASKfm and conducted a survey and about ASKfm user. We present 11 discourse types on ASKfm that occur alongside cyberbullying discourse. We suggest that users engage in these discourse types to self-disclose and seek social support and use the affordances of ASKfm to engage in such behaviors using affordances on the platform like self-directed questions and transition from anonymity to visibility by liking anonymously-asked questions. We discussed how ASKfm's semi-anonymous and non-anonymous affordances impact the types of discourse we observed, and the types of user behavior that emerged as a result. We make design recommendations that can potentially enhance user experience by decreasing the harm caused by cyberbullying, and enhancing it's social support features.

REFERENCES

[1] Nazanin Andalibi, Oliver L Haimson, Munmun De Choudhury, and Andrea Forte. 2016. Understanding Social Media Disclosures of Sexual Abuse Through the Lenses of Support Seeking and Anonymity. In *Proceedings of the 2016 CHI Conference on Human Factors in Computing Systems*. ACM, 3906–3918.

[2] Ask.fm. 2013. (2013). http://ask.fm/askfm/answer/14515248650

[3] Hazeline U Asuncion, Arthur U Asuncion, and Richard N Taylor. 2010. Software traceability with topic modeling. In *Proceedings of the 32nd ACM/IEEE International Conference on Software Engineering-Volume 1*. ACM, 95–104.

[4] Michael S Bernstein, Eytan Bakshy, Moira Burke, and Brian Karrer. 2013. Quantifying the invisible audience in social networks. In *Proceedings of the SIGCHI Conference on Human Factors in Computing Systems*. ACM, 21–30.

[5] Amy Binns. 2013. Facebookfis Ugly Sisters: Anonymity and Abuse on Formspring and Ask. fm. *Media Education Research Journal* (2013).

[6] David M Blei, Andrew Y Ng, and Michael I Jordan. 2003. Latent dirichlet allocation. *the Journal of machine Learning research* 3 (2003), 993–1022.

[7] Munmun De Choudhury and Sushovan De. 2014. Mental Health Discourse on reddit: Self-Disclosure, Social Support, and Anonymity.. In *ICWSM*. Citeseer.

[8] David Dearman and Khai N Truong. 2010. Why users of yahoo!: answers do not answer questions. In *Proceedings of the SIGCHI Conference on Human Factors in Computing Systems*. ACM, 329–332.

[9] Nicole B Ellison, Jessica Vitak, Rebecca Gray, and Cliff Lampe. 2014. Cultivating social resources on social network sites: Facebook relationship maintenance behaviors and their role in social capital processes. *Journal of Computer-Mediated Communication* 19, 4 (2014), 855–870.

[10] Amy L Gonzales. 2014. Text-based communication influences self-esteem more than face-to-face or cellphone communication. *Computers in Human Behavior* 39 (2014), 197–203.

[11] Samuel D Gosling, Peter J Rentfrow, and William B Swann. 2003. A very brief measure of the Big-Five personality domains. *Journal of Research in personality* 37, 6 (2003), 504–528.

[12] Ryan Grenoble. 2012. Amanda Todd: Bullied Canadian Teen Commits Suicide After Prolonged Battle Online And In School. (october 2012). http://www.huffingtonpost.com/2012/10/11/amanda-todd-suicide-bullying_n_1959909.html

[13] Erin E Hollenbaugh and Marcia K Everett. 2013. The effects of anonymity on self-disclosure in blogs: An application of the online disinhibition effect. *Journal of Computer-Mediated Communication* 18, 3 (2013), 283–302.

[14] Homa Hosseinmardi, Amir Ghasemianlangroodi, Richard Han, Qin Lv, and Shivakant Mishra. 2014a. Analyzing negative user behavior in a semi-anonymous social network. *arXiv preprint arXiv:1404.3839* (2014).

[15] Homa Hosseinmardi, Richard Han, Qin Lv, Shivakant Mishra, and Amir Ghasemianlangroodi. 2014b. Towards understanding cyberbullying behavior in a semi-anonymous social network. In *Advances in Social Networks Analysis and Mining (ASONAM), 2014 IEEE/ACM International Conference on*. IEEE, 244–252.

[16] Homa Hosseinmardi, Shaosong Li, Zhili Yang, Qin Lv, Rahat Ibn Rafiq, Richard Han, and Shivakant Mishra. 2014c. A comparison of common users across instagram and ask. fm to better understand cyberbullying. In *Big Data and Cloud Computing (BdCloud), 2014 IEEE Fourth International Conference on*. IEEE, 355–362.

[17] Ruogu Kang, Stephanie Brown, and Sara Kiesler. 2013. Why do people seek anonymity on the internet?: informing policy and design. In *Proceedings of the SIGCHI Conference on Human Factors in Computing Systems*. ACM, 2657–2666.

[18] Ruogu Kang, Laura Dabbish, and Katherine Sutton. 2016. Strangers on Your Phone: Why People Use Anonymous Communication Applications. In *Proceedings of the 19th ACM Conference on Computer-Supported Cooperative Work & Social Computing*. ACM, 359–370.

[19] Andreas M Kaplan and Michael Haenlein. 2010. Users of the world, unite! The challenges and opportunities of Social Media. *Business horizons* 53, 1 (2010), 59–68.

[20] April Kontostathis, Kelly Reynolds, Andy Garron, and Lynne Edwards. 2013. Detecting cyberbullying: query terms and techniques. In *Proceedings of the 5th Annual ACM Web Science Conference*. ACM, 195–204.

[21] Alex Leavitt. 2015. This is a Throwaway Account: Temporary Technical Identities and Perceptions of Anonymity in a Massive Online Community. In *Proceedings of the 18th ACM Conference on Computer Supported Cooperative Work & Social Computing*. ACM, 317–327.

[22] Tamar Lewin. 2010. Teenage insults, scrawled on web, not on walls. *The New York Times* (2010), A1.

[23] Alice E Marwick and danah boyd. 2011. I tweet honestly, I tweet passionately: Twitter users, context collapse, and the imagined audience. *New media & society* 13, 1 (2011), 114–133.

[24] Mary L McHugh. 2012. Interrater reliability: the kappa statistic. *Biochemia medica* 22, 3 (2012), 276–282.

[25] David Mimno, Hanna M Wallach, Edmund Talley, Miriam Leenders, and Andrew McCallum. 2011. Optimizing semantic coherence in topic models. In *Proceedings of the Conference on Empirical Methods in Natural Language Processing*. Association for Computational Linguistics, 262–272.

[26] Michael J Moore, Tadashi Nakano, Akihiro Enomoto, and Tatsuya Suda. 2012. Anonymity and roles associated with aggressive posts in an online forum. *Computers in Human Behavior* 28, 3 (2012), 861–867.

[27] J Brian Rollman, Kevin Krug, and Fredrick Parente. 2000. The chat room phenomenon: Reciprocal communication in cyberspace. *CyberPsychology and Behavior* 3, 2 (2000), 161–166.

[28] Morris Rosenberg, Carmi Schooler, and Carrie Schoenbach. 1989. Self-esteem and adolescent problems: Modeling reciprocal effects. *American sociological review* (1989), 1004–1018.

[29] Hope Jensen Schau and Mary C Gilly. 2003. We are what we post? Self-presentation in personal web space. *Journal of consumer research* 30, 3 (2003), 385–404.

[30] Sarita Yardi Schoenebeck. 2013. The Secret Life of Online Moms: Anonymity and Disinhibition on YouBeMom. com.. In *ICWSM*. Citeseer.

[31] L Smith-Spark. 2013. Hanna smith suicide fuels calls for action on ask. fm cyberbullying, cnn. (2013).

[32] Bongwon Suh, Lichan Hong, Peter Pirolli, and Ed H Chi. 2010. Want to be retweeted? large scale analytics on factors impacting retweet in twitter network. In *Social computing (socialcom), 2010 ieee second international conference on*. IEEE, 177–184.

[33] John Suler. 2004. The online disinhibition effect. *Cyberpsychology & behavior* 7, 3 (2004), 321–326.

[34] Catalina L Toma and Jeffrey T Hancock. 2013. Self-affirmation underlies Facebook use. *Personality and Social Psychology Bulletin* 39, 3 (2013), 321–331.

[35] Jessica Vitak and Jinyoung Kim. 2014. You can't block people offline: examining how Facebook's affordances shape the disclosure process. In *Proceedings of the 17th ACM conference on Computer supported cooperative work & social computing*. ACM, 461–474.

[36] Janis L Whitlock, Jane L Powers, and John Eckenrode. 2006. The virtual cutting edge: the internet and adolescent self-injury. *Developmental psychology* 42, 3 (2006), 407.

[37] Haejin Yun. 2006. *The creation and validation of a perceived anonymity scale based on the social information processing model and its nomological network test in an online social support community*. ProQuest.

[38] Wayne Xin Zhao, Jing Jiang, Jianshu Weng, Jing He, Ee-Peng Lim, Hongfei Yan, and Xiaoming Li. 2011. Comparing Twitter and traditional media using topic models. In *Advances in Information Retrieval*. Springer, 338–349.

Mean Birds: Detecting Aggression and Bullying on Twitter

Despoina Chatzakou[†], Nicolas Kourtellis[‡], Jeremy Blackburn[‡]
Emiliano De Cristofaro[♯], Gianluca Stringhini[♯], Athena Vakali[†]

[†]Aristotle University of Thessaloniki [‡]Telefonica Research [♯]University College London
deppych@csd.auth.gr, nicolas.kourtellis@telefonica.com, jeremy.blackburn@telefonica.com
e.decristofaro@ucl.ac.uk, g.stringhini@ucl.ac.uk, avakali@csd.auth.gr

ABSTRACT

In recent years, bullying and aggression against social media users have grown significantly, causing serious consequences to victims of all demographics. Nowadays, cyberbullying affects more than half of young social media users worldwide, suffering from prolonged and/or coordinated digital harassment. Also, tools and technologies geared to understand and mitigate it are scarce and mostly ineffective. In this paper, we present a principled and scalable approach to detect bullying and aggressive behavior on Twitter. We propose a robust methodology for extracting text, user, and network-based attributes, studying the properties of bullies and aggressors, and what features distinguish them from regular users. We find that bullies post less, participate in fewer online communities, and are less popular than normal users. Aggressors are relatively popular and tend to include more negativity in their posts. We evaluate our methodology using a corpus of 1.6M tweets posted over 3 months, and show that machine learning classification algorithms can accurately detect users exhibiting bullying and aggressive behavior, with over 90% AUC.

1 INTRODUCTION

Cyberbullying and cyberaggression are serious and widespread issues affecting increasingly more Internet users. Arguably, in today's hyper-connected society, bullying, once limited to particular places or times of the day (e.g., school hours), can instead occur anytime, anywhere, with just a few taps on a keyboard. Cyberbullying and cyberaggression can take many forms and definitions [19, 46, 52], however, the former typically denotes repeated and hostile behavior performed by a group or an individual and the latter intentional harm delivered via electronic means to a person or a group of people who perceive such acts as offensive, derogatory, harmful, or unwanted [19].

Only a few years ago, when Internet adoption was still limited, cyberbullying was not taken seriously: the typical advice was to "just turn off the screen" or "disconnect" [33]. However, as its proliferation and the extent of its consequences reach epidemic levels [4], this behavior can no longer be ignored: in 2014, about 50% of young social media users reported being bullied online in various forms [47]. Popular social media platforms like Twitter and Facebook are not immune [43], as racist and sexist attacks may even have caused potential buyers of Twitter to balk [51].

In this paper, we focus on these phenomena on Twitter. Despite the seriousness of the problem, there are very few successful efforts to detect abusive behavior on Twitter, both from the research community (see Section 2) and Twitter itself [50], due to several inherent obstacles. First, tweets are short and full of grammar and syntactic flaws, which makes it harder to use natural language processing tools to extract text-based attributes and characterize user interactions. Second, each tweet provides fairly limited context, therefore, taken on its own, an aggressive tweet may be disregarded as normal text, whereas, read along with other tweets, either from the same user or in the context of aggressive behavior from multiple users, the same tweet could be characterized as bullying. Third, despite extensive work on spam detection in social media [18, 48, 55], Twitter is still full of spam accounts [10], often using vulgar language and exhibiting behavior (repeated posts with similar content, mentions, or hashtags) that could also be considered as aggressive or bullying. Filtering out such accounts from actual abusive users may be a difficult task. Finally, aggression and bullying against an individual can be performed in several ways beyond just obviously abusive language – e.g., via constant sarcasm, trolling, etc.

Overview & Contributions. In this paper, we design and execute a novel methodology geared to label aggressive and bullying behavior in Twitter. Specifically, by presenting a principled and scalable approach for eliciting user, text, and network-based attributes of Twitter users, we extract a total of 30 features. We study the properties of bullies and aggressors, and what features distinguish them from regular users, alongside labels provided by human annotators recruited from CrowdFlower [13], a popular crowdsourcing platform. Such labels, contributed infrequently or at regular intervals, can be used to enhance an already trained model, bootstrapping the detection method and executed on large set of tweets.

We experiment with a corpus of 1.6*M* tweets, collected over 3 months, finding that bully users are less "popular" and participate in fewer communities. However, when they do become active, they post more frequently, and use more hashtags, URLs, etc., than others. Moreover, we show that bully and aggressive users tend to attack, in short bursts, particular users or groups they target. We also find that, although largely ignored in previous work, network-based attributes are actually the most effective features for detecting aggressive user behavior. Our features can be fed to classification algorithms, such as Random Forests, to effectively detect bullying

WebSci'17, June 25-28, 2017, Troy, NY, USA.

DOI: http://dx.doi.org/10.1145/3091478.3091487

and aggressive users, achieving up to 0.907 weighted AUC [21], 89.9% precision, and 91.7% recall. Finally, we discuss the effectiveness of our methods by comparing results with the suspension and deletion of accounts as observed in the wild for users who, though aggressive, remain seemingly undetected by Twitter. Our datasets are available to the research community upon request.

2 RELATED WORK

Over the past few years, several techniques have been proposed to measure and detect offensive or abusive content / behavior on platforms like Instagram [25], YouTube [11], 4chan [23], Yahoo Finance [17], and Yahoo Answers [28]. Chen et al. [11] use both textual and structural features (e.g., ratio of imperative sentences, adjective and adverbs as offensive words) to predict a user's aptitude in producing offensive content in YouTube comments, while Djuric et al. [17] rely on word embeddings to distinguish abusive comments on Yahoo Finance. Nobara et al. [36] perform hate speech detection on Yahoo Finance and News data, using supervised learning classification. Kayes et al. [28] find that users tend to flag abusive content posted on Yahoo Answers in an overwhelmingly correct way (as confirmed by human annotators). Also, some users significantly deviate from community norms, posting a large amount of content that is flagged as abusive. Through careful feature extraction, they also show it is possible to use machine learning methods to predict which users will be suspended.

Dinakar et al. [16] detect cyberbullying by decomposing it into detection of sensitive topics. They collect YouTube comments from controversial videos, use manual annotation to characterize them, and perform a bag-of-words driven text classification. Hee et al. [54] study linguistic characteristics in cyberbullying-related content extracted from Ask.fm, aiming to detect fine-grained types of cyberbullying, such as threats and insults. Besides the victim and harasser, they also identify bystander-defenders and bystander-assistants, who support, respectively, the victim or the harasser. Hosseinmardi et al. [25] study images posted on Instagram and their associated comments to detect and distinguish between cyberaggression and cyberbullying. Finally, authors in [44] present an approach for detecting bullying words in tweets, as well as demographics about bullies such as their age and gender.

Previous work often used features such as punctuation, URLs, part-of-speech, n-grams, Bag of Words (BoW), as well as lexical features relying on dictionaries of offensive words, and user-based features such as user's membership duration activity, number of friends/followers, etc. Different supervised approaches have been used for detection: [36] uses a regression model, whereas [14, 16, 54] rely on other methods like Naive Bayes, Support Vector Machines (SVM), and Decision Trees (J48). By contrast, Hosseinmardi et al. [24] use a graph-based approach based on likes and comments to build bipartite graphs and identify negative behavior. A similar graph-based approach is also used in [25].

Sentiment analysis of text can also contribute useful features in detecting offensive or abusive content. For instance, Nahar et al. [34] use sentiment scores of data collected from Kongregate (online gaming site), Slashdot, and MySpace. They use a probabilistic sentiment analysis approach to distinguish between bullies and non-bullies, and rank the most influential users based on a predator-victim graph built from exchanged messages. Xu et al. [56] rely on sentiment to identify victims on Twitter who pose high risk to themselves or others. Apart from using positive and negative sentiments, they consider specific emotions such as anger, embarrassment, and sadness. Finally, Patch [38] studies the presence of such emotions (anger, sadness, fear) in bullying instances on Twitter.

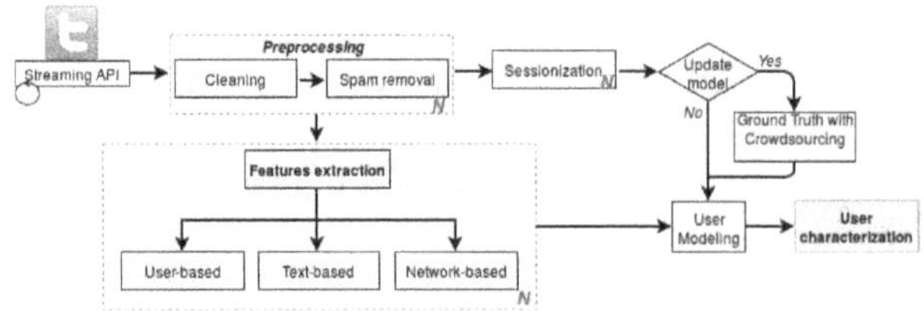

Figure 1: Overview of our methodology. *N* denotes the ability to parallelize a task on *N* processors.

Remarks. Our work advances the state-of-art on cyberbullying and cyberaggression detection by proposing a scalable methodology for large-scale analysis and extraction of text, user, and network based features on Twitter, which has not been studied in this context before. Our novel methodology analyzes users' tweets, individually and in groups, and extracts appropriate features connecting user behavior with a tendency of aggression or bullying. We examine the importance of such attributes, and further advance the state-of-art by focusing on new network-related attributes that further distinguish Twitter-specific user behaviors. Finally, we discuss the effectiveness of our detection method by comparing results with the suspension and deletion of accounts as observed in the wild for users who, though aggressive, remain seemingly undetected.

3 METHODOLOGY

Our approach to detect aggressive and bullying behavior on Twitter, as summarized in Figure 1, involves the following steps: (1) data collection, (2) preprocessing of tweets, (3) sessionization, (4) ground truth building, (5) extracting user-, text-, and network-level features, (6) user modeling and characterization, and (7) classification.

Data Collection. Our first step is to collect tweets and, naturally, there are a few possible ways to do so. In this paper, we rely on Twitter's Streaming API, which provides free access to 1% of all tweets. The API returns each tweet in a JSON format, with the content of the tweet, some metadata (e.g., creation time, whether it is a reply or a retweet, etc.), as well as information about the poster (e.g., username, followers, friends, number of total posted tweets).

Preprocessing. Next, we remove stop words, URLs, and punctuation marks from the tweet text and perform normalization – i.e., we eliminate repetitive characters; e.g., the word "yessss" is converted to "yes". This step also involves the removal of spam content, which can be done using a few different techniques relying on tweeting behavior (e.g., many hashtags per tweet) and/or network features (e.g., spam accounts forming micro-clusters) [18, 55].

Sessionization. Since analyzing single tweets does not provide enough context to discern if a user is behaving in an aggressive or bullying way, we group tweets from the same user, based on time clusters, into *sessions* and analyze them instead of single tweets.

Ground Truth. We build ground truth (needed for machine learning classification, explained next) using human annotators. For this

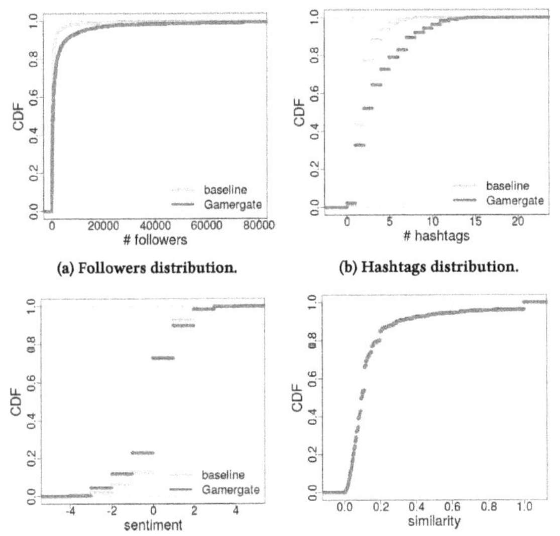

(a) Followers distribution. (b) Hashtags distribution.

(c) Sentiment distribution. (d) Similarity distribution.

Figure 2: CDF of (a) Followers, (b) Hashtags, (c) Avg. sentiment, (d) Portion of user's posts with similarity above 0.8.

we use a crowdsourced approach, by recruiting workers who are provided with a set of tweets from a user, and are asked to classify them according to predefined labels. If such an annotated dataset is already available, this step can be omitted.

Feature Extraction. We extract features from both tweets and user profiles. More specifically, features can be user-, text-, or network-based; e.g., the number of followers, tweets, hashtags, etc.

Classification. The final step is to perform classification using the (extracted) features and the ground truth. Naturally, different machine learning techniques can be used for this task, including probabilistic classifiers (e.g., Naïve Bayes), decision trees (e.g., J48), ensembles (e.g., Random Forests), or neural networks.

Scalability and Online Updates. An important challenge to address is supporting *scalable* analysis of large tweet corpora. Several of the above steps can be parallelized, e.g., over N subsets of the data, on N cores (Figure 1). Also, one can use different modeling algorithms and processing platforms (e.g., batch platforms like Hadoop vs. stream processing engines like Storm) if data are processed in batches or in a streaming fashion. Either way, some of the steps (e.g., annotation from crowd-workers) can be periodically executed on new data, and the model updated to handle changes in data and/or manifestation of new aggressive behaviors. Our pipeline design provides several benefits with respect to performance, accuracy, and extensibility, as it allows regular updates of the model, thus capturing previously unseen human behaviors. Moreover, we can plug-in new features, e.g., as new metadata is made available from the Twitter platform, or from new research insights. Finally, different components can be updated or extended with new technologies for better data cleaning, feature extraction, and modeling.

4 DATASET & GROUND TRUTH

In this section, we present the data used in our evaluation, and the way we process it to build ground truth.

4.1 Data Collection

Data was collected between June and August 2016, gathering two sets of tweets: (i) a **baseline** of 1M random tweets, (ii) a **hate-related**, i.e., a set of 650k tweets collected from the Twitter Streaming API using 309 hashtags related to bullying and hateful speech.

More specifically, we build the list of 309 hashtags as follows: we obtain a 1% sample of all public tweets in the given time window and select all tweets containing #GamerGate. The Gamergate controversy [30] is one of the most well documented and mature, large-scale instances of bullying/aggressive behavior that we are aware of. It originated from alleged improprieties in video game journalism, quickly growing into a larger campaign centered around sexism and social justice [6]. With individuals on both sides of the controversy using it, and extreme cases of cyberbullying and aggressive behavior associated with it (e.g., direct threats of rape and murder), #GamerGate serves as a relatively unambiguous hashtag associated with tweets that are likely to involve the type of behavior we are interested in. We use #GamerGate as a seed for a sort of snowball sampling of other hashtags likely associated with bullying and aggressive behavior; we also include tweets that have one of the 308 hashtags that appeared in the same tweet as #GamerGate. Indeed, when manually examining these hashtags, we see that they contain a number of hateful words or hashtags, e.g., #IStandWithHateSpeech, and #KillAllNiggers.

Apart from the hate-related set, we also crawl a random set of tweets to serve as a baseline, as it is less prone to contain any kind of offensive behaviors. As noted in our previous works [5, 6], there are significant differences among the two sets. To highlight such social and posting activity differences, we show the number of followers, the hashtag usage, and the expressed sentiment. We observe that users from the hate-related set have more followers compared to the baseline set. This could be because users with aggressive behavior tend to accumulate more popularity in their network (Fig. 2a). Also, baseline users tweet with fewer hashtags than users from the hate-related dataset (Fig. 2b), perhaps as the latter use Twitter as a rebroadcasting mechanism aiming at attracting attention to the topic. Finally, the hate-related tweets contain more negative sentiment since they are more offensive posts (Fig. 2c).

As expected, the hate-related dataset also contains activity of users who may not be aggressive or hateful, and in fact, may be driving metrics such as popularity in skewed ways. Therefore, to understand nuanced differences between aggressive or hateful users with normal users, we investigate in more detail behavioral patterns observed in this dataset in Section 5. More specifically, we analyze user behavior and profile characteristics based on labels (normal, bully, or aggressive) provided by human annotators.

4.2 Preprocessing

We perform several steps to prepare the data for labeling and build ground truth.

Cleaning. The first step is to clean the data of noise, i.e., removing numbers, stop words, and punctuations, as well as converting all characters to lower case.

Removing Spammers. Previous work has shown that Twitter contains a non-negligible amount of spammers [10], and proposed

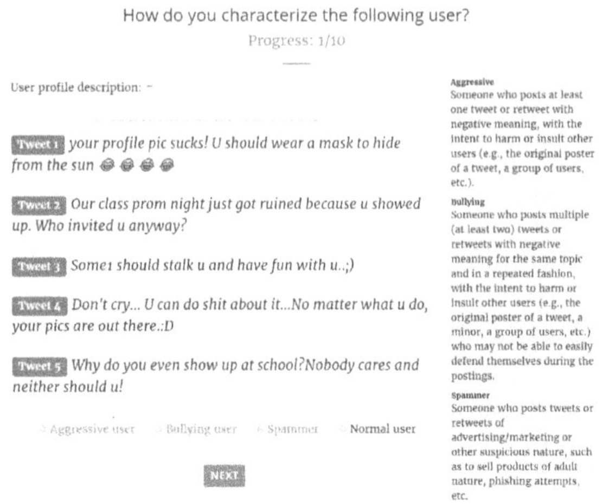

Figure 3: Example of the crowdsourcing user interface.

a number of spam detection tools [18, 55]. Here, we perform a first-level detection of spammers and remove them from our dataset. We use Wang et al.'s approach [55], relying on two main indicators of spam: (i) using a large number of hashtags in tweets (to boost visibility), and (ii) posting a large number of tweets highly similar to each other. To find optimal cutoffs for these heuristics, we study both the distribution of hashtags and duplication of tweets. For hashtags, we notice that the average number of hashtags within a user's posts ranges in 0 to 17. We experiment with different cutoffs and after a textual inspection on a sample of spam posts, we set the limit to 5 hashtags, i.e., users with more than 5 hashtags (on average) per tweet are removed. Next, we estimate the similarity of a user's tweets via the Levenshtein distance [35], i.e., the minimum number of single-character edits needed to convert one string into another, averaging it out over all pairs of the user's tweets. For a user's x tweets, we calculate the average intra-tweet similarity over a set of n similarity scores, where $n = x(x-1)/2$. If the average intra-tweet similarity is above 0.8, we exclude the user and their posting activity. Figure 2d shows that about 5% of users have a high percentage of similar posts and are removed from our dataset.

4.3 Sessionization

Cyberbullying usually involves *repetitive* actions, thus, we aim to study users' tweets *over time*. Inspired by Hosseinmardi et al. [25] – who consider a lower threshold of comments for media sessions extracted from Instagram to be presented in the annotation process – we create, for each user, sets of time-sorted tweets (sessions) by grouping tweets posted close to each other in time.

First, we remove users who are not significantly active, i.e., tweeting less than five times in the 3-month period. Then, we use a session-based model where, for each session S_i, the inter-arrival time between tweets does not exceed a predefined time threshold t_l. We experiment with various values of t_l to find an optimal session duration and arrive at a threshold of 8 hours. The minimum, median, and maximum length of the resulting sessions (in terms of the number of their included tweets) for the hate-related (i.e., Gamergate) dataset are, respectively, 12, 22, and 2.6k tweets. For the baseline set of tweets, they are 5, 44, and 1.6k tweets.

Next, we divide sessions in batches, as otherwise they would contain too much information to be carefully examined by a crowd-worker within a reasonable period of time. To find the optimal size of a batch, i.e., the number of tweets per batch, we performed preliminary labeling runs on CrowdFlower, involving 100 workers each, using batches of exactly 5, 5-10, and 5-20 tweets. Our intuition is that increasing the batch size provides more context to the worker to assess if a poster is acting in an aggressive or bullying behavior, however, too many tweets might confuse them. The best results with respect to labeling agreement – i.e., the number of workers that provide the same label for a batch – occur with 5-10 tweets per batch. Therefore, we eliminate sessions with fewer than 5 tweets, and further split those with more than 10 tweets (preserving the chronological ordering of their posted time). In the end, we arrive at $1,500$ batches. We also note that we maintain the same number of batches for both the hate-related and baseline tweets.

4.4 Crowdsourced Labeling

We now present the design of our crowdsourcing labeling process, performed on CrowdFlower.

Labeling. Our goal is to label each Twitter user – *not* single tweets – as *normal*, *aggressive*, *bullying*, or *spammer* by analyzing their batch(es) of tweets. Note that we also allow for the possibility that a user is spamming and has passed our basic spam filtering. Based on previous research [19, 46, 52], workers are provided with the following definitions of aggressive, bullying, and spam behaviors:

- *aggressor:* someone who posts at least one tweet or retweet with negative meaning, with the intent to harm or insult other users (e.g., the original poster of a tweet, a group of users, etc.);
- *bully:* someone who posts multiple tweets or retweets ($\geq$2) with negative meaning for the same topic and in a repeated fashion, with the intent to harm or insult other users (e.g., the original poster of a tweet, a minor, a group of users, etc.) who may not be able to easily defend themselves during the postings;
- *spammer:* someone who posts texts of advertising / marketing or other suspicious nature, such as to sell products of adult nature, and phishing attempts.

CrowdFlower Task. We redirect employed crowd workers to an online survey tool we developed. First, they are asked to provide basic demographic information: gender, age, nationality, education level, and annual income. In total, 30% are female and 70% male, while their claimed educational level is spread between secondary education (18.4%), bachelor degree (35.2%), master (44%), and PhD (2.4%). One third (35.5%) claim an income level below €10k, ~20% between €10k-€20k and the rest between €20k-€100k. Regarding age, 27% are 18-24, 30% are 25-31, 21% are 32-38, 12% are 39-45, and the remainder above 45 years old. They come from 56 different countries, with significant participation of users from USA, Venezuela, Russia, and Nigeria. Overall, the annotators from the top 10 countries contribute 75% of all annotations.

We then ask workers to label 10 batches, one of which is a control case (details below). We also provide them with the user profile description (if any) of the Twitter user they are labeling and the definition of aggressive, bullying, and spammer behaviors. Figure 3 presents an example of the interface. The workers rated

Type	Feature
User (total: 10)	avg. # posts, # days since account creation, verified account # subscribed lists, posts' interarrival time, default profile image? statistics on sessions: total number, avg., median, and STD. of their size
Textual (total: 9)	avg. # hashtags, avg. # emoticons, avg. # upper cases, # URLs avg. sentiment score, avg. emotional scores, hate score avg. word embedding score, avg. curse score
Network (total: 11)	# friends, # followers, hubs, (d=#followers/#friends), authority avg. power diff. with mentioned users, clustering coefficient, reciprocity eigenvector centrality, closeness centrality, louvain modularity

Table 1: Features considered in the study.

the instructions given to them, as well as the overall task, as very good with an overall score of 4 out 5.

Results. Overall, we recruit 834 workers. They are allowed to participate only once to eliminate behavioral bias across tasks and discourage rushed tasks. Each batch is labeled by 5 different workers, and, similar to [25], [36], a majority vote is used to decide the final label. We receive 1, 303 annotated batches, comprising 9, 484 tweets in total. 4.5% of users are labeled as bullies, 3.4% as aggressors, 31.8% as spammers, and 60.3% as normal. Overall, abusive users (i.e., bullies and aggressors) make up about 8% of our dataset, which mirrors observations from previous studies (e.g., in [28] 9% of the users in the examined dataset exhibits bad behavior, while in [2] 7% of users cheated). Thus, we believe our ground truth dataset contains a representative sample of aggressive/abusive content.

Annotator reliability. To assess the reliability of our workers, we use (i) the inter-rater reliability measure, and (ii) control cases. We find the inter-rater agreement to be 0.54. We also use control cases to ensure worker "quality" by manually annotating three batches of tweets. During the annotation process, each worker is given a set of batches to annotate, one of which is a randomly selected control case: the annotation of these control cases is used to assess their ability to adequately annotate for the given task. We find 66.5% accuracy overall (i.e., the percent of correctly annotated control cases). More specifically, 83.75% accuracy for spam, 53.56% for bully, and 61.31% for aggressive control cases.

5 FEATURE EXTRACTION

In this section, we focus on user-, text-, and network-based features that can be subsequently used in the modeling of user behaviors identified in the dataset. Next, we detail the features from each category, summarized in Table 1. To examine the significance of differences among the distributions presented next, we use the two-sample Kolmogorov-Smirnov test, a non-parametric statistical test, to compare the probability distributions of different samples. We consider as statistically significant all cases with $p < 0.05$.

5.1 User-based features

Basics. We experiment with various user-based features; i.e., features extracted from a user's profile. Features in this category include the number of tweets a user has made, the age of his account (i.e., number of days since its creation), the number of lists subscribed to, if the account is verified or not (i.e., acknowledged by Twitter as an account linked to a user of "public interest"), and whether or not the user still uses the default profile image. A representative example is shown in Figure 4a, which plots the CDF of the number of subscribed lists for each of the four behaviors we

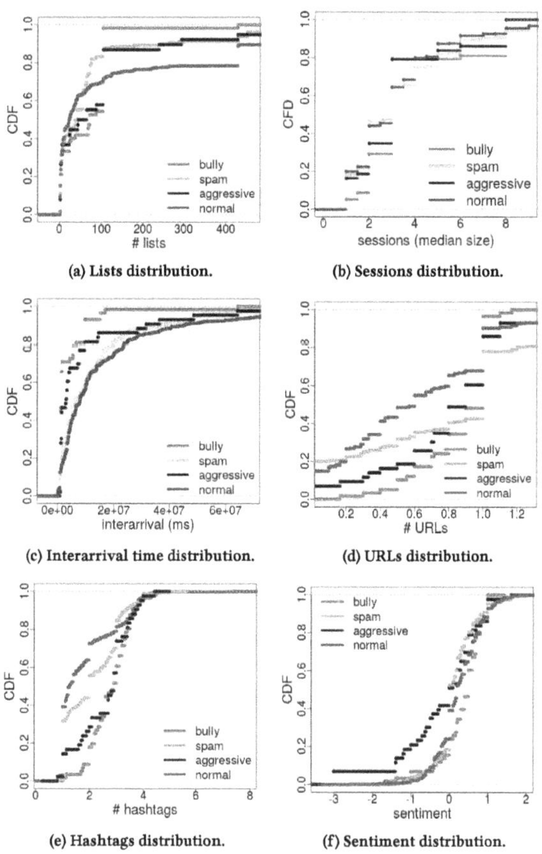

(a) Lists distribution. (b) Sessions distribution. (c) Interarrival time distribution. (d) URLs distribution. (e) Hashtags distribution. (f) Sentiment distribution.

Figure 4: (a) Lists, (b) Sessions size, (c) Interarrival time, (d) URLs, (e) Hashtags, and (f) Sentiment distribution.

examine (the maximum number of lists is 4, 327, but we trim the plot at 500 for readability). The median (max) number of lists for bullying, spam, aggressive, and normal users is 24 (428), 57 (3, 723), 40, (1, 075), and 74 (4, 327), respectively. We note the difference in the participation of groups from each class of users, with normal users signing up to more lists than the other types of users.

Session statistics. Here, we consider the number of sessions produced by a user from June to August and we estimate the average, median and standard deviation of the size of each users' sessions. Figure 4b shows the CDF of the median number of sessions for the 4 behavior classes. Comparing the distributions among the bullies and aggressors to the normal users, we observe that the differences are not statistically significant with D=0.16052 and D=0.14648 for bully vs. normal, and aggressors vs. normal, respectively.

Inter-arrival time. Figure 4c plots the CDF of users posts' inter-arrival time. We observe that bullies and aggressors tend to have less waiting time in their posting activity compared to the spam and normal users, which is in alignment with results in [25].

5.2 Text-based features

For text-based features, we look deeper into a user's tweeting activity by analyzing specific attributes that exist in his tweets.

Basics. We consider some basic metrics across a user's tweets: the number of hashtags used, uppercase text (which can be indicative of intense emotional state or 'shouting'), number of emoticons, and URLs. For each of these, we take the average over all tweets in a users' annotated batch. Figure 4d depicts the CDF of the average number of URLs for the different classes of users. The median value for bully, spam, aggressive, and normal users is 1, 1, 0.9, and 0.6, respectively. The maximum number of URLs between users also varies: for bully and aggressive users it is 1.17 and 2, respectively, while for spam and normal users it is 2.38 and 1.38. Thus, normal users tend to post fewer URLs than the other 3 classes. Also, from Figure 4e we observe that aggressive and bully users have a propensity to use more hashtags within their tweets, as they try to disseminate their attacking message to more individuals or groups.

Word embedding. Word embedding allows finding both semantic and syntactic relation of words, which permits the capturing of more refined attributes and contextual cues that are inherent in human language. E.g., people often use irony to express their aggressiveness or repulsion. Therefore, we use Word2Vec [32], an unsupervised word embedding-based approach to detect semantic and syntactic word relations. Word2Vec is a two-layer neural network that operates on a set of texts to: 1) initially establish a vocabulary based on the words included in such set more times than a user-defined threshold (to eliminate noise), 2) apply a learning model to input texts to learn the words' vector representations in a *D*-dimensional, user-defined space, and 3) output a vector representation for each word encountered in the input texts. Based on [32] 50-300 dimensions can model hundreds of millions of words with high accuracy. Possible methods to build the actual model are: 1) CBOW (i.e., Continuous bag of words), which uses context to predict a target word, and 2) Skip-gram, which uses a word to predict a target context. Skip-gram works well with small amounts of training data and handles rare words or phrases well, while CBOW shows better accuracy for frequent words and is faster to train.

Here, we use Word2Vec to generate features to better capture the context of the data at hand. We use a pre-trained model with a large scale thematic coverage (with 300 dimensions) and apply the CBOW model due to its better performance regarding the training execution time. Finally, having at hand the vector representations of all input texts' words, the overall vector representation of an input text is derived by averaging all the vectors of all its comprising words. Comparing the bully distribution with the normal one we conclude to D=0.094269 and p=0.7231, while in the aggressive vs. normal distribution comparison D=0.11046 and p=0.7024, thus in both cases the differences are not statistically significant.

Sentiment. Sentiment has already been considered during the process of detecting abusive behavior in communications among individuals, e.g., [34]. To detect sentiment, we use the SentiStrength tool [45], which estimates the positive and negative sentiment (on a [-4, 4] scale) in short texts, even for informal language often used on Twitter. First, however, we evaluate its performance by applying it on an already annotated dataset with 7,086 tweets [53]. The overall accuracy is 92%, attesting to its efficacy for our purposes. Figure 4f plots the CDF of average sentiment for the 4 user classes. Even though we observe a distinction among the aggressive and the rest of classes, this is not the case when comparing the remaining three classes, where similar behavior is observed concerning

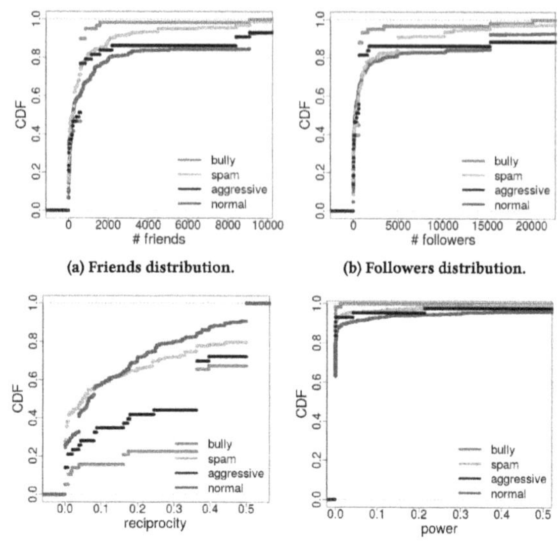

(a) Friends distribution. (b) Followers distribution. (c) Reciprocity distribution. (d) Power difference distribution.

Figure 5: (a) Friends, and (b) Followers distribution, (c) Avg. distribution for Reciprocities, and (d) Power difference.

the expressed sentiments. More specifically, comparing the distributions of the aggressive class with the normal, and bully with normal, they are statistically different (D=0.27425 and D=0.27425, respectively). We also attempt to detect more concrete emotions, i.e., anger, disgust, fear, joy, sadness, and surprise based on the approach presented in [7]. Comparing the distributions of the abusive classes with the normal, in most of cases we observe no statistical difference. For anger, even though the aggressive and normal distributions are statistically different (D=0.21515), the bully and normal users are not (D=0.080029 and p=0.88).

Hate and Curse words. Additionally, we wanted to specifically examine the existence of hate speech and curse words within tweets. For this purpose, we use the Hatebase database (HB) [22], which is a crowdsourced list of hate words. Each word in the HB is additionally scored on a [0, 100] scale indicating how hateful the word is. Finally, a list of swear words [37] is also used in a binary fashion; i.e., we set a variable to true if a tweet contained any word in the list, and false otherwise. Even though these lists can be useful in categorizing general text as hateful or aggressive, they are not well suited for classifying tweets as they are short and typically include modified words, URLs and emoticons. Overall, we find that bully and aggressive users have a minor bias towards using such words, but they are not significantly different from normal users' behavior.

5.3 Network-based features

Twitter social network plays a crucial role in diffusion of useful information and ideas, but also of negative opinions, rumors, and abusive language (e.g., [26, 39]). We study the association between aggressive or cyberbullying behavior and the position of users in the Twitter network of friends and followers. The network is comprised of about 1.2M users and 1.9M friend (i.e., someone who is followed by a user) or follower (i.e., someone who follows a user) edges, with 4.934 effective diameter, 0.0425 average clustering coefficient, and 24.95% and 99.99% nodes in the weakest and largest component, respectively. Users in such a network can have a varying degree of embeddedness with respect to friends or followers, reciprocity of connections, connectivity with different parts of the network, etc.

Popularity. The popularity of a user can be defined in different ways. For example, the number of friends or followers (out- or in-degree centrality), and the ratio of the two measures (since Twitter allows users to follow anyone without their approval, the ratio of followers to friends can quantify a user's popularity). These measures quantify the opportunity for a user to have a positive or negative impact in his ego-network in a direct way. Figures 5a and 5b indicate that bullies have fewer friends and followers than the other user categories, with normal users having the most friends.

Reciprocity. This metric quantifies the extent to which users reciprocate the follower connections they receive from other users. The average reciprocity in our network is 0.2. Figure 5c shows that the user classes considered have different distributions, with the bully and aggressive users being more similar (i.e., higher number of reciprocities) than the normal or spammers. Reciprocity as a feature has also been used in [24], but in an interaction-based graph using likes in posts. Here, we investigate the fundamental reciprocity in Twitter friendship; the first to do this in the context of bullying.

Power Difference. A recent study [41] found that the emotional and behavioral state of victims depend on the power of their bullies, e.g., more negative emotional experiences were observed when more popular cyberbullies conducted the attack, and the high power difference with respect to status in the network has been shown to be a significant characteristic of bullies [12]. Thus, we consider the power difference between a tweeter and his mentions. In fact, a further analysis of a user's mentioned users could reveal possible victims or bystanders of his aggressive or bullying behavior. To this end, we compute the difference in power a user has with respect to the users he mentions in his posts, in terms of their respective followers/friends ratio. Figure 5d shows the distribution of this power difference (we note that the maximum power difference is 20, but we trim the plot for readability). The difference in power between the aggressive (bully) and normal users is statistically significant (D=0.22133 and D=0.31676, respectively).

Centrality Scores. We also investigate users' position in their network through more elaborate metrics such as hub, authority, eigenvector and closeness centrality, that measure influence in their immediate and extended neighborhood, as well as connectivity.

Hubs and Authority. A node's hub score is the sum of the authority score of the nodes that point to it, and authority shows how many different hubs a user is connected with [29].

Influence. Eigenvector centrality measures the influence of a user in his network, immediate or extended over multiple hops. Closeness centrality measures the extent to which a user is close to each other user in the network. To calculate the last four measures, we consider both the followers and friends relations of the users under examination in an undirected version of the network. Figures 6a, 6b, and 6c show the CDFs of the hubs (max value: 0.861), authorities (max value: 0.377), and eigenvector (max value: 0.0041) scores for the four user classes. We observe that bullies have lower values in their hub and authority scores which indicates that they are not so popular in their networks. In terms of influence on their ego and extended network, they have behavior similar to spammers, while

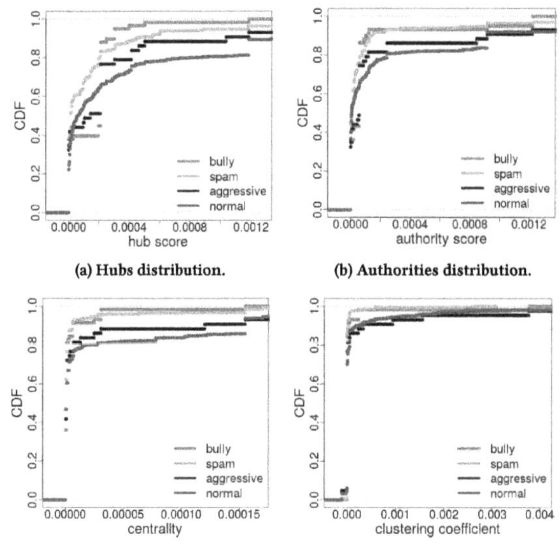

(a) Hubs distribution. (b) Authorities distribution. (c) Eigenvector distribution. (d) Clustering coef. distribution.

Figure 6: Avg. distribution for (a) Hubs, (b) Authorities, (c) Eigenvectors, and (d) Clustering Coefficient.

aggressors seem to have influence more similar to normal users. We omit the CDF of the closeness centrality measure because we cannot reject the null hypothesis that the distributions are different.

Communities. Past work [20] showed that bullies tend to experience social rejection from their environment and face difficulties in developing social relations. We examine the usefulness of this attribute and calculate the clustering coefficient which shows a user's tendency to cluster with others. Figure 6d plots the CDF of the clustering coefficient among the four classes. We observe that bullies, similar to the spammers, are less prone to create clusters in contrast to aggressive and normal users. Finally, we compute communities using the Louvain method [3] which is suitable for identifying groups on large networks as it attempts to optimize the modularity measure (how densely connected the nodes within a cluster are) of a network by moving nodes from one cluster to another. Overall, we observe a few communities with a high number of nodes (especially the network core) resulting in a feature which statistically differentiates bullies vs. normal users (D=0.206), but not aggressive vs. normal users (D=0.1166, p=0.6364).

6 MODELING AGGRESSORS & BULLIES

In this section, we present our efforts to model bullying and aggression behaviors on Twitter, using the features extracted and the labels provided by the crowdworkers as presented earlier.

6.1 Experimental Setup

We considered various machine learning algorithms, either probabilistic, tree-based, or ensemble classifiers (built on a set of classifiers whose individual decisions are then combined to classify data). Due to limited space, we only present the best results with respect to training time and performance, obtained with the Random Forest classifier. For all the experiments presented next, we use the WEKA data mining toolkit and repeated (10 times) 10-fold cross validation [27], providing the relevant standard deviation (STD). We do not balance the data to better match a real-world deployment.

Features selection. Most of the features presented in Section 5 are useful (stat. significant) in discriminating between the user classes. However, some are not useful and are excluded from the modeling analysis to avoid adding noise. Specifically, we exclude the following features from our analysis: *user-based* - verified account, default profile image, statistics on sessions, *text-based* - average emotional scores, hate score, average word embedding, average curse score, and *network-based* - closeness centrality and Louvain modularity.

Tree-based classifiers. Relatively fast compared to other classification models [42], tree classifiers have three types of nodes: (i) *root* node, with no incoming edges, (ii) *internal* nodes, with one incoming edge and two or more outgoing edges, (iii) *leaf* node, with incoming edge and no outgoing edges. The root and each internal node correspond to feature test conditions (each test corresponds to a single feature) for separating data based on their characteristics, while leaf nodes correspond to the available classes. We experimented with various tree classifiers: J48, LADTree, LMT, NBTree, Random Forest (RF), and Functional Tree; we achieved best performance with the RF classifier, which constructs a forest of decision trees with random subsets of features during the classification process. To build the RF model, we tune the number of trees to be generated as 10, and the maximum depth unlimited.

Evaluation. For evaluation purposes, we examine standard machine learning performance metrics: *precision* (prec), *recall* (rec), and weighted area under the ROC curve (AUC), at the class level and overall average across classes. Also, the overall kappa (compares an observed accuracy with an expected accuracy, i.e., random chance), the root mean squared error (RMSE), which measures the differences among the values predicted by the model and the actually observed values, and finally the accuracy values are presented.

Experimentation phases. Two setups are tested to assess the feasibility of detecting user behavior: (i) 4-classes classification: bully, aggressive, spam, and normal users, (ii) 3-classes classification: bully, aggressive, and normal users. This setup examines the case where we filter out spam with a more elaborate technique and attempt to detect the bullies and aggressors from normal users.

6.2 Classification Results

Detecting offensive classes. Here, we examine whether it is possible to distinguish between bully, aggressive, spam, and normal users. Table 2a overviews the results obtained with the RF classifier. In more detail, we observe that the classifier succeeds to detect **43.2%** (STD=0.042) of the bully cases, which is fair enough considering the small number of bully cases identified to begin with (only 4.5% of our dataset). In the aggressive case, we observe that recall is quite low, **11.8%** (STD=0.078). Based on the confusion matrix (omitted due to space limits), the misclassified cases mostly fall in either the normal or bullying classes, which aligns with the human annotations gathered during the crowdsourcing phase. Overall, the average precision is **71.6%**, and the recall is **73.32%**, while the accuracy is **73.45%**, with 0.4717 kappa and 0.3086 RMSE.

	Prec.	Rec.	AUC
bully	0.411	0.432	0.893
(STD)	0.027	0.042	0.009
aggressive	0.295	0.118	0.793
(STD)	0.054	0.078	0.036
spammer	0.686	0.561	0.808
(STD)	0.008	0.010	0.002
normal	0.782	0.883	0.831
(STD.)	0.004	0.005	0.003
overall (avg.)	0.718	0.733	0.815
(STD)	0.005	0.004	0.031

(a) 4-classes classification.

	Prec.	Rec.	AUC
bully	0.555	0.609	0.912
(STD)	0.018	0.029	0.009
aggressive	0.304	0.114	0.812
(STD)	0.039	0.012	0.015
normal	0.951	0.976	0.911
(STD)	0.018	0.029	0.009
overall (avg.)	0.899	0.917	0.907
(STD)	0.016	0.019	0.005

(b) 3-classes classification.

Table 2: Results on 4- and 3-classes classification.

Classifying after spam removal. In this experimental phase, we want to explore whether the distinction between bully/aggressive and normal users will be more evident after applying a more sophisticated spam removal process in the preprocessing step. To this end, we remove from our dataset all the cases identified by the annotators as spam, and re-run the RF modeling and classification. Table 2b shows that, as expected, for bully cases there is an important increase in both the precision (**14.4%**) and recall (**17.7%**). For aggressors, the precision and recall values are almost the same, indicating that further examination of this behavior is warranted in the future. Overall, the average precision and recall of the RF model is **89.9%** and **91.7%**, respectively, while the accuracy is **91.08%** with 0.5284 kappa value and 0.2117 RMSE. Considering a **0.907** AUC, we believe that with a more sophisticated spam detection applied on the stream of tweets, our features and classification techniques can perform even better at detecting bullies and aggressors and distinguishing them from the typical Twitter users.

Discussion on AUC. ROC curves are typically used to evaluate the performance of a machine learning algorithm [15] by testing the system on different points and getting pairs of true positive (i.e., recall) against false positive rates indicating the sensitivity of the model. The resulting area under the ROC curve can be read as the probability of a classifier correctly ranking a random positive case higher than a random negative case. Our model performs well in both setups (Tables 2a and 2b). In the aggressor case, even though the recall value is low, the AUC is quite high because the false positive rate is especially low, with 0.008 and 0.0135 for the 4-class and 3-class classification, respectively. We note that avoiding false positives is crucial to the successful deployment of any automated system aiming to deal with aggressive behavior. Ideally, our classification system's results would be fed to a human-monitored system for thorough evaluation of the suspected users and final decision to suspend them or not, to reduce false positives.

Features evaluation. Table 3 shows the top 12 features for each setup based on information gain. Overall, in both setups the most contributing features tend to be user- and network-based, which describe the activity and connectivity of a user in the network.

Balancing data. Based on [9], and similar to almost all classifiers, Random Forest suffers from appropriately handling extremely imbalanced training dataset (similar to our case) resulting in bias towards the majority classes. To address this issue, we over-sample (based on SMOTE [8], which creates synthetic instances of the minority class) and under-sample (a resampling technique without replacement) at the same time, as it has proven to result in better

Experiment	Feature (preserving order)
4-classes	#friends (11.43%), reciprocity (11.10%), #followers (10.84%) #followers/#friends (9.82%), interarrival (9.35%), #lists (9.11%) hubs (9.07%), #URLs (7.69%), #hashtags (7.02%) authority (6.33%), account age (4.77%), clustering coef. (3.47%)
3-classes	#followers/#friends (12.58%), #friends (12.56%), #followers (11.90%) interarrival (11.67%), reciprocity (11.01%), #lists (9.57%) hubs (8.41%), #hashtags (6.2%), #posts (6.01%) account age (4.13%), #URLs (3.73%), power difference (2.23%)

Table 3: Features evaluation.

	Prec.	Rec.	ROC
bully	1	0.667	0.833
aggressive	0.5	0.4	0.757
normal	0.931	0.971	0.82
overall (avg.)	0.909	0.913	0.817

Table 4: Classification on balanced data.

	active	deleted	suspended
bully	67.24%	32.76%	0.00%
aggressive	65.12%	20.93%	13.95%
normal	86.53%	5.72%	7.75%

(a) Status check on Nov 2016.

	active	deleted	suspended
bully	62.07%	37.93%	0.00%
aggressive	55.81%	25.58%	18.60%
normal	85.01%	6.86%	8.13%

(b) Status check on Feb 2017.

Table 5: Distribution of users' behaviors in twitter statuses.

overall performance [8]. Here, we focus on the 3-class experimentation setup, i.e., without considering the spam user class. After randomly splitting the data into 90% for training and 10% for testing sets, we proceed with the balancing of the training set. The resulting data distribution is 349, 386, and 340 instances for the bully, aggressive, and normal classes, respectively. We note there is no resampling of the test set. Table 4 shows the classification results. After balancing the data, the classifier detects **66.7%** and **40%** of the bully and aggressive cases, respectively, while overall, the accuracy is 91.25%, with 0.5965 kappa and 0.1423 RMSE.

6.3 Twitter Reaction to Aggression

Recently, Twitter has received a lot of attention due to the increasing occurrence of harassment incidents [51]. While some shortcomings have been directly acknowledged by Twitter [50], they do act in some cases. To understand the impact of our findings, we make an estimate of Twitter's current effectiveness to deal with harassment by looking at account statuses. Twitter accounts can be in one of three states: *active*, *deleted*, or *suspended*. Typically, Twitter suspends an account (temporarily or even permanently) if it has been compromised, is considered spam/fake, or if it is *abusive* [1].

After our initial experiments, we checked the current status of all labeled users in our dataset. The status check was performed over two time periods: at the end of November 2016 and February 2017. Tables 5a, 5b show the break down of account statuses for each label for the two time periods. From the more recent time period (February 2017), we observe that the majority of "bad" users in our dataset have suffered no consequences from Twitter: 55.81% of aggressive and 62.07% of cyberbullying accounts were still active. In particular, suspension (Twitter-taken action) and deletion (the user removing his account) statuses exhibit a stark contrast.

While 18.6% of aggressive users are suspended, *no* cyberbullying users are. Instead, bullies tend to delete their accounts proactively (~38%). Comparing the statuses of aggressive users between the two time periods, we see an increase (4.65%) in the percentage of those suspended. This is in alignment with Twitter's recent efforts to combat harassment cases, for instance, by preventing suspended users from creating new accounts [40], or temporarily limiting users for abusive behavior [49]. However, in both time periods, there are *no* suspended bully users. Again, bully users seem to delete their accounts, perhaps in an attempt to prevent suspension. Regardless of the reason, for these users we also observe a 5.17% increase in deleted accounts between the two time periods. The lack of suspension of bully users could because bullying often manifests in a hidden fashion, e.g., within seemingly innocuous criticisms, yet are repetitive (and thus harmful over time) in nature [31].

7 DISCUSSION & CONCLUSION

Although the digital revolution and the rise of social media enabled great advances in communication platforms and social interactions, wider proliferation of harmful behavior has also emerged. Unfortunately, effective tools for detecting harmful actions are scarce, as this type of behavior is often ambiguous in nature and/or exhibited via seemingly superficial comments and criticisms. Aiming to address this gap, this paper presented a novel system geared to automatically classify two kinds of harmful online behavior, cyberaggression and cyberbullying, focusing on Twitter.

We relied on crowd-workers to label 1.5*k* users as normal, spammers, aggressive, or bullies, from a corpus of ~10*k* tweets (distilled from a larger set of 1.6*M* tweets), using an efficient, streamlined labeling process. We investigated 30 features from 3 types of attributes (user, text, network based) characterizing such behavior. We found that bullies are less popular (fewer followers/friends, lower hub, authority, eigenvector scores) and participate in few communities. Although they are not very active as per number of posts overall, when they do become active, they post more frequently than typical users, and do so with more hashtags, URLs, etc. Based on the analysis in [5] they also are older Twitter users based on their account age.

Aggressive users show similar behavior to spammers in terms of number of followers, friends, and hub scores. Similar to bullies, they also do not post a lot of tweets, but exhibit a small response time between postings, and often use hashtags and URLs in their tweets. They also tend to have been on Twitter for a long time, like bullies. However, their posts seem to be more negative in sentiment than bullies or normal users. On the other hand, normal users are quite popular with respect to number of followers, friends, hubs, authorities. They participate in many topical lists, and use few hashtags and URLs. These observations are in line with the intuition that bully and aggressive users tend to attack, in rapid fashion, particular users or groups they target, and do so in short bursts, with not enough duration or content to be detected by Twitter's automated systems. In general, we find that aggressive users are more difficult to characterize and identify using a machine learning classifier than bullies, since sometimes they behave like bullies, but other times as normal or spam users.

We showed that our methodology for data analysis, labeling, and classification can scale up to millions of tweets, while our machine learning model built with a Random Forest classifier can distinguish between normal, aggressive, and cyberbullying users with high accuracy (> 91%). While prior work almost exclusively focused on user- and text-based features (e.g., linguistics, sentiment, membership duration), we performed a thorough analysis of network-based features, and found them to be very useful, as they actually are the most effective for classifying aggressive user behavior (half of the top-12 features in discriminatory power are network-based). Text-based features, somewhat surprisingly, do not contribute as much to the detection of aggression (with an exception of tweet characteristics, such as number of URLs, hashtags, and sentiment).

Finally, we discussed the effectiveness of our detection method by comparing prediction results of the examined users with the suspension and deletion of their accounts as observed in the wild. We found that bullies tend not to have been suspended, but instead, take seemingly proactive measures and delete their accounts. Contrary, aggressors are suspended more often than bullies or normal users, which is in line with recent Twitter efforts to combat harassment by preventing suspended users from creating new accounts [40] or temporarily limiting users for abusive behavior [49].

Acknowledgements This research has been funded by the European Commission as part of the ENCASE project (H2020-MSCA-RISE of the European Union under GA number 691025) and by the EPSRC under grant number N008448. We would also like to thank Andri Ioannou for her feedback throughout this project.

REFERENCES

[1] About suspended accounts. 2017. (2017). goo.gl/asJgpq.
[2] Jeremy Blackburn, Ramanuja Simha, Nicolas Kourtellis, Xiang Zuo, Matei Ripeanu, John Skvoretz, and Adriana Iamnitchi. 2012. Branded with a scarlet "C": cheaters in a gaming social network. In *WWW*.
[3] VD Blondel, JL Guillaume, R Lambiotte, and E Lefebvre. 2011. The Louvain method for community detection in large networks. *Statistical Mechanics: Theory and Experiment* 10 (2011).
[4] Cyberbullying Research Center. 2016. (26 November 2016). goo.gl/7kzSY0.
[5] Despoina Chatzakou, Nicolas Kourtellis, Jeremy Blackburn, Emiliano De Cristofaro, Gianluca Stringhini, and Athena Vakali. 2017. Hate is not Binary: Studying Abusive Behavior of #GamerGate on Twitter. In *ACM Hypertext*.
[6] Despoina Chatzakou, Nicolas Kourtellis, Jeremy Blackburn, Emiliano De Cristofaro, Gianluca Stringhini, and Athena Vakali. 2017. Measuring #GamerGate: A Tale of Hate, Sexism, and Bullying. In *WWW CyberSafety Workshop*.
[7] Despoina Chatzakou, Vassiliki Koutsonikola, Athena Vakali, and Konstantinos Kafetsios. 2013. Micro-blogging Content Analysis via Emotionally-Driven Clustering. In *ACII*.
[8] Nitesh V. Chawla, Kevin W. Bowyer, Lawrence O. Hall, and W. Philip Kegelmeyer. 2002. SMOTE: Synthetic Minority Over-sampling Technique. *Artificial Intelligence Research* 16, 1 (2002).
[9] Chao Chen, Andy Liaw, and Leo Breiman. 2004. Using random forest to learn imbalanced data. *University of California, Berkeley* (2004).
[10] C. Chen, J. Zhang, X. Chen, Y. Xiang, and W. Zhou. 2015. 6 million spam tweets: A large ground truth for timely Twitter spam detection. In *IEEE ICC*.
[11] Ying Chen, Yilu Zhou, Sencun Zhu, and Heng Xu. 2012. Detecting Offensive Language in Social Media to Protect Adolescent Online Safety. In *PASSAT and SocialCom*.
[12] Lucie Corcoran, Conor Mc Guckin, and Garry Prentice. 2015. Cyberbullying or Cyber Aggression?: A Review of Existing Definitions of Cyber-Based Peer-to-Peer Aggression. *Societies* 5, 2 (2015).
[13] CrowdFlower. 2017. (2017). crowdflower.com.
[14] Maral Dadvar, Dolf Trieschnigg, and Franciska Jong. 2014. Experts and machines against bullies: A hybrid approach to detect cyberbullies. In *Canadian AI*.
[15] Jesse Davis and Mark Goadrich. 2006. The relationship between Precision-Recall and ROC curves. In *Machine learning*.
[16] Karthik Dinakar, Roi Reichart, and Henry Lieberman. 2011. Modeling the detection of Textual Cyberbullying. *The Social Mobile Web* 11 (2011).
[17] Nemanja Djuric, Jing Zhou, Robin Morris, Mihajlo Grbovic, Vladan Radosavljevic, and Narayan Bhamidipati. 2015. Hate Speech Detection with Comment Embeddings. In *WWW*.
[18] Maria Giatsoglou, Despoina Chatzakou, Neil Shah, Christos Faloutsos, and Athena Vakali. 2015. Reteeting Activity on Twitter: Signs of Deception. In *PAKDD*.
[19] Dorothy Wunmi Grigg. 2010. Cyber-aggression: Definition and concept of cyberbullying. *Australian Journal of Guidance and Counselling* 20, 02 (2010).
[20] Laura D Hanish, Becky Kochenderfer-Ladd, Richard A Fabes, Carol Lynn Martin, Donna Denning, and others. 2004. Bullying among young children: The influence of peers and teachers. *Bullying in American schools: A social-ecological perspective on prevention and intervention* (2004).
[21] James A Hanley and Barbara J McNeil. 1982. The meaning and use of the area under a receiver operating characteristic (ROC) curve. *Radiology* 143, 1 (1982).
[22] Hatebase database. 2017. (2017). ttps://www.hatebase.org/.
[23] Gabriel Emile Hine, Jeremiah Onaolapo, Emiliano De Cristofaro, Nicolas Kourtellis, Ilias Leontiadis, Riginos Samaras, Gianluca Stringhini, and Jeremy Blackburn. 2017. Kek, Cucks, and God Emperor Trump: A Measurement Study of 4chan's Politically Incorrect Forum and Its Effects on the Web. In *ICWSM*.
[24] Homa Hosseinmardi, Richard Han, Qin Lv, Shivakant Mishra, and Amir Ghasemianlangroodi. 2014. Towards understanding cyberbullying behavior in a semi-anonymous social network. In *IEEE/ACM ASONAM*.
[25] Homa Hosseinmardi, Sabrina Arredondo Mattson, Rahat Ibn Rafiq, Richard Han, Qin Lv, and Shivakant Mishra. 2015. Analyzing Labeled Cyberbullying Incidents on the Instagram Social Network. In *In SocInfo*.
[26] Fang Jin, Edward Dougherty, Parang Saraf, Yang Cao, and Naren Ramakrishnan. 2013. Epidemiological Modeling of News and Rumors on Twitter. In *SNAKDD*.
[27] Ji-Hyun K. 2009. Estimating Classification Error Rate: Repeated Cross-validation, Repeated Hold-out and Bootstrap. *Comput. Stat. Data Anal.* 53, 11 (2009).
[28] Imrul Kayes, Nicolas Kourtellis, Daniele Quercia, Adriana Iamnitchi, and Francesco Bonchi. 2015. The Social World of Content Abusers in Community Question Answering. In *WWW*.
[29] Jon M. Kleinberg. 1999. Hubs, Authorities, and Communities. *Comput. Surveys* 31, 4es, Article 5 (1999).
[30] A. Massanari. 2015. #Gamergate and The Fappening: How Reddit's algorithm, governance, and culture support toxic technocultures. *New Media & Society* (2015).
[31] Lucy McMahon. 2000. Bullying and harassment in the workplace. *International Journal of Contemporary Hospitality Management* 12, 6 (2000).
[32] Tomas Mikolov, Kai Chen, Greg Corrado, and Jeffrey Dean. 2013. Efficient Estimation of Word Representations in Vector Space. *CoRR* abs/1301.3781 (2013).
[33] Meagan Miller. 2016. goo.gl/n1W6nt. (4 Oct 2016).
[34] Vinita Nahar, Sayan Unankard, Xue Li, and Chaoyi Pang. 2012. Sentiment Analysis for Effective Detection of Cyber Bullying. In *APWeb*.
[35] Gonzalo Navarro. 2001. A Guided Tour to Approximate String Matching. *Comput. Surveys* 33, 1 (2001).
[36] Chikashi Nobata, Joel Tetreault, Achint Thomas, Yashar Mehdad, and Yi Chang. 2016. Abusive Language Detection in Online User Content. In *WWW*.
[37] List of Swear Words & Curse Words. 2017. (2017). goo.gl/ur1Ind.
[38] Jerrad Arthur Patch. 2015. *Detecting bullying on Twitter using emotion lexicons.*
[39] J. Pfeffer, T. Zorbach, and K. M. Carley. 2014. Understanding online firestorms: Negative word-of-mouth dynamics in social media networks. *Journal of Marketing Communications* 20, 1-2 (2014).
[40] Pham, Sherisse. 2017. Twitter tries new measures in crackdown on harassment. CNNtech. (7 February 2017). goo.gl/nMi4ZQ.
[41] Stephanie Pieschl, Torsten Porsch, Tobias Kahl, and Rahel Klockenbusch. 2013. Relevant dimensions of cyberbullying - Results from two experimental studies . *Journal of Applied Developmental Psychology* 34, 5 (2013).
[42] J.R. Quinlan. 1986. Induction of Decision Trees. *Machine Learning* 1, 1 (1986).
[43] Rozsa, Matthew 2016. Twitter trolls are now abusing the company's bottom line. goo.gl/SryS3k. (2016).
[44] A Saravanaraj, J. I. Sheeba, and S. Pradeep Devaneyan. 2016. Automatic Detection of Cyberbullying from Twitter. *IJCSITS* 6 (2016).
[45] SentiStrength. 2017. http://sentistrength.wlv.ac.uk/. (2017).
[46] P.K. Smith, J. Mahdavi, M. Carvalho, S. Fisher, S. Russell, and N. Tippett. 2008. Cyberbullying: Its nature and impact in secondary school pupils. In *Child Psychology and Psychiatry*.
[47] stopbullying.gov. 2014. Facts About Bullying. (2014). goo.gl/in5JJB.
[48] Gianluca Stringhini, Christopher Kruegel, and Giovanni Vigna. 2010. Detecting spammers on social networks. In *ACSAC*.
[49] Aatif Sulleyman. 2017. Twitter temporarily limiting users for abusive behaviour. Independent. (16 February 2017). goo.gl/yfJrZn.
[50] The Guardian. 2015. Twitter CEO: We suck at dealing with trolls and abuse. goo.gl/6CxnwP. (2015).
[51] The Guardian. 2016. Did trolls cost Twitter 3.5bn and its sale? goo.gl/2IdA5W. (2016).
[52] Robert S. Tokunaga. 2010. Review: Following You Home from School: A Critical Review and Synthesis of Research on Cyberbullying Victimization. *Computers in Human Behavior* 26, 3 (2010).
[53] UMICH SI650 - Sentiment Classification. 2011. https://inclass.kaggle.com/c/si650winter11. (15 Apr 2011).
[54] Cynthia Van Hee, Els Lefever, Ben Verhoeven, Julie Mennes, Bart Desmet, Guy De Pauw, Walter Daelemans, and Véronique Hoste. 2015. Automatic detection and prevention of cyberbullying. In *Human and Social Analytics*.
[55] A. H. Wang. 2010. Don't follow me: Spam detection in Twitter. In *SECRYPT*.
[56] Jun-Ming Xu, Xiaojin Zhu, and Amy Bellmore. 2012. Fast Learning for Sentiment Analysis on Bullying. In *WISDOM*.

Stateless Puzzles for Real Time Online Fraud Preemption

Mizanur Rahman
Florida Int'l University, USA
mrahm031@fiu.edu

Ruben Recabarren
Florida Int'l University, USA
recabarren@gmail.com

Bogdan Carbunar
Florida Int'l University, USA
carbunar@gmail.com

Dongwon Lee
Penn State University, USA
dongwon@psu.edu

ABSTRACT

The profitability of fraud in online systems such as app markets and social networks marks the failure of existing defense mechanisms. In this paper, we propose **FraudSys**, a real-time fraud preemption approach that imposes Bitcoin-inspired computational puzzles on the devices that post online system activities, such as reviews and likes. We introduce and leverage several novel concepts that include (i) stateless, verifiable computational puzzles, that impose minimal performance overhead, but enable the efficient verification of their authenticity, (ii) a real-time, graph based solution to assign fraud scores to user activities, and (iii) mechanisms to dynamically adjust puzzle difficulty levels based on fraud scores and the computational capabilities of devices. FraudSys does not alter the experience of users in online systems, but delays fraudulent actions and consumes significant computational resources of the fraudsters. Using real datasets from Google Play and Facebook, we demonstrate the feasibility of FraudSys by showing that the devices of honest users are minimally impacted, while fraudster controlled devices receive daily computational penalties of up to 3,079 hours. In addition, we show that with FraudSys, fraud does not pay off, as a user equipped with mining hardware (e.g., AntMiner S7) will earn less than half through fraud than from honest Bitcoin mining.

KEYWORDS

Stateless Puzzle, Online Fraud Preemption

1 INTRODUCTION

The social impact of online services built on information posted by their users has also turned them into a lucrative medium for fraudulently influencing public opinion [8, 17, 21, 24]. The need to aggressively promote disinformation has created a black market for social network fraud, that includes fake opinions and reviews, likes, followers and app installs [4–6, 18, 22, 23, 25]. For instance, in § 3.1, we show that in fraud markets, a fake review can cost between $0.5 and $3 and a fake social networking "like" can cost

WebSci'17, June 25–28, 2017, Troy, NY, USA

DOI: http://dx.doi.org/10.1145/3091478.3091507

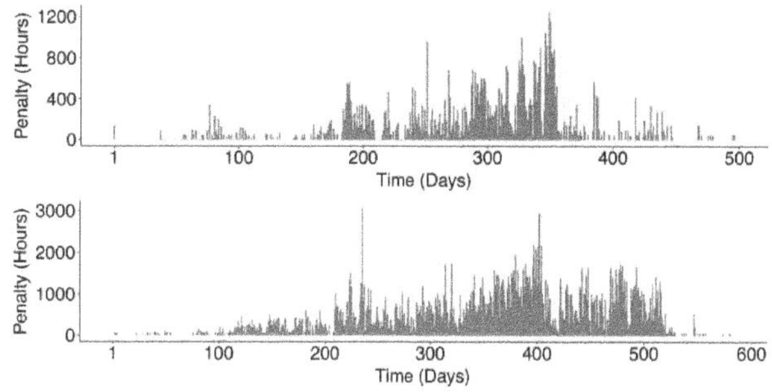

Figure 1: Timeline of daily penalties (in hours) assigned by FraudSys to the Google Play activities of two fraudsters we identified in Freelancer.com. FraudSys imposes daily penalties of up to 1,247 hours to the fraudster at the top and 3,079 hours for the fraudster at the bottom. As a result, the fraudsters need to consume significant computational resources, while their fraud is significantly delayed. This in turn reduces the number of payments they would receive, and impacts their profitability.

$2. The profitability of fraud suggests that current solutions that focus on fraud detection, are unable to control organized fraud.

In this paper we introduce the concept of *fraud preemption systems*, solutions deployed to defend online systems such as social networks and app markets. Instead of reacting to fraud posted in the past, fraud preemption systems seek to discourage fraudsters from posting fraud in the first place. We propose FraudSys, the first real-time fraud preemption system that reduces the profitability of fraud from the perspective of both crowdsourced fraud workers and the people who hire them. FraudSys imposes computational penalties: the activity of a user (e.g., review, like) is posted online only after his device solves a computational puzzle. Puzzles reduce the profitability of fraud by (i) limiting the amount of fraud per time unit that can be posted for any subject hosted on the online system, and (ii) by consuming the computational resources of fraudsters. For instance, Figure 1 shows the timelines of daily penalties assigned by FraudSys to two fraudsters detected in Google Play. Based only on the recorded activities, FraudSys frequently assigned hundreds of hours of daily computational penalties to a single fraudster.

Challenges. Implementing a fraud preemption system raises several challenges. First, FraudSys needs to detect fraud in real-time, whenever a user performs an online system activity. Once assigned, a puzzle cannot be rescinded. This is in contrast to existing systems (e.g., Yelp) that detect fraud retroactively and can update previous decisions when new information surfaces. Second, FraudSys needs to impose difficult puzzles on fraudsters, but minimally impact the experience of honest users. This is made even more complex by the fact that fraudsters can attempt to bypass detection and even obscure their true ability to solve puzzles. Third, a stateful FraudSys service that maintains state for millions of issued and active puzzles is expensive and vulnerable to DoS attacks.

Our Contributions. Through FraudSys, we introduce several innovative solutions. To address the first challenge, we exploit observations of fraudulent behaviors gleaned from crowdsourcing sites and online systems, to propose a real-time graph based algorithm to infer an *activity fraud score*, the chance that a user activity is fraudulent [§ 4.2]. More specifically, we introduce features that group fraudulent activities according to their human creator: FraudSys identifies densely connected components in the co-review graph of the subject targeted by the user activity, each presumably controlled by a different fraudster. It then quantifies the connectivity of the user account performing the action, to each component, and uses the highest connectivity as features that may indicate that the user account and the corresponding component are controlled by the same fraudster. FraudSys then leverages supervised learning algorithms trained on these features to infer the activity fraud score.

To address the second challenge, we develop adaptive hashrate inference techniques to detect the computational capabilities of even adversarial controlled devices to solve puzzles [§ 4.3], and devise mechanisms to convert fraud scores to appropriate temporal penalty and puzzle difficulty values [§ 4.3]. The puzzles assigned by FraudSys do not alter the online experience of users, as they are solved on their devices, in the background. However, the puzzles (1) significantly delay detected fraudulent activities, posted only when the device returns the correct puzzle solutions and (2) consume the computational resources of the fraudsters who control the devices.

To address the third challenge, we propose the notion of *stateless computational puzzles*, computational tasks that impose no storage overhead on the fraud preemption system provider, but enable it to efficiently verify their authenticity and the correctness of their solutions [§ 4.1]. Thus, the fraud preemption system can assign a puzzle to a device from which an activity was performed on the online system, without storing any state about this task. The device can return the results of the puzzle in 5 seconds or 1 day, and the provider can verify that the task is authentic, and its results are correct. This makes our approach resistant to DoS attacks that attempt to exhaust the provider's storage space for assigned puzzles.

We show that the computational penalty imposed by FraudSys on a fraudulent activity is a function of the capabilities of the device from which it is performed, and the probability that the activity is fraudulent. We introduce and prove upper bounds on the profitability of fraud and the amount of fraud that can be created for a single subject, per time unit [§ 5] . We evaluate FraudSys on 23,028 fraudulent reviews (posted by 23 fraudsters from 2,664 user accounts they control), and 1,061 honest reviews we collected from Google Play, as well as 274,297 fake and 180,400 honest likes from Facebook. Even with incomplete data, FraudSys imposes temporal penalties that can be as high as 3,079 hours per day for a single fraudster. We also show that fraud does not pay off. At today's fraud payout, a fraudster equipped with an AntMiner S7 (Bitcoin mining hardware) will earn through fraud less than half the payout of honest Bitcoin mining.

2 RELATED WORK

Computation Based Fraud Preemption. Dwork and Naor [12] were the first to propose the use of computation to prevent fraud, in particular spam, where the sender of an e-mail needs to include the solution to a "moderately hard function" computed over a function of the e-mail. Juels and Brainard [15] proposed to use puzzles to prevent denial of service attacks, while Borisov [11] introduced puzzles that deter Sybils in peer-to-peer networks. In Borisov [11], newly joined peers need to solve a puzzle to which all the other peers have contributed.

FraudSys not only seeks to adapt computational puzzles to prevent online system fraud, but also needs to solve the additional challenges of building puzzles whose difficulty is a function of the probability that an activity is fraudulent, while handling heterogeneous user devices (e.g., ranging from smartphones to machines that specialize in such puzzles).

Graph Based Fraud Detection. Graphs have been used extensively to model relationships and detect fraudulent behaviors in online systems. Ye and Akoglu [26] quantified the chance of a subject to be a spam campaign target, then clustered spammers on a 2-hop subgraph induced by the subjects with the highest chance values. Lu et al. [16] proposed a belief propagation approach implemented on a review-to-reviewer graph, that simultaneously detects fake reviews and spammers (fraudsters).

Mukherjee et al. [19] proposed a suite of features to identify reviewer groups, as users who review many subjects in common but not much else, post their reviews within small time windows, and are among the first to review the subject. Hooi et al. [14] have recently shown that fraudsters have evolved to hide their traces, by adding spurious reviews to popular items. To identify "camouflaged" fraud, Hooi et al. [14] introduced "suspiciousness" metrics that apply to bipartite user-to-item graphs, and developed a greedy algorithm to find the subgraph with the highest suspiciousness. Akoglu et al. [2] survey graph based online fraud detection. [13] provide a survey of community detection methods, evaluation scores and techniques for general networks.

Unlike previous work, FraudSys assigns fraud scores to individual user activities in *real time*, thus uses only partial information. To achieve this, FraudSys develops and leverages features that quantify the connectivity of the user activity to other groups of activities *previously* performed by other fraudsters on the same subject. Further, FraudSys also imposes computation and temporal penalties to discourage fraud creation.

3 SYSTEM AND ADVERSARY MODEL

Figure 2 illustrates the three main components of the system model. First, the online service (the *service*) hosts the system functionality, and stores information about user accounts and featured *subjects*. Subjects can be apps in stores like Google Play, or pages for businesses, accounts and stories in social networks like Facebook.

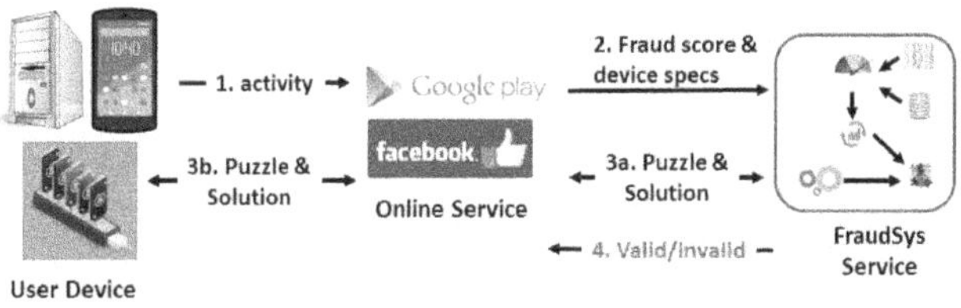

Figure 2: System model. The user performs actions on the online service, from a device that can range from a smartphone to a Bitcoin miner. The online service implements and posts the activity only if and after the FraudSys service validates it. The FraudSys functionality can be implemented by the online service or by a third party provider.

Second, the users: they register with the service, record profile information (e.g., name) and receive initial service credentials, including a unique id. Users can access the online service from a variety of devices. For this, they need to install a client (e.g., app) on each device they use. The online service stores and maintains information about each device that the user has used, e.g., to provide compatibility information on Google Play apps.

Users are encouraged to *act* on existing subjects. The activities include posting reviews, comments, or likes, installing mobile apps, etc. The online service associates statistics over the activities performed for each supported subject. The statistics have a significant impact on the popularity and search rank of subjects [1, 7], thus are targets of manipulation by fraudsters (see § 3.1).

The third component of the system model is the FraudSys service, whose goal is to validate user activities. For increased flexibility, Figure 2 shows FraudSys as an independent provider. However, FraudSys can also be a component of the online service.

3.1 Adversary Model

We consider two types of adversaries – adversarial owners and crowdsourced fraud workers.

Adversarial owners. Adversarial behaviors start with the subject owners. Adversarial owners seek to fraudulently promote their subjects (or demote competitor subjects) in order to bias the popularity and public opinion of specific subjects. For instance, fraudulent promotions seek to make subjects more profitable [3, 17], increase the "reachability" of malware (through more app installs), and boost the impact of fake news.

Fraud workers (= fraudsters). We assume that adversarial owners crowdsource this promotion task (also known as search rank fraud) to *fraud workers*, or fraudsters. In this paper we focus on two types of fraudulent activities: writing fake reviews in Google Play and posting fake "Likes" in Facebook. We have studied fraudster recruitment jobs in crowdsourcing sites and fraud posted in Google Play and Facebook. This has allowed us to collect fraud data (see § 6.1) and to identify several fraud behaviors: (i) more than one fraudster can target the same subject; (ii) user accounts controlled by a fraudster tend to have a significant history of common activities, i.e., performed on the same subjects; and (iii) accounts controlled by different fraudsters tend to have few common past activities.

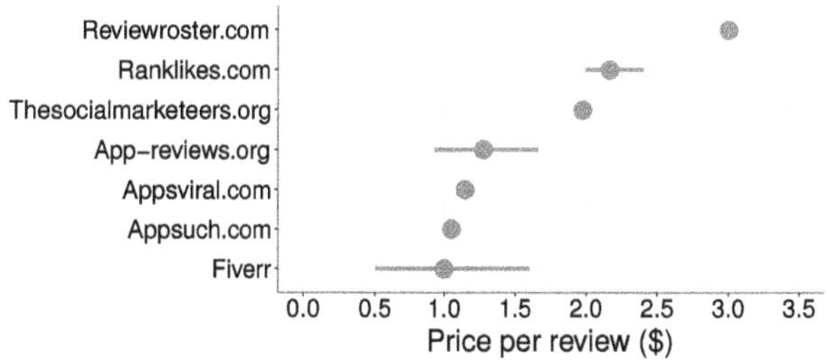

Figure 3: Price per review (minimum, average and maximum), for crowdsourcing sites that focus on app market fraud. The sites offer "fraud packages" and even discounts for bulk fake review purchases. A fake review costs between $0.5-$3.

Fraud incentives. We assume that fraud workers are rational, motivated by financial incentives. That is, given an original investment in expertise and equipment, a fraud worker seeks to maximize his revenue achieved per time unit. Figure 3 shows the minimum, average and maximum cost per fraudulent activity, as advertised by several crowdsourcing and fraud-as-a-service (FAAS) sites: a fake review for an app is worth between $0.5-$3, while a fake social networking "like" can cost $2. In contrast, an adversarial owner may have both financial incentives (e.g., increased market share for his subject, thus revenue), and external incentives (e.g., malware or fake news distribution).

3.2 Fraud Preemption System Definition

We introduce the concept of *fraud preemption systems*, that seek to restrict the profitability of fraud for both fraudsters and the people who hire the fraudsters (i.e., adversarial owners). Specifically, let $Sys = (\mathcal{U}, \mathcal{S}, \mathcal{F}, P)$ be a system that consists of finite sets of users ($\mathcal{U}$), subjects ($\mathcal{S}$) and fraudsters ($\mathcal{F}$) that interact through a set of procedures P. In the adversary model of § 3.1, we say that Sys is a (p,a)-*fraud preemption system* if it satisfies the following two conditions:

1. **Fraudster deterrence**: The average payout per time unit of any fraudster in $\mathcal{F}$ does not exceed p.
2. **Adversarial owner deterrence**: The average number of fraudulent activities allowed for any subject in $\mathcal{S}$ per time unit does not exceed a.

In addition, a puzzle-based fraud preemption system needs to satisfy the following requirements:

1. **Real-time fraud detection.** Detect fraud at the time it is created, with access to only limited information (i.e., no knowledge of the future).
2. **Penalty accuracy.** Impose difficult puzzles on fraudsters, but minimally impact the online experience of honest users.
3. **Device heterogeneity.** Both honest and fraudulent users may register and use multiple devices to access the online service. Malicious users may obfuscate the computational capabilities of their devices.
4. **Minimize system resource consumption.** The high number of issued, active puzzles will consume the resources of the FraudSys provider, and open it to DoS attacks.

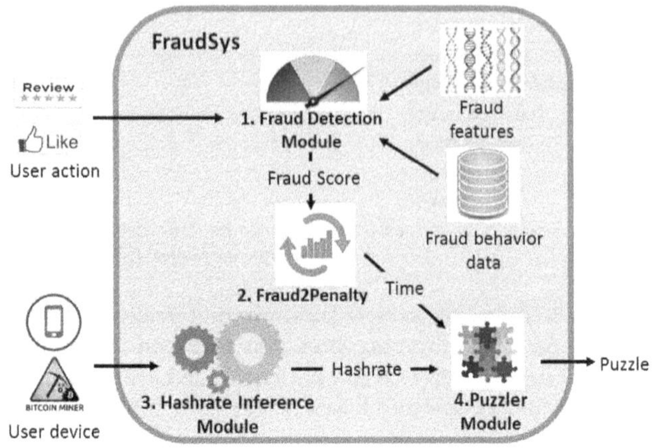

Figure 4: FraudSys architecture. The Fraud Detector module uses supervised learning to assign a fraud score to user activities. The Fraud2Penalty module converts the fraud score to a *time penalty*. The Hashrate Inference module estimates the computational capabilities of the user device. Finally, the Puzzler module generates a puzzle that the device should take approximately the time penalty to solve.

4 FRAUDSYS

We introduce FraudSys, a real-time fraud preemption system that requires users to verify commitment through an imposed resource consumption action for each activity they perform on the online system. Specifically, FraudSys requires the device from which the activity was issued, to solve a *computational puzzle*. FraudSys consists of the modules illustrated in Figure 4: The Fraud Detection module takes as input a user activity and the current state of the subject, and outputs a *fraud score*. The Fraud2Penalty module converts the fraud score to a *time penalty*: the time that the user's device will need to spend working on a computational puzzle. The Hashrate Inference module interacts with the user device in order to learn its puzzle solving capabilities. Finally, the Puzzler module uses the inferred device capabilities to generate a puzzle that the device will take a time approximately equal to *time penalty* to solve.

To address requirement #1, the Fraud Detection module exploits the fraudulent behaviors described in § 3.1. It builds *co-activity graphs* and extracts features that model the relationships between the user performing the activity and other users that have earlier performed similar activities for the same subject.

We address requirement #2 through a two-pronged approach. First, the Fraud Detection and Fraud2Penalty modules ensure that the difficulty of a FraudSys puzzle will be a function of the detected probability of fraud: activities believed to be honest will be assigned trivial puzzles, while increasingly fraudulent activities will be assigned increasingly difficult puzzles. Second, FraudSys does not change the experience of the user on the online system: the user writes the review or clicks on the like button, then continues browsing or quits the app. The assigned puzzle is solved in the background by the device on which the activity was performed. However, FraudSys delays the publication of the activity, until the device produces the correct puzzle solution.

Notation	Definition
U, D, S, A	user, device, subject, activity
T	time of puzzle issue
r	activity fraud score
Δ	puzzle difficulty
η_D	hashrate of device D
Γ	puzzle cookie
Π	puzzle
$target$	puzzle target value
τ	temporal penalty
q	number of shares (puzzle solutions)
K	secret key of FraudSys

Table 1: FraudSys symbol table.

To address requirement #3, the Hashrate Inference module estimates the hashrate of the device performing the activity, and provides the tool to punish devices that cheat about their puzzle solving capabilities. To solve requirement #4, the Puzzler module generates puzzles that outsource the storage constraints from the FraudSys service to the user devices that solve the puzzles. In the following we detail each FraudSys module, starting with the central puzzle creation module.

4.1 The Puzzler Module: Stateless Puzzles

Let U be a user that performs an activity A from a device D, on a subject S hosted by the online service. Table 1 summarizes the notations we use. The FraudSys service stores minimal state for each registered user, and *serializes* his activities, see Figure 5: the devices from which a user performs a sequence of activities on the online service, are assigned one puzzle per activity, each with its own timeout. The device needs to return the puzzle solutions before the associated timeout. To implement this, for each user U, the FraudSys service stores the following entry:

$$U, [\langle D_i, \eta_i \rangle]_{i=1..d}, timeout,$$

where, for each of the $i = 1..d$ devices registered by U, D_i is the device identifier and η_i is its hashrate (puzzle solving capabilities measure, see following), and $timeout$ is the latest time by which one of these devices needs to return puzzle solutions.

FraudSys builds on the computational puzzles of Bitcoin, see [20]. Let $H^2(M)$ denote the double SHA-256 hash of a message M. Then, the FraudSys puzzle issued to device D consists of a $target$ value and a fixed string F. We detail F shortly. To solve the puzzle, D needs to randomly choose 32 byte long *nonce* values until it finds at least one that satisfies:

$$H^2(nonce||F) < target \tag{1}$$

That is, the double hash of the *nonce* concatenated with F, needs to be smaller than the $target$ value, another 32 byte long value. A smaller $target$ implies a harder puzzle. The largest $target$ acceptable by the system is called *target_1*, or *target of difficulty 1*.

Bitcoin has two drawbacks. First, the current difficulty of Bitcoin puzzles requires computational capabilities that greatly exceed those of devices used to access online services. Second, Bitcoin requires the network to maintain state about issued puzzles. State storage exposes FraudSys to attacks, while not storing state

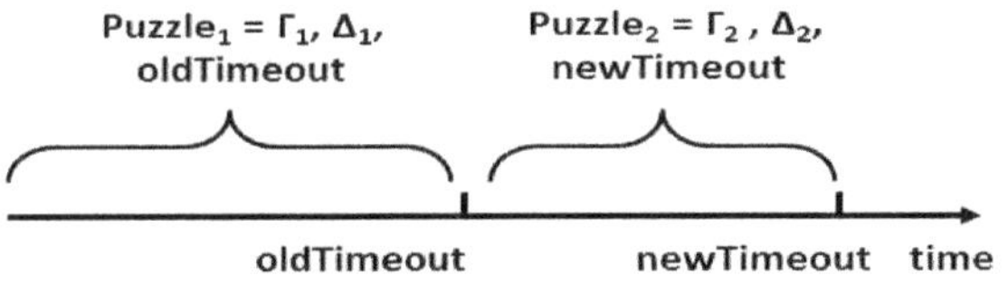

Figure 5: Puzzle serialization: a user can perform multiple activities, but each receives a different puzzle with its own timeout, authenticated through the cookie Γ.

can enable adversaries to lower the difficulty of their assigned puzzles. To address these problems we (i) change the *target_1* difficulty to allow trivial puzzles, and (ii) introduce *puzzle cookies*, special values that authenticate puzzles with minimal FraudSys state, see following.

Device hashrate and puzzle difficulty. We set the *target_1* value to be a 32 byte long value with one zero at the beginning, e.g., $2^{255} - 1$. In addition, the *hashrate* η_D of a device D is a measure that describes the ability of the device to solve puzzles. Since the puzzles need to be solved in a brute force approach, the hashrate is measured in hashes per second. A relevant concept is the notion of *difficulty*, denoted by Δ, a measure of how difficult it is to solve a puzzle whose input values hash below a given target. Its relationship to the above *target* value is given by:

$$\Delta = \frac{target\_1}{target} = \frac{2^{255} - 1}{target} \tag{2}$$

Given η_D, we derive the time τ taken by D to solve a puzzle with difficulty Δ, as follows. First, the number of hashes smaller than a given target is equal to the target. For instance, the number of hashes smaller than *target_1* is $2^{255} - 1$. Then, the probability p of finding an input that hashes to a value smaller than the target is equal to the target divided by the total number of hashes (2^{256}). Furthermore, the expected number of hashes, E, before achieving the target is given by $1/p$. Thus:

$$E = \eta_D \times \tau = \frac{2^{256}}{target} = \frac{2^{256}}{target\_1} \times \frac{target\_1}{target} \approx 2 \times \Delta$$

and conclude that

$$\tau = \frac{2 \times \Delta}{\eta_D} \tag{3}$$

For instance, the lowest puzzle difficulty is 1, which occurs when the *target* has a prefix of one zero and the device is expected to generate 2 hashes before solving the puzzle. Similarly, the maximum difficulty is $(2^{255} - 1)$, for a $target = 1$, when the device is expected to perform $\frac{2^{255}-1}{1} \times 2 \approx 2^{256}$ hashes.

The FraudSys puzzle and cookies. To minimize the storage imposed on the FraudSys service (see above), we leverage the cookie concept [10]. Algorithm 1 illustrates the puzzle creation, verification and computation components. The FraudSys service generates and stores a secret key K (line 2). When a user U performs an activity A from a device D on a subject S of the online service, the online service calls the BuildCookie function of the FraudSys service (lines 3-11). BuildCookie retrieves the hashrate of the device D from the record stored by FraudSys for U (line 4). It then computes the fraud score associated to the activity (line 5) then converts it to a time penalty τ (line 6). We describe this functionality in the next subsections. BuildCookie then uses a modified Equation 3 to compute the difficulty Δ that the puzzle should have (line 7). Δ is q times smaller than in Equation 3, as the puzzle solution consists of q shares, see SolvePuzzle. BuildCookie gets the current timeout *oldT* of U, and updates it to *newT* by adding the penalty τ to it (lines 8-9). It then computes the puzzle cookie Γ,

$$\Gamma = HMAC_K(U, D, S, A, timeout, \Delta)$$

as a keyed HMAC [9] over the user and device id, subject, activity, new timeout and puzzle difficulty (lines 9-10). BuildCookie sets U's timeout value to the updated *newT* value (line 11), then returns the following puzzle (line 12) to the online service that forwards it to device D (see Figure 2):

$$\Pi = \Gamma, \Delta, timeout.$$

The puzzle cookie ensures that an adversary that modifies the puzzle's difficulty or timeout, will be detected: the adversary does not know the key K, which is a secret of the FraudSys service. Puzzle cookies are unique with high probability, due to collision resistance properties of the HMAC, whose input is non-repeating.

Algorithm 1 FraudSys puzzle creation, verification and computation components.

1. Object **FraudSysService**
2. K: key;
3. Function **BuildCookie**(U, D, S, A, q)
4. η_D := getHashrate(U, D);
5. r := computeFraudScore(U, S, A);
6. τ := fraud2Penalty(r);
7. $\Delta := \eta_D \times \tau / 2q$
8. $oldT$:= getTimeout(U);
9. $newT := oldT + \tau$;
10. Γ := HMAC(K, U, D, S, $newT$, Δ, A);
11. setTimeout(U, $newT$);
12. return Γ, Δ, $newT$;
13. Function **VerifyPuzzle**(U, D, S, A, $timeout$, Γ, σ: share[q])
14. **if** (Γ != HMAC(K, U, D, S, A, $timeout$, Δ) return -1;
15. $target$:= getTarget(Δ);
16. **for** (i := 0; $i < q$; i++)
17. **if** ($H^2(\sigma[i] \mid\mid \Gamma) > target$) return -1;
18. waitUntil($timeout$); post A;
19. $\tau' := T_c - T$;
20. **if** (($\eta_D := 2\Delta/\tau') \geq \eta_{min}$)
21. updateHashrate(U, D, η_D);
22. Object **UserDevice**
23. Function **SolvePuzzle**(Γ, Δ, $timeout$, q)
24. $target$:= getTarget(Δ);
25. σ := new share[q]; i := 0;
26. **while** ($i < q$) **do**
27. $nonce$:= getRandom();
28. **if** ($H^2(nonce \mid\mid \Gamma) < target$)
29. $\sigma[i] := nonce$;
30. $i := i$+1;
31. return U, D, S, A, $timeout$, Γ, σ;

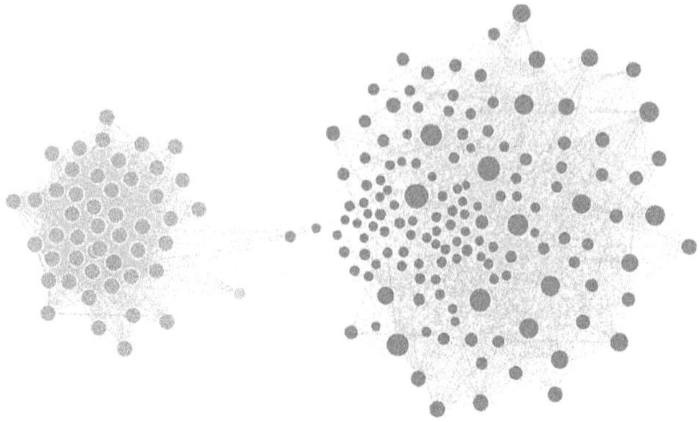

Figure 6: Visualization of the co-review graph of a fraudulent Google Play app. The nodes represent user accounts; edges connect nodes corresponding to accounts with common, past review activities. The nodes in each of the 2 clusters correspond to accounts controlled by the same fraudster.

Solving the puzzle. When the device D receives the puzzle, it needs to solve it: search for q *nonce* values that satisfy the inequality $H^2(nonce \parallel \Gamma) < target$, for a *target* corresponding to the difficulty Δ. Specifically, D invokes the SolvePuzzle function (lines 23-31), that needs to identify q *shares*, i.e., nonce values that satisfy the puzzle. q is a system parameter. The function first uses Equation 2 to retrieve the *target* value corresponding to the difficulty Δ (line 24). Then, it generates random *nonce* values until it identifies q values that satisfy the puzzle condition (lines 25-30). SolvePuzzle returns the identified shares (in the σ array), which are then sent to the online service and forwarded to the FraudSys server, along with the user, device and subject ids, activity, timeout and cookie of the received puzzle (see line 12 and Figure 2).

Verification of puzzle correctness. Upon receiving these values, the FraudSys server invokes the VerifyPuzzle function (lines 13-21), to verify its correctness as follows: (1) Reconstruct the puzzle cookie Γ based on the received values and the secret key K. Verify that this cookie is equal to the received Γ value (line 14). This ensures that all values, including the *timeout* have not been altered by an adversary; and (2) Verify that each of the q shares satisfy the puzzle (lines 15-17). If these verifications succeed, FraudSys waits until *timeout* expires to confirm the user action A, for posting by the online service (line 18). It then uses the time required by the device to solve the puzzle, to re-evaluate the hashrate of the device (lines 19-20). It updates the stored hashrate only if the new value is above a minimally accepted hashrate value (lines 20-21).

4.2 The Fraud Detection Module

To assign a fraud score to a user activity in real-time, the fraud detection module can only rely on the existing history of the user and of the subject on which the activity is performed. We propose an approach that builds on the *co-activity graphs* of subjects, where nodes correspond to user accounts that performed activities on the subject, and edges connect nodes whose user accounts have a history of activities that targeted the same subjects. Edge weights denote the size of that history. Figure 6 shows the co-review (where activities are reviews) graph of a fraudulent Google Play app, that

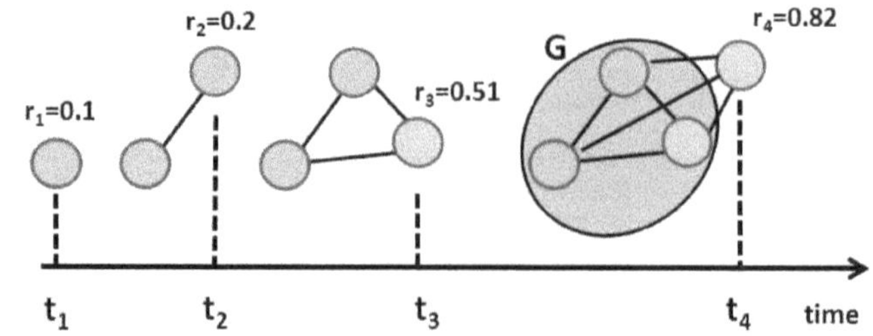

Figure 7: Fraud detection illustration: temporal evolution of the co-activity graph of a subject. The nodes represent user accounts that have performed an activity on the subject. Edges connect accounts with common past activities. As a new user account posts an activity, FraudSys assigns the activity a fraud score (the $r_1..r_4$ values), based on its connectivity to previous activities. Yellow nodes are considered fraudulent ($r > 0.5$).

received fake reviews from 2 fraud workers. Each cluster is formed by accounts controlled by one of the workers.

The fraud detection module leverages the adversary model findings (§ 3.1) that a fraudster-controlled user account that performs a new activity on a subject, is likely to be well connected to the co-activity graph of the subject, or at least one of its densely connected sub-graphs. Figure 7 illustrates this approach: Let U be a user account that performs an activity A for a subject S at time T. Let $G = (V, E)$ be the co-activity graph of S before time T. Let $G_T = (V_T, E_T)$ be the new co-activity graph of S, that also includes U, i.e., $V_T = V \cup U$. Given U, S and G, FraudSys extracts the following features, that model the relationship of U with S:

- **Connectivity features.** The percentage of nodes in V to whom U is connected. The average weight of the edges between U and the nodes in V. The average weight of those edges divided by the average weight of the edges in E. This feature will indicate if U increases or decreases the overall connectivity of G. The number of triangles in G_T that have U as a vertex. The average edge weight of those triangles.
- **Best fit connectivity features.** Since U may be controlled by one of multiple fraudsters who target S, U may be better connected to the subgraph of G controlled by that fraudster. Then, use a weighted min-cut algorithm to partition G into components $G_1, .., G_k$, such that any node in a component is more densely connected to the nodes in the same component than to the nodes in any of the other components. $G_1, .., G_k$ may contain user accounts controlled by different fraudsters, see Figure 6. Identify the component G_b, $b \in \{1, ..k\}$ to which U is the most tightly connected (according to the above connectivity features). Output the connectivity features between U and G_b.
- **Account based features.** The number of activities previously performed by U. The age of U: the time between U's creation and the time when activity A is performed on S. The *expertise* of U: the number of actions of U for subjects similar to S. Similarity depends on the online service, e.g., same category apps in Google Play, pages with similar topics in Facebook.

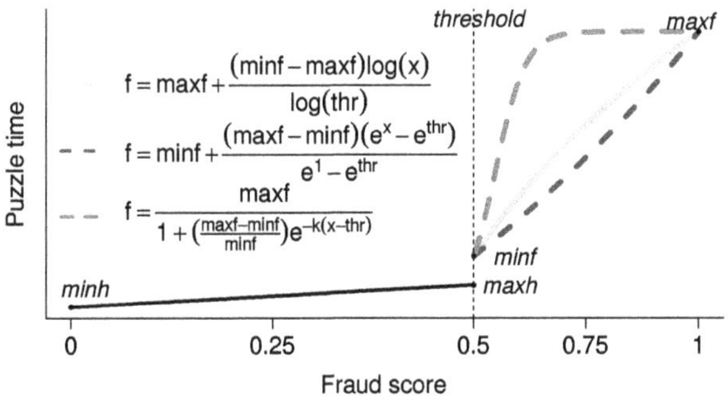

Figure 8: Comparison of functions to convert fraud scores (x axis) to time penalties (y axis). The logistic function (red dot-line) exhibits the required exponential increase.

The Fraud Detection module trains a probabilistic supervised learning algorithm on these features and uses the trained model to output the probability that a given activity is fraudulent. We detail the performance of various algorithms, over data that we collected from Google Play and Facebook, in § 6.

Per-fraudster timeout. We exploit the ability of the fraud detection module to identify accounts controlled by the same fraudster, to further restrict fraud. Specifically, instead of storing a *timeout* timestamp for each user account, FraudSys can store a single *timeout* per detected fraudster. Thus, FraudSys will accumulate penalties in a single, per-fraudster account. This facilitates Claim 2.

4.3 The Fraud2Penalty Module

Given the fraud score r of an activity of user U (output by the Fraud Detection module), performed from a device D associated with the account of U (see the model section), the Puzzler module generates a puzzle whose difficulty is a function of both r and the computational capability of D. We now describe the Fraud2Penalty module, that converts r into a time penalty. We have explored several functions to convert the fraud score r of a user activity to a time penalty. Let $minh$ and $maxh$, and $minf$ and $maxf$, denote the minimum and maximum times imposed on the device from which an honest, respectively fraudulent activity is performed. Let thr denote the threshold fraud score above which we start to consider a user activity as being fraudulent. We propose a conversion function that increases linearly when $r < thr$, and exponentially when $r > thr$. Specifically, we propose a flexible generalization of the logistic function (when $r > thr$), where the parameter k is the *growth rate*:

$$\begin{cases} \frac{maxh-minh}{thr} r + minh & 0 \le r \le thr \\ \frac{maxf}{1+(\frac{maxf-minf}{minf})e^{-k(r-thr)}} & thr \le r \le 1 \end{cases} \quad (4)$$

We have compared this logistic increase function with other functions, with the same linear increase in the honest region, but exponential $((maxf - minf)\frac{e^r - e^{thr}}{e^1 - e^{thr}} + minf)$ and logarithmic $((minf - maxf)\frac{log r}{log(thr)} + maxf)$ increase in the fraudulent regions. Figure 8 compares the logistic, exponential and logarithmic functions. It shows that unlike the exponential and logarithmic functions, the logistic function exhibits the desired rapid increase for fraud probability values above the threshold value. In § 6 we detail parameter values for the logistic conversion function,

4.4 The Hashrate Inference Module

New device registration. When a user registers a new device, the device sends its specs to the online service that forwards them to FraudSys. FraudSys leverages its list of profiled devices (see Table 2) to retrieve the hashrate of the profiled device with the most similar capabilities. FraudSys stores the new device along with this initial hashrate estimate under the id of the user that registers it (see the Puzzle module). Given this hashrate and the above time penalty, FraudSys uses Equation 3 to compute an initial puzzle difficulty.

Hashrate correction. The initial hashrate estimate of FraudSys may be incorrect. In addition, as discussed in the System Model, the user may be adversarial, thus attempt to provide an inaccurate view of the puzzle solving capabilities of his device. To address these problems, FraudSys employs an adaptive hashrate correction process. Specifically, an adversary with a more capable device than advertised (see e.g., Table 2) will solve the assigned puzzle faster. The incentive for this is a shorter wait time for his activity to post on the online service. If this occurs, FraudSys increases its device hashrate estimate to reflect the observed shorter time required by the device to solve the puzzle (see Algorithm 1, lines 19-20).

5 FRAUDSYS PROPERTIES

Claim 1. *A fraudster that performs a fraudulent activity with fraud score r from a device with hashrate η, is expected to compute* $\frac{\eta \times maxf}{1+(\frac{maxf-minf}{minf})e^{-k(r-thr)}}$ *double hashes.*

Proof. According to Equation 4, the time penalty assigned to a fraudulent activity with score r is $\tau = \frac{maxf}{1+(\frac{maxf-minf}{minf})e^{-k(r-thr)}}$. Then, Equation 3 ensures that the number of expected hashes that the device needs to perform to solve the puzzle of Equation 1 is $\eta \times \tau$, which concludes the proof. □

Let f be the number of fraud workers in the system (i.e., $f = |\mathcal{F}|$), τ be the average temporal penalty assigned by FraudSys to a fraudulent activity, and let p be the expected payout for a single fraudulent activity. We introduce then the following claim:

Claim 2. *FraudSys is a $(p/\tau, f/\tau)$-fraud preemption system.*

Proof. The best fit connectivity features of the Fraud Detection module (see § 4.2) enable FraudSys to detect activities performed from accounts controlled by the same fraudster. This, coupled with an extension of the *timeout* concept applied at the fraudster level (see § 4.2) ensures a serialization of fraudster activities. Then, the average number of fraudulent activities that a fraudster can post per time unit in FraudSys is $1/\tau$. This implies that, per time unit, the expected payout of a fraudster is p/τ, and a subject can be the target of at most f/τ fraudulent activities. This, according to the definition of § 3.2, completes the proof. □

5.1 Security Discussion and Limitations

The FraudSys puzzle not only ties the penalty computation to the user activity, but also addresses pre-computation, replay and guessing attacks: the adversary cannot predict the cookie value of its actions, thus cannot pre-compute puzzles and cannot reuse old cookies. It also offloads significant work from the FraudSys service, which no longer needs to keep track of puzzle assignments.

Device deception. An adversary with a specialized puzzle solving device (e.g., AntMiner) will be assigned puzzles with large difficulty values (see, e.g., Table 2), thus consume the same amount of time as when using a resource constrained device (e.g., a smartphone). The adversary can exploit this observation to avoid the implications of Claim 1: register a resource constrained device, but rely on a powerful back-end device to solve the assigned puzzles faster. The adversary has two options. First, report the solutions as soon as the back-end device retrieves them. In this case however, the adversary leaks his true capabilities, as FraudSys will update the adversary hashrate (Algorithm 1, line 20). Thus, subsequently, his assigned puzzles will have a significantly higher difficulty value. In a second strategy, the adversary estimates the time that his front-end device would take to complete the puzzle, then waits the remaining penalty time. In this case, the adversary incurs two penalties, the long wait time and the underutilized back-end device investment.

Adversary strategies: new user accounts. To avoid the implications of Claim 2, the adversary registers new user accounts. While new accounts are cheap, their freshness and lack of history will enable the account based features of the Fraud Detection module to label them as being likely fraudulent. As the adversary reuses such accounts, the connectivity features start to play a more important role in labeling their activities as fraudulent. Thus, the adversary has a small usable window of small penalties for new accounts.

While new honest accounts may also be assigned larger penalties for their first few activities, they will not affect the user experience: the user can continue her online activities, while her device solves the assigned puzzle in the background.

6 EMPIRICAL EVALUATION

6.1 Datasets

We have collected the following datasets of fraudulent and honest behaviors from Google Play and Facebook.

Google Play: fraud behavior data. We have identified 23 workers in Freelancer, Fiverr and Upwork, with proven expertise on performing fraud on Google Play apps. We have contacted these workers and collected the ids of 2,664 Google Play accounts controlled by them. We have also collected 640 apps heavily reviewed from those accounts, with between 7 and 3,889 reviews, of which between 2% and 100% (median of 50%) were written from accounts controlled by the workers. These apps form our gold standard *fraud app* dataset. We have also collected the 23,028 fake reviews written from the 2,664 fraudster controlled accounts for the 640 apps. Figure 6 shows the co-review graph of one of these apps, that received fake reviews from 2 of the identified 23 workers.

Device	Hashrate	Diff (5s)	(12hr)	(7 day)
Nexus 4	6.53 KH/s	16.32K	141.04M	1.97G
Nexus 5	13.26 KH/s	33.15K	286.41M	4.00G
LG Leon LTE	10.1 KH/s	25.25K	218.16M	3.05G
NVS 295	1.7MH/s	4.25M	36.72G	514.08G
Server	80 MH/s	200M	1.72T	24.19T
AntMiner	4.72 TH/s	11.8T	101.95P	1427P

Table 2: Hashrate profiling table for various device types (smartphone, tablet, PC and Bitcoin miner), along with difficulty values for penalty times of 5s, 12 hours and 7 days.

Google Play: honest behavior data. We have selected 925 candidate apps that have been developed by Google designated "top developers". We have removed the apps whose apks (executables) were flagged as malware by VirusTotal. We have manually investigated 601 of the remaining apps, and selected a set of 200 apps that (i) have more than 10 reviews and (ii) were developed by reputable media outlets (e.g., NBC, PBS) or have an associated business model (e.g., fitness trackers). We call these the gold standard *benign app dataset*.

We have identified 600 reviewers of these 200 benign apps and 140 reviewers of the 640 fraud apps (see above), such that each has reviewed at least 10 paid apps, i.e., paid to install the app, then reviewed it, and had at least 5 posts on their associated Google Plus (social network) accounts. These 740 user accounts form our gold standard *honest user dataset*. We have then retrieved and manually vetted 854 reviews written by the 600 honest reviewers for the 200 benign apps, and 207 reviews written by the 140 honest reviewers of the 640 fraud apps. Each selected review is informative, containing both positive and negative sentiment statements. We call the resulting dataset, the *honest review dataset*, with 1,061 reviews.

Facebook Like dataset. We have used a subset of the dataset from [8], consisting of 15,694 Facebook pages, that each has received at least 30 likes. The pages were liked from 13,147 user accounts, of which 6,895 are fraudster controlled, and 6,252 are honest. In total, these fraudsters have posted 274,297 fake likes, and the honest accounts have posted 180,400 honest likes.

6.2 Device Hashrate Profile

Strategy	FPR%	FNR%	Accuracy%
k-NN	1.41	4.45	97.92
SVM	5.8	11.3	92.40
Random Forest	3.44	6.46	95.69

Table 3: 10-fold cross validation results of supervised learning algorithms in fraud vs. honest Google Play review classification. k-NN achieves the lowest FPR and FNR.

We have profiled the hashrate of several devices, ranging from smartphones to a Bitcoin mining hardware (AntMiner S7: ARMv7 CPU, 254 Mb of RAM, 135 BM1385 chips @ 700MHz). Since Bitcoin mining requires capabilities far exceeding those of smartphones, we have implemented an Android app to evaluate the hashrate of several Android devices. Table 2 shows the hashrate values for the profiled devices, along with the corresponding difficulty (Δ) values for puzzles required to impose 5 second, 12 hour and 7 day

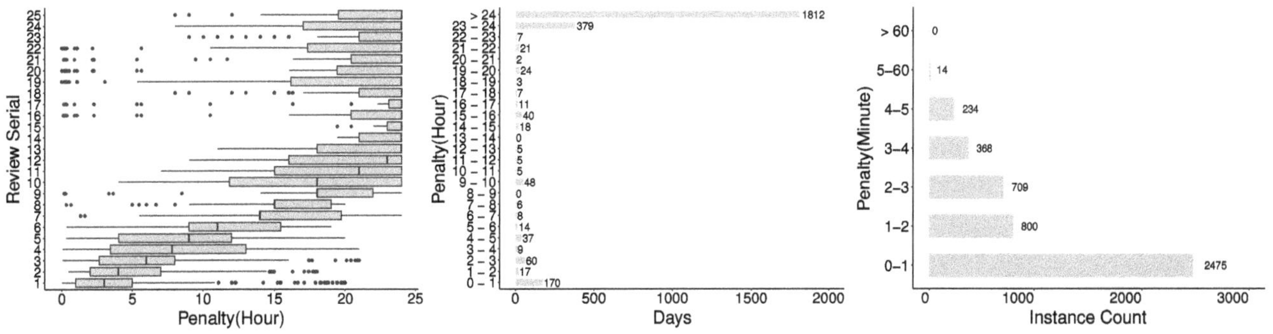

Figure 9: Stats over the Google Play data when *maxf* = 24h, *minh* = 2s, *maxh* = *minf* = 5min. (a) Evolution of average, 1st and 3rd quartile of the penalty imposed on the *i*-th fraud activity of a fraudster for the same subject. It shows a steep increase: the average penalty of the first three fraud activities for a subject sums to 15.34h, while the average penalty of the 12th activity exceeds 24h. (b) Distribution of per-fraudster daily penalties, over data from 23 fraudsters: in 1,812 days out of 2,708 days, the penalty assigned to a single fraudster exceeds 24 hours. (c) Distribution of penalties assigned to an honest review. Only 14 out of 4,600 honest review instances received a penalty exceeding 5 minutes, but still below 1 hour.

time penalties on such devices. We observe the significant gap between the hashrate of a smartphone (10-15 KH/s) and a specialized device (4.72 TH/s). This motivates the need for the puzzles issued by FraudSys to have different Δ values for various user devices. FraudSys maintains a similar table in order to be able to build appropriate puzzles for newly registered devices.

6.3 Fraud Penalty Evaluation: Google Play

Supervised learning algorithm choice. We first used 10 fold cross-validation to evaluate the ability of the Fraud Detection module to correctly classify the 23,028 fraudulent vs. 1,061 honest reviews of the Google Play dataset previously described. Table 3 shows the false positive (FPR) and negative (FNR) rates, as well as the accuracy achieved by the top 3 performing supervised algorithms. k-NN has the lowest FPR and FNR, for an accuracy of 97.92%. Thus, in the following experiments we use only k-NN.

Parameter evaluation. We have used the fraud and honest review datasets described earlier, to compute the temporal penalties imposed by FraudSys on fraudsters and honest users. We have performed the following experiments. In each experiment, we use the data of 22 fraud workers and 200 randomly chosen honest reviews (out of 1,061) to train the supervised learning algorithm (k-NN) then test the model on the data of the remaining fraud worker and on the remaining 861 honest reviews. Thus, we have performed 23 experiments, one for each worker.

We set the $maxf$ parameter such that the average daily payout of a fraudster is below the average Bitcoin mining payout with a last generation AntMiner device. Thus, this ensures that even such a powerful adversary has more incentive to do Bitcoin mining instead of search rank fraud. Specifically, the above AntMiner's current (Jan. 2017) average daily payout is 0.0037 BTC. At the current BTC to USD rate, this means $3.67 per day [1]. In addition, we have experimented with $maxf$ values ranging from 12 to 48 hours. The average penalty assigned by FraudSys to a fraudulent review is 8.01 hours when $maxf$=12h, 15.34h when $maxf$=24h, and 29.33h when $maxf$=48h. Figure 9a shows the median, first and third quartiles for the time penalty (in hours) imposed on the i-th fraudulent activity performed by a fraudster for a subject, when $maxf$= 24h: the 12th fake activity receives a median penalty of 24h.

Thus, we set $maxf$=24h, which is sufficient for Google Play reviews: A fraudster would be able to post on average less than 2 fake reviews per day, thus, even with a reward of $2 per fraud activity (see Figure 3), achieve a payout of around $3.15 per day, below the Bitcoin mining payout. In addition, we have set $minh$ = 2s. Figure 1 shows the penalty timelines of two workers when $minh$ = 2s, $maxh$ = $minf$ = 5 min, $maxf$ = 24 hours, thr = 0.5, and k = 30 (for a steep increase of time penalty with fraud score). We note that a $maxh$ = 5 min is not excessive: this penalty is not imposed on the user, but on his device. The user experience remains the same in the online service.

Each vertical bar shows the daily temporal penalty assigned to a single worker, over reviews posted from multiple accounts. The maximum daily penalty of the two workers is 1,247 hours and 3,079 hours respectively. We observe that each worker has many days with a daily penalty exceeding 24 hours.

Figure 9b shows for $maxh$ = $minf$ = 5min, the overall distribution of daily penalties assigned by FraudSys, over all the 23 fraud workers, in the above experiment. It shows that during most of the active days, fraud workers are assigned a daily penalty exceeding 24 hours. Figure 9c (also for $maxh$ = $minf$ = 5min) shows the distribution of per-review penalty assigned by FraudSys to honest reviews, shown over 4,600 (23 × 200) honest reviews. Irrespective of the $maxh$ value, only 14 honest reviews were classified as fraudulent, but assigned a penalty below 1 hour. We observed minimal changes in the distribution of penalties of fraudulent reviews when $maxh$ = $minf$ ranges from 5 to 15 minutes.

6.4 Fraud Penalty Evaluation: Facebook

We have performed a similar parameter analysis using the Facebook "like" dataset. Since this dataset lacks information about the fraudsters who control the accounts that posted fake likes, we focus on the penalties assigned by FraudSys to fake and honest likes.

[1]Historically speaking, the BTC to USD rate is increasing. The next generation AntMiner coming up this year is expected to be 3 times more capable.

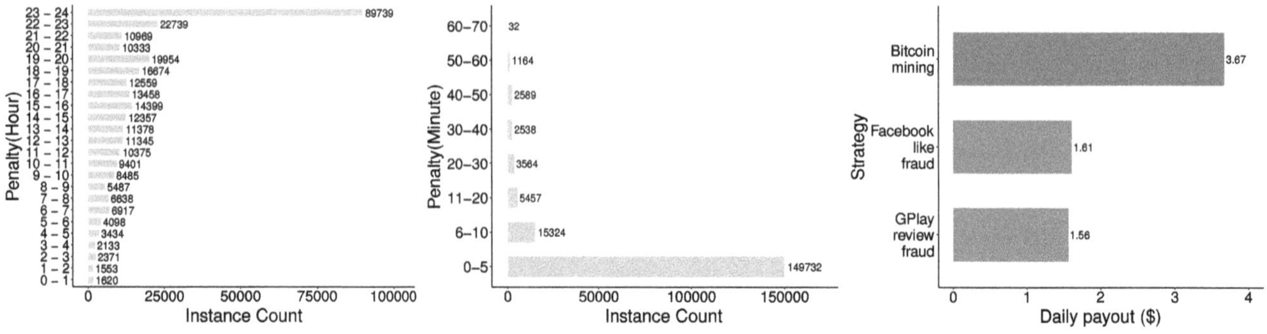

(a) (b) (c)

Figure 10: (a) Penalty distribution for the fake Facebook likes. 84% of the likes received a penalty that exceeds 12 hours, and the average fake like penalty is 19.32 hours. (b) Penalty distribution for the honest Facebook likes. 82.97% of the honest likes are assigned a penalty of under 5 min. The maximum penalty assigned to an honest like is 70 minutes. (c) Comparison of daily payouts provided by Bitcoin mining, writing fake reviews in Google Play and posting fake likes in Facebook, under FraudSys. Fraud does not pay off under FraudSys: the fraud payout is less than half the Bitcoin mining payout.

Figure 10a shows the distribution of penalties assigned to fake likes and Figure 10b shows the distribution of the honest likes. Compared to the results over the Google Play data, we observe a higher FPR, i.e., more honest likes with fraud level penalties. We posit that this is due to the fewer features that we can extract for the Facebook likes, as, unlike for Google Play reviews, we lack the time of the activity. Specifically, absence of like sequence information enables us to only extract features based on the last "snapshot" of the page, and not the current page snapshot when the like was posted.

However, 82.97% of the honest likes receive a penalty of under 5 mins and the maximum penalty assigned to an honest review is 70 mins. In addition, 84% of the fake likes receive a penalty that exceeds 12 hours, and the average penalty for a fake like is 19.32 hours. Figure 10c compares the daily payouts received by an AntMiner equipped fraudster who writes fake reviews in Google Play (at $1 per fake review), posts fake likes (at $2 per fake like), or honestly uses his device to mine Bitcoins. It shows that under FraudSys, fraud doesn't pay off: the Bitcoin mining payout is more than double the fraud payout for either fake reviews or likes.

7 CONCLUSION

We have introduced the concept of real-time fraud preemption systems, named as the FraudSys, that seek to restrict the profitability and impact of fraud in online systems. We propose and develop stateless, verifiable computational puzzles, that impose minimal overheads, but enable their efficient verification. We have developed a graph based, real-time algorithm to assign fraud scores to user activities and mechanisms to convert scores to puzzle difficulty values. We used data collected from Google Play and Facebook to show that our solutions impose significant penalties on fraudsters, and make fraud less productive than Bitcoin mining.

8 ACKNOWLEDGMENTS

This research was supported in part by NSF grants CNS-1527153, SES-1450619, CNS-1422215, IUSE-1525601, and Samsung GRO.

REFERENCES

[1] Google I/O 2013 - Getting Discovered on Google Play. www.youtube.com/watch?v=5Od2SuL2igA, 2013.
[2] L. Akoglu, H. Tong, and D. Koutra. Graph based anomaly detection and description: a survey. *Data Mining and Knowledge Discovery*, 29(3):626–688, 2015.
[3] M. Anderson and J. Magruder. Learning from the crowd: Regression discontinuity estimates of the effects of an online review database. *Economic Journal*, 122(563), 2012.
[4] AppReviews. http://www.app-reviews.org, 2016.
[5] AppSuch. http://www.appsuch.com, 2016.
[6] AppsViral. http://www.appsviral.com/, 2016.
[7] Apptamin. Optimize Your Google Play Store App Details Page. http://www.apptamin.com/blog/optimize-play-store-app/, 2016.
[8] P. R. Badri Satya, K. Lee, D. Lee, T. Tran, and J. J. Zhang. Uncovering fake likers in online social networks. In *Proceedings of the ACM CIKM*, 2016.
[9] M. Bellare, R. Canetti, and H. Krawczyk. Keying hash functions for message authentication. In *Proceedings of CRYPTO*, 1996.
[10] D. J. Bernstein. Syn cookies, 1996.
[11] N. Borisov. Computational puzzles as sybil defenses. In *Proceedings of the IEEE P2P*, 2006.
[12] C. Dwork and M. Naor. Pricing via processing or combatting junk mail. In *Proceedings of CRYPTO*, 1992.
[13] S. Fortunato and D. Hric. Community detection in networks: A user guide. arXiv:1608.00163, 2016.
[14] B. Hooi, H. A. Song, A. Beutel, N. Shah, K. Shin, and C. Faloutsos. Fraudar: Bounding graph fraud in the face of camouflage. In *Proceedings of ACM KDD*, 2016.
[15] A. Juels and J. Brainard. Client puzzles: A cryptographic counter-measure against connection depletion attacks. In *Proceedings of ISOC NDSS*, 1999.
[16] Y. Lu, L. Zhang, Y. Xiao, and Y. Li. Simultaneously detecting fake reviews and review spammers using factor graph model. In *Proceedings of the ACM WebSci*, 2013.
[17] M. Luca and G. Zervas. Fake it till you make it: Reputation, competition, and yelp review fraud. *Management Science*, 62(12), 2016.
[18] M. Motoyama, D. McCoy, K. Levchenko, S. Savage, and G. M. Voelker. Dirty jobs: The role of freelance labor in web service abuse. In *Proceedings of USENIX Security*, 2011.
[19] A. Mukherjee, B. Liu, and N. Glance. Spotting fake reviewer groups in consumer reviews. In *Proceedings of ACM WWW*, 2012.
[20] S. Nakamoto. Bitcoin: A peer-to-peer electronic cash system, 2008.
[21] M. Rahman, M. Rahman, B. Carbunar, and P. Chau. Fairplay: Fraud and Malware Detection in Google Play. In *Proceedings of SDM*, 2016.
[22] RankLikes. http://www.ranklikes.com/, 2016.
[23] ReviewRoster. http://www.reviewroster.com/, 2016.
[24] G. Stringhini, G. Wang, M. Egele, C. Kruegel, G. Vigna, H. Zheng, and B. Y. Zhao. Follow the green: growth and dynamics in twitter follower markets. In *Proceedings of ACM IMC*, 2013.
[25] TheSocialMarketeers. http://www.thesocialmarketeers.org/, 2016.
[26] J. Ye and L. Akoglu. Discovering opinion spammer groups by network footprints. In *Proceedings of ML-KDD*. 2015.

The Signals and Noise: Actionable Information in Improvised Social Media Channels During a Disaster

Xingsheng He[1,3], Di Lu[1], Drew Margolin[2], Mengdi Wang[1], Salma El Idrissi[2], Yu-Ru Lin[1]

[1]School of Computing and Information, University of Pittsburgh, Pittsburgh, PA 15260, USA
[2]Department of Communication, Cornell University, Ithaca, NY 14850, USA
[3]Department of Electronic Science and Technology, University of Science and Technology of China, Hefei, China

ABSTRACT

Web-based social and communication technologies enable citizens to self-organize relief efforts in response to crises.Th is work focuses on a question fundamental to the concept of collective intelligence: how effective are such self-organized channels, ungoverned by any central authority, in conforming to their intended function? In this study we examine the hashtag #PorteOuverte ("#OpenDoor") introduced during the 2015 Paris terrorist attacks, as an "improvised logistical channel" (ILC) to help individuals tofi nd a safe shelter near the attack sites. We analyze the dynamics and effectiveness of #PorteOuverte by comparing its proportion of relevant logistical messages – individuals requesting or offering shelter – to other messages such as those offering emotional consolation or commenting on the hashtag itself. Our results reveal that the vast majority of messages are not relevant, however the crowd senses and spreads relevant messages more than others. We further demonstrate that relevant messages can be automatically detected and thus algorithmic promotion may be possible.

KEYWORDS

collective intelligence, disaster response, social media, improvised logistical channel, crowd behaviors, self-organized systems

1 INTRODUCTION

Social media empowers individuals to spontaneously organize and perform actions traditionally performed by more formal institutions. One area where these citizen-based efforts have played a particularly important role is in disaster response [1, 12, 24, 25, 36]. Of particular importance are citizen efforts to offer or ask for concrete logistical assistance [9, 13, 21, 27, 28, 34, 37, 41, 49]. To date, however, research on the citizen efforts using technology to coordinate logistical support has focused on improving responses rather than understanding community dynamics. For example, researchers have provided techniques to improve the ability of formal relief organizations to respond to needs posted to social media [28, 41]) or for citizens tofi nd needed information [27, 37]. Little work has examined the dynamics of citizen efforts on their own with the aim of understanding how they operate and achieve their goals.

WebSci'17, June 25-28, 2017, Troy, NY, USA.
© 2017 ACM. 978-1-4503-4896-6/17/06...$15.00
DOI: http://dx.doi.org/10.1145/3091478.3091501

The #PorteOuverte hashtag, created in response to the November, 2015 terrorist attacks in Paris, provides an opportunity to observe such an effort.Th e hashtag, which means "open door," was used by individuals to offer shelter to strangers stranded by the attacks (see Fig. 1) and by individuals in need of shelter to request help and post their whereabouts. Such citizen-to-citizen coordination over social media during a disaster is not new [11, 12, 25, 27]. However, the crowd's creation of a specific, designated channel through which to accomplish this goal, similar to that afforded the study of political protests [30, 38], deserves attention. Via #PorteOuverte individuals not only communicated about logistical needs, they did so in an intentionally coordinated manner using a designated public channel.Th e channel bypassed formal organizations, however. It was comprised only of a simple, linguistic symbol. It thus placed the responsibility of coordinating vital resources on a self-organized conversation.

We refer to this spontaneous, crowd-based coordination of concrete resources as the use of an *improvised logistical channel* or *ILC*. We define ILCs as any **specified** means of **disseminating information** about who, where, or how individuals can take **concrete actions** to address a **novel or sudden** collective need that operates without the coordination of a central authority [19]. ILCs operate at the intersection of traditional public service and new media. Like traditional logistical infrastructure, an ILC has a designated use: to provide concrete, *actionable* information in times of distress. But unlike its more formal counterparts, an ILC can be created by anyone and disseminated in a cacophonous social space in which there is no formal mechanism of control.

In many ways hashtags are ideal candidates for ILCs. Like formal channels of communication such as radio or official websites, hashtags can rapidly draw attention to a particularfl ow of information [15]. Yet unlike these more formal channels, hashtags can be created cheaply by anyone through their use of natural language [5, 17, 23].Th ey are also easy to identify via searches [46] and spread easily through social networks [17, 32].Th us when confronting unforeseen disasters hashtags offer communities the ability quickly self-organize to share information and coordinate responses for which there may be little pre-existing infrastructure [25].

However, like their natural language cousins, thefl uid and uncontrolled nature of hashtags also makes them subject to an ongoing evolution that can undermine their logistical goals [5]. Hashtags can be re-purposed for a variety of social ends [45], lose their coherence [26], and even be "colonized" by messages designed to alter

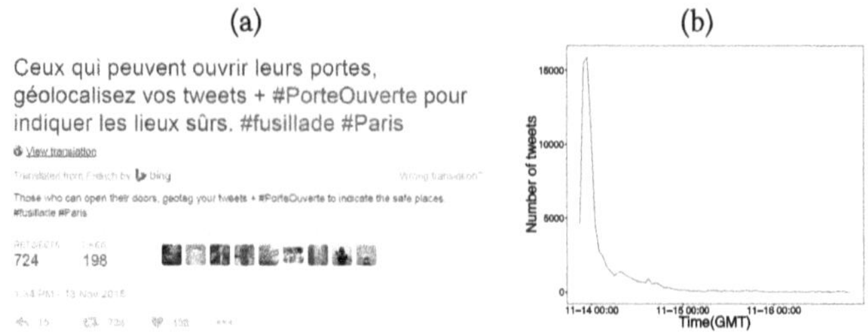

Figure 1: (a)Th efi rst tweet using the hashtag #PorteOuverte after the Paris attacks. (b)Th e hourly numbers of the original tweets containing the hashtag #PorteOuverte.

their meaning [10].Th e effectiveness of a hashtag as an ILC thus depends on the interplay of two competing dynamics: the need to spread *broadly* enough to be effective and the need to remain *specific* enough to be useful.

In this paper, we investigate #PorteOuverte hashtag as an ILC. We address three fundamental questions: (1) What portion of the messages sent to the channel addresses its intended purpose? (2) Of the messages sent to the channel, which types draw the most public attention? (3) Can relevant, logistical messages be automatically detected and selected for promotion?

This work thus initiates the theoretical study of hashtags as self-organized channels for addressing a communal need in the wake of a disaster. Ourfi ndings indicate that the channel is heavily polluted with irrelevant information, though the community makes efforts to distinguish and promote appropriate uses. Most interestingly, wefi nd that promotional and reflexive talk about the hashtag – celebrating it as an achievement – plays a substantial role in undermining its effectiveness.

2 BACKGROUND AND RELATED WORK

Social media has become increasingly important as a backchannel communication medium during emergencies and disasters [12, 22]. Social media enables individuals immediately proximate to or directly familiar with the disaster to communicate directly with one another and the public, improving both the speed and accuracy of information reported compared with messages from official accounts [24, 40]. Twitter in particular has been utilized for providing rapidly changing situational information about crises as they unfold [12, 39, 42].

At the same time, hashtags have emerged as an important technology for self-organized coordination [46]. Any user can create a novel hashtag to address a new situation or need [5]. Other users can disseminate the tag [32].Th e crowd can learn the tag's meaning from the manner in which others use it [26]. Hashtags also democratize discourse, allowing users to coordinate conversation without relying on formal leadership [23, 30]. Hashtags can thus support logistical crisis communication by allowing individuals to create specific channels to serve particular needs as an event unfolds [19].

Yet the open access and real-time adaptivity of hashtags can also be their downfall. Like natural language, hashtags are often used inconsistently [26].Th is tendency toward broad but inconsistent use can be problematic in the context of disasters where people tend to post a wide variety of message types [1, 4, 14, 29, 42]. While many messages are *informative* [22], meaning they provide situational information about the disaster, including updates regarding affected individuals, infrastructure, donations and volunteer activities, cautions, and other useful emergency information, many others are *non-informative* [22], such as those that provide emotional support or express general disaster related opinions [16, 29, 43].

A variety of recent research has attempted to distinguish useful disaster-related information in social media streams [44].These studies have primarily focused on external interventions to address specific problems, such as techniques that improve the effectiveness of relief organizations or match help requests to help offers [21, 27, 28, 37, 41]. Little work has focused on understanding the effectiveness and dynamics of the crowd's own self-organized efforts, however.

2.1 ResearchQuestions

Our study focuses on the ability of the #PorteOuverte hashtag to draw attention to messages relevant to matching individuals in need of shelter with other individuals offering shelter nearby. As described above, studies indicate that there are multiple, competing motivations for messages on social media during disasters such as sharing information, providing sympathy and solidarity, and giving general opinions [12, 22, 29].Th is leads to ourfi rst question:

RQ1: *What types of messages are sent to #PorteOuverte, and what is the proportion of messages that provide logistic information (relevant to the channel's intended purpose)?*

The proportion of relevant messages is also likely to be unstable over time. Speakers use "least effort" when expressing themselves [48].Th ey prefer terms that are specific but also widely recognized. The more broadly a symbol (e.g. word, hashtag) is used, the greater the incentive to tolerate its poor specificity to take advantage of its broad recognizability.Th is suggests that #PorteOuverte will draw more messages when users can observe that it is used as specifically intended, but as it becomes more widely diffused and recognized it will increasingly attract deviant messages designed to exploit the collective attention it receives. Hashtags in particular carry the risk of "colonization" by those who seek to co-opt or undermine their function once they are widely known [2, 10].Th us, #PorteOuverte might begin as an effective ILC and then lose its effectiveness over time. We thus ask:

RQ2: *How does the number and proportion of logistical messages sent to #PorteOuverte change over time?*

If the audience's reaction to the channel was entirely passive then the inflow of messages sent to #PorteOuverte would define the channel's effectiveness. However, social media users are not passive recipients but actively intervene in informationfl ows, particularly in disaster contexts [12, 37]. For example, while disasters often prompt the spread of false rumors, users often react by posting messages discouraging them [7, 35]. Similarly, users may overcome noise in the #PorteOuverte channel by rebroadcasting, via retweets, the relevant logistical messages over other kinds of messages[39]. We thus ask:

RQ3a: *What types of messages sent to #PorteOuverte are most retweeted by users?*

A related question is whether users are attending sufficiently to all logistical messages or only a select few.

RQ3b: *What portion of logistical messages sent to #PorteOuverte are retweeted by users?*

Ourfi nal question is whether simple tools can be developed to improve the integrity of the channel. Specifically, if logistically relevant messages can be detected algorithmically, it may be possible to implement automatedfi lters to maintain the proportion of relevant messages that pass through the channel at acceptable levels.

RQ4: *To what extent can logistically relevant messages be detected automatically?*

3 DATA COLLECTION

To collect all the original tweets using the hashtag #PorteOuverte, we used Twitter's advanced search function[1] to gather retrospectively tweets containing such a hashtag.

The data were collected in two steps: First, about two weeks after the Paris attacks, we requested through the Twitter advanced search service by specifying the hashtag as #PorteOuverte, the date as from 2015-11-12 to 2015-11-16 and the rest parameters as default in the web page interface.Th en we extracted all the tweet ids from the iteratively returned webpages. Second, after obtaining these tweet ids, we leveraged Twitter REST API to get more detailed information of each tweet. Fig. 1(a) shows thefirst tweet using #PorteOuverte.Th efi rst tweet posted on Friday, 13 Nov 2015 21:34:06 GMT created an online channel and advocated users who can offer help to use such a hashtag to provide offline shelters. Fig. 1(b) shows the hourly volume of original tweets, indicating that the majority of tweets appeared within thefi rst 24 hours after the attacks.

With the 75,547 original tweets returned from the Twitter advanced search service, wefi ltered out the tweets that only contain hashtags and the *conversational* tweets (i.e., tweets that replied to other tweets).Th efi nal data set contains 66,430 tweets in a period of 74 hours from the time the hashtag was created.

4 CATEGORIZING HASHTAG FUNCTIONS

Coding scheme derived from prior research. We seek to identify messages that relate specifically to the designated logistical purpose of #PorteOuverte – identifying safe shelters and individuals in need of a safe shelter – and distinguish these from other kinds of messages. Our coding procedure began with the baseline scheme provided by [29]. We examined the applicability of the scheme to #PorteOuverte tweets and then trained coders to apply the scheme and tested their reliability. We then made adjustments, in particular, by adding two new categories not observed in the prior work.

Qu et al. (2011) provided a six-category scheme for categorizing messages sent on Sina-Weibo related in the aftermath of the 2010 Yushu earthquake: *Situation updates, General disaster-related message, Action-related message, Emotional/Social-related message, Opinion-related message,* and *Off-topic.* Of specific interest is their distinction of action-related messages from both situational updates and general disaster information messages as those which aim to coordinate tangible resources in the affected region during and after disasters.

Open coding, pilot coding and code book. In ourfi rst step, one co-author labeled randomly selected 200 tweets from our dataset, according to the definitions from [29].Th e results indicated that the majority of messagesfi t the existing coding scheme. Nonetheless, we observed a significant number of tweets for a novel use – referencing the hashtag itself.Th is use was not identified by the study [29] as they examined all messages rather than those under a specific hashtag. In particular, many messages contained factual information about the hashtag with the intention of promoting its use, such as instructions and advocacy for its use. We categorized the messages as "containing *Information about the hashtag*".

Next, we conducted a pilot study in order to test whether our coding scheme is clear and sufficient to deliver reliable outcomes. We recruited two external coders along with four of our co-authors and conducted four sessions of pilot coding with 300 randomly selected tweets from our dataset. Each coder coded one batch of 100 tweets independently and therefore each batch was coded by at least two coders. We computed the inter-coder reliability for every two coders coded the same batch and the pairwise Cohen's kappa was relatively low ($\kappa = 0.35$) for some categories. (We computed the Cohen's kappa separately for each category as each tweet can have multiple categories.)

We found that the most disagreements among coders were caused by differing perceptions of *emotional/social-related* and *opinion-related* messages. In particular, many messages were highly emotional irrespective of their intention to provide support. Since social support has been considered as influential in buffering the effects of stress from disasters [3], we distinguished social support messages from those conveying emotion in a non-supportive way, such as anger at the government or terrorists.

We also discovered a novel kind of message related to the hashtag itself. A number of tweets used #PorteOuverte to refer to the phenomenon of the hashtag, that is, the fact that people self-organized through Twitter to offer one another assistance.Th ese messages often included emotional statements of awe or pride in humanity, as well as occasional statements of fear or scorn, and thus contained elements of social support and general opinion. However, they are also unique to the phenomenon of #PorteOuverte and its evolution as an improvised logistical channel. We thus distinguished these *Reflexive comments* from general messages of social support and opinion.

In addition, we found that categories in our code book are not mutually exclusive as a single tweet mayfi t more than one. We thus permitted each tweet in our dataset to be classified into more than one category as needed.

Based on these observations we refined our code book to clarify category boundaries, decomposing those two categories and reconstructing three new categories as *Social support, Reflexive comments* and *General opinion.* Table 1 lists the coding scheme and detailed selection criteria in ourfi nal code book with examples of tweets for each category. By conducting another round of pilot coding with three coders independently coding one batch of 100 tweets, we confirmed the results based on thefi nal coding scheme reached an acceptable inter-rater reliability (pariwise $\kappa > 0.75$ for all categories).

Coding process. We started the coding process with thefinal coding book (Table 1). We randomly sampled 14% tweets from our dataset with a uniform distribution across time.Th at is, we grouped all the tweets into different sessions using afi xed time (15-minute) window and randomly sampled tweets from each session.

[1] https://twitter.com/search-advanced

Category	Abbr.	Selection Criteria	Example
Logistical Information indicated by #PorteOuverte hashtag	*Log*	Offering or requesting help about accommodations aligning with the goal of #PorteOuverte activity	Hey tourists in #Paris if you need help or some place to sleep around Jussieu 5th arrondissement, my door is open. #PorteOuverte #OpenDoor
Information about #PorteOuverte hashtag	*Use*	Providing any type of information about the #PorteOuverte activity including the fact, news, advocation or instruction of the usage of #PorteOuverte	For people in Paris looking for a shelter use hashtag #PorteOuverte. Parisians will let you in their home.
Situational Updates of the attack	*Situ*	Providing factual information about what was happening in the attack area, such as information about including victim, injury, suspects, infrastructure, utilities, situational warning and cautions. Such information improves situational awareness of readers.	French army just stormed stadium but the terrorists had killed a lot of the hostage already! #ParisUnderAttack #porteouverte
Other General Information for the attack	*Gen*	Providing or requesting any other Paris attack related relief information, such as donation, mourning activities, embassy information or directions to other relief information resources	@**** American Embassy in #Paris +33143122222 #PorteOuverte
Social/Emotional Support	*S/E*	Providing social and emotional support, including mourning, blessing/praying, comforting, encouraging, and expressing concerns for or solidarity with victims.	Our thoughts go out to those suffering from the terrible #ParisAttacks. #porteouverte #PeaceForParis
Reflexive commentary on hashtag phenomenon	*Ref*	Referring to the #PorteOuverte hashtag as a social phenomenon or meme, including commenting on whether it is good or bad, how it makes the person feel etc.	The hashtag #PorteOuverte shows love and courage in the face of hatred and fear
General expression of opinion	*Exp*	Expressing opinions or feelings related to the attacks	We could make the world a better place if we all put our racial, #religious socio-political differences aside. #PorteOuverte #PrayForParis
Off-topic/Non Codeable	*off-topic*	The tweet does NOT contain any relevant information to Paris Attack or the coder cannot understand the content or infer the purpose	It was a day full of little brains trying tofi nd their place in -@*** 's majors. -#porteouverte

Table 1: Coding scheme for categorizing different types of tweets with hashtag #PorteOuverte.

We conducted two-round coding process. For thefi rst round we coded 10% and the second round we coded additional 4%.

The four co-authors who helped develop the code book as described above participated in this coding process as experienced coders. We provided coders with URL of each tweet instead of the plain text, so that through the browser all the contextual information of each tweet including the embedded tweets, pictures, videos, and replies are accessible to coders to help them precisely classify the type of information conveyed by the tweets. Each of the coders annotated a bulk of tweets independently and 9240 tweets were coded in total. To validate the accuracy of our coding process, we randomly selected three batches, each containing 100 tweets, to be coded by two coders.Th e pairwise agreement for every two coders who coded the same batch was relatively high (agreement=0.83). In particular, the pairwise inter-rater reliability for *Logistical information* tweets (Category *Log*), the focus of our study, reached 0.90.

5 ANALYSIS: FUNCTIONAL SIGNALS AND IMPACT

In this section we address RQ1, RQ2, RQ3a and RQ3b by examining the types and timing of messages users tweet and retweet through #PorteOuverte.

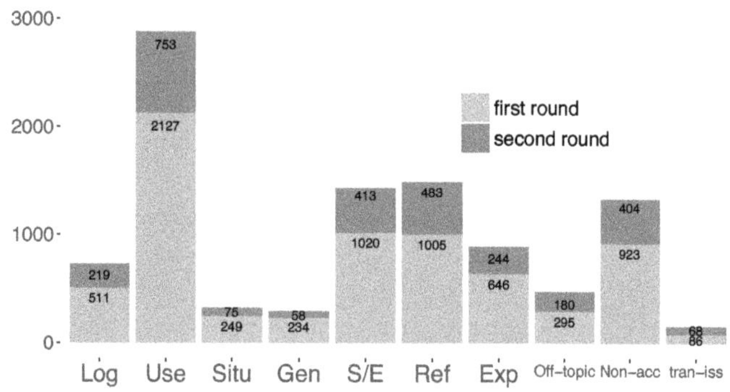

Figure 2: Category distribution of the #PorteOuverte tweets. "Non-acc" (abbr. for Non-accessible) are the tweets that can not be accessed from the webpages and "tran-iss" (abbr. for translation-issue) are the tweets that the coders have difficulty in understanding the translated content.

Content distribution (RQ1). We applied the classification scheme to the uniformly sampled tweets in a two-round coding process: Wefi rst coded 10% and then compared the coding results with the rest 4%. Overall, the coding results are consistent across different categories. For example, for the coded tweets, 7.74% and 8.42%

tweets were labeled as *Logistical information*, 15.45% and 15.88% tweets were labeled as *Social support* in thefi rst and second round, respectively. Fig. 2 gives the results of each round and shows the category distribution. Besides 475 tweets coded as *off-topic* and 154 tweets have the translation issue, most tweets fall into the seven categories: there are 324 *Situational updates* tweets, 292 *General information* tweets, 730 *Logistical information* tweets, 2880 *Information about the hashtag* tweets, 1433 *Social support* tweets, 1488 *Reflexive comments* tweets , and 890 *General opinion* tweets.

As shown in Fig. 2, the proportion of *Logistical information* tweets, those which are in alignment with the goal of the hashtag, occupied only a small portion of the channel.Th e modal category is *Information about the hashtag*, messages that are of uncertain usefulness.Th ese tweets that promote the hashtag may be of value in getting the word out about the existence of the channel, but too many *Information about the hashtag* tweets can also overwhelm the useful information. Furthermore, several other categories typically found in response to disasters (*Social support, General opinion*, and also *Situational updates*) also dominate relative to *Logistical information*. We also observed that, ironically, *Reflexive comments*, in which individuals celebrate the channel for its usefulness, also appears to drown out relevant information.

One possibility is that the channel is more accurately comprised of two channels: a useful, low-noise channel for individuals communicating logistical information in French and a more generic, high noise channel for those using other languages to talk about other things. As shown in Table 2, we do see differences in the channel's use based on languages; however, the results are not consistent with this characterization. First, we observed that the French-only tweets in the channel have improved, but still low, precision, as the proportion of *Logistical information* is still only (26.7%), with *Logistical information* plus *Information about the hashtag* still only combining to be just over half (53.6%). Moreover, French-only tweets are not particularly strong in recall, as only 71% of *Logistical information* tweets are in French. In other words, almost 1/3 of relevant messages would be missed if users of the channel focused only on French tweets. Furthermore, the channel's performance among these non-French tweets is very poor, as only 3.4% of non-French tweets to #PorteOuverte are relevant, *Logistical information* tweets.Th us, while there are important differences in the channel based on language use, it is not a case of two distinct channels with different applications, and so our subsequent analysis continues to focus on the channel as a whole.

Category trends (RQ2). Assessing the effectiveness of #PorteOuverte requires not only determining the overall mix of messages sent to it but also the timing of these different kinds of messages relative to one another. We summarize the temporal change of categories in Fig. 3 to help understand how the content and the ratios change as the events on the ground unfold.

As shown in Fig. 3 panel A, the hashtag, created at 11-13 21:34:06 GMT, began with an immediate spike triggered by the violent attacks. For roughly the next four hours a stream of *Logistical information* messages are sent through the channel. As indicated in panel B, over time, other types of information entered the channel but behaved differently.Th e most important information *Logistical information*, was, appropriately, the dominant form of information for thefi rst 30 minutes after the hashtag's creation. It was

Table 2:Th e number of French and non-French tweets in each category.Th e sum of all the categories may exceed the number of "on-topic tweets" as a tweet can be coded with multiple categories.

	# of tweets		# of retweets	
	Fr	Non-Fr	Fr	Non-Fr
on-topic tweets	1839	5405	38339	49817
Log	506	224	17464	13824
Use	549	2331	16322	23764
Situ	72	252	3527	3159
Gen	51	241	1020	2886
S/E	201	1232	2935	4190
Ref	451	1037	2234	6703
Exp	137	753	564	2366

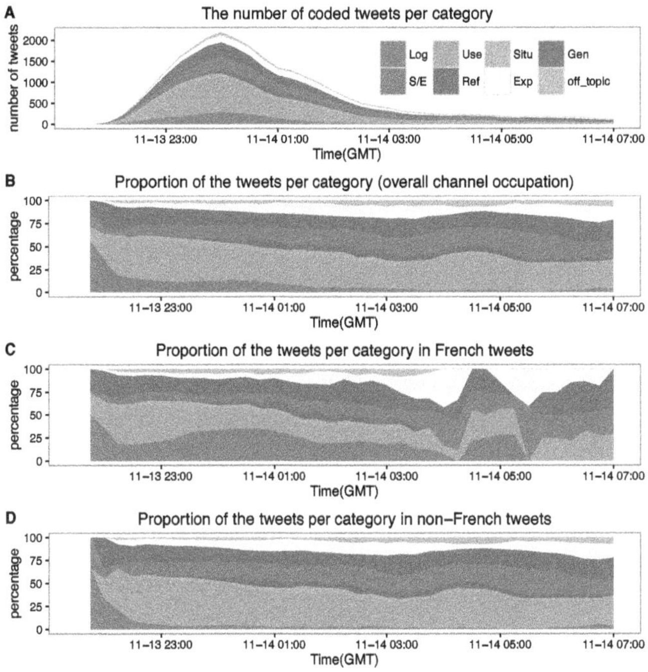

Figure 3:Th e number of coded tweets and the channel occupation of each category overtime.

quickly replaced by *Information about the hashtag*, however, which continued to dominate.

Similar to the previous content analysis, after its emergence the largest category remained *Information about the hashtag* while the channel was active. In addition, *Social support* and *General opinion* gradually became more dominant hours after the attacks as the logistical *Logistical information* messages began to wane. Nonetheless, our analysis indicates that noisy (*Social support, Reflexive comments, General opinion, off-topic*) information was prominent from the beginning (34% at 11-13 23:00), and increasingly squeezed the bandwidth as the evening wore on (45% at 11-14 01:00 and 54% at 11-14 03:00 GMT). As with the analysis of the overall proportions, the French-only tweets (panel C) were less noisy; nonetheless, *Logistical information* tweets were at no time more than 35% of the channel after thefi rst 30 minutes.

Comparing the raw number of *Logistical information* messages to their proportion provides further insight into whether these messages are interfering with the logistical coordination intended by #PorteOuverte. The number of *Logistical information* messages roughly indicates the number of individuals trying to use the channel for its intended purpose, while the proportion of noise indicates how hard it would be to find those messages. The problem is aggravated when the peaks of useful information (*Logistical information*) and proportion of noise coincide.

Results show that the proportion of noise is quite high even at the peak volume of actionable messages. Even excluding promotional use of the hashtag (*Information about the hashtag*), the peak of logistical messages, in terms of raw count, occurs between 11-13 23:34 and 11-13 23:49 GMT, when these messages are only a 13.67% share of the total, compared with 13.72% for *Social support*, 17.05% for *Reflexive comments*, and 7.17% for *General opinion*.

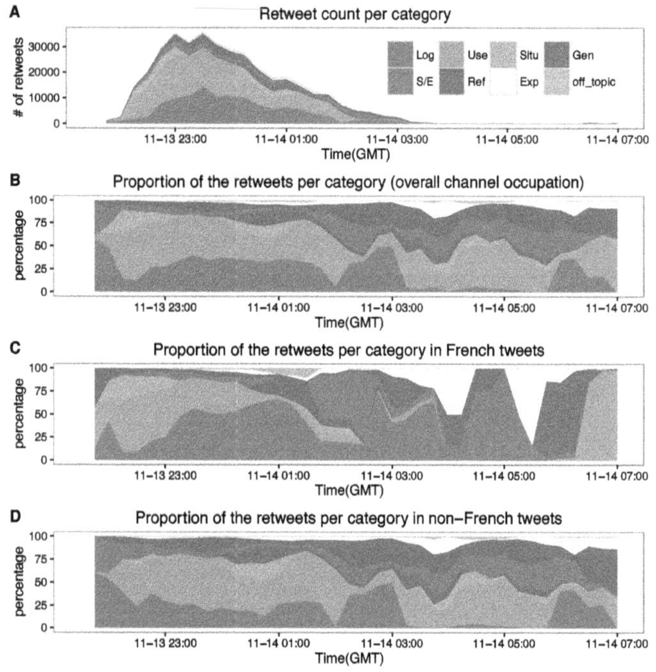

Figure 4: The retweet count and the channel occupation of each category overtime.

Whether this stream of irrelevant messages is problematic for the channel depends not only on its proportion but whether it is sufficient to distract from relevant information.

User attention (RQ3a). We began by analyzing the flow of vital *Logistical information* and noisy messages relative to users' attention for distinguishing them. At the peak time at which *Logistical information* messages were sent to #PorteOuverte the hashtag received approximately 4.8 tweets per second of which 13.67% were *Logistical information*. This means that a user would receive 1 logistically actionable message every 1.52 seconds, and need to discover and pick it out of an additional 6.32 messages received during this same 1.52-second interval. This rate is more than 100 times greater than the rate at which researchers have estimated information overload takes place, and more than twice the highest rate tested [31]. Thus, we conclude that even if these coarse calculations substantially underestimate users' attention or ability to navigate the channel, it was nonetheless substantially overloaded and any gain in the signal-to-noise ratio would appreciably improve the dissemination of relevant information.

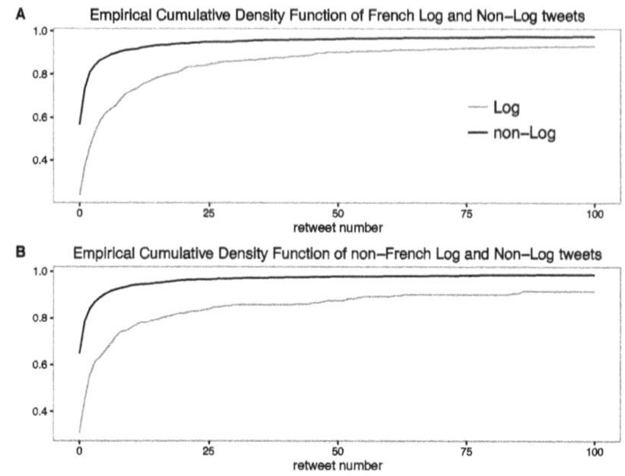

Figure 5: The ECDF of retweet numbers per tweet in the *Log* and Non-*Log* categories across different languages. Tweets with more than 100 retweets were not shown in the plots (less than 3% in Non-*Log* and 9% in *Log*).

To further examine user attention we consider the extent to which *Logistical information* tweets are identified by users for retweeting. Though Twitter does not re-post retweets directly into the channel the rate of retweets contributes to such tweets being identified as "Top" in Twitter's feed to the hashtag and also disseminates the tweet directly to the retweeting users' followers. Fig. 4 gives the attention each category gained over time and is more optimistic for the channel's effectiveness. Though the majority of tweets sent into the channel were not logistical, the audience did effectively select these relevant tweets for rebroadcasting such that, across Twitter, they ended up being a substantial portion of the #PorteOuverte messages disseminated. In particular, *Logistical information* tweets received an approximately fortyfold boost from retweets when the raw number of original *Logistical information* reached its peak. This enables this logistical information to populate about 37.42% of messages tagged with #PorteOuverte, even though they are only 13.67% of the original content tagged this way. Combined with the amplified *Information about the hashtag* tweets, this relevant information dominated until 11-14 03:00 GMT time, after the demand for *Logistical information* appeared to have subsided according to the raw count of original tweets. The effect is particularly dramatic for French-only tweets, which shows several bursts of retweets that drive the proportion of *Logistical information* to steadily grow and reaches as high as 66% when this channel was active. Thus, consistent with [24], self-organized participation in the channel is corrective against noise.

The unseen *Logistical information* (RQ3b). The preceding analyses indicate that though the channel is overloaded, the crowd has good precision in identifying relevant, logistical messages for rebroadcasting. This raises the question of whether this rebroadcasting effort is well distributed across all messages or focuses only on a few. In Fig. 5, we show the Empirical Cumulative Density Function of the retweets of *Logistical information* and

Non-*Logistical information* tweets. As in our previous analysis, *Log* tweets generally attracted more attention than non-*Logistical information* tweets. However, a considerable portion of valuable *Logistical information* tweets were not selected for re-broadcasting as 25% of *Logistical information* got no retweets at all and about half of *Logistical information* information got less that 4 retweets.

These results indicate that though the crowd attends to and selects for *Logistical information* messages, this attention is focused on only a subset of relevant messages. This phenomenon suggests that automated tools may help in identifying these messages and inspires us to develop an algorithmic approach that can automatically detect *Logistical information* tweets for better promotion under disasters.

6 MACHINE CLASSIFICATION

To answer **RQ4** – "*To what extent can logistically relevant messages be detected automatically?*" – we conducted experiments on various machine classification techniques. With the tweet labels obtained from the human coding process, the goal is to automatically detect the human-coded label(s) for a given tweet. We are interested more in the most relevant categories, *Log* and *Use*, which are central to the communication of the logistical messages, while we also tested our machine classification techniques on the other two categories *S/E* and *Ref*, for comparison.

Experiment setting. We operationalized the problem into a binary classification task with an objective to classify whether a given tweet was labeled with a particular category. For example, in the classification for category *Log*, we consider *Log*-labeled tweets as positive and otherwise negative. The binary classification setting enables us to examine each category separately and to study the most relevant categories in depth. The experiments used the first-round coded tweets (6,200 in total), and our text pre-processing step (see details below) resulted in 4,331 tweets. Table 3 lists the basic statistics in the experiment dataset.

Table 3: The number of tweets, proportion and positive-negative ratio for each category in the experiment dataset.

	# of tweets	Percentage	Ratio of +/-
Log	399	9.21%	1:10
Use	1814	41.88%	1:1.38
S/E	869	20.06%	1:3.98
Ref	922	21.29%	1:3.69

Text pre-processing. The text pre-processing step ensures the tweets used for experiments are interesting and avoids the results from being dominated by the peculiar or systematic features in the data. In the current work, we focused on how to automatically classify the event-related categories and excluded tweets annotated as *off-topic* (5.14%) or labeled as with translation-issue (1.67%) by annotators. In the real-world scenarios, both tweets with translation issue and *off-topic* tweets can be detected and filtered out by sophisticated translation systems (e.g. Google Translate[2]) or technical methods such as event-specific content segregation[18] or topical content distillation [47].

We also removed the token "#PorteOuverte" from each tweet as it appeared in all tweets. URLs and mention (@username) were replaced with standardized tokens and will be treated differently from other text tokens. We further filtered out tweets with less than two words as the semantics in such short tweets are often obscure. As tweets in our corpus were written in different languages, we translated all the tweets into English using Google Translate[2] and compared the translated data with non-translated ones. Tweets with translation issues were removed. We also applied standard text pre-processing such as removing punctuations and applied *Snowball Stemmer* for word stemming.

Feature engineering. Two types of features were extracted from each tweet as the input of the classification task.

Content features: features derived from the words appeared in the tweet text. We considered two alternatives: N-gram and word2vec [20]. N-gram is a continuous sequence of n words in a text. We extracted various N-gram features including *unigrams*, *bigrams*, and *trigrams*. The initially extracted N-grams resulted in a high-dimensional set of features (35,907 in total). To reduce the computational complexity and also to remove the noisy features, the dataset was pruned to ignore the infrequent terms (e.g., less than two times). We tested and compared several state-of-the-art methods to select the most discriminative features and decided to use the "Bi-Normal Separation" [8] over other commonly used metrics, such as "Information Gain," "Term Frequency" and "Chi-Squared." Finally, to further reduce the feature dimension, we applied the distributional representation method word2vec [20] to obtain the mean 100-dimensional vectors for each given tweet according to its contained words.

Contextual features: features describing the contextual information associated with the tweets. We extracted four types of contextual features to augment the content features: (1) ContainURL, (2) ContainMention, (3) ContainParisLocation, and (4) InParis. The first three features are binary features indicating whether the tweet contains a URL, an @-mention, or any identified location names in Paris, e.g., the name of a street or a subway station name. The street and subway station names were obtained from public website[3,4]. The last feature provides geographic proximity with respect to the event locus, Paris, with three categories: in Paris, not in Paris or unknown. Due to the sparseness of geo-codable tweets (only 0.3% tweets were posted with geotags), we extracted the geo-location from the users' profiles (available from 75% of users).

It is worth noting that the information about language and posting time of a tweet was excluded intentionally. While the goal of the classification is to distinguish the logistically relevant messages, our ultimate goal is to enhance the use of the ILCs during the course of the event and across communities. Thus, the machine classification should be built without the knowledge about the language and time of the tweets.

Training the classifiers. From the feature engineering, we obtained four combinations of features as the input of the classification: (1) N-gram alone, (2) word2vec alone, (3) N-gram with contextual features (N-gram-C), and (4) word2vec with contextual features (word2vec-C). We employed both traditional binary

[2] https://translate.google.com/

[3] http://www-groups.dcs.st-and.ac.uk/history/Societies/ParisNames.html

[4] https://en.wikipedia.org/wiki/List_of_stations_of_the_Paris_Metro

classifiers such as Naive Bayes, AdaBoost and Support Vector Machines (SVM), and a tree boosting classifier XGBoost [6], which has been shown to work better than other classifiers like Deep Neural Network in a moderate-size dataset.

Due to the imbalanced positive-negative class distributions in all categories (see Table 3), we have tested classifiers trained with data under various sampling strategies – ranging from a 1:1 under-sampling condition (where the negative instances were under-sampled to create a balanced positive-negative ratio) to a no-sampling condition to retain the original class ratios. Our comparison showed that the classification training with any under-sampling strategy did not have a significant effect (with only less than 1% or no improvement). Hence, we report and discuss the results based on the training data that retained the original class ratios.

Evaluation of the classifiers. The classification performance was evaluated using a 10-fold cross-validation. We report the standard evaluation metrics, including Precision, Recall, F-score and AUC (Area Under ROC curve).Th e AUC metric is particularly informative in the case of imbalanced class distribution.

Table 4: Classification performance (%), with 10-fold cross-validation, for different classifiers and across categories.

	Precision	Recall	F-Score	AUC	Method
Log	**93.67**	60.40	73.44	96.31	SVM
	93.60	58.64	72.11	95.96	AdaBoost
	64.40	**82.21**	72.24	94.90	NB
	91.06	68.92	**78.46**	**96.32**	XGBoost
Use	82.22	85.17	83.67	**93.59**	SVM
	82.47	**87.93**	85.11	93.03	AdaBoost
	80.61	84.34	82.43	91.22	NB
	82.82	87.85	**85.26**	93.34	XGBoost
S/E	**71.80**	51.20	59.81	**86.52**	SVM
	70.71	53.62	**60.99**	85.17	AdaBoost
	40.09	**73.30**	51.83	80.35	NB
	69.57	52.35	59.75	85.84	XGBoost
Ref	**72.15**	51.40	60.03	**86.60**	SVM
	71.80	53.58	61.36	86.20	AdaBoost
	49.26	**69.19**	57.55	82.93	NB
	71.48	54.12	**61.60**	86.50	XGBoost

Table 5: Classification performance in AUC (%), with 10-fold cross-validation, using different features with SVM.

	N-gram	N-gram-C	word2vec	word2vec-C
Log	94.60	95.61	95.89	**96.31**
Use	93.11	93.13	93.10	**93.14**
S/E	84.46	84.72	84.75	**86.52**
Ref	86.11	86.42	86.15	**86.60**

Table 6: Classification performance in AUC (%), testing with future data, using different features with SVM.

	N-gram	N-gram-C	word2vec	word2vec-C
Log	92.16	92.27	92.79	**93.10**
Use	90.02	91.94	90.39	**91.09**
S/E	82.02	83.10	83.28	**83.28**
Ref	81.55	84.85	85.05	**85.56**

6.1 Classification results

Table 4 shows the overall performance for different classifiers across different categories, with the best feature combination, word2vec-C, which captures both syntactic and semantic word relationships and performs the best across all different classifiers. All reported results are based on the translated texts, which have 1.12%–4.61% performance gains over the non-translated ones. As shown in Table 4, all the classifiers have reached to an AUC above 80%, indicating that the features that we selected have a good discriminating ability. In particular, we were able to obtain high precision in some cases (e.g., 93.67% when using SVM on *Log*), indicating the ability of a machine to correctly identify a specific kind of messages (e.g. logistical messages).

Classifier comparison. Based on the AUC metric (in Table 4), SVM and XGBoost perform the best across all categories. XGBoost achieves the best in *Log* and has similar performance with SVM in other categories. NB performs the worst in terms of AUC and F-score, but performs the best on Recall metric except for *Use*. Most of the classifiers (except for NB) have a Precision value higher than the Recall value, which indicates that the classifiers produced more false negative cases than false positive ones. Considering the F-score metric, XGBoost is the best except for *Use*, in which AdaBoost performs the best.

Feature comparison. As SVM performs the best overall, we use SVM to compare the strength of different types of features in the classification task. Table 5 provides a comparison of different features in terms of the AUC metric. Overall, the contextual features only bring 0.02–2.08% performance gain. For example, we found that in the *Log* classification, the additional gain for the contextual features is 1.06%, with InParis feature performs the best (0.6%). SVM with word2vec-C performs the best and the contextual features help improve the performance but not significantly.

Category comparison. From Table 4, we observe that the two most relevant categories, *Log* and *Use*, are more distinguishable in the classification task as they both have higher AUC than other two categories. We further look into some of the salient characteristics in each category.

The category *Log* has high AUC and Precision but low Recall, indicating the classifiers produce more false negative cases. Our further examination of the misclassified cases reveals several limitations including the location identification and label ambiguity. For example, two tweets are classified as negative (i.e., not *Log*) incorrectly: *"Shooting in Paris. If you can not go home and are on Paris-West, DM #PorteOuverte"* and *"#PorteOuverte #fusillade #Paris #RT a room available at Paris 15 for tourists or families in the..."*. These tweets contain the location names ("Paris-West" and "Paris 15") in Paris; however, our feature extraction failed to recognize the location names of these tweets, in part due to our limited location lexicons and informal names (e.g, "Paris 15") used in the tweets. Some false negative cases were produced because of the ambivalence in their labels. For example, the tweet (*"#PorteOuverte to Brochant do not hesitate. Tonight we are the France."*) was coded with two labels (*Log* and *S/E*) with each sentence signaling one category.Th e tweet is positive in the *Log* classification, but the second sentence has a considerable portion.Th erefore, the machine failed to classify this tweet correctly.

The classification of category *Use* also has high AUC, Precision and Recall. We observe that in this category, users tended to use similar words to promote the channel, e.g., *"If you're in Paris and you need a safe place to stay use the hashtag #PorteOuverte"* and *"If in Paris and need somewhere safe to go use the hashtag #PorteOuverte*). As a result, the content features (N-gram or word2vec) may capture the information of the category *Use* more easily than those in other categories.

Compared with category *Log* and *Use*, the classifications for category *S/E* and *Ref* are relatively hard. We observe that the tweets in the two categories often contain more diverse words.This can be further confirmed by the Bi-Normal Separation (BNS) scores of the content features in these categories.Th e mean BNS scores of the top 1000 N-grams in *S/E* and *Ref* are 0.52 and 0.58, respectively, much lower than the mean BNS scores for *Log* (1.02) and *Use* (0.77). This suggests that the content features in categories *S/E* and *Ref* may not be sufficiently discriminative for classification.

Testing with future data. In this section, we test the performance of the classifiers in a more realistic situation, which classify new tweets using previous ones.Th e whole dataset was sorted in chronological order and divided into two sets: thefi rst 80% as training and the remaining 20% as testing. We trained the same classifiers using the same feature combinations described earlier.Th e results are shown in Table 6. Overall, the results are similar to the cross-validation results shown previously (see Table 5): F-score and AUC decrease only slightly by less than 4%, indicating the effectiveness of the classifiers to be applied to the unseen, future data.

Overall, our experiment results indicate the capacity of using machine classification to distinguish the logistically relevant messages in the improvised #PorteOuverte channel, with possibility and insights to further improve the classification performance.

7 DISCUSSION AND FUTURE WORK

In this paper we investigated the potential effectiveness of an improvised logistical channel, #PorteOuverte. Moving beyond prior work on social media use after disasters [22, 29], we reported thefirst empirical assessment of the distribution of message types as they relate to the specific, logistical purpose of an improvised channel.

Channel content & effectiveness. Overall, our results indicate that #PorteOuverte was significantly hampered by noise. From early in the channel's history, and through its peak use, individual sent many more irrelevant messages to the channel than relevant ones.Th is problem was substantially worse for non-French tweets, a set of tweets that could not be ignored as they contained almost 1/3 of the relevant messages. In addition, the overall rate of tweets to the channel indicated that it was overloaded, and thus noise had a direct, unmitigated impact.

More encouragingly, the crowd was able to make substantial improvements to the raw messagefl ow. Crowd members "voted up" relevant tweets at a substantially higher rate than they did other message types.Th is was particularly effective among French-only tweets, where relevant retweets were modal in the channel and dominated on occasion. Unfortunately, the distribution of attention within the retweeted population is skewed, with some relevant offers and requests for logistical information receiving substantial attention while others received little.

Channel improvement. Our results also suggest ways that the channel can be improved through intervention. First, the crowd's attempt to intervene via retweets could be more systematically supported. As noted above, retweets do not re-post a tweet to the live feed from a hashtag, but rather "vote" it into the "Top" tweets. Promoters of ILCs may want to make such procedural nuances salient in their explanations of how to use a channel. Specifically, our results indicate that the "Top" feed is likely to contain substantially better precision and recall on relevant, logistical information than the "Live" feed. Secondly, our machine classification experiments indicate that there is an opportunity for substantial improvement through algorithmic intervention. In particular, logistical information can be identified automatically with good precision and thus promoted algorithmically. Promotional uses of the channel, which may or may not be of benefit depending on the state of the channel at a particular time, can also be identified.

Limitation and Future work. While the present work provides thefi rst attempt to understand hashtags as self-organized channels for addressing a logistical need in the wake of a disaster, our investigation is not conclusive.

First, our results indicate the capacity of supervised machine classification to distinguish the logistically relevant messages in the improvised #PorteOuverte channel; however, the labeled training data and the testing data are both from the same disaster. A practical system must detect logistical information in real time without waiting for relevant data to be labeled after a disaster strikes. Future research might consider testing the performance of machine classifiers in a practical cross-domain scenario [33] where the classifiers is trained on tweets from previous disasters and classify tweets of a new disaster event.

Secondly, the endogenous dynamics of the channel's growth also merit attention.Th e dominant message-type sent to #PorteOuverte, *Information about the hashtag*, is of ambiguous value. In particular, early in the channel's development it was likely that these messages helped to diffuse the idea of #PorteOuverte, indicating a "learning curve" for the audience regarding the improvised channel. At some point, however, it appears that these messages competed for and drew attention away from the relevant, logistical messages. Future work should consider modeling the dynamics of this natural tension between the need to promote the channel and the need to use it effectively. Results of our machine classification indicate that if these time points can be identified relevant messages could be promoted or suppressed automatically.

Further, our analysis indicates that individuals select some logistical tweets for rebroadcast but ignore others. Similar to research examining which notices from official authorities get the most reshares [39], future research might consider which kinds of logistical offers or requests draw the most user attention. In addition, our research uncovered a new kind of message, *Reflexive comments*, that emerged endogenously and created noise in the channel. Modeling how and when comments about the phenomenon begin to grow could be useful in anticipating the dynamics of future ILCs.

Nevertheless, the current work makes an important initial effort to understand the dynamic and effectiveness of hashtags as self-organized ILCs during and after disasters. It sheds a light towards a more effective mechanism to detect and disseminate logistical needs in self-organized channels on social media in the wake of disasters.

ACKNOWLEDGEMENTS

This work is part of the research supported by NSF Grants #1423697, #1634944 and #1634702, and the CRDF & CIS at the University of Pittsburgh. Xingsheng He also thanks the support of China Scholarship Council. Any opinions,fi ndings, and conclusions or recommendations expressed in this material do not necessarily reflect the views of the funding sources.

REFERENCES

[1] Adam Acar and Yuya Muraki. 2011. Twitter for crisis communication: lessons learned from Japan's tsunami disaster. *International Journal of Web Based Communities* 7, 3 (2011), 392–402.
[2] Jisun An, Haewoon Kwak, Yelena Mejova, De Oger, Sonia Alonso Saenz, and Braulio Gomez Fortes. 2016. Are you Charlie or Ahmed? Cultural pluralism in Charlie Hebdo response on Twitter. *arXiv preprint arXiv:1603.00646* (2016).
[3] Leonard Bickman and Jerome D Cook. 1986. Social support following a disaster. (1986).
[4] Axel Bruns, Jean E Burgess, Kate Crawford, and Frances Shaw. 2012. #qldfloods and @QPSMedia: Crisis communication on Twitter in the 2011 south east Queenslandfl oods. (2012).
[5] Paola-Maria Caleffi. 2015.Th e "hashtag": A new word or a new rule? 12, 2 (2015), 46–70.
[6] Tianqi Chen and Carlos Guestrin. 2016. Xgboost: A scalable tree boosting system. *arXiv preprint arXiv:1603.02754* (2016).
[7] Dharma Dailey and Kate Starbird. 2014. Visible Skepticism: Community Vetting after Hurricane Irene. In *ISCRAM 2014.* 777–781.
[8] George Forman. 2003. An extensive empirical study of feature selection metrics for text classification. *JMLR* 3, Mar (2003), 1289–1305.
[9] Huiji Gao, Xufei Wang, Geoffrey Barbier, and Huan Liu. 2011. Promoting coordination for disaster relief–from crowdsourcing to coordination. In *SBP 2011.* Springer, 197–204.
[10] Philip N. Howard and Samuel C. Woolley. 2016. Bots and Automation over Twitter during the US Election. (2016). http://politicalbots.org/wp-content/uploads/2016/11/Data-Memo-US-Election.pdf
[11] Qunying Huang and Yu Xiao. 2015. Geographic situational awareness: mining tweets for disaster preparedness, emergency response, impact, and recovery. *ISPRS International Journal of Geo-Information* 4, 3 (2015), 1549–1568.
[12] Muhammad Imran, Carlos Castillo, Fernando Diaz, and Sarah Vieweg. 2015. Processing social media messages in mass emergency: A survey. *Computing Surveys (CSUR)* 47, 4 (2015), 67.
[13] Peter M Landwehr and Kathleen M Carley. 2014. Social media in disaster relief. In *Data mining and knowledge discovery for big data.* Springer, 225–257.
[14] John Boaz Lee, Michael Ybañez, Marlene M De Leon, and Ma Regina E Estuar. 2013. Understanding the behavior offi lipino twitter users during disaster. *JoC* 3, 2 (2013), 37.
[15] Janette Lehmann, Bruno Gonalves, Jos J. Ramasco, and Ciro Cattuto. 2012. Dynamical classes of collective attention in twitter. In *WWW 2012.* ACM, 251–260.
[16] Yu-Ru Lin and Drew Margolin. 2014.Th e ripple of fear, sympathy and solidarity during the Boston bombings. *EPJ Data Science* 3, 1 (2014), 1–28.
[17] Yu-Ru Lin, Drew Margolin, Brian Keegan, Andrea Baronchelli, and David Lazer. 2013. #Bigbirds Never Die: Understanding Social Dynamics of Emergent Hashtags. In *ICWSM 2013.*
[18] Debanjan Mahata, John R Talburt, and Vivek Kumar Singh. 2015. From Chirps to Whistles: Discovering Event-specific Informative Content from Twitter. In *WebSci 2015.* ACM, 17.
[19] David J. Mendonca and William Al Wallace. 2007. A Cognitive Model of Improvisation in Emergency Management. *IEEE Transactions on Systems, Man, and Cybernetics - Part A: Systems and Humans* 37, 4 (July 2007), 547–561.
[20] Tomas Mikolov, Ilya Sutskever, Kai Chen, Greg S Corrado, and Jeff Dean. 2013. Distributed representations of words and phrases and their compositionality. In *NIPS 2013.* 3111–3119.
[21] Tahora H Nazer, Fred Morstatter, Harsh Dani, and Huan Liu. 2016. Finding requests in social media for disaster relief. In *ASONAM 2016.* IEEE, 1410–1413.
[22] Alexandra Olteanu, Sarah Vieweg, and Carlos Castillo. 2015. What to expect when the unexpected happens: Social media communications across crises. In *CSCW 2015.* ACM, 994–1009.
[23] Ruth Page. 2012.Th e linguistics of self-branding and micro-celebrity in Twitter: The role of hashtags. 6, 2 (2012), 181–201.
[24] Leysia Palen, Kate Starbird, Sarah Vieweg, and Amanda Hughes. 2010. Twitter-based information distribution during the 2009 Red River Valley flood threat. *ASIS&T* 36, 5 (2010), 13–17.
[25] Leysia Palen, Sarah Vieweg, Sophia B. Liu, and Amanda Lee Hughes. 2009. Crisis in a networked world features of computer-mediated communication in the April 16, 2007, Virginia Tech Event. 27, 4 (2009), 467–480.
[26] Lisa Posch, Claudia Wagner, Philipp Singer, and Markus Strohmaier. 2013. Meaning as collective use: predicting semantic hashtag categories on twitter. In *WWW 2013.* 621–628.
[27] Hemant Purohit, Carlos Castillo, Fernando Diaz, Amit Sheth, and Patrick Meier. 2013. Emergency-relief coordination on social media: Automatically matching resource requests and offers. *First Monday* 19, 1 (2013).
[28] Hemant Purohit, Andrew Hampton, Shreyansh Bhatt, Valerie L Shalin, Amit P Sheth, and John M Flach. 2014. Identifying seekers and suppliers in social media communities to support crisis coordination. *CSCW 2014* 23, 4-6 (2014), 513–545.
[29] YanQu , Chen Huang, Pengyi Zhang, and Jun Zhang. 2011. Microblogging after a major disaster in China: a case study of the 2010 Yushu earthquake. In *CSCW 2011.* ACM, 25–34.
[30] Raquel Recuero, Gabriela Zago, Marco T Bastos, and Ricardo Araflјo. 2015. Hashtags Functions in the Protests Across Brazil. *SAGE Open* 5, 2 (2015).
[31] Manuel Gomez Rodriguez, Krishna Gummadi, and Bernhard Schoelkopf. 2014. Quantifying information overload in social media and its impact on social contagions. In *ICWSM 2014.*
[32] Daniel M. Romero, Brendan Meeder, and Jon Kleinberg. 2011. Differences in the mechanics of information diffusion across topics: idioms, political hashtags, and complex contagion on twitter. In *WWW 2011.* ACM, 695–704.
[33] Koustav Rudra, Subham Ghosh, Niloy Ganguly, Pawan Goyal, and Saptarshi Ghosh. 2015. Extracting situational information from microblogs during disaster events: a classification-summarization approach. In *CIKM 2015.* ACM.
[34] Christopher Slagh. 2010. Managing chaos, 140 characters at a time: How the usage of social media in the 2010 Haiti crisis enhanced disaster relief. (2010).
[35] Kate Starbird, Jim Maddock, Mania Orand, Peg Achterman, and Robert M. Mason. 2014. Rumors, False Flags, and Digital Vigilantes: Misinformation on Twitter after the 2013 Boston Marathon Bombing. In *iConference 2014.* iSchools.
[36] Kate Starbird, Leysia Palen, Amanda L Hughes, and Sarah Vieweg. 2010. Chatter on the red: what hazards threat reveals about the social life of microblogged information. In *CSCW 2010.* ACM, 241–250.
[37] Kate Starbird and Jeannie Stamberger. 2010. Tweak the tweet: Leveraging microblogging proliferation with a prescriptive syntax to support citizen reporting. (2010).
[38] Zachary C Steinert-Threlkeld, Delia Mocanu, Alessandro Vespignani, and James Fowler. 2015. Online social networks and offline protest. *EPJ Data Science* 4, 1 (2015), 19.
[39] Jeannette Sutton, C. Ben Gibson, Nolan Edward Phillips, Emma S. Spiro, Cedar League, Britta Johnson, Sean M. Fitzhugh, and Carter T. Butts. 2015. A cross-hazard analysis of terse message retransmission on Twitter. *PNAS* 112, 48 (2015), 14793–14798.
[40] Jeannette Sutton, Leysia Palen, and Irina Shklovski. 2008. Backchannels on the front lines: Emergent uses of social media in the 2007 southern California wildfires. In *ISCRAM 2008.* 624–632.
[41] István Varga, Motoki Sano, Kentaro Torisawa, Chikara Hashimoto, Kiyonori Ohtake, Takao Kawai, Jong-Hoon Oh, and Stijn De Saeger. Aid is OutTh ere: Looking for Help from Tweets during a Large Scale Disaster.
[42] Sarah Vieweg, Amanda L Hughes, Kate Starbird, and Leysia Palen. 2010. Microblogging during two natural hazards events: what twitter may contribute to situational awareness. In *SIGCHI 2010.* ACM, 1079–1088.
[43] Xidao Wen and Yu-Ru Lin. 2016. Sensing Distress Following A Terrorist Event. In *SBP-BRiMS 2016.*
[44] Xidao Wen, Yu-Ru Lin, and Konstantinos Pelechrinis. 2016. PairFac: Event Analytics through Discriminant Tensor Factorization. In *CIKM 2016.*
[45] Lei Yang, Tao Sun, Ming Zhang, and Qiaozhu Mei. 2012. We know what@ you# tag: does the dual role affect hashtag adoption?. In *WWW 2012.* ACM, 261–270.
[46] Michele Zappavigna. 2015. Searchable talk: the linguistic functions of hashtags. 25, 3 (2015), 274–291. http://www.hca.westernsydney.edu.au/gmjau/?p=1762
[47] Hang Zhang and Vinay Setty. 2016. Finding diverse needles in a haystack of comments: social media exploration for news. In *WebSci 2016.* ACM, 286–290.
[48] G.K. Zipf. 1999. *The psycho-biology of language: An introduction to dynamic philology.* Routledge, London.
[49] Matthew Zook, Mark Graham, Taylor Shelton, and Sean Gorman. 2010. Volunteered geographic information and crowdsourcing disaster relief: a case study of the Haitian earthquake. *World Medical & Health Policy* 2, 2 (2010), 7–33.

The Effect of Collective Attention on Controversial Debates on Social Media

Kiran Garimella
Aalto University
Helsinki, Finland
kiran.garimella@aalto.fi

Gianmarco De Francisci Morales
Qatar Computing Research Institute
Doha, Qatar
gdfm@acm.org

Aristides Gionis
Aalto University
Helsinki, Finland
aristides.gionis@aalto.fi

Michael Mathioudakis
Aalto University
Helsinki, Finland
michael.mathioudakis@aalto.fi

ABSTRACT

We study the evolution of long-lived controversial debates as manifested on Twitter from 2011 to 2016. Specifically, we explore how the *structure of interactions* and *content of discussion* varies with the level of collective attention, as evidenced by the number of users discussing a topic. Spikes in the volume of users typically correspond to external events that increase the public attention on the topic – as, for instance, discussions about 'gun control' often erupt after a mass shooting.

This work is the first to study the dynamic evolution of polarized online debates at such scale. By employing a wide array of network and content analysis measures, we find consistent evidence that increased collective attention is associated with increased network polarization and network concentration within each side of the debate; and overall more uniform lexicon usage across all users.

1 INTRODUCTION

Social media are a major venue of public discourse today, hosting the opinions of hundreds of millions of individuals. Due to their prevalence they have become an invaluable instrument in the study of social phenomena and a fundamental subject of *computational social science*. In this work, we study discussions around issues that are deemed important at a societal level — and in particular, ones that are controversial. This work is a step towards understanding how the discussion about controversial topics on social media evolves, and more broadly how these topics shape the discussion at a societal and political level [1, 16, 23].

We study how online discussions around controversial topics change as interest in them increases and decreases. We are motivated by the observation that interest in enduring controversial issues is re-kindled by external events, e.g., when a major related story is reported. One typical example is the gun control debate in U.S., which is revived whenever a mass shooting occurs.[1] The occurrence of such an event commonly causes an increase in collective attention, e.g., in volume of related activity in social media.

Given a controversial topic, our focus is to analyze the interactions among users involved in the discussion, and quantify how certain structural properties of the interaction network vary with the change in volume of activity. Our main finding is that the polarization reflected in the network structure of online interactions is correlated with the increase in the popularity of a topic.

Differently from previous studies, we study the *dynamic* aspects of controversial topics on social media. While the evolution of networks and polarization on social media have been studied in the past [7, 21], they have not been studied in conjunction before. In addition, we seek to understand the *response* of social media to stimuli that cause increased interest in the topics, an issue that only very recently has seen some attention [30].

We take a longitudinal approach and collect data from Twitter that covers approximately five years. This dataset gives us a very fine-grained view of the activity on social media, including the structure of the interactions among users, and the content they produced during this period. We track four topics of discussion that are controversial in the U.S., that are recurring, and have seen considerable attention during the 2016 U.S. elections.

Our methodology relies on recent advances in quantifying controversy on social media [12]. We build two types of networks: an *endorsement* network from the retweet information on Twitter, and a *communication* network from the replies. We aggregate the data at a daily level, thus giving rise to a time series of interaction graphs. Then, we identify the sides of a controversy via graph clustering, and find the *core* of the network, i.e., the users who are consistently participating to the online discussion about the topic. Finally, we employ a wide array of measures that characterize the discussion about a topic on social media, both from the point of view of the network structure and of the actual content of the posts.

Apart from our main result — an increase in polarization linked to increased interest — we also report on several other findings. We find that most of the interactions during events of interest happen within the different controversy sides, and replies do not cross sides very often, in line with previous observations [31]. In addition, increased interest does not alter the fundamental structure

---

Contact authors: Kiran Garimella, Michael Mathioudakis.

WebSci'17, June 25-28, 2017, Troy, NY, USA.

978-1-4503-4896-6/17/06...$15.00
DOI: http://dx.doi.org/10.1145/3091478.3091486

[1] See, e.g., http://slate.me/1NswLLD.

of the endorsement network, which is hierarchical, with a disproportionately large fraction of edges linking the periphery to the core. This finding suggests that most casual users, who seldom participate in the discussion, endorse opinions from the core of the side they belong to. When looking at the content of the posts on the two sides of a controversy, we find a consistent trend of *convergence*, as the lexicons become both more uniform and more similar to each other. This result indicates that, while the discussion is still controversial, both sides of the debate focus over the same fundamental issues brought under the spotlight by the event at hand. Conversely, we do not find a consistent long-term trend in the polarization of discussions, which contradicts the common narrative that our society is becoming more divided over time. Finally, we perform similar measurements for a set of topics that are non-political and non-controversial, and highlight differences with the results for controversial discussions.[2]

2 RELATED WORK

A few studies exist on the topic of controversy in online news and social media. In one of the first papers, Adamic and Glance [2] study linking patterns and topic coverage of political bloggers, focusing on blog posts on the U.S. presidential election of 2004. They measure the degree of interaction between liberal and conservative blogs, and provide evidence that conservative blogs are linking to each other more frequently and in a denser pattern. These findings are confirmed by a more recent study of Conover et al. [7], who focus on political communication regarding congressional midterm elections. Using data from Twitter, they identify a highly segregated partisan structure (present in the retweet graph, but not in the mention graph), with limited connectivity between left- and right-leaning users. In another recent work, Mejova et al. [26] consider discussions of controversial and non-controversial news over a span of 7 months. They find a significant correlation between controversial issues and the use of negative affect and biased language. More recently, Garimella et al. [12] show that controversial discussions on social media have a well-defined structure, when looking at the *endorsement* network. They propose a measure based on random walks (RWC), which is able to identify controversial topics, and *quantify* the level of controversy of a given discussion via its network structure alone.

The aforementioned studies focus on static networks, which are a snapshot of the underlying dynamic networks. Instead, we are interested in network dynamics and, specifically, in how it responds to increased collective attention in the controversial topic.

Several studies have looked at how networks evolve, and proposed models of network formation [20, 21]. Densification over time is a pattern often observed [21], i.e., social networks gain more edges as the number of nodes grows. A change in the scaling behavior of the degree distribution has also been observed [3]. Newman et al. [29] offer a comprehensive review. Most of these studies focus on social networks, and in particular, on the friendship relationship. In our work, we are interested in studying an *interaction* network, which has markedly different characteristics.

[2]A limited subset of our results appeared in a poster at ICWSM 2017 [14].

There is a large amount of literature devoted to studying the evolution of networks. For an overview, see the book by Dorogovtsev and Mendes [10]. However, none of these previous studies has devoted much attention to the evolution of interaction networks for controversial topics, especially when tracking topics for a long period of time.

DiFonzo et al. [9] report on a user study that shows how the network structure affects the formation of stereotypes when discussing controversial topics. They find that segregation and clustering lead to a stronger "echo chamber" effect, with higher polarization of opinions. Our study examines a similar correlation between polarization and network structure, although in a much wider context, and focusing on the influence of external events.

Garimella and Weber [15] study polarization on Twitter over a long period of time, using content and network-based measures for polarization and find that over the past decade, polarization has increased. We find no consistent trend among the topics we study.

Perhaps the closest work to this paper is the work by Smith et al. [31], who study the role of social media in the discussion of controversial topics. They try to understand how positions on controversial issues are communicated via social media, mostly by looking at user level features such as retweet and reply rates, url sharing behavior, etc. They find that users spread information faster if it agrees with their position, and that Twitter debates may not play a big role in deciding the outcome of a controversial issue.

However, there are differences with our work: (i) they study one local topic (California ballot), over a small period of time, while we study a wide range of popular topics, spanning multiple years; and (ii) their analysis is mostly user centric, whereas we take a global viewpoint, constructing and analyzing networks of user interaction.

The effect of external events on social networks. A few studies have examined the effects of events on social networks. Romero et al. [30] study the behavior of a hedge-fund company via the communication network of their instant messaging systems. They find that in response to external shocks, i.e., when stock prices change significantly, the network "turtles up," strong ties become more important, and the clustering coefficient increases. In our case, we examine both a communication network and an endorsement network, and we focus on controversial issues. Given the different setting, many of our findings are quite different.

Other works, such as the ones by Lehmann et al. [19] and Wu and Huberman [32], examine how collective attention focuses on individual topics or items and evolves over time. Lehmann et al. [19] examine spikes in the frequency of hashtags and whether most frequency volume appears before or after the spike. They find that the observed patterns point to a classification of hashtags, that agrees with whether the hashtags correspond to topics that are endogenously or exogenously driven. Wu and Huberman [32], on the other hand, examine items posted on digg.com and how their popularity decreases over time.

Morales et al. [27] study polarization over time for a single event, the death of Hugo Chavez. Our analysis has a more broad spectrum, as we establish common trends across several topics, and find strong signals linking the volume of interest to the degree of polarization in the discussion.

Table 1: Keywords for the controversial topics.

Topic	Keywords	#Tweets	#Users
Obamacare	obamacare, #aca	866 484	148 571
Abortion	abortion, prolife, prochoice, anti-abortion, pro-abortion, planned parenthood	1 571 363	327 702
Gun Control	gun control, gun right, pro gun, anti gun, gun free, gun law, gun safety, gun violence	824 364	224 270
Fracking	fracking, #frack, hydraulic fracturing, shale, horizontal drilling	2 117 945	170 835

Andris et al. [4] study the partisanship of the U.S. congress over a long period of time. They find that partisanship (or non-cooperation) in the U.S. congress has been increasing dramatically for over 60 years. Our study suggests that increased controversy is linked to an increase in attention on a topic, whereas we do not see a global trend over time.

3 DATASET

Our study uses data collected from Twitter. Using the repositories of the Internet Archive,[3] we collect a 1% sample of tweets from September 2011 to August 2016,[4] for four topics of discussion, related to 'Obamacare', 'Abortion', 'Gun Control', and 'Fracking'. These topics constitute long-standing controversial issues in the U.S.[5] and have been used in previous work [25]. For each topic, we use a keyword list as proposed by Lu et al. [25] (shown in Table 1), and extract a base set of tweets which contain at least one topic-related keyword. To enrich this original dataset, we use the Twitter REST API to obtain all tweets of users who have participated in the discussion at least once.[6] Admittedly, this dataset might suffer from sampling bias, however the topics are specific enough that the distortion should be negligible [28]. There might also be recency bias due to the addition of the latest tweets of the users. However, the data does not show any clear trend in this sense (see Figure 1). In addition, given that we rely on detecting volume peaks, the trend does not affect our analysis. Table 1 shows the final statistics for the dataset.

We infer two types of interaction network from the dataset: (*i*) a retweet network – a directed endorsement network of users, where there is an edge between two users ($u \rightarrow v$) if u retweets v, and (*ii*) a reply network – a directed communication network of users, where an edge ($u \rightarrow v$) indicates that user u has replied to a tweet by user v. Note that replies are characterized by a tweet starting with `'@username'` and do not include mentions and retweets.[7]

[3]https://archive.org/details/twitterstream
[4]To be precise, we have data for 57 months from that period
[5]According to http://2016election.procon.org.
[6]Up to 3200 due to limits imposed by the Twitter API.
[7]See also https://support.twitter.com/articles/14023 for terminology related to different types of Twitter messages.

Polarized networks, especially the ones considered here, can be broadly characterized by two opposing *sides*, which express different opinions on the topic at hand. It is commonly understood that retweets indicate endorsement, and endorsement networks for controversial topics have been shown to have a bi-clustered structure [7, 12], i.e., they consist of two well-separated clusters that correspond to the opposing points of view on the topic. Conversely, replies can indicate discussion, and several studies have reported that users tend to use replies to talk across the sides of a controversy [6, 24]. These two types of network capture different dynamics of activity, and allow us to tease apart the processes that generate these interactions.

In this paper, we build upon the observation that the clustering structure of retweet networks reveals the opposing sides of a topic. In particular, following an approach from previous work [12], we collapse all retweets contained in the dataset of each topic into a single large static retweet network. Then, we use the METIS clustering algorithm [17] to identify two clusters that correspond to the two opposing sides. This process allows us to identify more consistent sides for the topic. We evaluate the sides by manual inspection of the top retweeted users, URLs, and hashtags. The results are consistent and accurate, and can be inspected online.[8]

Let us now consider the temporal dynamics of these interaction networks. Given the traditional daily news reporting cycle, we build the time series of networks with the same daily granularity. This high resolution allows us to easily discern the level of interest in the topic, and possibly identify spikes of interest linked to real world external events, as shown in Figure 1. These spikes usually correspond to external newsworthy events, as shown by the annotations. These results support the observation that Twitter is used as an *agorá* to discuss the daily matters of public interest [8].

As shown in Figure 1, the size of the active network for each day varies significantly. There is, however, a *hard core* set of active users who are involved in the discussion of these controversial topics most of the time. Therefore, to understand the role of these more engaged users, we define the 'core network' as the one induced by users who are active for more than 3/4 of the observation time. Specifically, to build a *core* set of users, we first identify two subsets – one consisting of those users who generated or received a retweet at least once per month for 45 months; and another one defined similarly for replies. We define the core set of users as the union of the aforementioned two sets. Nodes of a network that do not belong to the core are said to belong to the *periphery* of that network. The size of the core ranges from around 600 to 2800 nodes for the four topics. For any given day, the core accounts for at most around 10% of the active users.

3.1 Notation

The set of retweets that occur within a single day d gives rise to one retweet network N_d^{rt}. Each user associated with a retweet is represented with one node in the network. There is a directed edge from user u to user v only when user u has retweeted at least one tweet authored by user v. Correspondingly, the set of replies that occur within a single day give rise to a reply network N_d^{re}. In addition, each node u in the network is associated with a binary

[8]https://mmathioudakis.github.io/polarization/

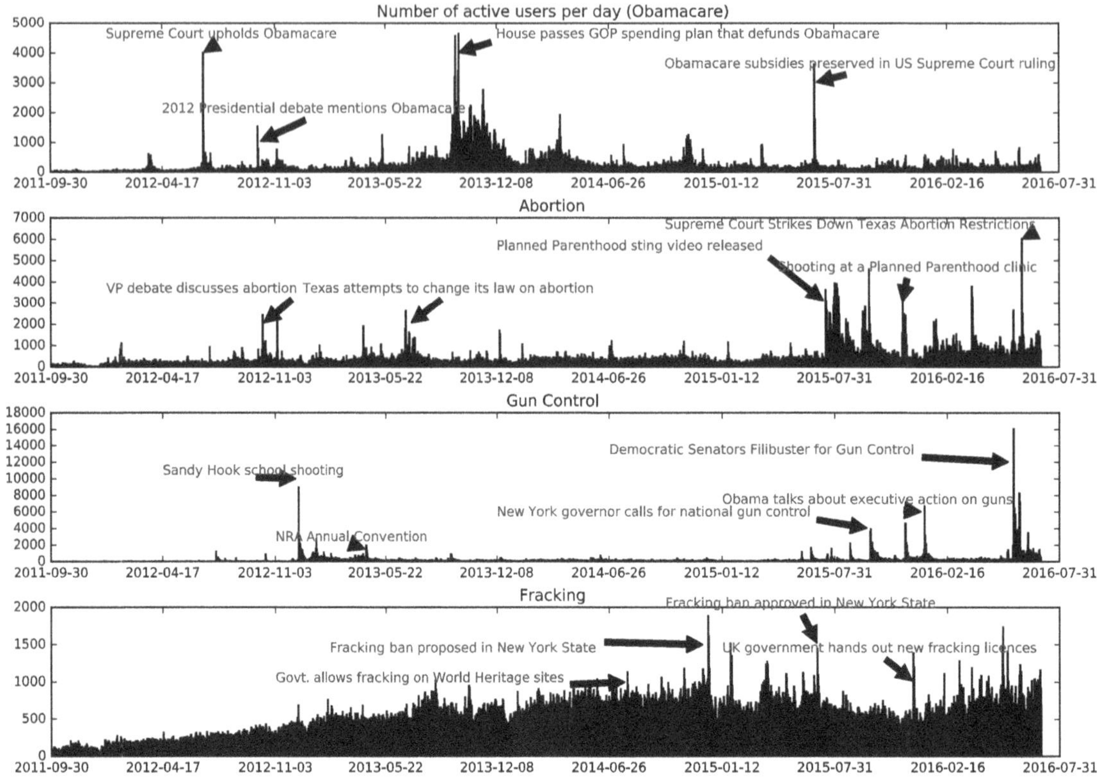

Figure 1: Daily trends for number of active users for the four controversial topics under study. Clear spikes occur at several points in the timeline. Manually chosen labels describing related events reported in the news on the same day are shown in blue for some of the spikes.

attribute $c(u) \in \{\texttt{true}, \texttt{false}\}$ that indicates whether the node is part of the core, and an attribute $s(u) \in \{1, 2\}$ that represents the side the node belongs to. In some cases, we consider undirected versions of the networks defined above. In such cases, we write G_d^{rt}, G_d^{re} to denote the undirected graphs corresponding to N_d^{rt}, N_d^{re}, respectively.

Besides these two types of network, for each day we consider the set of tweets that were generated on that day. Every tweet m is associated with an attribute $s(m) \in \{1, 2\}$ that indicates the side its author belongs to. Moreover, every tweet m is associated with the list of words $w(m)$ that occur in its text. This information gives rise to two unigram distributions W_d^1 and W_d^2, one for each side. Each distribution expresses the number of times each word appears in the tweets of nodes from each side.

4 MEASURES

For each day d, we employ a set of measures on the associated networks N_d^{rt}, N_d^{re}, and unigram distributions W_d^1 and W_d^2. We describe them below.

Polarization. We quantify the polarization of a network N_d by using the random-walk controversy (RWC) score introduced in previous work [12]. Intuitively, the score captures whether the network consists of two well-separated clusters.

Clustering coefficient. In an undirected graph, the clustering coefficient $cc(u)$ of a node u is defined as the fraction of closed triangles in its immediate neighborhood. Specifically, let d be the degree of node u, and T be the number of closed triangles involving u and two of its neighbors, then

$$cc(u) = \frac{2T}{d(d-1)}.$$

In our case, we consider the undirected graph G_d and compute the average clustering coefficient of all nodes that belong to each *side* – then take the mean of the two averages as the clustering coefficient of the network.

In order to control for scale effects, i.e., correlation between the size of the network (as determined by the volume of users active on day d) and the clustering coefficient, we employ a normalizer for the score. More in detail, we use an Erdős-Rényi graph as null model (with edges drawn at random among pair of nodes), and normalize the score by the expected value for a null-model graph of the same size. Unless otherwise specified, we apply the same type of normalization for all the methods defined below.

Tie strength. For each node u in a graph G_d, we consider all nodes v it is connected to across all days, and order them decreasingly by the number of occurrences $|\{d : (u, v) \in G_d\}|$. That is, the node v at the top of the list for u is the node to which v connects the most consistently throughout the time span of the dataset. Then, we define the *strong ties* of a node u as the top 10% of the nodes ordered as described above. For a given day d, we define the tie strength of a node as the number of strong ties it is connected to in the corresponding graph G_d. The tie-strength measure for the day is defined as the average tie strength for all nodes on either side. As described for the previous measure above, we normalize the reported measure by the expected value for a random graph with the same number of nodes and edges.

Cross–side openness. This measure reports the number of edges that connect nodes from opposing sides, and captures the inter-side interaction happening in the network on a given day. Formally, it is defined as

$$CSO = |\{(u, v) \in G_d : s(u) \neq s(v)\}|.$$

We apply the same normalization as described above.

Sides edge composition. For a given network, we distinguish two types of edges: *within-sides*, where both adjacent nodes belong to the same side, and *across-sides*, where the adjacent nodes belong to different sides. For each day and network, we track the fraction of the two types of edges.

Core–periphery openness. This measure is defined as the number of edges that connect a node from the core to the periphery. It captures the amount of interaction between the hard core users and the casual ones. Formally,

$$CPO = |\{(u, v) \in G_d : c(u) \wedge \neg c(v)\}|.$$

Bimotif. For a network N_d, we define the bimotif measure as the number of directed edges $(u, v) \in N_d$ for which the opposite edge (v, u) also appears in the network

$$Bimotif = |\{(u, v) \in N_d : (v, u) \in N_d\}|.$$

This measure captures the mutual interactions happening within the network. It is also known as 'reciprocity' in the literature.

Core Density. This measure captures the number of edges that connect exclusively members of the core

$$CoreDens = |\{(u, v) \in N_d : c(u) \wedge c(v)\}|.$$

Core–periphery edge composition. For a given network, we distinguish three types of edges: *core–core*, where both adjacent nodes belong to the core we have identified, *core–periphery*, where one node belongs to the core and one to the periphery, and *periphery–periphery*, where both nodes belong to the periphery. For each day and network, we track the fraction of each type of edges.

Cross–side content divergence. This measure captures the difference between the word distributions W_d^1 and W_d^2, and is based on the Jensen-Shannon divergence [22]. The Jensen-Shannon divergence is undefined when one of the two distributions is zero at a point where the other is not. Thus, we smooth the distributions by adding Laplace counts $\beta = 10^{-5}$ to avoid zero entries in either distribution.

The traffic volume on a given day can increase the vocabulary size, and thus induce an unwanted bias in the measure. In order to counter this bias, we employ a sampling procedure similar to bootstrapping from the two distributions. For each smoothed distribution W_d^1 and W_d^2, we sample with replacement $k = 10\,000$ words at random, and compute the Jensen-Shannon divergence of these equal-sized samples. We repeat the process 100 times and report the average sample Jensen-Shannon divergence as the 'cross-side content divergence' for day d. Intuitively, the higher its value, the more different the word distributions across the two sides.

Within-side entropy. This measure captures how 'concentrated' each of the two distributions W_d^1 and W_d^2 is. For each side, we compute the entropy for each distribution. The higher its value, the more widely spread is the corresponding distribution. We use the same bootstrap sampling method described above to avoid bias due to activity volume.

Topic variance. This measure captures, to some extent, *what* is being talked on the two sides of the discussion. We extract a large number of topics by using Latent Dirichlet Allocation (k=100) on the complete tweet corpus. We then compute the distribution of topics in each bucket. This distribution gives an estimate on which of the 100 topics are being talked about in the bucket. We report the variance of this distribution. If the distribution is focused on a small number of topics, the variance is high. Conversely, a low variance indicates a uniform distribution of topics.

Sentiment variance. This measure captures the variance of sentiment valence (positive versus negative) in all the tweets of one day d [12].

Psychometric analysis. To understand the if there are behavioral changes in terms of content generated and shared by users with increasing activity, we use the Linguistic Inquiry and Word Count (LIWC) dictionary,[9] which identifies emotions in words [18]. We measure the fraction of tweets containing the LIWC categories: anger, sadness, posemo, negemo, and anxiety.

4.1 Analysis

We explore how the aforementioned measures vary with the number of active users in the networks, which is a proxy for the amount of collective attention the topic attracts. We sort the time series of networks by volume of active users, and partition it into ten quantiles (each having an equal number of days), so that days of bucket i are associated with smaller volume than those of bucket j, for $i < j$. For each bucket, we report the mean and standard deviation of the values for each measure, and observe the trend from lower to higher volume.

Note that the measures presented in this section are carefully defined so that their expected value does not depend on the volume of underlying activity (i.e., number of network nodes and edges or vocabulary size).

5 FINDINGS

In what follows, we report our findings on the measures defined in Section 4 — starting from the ones related to the retweet and reply networks (Section 5.1), then proceeding to the ones related to content (Section 5.2) and network cores (Section 5.3). We provide additional analysis for the periods around the spikes in interest (Section 5.4), as well as for the evolution of measures over time (Section 5.5).

[9]http://liwc.net

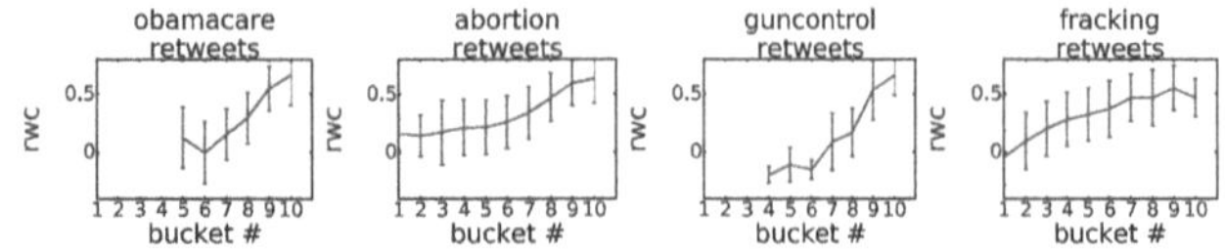

Figure 2: RWC score as a function of the activity in the retweet network. An increase in interest in the controversial topic corresponds to an increase in the controversy score of the retweet network.

5.1 Network

We observe a significant correlation between RWC score and interest in the topic. Figure 2 shows the RWC score as a function of the quantiles of the network by retweet volume (as explained in the previous section). There is a clear increasing trend, which is consistent across topics. This trend suggests that increased interest in the topic is correlated with an increase in controversy of the debate, and increased polarization of the retweet networks for the two sides. Conversely, reply networks are sparser and more disconnected, thus, the RWC score is not meaningful in this case (not shown due to space constraints). This difference is expected, and was already observed in the work that introduced RWC [12].

A similar result can be observed for the clustering coefficient, as shown in Figure 3. As the interest in the topic increases, the two sides tend to *turtle up*, and form a more close-knit retweet network. This result suggests that the *echo chamber* phenomenon gets stronger when the discussion sparks. Our finding is also consistent with results by Romero et al. [30]. As for the previous measure, the clustering coefficient does not show a significant pattern for the reply networks. Replies are often linked to dyadic interactions, while the clustering coefficient measures triadic ones, so we expect such a difference between the two types of network.

In line with the above results, tie strength is correlated with retweet volume, as indicated by Figure 4. When the discussion intensifies, users tend to endorse the opinions of their closest friends, or their trusted sources of information. Again, this observation indicates a closing up of both sides when the debate gets heated. Interestingly, a similar trend is present for the reply network, as shown in Figure 5. Differently from previous work, we find an increase of communication of users with their strong ties, rather than with weak ties or users of the opposing side. We also observe an increase in back-and-forth communication, indicating a dialogue between users of the same side. Figure 6 shows an increase in bimotifs in the reply network when the discussion intensifies. This measure is inconclusive for the retweet network, for the reasons mentioned above.

Finally, when calculating the fractions of *within-side edges* and *across-side edges* for *across sides edge composition*, we find that reply networks typically contain higher proportions of across-side activity compared to retweet networks, consistently with earlier work. In fact, for retweet networks, almost all edges are classified as *within-side edges*. Interestingly, we also find that these proportions do not change significantly as the volume increases. The same is true for the *cross-side openness* measure (not shown).

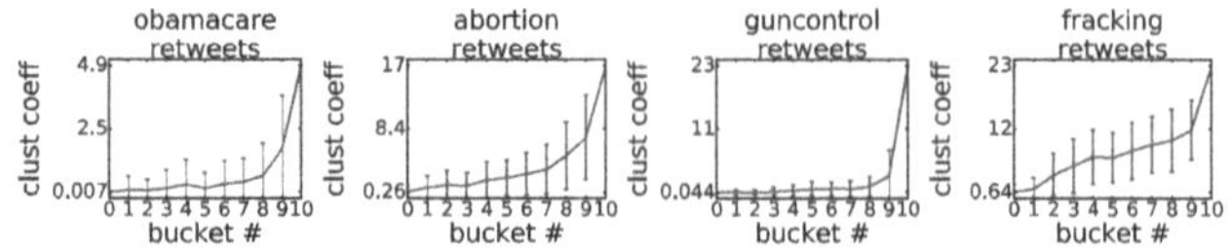

Figure 3: Average clustering coefficient of as a function of the activity in the retweet network. Spikes in interest correspond to an increase in the clustering coefficient on both sides of the discussion, which indicates the retweet networks tend to close up.

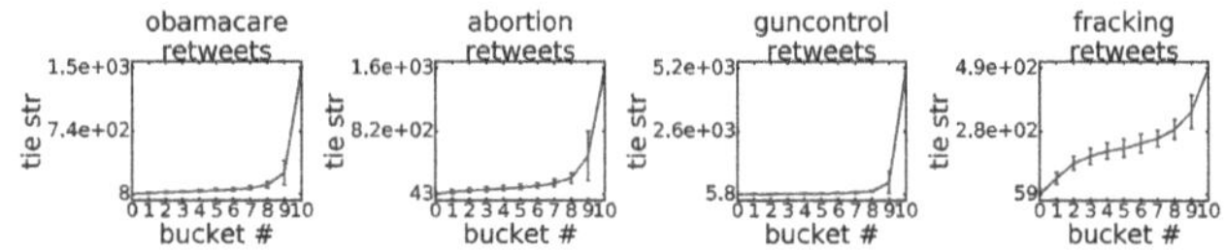

Figure 4: Tie strength as a function of the activity in the retweet network. Spikes in activity correspond to more interaction with stronger ties, which indicates a closing up of the retweet network.

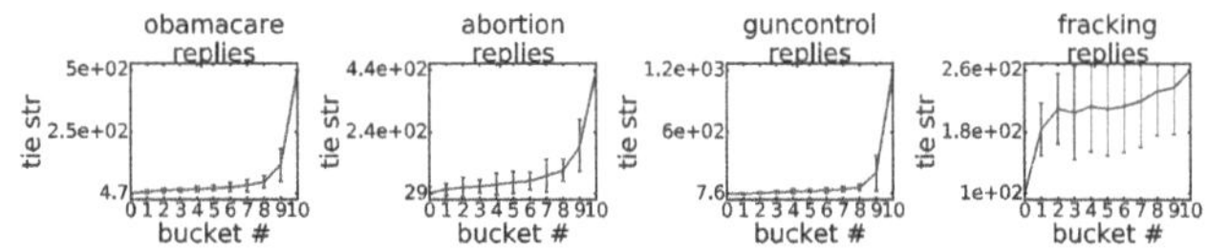

Figure 5: Tie strength as a function of the activity in the reply network. Users tend to communicate proportionally more with closer ties when interest spikes, which reveals a further closing up of the network.

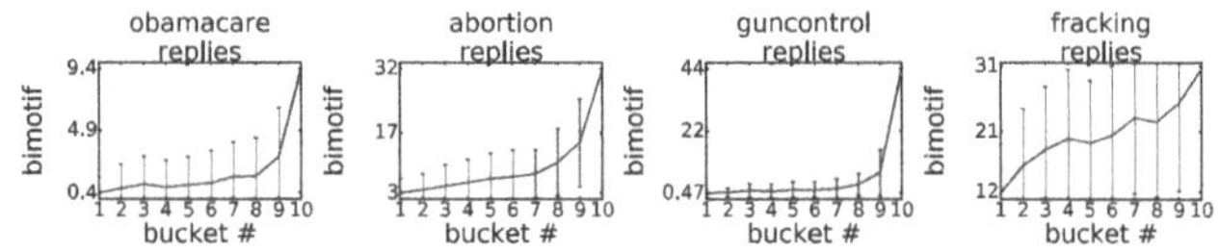

Figure 6: Bimotifs as a function of the activity in the reply network. Users tend to reciprocate the communication more as the discussion intensifies.

5.2 Content

Let us now switch our attention to the content measures. Recall that for these measures we do not distinguish between retweet and reply networks, but only between the two sides of the discussion. The main observation is that the Jensen-Shannon divergence between the two sides decreases, as shown by Figure 7. This decrease indicates that the lexicon of the two sides tends to converge. The cause of this phenomenon might be the participation of casual users to the discussions, who contribute a more general lexicon to the discussion. Alternatively, the cause might be in the event that sparks the discussion, which brings the whole network to adopt similar lexicon to speak about it, i.e., there is an event-based convergence.

To further examine the cause of the convergence of lexicon, we report the entropy of the unigram distribution. Figure 8 shows that the entropy for one of the sides increases as interest increases

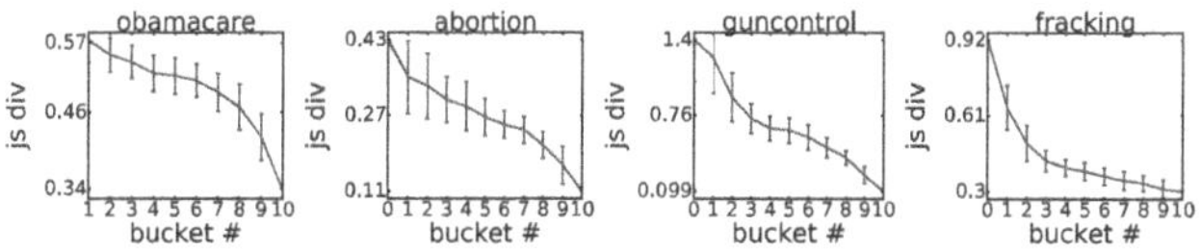

Figure 7: Jensen-Shannon divergence of the lexicon between the two sides as a function of network activity. As the interest in the topic rises, the lexicon used by the two sides tends to converge.

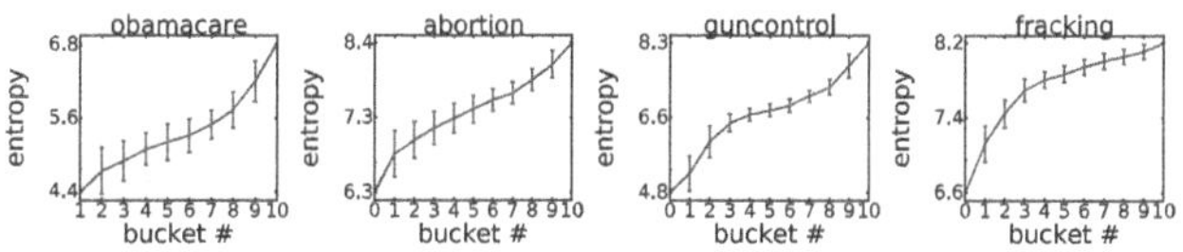

Figure 8: Entropy of the distribution over the lexicon for one side of the discussion as a function of the activity in the network (the other side shows similar patterns). As the interest increases, the entropy increases, thus indicating the use of a wider lexicon.

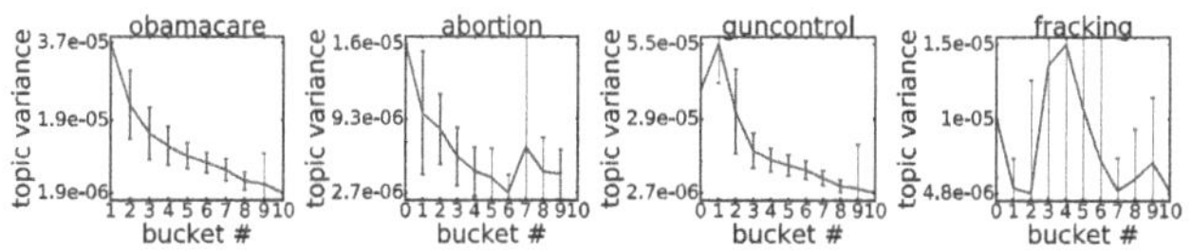

Figure 9: Variance of the topic distribution. As the interest increases, variance decreases, indicating that a wider range of topics are being discussed.

(results for the other side show similar trends). Thus, we find that the lexicon is more uniform and less skewed, which supports the hypothesis that a larger group of users brings a more general lexicon to the discussion, rather than the alternative hypothesis of event-based convergence.

To investigate *what* causes the lexicon to be generalized, we compute the variance of the topic distribution for each bucket. As we see from Figure 9, the variance decreases with increased activity, meaning that the topic distribution becomes more uniform[10]. This result provides evidence that users do indeed discuss a wider range of topics when there is a spike in activity.

Finally, we also examine how the sentiment and other linguistic cues change with interest. We measure the variance in sentiment, fraction of tweets containing various LIWC categories, such as anger, sadness, positive and negative emotion, and anxiety. Previous work shows that sentiment variance is a measure able to separate controversial from non-controversial topics [12] and linguistic patterns of communication change during shocks [30]. However, we do not see any consistent trend. We hypothesise that this might be due to the noise in language (slang, sarcasm, short text, etc) on social media.

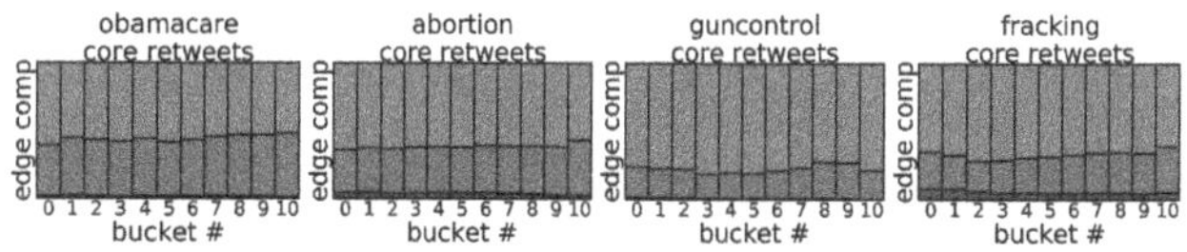

Figure 10: Edge composition as a function of network activity in the retweet network. As the interest increases, there are no major changes in the fractions of core-core (blue), core-periphery (green), and periphery-periphery (red) edges.

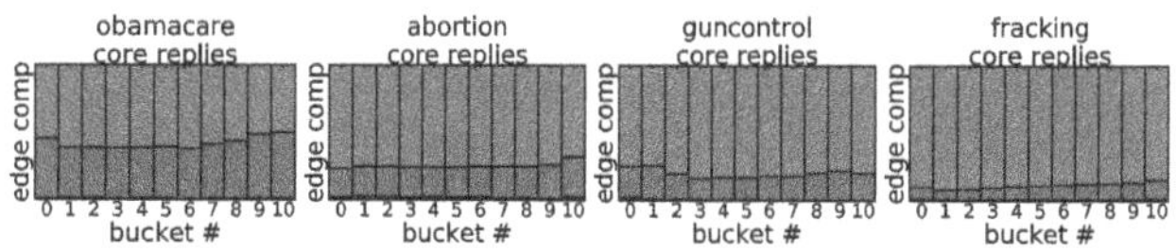

Figure 11: Edge composition as a function of network activity in the reply network. As the interest increases, there are no major changes in the fractions of core-core (blue), core-periphery (green), and periphery-periphery (red) edges.

5.3 Core

Looking at the fractions of the different types of edges (core–core, core–periphery, and periphery–periphery) across the volume buckets in Figures 10 and 11, we see that the composition of edges does not change significantly with increase collective attention. This result suggests that the discussion grows in a self-similar way.

A disproportionately large fraction of edges link the periphery to the core, when taking into account the core size, as seen in Figure 10. During a spike in interest, most casual users, who seldom participate in the discussion, endorse opinions from the core of the side they belong to (red bars). For replies, we see a similar trend with respect to activity volume in Figure 11. In general, the core is less prevalent in the discussion, as shown by the lower fraction of core-periphery edges (green bars).

However, when looking at the *core–periphery openness* (Figures 12 and 13), we see that the *normalized* number of edges between core and periphery increases, i.e., the number of edges between core and periphery increases compared to the expected number based on a random-graph null model. To interpret this result, note that when the network grows, given that the periphery is much larger than the core, most edges for the null model are among periphery nodes. Therefore, the interaction networks show a clear hierarchical structure when growing.

5.4 Local analysis

So far, we have analyzed global trends across the time series. We now focus on local trends, to drill down on what happens around the spikes, and look at local variations of the measures just before and after the spike. We mark a day in the time series as a spike if the volume of active users is at least two standard deviations above the mean. Table 2 shows the Pearson correlation between various measures and network activity, one week before and after the spike. The trends observed globally still hold. There is a positive correlation of RWC with activity, which adds more evidence to our

[10]The term 'fracking' is also sometimes used as an expletive, which might explain why the effects we measure are not as pronounced for this topic as the other ones. E.g. see https://twitter.com/KitKat0122/status/19820978435522561

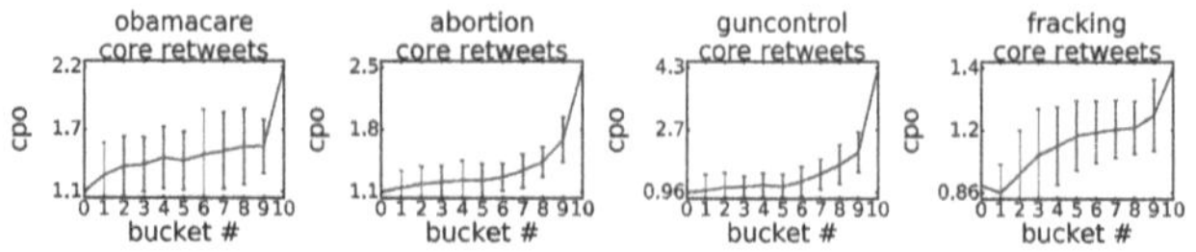

Figure 12: Core–periphery openness as a function of activity in the retweet network. As the interest increases, the number of core-periphery edges, normalized by the expected number of edges in a random network, increases. This suggests a propensity of periphery nodes to connect with the core nodes when interest increases.

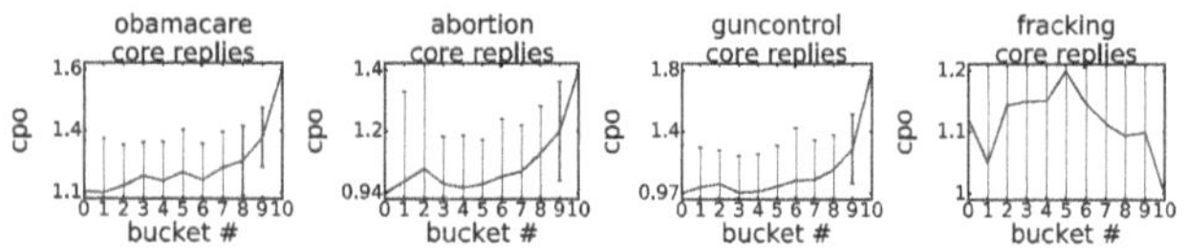

Figure 13: Core-periphery openness as a function of activity in the reply network. As the interest increases, the number of core-periphery edges, normalized by the expected number of edges in a random network, increases for most topics. This suggests a propensity of periphery nodes to connect with the core nodes when interest increases.

Table 2: Pearson correlation of various measures with volume one week before, during and after a spike in interest. All values except those marked with an asterisk (*) are significant at $p < 0.05$.

Measure	Obamacare	Gun Control	Abortion	Fracking
RWC	0.20	0.21	0.19	0.23
Openness	-0.09*	0.81	0.23	0.08
Bimotif	0.27	0.36	0.33	0.23
Tie Strength	0.96	0.98	0.95	0.86
JSD	-0.66	-0.86	-0.63	-0.46
Entropy	0.42	0.46	0.67	0.26
Frac. RT	0.15*	0.6	0.59	0.56
Frac. Men.	0.20	0.71	0.54	0.51
Frac. URL	0.32	0.36	0.39	0.40

finding that polarization increases during spikes. The trends for bimotif, tie strength, and content divergence also persist, and are much stronger locally.

In addition to the previous measures, we also analyze other content features, such as the fraction of retweets, replies, mentions, and URLs around the spike. Interestingly, we find strong positive correlation of retweets, mentions, and URLs with volume, which indicates that discussion and endorsement increase during a spike. This finding is consistent with the ones by Smith et al. [31], who find that users tend to add URLs to their tweets when discussing controversial topics. Note that these additional content measures are only indicative for the local analysis, and do not produce consistent results at the global level.

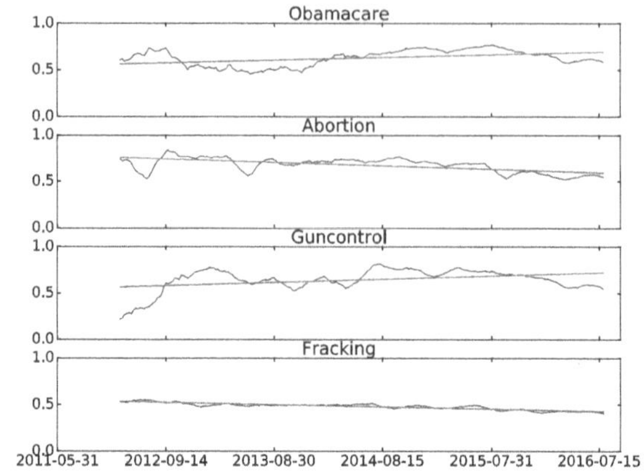

Figure 14: Long-term trends of RWC (controversy) score in our dataset. No consistent trend can be observed, which contradicts the narrative that social media is making our society more divided.

5.5 Evolution over time

Let us now focus on how the measures change throughout time. The longitudinal span of the dataset of five years allows us to track the long-term evolution of discussion on controversial topics. A common point of view holds that social media is aggravating the polarization of society and exacerbating the divisions in it [5]. At the same time, the political debate (in U.S.) itself has become more polarized in recent years [4]. However, we do not find conclusive evidence for this argument with our analysis on this dataset.

Figure 14 shows the long-term trends of the RWC measure for the four topics. The trend is downwards for 'abortion' and 'fracking', while it is upwards for 'obamacare' and 'gun control'. One could argue that the latter topics are more politically linked to the current administration in U.S., and for this reason have received increasing attention with the elections approaching. However, the only safe conclusion that can be drawn from this dataset is that there is no clear signal. The figure suggests that social media, and in particular Twitter, are better suited at capturing the 'twitch' response of the public to events and news. In addition, while our dataset spans a quite long time span for typical social media studies, it is still much shorter than other ones used typically in social science (coming from, e.g., census, polls, congress votes). This limit is intrinsic of the tool, given that social media have risen in popularity only relatively recently (e.g., Twitter is 10 years old).

5.6 Non-controversial topics

For comparison, we perform measurements over a set of non-controversial topics, defined by the hashtags *#ff*, standing for 'Follow Friday', used every Friday by users to recommend interesting accounts to follow; *#nba* and *#nfl*, used to discuss sports games; *#sxsw*, used to comment on the *South-by-South-West* conference; *#tbt*, standing for 'Throwback Thursday', used every Thursday by users to share memories (news, pictures, stories) from the past.

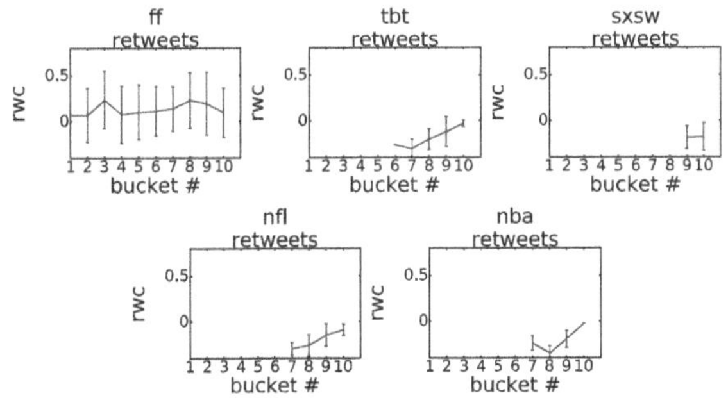

Figure 15: Non-controversial topics: RWC score as a function of the activity in the retweet network.

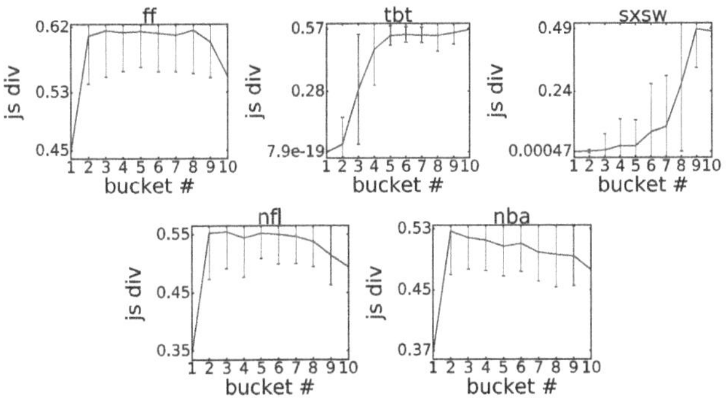

Figure 16: Non-controversial topics: Jensen-Shannon divergence of the lexicon between the two sides as a function of network activity. As the interest in the topic rises, the lexicon used by the two sides tends to converge.

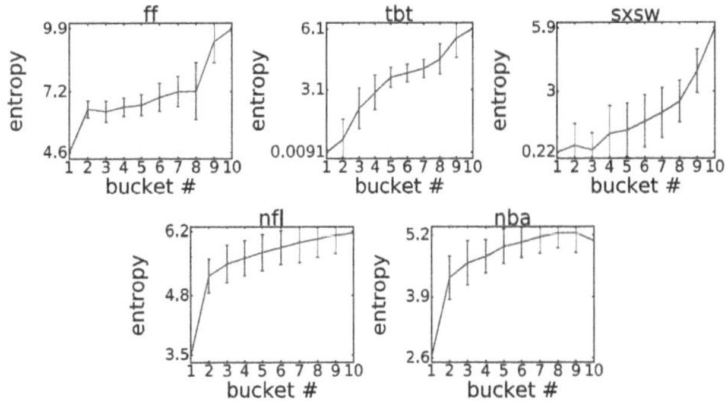

Figure 17: Non-controversial topics: Entropy of the distribution over the lexicon for one side of the discussion as a function of the activity in the network (the other side shows similar patterns).

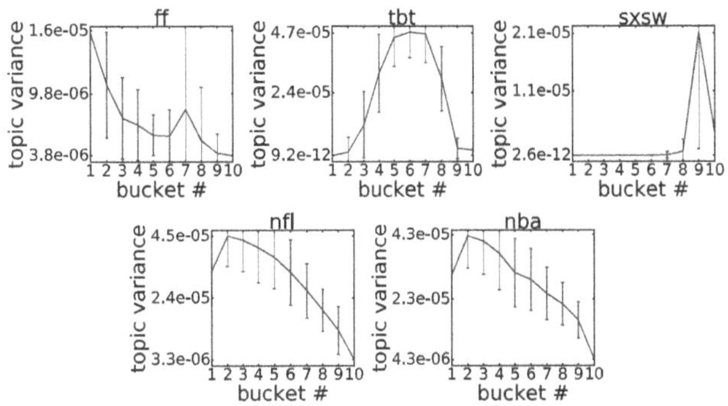

Figure 18: Non-controversial topics: Variance of the topic distribution. As the interest increases, variance decreases, indicating that a wider range of topics are being discussed.

We find that several structural measures, namely *clustering coefficient, tie strength,* and *bimotif,* behave similarly to the controversial topics, in that they obtain increased values for increased volume of activity. This result is in accordance with the ones by Romero et al. [30]. Conversely, the values of the RWC measure typically remain in ranges that indicate low presence of controversy, even as the volume of activity spikes (Figure 15). Additionally, with the definition of 'core' introduced above, we could only identify a negligibly small core for these topics (i.e., found very few users who were consistently active on these topics).

Finally, in terms of content measures we find that, as for the controversial topics, the entropy of the lexicon increases with volume (Figure 17). Topic variance also decreases with volume in most cases, meaning that a wider range of topics are discussed (Figure 18). On the contrary, the Jensen-Shannon divergence stays at relatively constant values across volume levels (Figure 16). It thus behaves differently compared to controversial topics (Figure 7). This result is to be expected, as the two 'sides' identified by METIS on the networks of non-controversial topics are not as well defined as they are in the case of controversial topics.

6 CONCLUSION

The evolution of networks is a well-studied phenomenon in social sciences, physics, and computer science. However, the evolution of *interaction* networks has received substantially less attention so far. In particular, interaction networks related to discussions of controversial topics, which are important from a sociological point of view, have not been analyzed before. This study is a first step towards understanding this important social phenomenon.

We analyzed four highly controversial topics of discussion on Twitter for a period of five years. By examining the endorsement and communication networks of users involved in these discussions, we found that spikes in interest correspond to an increase in the controversy of the discussion. This result is supported by a wide array of network analysis measures, and is consistent across topics. We also found that interest spikes correspond to a convergence of the lexicon used by the opposite sides of a controversy, and a more uniform lexicon overall. The code and datasets used in the paper are available on the project website.[8]

Implications of this work relate to the understanding of how our society evolves via continuous debates, and how culture wars develop [1, 16, 23]. It is often argued that technology, and social media in particular, is having a negative impact on our ability to relate to the unfamiliar [5], due to the "echo chamber" and "filter bubble" effects. However, while we found instantaneous temporary increase in controversy in relation to external events, our study did not find evidence of long term increase in polarization of the discussions, neither after these events nor as a general longitudinal trend. At the same time, investigating how to reduce the polarization of these discussions on controversial topics is a research-worthy problem [11, 13], and taking into account the dynamics of the process is a promising direction to explore.

Our observations pave the way to the development of models of evolution for controversial interaction networks, similarly to how studies about measuring the Web and social media were the stepping stone to developing models for them. A logical next step for this line of work is to investigate how to use early signals from social media network structure and content to predict the impact of an event. Equally of interest is whether the observations made in this study translate to other social media beside Twitter, for instance, Facebook or Reddit. Finally, while we did not find any consistent long-term trend in the polarization of the discussions, it is worth continuing this line of investigation, as the effects of increased polarization might not be easily discoverable from social-media analysis alone.

Acknowledgements. This work has been supported by the Academy of Finland project "Nestor" (286211) and the EC H2020 RIA project "SoBigData" (654024).

7 REFERENCES

[1] Alan Abramowitz and Kyle Saunders. 2005. Why can't we all just get along? The reality of a polarized America. In *The Forum*, Vol. 3. bepress, 1–22.

[2] Lada A Adamic and Natalie Glance. 2005. The political blogosphere and the 2004 US election: divided they blog. In *LinkKDD*. 36–43.

[3] Yong-Yeol Ahn, Seungyeop Han, Haewoon Kwak, Sue Moon, and Hawoong Jeong. 2007. Analysis of topological characteristics of huge online social networking services. In *WWW*. ACM, 835–844.

[4] Clio Andris, David Lee, Marcus J Hamilton, Mauro Martino, Christian E Gunning, and John Armistead Selden. 2015. The rise of partisanship and super-cooperators in the US House of Representatives. *PloS one* 10, 4 (2015), e0123507.

[5] Yochai Benkler. 2006. *The wealth of networks: How social production transforms markets and freedom.* Yale University Press.

[6] Alessandro Bessi, Guido Caldarelli, Michela Del Vicario, Antonio Scala, and Walter Quattrociocchi. 2014. Social determinants of content selection in the age of (mis) information. In *SocInfo*. Springer, 259–268.

[7] Michael Conover, Jacob Ratkiewicz, Matthew Francisco, Bruno Gonçalves, Filippo Menczer, and Alessandro Flammini. 2011. Political Polarization on Twitter. In *ICWSM*.

[8] Gianmarco De Francisci Morales, Aristides Gionis, and Claudio Lucchese. 2012. From Chatter to Headlines: Harnessing the Real-Time Web for Personalized News Recommendation. In *WSDM*. 153–162.

[9] Nicholas DiFonzo, Jerry Suls, Jason W Beckstead, Martin J Bourgeois, Christopher M Homan, Samuel Brougher, Andrew J Younge, and Nicholas Terpstra-Schwab. 2014. Network structure moderates intergroup differentiation of stereotyped rumors. *Social Cognition* 32, 5 (2014), 409.

[10] Sergei N Dorogovtsev and José FF Mendes. 2013. *Evolution of networks: From biological nets to the Internet and WWW.* OUP Oxford.

[11] Kiran Garimella, Gianmarco De Francisc iMorales, Aristides Gionis, and Michael Mathioudakis. 2017. Mary, Mary, Quite Contrary: Exposing Twitter Users to Contrarian News. In *WWW*. 201–205.

[12] Kiran Garimella, Gianmarco De Francisci Morales, Aristides Gionis, and Michael Mathioudakis. 2016. Quantifying Controversy in Social Media. In *WSDM*. ACM, 33–42.

[13] Kiran Garimella, Gianmarco De Francisci Morales, Aristides Gionis, and Michael Mathioudakis. 2017. Reducing Controversy by Connecting Opposing Views. In *WSDM*. ACM, 81–90.

[14] Kiran Garimella, Gianmarco De Francisci Morales, Aristides Gionis, and Michael Mathioudakis. 2017. The Ebb and Flow of Controversial Debates on Social Media. In *ICWSM*.

[15] Kiran Garimella and Ingmar Weber. 2017. A Long-Term Analysis of Polarization on Twitter. In *ICWSM*.

[16] Benjamin Highton and Cindy D Kam. 2011. The long-term dynamics of partisanship and issue orientations. *The Journal of Politics* 73, 01 (2011), 202–215.

[17] George Karypis and Vipin Kumar. 1995. METIS - Unstructured Graph Partitioning and Sparse Matrix Ordering System. (1995).

[18] Adam DI Kramer, Jamie E Guillory, and Jeffrey T Hancock. 2014. Experimental evidence of massive-scale emotional contagion through social networks. *Proceedings of the National Academy of Sciences* 111, 24 (2014), 8788–8790.

[19] Janette Lehmann, Bruno Gonçalves, José J. Ramasco, and Ciro Cattuto. 2012. Dynamical Classes of Collective Attention in Twitter. In *WWW*. ACM, 251–260.

[20] Jure Leskovec, Lars Backstrom, Ravi Kumar, and Andrew Tomkins. 2008. Microscopic evolution of social networks. In *KDD*. ACM, 462–470.

[21] Jure Leskovec, Jon Kleinberg, and Christos Faloutsos. 2005. Graphs over time: densification laws, shrinking diameters and possible explanations. In *KDD*. ACM, 177–187.

[22] Jianhua Lin. 1991. Divergence measures based on the Shannon entropy. *IEEE Transactions on Information theory* 37, 1 (1991), 145–151.

[23] Kara Lindaman and Donald P Haider-Markel. 2002. Issue evolution, political parties, and the culture wars. *Political Research Quarterly* 55, 1 (2002), 91–110.

[24] Zhe Liu and Ingmar Weber. 2014. Is Twitter a public sphere for online conflicts? A cross-ideological and cross-hierarchical look. In *SocInfo*. Springer, 336–347.

[25] Haokai Lu, James Caverlee, and Wei Niu. 2015. BiasWatch: A Lightweight System for Discovering and Tracking Topic-Sensitive Opinion Bias in Social Media. In *CIKM*. ACM, 213–222.

[26] Yelena Mejova, Amy X Zhang, Nicholas Diakopoulos, and Carlos Castillo. 2014. Controversy and Sentiment in Online News. *Symposium on Computation + Journalism* (2014).

[27] AJ Morales, J Borondo, JC Losada, and RM Benito. 2015. Measuring political polarization: Twitter shows the two sides of Venezuela. *Chaos* 25, 3 (2015).

[28] Fred Morstatter, Jürgen Pfeffer, Huan Liu, and Kathleen M Carley. 2013. Is the sample good enough? Comparing data from Twitter's streaming API with Twitter's firehose. *arXiv:1306.5204* (2013).

[29] Mark Newman, Albert-Laszlo Barabasi, and Duncan J Watts. 2011. *The structure and dynamics of networks.* Princeton University Press.

[30] Daniel M Romero, Brian Uzzi, and Jon Kleinberg. 2016. Social Networks Under Stress. In *WWW*. 9–20.

[31] Laura M Smith, Linhong Zhu, Kristina Lerman, and Zornitsa Kozareva. 2013. The role of social media in the discussion of controversial topics. In *SocialCom*. IEEE, 236–243.

[32] Fang Wu and Bernardo A. Huberman. 2007. Novelty and collective attention. *Proceedings of the National Academy of Sciences* 104, 45 (2007), 17599–17601.

Predicting Trust Relations Within a Social Network: A Case Study on Emergency Response

Nikhita Vedula
Department of Computer Science and Engineering
Ohio State University
vedula.5@osu.edu

Srinivasan Parthasarathy
Department of Computer Science and Engineering
Ohio State University
srini@cse.ohio-state.edu

Valerie L. Shalin
Department of Psychology and Kno.e.sis
Wright State University
valerie@knoesis.org

ABSTRACT

Trust is a fundamental construct underpinning modern society and the social exchanges it contains. The rise of Web 2.0 technologies and the increased use of online social networks, promotes the study of trust among users. Drawing on social and psychological theory, we detect pairwise and global trust relations between users in the context of emergent real-world crisis scenarios. In such situations and scale, seeking explicit pairwise trust assessments between users is impractical. Instead, in an unsupervised manner we integrate the implicit factors of social influence exerted by each user over the network, the underlying network structural topology and the affective valence expressed by the users in the textual content they communicate. A key finding is the importance of modeling influence and affective valence in such exchanges and their role in detecting stable trust relationships. We extensively evaluate these ideas and demonstrate significant gains over competitive baselines across multiple datasets drawn from both crisis and non-crisis scenarios, including those with normative ground truth.

ACM Reference format:
Nikhita Vedula, Srinivasan Parthasarathy, and Valerie L. Shalin. 2017. Predicting Trust Relations Within a Social Network: A Case Study on Emergency Response. In *Proceedings of WebSci '17, Troy, NY, USA, June 25-28, 2017,* 10 pages.
https://doi.org/http://dx.doi.org/10.1145/3091478.3091494

1 INTRODUCTION

Trust is a vital social construct that has drawn attention from multiple areas of research including sociology, psychology, management, economics, political science and computer science. The economist Arrow [33] identifies trust as "a lubricant of the social system", while computer scientists such as Massa et al [41] define it as a user's opinion on another user's characteristics. With the rise of Web 2.0 technologies, trust has emerged as a key concept in social network and social media analysis, reflecting credibility and reliability for the multitude of online participants and data [17].

WebSci '17, June 25-28, 2017, Troy, NY, USA

ACM ISBN 978-1-4503-4896-6/17/06...$15.00
https://doi.org/http://dx.doi.org/10.1145/3091478.3091494

In particular, wireless technologies and social networking tools (e.g. Facebook) have created *citizen sensing*, appearing in CNN iReports and Twitter event commentary. Clearly, the organizational effectiveness of such resources depends on the filtering, integration and dissemination of *trustworthy* information [47]. Emergency response provides an ideal domain for examining citizen sensing [11]. Citizen response can have an enormous influence on the societal impact (cost, recovery) of a disaster. Victims and their neighbors share timely information (e.g. flood level, road blockages) and offer resources (e.g. vehicles, food and supplies) on social media, leading to the prioritization of relief effort ranging from critical infrastructure repair to saving lives in affected areas. Affordability, reach, proximity and timeliness make social media such as Twitter an attractive resource for capturing public observations and activity during emergencies [40]. However, message recipients such as response agencies must trust citizen sources to provide reliable information, and must rapidly vet and separate noise (inaccurate information from unreliable sources or ambiguities from reliable sources) from the informative signal. A trust ranking of participants in social networks can promote reliance on trustworthy citizens to improve disaster response and recovery efforts [56].

Our primary focus here is on trust among users as opposed to trust in *facts*, e.g. road closures. We adopt the notion of interpersonal trust proposed by Kelton et al [31] who consider dyadic trust as a social tie between two individuals. We only consider information that is available or can be inferred from the social network and do not take into account any detail regarding background or previous history of entities. We develop an unsupervised algorithm to predict user trust relationships in social networks, using both structural properties of the network and information content posted by members of these networks.

A key contribution of our work is a robust method that takes into account indicators of influence as a proxy for how much one user trusts another: structural cohesion within a network, and valence-enhanced content (sentiment expressed related to the concept being sensed). Taking valence into account provides a robust and stable model of trust in such an analysis. To the best of our knowledge, *this is the first unsupervised effort taking into account social theories* related to influence, passive cohesiveness (structural cohesion) and active cohesiveness (valence and content) and their role on interpersonal trust. We show that our method detects pairwise and global user trust relations on a range of real-world crisis and non-crisis datasets and outperform extant state-of-the-art methods. We also find it effective in *dynamically* identifying trustworthy users in situations of crisis or emergency.

2 METHODOLOGY

Informally, we seek to develop a model to infer trust among users within a network and also identify highly trusted users or organizations within a social network. Specifically, we focus on the social network *Twitter.*

2.1 Problem Statement

Formally, we assume the social network of interest is represented as a bipartite graph $G = (U \cup T, E)$, where U and T are two disjoint sets and E is the set of edges or interactions between them. U represents the set of individuals or users in the network and T refers to the set of general topics expressed by the users in their textual content. Topics are extracted after aggregating the text posted by the users, by employing standard topic modeling algorithms based on Latent Dirichlet Allocation [9] or Non-Negative Matrix Factorization [59]. The trust prediction algorithm aims to predict the pairwise trust value between every pair of users, and generate an aggregated rank ordering of network users based on this trustworthiness score.

Our solution desiderata include the goals of efficacy and efficiency: Efficacy in effectively identifying and ranking trustworthy users and efficiency in being able to compute these in real-time emergent situations (e.g. during or shortly after a disaster). We discuss below three elements informed by social and psychological theory, that we believe play a role in developing trust between two users in a social network, and we measure these elements to determine a trust metric among users.

2.2 Influence

Theory: Leading sociologists note that trust is integral to social influence [16, 37, 50]. A messenger more easily influences or persuades a recipient to respond in a certain manner if that recipient trusts the original messenger. While trust itself is difficult to measure outside of specific experimental paradigms (for instance Berg's trust game [8], which addresses this problem from the perspective of behavioral economics), several researchers have tackled the problem of detecting *influential* users within a social network.

Here we exploit influence as a proxy for pairwise trust relationships. Theory suggests a strong correlation between the trust of a user x on a user y and the observed influence of user y on user x. Intuitively, users trust the users who influence them to re-post (or retweet) a particular post or tweet on a certain topic. The available measures of influence include the use of the structure of the network such as page-rank style [44], the dynamics of the network interaction [15], the frequency with which the users' posts are re-posted while accounting for user passivity and prior content history of the users' posts [48] or by taking into account the local neighborhood of the posting user via viewpoint analysis [4].

Implementation: Guided by the above theory and the available measures of social influence, we settled on the Influence-Passivity algorithm [48]. It is simple and also accounts for user passivity i.e. the likelihood of a user reacting to a messenger. Passivity is an essential constituent of the influence computation because intuitively, the retweeting or re-posting of a user's tweet should carry more weight from a typically passive user (who rarely retweets) than from a relatively active or frequent retweeter. The resulting HITS-style algorithm [34] calculates a global influence and passivity score for each user.

We first construct a weighted, directed, unipartite graph $H = (U, E_h, W_h)$ consisting of all the users in set U of our bipartite graph described above, joined by a set of edges E_h and a set of edge weights W_h. Edge (i, j) exists between a user i and user j in the graph if user j re-posts or shares in some way (or retweets) a post (or tweet) posted by user i at least once. Weight w_{ij} on edge $e = (i, j)$ represents the ratio of influence that i exerts on j to the total influence i attempted to exert on j. It is expressed as $w_e = \frac{S_{ij}}{Q_i}$ where Q_i is the number of posts that user i creates and S_{ij} is the number of posts i created and j re-posted or retweeted.

The influence function $Infl_i : U \longrightarrow [0, 1]$ that represents node i's influence on the network is calculated as:

$$Infl_i = \sum_{j:(i,j) \in E} u_{ij} Passiv_j$$

$$Passiv_i = \sum_{j:(j,i) \in E} v_{ji} Infl_j$$

$$u_{ij} = \frac{w_{ij}}{\sum_{(k,j) \in E} w_{kj}} \text{ and } v_{ji} = \frac{1 - w_{ji}}{\sum_{(j,k) \in E} (1 - w_{jk})}$$

Here u_{ij} represents the amount of influence user j accepted from user i normalized by the total influence j accepted from all users in the network. v_{ji} represents the influence that user i rejected from j normalized by the total influence rejected from j by all users in the network.

2.3 Social Cohesion

Theory: Social cohesion theory posits that a necessary and sufficient condition for individuals to work as a group is cohesive social relationships among individuals within the group. While social relationships exist for different reasons (e.g. kinship ties or similar social values), we focus on a group's structural cohesion, the collective result of those various social relationships. Sociologists and public policy experts believe that if common values, *trust* or a shared sense of place emerge, they will do so as a function of structural (cohesive) engagement [37]. Similar ideas are also posited by Golbeck and Ziegler et al [20, 60]. We adopt the definition by Lott and Lott [39] that interprets cohesiveness as a function of interpersonal attraction between individuals. In other words, cohesiveness relates to the members of a group who share emotional and behavioral characteristics with one another and the group as a whole [39, 46].

Implementation: We compute the Jaccard similarity metric [13, 19] between the neighborhoods of pairs of users in the bipartite network. This approximates the number of triads each pair belongs to, or the local triangle density. The notion of triads has been widely used to characterize community cohesiveness within a network [23, 24]. Such measures are also easy to approximate efficiently [49]. Based on the above theoretical insights, two users can be said to belong to a 'group' or possess some similar behavioral characteristics if they share common contextual interests. Specifically, we associate with each user x a *vector* V_x of topic identifiers to which x has a directed edge i.e. all topics on which a user shares text online. The Jaccard similarity between the users x and y is then:

$$Jacc(x, y) = \frac{|V_x \cap V_y|}{|V_x \cup V_y|}$$

In measuring shared topic interests among users we rely on what the social science literature refers to as passive cohesive interactions [37, 39]. We next examine the role of active relationships, which account for specific content, popularity of said content and the emotional attachment (sentiment/valence) associated with such content by actors within such networks.

2.4 Valence

Theory: We hypothesize that a critical dimension in the trust equation is the positive interactions, i.e. supportive exchanges among individuals and more broadly among communities, or "active social relationships". Such contacts and connections reflect trust as they offer people and organizations mutual support, information and credit. This is particularly relevant during times of need; such as those that arise in crisis and disaster settings [37]. The Jaccard measure just described largely reflects similarity between users in the social network based on structural cohesion. It does not account for the popularity of certain topics that the users talk about, nor as suggested by Lott and Lott [39] does it account for emotional content (valence ranging from positive to negative) and interpersonal agreement among users. We note that to the best of our knowledge, while the corresponding social theory exists, none of these have been examined in the context of online social networks. To overcome the limitations of the Jaccard measure, we propose a more nuanced measure that takes into account the relative *popularity* of the topics that the tweets or text of the users primarily describe, the valence of a user with respect to a particular topic and the agreement among them.

Implementation: We introduce the notion of a *shared* topic (or context) between two users in U as any topic in T to which both users in graph G have a directed edge. Our implementation accounts for a number of confounding influences on apparent sharing. We distinguish between shared topics according to their relative popularity, i.e their in-degree in the bipartite graph. Intuitively, as the in-degree of a topic (the number of users talking about it) increases, the extent to which we can infer about the relative similarity of two users who post on that topic reduces. Two users who post on a rare topic are more likely to have an affinity or an interest towards that topic and consequently towards each other and therefore, a stronger trust relationship. Nevertheless, a pair of users posting on a popular topic may be doing so precisely because of its popularity or it being the current trend (see Figure 1(a)). User baseline activity level is also relevant. If two users post frequently on numerous or diverse topics, sharing a topic may not attest as much to their similarity (see Figure 1(b)) as for a pair of less active users sharing a common topic. Figure 1(c) thus represents the case in which the pair of users x and y have the strongest likelihood of being similar to each other (and consequently trusting each other) based on their textual content. We now formalize the notion of *degree discounting* to capture the above ideas as follows:

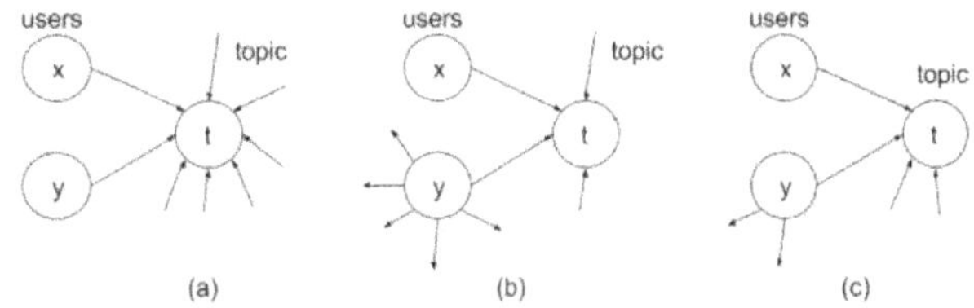

Figure 1: Content based user similarity, based on degree discounting

(1) When two users x and y share a topic t, the contribution of t to the similarity between x and y is inversely related to the in-degree of t.
(2) The out-link similarity between two users x and y is inversely related to the out-degrees of x and y.

$$sim_d(x, y) = \frac{1}{\sqrt{D_o(x,x)}\sqrt{D_o(y,y)}} \sum_t \frac{A(x,t)A(y,t)}{\sqrt{D_i(t,t)}}$$

$sim_d(x, y)$ is the degree-discounted out-link similarity between users x and y. A is the adjacency matrix of the bipartite graph G. D_o is the diagonal matrix of users' out-degrees and D_i is the diagonal matrix of topics' in-degrees in G. t represents a shared topic between x and y, and can be defined in two ways: i) *without valence:* the pair of users merely post text or tweets on t, and ii) *with valence:* they not only post on t but also express the same dominant valence towards it (positive, negative or neutral) in their text.

The inclusion of valence expressed by the users on a particular topic lends more validity to pairwise user similarity and may reflect greater trust between a pair of users, reflecting the theoretical notion of interpersonal emotional agreement. A user x likely has greater trust in a user y who shares x's opinion on a particular event or topic. To quantify the overall opinion or valence within the textual content expressed by each user on each topic, we use a widely used tool called SentiStrength [55]. It builds a simple discriminative predictor based on psychological theories of emotive strength, exploiting de-facto grammar and spelling styles (e.g. informal spellings, social media specific linguistic terms, idioms and emoticons). We found this tool to be more effective than traditional ones such as LIWC [45] and ANEW [10] that are better suited to longer and more linguistically standard pieces of text.

2.5 Putting It All Together

To combine the three measures or quantities (influence, cohesion and valence), we first did a systematic study across a range of datasets described in Tables 1 and 2. We observed that each of these measures are well estimated by a Gaussian distribution suggesting that a natural way to standardize these quantities is to employ z-score normalization [35].

Once each measure is normalized we determine the regularization coefficients (via a parametric grid search as described in the next section) employed in the overall trust equation as follows:

$$Trust(x, y) = \alpha Infl(y, x) + \beta Jacc(x, y) + \gamma sim_d(x, y)$$

$Trust(x, y)$ represents the pairwise trust of user x on user y. α, β and γ are regularization parameters representing the factor weights and are tuned empirically such that $\alpha + \beta + \gamma = 1$.

After computing the value of pairwise trust for every pair of users, we assign a global trust score $GTrust(x)$ to each user x in the following way:

$$GTrust(x) = \frac{\sum_{y \in T_x} Trust(y,x)}{|T_x|}$$

T_x = a set of users that have a non-zero pairwise trust score with user x, $|T_x|$ = cardinality of set T_x.

Based on these global trust scores assigned to users, we generate a trust-based ranking of all the users in the dataset. The relative order of $GTrust$ values provides a notion of ordinality regarding the overall trust a user enjoys within these network contexts. Depending on the values of α, β and γ employed to compute pairwise trust, we obtain multiple distinct trust-based user rankings.

Complexity Considerations: In order to compute a trust score between all pairs of users in the social network, a $O(n^2)$ complexity is unavoidable. Particularly for larger datasets with millions or billions of users, computing trust between every pair of users in the network will not scale, so pairwise trust might need to be only computed for a sample of users. For discovering the top trustworthy users one can potentially employ a smart sampling strategy where the trust for each user is accumulated over a sample of other users that interact with that user. Strategies such as those employed in similarity search problems [13, 19] can also be leveraged.

In our algorithm, the complexity of computing individual factors is as follows: Computing influence has the same complexity as the HITS algorithm [34] i.e. $O(E)$ per iteration; in our experiments we typically converge in less than 30 iterations. The complexity of determining the structural cohesion of two users as well as the valence step is bounded again by $O(E)$ (although in practice it is much less with our proposed optimizations). The complexity of parametric tuning (for each of the factors of influence, cohesion, and valence) can potentially be expensive. However, as discussed next, our results strongly suggest a robust weighting scheme highlighting the importance of influence, followed by content valence, followed by passive social cohesion.

3 EVALUATION

3.1 Datasets and Ground Truth

The datasets we employ in this study are described in Tables 1, 2 and 3. All social media data were collected using Twitter's Streaming API. Because ground truth for each pairwise trust relationship from social media data is difficult to obtain without a dedicated social survey instrument, we also include results on two datasets with normative ground truth: i) a Film DVD review dataset collected by Guo et al [26] in December 2013 by crawling 17 categories of film DVDs from the dvd.ciao.co.uk website; and ii) a dataset made available by Massa et al from the Epinions product rating and review website [42]. Both these datasets provide authentic ground truth information as a list of pairs of users who trust each other (scaled values from 1 to 5). We construct a bipartite graph for these two datasets as described in Section 2. Because there is no direct measure of re-posting or retweeting associated with these two datasets, for the purpose of computing influence we assume that a user x functionally 'retweets' a user y if x rates y's reviews more than three times. For contextual information, we used the provided genre of each film and the provided category of each product

Dataset	#Users	#Topics	#Nodes	#Edges	#Tweets
India Anti-Corruption	2104	15	2119	7180	100K
Mumbai Blast	581	10	591	932	10K
Phone and Tablet	9939	15	9954	16265	100K
Houston Floods	986	15	971	875	100K
Hurricane Irene	50561	20	50541	17593	200K
Nice Attack	253243	20	253223	166943	800K

Table 1: Bipartite graph statistics of social media datasets

Dataset	#Users	#Topics	#Nodes	#Edges	#Trust relations
CiaoDVD	7375	17	7392	111781	40133
Epinions	114467	27	114494	442787	717667

Table 2: Bipartite graph statistics of non-social media datasets with ground truth trust relations

Dataset	Timeline
India Anti-Corruption	April 4, 2011 to December 28, 2011: Protests against political corruption in India (https://en.wikipedia.org/wiki/2011_Indian_anti-corruption_movement)
Mumbai Blast	July 13, 2011: A series of three coordinated bombings in Mumbai (https://en.wikipedia.org/wiki/2011_Mumbai_bombings)
Hurricane Irene	August 21, 2011 to August 30, 2011: A tropical cyclone on US East Coast that grew into a hurricane (https://en.wikipedia.org/wiki/Hurricane_Irene)
Phone and Tablet	All tweets related to phones and tablets, during the day of April 15, 2013
Houston Floods	April 15, 2016 to April 23, 2016: Snowstorm leading to severe floods (https://en.wikipedia.org/wiki/2016_Texas_floods)
Nice Attacks	July 14, 2016: A cargo truck driven into a crowd, followed by a gunfire which led to an emergency (https://en.wikipedia.org/wiki/2016_Nice_attack)

Table 3: Timeline and details of each Twitter dataset

respectively, as topics. Additionally, we used user provided ratings to estimate the user valence towards a particular film or product. A user rating of 4 or more (out of 5) was taken as the expression of positive valence, 2 or less was taken as negative valence and a rating of 3 was assumed to be neutral.

3.2 Factor Analysis and Impact of Valence

Metrics: We begin by comparing our global trust-based user ranking (details in Section 2.5) at various parameter value settings against the ground truth user trust ranking for the CiaoDVD and Epinions datasets. This provides an independent assessment of our method on datasets with factual ground truth. For this, we made use of the standard information retrieval metric of Normalized Discounted Cumulative Gain (NDCG) [28]. NDCG is often the measure

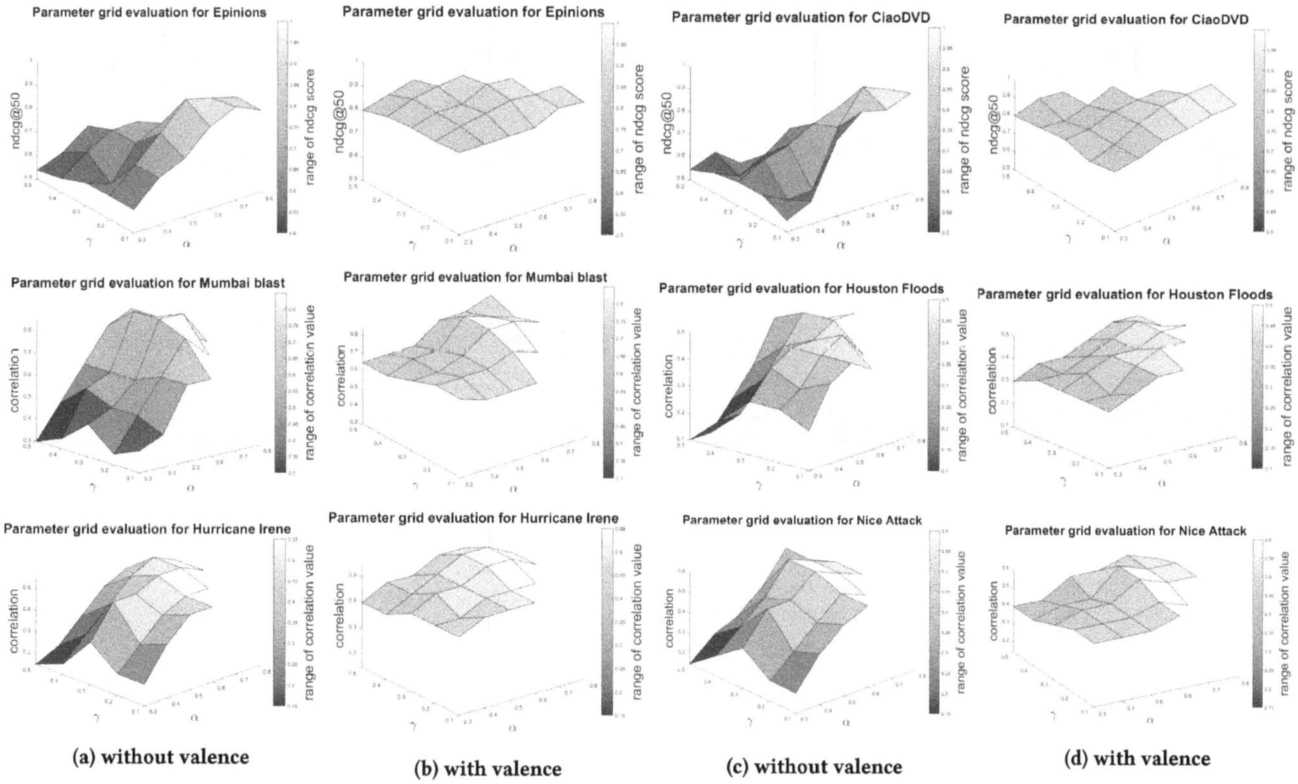

Figure 2: The first row of sub-figures shows the NDCG scores of various rank orders for the parameter grid against ground truth for CiaoDVD and Epinions. The next 2 rows show correlation between the pairwise trust score and conversation length for the parametric grid for social media datasets; in both cases using content-based similarity without and with valence

Dataset	α	β	γ
India Anti-Corruption	0.6	0.05	0.35
Mumbai Blast	0.65	0.05	0.3
Phone and Tablet	0.7	0.2	0.1
Houston Floods	0.65	0.1	0.25
Hurricane Irene	0.65	0.05	0.3
Nice Attacks	0.7	0.05	0.25
CiaoDVD	0.7	0.1	0.2
Epinions	0.65	0.1	0.25

Table 4: Best parametric settings for different datasets

of choice for comparing ranked lists since it emphasizes high fidelity with ground truth ranking at the top of the list [28], which aligns with our goals for identifying top trusted users in emergent situations. The NDCG score at a rank position k (we used $k = 50$ in our experiments) is defined as:

$$DCG_k = \sum_{i=1}^{k} \frac{2^{imp_i - 1}}{log_2(i+1)}$$

$$NDCG_k = \frac{DCG_k}{ideal_k}$$

where imp_i is an integer (between -2 and 2 based on the position of the user in the original rank list) representing the importance of user i, DCG_k is the discounted cumulative gain at rank k and $ideal_k$ is the ideal ground truth ranking.

For social media data, ground truth information on pairwise trust is difficult to obtain, which requires us to identify an approximation to ground truth. Adali et al [1, 2], recommend the use of the length of conversation between pairs of users as an approximate measure of the mutual trust between them. We acknowledge that there can be two limitations of such an approximation. First, the absence of dialogue online between a pair of users does not imply a lack of trust (false negatives). Roughly 35% of the users on average do not engage in active conversation during the respective time period of the events. Second, conversation length could also reflect discord as opposed to agreement or trust (false positives). We manually scrutinized the crisis related Twitter data in detail and found no evidence of lengthy discordant conversations; contextually, in such situations, discord is unlikely to occur. The conversation lengths in the datasets range from 2 to 13.6 on average. We computed the Pearson correlation coefficient between the length of a conversation between a pair of users (i.e. the number of times they replied to each others tweets during the time period of the particular event), and the corresponding trust score obtained by our methodology. As Table 7 and the last two rows of Figure 2 show, moderate (0.45) to strong (0.85) correlations were obtained between trust scores and conversation length, which indicates that this metric can be a suitable approximation despite the limitations noted above. We also note that conversation length was not used for computing any

WebSci '17, June 25-28, 2017, Troy, NY, USA

of the factors in our trust equation, it is an independent measure of quality.

Results: Figure 2 illustrates a series of surface heat plots varying two parameters: α and γ (β can be inferred from them). The first row of plots shows the variation in NDCG scores while the next two rows of plots show the variation in the correlation between pairwise trust score and conversation length, as the parametric values are varied, with and without valence. We find that the *inclusion of valence reduces the sensitivity of the method to parametric tuning in both cases.* Without valence, the NDCG scores range from 0.55-1 with high fluctuations on small parametric changes, whereas with valence the decision surface is more stable (the NDCG scores range from 0.75-1). We found the best NDCG score of 0.955 for CiaoDVD and 0.913 for Epinions (see Table 4 for parameter values). The surface plots for the social media datasets show similar trends: i) moderate (0.45) to strong (0.85) correlation between obtained trust values and conversation length demonstrating the effectiveness of our method; and ii) valence plays a critical role in a performance improvement and stabilizing the sensitivity of the method to parametric changes i.e. reducing fluctuation in correlation scores for small parametric changes. For the social media datasets, the best correlation values obtained by our method can be viewed in Table 7.

For each dataset, the best parametric setting is noted in Table 4, used henceforth for all experiments unless otherwise stated. Scanning through this table, it is clear that influence is the strongest factor contributing to an accurate ranking; α values typically range between 0.6 and 0.7. Content-based user similarity conditioned on topic popularity and valence weighted by γ follows, with parameter values typically between 0.2 and 0.3. Finally, structural cohesion had a non-trivial but muted role with β values up to 0.2.

3.3 Comparative Analysis

Baselines: We evaluated our method's performance on the CiaoDVD and Epinions datasets against the following unsupervised baseline trust computation algorithms: EigenTrust by Kamwar et al [29], TidalTrust by Katz et al [30] and an atomic trust propagation based approach by Guha et al [25]. We additionally include as baselines algorithms that only compute social influence to evaluate how they fare against trust computation; namely, a topic-aware influence maximization approach [3] called INFLEX, and a modification of our method to consider only the influence component i.e. setting the value of the parameter α to 1. Although our method is unsupervised, for the sake of completeness we further compare our method with a recently proposed supervised algorithm ETD [7], which also uses emotional information to aid in trust prediction, and is shown to outperform other supervised trust prediction methods [27, 38]. While such algorithms are hard to deploy in a social media setting (as obtaining ground truth for trust relationships is difficult), and moreover expensive to compute, they provide a challenging baseline.

Results: In Figure 3, the x axis represents the rank at which we compute the NDCG score between the global ranking developed by the trust algorithm and the ground truth trust ranking, and the y axis represents the value of the NDCG score. Since we lacked the timestamp at which users posted and rated reviews for the CiaoDVD dataset, which is required for influence maximization

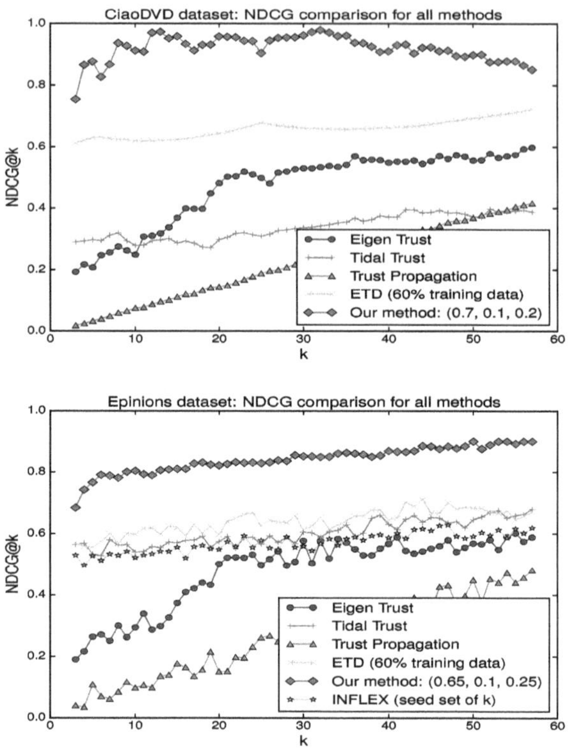

Figure 3: Comparison of NDCG score at various ranks for our algorithm against baselines, for CiaoDVD and Epinions.

algorithms, we could not run the INFLEX algorithm on this dataset. We observe that our method outperforms the baseline techniques, including the supervised method, giving a consistently high NDCG score > 0.75.

In order to assess the quality of pairwise user trust relations our algorithm is able to detect, we next compute the F-measure or F-score for the baseline algorithms and our method as follows:

$$P = \frac{TP}{TP+FP}$$
$$R = \frac{TP}{TP+FN}$$
$$Fscore = \frac{2PR}{P+R}$$

Here, TP stands for the number of pairwise user trust relations correctly recognized by the algorithm (true positives), FP represents the number of relations identified as trusted by the algorithm, but which are either distrust relations or those for which ground truth is not available (false positives) and FN stands for the number of pairwise trust relations the algorithm failed to recognize (false negatives). P and R represent the precision and recall respectively. We consider a reasonable trust relation to exists between two users if the value of the (normalized) pairwise trust between them is ≥ 0.5.

We find from Tables 5 and 6 that our unsupervised framework *outperforms all baseline algorithms significantly with respect to NDCG scores at rank 50,* for both the social media and non-social media datasets. Adding content and valence information while computing trust does improve NDCG scores, showing that it is insufficient to consider only influence propagation while computing trust. Since EigenTrust, INFLEX and the influence component of our method (α set to 1) only compute a global and not pairwise trust score for each user, we are unable to compute an F-score for them. *With respect to the available F-scores, our method outperforms all unsupervised baselines and is comparable to the supervised ETD approach*, when it trains on 60% of pairwise trust values (it outperforms the ETD approach with 30% training data). Clearly, it is impractical to obtain such a large fraction of ground truth pairwise trust data from even a moderately sized social network.

Algorithm	Dataset	NDCG@50	F-score
EigenTrust	CiaoDVD	0.523	N/A
TidalTrust	CiaoDVD	0.35	0.43
TrustPropagation	CiaoDVD	0.33	0.21
ETD-T60 (T30)	CiaoDVD	0.69 (0.489)	0.78 (0.53)
Our method (α = 1)	CiaoDVD	0.686	N/A
Our method	CiaoDVD	**0.955**	**0.84**
EigenTrust	Epinions	0.494	N/A
TidalTrust	Epinions	0.586	0.465
TrustPropagation	Epinions	0.371	0.237
ETD-T60 (T30)	Epinions	0.645 (0.51)	**0.816** (0.52)
INFLEX	Epinions	0.579	N/A
Our method (α = 1)	Epinions	0.658	N/A
Our method	Epinions	**0.913**	0.805

Table 5: NDCG at rank 50 and F-score values for different algorithms for CiaoDVD and Epinions. ETD results are reported with 30% (T30) and 60% training (T60) data.

Algorithm	Avg NDCG@50 for Twitter datasets	Avg F-score for Twitter datasets
EigenTrust	0.444	N/A
TidalTrust	0.549	0.511
TrustPropagation	0.321	0.303
INFLEX	0.647	N/A
Our method	**0.876**	**0.803**

Table 6: NDCG scores at rank 50 and F-scores averaged across the Twitter datasets, for the unsupervised algorithms using conversation length as ground truth.

Dataset	Corr (Tidal Trust)	Corr (Trust Propagation)	Corr (Our Method)
India Anti-Corruption	0.35	0.16	**0.507**
Mumbai Blast	0.521	0.187	**0.849**
Phone/Tablet	0.309	0.083	**0.4614**
Houston Flood	0.267	0.111	**0.484**
Hurricane Irene	0.222	0.091	**0.518**
Nice Attacks	0.313	0.181	**0.565**

Table 7: Correlation between pairwise trust score and conversation length between pairs of users during that time period, using different algorithms

For social media datasets, in Table 7 we report the correlation between conversation length and pairwise trust scores computed by our method and the unsupervised baselines (supervised baselines are not feasible because we lack pairwise trust ground truth). As before, we observe that our method outperforms the baselines significantly.

3.4 Performance Enhancements and Scalability

Benefits of Degree-Discounting: Here we examine the benefits of accounting for degree-discounting while computing pairwise user trust (Figure 1). The user trust relations obtained without this optimization achieve an NDCG@50 score of 0.76 and an F1-score of 0.424 on the CiaoDVD dataset. Adding degree discounting without valence yields an NDCG@50 score of 0.82 and F1-score of 0.63 respectively. Further, adding valence yields an NDCG@50 score of 0.955 and an F1-score of 0.84 respectively. Similar benefits were observed in other datasets.

Execution Time: We present an analysis of the total runtime of our method amortized over the number of user pairs in Table 8. We note that using SentiStrength for detecting valence (which can process about 10K tweets per second), the efficiency of computing pairwise trust is comfortably able to handle the influx of tweets associated with an event even at full firehose (several hundred million tweets a day) rates.

Dataset	Runtime per pair of users
India Anti-Corruption	0.000854 sec
Mumbai Blast	0.0034 sec
Phone and Tablet	6.56×10^{-4} sec
Houston Floods	0.000296 sec
Hurricane Irene	6.689×10^{-5} sec
Nice Attacks	4.659×10^{-6} sec
CiaoDVD Film	0.000199 sec
Epinions	9.616×10^{-6} sec

Table 8: Runtime for pairwise trust value computation and parameter tuning, amortized over number of user pairs

3.5 Case Study: Crisis Response

Here, we examine the kinds of individual users or organizations on Twitter who were identified by our algorithm as being highly trustworthy during various hazards, and also track the change in their overall trustworthiness across different temporal phases of the hazard occurrence, i.e. before the hazard, during its worst impact and immediately after it has subsided at the affected area. Due to space constraints, we only display results for three hazard datasets in Table 9. Users common across columns are represented in the same color (except black) so that we can track how their trust ranking changes across the three phases of the hazard. Top trustworthy users unique to each phase are colored in black.

Observations: Several users in Table 9 are well known personalities or reputed organizations and are thus likely to be highly

Before	During	After
mashable	cnnbrk	cnnbrk
lfmccullough	BreakingNews	BreakingNews
richmintz	USArmy	BarackObama
Reuters	CharityIdeas	nytimes
FrommersTravel	severestudios	HumaneSociety
nydailynews	shibanijoshi	RedCross
6abc	JimCantore	JimCantore
travelingmoms	xanpearson	*atmanes*
severestudios	CraigatFEMA	CraigatFEMA
BreakingNews	MikeBloomberg	*Fanua*
Daily_Press	*atmanes*	RedCrossPhilly
cnnbrk	*Fanua*	SamaritansPurse
funnyordie	HumaneSociety	RedCrossSAZ
afreedma	BarackObama	mashable
BarackObama	RedCross	USGS

(a) Hurricane Irene

Before	During	After
GlitchxCity	Breaking911	Breaking911
Sportsnaut	NWSHouston	NWSHouston
TriCityHerald	AlertHouston	BarackObama
Nick_Anderson_	WSOCWeather	AlertHouston
HOUBizJournal	StormViewLIVE	*TexasTsunami*
StarfishGawdess	BarackObama	RedCross
Breaking911	ArchCollegeTAMU	ArchCollegeTAMU
BarackObama	JohnCornyn	WSOCWeather
JohnCornyn	*TexasTsunami*	JohnCornyn
NWSHouston	GlitchxCity	GlitchxCity

(b) Houston Floods

Before	During	After
ScepticGeek	ndtv	mid_day
AltCricket	mid_day	ndtv
acarvin	rameshsrivats	[illegible]
dina	maheshmurthy	rameshsrivats
maheshmurthy	AnupamPKher	*ashwinsid*
[illegible]	[illegible]	Netra
mid_day	fakingnews	fakingnews
ndtv	PatrickMeier	maheshmurthy
timesofindia	*ashwinsid*	PatrickMeier
guardian	Netra	ScepticGeek

(c) Mumbai Blast

Table 9: Top trustworthy users with global trust score> 0.7 for different datasets. The same color is used for users reappearing across the phases of a disaster. Newly emergent trustworthy users are italicised.

trusted. These include journalists and news agencies (*cnnbrk, BreakingNews, Breaking911, ndtv*), key weather related officials and services (*NWSHouston, CraigAtFEMA, JimCantore*), entertainment related (*mashable, funnyordie, GlitchxCity*), political and social figures (*BarackObama, xanpearson, dina*) and relief organizations (*SamaritansPurse, RedCross, HumaneSociety*). This lends credibility to our analysis.

Moreover, certain users were not previously well known in any field, yet our algorithm identified them as commanding a high trust value during the time period of these events. Such users have been highlighted in italics in Table 9. On examining their tweet logs, we found that the Twitter user *TexasTsunami* provided assistance to the Houston flood victims and tweeted some strong statements such as *"I know it is ILLEGAL to give a hungry man a sandwich here in Houston. Is it legal to assist flood victims?"*, which popularized him and increased his trust level on topics related to the flood (though he wasn't as popular as the other highly trusted users). Similarly, user *atmanes* helped a taxi service in transporting animals, while user *Fanua* repeatedly re-tweeted several reliable news sources regarding Hurricane Irene, which increased the trust of other users towards them during this time. User *ashwinsid* provided transport to stranded victims of the Mumbai blast. Thus, *our approach not only captures trusted users who are well known or popular but also effectively identifies emergent trustworthy users* who were neither well known nor previously popular – during and immediately after an emergency situation. This is particularly relevant for our ongoing efforts in identifying trustworthy "good samaritan" citizen sensors both during and immediately after a disaster occurs.

Role of Valence: Valence is crucial in recognizing emergent trustworthy users. Without valence, we observed that good samaritan, trustworthy users *(atmanes, Fanua, TexasTsunami, ashwinsid)* could only be detected in one of the datasets (Mumbai Blast), and that too only in the top 60 trustworthy users (and not in the top 10 or 15).

Dynamics of Trust: Finally, we perceive intuitive trends in connection with the changes in highly trusted users over the three phases of the disaster previously outlined. From Table 9 we note that before the hurricane or flood struck the respective affected area, the highly trusted users were from a wide variety of fields such as travel, sports or entertainment blogs along with key political figures and news channels. However, we see a significant variation during and immediately after the disaster. News channels, reporters and weather related user accounts rise to the top of the list. New trustworthy users start emerging in the 'during' phase and their trust scores rise as the disaster progresses to the 'immediately after' phase, which is when they primarily provide voluntary assistance to affected victims. Additionally, relief and humanitarian organizations such as the *RedCross* are highly trustworthy shortly after the disaster.

4 RELATED WORK

Existing literature addresses the challenge of identifying or predicting the credible aspects of data and entities, under a social model of trust [54]. A simple strategy to encode a pre-defined notion of trust involves learning the encoding (via regression or classification) from a labeled set of specific interactions and their associated values obtained from a domain expert. Subsequently the learned model automatically categorizes the trust values associated with other relationships within the network. Both the biological and social network analysis literatures rely on the local topology within the network to assess the confidence associated with a specific relationship [18]. However, topological signals alone may be insufficient. For example, Palen et al [56] imply that content and context, and metrics such as re-tweeting by others reflect a notion of trust between the user and her immediate followers. Some of these signals can be directly recovered from the data (e.g. location-specific tags from Twitter, volunteered GIS information etc.) but others must be inferred through suitable content analysis and other methods [43].

We have hypothesized that the idea of expertise or influence can serve as a prominent contributor to trust. Influence can often be estimated from the structure of the global network, as in Twitter-Rank [57] and Trust-Rank [58], or the local network via viewpoint-based methods [4]. A large body of work has focused on studying diffusion and influence specifically on Twitter, using measures of influence such as number of followers, page-rank, number of retweets and number of mentions [12, 36, 57]. The influence-passivity algorithm by Romero et al [48] which we employ in this work also makes use of Twitter retweets and URLs, however it also simultaneously accounts for the passivity of network users as well, which can be important as explained in Section 2.

Social influence coupled with contextual information has been used in the literature in the problem of influence maximization [3, 6, 14, 32], where the objective is to identify seed users such that the number of users they influence in the network is maximized. We note that though influence plays a crucial role in our algorithm in quantifying trust, our work is distinct from these efforts in that we do not aim to study influence (and consequently, trust) propagation through the network or find the set of users with the maximum overall trust reach. We study both pairwise trust relations among users as well as identify users who are globally trusted. Having said that, we do compare our work against the topic-aware influence maximization algorithm by Aslay et al [3] and find that along with influence and context, shared content and valence information play a non-trivial role in discerning trust among users (Sections 3 and 3.5).

One may not have enough data or domain knowledge to assess a meaningful trust value for all of the entities and relationships in the network. Hence, propagating trust values across entities using a set of rules [25] may be essential to obtain a completely specified trust network. Golbeck and Hendler [22] describe some of the challenges with trust propagation (including conflict resolution) based on the underlying model of trust and highlight the following properties regarding trust propagation: asymmetry (person A may trust person B but not vice-versa), transitivity (if person A trusts person B and person B trusts person C, a trust relationship can be inferred between A and C) and composability (a user should aggregate trust values received from different paths). The TidalTrust algorithm [21] propagates trust ratings along a path between a source and a sink in Friend-Of-A-Friend based social networks using a Breadth-First search. EigenTrust [29] and MoleTrust [41] are peer-to-peer algorithms for determining peer trustworthiness.

A crucial dimension to the study of trust is the fact that trust is context-dependent; different users may be trusted differently on different contexts or topics. Tang et al [53] in their work on mTrust develop a topic-specific tensor representation in which a user probabilistically trusts another on a certain topic. In our work, we incorporate contextual information as a contributor to pairwise user trust scores but we do not currently compute topic-specific user trust values. We also utilize the idea that similarity in emotion expressed by users can be a crucial signal of the trust between them, which has also been studied in [7].

Finally, the notion of structural similarity between users has a role to play in shaping their trust relationships. Tajfel [51] defines the concept of social identity as "the individual's knowledge that he belongs to certain social groups together with some emotional and value significance to him of this group membership". Such shared identity among members of a group can in turn lead to cohesiveness, uniformity and the motivation to sustain the reputation of their associated identity, which can consequently increase the feeling of mutual trust and affinity among the group members. In the literature, Golbeck [20] supports the idea of a positive correlation between user profile similarity and personalized trust values, while Yeung et al [5] find similarities in user trust networks on product review sites. Tang et al [52] model the effects of homophily in trust prediction with a low rank matrix factorization model. We incorporate this concept into our trust calculation by increasing the pairwise trust score between users if they belong to a "group", i.e. if they share a common context.

5 CONCLUDING REMARKS

We present a simple unsupervised approach to computing interpersonal trust among users within a social network, bringing to bear theoretical ideas from psychology and sociology as they relate to influence, passive (structural) and active cohesiveness (content and valence). In our empirical analysis we sought to answer three questions: i) Which among the three factors (influence, structural cohesion, affective valence) are most important to estimate trust relationships among users in a social network? ii) How robust is the method in predicting trust with and without valence? iii) How does real-world performance of the method compare to baselines and can it be useful in emergent settings?

Consistent with the literature, although we find influence to be the principal factor contributing to recognizing trustworthy users in social media, we demonstrate that the presence of valence or sentiment while calculating trust adds significantly to the stability of the response surface, and to performance. Structural cohesion, while still useful has less of an impact than the other two factors, especially in the case of ephemeral (Mumbai attacks, Nice attacks, Hurricane Irene and Houston Floods) and political movement events (India Anti-Corruption). This may be related to the type of event, because structural cohesion plays a stronger role than valence-enhanced content on the Phone and Tablet dataset. Finally, we demonstrate that our method is able to develop a trust based ranking of users that comprehensively outperforms strong baselines on a range of real-world datasets. We also demonstrate the efficacy of the methodology for the dynamic identification of trusted users in emergent crisis settings.

Future Work: We plan to further examine the temporal dynamics in user trust relations. We are enhancing our evaluation to examine broad spectrum effects of our trust inference procedure, in particular the propagation of trust when limited ground truth is available to our method (unavoidable with social media data). We also plan to model user trust relations over a hierarchy of topics and use more sophisticated techniques such as word embeddings for valence. Although our results reveal reasonably stable parametric settings for influence, cohesion and valence-enhanced content across datasets, there is some variance. We would like to develop a method to auto-tune the parameters of our method in the future. We also plan to enhance our study with a detailed survey instrument that polls individual users regarding their trust relationships. Such ground truth can provide a broader evaluation for not just the top trustworthy users but also on pairwise relationships across a larger sample of users.

6 ACKNOWLEDGMENTS

This work is supported by the National Science Foundation Grant EAR-1520870. Any opinions, findings, and conclusions or recommendations expressed in this material are those of the author(s) and do not necessarily reflect the views of the National Science Foundation. The authors also thank Jiongqian Liang, T.K. Prasad and A. Sheth for useful comments on earlier drafts of this work.

REFERENCES

[1] Sibel Adali, Robert Escriva, Mark K Goldberg, Mykola Hayvanovych, Malik Magdon-Ismail, Boleslaw K Szymanski, William A Wallace, and Gregory Williams. 2010. Measuring behavioral trust in social networks. In *IEEE ISI*.

[2] Sibel Adali, Fred Sisenda, and Malik Magdon-Ismail. 2012. Actions speak as loud as words: Predicting relationships from social behavior data. In *WWW*.

[3] Cigdem Aslay, Nicola Barbieri, Francesco Bonchi, and Ricardo A Baeza-Yates. 2014. Online Topic-aware Influence Maximization Queries.. In *EDBT*. 295–306.

[4] Sitaram Asur and Srinivasan Parthasarathy. 2009. A viewpoint-based approach for interaction graph analysis. In *SIGKDD*.

[5] Ching-man Au Yeung and Tomoharu Iwata. 2011. Strength of social influence in trust networks in product review sites. In *WSDM*.

[6] Nicola Barbieri, Francesco Bonchi, and Giuseppe Manco. 2013. Topic-aware social influence propagation models. *Knowledge and information systems* (2013).

[7] Ghazaleh Beigi, Jiliang Tang, Suhang Wang, and Huan Liu. 2016. Exploiting emotional information for trust/distrust prediction. In *SIAM*.

[8] Joyce Berg, John Dickhaut, and Kevin McCabe. 1995. Trust, reciprocity, and social history. *Games and economic behavior* (1995).

[9] David M Blei. 2012. Probabilistic topic models. *Commun. ACM* (2012).

[10] Margaret M Bradley and Peter J Lang. 1999. *Affective norms for English words.* Technical Report. C-1, the center for research in psycho physiology, University of Florida.

[11] Carlos Castillo. 2016. *Big Crisis Data.* Cambridge University Press.

[12] Meeyoung Cha, Hamed Haddadi, Fabricio Benevenuto, and P Krishna Gummadi. 2010. Measuring user influence in twitter: The million follower fallacy. *ICWSM* (2010).

[13] Moses S Charikar. 2002. Similarity estimation techniques from rounding algorithms. In *STOC*.

[14] Wei Chen, Tian Lin, and Cheng Yang. 2014. Efficient topic-aware influence maximization using preprocessing. *CoRR, abs/1403.0057* (2014).

[15] Pedro Domingos and Matt Richardson. 2001. Mining the network value of customers. In *SIGKDD*.

[16] Rino Falcone and Cristiano Castelfranchi. 2001. Social trust: A cognitive approach. In *Trust and deception in virtual societies*.

[17] BJ Fogg and Hsiang Tseng. 1999. The elements of computer credibility. In *SIGCHI*.

[18] Santo Fortunato. 2010. Community detection in graphs. *Physics reports* (2010).

[19] Aristides Gionis, Piotr Indyk, Rajeev Motwani, and others. 1999. Similarity search in high dimensions via hashing. In *VLDB*.

[20] Jennifer Golbeck. 2009. Trust and nuanced profile similarity in online social networks. *TWEB* (2009).

[21] Jennifer Golbeck and James Hendler. 2006. Filmtrust: Movie recommendations using trust in web-based social networks. In *IEEE CCNC*.

[22] Jennifer Golbeck and James Hendler. 2006. Inferring binary trust relationships in web-based social networks. *TOIT* (2006).

[23] Debra S Goldberg and Frederick P Roth. 2003. Assessing experimentally derived interactions in a small world. *Proceedings of the National Academy of Sciences* (2003).

[24] Mark S Granovetter. 1973. The strength of weak ties. *American journal of sociology* (1973).

[25] Ramanthan Guha, Ravi Kumar, Prabhakar Raghavan, and Andrew Tomkins. 2004. Propagation of trust and distrust. In *WWW*.

[26] G. Guo, J. Zhang, D. Thalmann, and N. Yorke-Smith. 2014. ETAF: An Extended Trust Antecedents Framework for Trust Prediction. In *ASONAM*.

[27] Cho-Jui Hsieh, Kai-Yang Chiang, and Inderjit S Dhillon. 2012. Low rank modeling of signed networks. In *ACM SIGKDD*.

[28] Kalervo Järvelin and Jaana Kekäläinen. 2002. Cumulated gain-based evaluation of IR techniques. *TOIS* (2002).

[29] Sepandar D Kamvar, Mario T Schlosser, and Hector Garcia-Molina. 2003. The eigentrust algorithm for reputation management in p2p networks. In *WWW*.

[30] Yarden Katz and Jennifer Golbeck. 2006. Social network-based trust in prioritized default logic. In *AAAI*.

[31] Kari Kelton, Kenneth R Fleischmann, and William A Wallace. 2008. Trust in digital information. *JASIST* (2008).

[32] David Kempe, Jon Kleinberg, and Éva Tardos. 2003. Maximizing the spread of influence through a social network. In *SIGKDD*.

[33] Arrow Kenneth and others. 1974. The limits of organization. *N–Y.: Norton* (1974).

[34] Jon M Kleinberg. 1999. Authoritative sources in a hyperlinked environment. *JACM* (1999).

[35] Erwin Kreyszig. 1979. *Advanced Engineering Mathematics.* John Wiley & Sons.

[36] Haewoon Kwak, Changhyun Lee, Hosung Park, and Sue Moon. 2010. What is Twitter, a social network or a news media?. In *WWW*.

[37] Christian Albrekt Larsen. 2013. *The rise and fall of social cohesion: The construction and de-construction of social trust in the US, UK, Sweden and Denmark.* Oxford University Press.

[38] Jure Leskovec, Daniel Huttenlocher, and Jon Kleinberg. 2010. Predicting positive and negative links in online social networks. In *WWW*.

[39] Albert J Lott and Bernice E Lott. 1965. Group cohesiveness as interpersonal attraction: a review of relationships with antecedent and consequent variables. *Psychological bulletin* (1965).

[40] Winter Mason. 2010. Crisis mapping as Collective Problem Solving. *ACM Transactions on Applied Perception* (2010).

[41] Paolo Massa and Paolo Avesani. 2005. Controversial users demand local trust metrics: An experimental study on epinions.com community. In *National Conference on AI*.

[42] Paolo Massa, Kasper Souren, Martino Salvetti, and Danilo Tomasoni. 2001. Trustlet, open research on trust metrics. *Scalable Computing: Practice and Experience* (2001).

[43] Meenakshi Nagarajan, Karthik Gomadam, Amit P Sheth, Ajith Ranabahu, Raghava Mutharaju, and Ashutosh Jadhav. 2009. *Spatio-temporal-thematic analysis of citizen sensor data: Challenges and experiences.*

[44] Lawrence Page, Sergey Brin, Rajeev Motwani, and Terry Winograd. 1999. The PageRank citation ranking: bringing order to the web. (1999).

[45] James W Pennebaker, Martha E Francis, and Roger J Booth. 2001. Linguistic inquiry and word count: LIWC 2001. *Mahway: Lawrence Erlbaum Associates* (2001).

[46] Hemant Purohit, Yiye Ruan, David Fuhry, Srinivasan Parthasarathy, and Amit P Sheth. 2014. On Understanding the Divergence of Online Social Group Discussion. *ICWSM* (2014).

[47] Gene I Rochlin. 2004. Mind the gap: The growing distance between institutional and technical capabilities in organizations performing critical operations. In *Intelligence and Security Informatics*.

[48] Daniel M Romero, Wojciech Galuba, Sitaram Asur, and Bernardo A Huberman. 2011. Influence and passivity in social media. In *ECML PKDD*.

[49] Venu Satuluri and Srinivasan Parthasarathy. 2012. Bayesian locality sensitive hashing for fast similarity search. *VLDB Endowment* (2012).

[50] Piotr Sztompka. 1999. Trust: A sociological theory. In *Cambridge University Press*.

[51] Henri Tajfel. 2010. Social identity and intergroup relations. In *Cambridge University Press*.

[52] Jiliang Tang, Huiji Gao, Xia Hu, and Huan Liu. 2013. Exploiting homophily effect for trust prediction. In *WSDM*.

[53] Jiliang Tang, Huiji Gao, and Huan Liu. 2012. mTrust: discerning multi-faceted trust in a connected world. In *WSDM*.

[54] Jiliang Tang and Huan Liu. 2015. *Trust in Social Media: Synthesis Lectures on Information Security, Privacy, and Trust.* Morgan & Claypool Publishers.

[55] Mike Thelwall, Kevan Buckley, and Georgios Paltoglou. 2012. Sentiment strength detection for the social web. *JASIST* (2012).

[56] Sarah Vieweg, Amanda L Hughes, Kate Starbird, and Leysia Palen. 2010. Microblogging during two natural hazards events: what Twitter may contribute to situational awareness. In *SIGCHI*.

[57] Jianshu Weng, Ee-Peng Lim, Jing Jiang, and Qi He. 2010. Twitterrank: finding topic-sensitive influential twitterers. In *WSDM*.

[58] Baoning Wu, Vinay Goel, and Brian D Davison. 2006. Topical trustrank: Using topicality to combat web spam. In *WWW*.

[59] Wei Xu, Xin Liu, and Yihong Gong. 2003. Document clustering based on non-negative matrix factorization. In *SIGIR*.

[60] Cai-Nicolas Ziegler and Jennifer Golbeck. 2007. Investigating interactions of trust and interest similarity. *Decision support systems* (2007).

Privacy for Children and Teenagers on Social Networks from a Usability Perspective: A Case Study on Facebook

Cristiana S. Silva
Pontifícia Universidade Católica de Minas Gerais
Brazil
cristiana.sant.silva@gmail.com

Glívia A. R. Barbosa
Centro Federal de Educação Tecnológica de Minas Gerais
Brazil
gliviabarbosa@decom.cefetmg.br

Ismael S. Silva
Centro Federal de Educação Tecnológica de Minas Gerais
Brazil
ismaelsantana@decom.cefetmg.br

Tatiane S. Silva
Faculdade de Ciências Médicas
Brazil
tatabernado@hotmail.com

Fernando Mourão
Seek AI Labs
Brazil
fernando.mourao@catho.com

Flávio Coutinho
Centro Federal de Educação Tecnológica de Minas Gerais
Brazil
coutinho@decom.cefetmg.br

ABSTRACT

Children and teenagers comprise a user group particularly susceptible to privacy infringement risks in Online Social Networks (OSNs). In this sense, the usability of privacy controls should be appropriate to such users. This study aims to characterize, through a case study on Facebook, how children and teenagers deal with privacy features on OSNs and whether the available privacy controls help this user group to manage the privacy levels of their personal data. The case study considered children and teenagers in Brazil, the top-3 country on the number of Facebook users. The results indicated that there are usability violations that hinder this group from adjusting privacy settings, compromising its privacy and security on OSNs. These results are relevant and not limited to the context of Brazil, because they warn us about the vulnerability of children and teenagers on OSNs, as well as they evince the role of usability in privacy controls.

KEYWORDS

Privacy; Usability; Online Social Networks; Children; Teenagers.

1 INTRODUCTION

Online Social Networks (OSNs) have become increasingly popular. Indeed, researches indicate that 29% of the global population has connected to OSNs in 2014, and such percentage would reach 31% of the population by the end of 2015 (i.e., more than two billion people) [8,15]. This growing relevance has made OSNs an important Web environment to mediate interactions among people from different regions, cultures, beliefs and ethics.

Along with all potential benefits this type of environment may offer to its users, there are also concerns about the privacy of users [19, 39]. Privacy is a critical issue in this context since, in most cases, the shared content (e.g., location, photos, and videos) refers to personal information that, without proper control, may expose users to unauthorized or malicious people [19]. A user group particularly vulnerable to such privacy violations comprises children and teenagers, who usually share personal data publicly and that are more easily induced or duped by malicious users [3,12,13,27].

Aiming to enhance the privacy of users on OSNs, several designers and researchers in the area of Human-Computer Interaction (HCI) have focused their efforts on evaluating and proposing mechanisms of privacy settings to these networks [18,23,35,39]. However, distinct researches have shown that the current configuration templates fail to offer proper protection to all distinct user profiles, reflecting a disparity between the desired and the actual privacy [26,39].

As reported by Villela and Prates [39], this disparity occurs because the interfaces do not indicate clearly to users the mechanisms for managing the privacy levels of their personal data. In other words, the usability of privacy settings may not suit configuration needs of all user groups existing in OSNs [4]. This fact applies in particular to the group of users composed by children and teenagers [17,20,27,28].

Despite the existence of laws that control children's and teenagers' access to OSNs (e.g., the Children's Online Privacy Protection Act - COPPA [3]), studies indicate that this group of users is representative on OSNs, in most cases, without the supervision of an adult [27]. This scenario reinforces the need for adapting privacy setting resources to this user group.

WebSci '17, June 25-28, 2017, Troy, NY, USA
© 2017 Association for Computing Machinery.
ACM ISBN 978-1-4503-4896-6/17/06...$15.00
http://dx.doi.org/10.1145/3091478.3091479

Furthermore, it is relevant to assess how the usability of privacy controls in OSNs reflects on the perception and usage of such resources by children and teenagers. Researches on this direction are crucial to alert about vulnerabilities that this user group may be subject, as well as to improve usability of existing privacy controls and to assist in the development of new solutions that maximize the privacy of children and teenagers in OSNs [17, 20].

Therefore, this work aims to evaluate and characterize how children and teenagers have been dealing with privacy settings on their profiles in OSNs and whether the usability of the privacy control resources is appropriate to this user profile. In this sense, we conducted a case study on Facebook, considering children and teenagers from Brazil (i.e., users between 6 and 17 years, as defined in Article 2 of the Law 8069 from the Brazilian Statute of the Child and Adolescent - 1990[1]).

We chose Facebook for our analyses due to two main reasons. First, it is the most used OSN in the world [15,16]. Second, although Facebook's usage policy requires all users to be over the age of 13[2], recent surveys point out that children under this minimum age make use of Facebook [3]. We focus on Brazilian users, since Brazil figures among the top-3 countries on the number of Facebook users. Also, it was found that approximately 30% of Brazilian users of Facebook are under the age of 17 [7,8,9]. Finally, we highlight as a relevant motivation for this study the frequent risks to which this user group is subject in Brazil (e.g., cases of pedophilia through OSNs [32] and exposure of intimacy by teenagers with unknown [2]).

The methodology we proposed to achieve our goals consists in an approach split in three steps. Initially, an inspection in Facebook's privacy control resources was performed to verify the adequacy to the usability principles proposed by Nielsen [29], considering children and teenagers users. Later, through questionnaires, we verified the perception that these users have about privacy. Finally, we triangulated the results to verify how the usability of privacy controls impacts the usage of such resources by children and teenagers. The main results indicated that usability problems had indeed influenced the limited degree of knowledge and use that children and teenagers had made of security and privacy settings on Facebook.

In summary, this work has practical and scientific contributions to HCI and studies about privacy in OSNs, which are not limited to Brazilian context. In practical terms, we alert interface designers about the relevance of usability in privacy settings of OSNs. Additionally, the reported results may provide parameters to improve or to create privacy mechanisms in these virtual environments, with increased usability, for children and teenagers. Regarding scientific contributions, this work brings up the conversation on the importance of proposing and evaluating novel interfaces for privacy settings aimed at such target group. Discussions on this direction reinforce the important role of initiatives such as: (1) User Experience (UX) for teenagers [17]; (2) Usability Guidelines for children [20]; and (3) interface design and interaction for children [28].

[1] Brazilian Statute of the Child and Adolescent. Law N° 8.069. 13 Jul. 1990. Available in: http://www.planalto.gov.br/CCIVIL_03/leis/L8069.htm.

[2] https://www.facebook.com/help/210644045634222

2 RELATED WORKS

Privacy in OSNs is a complex issue that has been investigated by researchers at HCI and related areas considering different perspectives. One investigation thread includes, for example, works that aim to characterize the general perception and usage of privacy settings in these networks [1,26,35].

In Albesher and Alhussain [1], the authors investigate the efficiency of Facebook's privacy mechanisms to control the interaction among users. The authors also discuss the importance of regularly reviewing these controls, as well as the privacy policies in order to maintain them suitable to the diversity of needs defined by the current users.

In turn, Liu et al. [26] call attention to the fact that not always the privacy controls are compatible with the needs and demands of users. From a questionnaire applied to 200 Facebook users, the authors found that the expectation of the users about how to configure privacy does not match how that feature is implemented by the system. Hence, users feel exposed in ways they would like to preserve. The authors recommend new investigations in this context by exploring different user profiles. The goal is to characterize and to understand the real demands of distinct profiles and, later, to address these requirements through the interface and interaction models proposed for privacy setting.

Finally, Rodrigues et al. [35] assess the usability and accessibility of Facebook's privacy settings and the emotional impact that these aspects might cause to OSN users. The study showed that Facebook presents quality of use barriers to control privacy, which have impacted on the user emotions so that these users have made a wrong use of the available resources to safeguard privacy.

Aiming to minimize the problems raised by the literature about privacy controls on OSNs, another research thread propose tools that seek to customize these controls to the user needs [24,14,22]. For instance, in Jakob et al. [22], the authors propose a "Privacy Smart Wizard" for Facebook that partly automates the assignment of sharing permissions on user profiles. The suggested assignment is based on the content of the information being shared and Facebook sharing policies. In that sense, the wizard attempts to guide users to the most appropriate visibility according to each content being shared. The authors argue that the proposed mechanism proved to be effective in real scenarios.

The third thread of research efforts focuses on analyzing privacy under the lens of segmented user groups, such as children and teenagers [3,21,37]. In Boyd et al. [3], the authors alert to the risks of security and privacy that children are subject when lying about their age in OSNs, even with parents' permission. The study indicates that many parents consent to this lie but do not monitor their kids properly when browsing in OSNs. Thus, these children usually neglect their security and privacy and become vulnerable to malicious people.

Hinduja and Patchin [21] empirically assessed which personal information (e.g., full name, profile photo, education, and phone number) that teenagers expose on MySpace. The results indicated that, except profile photo, most participants are aware of privacy risks and less than 20% of them expose data such as full name, education, and phone number. However, the authors alert that more than half of the participants use personal photos to compose the public profile and this information is a visual identification that must be controlled.

Similarly, Souza and Dick [37] examined what information children share on MySpace and what their level of understanding on privacy issues. The authors concluded that the amount of personal information exposed by this user group is related to at least two main factors: (1) the knowledge level the users have about privacy and (2) the adequacy of privacy controls to user needs. This conclusion stems from the observation that children who better understand the concept of privacy and handle the MySpace interface without difficulties are less likely to share personal information in OSNs.

Since the perception of privacy on social networks is influenced by culture, several studies attempt to understand how people from different countries deal with this issue [11,25,38]. An example is the research conducted by Tsoi and Chen [38], in which the authors presented significant differences among users in Hong Kong and France with regard to the usage patterns on OSNs and their respective privacy settings. The results were derived using questionnaires and focus groups of users from each country.

Following this line, distinct Brazilian researchers also have focused on evaluating and proposing mechanisms that allow privacy control in OSNs [34,40,39]. We highlight that, although these works analyze the privacy issue under a cultural perspective, their contributions are not limited to the culture investigated. Understanding aspects such as cultural and physical or psychological conditions is important to propose proper technological solutions that suit all user profiles [40,33,10].

Although different privacy-related aspects have been investigated, we did not find any work in the literature that conducted the proposed analysis addressing privacy for children and teenagers in OSNs under the lens of usability. Besides, a case study on Facebook with children and teenagers from Brazil, such as the one conducted here, roots significant discussions for the entire HCI community and for professionals who investigate and design aspects related to usability and privacy in OSNs. Our analyses bring out how usability issues may impact the perception and usage of privacy controls in these networks.

3 METHODOLOGY

The proposed methodology consists in, initially, conducting a usability inspection based on heuristics proposed by Nielsen [29], in which experts in HCI evaluated the Facebook privacy controls. We performed such inspection with the assistance of an Occupational Therapist, specialist in educational psychology of children and young people, in order to verify the adequacy of these features to the intellect and usage patterns of children and teenagers.

Later, we carried out an assessment with this group of users through the questionnaire method to detect how they use these features and how vulnerable they are in Facebook. Finally, we triangulated the results to make it possible to verify how the usability of Facebook's privacy settings has impacted on the safety of children and teenagers.

Triangulation refers to a procedure of research performed by comparing data extracted by different methods, and its purpose is to check the validity of the results in a scientific research [5]. In this case, validation is to seek different interpretations of the same research question [5].

In the following section, we detail the analyses, as well as the main results and conclusions related to each step of our methodology.

4 ANALYSIS OF USABILITY ON FACEBOOK'S PRIVACY SETTINGS THROUGH EXPERTS PERSPECTIVE

A well-known method to evaluate the usability of system interfaces consists of performing a Heuristic Evaluation (HE) [30]. HE is an inspection method conducted by experts in HCI to identify potential usability problems. Through this method, the expert judges the compliance of the interface concerning a set of 10 usability heuristics proposed by Nielsen [29]. Such heuristics are described below:

H1 - Visibility of system status;
H2 - Match between system and the real world;
H3 - User control and freedom;
H4 - Consistency and standards;
H5 - Help users recognize, diagnose, and recover from errors;
H6 - Error prevention;
H7 - Recognition rather than recall;
H8 - Flexibility and efficiency of use;
H9 - Aesthetic and minimalist design;
H10 - Help and documentation.

For each problem identified, the evaluator associates one or more infringed heuristics and assigns a degree of severity. The severity scale ranges from 0 to 4, where the higher the value, the more serious the usability issue [29,30].

Aiming to identify potential usability problems in Facebook's privacy mechanisms for Brazilian children and teenagers, we performed a HE considering 12 distinct interaction scenarios representing different possibilities of privacy settings. They were (1) set the visibility of user profile; (2) configure who can contact the user to send friend requests; (3) configure who can look the user up on Facebook; (4) configure who can add content in the user timeline; (5) set who can see the posts in the user's timeline; (6) manage marks of others; (7) manage suggestions from others; (8) set up a shortlist of friends who can see only publications and public information; (9) block a user; (10) block an application invitation; (11) block an event invitation; and (12) block an application.

We conducted this evaluation in the first half of March 2016 with two evaluators with experience in applying HE. The results were validated by an expert in HCI (i.e., a professional with more than seven years of experience) and an Occupational Therapist, specialized in educational psychology of child and young people, with more than five years of experience in the field. The Therapist had an important role in the process, helping HCI evaluators to justify why the usability problems identified affected the interaction of children and teenagers during the evaluation. The following section summarizes the main results achieved in this step.

4.1 Analysis of the Raised Problems

Through the evaluation, we found a total of 12 problems that violated at least one usability heuristic. Further, 83% of them were classified with severity 3 (i.e., big problems), 8% with severity 4 (i.e., catastrophic problems) and 9% with severity 2 (i.e., minor problems).

Among the identified problems, we highlight one about the option to configure who can view the user's publications. We found that the system limits this setting only to future publications (i.e., publications carried out after modifying this setting). Plus, Facebook does not offer a general option to configure the visualization of all publications, including the past ones. This behavior may raise doubts on users, exposure problems and hamper users who want to set the view permissions for all previous publications. In this case, Facebook requires configuring the view permission of each publication at a time.

Another noteworthy problem relates to the option to configure who can look the user up on Facebook by e-mail. The system offers only the general options: "Everyone", "Friends" and "Friends of Friends", not providing an alternative path for blocking a specific user. Such option would facilitate the understanding and use of this functionality.

Since each problem may be associated with the absence of one or more usability heuristics and the same heuristic may be violated by different problems, we checked the frequency that each heuristic was violated in the evaluation, such as shown in Fig. 1. We observe that heuristics H3, H8, and H2 have had the highest violation frequencies along different problems, presenting frequencies of 92%, 83%, and 50%, respectively.

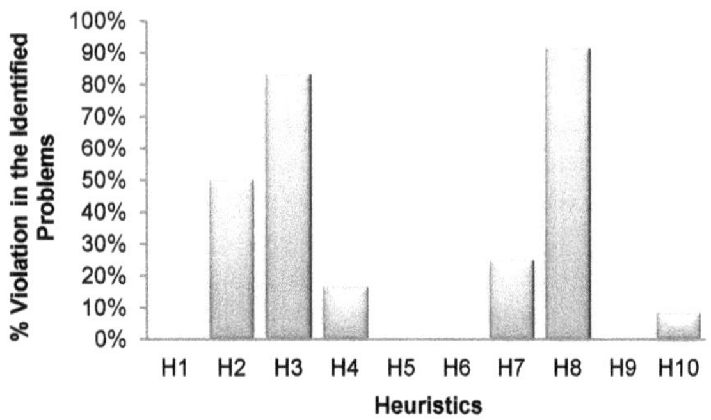

Figure 1: Violation frequency of usability heuristics in Facebook privacy settings.

The violation frequency of these three heuristics may be explained by an intrinsic relationship among them. Whether the designer does not use elements in the interface to allude the real world (H2), users can not interact with the interface efficiently (H3, H8). In addition, users become discouraged to use functionality when the interface exhibits little flexibility (H8). Such problems may compromise the perception of privacy and use of privacy control mechanisms on Facebook [29,30,20].

Taking into consideration the focus of this research, when dealing with children and teenagers, these problems become even worse, since this group is usually impatient to deal with this type of difficulties during privacy settings [17,20]. This scenario reduces the chances of children and teenagers to protect themselves from privacy risks on Facebook.

In turn, Heuristics H4, H7 and H10 have presented, respectively, 17%, 25% and 8% of incidence rates in the problems. Although these heuristics had a lower frequency of violations, we cannot ignore their impact on Facebook privacy settings. Violations of H4 and H7 indicate that users may struggle to recognize the possibilities of interaction in the privacy setting process, since the mechanisms offered do not follow a consistent pattern. Consequently, if users have difficulty in understanding and using the settings and do not have a help option or an adequate documentation to assist him/her, he/she may get frustrated and give up on using the functionality [20,29]. Again, these problems worsen since children and teenagers are shortsighted and easily frustrated by difficulties [17,20]. Thus, these users may choose to ignore the privacy setting possibilities, becoming vulnerable on Facebook.

In summary, we conclude that Facebook presents several usability violations that may limit the user's autonomy, discouraging them to set privacy settings properly. Particularly, this lack of freedom and motivation may compromise the safety of children and teenagers in the network.

5 PERCEPTION OF PRIVACY ON FACEBOOK: CHILDREN AND TEENAGERS VIEWPOINTS

In this step, we conducted a survey with the participants with two goals. First, we intended to investigate the perception of children and teenagers about privacy on Facebook. Second, we aimed at checking whether the usability problems identified in the previous step were, indeed, experienced by the participants. The survey comprised a questionnaire with 29 multiple-choice questions and 1 open question. We grouped the questions so that it was possible to identify: (1) the participant's profiles, (2) account details and Facebook friends, (3) the published content and (4) how each participant deals with privacy on Facebook.

The survey took place from 03/16/2016 to 03/29/2016, with Brazilian children and teenagers. It was conducted and analyzed by three authors of this study, two of them experts in HCI and an Occupational Therapist specialized in educational psychology of children and young people. Such as in the evaluation by inspection (i.e., the first step of the proposed methodology), the role of the expert in educational psychology was important to assist both participants and HCI experts in conducting the survey, as well as in analyzing the data. Thus, we focused the evaluation on the perception and use of the privacy settings of Facebook for children and teenagers.

A total of 142 distinct children and teenagers answered the questionnaire. Despite not being statistically representative, this number allows us to assess the perception and use of privacy settings on Facebook for that audience [31].

5.1 Participant Profiles

Regarding age, 75% of the participants were in the age group of 15 to 16, 9% of them were 10 years, 8% were 11 years and 8% were 14 years. Further, 75% of the participants were female and 25% male. Considering education, we found that most of the participants (58%) were in high school, 25% had completed the primary school only, and 17% were taking elementary level. This data indicates that the participant group had a minimum education degree expected to understand and discern the privacy issues raised in this work.

Participants were asked about OSNs they were using at the moment of the survey and about those they had used before. Fig. 2 summarizes this data and shows Facebook as the social network most used by the participants (100% of them).

Regarding the mean lifetime of the participants on Facebook, we found that all of them had accounts in this OSN for at least two years. The gathered data also points out that all participants accessed Facebook at least twice per week, while 58% of them accessed it daily, mainly, through mobile devices, for at least 1 hour.

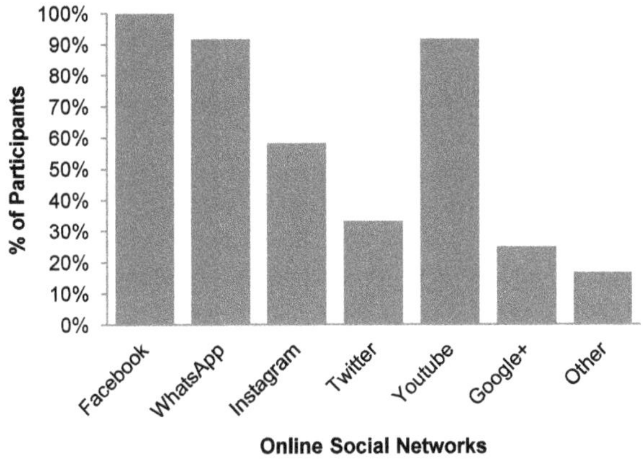

Figure 2: Online Social Networks used by the survey participants.

5.2 Contacts and Publications on Facebook

Initially, participants were asked to answer how many friends they kept on Facebook. Fig. 3 presents this information, indicating that most of the participants (67%) had more than 500 friends on Facebook and 33% had between 201 and 500 contacts in this OSN.

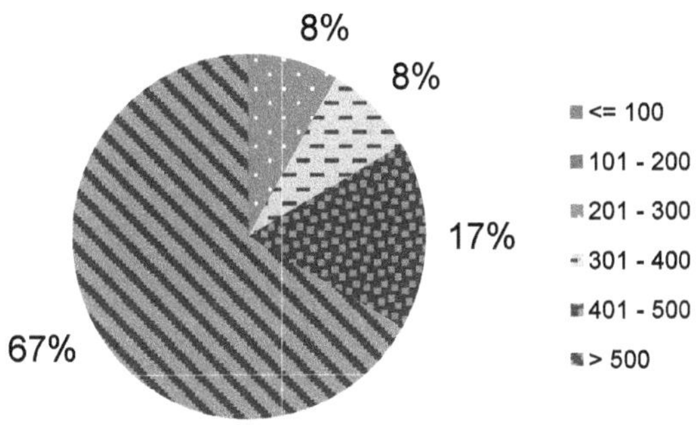

Figure 3: Number of friends that each participant has on Facebook.

By analyzing the number of friends distributed by the participant ages, as shown in Fig. 4, we note that all participants between 10 and 11 years had 401-500 friends on Facebook and all teenagers aged 14 were connected to more than 500 people.

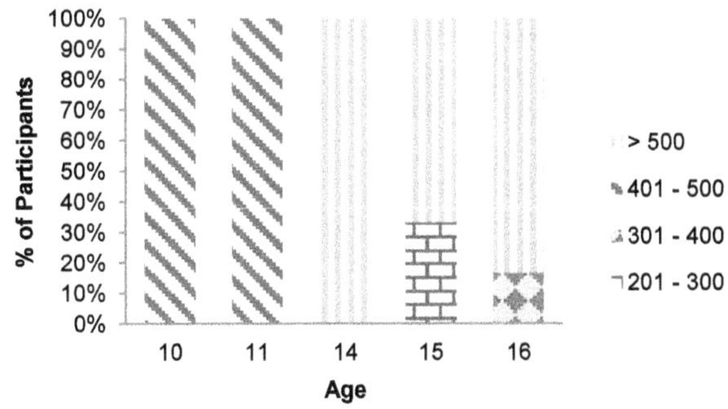

Figure 4: Age versus number of friends on Facebook.

Regarding the high number of friendships established on Facebook, we asked participants whether they knew all their Facebook friends personally. Results showed that 92% of them declared not knowing the entirety of their Facebook friends personally. This information brings attention to the fact that malicious users may take advantage of this situation to commit crimes, such as harassment, abuses (e.g., cyber bullying), or even public humiliation or threats. That may represent a dangerous behavior, because 25% of these children and teenagers declared that they interact actively (e.g., exchanging text messages or pictures) with those personally unknown contacts.

The previously found fact is a warning to the issue of security and privacy of these children and teenagers on Facebook. A large number of people may have access to personal data and information of these users, who represent a more vulnerable group for malicious people [3,12,13,27]. This observation reinforces the importance of enhancing usability on this type of virtual environment so that children and teenagers can understand and feel motivated to use the mechanisms that allow them to set privacy on Facebook properly.

Participants were also asked about the type of content they publish on Facebook. Fig. 5 shows that 25% of the participants admits publishing personal data such as name, address, and telephone number. This behavior demonstrates that some children and teenagers have no perception of the risks they may be exposed, since this personal data may be used to harm them.

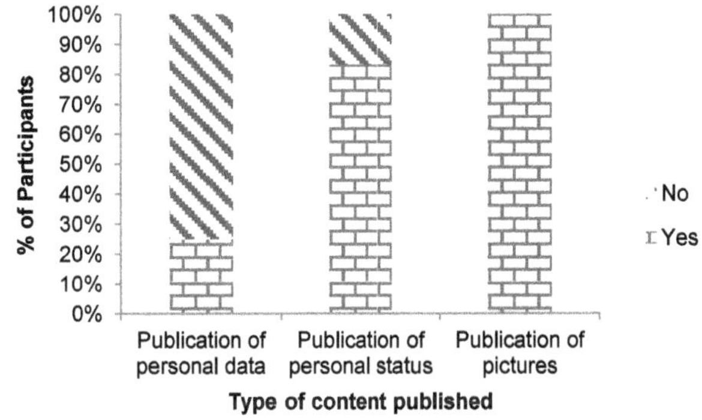

Figure 5: Type of content published on Facebook.

In addition to personal data, participants also indicated they published content that express their personal status (e.g., joys, sorrows, achievements, travels) and pictures, which further expose them on the OSN. By disclosing their personal status to any person, the user is more likely to be a victim of criminals who may take advantage of a moment of weakness to get closer. Further, by exposing personal pictures, users ease the action of such criminals to view and recognize their victims, the places they frequent or even their material possessions [3,12,13,27].

This behavior becomes more serious when considering the visibility of the content published. It was found that although half of the participants limit access to publications only to friends, 42% reported that the visibility of the content published in their timeline is public. Also, 8% of participants said they did not know the visibility of the content published by them. Despite being a small percentage, this information is relevant because it demonstrates that there still are people, within the profile analyzed in this research, who are unaware of the existence of visibility control for content on Facebook. The limited use and even ignorance of this control mechanism may be justified by the usability problems exemplified in the evaluation by inspection section.

After analyzing the interaction with Facebook contacts, as well as the type and visibility of the content published by each participant, we could characterize two issues: (1) the perception and use of privacy settings by children and teenagers and (2) the privacy problems already experienced by these users. The next section discusses the results of this characterization.

5.3 Privacy on Facebook

Initially, we asked participants whether they were concerned about security and privacy on Facebook and whether they knew the privacy policy of that OSN. Among all participants, 68% said they worried about their privacy. However, 80% stated that they had no knowledge (i.e., had not read) about the privacy policy of Facebook. This information may help explain the fact that less than 50% of the participants claim to know or use all the privacy settings available on Facebook, as presented in Fig. 6.

Fig. 6 lists the main privacy controls offered by Facebook and indicates the percentage of participants who know or use each one of these features. Note that, for example, the setting "*Control the restricted list of friends that can only see the information and posts you made public*", that is useful to limit the content to a particular group of trustful friends, is known and used by only 18% of the participants.

Another important configuration is the "*Control who can add things to your timeline*". This feature also had low awareness level, since only 25% of the participants have heard about it. This setting allows users to avoid possible embarrassments with undesirable content such as insults and threats.

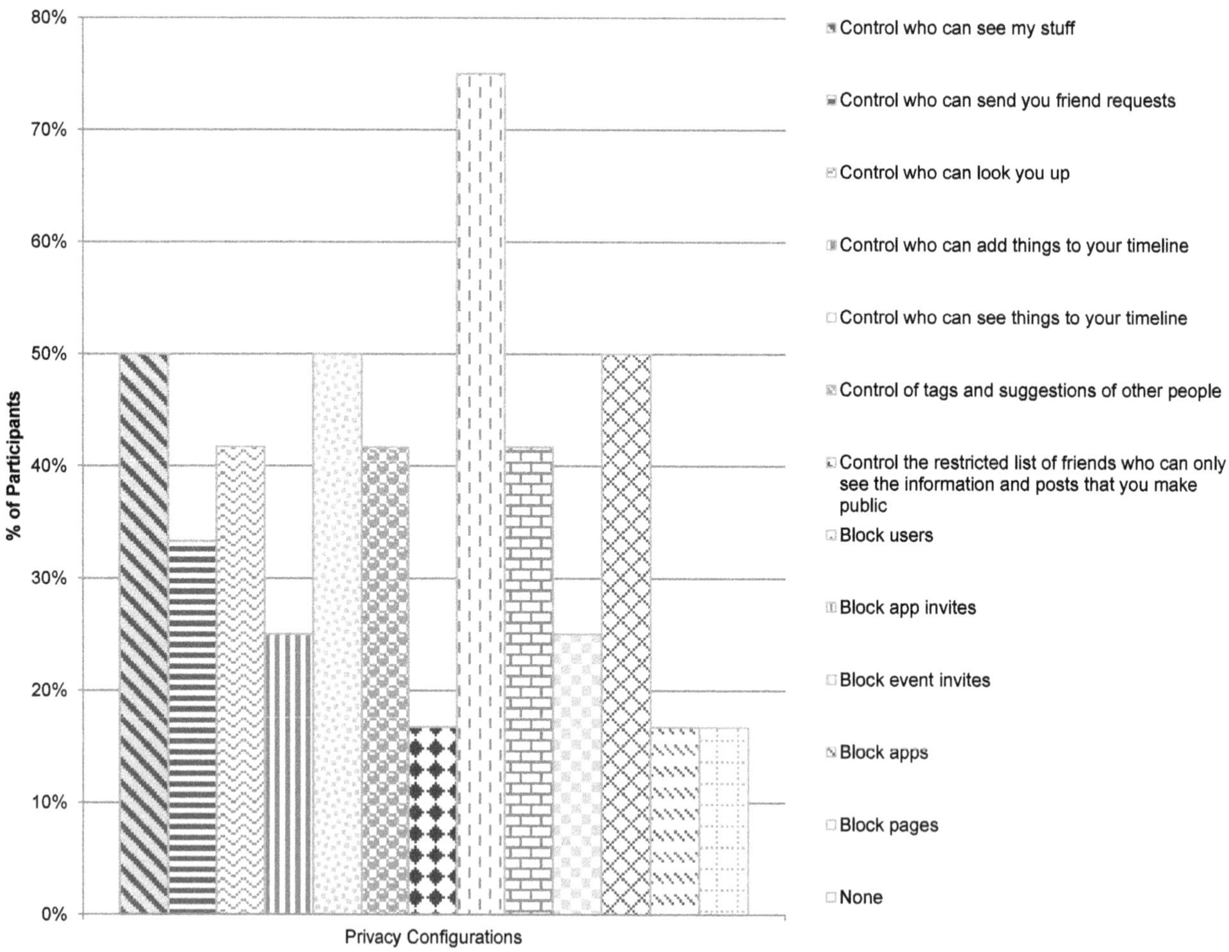

Figure 6: Facebook's privacy configurations used by the participants.

As aforementioned, participants were asked whether they had experienced privacy problems on Facebook. Such as shown in Fig. 7, 50% of them had endured some privacy violation. Further, 33% had their account hacked, and at least 8% had suffered some type of harassment or abuse (e.g., cyberbullying) and problems with fake accounts on Facebook.

By contrasting the profile visibility of the participants against the type of privacy violation, we may conclude, with the help of Fig. 8, that children and teenagers holding a public profile suffered different kinds of privacy violations.

At the end of this step, we observed that the most participants of this survey claimed to worry about their safety and privacy on Facebook. However, less than half of them knew or used the main privacy controls available in this OSN. The lack of knowledge may influence the limited use or even the non-use of important privacy settings on Facebook.

This limited use is a warning because, as previously reported, children and teenagers are potentially more vulnerable in OSNs. Further, since they make their profile public, add and interact with strangers and share personal information such as data, pictures, and "personal states" they increase the chances of suffering privacy violations, as indeed occurred with at least 50% of the participants.

The results of this evaluation not only draw attention of parents and guardians in relation to the care that must be taken during the access of their children and teenagers to OSNs, but also of their developers, since the supply of lighter and appropriate privacy settings may increase the safety and privacy of children and teenagers in these social networks.

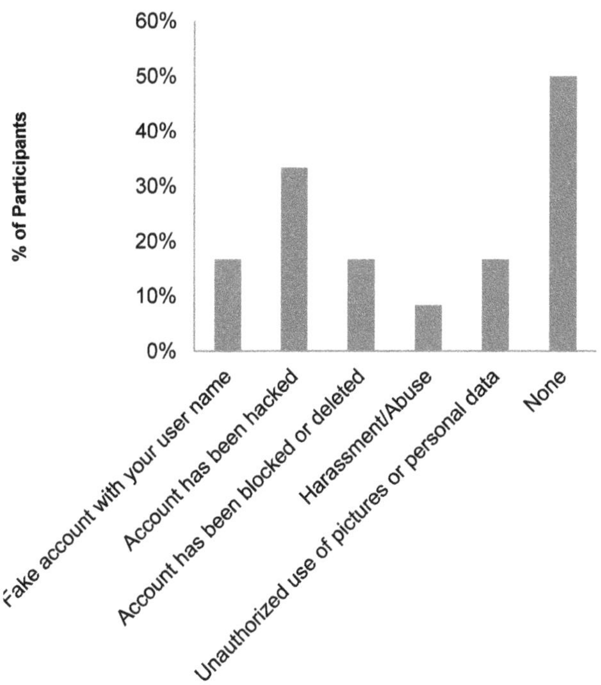

Figure 7: Type of privacy violation that participants had suffered on Facebook.

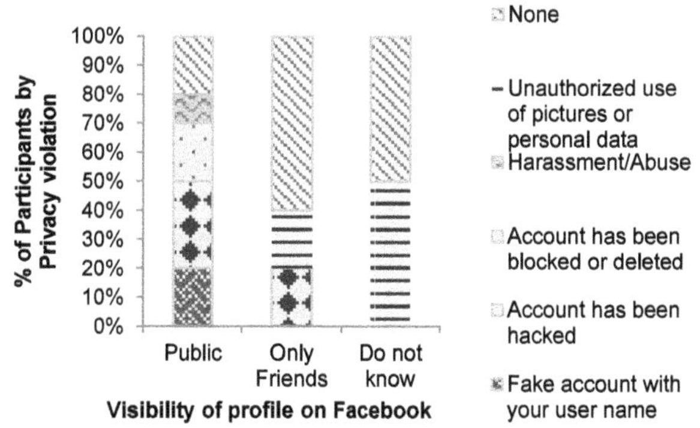

Figure 8: Profile visibility versus privacy violation.

6 TRIANGULATION AND DISCUSSIONS OF RESULTS

Aiming to assess how the usability of Facebook's privacy settings has impacted the safety of Brazilian children and teenagers, the last step of this research consisted of applying the triangulation technique. We applied such technique on the results of usability inspection and on the data collected with questionnaire with participants of the survey.

The results indicate that violations of the usability heuristics H2, H4, H7, and H10 may explain the fact that most participants in this case study do not know the privacy policy of Facebook and are making a limited use of the controls offered by the system.

By violating heuristics H2, H4, H7, and H10, Facebook does not use interface elements consistent with the expectation and experience of children and teenagers. As all these heuristics aim to ensure ease of use, efficiency, productivity, and user satisfaction, by violating them, Facebook prevents this group from making productive use of privacy mechanisms. Thus, these users find it difficult to recognize and use the privacy setting options, as well as to look for help through the System Help Resources [29,30,20]. Indeed, children and teenagers do not feel guided and motivated to apply privacy controls due to barriers found in the available interface for these settings. Consequently, such difficulties may hamper, or even prevent, privacy settings to be applied properly.

In summary, triangulation shows that usability problems reflect the use that children and teenagers make of privacy features on Facebook. Further, this research has shown that, in fact, the limited use of privacy controls compromises the safety of this user group. At least 50% of the participants admitted facing problems with violation of privacy. Thus, the poor usability of resources to configure privacy increases the vulnerability of children and teenagers on Facebook.

7 CONCLUSIONS AND FUTURE WORKS

This study aimed to assess and characterize how children and teenagers have dealt with the privacy controls on their profiles on OSNs and whether the usability of these controls is appropriate to this user group. In this sense, we conducted a case study on Facebook, considering Brazilin children and teenagers, since Brazil figures among the top-3 countries on the number of Facebook users.

The results indicated how usability problems have influenced the limited degree of knowledge and use of the security and privacy settings on Facebook by Brazilian children and teenagers.

Although the case study has been conducted on Facebook, considering the profile of children and teenagers in Brazil, the results presented and discussed in this paper are relevant and not limited to the context of that country. The relevance of this research can be supported by arguments presented in Wilson et al. [40] and Willinger et al. [33], where the authors list the research challenges related to OSNs. According to these authors, proper solutions to address demands of different user profiles, in all situations, must focus on dynamic and behavioral aspects during the use of this type of system. Further, it is important to characterize and understand how the various profiles of users are actually interacting with the OSN, to verify and address the problems that may be affecting the quality of this interaction [40,33].

Therefore, this work presents practical and scientific/methodological contributions. In scientific terms, this work is important because it discusses the relevance of proposing and evaluating interfaces for privacy settings considering children and teenagers. It is noteworthy that the methodology here proposed can be reproduced in the evaluation of other social networks, considering the usability of distinct privacy features and other user profiles.

Regarding practical contributions, this work raises awareness for interface designers about the importance of usability in the privacy controls of OSNs. Additionally, the reported results may provide parameters to improve and create privacy mechanisms, with increased usability, in this virtual environment for children and teenagers.

As further work, we propose to create an interface design with improvements and a set of best practices that describe the most appropriate privacy features for children and teenagers. Another promising direction is the evaluation of privacy mechanisms in OSNs from the perspectives of other profiles, such as people with disabilities and older adults.

REFERENCES

[1] Abdulmohsen Albesher and Thamer Alhussain. 2013. Privacy and security issues in social networks: an evaluation of Facebook. In Proceedings of the 2013 International Conference on Information Systems and Design of Communication (ISDOC '13). ACM, New York, NY, USA, 7-10. DOI=http://dx.doi.org/10.1145/2503859.2503861

[2] Ocimara Balmant, O. 2012. Cresce exposição de jovens na internet. O Estado de São Paulo, Caderno Vida, p.27, 02 dez 2012. Estadão Geral. Available in: < http://www.estadao.com.br/noticias/geral,cresce-exposicao-de-jovens-na-internet-imp-,968026>. Last access: Dec – 23, 2016

[3] Danah Boyd, Eszter Hargittai, Jason Schultz, and John Palfrey. 2011. Why Parents Help Their Children Lie to Facebook: Unintended Consequences of the 'Children's Online Privacy Protection Act'. First Monday, 16(11), November 7, 2011.

[4] Parmit Chilana, Christina Holsberry, Flavio Oliveira, and Andrew Ko. 2012. Designing for a billion users: a case study of facebook. In CHI '12 Extended Abstracts on Human Factors in Computing Systems (CHI EA '12). ACM, New York, NY, USA, 419-432. DOI: http://dx.doi.org/10.1145/2212776.2212819

[5] Jeasik Cho, and Allen Trent. (2006). Validity in qualitative research revisited. Qualitative Research, 6(3):319--340.

[6] comScore. 2012(a). Facebook Blasts into Top Position in Brazilian Social Networking Market Following Year of Tremendous Growth. Available in: <http://goo.gl/TcXcM>. Last access: Dec – 23, 2016.

[7] comScore. 2012(b). Argentina Ranks First in Worldwide Desktop Social Networking Engagement at Nearly 10 Hours per Visitor Each Month. Available in: <http://goo.gl/cLLzM>. Last access: Dec – 23, 2016.

[8] comScore. 2015. Brazil Digital Future in Focus. Available in: <https://www.comscore.com/Insights/Presentations-and-Whitepapers/2015/2015-Brazil-Digital-Future-in-Focus>. Last access: Dec – 23, 2016.

[9] Consumer Reports News. 2012. Facebook may let children under age 13 use the site. Available in: <https://goo.gl/KfTtZl> Last access: Dec – 23, 2016.

[10] Sérgio R. P. da Silva, and Roberto Pereira. 2008. Aspectos da interação humano-computador na web social. In Proceedings of the IX Simpósio Brasileiro de Fatores Humanos em Sistemas Computacionais – IHC 2008, Outubro de 2008, pp.350-553.

[11] Ratan Dey, Zubin Jelveh, and Keith Ross. 2012. Facebook users have become much more private: A large-scale study. In Proceedings of the 4th IEEE International Workshop on Security and Social Networking. IEEE, pp. 346-352.

[12] Ratan Dey, Cong Tang, Keith Ross, and Nitesh Saxena. 2012. Estimating age privacy leakage in online social networks. In Proceedings of the IEEE INFOCOM 2012, Orlando, FL, USA, 2836-2840.

[13] Ratan Dey, Yuan Ding, and Keith W. Ross. 2013. Profiling high-school students with facebook: how online privacy laws can actually increase minors' risk. In Proceedings of the 2013 conference on Internet measurement conference (IMC '13). ACM, New York, NY, USA, 405-416. DOI=http://dx.doi.org/10.1145/2504730.2504733

[14] Imen Ben Dhia, Talel Abdessalem, and Mauro Sozio. 2012. Primates: a privacy management system for social networks. In Proceedings of the 21st ACM international conference on Information and knowledge management (CIKM '12), NY, USA, 2746-2748. DOI=http://dx.doi.org/10.1145/2396761.2398748

[15] Maeve Duggan, Nicole b. Ellison, Cliff Lampe, Amanda Lenhart, and Mary Madden. 2015. Social Media Update 2014. In Pew Internet and American Life Project. Available in: <http://www.pewinternet.org/2015/01/09/social-media-update-2014/>, Last access: Dec – 23, 2016.

[16] Maeve Duggan, Nicole b. Ellison, Cliff Lampe, Amanda Lenhart and Mary Madden. 2015. Mobile Messaging and Social Media 2015. In Pew Research Center. Available in: <http://www.pewinternet.org/2015/08/19/mobile-messaging-and-social-media-2015/>, Last access: Dec – 23, 2016.

[17] Dan Fitton, Beth Bell, Janet C. Read, Ole Iversen, Linda Little, and Matthew Horton. 2014. Understanding teen UX: building a bridge to the future. In Extended Abstracts on Human Factors in Computing Systems (CHI EA '14). ACM, New York, NY, USA, 79-82. DOI=http://dx.doi.org/10.1145/2559206.2559232

[18] Philip WL Fong, Mohd Anwar, and Zhen Zhao. 2009. A privacy preservation model for facebook-style social network systems. In Computer Security - ESORICS, Springer Berlin Heidelberg, 303-320.

[19] Alastair J. Gill, Asimina Vasalou, Chrysanthi Papoutsi, and Adam N. Joinson. 2011. Privacy dictionary: a linguistic taxonomy of privacy for content analysis. In Proceedings of the SIGCHI Conference on Human Factors in Computing Systems (CHI '11). ACM, New York, NY, USA, 3227-3236. DOI=http://dx.doi.org/10.1145/1978942.1979421

[20] Shuli Gilutz, and Jakob Nielsen. 2002. Usability of Websites for Children: Children (Ages 3-12) on the Web - 70 Design Guidelines. 3rd Edition. Nielsen Norman Group. Available in: <www.nngroup.com/reports/kids/>. Last access: Dec – 23, 2016

[21] Sameer Hinduja, and Justin W. Patchin. 2008. Personal information of adolescents on the Internet: A quantitative content analysis of MySpace. Journal of Adolescence, 31(1), 125-146.

[22] Michal Jakob, Zbynek Moler, Michal Pechoucek, and Roman Vaculin. 2011. Intelligent Content-Based Privacy Assistant for Facebook. In Proceedings of the 2011 IEEE/WIC/ACM International Conferences on Web Intelligence and Intelligent Agent Technology - Volume 01 (WI-IAT '11), Vol. 1. IEEE Computer Society, Washington, DC, USA, 499-500. DOI=http://dx.doi.org/10.1109/WI-IAT.2011.67

[23] Manoel Pereira Junior, Simone Isabela de Rezende Xavier, and Raquel Oliveira Prates. 2014. Investigating the Use of a Simulator to Support Users in Anticipating Impact of Privacy Settings in Facebook. In Proceedings of the 18th International Conference on Supporting Group Work (GROUP '14). ACM, New York, NY, USA, 63-72. DOI=http://dx.doi.org/10.1145/2660398.2660419

[24] Michaela Kauer, Benjamin Franz, Thomas Pfeiffer, Martin Heine, and Delphine Christin. 2013. Improving privacy settings for facebook by using interpersonal distance as criterion. In CHI '13 Extended Abstracts on Human Factors in Computing Systems (CHI EA '13). ACM, New York, NY, USA, 793-798. DOI: http://dx.doi.org/10.1145/2468356.2468498

[25] Hanna Krasnova, and Natasha F. Veltri. 2010. Privacy Calculus on Social Networking Sites: Explorative Evidence from Germany and USA, In Proceedings of the 43rd Hawaii International Conference on System Sciences (HICSS), IEEE, 1-10.

[26] Yabing Liu, Krishna P. Gummadi, Balachander Krishnamurthy, and Alan Mislove. 2011. Analyzing facebook privacy settings: user expectations vs. reality. In Proceedings of the 2011 ACM SIGCOMM conference on Internet measurement conference (IMC '11). ACM, New York, NY, USA, 61-70. DOI=http://dx.doi.org/10.1145/2068816.2068823

[27] Sonia Livingstone, Kjartan Ólafsson, and Elisabeth Staksrud. 2011. Social networking, age and privacy. EU Kids Online, London, UK. Available in: <http://eprints.lse.ac.uk/35849/>. Last access: Dec – 23, 2016.

[28] Amanda Meincke Melo, and M. Cecília C. Baranauskas. 2003. Design with children: a Semiotic approach. In Proceedings of the Latin American conference on Human-computer interaction (CLIHC '03). ACM, New York, NY, USA, 69-78.

[29] Jakob Nielsen. 1993. Usability Engineering. Morgan Kaufmann Publishers Inc., San Francisco, CA, USA

[30] Jakob Nielsen. 1994. Usability inspection methods. In Conference Companion on Human Factors in Computing Systems (CHI '94), NY, USA, 413-414. DOI=http://dx.doi.org/10.1145/259963.260531

[31] Jakob Nielsen. 2000. Why you only need to test with 5 users. 2000. Available in: <https://www.nngroup.com/articles/why-you-only-need-to-test-with-5-users/>. Last access: Dec 23, 2016.

[32] TEMPO (Jornal). 2014. Pedófilo se passa por atriz de Chiquititas para abordar crianças. . Available in: <http://www.otempo.com.br/capa/brasil/ped%C3%B3filo-se-passa-por-atriz-de-chiquititas-para-abordar-crian%C3%A7as-1.906223>. Last access: Dec – 23, 2016.

[33] Walter Willinger, Reza Rejaie, Mojtaba Torkjazi, Masoud Valafar, and Mauro Maggioni. 2010. Research on online social networks: time to face the real challenges. SIGMETRICS Perform. Eval. Rev. 37, 3 (January 2010), 49-54. DOI=http://dx.doi.org/10.1145/1710115.1710125

[34] João Paulo Pesce, Diego Las Casas, Gustavo Rauber, and Virgílio Almeida. 2012. Privacy attacks in social media using photo tagging networks: a case study with Facebook. In Proceedings of the 1st Workshop on Privacy and Security in Online Social Media (PSOSM '12). ACM, New York, NY, USA, Article 4 , 8 pages. DOI=http://dx.doi.org/10.1145/2185354.2185358

[35] Kamila R. H. Rodrigues, Maíra C. Canal, Rogério A. C. Xavier, Tatiana S. Alencar, and Vânia P. A. Neris. 2012. Avaliando aspectos de privacidade no Facebook pelas lentes de usabilidade, acessibilidade e fatores emocionais. In Companion Proceedings of the 11th Brazilian Symposium on Human Factors in Computing Systems (IHC '12). Brazilian Computer Society, Porto Alegre, Brazil, Brazil, 75-76.

[36] Alan Rubel, and Ryan Biava. "A framework for analyzing and comparing privacy states." Journal of the Association for Information Science and Technology 65.12 (2014): 2422-2431.

[37] Zaineb de Souza, and Geoffrey N. Dick. 2009. Disclosure of information by children in social networking - Not just a case of "you show me yours and I'll show you mine". International Journal of Information Management. (2009), 255-261

[38] Ho Keung Tsoi, and Li Chen. From privacy concern to uses of social network sites: A cultural comparison via user survey. 2011. In Proceedings of the Privacy, Security, Risk and Trust (PASSAT) and 2011 IEEE Third Inernational Conference on Social Computing (SocialCom), vol., no., pp.457-464, 9-11 Oct. 2011. DOI: 10.1109/PASSAT/SocialCom.2011.71.

[39] Maria Lúcia B. Villela and Raquel O. Prates. 2015. Supporting Designers in Modeling Privacy for Social Network Sites. In Proceedings of 15th Brazilian Symposium on Human Factors in Computing Systems. (IHC'15). November 03-06, 2015.

[40] Christo Wilson, Bryce Boe, Alessandra Sala, Krishna P.N. Puttaswamy, and Ben Y. Zhao. 2009. User interactions in social networks and their implications. In Proceedings of the 4th ACM European conference on Computer systems (EuroSys '09). ACM, New York, NY, USA, 205-218. DOI=http://dx.doi.org/10.1145/1519065.1519089

Closed-Loop Opinion Formation

Larissa Spinelli
Boston University
lspinell@bu.edu

Mark Crovella
Boston University
crovella@bu.edu

ABSTRACT

When information sources are moderated by recommender systems, so-called "filter bubbles" may restrict the diversity of content made available to users, potentially affecting their opinions. User opinions may in turn affect the output of recommender systems. In this work we ask how the dynamical system defined by user and recommender systems behaves, as each element evolves in time. In particular, we look at whether the use of recommender system can affect user experience and user opinions in a systematic way. We define and analyze three metrics to understand those effects – intensity, simplification, and divergence – and we explore both link-based and ratings-based recommender systems. Our results suggest that previous studies of this problem have been too simplistic, and that user opinions can evolve in complex ways under the influence of personalized information sources.

CCS CONCEPTS

• **Information systems** → *Collaborative filtering*;

KEYWORDS

Filter Bubble, User Experience, Metrics

1 INTRODUCTION

Recommender systems are an increasingly prevalent part of online services, and increasingly mediate access to online resources. Recommender systems are found in systems for online-shopping, video streaming, news feeds, search queries and social media. Recommender systems are employed not just to explicitly give recommendations, but to implicitly guide users, as in the selection and ordering of items in a Facebook news feed.

The term *filter bubble* refers to a narrowed access of information caused by personalization, often in combination with search engines [22]. The term and associated literature raises the concern that recommender systems may have an effect on society, for example by influencing user opinions. Given the prevalence of recommender systems, it is natural to ask whether they can have an effect on user opinions, and what the nature of that effect is.

In this paper we take this question a step further, and ask how user opinions *and* recommender systems together change as they interact over time. This question arises because many recommender systems are adaptive, making and incorporating observations of users preferences and choices, even as the users are themselves reacting to the recommended items (again, take as an example a Facebook news feed). This constitutes a kind of closed loop, or dynamical system. The central question we ask is: how do user opinions evolve when users and recommender systems each take input from the other, over time?

To answer this question requires significantly abstracting both recommender systems and users in a manner that captures essential properties. Taking recommender systems first, these are usually classified according to how the recommendations are made [2]: *content-based filtering* systems recommend items based on features of the previous items evaluated by the user, while *collaborative filtering* systems recommend items that people with similar tastes and preferences had evaluated before. Since the latter are based on the opinions of users, our focus is on collaborative filtering systems. We use two different models of collaborative filtering to compare results and explore differences: link based systems and ratings based systems. Link based systems are exemplified by online retailers, which rely on the past records of purchases by the set of all users. Ratings based systems are exemplified by movie, music, and hotel sites sites that recommend new (or previously seen) experiences for a user based on their explicit feedback. These two types of systems are often addressed using the *neighbor* approach and *latent factor* models, respectively [24].

Turning to user modeling, the central effect to be captured is how user opinion about an item is affected by the fact the item has been presented to the user by the recommender system. Here, we study a range of options, from the case where the user's reaction is random, to cases in which users have maximally negative or maximally positive reactions to the item presented. These reactions are captured by the recommender system and used to update its knowledge base.

While there is little work to date that has addressed this question in the form that we pose it, parts of our study have connection to the work in [8]. That paper constructed abstractions of three link based recommender systems, and analyzed the effects on user opinion under certain assumptions. Part of our work looks more deeply at the same systems, examining the effect of key assumptions, and shows effects that differ considerably from what is predicted in [8]. However our work also goes beyond link based systems to ratings based systems, where we find that the set of phenomena (system metrics) to be studied are more diverse.

Beyond abstracting the key system elements, we also must identify the properties of user opinions that are of interest. We study three key properties of the evolving set of user opinions: the *intensity* of individual user's opinions, the *simplicity* of individual user's opinions, and the *divergence* of the opinions of the entire set of users. We make these concrete in the form of specific metrics.

WebSci'17, June 25-28, 2017, Troy, NY, USA.
 978-1-4503-4896-6/17/06...$15.00
DOI: http://dx.doi.org/10.1145/3091478.3091483

Our results show a surprisingly subtle interaction between properties of recommender system algorithms, actions of users, and initial system state. We show that small differences in algorithms (e.g., whether an algorithm returns the "best" item or merely a "good" item) have a strong effect on whether user opinions undergo simplification as they evolve. We show that the initial distribution of opinions can determine whether users become simplified over time. And we show that recommender systems can cause user opinions to diverge and simplify, but generally only if the recommender system accurately predicts user preferences. On the other hand, we show that a recommender system does not necessarily increase the intensity of user opinions, as long as the system makes good recommendations to the user. We conclude that there is striking richness of interactions that are observed when user opinions and recommender systems form a dynamical system, despite the high level of abstraction necessary for a study like ours. Furthermore, the nature of the effects observed suggests that the increasing prevalence of recommender systems deserves attention and care.

2 FRAMEWORK

We formalize the problem as follows. We consider a system of n *users* and m *items.* Items are objects over which the user has an opinion or has a connection with, e.g., products, movies, books, or news articles.

The knowledge used by the recommender system is held in an $n \times m$ matrix $\mathbf{M}$. In link-based systems, entries in $\mathbf{M}$ are in $\{0, 1\}$, while in ratings based systems entries in $\mathbf{M}$ are in $\mathbb{R}$. In ratings systems, $\mathbf{M}$ is only partially known. In that case, let Ω denote the index set $\{(i_1, j_1), (i_2, j_2), \ldots\}$ of known (observed) entries of $\mathbf{M}$ and $\bar{\Omega}$ the index set of unknown entries of $\mathbf{M}$. We use $\mathbf{M}^{\Omega}$ to denote the known entries of $\mathbf{M}$.

In a ratings-based system, a matrix completion algorithm decomposes $\mathbf{M}$ into matrices $\mathbf{X}$ and $\mathbf{Y}$ (k by n and k by m respectively) for a given latent space dimension k such that $\mathbf{C} = \mathbf{X}^T\mathbf{Y}$ and $||\mathbf{M}^{\Omega} - \mathbf{C}^{\Omega}||_2$ is minimized.

We model a user's set of preferences or opinions as an s dimensional vector $\mathbf{u_i} \in \mathbb{R}^s$. We think of this vector as the location of the user in a "preference space." This abstract representation can capture a variety of user characterizations. For instance, in a link based system, (such as specified in [8]) the user vector can be interpreted as a distribution over categories of items to which the user is linked. On the other hand, for a ratings based system using matrix completion $\mathbf{u_i}$ can represent the completed vector of items opinions, i.e., $\mathbf{u_i} = \mathbf{c_i}$ (i-th row of $\mathbf{C}$) or it can represent the projection of the user's ratings in the latent space, $\mathbf{u_i} = \mathbf{x_i}$ (i-th row of $\mathbf{X}$).

Dynamical System. The process we study in this paper is a dynamical system. Hence we introduce time indexing, where $\mathbf{M_t}$ and $\mathbf{u_{it}}$ denote respectively the state of $\mathbf{M}$ and $\mathbf{u_i}$ at time t. The conceptual approach we take is described abstractly as follows.

Let $f(i, \mathbf{M})$ represent a recommender system algorithm; f returns the next item r suggested for user i. Let $g(i, r)$ represent the response of the user to the recommendation; this can be either a rating for the item r or the decision to link to item r (e.g., to purchase item r). This action then provides additional knowledge for the recommender system. Hence after a user has responded to an item, $\mathbf{M}_{t+1}(i, r)$ is set to $g(i, r)$, and Ω is updated to include (i, r).

In this setting we are interested in the dynamical system $\{\mathbf{M}_t\}, t = 0, 1, \ldots$ whose dynamics are governed by

$$\mathbf{M}_{t+1}(i, r) = g(i, f(i, \mathbf{M}_t)).$$

Denote by *Pref*$(i, \mathbf{M})$ the function that computes the user preference vector $\mathbf{u_i}$. The principal characterization of the system we use is via $\mathbf{u}_{it} = Pref(i, \mathbf{M}_t)$.

This general framework allows for a wide variety of investigations. To assess the impact of recommender system algorithms, we consider two different f functions. The two f functions return either the top rated, or a randomly chosen, item for that user. We also consider a range of g functions, which reflect the degree to which whether users tend to be favorably, or even unfavorably, influenced by the recommended items.

Metrics. Previous opinion formation studies have modeled user opinions as scalar values, leading to a one-dimensional representation of user preferences [8]. Nonetheless, empirical studies show that user opinions are better characterized as occupying a higher-dimensional space, e.g., 20 to 40 dimensions [4]. Hence the set of user preferences can be viewed as cloud of points, which we consider to be centered at the origin.

While one-dimensional views of user preferences lead to the single metric of *polarization* to describe opinion dynamics, the more realistic multidimensional view of user preferences provides the basis for a more diverse set of relevant metrics. We introduce three definitions that generalize polarization in different ways to describe how user preferences may evolve over time.

First, we define **intensity** as a per-user metric that captures the strength of a user's preferences. In our point-cloud view, intensity could be conceived of as the distance of the user point from the origin. Hence, given a user i at point $\mathbf{u_{it}}$ at time t, if at time $t' > t$, we have $||\mathbf{u_{it'}}|| > ||\mathbf{u_{it}}||$, we say the user's intensity has increased.

Second, we define **simplification** as a per-user metric that captures the diversity of items that the user prefers, i.e., the spread of user preferences as a distribution. Hence simplification consists of a reduction in the entropy of the user's vector as a distribution, $H(\mathbf{u_i})$. For a given user i

$$H(\mathbf{u_i}) = -\sum_{j=1}^{s}\left(\frac{\mathbf{u_i}[j]}{\sum_{l=1}^{s}\mathbf{u_i}[l]}\right)\log_s\left(\frac{\mathbf{u_i}[j]}{\sum_{l}^{s}\mathbf{u_i}[l]}\right)$$

Then, for a user i at point $\mathbf{u_{it}}$ at time t, if at time $t' > t$, we have $H(\mathbf{u_{it'}}) < H(\mathbf{u_{it}})$, we say the user's opinions have undergone simplification. We also use the term *diversification* as the opposite of simplification, i.e., an increase the entropy of the user's preference vector.

Finally, we define **divergence** as a property of a set of users that captures the similarities among the users' preference vectors, i.e., the degree two which any two user's preferences are alike. To measure this we use the average correlation coefficient over all pairs of user preference vectors, $\bar{\rho} = \frac{2}{n^2-n}\sum_{i>j}\rho(\mathbf{u_i}, \mathbf{u_j})$ where ρ is the standard correlation coefficient. Then, if we have for a set of users at time $t' > t$ that $\bar{\rho}_{t'} < \bar{\rho}_t$ we say that the user set has increased divergence.

3 LINK BASED SYSTEMS

A large class of recommender systems can be abstracted using a graph; we call these *link based* systems. A link based system is modeled as a bipartite graph $G = (V_1, V_2, E)$, where nodes in V_1 represent users, nodes in V_2 represent items, and E is the set of edges, i.e., connection among those nodes. In such a system the recommender algorithm is a function f that takes as input G and a node $i \in V_1$ and outputs a node $j \in V_2$. The representation of those connections varies with the specificity of each system. Edges can be unweighted to simply represent viewing of a video or purchase of an product such as at [8], or weighted edges representing scores or ratings such as at [7].

In this section we study three abstractions of link based systems introduced in [8]. Our goal is twofold: first, we use these as a comparison case for our study of ratings based systems in the next section; and second we seek to extend and probe the limits of the analysis performed in [8].

3.1 Polarization: theoretical analysis

In [8], the authors investigate whether certain link based recommender systems have a polarization effect, i.e., whether the recommender system dynamics result in an increased divergence of opinions.

The authors analyzed three random-walk based recommender algorithms inspired by well-known algorithms from literature: SALSA [16] (*SimpleSALSA*), Item-based Collaborative Filtering [17] (*SimpleICF*), and Personalized PageRank [21] (*SimplePPR*), described in more detail below. We follow their framework, in which items have labels $l \in \{\text{"RED"}, \text{"BLUE"}\}$, and there are an equal number of items of each label. That is, $|V_1| = n$ and $|V_2| = m = 2w$ with w items of each label.

These analyses considered cases in which users respond either with or without what was termed *biased assimilation.* In that context biased assimilation specifically means that the probability that a user i accepts an item recommendation is proportional to the quantity of items that i has of that label. On the other hand, without biased assimilation the probability that a user accepts a given recommendation is label-independent. Specifically, let x_i be the fraction of "RED" items owned by i. A recommender algorithm is polarizing with respect to i if: (1) when $x_i > \frac{1}{2}$ the probability that than a recommended item accepted by user i is "RED" is greater than x_i, and (2) when $x_i < \frac{1}{2}$, the probability that the recommended item accepted by user i is "RED" is less than x_i.

The authors in [8] conclude through analysis that *SimpleSALSA* and *SimpleICF* are polarizing only if users respond with biased assimilation; in contrast, *SimplePPR* is always polarizing. That analysis includes three assumptions: (1) the number of "RED" and "BLUE" items is equal; (2) the set of items is arbitrarily large (i.e., they study the system properties as $m \to \infty$); and (3) the recommender system may recommend the same item multiple times, even if the user has already linked to it. The third assumption is not explicitly stated but is implicit. One of the goals of this section is to show that analysis of these algorithms are quite sensitive to these assumptions and that as a result, conclusions about polarization are necessarily more nuanced.

3.2 Model

We encode the link based model in a binary matrix $\mathbf{M}$ such that $\mathbf{M}(i,j) = 1$ iff there exists an edge $e_{ij} \in E$ that connects $i \in V_1$ to $j \in V_2$. Once that there are equal quantities of items of each label we fixed the item label with respect of its position in $\mathbf{M}$, for instance, the first $\frac{m}{2}$ items have "RED" label and consequently last $\frac{m}{2}$ items have label "BLUE".

The recommender algorithms studied in [8] were defined in terms of a random walk on G. However, analysis becomes clearer if we express the algorithms in terms of a Markov chain. Let $\mathbf{P}_{\mathbf{V_i},\mathbf{V_j}}$ be the transition matrix between elements $i' \in V_i$ to $j' \in V_j$. So, $\mathbf{P}_{\mathbf{V_1},\mathbf{V_2}}$ is n by m matrix can be calculated from $\mathbf{M}$ such that each element $p_{ij} = \frac{m_{ij}}{\sum_j m_{ij}}$ and $\mathbf{P}_{\mathbf{V_2},\mathbf{V_1}}$ is m by n matrix such that $p_{ij} = \frac{m_{ji}}{\sum_i m_{ji}}$. Since G is bipartite $\mathbf{P}_{\mathbf{V_1},\mathbf{V_1}} = 0$ and $\mathbf{P}_{\mathbf{V_2},\mathbf{V_2}} = 0$. Thus:

$$\mathbf{P} = \begin{bmatrix} 0 & \mathbf{P}_{\mathbf{V_1},\mathbf{V_2}} \\ \mathbf{P}_{\mathbf{V_2},\mathbf{V_1}} & 0 \end{bmatrix}$$

We can now rewrite the random-walk based recommender algorithms as Markov chain based algorithms as follows.

Algorithm 1 *SimpleSALSA* using transition matrix $\mathbf{P}$

Require: $\mathbf{M}$ and a user i .
1: Compute $\mathbf{P}^3$, a three-step transition on the transition matrix $\mathbf{P}$
2: Choose an item j according to the distribution $\mathbf{P}^3(i, \cdot)$.
3: Return j

Algorithm 2 *SimpleICF* using transition matrix $\mathbf{P}$

Require: $\mathbf{M}$ and a user i.
1: Compute $\mathbf{P}^2$, a two-step transition on the transition matrix $\mathbf{P}$
2: Choose k according to the distribution $\mathbf{P}(i, \cdot)$
3: Compute $j = \arg\max_s \mathbf{P}^2(k, s)$
4: Return j

Algorithm 3 *SimplePPR* using transition matrix $\mathbf{P}$

Require: $\mathbf{M}$ and a user i.
1: Compute $\mathbf{P}^3$, a three-step transition on the transition matrix $\mathbf{P}$
2: Compute $j = \arg\max_k \mathbf{P}^3(i, k)$
3: Return j

Note that none of these algorithms are prevented from recommending an item to which the user has already linked. While some systems such as music recommenders may suggest items multiple times, for many other systems it is not desirable to recommend items that have already been purchased or viewed (e.g., books, movies, news articles).

To study the case in which repeated recommendation of an already-linked item is not allowed, we adjusted the above algorithms during simulation. In each case we simply ensured that the algorithm did not return an item that had been already linked by the user. Denoting Ω as the set of items already linked, we ensure that each item k such that $(i, k) \in \Omega$ is removed from the distribution used in *SimpleSALSA* and eliminated from consideration in the arg max computations in *SimpleICF* or *SimplePPR*. In such cases, to ensure that a recommendation is always possible, we replace the zeros in $\mathbf{P}$ with a small value $0 < \epsilon \ll 1$.

3.3 Simulation and Analysis

We would like to understand the role of each factor – recommender algorithm, user behavior, and initial system settings – in the formation of user opinion in the linked model G.

For this, we use simulation consisting of the following steps: (i) First, initialize $\mathbf{M}$ according to a probability distribution $q(\cdot)$; (ii) Provide recommendations for all users according to Algorithm 1, Algorithm 2 or Algorithm 3; (iii) For each user, accept the suggested recommendation with some probability p, where p can be a fixed probability (when users respond without biased assimilation), or can vary with the fraction of items with same label that the user has (for biased assimilation). (iv) The matrix $\mathbf{M}$ is updated synchronously with the accepted items . The system evolves (repeating steps (ii) to (iv)) for $T = 1000$ timesteps. We repeat each simulation 30 times and report confidence intervals.

For simulations in this section we define user preference $\mathbf{u_i}$ as a vector consisting of the distribution c_{li} of items the user i is linked to over all labels l. We use two metrics: (i) average user entropy, i.e. $E[H(\mathbf{u_i})] = \frac{1}{n}\sum_i H(\mathbf{u_i})$ where $H(\mathbf{u_i}) = -\sum_{l=1}^{s} c_{li}\log_s(c_{li})$ (ii) the system entropy $H(\mathbf{U})$, where

$$H(\mathbf{U}) = -\sum_{l=1}^{s}\left(\frac{\sum_i c_{li}}{n}\right)\log_s\left(\frac{\sum_i c_{li}}{n}\right).$$

Hence the property we study is simplification (as defined above) which in this case measures the tendency for users to link primarily to one label type versus the other. We use simplification rather than polarization because it measures the degree to which user opinions become more extreme in cases where there may be more than two labels, and hence is more general than polarization.

3.3.1 Case Study 1: including already-linked items. Our first set of results studies the case in which the system is allowed to recommend an already-linked item. The settings simulated were 4700 users and 3700 items. Each user was initialized with an average of 40 known items uniformly distributed between labels. Those settings are inspired in by **MovieLens** [23] dataset. The label-independent acceptance probability for non-biased user responses was $p = 1.0$, i.e., the user always accepts the recommended item.

Figure 1a and Figure 2a show the simplification effects for Case Study 1 over 1000 steps. The figure shows that none of the 3 algorithms show significant variation over time, with or without biased assimilation. This is surprising because the theoretical analysis of [8] suggests that *SimpleSALSA* and *SimpleICF* should have distinct behavior (not polarizing and polarizing) when comparing label-independent and biased assimilation.

However, a closer look at those simulation outcomes revealed that they were mostly outputting the same recommendation over time.

A simple inspection of the *SimpleICF* and *SimplePPR* algorithms and their respective random process reveals that without constraints preventing the repetition of the same item, and given a finite number of users and items, the selection step (through the arg max computation at line 2) of *SimplePPR* and *SimpleICF* is likely to always return the same item; consequently few or no updates are made on $\mathbf{M}$, explaining the constant entropy measured. In contrast, when an infinite number of items and users is considered a higher randomness in the selection step is expected. Therefore,the chances of return the same item is reduced.

This leads to two conclusions: (1) the simplification (or polarization) effects of a real (finite) recommender system are different than those of a idealized infinite system; and (2) the previous conclusions that *SimpleSALSA* and *SimpleICF* can be non-polarizing in some cases need to be re-examined for realistic systems.

3.3.2 Case Study 2: no already-linked items. Next, in Case Study 2 we look at how results change when the system is not allowed to repeat already-linked items. In all other respects, simulation settings are the same as Case 1.

The simplification of user preference in Case Study 2 is shown in Figure 1b. The figure shows that (i) without biased assimilation all algorithms have a diversification effect; (ii) with biased assimilation *SimpleSALSA* lead to simplification, *SimpleICF* has an initial diversification followed by a simplification effect and, *SimplePPR* leads to a diversification effect. This shows that when linked items are not repeated, results are very different from those in Case Study 1, and from the systems analyzed in [8].

We also analyze for Case Study 2 the simplification of the system, i.e. the diversity of the combined preferences of all users as it evolves over time. Figure 2b shows that for*SimpleSALSA* and *SimplePPR* the system has a similar and almost constant effect regardless of whether users respond in a label independent way or with biased assimilation. However, *SimpleICF* suffers a simplification effect when there is biased assimilation.

The diversification effects for biased assimilation in Figure 1b for the initial steps of *SimpleICF* and *SimplePPR* may seem counterintuitive, but they can be understood as resulting from the less-diverse set of recommendations that those algorithms provide to the user. These algorithm provide less diverse recommendations as a result of the arg max step that each employs. We note that the most well connected items are those most likely to be recommended because of their higher values in $\mathbf{P}^2$ or $\mathbf{P}^3$. Although initially there is on average the same quantity of items of each label there are also well connected items of both labels due to randomness in the connection pattern. As a result, the lower randomness of recommendations in *SimpleICF* and *SimplePPR* often results in the system recommending the same item repeatedly until the user accepts it. This leads initially to each user linking to items with both labels approximately equally, regardless of whether the user's assimilation is biased or unbiased. However, after some number of simulation steps (approximately 200 steps) the increase of density leads to an increase of the randomness output from *SimpleICF*. I that case, biased assimilation is able to cause a user to acquire more items of one label than another, resulting in simplification of user preference. Furthermore the greater randomness of *SimpleSALSA* causes a similar biased consumption effect resulting in simplification of individual users' opinions. This is further confirmed by the fact that the overall system sees no change in the label distribution as shown in Figure 2b under *SimpleSALSA*.

In summary, this section shows that the tendency of user preferences to simplify or diversify depends on a delicate interplay of the diversity of items suggested by the recommender system and the extent to which users exhibit biased assimilation.

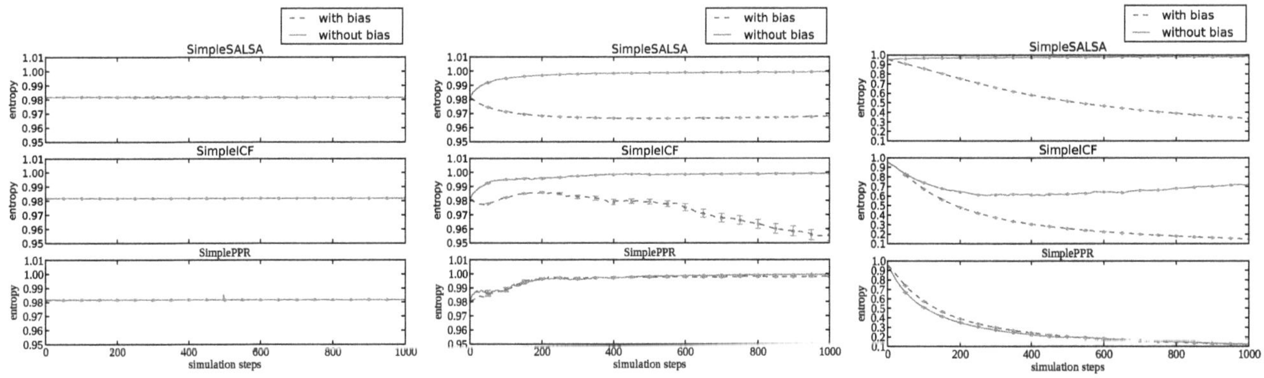

(a) Case Study 1 (b) Case Study 2 (c) Case Study 4

Figure 1: Average Entropy: User's Preference

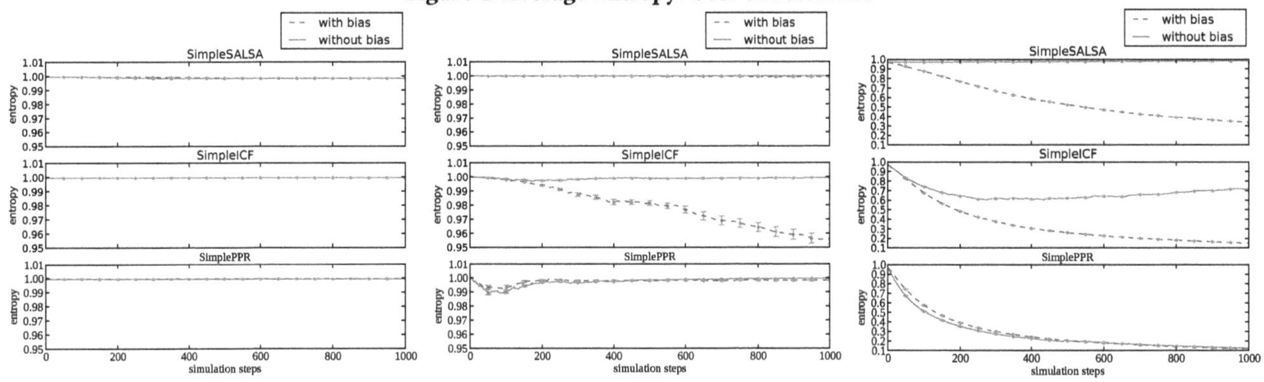

(a) Case Study 1 (b) Case Study 2 (c) Case Study 4

Figure 2: Average Entropy: System' Preference

3.3.3 Case Study 3: Variations. To test whether our results in Case Study 2 are representative, we vary the simulation parameters from Study Case 2. In particular, we study the effects of varying;

(1) The percentage of items to which each user is initially linked. Previous cases used 1.08%, here we also explored 10%;
(2) The label-independent probability of accepting an item in the unbiased biased case. Previous results used $p = 1.0$, here we range p in $\{0.6, 0.8\}$.

None of the above variations affected significantly the trends results presented in Study Case 2, regardless of recommender algorithm or biased/unbiased assimilation. Rather than presenting all results in full, we summarize their similarity by presenting statistics in Table 1. The table shows the coefficients of linear regression lines fit to each individual algorithm and response variation. Specifically, Table 1 presents the slopes (noted as s) and intercept points (noted as i) for algorithms *SimpleSALSA*, *SimpleICF* and *SimplePPR* (noted respectively as $f = \{1, 2, 3\}$). In the Table the percentage of initial items is denoted as $q(\%)$, the number of users is n, the number of items is m, and the user response probability or biased response indicator is denoted as $g(p)$. Across almost all variants in Table 1 we observe similar slopes and intercept points.

3.3.4 Case Study 4: non-uniform initialization. The case studies above demonstrate how different algorithms and user responses

Table 1: Case Study 3: Comparison over parameter variations.

n	m	$q(\%)$	f	$g(p)$	slope	intercept
4700	3700	1.08	1	0.6	8.4e-06	0.99
4700	3700	1.08	2	0.6	8.4e-06	0.99
4700	3700	1.08	3	0.6	6.8e-06	0.99
4700	3700	1.08	1	0.8	7.5e-06	0.99
4700	3700	1.08	2	0.8	7.8e-06	0.99
4700	3700	1.08	3	0.8	1.3e-05	0.99
4700	3700	1.08	1	1.0	6.6e-06	0.99
4700	3700	1.08	2	1.0	6.7e-06	0.99
4700	3700	1.08	3	1.0	1.1e-05	0.99
4700	3700	1.08	1	bias	-5.3e-06	0.98
4700	3700	1.08	2	bias	-3.2e-05	0.99
4700	3700	1.08	3	bias	7.4e-06	0.99
4700	3700	12	1	1.0	9.5e-07	0.99
4700	3700	12	2	1.0	5.7e-07	0.99
4700	3700	12	3	1.0	1.0e-06	0.99
4700	3700	12	1	bias	-2.1e-07	0.99
4700	3700	12	2	bias	-7.2e-07	0.99
4700	3700	12	3	bias	7.4e-07	0.99

evolve in a system in which links to items of different labels are initially uniformly-distributed. We undertake Case Study 4 in order to better understand the role played by the initial distribution of item labels. The setting of Case Study 4 is the same as Case Study 2 except for the initialization step. Each user is still linked on average to 40 items but on average 60% of those links are to items with the first label ("RED") and 40% are to items with the second label. Figure 1c and Figure 2c shows the simplification effects over time at the user and system level respectively when there is a uneven starting link distribution and no repeat items are allowed. The figures show first of all that the degree of simplification in this case is dramatically larger than in any of the balanced-link cases. This shows the very strong effect that the initial preferences of users have on the evolution of the system. Second, the figures show that the high levels of simplification are visible both at the user level and at the system level. Overall, the fraction of links that are to RED items grows dramatically at the system level. Third, with respect to the behavior of various algorithms, we note the following. Without biased assimilation *SimpleSALSA* still has a diversification effect on both user's and system level effect measured by the increase of average entropy. However when the user's response is biased the *SimpleSALSA* results in significant simplification at both the user and system level. On the other hand, *SimpleICF* and *SimplePPR* always result in very signficant simplification at the user and system level regardless of the user's response behavior.

The dramatic change of behavior of *SimpleICF* and *SimplePPR* when starting preferences are unbalanced is once more explained by the selection step (through the arg max computation at line 2). When there are initially more links to items of one label the most well connected items are also from that label, creating a cycle of same-label recommendations.

3.4 Discussion

The failure of the theoretical analysis to consistently match any set of results in our case studies reveals how sensitive the analysis of system dynamics in [8] is to assumptions and initial state. This can be seen intuitively as well. For example, the operation of *SimpleSALSA* is just to take three steps in a Markov Chain starting from a random state. Intuitively this results in an output vector that interpolates between the initial state and the steady state of the chain. The extreme symmetry of the initial system setup in [8] suggests that the steady state is the uniform distribution (considered separately over users and items). Creating a new link according to this distribution will move the system to an ever more uniformly connected state – hence the decrease in polarization shown in Figure 1a and Figure 2a which agrees with the analytical results in [8]. However, the same analysis suggests that the analytical results are strongly dependent on the initial linking pattern, as an imbalance in that pattern will result in an imbalanced steady state, and hence the addition of links in an imbalanced fashion as well.

Our analysis also shows the key role played by diversity of recommendations. Both *SimpleICF* and *SimplePPR* attempt to provide a notion of "best" recommendation through the use of the arg max step. On the other hand, *SimpleSALSA* only tries to provide a "good" recommendation (with high probability). While providing the "best" recommendation may seem more optimal in some sense, *SimpleSALSA* shows a much smaller tendency to simplify user preferences, particularly when user preferences start out in an imbalanced state (which seems the likely case in practice).

4 RATINGS BASED SYSTEMS

The link based systems considered in the previous section are relatively easy to analyze and interpret. However, in many recommender systems the relation between a user and an item goes beyond a simple binary connection and is expressed in some form of numerical rating. We term such systems as *ratings based systems.* A recommender algorithm in that scenario aims to predict the ratings of the unevaluated items – i.e., anticipate how the user will evaluate the remaining unevaluated items.

One of the main methods used by rating based systems is to provide recommendations using latent factor models [24]. Latent factor models estimate the ratings relations between users and items by modeling each in a latent space. The latent vectors are are learned from the data. Ratings are then estimated using inner product of user and item vector in the latent space. This estimation process can be also understood as *matrix completion.*

In a system where user preferences are real-valued, there are a wider array of metrics that are important and can be considered. Our goal in this section is to understand not just how simplification evolves (as in the last section) but also how intensity and diversity evolve in time.

4.1 Model

Let $\mathbf{M} \in \mathbb{R}^{n \times m}$ be a ratings matrix of n users over m items, λ_{MIN} be the minimum ratings value, λ_{MAX} be the maximum ratings value, and a the completion algorithm that decomposes $\mathbf{M}$ into the factors $\mathbf{X}$ and $\mathbf{Y}$ where $\mathbf{C} = \mathbf{X}^{\mathbf{T}}\mathbf{Y}$.

Once $\mathbf{C}$ is computed, a typical way to provide a recommendation r to a user i is using an algorithm f that recommends the unevaluated item $C(i, j)$ with highest predicted rating. We denote that algorithm as *RecBEST*; it is described below (Algorithm 4).

As a comparative case we define *RecRAN* (Algorithm 5) to be the recommender algorithm f that simply recommends a random unevaluated item.

Algorithm 4 RecBEST using C

Require: C, Ω and a user i .

1: Compute $j = \arg\max_j C[i, j]$ such that $(i, j) \in \bar{\Omega}$.

2: Return j

Algorithm 5 RecRAN using C

Require: C, Ω and a user i .

1: Choose randomly j such that $(i, j) \in \bar{\Omega}$.

2: Return j

We seek to capture a range of possibilities for the response of a user to a recommendation. These essentially reflect how a user's opinion changes in response to evaluating an item (e.g., viewing a movie or reading a book). We model the user response $g_x(i, r)$ as a probabilistic function of $x \in [0, 1]$. The user signals her evaluation by providing either a rating of λ_{MAX} or λ_{MIN}. The parameter x determines how often a user tends to be positive about a recommended item. That is, for a given user i and a recommendation r, $\mathbf{M}$ will be updated accordingly to $g_x(i, r)$, i.e., $M(i, r) = g_x(i, r)$, where:

$$g_x(i,r) = \begin{cases} \lambda_{MAX}, & \text{with probability } x \\ \lambda_{MIN}, & \text{with probability } (1-x) \end{cases} \quad (1)$$

4.2 Datasets

The previous section showed that system dynamics can be strongly influenced by the initial system state. Hence we conclude that it is important to initialize the system in a realistic manner. As a result we use previously captured datasets as the system initialization in this section. We use three datasets that include ratings relations between users and items to define the starting point matrix **M** and initial Ω.

The **MovieLens** dataset is collected from a non-commercial web movie recommender [23]. We selected a relatively dense subset of this dataset, consisting of users that have at least 40 ratings, which we denote as `dataML`. In total `dataML` has 4736 users, 3706 movies, and 962682 ratings. Additionally we scaled the ratings to center them at zero, changing the initial range from [1:5] to [-2:2].

The **MovieTweetings** dataset is collected from well-structured movie evaluation tweets on Twitter from 2013 until 2015 [9]. We selected a relatively dense subset of this dataset of movies that have at least 10 ratings and users that have at least 40 ratings, which we denote `dataMT`. This dataset has 2604 users, 3703 movies and 218302 ratings. We centered the ratings in `dataMT` by rescaling them from [1:10] to [-5:5].

The **BookCrossing** was collected in a 4-week crawl from the Book-Crossing community [28]. We used a relatively subset of this data excluding null inferred ratings and selecting user with at least 40 ratings over books with at least 5 ratings, which we denote `dataBX`. This dataset has 294 users, 2764 books, and 20040 ratings rescaled from [1:10] to [-5:5].

4.3 Simulations

We again study the closed-loop dynamics between recommender system and users in simulation.

In our simulations all matrix completion procedures were performed using LMaFit [26] with a latent space $k = 20$. We define the user preference vector as the completed vector of item opinions ($\mathbf{u_i} = \mathbf{c_i}$) and observe how $\mathbf{u_i}$ evolves over time through an individual dynamic simulation, i.e., just one user evolves in time while other user ratings are not changed. We observe how the user preference evolves in the dynamical system at an individual level (through intensity and simplification) as well as at a system level (through divergence).

We analyzed the recommender algorithms $f \in \{RecBEST, RecRAN\}$. over the probabilistic users response $g_x(i,r)$ for $x \in \{0.0, 0.1, \ldots, 1.0\}$. Using those settings we evolved each user for $T = 400$ iterations where at each step a new recommendation was made and evaluated by the user according to rating policy g_x. Furthermore some individual and collective metrics were computed from $\mathbf{u_i}$ at each step. This framework for our analysis is described in Algorithm 6.

4.3.1 Intensity. First we consider how the intensity of the user preference vector varies over time and how the choice of user response and recommender system influence in those changes.

Figure 3 captures the intensity measures computed for all of our simulations. Each square from each plot of Figure 3 represents one

Algorithm 6 Ratings based dynamical system

Require: A partially-observed matrix of ratings $\mathbf{M}^{\Omega}$; a recommender system algorithm f; a user response function g_x; a preference space size k; and a number of iterations T.

for $i \in$ *Users* **do**
    R = M
    for (step=1:T) **do**
        $(\mathrm{X}, \mathrm{Y}) = \mathrm{LMaFit}(\mathrm{R}, k, \Omega)$
        $\mathrm{C} = \mathbf{X^T Y}$
        $j = f(\mathrm{C}, i, \Omega)$
        $\mathrm{R}(i,j) = g_x(i,j)$
        $\Omega = \Omega \cup (i,j)$
        Output Intensity and Simplification of $\mathbf{c_i}$
        $S(\text{step}, \mathrm{i}) = \mathbf{c_i}$
    end for
end for
for (step=1:T) **do**
    Output Divergence of S(step)
end for

metric observation, while the color of the square indicates the metric value as indicated in the color map. Furthermore, the x-axis in each plot represents the simulation step (ranging from 1 to 400) and, the y-axis in each plot represents the probability with which the user response g_x was set. Thus each horizontal set of points represent one particular simulation. Each plot of Figure 3 represents a set of simulations results from a given algorithm and dataset. Different set of plots rows correspond to the dataset used to initialize M – respectively `dataML` , `dataMT` or `dataBX` . The first two columns of plots group simulation results from *RecBEST* and *RecRAN* respectively. The last column shows the pointwise subtraction of *RecRAN* from *RecBEST* for comparative purposes.

The reason for the last column of plots is that the *RecRAN* simulations measure the effects on user opinion when randomly chosen items are evaluated by the user according to the rating policy g_x. Thus, this case can be considered to capture the effect of a user viewing and rating items without the influence of a recommender system, but rather in completely random fashion. Therefore the subtraction of the simulations results (*RecBEST* - *RecRAN*) – noted in this work as *BEST-RAN* – is a measure of influence of the recommender system *algorithm* on user opinion.

All the intensity observations represented at Figure 3 were computed by averaging the norm of the users preference vectors for a given time step.

The figure show a number of results. First, for both algorithms (*RecBEST* and *RecRAN*) and for all datasets, regardless of the user's response, we can observe a general increase in intensity over time – marked by the vertical increase of average norm value when the time color indicators also increases.

Second, for *RecBEST* (first column) the increase in intensity of opinion is maximized for probabilities x intermediate between 0 and 1. The *RecBEST* system increases intensity the least when $x = 1$, the user always agrees with the system and rates the items presented highly.

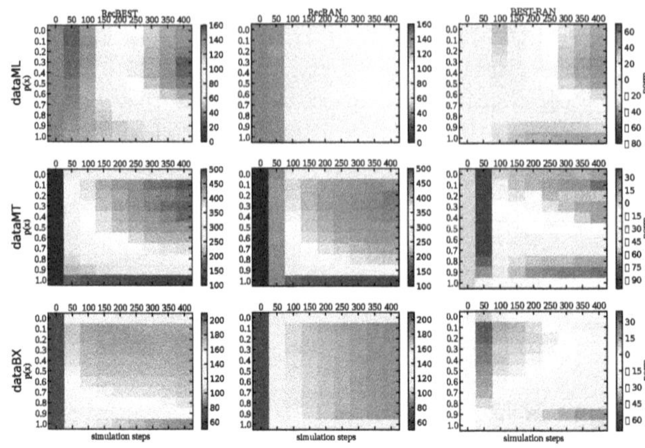

Figure 3: Average Norm of User's Preference

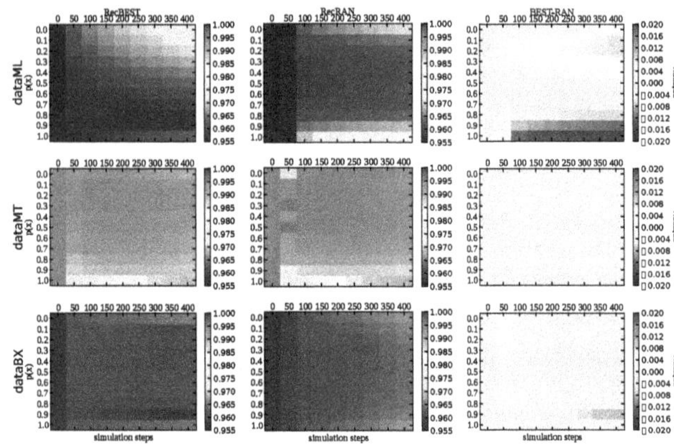

Figure 4: Average Entropy of User's Preference

These two effects together mean that for *BEST-RAN* (third column) there is a generally decreasing relationship between the user opinion intensity and the degree to which the user agrees with the recommender algorithm. In other words, when the user agrees with the recommendations made by the system, the user's opinion intensity increases, but the increase is lower than if there had not been a recommender system in the loop. On the other hand, when the user disagrees with the recommender system, the user's intensity of opinions increases more than if there had been no recommender system in the loop. We conclude from this that a recommender system does not necessarily increase the *intensity* of user opinions, as compared to random recommendations, as long as the system makes good recommendations to the user.

4.3.2 Simplification. Our second analysis concerns how the user's preference vector behaves over time as a distribution, which is captured as simplification (or diversification) of opinions. Figure 4 compiles the results from the simplification measures of the user preference vector. The figure uses the same representation for squares, colors, plots and plot positions as Figure 3.

The figure shows a number of effects in opinion dynamics. First of all, for both algorithms (*RecBEST* and *RecRAN*) and for all datasets regardless the user response, we can observe a general increase of entropy over time. In another words, user opinions get more diverse under the influence of either a recommender system or a random presentation of items.

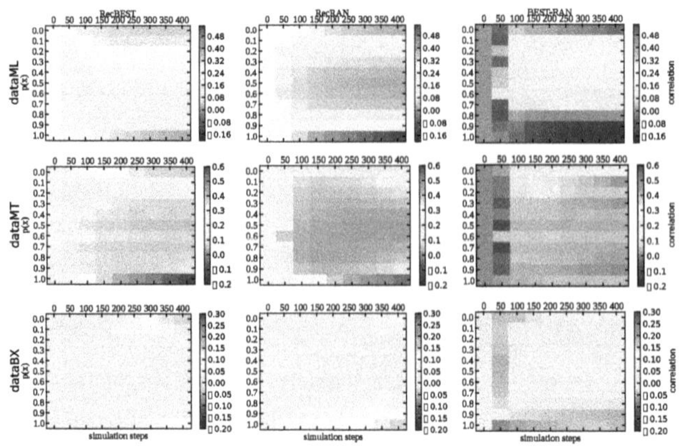

Figure 5: Average Correlation Coefficient of User's Preference

Second, the influence of dataset (i.e., system initialization) has a much stronger effect on diversity (as compared to, eg, intensity). The changes in diversity are highly varied across datasets (although diversity always increases).

However, the third column (*BEST-RAN*) shows that the relative influence of the recommender algorithm *RecBEST* over users for `dataML` and `dataMT` is that when y increases, the average entropy decreases. This means that, when the user agrees more with the recommendations its opinions become simpler, as compared to a random presentation of items. Even for `dataBX`, where there is no strong correlation between the influence of the recommender system and the user response g_x, user opinion always becomes simpler under the influence of the recommender system than under a random item presentation.

These results emphasize the importance of comparing the effect of a recommender system to an alternative. While a dynamical system involving a recommender system tends to result in diversified user opinions, the same is true of a dynamical system that does not involve a recommender system. Only by comparing the two do we see how the recommender system decreases the diversity of user opinion.

4.3.3 Divergence. Our last analysis is with regard to how closed loop dynamics shapes the user preference vectors as a set. We want to understand the conditions under which the user preference vectors become more similar to the others, i.e. we want to observe when there is loss or increase of individuality from the user preference vectors set.

Figure 5 presents the average correlation of user preference vectors, with plots using the same representation for squares, colors, plots and plot positions as in previous figures.

We note that for both algorithms (*RecBEST* and *RecRAN*) and for all datasets, the average correlation coefficient decreases for intermediate values of x, while it increases when x is close to either 0 or 1. Thus, unless the user does not fully agree or disagree with most recommendations, the set of user opinions tends to diverge. However, the influence of the recommender system as compared to random recommendations, as shown in the third column (*BEST-RAN*) is quite different. That column shows that as the user's agreement with recommendations increases, there is a consistent increase in opinion divergence. This effect is strong enough that opinions always increase in divergence, compared to random item presentations, when the user fully agrees with the recommendations made by the recommender system.

4.4 Discussion

The conclusions from this section and the previous section together show consistencies that reinforce a number of high level conclusions. The principal conclusion concerns the tendency of recommender systems to simplify user opinions. This tendency is observed generally over both link based and ratings based systems, although it comes with some caveats. First, recommender systems that recommend the "best" item at any given time (eg, *SimpleICF*, *SimplePPR*, and *RecBEST*) have a much stronger simplifying effect than systems that return "good" recommendations according to some probability (*SimpleSALSA*). Furthermore, the simplifying effect is strongest when the recommender system does a good job of predicting user preference (e.g., when $x = 1$ in *RecBEST*).

Second, the initial state of the system when the recommender system starts has a strong effect on the eventual outcome. In the case of *RecBEST*, opinion diversity is strongly affected by the dataset used, and in the cases of *SimpleICF* and *SimplePPR* the simplification effect is highly pronounced when the system does not state in a perfectly balanced configuration.

Turning to the other metrics, our results suggest that the ratings based system tends to cause user opinions to collectively diverge and to become individually less diverse, but *only* when the system accurately predicts the user's preferences. If the system is less effective in this regard, it can cause the opposite effect, namely, the to cause user opinions to become more similar to each other, and to become individually more diverse. On the one hand, the conclusion that opinions can diverge and become less diverse is potentially concerning, but the realization that the recommender system must be quite accurate for this to happen raises questions about whether this effect is likely to occur in practice.

5 RELATED WORK

Although a number of papers have addressed the individual components of the dynamics between recommender systems and user opinion formation or the social implications of that dynamic, few of them have addressed the problem in whole.

In this section we review three works that have addressed the dynamics of opinion formation by recommender systems, and we review key prior work that has explored individual components of that dynamics.

As discussed extensively in the body of the paper, the authors in [8] explore the causes of polarization through an opinion formation process based on averaging of users opinions. They show that the opinion in the group polarizes when users have biased assimilation responses. Additionally, they expand the opinion formation process analysis to a recommender system model analyzing the biased assimilation response. As we covered in Section 3 our results generalize that work and show that in many realistic settings, the conclusions therein do not apply.

Bakshy, Messing and Adamic carry out an empirical analysis of the ideological diversity of news exposure on Facebook in [3]. They measure the diversity of news (through political alignment) shared between friends and measure the potential for cross-cutting – i.e. how much a user from a given political alignment (conservative, moderate or liberal) is exposed to news of a different political alignment. They concluded that the individual's social network itself is the most important factor in limiting their exposure to diversity. However, is the user's choices about what to consume (i.e. which links to click) more than the newsfeed ranking algorithms that contribute to the news diversity consumed. Although [3] recognized the dynamics between news feed (recommender system) and users, their analysis focuses only on the user's exposure to diversity when user opinion (political affiliation) is held constant in their model.

Koren in [15] proposes a recommender system based in collaborative filtering that incorpores temporal dynamics. Using his recommender system he splits the prediction score between factors dependent or independent of the interaction of users and items and performs an analysis of rating drifting on a Netflix dataset. Although [15] studies the dynamics of recommender systems and how much the interaction of user and items can affects the prediction score over time, his analysis is focused in the recommender system itself and doesn't explore the user's opinion formation.

Opinion Formation. Next, we turn to work that addresses individual aspects of our study. Prior work in opinion formation has taken several approaches to understand how opinions can evolve in a network according to a given model of information propagation.

One line of work examines the direct influence of neighbors and self beliefs in opinion formation; this is studied in [6] where a repeated averaging model is used to analyze consensus. An alternative approach, taken by [5] uses game theory as opinion formation process. Both works present boundaries for the cost to reach consensus in their models. Finally, in [19] Mas and Flache propose a peer-to-peer interaction model that can explain polarization of opinion with homophily and without negative influence (disliking of dissimilar others). Although these models are concerned with some of the same phenomena as our study (eg, polarization) they do not include a recommender system as an external agent.

Filter Bubble. Finally, attention has recently been drawn to the situation in which there is a narrowing of access to information by users in online systems. The focus here has primarily been on personalization and recommender engines. This effect has been dubbed a "filter bubble" by Pariser in [22]. Following this line, researchers have analyzed interactions between users and recommender systems to detect filter bubbles. The authors in [11] and [13] explore the factors that trigger personalization on results of search queries. Furthermore online price discrimination was exposed by [12] and online ad delivery discrimination was exposed by Sweeney in [25]. These are examples in which information content is filtered and throttled in a fashion that is undesirable.

The authors in [29] investigate the different types of personalization in communication and they claim that at present, there is no empirical evidence that warrants any strong worries about filter bubbles however, they agree that this could be a future problem if personalization technology improves.

Another line of work related to the filter bubble phenomenon tries to understand the role played by recommender algorithms in decreasing recommendations diversity and thus potentially limiting user experience.

Knijenburg et al in [14] claims that for solve the Filter Bubble problem it is necessary to build a recommender system with a different goal than simply recommending good items. The authors of [14] then proposes a idea of a new recommender system – named "Recommender System for Self-Actualization" – that aims to support the users in developing, exploring and understand their unique taste.

Graells-Garrrido et al in [10] proposes a content recommender on Twitter that uses graphical tools and gap indicators to stimulate diversity and connect people of opposite views. Other researchers such as [18], [1], [27] and [20] suggest the inclusion of "serendipitous" recommendations in order to promote diversification. While these suggestions are consistent with our observation that "best" recommendations are not always the most beneficial for user opinion formation, they also do not consider how opinions and recommender systems evolve together over time.

6 CONCLUSIONS

In this paper we studied the closed-loop dynamics between recommender systems and users across a wide variety of system models and configurations. We proposed three metrics – intensity, simplification and divergence – to capture important properties of user opinions as they evolve in such a system. By studying a wider range of settings, we extend previous work [8] and show that its conclusions do not always generalize to more typical settings (eg., when already-linked items may not be recommended, or when the system starts with nonuniform user preferences). Further, comparing results for link based and ratings based systems, we identify common features of recommender systems that tend to simplify user opinions. We also show that under certain circumstances, recommender systems can act to cause user opinions to diverge and become less diverse, but this is not always the case, and more study is needed to determine whether in practice the conditions necessary for divergence and simplification of opinions do actually occur.

Our work has a number of limitations that suggest the need for future study; in particular, further theoretical analysis of both link based and ratings based dynamics seems worthwhile and potentially feasible. Nonetheless, our results show that the dynamics of recommender systems over time are complex and varied, and that there is potential for such systems to affect user opinions in subtle ways. Combined with the increasing prevalence of recommender systems, our results suggest that better understanding of closed loop opinion formation is an ongoing and important problem.

7 ACKNOWLEDGMENTS

This material is based upon work supported by the National Science Foundation under grant numbers IIS-1421759 and CNS-1618207.

REFERENCES

[1] Zeinab Abbassi, Sihem Amer-Yahia, Laks V.S. Lakshmanan, Sergei Vassilvitskii, and Cong Yu. 2009. Getting Recommender Systems to Think Outside the Box. In *Proceedings of RecSys*. ACM, New York, NY, USA, 285–288.

[2] Gediminas Adomavicius and Alexander Tuzhilin. 2005. Toward the next generation of recommender systems: A survey of the state-of-the-art and possible extensions. *IEEE TRANSACTIONS ON KNOWLEDGE AND DATA ENGINEERING* 17, 6 (2005), 734–749.

[3] Eytan Bakshy, Solomon Messing, and Lada Adamic. 2015. Exposure to ideologically diverse news and opinion on Facebook. *Science* (07 May 2015), aaa1160+.

[4] Robert M. Bell and Yehuda Koren. 2007. Lessons from the Netflix Prize Challenge. *SIGKDD Explor. Newsl.* 9, 2 (Dec. 2007), 75–79.

[5] Kshipra Bhawalkar, Sreenivas Gollapudi, and Kamesh Munagala. 2013. Coevolutionary Opinion Formation Games. In *Proceedings of the Forty-fifth Annual ACM Symposium on Theory of Computing*. ACM, New York, NY, USA, 41–50.

[6] David Bindel, Jon M. Kleinberg, and Sigal Oren. 2012. How Bad is Forming Your Own Opinion? *CoRR* abs/1203.2973 (2012).

[7] Colin Cooper, Sang Hyuk Lee, Tomasz Radzik, and Yiannis Siantos. 2014. Random Walks in Recommender Systems: Exact Computation and Simulations. In *Proceedings of WWW*. International World Wide Web Conferences Steering Committee, Republic and Canton of Geneva, Switzerland, 811–816.

[8] Pranav Dandekar, Ashish Goel, and David T. Lee. 2013. Biased assimilation, homophily, and the dynamics of polarization. *Proceedings of the National Academy of Sciences* 110, 15 (2013), 5791–5796.

[9] Simon Dooms, Toon De Pessemier, and Luc Martens. 2013. MovieTweetings: a Movie Rating Dataset Collected From Twitter. In *CrowdRec at RecSys 2013*. https://github.com/sidooms/MovieTweetings

[10] Eduardo Graells-Garrido, Mounia Lalmas, and Daniele Quercia. 2013. Data Portraits: Connecting People of Opposing Views. *CoRR* abs/1311.4658 (2013).

[11] Aniko Hannak, Piotr Sapiezynski, Arash Molavi Kakhki, Balachander Krishnamurthy, David Lazer, Alan Mislove, and Christo Wilson. 2013. Measuring Personalization of Web Search. In *Proceedings of WWW*. ACM, New York, NY, USA, 527–538.

[12] Aniko Hannak, Gary Soeller, David Lazer, Alan Mislove, and Christo Wilson. 2014. Measuring Price Discrimination and Steering on E-commerce Web Sites. In *Proceedings of IMC*. ACM, New York, NY, USA, 305–318.

[13] Chloe Kliman-Silver, Aniko Hannak, David Lazer, Christo Wilson, and Alan Mislove. 2015. Location, Location, Location: The Impact of Geolocation on Web Search Personalization. In *Proceedings of ACM IMC*. ACM, New York, NY, USA, 121–127.

[14] Bart P Knijnenburg, Saadhika Sivakumar, and Daricia Wilkinson. 2016. Recommender systems for self-actualization. In *Proceedings of the 10th ACM Conference on Recommender Systems*. ACM, 11–14.

[15] Yehuda Koren. 2010. Collaborative filtering with temporal dynamics. *Commun. ACM* 53, 4 (2010), 89–97.

[16] Ronny Lempel and Shlomo Moran. 2001. SALSA: the stochastic approach for link-structure analysis. *ACM Transactions on Information Systems (TOIS)* 19, 2 (2001), 131–160.

[17] G. Linden, B. Smith, and J. York. 2003. Amazon.com recommendations: item-to-item collaborative filtering. *Internet Computing, IEEE* 7, 1 (Jan 2003), 76–80.

[18] Valentina Maccatrozzo. 2012. Burst the Filter Bubble: Using Semantic Web to Enable Serendipity.. In *International Semantic Web Conference (2) (Lecture Notes in Computer Science)*, Philippe Cudré-Mauroux, Jeff Heflin, Evren Sirin, Tania Tudorache, Jérôme Euzenat, Manfred Hauswirth, Josiane Xavier Parreira, Jim Hendler, Guus Schreiber, Abraham Bernstein, and Eva Blomqvist (Eds.), Vol. 7650. Springer, 391–398.

[19] Flache A Mäs M. 2013. Differentiation without Distancing. Explaining Bi-Polarization of Opinions without Negative Influence. *PLoS ONE* 11, 8 (2013).

[20] Kenta Oku and Fumio Hattori. 2011. Fusion-based Recommender System for Improving Serendipity. In *1st International Workshop on Novelty and Diversity in Recommender System (DiveRS 2011)*.

[21] Lawrence Page, Sergey Brin, Rajeev Motwani, and Terry Winograd. 1999. The PageRank citation ranking: bringing order to the web. (1999).

[22] E. Pariser. 2011. *The Filter Bubble: What the Internet Is Hiding from You*. Penguin Group USA.

[23] GroupLens Research Project. 2003. MovieLens dataset ml-1m. http://grouplens.org/datasets/movielens/

[24] Francesco Ricci, Lior Rokach, Bracha Shapira, and Paul B. Kantor. 2010. *Recommender Systems Handbook* (1st ed.). Springer-Verlag New York, Inc., New York, NY, USA.

[25] Latanya Sweeney. 2013. Discrimination in Online Ad Delivery. *Queue* 11, 3, Article 10 (March 2013), 20 pages.

[26] Zaiwen Wen, Wotao Yin, and Yin Zhang. 2012. Solving a low-rank factorization model for matrix completion by a nonlinear successive over-relaxation algorithm. *Mathematical Programming Computation* 4, 4 (2012), 333–361.

[27] Yuan Cao Zhang, Diarmuid Ó Séaghdha, Daniele Quercia, and Tamas Jambor. 2012. Auralist: Introducing Serendipity into Music Recommendation. In *Proceedings of the ACM WSDM*. ACM, New York, NY, USA, 13–22.

[28] Cai-Nicolas Ziegler, Sean McNee, Joseph Konstan, and Georg Lausen. 2005. Improving Recommendation Lists Through Topic Diversification. In *14th WWW*. ACM, Chiba, Japan.

[29] Frederik J. Zuiderveen Borgesius, Damian Trilling, Judith Moeller, BalÃązs Bodó, Claes H. de Vreese, and Natali Helberger. 2016. Should We Worry About Filter Bubbles? *Internet Policy Review. Journal on Internet Regulation* 5, 1 (2016), 102–114.

"(Weitergeleitet von Journalistin)": The Gendered Presentation of Professions on Wikipedia

Olga Zagovora
GESIS - Leibniz Institute for the Social Sciences
Cologne, Germany
olga.zagovora@gesis.org

Fabian Flöck
GESIS - Leibniz Institute for the Social Sciences
Cologne, Germany
fabian.floeck@gesis.org

Claudia Wagner
GESIS - Leibniz Institute for the Social Sciences and U. of Koblenz-Landau
Cologne/Koblenz, Germany
claudia.wagner@gesis.org

ABSTRACT

Previous research has shown the existence of gender biases in the depiction of professions and occupations in search engine results. Such an unbalanced presentation might just as likely occur on Wikipedia, one of the most popular knowledge resources on the Web, since the encyclopedia has already been found to exhibit such tendencies in past studies. Under this premise, our work assesses gender bias with respect to the content of German Wikipedia articles about professions and occupations along three dimensions: used male vs. female titles (and redirects), included images of persons, and names of professionals mentioned in the articles. We further use German labor market data to assess the potential misrepresentation of a gender for each specific profession. Our findings in fact provide evidence for systematic over-representation of men on all three dimensions. For instance, for professional fields dominated by females, the respective articles on average still feature almost two times more images of men; and in the mean, 83% of the mentioned names of professionals were male and only 17% female.

KEYWORDS

Wikipedia; gender inequality; professions; gender bias

ACM Reference format:
Olga Zagovora, Fabian Flöck, and Claudia Wagner. 2017. "(Weitergeleitet von Journalistin)": The Gendered Presentation of Professions on Wikipedia. In *Proceedings of WebSci '17, Troy, NY, USA, June 25-28, 2017*, 10 pages.
https://doi.org/http://dx.doi.org/10.1145/3091478.3091488

Figure 1: Screenshots of all images present in the German Wikipedia article "Journalist" as of Feb. 2017.

1 INTRODUCTION

An experiment by Chambers [5] conducted in 1983 brought forth an interesting **observation**: Given the request to draw a picture of a "scientist", only 28 (0.06%) of 4807 children depicted a female scientist. However, at the time of the study female researchers already made up 14% of STEM professionals in the United States [26]. More recently, a study [17] unveiled that a Google search for profession names returns more images of men in the top results than one would expect from the actual gender distribution in the queried profession, i.e., it occurred even if the field was not dominated by men.

These observations highlight an important **issue**: Professions and occupations[1] are a central part of societal life; and the mental pictures we hold of these professions shape our opinions about and our attitudes towards them. While this holds true for several perceived features of a person in a profession, like their race or political convictions, gender is one of the most defining characteristic of a stereotype [12], and also one that has sparked great disputes.

Information that (mis)represents a given state of affairs may endorse existing or create new stereotypes in the reader or viewer [3] which potentially impact their behavior. Cultivation theory has long suggested that prolonged exposure to biased information may shift individuals' perceptions over time [4] and even different gender ratios in image search results affect participants's perception of gender proportions in professions slightly but notably [17]. In respect to professions and gender, a potential **effect** is that in particular young people can be influenced in their career decisions, after being exposed to such information – conceivably avoiding an

[1] In the remainder of this paper, we will refer to both solely as "professions", unless specifically distinguished.

ACM ISBN 978-1-4503-4896-6/17/06...$15.00
https://doi.org/http://dx.doi.org/10.1145/3091478.3091488

ostensibly (fe)male-dominated trade, even if they have a natural predisposition for it [8].

Sources for such distorted views of a profession can be peers or the mass media - yet today, the Web has arguably become one of the main reference points for personal research, including when acquiring general knowledge about professions. And very frequently, Web surfers end up informing themselves from related **articles on Wikipedia**, the world's largest and most popular online encyclopedia. In 2016 for instance, articles in the category "Occupations" on the English Wikipedia received 368,512,005 unique hits together (of 93 billion in total) and the corresponding category "Beruf" on the German Wikipedia accumulated 30,669,129 unique hits (of 12 billion total)[2]. Apparently, *a sizable proportion of Internet users is hence exposed to, and probably influenced by, the presentation of facts about professions on Wikipedia, and the way gender is portrayed in those professionals fields.*

At the same time, the encyclopedia has already been found to exhibit considerable gender biases in past studies [7, 14, 28] and a similar distortion in its profession articles is entirely possible. The article "Journalist" on the German Wikipedia (Figure 1) is a showcase of how visible gender disparities can become on Wikipedia. Throughout the article, there are many images depicting men and only two images depicting women. Further, considerably fewer female than male journalists are mentioned in the text by name. Lastly, the common female form "Journalistin" doesn't even exist as an article, instead redirecting to the male form "Journalist".

The objectives of our study, are hence to reveal (i) how (im)-balanced the gender presentation is on the profession pages of Wikipedia and (ii) test if any imbalance can be explained by underlying labor market data or other facts which could serve to rebut an inherent gender bias of Wikipedia. We focus on the German Wikipedia as it is less studied than its English counterpart and because the language features a large set of female vs. male profession descriptors for analysis, as gender-specific versions exist for almost all profession names.

As illustrated through the "Journalist" example, we focus on three dimensions of profession articles: we (i) study redirections[3] between neutral, male and female profession descriptors, and we analyze (ii) the ratios of male and female images as well as (iii) the ratios of mentioned male and female names of professionals. Our work shows that for most professions for which a male and a female title exists in the German language, only the male title has a corresponding article. In the articles, almost four times more images depicting men than women were encountered. Articles about professions also tend to mention more men. In fact, 75% of all articles have proportions of mentioned men from 0.8 to 1.0. Moreover, 83% men and only 17% women were mentioned on average in the articles. To explain the male bias in the German Wikipedia, we compared it with the Google bias and offline imbalances in the labor market, indicating that Wikipedia not only inherits gender inequalities from other sources but also aggravates skewed gender ratios in many cases.

[2]According to the Wikimedia pageviews API as of 28.02.17

[3]A redirection automatically forwards from a requested lemma to the redirection target, another lemma/article. At the target page, a tiny notification "redirected from X" (EN) or "weitergeleitet von X" (DE) appears, cf. top of Fig.1.

2 DATA COLLECTION

In order to conduct our analyses, several datasets had to be collected and prepared.

Seed dataset of profession names. An official list of professions from the German Federal Employment Agency ("Bundesagentur für Arbeit")[4] was retrieved in order to create a comprehensive seed list of corresponding male-female pairs of profession names.

We parsed the profession descriptors using the grammatical rules of the German language including corresponding suffixes in order to create appropriate male and female forms of job titles. 4274 pairs were generated, such as "Lehrer"-"Lehrerin", "Krankenpfleger"-"Krankenschwester", "Entbindungspfleger"-"Hebamme" etc. Further, we extracted 183 gender-neutral profession labels from the initial professions list, e.g., "PR-Fachkraft", "Fotomodell", "Aufsichtsperson". The complete lists were manually cross-validated by two of the authors.

Wikipedia profession articles dataset. To map the seed list of profession names to Wikipedia articles we extracted all articles belonging to the German Wikipedia categories "Profession" (DE[5]: "Beruf"), "(Public) position" (DE: "Amt"), "Person by occupation" (DE: "Person nach Tätigkeit"), and any of their subcategories down to the 5th depth level.[6] This was done as (i) profession labels can be homonyms and hence match a seed list entry to a non-profession article and (ii) to find a comprehensive, yet still clearly profession-related set of articles to compute a more relaxed matching method with. We then constructed the intersection of the set of profession names from the seed list with the profession article title set, by applying a relaxed string-matching: the Levenshtein distance and ratio (the match proportion of two words) were calculated between each profession name and each article title. If the Levenshtein distance was at most 2 or the Levenshtein ratio was at least 0.8, the corresponding pairs of words were matched. Hence, we were able to find profession articles with titles written in a slightly different manner. In order to avoid inappropriate matches (e.g., profession "Bäcker" and name "Säcker"), all matched pairs were manually validated. We proceeded to add 22 professions from the seed list that we identified by hand to have a matching article in Wikipedia, but lacking the appropriate category label.

For each matched article title, additional information regarding its redirection was stored, i.e., whether the original lemma redirected to another article - and to which one.

As a result, a high-quality list of unique, non-redirect Wikipedia articles (885 entries) about professions was collected.[7] An additional 820 lemmas that matched with the seed list were redirects.

Gender-specific person names. To identify if and how many female or male persons are mentioned in a profession article, we applied a two-pronged approach.

First, all internal links in the profession articles were collected which point to articles about persons either in the Wikipedia-categories "Woman" (DE: "Frau") or "Man" (DE: "Mann") using

[4]Retrieved from http://berufenet.arbeitsagentur.de/berufe/berufe-beschreibungen.html on 15.06.15

[5]Henceforth "DE" is used as an abbreviation for "German".

[6]Accessed on 07.02.16 from https://de.wikipedia.org/w/api.php

[7]One reason for the relatively small overlap is that the seed list is exhaustive and contains many specialized professions that seem not to be "notable" enough for the DE Wikipedia.

the MediaWiki API[6] - these were each counted as one mention of a person with the Category-derived gender.

Second, the Named Entity Recognition method proposed by Al-Rafou et al. [1] was applied to the complete article text content, yielding all Entity Names of class "Person" that were identified. Then, for each found person mention, the gender was identified according to the first name. To make gender identification more accurate, several vocabularies [16, 20] were used. The results obtained by these two methods were combined for each article, producing an overall dataset of 5085 identified person labels (4272 men and 813 women). For cases where the two datasets clashed in the determination of the gender (2.77%), we were able to identify the correct genders automatically since persons from the first dataset are readily gendered. The end-result allowed us to reliably assess the number of female or male individuals mentioned.

Images of persons. The MediaWiki API[6] was used to retrieve all images contained in the articles. Only images wider than 100 pixels were stored, assuming that small images are either icons or too small to recognize the gender. A manual corroboration of this assumption with about 80 pictures yielded zero false positives for this filter. Files with the following formats were also excluded: "svg"-files are vector images used solely for schemas and icons, and "ogg", "ogv" are video and multimedia text formats. Thus, 906 images were collected from 345 profession articles. The remaining articles did not contain (suitable) images.

Labor market statistics. Gender-specific employment statistics were obtained from the "Statistics of the Federal Employment Agency" (DE: "Statistik der Bundesagentur für Arbeit"). The statistics consist of absolute numbers of men and women involved in profession subgroups as of June 30, 2015. Some examples of profession subgroups are: "8445; (Fremd-) Sprachenlehrer/innen" and "8442; Berufe in der Religionspädagogik". Each profession in our seed dataset is annotated with a specific classification number by the Employment Agency, enabling the assignation to its respective profession group according to an accompanying profession directory (DE: "Klassifikation der Berufe 2010 - alphabetisches Verzeichnis der Berufsbenennungen") E.g., "8445x" is the encoding of all professions in subgroup "(Fremd-) Sprachenlehrer/innen". In this way we could match 871 of the 885 article-mapped professions to their respective labor market statistics including gender distributions.

Google hits. By using each of the female and male profession labels as a search query term, we collected the amount of Google search results (hits) generated through the Google Web Search API[8] to gauge the number of Web resources featuring these descriptions. The search scope was restricted to the German language using the corresponding parameter in the API query, as some search terms could also be valid English words, for example.

3 RESEARCH METHOD

To assess whether and to what extent the German Wikipedia exhibits a gender imbalance with respect to professions, the collected articles have been analyzed along three dimensions: (i) gender inclusiveness in job titles and a corresponding redirection analysis, (ii) analysis of male-female image proportions, and (iii) the balance of male-female mentions. We present these dimensions in the following subsections.

3.1 Redirection analysis

The following analysis was inspired by the scenario of a user wanting to inform herself about a specific profession and entering the respective (fe)male form in Wikipedia's search bar or directly navigating to de.wikipedia.org/wiki/<profession_title>. We were interested in how many cases such a search will lead to either no results or a redirect to the opposite gender form or a neutral page – with redirects happening immediately after visiting a target article address, being indicated with an unobtrusive disclaimer, and hence possibly going unnoticed.

For each of the female-male pairs in our profession list (and the neutral labels), we applied these rules to sort each profession into distinct classes, indicating a potential skewness, or bias[9], towards men or women:

(1) If articles/lemmas do not exist at all on Wikipedia for a profession in our seed list – *no evidence*;
(2) If (non-redirect) profession articles with both gender titles exist (i.e., male and female titles) – *neutral*;
(3) If a profession article with a male / female title exists without the other gender form existing as an article – *male bias* or *female bias*;
(4) If only an article with a neutral title exists – *neutral*.
(5) If a profession lemma exists, but redirects to the other gender – bias in favor of the redirection target (i.e., *male bias* or *female bias*);
(6) If a profession lemma with a male or female title redirects to the neutral form or field name – *neutral*;
(7) If a profession lemma exists, but redirects to some article whose title is not in our seed dataset – *other*.

After assigning professions to these bias groups, we can assess whether professions are more likely to be presented via male, female or neutral profession names. However, the non-existence of one gender form can have a host of reasons, based, e.g., on the fact that virtually no (wo)men are employed in a specific profession. Also, we were interested how idiosyncratic the profession representation of Wikipedia is in comparison with the Web in general. For the latter, we compared the amount of results found through the Google search engine for each profession label to Wikipedia. For the former, we made use of the German labor market statistics.

Google hits. As a starting hypothesis, we presume that profession titles that appear on Wikipedia are more popular on the Web, meaning that there are more sources on the Web about them than about the corresponding profession titles of the opposite gender. Consequently, one should observe more search hits for profession titles represented on Wikipedia than for those that are not. As a proxy, we look into the number of hits returned by the Google search engine. For each profession, the number of hits was stored for female and male job titles. In order to assess if the difference

[8] Accessed on 09.02.16 from http://ajax.googleapis.com/ajax/services/search/web?v=1.0&hl=de&btnG=Google+Search&q=; the API results are not subject to custom personalization.

[9] Note that we do not associate "bias" here with any deliberate attempt to systematically discriminate, cf. discussion.

between Google hits for female and male titles is significant, a two-sided Mann-Whitney rank-sum test was utilized.

Next, we examined whether one can describe the relationship between the number of Google hits and the redirection bias of a profession. First, for each profession, the normalized difference between hits for male and corresponding female job titles was estimated using the following formula:

$$Normalized\_difference_i = \frac{Hits_{male_i} - Hits_{female_i}}{Hits_{male_i} + Hits_{female_i}} \quad (1)$$

where $Hits_{male_i}$ is the number of hits returned for male title of profession i, $Hits_{female_i}$ is the number of hits returned for the corresponding female title of profession i. A positive difference indicates that more search results have been returned for the male profession title than for the corresponding female title, while a negative difference indicates the contrary. The difference approaches zero if both gendered profession titles returned the same amount of search results.

Then, two logistic regression models were fitted in order to predict the redirection bias using Google hits for profession names. The first model uses the state of being in the male bias group as a dependent variable; the second model deals with female bias instead. The regression functions for both models are given by:

$$p_i = \frac{1}{1 + e^{-(\beta_0 + \beta_1 x_{1,i} + \beta_2 x_{2,i})}} \quad (2)$$

where $x_{1,i}$ is the normalized difference of Google hits of profession i, and $x_{2,i}$ is the Google hits for male title of profession i.

Labor Market. For the next analysis, each profession was coupled with the corresponding number of employed people per gender as per the labor market statistics collected. For each profession, the percentage of women involved was obtained. Then, the dependence between the percentage of women involved in the profession and the redirection bias group of the profession was tested. The null hypothesis is that two sets of measurements are drawn from the same distribution, i.e., the percentage of women involved in profession of the first bias group is drawn from the same distribution as the percentage from the second bias group. The alternative hypothesis is that values in one sample are more likely to be larger than the values in the other sample.

The Wilcoxon rank-sum test was used for each pair of the bias groups (male-female bias, male-neutral bias, neutral-female bias) in order to find profession groups which show significant differences in the percentage of employed women. Bonferroni correction [9] was used in order to control for the family-wise error rate. To describe the relations between the bias groups using the percentage of women involved in professions, logistic regression models were fitted. Analogously to the analysis of Google results, we predict whether a profession is in the female\neutral\male bias group. The explanatory variable is the percentage of women involved in a profession. Since not all bias groups show significant differences between distributions of values, we fit our models only between those which do.

3.2 Images analysis

To identify the gender of people on an extracted picture, a CrowdFlower[10] task was set up. First, CrowdFlower workers were to identify whether the image shows one or several persons, or none. If the image depicted more than one person, workers were asked to identify whether s/he was depicted in a dominant way, as we are interested only in the gender of the main person. For every image with one person or where one person is dominant, workers were asked to identify the gender of that individual. Otherwise, they were asked to identify the gender of the majority of people on the photo. For non-recognizable gender or an equal number of men and women, corresponding options were offered.

Images depicting one (fe)male, one dominant (fe)male, and images with (fe)male majority were assigned the label "female" and "male", respectively. Images where gender was not recognizable and with equal number of men and women were assigned two separate labels.

Each image was classified by at least three different workers. In order to control the reliability of all responses, the CrowdFlower accuracy threshold for workers was defined as 70% in the setting of the task. We also manually labeled 15% of the images such that one of 10 images shown to a CrowdFlower contributor would be from the labeled set - this was used as an additional worker accuracy control. If the accuracy of a worker fell below the accuracy threshold, the contributor would be removed from the job and her answers would not be taken into account.

Further, for the whole CrowdFlower task the worker agreement per Fleiss' kappa [23] was estimated. This allowed us to measure the degree to which the observed amount of agreement among workers exceeds what would be expected if all workers made their choices completely randomly. General reliability of agreement between CrowdFlower contributors was achieved with a 0.75 Fleiss' kappa score. Thus, we can assume that within our task relatively high agreement was achieved.

After gathering all answers for all images, the majority answer was used to label the image.

Labor Market. In order to test whether images from the profession articles reflect labor market statistics, professions were divided into two groups: professions with female (> 50% women) and male majority according to the labor market statistics. Then, the statistical significance of the difference between distributions of image groups were tested using chi-square independence tests with Monte Carlo p-value simulations [22].[11] We also explored how distribution of image categories would look like if one restricts professions to those with more than 70% men or women, respectively.

Next, the strength of relation was examined between the number of images depicting a particular gender in the article and the labor market statistics of profession. The Spearman's rank correlation was utilized.

We also tested whether distributions of image categories are significantly different for articles with male, female and neutral titles. The images were grouped according to the gender of article titles and chi-square tests were applied.

[10] https://www.crowdflower.com/

[11] The simulations were used since some image categories have small numbers, possibly making p-values unreliable.

Analogously, we analyzed whether distributions of image categories are significantly different for professions which were assigned to different redirection bias groups.

3.3 Mentioned people analysis

Articles that did not mention any persons per our name dataset were excluded from the analysis, leaving 411 articles. Then, for each article, the proportion of mentioned men was calculated.

First, the dependency between the proportion of mentioned men and the gender of the article title was tested, by examining if articles with male title have a higher proportion of mentioned men than articles with female titles. To this end, three rank-sum tests (i.e., one for each pair of article groups) with p-value correction [19] were performed.

Second, we tested the dependency between the proportion of mentioned men and redirection bias group of profession. Thus, analogously to the previous analysis, the professions were grouped and then rank-sum tests were applied between proportions of mentioned men in each of the groups.

Labor Market. Third, we examined whether the proportions of mentioned men in the profession articles reflect labor market statistics. The professions were divided in two groups: professions with more than 50% men and more than 50% women. If proportions of mentioned men in the profession articles reflect the labor market, one would observe a high proportion of mentioned men in the group of professions with male majority and low proportion of mentioned men in the group of professions with female majority. Next we analyzed the strength of the relation between the percentage of mentioned men/women in an article and the percentage/number of employed men/women in a profession. To this end, the Spearman's rank correlation was utilized.

4 RESULTS

Our results on gender inequality in Wikipedia's profession presentations are outlined for the three distinct dimensions.

4.1 Redirection analysis

Most of the pages (885) about professions we found on Wikipedia have male titles (831), compared to much fewer female titles (25). A few articles about professions have neutral profession names (36). Hence, at first glance, the Wikipedia community is more male profession-oriented. For corresponding male-female profession title pairs , we encounter eight "neutral" professions (i.e., 16 articles) that have corresponding articles for both gender versions. Articles with a neutral profession title were also assigned to the neutral group.

Among the 820 redirects, 5 are from the male to the female label of a profession, 214 redirect from female to male labels, and 3 redirect from neutral to male labels; other redirects are either to broader fields of professions or titles that are synonyms. For example, going to the Wikipedia article "Sekretärin" (EN: female secretary), will automatically redirect to the article "Sekretär"(EN: male secretary), and thus, one never reaches a Wikipedia page "Sekretärin".

As a bottom line, the combination of redirects and existing pages of corresponding male-female profession names reveals 812 male bias cases, 6 cases of female bias, and 55 neutral cases. I.e., 812 professions have only an article with male title or a female title lemma redirect to an article with the corresponding male title, 6 professions have only an article with female title or a male title lemma redirect to the corresponding female title, 55 professions have either an article with neutral title or articles with both male and female titles. Thus, we observe evidence for gender disparity among article titles chosen by the Wikipedia editors.

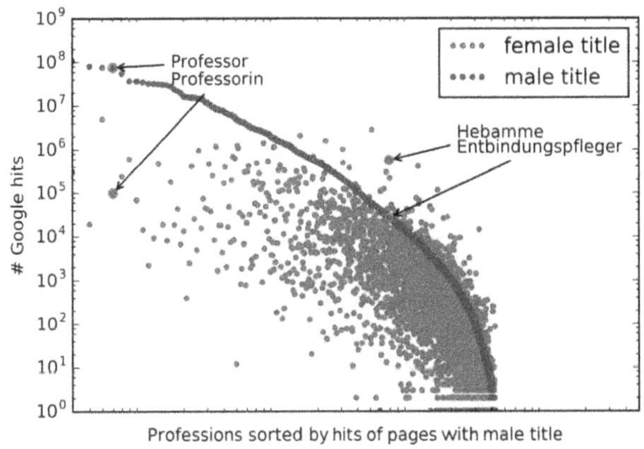

Figure 2: Distribution of Google hits for profession names, sorted according to amount of hits (log) for male profession names. One can see that most female titles have fewer Google results than corresponding male titles. For instance, "Professor" has more Google hits than the female "Professorin". The female profession names are more popular than the male ones for only a few professions, e.g., "Hebamme" (EN: midwife) vs. "Entbindungspfleger" (EN: male midwife).

Google hits. Figure 2 shows the distribution of Google hits for the profession names in our dataset. One can see that male profession names tend to be more popular than female names ($z = 28.6, p^{***}$) on Google. This indicates that the German speaking Web features more sources for male than female profession names, potentially reflected on Wikipedia.

Next we explored the normalized difference between Google hits of male and female profession titles for three groups separately: all professions with male, female, and neutral redirection bias identified previously. Our results indicate that a logistic regression model (Table 1) can indeed predict if a profession has a male or female redirection bias, based on the normalized difference of Google hits. The coefficients reveal that with a one-unit increase in the normalized difference of Google hits, odds of a profession having a male bias on Wikipedia increases by a factor of 11.48, whereas the probability of having a female bias decreases. In other words, it is more likely that professions have only a Wikipedia article with a female profession title (female bias group) when the female profession name has a greater number of Google hits than the male profession name. This indicates that the male skew of the German speaking Web is indeed mirrored on Wikipedia.

Labor Market. Next we investigated if the gender over- or under-representation in profession titles on Wikipedia can be explained by labor market statistics. We hypothesized that professions which are dominated by women nowadays will be found in the

Table 1: Logistic regression for Google hits. (Results of the best fitted logistic regression models) Model 1 stands for a logit model with binary outcome of a profession being in the female bias group or not. We see an 11.48 factor increase in the odds of being in a female bias group for a one-unit increase in the "Normalized Google difference" (NGD) score, since $exp(2.44) = 11.48$. Model 2 is the logit model with the binary outcome of a profession being in the male bias group. The coefficient for NGD reveals a 0.0026 factor increase (or $1/0.0026 = 384$ factor decrease) in the odds of being in a male bias group for a one-unit increase in the NGD score since $exp(-5.93) = 0.002654$. For example, both regression models will predict a female bias when the value of normalized Goggle difference equals -1 and male bias when the value equals 1.

	coef.	p	95% conf.int.
Model 1		Accuracy: 0.971	Pseudo R-squared:0.21
Normalized Google difference	2.44	0.0000	[1.68, 3.20]
Google hits for male name	0.00	0.9949	[0.00, 0.00]
(Intercept)	2.41	0.0000	[1.92, 2.90]
Model 2		Accuracy: 0.995	Pseudo R-squared:0.62
Normalized Google difference	-5.93	0.006	[-10.13, -1.73]
Google hits for male name	-2.07e-5	0.558	[-9.02e-3, 4.87e-5]
(Intercept)	-5-55	0.001	[-8.87, -2.24]

"female bias" group, whereas professions dominated by men will be found in the the "male bias" group we created. To this end, the dependence between the percentage of women involved in a profession and the redirection bias was analyzed. We observed statistically significant differences in terms of percentage of women involved in a profession between: (1) the male and female bias groups ($z = -3.32, p^{**}$), and (2) neutral and female bias groups ($z = -3.35, p^{**}$). In other words, professions which are represented by only articles with female titles (i.e., female bias) show a significantly higher percentage of employed women than other professions, i.e., between 82 and 100 percent of women, whereas professions that are represented by only articles with male title tend to have from 10 to 60 percent of women. There was no significant difference between the underlying distributions of the percentage of women involved in professions which are in the male bias and neutral groups.

Nevertheless, one can glean from Figure 3 that some professions with 80-100 percent of women are in the male bias group. For example, in the profession "Gesundheits- und KrankenpflegerIn" (EN: health and nursing staff) one encounters about 85% women and the Wikipedia page with the female title "Gesundheits- und Krankenpflegerin" automatically redirects to the respective male form "Gesundheits- und Krankenpfleger", hence the profession is in the male bias group. Another example is profession "Sekretär/in" (EN: secretary) whose workforce is constituted of about 88% women in Germany and only features the male article "Sekretär". Thus, we cannot claim that the Wikipedia community, e.g., decided to use only female profession names as article titles for professions with a majority of women in the labor market. We can only conclude that existing professions with only a female profession article are more likely to have higher percentage of women in the labor market than professions with only a male profession article.

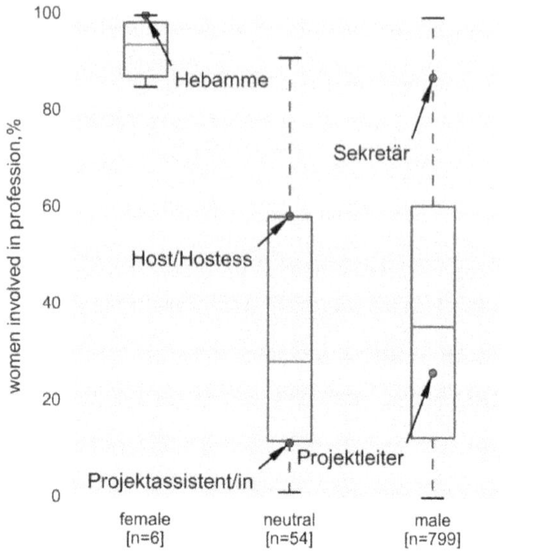

Figure 3: Percentage of women involved in professions (German labor market). Data is grouped by redirection bias of professions. The statistics from the German labor market were associated with 859 professions (799 male bias, 54 neutral, and 6 female bias). For some generic labels (e.g., DE: "Leiter", EN: "head", "leader"), no labor market statistics exist. One can see that professions with a female redirection bias on Wikipedia are indeed dominated by women in the German labor market, while there is no clear relation with the labor market statistics for the other two groups.

Second, the logistic regression model was fitted in order to describe relations between the redirection bias groups using the percentage of women involved. Because professions from the neutral and male bias groups do not show significant differences, we fit a logistic regression which will predict whether a profession is in the female bias group or not – i.e., the neutral and male bias groups were processed together. The logistic regression coefficients (Table 2) reveal that a one-unit increase in the percentage of employed women will result in a 44% increase in the odds of being in the female bias group (versus being in the male bias or neutral groups).

Table 2: Logistic regression for the labor market. (Results of the best fitted logistic regression model). The binary dependent variable represents a profession being in the female bias group. The coefficient for "Percentage of involved women" reveals that we will see a 44% increase in the odds of being in a female bias group for a one-unit increase in percentage of involved women, since $exp(0.364) = 1.44$. For example, the probability of a profession being in the female bias group for a profession with 20% women in Germany equals $5.3e - 13$ and 0.55 if a profession has 98% women.

	coef.	p	95% conf.int.
		Accuracy: 0.99	Pseudo R-squared:0.61
Percentage of involved women	0.36	0.008	[0.10, 0.63]
(Intercept)	-35.53	0.005	[-60.44, -10.62]

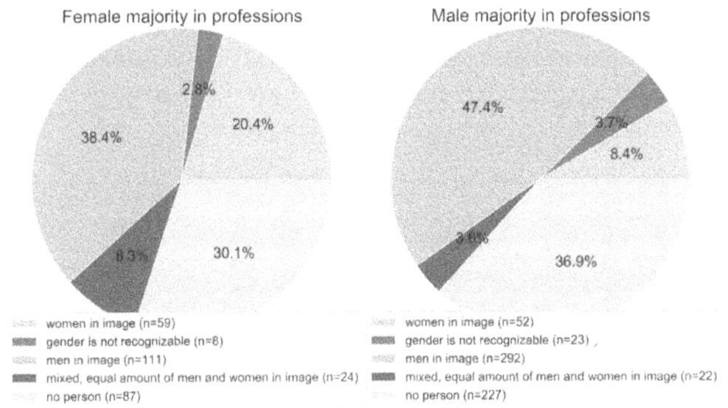

Figure 4: Distribution of image categories, grouped by gender of majority in the labor market. Professions with a female employment majority have almost two times more images depicting men than women, whereas professions with male majority feature even fewer images depicting women, around 5.6 times less.

The output indicates that the percentage of employed women is significantly associated with the probability of being in the female bias group, yet this relation shows itself only at very high values of female employment ratios. For example, we have an estimated probability of 0.001 for being in the female bias group for a profession with 80% employed women. The estimated probability is instead 0.63 for a profession with 99% employed women. That means that only professions with very high (> 97%) percentages of employed women will be likely to have only an article with a female title.

Results of rank-sum tests and fitted logistic regression model support the hypothesis that professions with higher percentages of women have only a female page (i.e., professions from female bias redirection group). At the same time, the threshold of percentage of employed women, where one observes increase in likelihood of profession to be in the female bias, is very high (about 97% employed women). However, we cannot identify a significant difference between the male and neutral bias groups. The relation between these groups cannot be described using the percentage of employed women in the labor market.

4.2 Images analysis

The aggregated results for all 906 labeled images were as follows: (1) almost half (44.8%) of the images show men, whereas only 12.4% of images show women; (2) an equal amount of men and women is observed only in a few images (5.1%); (3) almost a third (34.3%) of the images depicts no person; (4) gender is not recognizable for 3.4% of the images.

The analysis of images, grouped by gender of article title (profession name) where the images were encountered reveals a significant difference in image composition. Articles with a female title have almost 10 times more images depicting women than men, whereas articles with a male title have 4 times more images depicting men than women. Articles with a neutral title have 6 times more images depicting men than women. Thus, articles with female and male titles both show a respective gender inclination. While men are vastly underrepresented in articles with female titles, the underrepresentation of women in articles with male and neutral titles

Table 3: Spearman's rank correlation coefficients between the number of images in Wikipedia article about a profession and the labor market statistics of the profession.

Images	Labor market	Corr.
percentage of img depicting men	percentage of women	-0.3***
percentage of img depicting women	percentage of women	0.34***
percentage of img depicting women	number of women	0.17**
percentage of img depicting men	number of men	0.013

exists, but is much weaker. We observed the same tendencies when grouping images by redirection bias of profession. Professions with only an article with a female title on Wikipedia have most images depicting women (75% of images). Nevertheless, professions from "male bias" and "neutral bias" redirection groups are not gender neutral in terms of image representations, as the majority of images depicts men (44.4% and 52% of all images, correspondingly).

Labor Market. Professions were divided into two groups: professions with female majority and such with male majority (>50%). Figure 4 shows the distribution of image categories, grouped by gender of majority in the labor market. One can see that there are almost two times more images depicting men (38.4%) than women (20.4%) in professions with more than 50% women in labor market (female majority group). At the same time, there are almost 6 times more images depicting men (47.4%) than women (8.4%) in professions with male majority. In both groups we observe that the majority of images depict men. Therefore, we can conclude that profession images on Wikipedia do not reflect the labor market statistics. We also looked at groups with more than 70% men and women in the labor market.

An analysis of the images, grouped by gender of majority (>50%) according to the labor market statistics, reveals a significant difference in image composition. Professions with more than 50% women in the labor market have 2 times less images depicting women than men, whereas professions with more than 50% men in the labor market have almost 6 times less images depicting women than men. In other words, a majority of one gender in the labor market does not imply a majority of the same gender in images.

Results of Spearman's rank correlation (Table 3) reveal a moderate positive correlation ($\rho = 0.34$) between the percentage of images depicting women in an article and the percentage of women in the corresponding profession, and a moderate positive correlation ($\rho = 0.3$) between the percentage of images depicting men in an article and the percentage of men in the profession. Thus, professions with higher percentage of images depicting women/men exhibit a moderately higher percentage of women/men in the labor market.

4.3 Analysis of mentioned names

There are 411 articles about professions which mention at least one person. The articles mention overall 5085 persons (4272 men and 813 women). 10.4 men and 1.9 women were mentioned on average in the articles. The mean proportion of mentioned men per article is 0.83 and the median proportion is 0.98. In other words, out of all people mentioned in an article, 83% of them are men and only 17% of them are women on average.

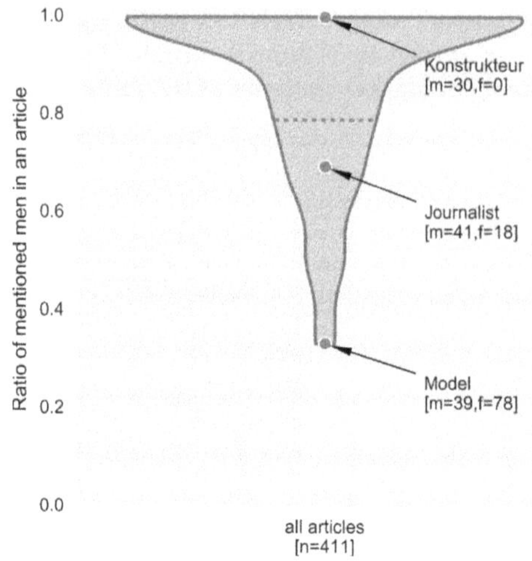

Figure 5: Mentioned men proportions. Violin plot of the distribution of proportional mentions of male names in articles. The violin plot features a kernel density estimation of the underlying distribution. The shape of the violin plot represents the density: the wider the violin plot, the greater the number of articles with a particular proportion of men. The solid red line represents the median; the dotted line shows the 3rd quartile (1st quartile line hidden). The violin plot represents data points which are distributed within two standard deviations of the mean, outliers are removed. One can see that ½ of articles mention only men in the articles, ¾ of articles mention 80-100% men and only 0-20% women. Moreover, only a few articles mention either an equal number of men and women or more women than men.

Figure 5 shows the distribution of men proportions. As one can see, 50% of articles have a proportion of mentioned men close to 1.0 and 75% of articles have a proportion of mentioned men from 0.8 to 1.0. The article "Konstrukteur" (EN≈ "design engineer") for example mentions 30 persons, all of them men, the article "Journalist" mentions 41 men and 18 women, and the article "Model" 39 men and 78 women. Articles which mention an equal number of men and women are considered gender neutral. Consequently, all articles with > 50% male names are male-biased with the remainder being female-biased in our consideration. One can see from Figure 5 that most articles have a proportion higher than 0.5. In particular, 92.5% of the articles are male-biased, 3.1% of the articles are female-biased, and 4.4% of the articles are gender-equal.

Lastly, we grouped articles according to the gender of the article title and found that the distribution of proportions of mentioned men was significantly different (p^*) between articles with male and female titles. Proportions of mentioned men in articles with male titles (median is 0.98) are more likely to be larger than the proportions in articles with female title (median is 0.65).

Labor Market. The difference in proportions of mentioned men was explored between professions with male and female majorities.

Three quarters of articles among professions with female majority in the labor market mention 68%-100% men and 0-32% women. This implies that the largest part of the articles for professions with female majority expose male bias; this is despite the fact that compared to professions with male majority, female majority articles still feature a significantly lower proportion of mentioned men (medians are 0.88 and 0.98, p^{***} for male majority professions) .

Table 4: Spearman's rank correlation coefficients between the number of mentioned men/women in a Wikipedia article about a profession and the labor market statistics of the profession.

Mentioned people	Labor market	Corr.
percentage of mentioned women	percentage of women	0.27***
percentage of mentioned men	percentage of men	0.27***
percentage of mentioned women	number of women	0.17***

Results of Spearman's rank correlation (Table 4) reveal weak positive correlation ($\rho = 0.27$) between the percentage of mentioned women or men and the percentage of women or men in the labor market correspondingly. In other words, the higher is the percentage of women in a profession, the higher is the percentage of mentioned women in the article about the profession, and the other way around. In summary, one can conclude that for some professions the percentage of mentioned men or women reflects the labor market statistics in terms of gender proportions.

5 RELATED WORK

Due to the increasing importance of online media, much research is concerned with an assessment of bias in Wikipedia and on the Web in general. For example, Reagle and Rhue [24] compared biographical articles from the English Wikipedia edition and the online Encyclopedia Britannica with respect to coverage, gender representation, and article length. Authors concluded that Wikipedia provided better coverage and longer articles. While Wikipedia has more articles on women than Britannica in absolute terms, Wikipedia articles on women are missing more often than are articles on men, when compared to Britannica. Wagner et al.[28] studied coverage of famous women in Wikipedia articles and the way women are portrayed in the online encyclopedia. The authors found that, despite good coverage of famous women in many Wikipedia language editions, the ways in which women and men are portrayed differ significantly. For example, romantic relationships and family-related issues are much more frequently discussed about women than men. In [11, 28, 29] differences between descriptions of male and female biographies in terms of network structure, topical focus, structural properties and language were researched. Thus, several studies suggest that gender bias on Wikipedia can be assessed using articles with biographies.

Several studies [7, 18] have tried to explain gender imbalance by studying how conflict-related behaviors (e.g., reverts) affect male and female editors. Collier and Bear [7] studied reasons for why female contributors stop contributing, indicating that the gender contribution gap is due to responses to conflicts. In [13, 15] authors found that significant Internet experiences and beliefs about one's competence explain a large share of the gender gap. According to [14] only 16.1% of editors on Wikipedia are women. Antin et al.[2] studied differences between men and women's editing activity in terms of the number and size of the revisions they make.

Bernacchi [27] performed a visual exploration of the gender issue on Wikipedia by studying the articles "Man" and "Woman" in several language editions of Wikipedia. The researchers compared sizes of articles, numbers of edits per article, changes in TOC structures, network structures of related articles and intersection of used concepts, topics coverage, revisions in terms of vandalism and deleted content. However, profession-related gender bias on Wikipedia and corresponding aspects remain uncovered, to the best of our knowledge.

Kay et al. [17] studied the gender bias in image search results and found that manipulated search results have a small significant effect on people's gender ratio perception (cf. Section 1).

6 DISCUSSION

In general, we observe a strong overrepresentation of male titles, images and mentioned names on the German Wikipedia that cannot be explained in its entirety by labor market statistics.

The analysis of article titles and redirections reveals that most professions are represented only via an article with a male form of the profession. Moreover, most encountered redirections are from female to male titles. This evidence supports the existence of gender disparity along article titles in the professional domain. Choices of article titles mostly reflect the general popularity of male over female profession names on the German speaking Web, with some exceptions. Turning to the labor market statistics, we observe a relation between the percentage of women involved in a profession and the probability of having only a female article on Wikipedia. However, only professions with a distinctly larger female ratio in the workforce are likely to be represented only by a female article. On the other hand, using labor market statistics, we cannot well distinguish between professions with both male and female lemmata versus professions represented only by a male title, as the male redirection/representation bias on Wikipedia does not only appear for "male" professions as measured by true employment.

Regarding depictions, almost four times more images of men than women are used to describe the professions. We find that almost half of the images from the profession articles depict men and only around 12% show women. We observe a significantly higher number of images depicting men in professions, regardless of female majority or male majority in the labor market for that profession. Only for articles under female lemmas and professions which have only a female article on Wikipedia do we find a significantly higher number of images depicting women than men.

Along the mentioned people dimension, an imbalance towards male names (more than 50% men) was observed in 92.5% of the articles. Only very few articles mention exhibit either (a near) equal number of men and women or more women than men. Particularly, out of all mentioned people, we observed ¾ of articles with 79-100% men and 0-21% women. Less than 50% men (i.e., female bias) were mentioned in 3.1% of the articles and equal representation was observed in 4.4%. Analyses of the articles with female title and articles of professions with female majority in the labor market revealed significantly lower proportions of mentioned men. Nevertheless, even for groups where the difference of proportions was significant, a male bias was observed in the larger part of articles from these profession groups.

Interpreting these results, one major reason for why male lemmas and redirects dominate in (the profession articles of) the German Wikipedia is certainly the existence of the "Generisches Maskulinum", i.e., the traditional German language tendency to refer to a group of mixed or unknown gender with the male descriptor. We have also found several discussions on the talk pages of the respective articles studied here that point to a deliberate decision to "simplify" the navigation structure of Wikipedia by agreeing on the guideline to put all profession names under their generic masculine name. This "bias" as we have called it hence doesn't automatically indicate a deliberate prejudiced ideology against female descriptors. Yet, the effect on a reader is the same: she is being redirected or cannot find results for female profession name forms, which certainly influences her perception of how society views certain professions; also reinforcing the use of the generic masculine form that has been criticized in the German-speaking public discourse. A simple solution would be to host all articles under a gender-neutral lemma (as is practice already for some profession as we have seen), reachable via redirect from the male and female lemmas - the description of the profession througout the article then has to be simply adapted to a neutral/both-gender form (e.g., with the "/In" suffix).

Regarding images and names, another reason for male overrepresentation is presumably that, especially in long-established professions like "smith", many older depictions and records exist that contain for the most part men – and as prominence often is achieved post-mortem, names of famous representatives of a trade are more likely to be mentioned by name in reference works, reflecting a historic imbalance towards working men. Nonetheless, the biases we unveiled also appear in some more modern professions. And, if we again consider solely the effect on the reader, in such cases a more recent focus on the occupational field might be useful, for example by concentrating the lede and starting sections on the contemporary state of a profession before covering its history. To control for history effects, future work might filter out entity-matched persons by their date of birth, and specifically identify paragraphs that refer to historical aspects of a profession.

Regarding possible reasons for the observed imbalances, previous research [7, 14] has revealed that a dominant majority of editors in Wikipedia is male. Wikipedia further contains fewer and less extensive articles about women or topics important to women [18], indicating that male editors might not be suited to entirely represent the female world view and interests. Over the last years, the Wikimedia Foundation has made many attempts to attract more female editors [6, 21], although with mixed success. Yet, the gender of editors is likely not the only factor behind the described imbalances. Just as many historical reference works already contain a male-dominant description, Wikipedia might reflect and in some cases inherit biases from other media and the references contained therein. We observed evidence for a male bias on the German speaking Web, i.e., for most of professions one can find much more sources for male than female professions. Moreover, several studies [10, 25] reveal gender bias and stereotypes in mass media. I.e., apart from gender equality of the editor base, having transparent guidelines and rules towards representative equality in article content might prove just as useful to decrease gender disparities of individual articles; defining clear target audience groups and contemplating suitability of the content for those readers might likewise be helpful.

The method proposed in our research can in principle be applied for the analysis of gender inequalities in different Wikipedia editions. The image and mentioned people analysis methods can be applied to any language; the image analysis could in future work even be fully automated given the availability of reliable algorithmic tools. And while the redirection analysis can only be applied to languages with masculine and feminine grammatical genders, this leaves several candidate languages. A cross-language analysis extension is a promising goal for future work, by matching the respective profession pages, in order to compare biases over editions. Results could be compared to external country-wise data like the Global Gender Gap Index for each country associated with a Wikipedia edition.

7 CONCLUSION

This study presents a computational approach to gender bias assessment along three distinct dimensions using Wikipedia profession articles. We made use of crowdsourcing to complement our analysis with high-quality data and compared against publicly available labor market data.

The results indicate clear gender presentation imbalances on all the three dimensions studied (titles, mentioned persons, images). A notable portion cannot be explained simply by underlying labor market conditions, and many choices of representation seem to be made out of tradition or based on historic reference material.

This work has the potential to provide aides and inform guidelines for the Wikipedia community to identify and address gender disparities. Likewise, the outlined approach could be implemented in a software tool supporting Wikipedia editors in writing articles. The analysis procedure is likely reproducible for other Wikipedia language editions. Lastly, a careful consideration and possible evaluation of the effects of gender imbalance in profession articles especially on younger readers seems worthwile, given our results.

The data and code are available online on GitHub.[12]

REFERENCES

[1] Rami Al-Rfou, Vivek Kulkarni, Bryan Perozzi, and Steven Skiena. 2015. Polyglot-NER: Massive Multilingual Named Entity Recognition. In *Proceedings of the 2015 SIAM International Conference on Data Mining*. SIAM, 586–594.

[2] Judd Antin, Raymond Yee, Coye Cheshire, and Oded Nov. 2011. Gender Differences in Wikipedia Editing. In *Proceedings of the 7th International Symposium on Wikis and Open Collaboration (WikiSym '11)*. ACM, 11–14. https://doi.org/10.1145/2038558.2038561

[3] Florian Arendt and Temple Northup. 2015. Effects of Long-Term Exposure to News Stereotypes on Implicit and Explicit Attitudes. *International Journal of Communication* 9, 0 (2015), 21. http://ijoc.org/index.php/ijoc/article/view/2691

[4] Sherryl Browne Graves. 1999. Television and Prejudice Reduction: When Does Television as a Vicarious Experience Make a Difference? *Journal of Social Issues* 55, 4 (1999), 707–727. https://doi.org/10.1111/0022-4537.00143

[5] David Chambers. 1983. Stereotypic images of the scientist: The draw- a-scientist test. *Science Education* 67, 2 (1983), 255–265. https://doi.org/10.1002/sce.3730670213

[6] Giovanni Luca Ciampaglia and Dario Taraborelli. 2015. MoodBar: Increasing New User Retention in Wikipedia Through Lightweight Socialization. In *Proceedings of the 18th ACM Conference on Computer Supported Cooperative Work & Social Computing (CSCW '15)*. ACM, 734–742. https://doi.org/10.1145/2675133.2675181

[7] Benjamin Collier and Julia Bear. 2012. Conflict, Criticism, or Confidence: An Empirical Examination of the Gender Gap in Wikipedia Contributions. In *Proceedings of the ACM 2012 Conference on Computer Supported Cooperative Work (CSCW '12)*. ACM, 383–392. https://doi.org/10.1145/2145204.2145265

[8] Shelley J. Correll. 2001. Gender and the Career Choice Process: The Role of Biased Self-Assessments. *Amer. J. Sociology* 106, 6 (May 2001), 1691–1730. https://doi.org/10.1086/321299

[9] Olive Jean Dunn. 1959. Estimation of the Medians for Dependent Variables. *The Annals of Mathematical Statistics* 30, 1 (1959), 192–197.

[10] Liye Fu, Cristian Danescu-Niculescu-Mizil, and Lillian Lee. 2016. Tie-breaker: Using language models to quantify gender bias in sports journalism. (July 2016). http://arxiv.org/abs/1607.03895 arXiv: 1607.03895.

[11] Eduardo Graells-Garrido, Mounia Lalmas, and Filippo Menczer. 2015. First Women, Second Sex: Gender Bias in Wikipedia. In *Proceedings of the 26th ACM Conference on Hypertext & Social Media (HT '15)*. ACM, 165–174. https://doi.org/10.1145/2700171.2791036

[12] A. G. Greenwald and M. R. Banaji. 1995. Implicit social cognition: attitudes, self-esteem, and stereotypes. *Psychological Review* 102, 1 (1995), 4–27.

[13] Eszter Hargittai and Aaron Shaw. 2015. Mind the skills gap: the role of Internet know-how and gender in differentiated contributions to Wikipedia. *Information, Communication & Society* 18, 4 (2015), 424–442. https://doi.org/10.1080/1369118X.2014.957711

[14] Benjamin Mako Hill and Aaron Shaw. 2013. The Wikipedia Gender Gap Revisited: Characterizing Survey Response Bias with Propensity Score Estimation. *PLOS ONE* 8, 6 (2013), e65782. https://doi.org/10.1371/journal.pone.0065782

[15] Marit Hinnosaar. 2015. Gender Inequality in New Media: Evidence from Wikipedia. (May 2015). https://doi.org/10.2139/ssrn.2617021 Available at SSRN: https://ssrn.com/abstract=2617021.

[16] Fariba Karimi, Claudia Wagner, Florian Lemmerich, Mohsen Jadidi, and Markus Strohmaier. 2016. Inferring Gender from Names on the Web: A Comparative Evaluation of Gender Detection Methods. In *Proceedings of the 25th International Conference Companion on World Wide Web*. ACM, 53–54. https://doi.org/10.1145/2872518.2889385

[17] Matthew Kay, Cynthia Matuszek, and Sean A. Munson. 2015. Unequal Representation and Gender Stereotypes in Image Search Results for Occupations. In *Proceedings of the 33rd Annual ACM Conference on Human Factors in Computing Systems (CHI '15)*. ACM, 3819–3828. https://doi.org/10.1145/2702123.2702520

[18] Shyong (Tony) K. Lam, Anuradha Uduwage, Zhenhua Dong, Shilad Sen, David R. Musicant, Loren Terveen, and John Riedl. 2011. WP:Clubhouse?: An Exploration of Wikipedia's Gender Imbalance. In *Proceedings of the 7th International Symposium on Wikis and Open Collaboration (WikiSym '11)*. ACM, 1–10. https://doi.org/10.1145/2038558.2038560

[19] Paul L. MacDonald and Robert C. Gardner. 2000. Type I Error Rate Comparisons of Post Hoc Procedures for I x J Chi-Square Tables. *Educational and Psychological Measurement* 60, 5 (2000), 735–54.

[20] Jörg Michael. 2007. 40000 Namen, Anredebestimmung anhand des Vornamens. *c't* 07, 17 (2007), 182–183. http://www.heise.de/ct/ftp/07/17/182/

[21] Jonathan T. Morgan, Siko Bouterse, Heather Walls, and Sarah Stierch. 2013. Tea and Sympathy: Crafting Positive New User Experiences on Wikipedia. In *Proceedings of the 2013 Conference on Computer Supported Cooperative Work (CSCW '13)*. ACM, 839–848. https://doi.org/10.1145/2441776.2441871

[22] B. V. North, D. Curtis, and P. C. Sham. 2002. A Note on the Calculation of Empirical P Values from Monte Carlo Procedures. *American Journal of Human Genetics* 71, 2 (2002), 439–441. http://www.ncbi.nlm.nih.gov/pmc/articles/PMC379178/

[23] D.M.W. Powers. 2011. Evaluation: from Precision, Recall and F -measure to ROC, Informedness, Markedness and C orrelation. *Journal of Machine Learning Technologies* 2, 1 (2011), 37–63. http://en.journals.sid.ir/ViewPaper.aspx?ID=436993

[24] Joseph Reagle and Lauren Rhue. 2011. Gender Bias in Wikipedia and Britannica. *International Journal of Communication* 5, 0 (2011), 21. http://ijoc.org/index.php/ijoc/article/view/777

[25] Stacy L Smith, Marc Choueiti, and Stephanie Gall. 2010. *Gender inequality in popular films: Examining on screen portrayals and behind-the-scenes employment patterns in motion pictures released between 2007–2009.* Los Angeles, CA: Annenberg School for Communication & Journalism.

[26] U.S. Census Bureau. 1983. 1980, Census of the population. Detailed Occupation and Years of School Completed by Age, for the Civilian Labor Force; by Sex, Race, and Spanish Origin. U.S. Department of Commerce. (1983).

[27] Viola Bernacchi. 2015. *Gender imbalance and Wikipedia.* Ph.D. Dissertation. Polytechnic University of Milan, Italy.

[28] Claudia Wagner, David Garcia, Mohsen Jadidi, and Markus Strohmaier. 2015. It's a Man's Wikipedia? Assessing Gender Inequality in an Online Encyclopedia. In *Ninth International AAAI Conference on Web and Social Media.* http://www.aaai.org/ocs/index.php/ICWSM/ICWSM15/paper/view/10585

[29] Claudia Wagner, Eduardo Graells-Garrido, David Garcia, and Filippo Menczer. 2016. Women through the glass ceiling: gender asymmetries in Wikipedia. *EPJ Data Science* 5, 1 (2016). https://doi.org/10.1140/epjds/s13688-016-0066-4

[12] https://github.com/gesiscss/Wikipedia-Language-Olga-master/

Where Could We Go? Recommendations for Groups in Location-Based Social Networks

Frederick Ayala-Gómez
Eötvös Loránd University,
Faculty of Informatics
Budapest, Hungary
fayala@caesar.elte.hu

Bálint Daróczy
Inst. Computer Science and Control,
Hungarian Academy of Sciences
(MTA SZTAKI)
Budapest, Hungary
daroczyb@ilab.sztaki.hu

Michael Mathioudakis
Computer Science Department
Aalto University
Espoo, Finland
michael.mathioudakis@aalto.fi

András Benczúr
Inst. Computer Science and Control,
Hungarian Academy of Sciences
(MTA SZTAKI)
Budapest, Hungary
benczur@sztaki.mta.hu

Aristides Gionis
Computer Science Department
Aalto University
Espoo, Finland
aristides.gionis@aalto.fi

ABSTRACT

Location-Based Social Networks (LBSNs) enable their users to share with their friends the places they go to and whom they go with. Additionally, they provide users with recommendations for Points of Interest (POI) they have not visited before. This functionality is of great importance for users of LBSNs, as it allows them to discover interesting places in populous cities that are not easy to explore. For this reason, previous research has focused on providing recommendations to LBSN users. Nevertheless, while most existing work focuses on recommendations for individual users, techniques to provide recommendations to groups of users are scarce.

In this paper, we consider the problem of recommending a list of POIs to a group of users in the areas that the group frequents. Our data consist of activity on Swarm, a social networking app by Foursquare, and our results demonstrate that our proposed *Geo-Group-Recommender* (GGR), a class of hybrid recommender systems that combine the group geographical preferences using Kernel Density Estimation, category and location features and group check-ins outperform a large number of other recommender systems. Moreover, we find evidence that user preferences differ both in venue category and in location between individual and group activities. We also show that combining individual recommendations using group aggregation strategies is not as good as building a profile for a group. Our experiments show that (GGR) outperforms the baselines in terms of precision and recall at different cutoffs.

CCS CONCEPTS

•Information systems →Location based services; Personalization; Recommender systems;

KEYWORDS

Group Recommendation; Location-Based Social Networks; Recommender Systems

1 INTRODUCTION

Location-Based Social Networks (LBSNs) are platforms that enable people to share online their whereabouts (the places they visit and whom they visit them with) – and, in turn, learn the whereabouts of their online friends. This is achieved via *check-ins*, i.e., posts that contain the location (latitude, longitude) of a user and the exact venue, e.g., a restaurant. Using this information users get to know where their friends are. Additionally, check-ins create a timeline of the places that users have visited. Utilizing check-in information, LBSNs recommend venues as Point of Interests (POIs) that users might like to visit.

Recommendations for new places to visit are of major importance for users of LBSNs. For example, in metropolitan areas or while on holidays, users often wish to discover new places that they would be interested in – yet such information is often not readily available. Note that the task of recommending new POIs is different than that of recommending other types of items (e.g., movies, news) in that geography also comes into play. Recalling Tobler's first law of geography: "everything is related to everything else, but near things are more related than distant things" [26].

In this work, we focus on a particular variant of the recommendation task: one that seeks to *recommend a new POI to a group of users*. To see why this task deserves particular attention, consider that, when users choose a venue to visit with somebody else (e.g., friends or family), their venue of choice can generally be different than if they do so alone. For example, consider a person that is a big fan of hamburgers – but hangs out with friends who prefer sushi. Such situations of conflicting tastes and interests pose a challenge for the recommendation task: what POIs to recommend for a group of users if the individual preferences differ? Moreover, note that we restrict ourselves in recommending *new POIs* (i.e., ones that the group has not visited in the past), as such recommendations are of most practical interest (compared to recommending POIs that

WebSci'17, June 25-28, 2017, Troy, NY, USA.

978-1-4503-4896-6/17/06...$15.00
DOI: http://dx.doi.org/10.1145/3091478.3091485

the group has already visited) and most commonly deployed on real-world LBSNs (like Foursquare).

The problem of group recommendations has been studied before, but in different settings. For instance, there is work on recommending relevant music [18], movies [21], holidays [19], news [9]. In the setting of LBSNs, on the other hand, most earlier work has focused on recommendations for individual users [4].

To address the gap in the literature, our work addresses the following research questions.

RQ1: How do groups behave in LBSNs?
RQ2: How do preferences change when users are alone vs. when they are in a group?
RQ3: How to recommend items in the areas that a group frequents?

For all questions above, our analysis is based on a new dataset from Swarm, a LBSN developed by Foursquare. The data cover activity in three major cities: Istanbul, Izmir and Mexico City. The code used for data collection, analysis, experimentation, and the dataset are available for academic purposes[1].

With respect to **RQ3**, the use case scenario is that of a group of users who plan to meet and look for recommendations for a new place to try: in a first step, they are prompted by the system to select an area among the ones they have been to in the past; in a second step, the system provides them with recommendations for the selected area. The techniques we study implement the latter (second) step. For all techniques, individual and group preferences are assumed known and a single venue is recommended. Moreover, the group is passive towards the provided recommendation – i.e., there is no interaction between the users and the recommender system to shape the recommendation (e.g., via voting and a concensus mechanism).

We experiment with a large number of techniques drawn from the literature; and present *Geo-Group-Recommender* (GGR), a hybrid recommender system that combines collaborative and content filtering together with a geographical Kernel Density Estimation. Our results show that the proposed recommender system outperforms existing systems and other baselines.

2 BACKGROUND AND PRIOR WORK

The problem of recommending venues for individual users in LBSNs has been widely studied. A recent survey can be found in [4]. State of the art models like Fused Matrix Factorization Framework with the Multi-center Gaussian Model (FMFMGM) [7] and GeoSoCa [27] exploit geographical and social information of users. The idea of including the location preferences in the collaborative filtering learning is presented in GeoMF [15]. Research on recommending venues to groups is still scarce but emerging and promising.

2.1 Group recommendations

Recommender systems for groups are surveyed in [17]. The authors highlight that the use case of the recommender system greatly affects the design. They characterize group recommender systems by considering the following dimensions and we highlight in bold those that apply to our case: (*i*) **individual preferences are known** vs. developed over time; (*ii*) recommended items are experienced by the group vs. **presented as options in a list**; (*iii*) **the group is passive** (e.g., users are not voting) vs. active (e.g., the system helps create consensus) and (*iv*) **recommending a single item** vs. a set.

A summary of different strategies to combine individual preferences to generate group recommendations can be found in [17]. A brief summary of the methods is the following: Average Individual Ratings (AIR) considers the average rating of each item; Average Without Misery (AWM) assigns to items the average of their individual ratings under a certain threshold; Least Misery (LM) considers the minimum of their individual ratings. The authors also present more elaborate methods like graph-based ranking [13], Spearman footrule rank [2], Nash equilibrium [6] and purity and completeness [25].

2.2 Groups in LSBNs

The behavior of groups in LBSNs has been researched for different tasks. For instance, [16] studies companion recommendations where the task is to find friends interested in joining certain POI. [1] focus on recommending an itinerary for touristic groups visiting a city. However, there is scarce research work specialized in POIs recommendation for groups.

Comparing users and groups behavior in LSBN is investigated in [5] using data from Foursquare (i.e. Swarm) and Telecommunications networks. The authors show that the category of the venue and location affects the propensity for groups to meet and discuss that this behavior could affect the POIs recommendation task. Our work is complementary in the following aspects. We analyze check-ins that explicitly mention friends that are together instead of co-located within an hour. We study the behavior of Swarm users from other cities than New York. To measure the category preferences of users and groups, we use Kendall-tau as a ranking correlation metric. Our behavior analysis includes time and distance between check-ins. We use all the POIs check-ins by using clusting with DBSCAN instead of just the top POIs for users and groups. Finally, the authors in [5] did not research the performance of recommender systems for groups in LBSN.

The authors in [23] study group behavior and recommending POIs to groups in LBSNs. To detect the groups, they identify the connected components based on time, location and friends network of the Gowalla dataset. A major drawback of the dataset is that it lacks information about the location itself (e.g., category, popularity). The Gowalla check-ins contains just the latitude, longitude and ID for the POI. To overcome this, the authors retrieve POI around the latitude and longitude using the Foursquare API and then aggregate the categories. Also, check-ins are spread around the world and the authors do not mention any geographical scope limitation for their experiments.

Their model, called Collaborative Group Activity Recommender (CGAR), represents group and location activities as topic models that are combined using collaborative filtering techniques. Their model includes latent variables for activity preference and community influence, that express whether an activity at a location is more interesting for one group than to another, as well as how user communities influence the preference of locations. They highlight

[1] https://github.com/frederickayala/lbsn_group_recsys

that preferences between users and groups differ and show that their model personalizes category preferences better than regular strategies to combine individual recommendations (i.e., aggregating by average). Their model outperforms baselines (i.e., CTR, MF) in Mean Recall@K(50-1000), Mean Rating Prediction Accuracy and Mean Root Mean Squared Error.

The main differences between [23] and our work are the following. First, we use a dataset collected from Swarm that does not require any additional technique for detecting groups. Also, our collected dataset contains information about the POI so there is no need to crawl for the venues information. To improve the quality of our results, we include a cleaning step to remove bots and very active users. We present a more comprehensive analysis that highlights not only the category preferences but also the location and time preferences. Recommendations are usually presented in the shape of a ranked lists with few POIs. This is why we evaluate our recommender on the TOP K recommendation setting where K is in the range of [5,50] instead of [50,1000]. Another difference is that we focus on recommending items near the areas where the group check-ins are more concentrated and for three major cities (i.e., Istanbul, Izmir and Mexico City). We tried different recommender systems to generate a ranked list of possible POIs. Finally, we fit a Kernel Density Estimation with Gaussian Kernel per group to prioritize the POIs near the area of recommendation.

Table 1 highlights the differences of *Geo-Group-Recommender* (GGR – our model) in comparison to CGAR and recent LBSN recommender systems for individual users.

Model	Categories	Geography	Social	Group	TOP K @	Prioritize POIs
GGR (Ours)	Yes	Yes	No	Yes	5-50	Group Geo Density
CGAR [23]	Yes	No	Yes	Yes	50-1000	No
GeoMF [15]	No	Yes	No	No	5-100	User Geo Density, POI influence
GeoSoCa [27]	Yes	Yes	Yes	No	2-50	User Social Network
FMFMGM [7]	No	Yes	Yes	No	5-10	No

Table 1: Model Comparison

2.3 Recommender systems

A recent survey on recommender systems can be found in [24]. We are interested in methods that can be used when the user-item consumption lacks explicit ratings (e.g. 1-5 stars). For this purpose, we use implicit matrix factorization with two optimization methods (i.e. Implicit Alternating Least Squares (iALS) [22] and Stochastic Gradient Descent (SGD) for collaborative filtering [14]. We use other models that learn item and user similarities based on a distance metric and Nearest Neighbour methods [14], as well as ones based on item popularity.

2.4 Kernel Density Estimation

As mentioned in [4] and [27], Kernel Density Estimation (KDE) is used in several LBSNs recommender systems. KDE is calculated using the equation

$$f(x) = \sum_{i=1}^{n} K(x, x_i; h), \tag{1}$$

where X is a set that contains samples $x_1, x_2, \ldots, x_n$ from the corresponding probability distribution. K is the kernel and h is the smoothing parameter called bandwidth. In our experiments, K is the Gaussian Kernel

$$K(x, x_i; h) \sim \exp\left(-\frac{(x - x_i)^2}{2h^2}\right). \tag{2}$$

3 DATA

We require a dataset with the LBSN activity of users both when they are alone and when they are in a group. The datasets used in [3], [8], [11], [5] and [20] contain information about the activity of individual users and their friends, but no group information – and some lack detailed information about the venue.

To create such a dataset, we collect data related to the popular LBSN Swarm, a platform that enables users to indicate the venue they are *checking-in*. On Swarm, users are able to mention with whom they visit a venue and share publicly their check-ins in other social networks, like Twitter. This gives us the opportunity to collect data related to both individual and group activity.[2]

Towards that end, we deploy a crawler that uses the Twitter API to search for public tweets that contain group check-ins. Then, in snowballing fashion, we collect the latest 200 tweets of each user that is mentioned in a group check-in and extract their public check-ins contained therein. Figure 1 is a visualization of this recursive process.

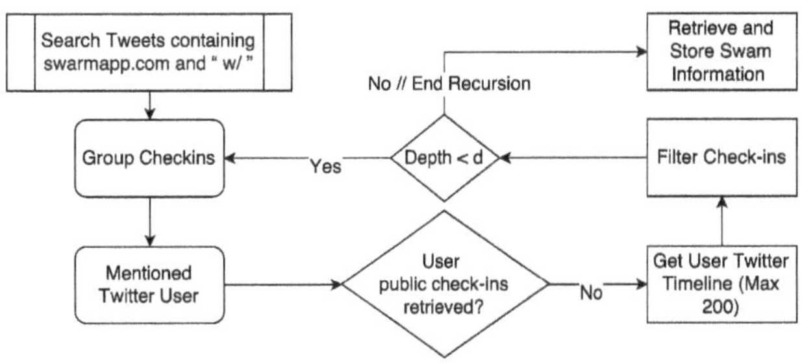

Figure 1: The crawling process of Swarm check-ins. Additionally, the lookup endpoint of the Twitter API allow us to constrain the search to a specific location by defining the geographical center and a radius.

Our recursive crawl is constrained by a stopping condition that specifies the maximum depth d the crawler can reach from the original group check-in. Depth 0 corresponds to the check-ins retrieved in the first pass over tweets, depth 1 to the check-ins of the users who are mentioned in a group check-in from depth 0, depth 2 to the check-ins of the users who are mentioned in a group check-in from depth 1, and so on.

[2] In what follows, we'll be using the term 'group' to refer to sets of at least two (2) users – and distinguish it from the term 'individual', which refers to a singleton set (one user).

We completed two crawls with no location constraint at depth 2 and 3. Subsequently, we identified the city with most check-ins for each country and performed a crawl constrained to the geographical coordinates of the city. To do that, we used the geographic coordinates that are associated with tweets and indicate the location of the user the moment when they generated the tweet. Since not all tweets are tagged with such geographic coordinates (due to the different privacy choices of Twitter users), for many cities we were not able to retrieve a sufficient number of tweets – and thus neither check-ins.

At the end of all crawls, we had a global dataset with approximately 143 K users, 522 K venues, 780 categories, 453 K groups, 5.6 M check-ins and 1 M group check-ins. Figure 2 shows a map with the check-ins around the globe. The data collection was done between September and October 2016.

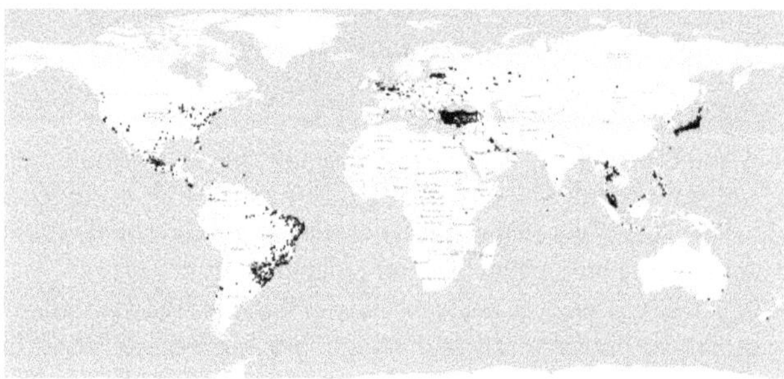

Figure 2: Map of the check-ins of all the collections together.

The top 10 cities from the collection are presented in Table 2. The names of the cities were obtained by assigning to each check-in the closest city from the Geonames database.[3] For this purpose, we used R-Trees [12].

City	Total Check-ins	Total Venues	Total Categories	Group Check-ins	Group Venues	Group Categories
Istanbul	483,214	25,953	402	43,096	8,072	297
Izmir	369,627	16,306	378	37,105	4,865	263
Mexico City	95,422	15,805	354	12,612	4,839	271
Kuala Lumpur	69,861	12,376	359	3,553	1,843	203
Bursa	59,931	4,465	283	5,459	1,218	164
Aydn	58,864	5,386	305	6,127	1,562	181
Izmit	45,575	2,961	255	4,189	818	128
Antalya	41,408	3,855	277	6,495	1,245	164
Mugla	40,148	3,520	276	5,121	1,129	173
Mytilene	40,027	2,662	219	3,220	796	131

Table 2: Top 10 cities in the data collection.

To improve the quality of our experiments, we remove possible biases caused by bots and very active users. Bots and very active users have a big geographical dispersion in their check-ins. We filtered the dataset by removing the last quartile of the users according to the standard deviation of their geographical mobility. Also, we removed approximately 2.3 M check-ins of irrelevant categories to our research (i.e., *Residence, States & Municipalities, Professional & Other Places* and *Event, College & University, Travel & Transport*).[4]

[3] http://download.geonames.org/export/dump/

[4] More information about the categorization of venues can be found in the Foursquare documentation. https://developer.foursquare.com/categorytree

4 EXPLORATION OF GROUP BEHAVIOR

In this section, we provide an exploration of the dataset, in terms of statistics that describe various aspects of group behavior.

4.1 Group Size and Activity Dispersion

We investigate group sizes as well as the distance and time between their check-ins. Figure 3 shows the group size frequency. We filter the groups with maximum 12 participants. Figure 4 presents the time and distance between check-ins for users and groups. We removed the last quartile of time and distance.

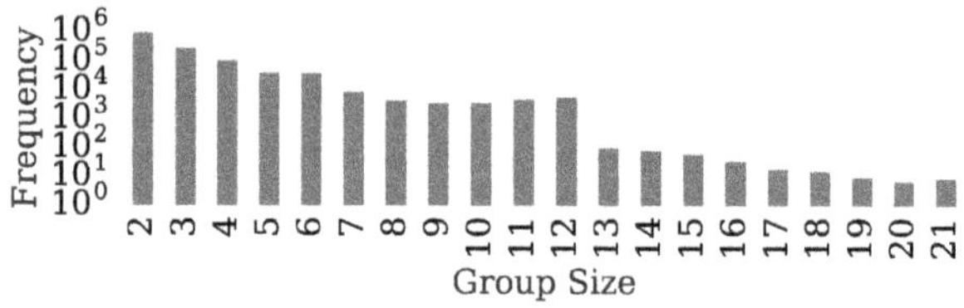

Figure 3: Group size check-in frequency (logarithmic scale).

4.2 Category Preferences

Next, we analyze the preferences of individuals and groups for venues of different categories and identify differences between the two. For category preferences we construct one ranked list of the preferred categories for individuals and one groups – and compare them using the Kendall-tau ranking correlation coefficient.

We compare the preferences at three levels: global, per city, per user. By comparing the most frequent categories for users and groups globally, the global Kendall-tau is 0.82. Figure 5 presents the Kendall-tau at the city and user level. In Figure 6 we give examples of a city and a user by parallel coordinates.

For the categorical information we use the Foursquare category tree to compute the similarity. This helps us find similar venues among different depths of the category hierarchy. For instance, if a venue is a "mexican restaurant" and another is "mediterranean restaurant" there will be some similarity between the venues because both are in the "food" main category.

4.3 Location Preferences

Figure 4 suggests that individual and group check-in behavior is different in frequency and distance spread. Next we investigate if the areas where individuals usually check-in are the same for the group.

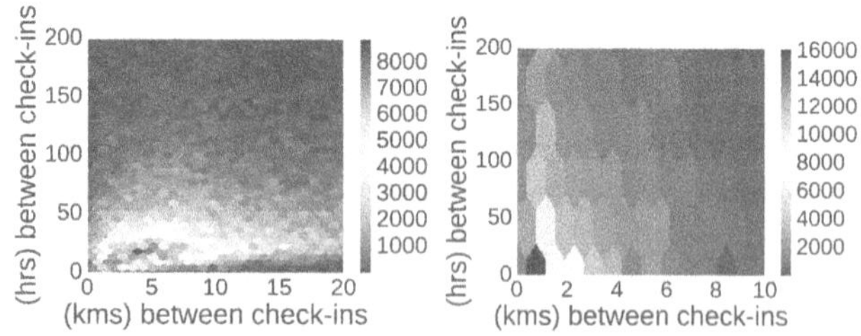

Figure 4: Frequency of time and distance between check-ins for users (left) and groups (right).

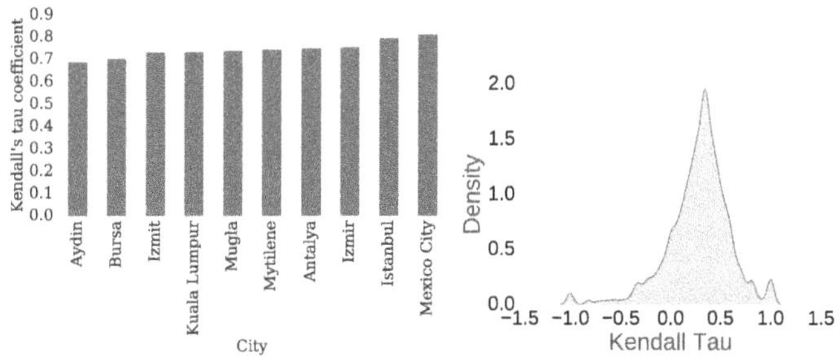

Figure 5: Kendall-tau for user and group category preferences. Left: average by city; Right: distribution on users.

To measure how much users travel to meet with a group, we first need to identify the areas where users and groups are. A well-known technique that enables us to do this is DBSCAN [10]. We use the *Vincenty distance* as the metric to identify the clusters. Figure 7 shows the user and group check-in clusters as well as their distance.

With the identified clusters, we can define a weighted average of movement for user to the groups. The following are the steps required for the whole analysis. In Step 1, for each user, we compute the centers c_u of the geographical clusters of their check-ins and the total check-ins per cluster w_u. In Step 2, for each group, we compute the centers c_g of the geographical clusters of their check-ins and the total check-ins per cluster w_g. In Step 3, we compute the weighted average distance as

$$d(c_u, c_g) = \frac{\sum_{c_{ui}} \sum_{c_{gj}} w_{ui} w_{gj} d_{vinc.}(c_{ui}, c_{gj})}{\sum_{c_{ui}} \sum_{c_{gj}} w_{ui} w_{gj}}. \tag{3}$$

We want to allow clusters to form where the POIs are at maximum 1.5 km (i.e., about 10 blocks) away from each other – and, if a POI is too far away, we consider it as an independent cluster. We used an *epsilon* of 1.5 km and *minimum points* of 1 as the parameters for the DBSCAN clustering.

Figure 8 shows the KDE for the weighted average traveling distance that users need to move to meet with the groups.

To use the geographical feature in the recommender systems we projected the latitude and longitude from the World Geodetic System (i.e., WGS84 Model) to a sphere in the Cartesian coordinate system.

5 RECOMMENDATION ALGORITHMS

We experiment with a large set of recommender systems from the literature that we use as baselines. Then, for each recommender system we create variants that differ along three dimensions. Firstly, they differ in whether we include a pre-processing step that filters POIs near the areas where the group has already been. Secondly, they differ in whether we include as features the category and location of the POI to the recommender system. Thirdly, they differ in whether the recommender system is trained using individual user check-ins or group check-ins. The variants that include the pre-processing step, category and location features and are trained on the group check-ins are collectively reffered to as *Geo-Group-Recommender* (GGR)

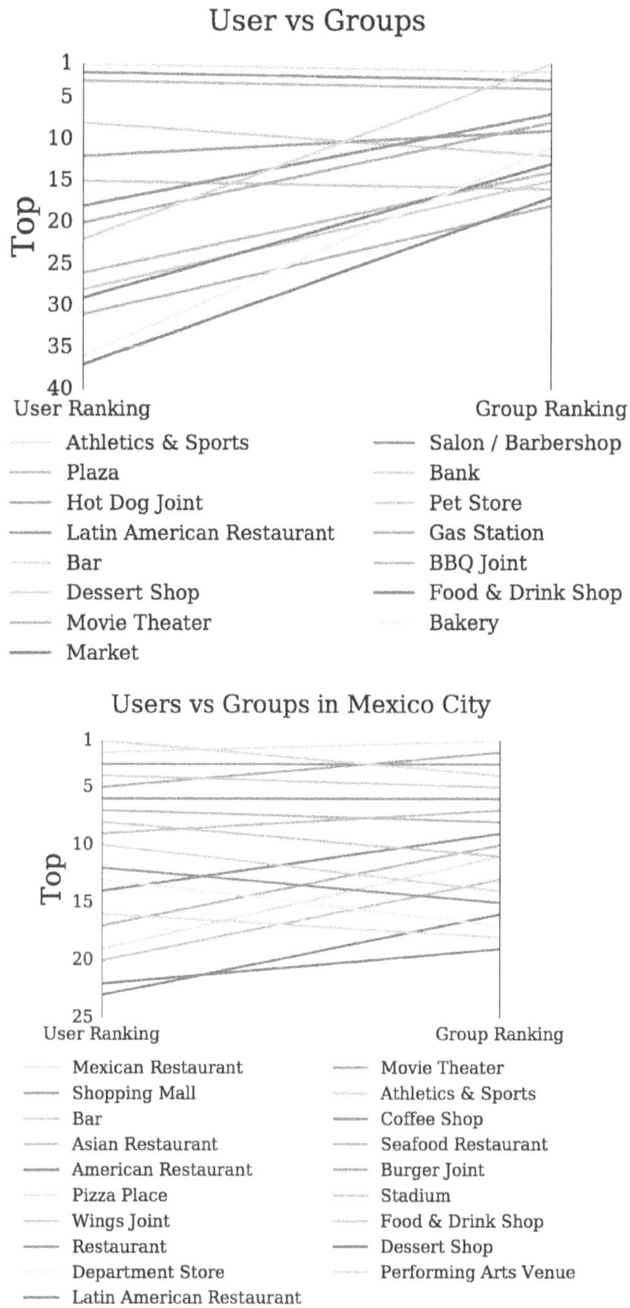

Figure 6: Category comparison using the check-ins of a single user and her groups. The Kendall-tau is 0.1(top). Total check-ins count for all the users and groups in Mexico City. The Kendall-tau is 0.8(bottom).

The motivation for the first type of variant is that, based on the inter-distance distribution of Figure 4, we know that groups do not travel much between their check-ins. Therefore, it is natural to narrow geographically the recommendations for the groups, we do this by fitting a Gaussian KDE. KDE helps us to differentiate the dense areas for a group based on the geographical check-in

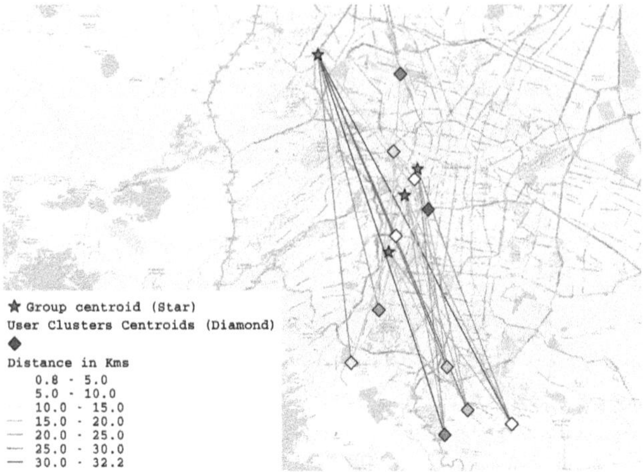

Figure 7: A map of Mexico City with an example of a user and her groups location preferences. The *diamond* shape are the centroids of the user check-in clusters. The *star* shape are the centroids of the group cluster.

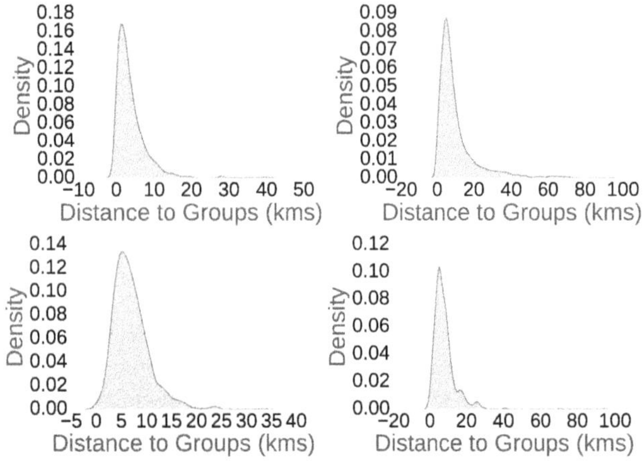

Figure 8: The KDE of users individual location preference vs. group location preference in four major cities. Lower means that the user had to travel less to meet the groups. From left to right and top to bottom: Istanbul, Izmir, Mexico City and Kuala Lumpur.

distribution, as shown in Figure 9 for one group. Specifically, we fit a KDE for each group using the check-ins in the training dataset. Subsequently, we compute a density score at the location of each venue, and keep as candidates for recommendation only the venues in the highest (densest) quartile. These POIs are then passed to the recommender system for ranking. The variants that include this pre-processing contain the keyword *KDE* in their name.

The second type of variant includes also category and/or geolocation features. These variants are denoted with *GEO* and *CAT* in their acronym.

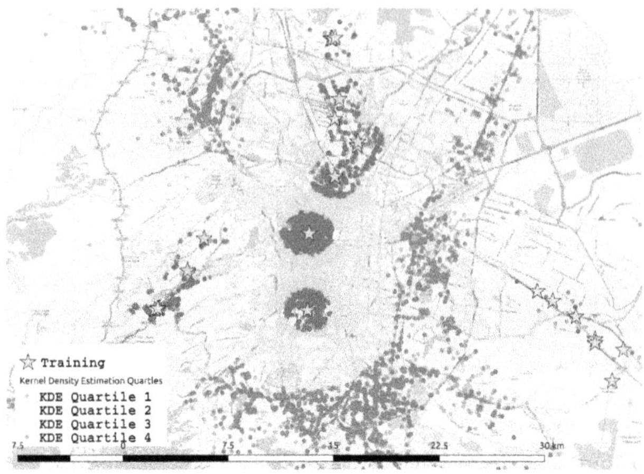

(a) A Map showing the POIs that could be recommended in Mexico City colored by the KDE score for a particular group. The *star* shapes represent the check-ins used to fit the KDE. In our experiments, we used a fixed bandwidth of 0.2 and picked venues at the 4th quartile as POIs candidates.

Figure 9: Example of pre-processing of geographical information to calculate the KDE for a particular group. Please view in color print.

Model	Acronym
IALS Matrix Factorization [22]	IALS
KDE ∩ IALS Matrix Factorization	KDE IALS
SGD Matrix Factorization [14]	SGD
KDE ∩ SGD Matrix Factorization	KDE SGD
Item To Item [24]	ITEM-ITEM
KDE ∩ Item To Item	KDE ITEM-ITEM
Popularity Recommender [24]	POP
KDE ∩ Popularity Recommender	KDE POP
Content Based Recommender [24]	CB
KDE ∩ Content Based Recommender	KDE CB

Table 3: Models used to generate recommendations.

Among the third type of variants we distinguish three subtypes depending on the aggregation function of individual preferences. Specifically, the recommender systems generate a rating $r_{u,i}$ for each pair of user u and candidate venue i that are combined with one of the following aggregation schemes [24]:

- average individual ratings (AIR), which considers the average rating of each item,

$$\hat{r}(G, i) = \frac{\sum_{u \in G} r_{u,i}}{|G|}, \tag{4}$$

- average without misery (AWM), which assigns to items the average of their individual ratings under a certain threshold,

$$\hat{r}(G, i; s) = \frac{\sum_{u \in G; r_{u,i} > s} r_{u,i}}{|G|} \tag{5}$$

- and average least misery (ALM), which considers the minimum of their individual ratings,

$$\hat{r}(G, i) = \frac{\sum \min_{u \in G} r_{u,i}}{|G|}. \tag{6}$$

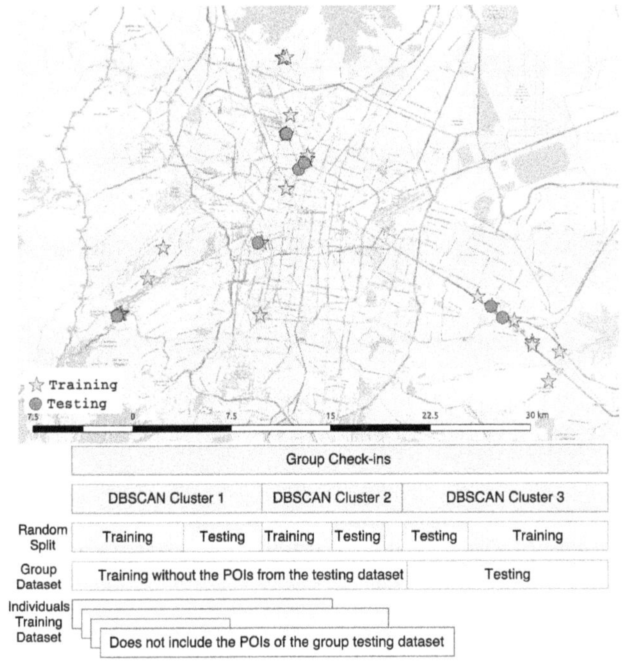

Figure 10: Random split per group and cluster. An example of the group check-ins split is shown at the top and the data split at the bottom.

Table 3 includes the names of the recommender systems that differ along the first two dimensions. Recommender systems that are trained on individual user check-ins have one of the three acronyms (i.e. AIR, AWM, ALM) appended to their name.

Evaluation Methodology

Our experiments focus on the cities with most of the group check-ins – i.e., Istanbul, Izmir and Mexico City. We split the check-ins per group cluster (i.e. clusters detected by DBSCAN) to create two datasets. The training set contains (apprx. 70%) of check-ins at the group cluster and the remaining comprises the testing set (apprx. 30%). Group clusters with size lower than the median were added to the training set. We combined all the group cluster splits to create one global training and one testing dataset. Figure 10 describes this process.

We used Turi's GraphLab Create[5] implementation of the recommender systems listed in Table 3. We used GraphLab's built-in function for tuning the parameters of the models. For this purpose, we used 5% of the training dataset as a validation set. The experiments were conducted in a single machine with 40 cores and 200 GB of RAM and ran for a day.

For performance metrics we use precision and recall at different cutoffs K (i.e. 5, 10, 20, 30, 40, 50),

$$\text{Precision@}K = \frac{\text{Visited POIs in Cluster} \cap \text{Recommended POIs}}{\text{Recommended POIs}},$$

and

$$\text{Recall@}K = \frac{\text{Visited POIs in Cluster} \cap \text{Recommended POIs}}{\text{Visited POIs in Cluster}}.$$

[5]https://turi.com/

6 RESULTS

Building upon the discussion of Sections 4 and 5, we now provide answers to the research questions we set in the beginning of this work.

6.1 RQ 1: Group Behavior

Observation 1: *Groups move less than users and their check-ins are less frequent.*

Based on the analysis of time and distance between check-ins we observed that 75% of the user check-ins occur between 2.5 days and within a distance of 10 kms. However, 75% of the groups check-ins happen between 8 days and within 5 kms. 50% of the groups move just 1 km between their check-ins.

Observation 2: *Groups in LBSNs are small.*

Most of the check-ins are made of groups of two people. Groups with size greater than 12 people are rare.

6.2 RQ 2: Individual vs. Group Preferences

Observation 3: *Group prefer other areas than their members.*

In Figure 8 we can observe that users needs to travel to parts of the city that they are not usually going. The KDE of the average weighted distance saturates between 5-10 kms.

Observation 4: *Groups prefer other types of venues than their members.*

In Figure 5 (right) we observe that top categories for users are different than groups. The Kendall-tau most dense part is around 0.4.

6.3 RQ 3: POI Recommendation

Our main result is the comparison of recommender system algorithms in different large cities. GGR models are top performers and the types of recommender systems perform differently among cities. Figure 11 shows the results for Istanbul, where KDE IALS performs best for both precision and recall. Figure 12 shows the results for Izmir, where in contrast, KDE SGD GEO performs best for both precision and recall. Finally for Mexico City (Figure 13), KDE IALS again performs best for recall@5-10 while KDE SGD CAT for recall@20-50. Best performing methods are the same for precision as well.

Observation 5: *Training recommender systems for groups works better than combining individual recommendations.*

By answering **RQ1** and **RQ2** we show that the behavior of users and groups is different. This is the reason why combining individual recommendations by averaging under-performs the group models. A better approach is to train a model based on groups information only. The results for comparing iALS for groups vs. aggregating for individual users in Figure 14 show the superiority of group-based over individual recommendations.

Observation 6: *A Geographical KDE improves the performance of new POIs recommendation in the area where the group check-ins.*

Using the geographical KDE prioritize new POIs around the group preferred areas. This improves the models for all the cities, as seen in Figs. 11–13.

Observation 7: *Geography and Categorical Features are important.*

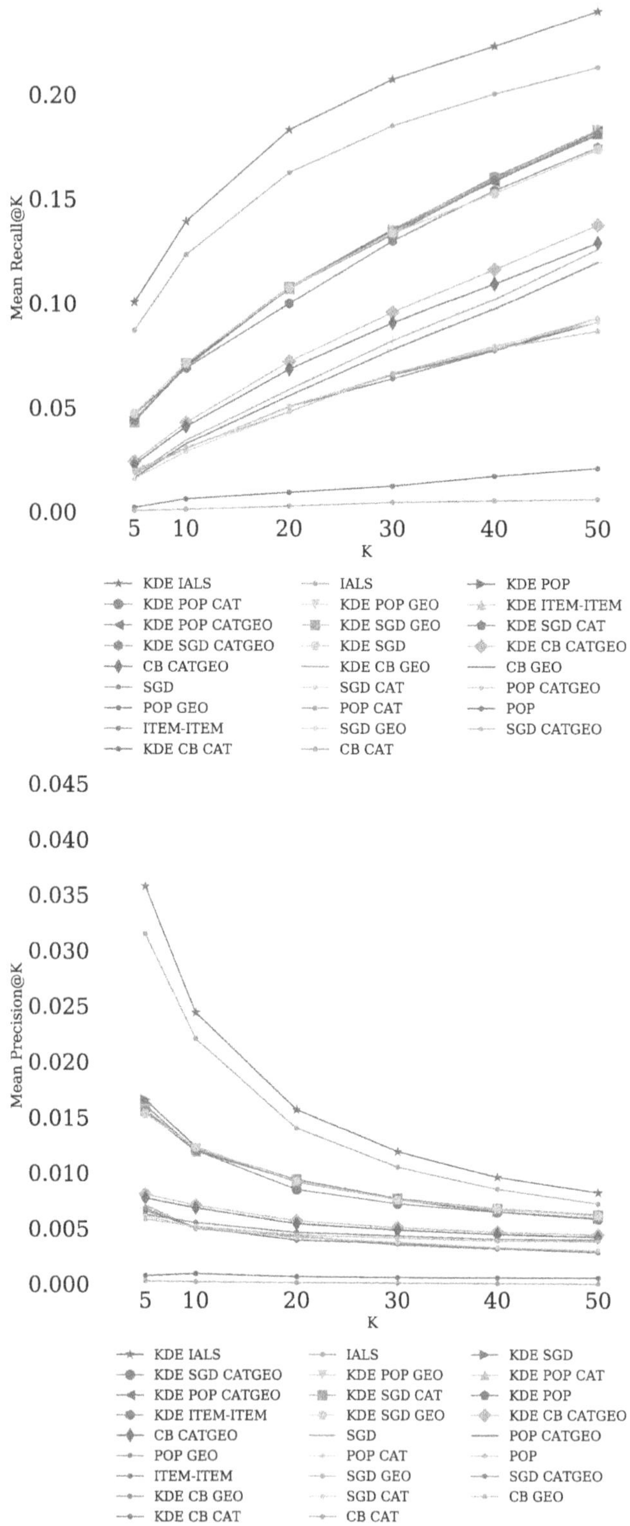

Figure 11: Istanbul Recall@K(top) and Precision@K(bottom). The legends are sorted by the best performance models from left to right and top to bottom.

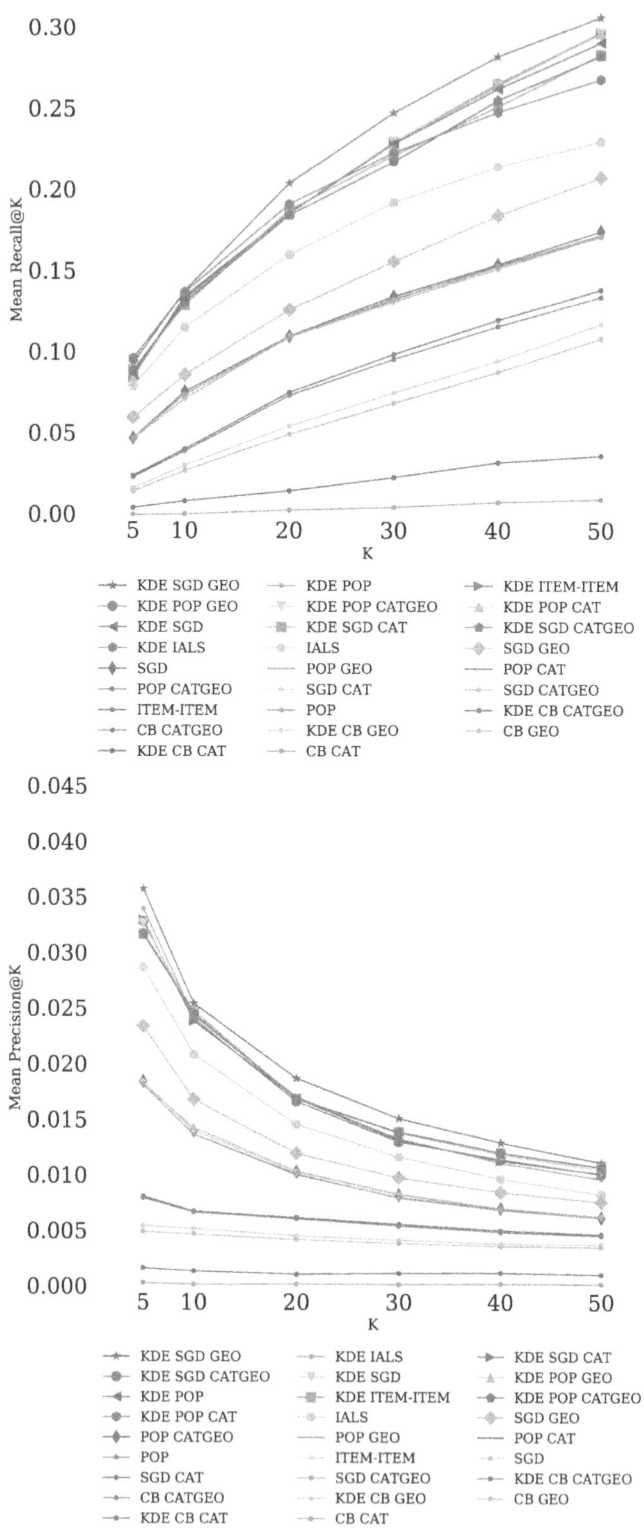

Figure 12: Izmir Recall@K(top) and Precision@K(bottom). The legends are sorted by the best performance models from left to right and top to bottom.

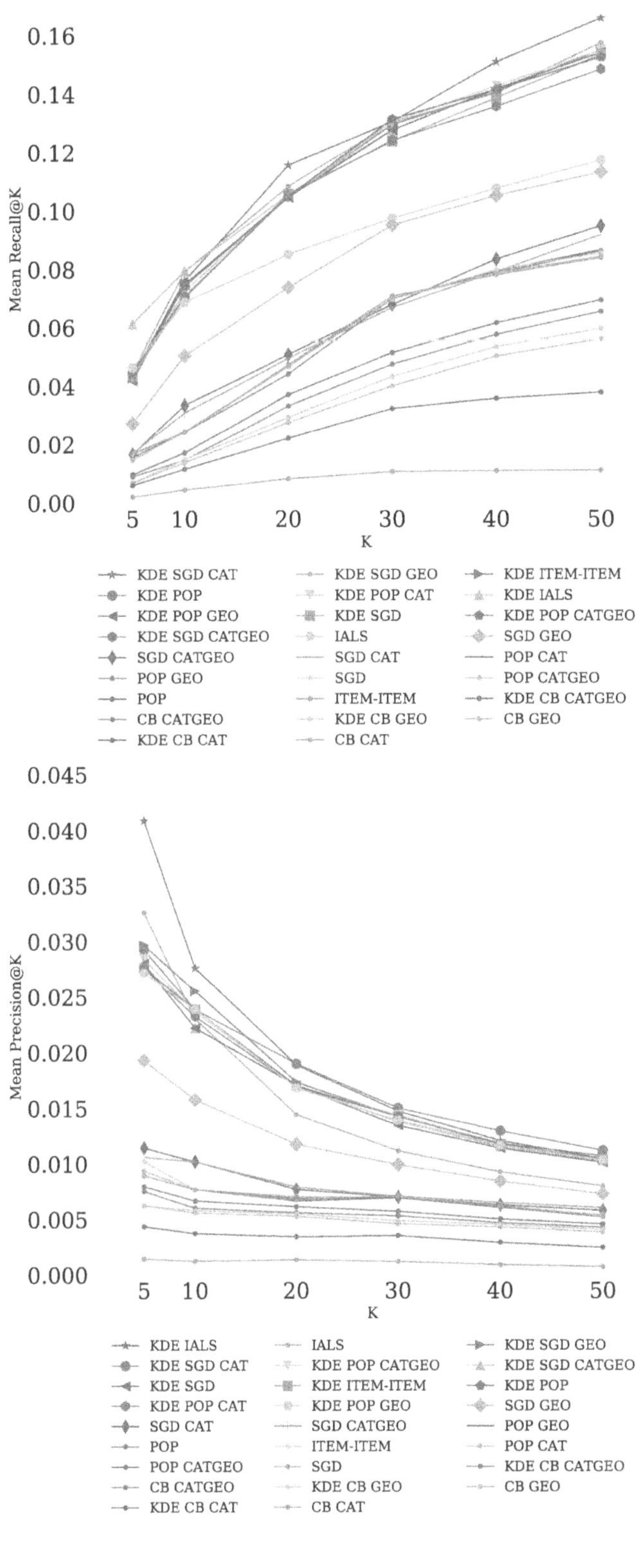

Figure 13: Mexico City Recall@K(top) and Precision@K(bottom). The legends are sorted by the best performance models from left to right and top to bottom.

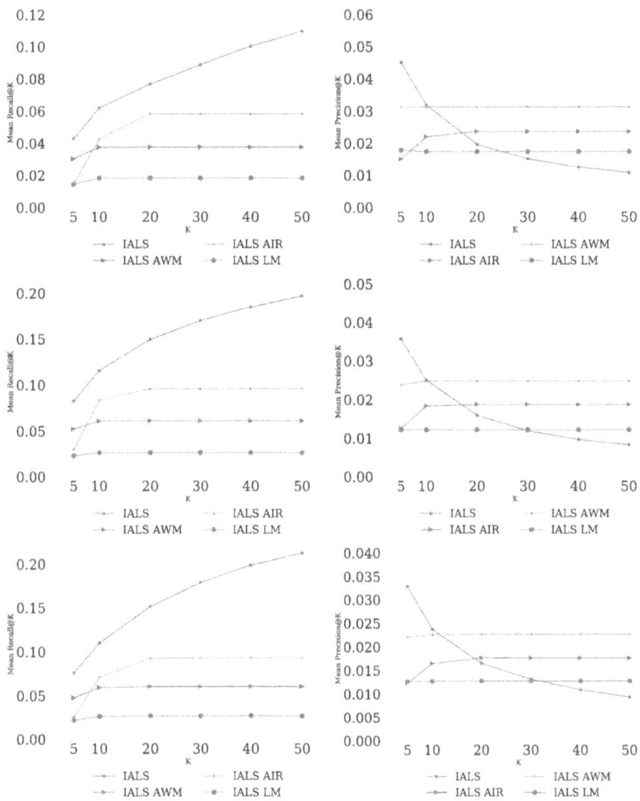

Figure 14: Combining individual iALS recommendations by equations(4–6) under-perform the group model. From top to bottom: Mexico City; Istanbul; Izmir. Left: Recall; Right: Precision.

In addition to geographical KDE, in our experiments the SGD, POP and CB models with either categorical or geographical information performed better than the same model without these features.

7 DISCUSSION

7.1 Implications

When groups decide where to go, they could save time if they receive a tailored top list of venues. The recommended list should be in-line with the group preferences in order to be useful and reasonable. Our findings suggest that this is feasible for the areas that we know a group has been to in the past. However, there are other possible POIs recommendations for groups. For example, we could recommend a new area in the city with venues that they might like. Or, we could recommend individuals to go together for the first time to a place.

7.2 Future Work

Our data collection was limited to publicly available data from Swarm and Twitter and the check-ins were extracted from the latest 200 tweets of the users. Our crawling strategy collected data from cities of Istanbul, Izmir and Mexico City. Other cities like New York where Swarm is very popular did not appear in our collection.

We could not retrieve the entire social graph for the users. Using such information (e.g. POIs popularity, areas and categories in the users ego network) would give rise to other ways to combine user preferences into group recommendations. Future work could be to understand the reasons why the models perform different for the different cities. Possible reasons are differences in the sizes of the cities, how easy is to move inside a city, the lack of data for groups (i.e. cold start problem) or even natural boundaries (e.g. rivers, mountains). Collecting more data could help to generalize our findings among different cultures, nations, urban or rural areas.

8 CONCLUSIONS

Our research work presents empirical findings on recommending new POIs to groups. To the best of our knowledge, this is the first study that uses group information in LBSNs without using specific assumptions and heuristics to detect the groups. Our experiments on over 5.6 M user check-ins and 1 M group check-ins show that users and groups prefer different geographical areas and categories. We show that recommending POIs near the areas were groups move is feasible. A major finding is that training a model using group profiles performs better than combining individual recommendations and that the GGR models generally are top performers.

9 ACKNOWLEDGMENTS

The publication was supported by the PIAC_13-1-2013-0205 project of the Research and Technology Innovation Fund, by the Momentum Grant of the Hungarian Academy of Sciences and by the Mexican Postgraduate Scholarship of the Mexican National Council for Science and Technology (CONACYT) and by the European Institute of Innovation and Technology (EIT) Digital Doctoral School. This work has been supported by the Academy of Finland project "Nestor" (286211) and the EC H2020 RIA project "SoBigData" (654024). Special thanks to Turi for the GraphLab Academic License.

REFERENCES

[1] Aris Anagnostopoulos, Reem Atassi, Luca Becchetti, Adriano Fazzone, and Fabrizio Silvestri. 2016. Tour recommendation for groups. *Data Mining and Knowledge Discovery* (2016), 1–32. DOI:http://dx.doi.org/10.1007/s10618-016-0477-7
[2] Linas Baltrunas, Tadas Makcinskas, and Francesco Ricci. 2010. Group Recommendations with Rank Aggregation and Collaborative Filtering. In *Proceedings of the Fourth ACM Conference on Recommender Systems (RecSys '10)*. ACM, New York, NY, USA, 119–126. DOI:http://dx.doi.org/10.1145/1864708.1864733
[3] Jie Bao, Yu Zheng, and Mohamed F. Mokbel. 2012. Location-based and preference-aware recommendation using sparse geo-social networking data.. In *SIGSPATIAL/GIS*, Isabel F. Cruz, Craig Knoblock, Peer Krger, Egemen Tanin, and Peter Widmayer (Eds.). ACM, 199–208. http://dblp.uni-trier.de/db/conf/gis/gis2012.html
[4] Jie Bao, Yu Zheng, David Wilkie, and Mohamed Mokbel. 2015. Recommendations in Location-based Social Networks: A Survey. *Geoinformatica* 19, 3 (July 2015), 525–565. DOI:http://dx.doi.org/10.1007/s10707-014-0220-8
[5] Chlo Brown, Neal Lathia, Cecilia Mascolo, Anastasios Noulas, and Vincent Blondel. 2014. Group Colocation Behavior in Technological Social Networks. *PLOS ONE* 9, 8 (08 2014), 1–9. DOI:http://dx.doi.org/10.1371/journal.pone.0105816
[6] Lucas Augusto Montalvão Costa Carvalho and Hendrik Teixeira Macedo. 2013. Users' Satisfaction in Recommendation Systems for Groups: An Approach Based on Noncooperative Games. In *Proceedings of the 22Nd International Conference on World Wide Web (WWW '13 Companion)*. ACM, New York, NY, USA, 951–958. DOI:http://dx.doi.org/10.1145/2487788.2488090
[7] Chen Cheng, Haiqin Yang, Irwin King, and Michael R Lyu. 2012. Fused Matrix Factorization with Geographical and Social Influence in Location-Based Social Networks.. In *Aaai*, Vol. 12. 1.
[8] Eunjoon Cho, Seth A. Myers, and Jure Leskovec. 2011. Friendship and Mobility: User Movement in Location-based Social Networks. In *Proceedings of the 17th ACM SIGKDD International Conference on Knowledge Discovery and Data Mining (KDD '11)*. ACM, New York, NY, USA, 1082–1090. DOI:http://dx.doi.org/10.1145/2020408.2020579
[9] Berardina De Carolis. 2011. *Adapting News and Advertisements to Groups*. Springer London, London, 227–246. DOI:http://dx.doi.org/10.1007/978-0-85729-352-7_11
[10] Martin Ester, Hans-Peter Kriegel, Jörg Sander, and Xiaowei Xu. 1996. A Density-Based Algorithm for Discovering Clusters in Large Spatial Databases with Noise. In *Proc. of 2nd International Conference on Knowledge Discovery and Data Mining (KDD-96)*. 226–231.
[11] Huiji Gao, Jiliang Tang, Xia Hu, and Huan Liu. 2013. Exploring temporal effects for location recommendation on location-based social networks.. In *RecSys*, Qiang Yang, Irwin King, Qing Li, Pearl Pu, and George Karypis (Eds.). ACM, 93–100. http://dblp.uni-trier.de/db/conf/recsys/recsys2013.html
[12] Antonin Guttman. 1984. *R-trees: a dynamic index structure for spatial searching*. Vol. 14. ACM.
[13] Heung-Nam Kim, Mark Bloess, and Abdulmotaleb El Saddik. 2013. Folkommender: a group recommender system based on a graph-based ranking algorithm. *Multimedia Systems* 19, 6 (2013), 509–525. DOI:http://dx.doi.org/10.1007/s00530-012-0298-5
[14] Yehuda Koren, Robert Bell, Chris Volinsky, and others. 2009. Matrix factorization techniques for recommender systems. *Computer* 42, 8 (2009), 30–37.
[15] Defu Lian, Cong Zhao, Xing Xie, Guangzhong Sun, Enhong Chen, and Yong Rui. 2014. GeoMF: joint geographical modeling and matrix factorization for point-of-interest recommendation. In *Proceedings of the 20th ACM SIGKDD international conference on Knowledge discovery and data mining*. ACM, 831–840.
[16] Yi Liao, Wai Lam, Shoaib Jameel, Steven Schockaert, and Xing Xie. 2016. Who Wants to Join Me?: Companion Recommendation in Location Based Social Networks. In *Proceedings of the 2016 ACM International Conference on the Theory of Information Retrieval (ICTIR '16)*. ACM, New York, NY, USA, 271–280. DOI:http://dx.doi.org/10.1145/2970398.2970420
[17] Judith Masthoff. 2015. *Group Recommender Systems: Aggregation, Satisfaction and Group Attributes*. Springer US, Boston, MA, 743–776. DOI:http://dx.doi.org/10.1007/978-1-4899-7637-6_22
[18] Joseph F. McCarthy and Theodore D. Anagnost. 1998. MusicFX: An Arbiter of Group Preferences for Computer Supported Collaborative Workouts. In *Proceedings of the 1998 ACM Conference on Computer Supported Cooperative Work (CSCW '98)*. ACM, New York, NY, USA, 363–372. DOI:http://dx.doi.org/10.1145/289444.289511
[19] Kevin McCarthy, Lorraine McGinty, Barry Smyth, and Maria Salamó. 2006. The Needs of the Many: A Case-based Group Recommender System. In *Proceedings of the 8th European Conference on Advances in Case-Based Reasoning (ECCBR'06)*. Springer-Verlag, Berlin, Heidelberg, 196–210. DOI:http://dx.doi.org/10.1007/11805816_16
[20] Anastasios Noulas, Salvatore Scellato, Cecilia Mascolo, and Massimiliano Pontil. 2011. An Empirical Study of Geographic User Activity Patterns in Foursquare.. In *ICWSM*, Lada A. Adamic, Ricardo A. Baeza-Yates, and Scott Counts (Eds.). The AAAI Press. http://dblp.uni-trier.de/db/conf/icwsm/icwsm2011.html
[21] Mark O'Connor, Dan Cosley, Joseph A. Konstan, and John Riedl. 2001. PolyLens: A Recommender System for Groups of Users. In *Proceedings of the Seventh Conference on European Conference on Computer Supported Cooperative Work (ECSCW'01)*. Kluwer Academic Publishers, Norwell, MA, USA, 199–218. http://dl.acm.org/citation.cfm?id=1241867.1241878
[22] István Pilászy, Dávid Zibriczky, and Domonkos Tikk. 2010. Fast als-based matrix factorization for explicit and implicit feedback datasets. In *Proceedings of the fourth ACM conference on Recommender systems*. ACM, 71–78.
[23] Sanjay Purushotham, C.-C. Jay Kuo, Junaith Shahabdeen, and Lama Nachman. 2014. Collaborative Group-activity Recommendation in Location-based Social Networks. In *Proceedings of the 3rd ACM SIGSPATIAL International Workshop on Crowdsourced and Volunteered Geographic Information (GeoCrowd '14)*. ACM, New York, NY, USA, 8–15. DOI:http://dx.doi.org/10.1145/2676440.2676442
[24] Francesco Ricci, Lior Rokach, and Bracha Shapira. 2015. *Recommender Systems Handbook* (2nd ed.). Springer Publishing Company, Incorporated.
[25] Maria Salamó, Kevin Mccarthy, and Barry Smyth. 2012. Generating Recommendations for Consensus Negotiation in Group Personalization Services. *Personal Ubiquitous Comput.* 16, 5 (June 2012), 597–610. DOI:http://dx.doi.org/10.1007/s00779-011-0413-1
[26] Waldo R Tobler. 1970. A computer movie simulating urban growth in the Detroit region. *Economic geography* 46, sup1 (1970), 234–240.
[27] Jia-Dong Zhang and Chi-Yin Chow. 2015. GeoSoCa: Exploiting Geographical, Social and Categorical Correlations for Point-of-Interest Recommendations. In *Proceedings of the 38th International ACM SIGIR Conference on Research and Development in Information Retrieval (SIGIR '15)*. ACM, New York, NY, USA, 443–452. DOI:http://dx.doi.org/10.1145/2766462.2767711

Using Twitter Data to Estimate the Relationships between Short-term Mobility and Long-term Migration

Lee Fiorio
University of Washington
Seattle, USA
fiorio@uw.edu

Guy Abel
Shanghai University
Shanghai, China
guy.abel@shu.edu.cn

Jixuan Cai
Chinese University of Hong Kong
Hong Kong, China
caijixuan@link.cuhk.edu.hk

Emilio Zagheni
University of Washington
Seattle, USA
emilioz@uw.edu

Ingmar Weber
Qatar Computing Research Institute
Doha, Qatar
iweber@hbku.edu.qa

Guillermo Vinué
Austrian Academy of Sciences
Vienna, Austria
guillermo.vinue.visus@oeaw.ac.at

ABSTRACT

Migration estimates are sensitive to definitions of time interval and duration. For example, when does a tourist become a migrant? As a result, harmonizing across different kinds of estimates or data sources can be difficult. Moreover in countries like the United States, that do not have a national registry system, estimates of internal migration typically rely on survey data that can require over a year from data collection to publication. In addition, each survey can ask only a limited set questions about migration (e.g., where did you live a year ago? where did you live five years ago?). We leverage a sample of geo-referenced Twitter tweets for about 62,000 users, spanning the period between 2010 and 2016, to estimate a series of US internal migration flows under varying time intervals and durations. Our findings, expressed in terms of 'migration curves', document, for the first time, the relationships between short-term mobility and long-term migration. The results open new avenues for demographic research. More specifically, future directions include the use of migration curves to produce probabilistic estimates of long-term migration from short-term (and vice versa) and to nowcast mobility rates at different levels of spatial and temporal granularity using a combination of previously published American Community Survey data and up-to-date data from a panel of Twitter users.

CCS CONCEPTS

•**Applied computing → Sociology;** •**Human-centered computing →** *HCI theory, concepts and models;*

KEYWORDS

Twitter, Migration, Mobility, Demographic research

WebSci'17, June 25-28, 2017, Troy, NY, USA.
© 2017 ACM. 978-1-4503-4896-6/17/06...$15.00
DOI: http://dx.doi.org/10.1145/3091478.3091496

1 INTRODUCTION

Over the last fifty years, migration has played an increasingly important role in population change [16, 25]. Global international migration flows have steadily grown by 7.3 million between 1995-2000 and 2005-2010 [1] and have been at the center of recent political debates across the globe. For example, the Arab and middle East unrest are causing a refugee crisis, with impact on the stability of European societies [10]. Rapid urbanization in China has led to a large number of new immigrants without urban *Hukou* – a record in the Chinese government system of household registration. As a result, there is a large number of immigrants in cities, who hardly enjoy urban welfare [4]. Long-term migration and short-term mobility are also fundamental drivers of the spread of infectious diseases [2, 9].

Despite the growing need for timely and high-quality migration data, measuring geographic mobility and its relationship to long-term migrations remains an elusive goal for demographers. There are two main types of challenges. First, different countries use different definitions of migration. Some countries collect information on immigrants, other on emigrants. Some countries define a migrant as someone who has relocated to a new residence for a period of at least 3 months. Others use temporal frameworks of 6 months or a year. Some statistical offices produce estimate using data from registrations systems. Others rely on surveys. In other words, migration data are often inconsistent across countries. The second main challenge is that data collection and modeling of long-term migration are typically unrelated to the study of short-term mobility, and vice versa. Similarly, researchers who study internal migration typically tie their models to international migration processes only rarely. The lack of interaction between approaches and communities is mostly motivated by the absence of appropriate data that could enable researchers to cross bridges and model migration and mobility at various temporal and spatial scales, within a unified framework.

The primary focus of this paper is to contribute to ongoing work in designing and assessing methodologies for harmonizing migration estimates. In particular, we use geo-referenced Twitter data as a test-bed of migration theory and investigate the link between short-term mobility and long-term migration among a robust sample of social media users followed over several years. By calculating different kinds of migration rates using the same sample of users, we can test for systematic variation in migration estimates along these dimensions. From these experiments, we can further refine tools to harmonize migration estimates, when they are inconsistent or sparse, and develop tools to produce more timely estimates (i.e. "now-casts") of migration. Broadly speaking, we use estimates of migration and mobility generated from a panel of Twitter users to demonstrate the ways in which migration rates calculated using different transition intervals and durations can be modeled along a single curve and be linked together with quantifiable uncertainty. This has important implications for the study long-term migration from short-term migration (or vice versa) when certain kinds of data are sparse.

2 BACKGROUND

The Balancing Equation, the most fundamental formula in demography, states that population change can be expressed as a function of three basic processes: fertility, mortality and migration. It is the role of the demographer to investigate these processes and their trends, either historical or contemporary, and to make projections [27]. As population processes, fertility, mortality and migration all exist at the nexus of biology and sociology, but it is common for demographers to parse the biological from the sociological by creating models that treat a well-defined biological outcome (e.g. total number of births) as the response variable and socio-economic/socio-cultural characteristics (e.g. GDP, or female secondary education) as predictors [3, 7, 24]. Unlike fertility and mortality, however, it is difficult to reduce migration to a strictly biological population process [21]. Even the most basic contemplation of migration quickly leads to tricky ontological questions – what is a migrant? what is a migration? – that are more overtly sociological and political in nature and that necessitate a theoretical framework for understanding the relationship between people, time and space.

The definitional issues entailed in studying migration mean that there has been comparatively less work refining the methodologies for measuring migration and, as a result, migration data are more difficult to use and to compare across contexts. Estimates of migration are sensitive to the definitions of time and space, and reconciling inconsistent migration rates is a prevalent and enduring problem in the study of migration [20, 22, 23]. While efforts have been made to impose standards in certain settings, such as the attempt by European Union policy makers at regulating international migration rates estimated by member states [5], transformations of migration statistics to meet such requirements are frequently applied post hoc thus highlighting the need for sound harmonization methodologies [20].

In migration research, a significant obstacle has often been a lack of empirical data from which to test for systematic differences between inconsistent migration statistics. Though a migration rate that uses a six month threshold to define residence and a migration rate that uses a one year threshold to define residence are observations of the same underlying process (i.e. the movement of individuals or households in space), it is rare for a single survey to produce multiple estimates of migration for comparison and calibration. At the same time, the increasing availability of geo-referenced user-generated content from social media data is offering new opportunities to study migrations in new ways [8, 17, 28]. With a sufficiently large sample of users and many geo-referenced posts from those users, it becomes possible to convert their activity into streams of individual movement which can then be aggregated into migration rates and migration flows using any number of temporal or spatial criteria of the researchers' choosing [11, 13, 14].

2.1 Conceptualizing Migration

People move around in time and space. Migration literature has historically distinguished between two perspectives from which to observe movement, that of the migration event or movement and that of the migrant or mover [6]. The former consists of event data describing the timing of a move, while the latter consists of stock data describing whether or not an individual has experienced a move (these data are usually counts of the number of foreign born). Other scholars, including Rees ([1977]), have included a third type of migration data, transition data, which describes the case where migration is assessed based on residence at two discrete points in time. Most migration data collected by government agencies and used in demographic projections is transition data. Transition data are sensitive to two kinds of temporal variation. In this paper we set aside issues of geographic scale and focus on temporal dimensions of migration measurement which come in two forms: duration and interval.

2.2 The Concept of Duration

Perhaps the least standardized aspect of migration measurement is duration. Duration can be understood as the minimum length of residence necessary to qualify as a migrant rather than as a visitor or tourist. There is no standard in the European context [26] with a variety of durations used (3 months, 6 months, 1 year).

Methodologically, duration is the most crucial element in converting discrete geo-located data into migration estimates [15]. A standalone geo-located data point can tell us where a particular person was at a specific point in time, but it tells us nothing about how long the person remained at that location. For this reason, it is necessary to group geo-located data points together based on their temporality in order to establish an estimate of where each person spent their time.

Figure 1 illustrates our method for imputing residence and migration using this conceptualization of "duration". First we choose two reference points, t and $t+$. We then select the tweets that occurred within some buffer, d, around each reference point. The residence of a user over duration d is determined as the modal tweet location of the user. To avoid double counting tweets, d is never larger than the time between the two reference points.

The intuition about the relationship of duration on migration rates is as follows: the shorter the duration, the larger the amount of short term migration will be captured, and so the higher the rate of migration. If the duration is two weeks for example, then a good deal of vacations, business trips and other kinds of non-permanent travel will be observed in the estimate, regardless of the distance between the two points in time. If, for example, one wanted to estimate the migration rate between July 1st, 2010 and July 1st, 2011, we expect to estimate a higher rate of migration if we use a two week duration to impute location than if we use a month

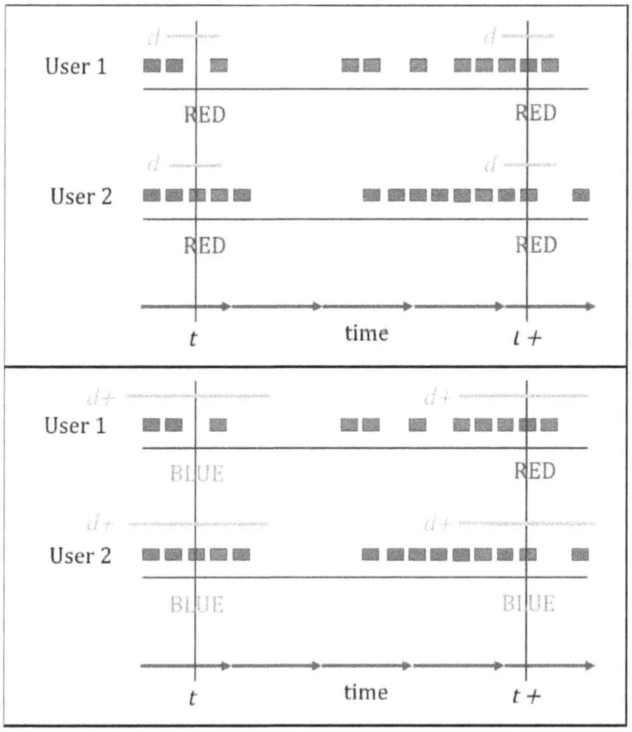

Figure 1: *Illustrative example of the concept of duration. Between time t and t+, two users tweet from either location blue or red. The location assigned to each user (color-coded text in caps) depends on modal location of tweets occurring within the duration (horizontal gray lines) or buffer around the two reference points, t and t+. The data points are the same in the top and bottom panels, but the duration used to identify the location of residence is shorter in the top panel.*

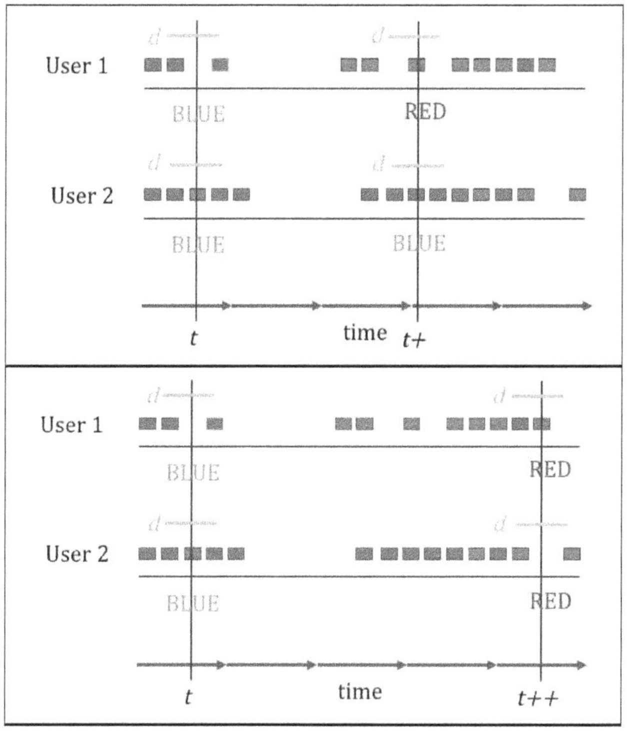

Figure 2: *Illustrative example of the concept of interval. Between time t and t+, two users tweet from either location blue or red. Holding duration constant, the location assigned to each user (color-coded text in caps) is a function of the interval, the time between t and t+ or t++ (vertical gray lines). The data points are the same in the top and bottom panels, but the interval used to identify the location of residence is shorter in the top panel.*

duration. We also expect that as durations grow very large, the negative effect on migration rates should diminish. That is, the change in migration rate should flatten out at large durations. We expect that this will happen because we hypothesize that the distribution of non-permanent trips approximates a negative exponential: the difference between the number of two-week trips and four-week trips is greater than the difference between the number of 30-week trips and 32-week trips. Therefore, the difference between migration rates estimated using two- and four-week intervals should be greater than the difference between migration rates estimated using 30- and 32-week intervals. In summary, we hypothesize that, holding the interval constant, migration rates should fall as the duration increases, eventually flattening out.

2.3 The Concept of Interval

The concept of interval is more straightforward. In order to determine whether a migration transition took place, it is necessary to select two points in time and compare the estimated location of residence. The interval is the temporal distance between two points of comparison. A common way for migration data to be collected via survey is to ask respondents a question similar to "where did you live five years ago?" Five years in this example would be the interval. In such a question, no data on duration is explicitly collected, though arguably some notion of duration is implied by the concept of "to live"/"residency". That is, even if a respondent was on vacation precisely five years before completing a questionnaire with this question, chances are that the respondent will answer with their place of residence five years ago and not with the location where they traveled to on vacation. This does not mean that duration is the same as the interval in these types of survey questions, just that we can expect the duration to be sufficiently large as to capture some sense of "residency".

Figure 2 illustrates the concept of interval as it relates to our method of estimating migration. First, we fix one reference point at time *t* and impute a location for this time based on the modal location of tweets that occurred within duration *d*. Then, we select a second reference point at time t+ and impute a location. To estimate whether a migration occurred for a given person, we compare their imputed locations at the two reference points. As we increase the interval, we keep the left hand reference point, *t*, fixed while shifting the right hand reference point forward in time, i.e. to *t++*. While the decision to fix the left hand reference point was predicated on goal of eventually being able to forecast long term migration from short term migration, it would be just as easy to fix the right hand reference point and work backwards in time. Results from our analysis would be the same.

The intuition about the relationship between interval and migration estimates is as follows: the larger the interval, the longer the period of exposure, and the higher the migration rate. Here it is helpful to think about migration as a risk. Exposure to the risk of migrating accumulates over the interval, so that longer intervals should produce higher rates of migration. That being said, with larger intervals also comes the increased possibility that moves go unobserved. If a person moves from place A to place B to place C over an interval, we would only capture A and C or A and B (depending on the duration and the timing of the moves). Similarly, in the case of return migration, when a person moves from place A to place B to place A, we might capture A and A (depending on the duration and on the timing of the move) and not classify this person as a migrant. Because the risk of return migration also increases with time, we expect the positive relationship between interval and migration rate to be slightly diminishing at large intervals. In summary, we hypothesize that, holding the duration constant, migration rates should rise as the interval increases, but the rate of increase should diminish at larger intervals.

2.4 Linking Duration and Interval

The ultimate goal of this research is to examine the joint effect of duration and interval on migration rates and to assess the potential for estimating long-term migration from short-term mobility and vice versa. When attempting to estimate migration rates from discrete individual-level geo-location data, short-term moves will always be mixed in with long-term moves. It is difficult if not impossible to infer a person's intent to stay in a location based on their (geo-locational) tweeting behavior. A migration rate estimated using a three month interval and a one month duration, for example, will count a relatively large number of individuals as migrants: people who have traveled from place A to place B for a short trip but who will return to A as well as people who have permanently moved from A to B. The question becomes whether one kind of movement is noise to the other's signal or whether short-term mobility and long-term migration can provide information about each other.

In literature on migration there is a theoretical connection between short-term mobility and long-term migration. At the most basic level, greater connectivity and commonality between two places (e.g. capital flows or a shared language) is associated with higher degrees of migration [19]. Similarly, short-term mobility might signal the existence or even presage changing patterns in long-term migration. For example, it is not uncommon that economic migrants who intend to stay abroad for only a short period end up becoming permanent residents of their new country. Alternatively, it is possible that a person who travels to a particular place frequently for business or pleasure simply decides to relocate to that place. Increased short-term mobility between two places results in greater exposure to possible long-term migrants, but the precise relationship has not been explored in the literature.

The growing wealth of social media data provides the means for testing theories about the relationship between short-term mobility and long-term migration in a way that could not be done before. Our analysis is largely exploratory in this sense; however, our basic intuition is as follows: all movements can be plotted along a single curve and that the shape of the curve contains information about the relationship between short-term mobility and long-term migration in whatever context the rates have been estimated.

Our conceptual approach towards understanding the relationship between short-term mobility and long-term migration is to investigate the joint effect of duration and interval on migration estimates. Though conceptually distinct, duration and interval are co-dependent in the sense that duration can never be larger than interval and interval can never be smaller than duration. One method for estimating a curve covering short-term mobility estimates (i.e. estimates with small duration and small interval) and long-term migration (i.e. estimates with large duration and large interval) is to plot a curve using estimates for which duration always equals interval. We hypothesize that such a curve would decrease over short intervals until they reach an inflection point and begin to rise. Demonstrating the possibility of plotting such a curve would be a significant contribution to migration literature in that it would suggest that researchers could then study the nature of these curves (e.g. their shape, the location of their inflection points, and so on) as they relate to different patterns in short- and long-term movement.

3 DATA AND METHODOLOGY

The bulk of data collection occurred in real time from January 2010 to March 2013. In particular we use, as seed, data that were collected for a previous study (see [28]). We then took a subset of the data that includes the geographic coordinates from users who posted geolocated tweets in the U.S. over the period. This resulted in 12.5 million tweets with latitude and longitude from a sample of 62,381 Twitter users. Further data collection was performed in September 2016 by querying individual user timelines from our sample using the Twitter API. This allowed us to collect geo-tagged tweets from the same group of users, but that were posted more recently, since March 2013. We ended up with a total of 15.3 million geolocated tweets. Because the API only provides access to the 3,200 most recent tweets and because geo-tagged tweets are relatively rare, the majority of tweets in the analysis were posted over the original time frame. Duplicates of the original tweets were detected by the unique tweet ID and removed. By using a sample of users who posted over a long period of time and who opened their accounts several years ago, we believe that we are reducing the likelihood of having bots in our sample. In other words, we could have chosen to have a larger sample of users, but we preferred to have a smaller sample of "trusted" users who post on a regular basis. For this analysis, we focused on the U.S., partially because for this first analysis we wanted to avoid the need to model differential usage of Twitter and differences in selection bias across countries.

To make sure that our one-week bins add up to months and years, we made it so each month has exactly four "weeks". We did this by by classifying the first eight days of each month as week one, the next seven days as week two, the next eight days as week three and the remaining days (either eight, seven or five) as week four. While this means that there is some inconsistency in our unit of time, we argue that any impact on our results is minimal, especially at large intervals and/or durations. From this point on, "week" will refer to a quarter of a month. A year using this schema has 48 weeks.

Tweets are converted into migration flows using the following steps:

(1) Each tweet is geocoded to the US county level by the latitude and longitude and assigned to one of the nine US Census Divisions or to a tenth overseas "division" if the tweet originates from outside the US.
(2) Each tweet is placed in a one week bin based on its time stamp. This allows for more efficient aggregation in later steps. An example of user time lines of state-level movement are visualized in Figure 3 which shows flows of our sampled Twitter users in and out of Arkansas.
(3) The tweets are grouped by user ID to create user-specific time lines.
(4) Twitter users are assigned a location based on the modal location of their tweets during a specified duration around each reference date. For example, if we want to know the location of a given user on March 1st, 2011, and the specified duration is three months, we would determine which of the divisions contained the majority of that user's tweets in the six weeks before and after March 1st, 2011. If there is a tie between two or more locations, we assign the location that occurred first over the duration.
(5) Users are categorized based on whether they changed locations over the interval, i.e. whether the modal location at reference point *t* is different from the modal location at reference point *t+1*.
(6) Finally, we sum across all eligible users to create counts of movers and non-movers for each division by specified start date, interval and duration. We then use these counts to calculate migration rates. In the analysis that follows, we aggregate the flows between the nine different regions to estimates of the division-level internal migration rate within the US. In future iterations of this project, it is possible to investigate patterns in the rates calculated between individual pairs of divisions.

It should be noted that the tweeting behavior of users is highly irregular with respect to time. There may be users in the data set who only posted a minimal number of geo-tagged tweets and who did so in the span of a month or two in 2011, for example. When estimating rates, any user for which there is insufficient data (i.e. zero tweets during the specified duration for one or both reference points) is excluded from both the numerator and the denominator of the estimated rate. This means that information from a user might appear in the migration rate estimated between reference point *t* and *t+* but be excluded in the migration rate estimated between *t* and *t++*. Similarly, a user might be excluded in the estimate of migration rate *t* and *t+* using duration *d* but be included using duration *d+*. We proceed with our analysis under the assumption that the pattern at which users are included or not included in our rates does not vary systematically with the rates. There may be cases when this assumption may not hold; however, we argue that in this initial exploration of migration curves, the added benefit of including as many users as possible in our analysis is worth the cost.

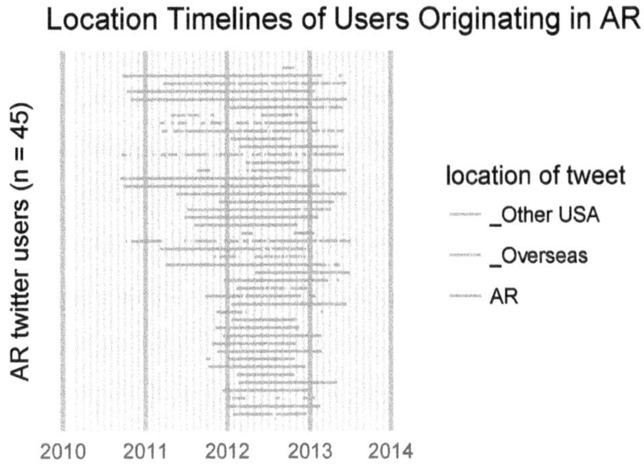

Figure 3: ***Graphical representation of Twitter-estimated migration histories of users originating in Arkansas. Each line represents one user and is color-coded by the estimated location of the user over time (in AR, in a different US state, outside the US).***

4 RESULTS

With data spanning close to six years, there are a large number of migration estimates we can calculate using different combinations of start date, interval and duration. We have calculated migration rates and flows between each of the nine US Census Divisions[1]. For any set of estimates, there are a total of 72 flows, one for each directional pair of divisions (9x8).

4.1 Larger Duration: Smaller Mobility Rate

Our first hypothesis is that there is a negative but diminishing relationship between duration and estimated migration rate. We expect that, as the duration grows, the amount of non-permanent mobility (e.g. holidays, business trips) observed in our estimate will decrease; however, as the duration increases past a certain point, we predict that the changes should flatten out. To test this hypothesis, we estimated a series of migration rates holding the interval constant at 72 weeks (a year and a half) while increasing the duration from two to 72, in two-week increments. To generate multiple estimates for each duration, we shifted the left hand reference date from January 1st 2011 to September 2012 in 6 week increments. This resulted in 15 estimates for all 36 durations for a total of 540 migration estimates.

Results from this analysis are plotted in Figure 4. The blue line shows the estimates of the trend in the data points, from a non-parametric smoother, together with the associate 95% confidence intervals. It is clear from this plot that our hypothesis is largely validated. The relationship between duration and migration rate

[1] https://www2.census.gov/geo/pdfs/maps-data/maps/reference/us_regdiv.pdf

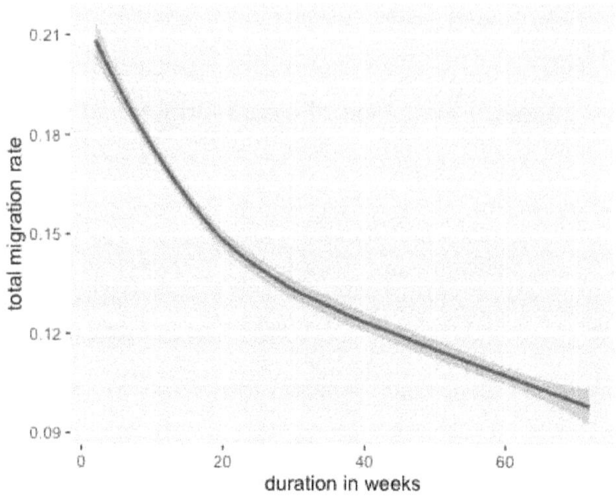

Figure 4: ***Plot of estimated migration rate as a function of duration length, holding interval constant.***

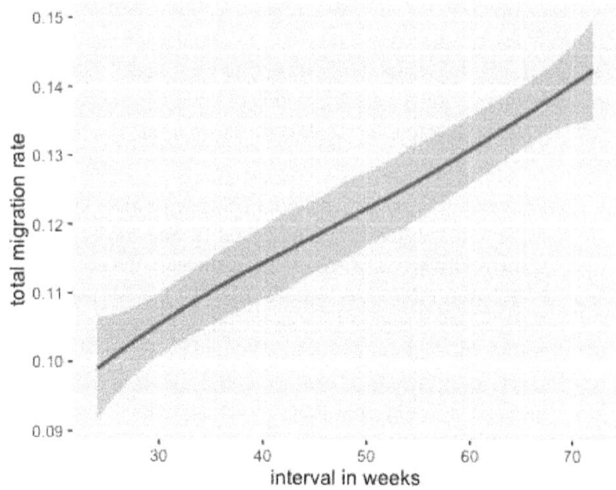

Figure 5: ***Plot of estimated migration rate as a function of interval length, holding duration constant.***

is negative and diminishing. Yet, the plot does not flatten out like we expected. Even at the right hand side where the durations are very large (larger than a year) we still see a fairly pronounced negative relationship. It is unlikely that there are many users who are counted as migrants at a one year duration but who are no longer counted as migrants at one year+one month durations. Perhaps users that tweet infrequently–who are only counted when durations are large–have lower migration propensities than users that tweet frequently. In other words, for very large durations, the data may be more noisy. Future work with larger samples is needed to test the robustness of the trend for large values of duration.

It should be noted here that there appears to be a slight elbow in the trend line between five and six months (20 and 24 weeks). The trend line and information about potential inflection points can be used to evaluate the ideal duration for calculating long-term migration. An unanswered question in the literature is related to the evaluation of the point at which the marginal impact of an increased duration falls below some threshold of acceptable variance. Findings from the duration analysis presented here suggest that the differences between rates estimated with less than six month durations are larger than the differences between rates estimated with more than six month durations. We are not offering a definitive answer, as our results are potentially subject to a number of biases (e.g., Twitter users are not representative of the underlying population, and there may be platform-specific biases in behavior, especially with respect to the use of geolocation). However, we believe that this is a good starting point for further developments using other data sources, and for geographic areas outside of the US.

4.2 Larger Interval: Larger Mobility Rate

Our second hypothesis is that there is a positive relationship between interval and migration rate, but due to return migration, this relationship is diminishing. To test this hypothesis, we estimated a series of migration rates holding the duration constant at 24 weeks (six months) while increasing the interval from 24 to 72, in six-week increments. To generate multiple estimates for each interval, we shifted the left hand reference date from January 1st 2011 to September 2012 in 6-week increments. This resulted in 15 estimates for all nine intervals for a total of 135 estimates.

Figure 5 shows results from this analysis. Here we have evidence that the relationship between interval and migration rate is positive as we expected, but there is no evidence from this plot that the relationship is diminishing. It should be noted that the largest interval in this analysis, 1.5 years, is relatively small. It is not uncommon for migration estimates to be generated from survey questions that ask respondents about their locations two, five, or even ten years before. The amount of return migration that would occur over an 18-month period is likely not very high, and therefore it arguably makes sense that this plot does not show the relationship between interval and migration as diminishing.

Results from this section of the analysis are promising for the prospect of improving data harmonization. The plot clearly suggests that it may be possible to estimate long-term migration from short- to medium-term migration. Certainly two migration rates, one that uses a six-month interval and a second one that uses a one-year interval could be combined to produce an estimate of the migration rate at one and a half years. In future analyses, the interval can be expanded to explore whether the linear relationship between interval and migration rate holds. This would lead to the development of conversion scales that enable researchers to "translate" expected values of migration rates across different definitions of interval.

4.3 Joint Effect of Duration and Interval

Our third hypothesis was that short- and long-term rates of movement could be plotted along a single curve by estimating a series of rates for which duration and interval are always equal. We further hypothesized that this curve would be shaped like a 'U' – declining and then rising as the estimates move from short-term mobility to

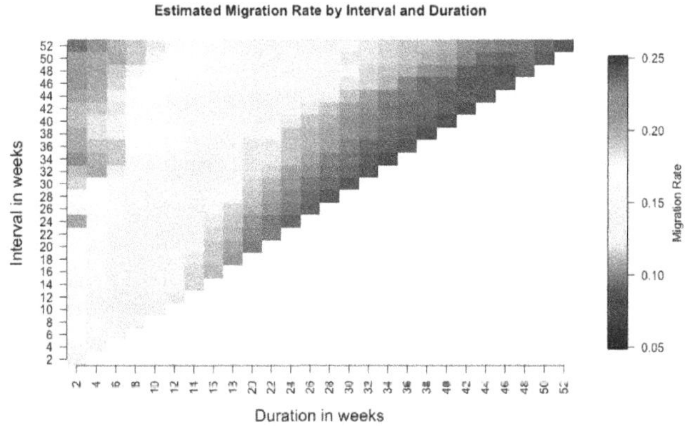

Figure 6: ***Plot of estimated migration rate as a function of interval and duration length. Rates were estimated fixing July 1st 2012 as the starting point.***

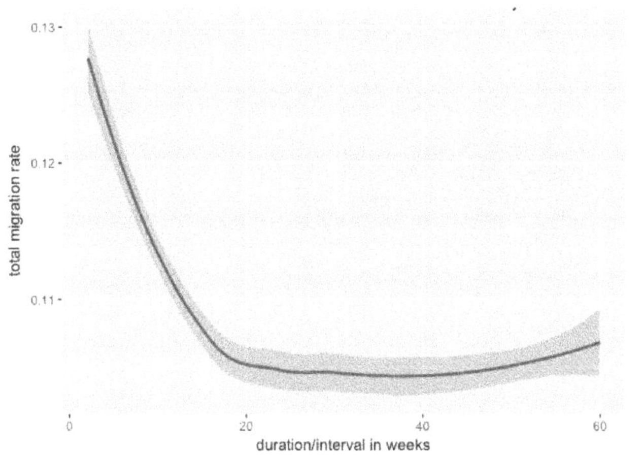

Figure 7: ***Plot of estimated migration rate as a function of duration and interval, where duration = interval.***

long-term migration. To explore the underlying intuition of this hypothesis, we first estimated 351 migration rates with start date July 1st 2011: one for each possible interval-duration pair (2 to 72 by 2) x (2 to 72 by 2) such that interval would always be greater than or equal to duration. The results from this initial analysis are visualized as a contour plot in Figure 6. This plot demonstrates that for nearly all columns (intervals) migration rates increase, and that for nearly all rows (durations) migrations rates decrease, but the two interact in interesting ways.

The next step towards testing our hypothesis involves plotting a single curve using rates for which duration and interval are equal. These rates are equivalent to those plotted along the diagonal of Figure 6. We estimated a large set of such rates using values from two weeks to 60 weeks by increments of two. To ensure that there would be multiple observations of each value, we shifted the left hand start date from January 1st 2010 to January 1st 2011 in one-month intervals. This resulted in 12 estimates of 30 interval-duration lengths, or 360 total estimates.

Results from this analysis are shown in Figure 7, which include the trend line as well as 95% confidence intervals. Once again, our hypothesis regarding the shape of this curve is mostly confirmed. Migration rates decline and then, at some point, begin to increase. What is unexpected, however, is the long trough between 20 and 50 weeks for which the rates stay relatively constant.

5 DISCUSSION AND FUTURE DIRECTIONS

This paper has demonstrated a new use of geo-tagged social media data for exploring unanswered questions related to migration theory. These theoretical questions regarding the relationship between short-term mobility and long-term migration can only be tested empirically using high-volume geo-coded data that come most readily from social media sources. In the analysis above, we have demonstrated that interval and duration behave in ways consistent with our intuitions and migration theory. Importantly, these hypotheses could not have been tested with traditional data sources. Social media data offer new opportunities to validate or confute theories using empirical information. Geo-located social media data suffer from a number of biases and potential issues that may be platform-specific [12, 18]. Nonetheless, data from social media allow for first-approximation type of analyses on which the research community can build. Preliminary findings can potentially lead to the design of new surveys and new data collection strategies.

The analysis that we presented in this paper is motivated by the desire to address an important question related to the theory of migration and mobility. Although the perspectives and approaches that we used mainly come from the toolbox of demographers and geographers, our work resonates well with recent developments in the area of social media analysis and is likely to provide further momentum to a growing field that addresses modeling and understanding human mobility using social media data [13, 14].

Some methods that we used could be refined and the sensitivity of our results to different modeling choices could be tested. For example, we inferred a user's home location based on the modal location of tweets over the course of a defined period of time, which is arguably the most obvious choice. However, one could also use other metrics that include the number of distinct days in a location, the day of the week, and the time of the day [12].

We think of this study as a further step towards a better understanding of human mobility at various temporal and spatial scales. We believe that the research community working with social media data has an unprecedented opportunity to build a unified framework for mobility and migration. This would lead to improved understanding of human movements as well as translate into useful tools for data harmonization that would be very relevant for national statistical offices.

ACKNOWLEDGMENTS

Partial support for this research came from a Eunice Kennedy Shriver National Institute of Child Health and Human Development research infrastructure grant, No.: R24 HD042828, and a Shanahan Endowment Fellowship and a Eunice Kennedy Shriver National Institute of Child Health and Human Development training grant, No.: T32 HD007543, to the Center for Studies in Demography and Ecology at the University of Washington.

REFERENCES

[1] Guy J Abel and Nikola Sander. 2014. Quantifying global international migration flows. *Science* 343, 6178 (2014), 1520–1522.
[2] Duygu Balcan, Vittoria Colizza, Bruno Gonçalves, Hao Hu, José J Ramasco, and Alessandro Vespignani. 2009. Multiscale mobility networks and the spatial spreading of infectious diseases. *Proceedings of the National Academy of Sciences* 106, 51 (2009), 21484–21489.
[3] Stuart Basten, Tomáš Sobotka, Krystof Zeman, M Jalal Abassi-Shavazi, Alicia Adsera, Jan Van Bavel, Caroline Berghammer, Minja Kim Choe, Tomas Frejka, Henri Leridon, et al. 2014. Future fertility in low fertility countries. (2014).
[4] Fang Cai. 2011. Hukou system reform and unification of rural–urban social welfare. *China & World Economy* 19, 3 (2011), 33–48.
[5] European Commission. 2007. Regulation (EC) No 862/2007 of the European Parliament and of the Council of 11 July 2007 on Community statistics on migration and international protection. (2007). http://eur-lex.europa.eu/LexUriServ/LexUriServ.do?uri=OJ:L:2007:199:0023:0029:EN:PDF.
[6] Daniel Courgeau. 1973. Migrants et migrations. *Population (french edition)* (1973), 95–129.
[7] A Garbero and E Pamuk. 2014. Future mortality in high mortality countries. (2014).
[8] Michael F Goodchild. 2007. Citizens as sensors: the world of volunteered geography. *GeoJournal* 69, 4 (2007), 211–221.
[9] Brian D Gushulak and Douglas W MacPherson. 2004. Globalization of infectious diseases: the impact of migration. *Clinical Infectious Diseases* 38, 12 (2004), 1742–1748.
[10] Randall Hansen and Shalini Randeria. 2016. Tensions of refugee politics in Europe. *Science* 353, 6303 (2016), 994–995.
[11] Bartosz Hawelka, Izabela Sitko, Euro Beinat, Stanislav Sobolevsky, Pavlos Kazakopoulos, and Carlo Ratti. 2014. Geo-located Twitter as proxy for global mobility patterns. *Cartography and Geographic Information Science* 41, 3 (2014), 260–271.
[12] Brent Hecht and Monica Stephens. 2014. A Tale of Cities: Urban Biases in Volunteered Geographic Information. In *ICWSM*.
[13] Andrea Hess, Karin Anna Hummel, Wilfried N. Gansterer, and Günter Haring. 2015. Data-driven Human Mobility Modeling: A Survey and Engineering Guidance for Mobile Networking. *ACM Comput. Surv.* 48, 3 (Dec. 2015), 38:1–38:39.
[14] Raja Jurdak, Kun Zhao, Jiajun Liu, Maurice AbouJaoude, Mark Cameron, and David Newth. 2015. Understanding human mobility from Twitter. *PloS one* 10, 7 (2015), e0131469.
[15] Kenneth C Land. 1969. Duration of residence and prospective migration: Further evidence. *Demography* 6, 2 (1969), 133–140.
[16] Ronald Lee. 2011. The outlook for population growth. *Science* 333, 6042 (2011), 569–573.
[17] Yu Liu, Zhengwei Sui, Chaogui Kang, and Yong Gao. 2014. Uncovering patterns of inter-urban trip and spatial interaction from social media check-in data. *PloS one* 9, 1 (2014), e86026.
[18] Momin Malik, Hemank Lamba, Constantine Nakos, and Jürgen Pfeffer. 2015. Population bias in geotagged tweets. In *ICWSM Workshop on Standards and Practices in Large-Scale Social Media Research*. 18–27.
[19] Douglas S Massey, Joaquin Arango, Graeme Hugo, Ali Kouaouci, Adela Pellegrino, and J Edward Taylor. 1993. Theories of international migration: A review and appraisal. *Population and development review* (1993), 431–466.
[20] Beata Nowok and Frans Willekens. 2011. A probabilistic framework for harmonisation of migration statistics. *Population, Space and Place* 17, 5 (2011), 521–533.
[21] Philip H Rees. 1977. The measurement of migration, from census data and other sources. *Environment and Planning A* 9, 3 (1977), 247–272.
[22] Andrei Rogers, James Raymer, and K. Bruce Newbold. 2003. Reconciling and translating migration data collected over time intervals of differing widths. *The Annals of Regional Science* 37, 4 (2003), 581–601.
[23] Peter A. Rogerson. 1990. Migration analysis using data with time intervals of differing widths. *Papers of the Regional Science Association* 68, 1 (1990), 97–106.
[24] Susheela Singh and John Casterline. 1985. The socio-economic determinants of fertility. (1985).
[25] J Edward Taylor and Philip L Martin. 2001. Human capital: Migration and rural population change. *Handbook of agricultural economics* 1 (2001), 457–511.
[26] Xavier Thierry, Anne Herm, Dorota Kupiszewska, Beata Nowok, and Michel Poulain. 2005. How the UN recommendations and the forthcoming EU regulation on international migration statistics are fulfilled in the 25 EU countries. In *XXV International Population Conference, Tours*. 18–23.
[27] Kunniparampil Curien Zachariah, My T Vu, et al. 1988. *World Population Projections: 1987.* JSTOR.
[28] Emilio Zagheni, Venkata Rama Kiran Garimella, Ingmar Weber, et al. 2014. Inferring international and internal migration patterns from twitter data. In *Proceedings of the 23rd International Conference on World Wide Web*. ACM, 439–444.

ELEVATE: A Framework for Entity-level Event Diffusion Prediction into Foreign Language Communities

Govind
Université de Caen Normandie
Caen, France
govind@unicaen.fr

Marc Spaniol
Université de Caen Normandie
Caen, France
marc.spaniol@unicaen.fr

ABSTRACT

The accessibility to news via the Web or other "traditional" media allows a rapid diffusion of information into almost every part of the world. These reports cover the full spectrum of events, ranging from locally relevant ones up to those that gain global attention. The societal impact of an event can be relatively easily "measured" by the attention it attracts (e.g. in the number of responses it receives and/or provokes) in the news or social media. However, this does not necessarily reflect its inter-cultural impact and its diffusion into other communities. In order to address the issue of predicting the spread of information into foreign language communities we introduce the ELEVATE framework. ELEVATE exploits entity information from Web contents and harnesses location related data for language-related event diffusion prediction. Our experiments on event spreading across Wikipedia communities of different language demonstrate the viability of our approach and improvement over state-of-the-art approaches.

KEYWORDS

Societal Events Analysis, Multilingual Web Data

ACM Reference format:
Govind and Marc Spaniol. 2017. ELEVATE: A Framework for Entity-level Event Diffusion Prediction into Foreign Language Communities. In *Proceedings of WebSci '17, Troy, NY, USA, June 25-28, 2017*, 10 pages.
https://doi.org/http://dx.doi.org/10.1145/3091478.3091481

1 INTRODUCTION

1.1 Motivation and Problem

With the availability of world-wide media coverage virtually all over the planet, happenings of various kinds have an almost global diffusion. This reaches from "relatively" minor incidents, e.g. an Oscars mix-up, with a mostly local perception up to globally registered events, such as the Executive Order 13769 aka the "Muslim travel ban"[1]. The effect of happenings like the before mentioned can also be recognized as the "seismic waves" in cyberspace. While a smaller incident might trigger short term reactions in social media only, the impact of a more sweeping one eventually triggers a so-called "sh**storm" or might also find its way into Wikipedia. In particular, we consider an event as "societal relevant" if the user community of Wikipedia creates a corresponding entry.

The aftermath of a societal relevant event is not necessarily limited to a single community, but might also influence others. For instance the before mentioned Executive Order 13769 has so far been translated into more than 25 additional languages. Among these languages are - of course - also those, which are predominantly spoken in the affected countries, including Arabic. The key question, however, still remains: how to automatically assess the impact of societal relevant events with respect to their diffusion potential into foreign language communities? Our hypothesis therefore is: based on the origin of entities associated with an event, we are assuming a predictable information diffusion into the corresponding languages.

1.2 Approach and Contribution

With the availability of knowledge bases (KBs) such as DBpedia [4] or YAGO [15, 33] there are freely available information sources that provide a wealth of knowledge about named entities. Further, with the emergence of scalable tools for interlinking text documents with Linked Open Data (LOD) like AIDA [16, 40] or DBpedia spotlight [24] there are efficient means to give semantics to plain natural text by raising it to the entity-level. By doing so, we are then able to exploit the knowledge captured in KBs and derive valuable background information about the entities involved. In our setting, the information utilized includes the country to which an entity is associated with and the predominant language of this country.

In this paper, we introduce the ELEVATE (Entity-LEVel AnalyTics for Event diffusion prediction) framework. To this end, we investigate the diffusion of unscheduled, or, so-called "unforeseeable" events. These kind of events cover a wide spectrum, such as natural disasters, conflicts, political actions, etc. Specifically, ELEVATE semantically analyses the Web contents by exploiting the information about the entities contained. Figure 3 depicts the conceptual approach of the ELEVATE framework (cf. Section 3.2 for details). Based on the aggregated entity information it incorporates a diffusion model that has been trained and tested in order to accurately predict an event's impact onto foreign language communities. Other than existing methods, our approach is "purely" semantic, which derives all its knowledge from the YAGO knowledge base.

In summary, the salient contributions of this paper are:

- defining a prediction model of event impact,
- utilizing LOD for entity-level (semantic) analysis of the Web contents,

[1] https://en.wikipedia.org/wiki/Executive_Order_13769

ACM ISBN 978-1-4503-4896-6/17/06...$15.00
https://doi.org/http://dx.doi.org/10.1145/3091478.3091481

- experimentation with a multi-label classifier for identifying spread patterns in order to improve recall by simultaneously maintaining precision,
- a comprehensive experimental study on events in Wikipedia covering a time span of almost two decades demonstrating the high quality of our method.

2 COMPUTATIONAL MODEL

A societal event $e \in E$ receives reactions on the Web in form of contents of varying nature like the Wikipedia pages, tweets, blogs and news stories etc. Moreover the Web contents exist in multiple languages. We consider any publicly accessible resource on the Web with uniform resource identifier (URI) as a candidate for the Web content. The set of predominant languages on the Web is denoted by L. A Web content $w \in \mathcal{W}$ about an event e in language $l \in L$ is denoted by w_e^l. All the Web contents associated with an event e are represented by set W_e as shown in equation 1. The named entities $n \in \mathcal{N}$ are the real world objects having abstract or physical existence e.g. persons, locations, organizations etc. A named entity n in the language l is represented by n^l. N_j represents instances of the entity n_j in different languages as shown in equation 2. The named entities associated with a Web content w_e^l are language dependent and given by $\eta(w_e^l)$ as shown in equation 3.

$$W_e = \{w_e^{l_1}, w_e^{l_2}, \dots w_e^{l_p} | l_1, l_2, \dots, l_p \in L\} \quad (1)$$

$$N_j = \{n_j^{l_1}, n_j^{l_2}, \dots n_j^{l_q} | l_1, l_2, \dots, l_q \in L\} \quad (2)$$

$$\eta(w_e^l) = \{N_1, N_2 \dots N_r | r \in [1, |\mathcal{N}|]\} \quad (3)$$

We define the graphs G_{link} and G_{sem} for our link-based and entity-level (semantic) prediction models respectively. The graph $G_{link} = (V_{link}, E_{link})$ is a directed graph with vertices comprised of the Web contents and named entities i.e. $V_{link} \subseteq \mathcal{W} \cup \mathcal{N}$. The graph G_{link} can be constructed using the inlinks and outlinks associated with the Web contents. It consists of two types of edges namely inter-language edges and mention edges. An edge is an inter-language edge if it connects two nodes representing the same named entity or Web content but in different languages. A mention edge connects a Web content to a named entity or vice versa, depending on what type of association between the Web content and named entity is considered. When the graph is being constructed using the outlinks then there will be a mention edge from the Web content to the named entity if the corresponding named entity is mentioned in this Web content. On the other hand, when the graph is being constructed based on the inlinks then there will be a mention edge from the named entity to the Web content if the named entity is referring to it. So the edge set is $E_{link} \subseteq \{(\mathcal{W} \times \mathcal{N}) \cup (\mathcal{N} \times \mathcal{N}) \cup (\mathcal{W} \times \mathcal{W})\}$ in case of outlinks and $E_{link} \subseteq \{(\mathcal{N} \times \mathcal{W}) \cup (\mathcal{N} \times \mathcal{N}) \cup (\mathcal{W} \times \mathcal{W})\}$ in case of inlinks. Thus, edges connecting two nodes representing the same named entity or Web content in different languages are bidirectional.

The Graph $G_{sem} = (V_{sem}, E_{sem})$ is a directed graph with vertices comprised of the Web contents and named entities, and edges representing outlink-based association of the Web contents to named entities i.e. $V_{sem} \subseteq \mathcal{W} \cup \mathcal{N}$ and $E_{sem} \subseteq \mathcal{W} \times \mathcal{N}$. It is worth mentioning that the graph G_{sem} is less complex in structure than the graph G_{link} as it contains the outlink-based mention edges only and is bipartite in nature. The snapshots of the graphs G_{link} and G_{sem} at time $t \in T$ are denoted by G_{link}^t and G_{sem}^t respectively. Language $l_e^0 \in L$ denotes the Web content's language where an event e is being mentioned first. By $t_e^0 \in T$ we define the time of its premier appearance. For the sake of readability, in the following we refer to l_e^0 and t_e^0 by l^0 and t^0, respectively. For the same reason, subsequently G_{link}^t is referred by G_{link} as well as G_{sem}^t is referred by G_{sem}. The event spread $\psi(e)$ is the set of all languages in which there exist Web contents for an event e with $t^0 + \tau_\Delta$ specifying the time passed by after the event's first appearance (cf. Equation 4).

$$\psi(e) = \{l | \exists w_e^l \in W_e \text{ at } t^0 + \tau_\Delta, l \in L - \{l^0\}\} \quad (4)$$

Problem Definition. *Given a snapshot at time $t \in T$ of graph $G \in \{G_{link}, G_{sem}\}$ for an event e, predict the spread $\psi(e)$ i.e. the set of languages in which the event will appear eventually on the Web.*

We describe various approaches for event spread prediction in the following section. The generic prediction process involves four steps to compute the event spread $\psi(e)$. It starts with extraction of the available information for an event from a Web content W_e. This can be entities, inlinks and/or outlinks related to an event describing Web content W_e. Then in the second step, additional information sources based on the model type are explored in order to discover an event's associations with different languages. In the third step, each language is scored based on the findings from previous step. In the last step, for each model the event spread $\psi(e)$ is computed by picking the most relevant languages from the scored candidates.

3 EVENT SPREADING

Our hypothesis is, that the impact of societal relevant events can be assessed by the amount of reactions they trigger in the media as well as on the Web. Further, we assume that there are - like in the real world - inter-dependencies between the different actors involved and their impact on the resulting diffusion.

In order to predict the diffusion of event into foreign languages we investigate two conceptually different model types: link-based and entity-level (semantic). Each model exploits for a given event $e \in E$ the temporal snapshot $t \in T$ of graph $G \in \{G_{link}, G_{sem}\}$. Further, there is one language $l^0 \in L$, which can be identified as the premier language of appearance.

Link-based prediction: Based on the initial occurrence of the event e at time t^0 in language l^0, we can construct a link-based graph $G_{link} = (V_{link}, E_{link})$ at subsequent snapshots $t' = t^0 + \tau_{5\ days}$, $t'' = t^0 + \tau_{10\ days}$ and $t''' = t^0 + \tau_{20\ days}$. Thus, we obtain a representation of all other Web contents $w \in \mathcal{W}$ which is referring to or being referred by the event appearance $w_e^{l^0}$ in the premier language via a hyperlink. On top of the induced graphs at the time points t', t'' and t''' we gain per language information on the "importance" of an event based on the inlinks it receives and likewise in case of outlinks. Thereby, the languages with strong presence among the referring and referred Web pages $w \in \mathcal{W}$ for $w_e^{l^0}$ can be considered as candidates for the spread in near future. Figure 1 depicts the elements of the outlink-based construction of the graph G_{link} at a snapshot $t' > t^0$ in a graphical fashion. In a similar way, the graph G_{link} can be constructed using the inlinks as formalized in the previous section.

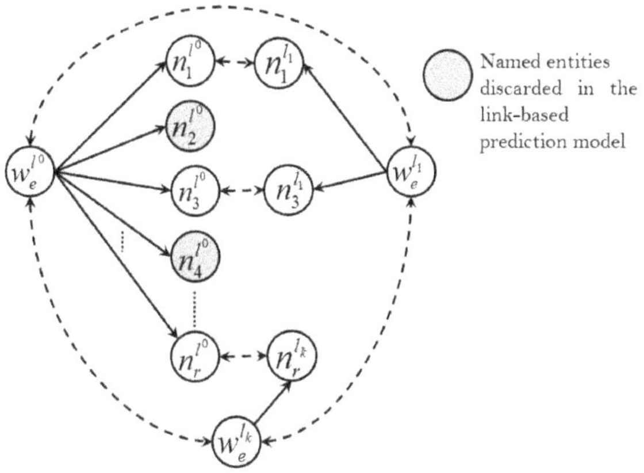

Figure 1: Outlink-based graph G_{link} at snapshot t'

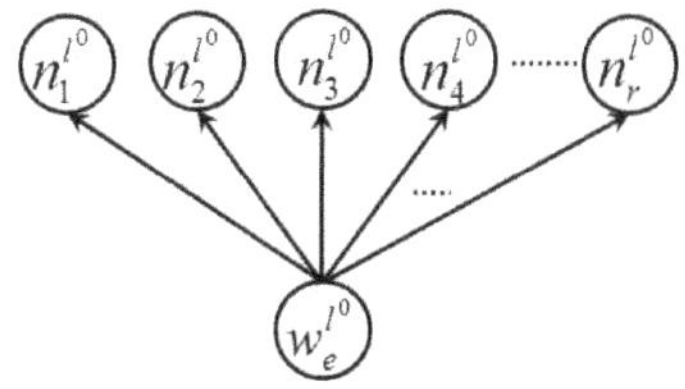

Figure 2: Entity-level (semantic) graph G_{sem} at snapshot t'

Entity-level prediction: As in the previous case, we construct graph based on the initial occurrence of the event e at time t^0 in language l^0 at the subsequent snapshots $t' = t^0 + \tau_{5\ days}$, $t'' = t^0 + \tau_{10\ days}$ and $t''' = t^0 + \tau_{20\ days}$. In contrast to before, we now construct a "semantically induced" graph $G_{sem} = (V_{sem}, E_{sem})$ which is solely induced via the named entities n mentioned in the event's Web page w. At this point, we are "lifting" the event to the entity-level only (without considering the Web graph structure). The core concepts of the entity-induced graph at a snapshot $t' > t^0$ are highlighted in Figure 2.

It is worth mentioning, that any implementation using the link-based prediction model requires "full world knowledge" in the sense that the entire Web graph must be known upon creation of the induced graph G_{link}. In contrast, the entity-level prediction model solely relies on the Web page w of an event e in the language of first occurrence l^0 and the named entities $n \in \mathcal{N}$ it contains. As such, the link-based prediction model has a clear competitive advantage over the entity-level model as it benefits from the inlinks and outlinks as a signal of "authority" and full contextual knowledge.

In the following we introduce in detail the aforementioned event spreading models. To this end, we present various different implementations in order to pinpoint specific characteristics of the underlying model.

3.1 Link-based Prediction Model

In the link-based prediction model we exploit the "neighborhood" of an event. To this end, we incorporate all pages connected to an event's Wikipedia page and induce a sub-graph associated with an event e_i. This subgraph is built upon the interwiki-language links to the same event in other languages ($w_{e_i}^l$) and the associated named entities ($\eta(w_{e_i}^l)$). In order to express an event's importance, their are two notions of authority: outlink-based and inlink-based referral, which will both be investigated in the experimental section. The resulting sub-graph, thus, consists of a set of event related Web contents (in our case from Wikipedia) and entities linked to them.

The link-based prediction model now builds the aforementioned graph. In particular, we induce the connected sub-graph of an event e_i comprising all the corresponding event pages in different languages accessible via the interwiki-links, as well as the entities $\eta(w_{e_i}^l)$ associated with all the before mentioned pages. In order to identify a coherent subsection of the cross-language connections and to eliminate outliers (e.g. pages that link to an event without any other connection to the events and/or entities of this event's neighborhood) we set the scope of the graph onto those entities n that are linked with at least two different language versions of the very same event e_i (formally $n \in \eta(w_{e_i}^{l_1})$ and $n \in \eta(w_{e_i}^{l_2})$ for $l_1, l_2 \in L$). Thus, all those named entities connected to just one language version of an event are discarded, because they do not contribute to the spread of event e_i. As a result, we obtain the graph G_{link} as highlighted in Figure 1 (bold lines indicate those neighborhood relations taken into consideration for prediction, while dashed lines indicate the corresponding translations of an event e_i into foreign languages incorporated for setting the scope). The grey nodes in Figure 1 are the named entities which are discarded because they are linked to only one language version of event e_i.

Based on the previous graph, we adapted several graph link prediction methods incorporating the node proximity measures. The underlying assumption is that the event (represented by its Wikipedia page), its translations into foreign languages and the entities (again connected via interwiki-links) form a "topological" cluster of this event. The intuition behind this approach is that an event e_i originating in the language l^0 - if found via an interwiki-link in a different language l_k - will cover a large amount of common context (in our context the named entities $n \in \mathcal{N}$). To this end, we identified and employed two similarity based measures namely common neighbors [25] and the Adamic/Adar [1].

Common neighbors (referred to in the following as CN) is formally defined by the equation 5 where x and y are nodes in the graph, and Γ represents the neighborhood of a node. In our case, the nodes x and y are the Wikipedia pages corresponding to an event in different languages. The neighborhood of an event e_j first mentioned in l^0 is the set of named entities in its context i.e. $\eta(w_{e_j}^{l^0})$. Thereby, the common neighbors of an event e_j in the language of first appearance l^0 and the event's counterpart(s) in some other language $l_j \in L$ are the entities $n \in \eta(w_e^{l^0})$ which have presence in both the languages l^0 and l^j (formally $n \in \eta(w_{e_i}^{l^0})$ and $n \in \eta(w_{e_i}^{l_j})$ for $l_j \in L$).

$$CN(x, y) = |\Gamma(x) \cap \Gamma(y)| \tag{5}$$

Adamic/Adar (referred to in the following as AA) is formally defined by equation 6. This approach is a weighted reformulation of the common neighbors and has shown improvements over the previous approach [20].

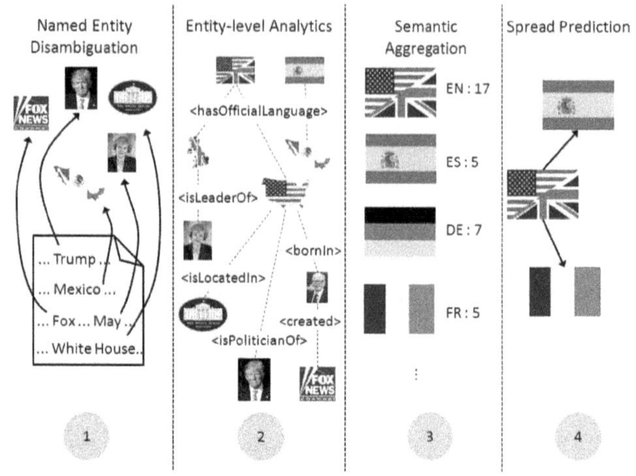

Figure 3: Conceptual approach of the ELEVATE pipeline illustrating the event on the "US-Mexico diplomatic crisis in 2017". (Graphical elements via Wikimedia Commons)

$$AA(x,y) = \sum_{z \in \Gamma(x) \cap \Gamma(y)} \frac{1}{log(|\Gamma(z)|)} \quad (6)$$

To this end, we score all the languages $l_j \in L - l^0$ for the event e_i using above described measures. It should be noted that existence of $w_{e_i}^{l_j}$ is not necessary for scoring a language l_j because all we need is the entities n from $\eta(w_{e_i}^{l^0})$ which exist in l_j. The aforementioned measures can be employed to compute the language scores based on the inlinks and outlinks separately.

3.2 Entity-level (Semantic) Prediction Model

The semantic prediction model aims at exploiting information about the named entities mentioned in a Web content in order to derive their geographical provenance. The entity information is a valuable source in order to interlink Web contents with countries and, thus, languages. Figure 3 depicts the ELEVATE pipeline, which consists of the following four steps:

Step 1:

Initially, we build a sub-graph of G_{sem} corresponding to the Web content of event e in language l^0. To accomplish this, we process the Web contents in order to extract the named entities contained. To this end, we employ a state-of-the-art standard named entity disambiguation tool, AIDA [16, 40]. In the case of Wikipedia this process can be further simplified by exploiting the linked Wikipedia pages and directly mapping them on the corresponding canonicalized entity in YAGO [15, 33].

Step 2:

Subsequently, we derive geographical information about the disambiguated entities associated with event e in previously built graph. For this purpose, we employ country and organization centric YAGO relations, such as `isLocatedIn` or `livesIn` (cf. Table 1 for the full list of relations). The process of extracting the countries associated with the entities is explained in detail in Section 3.2.1.

Step 3:

Based on the countries extracted in the previous step, we are now able to identify the languages associated with the entities mentioned and aggregate those scores. While there are in many cases several official languages associated with a country, we focus on the predominant language spoken in each of the countries mentioned. To this end, we automatically extracted from Wikipedia's "List of official languages by country and territory"[2] where for each country the first language is mentioned. The resulting mapping between countries and languages is available from the project page of ELEVATE[3].

Step 4:

The final process then is the actual prediction based on the before aggregated entity-specific language scores. As a result, we obtain for each event e a language score vector. This vector is subsequently used in order to predict the "spread" $\psi(e)$ of this event into other foreign language communities. For that purpose, we tested and evaluated two different strategies: an adjusted thresholding based method and multi-label based classification approach. Both strategies are explained in detail in Section 3.3.

Relation Type	YAGO Relation
Country centric	`<isCitizenOf>`
	`<diedIn>`
	`<isLocatedIn>`
	`<isLeaderOf>`
	`<isPoliticianOf>`
	`<wasBornIn>`
	`<livesIn>`
Organization centric	`<owns>`
	`<created>`
	`<worksAt>`

Table 1: YAGO relations used for entity-level analytics

3.2.1 Country Extraction. Each language is scored based on its direct or implicit connection to the entities. The language extraction process comes into place, once the mentions of named entities have been mapped onto canonical entities. To this end, the connections of the entities to different languages are discovered using the semantic relations listed in Table 1 from the YAGO knowledge base.

The connections of entities to the languages can be direct by explicitly referring to the associated language or indirect by referring to the another entity from which country and/or language related information can be found. To this end, we transitively traverse the before mentioned relations. Here, we apply two conceptually different strategies:

- Full exploration of languages
- Closest language discovery

When fully exploring the languages associated with the named entities mentioned, we traverse the entire knowledge base utilizing our semantic relations. This results in an exhaustive search and requires tracing of the explored path in order not to get stuck in a loop (similar to depth-first-search with loop avoidance). The pseudo code in Algorithm 1 presents the implemented strategy. Naturally, this exploration strategy is susceptible to "semantic-drift"

[2] https://en.wikipedia.org/wiki/List_of_official_languages_by_country_and_territory
[3] https://spaniol.users.greyc.fr/research/ELEVATE/

and might interlink several countries (and thus languages) that only have very loose ties with the original entity. In order to avoid this kind of unwanted expansion, we have also developed a strategy that aims at discovering the closest language, only. This approach is comparable to a breadth-first-search with a stopping criterion once a country-related entity information has been found. The pseudo code in Algorithm 2 presents the implemented strategy. It is worth to mention that the algorithm does not immediately stop once a country-related entity information has been found, but further explores all other so far discovered entities "on the same level" for corresponding information. This has been done in order to treat entities on each level similarly and avoid misconception due to randomness in expansion. As a result, it is well possible that this algorithm also discovers more than one (different) language information per entity. Apart from above stated two schemes, a basic approach of directly mapping the country name in the event's page to its major language is also experimented.

```
Data: Entity n
Result: Related language set langs and their scores
Stack S= empty
S.push(n)
while S is not empty do
    entity = S.pop()
    if entity is already visited then
        Do not explore
    else
        if entity is a country then
            official_lang = entity official language
            if official_lang is already in langs then
                Increment official_lang score in scores
            else
                Add official_lang to langs
                Assign official_lang score to 1 in scores
            end
            Mark entity visited
        else
            Explore Yago for entity with following predicates:
            (isCitizenOf, diedIn, isLocatedIn, isLeaderOf,
            isPoliticianOf, wasBornIn, livesIn, owns, created,
            worksAt)
            Push explored entities to S
        end
    end
end
```

Algorithm 1: Full exploration of languages

3.3 Spread Prediction

The final process of the above described prediction models involve computation of the spread $\psi(e)$ for each event e from all the scored candidate languages. For this purpose, we employ two techniques namely adjusted threshold and multi-label classification which are described subsequently.

3.3.1 Adjusted Threshold. The thresholding is used to compute the spread $\psi(e)$ by only selecting the top Θ languages from the available set of scored candidates. Here, specifying a suitable threshold

```
Data: Entity n
Result: Related language set langs and their scores
Queue Q = empty
Initialize cutoff level cutoff = ∞
Q.enqueue(n)
while Q is not empty do
    entity = queue.dequeue()
    if entity is already visited or entity level ≥ cutoff then
        Do not explore
    else
        if entity is a country then
            official_lang = entity official language
            if official_lang is already in langs then
                Increment official_lang score in scores
            else
                Add official_lang to langs
                Assign official_lang score to 1 in scores
            end
        else
            if cutoff is -1 then
                Explore Yago for entity with following
                predicates: (isCitizenOf, diedIn, isLocatedIn,
                isLeaderOf, isPoliticianOf, wasBornIn, livesIn,
                owns, created, worksAt)
                Enqueue explored entities to Q
            else
                Do not explore
            end
        end
    end
end
```

Algorithm 2: Closest language discovery

value is crucial as it has a strong effect on the event's spread. Not relying on the heuristic values, we compute the threshold based on the average spread onto other languages in the ground truth. In order to avoid over-fitting we perform the k-fold cross-validation where we learn the threshold using $k-1$ folds and predict the spread for events in the remaining fold.

3.3.2 Multi-label Classification. Intuitively the aforementioned thresholding scheme has the risk of picking the irrelevant languages when there is low variance or no difference at all in the scores of candidate languages. When there is sparsity in the available features (i.e. hyperlinks and entities in our case) it is likely to be the frequent situation that the prediction models assign more or less the same scores to all the candidate languages.

Thus, we model the spread $\psi(e)$ computation for an event e as a machine learning problem and specifically multi-label classification where the labels represent the languages of spread. The scores assigned to different languages by the previously described prediction models are utilized as the features. The spread of the event can be in any of the language $l \in P$ where $P = \{L - l^0\}$. Let $x \in \mathbb{R}^{|P|}$ represents the feature vector for some event e then our goal is to compute the vector $f(x) \in \mathbb{R}^{|P|}$ where $f_i(x)$ determines the membership of x in the target class $i \in P$. We use the one-against-all problem transformation method to transform the multi-label classification into a set of binary classification problem instances. We employ the support vector machine [10] for classification purpose which is considered as a strong choice for large scale multi-label classification. One binary classifier for the individual class is trained to separate the members of that class from the members of all others classes. Given a training set of feature vectors $X \in \mathbb{R}^{|E| \times |P|}$ and corresponding set of class-label vectors $Y \in \{0,1\}^{|E| \times |P|}$, a decision function f is built for each class labels by considering the instances belonging to that class as the positive examples and all the others as negative. The decision function $f_i(x)$ is formalized in equation 7 for a class label i and the test instance x on binary training set of instance-label pairs $(x_j, y_j), j = 1 \ldots |E|$ where $x_j \in \mathbb{R}^{|P|}$ and $y_j \in \{-1, 1\}$.

$$f_i(x) = sign\Big[\sum_{j=1}^{|E|} \alpha_j y_j K(x_j, x) + b_i\Big], \alpha_j \geq 0 \quad (7)$$

$$K(x_j, x) = \phi(x_j)^T \phi(x) \quad (8)$$

Where b_i is a bias parameter for the class i and $K(x_j, x)$ is a non-linear kernel function defined by equation 8. $\phi(x)$ defines a feature mapping from the input space to the feature space. To this end, one classifier is trained for each language which learns the pattern of occurrence for this language based on the provided language score feature vectors. In total there will be $|L| - 1$ classifier that will decide the spread of an event.

4 EXPERIMENTAL EVALUATION

We will now explain the setting of our experiments. To this end, we introduce the experimental set up before presenting the evaluation methods, experimental results and findings.

4.1 Experimental Setup

In order to conduct our experiments we aim at investigating the societal relevant events. One, if not the, most important source for these kind of information is Wikipedia. To this end, we employ the Wikipedia portal of current events[4], which records events of the aforementioned kind around the world on a daily basis. From this Web source, we automatically extracted all current events linked to their own Web page. In the following subsections, we will in detail explain the creation of our experimental data set.

4.1.1 Event Types. Wikipedia covers a wide spectrum of the societal relevant events. These events can be broadly classified into two different types:

- Foreseeable (predicted and scheduled) events
- Unforeseeable (unscheduled) events

The mentioned event types are conceptually very different. The foreseeable events include, but are not limited to, e.g. Olympic Games, periodic elections, Cosmic constellations, etc. These events allow a long look ahead period. As such, these kind of events are commonly anticipated and - as a consequence - listed in Wikipedia a long time before the actual event takes place. Hence, the event's details is subsequently refined over a long period of time (potentially spanning years). In contrast, the unforeseeable events cover a wide spectrum of events, such as natural disasters, conflicts, political actions, etc. These kind of events are, in general, non-predictable and hence get listed in Wikipedia temporally close to the actual occurrence. One can thus observe, that foreseeable are less dynamic than unforeseeable events. In our experiments we focus on those events that are "unforeseeable".

4.1.2 Unforeseeable Events Extraction. In order to extract unforeseeable societal relevant events, we employed Wikipedia's Current events portal[4]. This page lists the chronological order of events covered in Wikipedia. The contents relevant to our experiments cover each day in the time span form 2001 to 2016 retrieved via MediaWiki action APIs [5]. Spanning the 16 years of our experimental time frame, the Wikipedia "Current events Portal" contains links to more than 3,400 unique events. These events unroll across multiple languages which results in more than 43,800 Wikipedia event pages in different languages.

When using information from Wikipedia's "Current events Portal" one has to consider that the page not only contains the links to the events themselves, but also links to other related named entities (such as persons, countries, etc.). In order now to extract from all entities pointed to, those, that represent events, we employed Wikipedia's categorical system. The Wikipedia pages associated with the societal events tend to belong to the categories indicating time, geographical region and/or eventuality nature (e.g. *2017 in American politics, Conflicts in 2017* etc.). The events from year Y are highly likely to belong to one of the categories matching the regular expression "[[Y in %][% in Y]]". By employing this method, we are therefore able to identify the event pages (out of the set all entity pages linked from the portal page).

After having obtained the event pages based on the aforementioned process, the final step is the identification of those which are related to unforeseeable events. To this end, we consider an event as unforeseeable only if it is mentioned on current events portal in the same year as its page creation year on the Wikipedia. This filtering criteria captures the intuition that the event pages related to unforeseeable (unscheduled) events are created close to their actual occurrence in contrast to foreseeable (predicted and scheduled) events where pages are created far ahead of actual occurrence.

4.1.3 Experimental Data Set. From the previously described approach, we obtained more than 1,400 unforeseeable events from Wikipedia between January 2001 and May 2016. In order to perform our predictions, we consider those languages in Wikipedia that have a sufficiently large coverage. Therefore, we identified from the List of Wikipedias[6] those versions that contain more than 25,000 distinct pages (as of January 12, 2017). This lead to a total amount of 102 languages in our data set. Thus, predictions are possible for up to 101 languages (excluding the language of event origin).

It is safe to assume that the event pages in Wikipedia (in their nature as a Web encyclopedia) are monotonically increasing contents. This means, once an event in Wikipedia has been created, it is (in general) not going to be reversed anymore, but - potentially - refined and, thus, increasing in terms of contents, hyperlinks and entities contained. Table 2 confirms this hypothesis. Further, it is evident to see, that the interwiki-links among the event pages at the

[4] https://en.wikipedia.org/wiki/Portal:Current_events

[5] https://www.mediawiki.org/wiki/API:Main_page

[6] https://en.wikipedia.org/wiki/List_of_Wikipedias

	5 days		10 days		20 days	
	Total	Average	Total	Average	Total	Average
Outlinks	76988	55	91134	65	105447	75
Inlinks	9386	7	13900	10	18384	13
Entities	23350	17	26635	19	30285	22
Countries	2433	2	2588	2	2945	2

Table 2: Temporal evolution of prediction parameters

latest time point of our data set constitute "ground truth" of event-spread among languages. The latter observation also indicates that the knowledge about interwiki-links is a very strong indicator of language diffusion (which, in general, results in advantages of link-based approached over semantic approaches). Quality of the data set has been manually evaluated and is found to be over 95 percent accurate. The extracted ground truth events data set is available at the project page of ELEVATE[3].

4.2 Evaluation Methods

We performed extensive experiments on the dataset we introduced before. To this end, we conducted the 10-fold cross-validation experiments applying the previously presented (cf. Section 3) link-based as well as the entity-level (semantic) spreading models. We use the support vector machine library LIBSVM [8] for the classification purpose because of its open source availability. We evaluated different non-linear kernel functions namely the radial basis function and the polynomial kernel function on our dataset, and choose the polynomial kernel because of its best performance among the two. To this end we utilize a polynomial kernel of degree 3 with γ and the cost parameter c tuned for the maximization of F1 score.

We distinguish in our experiments between the different time points of observation. In particular, we consider $t^0 + \tau_{5\ days}$, $t^0 + \tau_{10\ days}$ and $t^0 + \tau_{20\ days}$ after the first appearance of an event in Wikipedia. These time points have been chosen in order to capture the different dynamics an event attracts after its emergence: while events shortly after their emergence (e.g. $t^0 + \tau_{5\ days}$) have not necessarily received their full "attention", the coverage becomes fairly "mature" in due time (e.g. $t^0 + \tau_{20\ days}$). Table 2 depicts the evolution of various core parameters along the temporal dimension where average values are rounded off. It is worth to mention that - not surprisingly - for all of the observed parameters the absolute number of occurrences monotonically increases, which confirms our assumption about the archive-like character of Wikipedia.

4.3 Prediction Results

In this section we present the scores for several tried combination of the methods resulted from the underlying data set features employed and the aforementioned prediction models on top. To this end we have a total of four link-based models and three entity-level models. The evaluated link-based models are the common neighbors count with inlinks ($Inlinks_{CNC}$), Adamic/Adar with inlinks ($Inlinks_{Adamic}$), common neighbors count with outlinks ($Outlinks_{CNC}$) and Adamic/Adar with outlinks ($Outlinks_{Adamic}$). The entity-level models are the direct mapping of country names onto their major language, full exploration of all languages and discovery of the "closest" language(s) connected to the associated entities referred to as *DirectMapping*, $Entitites_{DFS}$ and $Entities_{BFS}$, respectively. Further the adjusted thresholding and multi-label classification are examined for each method. We report the micro-averaged and macro-averaged precision, recall and F1 for three snapshot. Along with this, we report the number of classifications made by each approach denoted by *#PC* which is 11,057 in ground truth. The knowledge base (in our case YAGO) provides support for semantic relations among the named entities represented in 10 major languages only. There exist 1,049 events which first appeared in English and another 362 events in a non-English language. For the non-English languages we observe a resource scarcity in the knowledge base, which is due to YAGO's limitation on core facts extracted from 10 frequently used languages. Out of all events emerging in a non-English language, this results in 197 events in the languages not covered by YAGO. To overcome this shortcoming affecting the processing by semantic methods, we implement the spread onto English as default. In addition to the above methods, we also provide a "naive" baseline called *Random*. This method randomly selects a number of Θ languages (based on the average event spread) from the 101 languages under consideration. As *Random* does not use any temporally evolving event characteristics, the predictions made by this method are independent of time.

4.3.1 Threshold based Prediction. As observed in macro-average scores reported in Table 3, the three entity-level approaches namely *DirectMapping*, $Entities_{DFS}$ and $Entities_{BFS}$ are best in precision across all three snapshots (i.e. $t^0 + \tau_{5\ days}$, $t^0 + \tau_{10\ days}$ and $t^0 + \tau_{20\ days}$). Moreover $Entities_{DFS}$ and $Entities_{BFS}$ perform better than inlink-based methods in F1, only losing to the link-based approaches $Outlinks_{Adamic}$ and $Outlinks_{CNC}$. Adamic/Adar performs slightly better than the common neighbors based approaches.

From the micro-average scores in Table 4, it can be noted that *DirectMapping* is best in precision due to the fact that it makes very concise predictions, because the presence of country names provides a strong clue for event spread in languages associated with this country. $Etities_{DFS}$ and $Entities_{BFS}$ perform lower than link-based methods in recall and F1 which is attributed to sparsity in entity information. It is worth noting that $Entities_{DFS}$ (full exploration of all languages) has best recall among the entity-level methods but loses in precision due to the noise induced from a "semantic drift". In contrast, $Entities_{BFS}$ makes the concise prediction by avoiding this drift and, thus, has better precision. In general outlink-based methods are better in F1, but use much more information that may not be available. As such, the link-based methods have a competitive advantage of having access to the full world knowledge in contrast to the entity-level methods which are limited to the sparse entity information.

4.3.2 Multi-label Classification based Prediction. By transformation of the spread prediction problem as multi-label classification, the classifier learns to predict the languages in the event spread. As the features and output labels both are languages, the classifier is actually also learning the pattern of occurrence of a language with others. The entity-level methods has benefited more as compared to the link-based methods by this setting. Across different snapshots we observe an average improvement of 2%, 4%, 2% in macro-F1 and 6%, 3%, 3% in micro-F1 for *DirectMapping*, $Entities_{DFS}$, $Entites_{BFS}$ respectively when compared to the adjusted thresholding based

	5 days				10 days				20 days			
Method	Precision	Recall	F1	#PC	Precision	Recall	F1	#PC	Precision	Recall	F1	#PC
Random	0.07736	0.07691	0.07714	11288	0.07736	0.07691	0.07714	11288	0.07736	0.07691	0.07714	11288
$Inlinks_{CNC}$	0.23571	0.21023	0.22224	5045	0.25685	0.24077	0.24855	5875	0.28541	0.27803	0.28167	6607
$Inlinks_{Adamic}$	0.23553	0.21011	0.22210	5045	0.25685	0.24151	0.24894	5875	0.28470	0.27854	0.28159	6607
$Outlinks_{CNC}$	0.33301	0.42227	0.37236	10568	0.34840	0.45237	0.39363	10845	0.36049	0.46988	0.40798	11049
$Outlinks_{Adamic}$	0.33230	**0.42473**	**0.37287**	10568	0.34928	**0.45498**	**0.39518**	10845	0.36182	**0.47766**	**0.41175**	11049
DirectMapping	0.35574	0.11457	0.17332	1571	0.36171	0.12032	0.18058	1677	0.36565	0.12337	0.18449	1770
$Entities_{DFS}$	0.48845	0.22548	0.30854	4612	0.48580	0.23545	0.31718	4886	0.48444	0.24076	0.32166	5087
$Entities_{BFS}$	**0.53199**	0.19554	0.28597	2842	**0.53082**	0.20154	0.29215	3068	**0.53368**	0.20823	0.29958	3234

Table 3: Macro-average scores for the adjusted threshold based models (#PC: number of predictions)

	5 days				10 days				20 days			
Method	Precision	Recall	F1	#PC	Precision	Recall	F1	#PC	Precision	Recall	F1	#PC
Random	0.07736	0.07891	0.07813	11288	0.07736	0.07891	0.07813	11288	0.07736	0.07891	0.07813	11288
$Inlinks_{CNC}$	0.42002	0.19164	0.26320	5045	0.41260	0.21927	0.28636	5875	0.41305	0.24686	0.30903	6607
$Inlinks_{Adamic}$	0.41962	0.19146	0.26295	5045	0.41260	0.21927	0.28636	5875	0.41184	0.24613	0.30812	6607
$Outlinks_{CNC}$	0.34832	**0.33291**	**0.34044**	10568	0.35832	0.35152	0.35489	10845	0.36429	0.36409	0.36419	11049
$Outlinks_{Adamic}$	0.34756	0.33219	0.33970	10568	0.35924	**0.35242**	**0.35580**	10845	0.36564	**0.36545**	**0.36554**	11049
DirectMapping	**0.58498**	0.08311	0.14555	1571	**0.57662**	0.08746	0.15188	1677	**0.56836**	0.09098	0.15686	1770
$Entities_{DFS}$	0.36362	0.15172	0.21411	4612	0.35612	0.15744	0.21835	4886	0.35286	0.16266	0.22268	5087
$Entities_{BFS}$	0.49859	0.12819	0.20394	2842	0.48175	0.13371	0.20932	3068	0.47835	0.14000	0.21661	3234

Table 4: Micro-average scores for the adjusted threshold based models (#PC: number of predictions)

	5 days				10 days				20 days			
Method	Precision	Recall	F1	#PC	Precision	Recall	F1	#PC	Precision	Recall	F1	#PC
$Inlinks_{CNC}$	0.18634	0.20129	0.19353	7055	0.20312	0.22926	0.21540	8336	0.23301	0.25911	0.24537	9220
$Inlinks_{Adamic}$	0.21763	0.18534	0.20020	6028	0.22731	0.20412	0.21509	7011	0.25686	0.23574	0.24585	7687
$Outlinks_{CNC}$	0.27909	**0.38017**	0.32188	14169	0.28725	0.39046	0.33100	14320	0.28945	**0.41396**	0.34069	14533
$Outlinks_{Adamic}$	0.30896	0.37136	0.33730	13315	0.30479	**0.40219**	0.34678	14153	0.30112	0.40503	0.34543	14282
DirectMapping	0.31113	0.14553	0.19830	3538	0.31941	0.14587	0.20028	3529	0.32077	0.14912	0.20359	3755
$Entities_{DFS}$	**0.49333**	0.27747	**0.35517**	7179	**0.47678**	0.28490	**0.35667**	7509	**0.47549**	0.28420	**0.35576**	8210
$Entities_{BFS}$	0.45635	0.23128	0.30698	5413	0.46679	0.22763	0.30603	5408	0.46420	0.23649	0.31334	5702

Table 5: Macro-average scores for the machine learning approach (#PC: number of predictions)

	5 days				10 days				20 days			
Method	Precision	Recall	F1	#PC	Precision	Recall	F1	#PC	Precision	Recall	F1	#PC
$Inlinks_{CNC}$	0.36173	0.22242	0.27546	7055	0.36972	0.26865	0.31119	8336	0.35944	0.28888	0.32032	9220
$Inlinks_{Adamic}$	0.41291	0.21693	0.28442	6028	0.39752	0.24294	0.30157	7011	0.40757	0.27310	0.32705	7687
$Outlinks_{CNC}$	0.29162	**0.36012**	0.32227	14169	0.29825	0.37230	0.33119	14320	0.30544	**0.38694**	**0.34140**	14533
$Outlinks_{Adamic}$	0.30079	0.34905	**0.32313**	13315	0.30460	**0.37578**	**0.33647**	14153	0.30647	0.38154	0.33991	14282
DirectMapping	**0.44686**	0.13779	0.21063	3538	**0.44092**	0.13561	0.20743	3529	**0.42104**	0.13779	0.20763	3755
$Entities_{DFS}$	0.32888	0.20584	0.25320	7179	0.32028	0.20970	0.25345	7509	0.30134	0.21607	0.25168	8210
$Entities_{BFS}$	0.37761	0.17819	0.24212	5413	0.36890	0.17392	0.23639	5408	0.36584	0.18193	0.24301	5702

Table 6: Micro-average scores for the machine learning approach (#PC: number of predictions)

performance. The driving factor behind this improvement is the improved recall as observed on Table 5 and 6.

The link-based methods do not improve except slight improvement in micro-F1 of the inlink-based methods. This behavior is generated because of the noise in features of the link-based methods. To explain it, let us take example of an event "AlphaGo versus Lee Sedol". This is an event which has a spread in around 10 languages. The feature set generated using the entity-level method $Entities_{BFS}$ has less than 10 languages which includes some of the most relevant languages to the event (Korean, Japanese, Chinese). On the other hand, the link-based method *outlinksAdamic* generates more than 70 features which includes irrelevant languages like Macedonian, Scottish etc. This makes the training data generated by the link-based methods more noisy and hinders the classifier to learn unambiguous patterns and leads to drop in the performance when compared to the adjusted thresholding approach.

4.4 Findings

In the previous subsections we highlighted the key results from our experiments. As indicated, we performed extensive results on a large number of events captured in English as well as non-English languages. From the threshold adjusted experiments we were able to confirm our hypothesis that entities are an excellent indicator in order to "locate" an events impact, which is reflected precision scores. In order to improve the recall without suffering a big loss in precision, we applied machine learning for multi-label based classification. In fact, this approach drastically increased the number of predictions by inferring common diffusion patterns (cf. Table 7

	Adjusted Thresholding			Multi-label classification		
	5 days	10 days	20 days	5 days	10 days	20 days
$Inlinks_{CNC}$	75	77	77	90	91	89
$Inlinks_{Adamic}$	82	84	82	93	93	92
$Outlinks_{CNC}$	79	82	84	94	96	96
$Outlinks_{Adamic}$	85	88	91	96	96	95
$DirectMapping$	59	59	59	87	88	88
$Entities_{DFS}$	57	57	57	93	93	92
$Entities_{BFS}$	58	58	58	90	89	91

Table 7: Number of predicted languages per method

for details about the number of languages covered in the different prediction methods). Regarding the ground truth of 11,057 spreads, we consider the aforementioned approach as a suitable balance between precision and recall. In conclusion, the most important findings from the experiments with our ELEVATE framework are the following:

- predictions based on ELEVATE solely rely on semantic information without the need of exploiting neighborhood dependencies that require "'full world knowledge",
- the ELEVATE framework scores best among all competitors on macro precision showing that entity information really capture the "semantics" of an event,
- when applying machine learning for multi-label classification ELEVATE is able to significantly increase the number of predictions, which helps to increase recall by simultaneously preserving a high quality of precision.

5 RELATED WORK

The state of the art and related studies with reference to our work can be put into the following groups:

Societal Event Analytics. Societal event analytics deals with the detection, prediction and analysis of the events from the Web data. Prior related works include mining the Web data to analyze and predict the behavior of crowd. In [18], the authors investigate predictive signals in the Web data collected from 300,000 sources to predict the upcoming societal events. Evidential increase in the likelihood of occurrence of the protests, disease epidemics and other societal events can be observed from the news stories and social media [28]. Recently social media has witnessed a tremendous interest for the event analytics because of its real time nature. Wikipedia has been intensively studied in its nature as a collaboratively curated encyclopedic information platform [2, 14, 23, 26, 38]. Various studies are conducted on Wikipedia data for detecting the trending topics/pages. Most of such studies considered the page views statistics for predicting the trends. In [2], authors propose a model WikiTopics which provides the textual explanation about which articles on Wikipedia are trending and for what reason. In [26], authors used Wikipedia page views data to aid the event detection on Twitter. [13] investigated the events and entity related information flow between the news and articles on Wikipedia. In addition, Twitter has been widely used for detecting the societal events and popular trends [3, 27]. It has served as a source for analyzing the variety of societal happenings from detecting earthquake[30] to a small scale incident [31]. [27] presents an algorithm based on locality-sensitive hashing to detect first story from tweets stream with low computational cost. To the best of our knowledge no study has been performed on the entity-level event diffusion prediction.

Future Link Prediction. Future link prediction has been applied to solve variety of tasks from the disparate fields where underlying data is of the form of network [37]. Particularly it has been used to analyze the social networks such as collaboration in co-authorship networks [21], detecting the links in terrorists association networks [9] and recommendation in the social networks. More recent work involves suggesting who to follow and why in the social networks [5], and link prediction in coupled networks [12]. Link prediction methods are broadly categorized in three types namely similarity based methods, maximum likelihood methods and probabilistic methods [22]. Our decision to employ the local similarity based methods is driven by their effectiveness [21] and simplicity in computation. The methods based on node neighborhoods include common neighbors, Jaccard coefficient [17], Adamic/Adar [1] and preferential attachment etc[19]. These methods use the local information to the node in order to predict its likelihood of forming a link with other nodes in the graph. To this end, the indices are computed using local neighborhood information only.

Knowledge Based Models. Using the knowledge bases and other openly available world knowledge like Wikipedia, has been proven to improve across a variety of tasks in information retrieval [11] and natural language processing [32]. With the availability of the knowledge bases like DBpedia [4], Yago [15, 33], FreeBase [6] which provide expansion of knowledge in spatial and temporal dimension, plethora of tasks from the diverse disciplines have benefited. Few recent studies include automatic selection of meaningful concepts for detection of complex events [39], disambiguation of named entities [36] and topic classification in the social media [7]. However, none of them addresses the issue of event diffusion on the Web.

Multi-label Classification. Multi-label classification involves the learning of multiple labels from a set of given examples, in contrast to the single-label classification where each example is associated with single label. Multi-label classification has been increasingly becoming need for many real world modern problems such as protein function categorization, music genre classification and scene classification [35]. There are two ways of approaching a multi-label classification problem namely by transformation or adaptation. Problem transformation methods transform the problem in binary classification whereas in contrast adaptation methods deal the problem in full form which involves more complexity. We use one-against-all SVM [29] transformation as described in Section 3.3.2 because it is considered most suitable for the large scale classification [34].

6 CONCLUSIONS AND FUTURE WORK

In this paper, we presented the ELEVATE system in order to address the issue of predicting the spread of information into foreign language communities. Our unique method introduces a novel method of exploiting entity information from Web contents and harnessing the location related data for language-related event diffusion prediction. In our comprehensive experiments on unforeseeable events covered in Wikipedia, we show that the exploitation of entity information allows a highly accurate prediction of spread into communities of different language. In particular, ELEVATE doesn't require "full world knowledge" based on inlinks, which is required for the link-based approaches, but impractical in practice. By automatically learning typical patterns of diffusion we are furthermore able to increase the number of predictions (recall), by simultaneously preserving a high quality of precision.

As for future work, we will look into event spreading in Web contents beyond Wikipedia. To this end, we will study event patterns in social media (such as twitter) and apply our framework to these contents. In addition, we will also consider additional parameters, such as the event type in order to improve prediction the spread diffusion even further.

REFERENCES

[1] Lada A Adamic and Eytan Adar. 2003. Friends and neighbors on the Web. *Social Networks* 25, 3 (2003), 211 – 230. https://doi.org/10.1016/S0378-8733(03)00009-1

[2] Byung Gyu Ahn, Benjamin Van Durme, and Chris Callison-Burch. 2011. WikiTopics: What is Popular on Wikipedia and Why. In *Proceedings of the Workshop on Automatic Summarization for Different Genres, Media, and Languages (WASDGML '11)*. Association for Computational Linguistics, Stroudsburg, PA, USA, 33–40. http://dl.acm.org/citation.cfm?id=2018987.2018992

[3] Farzindar Atefeh and Wael Khreich. 2013. A survey of techniques for event detection in Twitter. *Computational Intelligence* 31, 1 (2013), 132–164.

[4] S. Auer, C. Bizer, G. Kobilarov, J. Lehmann, R. Cyganiak, and Z. G. Ives. 2007. DBpedia: A Nucleus for a Web of Open Data. In *ISWC/ASWC*. 722–735.

[5] Nicola Barbieri, Francesco Bonchi, and Giuseppe Manco. 2014. Who to Follow and Why: Link Prediction with Explanations. In *Proceedings of the 20th ACM SIGKDD International Conference on Knowledge Discovery and Data Mining (KDD '14)*. ACM, New York, NY, USA, 1266–1275. https://doi.org/10.1145/2623330.2623733

[6] Kurt Bollacker, Colin Evans, Praveen Paritosh, Tim Sturge, and Jamie Taylor. 2008. Freebase: A Collaboratively Created Graph Database for Structuring Human Knowledge. In *Proceedings of the 2008 ACM SIGMOD International Conference on Management of Data (SIGMOD '08)*. ACM, New York, NY, USA, 1247–1250. https://doi.org/10.1145/1376616.1376746

[7] Amparo E. Cano, Andrea Varga, Matthew Rowe, Fabio Ciravegna, and Yulan He. 2013. Harnessing Linked Knowledge Sources for Topic Classification in Social Media. In *Proceedings of the 24th ACM Conference on Hypertext and Social Media (HT '13)*. ACM, New York, NY, USA, 41–50. https://doi.org/10.1145/2481492.2481497

[8] Chih-Chung Chang and Chih-Jen Lin. 2011. LIBSVM: A library for support vector machines. *ACM Transactions on Intelligent Systems and Technology* 2 (2011), 27:1–27:27. Issue 3. Software available at http://www.csie.ntu.edu.tw/~cjlin/libsvm.

[9] Clauset Aaron, Moore Cristopher, and Newman M. E. J. 2008. Hierarchical structure and the prediction of missing links in networks. *Nature* 453, 7191 (may 2008), 98–101. https://doi.org/10.1038/nature06830 10.1038/nature06830.

[10] Corinna Cortes and Vladimir Vapnik. 1995. Support-Vector Networks. *Machine Learning* 20, 3 (1995), 273–297. https://doi.org/10.1023/A:1022627411411

[11] Jeffrey Dalton, Laura Dietz, and James Allan. 2014. Entity Query Feature Expansion Using Knowledge Base Links. In *Proceedings of the 37th International ACM SIGIR Conference on Research & Development in Information Retrieval (SIGIR '14)*. ACM, New York, NY, USA, 365–374. https://doi.org/10.1145/2600428.2609628

[12] Yuxiao Dong, Jing Zhang, Jie Tang, Nitesh V. Chawla, and Bai Wang. 2015. CoupledLP: Link Prediction in Coupled Networks. In *Proceedings of the 21th ACM SIGKDD International Conference on Knowledge Discovery and Data Mining (KDD '15)*. ACM, New York, NY, USA, 199–208. https://doi.org/10.1145/2783258.2783329

[13] Besnik Fetahu, Abhijit Anand, and Avishek Anand. 2015. How much is Wikipedia Lagging Behind News?. In *Proceedings of the ACM Web Science Conference*. ACM, 28.

[14] Ana Freire, Matteo Manca, Diego Saez-Trumper, David Laniado, Ilaria Bordino, Francesco Gullo, and Andreas Kaltenbrunner. 2016. Graph-Based Breaking News Detection on Wikipedia. *Wiki Workshop, ICWSM 2016* 6 (2016), 1.

[15] J. Hoffart, F. M. Suchanek, K. Berberich, and G. Weikum. 2013. YAGO2: A spatially and temporally enhanced knowledge base from Wikipedia. *Artificial Intelligence* 194 (2013), 28–61.

[16] J. Hoffart, M. Amir Yosef, I. Bordino, H. Fürstenau, M. Pinkal, M. Spaniol, S. Thater, and G. Weikum. 2011. Robust Disambiguation of Named Entities in Text. In *Conference on Empirical Methods in Natural Language Processing (EMNLP)*. 782–792.

[17] Paul Jaccard. 1901. Étude comparative de la distribution florale dans une portion des Alpes et des Jura. *Bulletin del la Société Vaudoise des Sciences Naturelles* 37 (1901), 547–579.

[18] Nathan Kallus. 2014. Predicting Crowd Behavior with Big Public Data. In *Proceedings of the 23rd International Conference on World Wide Web (WWW '14 Companion)*. ACM, New York, NY, USA, 625–630. https://doi.org/10.1145/2567948.2579233

[19] Myunghwan Kim and Jure Leskovec. *The Network Completion Problem: Inferring Missing Nodes and Edges in Networks*. 47–58. https://doi.org/10.1137/1.9781611972818.5 arXiv:http://epubs.siam.org/doi/pdf/10.1137/1.9781611972818.5

[20] David Liben-Nowell and Jon Kleinberg. 2007. The link-prediction problem for social networks. *Journal of the American Society for Information Science and Technology* 58, 7 (2007), 1019–1031. https://doi.org/10.1002/asi.20591

[21] David Liben-Nowell and Jon Kleinberg. 2007. The link-prediction problem for social networks. *journal of the Association for Information Science and Technology* 58, 7 (2007), 1019–1031.

[22] Linyuan Lü and Tao Zhou. 2011. Link prediction in complex networks: A survey. *Physica A: Statistical Mechanics and its Applications* 390, 6 (2011), 1150 – 1170. https://doi.org/10.1016/j.physa.2010.11.027

[23] David J McIver and John S Brownstein. 2014. Wikipedia usage estimates prevalence of influenza-like illness in the United States in near real-time. *PLoS Comput Biol* 10, 4 (2014), e1003581.

[24] Pablo N. Mendes, Max Jakob, Andrés García-Silva, and Christian Bizer. 2011. DBpedia Spotlight: Shedding Light on the Web of Documents. In *Proceedings of the 7th International Conference on Semantic Systems (I-Semantics '11)*. ACM, New York, NY, USA, 1–8.

[25] M. E. J. Newman. 2001. Clustering and preferential attachment in growing networks. *Phys. Rev. E* 64 (Jul 2001), 025102. Issue 2. https://doi.org/10.1103/PhysRevE.64.025102

[26] Miles Osborne, Saša Petrovic, Richard McCreadie, Craig Macdonald, and Iadh Ounis. 2012. Bieber no more: First story detection using Twitter and Wikipedia. In *SIGIR 2012 Workshop on Time-aware Information Access*. ACM.

[27] Saša Petrović, Miles Osborne, and Victor Lavrenko. 2010. Streaming First Story Detection with Application to Twitter. In *Human Language Technologies: The 2010 Annual Conference of the North American Chapter of the Association for Computational Linguistics (HLT '10)*. Association for Computational Linguistics, Stroudsburg, PA, USA, 181–189. http://dl.acm.org/citation.cfm?id=1857999.1858020

[28] Kira Radinsky and Eric Horvitz. 2013. Mining the Web to Predict Future Events. In *Proceedings of the Sixth ACM International Conference on Web Search and Data Mining (WSDM '13)*. ACM, New York, NY, USA, 255–264. https://doi.org/10.1145/2433396.2433431

[29] Ryan Rifkin and Aldebaro Klautau. 2004. In Defense of One-Vs-All Classification. *J. Mach. Learn. Res.* 5 (Dec. 2004), 101–141. http://dl.acm.org/citation.cfm?id=1005332.1005336

[30] Takeshi Sakaki, Makoto Okazaki, and Yutaka Matsuo. 2010. Earthquake Shakes Twitter Users: Real-time Event Detection by Social Sensors. In *Proceedings of the 19th International Conference on World Wide Web (WWW '10)*. ACM, New York, NY, USA, 851–860. https://doi.org/10.1145/1772690.1772777

[31] Axel Schulz, Benedikt Schmidt, and Thorsten Strufe. 2015. Small-Scale Incident Detection Based on Microposts. In *Proceedings of the 26th ACM Conference on Hypertext & Social Media (HT '15)*. ACM, New York, NY, USA, 3–12. https://doi.org/10.1145/2700171.2791038

[32] Michael Strube and Simone Paolo Ponzetto. 2006. WikiRelate! Computing Semantic Relatedness Using Wikipedia. In *Proceedings of the 21st National Conference on Artificial Intelligence - Volume 2 (AAAI'06)*. AAAI Press, 1419–1424. http://dl.acm.org/citation.cfm?id=1597348.1597414

[33] F. M. Suchanek, G. Kasneci, and G. Weikum. 2007. YAGO: A Core of Semantic Knowledge - Unifying WordNet and Wikipedia. In *16th International World Wide Web Conference (WWW 2007)*. ACM, 697–706.

[34] Lei Tang, Suju Rajan, and Vijay K. Narayanan. 2009. Large Scale Multi-label Classification via Metalabeler. In *Proceedings of the 18th International Conference on World Wide Web (WWW '09)*. ACM, New York, NY, USA, 211–220. https://doi.org/10.1145/1526709.1526738

[35] Grigorios Tsoumakas and Ioannis Katakis. 2006. Multi-label classification: An overview. *International Journal of Data Warehousing and Mining* 3, 3 (2006).

[36] Ricardo Usbeck, Axel-Cyrille Ngonga Ngomo, Michael Röder, Daniel Gerber, Sandro Athaide Coelho, Sören Auer, and Andreas Both. 2014. *AGDISTIS - Graph-Based Disambiguation of Named Entities Using Linked Data*. Springer International Publishing, Cham, 457–471. https://doi.org/10.1007/978-3-319-11964-9_29

[37] Peng Wang, BaoWen Xu, YuRong Wu, and XiaoYu Zhou. 2015. Link prediction in social networks: the state-of-the-art. *Science China Information Sciences* 58, 1 (2015), 1–38. https://doi.org/10.1007/s11432-014-5237-y

[38] Stewart Whiting, Joemon Jose, and Omar Alonso. 2014. Wikipedia As a Time Machine. In *Proceedings of the 23rd International Conference on World Wide Web (WWW '14 Companion)*. ACM, New York, NY, USA, 857–862. https://doi.org/10.1145/2567948.2579048

[39] Y. Yan, Y. Yang, D. Meng, G. Liu, W. Tong, A. G. Hauptmann, and N. Sebe. 2015. Event Oriented Dictionary Learning for Complex Event Detection. *IEEE Transactions on Image Processing* 24, 6 (June 2015), 1867–1878. https://doi.org/10.1109/TIP.2015.2413294

[40] M. A. Yosef, J. Hoffart, I. Bordino, M. Spaniol, and G. Weikum. 2011. AIDA: An Online Tool for Accurate Disambiguation of Named Entities in Text and Tables. In *Proc. of the 37th Intl. Conference on Very Large Databases (VLDB 2011), August 29 - September 3, Seattle, WA, USA.* 1450–1453.

Predicting Rising Follower Counts on Twitter Using Profile Information

Juergen Mueller
University of Kassel
Research Center for Information System Design (ITeG)
Pfannkuchstr. 1
34121 Kassel, Germany
mueller@cs.uni-kassel.de

Gerd Stumme
University of Kassel
Research Center for Information System Design (ITeG)
Pfannkuchstr. 1
34121 Kassel, Germany
stumme@cs.uni-kassel.de

ABSTRACT

When evaluating the cause of one's popularity on Twitter, one thing is considered to be the main driver: Many tweets. There is debate about the kind of tweet one should publish, but little beyond tweets. Of particular interest is the information provided by each Twitter user's profile page. One of the features are the given names on those profiles. Studies on psychology and economics identified correlations of the first name to, e.g., one's school marks or chances of getting a job interview in the US. Therefore, we are interested in the influence of those profile information on the follower count. We addressed this question by analyzing the profiles of about 6 Million Twitter users. All profiles are separated into three groups: Users that have a first name, English words, or neither of both in their name field. The assumption is that names and words influence the discoverability of a user and subsequently his/her follower count. We propose a classifier that labels users who will increase their follower count within a month by applying different models based on the user's group. The classifiers are evaluated with the area under the receiver operator curve score and achieves a score above 0.800.

CCS CONCEPTS

• **Information systems** → **Probabilistic retrieval models**; **Information extraction**; **Clustering and classification**; • **Computing methodologies** → *Machine learning*; • **Human-centered computing** → *Social media*;

KEYWORDS

Prediction; Correlational Analysis; Classification; Social Network Analysis; Experimental Study; Onomastics

ACM Reference format:
Juergen Mueller and Gerd Stumme. 2017. Predicting Rising Follower Counts on Twitter Using Profile Information. In *Proceedings of WebSci '17, Troy, NY, USA, June 25-28, 2017,* 10 pages.
https://doi.org/10.1145/3091478.3091490

ACM ISBN 978-1-4503-4896-6/17/06...$15.00
https://doi.org/10.1145/3091478.3091490

1 INTRODUCTION

Twitter is with 320 million monthly active users [29] one of the largest online social networks. It is important to follow the "right" users to maximize the user experience. But, what are the "right" users? Most scientists deem those users as "right" that produce a huge amount of interesting tweets—measured by their retweet, mention, and favorite rate—and those that have a huge follower count [1, 4, 6, 8, 12–14, 21, 23, 30]. This assumption is supported by a strong correlation between the number of tweets and the number of followers that are observed on Twitter by Beevolve[1] in October 2012 as shown in Figure 1.

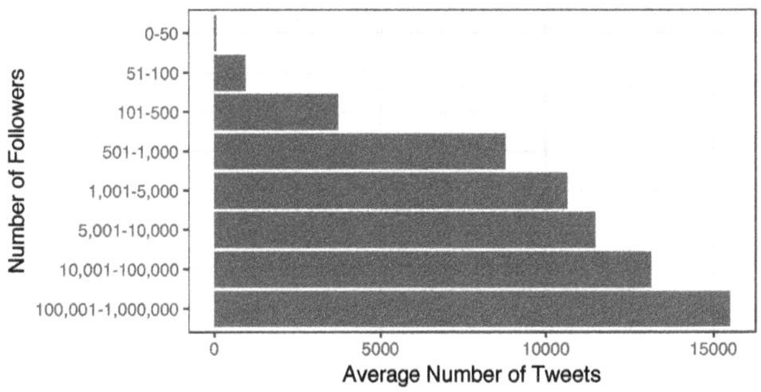

Figure 1: Average number of tweets versus follower count (Source: Beevolve).

With this assumption in mind, one could wonder whether these traits cover the manual discovery of new users to follow. Twitter offers only a text-based search to discover those users (recommended users aside). The search function focuses on the text information, given on a user's profile page. This means that a good selection of descriptive should increase visibility, because those terms are more likely to be entered in the search function.

The name is of interest, because studies in psychology and economics have identified correlations related to one's first name. Having a popular name helps to obtain good marks at school [16], while having a distinctively black name reduces your chances of getting a job interview [5, 10]. Some names are strong signals for one's ideology and, consequently, could attract more likeminded people [22]. Therefore, our aim is to analyze the impact that the profile information as well as the content of name field have on the

[1] Source: http://beevolve.com/twitter-statistics

follower count. Understanding the influence of those information on the popularity can be used to increase the discoverability.

In this paper, we first identify the influence of the content of the real name field of a Twitter user has on her/his follower count. Then we identify those profile features that have the strongest relation to the increase of the follower count of that user. We will use those features in a novel user classifier that labels those users that are likely to gain more traction on Twitter—i.e., increase their follower count within a month. These users are of interest, because they could become the stars of tomorrow. The recommender utilizes only that information given in the user profile of the Twitter users. We do so, because of the following reasons:

(1) It reflects the way a user would scan the network for potential users to follow using the search feature rather than the timeline.
(2) It enables us to cover far more users than if we would include the status messages as well. The reason for this is that the Twitter API rate allows far more queries for different user profile information than it does for the timeline information of dedicated users. For instance, we could get all profile information from the dataset used for this paper within 6 days—crawling the tweets would take about 68 months.

Accordingly, we focus on those data that are accessible using the user profile information for answering the following research questions:

(1) What is the relation of the real name field and the popularity of a Twitter user?
(2) Which information from a user profile has the strongest relation to the popularity-gain of the users?
(3) Can we classify users that are about to increase their follower count?

We will address each of those research questions in an experiment that will be described in this paper.

For this work, we refer to the content of the real name field on a profile page of a Twitter users as that users' name. A Twitter user always has a second name that is used as human-readable unique identifier (see Figure 2). This name is called username and is referred to in some literature as screen name. It is prefixed with an @-sign and not the content of our study.

We propose an approach to label users that will or will increase their follower count within the next month. It uses a different classification model based on the content of the users' name. It differs between three types of user name contents: Contains a given name, contains English words, and contains neither of both. Each group's classifier can use a different model (e.g., Gradient Boosting Machine, Naive Bayes, etc.) that is trained with distinct parameters and features based on the corresponding group. We can obtain classification results of above 0.800 across all groups as measured by the area under the receiver operator curve (AUC) based on the classification probability.

The remainder of this paper is structured as follows: First, we will lay out the previous work on popularity-prediction as well as findings about given names in the following section. We then describe the used data of Twitter, English words, and names in the data section. Our first research question is addressed in Section 4, where we analyze the relation between the real name field and the follower count. The main contribution of this paper is presented in Section 5 where we discuss our second research question, where we identify those profile features that have a statistical significant relation with an increase of the follower count. All findings are then applied in Section 6, where we present our classifier that assigns users to two categories: users that will increase their follower count and users that will not. Finally, we end our paper with the conclusions section.

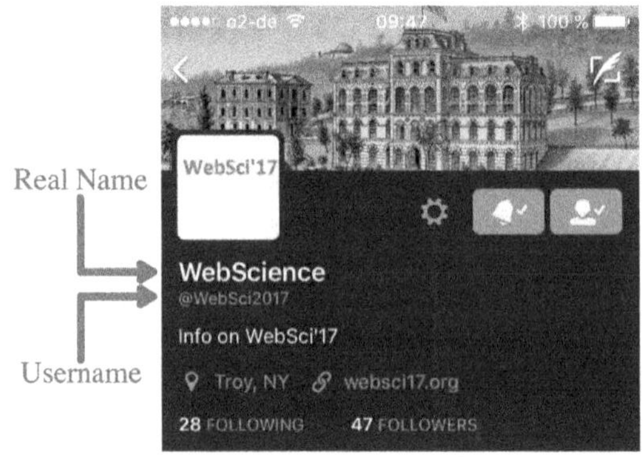

Figure 2: Example of a Twitter profile, highlighting the real name (i.e., "WebScience") and the username (i.e., "@WebSci2017") of the user account of 9th International ACM Web Science Conference 2017.

2 RELATED WORK

Following Riquelme and González-Cantergiani [24], "popularity" describes the number of channels over which a user can reach other users [24]. Mostly, this refers to direct follow-up relationships, but extends to mentions of the author and replies to and retweets of the author's tweets. Popularity gets easily confused with the broader term "influence". Influential users are those users that can affect other users. Basically, it is beneficial for them to be popular (well connected) and have a decent amount of interesting output (i.e., tweets or retweets). Surprisingly, to the best of our knowledge, one channel is left out by the literature: lists. Twitter allows each user to create lists of users. A list can, for example, summarize all researches a given user knows on Twitter. They can be used to get a view on only the tweets of the users in the given list. It is worth mentioning that a user does not need to actively follow those users, i.e., it can contain tweets that are not part of the user's timeline. Therefore, we add this feature in our experiments.

In their survey on influence on Twitter, Riquelme and González-Cantergiani [24] provide a good overview over influence metrics. The survey serves as toolkit to select the proper metrics for one's research. The authors describe eight different popularity measures. The simplest is to count only follow-up relations, but there are more complex ones, like the FollowerRank [7, 20], the Tweet-Follower-Followee ratio (TFF) [6], and the Popularity measure [1]. Those measures weight the follower count with the friend count. There are further metrics by Srinivasan et al. [25] that consider the number of users that mention, reply to, or retweet the author's tweets.

However, FollowerRank, TFF, and the Popularity can be influenced by the given user by changing the number of users s/he follows. The measures by Srinivasan et al. [25] are not feasible with only Twitter API access, because it would require crawling the mutual follow-relation of all users, which is very time-consuming. A detailed dump of Twitter data would be needed to get the required information. Further, Riquelme and González-Cantergiani [24] write that—even with this level of access—computational issues can occur. Therefore, we will focus in this paper on the most simple measure, the follower count. It is not changeable by the given user and can be retrieved using the Twitter API within reasonable time-bounds.

The popularity of a Twitter user can be part of her/his influence. Consequently, the popularity is one factor to be used on influence tracking systems. One such system is InfluenceTracker by Razis and Anagnostopoulos [23]. The authors describe the way their monitoring services ranks influential Twitter users by relying on the following characteristics: (1) TFF ratio: The authors argue that a user that follows more users than s/he has followers is a viewing user rather than a composing one. (2) Tweets Creation Rate (TCR): The frequency of newly created tweets is added to identify more influential user if two users have the same TFF ratio. It is computed using the distance in hours between the 100 most recent tweets. (3) The authors present an h-index for retweets and Favorites. It is—as the TCR—calculated based on the 100 most recent tweets. This index should reflect the assessment of a user's tweet by others. The authors use those three scores to compute an influence metric for every user. Amongst those, the TFF ratio takes the popularity of the user into account. However, as already mentioned at the popularity measures, this measure is under partial control of the user (s/he controls the number of friends).

Suh et al. [26] conducted a large-scale analysis of Twitter data to identify those features that affect the retweet-ability of tweets the most. They considered the number of URLs, hashtags, and mentions of any given tweet as content feature and the number of followers and friends, the age in days of the account, the number of tweets, favorites, and retweets as contextual features. They discovered that the number of URLs and hashtags from the content features as well as the age and the number of follower and friends to be good predictors for the retweet-ability. Interestingly, the authors noted that the number of tweets was marginally a bad predictor. We will adopt some of their features for our analysis, but will also extend them by others that where left out by Suh et al. [26].

Bandari et al. [4] went one step further and tried to predict the popularity of tweets. They focused on news stories and identified criteria using classification and regression methods that make a tweet more retweet-able. They selected as features the news category, the tone of language (i.e., subjective or objective), the mentioned users, as well as the source of the tweet. The authors were not able to predict the exact numbers of retweets using regression and obtained an accuracy of 85 % using classification. They classified their data into three classes: low, medium, and high spread. This is a good decision, because this enables to reduce the effects of outliers. However, the authors give no information about the accuracy per class. It is likely that most accuracy is achieved in the biggest class for low spread. Nevertheless, we will adopt the classification approach used in this work and focus on classification, rather than regression for our predictor.

Tsur and Rappoport [28] proposed an adapted Gradient Boosted Trees approach to predict the future popularity of hashtags. The authors extract several hashtag-related features from a huge dataset of tweets, like the length of the hashtag, the number of words in it, or the number of upper-cased letters. Their approach could obtain quite low error rates. However, as the previous approaches, we cannot transfer their finding, because it focusses solely on the tweets content.

Hutto et al. [15] done a longitudinal study on follower count changes using a dataset of 507 users. Their study focuses on social behavior, message content, and network structure. They also included some profile information as the presence of a location or URL into their study. However, their sample is rather small and their focus lies more on the tweets than on the profile data.

Martín et al. [18] conducted a focused experimental study to isolate on the influence of the number of hashtags per tweet on the follower count. They used data from 502891 users and grouped them into a control and experimental group based on the presence of hashtags in the tweet. Their experiments show that users with hashtags increased their follower count by 2.88 and users without hashtags increased it by 0.88. However, like the study of Hutto et al. [15], their findings focus solely on the tweets.

In addition to current research, we want to add profile information as well as the name of the Twitter users to our experiments. To the best of our knowledge, no prior work has considered the influence of those features on a user's popularity. Those features are promising, given that for example Gaudeul and Giannetti [11] have discovered that disclosing the real name leads to smaller, but more productive networks.

Kaiser [16] found out that teachers have negative prejudices regarding certain names like "Kevin" and "Chantal" in Germany. Similar results were obtained in the United States by Anderson-Clark et al. [3] who found an effect for ethnic first names. Such negative prejudices can have direct negative consequences on the student's evaluation and are most likely the effect of the halo effect [2, 27]. The halo effect is a cognitive bias that leads people to evaluate others based on their prejudices. An effect that is not limited to the classroom. Therefore, we will identify whether a un/popular name has on the popularity of a user.

Additionally, Fryer and Levitt [10] have tested the influence of distinctively black names on the economic outcome—that is one's chance to get a job. A distinctively black name was modeled using the share of blacks using a given name per birth certificates registered in California and Massachusetts. Prior findings suggested that distinctively black names are a disadvantage during job application and lead to higher rejection rates [5]. However, Fryer and Levitt [10] could not find negative effects of black names over white ones for later live outcomes after controlling the circumstances of birth. One of their explanations for their contradicting finding was that the disadvantage of black names holds only till the callback decision. A racist employer will not hire a black person, with or without a black name. However, the situation on Twitter is different, because a user's true identity is probably never revealed.

Coffey and McLaughlin [9] have done a similar study where they conducted an empirical test with the hypothesis of whether masculine names help women to be successful in legal careers. The masculinity of a name was modeled by computing the share of men that use a given female name as well per South Carolina's voter registration dataset. They found a statistical significantly higher number of masculine names amongst South California Bar Association members; however, their finding is unable to pin down the source of this inequality.

Finally, Oliver et al. [22] found out that many parents try to signal their ideology by given certain names to their offspring using the same birth certificate data from California as Fryer and Levitt [10] did. It is consequently very likely that users with ideology carrying names (e.g., a liberal one) attracts other users with the same ideology, because of the homophily effect [19], which describes a tendency of individuals to connect with similar ones.

3 DATA

We use three types of data to conduct our experiments: The Twitter dataset, a dataset to identify the presence of English words in the name field, and a dataset to identify given names in the same field. All three datasets are described in the following.

3.1 Twitter Data

We use the social graph dataset[2] from Kwak et al. [17] to get a list of user identifiers to crawl. The original dataset was collected between June 6th and June 31st of 2009 and contains all Twitter users at the time (41.7 million). We crawled the users using their unique identifier with the Twitter API between September 12th and October 2nd of 2016. We could access only 30.5 of the 41.7 million users—a reduction of 26.6 %. One reason for the decreased number of accessible users could be that the dataset was collected in 2009 and many users deactivated their account since then.

Amongst the collected users were 3760586 protected and 57087 verified profiles. Protected users are users that have set their tweet privacy level to protected, meaning that only approved users can view their tweets. Users in this group do not contribute in the usual public way to the network and are likely to be followed by actual "offline" friends. A protected user must manually confirm every follower. Therefore, the follower counts of those users are different from the follower counts of "regular users". Verified users are users that are confirmed by Twitter. Users in this group are already well known from outside of Twitter and, consequently, are being followed for their outside activity. Therefore, we decided to remove both user groups from the sample. We further removed any user account from our sample that has not sent any tweet within the past year. We consider those users as abundant—the owner has likely forgotten to delete his/her account. These reductions lead to a remaining dataset of 3131421 users.

During our experiments, we assign every user to one of three groups based on the content of the real name field: "Contains Name", "Contains Words", and "Custom Content" (see Section 4.1). The descriptive statistics of the remaining user profiles in Table 1 shows that the collected accounts are more than 7 years old. Surprisingly, the newest account was 334 days old, which should not be the case given that the dataset was originally collected in 2009. Obviously, Twitter reassigns old user IDs after some time. The collected users contributed with a median of 599 tweets to the social network. More than half of the users in the dataset have less than 112 followers, which indicates that we have a lot of non-prominent users in the dataset. We further had 1899209 users that still use the default profile settings and 444045 use the default profile image (an egg on a colored background). 4127518 users provide a description, 4598818 a location, and 2241756 a URL. As shown in Figure 3, the distribution of the follower counts in our data sample follows a power law distribution, which is in line with publications of Twitter researchers [12]. The mean follow count is 792.251, while the median is at 50.

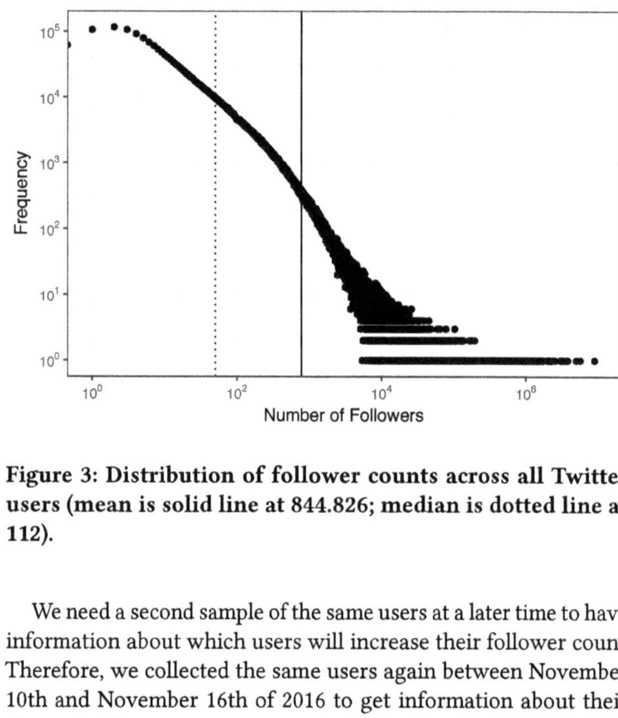

Figure 3: Distribution of follower counts across all Twitter users (mean is solid line at 844.826; median is dotted line at 112).

We need a second sample of the same users at a later time to have information about which users will increase their follower count. Therefore, we collected the same users again between November 10th and November 16th of 2016 to get information about their changed follower counts. We then compared the follower counts of both crawls and mark every user that could improve his/her follower count during that time with a flag. This resulted in 2789168 (43.9 %) flagged users that improved their follower count. Table 2 shows some descriptive statistics about the follower count of both crawls as well as the change of it.

3.2 English Wordlist

We used the English wordlist[3] from SIL International to identify the presence of English words in the name field of a Twitter users. It is a collection of 109582 English words and was originally obtained from the Interocitor bulletin board in Dallas (214-258-1832).

3.3 Name Data

The text in a Twitter user's name field where converted to ASCII, lower-cased, separated by non-letters, and then matched against

[2]Source: http://an.kaist.ac.kr/traces/WWW2010.html

[3]Source: http://sil.org/linguistics/wordlists/english

Table 1: Descriptive statistics about the interval level measures of the dataset showing the mean, standard deviation (SD), median, lower and upper bound of the 95 % confidence interval (CI), minimum (Min), and maximum (Max) value (N = 6354052).

Profile Feature	Mean	SD	Median	95 % CI	Min	Max
Followers Count	844.825	14263.897	112	[5, 2030]	0	13359378
Friends Count	477.172	3166.262	194	[12, 1619]	0	3106717
Tweet Count	4777.485	16056.563	599	[5, 22298]	0	4345445
Favorited Count	794.268	4665.824	36	[0, 3262]	0	1266503
Listed Count	16.698	955.009	2	[0, 63]	0	2386908
Description URL Count	0.042	0.239	0	[0, 0]	0	7
Description Hashtag Count	0.125	0.737	0	[0, 0]	0	30
UTC Offset	-2.411	4.502	-4	[-7, 8]	-11	13
Age in Days	2720.865	77.124	2713	[2632, 2888]	334	3817
Inactivity in Days	67.801	96.327	15	[0, 295]	0	365

Table 2: Descriptive statistics about the follower counts accross the two samples (N = 6354052).

Follower Count	Mean	SD	Median	95 % CI	Min	Max
First Dataset	844.825	14263.897	112.000	[5.000, 2030.000]	0.000	13359378.000
Second Dataset	856.920	14480.515	113.000	[6.000, 2058.000]	0.000	13395833.000
Absolute Change	12.095	500.767	0.000	[-5.000, 23.000]	-126099.000	437959.000
Relative Change	0.989	0.196	1.000	[0.917, 1.032]	0.000	315.000

the names that are provided in Behind the Name.[4] It is a website that tries to colect all names in order to make them accessible for the public. We collected 19766 distinct names from which 10467 are male, 8351 are female, and 948 are used by both genders. Additionally, we collected data about name impressions to cover the subjective impressions of names. These data are important to check for effects like negative prejudices for certain names as in the findings of Kaiser [16]. They were created using the feedback of the Behind the Name users and consists of the following data (counts are given in the parentheses): good vs. bad (7666/1390), masculine vs. feminine (6325/6471), classic vs. modern (8127/1771), mature vs. youthful (5283/3624), formal vs. informal (6473/3080), upper-class vs. common (6640/2125), urban vs. natural (2076/6054), wholesome vs. devious (7651/1387), strong vs. delicate (8143/1523), refined vs. rough (7070/2316), strange vs. boring (11286/164), simple vs. complex (4037/5214), serious vs. comedic (7328/1679), and nerdy vs. unintellectual (5664/1577). A name that is present in one of those list is associated by the Behind the Name community with the respective trait.

4 EXPERIMENT 1 – EFFECTS OF NAMES ON POPULARITY

Our first experiment focuses on the question of whether the presence of given names or English words in the real name field of a Twitter users profile improves his or her popularity. Having well known words or names in there should increase the discoverability of a user and, therefore, his/her chance of more followers.

[4]Campbell, Michael D. "Behind the Name: the Etymology and History of First Names." http://behindthename.com

4.1 Used Data

We want to measure the effect of the name field on the follower count of a Twitter user. Therefore, we will parse the name fields and assign every Twitter user to one of three groups:

(1) Contains Name: This group contains users that have a given name in their name field that we could match to the Behind the Name data.
(2) Contains Words: This group contains all users that are not in the first group, but have at least one English word from the SIL list in their name field.
(3) Custom Content: This group contains all users that are neither in the first nor in the second group.

Table 3 shows some descriptive statistics about the follower count for all three groups. Users with given names have the fewest followers with a median 97 and a mean of 619.549. Users that have English words in their real name field are—with a median of 289 and a mean of 2320.123—the most followed group by far. Users from the "Custom Content" group are—with a median of 130 and a mean of 1040.749—between the other two groups

4.2 Design and Procedure

We will conduct a one-way analysis of variance (ANOVA) on the follower count of the users from the "Contains Name", "Contains Word", and "Custom Content" groups using SPSS version 24. We want to find out whether there is a statistical difference between these groups regarding their follower count.

Further, we want to identify whether there is a statistically significant difference between the follower counts of each group. Therefore, we will add a Tukey post-hoc test to find the differences between the groups if the ANOVA finds a difference in the groups.

Table 3: Descriptive statistics about the follower counts accross the groups.

User Group	N	Mean	SD	Median	95 % CI	Min	Max
Custom Content	1495530	1040.749	19476.297	130	[6, 2413]	0	13359378
Contains Words	471312	2320.123	24841.446	289	[10, 7420]	0	8988128
Contains a Name	4387210	619.549	9938.525	97	[5, 1503]	0	5670985
Overall	6354052	844.826	14263.900	112	[5, 2030]	0	13359378

4.3 Results

The one-way ANOVA results presented in Table 4 show that there is a statistically significant difference between our experimental groups ($F(2, 6354049) = 3212.414, p = 0.000$).

A Tukey HSD post hoc test reveals that the followers count is statistically significantly higher for users with English words ($2320.123 \pm 24841.446, p = 0.000$) and lower for those with given names in their name field ($619.549 \pm 9938.525, p = 0.000$) compared to the users with custom content in their name field (1040.749 ± 19476.297). There is a statistically significant difference between those users with English words and given names in their name field as well ($p = 0.000$).

Table 4: Results from the analysis of variance (ANOVA) for the followers count showing the sum of squares (SS), degrees of freedom (df), mean square (MS), and F-value.

Source	SS	df	MS	F
Between	1.306e12	2	6.529e11	3212.414
Within	1.291e15	6354049	2.033e08	
Total	1.293e14	6354051		

Significant at $p < 0.001$.

4.4 Discussion

Twitter uses the name field as part of its user search feature.[5] Our hypothesis is that having known terms in there should consequently increase the chance to be found by it. Consequently, having English words and given names makes it easier to be found using text search. However, this should not directly translate in huge follower counts as Gaudeul and Giannetti [11] pointed out: Disclosing your given names results in smaller, but more profitable networks.

This hypothesis is confirmed by the one-way ANOVA with Tukey HSD post-hoc test. Users that have English words in their name field have statistically significant higher follow counts. On the other hand, users that have a given name in their name field have less followers, which is in line with the finding of Gaudeul and Giannetti [11]. A difference that will implicitly be used by our later experiments where we want to predict an increase of the follower count based on the content of the real name field.

The high follower counts of users with "Custom Content" can be explained by other languages—our experiments only considers English words. Therefore, "Custom Content" refers not only to misspelled or Emoji names, but could include valid words from other languages as well. Those in turn, are easy to discover by the search function.

While we observed statistically significant differences in the follower counts amongst the groups, we do not know where they come from. However, the presence of this difference could be used to predict popular users. The feature is easy to extract from the user profile data and can serve as a feature in a popularity predictor.

[5]Source: https://dev.twitter.com/rest/reference/get/users/search

5 EXPERIMENT 2 – IDENTIFYING PREDICTIVE FEATURES

Our second experiment tries to identify user profile features that have the strongest statistical relation with the change of the follower count. In other words, what features are the best proxy to predict an increase of the follower count.

5.1 Used Data

During this experiment, we used the second crawl of the users to access the information about their change of the follower count. Further, we add the subjective name features from Behind the Name to the users from the "Contains Name" group to identify the influence of the perception of a given name to the follower count. Additionally, we add the share of English words in the real name field to all users except of those from the "Custom Content" group.

We mark with a flag, called *follower count increased flag* in the sequel, all users with an increased follower count in the second crawl. Then the dataset is randomly split into halves while preserving the relative ratio of the follower count increased flag. We will use the first partition to identify features with a statistical significant effect on the flag during this experiment—the second partition will be used later in the following experiment.

5.2 Design and Procedure

We will conduct a binary logistic regression on the follower count increased flag for users in the "Contains Name", "Contains Word", and "Custom Content" groups separately using SPSS version 24.

We want to identify which profile features have a statistical significant relation with the follower count increased flag. The results from our first experiment showed that users from all three groups show a different pattern in their follower count. Therefore, we want to identify the features for every group separately. We will use this detailed information in our third and last experiment where we present our popularity predictor.

5.3 Results

A binary logistic regression for every user group was performed to identify the effects of all user profile features as well as the Behind the Names data on the follower count changed flag.

The variation in the follower count that can be explained by the models are presented in Table 5. Therein, our models can explain about 21.0 % (Nagelkerke R^2) of the variation of users with custom content, 23.8 % for users with English word in their name, and 20.5 % for users with names in their real name field.

Table 5: Amount of variation in the dependent variables that can be explained by the models of every user group.

User Group	Nagelkerke R^2
Custom Content	0.210
Contains Words	0.238
Contains Names	0.205

The effect sizes are presented in Table 6. We limited the presented variables to those that are statistically significant for space reasons.

The logistic regression model for users with custom content in their name contains all variables. The biggest effects come from two distinct areas: The degree of customization of the user profile and the presence of additional meta information. On the one hand, the likelihood of additional followers increases if a user uses the default profile settings (+10.7 %), provides a description (+23.8 %), location (+10.4 %), or URL (+24.7 %). On the other hand, the likelihood of additional followers decreases dramatically if the user did not provide a custom profile image (−58.2 %).

The logistic regression model for users with English words in their name contains all possible variables as well. In this group, the likelihood of additional followers increases if a user uses the default profile settings (+10.3 %), provides a description (+25.0 %), location (+9.2 %), or URL (+56.1 %). The likelihood of additional followers decreases dramatically as well if the user did not provide a custom profile image (−58.9 %). Further, the fraction of English words in the name field decreases the likelihood that the follower count increases by 17.1 %.

The logistic regression model for users with English words in their name contains all possible profile information variables. Amongst the statistical not significant ones are the impressions boring ($p = 0.348$), common ($p = 0.982$), complex ($p = 0.762$), delicate ($p = 0.151$), informal ($p = 0.176$), natural ($p = 0.438$), refined ($p = 0.088$), simple ($p = 0.303$), upper-class ($p = 0.264$), urban ($p = 0.207$), and wholesome ($p = 0.378$). In this group, the likelihood of additional followers increases if a user uses the default profile settings (+12.8 %), provides a description (+28.1 %), location (+5.6 %), or URL (+17.5 %). The absence of a custom profile image (−58.3 %) as well as the fraction of English words (−6.6 %) in the real name field decreased the likelihood of additional followers. The biggest changes amongst the name-related features are obtained for names that are perceived as female (−5.6 %) or give a feminine impression (−5.6 %).

Table 6: The contribution of each independent variable to the models and its statistical significance as determined by a Wald test. The results are separated by user group (G) and show the significance as well as the β value, its standard error (SE), and the effect size (e^β).

G	Variable	β	SE	e^β
Custom Content	Age in Days	0,000***	0,000	1,000
	Inactivity in Days	-0,009***	0,000	0,991
	Tweet Count	0,000**	0,002	1,000
	Favorited Count	0,000***	0,000	1,000
	Friends Count	0,000***	0,000	1,000
	Listed Count	0,002***	0,000	1,002
	Description URL Count	0,036***	0,000	1,037
	Description Hashtag Count	0,013***	0,000	1,013
	Has Default Profile	0,102***	0,000	1,107
	Has Default Profile Image	-0,872***	0,000	0,418
	Has Description	0,214***	0,000	1,238
	Has Location	0,099***	0,000	1,104
	Has URL	0,221***	0,000	1,247
Contains Words	Age in Days	0,000***	0,000	1,000
	Inactivity in Days	-0,010***	0,000	0,990
	Tweet Count	0,000***	0,000	1,000
	Favorited Count	0,000***	0,000	1,000
	Friends Count	0,000***	0,000	1,000
	Listed Count	0,003***	0,000	1,003
	Description URL Count	-0,032**	0,002	0,969
	Description Hashtag Count	-0,010**	0,002	0,990
	Has Default Profile	0,098***	0,000	1,103
	Has Default Profile Image	-0,889***	0,000	0,411
	Has Description	0,223***	0,000	1,250
	Has Location	0,088***	0,000	1,092
	Has URL	0,445***	0,000	1,561
	Name Countains Words	-0,187***	0,000	0,829
Contains Names	Age in Days	0,001***	0,000	1,001
	Inactivity in Days	-0,009***	0,000	0,991
	Tweet Count	0,000***	0,000	1,000
	Favorited Count	0,000***	0,000	1,000
	Friends Count	0,000***	0,000	1,000
	Listed Count	0,001***	0,000	1,001
	Description URL Count	0,055***	0,000	1,056
	Description Hashtag Count	0,029***	0,000	1,029
	Has Default Profile	0,120***	0,000	1,128
	Has Default Profile Image	-0,898***	0,000	0,407
	Has Description	0,248***	0,000	1,281
	Has Location	0,055***	0,000	1,056
	Has URL	0,161***	0,000	1,175
	Name is Male	-0,011*	0,023	0,989
	Name is Female	-0,058***	0,000	0,944
	Impression: bad	-0,027**	0,001	0,973
	Impression: classic	0,010**	0,001	1,010
	Impression: comedic	-0,011**	0,007	0,989
	Impression: devious	0,022**	0,008	1,022
	Impression: feminine	-0,058***	0,000	0,944

– Continued on next page –

Table 6 – Concluded from previous page

G	Variable	β	SE	e^{β}
Contains Names	Impression: formal	0,011**	0,001	1,011
	Impression: good	-0,026***	0,000	0,975
	Impression: masculine	-0,033***	0,000	0,968
	Impression: mature	-0,010**	0,001	0,990
	Impression: modern	-0,032***	0,000	0,969
	Impression: nerdy	0,011***	0,000	1,011
	Impression: rough	-0,019***	0,000	0,981
	Impression: serious	0,015***	0,000	1,015
	Impression: strange	0,012***	0,000	1,012
	Impression: strong	0,007*	0,028	1,007
	Impression: unintellectual	0,013*	0,016	1,014
	Impression: youthful	0,009*	0,015	1,009
	Name Contains Words	-0,068***	0,000	0,934

*** Significant at $p < 0.001$
** Significant at $p < 0.010$
* Significant at $p < 0.050$

5.4 Discussion

In Section 2, we pointed out that there is one user-relation missing in the current literature: the listed count. So, how does the list count performs in our analysis. Not so well. It is a statistical significant variable and its effect size is higher than those of the follower, friend, and tweet count in all three groups. However, the effect size is still quite low.

We can see some analogies, while comparing our results with those from tweet-based popularity predictions (those that extend their variables to profile information). Suh et al. [26] found a statistical significant effect for follower and friends count, the age of the account in days, and the presence of a URL, which is in line with our results. However, in our results, only the presence of a URL has a relevant effect size (different from 1.000). Hutto et al. [15] conducted another study involving profile information. They identified the description length as well as the presence of a URL and a location. We have not included the length of the description into our model, but its presence. All three variables are indeed statistical significant and have a relevant effect size in our models.

Our analysis also shows that the subjective impression of a name matters. In most cases the effects are rather small, except for names that are perceived as "female" or "feminine". Those perceptions reduce the likelihood of additional followers. This indicates a slight discrimination of women on Twitter, probably comparable to those found by Coffey and McLaughlin [9] in legal careers. Our data allow no comparison with the findings about distinctively black names; however, we have some information about names that are perceived as bad or rough (with a decreasing effect) and names that are perceived as strange or unintellectual (with an increasing effect). Especially the later ones indicate that negative prejudices about names do not necessarily translate into direct negative consequences.

Our analysis show that we can model the flag about the increase of the follower count for each user group using a different set of variables. All user groups share a strong core of five variables, consisting of the flags for default profile and profile image as well as the presence of a description, location, and URL. The fraction of English word in the name field is also a good additional predictor for users of the "Contains Words" group. Users from the "Contains Names" group extend the list of predictors by some name related variables.

6 EXPERIMENT 3 – CLASSIFYING USERS

Our final experiment focuses on the question of whether we can correctly predict if the follower count of a Twitter user will increase based on her/his profile information within a time-span of one month. We will predict only if the follower count of a Twitter user will increase. It will not reflect the magnitude of the change. The work of Bandari et al. [4] already shows that a regression model is not very promising. Further, there is no scientific way to set clear ranges.

6.1 Used Data

We use the same data that was used during experiment 2. The first partition of the data will be used to find good parameters for every model during a grid search approach and to train the best model of each group using the found parameters. The second partition will we used in the second part of this experiment to evaluate the performance of the trained models.

6.2 Design and Procedure

We conducted our experiments with GNU R 3.3.3[6] using the caret package in version 6.0-73.[7] We test a broad selection of classification models that are available in caret: C5.0, Gradient Boosting Machine, k-Nearest Neighbors, Naive Bayes, Neural Network, and Random Forest. We start by conducting a grid search approach on all models using the first partition of the user data. The best configuration of each model is used to compare all models against each other to select the best model for every group. We then train those selected models using the first partition of the data and use them to classify the data in the second partition of the dataset. Our classifier then first identifies the group a given user belongs to by analyzing the content of the real name field. The model that was trained for the assigned group is then used to classify the user.

The classification will be evaluated using the area under the receiver operator curve (AUC) with a 10-fold cross-validation with five repeats. We will compare this approach with a general solution that applies the same model on all data as well as a random classifier that serves as a lower baseline.

6.3 Results

Table 7 shows the results from the grid search. Shown are only the parameter and AUC scores of the best found configuration.

The parameters of some models seem to be equal across all groups as the Naive Base without Laplace correction, kernel, and bandwidth adjustment. Others do have quit similar configurations across all groups as the C5.0 classifier which has 25 boosting iterations, no winnowing, but with differences in the used model or the Gradient Boosting Machine with a tree depth of 15, a shrinkage of

[6] Source: https://r-project.org
[7] Source: https://github.com/topepo/caret

Table 7: Detailed results for all prediction models on every group showing the best found parameter as well as the accuracy under the receiver operator curve (AUC) value.

Group	Model	Parameter	AUC
Custom Content	C5.0	boosting iterations: 25; model: tree; winnowing: FALSE	0.809
	Gradient Boosting Machine	boosting iterations: 1600; maximux tree depth: 15; shrinkage: 0.025	0.815
	k-Nearest Neighbors	k: 135	0.764
	Naive Bayes	Laplace correction: FALSE; kernel: TRUE; bandwidth adjustment: TRUE	0.761
	Neural Network	hidden units: 11; decay weigth: 1.1	0.762
	Random Forest	randomly selected predictors: 3	0.808
Contains Words	C5.0	boosting iterations: 25; model: rules; winnowing: FALSE	0.833
	Gradient Boosting Machine	boosting iterations: 1100; maximux tree depth: 15; shrinkage: 0.025	0.838
	k-Nearest Neighbors	k: 100	0.762
	Naive Bayes	Laplace correction: FALSE; kernel: TRUE; bandwidth adjustment: TRUE	0.782
	Neural Network	hidden units: 3; decay weigth: 1.2	0.775
	Random Forest	randomly selected predictors: 3	0.832
Contains Names	C5.0	boosting iterations: 25; model: tree; winnowing: FALSE	0.806
	Gradient Boosting Machine	boosting iterations: 1600; maximux tree depth: 15; shrinkage: 0.025	0.813
	k-Nearest Neighbors	k: 135	0.777
	Naive Bayes	Laplace correction: FALSE; kernel: TRUE; bandwidth adjustment: TRUE	0.755
	Neural Network	hidden units: 13; decay weigth: 1.1	0.773
	Random Forest	randomly selected predictors: 7	0.805

Table 8: Overall results for all prediction models using the accuracy under the receiver operator curve (AUC).

Group	Model	AUC
Custom Content	Gradient Boosting Machine	0.815
Contains Names	Gradient Boosting Machine	0.812
Contains Words	Gradient Boosting Machine	0.838
Overall		0.816

0.025, but a different number of boosting iterations. The obtained AUC scores are in a range between 0.761 by the Naive Bayes on the "Custom Content" group and 0.838 by the Gradient Boosting Machine on the "Contains Words" group. k-Nearest Neighbors, Naive Bayes, and Neural Network perform bad across all groups with AUC scores bellow 0.800, while the C5.0, Gradient Boosting Machine, and Random Forest perform comparable well in all groups with Gradient Boosting Machine being consistently the best model.

Therefore, a Gradient Boosting Machine will be used during our evaluation for all groups, but it will differ in the used parameters and used portion of the train data.

Table 8 shows the AUC results of the final classification task. A Gradient Boosting Machine was used for every group, using a different parameter set as well as a different feature set, based on the assigned group. The best score was obtained with 0.838 for users in the "Contains Words" group, followed be the "Custom Content" group with 0.815, and the "Contains Name" group with 0.812. The group-wise scores are in line with the scores from the training stage in Table 7 and essentially the same for all groups except of a tiny difference of 0.001 in the "Contains Names" group.

Given the low variance between those results, one might raise the question of whether the distinction of the three groups brings any benefits. However, using the most general model from the "Custom Content" group for all data results in lower AUC scores for the remaining groups (i.e., 0.813 for "Contains Words" and 0.812 for "Contains Names").

6.4 Discussion

Our proposed model performs well on all three experimental groups. We were able to classify especially users from the "Contains Words" group better than those from the other groups.

We see a clearly better outcome while comparing our results with the random baseline, which would obtain an AUC score of 0.500 across all groups. Therefore, we can say that our classifier is far better than if we would guess which user will increase his/her follower count by random. However, we should keep in mind that the random classifier is a poor classifier and can serve only as a lower bound.

We can further compare our approach to a simple model that classifies all users with the same model—and by doing so, ignoring all additional name field-related features for the model. This comparison leads to some interesting results. The classification of users in the "Contains Words" group obtained far better scores with our approach, which lead to a reduction of the classification error rate of 13.4 %. This group benefits the most from the name field-based distinction of the groups. However, we can see no relevant improvement for users in the "Contains Names" group. This is surprising, given that this model had a bunch of additional statistical significant variables with a decent effect size to draw from (see Table 6). We should spend more research in finding good ways to use those effects for our classification.

7 CONCLUSIONS

A key feature of our proposed approach is the incorporation of the content of the name field, which was to the best of our knowledge never used before. We used the presence of English words and given names to form three groups (i.e., "Custom Content", "Contains Words", and "Contains Names"). We combined the found names with meta-information from Behind the Name to add more details about those names. Our experiments show that adding those features that stem from the content of the name field leads to better outcomes for the prediction of an increase in follower counts.

Our experimental study identified multiple predictors from the profile information of a Twitter user that can be used to predict an increase of the follower count. Focusing on variables that are given in the profile information enables far bigger studies than those that use the content of the tweets as it is the case in the studies of Hutto et al. [15] and Martín et al. [18]—because of the rate limitations of the Twitter API.

One limitation of our approach is that it focusses solely on words of the English language. Users with words from other languages are likely to be assigned to the "Custom Content" group, which is especially interesting given the spread of languages like Spanish, which is also a very common language on Twitter. One could try to evaluate the "lang"-Field of the Twitter profile, which conveys the self-declared user interface language. However, most users in our data have set their interface to English with only a marginally difference for users in the "Custom Content" group (i.e., 81.12 % in the "Custom Content", 90.39 % in the "Contains Words", and 89.98 % in the "Contains Names" group). Therefore, it would be more promising to detect the language of a user using machine learning in order to make further distinctions on the language.

Another limitation of our approach is that it predicts only if a user increases her/his follower count. Further research is needed to find a way to map the change into classes.

Finally, we would like to point out that our model is based on statistical differences and we do not yet have a clear indication where they come from. Our hypothesis is that more familiar content in the user profiles lead to better discoverability. For instance, the effect size of the default profile flag indicates that users with default profiles (without a description, location, URL, or profile image) are seen a less invested in Twitter and, therefore, less interesting to follow. Therefore, it would be of interest to conduct further social research to identify those causes.

REFERENCES

[1] Abolfazl Aleahmad, Payam Karisani, Maseud Rahgozar, and Farhad Oroumchian. 2015. OLFinder: Finding Opinion Leaders in Online Social Networks. *Journal of Information Science* 42, 5 (Sept. 2015), 659–674.

[2] Gordon W. Allport. 1979. *The Nature of Prejudice: 25th Anniversary Edition.* Basic Books, New York, NY, USA, Chapter Patterning and Extent of Prejudice, 68–81.

[3] Tracy N. Anderson-Clark, Raymond J. Green, and Tracy B. Henley. 2008. The Relationship Between First Names and Teacher Expectations for Achievement Motivation. *Journal of Language and Social Psychology* 27, 1 (March 2008), 94–99.

[4] Roja Bandari, Sitaram Asur, and Bernardo Huberman. 2012. The Pulse of News in Social Media: Forecasting Popularity. In *6th International Conference on Web and Social Media (ICWSM-12), Proceedings.* AAAI, Palo Alto, CA, USA, 26–33.

[5] Marianne Bertrand and Sendhil Mullainathan. 2003. *Are Emily and Greg More Employable than Lakisha and Jamal? A Field Experiment on Labor Market Discrimination.* Working Paper 9873. National Bureau of Economic Research.

[6] Carolina Bigonha, Thiago N. C. Cardoso, Mirella M. Moro, Marcos A. Gonçalves, and Virgílio A. F. Almeida. 2012. Sentiment-based Influence Detection on Twitter. *Journal of the Brazilian Computer Society* 18, 3 (Sept. 2012), 169–183.

[7] Rafael Cappelletti and Nishanth Sastry. 2012. IARank: Ranking Users on Twitter in Near Real-Time, Based on Their Information Amplification Potential. In *1st International Conference on Social Informatics (SocialInformatics 2012), Proceedings.* IEEE, New York, NY, USA, 70–77.

[8] Martin J. Chorley, Gualtiero B. Colombo, Stuart M. Allen, and Roger M. Whitaker. 2015. Human Content Filtering in Twitter: The Influence of Metadata. *International Journal of Human-Computer Studies* 74 (Feb. 2015), 32–40.

[9] Bentley Coffey and Patrick A. McLaughlin. 2009. Do Masculine Names Help Female Lawyers Become Judges? Evidence from South Carolina. *American Law and Economics Review* 11, 1 (Aug. 2009), 112–133.

[10] Roland G. Fryer and Steven D. Levitt. 2004. The Causes and Consequences of Distinctively Black Names. *The Quarterly Journal of Economics* 119, 3 (Aug. 2004), 767–805.

[11] Alexia Gaudeul and Caterina Giannetti. 2015. *Privacy, Trust and Social Network Formation.* Jena Economic Research Papers 2015-023. Friedrich-Schiller-University Jena.

[12] Pankaj Gupta, Ashish Goel, Jimmy Lin, Aneesh Sharma, Dong Wang, and Reza Zadeh. 2013. WTF: The Who to Follow Service at Twitter. In *22nd International Conference on World Wide Web (WWW 2013), Proceedings.* ACM, New York, NY, USA, 505–514.

[13] John Hannon, Mike Bennett, and Barry Smyth. 2010. Recommending Twitter Users to Follow Using Content and Collaborative Filtering Approaches. In *4th Conference on Recommender Systems (RecSys 2010), Proceedings.* ACM, New York, NY, USA, 199–206.

[14] Liangjie Hong, Ovidiu Dan, and Brian D. Davison. 2011. Predicting Popular Messages in Twitter. In *20th International Conference Companion on World Wide Web (WWW 2011), Proceedings.* ACM, New York, NY, USA, 57–58. Poster.

[15] Clayton J. Hutto, Sarita Yardi, and Eric Gilbert. 2013. A Longitudinal Study of Follow Predictors on Twitter. In *32nd Conference on Human Factors in Computing Systems (CHI 2013), Proceedings.* ACM, New York, NY, USA, 821–830.

[16] Astrid Kaiser. 2009. Vornamen: Nomen est omen? [Given Names: Nomen est omen?]. *Oberfränkischer Schulanzeiger* 12 (Dec. 2009), 15–18.

[17] Haewoon Kwak, Changhyun Lee, Hosung Park, and Sue Moon. 2010. What is Twitter, a Social Network or a News Media?. In *19th International Conference on World Wide Web (WWW 2010), Proceedings.* ACM, New York, NY, USA, 591–600.

[18] Eva García Martín, Niklas Lavesson, and Mina Doroud. 2016. Hashtags and Followers. *Social Network Analysis and Mining* 6, 1 (March 2016), 12.

[19] Miller McPherson, Lynn Smith-Lovin, and James M. Cook. 2001. Birds of a Feather: Homophily in Social Networks. *Annual Review of Sociology* 27 (Aug. 2001), 415–444.

[20] Rinkesh Nagmoti, Ankur Teredesai, and Martine De Cock. 2010. Ranking Approaches for Microblog Search. In *International Conference on Web Intelligence and Intelligent Agent Technology (WI-IAT 2010), Proceedings*, Vol. 1. IEEE, New York, NY, USA, 153–157.

[21] Tomoya Noro, Fei Ru, Feng Xiao, and Takehiro Tokuda. 2013. Twitter User Rank Using Keyword Search. In *Information Modelling and Knowledge Bases XXIV (Frontiers in Artificial Intelligence and Applications)*, Vol. 251. IOS Press, Amsterdam, Netherlands, 31–48.

[22] J. Eric Oliver, Thomas Wood, and Alexandra Bass. 2015. Liberellas Versus Konservatives: Social Status, Ideology, and Birth Names in the United States. *Political Behavior* 38, 1 (March 2015), 55–81.

[23] Gerasimos Razis and Ioannis Anagnostopoulos. 2014. InfluenceTracker: Rating the Impact of a Twitter Account. In *Artificial Intelligence Applications and Innovations.* IFIP Advances in Information and Communication Technology, Vol. 437. Springer, Berlin / Heidelberg, Germany, 184–195.

[24] Fabián Riquelme and Pablo González-Cantergiani. 2016. Measuring User Influence on Twitter: A Survey. *Information Processing & Management* 52, 5 (Sept. 2016), 949–975.

[25] MS Srinivasan, Srinath Srinivasa, and Sunil Thulasidasan. 2014. A Comparative Study of Two Models for Celebrity Identification on Twitter. In *20th International Conference on Management of Data (COMAD 2014), Proceedings.* Computer Society of India, Mumbai, India, India, 57–65.

[26] Bongwon Suh, Lichan Hong, Peter Pirolli, and Ed H. Chi. 2010. Want to be Retweeted? Large Scale Analytics on Factors Impacting Retweet in Twitter Network. In *2nd International Conference on Social Computing (SocialCom 2010), Proceedings.* IEEE, New York, NY, USA, 177–184.

[27] Edward L. Thorndike. 1920. A Constant Error in Psychological Ratings. *Journal of Applied Psychology* 4, 1 (March 1920), 25–29.

[28] Oren Tsur and Ari Rappoport. 2015. Don't Let Me Be #Misunderstood: Linguistically Motivated Algorithm for Predicting the Popularity of Textual Memes. In *9th International Conference on Web and Social Media (ICWSM-15), Proceedings.* AAAI, Palo Alto, CA, USA, 426–435.

[29] Twitter, Inc. 2015. Annual Report 2016. San Francisco, CA, USA.

[30] Jianshu Weng, Ee-Peng Lim, Jing Jiang, and Qi He. 2010. TwitterRank: Finding Topic-sensitive Influential Twitterers. In *3rd International Conference on Web Search and Data Mining (WSDM 2010), Proceedings.* ACM, New York, NY, USA, 261–270.

Sharing Means Renting?: An Entire-marketplace Analysis of Airbnb

Qing Ke
Indiana University, Bloomington
qke@indiana.edu

ABSTRACT

Airbnb, an online marketplace for accommodations, has experienced a staggering growth accompanied by intense debates and scattered regulations around the world. Current discourses, however, are largely focused on opinions rather than empirical evidences. Here, we aim to bridge this gap by presenting the first large-scale measurement study on Airbnb, using a crawled data set containing 2.3 million listings, 1.3 million hosts, and 19.3 million reviews. We measure several key characteristics at the heart of the ongoing debate and the sharing economy. Among others, we find that Airbnb has reached a global yet heterogeneous coverage. The majority of its listings across many countries are entire homes, suggesting that Airbnb is actually more like a rental marketplace rather than a spare-room sharing platform. Analysis on star-ratings reveals that there is a bias toward positive ratings, amplified by a bias toward using positive words in reviews. The extent of such bias is greater than Yelp reviews, which were already shown to exhibit a positive bias. We investigate a key issue—commercial hosts who own multiple listings on Airbnb—repeatedly discussed in the current debate. We find that their existence is prevalent, they are early-movers towards joining Airbnb, and their listings are disproportionately entire homes and located in the US. Our work advances the current understanding of how Airbnb is being used and may serve as an independent and empirical reference to inform the debate.

CCS CONCEPTS

• **Information systems → Reputation systems**; • **Applied computing → Law, social and behavioral sciences**;

KEYWORDS

Airbnb; measurement; sharing economy; online marketplace

1 INTRODUCTION

Recent years have seen a proliferation of online peer-to-peer marketplaces [10]. Examples abound and the services covered range from personal loans (Prosper, LendingClub, SocietyOne) and ride (Uber, Lyft) to household tasks (TaskRabbit) and accommodations (Airbnb). Enabled by the Internet and information technology, these marketplaces aim to match sellers who are willing to share underutilized goods or services with buyers who need them [3, 29]. Such marketplaces are thus often referred to as examples of the so-called "sharing economy" [6, 25, 33]. Airbnb, a primary example of this type of marketplaces, connects hosts who have spare rooms with guests who need accommodations. Founded in 2008, it now has more than two million listings located in more than 191 countries, and has accumulated more than 60 million guests.[1]

Accompanied by its rapid growth, Airbnb has confronted intense debates, regulatory challenges, and battles. Advocates argue that the platform enables many householders to become small business owners and reduce their rental burden. It may also make travelers pay less than hotel prices and have a more local and authentic experience, exemplified by its slogan "live there." Opponents argue that many hosts rent their entire homes for short-terms, which is illegal in many cities [17, 30, 31]. This usage also involves two other critical issues. First, entire homes that are used for short-term rentals on Airbnb may be taken down from local housing markets, which may drive the rents up. A recent study, however, suggested that this might not be the case [32]. Second, the coming-in of more travelers may be disruptive to residential neighborhoods. Another argument from opponents is that some hosts who own a large number of listings may be operating business on Airbnb but may fail to fulfill their tax obligations. This gives them advantages over hotels and makes them "free riders," because accommodation taxes collected from hotels are often used for tourism promotions that benefit all accommodation suppliers [17].

Although much debated, to what extent the discussed arguments are empirically grounded remains to be seen. To this end, here we present the first large-scale data-driven study on Airbnb, focusing on the entire market. By measuring key characteristics directly related to these arguments, we paint a more complete yet complicated picture of Airbnb. First, regrading the issue of short-term rentals of entire homes, we document that across many countries, entire homes account for the majority of listings; 68.5% of all listings are entire homes and only 29.8% are private rooms. Although we do not further quantify the extent to which they are used for short-term rentals—a limitation of our work—simply due to the unavailability of proprietary data from Airbnb on listing bookings, we note that the statistics of room types have changed from 2012 when 57% are entire homes and 41% are private rooms [17]. This change suggests that Airbnb has been becoming more like a rental marketplace rather than a spare-room sharing platform. Moreover, listings owned by business operators may more likely be rented in short-terms, compared with other ordinary hosts.

[1] https://www.airbnb.com/about/about-us

WebSci '17, June 25-28, 2017, Troy, NY, USA

ACM ISBN 978-1-4503-4896-6/17/06...$15.00
https://doi.org/http://dx.doi.org/10.1145/3091478.3091504

Table 1: Statistics of our data set about Airbnb

Countries		193
Listings	Active	2,018,747
	Unavailable	284,039
	Total	2,302,786
Users	Hosts	1,313,626
	Guests	11,150,017
	Total	12,156,178*
Reviews		19,377,978
Note:	* 307,465 users are both hosts and guests	

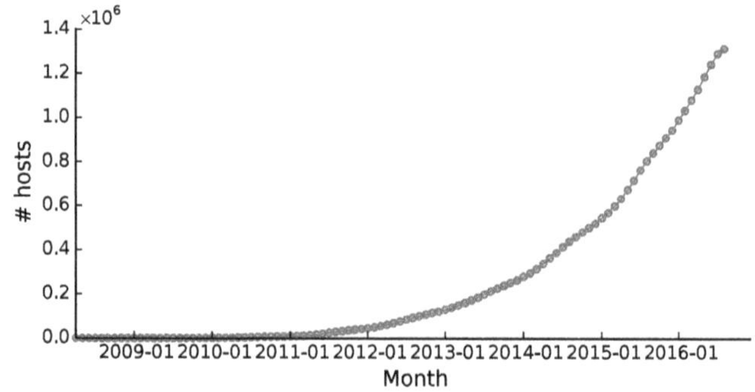

Figure 1: Cumulative number of hosts.

Second, regarding the issue of business operators, we characterize in a great detail who they are and what their listings are. Our results suggest a heavier usage from business operators than previously thought. The number of listings owned by a host is distributed according to a power-law, spanning three orders of magnitude. One third of all listings are owned by 9.4% of hosts, each of whom has at least three listings, and one host even owns 1,800 listings. Furthermore, we show that business operators are early-movers towards joining Airbnb and behave more professionally than ordinary hosts and that their listings are disproportionately of the entire home type and located in the US. These results reinforce the rental marketplace notion of Airbnb.

Third, our analysis reveals predominantly positive star-ratings of listings, which is different from previously observed J-shaped distribution. This positivity bias is consistent with a bias toward using positive words in reviews, and the extent is greater than Yelp reviews. These results may suggest that many guests had overall positive experiences during their stays, corroborating advocates' argument on traveler experiences. It can also indicate the presence of selection bias in review behaviors [14]—only those who had great experiences chose to give reviews.

Taken together, we believe that our work significantly advances the current understanding of how Airbnb is being used. Our main contributions in this work are:

- We crawl Airbnb listing data on a global scale. (§ 2)
- We analyze geolocations, room types, star-ratings, and reviews of listings. (§ 3)
- We characterize hosts who own multiple listings on Airbnb and those listings owned by them. (§ 4)
- We investigate factors linked to listings' future rental performance. (§ 5)

2 DATA

2.1 Data Collection

On Airbnb, each listing has a web page showing its details such as room type, price, reviews from previous guests, host information, etc. For example, the listing called "Van Gogh's Bedroom" can be visited at https://www.airbnb.com/rooms/10981658. The main goal of our data collection is to accumulate as many listings as possible, so that we can perform a systematic analysis. There are two steps in the data collection process: (1) accumulating listing IDs; and (2) downloading their HTML files and reviews. We describe them in detail below, and before that, let us present in Table 1 some summary statistics about the collected data set. To our best knowledge, these are the first public and exact statistics about the Airbnb marketplace.

In the first step, we accumulated listing IDs by exploiting the hierarchical structure of the Airbnb site map, which has three levels: country, regions in the country, and search results of listings in the region. The top level at `/sitemaps` lists 152 countries, each of which has a hyperlink pointing to the web page that lists regions in the country. All the regions in Australia, for example, are listed at `/sitemaps/AU`. Each region, again, has a hyperlink pointing to the page of search results of listings in the region. Our script followed all these hyperlinks and obtained 83,174 regions in 152 countries. Then for each region, our script visited its search page and saved all the listing IDs there. We repeated this search process 7 times, with each new search resulting in a smaller number of new IDs. The only constraint stopping us from more searches is the availability of computing and storage resources. In total, we accumulated 2,302,786 unique listings.

In the second step, for each listing, our script visited its web page, saved the HTML file, and collected all the reviews. As we are also interested in rental performances of listings, we repeated this step 3 times—after the 1st, 2nd, and 7th search. The statistics in Table 1 and the analyses presented in § 3 and § 4 are based on the latest crawl. We found 284,039 (12.3%) listings were unavailable, by which we mean visiting them redirected to a search page with a message saying "the listing is no longer available." As an example, see `/rooms/11599049`.

The entire data collection process was performed between May and September, 2016. Note that we followed the crawler-etiquette described in Airbnb's `robots.txt`:[2] None of the three directories we visited—`/sitemaps`, `/s/`, and `/rooms/{listing ID}`—are specified as disallowed in the file.

2.2 Summary Statistics Analysis

We compare the statistics in Table 1 with official ones. The only official but approximate numbers we found were already mentioned in § 1: 191+ countries, 2*M*+ listings, and 60*M*+ total guests. Our obtained number of countries and listings seem to be comparable to official ones. We note, however, that the number of guests (11*M*) is much smaller than the official one (60*M*). One obvious reason is that here we have only counted those guests who have left at least

[2] https://www.airbnb.com/robots.txt

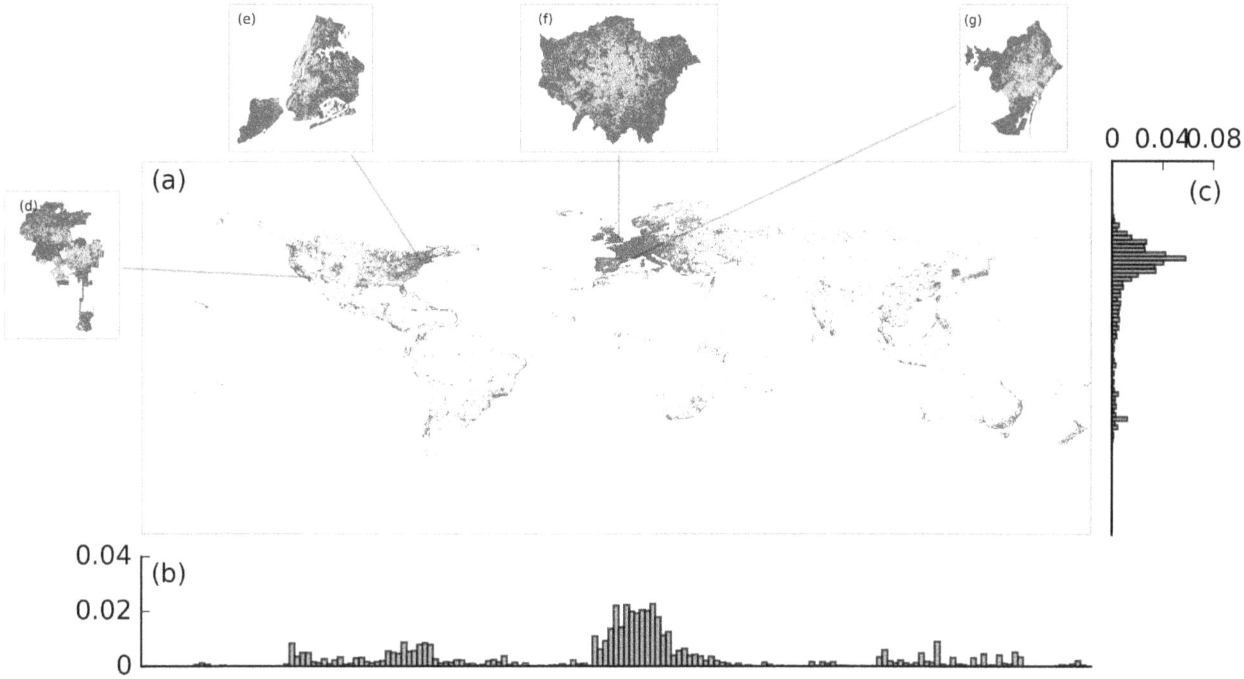

Figure 2: Geolocations of Airbnb listings. (a) Dot plot of all the 2,018,747 active listings; (b–c) Histogram of longitude and latitude; (d–g) Dot plot of listings in the city of Los Angeles, New York, London, and Barcelona. See Appendix A for the copyright of city maps.

one review captured in our data set but not every guest has given reviews.

Next, we provide estimations of some statistics that are still unknown or may be outdated. First, 307,465 users are both hosts and guests, accounting for 23.4% of all hosts, counted based on the observation that they own listings and give reviews to other listings. This gives one answer to the Quora question.[3] Second, Fig. 1 presents the cumulative number of hosts in each month from March 2008 to August 2016, constructed using the month information that indicates when they joined Airbnb. We see that an exponential growth of number of hosts started from around 2012. Third, we make an estimate of an important statistic—the guest-to-host review rate—meaning the fraction of stays where guests have left reviews to their hosts after the conclusion of their stays. We approximate it as

$$\begin{aligned}\text{guest-to-host review rate} &= \frac{\#\text{ stays with reviews left}}{\#\text{ total stays}} \\ &\approx \frac{19,102,711}{102,718,148} = 18.6\%.\end{aligned} \tag{1}$$

Here the number of stays with reviews left is simply the number of reviews (excluding automatic reviews, cf. § 3.4), and the total number of stays is estimated by extrapolating the distribution of number of reviews per guest showed in Fig. 5(a) from the $11M$ guests to the entire population of $60M$ guests. Our estimate has already been significantly smaller than the reported 72% in 2012 by Airbnb's CEO Brian Chesky.[4] It remains to be seen how accurate our estimation is and how the one disclosed in early days is different from the one nowadays.

3 MEASURING AIRBNB LISTINGS

3.1 Geolocations

Let us start with where Airbnb listings are located—a question repeatedly asked by hoteliers, policy-makers, and other stakeholders (e.g., [30]). Using each listing's approximate geolocation information in latitude/longitude values provided by Airbnb, we present in Fig. 2(a) a dot plot showing geolocations of all active listings across the world. We see that listings are globally distributed. To understand their geographic concentration, Figs. 2(b) and (c) respectively show the histograms of longitude and latitude values. We observe that, on the continental level, listings are heavily located in Western Europe, North America, East and South Asia, and Pacific Asia. Focusing on the country level, Airbnb has reached a world-wide yet heterogeneous coverage. US is the largest market for Airbnb, with 308,714 listings totaling for 15.29% of all listings, followed by France (11.82%), Italy (10.07%), Spain (6.16%), and United Kingdom (3.93%). Figure 3(b) lists the top 30 countries, which in total account for 83.55% of all listings. Meanwhile, many countries have only hundreds of listings, and there are no listings in a lot of African countries.

[3]https://www.quora.com/What-percentage-of-Airbnb-hosts-are-also-guests

[4]https://www.quora.com/What-percent-of-Airbnb-hosts-leave-reviews-for-their-guests/answer/Brian-Chesky?srid=uU9cX

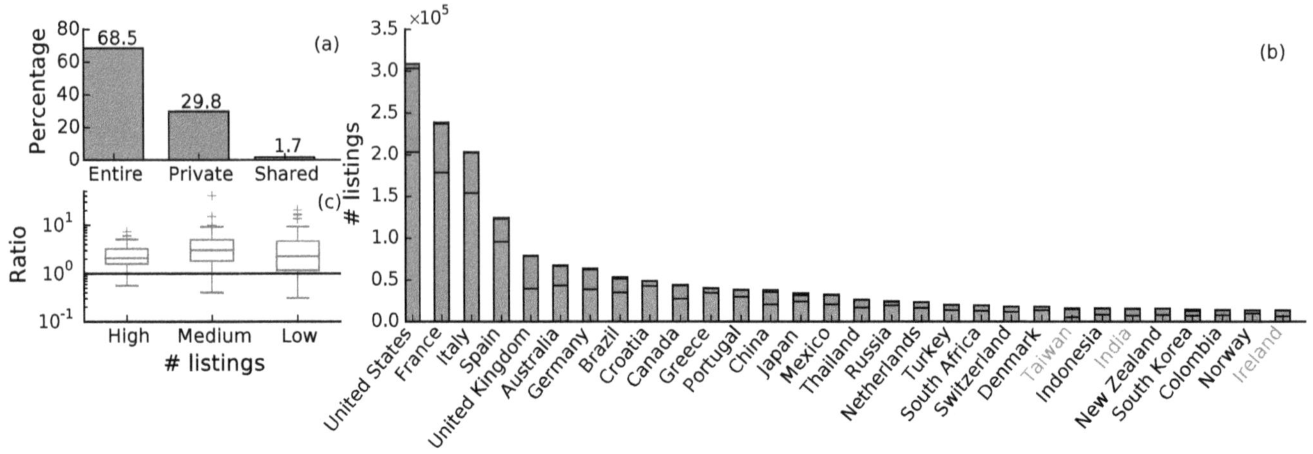

Figure 3: Room types of Airbnb listings. (a) Distribution of room types of all active listings; (b) Number of listings by room type in the top 30 countries with the highest number of listings. Countries with smaller number of entire homes than private rooms are marked red; (c) Distribution of the ratio between entire homes and private rooms in countries with high, medium, and low number of listings.

Focusing on cities, Figs. 2(d)–(g) respectively display locations of listings in the city of Los Angeles, New York, London, and Barcelona. As here we are interested in the global distribution, we leave the detailed study of how listings are located within cities as future work. Some studies have done so focusing on London [28] and Barcelona [16].

3.2 Room Types

Next, we study the distribution of the three types of rooms of Airbnb listings: *entire home/apartment*, *private room*, and *shared room*. As suggested by their names, entire home means that the host will not be present in the home during one's stay; private room means that the guest will occupy a private bedroom and share other spaces with others; and shared room means the guest will share the bedroom with other guests. While the latter two types of listings may align with the symbolism of the sharing economy that hosts occasionally share their spare rooms, it is the type of entire home that (1) directly contrasts with such symbolism; and (2) becomes the necessary condition for hosts to convert residential houses into short-term rentals and for business operators to conduct business by renting out their numerous properties. Hosts who use entire homes in such ways have become one of the main targets of regulations in some cities. For instance, the New York State Legislature recently passed a bill that subjects hosts to fines when they rent their entire homes for less than thirty days,[5] and the bill was recently signed by New York Governor Andrew M. Cuomo.[6] The statistics about room types are therefore among the key characteristics mentioned in many reports by various interest groups (e.g., [30]), yet they are still unknown at the entire-marketplace level.

Figure 3(a) shows that on the entire market, 68.5% of listings are entire homes, while only 29.8% are private rooms; Airbnb has 1.3 times more entire homes than private rooms. These statistics are in contrast with the ones back in 2012 when 57% were entire homes and 41% were private rooms [17]. Such change indicates that Airbnb, a primary example of the "sharing economy," is more like a rental marketplace rather than a spare-room sharing platform.

We investigate variations of the room type distribution across countries. Figure 3(b) shows the number of the three types of listings in the top 30 countries with the largest number of listings. Among them, 27 countries have more entire homes than private rooms. In the US, which has the largest number of listings, 65.8% are entire rooms, and the ratio between number of entire homes and private rooms reaches 2. The only three countries or regions where there are more private rooms than entire homes are Taiwan (0.57), India (0.91), and Ireland (0.96), though the ratio is close to one for the latter two countries. We further calculate the ratio for each of the 150 countries with more than 100 listings (Countries with small number of listings have large fluctuations of the ratio.), and show in Fig. 3(c) the distributions of the ratio for the three equally-sized groups of countries, based on their total number of listings. We see that the ratio is greater than one across many countries and even larger for countries with smaller number of listings.

3.3 Star-ratings

We now focus on star-ratings and reviews, which are the reputation system of Airbnb and important sources of information for guests to pick listings [24]. At the conclusion of each stay, both the host and guest can give reviews to and rate each other at a scale from 1 to 5 stars with a unit of 0.5 star. Each listing will receive an average star-rating once it is rated by at least 3 guests.[7] The star-rating of each individual review, however, is not publicly disclosed.

Figure 4(a) shows a bimodal distribution of star-ratings over all listings. More than half of them (54.6%) have not received their ratings, and 40.6% have 4.5 or 5 stars. These three categories of listings account for over 95% of all listings, and the number of

[5] http://www.forbes.com/sites/briansolomon/2016/06/17/new-york-wants-to-fine-airbnb-hosts-up-to-7500

[6] http://www.nytimes.com/2016/10/22/technology/new-york-passes-law-airbnb.html

[7] https://www.airbnb.com/help/article/1257/how-do-star-ratings-work

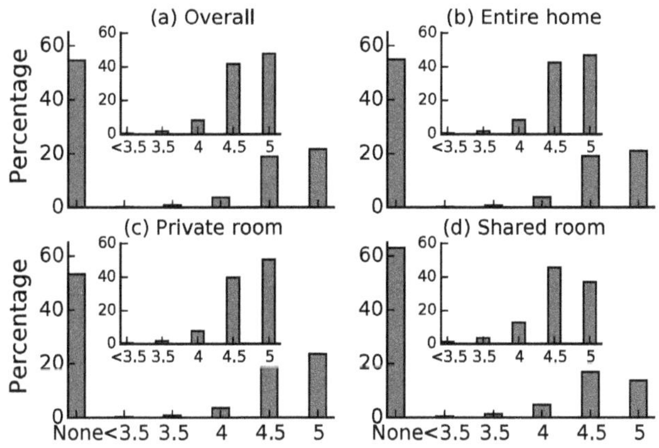

Figure 4: Distribution of star-ratings.

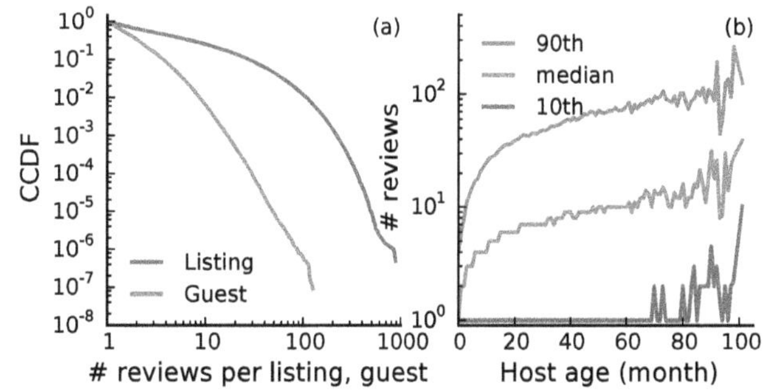

Figure 5: Review counts on Airbnb. (a) Distribution of number of reviews per listing and guest; (b) Number of reviews of listings with different host ages.

listings with 3.5 or lower stars is essentially negligible. Focusing on listings that have received star-ratings, Fig. 4(a) inset shows that star-ratings are overwhelmingly positive; 89.5% of them have 4.5 or 5 stars, and the mean (median) rating is 4.67 (4.5). These results are consistent with a previous small-scale study [35]. However, this heavily skewed distribution is sightly different from previously observed J-shaped distribution of product reviews [18]. In particular, such distribution suggests that the number of 1-star products is high, which is not the case for Airbnb listings.

We explore variations of this distribution by room type. Figures 4(b)–(d) respectively show the star-rating distributions of entire homes, private rooms, and shared rooms. Although, for shared rooms, 4.5-star listings are of a higher fraction than 5-star listings, there is very limited variation of the distribution: The majority of listings, irrespective of room type, have either no or very high ratings. This, on the one hand, suggests that many guests had great experiences during their stays, but makes star-ratings less informative and distinguishable for future guests to choose among potential listings, on the other.

3.4 Reviews

There are 19, 377, 978 reviews given by 11, 150, 017 guests. We are aware that Airbnb will post an automatic review if a host cancels a reservation, serving as one penalty for the cancellation.[8] We find 275, 267 automatic reviews, amounting to 1.4% of all reviews. This provides an upper bound of the cancellation rate by hosts, as not every stay yields a review. We removed all automatic reviews before further analysis.

3.4.1 Distribution of Review Counts. On the Airbnb review system, which is different from others like Yelp, only guests who concluded their stays can give reviews. This makes the number of reviews a listing has received a proxy of its business attention, although the review rate and number of stayed nights associated with each review may be different. Therefore, we analyze how reviews are distributed among listings, showing in Fig. 5(a) the survival distribution. We shift it by one to make the zero-review data point visible in the logarithmic scale. We see that although Airbnb is a relatively young marketplace, reviews have already been heterogeneously distributed among listings. About 35.7% listings do not have reviews, and respectively 12.2% and 7.4% listings have one and two reviews. The remaining 44.6% listings, each of which has at least three reviews, account for 93.6% reviews. In § 5, we demonstrate the presence of the rich-get-richer mechanism in explaining the growth of reviews.

We next analyze the relation between listing age and number of reviews. As we do not know when each listing was established, nor do we know when each and every review was given, we use the Airbnb age of its host—the number of months passed since they joined Airbnb—as a proxy of the listing age. Focusing on listings with at least one review, Fig. 5(b) shows the 10th, 50th, and 90th percentile of number of reviews of listings grouped by host age. We observe that (1) the number of reviews in general increases with host ages; (2) even for hosts who joined Airbnb for years, the median number of reviews still remains in the order of ten; and (3) the review count is heterogeneously distributed even for hosts who joined Airbnb in the same month.

Figure 5(a) also shows a heavy-tailed distribution of number of reviews per guest. Respectively 66.3% and 17.8% guests have given one and two reviews, while only 0.63% guests have left at least 10 reviews.

3.4.2 Review Content. We start investigating text content of reviews with what languages are used. Using the `langdetect` language detection library,[9] we found 49 languages used. Table 2 reports the percentages of reviews written in the top 10 most used languages. English dominates this ranking, with 72.8% of reviews using it, followed by French, Spanish, German, and Italian. From now on, we focus on the 14, 094, 229 English reviews.

Positive/Negative words: Recall that a vast majority (89.5%) of listings have 4.5 or 5 stars (Fig. 4(a) inset). This raises the question of whether this strongly skew toward positive star-ratings is consistent with a usage bias toward positive vocabulary. To answer this, we use a recently released resource that contains norms of almost 14*K* English words [34], each of which has a valence score from 1 to 9, where valence greater than 5 means positive words

[8] https://www.airbnb.com/help/article/314/why-did-i-get-a-review-that-says-i-canceled

[9] https://pypi.python.org/pypi/langdetect

Table 2: Top 10 languages used in reviews

Language	%	Language	%
English	72.8	Chinese (Simplified)	1.6
French	10.3	Korean	1.3
Spanish	3.8	Portuguese	1.0
German	3.5	Dutch	0.9
Italian	2.3	Russian	0.9

and smaller than 5 negative words. We calculate the ratio of the frequency of positive and negative words in Airbnb reviews. To compare the skewness, we also calculate the ratio for $2.7M$ Yelp reviews.[10] Table 3 shows that the ratio doubles for Airbnb reviews. This confirms a bias toward using positive words, and the extent is even greater than reviews on Yelp, which already exhibits a positive bias [20]. Given that Airbnb is a P2P platform where hosts can also choose which guests to accommodate, this finding may open up further investigations into user behaviors on different platforms.

4 MEASURING MULTI-LISTING HOSTS

In this section, we investigate a key issue repeatedly discussed in the current debate—the existence of hosts who own multiple listings on Airbnb. Hereafter, we call them "multi-listers." Note that they may have different names in various reports, such as "commercial hosts," "professional hosts," and "business operators," all attempting to capture the possibility that they may operate business on Airbnb, as an ordinary host is less likely to own numerous listings. Despite being a critical issue, there has been no systematic analysis about multi-listers and their listings.

4.1 Existence of Multi-listers

Recall that there are 2, 018, 747 active listings owned by 1, 313, 626 hosts (Table 1), thus on average every host owns 1.54 listings. Figure 6(a) shows the survival distribution of number of owned listings per host. We observe a somewhat surprising heavy-tailed distribution that spans more than three orders of magnitude, similar to what have been observed in many complex systems [1]. We fit the empirical distribution with a power-law function $p(x) = \frac{\alpha-1}{x_{\min}}\left(\frac{x}{x_{\min}}\right)^{-\alpha}$ using the methods developed in refs [2, 4], and obtain $\alpha = 2.65$ and $x_{\min} = 15$. These results not only demonstrate the existence of "super multi-listers"—hosts who can own up to 1, 800 listings, but also indicate that the existence of multi-listers is prevalent. Simply put, although the vast majority of hosts have a small number of listings, there is a consistent number of hosts who own a large number of listings. In particular, 1, 030, 134 (78.4%) and 159, 627 (12.2%) hosts respectively own one and two listings, and the remaining 9.43% hosts own 33.16% of all listings.

To further characterize multi-listers and their listings, we need to answer a key question—which threshold of number of owned listings per host allows us to separate hosts into two groups and then compare them. Previous literature have not reached a consensus about this. The New York State Attorney General, for example, defined "commercial hosts" as those who have three or more unique listings [30]. Li *et al.* defined "professional hosts" as those who have two or more listings [23]. Here, we argue that a typical threshold value may not be well-defined, as Fig. 6(a) clearly suggests that the number of owned listings is a multi-scale phenomenon. Moreover, as we shall show, focusing on a particular value loses the whole picture and can even be misleading.

[10] https://www.yelp.com/dataset_challenge/

Table 3: Ratio of frequency of positive and negative words used in Airbnb and Yelp reviews

	Airbnb reviews	Yelp reviews
Ratio	13.749	6.705

Instead, we simply increase the threshold and study how various measures of interest change accordingly. Specifically, for a given threshold, we characterize (1) the subset of hosts whose number of owned listings *exceeds* the given threshold; and (2) the subset of listings owned by those hosts. If the threshold is zero, we simply focus on all hosts and all listings.

4.2 Listings Owned by Multi-listers

Figures 6(b)–(e) present the characterization results for listings owned by multi-listers. Figure 6(b) shows the percentages of listings in 5 countries, United States (US), Spain (ES), Croatia (HR), Italy (IT), and Australia (AU), selected because they have the largest number of listings when the threshold is 20. We observe that as we increase the threshold, listings owned by multi-listers are disproportionately located in the US. We also see that a decreasing portion of listings are from Italy, while Spain and Croatia have an increasing portion. Figure 6(b) (and Fig. 6(d)) also illustrates why focusing on a particular threshold can be misleading. For example, if one focused on a particular value (1 or 2), one would have concluded that the number of US listings owned by multi-listers is proportional to total listings in the US, which is not the case.

Figure 6(c) focuses on how the total number of listings and number of reviews received by them change as we increase the threshold. We observe a faster decrease of review counts, indicating that the average number of reviews per listing decreases. When the threshold is 0, on average a listing has 9.6 reviews, which decreases to 2.6 when the threshold reaches 20. Therefore, listings owned by multi-listers are less reviewed.

Figure 6(d) shows that an increasing portion of listings are entire homes as the threshold increases. When the threshold is 20, more than 92% of listings are entire homes, compared to 68.5% on the entire market. This confirms the previous conjecture that commercial hosts seek to rent out their entire home properties.

Figure 6(e) answers the question of how far away the listings owned by a single host. Using listings' latitude/longitude values, we calculate, for each host, the maximum distance among all pairwise distances between two of their listings, capturing the geographical diameter of their "managerial" activities. Figure 6(e) shows that the median of the distribution of maximum distance over all hosts whose number of listings exceeds a given threshold, though keeps increasing, is in the order of $10km$. This suggests that listings owned by multi-listers may locate within a city and that they may operate business locally.

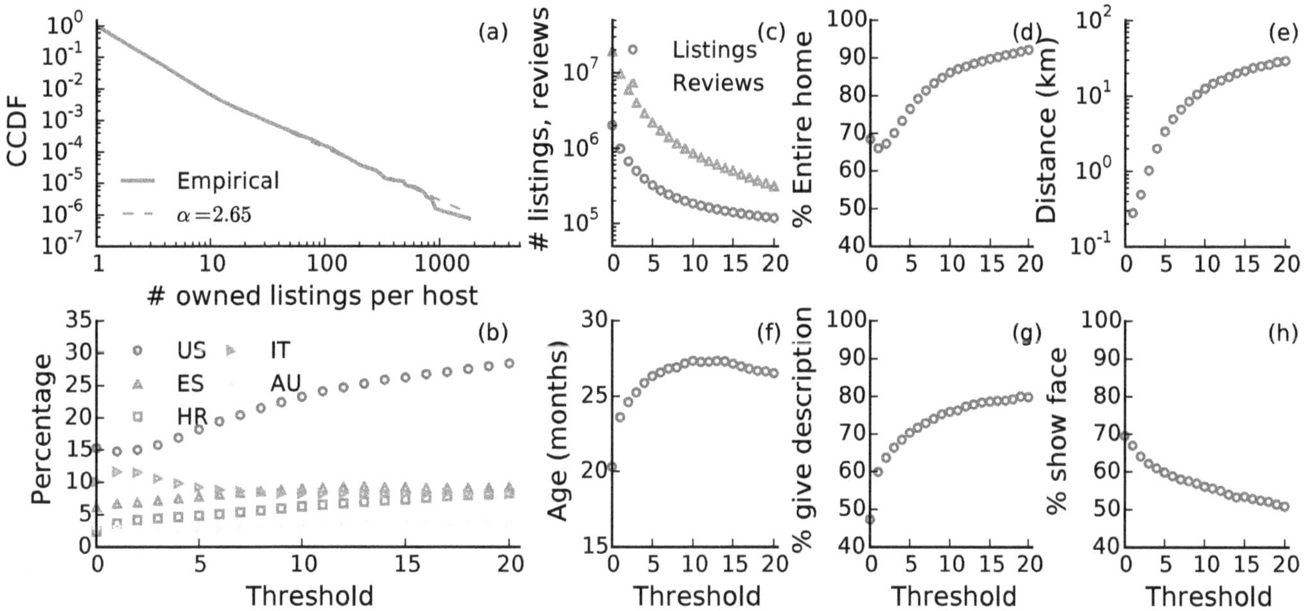

Figure 6: Characterizing multi-listers and their listings. (a) Survival distribution of number of owned listings per host. From (b) to (h), we focus on (1) the subset of hosts whose number of owned listings *exceeds* a threshold; and (2) the subset of listings owned by those hosts, and show how various measures change as we increase the threshold. (b) Percentage of listings located in 5 countries; (c) Number of listings and their total reviews; (d) Percentage of entire homes; (e) The median of the distribution of the maximum distance between pairs of listings owned by a host; (f) Mean Airbnb age of hosts; (g) Percentage of hosts who give descriptions; (h) Percentage of hosts whose profile photos have facial features.

4.3 Multi-listers

Figures 6(f)–(h) show the characterization results for multi-listers. First, Fig. 6(f) demonstrates that multi-listers are early-movers towards joining Airbnb, as their mean Airbnb age is larger than other hosts.

Figure 6(g) focuses on the percentages of hosts who give descriptions in the space-limited "Your Host" section on listings' web pages. Presenting self-description is one important way to establish trust between guests and hosts. Surprisingly, only 47.3% of all hosts have given descriptions (threshold 0), and multi-listers are more likely to do so. Using the method described in ref. [26] and setting the threshold to 10, we find the top 10 overrepresented words used in multi-listers' descriptions are "https," "vacation," "wildschönau," "properties," "rentals," "team," "villas," "rental," "apartments," and "services," indicating that they use the description section to advertise their listings.

Figure 6(h) examines another way to establish trust—showing faces in profile photos. Using a service provided by Face++ to detect whether there are facial features presented in a given photo,[11] we find that for 69.5% of all hosts, there are faces detected in their profile photos. Multi-listers are less likely to show faces in their photos, and a manual inspection reveals that many of them use company's logos as profile photos.

[11]http://www.faceplusplus.com/detection_detect/

5 MODELING REVIEW GROWTH

In the last section, we have found notable differences between multi-listers and other hosts. This raises the question of whether the differences are linked to listings' future rental performances. To answer this, we approximate performances with number of new reviews, as we do not know listings' actual booked nights. For each listing, we calculate the number of new reviews it has received in one month, which is our response variable. The first two columns in Table 4 list predictors and their definitions. Instant Book is a listing feature, meaning that a potential guest can book the listing without the host's approval.[12] The superhost badge is awarded to a host if they satisfies a series of requirements set by Airbnb.[13] Response time of a host is transformed into numerical values, so that a faster response corresponds to a larger value.

We fit a linear regression model by ordinary least squares (OLS) to understand factors linked to the growth of reviews. The last column in Table 4 presents the regression results. Other predictors being the same, listings with more existing reviews will have more new reviews, demonstrating the presence of the rich-get-richer mechanism that has been found to explain the growth of numerous systems [27]. Listings whose ratings have one more star will have 0.169 more review. A private room will gain 0.112 more review than an entire home, while a shared room will have 0.091 less review than an entire home. A listing that can be instantly booked will have 0.272 more review than those without the Instant Book feature.

[12]https://www.airbnb.com/help/article/187/what-is-instant-book
[13]https://www.airbnb.com/superhost

Table 4: Regression results for monthly new reviews

reviews	Number of reviews	0.037***
		(0.0001)
rating	Star-rating	0.169***
		(0.001)
room_type	Room type	
	private	0.112***
		(0.003)
	shared	−0.091***
		(0.011)
amenities	# available amenities	0.017***
		(0.0003)
instant_book	Instant book is allowed	
	1	0.272***
		(0.003)
photos	Number of photos	−0.002***
		(0.0001)
host_age	Host age	−0.018***
		(0.0001)
host_super	Host is a superhost	
	1	0.259***
		(0.005)
host_desp	Host gives descriptions	
	1	0.040***
		(0.003)
host_resp_rate	Host response rate	0.229***
		(0.013)
host_resp_time	Host response time	0.220***
		(0.002)
host_nlisting	# owned listings	−0.001***
		(0.00002)
Constant		−0.446***
		(0.011)
Observations		1,140,488
Adjusted R^2		0.388
Note:		*p<0.1; **p<0.05; ***p<0.01

Being a superhost, giving descriptions, maintaining high response rate, responding in short time, and owning a smaller number of listings all have positive effects on review growth, though the effect is small for the number of owned listings.

6 RELATED WORK

There is a growing interest in Airbnb and other sharing economy platforms from diverse disciplines, ranging from computer science to economics to law. Empirical studies have focused on, for example, star-ratings of listings [35] and geolocations of listings within cities [16, 28]. Our focus here is the entire Airbnb platform. There are studies that have reported the presence of discrimination on Airbnb [8, 9]. Some work have investigated factors associated with listings' price, such as the receipt of star-ratings [15] and race [21] and personal photos [11] of their hosts. The impact of Airbnb on hotel industry revenue [36, 37] and on tourism industry employment [12] has been investigated. Discussions about regulations of Airbnb have also generated much attention [5, 7]. Li *et al.* investigated differences in performances and behaviors between professional hosts—those who own two or more listings—and non-professional hosts on Airbnb [23]. Our analysis, however, reveals the lack of threshold that allows us to separate professional and non-professional hosts. Studies focusing on the motivations behind joining Airbnb to provide hospitality have pointed out that monetary compensation and sociability are two important aspects [19, 22]. Fradkin *et al.* experimentally investigated the determinants and bias in the Airbnb review system [14]. Fradkin proposed ranking algorithms for the Airbnb search engine [13].

7 CONCLUSION AND FUTURE WORK

In this work, we have presented the first large-scale data-driven study on Airbnb. After crawling the largest ever number of Airbnb listings, we have measured their geolocations, room types, star-ratings, and reviews. We have also characterized in a great detail hosts who own multiple listings as well as their listings. We have built a linear regression model to understand factors linked to the growth of reviews. As these aspects are among the key points discussed in the ongoing debate and among important features in the sharing economy, we believe that our work provides valuable insights for various stakeholders and may serve as a public and empirical reference to inform the debate.

One major limitation of our work is that we do not measure listing occupancy. Therefore we do not know to what extent a listing is rented in short-terms or what revenue differences are between multi-listers and ordinary hosts. We notice that it is feasible to crawl listing calendar data. However, one issue of using such data is that, given a listing is unavailable on some dates, we cannot tell if it is rented out or simply blocked by the host for not renting. Another technical challenge is to large-scale monitor the calender data on a daily basis. Future work may do so on a small scale. Other future work include studying geolocation at a finer level, measuring hosts' behavioral changes, and understanding the effect of review content on listings' future rentals.

A COPYRIGHT OF CITY MAPS

Los Angeles: shapefile from https://goo.gl/SxFhCx. **New York City**: shapefile from https://goo.gl/Isb4rf. **London**: shapefile from https://goo.gl/bWn9ua; copyright: "Contains National Statistics data ©Crown copyright and database right [2015]" and "Contains Ordnance Survey data ©Crown copyright and database right [2015]". **Barcelona**: shapefile from https://goo.gl/bYOhWL.

ACKNOWLEDGMENTS

I thank the anonymous referees for their comments and suggestions and Center for Complex Networks and Systems Research and School of Informatics and Computing at Indiana University for excellent computing resources.

REFERENCES

[1] Réka Albert and Albert-László Barabási. 2002. Statistical mechanics of complex networks. *Reviews of Modern Physics* 74 (2002), 47–97. Issue 1. https://doi.org/10.1103/RevModPhys.74.47

[2] Jeff Alstott, Ed Bullmore, and Dietmar Plenz. 2014. powerlaw: A Python Package for Analysis of Heavy-Tailed Distributions. *PLoS ONE* 9, 1 (2014), e85777. https://doi.org/10.1371/journal.pone.0085777

[3] Eduardo M. Azevedo and E. Glen Weyl. 2016. Matching markets in the digital age. *Science* 352 (2016), 1056–1057. Issue 6289. https://doi.org/10.1126/science.aaf7781

[4] Aaron Clauset, Cosma Rohilla Shalizi, and M. E. J. Newman. 2009. Power-law distributions in empirical data. *SIAM Rev.* 51, 4 (2009), 661–703. https://doi.org/10.1137/070710111

[5] Molly Cohen and Arun Sundararajan. 2015. Self-Regulation and Innovation in the Peer-to-Peer Sharing Economy. *U Chi L Rev Dialogue* 82 (2015), 116.

[6] Michael A. Cusumano. 2015. How Traditional Firms Must Compete in the Sharing Economy. *Commun. ACM* 58, 1 (2015), 32–34. https://doi.org/10.1145/2688487

[7] Benjamin G. Edelman and Damien Geradin. 2015. Efficiencies and Regulatory Shortcuts: How Should We Regulate Companies like Airbnb and Uber? (2015). https://ssrn.com/abstract=2658603.

[8] Benjamin G. Edelman and Michael Luca. 2014. Digital Discrimination: The Case of Airbnb.com. (2014). Harvard Business School NOM Unit Working Paper No. 14–054.

[9] Benjamin G. Edelman, Michael Luca, and Dan Svirsky. 2017. Racial Discrimination in the Sharing Economy: Evidence from a Field Experiment. *American Economic Journal: Applied Economics* 9, 2 (2017), 1–22. https://doi.org/10.1257/app.20160213

[10] Liran Einav, Chiara Farronato, and Jonathan D. Levin. 2016. Peer-to-Peer Markets. *Annual Review of Economics* 8, 1 (2016), 615–635. https://doi.org/10.1146/annurev-economics-080315-015334

[11] Eyal Ert, Aliza Fleischer, and Nathan Magen. 2016. Trust and Reputation in the Sharing Economy: The Role of Personal Photos on Airbnb. *Tourism Management* 55 (2016), 62–73. https://doi.org/10.1016/j.tourman.2016.01.013

[12] Bin Fang, Qiang Ye, and Rob Law. 2016. Effect of sharing economy on tourism industry employment. *Annals of Tourism Research* 57 (2016), 264–267. https://doi.org/10.1016/j.annals.2015.11.018

[13] Andrey Fradkin. 2015. Search Frictions and the Design of Online Marketplaces. (2015). http://andreyfradkin.com/assets/SearchFrictions.pdf.

[14] Andrey Fradkin, Elena Grewal, Dave Holtz, and Matthew Pearson. 2015. Bias and Reciprocity in Online Reviews: Evidence From Field Experiments on Airbnb. In *Proceedings of the 16th ACM Conference on Economics and Computation*. 641–641. https://doi.org/10.1145/2764468.2764528

[15] Dominik Gut and Philipp Herrmann. 2015. Sharing Means Caring? Hosts' Price Reaction to Rating Visibility. *European Conference on Information Systems 2015 Research-in-Progress Papers* (2015). Paper 54.

[16] Javier Gutierrez, Juan Carlos Garcia-Palomares, Gustavo Romanillos, and Maria Henar Salas-Olmedo. 2016. Airbnb in tourist cities: comparing spatial patterns of hotels and peer-to-peer accommodation. (2016). arXiv:1606.07138.

[17] Daniel Guttentag. 2015. Airbnb: disruptive innovation and the rise of an informal tourism accommodation sector. *Current Issues in Tourism* 18, 12 (2015), 1192–1217. https://doi.org/10.1080/13683500.2013.827159

[18] Nan Hu, Jie Zhang, and Paul A. Pavlou. 2009. Overcoming the J-shaped distribution of product reviews. *Commun. ACM* 52, 10 (2009), 144–147. https://doi.org/10.1145/1562764.1562800

[19] Tapio Ikkala and Airi Lampinen. 2015. Monetizing Network Hospitality: Hospitality and Sociability in the Context of Airbnb. In *Proceedings of the 18th ACM Conference on Computer Supported Cooperative Work & Social Computing*. 1033–1044. https://doi.org/10.1145/2675133.2675274

[20] Dan Jurafsky, Victor Chahuneau, Bryan R. Routledge, and Noah A. Smith. 2014. Narrative framing of consumer sentiment in online restaurant reviews. *First Monday* 19, 4 (2014), 4944. https://doi.org/10.5210/fm.v19i4.4944

[21] Venoo Kakar, Julisa Franco, Joel Voelz, and Julia Wu. 2016. Effects of Host Race Information on Airbnb Listing Prices in San Francisco. (2016). https://ideas.repec.org/p/pra/mprapa/69974.html.

[22] Airi Lampinen and Coye Cheshire. 2016. Hosting via Airbnb: Motivations and Financial Assurances in Monetized Network Hospitality. In *Proceedings of the 2016 CHI Conference on Human Factors in Computing Systems*. 1669–1680. https://doi.org/10.1145/2858036.2858092

[23] Jun Li, Antonio Moreno, and Dennis J. Zhang. 2015. Agent Behavior in the Sharing Economy: Evidence from Airbnb. (2015). Ross School of Business Paper No. 1298. http://ssrn.com/abstract=2708279.

[24] Michael Luca. 2016. Designing Online Marketplaces: Trust and Reputation Mechanisms. (2016). https://doi.org/10.3386/w22616 NBER Working Paper No. 22616.

[25] Arvind Malhotra and Marshall Van Alstyne. 2014. The Dark Side of the Sharing Economy . . . and How to Lighten It. *Commun. ACM* 57, 11 (2014), 24–27. https://doi.org/10.1145/2668893

[26] Burt L. Monroe, Michael P. Colaresi, and Kevin M. Quinn. 2008. Fightin' Words: Lexical Feature Selection and Evaluation for Identifying the Content of Political Conflict. *Political Analysis* 16, 4 (2008), 372–403. https://doi.org/10.1093/pan/mpn018

[27] Matjaž Perc. 2014. The Matthew effect in empirical data. *Journal of The Royal Society Interface* 11, 98 (2014), 20140378. https://doi.org/10.1098/rsif.2014.0378

[28] Giovanni Quattrone, Davide Proserpio, Daniele Quercia, Licia Capra, and Mirco Musolesi. 2016. Who Benefits from the "Sharing" Economy of Airbnb?. In *Proceedings of the 25th International Conference on World Wide Web*. 1385–1394. https://doi.org/10.1145/2872427.2874815

[29] Alvin E. Roth. 2015. *Who Gets What—and Why: The New Economics of Matchmaking and Market Design.*

[30] Eric T. Schneiderman. 2014. Airbnb in the city. (October 2014). https://ag.ny.gov/pdfs/AIRBNB REPORT.pdf.

[31] David Streitfeld. 2014. Airbnb Listings Mostly Illegal, New York State Contends. (2014). http://www.nytimes.com/2014/10/16/business/airbnb-listings-mostly-illegal-state-contends.html.

[32] Ariel Stulberg. 2016. Airbnb Probably Isn't Driving Rents Up Much, At Least Not Yet. (August 2016). http://fivethirtyeight.com/features/airbnb-probably-isnt-driving-rents-up-much-at-least-not-yet/.

[33] Arun Sundararajan. 2016. *The Sharing Economy.*

[34] A. B. Warriner, V. Kuperman, and M. Brysbaert. 2013. Norms of valence, arousal, and dominance for 13,915 English lemmas. *Behavior Research Methods* 45, 4 (2013), 1191–1207. https://doi.org/10.3758/s13428-012-0314-x

[35] Georgios Zervas, Davide Proserpio, and John Byers. 2015. A First Look at Online Reputation on Airbnb, Where Every Stay is Above Average. (2015). http://ssrn.com/abstract=2554500.

[36] Georgios Zervas, Davide Proserpio, and John Byers. 2016. The Rise of the Sharing Economy: Estimating the Impact of Airbnb on the Hotel Industry. (2016). Boston U. School of Management Research Paper No. 2013-16.

[37] Georgios Zervas, Davide Proserpio, and John W. Byers. 2015. The Impact of the Sharing Economy on the Hotel Industry: Evidence from Airbnb's Entry Into the Texas Market. In *Proceedings of the Sixteenth ACM Conference on Economics and Computation*. 637–637. https://doi.org/10.1145/2764468.2764524

Understanding Citizens' and Local Governments' Digital Communications during Natural Disasters: The Case of Snowstorms

Lingzi Hong
iSchool
University of Maryland
lzhong@umd.edu

Cheng Fu
Department of Geographical Sciences
University of Maryland
cfu@umd.edu

Paul Torrens
Deparment of Computer Science and Engineering
New York University
torrens@nyu.edu

Vanessa Frias-Martinez
iSchool
University of Maryland
vfrias@umd.edu

ABSTRACT

A growing number of citizens and local governments have embraced the use of Twitter to communicate during natural disasters. Studies have shown that online communications during disasters can be explained using crisis communication taxonomies. However, such taxonomies are broad and general, and offer little insight into the detailed content of the communications. In this paper, we propose a semi-automatic framework to extract and compare, in retrospect, the digital communication footprints of citizens and governments during disasters. These footprints, which characterize the topics discussed during a disaster at different spatio-temporal scales, are computed in an unsupervised manner using topic models, and manually labelled to identify specific issues affecting the population. The end objective is to offer detailed information about issues affecting citizens during natural disasters and to compare these against local governments' communications. We evaluate the framework using Twitter communications from 18 snowstorms (including two blizzards) on the US east coast.

CCS CONCEPTS

• **Information systems** → **Data analytics**; **Social networks**; *Geographic information systems*; • **Computing methodologies** → **Information extraction**; **Topic modeling**;

KEYWORDS

crisis communication, disaster analytics, topic models,spatio-temporal analysis

1 INTRODUCTION

Natural disasters such as snowstorms, floods or tornados affect millions of citizens every year [4, 36]. The use of social media during such events has been extensively studied in the literature, with a heavy focus on Twitter. Researchers have analyzed the use of Twitter as an information spreading tool during disasters [31]; as a platform to generate situational awareness for humanitarian response [34]; as a way for governments to connect and engage with citizens [37]; or to extract and classify *information nuggets* in an automatic manner [15].

A growing number of citizens and local government agencies recognize its importance and embrace the use of social media platforms such as Twitter during natural disasters [37]. Most of the work in understanding citizens' and governments' digital communications during natural disasters has focused on using taxonomies with pre-defined sets of crisis communication categories [26, 30]. For example, two of the pre-defined categories in crisis communications are direct experience and media sharing which reflect a common human behavior during natural disasters, that of sharing what is seen. Such categorization is highly useful to understand behaviors from a sociological perspective, but it does not provide insights into the types of issues being discussed.

In this paper, we present an approach to extract and compare, in retrospect, the communication footprints of citizens and local governments during natural disasters. Our objective is twofold: first, we are interested in gaining more insight into the specific types of issues citizens and local governments discuss through social media. We propose to do this by freely exploring the topics discussed online, rather than using a pre-determined taxonomy of categories. For these topics to be meaningful, we also need to be able to frame them within various spatio-temporal scales that characterize different time periods and regions affected by the disaster. Second, we are interested in comparing the official communications from local governments with the citizens' digital communications. Ultimately, although not the focus of this paper, such comparisons could be used to analyze whether local governments' social media strategies are covering the information that citizens seek online during disasters.

With that purpose in mind, we present a framework to extract, with limited human supervision, a set of insightful topics shared online by citizens or local governments at fine-grained spatio-temporal scales during natural disasters. Broadly speaking, the framework uses geolocated tweets collected during several occurrences of a given type of natural disaster to identify, in retrospect, the issues discussed online at two spatial scales: counties and roads; and during

WebSci'17, June 25-28, 2017, Troy, NY, USA.
 ACM ISBN 978-1-4503-4896-6/17/06...$15.00
DOI: http://dx.doi.org/10.1145/3091478.3091502

three periods: before, during and after the disaster took place. Since the collection of geolocated tweets can include tweets potentially not related to the disaster, the framework uses hashtagged tweets, collected during the same natural disaster, as a gold standard of what disaster-related tweets look like, and ranks the geolocated tweets based on their similarity with respect to the gold standard. The similarity is computed using a language-based technique known as *ranking by cross-entropy* [3] that ranks each tweet by its similarity to the n-gram probabilistic distribution of the gold standard. The final subset of disaster-related tweets is selected from the ranked pool as the set of tweets with the largest topic coherence and interpretability when topics are extracted using Single-topic Latent Dirichlet Allocation (ST-LDA)[5, 13], a fully unsupervised topic modeling technique that creates probabilistic associations of words to topics and assigns a unique topic per tweet.

The resulting topics are manually labelled by annotators and the framework computes the *digital communication footprints* that characterize the types and distribution of topics for local governments and citizens, using only tweets with high topic membership probabilities. Finally, the framework analyzes the footprints observed in citizens' and local governments' digital communications and compares similarities and differences across space and time.

The proposed framework advances the state of the art in several fronts: (1) it extracts and compares, in a semi-automatic manner, digital communication footprints that characterize the types of topics local governments and citizens discuss online at different spatio-temporal scales. The objective is to extract and compare, in retrospect, detailed topics rather than general, pre-defined categories that albeit useful from a sociological point of view, do not provide insights into the specific types of issues discussed online [30]; (2) it requires a small amount of manual work carried out by annotators labeling the topics extracted by ST-LDA in a fully unsupervised manner; compared to previous automatic approaches of tweet classification during disasters that require massive labelings of individual tweets to train the classifiers [26]; and (3) it presents a novel approach to select tweets relevant to a natural disaster using a *ranking by cross-entropy* technique combined with topic models that eliminates the need to manually pre-define a set of keywords to identify tweets related to disasters [25]. We will also show that this technique provides a ranking that results in more cohesive and informative topics than using keyword-based rankings.

2 RELATED WORK

Social media, with a heavy focus on Twitter, has been extensively used in the past to retrieve information being exchanged during natural disasters [1, 31, 34]. Some approaches focus on understanding communication patterns via the analysis of tweeting behaviors [7, 11]; on studying the types of information being exchanged [25, 32]; or on understanding whether Twitter can be used as a proxy for damage assessment during disasters [18]. A complementary line of research has also analyzed official and media responses to natural disasters, and how these might differ with respect to citizens' responses across various types of disasters [6, 26]. The approach presented in this paper, is based on the fact that all the previous findings show that Twitter, with all of its limitations, can be used as a tool to understand communications during natural disasters, both in terms of behaviors and content being exchanged. Unlike previous comparative analyses that focus on the use of pre-defined taxonomies to characterize communications during disasters, our approach presents a framework that extracts detailed information using topic modeling techniques that allow to freely explore, in retrospect, the topics discussed online at various spatio-temporal scales [17].

From an analytical point of view, most of the work in this area has either focused on collecting tweets via hashtags and analyzing communication patterns and content during disasters [8, 29, 33]; on collecting geolocated tweets and/or tweets with disaster-related keywords and developing automatic classifiers to extract the tweets that are talking about the disaster [2, 15, 16, 25] or on a combination of both [19]. In this paper, we present a solution that uses both hashtagged and geolocated tweets, but that unlike previous approaches does not require the labeling of massive amounts of tweets to train automatic tweet classifiers. We achieve this by using unsupervised topic models and manual topic labeling to both extract disaster-related tweets and to analyze the types of topics discussed online during disasters.

3 THE FRAMEWORK

In this section we present the framework to extract digital communication footprints from the twitter activity of local governments and citizens during natural disasters, and to analyze their similarities and differences. The framework has four sequential components (see Figure 1): (1) data preparation, to clean and prepare the tweet datasets from local governments and citizens; (2) tweet ranking and selection, to determine the geolocated tweets that could be potentially related to the natural disaster; (3) topic identification, to extract and annotate the topics communicated online by local governments and by citizens; and (4) computation of digital communication footprints, to characterize and compare the distribution of topics discussed online by local governments and citizens at two spatial scales: counties and roads; and during three time periods: before, during and after the natural disaster.

In the next sections, we describe each component in detail and evaluate the framework for a specific type of natural disaster: snowstorms. The underlying hazards of snowstorms are varied, including vehicle accidents due to icy conditions on roads or power outages, and disrupt the lives of citizens even when their cities are, in principle, well prepared to cope with them [28]. We evaluate the framework on the snowstorms that took place across 24 counties in the state of Maryland for two winters from November, 2014 till April, 2016. This period was very harsh with 18 snowstorms including two blizzards. We define as snowstorms periods of one or more consecutive days when the snowfall was disruptive *i.e.,* when the snow depth provided by the National Oceanic and Atmospheric Administration was of at least $2in$ [24]. Although the evaluation focuses on snowstorms, the framework can be used to extract and compare, in retrospect, digital communication footprints from local governments and citizens for any type of acute event were both local agencies and the population participate and as long as it has one or multiple hashtags associated to it.

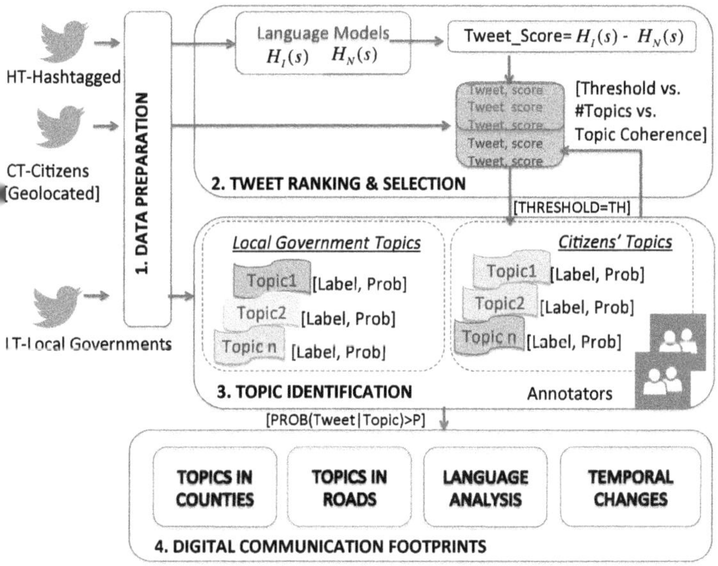

Figure 1: Overview of the proposed Framework.

4 DATA PREPARATION

The framework uses three data sources: geolocated tweets from citizens (CT), hashtagged tweets (HT), and tweets from local government agencies (LT). All these data sources are collected using Twitter's streaming API. The framework uses the geolocated tweets (CT) to extract the digital communication footprints of the citizens affected by the snowstorms at two spatial scales: counties and roads; and three time periods: before, during and after the natural disaster. CT was collected during the 2014-2016 winter seasons for the 24 counties in the state of Maryland using a bounding box over the whole state. Since the bounding box covered some areas outside of the limits of the state, we used the state's shapefile [9] to filter out tweets outside of its geographical boundary. We collected a total of $723,033$ geolocated tweets. However, since we are only interested in tweets published during disruptive snowstorms, we only kept tweets from CT that were posted on days when there was snow and its depth was of, at least, $2in$. To analyze the digital communications before and after the snowstorms took place, we also kept CT tweets published two days before and two days after each snowstorm. Finally, since we are interested in modeling the online voice of *average* citizens during the snowstorms, it is important to eliminate from CT all accounts potentially representing organizations or spammers. For that purpose, we retrieved the number of followers and followees for each twitter account in CT and filtered out accounts whose: (1) number of followers and followees were two standard deviations larger than the average values [38]; and (2) whose ratio of followees over followers was smaller than two standard deviations from the average value of the dataset [39]. The final size of CT after applying the described filters was of $169,987$ tweets.

The framework also requires all the hashtagged tweets (HT) associated to the area affected by the natural disaster under study. This second dataset is used in the Tweet Ranking and Selection component of the framework as a gold standard of the language employed and the topics discussed during the natural disaster. To collect HT during the snowstorms, we manually curated a list of 12 hashtags that were used during the 2014-2016 snowstorms in Maryland (MD) and collected all the tweets that had at least one of the hashtags in the text of the tweet. Some examples of the collected hashtags include #mdblizzard or #mdsnow. We did not collect more generic hashtags (*e.g., #blizzard*) since they could represent topics and language from other regions. The final HT dataset contained a total of $96,423$ hashtagged tweets.

The framework also requires a dataset with the tweets generated by local government agencies (LT) in the area where the natural disaster takes place. To carry out this data collection for the snowstorms, we computed a curated list of 83 Twitter handles representing local government agencies from the 24 counties in the state of Maryland; and collected all their tweets for the 2014-2016 winter seasons. Similarly to CT, we only kept LT tweets that were published either two days before, during, or two days after a snowstorm with a depth of at least $2in$. The final size of LT was $18,688$ tweets.

Local government tweets are typically not geolocated. However, we need to assign a location to be able to compare the digital communication footprints of local governments and citizens at two spatial scales: counties and roads. As a result, an official tweet will be assigned a location based on the location of the agency itself. For example, if the local agency is the Allegany County Department of Emergency Services (@Allegany911), the location assigned to the tweets generated by this account will be Allegany county. On the other hand, the tweets created by local transportation agencies are associated to roads. For example, tweets by Montgomery County's Highway Service (@MontCo_Highways) would be used to compute the digital footprints on roads.

Finally, we clean the text of all the collected tweets as follows: we eliminate stop words, emoticons, and tweets with less than 4 words; we maintain retweets because they are indicative of individuals agreeing with a message; we replace specific numbers and road names with the generic words *number* and *roadname* since these are frequent in our tweets but hard to model due to the different types of addresses, numbers and roads involved; we replace links with the word *link* to keep track of media being shared; and we lemmatize all words using NLTK's WordNet [21]. As opposed to stemming, lemmatization (which reduces words to lemmas, or dictionary forms) has been frequently used with topic models providing good results [35]. The final size of the CT dataset after this cleaning was $163,019$ tweets since there were $\approx$ 6000 tweets with less than four words. HT and LT kept the same number of tweets. It is important to clarify that, by exclusively using geolocated tweets from citizens to compare against local governments' tweets, we acknowledge that we are only able to capture the voice of those who have geolocation enabled on their Twitter accounts. Although that is a limitation, it is the unique way to extract local information that is meaningful and actionable at the granular spatial scales we are interested in studying. Other approaches with larger, non-geolocated, datasets could provide potentially additional information; however, it would come at the cost of loosing the local scale, which is the focus of this research.

5 TWEET RANKING AND SELECTION

CT contains tweets that were published by citizens during snowstorms. However, it is highly probable that not all the collected tweets are talking about the snowstorms. This framework component focuses on: (1) the ranking of the *CT* tweets with respect to their similarity to snowstorm-related tweets; and (2) the computation of the threshold to select the final subset of ranked *CT* tweets that potentially talk about snowstorms (see Tweet Ranking in Figure 1). This component is exclusively executed on *CT* since local governments' tweets during a disaster (*LT*) typically focus on disaster-related topics [14].

The framework performs the ranking process using the hashtagged tweets (*HT*) as a gold standard of what snowstorm-related tweets might look like. By comparing the *CT* tweets against the ground truth, the framework can assign a similarity score to each geolocated tweet and rank them. Specifically, the framework uses a method called *ranking by cross-entropy* [3]. This method uses all the hashtagged tweets (*HT*) to compute an *in-domain* language model that characterizes the frequency of different n-grams in tweets that talk about snowstorm-related topics. *HT* tweets are considered to be *in-domain* as opposed to more generic tweets that can talk or not about snowstorms, which the method will refer to as *general-domain* tweets. The method also computes the language model for the *general-domain* *CT* tweets, that can talk about any topic, calculating the frequency distribution of n-grams across all the *CT* tweets. These two language models are used to compute, for each *CT* tweet, the difference between the tweet's perplexity using the in-domain model and the tweet's perplexity using the general-domain model. The idea behind this scoring is that tweets that are highly similar to in-domain (snowstorm) tweets and highly dissimilar to the general-domain tweets will be ranked highly. Formally, given a string s with empirical n-gram distribution p in a language model q, we calculate its perplexity as: $P(s) = 2^{H(s)}$ where $H(s)$ is the cross-entropy of the string s computed as $H(s) = -\sum_x p(x) \log q(x)$. This process results in a list of ranked *CT* tweets based on their perplexity score, from smaller (most similar) to larger (most different) values. The framework uses the SRI Language Modeling Toolkit with one to four n-grams to compute the language models [22]. To account for the sparsity and the fact that many words are not present in our datasets, we use the interpolated modified Kneser-Ney discount when building the language models.

Next, the framework performs the computation of the threshold that determines the percentage of tweets from the ranked pool to be selected as snowstorm-related tweets. Since the final goal of the framework is to extract the topics discussed online during snowstorms, we use the quality of the topics obtained as a measure of how good the selection of in-domain, snowstorm-related tweets is. The underlying assumption is that if the *CT* tweets selected are snowstorm-related tweets, then the quality of the topics extracted by the topic modeling technique will be high; while if the selected *CT* tweets are mostly noisy *i.e.,* not related to snowstorms, then the quality of the topics would be low. To determine the best threshold value, the framework uses the PMI score (point-wise mutual information) as a measure of the quality and interpretability of the topics extracted using ST-LDA over the *CT* tweets [5, 13]. This measure has been showed to best model topic coherence and interpretability when compared to other topic scoring methods [23]. Specifically, the method computes the PMI score for various combinations of threshold values (th) and numbers of topics (K) and selects the final th and K based on the largest PMI achieved. Formally, the framework computes the PMI for each topic and averages across all topics. The PMI for a topic is computed as $PMI(x, y) = \log \frac{p(y,x)}{p(y)}$ where x and y are word n-grams from the top t most frequent words for that topic, and the PMI measures the probability of co-occurrence of those two words. Details about topic identification with ST-LDA are described in the next component of the framework.

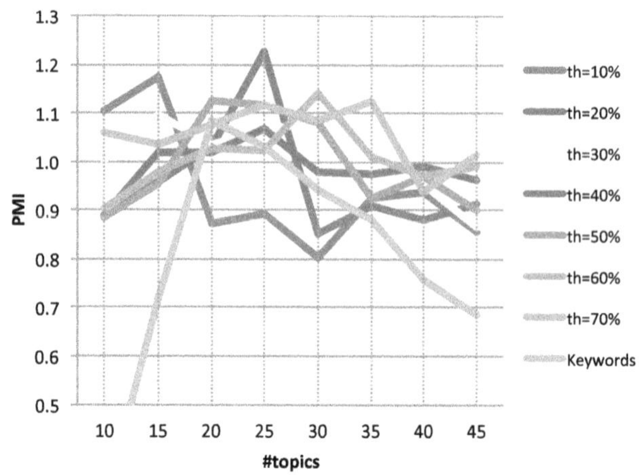

Figure 2: PMI values for various threshold (*th*) and number of topics (*K*) combinations; and for the keywords approach.

Figure 2 shows the results of the ranking process and threshold-based tweet selection using the *CT* and *HT* datasets containing snowstorm tweets across the 24 counties in the state of Maryland. Each data point represents the PMI for a given combination of threshold and number of topics, and is computed as the average PMI across all the topics when the top 10 1-gram words are considered. We show results for $K = 10$ to $K = 45$ different topics and threshold values from 10% to 70% (other values perform worse and are thus not shown). We observe that the best values for our dataset were 25 topics and a threshold of 20% *i.e.,* selecting the top 20% of the ranked tweets as being snowstorm related and extracting 25 topics provides the most coherent and interpretable set of topics discussed online during snowstorms.

Computing the two language models for the ranking process is computationally expensive. One could argue that a keyword-based approach would be a much more efficient way to select the subset of *CT* tweets related to snowstorms. To assess this hypothesis, we compare the performance of both approaches as follows. We collected snowstorm-related keywords using two sources: (1) words provided by five individuals who were asked to create a list of words they would use on Twitter to talk about their experiences during the 2014-2016 snowstorms (filtering out repeated words); and (2) a list of 380 disaster-related words from the dataset published in [25]. The total set of keywords collected was of 419. We used this set of keywords to filter out the *CT* tweets that did not contain any of these words in their text; and computed the PMI for the same sets of topics (K values) reported in Figure 2. As the green line in the Figure shows, the keyword-based PMI values are worse than the proposed ranking-selection approach for most of the thresholds explored. The best result for the keyword-based approach (with $K = 20$) gives a $PMI = 1.08$, which is much worse than the best result for the proposed ranking approach with a $PMI = 1.23$ (with $K = 25$ and $th = 20\%$). This result shows that our ranking and selection approach helps in identifying a subset of disaster-related tweets that result in more coherent and interpretable topics than when using tweets exclusively selected via keywords. Given that the keyword list we used is quite comprehensive, we argue that this finding could be related to the fact that Twitter language is very informal and words are prone to polysemy (*e.g.,* Jonas: the name of a snowstorm and a music band); as well as to slang (*e.g.,* crash: fall asleep or accident). Using such informal language as keywords, we could be labeling as snowstorm-related tweets, tweets that are not in reality.

6 TOPIC IDENTIFICATION

This component focuses on identifying the topics discussed online by local governments and citizens. The framework runs two steps: (1) topic extraction and (2) topic labeling. The topic extraction is executed using Single-topic Latent Dirichlet Allocation (ST-LDA), a variant of the topic modeling technique LDA. Similarly to LDA, it considers each tweet as a document and clusters them automatically into latent topics based on word co-occurrence. However, acknowledging the fact that the length of a tweet does not allow for a lot of issues to be discussed, it exclusively assigns a unique topic per tweet [13]. ST-LDA also computes, for each tweet, the topic membership probability, which can be used as a measure of how representative of a topic a given tweet is. Two separate topic models are run, one for the local governments' tweets (LT) and another one for the citizens' tweets (CT). The reason for this is that the number of tweets by local governments is typically much smaller than the volume of citizen tweets, and as a result, local government's topics could be hindered by the citizens' ones if a unique ST-LDA is used [10]. The models are run for various number of topics K, and the final value is selected based on the coherence and interpretability of the topics, which is measured by the PMI over the top ten most frequent words in each topic.

The topic extraction for the citizens' tweets is incorporated in the Tweet Ranking and Selection component described in the previous section. Recall that the topic extraction is used to select the snowstorm-related tweets from the CT pool, and that the most coherent set of topics was obtained for $K = 25$. On the other hand, the topics discussed by local governments are extracted applying ST-LDA over all the tweets in LT; which, using the best PMI value, resulted in $K = 45$ deemed as the most coherent and interpretable set of topics.

Once local governments' and citizens' topics are extracted, these need to be labeled to identify the types of issues discussed online during disasters. For that purpose, we recruited four annotators who were given access to the top ten words per topic and, for completeness, to the full set of words and their topic membership probabilities, prior lemmatization. Each topic had on average 96 words. Each annotator was asked to assign a label (of maximum five words) to each of the 25 citizen topics and 45 local government topics. If they believed a pair of citizen and local government topics were similar, they were required to provide the same labels. It is important to highlight that annotators were trained to understand the task, but were not offered any guidance in terms of labels or topics they should identify. From that perspective, the labeling was completely unsupervised and bottom-up, and did not include any bias as of what types of topics should be found in the online communications. However, that freedom implied that annotators could be using different words to refer to the same topic *e.g.,* "complaints school delays" versus "venting school closed". To bridge those differences, we designed a protocol by which once all labeling was done, annotators met and discussed their labels in person so as to evaluate whether they were referring to the same topics or not, and achieve a final agreement over the names of the labels assigned (categories). Due to the nature of this protocol, we did not use crowdsourced platforms for the labeling, since we required annotators to be able to meet in person. Finally, we computed the inter-annotator agreement using Fleiss' Kappa since we had multiple annotators [12]. The test gave a strong inter-rater reliability of $\kappa = 0.78$.

Table 1 shows the topics identified by the annotators. For discussion purposes, we have grouped some of the topics into themes that bring together issues that were highly related. For example, the topics of "traffic accidents" and "driving conditions" were grouped together in the "Traffic" theme that includes two topics: accidents and driving conditions. Topics that were not grouped have the same theme and topic name in the Table. Overall, there were seven general themes identified namely, economic and social factors, government offices and schools, traffic, public transportation, preparedness, response and weather information. The table shows whether the topic was exclusive to citizens $[CT]$, to local governments $[LT]$ or shared by both $[CT, LT]$; and it also displays, for each theme and topic, two top ranked tweets based on their topic membership probability. Next, we describe each theme in detail. The discussion about how each topic is used by local governments or citizens is covered in the next section.

The *economic and social factors* topic is mostly represented by words reflecting thoughts and opinions around the impact of snowstorms on citizens' daily routines using terms related to work, money and access to food stores and supplies. This topic, which is exclusive to citizens, had top ranked tweets expressing opinions about the impact of snowstorms on the local economy *e.g.,* companies forcing their employees to go to work under harsh weather conditions; about citizens having a hard time finding food supplies in stores; or about citizens spending the snowstorms working from home, or eating and drinking with family and friends.

The second general theme identified was *government offices and schools*. This theme covered two topics: (1) information about delays and closures, and (2) citizen complaints about official decisions with respect to offices' or schools' schedule changes. The words in the first topic were related to updates and schedules including times and places such as elementary schools, colleges or government offices. On the other hand, the second topic was represented by complaint, decision and choice words, verb negations as well as by local government agency names. Some of the top tweets in this topic show citizen tweets asking their local governments to reconsider

Table 1: Themes and topics for citizens' tweets [CT], local governments' tweets [LT] or both [CT,LT] and sampled top ranked tweets.

Themes	Topics	Top Tweets
Economic and Social Factors	Economic and Social Factors [CT]	a. Sears has no love for their employees making me work in this bullshit weather b. [...] If you are on verge of suicide, go grocery shopping at Walmart before [...] the snow
Gov.Offices and Schools	Delays and Closures [CT,LT]	a. UPDATE: Anne Arundel County Government Offices Will Be closed Today b. Due to the inclement weather, all BCPSchools [...] will be closed Friday [...]
	Complaints [CT]	a. Mcps is the type of county that would still give school even with this weather on Tuesday b. Howard it's too cold, kids can't go outside in this, 2 hour delay please
Public Transportation	Delays and Closures [CT,LT]	a. MARC Train service is closed Thursday snow is expected [...][link] b. RTA bus service remains suspended & will not operate 1/25 [...] for service updates visit [link]
	Private Options [CT]	a. If anyone wants to make $1 billion, be an Uber driver in Baltimore [...] 4x surge pricing b. How did I get an Uber_Maryland today without Surge pricing? [...] Thank you Uber
Traffic	Accidents [CT,LT]	a. Accident in #BaltimoreCity on I83 NB between Northern Pkwy and Ruxton Rd b. Disabled snow plow in #GlenBurnie on Baltimore Annapolis Blvd near Marley Neck Rd
	Driving Conditions [CT,LT]	a. Snow on roadway on I-695 Outer Loop at X16 b. Icy conditions in #Bethesda on The Beltway Inner Loop at I-270 Spur and before Connecticut Ave
Preparedness	Preparedness [LT]	a. Not sure what you should have in your emergency kit? Free checklist from APHA's b. Protect your pipes against freezing by letting a thin stream of water flow through faucet
Response	Snow Removal [CT,LT]	a. 98% of County roads plowed at least once. Constant work continues to the 2,600 miles [...] b. Thank you MCPS for not plowing your parking lots
	Emergency Services [LT]	a. MCFRS Emergency Communications on 'CONDITION RED' due to heavy call volume [...] b. For an emergency during the #WinterStorm call 911. For non-emergencies call 410-887-2222 [...]
Weather Info	Weather Info [CT,LT]	a. Snow totals for AACO are up. Now in the 8-10 inch range b. Old Village and Mechanicsville Road (picture was taken around 8:30 a.m.) this morning

delay or closure decisions given the harsh weather conditions (see Table 1).

The third theme identified was *public transportation*. This theme grouped two topics, delay and closure information and private transportation options. The first topic focuses on words explaining changes in schedules or closures in trains, metro, light rail or buses. Table 1 shows an example from Baltimore's Department of Transportation announcing the closure of several services due to snow. The second topic in this theme, exclusive to citizens, was represented by words related to private transportation alternatives and its implications; including words such as Uber, Lyft, service, or price surges during snowstorms.

Another theme identified was *traffic*. Our annotators labeled two distinct topics in this domain: road accidents and driving conditions. The topic of road accidents included words related to cars, accidents and road numbers and names; while the driving conditions topic gathered words mostly around speed, ice, snow, and road names and numbers. Examples of some of the top ranked tweets are showed in the table. The topic of *preparedness*, exclusive to local governments, mostly reflected advisory and safety words about how to cope with harsh weather conditions. Some top tweets offered information about emergency kits or about how to protect home pipes under freezing conditions.

The theme of *response* included two topics: snow removal and emergency services; the latter exclusive to local governments. The first topic was represented by snow plowing related words, announcement and update words, locations and times. Table 1 shows a tweet from Baltimore County explaining that most of its roads have been plowed. As for emergency services, most words were related to emergency-specific phone numbers and their status. Finally, the last topic identified, *weather information*, had words mostly related to weather conditions including snow depth, temperatures and links to pictures showing those conditions during the snowstorms.

7 DIGITAL COMMUNICATION FOOTPRINTS

Once topics have been identified, the framework focuses on the computation of the digital communication footprints during disasters for local governments and citizens at various spatio-temporal scales. Specifically, the framework performs four retrospective analyses: (1) comparison of theme and topic usage by local governments and citizens in counties, (2) comparison of theme and topic usage by local governments and citizens in roads, (3) language used in citizens' communications, and (4) changes in local governments' and citizens' themes and topics before, during and after snowstorms.

For the spatial analysis, the footprints are computed by counting the number of tweets per topic identified for each of the 24 counties in Maryland and for the roads in the state. The objective is to understand the topic distribution for a given spatial scale; and to compare across local governments and citizens. To carry out the analysis, the framework assigns each geolocated tweet in CT to the county whose geographical boundaries contain the geolocation of the tweet; and to the road whose boundaries, with a $2m$ buffer, include the location of the tweet. TIGER/Line shapefiles are used to extract the exact boundary information [9] for the 24 counties and for five types of roads: interstates, freeways, principal arterials, minor arterials and collector streets. As explained earlier, local government tweets in LT are not geolocated and as a result are assigned to the county of

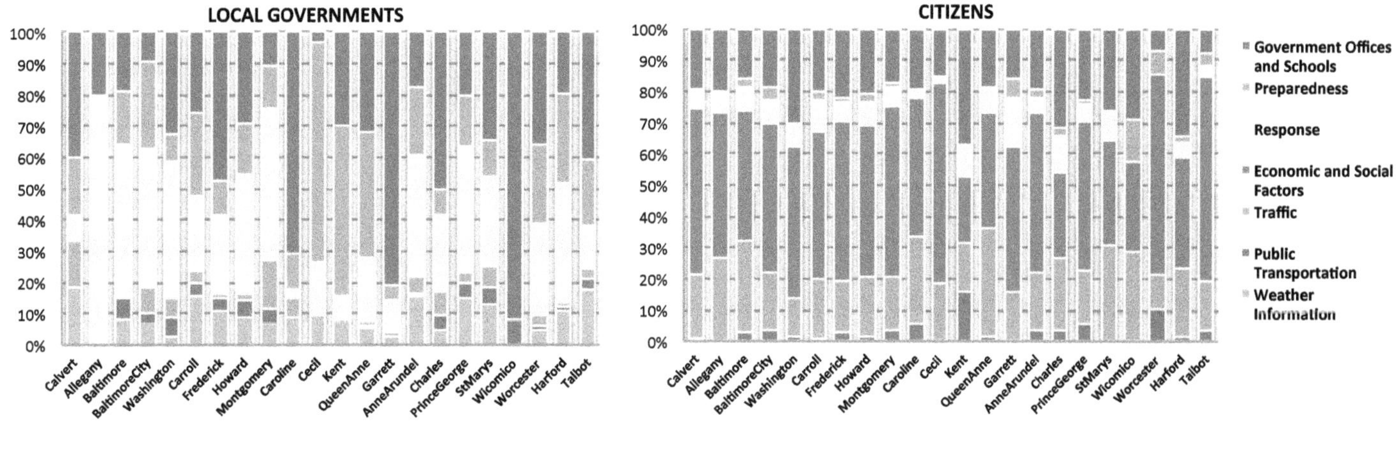

Figure 3: Digital Communication Footprints of Local Governments and Citizens for each county in the state of Maryland.

the agency represented by the twitter handle; or to roads (without a specific type) if the twitter account is from a local transportation agency. We also present a language analysis to further understand the thought processes behind the topics discussed online by citizens. Finally, we discuss the results of the temporal analysis, focused on exploring differences in topic usage before, during and after disasters take place.

Rather than using all the tweets in CT and LT to compute the digital communication footprints, the framework only uses tweets whose topic membership probability is sufficiently large to guarantee representativity for that topic. This approach eliminates from the footprints tweets that have been assigned to a topic with very little certainty. Specifically, the framework requires the topic membership probability assigned by ST-LDA to each tweet to be of at least $p > .75$ to be counted as a communication with that topic label. Such p value guarantees a maximum error of $e = 1 - p \leq .25$ in tweet to topic associations. That error value is a lower bound, since the average topic membership probability for tweets whose $p > .75$ in CT and LT is 0.96 ($e \leq 0.04$), which is comparable to error rates achieved when identifying topics using classifiers trained with labeled tweets [25]. After applying the probabilistic filter, the total number of tweets in counties was of $148,103$. To guarantee analytical significance, we eliminated from the analysis counties with less than 50 tweets throughout all the snowstorms, which excluded two counties: Somerset and Worcester. As for roads, we collected 7904 tweets from both CT and LT. CT tweets covered 31% of all road segments in the state of Maryland, almost evenly distributed across all five types of roads. Next, we describe each analysis in detail.

7.1 Themes and Topics in Counties

Figure 3 shows the digital communication footprints of local governments and citizens for all the counties in Maryland. The counties on the x-axis are ordered by the median amount of snow throughout the 18 snowstorms in our dataset. Each bar in the histogram represents the digital communication footprint for a county, with the percentage of the overall communication (y-axis) associated to each theme. An important first observation is that the types of themes discussed by citizens and local governments are largely different; and that the amount of snow does not appear to play a role in the theme choice. Local governments tend to focus their online communications on three themes: Government Offices and Schools, Response and Preparedness, representing an average of 30.1%, 26.6% and 16.9% of their total communications, respectively. Hierarchical clustering of the local government county footprints grouped together urban counties such as Montgomery or Prince George, characterized by higher response communication volumes than their rural counterparts (using the 2013 urban-rural classification scheme by the NCHS/CDC); which might be indicative of urban counties being more informative about their decisions to cope with snowstorms. On the other hand, citizens mostly use Twitter to talk about Economic and Social factors (47.6%), Government Offices and Schools (19.8%), and Traffic (18.8%), with no clear clusters differentiating urban and rural citizen communications. These findings suggest that while local governments mostly use Twitter to prepare the community for the snowstorms and to inform them about how they are responding; citizens use Twitter as both a social network: discussing and sharing thoughts about the economic and social impact of the snowstorms, and as a news platform: sharing news about closures, delays or driving conditions [20].

Next, we look in depth into the use of topics within the themes shared by local governments and citizens in their communications. Figure 4 represents the difference between official and citizen footprints for the topics in the Government Offices and Schools theme. The differences are computed subtracting from the local governments' percentage of tweets per topic, the percentage of citizen tweets for that same topic. Positive values imply that local governments dominate the topic while negative values represent citizens talking more about that topic. Situations were the topic is exclusive to either local governments or citizens are clarified in the discussion. Figure 4 shows that while for most of the counties the topic of delays and closures is dominated by local government agencies, possibly making official announcements (with average 23% more communications than citizens); the topic of complaints is exclusive

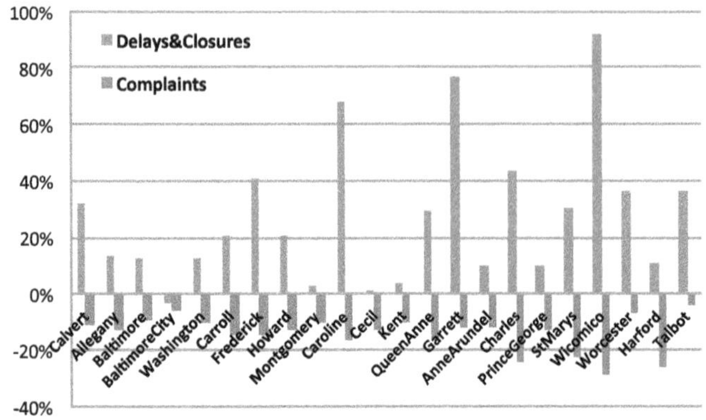

Figure 4: Government Offices and Schools: topic differences between local government and citizen communications.

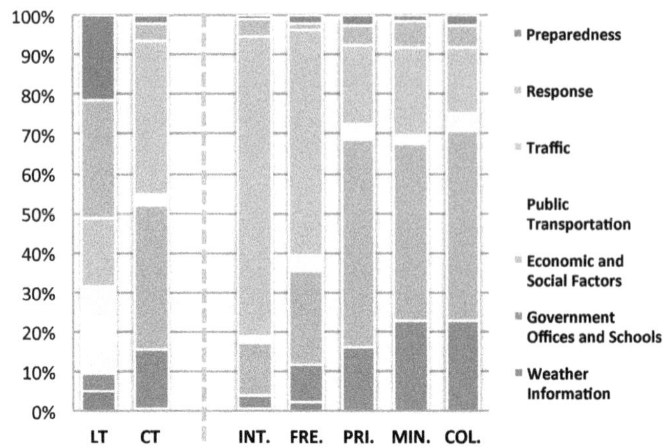

Figure 5: Distribution of themes and topics on roads. Two bars on the left show the average footprint across all types of roads; five bars to the right show footprints per type of road: interstate, freeway, principal and minor arterials and collector

to citizens demanding their local governments different scheduling decisions (with average communication volumes of 12%).

Similar analyses showed that for the Traffic theme, accident reporting online is done almost equally by citizens and local governments for most of the counties. However, citizens dominate the conversation with respect to reporting driving conditions, with an average of 16% more communications than their local governments. The topic of delays and closures in the Public Transportation theme has local governments talking slightly more about it than citizens, possibly making official announcements (4% higher volumes on average); while citizens were the only ones to talk about the private options topic, with a conversation around Lyft and Uber when public transportation was not an option. In the Response theme, the topic of emergency services is exclusive to local governments who share information about how to use these types of services during snowstorms; while local governments also lead communications about snow removal in their communities (7% larger). Finally, the weather information topic was common for both local governments and citizens, with only 1% more official communications.

7.2 Themes and Topics in Roads

Figure 5 shows the digital communication footprints for local governments and citizens on roads. The first two bars on the left, represent the average footprint across all types of roads for local government (*LT*) and citizen (*CT*) communications. We observe that, similarly to the county communication footprints, local government communications focus on preparedness and response, possibly offering pre-snowstorm advice and updates about snow removal strategies. However, we also observe that the official discourse on roads puts a lot of weight on communications about traffic and public transportation, with tweets spreading details about accidents or driving conditions; and offering information about delays and closures of public transportation services. On the other hand, citizen communications on roads still focus on economic and social factors (35%), and government offices and schools (14%). However, citizen traffic-related communications have almost doubled with respect to their county communications, from 18% to 35%. Looking in depth into the citizens' communication footprints for each type of road (Figure 5, five bars to the right), we observe that the distribution of topics changes from larger roads (interstates, *INT.* or freeways *FRE.*) to smaller roads (principal and minor arterials *PRI.,MIN.* or collectors *COL.*). Interestingly, while citizens mostly focus on sharing accident information and driving conditions with others when they are on large interstates or freeways (65% average communications on the traffic theme), the discourse changes towards economic and social factors (48%) when we move to smaller arterial and collector roads. This reflects that citizens' communications during snowstorms change depending on the physical spaces they occupy. Driving in large roads during snowstorms encourages a utilitarian approach with drivers sharing useful information (Twitter as a news platform) while smaller roads bring them back to opinion and thought sharing (Twitter as a social network).

7.3 Language Analysis

Understanding the types of topics discussed online by citizens is highly relevant for local governments wishing to serve their populations during snowstorms. However, since topics simply provide lists of words, it would be important for local governments to gain more insights into the potential emotions and thought processes behind the citizen communications shared online. To carry out this analysis, the framework uses the psycholinguistic lexicon LIWC, which has been extensively validated in determining mental states for different types of text sources [27]). Specifically, the framework puts in a document all the citizens' tweets for each theme and topic identified (across counties and roads) and analyzes the following LIWC dimensions per topic: positive and negative emotion, anxiety and anger from *affect words*; insight, cause, discrepancies and tentativeness from *cognitive processes*; seeing and hearing from *perpetual processes*; and work, leisure, home and money from *personal concerns*.

Figure 6 shows a radar chart with the LIWC dimension values for the most popular citizen themes and topics. Each line in the chart represents the distribution of the values for a given topic. The line for economic and social factors shows that there is a heavy use of

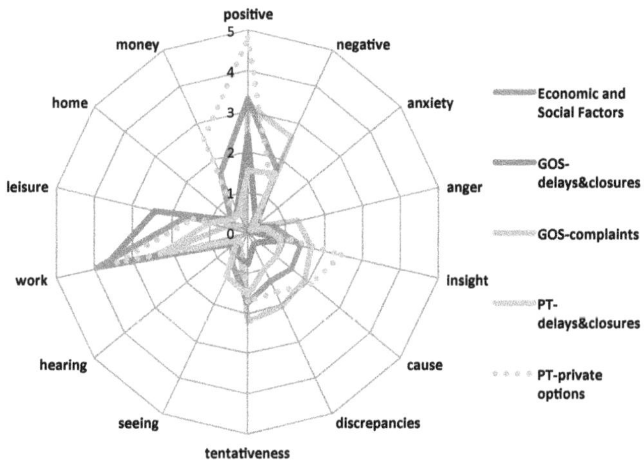

Figure 6: LIWC dimension values for citizen topics.

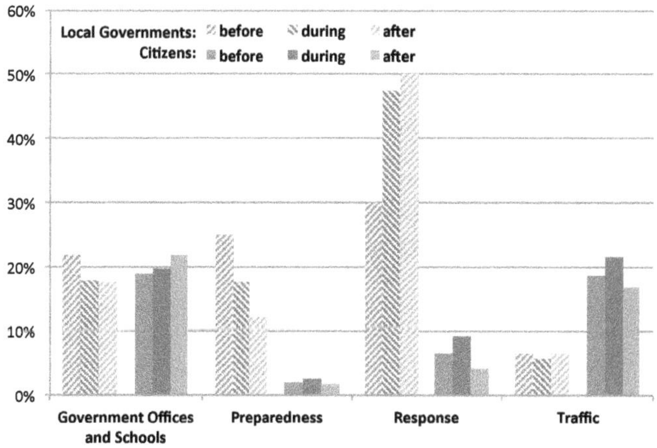

Figure 7: Percentage of tweets per topic and time period for local governments (texture bars) and citizens (solid bars).

work, money and leisure-related words (with values of 3.9, 1.8 and 1.6, respectively), with a mix of positive and negative emotions, and a heavy use of words related to tentativeness, discrepancy, causal effects and insights. This reflects very well the nature of the topic, with individuals sharing strong positive and negative opinions about the impact of the snowstorms on their daily routines *e.g.,* staying at home with the family versus going to work under harsh weather conditions.

The line for government offices and schools (*GOS*) shows that communications about delays and closures (*GOS-delays&closures*) are mostly represented by work and leisure related words mixed with positive emotions (3.6, 2.4 and 2.5, respectively), implying that, in general, the population accepts the closures as something positive and leisurely *e.g., staying at home*. On the other hand, the topic about complaints with respect to closures (*GOS-complaints*) shows a heavy use of angry, tentative, causal and discrepancy words probably reflecting anger, confusion and uncertainty about how to plan a day when schools and offices are closed. Public transportation topics (*PT-delays&closures* and *PT-private options*) also show a peak in the use of work related words, probably reflecting people's concerns about reaching work on time; additionally, a very high peak (4.9 and 2.5) for positive emotion and insight words is observed when talking about private transportation alternatives, which might be indicative of the fact that people are very happy to have other transportation options when public transportation is not fully working. Finally, the traffic topics (not shown in graph for clarity), reflected a heavy use of work-related and negative emotion words (3.5 and 3.2) when citizens were reporting driving conditions; while causal and negative words were mostly present when reporting accidents (2.1 and 2.3).

7.4 Temporal Changes

In this component, the framework evaluates whether the communication patterns of local governments and citizens change over time as the snowstorm evolves. Specifically, it computes the percentage of tweets per topic communicated by local governments and citizens in three distinct time periods: two days before a snowstorm, snowstorm days and two days after a snowstorm. Figure 7 shows the percentage of local governments' tweets (texture bars) and citizens' tweets (solid bars) for the topics that showed a distinct change across time periods.

We can observe that local governments' tweets talking about delays and closures of offices and schools are slightly larger before the snowstorms than during or after (from 21% to 18% of the total communications), probably related to the fact that official closure announcements are typically made before the snowstorm fully develops. The opposite trend is observed for citizens' communications about government offices and schools which increase during and after the snowstorms (from 18% to 22%), probably reflecting continued discussions about closure decisions. Preparedness communications from local governments show a large, decreasing trend in volumes (from 22% to 11%), which might indicate that local governments focus on spreading information about how to prepare for the snowstorm well in advance; while no significant change is observed in citizens' preparedness communications. On the other hand, local governments' response communications heavily increase (from 29% to 49%) during and after the snowstorms take place, indicating that local governments share updates about snow removal and information on emergency services mostly once the snowstorm has reached their geographical boundaries and several days later; while citizen tweets focus on communicating about response topics mostly during snowstorms (9%). Finally, citizen tweets showed that traffic information was mostly posted during snowstorms, reflecting the use of Twitter by citizens as a (real-time) news sharing platform; while local governments' traffic communications did not show any significant change.

8 CONCLUSIONS

We have presented a semi-automatic framework to extract and compare, in retrospect, the digital communication footprints of citizens and local governments during snowstorms at various spatio-temporal scales. The framework uses a fully unsupervised ST-LDA model to select disaster-related tweets and to extract the topics that are discussed online during snowstorms; together with human annotators to give labels and meaning to the topics identified. We acknowledge that by exclusively using geolocated tweets from citizens to compare against local governments' tweets, we are only able to capture the voice of those who have geolocation enabled on their Twitter accounts. Although that is a limitation, it is the unique way to extract local information that is meaningful and actionable at the granular spatio-temporal scales we are interested in studying.

Our analysis of tweets from 18 snowstorms shows that the digital communication behaviors of citizens and local governments are vastly different. While citizens use Twitter heavily to share thoughts and opinions about the implications of the snowstorms; and to a lesser degree, to exchange information about delays, closures and traffic conditions, local governments heavily focus on preparedness and response.

Although the evaluation focuses on snowstorms, the framework can be used to extract and compare, in retrospect, digital communication footprints from local governments and citizens for any type of acute event were both local agencies and the population participate online via Twitter. In the future, we plan to use the proposed framework to analyze whether local governments' social media strategies are covering the information that citizens seek online during disasters; and to provide information to help local governments cater their social media messages to citizens' needs.

REFERENCES

[1] Adam Acar and Yuya Muraki. 2011. Twitter for crisis communication: lessons learned from Japan's tsunami disaster. *International Journal of Web Based Communities* 7, 3 (2011), 392–402.

[2] Zahra Ashktorab, Christopher Brown, Manojit Nandi, and Aron Culotta. 2014. Tweedr: Mining twitter to inform disaster response. *International Community on Information Systems for Crisis Response and Management* (2014).

[3] A. Axelrod, X. He, and J. Gao. 2010. Domain Adaptation via Pseudo In-domain Data Selection. *Annual Meeting of the Association for Computational Linguistics ACL* (2010).

[4] R.W. Belter and M.P. Shannon. 1993. Impact of natural disasters on children and families. In *Children and disasters*. Springer, 85–103.

[5] David M Blei, Andrew Y Ng, and Michael I Jordan. 2003. Latent dirichlet allocation. *Journal of machine earning research* 3, Jan (2003), 993–1022.

[6] A. Bruns, J.E. Burgess, K. Crawford, and F. Shaw. 2012. # qldfloods and@ QPSMedia: Crisis communication on Twitter in the 2011 south east Queensland floods. http://www.cci.edu.au/floodsreport.pdf[Accessed March-2-2017]. (2012).

[7] Axel Bruns and Jean E Burgess. 2012. Local and global responses to disaster:# eqnz and the Christchurch earthquake. In *Disaster and emergency management conference*, Vol. 2012. 86–103.

[8] Axel Bruns and Stefan Stieglitz. 2012. Quantitative approaches to comparing communication patterns on Twitter. *Journal of Technology in Human Services* 30, 3-4 (2012), 160–185.

[9] CensusBureau. 2016. USA County Shapefiles. https://www.census.gov/cgi-bin/geo/shapefiles/index.php. (2016).

[10] Enhong Chen, Yanggang Lin, Hui Xiong, Qiming Luo, and Haiping Ma. 2011. Exploiting probabilistic topic models to improve text categorization under class imbalance. *Information Processing & Management* 47, 2 (2011), 202–214.

[11] F. Cheong and C. Cheong. 2011. Social media data mining: A social network analysis of tweets during the 2010-2011 Australian floods. *Pacific Asia Conference on Information Systems* (2011).

[12] J. L. Fleiss. (1971). Measuring nominal scale agreement among many raters. *Psychological Bulletin* ((1971)), 378.

[13] L. Hong, W. Yang, P. Resnik, and V. Frias-Martinez. 2016. Uncovering Topic Dynamics of Social Media and News: the Case of Ferguson. *International Conference on Social Informatics* (2016).

[14] Amanda L Hughes, Lise AA St Denis, Leysia Palen, and Kenneth M Anderson. 2014. Online public communications by police & fire services during the 2012 Hurricane Sandy. In *CHI Conference on Human Factors in Computing Systems*.

[15] Muhammad Imran, Shady Elbassuoni, Carlos Castillo, Fernando Diaz, and Patrick Meier. 2013. Practical Extraction of Disaster-relevant Information from Social Media. In *World Wide Web Conference*.

[16] Muhammad Imran, Shady Mamoon Elbassuoni, Carlos Castillo, Fernando Diaz, and Patrick Meier. 2013. Extracting information nuggets from disaster-related messages in social media. *International Community on Information Systems for Crisis Response and Management* (2013).

[17] K. Kireyev, L. Palen, and K. Anderson. 2009. Applications of topics models to analysis of disaster-related twitter data. In *NIPS Conference on Neural Information Processing Systems*.

[18] Yury Kryvasheyeu, Haohui Chen, Nick Obradovich, Esteban Moro, Pascal Van Hentenryck, James Fowler, and Manuel Cebrian. 2016. Rapid assessment of disaster damage using social media activity. *Science* 2, 3 (2016).

[19] Shamanth Kumar, Geoffrey Barbier, Mohammad Ali Abbasi, and Huan Liu. 2011. TweetTracker: An Analysis Tool for Humanitarian and Disaster Relief.. In *International Conference on Web and Social Media ICWSM*.

[20] Haewoon Kwak, Changhyun Lee, Hosung Park, and Sue Moon. 2010. What is Twitter, a social network or a news media?. In *World Wide Web Conference*.

[21] Edward Loper and Steven Bird. 2002. NLTK: The natural language toolkit. In *Annual Meeting of the Association for Computational Linguistics ACL Workshop*. Association for Computational Linguistics, 63–70.

[22] R. Moore and W. Lewis. 2010. Intelligent Selection of Language Model Training Data. *Annual Meeting of the Association for Computational Linguistics ACL* (2010).

[23] David Newman, Jey Han Lau, Karl Grieser, and Timothy Baldwin. 2010. Automatic Evaluation of Topic Coherence *(Human Language Technology Conference)*.

[24] NOAA. 2017. http://www.nohrsc.noaa.gov/. (2017). [Accessed March-2-2017].

[25] Alexandra Olteanu, Carlos Castillo, Fernando Diaz, and Sarah Vieweg. 2014. CrisisLex: A Lexicon for Collecting and Filtering Microblogged Communications in Crises.. In *International Conference on Web and Social Media ICWSM*.

[26] Alexandra Olteanu, Sarah Vieweg, and Carlos Castillo. 2015. What to expect when the unexpected happens: Social media communications across crises. In *Computed-Supported Cooperative Work and Social Computing CSCW*.

[27] James W Pennebaker, Martha E Francis, and Roger J Booth. 2001. Linguistic inquiry and word count: LIWC. *Lawrence Erlbaum Ass.* 71 (2001).

[28] John F Jr. Rooney. 1967. The urban snow hazard in the United States: An appraisal of disruption. *Geographical Review* (1967), 538–559.

[29] H.M. Saleem, Y. Xu, and D. Ruths. 2014. Effects of disaster characteristics on Twitter event signature. *Procedia Engineering* 78 (2014), 165–172.

[30] F. Shaw, J. Burgess, K. Crawford, and A. Bruns. 2013. Sharing News, Making Sense, Saying Thanks: Patterns of Talk on Twitter during the Queensland Floods. *Australian Journal of Communication* (2013).

[31] Kate Starbird and Leysia Palen. 2010. *Pass it on?: Retweeting in mass emergency*. International Community on Information Systems for Crisis Response and Management.

[32] Kate Starbird and Jeannie Stamberger. Tweak the tweet: Leveraging microblogging proliferation with a prescriptive syntax to support citizen reporting. In *International Community on Information Systems for Crisis Response and Management*.

[33] T. Terpstra, A de Vries, R Stronkman, and GL Paradies. 2012. *Towards a realtime Twitter analysis during crises for operational crisis management*. Simon Fraser University.

[34] Sarah Vieweg, Amanda L Hughes, Kate Starbird, and Leysia Palen. 2010. Microblogging during two natural hazards events: what twitter may contribute to situational awareness. In *CHI Conference on Human Factors in Computing Systems*. 1079–1088.

[35] Christian Wartena and Rogier Brussee. 2008. Topic detection by clustering keywords. In *DB and Expert Systems Applications*.

[36] Andrew Worthington and Abbas Valadkhani. 2004. Measuring the impact of natural disasters on capital markets: an empirical application using intervention analysis. *Applied Economics* 36, 19 (2004), 2177–2186.

[37] C. Wukich and I. A. Mergel. 2014. Closing the Citizen-Government communication gap: Content,audience, and network analysis of government tweets. *Socal Science Research Network Working Paper* (2014).

[38] Sarita Yardi, Daniel Romero, Grant Schoenebeck, and others. 2009. Detecting spam in a twitter network. *First Monday* 15, 1 (2009).

[39] Louis Yu, Sitaram Asur, and Bernardo A Huberman. 2011. What Trends in Chinese Social Media. In *CoRRabs/1107.3522*.

Breaking Cycles in Noisy Hierarchies*

Jiankai Sun
The Ohio State University
sun.1306@osu.edu

Deepak Ajwani
Nokia Bell Labs, Ireland
deepak.ajwani@nokia-bell-labs.com

Patrick K. Nicholson
Nokia Bell Labs, Ireland
pat.nicholson@nokia-bell-labs.com

Alessandra Sala
Nokia Bell Labs, Ireland
alessandra.sala@nokia-bell-labs.com

Srinivasan Parthasarathy
The Ohio State University
srini@cse.ohio-state.edu

ABSTRACT

Taxonomy graphs that capture hyponymy or meronymy relationships through directed edges are expected to be acyclic. However, in practice, they may have thousands of cycles, as they are often created in a crowd-sourced way. Since these cycles represent logical fallacies, they need to be removed for many web applications. In this paper, we address the problem of breaking cycles while preserving the logical structure (hierarchy) of a directed graph as much as possible. Existing approaches for this problem either need manual intervention or use heuristics that can critically alter the taxonomy structure. In contrast, our approach infers graph hierarchy using a range of features, including a Bayesian skill rating system and a social agony metric. We also devise several strategies to leverage the inferred hierarchy for removing a small subset of edges to make the graph acyclic. Extensive experiments demonstrate the effectiveness of our approach.

CCS CONCEPTS

•Theory of computation → *Network flows;* **•Computing methodologies** → *Ontology engineering;* **•Information systems** → Data cleaning;

KEYWORDS

Directed Acyclic Graph, Graph Hierarchy, TrueSkill, Social Agony, Cycle Edges

ACM Reference format:
Jiankai Sun, Deepak Ajwani, Patrick K. Nicholson, Alessandra Sala, and Srinivasan Parthasarathy. 2017. Breaking Cycles in Noisy Hierarchies. In *Proceedings of WebSci'17, June 25-28, 2017, Troy, NY, USA.*, , 10 pages.
DOI: http://dx.doi.org/10.1145/3091478.3091495

1 INTRODUCTION

A large number of applications in information science, in fields such as AI, semantic web, biomedical informatics, library science and information architecture, rely on ontological knowledge such as taxonomies and meronomies. Taxonomies capture generalization/specification of semantic concepts and categories and meronomies capture "has a" and "is a part of" relationship. Thus, the taxonomy and meronomy graphs (as well as graphs representing many other ontological relationships) should ideally be acyclic as cycles represent logical contradictions.

However, many large ontological knowledge bases are created either in (i) crowd-sourced way (e.g., Wikipedia categories [39]) or (ii) using automated text analytics tools (e.g, Yago [13, 31]). The creation process often results in inconsistencies and errors. As a result, the directed graphs capturing these ontological relations, can have a large number of cycles. For instance, the popular skos:broader category[1] is not guaranteed to be transitive and irreflexive and, as a result, it has various cycles that can "represent a potential problem for many web applications" [2]. In fact, there exists a body of work [5, 9, 20, 24, 26, 29, 33, 34, 38, 42] that has identified and recognized the presence of cycles in the hierarchical relations as one of the main problems for many web applications dealing with ontologies, such as United Medical Language System (UMLS) Metathesaurus graph and DBpedia taxonomy graph. For example, the unsupervised learning approach proposed by Fossati et al. [9], to automatically derive a taxonomy for a DBpedia entity from a prominent subset of the Wikipedia category graph, requires that the Wikipedia category graph is a directed acyclic graph (DAG), which can ensure a strict hierarchy. To support these web applications, there is a need for a principled technique to reduce a directed graph modeling a hierarchical relationship into a DAG, which only includes acyclic relationships.

In addition to removing logical contradictions, a DAG with strict hierarchy, can also benefit many applications to be computationally more efficient. This is because a DAG supports faster traversals (e.g., for computing descendants and transitive closure) compared to general directed graphs.

The problem of reducing graphs modeling hierarchical relations into DAGs is also relevant in many other domains. For instance, in synchronous dataflow (SDF) scheduling (an important problem in design automation for communication and digital signal processing systems [14, 15]), the existence of cycles in SDF graphs prevents or greatly restricts applications of many useful optimization techniques that are available for acyclic SDF graphs, because cyclic data dependences can cause deadlocks when scheduling tasks.

In this paper, we propose techniques to remove the cycles while preserving the logical structure (hierarchy) of a directed graph as

*This Work was conducted while the first author was doing internship at Nokia Bell Labs, Ireland.

WebSci'17, June 25-28, 2017, Troy, NY, USA.

978-1-4503-4896-6/17/06...$15.00
DOI: http://dx.doi.org/10.1145/3091478.3091495

[1] https://www.w3.org/2009/08/skos-reference/skos.html
[2] https://www.w3.org/TR/skos-reference/#L2484

much as possible. Despite the proliferation of applications relying on ontologies capturing hierarchical relationships, there is hardly any solution for this problem that is principled, fast and fully automated. Existing approaches for this problem fall into the following categories:

- Simple DFS or BFS based heuristic (e.g., [9, 33, 34, 42]) to eliminate cycles (e.g., remove back edges in DFS)
- Theoretical solutions that model the problem in terms of variants of minimum-feedback arc set problem [18] or other NP-hard optimization problems
- Complex domain-specific algorithms (e.g. [24, 26]) that eliminate cycles based on many criteria, including redundancy and confidence of sources asserting the relations

While the first set of techniques are fast and automated, they are not principled – the edges removed heavily depend on the order of traversal, independent of other structural properties (For example in Figure 1, edge (C, B) will be deleted if DFS starts from node A, otherwise edge (B, C) will be the back edge). As a result, they often eliminate a large number of edges relevant for the taxonomy structure. The second set of techniques have a theoretical basis, but they are too slow in practice. Also, since minimum feedback arc set problem is APX-hard [17], one has to rely on approximation algorithms [8] with poor worst-case guarantees or heuristics (e.g., [2, 21, 30]). As such, it is not clear how well these techniques can preserve the logical structure of taxonomy while removing the cycles. The last set of techniques are (i) typically domain-specific, (ii) require significant manual intervention making it difficult to scale and (iii) depend on additional information (e.g., number of sources asserting each relation and confidence on sources) that is not easily available.

Figure 1: DFS-based Approach Toy Example

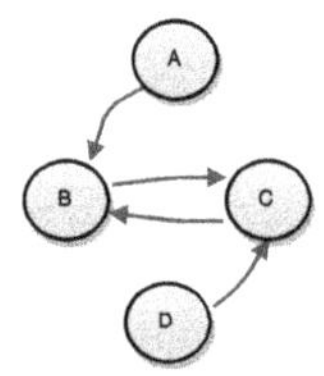

To overcome the above limitations, we propose to remove cycle edges via graph hierarchy. The graph hierarchy can be inferred by a Bayesian skill rating system (*TrueSkill*) [12] or Social agony (*SocialAgony*) [11], without any manual intervention. Several strategies are then devised to remove cycle edges based on their corresponding nodes' ranking scores in the hierarchy. To summarize, the key contributions of this article are:

- We address the problem of breaking cycles from directed graphs, while preserving the underlying hierarchy of the ontological relation as much as possible. To this end, we propose an ensemble of strategies, based on inferring the underlying graph hierarchy, to select edges for removal from the graph.
- To infer graph hierarchy, we (i) model it as a competition problem and leverage TrueSkill to solve it and (ii) model it as the problem of minimizing agony in social networks and leverage SocialAgony to solve it.
- We show extensive experimental results on real and synthetic data sets demonstrating the effectiveness of our approaches.

The rest of this article is organized as follows: In section 2, we describe related work. In section 3, we discuss ways to infer graph hierarchy and strategies to remove cycle edges via graph hierarchy. Section 4 reports on our empirical results. Finally, we conclude in Section 5.

2 RELATED WORK

We categorize the related work as follows:

2.1 Simple Heuristics Based on BFS or DFS

Owing to their simplicity, speed and domain independence, simple heuristics based on Depth-First Search (DFS) (e.g., [33, 34, 42]) or Breadth-First Search (BFS) (e.g., [9]) have been used to remove cycles. Assuming edges in taxonomy graph point from specific to general concepts, DFS based approaches perform a DFS starting from the most specific concepts (zero in-degree) in the hierarchy and then remove the back edges. In contrast, a BFS based approach traverses the graph in a breadth-first manner (though still from the most specific concept l) and removes the edges (u, v) with $d(u) \geq d(v)$. Here, (u, v) is a directed edge from u to v, and $d(u)$ is the unweighted distance from l to u that is computed during the BFS traversal. Note that this can potentially remove many non-cycle edges as well and even from cycles, it may remove more edges than is strictly necessary. Take Figure 2 as an example: a BFS will start from a leaf node A, and will remove non-cycle edge (C, B) and both cycle edges (D, E) and (E, D).

The main problem with these heuristics is that there is no intuitive or empirical evidence that edges deleted this way are actually the appropriate edges to be removed. In our experiments, we found that these heuristics removed a large number of edges that were relevant for the taxonomy hierarchy, based on a manual insepection of the removed edges. The selection of edges to remove solely depends on the order in which the graph is traversed and is independent of other structural properties of the nodes.

Figure 2: BFS-based Approach Toy Example

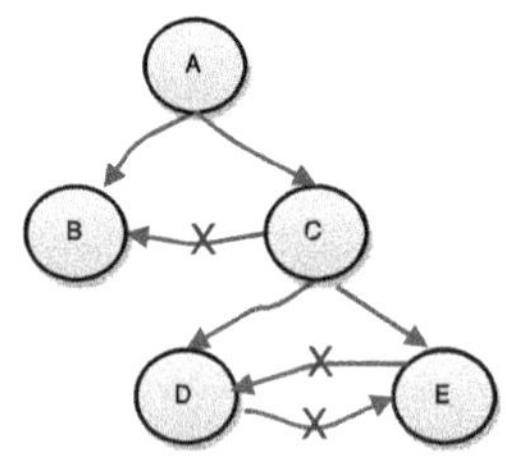

2.2 Minimum Feedback Arc Set

Theoretically, one can consider the problem of maximizing the size of the acyclic subgraph or minimizing the number of edges removed to make the graph acyclic. This is the popular minimum feedback arc set (MFAS) problem and it is on the original list of Richard M. Karp's 21 NP-complete problems [18]. In fact, the MFAS problem is APX-hard: Unless $P = NP$, the MFAS problem does not have a polynomial-time approximation scheme (PTAS) [17]. Heuristic approaches are proposed to gradually build the feedback edge set by always removing the edge that breaks the most of the remaining simple cycles(e.g., [21]).

To avoid enumerating all simple cycles of a graph, there exists a greedy local heuristic method that only uses local information to make greedy choices [6, 7]. Score functions are defined based on local information (in- and out-degree of nodes). Such score functions are defined as: $score(i) = |d_i^{in} - d_i^{out}|$ or $score(i) = max(\frac{d_i^{in}}{d_i^{out}}, \frac{d_i^{out}}{d_i^{in}})$, where $score(i)$ is the score of a node i (a higher score means node i is more asymmetric regarding to its in- and out-degrees), and d_i^{in} (resp. d_i^{out}) are the in-degree (resp. out-degree) of node i. The node with the highest score is selected, then all of its in- or out-edges are removed, whichever edge set is of smaller cardinality.

MFAS heuristics (e.g., [6, 7, 21, 27, 35]) do not offer any guarantees on the number of edges removed and in the worst case, the gap between the heuristic solution and the optimal solution can be extremely large. Furthermore, even if an exact algorithm (e.g., [2]) can be used, there is no evidence to suggest that it preserves the logical hierarchy structure or that minimizing the edges to remove is the correct objective to optimize for cleaning the ontologies with hierarchical relations. Take Figure 3 for example, the edge (*Programming Language,Computer Science*) will be removed according to the above greedy local heuristic method. However, edges (*Computer Science*, Python) and (*Computer Science, Java*) should be removed to maintain the correctness of this graph's logical structure.

Figure 3: Minimum Feedback Arc Set Toy Example

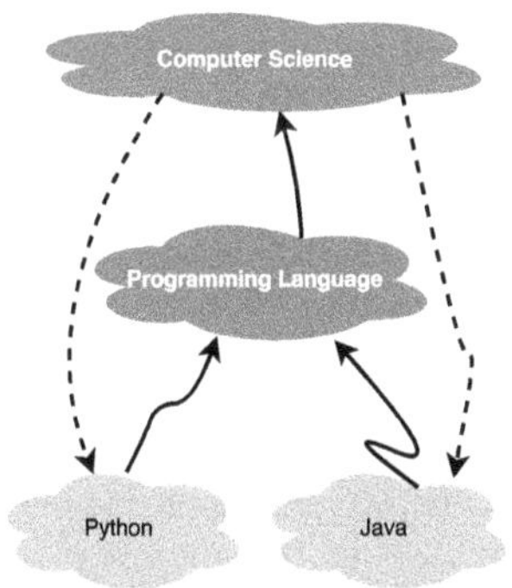

2.3 Domain-specific Algorithms

Many other algorithms have been proposed for the problem of eliminating cycles for specific domains. However, these techniques rely on manual intervention and/or additional information that is often not available.

For UMLS Metathesaurus graph, solutions [24, 26] have been proposed for eliminating inappropriate edges causing circular hierarchical relations. The algorithm proposed by Bodenreider [26] is relatively complex and for complex cycles, it requires manual intervention [24] by domain experts, which is not scalable. The technique by Mougin and Bodenreider [24] uses a set of heuristics and rules to identify and eliminate all cycles from the UMLS graph. For example, criteria redundancy (i.e. the number of sources asserting each relation) and criteria confidence can be exploited to determine relations. However, this information about number and confidence of sources is not easily available for many ontological knowledge bases.

For synchronous data flow graphs, Bhattacharyya et al. and Hsu et al. [3, 14, 15] proposed the loose interdependence algorithm framework (LIAF) to decompose and break cycles. This framework relies on a very specific property of SDF graphs, namely, that for each strongly connected component (SCC)[3] of the SDF graph, there exists a set of edges with sufficient delays (an edge in an SDF graph is associated with a delay that can also be interpreted as the number of initial tokens) whose removal reduces the number of nodes in the SCC of the remaining graph. In fact, the algorithm recursively eliminates such edges to get rid of all cycles in the input SDF graphs (removed edges become inter-iteration edges). However, in our scenario of large ontological knowledge graphs, no such delay measure is known to exist and there is no corresponding notion of iterations, so these algorithms are not applicable.

Some approaches [20] transform the SCCs in the hierarchical relationships (broader/narrower, whole/part, generic/specific, instance of) into *related* relationship between the concepts. While this may be sufficient for some applications, many applications will end up simply ignoring the *related* relationship edges and the large number of corresponding direct and implied relations, leading to inaccurate results.

3 OUR APPROACH

In this section, we propose graph hierarchy based strategies to break cycles from a directed graph, while preserving the underlying hierarchy of the relations as much as possible. Consider a ranking function f that assigns a ranking score to each node in the graph. A higher ranking score implies that the corresponding node is higher up (e.g., more general) in the hierarchy. Given such a ranking, the edges which violate the hierarchy (i.e., edges from a higher/general group to a lower/specific group) are potential candidates for removal. Thus in our approach, there are two sub-tasks involved:

- Inferring graph hierarchy (or finding a ranking function)
- Proposing strategies to select violation edges as candidates for removal

3.1 Inferring Graph Hierarchy

One way to infer graph hierarchy is through PageRank [28]. The relative importance inferred by PageRank is considered as corresponding nodes' ranking score in the graph hierarchy. However, nodes' ranking scores in graph hierarchy are not always consistent with their PageRank values even in a DAG. Take Figure 4 as an example, node C has the highest PageRank value, but it is neither the highest, nor the lowest node in the actual graph hierarchy.

3.1.1 TrueSkill. TrueSkill [12] is a Bayesian skill rating system which is designed to calculate the relative skill of players from the set of generated competitions in multi-player games. Liu et al. [22, 23] introduced a two-player and no-draw version of TrueSkill to estimate question difficulty level in community question answering

[3]A directed graph is strongly connected if there is a path between all pairs of vertices. An SCC of a directed graph is a maximal strongly connected subgraph. SCCs can be detected by the work of Nuutila et al. [25].

Figure 4: Illustrating issues of using PageRank to infer graph hierarchy (damping parameter $d = 0.85$)

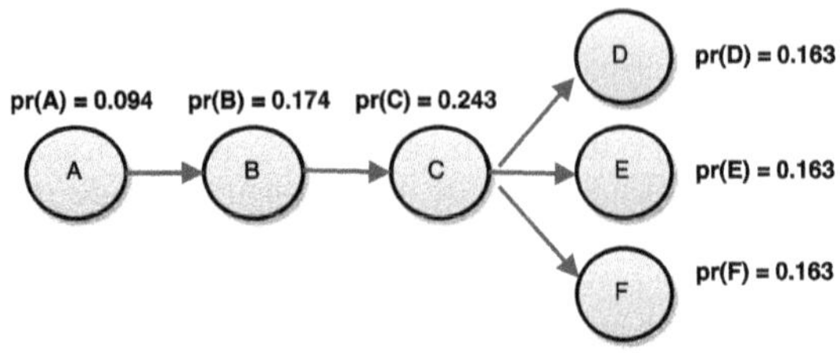

services. It assumes that the practical performance of each player in one game follows a normal distribution $\mathcal{N}(\mu, \sigma^2)$, where μ is the average skill of the player and σ means a system's uncertainty of the estimated skill level. Intuitively, if a system learns more about the skill of one player from more data, the standard deviation σ (uncertainty) will decrease. The skill of each player will slightly change after each game in TrueSkill. The measure $\mu - 3\sigma$ is used to rank players to ensure that top ranked players are highly skilled with high certainty [12, 22, 23].

We transform a directed graph $G = (V, E)$ into a multiplayer tournament with $|V|$ players and $|E|$ competitions. For each edge $(u, v) \in E$, we consider that u loses the competition between u and v. Based on the current estimated skill levels of two players (u and v) and the outcome of a new game between them (edge (u, v)), the TrueSkill model updates the skill level μ and σ intuitively based on whether the outcome of the new competition is expected or unexpected:

- If player v has a higher skill level than u, then the outcome of edge (u, v) is expected, and it will cause small updates in skill level μ and σ.
- If player u has a higher skill level than v, then the outcome of edge (u, v) is unexpected, and it will cause large updates in skill level μ and σ.

As far as we know, we are the first one to consider the problem of inferring graph hierarchy as a competition problem. A node v's ranking score in the graph hierarchy inferred by TrueSkill is defined as:

$$f_{ts}(v) = \mu_v - 3\sigma_v \quad (1)$$

3.1.2 Social Agony. Social agony proposed by Gupte et al. [11] assumes that the existence of a link indicates a rank recommendation. A link $u \Rightarrow v$ indicates a recommendation of v from u. If there is no reverse link from v to u, it could indicate that v is higher up in the hierarchy than u. It's assumed that in social networks such as Twitter, agony can be caused when people follow other people who are lower in the hierarchy.

Given a network $G = (V, E)$ which contains cycles, each node v has a rank $r(v)$. Higher ranking nodes are less likely to connect to lower ranking nodes. Hence, directed edges that go from higher ranking nodes are less prevalent than edges that go in reverse direction. If $r(u) > r(v)$, then edge $u \Rightarrow v$ causes agony to the node u and the amount of agony depends on the difference between their ranks.

There are many choices for defining agony. The simplest way is to define a constant value for any edge that violates the hierarchy. If it is set as a constant 1, then this problem is equivalent to a minimum feedback arc set problem as we discussed earlier. A more practical variant is to penalize the violating edges by the severity of their violation, which means that edges that respect the hierarchy receive a penalty of 0 and penalty increase linearly as the violation becomes more severe. Gupte et al. [11] defined the agony to u caused by edge (u, v) is equal to $max(r(u) - r(v) + 1, 0)$.

The agony in the network relative to the ranking r is the sum of agony on each edge: $A(G, r) = \sum_{(u,v) \in E} \max(r(u) - r(v) + 1, 0)$. Since nodes typically minimize their agony, the problem is changed to find a ranking r that minimize the total agony in the graph: $A(G) = \min_{r \in Rankings}(\sum_{(u,v) \in E} \max(r(u) - r(v) + 1, 0))$.

Gupte et al. [11] provided an $O(nm^2)$ algorithm to minimize the agony of the graph, which has n vertices and m edges. A faster discovery algorithm with the computational complexity of $O(m^2)$ was introduced by Tatti [36, 37].

A node v's ranking score in the graph hierarchy inferred by social agony is defined as:

$$f_{agony}(v) = r(v) \quad (2)$$

3.2 Strategies to select violation edges

In this section, we will introduce strategies to select edges to remove and break cycles in the graph.

Our first strategy is to select the edge which violates the graph hierarchy the most in a simple cycle (a closed path where no node appears twice, except that the first and last node are the same). Consider a simple cycle $s = (v_1, v_2, ..., v_l, v_1)$, and let $i = argmax(f(v_i) - f(v_{(i+1)\%l}))$, then edge $(v_i, v_{(i+1)\%l})$ is the one which violates the graph hierarchy the most and will be added to the set of edges to be removed. Note that removal of one edge in a simple cycle may break many other cycles at the same time, since the removed edge could be a part of multiple simple cycles. Hence it is necessary to track all simple cycles that the target edge is involved in. A major challenge in using this strategy is the time complexity to find all simple cycles in a directed graph. The time complexity for finding all simple cycles introduced by Donald [16] is $O((|V| + |E|)(|C| + 1))$ for $|V|$ nodes, $|E|$ edges and $|C|$ simple cycles. It can be computationally expensive for large graphs.

To be more efficient, we propose to simplify the input graph before using any strategy for selecting edges to break cycles. The simplification includes removing self-loops, dividing the graph into SCCs, and then dropping the trivial SCCs (a trivial SCC consists of a single node). For a non trivial SCC scc_i, several heuristic solutions to reduce scc_i to a DAG are proposed as follows:

- *Forward*: Select the node v which has the *highest* ranking score $f(v)$ in scc_i and then remove its all *out* edges in scc_i: $\{(v, u), \forall(v, u) \in scc_i\}$.
- *Backward*: Select the node v which has the *lowest* ranking score $f(v)$ in scc_i and then remove its all *in* edges in scc_i: $\{(u, v), \forall(u, v) \in scc_i\}$.
- *Greedy*: Select the edge which violates the hierarchy the most to remove. The violation of hierarchy on an edge (u, v) is defined as $max(f(u) - f(v), 0)$.

We iteratively use the above simplification processes and heuristic solutions to break cycles in the graph until the graph becomes a *DAG*. It is easy to notice that processes for each SCC are independent from each other, and they can be parallelized to improve efficiency.

Since each node's hierarchical ranking score can be inferred by TrueSkill and Social Agony, we have 6 combinations to remove cycle edges:

- TS_G: Use TrueSkill (*TS*) to infer the graph hierarchy, and strategy *Greedy* is applied to remove cycle edges.
- TS_B: Same as TS_G, except strategy *Backward* is applied to remove cycle edges.
- TS_F: Same as TS_G, except strategy *Forward* is applied to remove cycle edges.
- SA_G: Same as TS_G, except use Social Agony (*SA*) to infer the graph hierarchy.
- SA_B: Same as TS_B, except use *SA* to infer graph hierarchy.
- SA_F: Same as TS_F, except use *SA* to infer graph hierarchy.

We use a voting schema (*H_Voting*) to ensemble the above 6 approaches for breaking cycles in a graph. For each cycle edge e, its voting score is $\sum_m (I_m(e))$, where $m \in \{TS\_G, TS\_F, TS\_B, SA\_G, SA\_F, SA\_B\}$ and $I_m(\cdot)$ is an indicator function. If edge e is removed by method m, $I_m(e) = 1$, otherwise $I_m(e) = 0$. Thus, *H_Voting* selects the edge with the highest voting score for removal.

4 EXPERIMENTS

4.1 Datasets

In this section we describe the datasets used in our experiments. We experiment not only with real-world datasets but also synthetic (random) graphs in order to demonstrate the robustness of our approach.

We use the following real-world graphs:

- *arXiv*: The Arxiv HEP-PH citation graph[4] is extracted from arXiv[5] and covers all citations from Jan. 1993 to Arpril 2003. If a paper i cites paper j, the graph contains a directed edge from i to j.
- *EU_Email*: The EU email community network graph[6] is generated using email data from a large European research institution. If a node i sent at least one message to j, then there is a directed edge from i to j.
- *Web_Google*: The Google web graph[7] is generated by representing web pages as nodes and hyperlinks between web pages as directed edges.
- *Wiki_Vote/Wiki_Talk*: Wikipedia vote/talk network graph[8] contains all the Wikipedia voting/talk data from the inception of Wikipedia till Jan. 2008. If user i voted/edited the talk page on/of user j, there is a directed edge from i to j in the graph.
- *Stackoverflow_Q2A*: The Stack Overflow network[9] contains interactions between users and questions on the stack exchange web site Stack Overflow. If user j has answered user i's question, there is a directed edge from i to j in the Stackoverflow_Q2A graph.
- *DBP_2014, DBP_2015, DBP_2016*: These three category graphs from DBpedia[10] are extracted from relationships of categories published in 2014, Oct. 2015, and April. 2016 respectively. If i is a sub-category of category j, there is a directed edge from i to j in corresponding category graph.

In addition, we also consider two graph datasets that have no cycle edges: a patent citation graph (*Cit-Patents*)[11] and the NCBI taxonomy graph (*NCBI-Taxo*) [12]. The Cit-Patent data set spans from January 1, 1963 to December 30, 1999, and includes all the utility patents granted during that period. In the Cit-Patent graph, if a patent i cites patent j, there is a directed edge from i to j. In NCBI-Taxo graph, there is a directed edge from more specific nodes to more general nodes. There is a self loop for the root node. Hence the out-degree of each node in NCBI-Taxo graph is 1.

Condensation graphs: For graphs containing cycles such as *arXiv*, *EU_Email*, etc., we use their corresponding **condensation graphs** in our experiments. The condensation graph CG of graph G is a cycle-free graph that is generated by contracting each SCC in G to a single node. Statistics of these condensation graphs are shown in Table 1.

Table 1: Statistics of Datasets

Dataset	# nodes	# edges
Cit-Patents	3,774,768	16,518,948
NCBI-Taxo	1,553,020	1,553,019
arXiv	20,085	130,469
EU-Email	230,795	223,004
Web_Google	371,603	519,304
Wiki_Vote	5,816	19,540
Gnutella	48,438	55,349
Wiki_Talk	2,394,385	5,021,410
Stackoverflow_Q2A	2,021,984	3,345,760
DBP_2014	5,502,627	20,854,028
DBP_2015	6,092,789	24,173,109
DBP_2016	6,263,925	25,211,684

Random Graphs: To provide evidence that our techniques are not merely exploiting structural properties of these particular real-world graphs, we also generated several random DAGs for our experiments. This follows the DAG(n, M) model from the random graph literature (see e.g., [1]). The following procedure is applied to generate a random DAG $RG = (N, M)$:

- Generate $|N|$ nodes with node ids in the range $[1, |N|]$.
- Randomly select $|M|$ pairs of nodes as edges in M. For each pair $\{u, v\}$, add (u, v) to M if $id(u) < id(v)$ and (v, u) otherwise.
- Randomly permute the node ids for each node in N, so that node ids do not imply anything about the order information.

[4] https://snap.stanford.edu/data/cit-HepPh.html
[5] https://arxiv.org/
[6] https://snap.stanford.edu/data/email-EuAll.html
[7] https://snap.stanford.edu/data/web-Google.html
[8] https://snap.stanford.edu/data/wiki-Vote.html and https://snap.stanford.edu/data/wiki-Talk.html
[9] https://snap.stanford.edu/data/sx-stackoverflow.html
[10] http://downloads.dbpedia.org/
[11] https://snap.stanford.edu/data/cit-Patents.html
[12] https://www.ncbi.nlm.nih.gov/taxonomy

4.2 Experimental Setup

Since there are few large real taxonomy graphs with ground truth publicly available, we consider the following set up to evaluate the different approaches: We consider a large real or synthetic DAG and introduce cycles in it by inserting edges that violate the partial ordering induced by the DAG. The goal for the various approaches is to identify the set of edges that were inserted. In particular, we evaluate the performance of different approaches by considering the set of newly inserted cycle-introducing edges as the ground truth and computing *precision*, *recall*, and *F1-score* with respect to this ground truth.

To introduce cycles, we repeatedly perform the following step: randomly select a node pair (u, v) and if u can reach v in the input DAG, then we insert the edge (v, u) into the cycle-introducing edge set T. In some experiments, we also constrain the shortest path length of $u \rightarrow v$ to be no larger than a threshold d. Once we have the required number of edges in T, we insert these edges into the input DAG. Hence, edges in T are labeled as *noisy edges* which can be used for evaluation.

Baselines to Remove Cycle Edges:

Three baseline approaches are used in our experiments:

- *DFS*: use DFS to detect and remove back edges
- *PR*: use PageRank to infer graph hierarchy, and strategy *Greedy* is applied to break cycles.
- *MFAS*: a local greedy implementation of minimum feedback arc set problem, as described in section 2.

In addition to the precision, recall and F1-score obtained using the above setup, we also consider auxiliary measures such as the number of edges removed to make the graph acyclic.

4.3 Experimental Results

First, we consider the general case where there are no constraints on the length (d) of the cycle. Figure 5 presents our results on random DAGs (with $RG(n, m)$ representing a random DAG with n nodes and m edges, where 1K is used as shorthand for 1000). We inserted 1500[13] random edges into these graphs to create cycles[14], and the goal is to identify and remove these edges in order to break the cycles. We observe that the different approaches achieve very different precision, recall and overall F1 score. Our proposed voting approach, *H_Voting*, achieves the best F1 score across the entire range of different random DAGs. Note that our approach is much more accurate for these graphs than the traditional heuristics based on *DFS* and *MFAS* on random DAGs.

Next, we consider the real-world graphs, and, as before, insert 1,500 random edges to create cycles. As shown in Figure 6, there is no consistent winning strategy. While most approaches based on TrueSkill and Social agony achieve fairly similar performance on *Cit-Patents*, TS-B achieves the best F1 score on the tree-like NCBI taxonomy graph[15]. We note that *H_Voting* achieves the best F1 score (around 0.9) on the *arXiv* condensation graph and is among the top-3 over all settings, both in terms of precision and F1. In contrast, the F1 score of *DFS* based heuristic is 0.12 for *Cit-Patents*, 0.17 for *NCBI-Taxo* and 0.02 for *arXiv*.

4.4 Number of Edges to be Removed

In addition to precision, recall and F1 score, another important performance measure is the number of edges removed. Although there is no empirical evidence that removing fewer edges causes less damage to the logical hierarchy of the ontological relation, we still want as few edges to be removed as possible. In particular, this is the measure that is directly optimized by the minimum feedback arc set (*MFAS*) problem.

For brevity, we only report the number of edges that are removed from graphs $RG(3K, 15K)$, $RG(30K, 150K)$, and $RG(10K, 150K)$ in Table 2. In these cases, 1500 random edges were inserted to introduce cycles. We note that TS_G, SA_G, and *H_Voting* remove fewer edges compared to other approaches. Furthermore, the number of removed edges is close to 1500, which is the number of edges in the ground truth. Interestingly, the number of edges removed by TS_G, SA_G, and *H_Voting* is considerably smaller than by the greedy heuristic for *MFAS*, which is directly minimizing the number of removed edges. The results in other settings are similar. The corresponding precision, recall and F1 scores are shown in Figure 5, and indicate that strategies that remove fewer edges also have higher F1 scores.

Table 2: # edges to be removed

# edges to be removed	RG(3K,15K)	RG(30K,150K)	RG(10K,150K)
DFS	6,057	17,587	54,774
PR	3,337	5,155	8,478
MFAS	2,423	3,378	4,584
TS_B	2,431	3,622	3,865
TS_F	2,307	3,232	3,736
SA_F	2,175	2,077	2,707
SA_B	2,193	1,881	2,566
TS_G	1,860	1,544	1,597
SA-G	1,691	1,506	1,531
H_Voting	1,649	1,502	1,513

4.5 Sensitivity to Number of Noisy Edges

Next, we test the sensitivity of H_Voting to the number of noisy edges in the hierarchical relationship. For this, we consider small ($RG(3K, 15K)$), medium ($RG(3K, 30K)$) and a large ($RG(3K, 45K)$) random DAGs. Figure 7 shows how the precision ("-p" in legend), recall ("-r") and F1 ("-f1") scores vary on these graphs as the fraction of noisy edges is increased (e.g., a fraction of 0.1 in the x-axis corresponds to adding $1.5K$, $3K$, and $4.5K$ noisy edges in $RG(3K, 15K)$,$RG(3K, 30K)$, and $RG(3K, 45K)$, respectively, for introducing cycles). As expected, the accuracy scores decrease as the fraction of incorrect edges is increased. But more importantly, we find that the accuracy of our approaches becomes more robust to noise as the graph size increases. For instance, when 30% ($13.5K$) extra noisy edges are added to $RG(3K, 45K)$, *H_Voting* is still able to achieve a F1 score of around 0.8 and recall of around 0.9. This gives us confidence that in large real-world graphs, *H_Voting* can accurately identify the edges to remove, even in scenarios with large amounts of noise.

[13] We have tested the performance on a varying number of edges as shown in Section 4.5. In the interest of space, we report only the performance for 1500 extra edges. Other settings yield similar results.

[14] The maximum number of big SCCs generated is 1500

[15] After removal of the only self-loop edge.

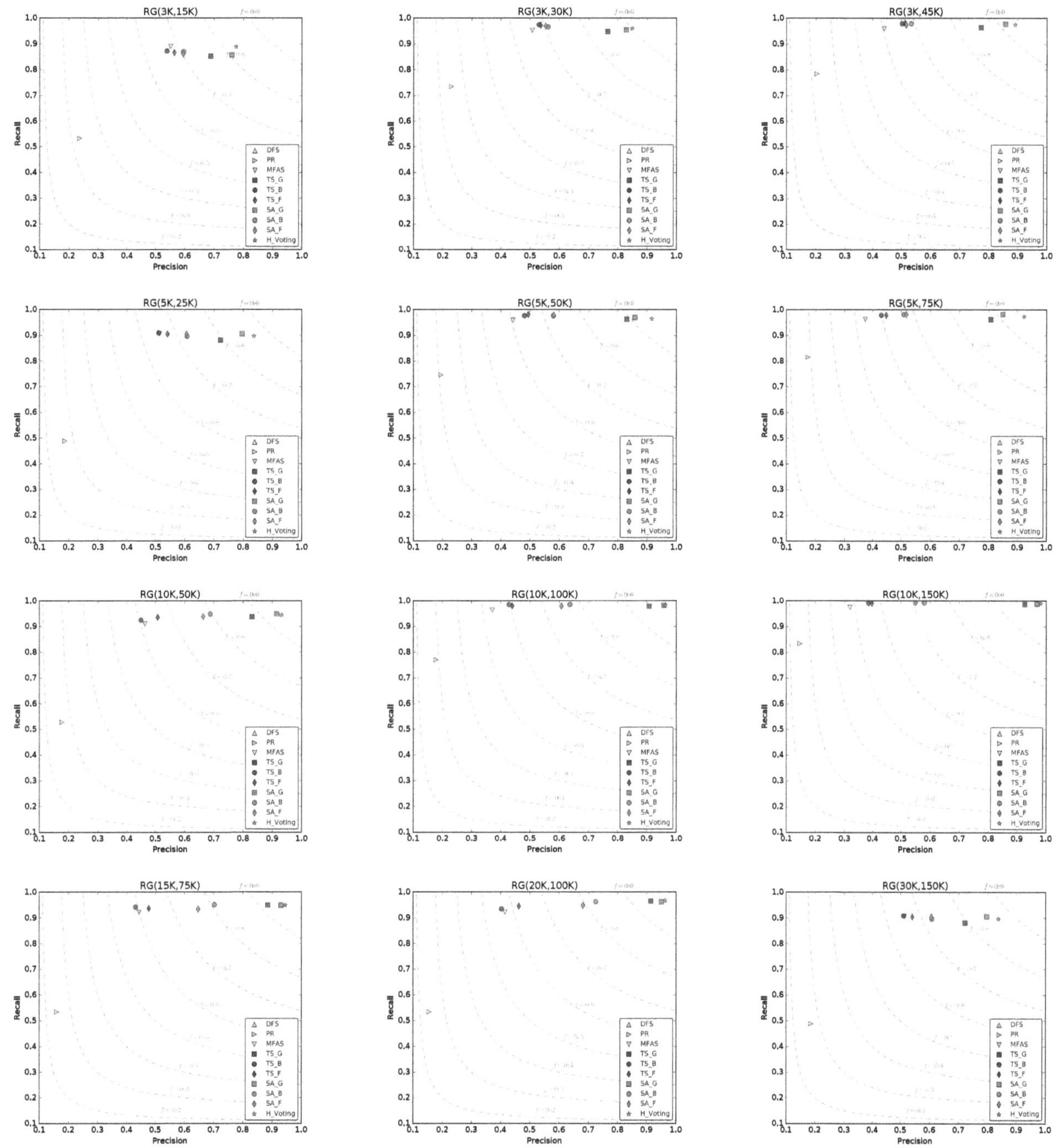

Figure 5: Performance (precision,recall,f-1 score) on different sizes of random generated graphs (path length control parameter *d* is unlimited). We can observe that our proposed voting approach, *H_Voting*, achieves the best F1 score across the entire range of different random DAGs.

4.6 Special case of constrained cycle length

To further understand why the TrueSkill and Social agony based approaches are more accurate than the traditional heuristics based on *MFAS*, *DFS* or *Pagerank*, we consider the special case in which cycles are constrained to be of length at most two. We consider a range of real-world graphs and insert 1,500 random edges to introduce cycles. Note that it is easy to obtain high accuracy in this setting, as even randomly selecting one of the two edges from every simple cycle achieves an expected 0.5 precision and recall. As expected, we observe from Figure 8 that generally, most approaches achieve

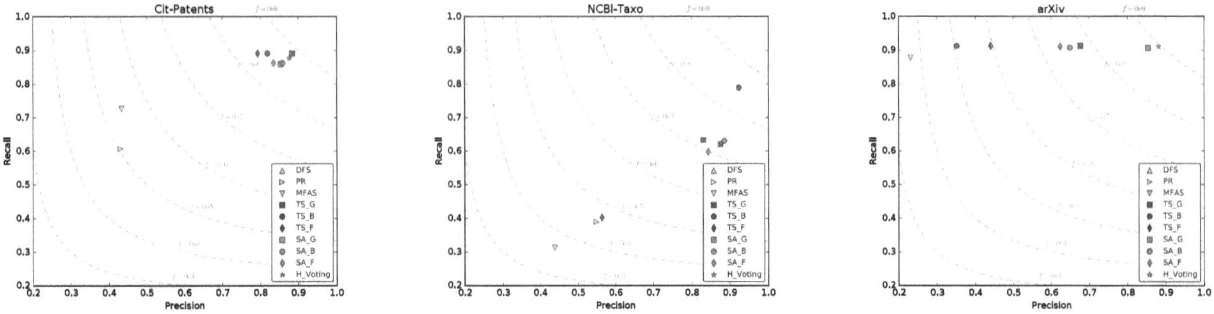

Figure 6: Performance (precision,recall,f-1 score) on different datasets' corresponding graphs (condensation graph for *arXiv*); path length control parameter d is unlimited

Figure 7: Sensitivity to Extra Edges Added

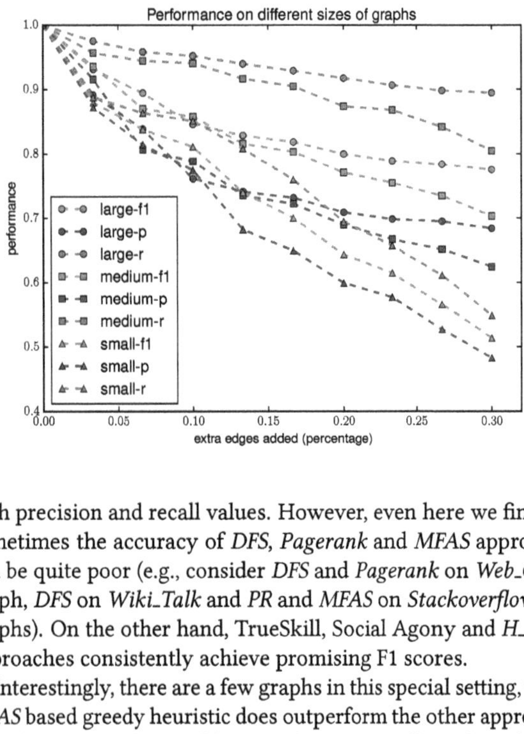

high precision and recall values. However, even here we find that sometimes the accuracy of *DFS*, *Pagerank* and *MFAS* approaches can be quite poor (e.g., consider *DFS* and *Pagerank* on *Web_Google* graph, *DFS* on *Wiki_Talk* and *PR* and *MFAS* on *Stackoverflow_Q2A* graphs). On the other hand, TrueSkill, Social Agony and *H_Voting* approaches consistently achieve promising F1 scores.

Interestingly, there are a few graphs in this special setting, where *MFAS* based greedy heuristic does outperform the other approaches slightly (e.g., *Web_Google*) or performs as well as the other approaches. To understand this, consider Figure 9, where edge (B, A) is the randomly added edge that generates a SCC in the corresponding graph. A node i's ratio value is defined as $r(i) = \frac{d_i^{in}}{d_i^{out}}$. In this example $r(B) \gg 1$ and $r(A) \ll 1$. Then edge (B, A) will be selected as the edge to be removed based on the local greedy implementation of *MFAS*. The average ratio value of source nodes such as B in Figure 9 is 14, 13.23, and 13.97 in *EU-Email*, *Web_Google* and *Wiki_Vote* graph respectively. And the average ratio value of target nodes such as A in Figure 9 is 0.076, 0.85, and 0.0664 in *EU-Email*, *Web_Google* and *Wiki_Vote* graph respectively. As a result, the greedy *MFAS* heuristic correctly picks up edge (B, A) for removal in many of these graphs. However, in graphs with larger simple cycles, these heuristics suffer from very poor precision (as already noted in Section 4.3).

Figure 9: A toy scenario in which MFAS can outperform other strategies.

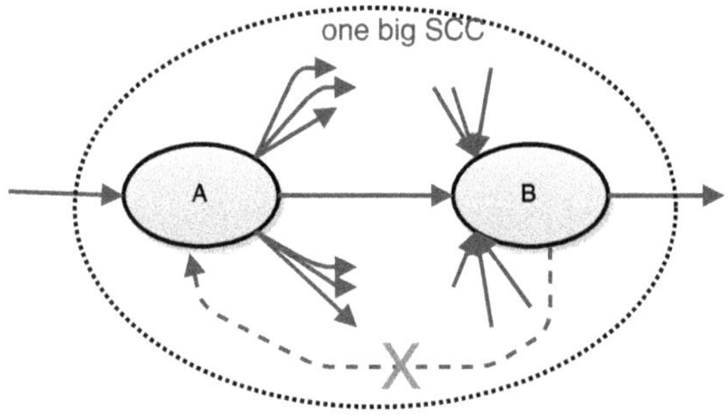

4.7 Performance on Wikipedia Category Graph

We apply our approach to remove cycle edges in the Wikipedia category graphs. Note that this is a graph extracted from a 2014 snapshot of the popular skos:broader relationships in DBpedia. First, we note that even though skos:broader captures the hierarchical specific/general relationship, it has a large number of cycles forming many SCCs (c.f. Table 3). This is because it is created in a crowd-sourced way and its creators often misinterpret the granularity of concepts. For instance, the concept United Nations can refer to its headquarter in New York or it can refer to the intergovernmental organization, creating a cycle United Nations → New York → United States of America → United Nations. The results are similar for later snapshots of Wikipedia categories.

Table 3: Statistics of big SCCs in DBpedia

DBpedia	2014
# SCCs	534
# nodes in SCCs	8,939
# edges in SCCs	24,178
# nodes in the biggest SCC	6,741
# edges in the biggest SCC	20,979

Since we don't have a good ground truth for edges to remove in this dataset (there are a large number of cycles destroyed, new

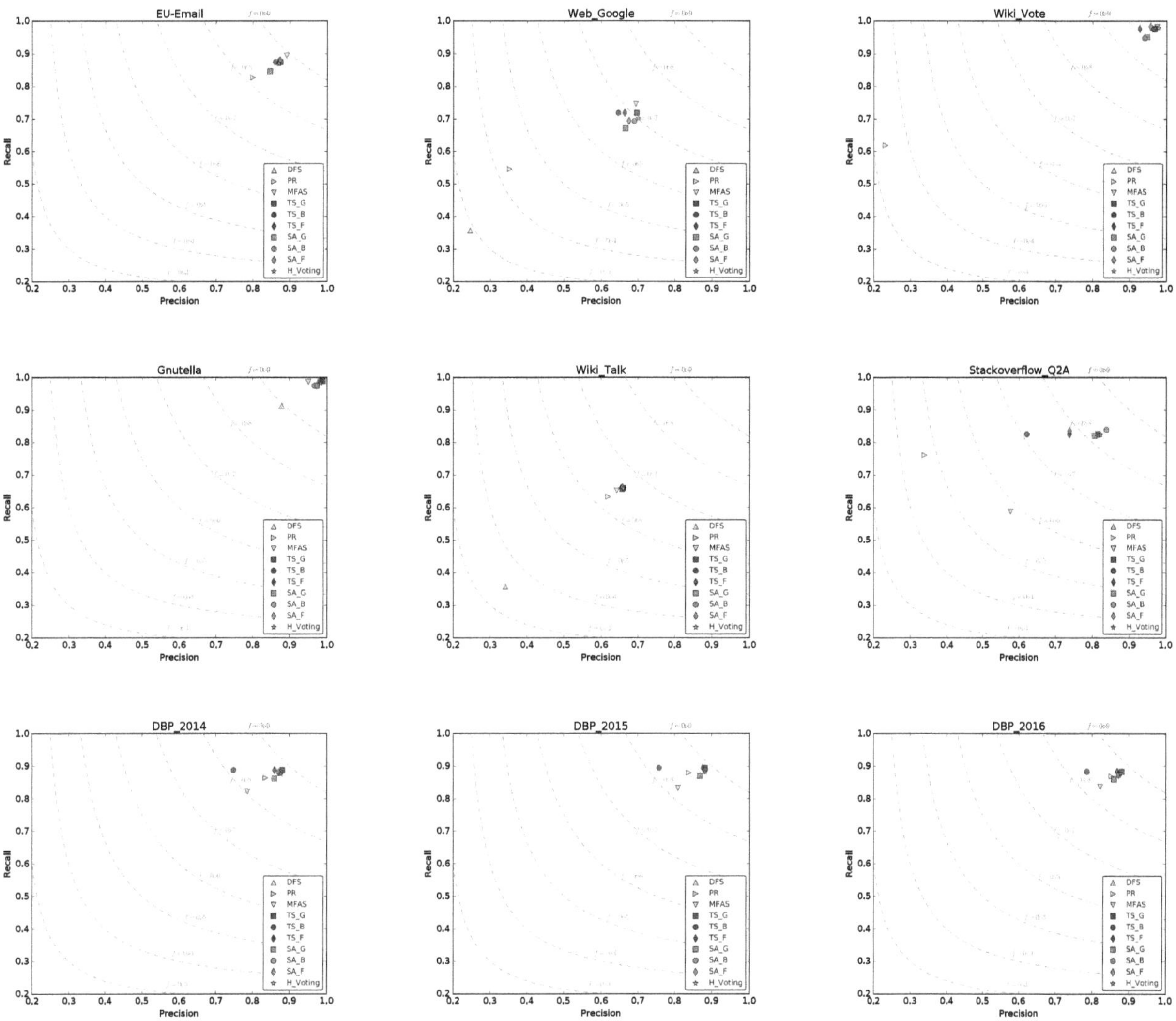

Figure 8: Performance (precision,recall,f-1 score) on different datasets' corresponding condensation graphs (path length control parameter $d = 2$)

cycles created and many new nodes and edges created from one snapshot to another), we focus on the number of edges that are removed by different approaches. We observe from Table 4 that, similar to the results on random DAGs in Section 4.4, *H_Voting* and SA_G break cycles in *DBP_2014* graph by removing considerably fewer edges compared to other approaches.

Table 4: # edges to be removed

# edges to be removed	DBP_2014 Category Graph
MFAS	4,075
PR	3,920
DFS	3,602
TS_F	3,030
TS_B	2,501
TS_G	2,479
SA_F	1,737
SA_B	1,730
H_Voting	1,713
SA_G	1,672

5 CONCLUSION

In this paper, we address the problem of breaking cycles while preserving the logical structure (hierarchy) of the directed graph as much as possible. We propose approaches that explicitly focus on inferring the graph hierarchy using TrueSkill and Social Agony. We leverage this inferred hierarchy using an ensemble approach to identify the edges to be removed. We show that our approaches achieve significantly better accuracy compared to the traditional heuristics based on DFS and MFAS and at the same time, they are fast, scalable and fully automated. Thus, they can support a large and growing number of applications that rely on clean ontological knowledge bases representing hierarchical relations.

Future work. In this study, the issue of breaking cycles from directed graphs is addressed from a heuristic perspective. An alternative is to consider model based approaches to predict the edge in a SCC that has the highest probability of being removed. The required features for the prediction model can be extracted from graph embedding methods, such as node2vec[10], or low rank representations of adjacency matrices, decomposed by matrix factorization (a widely used technique in recommender systems [4, 19, 32, 40, 41]). Furthermore, other measures, such as deviation to dominant structural role, and deviation to transitive closure, may also prove to be very useful both for the heuristic and model-based approaches. However, significant effort is required to compute these measures for large graphs in a fast and scalable way.

Acknowledgments This work is supported by the National Science Foundation of United States under grant CCF-1645599 and IIS-1550302. All content represents the opinion of the authors, which is not necessarily shared or endorsed by their respective employers and/or sponsors.

REFERENCES

[1] Deepak Ajwani and Tobias Friedrich. 2010. Average-case analysis of incremental topological ordering. *Discrete Applied Mathematics* 158, 4 (2010), 240–250.
[2] Ali Baharev, Hermann Schichl, and Arnold Neumaier. 2015. An exact method for the minimum feedback arc set problem. (2015).
[3] Shuvra S Bhattacharyya, Praveen K Murthy, and Edward A Lee. 1996. *Software Synthesis from Dataflow Graphs.* Vol. 360. Springer Science & Business Media.
[4] Peizhe Cheng, Shuaiqiang Wang, Jun Ma, Jiankai Sun, and Hui Xiong. 2017. Learning to Recommend Accurate and Diverse Items. In *Proceedings of the 26th International Conference on World Wide Web (WWW '17).* 183–192.
[5] James J Cimino. 1998. Auditing the unified medical language system with semantic methods. *Journal of the American Medical Informatics Association* 5, 1 (1998), 41–51.
[6] Peter Eades and Xuemin Lin. 1995. A new heuristic for the feedback arc set problem. *Australasian Journal of Combinatorics* (1995), 15–25.
[7] Peter Eades, Xuemin Lin, and William F Smyth. 1993. A fast and effective heuristic for the feedback arc set problem. *Inform. Process. Lett.* 47, 6 (1993), 319–323.
[8] G. Even, J. (Seffi) Naor, B. Schieber, and M. Sudan. 1998. Approximating Minimum Feedback Sets and Multicuts in Directed Graphs. *Algorithmica* 20, 2 (1998), 151–174.
[9] Marco Fossati, Dimitris Kontokostas, and Jens Lehmann. 2015. Unsupervised Learning of an Extensive and Usable Taxonomy for DBpedia. In *Proceedings of the 11th International Conference on Semantic Systems (SEMANTICS '15).* 177–184.
[10] Aditya Grover and Jure Leskovec. 2016. node2vec: Scalable feature learning for networks. In *Proceedings of the 22nd ACM SIGKDD International Conference on Knowledge Discovery and Data Mining.* ACM, 855–864.
[11] Mangesh Gupte, Pravin Shankar, Jing Li, S. Muthukrishnan, and Liviu Iftode. 2011. Finding Hierarchy in Directed Online Social Networks. In *Proceedings of the 20th International Conference on World Wide Web (WWW '11).* New York, NY, USA, 557–566.
[12] Ralf Herbrich, Tom Minka, and Thore Graepel. 2007. TrueSkill™: A Bayesian Skill Rating System. In *Advances in Neural Information Processing Systems (NIPS)*, P. B. Schölkopf, J. C. Platt, and T. Hoffman (Eds.). 569–576.
[13] Johannes Hoffart, Fabian M Suchanek, Klaus Berberich, and Gerhard Weikum. 2013. YAGO2: A spatially and temporally enhanced knowledge base from Wikipedia. *Artificial Intelligence* 194 (2013), 28–61.
[14] Chia-Jui Hsu and Shuvra S Bhattacharyya. 2007. *Cycle-breaking techniques for scheduling synchronous dataflow graphs.* Technical Report.
[15] Chia-Jui Hsu, Ming-Yung Ko, Shuvra S Bhattacharyya, Suren Ramasubbu, and José Luis Pino. 2007. Efficient simulation of critical synchronous dataflow graphs. *ACM Transactions on Design Automation of Electronic Systems (TODAES)* 12, 3 (2007), 21.
[16] Donald B Johnson. 1975. Finding all the elementary circuits of a directed graph. *SIAM J. Comput.* 4, 1 (1975), 77–84.
[17] Viggo Kann. 1992. *On the approximability of NP-complete optimization problems.* Ph.D. Dissertation.
[18] Richard M. Karp. 1972. *Reducibility among Combinatorial Problems.* Boston, MA, 85–103.
[19] Y. Koren, R. Bell, and C. Volinsky. 2009. Matrix Factorization Techniques for Recommender Systems. *Computer* 42, 8 (Aug 2009), 30–37.
[20] Javier Lacasta, Javier Nogueras-Iso, and Francisco Javier Zarazaga-Soria. 2010. *Terminological Ontologies - Design, Management and Practical Applications.* Semantic Web and Beyond: Computing for Human Experience, Vol. 9. Springer.
[21] Wooyoung Lee and Dale F Rudd. 1966. On the ordering of recycle calculations. *AIChE Journal* 12, 6 (1966), 1184–1190.
[22] Jing Liu, Young-In Song, and Chin-Yew Lin. 2011. Competition-based User Expertise Score Estimation. In *Proceedings of the 34th International ACM SIGIR Conference on Research and Development in Information Retrieval (SIGIR '11).* New York, NY, USA, 425–434.
[23] Jing Liu, Quan Wang, Chin-Yew Lin, and Hsiao-Wuen Hon. 2013. Question Difficulty Estimation in Community Question Answering Services. In Proceedings of the 2013 Conference on Empirical Methods in Natural Language Processing, 85–90.
[24] Bodenreider Olivier Mougin Fleur. 2005. Approaches to Eliminating Cycles in the UMLS Metathesaurus: Nave vs. Formal. *American Medical Informatics Association Annual Symposium Proceedings* (2005), 550–554.
[25] Esko Nuutila and Eljas Soisalon-Soininen. 1994. On Finding the Strongly Connected Components in a Directed Graph. *Inf. Process. Lett.* 49, 1 (Jan. 1994), 9–14.
[26] Bodenreider Olivier. 2001. Circular Hierarchical Relationships in the UMLS: Etiology, Diagnosis, Treatment, Complications and Prevention. *Proceedings of the American Medical Informatics Association Symposium* (2001), 57–61.
[27] Tatiana Orenstein, Zvi Kohavi, and Irith Pomeranz. 1995. An optimal algorithm for cycle breaking in directed graphs. *Journal of Electronic Testing* 7, 1 (1995), 71–81.
[28] Lawrence Page, Sergey Brin, Rajeev Motwani, and Terry Winograd. 1999. *The PageRank citation ranking: Bringing order to the web.* Technical Report. Stanford InfoLab.
[29] Domenico M Pisanelli, Aldo Gangemi, and Geri Steve. 1998. An ontological analysis of the UMLS Metathesaurus.. In *Proceedings of the AMIA symposium.* American Medical Informatics Association, 810.
[30] Youssef Saab. 2001. A Fast and Effective Algorithm for the Feedback Arc Set Problem. *Journal of Heuristics* 7, 3 (May 2001), 235–250.
[31] Fabian M Suchanek, Gjergji Kasneci, and Gerhard Weikum. 2007. Yago: a core of semantic knowledge. In *Proceedings of the 16th international conference on World Wide Web.* ACM, 697–706.
[32] Jiankai Sun, Shuaiqiang Wang, Byron J. Gao, and Jun Ma. 2012. Learning to Rank for Hybrid Recommendation. In *Proceedings of the 21st ACM International Conference on Information and Knowledge Management (CIKM '12).* 2239–2242.
[33] Osma Suominen and Eero Hyvönen. 2012. Improving the Quality of SKOS Vocabularies with Skosify. In *Proceedings of the 18th International Conference on Knowledge Engineering and Knowledge Management (EKAW'12).* 383–397.
[34] Osma Suominen and Christian Mader. 2014. Assessing and Improving the Quality of SKOS Vocabularies. *Journal on Data Semantics* 3, 1 (2014), 47–73. DOI: http://dx.doi.org/10.1007/s13740-013-0026-0
[35] Roberto Tamassia. 2007. *Handbook of Graph Drawing and Visualization (Discrete Mathematics and Its Applications).* Chapman & Hall/CRC.
[36] Nikolaj Tatti. 2014. *Faster Way to Agony Discovering hierarchies in directed graphs.* Berlin, Heidelberg, 163–178.
[37] Nikolaj Tatti. 2015. Hierarchies in Directed Networks. In *2015 IEEE International Conference on Data Mining.* 991–996.
[38] Hahn Udo and Stefan Schulz. 2004. Boosting the Medical Knowledge Infrastructurefi!?A Feasibility Study on Very Large Terminological Knowledge Bases. *Proc Symp on Engineering of Intelligent Systems* (2004).
[39] Denny Vrandečić and Markus Krötzsch. 2014. Wikidata: a free collaborative knowledgebase. *Commun. ACM* 57, 10 (2014), 78–85.
[40] Shuaiqiang Wang, Jiankai Sun, Byron J. Gao, and Jun Ma. 2012. Adapting Vector Space Model to Ranking-based Collaborative Filtering. In *Proceedings of the 21st ACM International Conference on Information and Knowledge Management (CIKM '12).* 1487–1491.
[41] Shuaiqiang Wang, Jiankai Sun, Byron J. Gao, and Jun Ma. 2014. VSRank: A Novel Framework for Ranking-Based Collaborative Filtering. *ACM Trans. Intell. Syst. Technol.* 5, 3, Article 51 (July 2014), 24 pages.
[42] Torsten Zesch and Iryna Gurevych. 2007. Analysis of the Wikipedia Category Graph for NLP Applications. In *Proceedings of the TextGraphs-2 Workshop (NAACL-HLT).* Association for Computational Linguistics, Rochester, 1–8.

ϵ-WGX: Adaptive Edge Probing for Enhancing Incomplete Networks

Sucheta Soundarajan
Syracuse University
susounda@syr.edu

Tina Eliassi-Rad
Northeastern University
eliassi@ccs.neu.edu

Brian Gallagher
Lawrence Livermore National Laboratory
bgallagher@llnl.gov

Ali Pinar
Sandia National Laboratories
apinar@sandia.gov

ABSTRACT

No matter how meticulously constructed, network datasets are often partially observed and incomplete. For example, most of the publicly available data from online social networking services (such as Facebook and Twitter) are collected via apps, users who make their accounts public, and/or the resources available to the researcher/practitioner. Such incompleteness can lead to inaccurate findings. We introduce the *Adaptive Edge Probing* problem. Suppose that one has observed a networked phenomenon via some form of sampling and has a budget to enhance the incomplete network by asking for additional information about specific nodes, with the ultimate goal of obtaining the most valuable information about the network as a whole. Which nodes should be further explored? We present ϵ-WGX, a network-based explore-exploit algorithm for identifying which nodes in the incomplete network to probe. Aggregated over multiple datasets and a wide range of probing budgets, we find that ϵ-WGX outperforms other explore-exploit strategies and baseline probing strategies. For example, for the task of adding as many nodes as possible, over incomplete networks observed via four popular sampling methods, ϵ-WGX outperforms the best comparison strategy by 12%-23% on average.

KEYWORDS

incomplete networks, adaptive probing, graph exploration

1 INTRODUCTION

Collecting network data is expensive, time-consuming, and labor intensive, so most network analyses are conducted on incomplete, partially observed graphs. For example, many researchers obtain graphs from online data repositories for their experiments or collect a limited amount of data through APIs. However, these graphs are often poor representations of the fully observed graph. Having access to more complete data would lead to more accurate analyses, but data acquisition is costly.

A great deal of work has been devoted to the network sampling problem, but here we consider a different problem: If a researcher or analyst is given an incomplete network dataset (e.g., one that was collected by a different individual for some other purpose), how can that person collect a small amount of additional data to best enhance the incomplete network?

Problem Overview. We define the *Active Edge Probing* (AEP) problem as follows: Suppose one obtains an incomplete network $\hat{G}$ that is part of a larger network G, without knowledge of or control over how $\hat{G}$ was generated or observed. Given some amount of budget to obtain more information, which nodes in $\hat{G}$ should one choose to further explore? The specific model for this exploration depends largely on the data collection process (see the discussion below about Probing Models).

Applications. Consider the common case where an organization has access to data within its boundaries, but limited data outside these boundaries. There are many such examples: for instance, a micro-loan company may obtain each applicant's Facebook account, and use his/her social network to make credit decisions about the applicant. In this case, the company wishes to close wedges in the incomplete network, for example by providing some incentive to external users to obtain their data. Alternatively, consider an Internet mapping organization that wishes to identify as many machines as possible in the network. Incomplete maps of the Internet exist, and additional data may be collected by placing monitoring hardware on specific machines/routers. This is an expensive process, so sampling decisions must be made judiciously.

Probing Models. We have observed that the ideal probing algorithm varies substantially depending on the probing model, which describes the information that is returned in response to a query. For example, in response to a query on a node, an API might return all of that node's neighbors, the node's most recent communication, or k random neighbors. In this paper, we consider the case in which a query returns a single random edge adjacent to the queried node. For instance, a probe might represent acquiring an additional random retweet for a Twitter user. This retweet may correspond to an edge already observed. For discussion of other models, refer to our earlier node probing work in [17].

Proposed Method, ϵ-WGX. To solve the AEP problem, we present ϵ-*WGX* (Weighted Graph eXplore), an explore-exploit strategy that takes advantage of the networked representation of the data to determine which node to probe. The strength of ϵ-WGX

WebSci'17, June 25-28, 2017, Troy, NY, USA.
 978-1-4503-4896-6/17/06...$15.00
DOI: http://dx.doi.org/10.1145/3091478.3091492

is that it does not require background information about (1) how the incomplete network was generated, (2) the underlying network structure of the fully observed graph G, or (3) which nodes are good choices for a specific goal/reward.

We compare ϵ-WGX to several baseline strategies, including structural and explore-exploit strategies. We conduct experiments on ten real networks. In this work, we consider three probing goals: (1) Adding as many new nodes as possible to the observed network, (2) adding as many triangles as possible to the observed network, and (3) adding as many new nodes of a certain type to the observed network. Aggregated across sampling methods, networks, and reward functions, ϵ-WGX regularly outperforms the baseline strategies and the other explore-exploit algorithms – e.g., by an average of at least 12% - 23% on the task of adding as many nodes as possible to the incomplete network.

At a high-level, our goals might be considered similar to the goals of network sampling and link prediction. However, ϵ-WGX differs from existing network sampling methods in that it is a general method in which the user specifies the goal of the data collection (e.g., observing new nodes or adding additional triangles to the network). Additionally, rather than sampling a network from scratch, it supplements an existing incomplete network observation. Depending on the probing goal (e.g., adding triangles to the observed network), ϵ-WGX may appear to be similar to link prediction. However, in such cases, link prediction methods are limited to adding edges *within* the initially observed network, while ϵ-WGX attempts to optimize the *entire* observed network with respect to a feature of interest. ϵ-WGX might thus learn that the initial observation is in a triangle-poor region of the network, and moving to a more triangle-dense region of the network would lead to more triangles than adding edges within the initial observation.

Contributions. Our contributions are as follows:

(1) *A new research direction:* We formalize the *Adaptive Edge Probing* (AEP) problem, which is important to a variety of applications in complex network analysis and graph mining.

(2) *An original algorithm for the explore-exploit formulation:* We propose the ϵ-WGX algorithm, which outperforms other explore-exploit strategies at the AEP problem.

(3) *A thorough empirical study:* Our experiments on various data sets and objective functions show that ϵ-WGX regularly outperforms other approaches.s

(4) *A theoretical analysis of regret:* We prove that ϵ-WGX has linear regret, meaning that it performs a constant factor worse than optimal. Although this regret is large, we argue that it is necessary, because the problem setting leads to rewards that are rapidly changing.

2 PROBLEM STATEMENT

In the AEP problem, we want to analyze a graph G, which is a fully observed, networked representation of some social or physical phenomena. But we have access to $\hat{G}$, which is a partially observed version of G. A node or edge is 'observed' if it appears in $\hat{G}$. To improve the accuracy of our analysis, we have a budget b, which can be used to obtain additional data to enhance $\hat{G}$. Each unit of budget is equal to probing a selected node in $\hat{G}$. The probe involves going to the source of the data and receiving a random edge adjacent to the selected node in the fully observed graph G. Note that this is not the link prediction problem, as we only specify one node (rather than querying for an edge between two specified nodes), and may obtain an edge leading to a previously-unseen node.

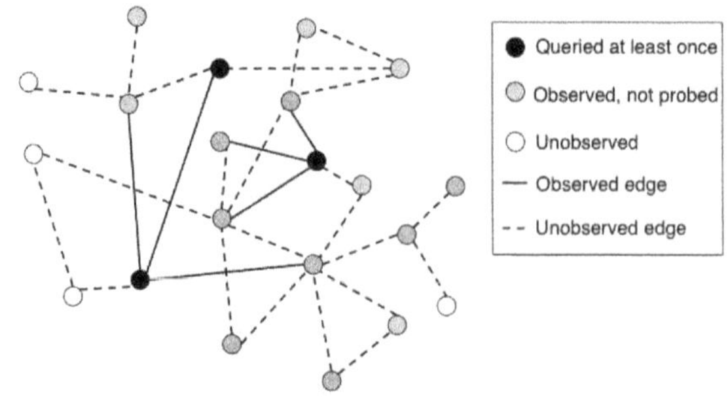

Figure 1: Example of an incomplete graph $\hat{G}$ after some probes have been conducted. Black nodes have been probed at least once, gray nodes have been observed but not yet probed, and white nodes exist in the underlying 'whole' graph, but have not yet been observed.

Definition 1. *Adaptive Edge Probing (AEP) Problem.*
We assume that we are given:

- *An incomplete graph* $\hat{G} = (\hat{V}, \hat{E})$
- *Probing budget* $b \in \mathbb{N}$
- *A global reward function* $g : H \subset G \to \mathbb{R}$, *which measures the quality of an observed network with respect to a specific goal (e.g., if the goal is to observe as many nodes as possible, how many nodes are in* H*?).*
- *A local reward function* $f : (H, e) \to \mathbb{R}$, *where* H *is an observed network and* e *is an edge.* f *quantifies the value of edge* e *in graph* H. *As discussed in Section 4, the local reward function is related to the global reward function, but does not simply measure the improvement in* g *after an edge is observed.*

We are allowed to perform b *iterations of probing. Let* $\hat{G_k}$ *be the graph observed after* k *iterations of probing. In iteration* k, *a probe consists of selecting a node* u *from* $\hat{G}_{k-1}$. *The result of probing a node* u *is an edge, which is selected uniformly at random from among all of* u*'s neighbors in* G, *including edges seen before. The goal is to select* b *nodes for probing such that* $g(\hat{G_b})$ *is maximized.*

As an example, consider the graph depicted in Figure 1. Black nodes have been probed at least once, and so each black node has at least one observed edge incident to it. However, it is not necessarily the case that all edges adjacent to a probed node have been observed. The observed graph additionally contains gray nodes, which have been observed but not yet probed. The underlying graph contains white nodes, which the observer is unaware of. The challenge is to determine which of the observed (black or gray) nodes should be probed next so as to improve the value of the global reward function by the greatest amount.

Challenges. There are two major challenges in designing a successful probing strategy. (1) For a reward function (such as maximizing the number of nodes in the network $\hat{G_b}$), it is not immediately clear how one should select nodes based only on their structural profile in $\hat{G}$. As we will see, the success of such a strategy can vary across datasets, how the data were observed, probing budgets, and certainly by the application of interest. (2) Since a probe can return an already known edge, the probing strategy must determine when to stop probing a node.

3 PRELIMINARIES

3.1 Explore-Exploit Algorithms

Explore-exploit algorithms are common in settings where one must choose from among a variety of options, each with a different payoff, without prior knowledge of which option is best. Multi-armed bandit algorithms are a popular class of algorithms within this broad category. The simplest solution to the multi-armed bandit problem is the ϵ-greedy algorithm [20]. In this method, one explores with probability ϵ (i.e., selects an arm uniformly at random), and exploits with probability $1 - \epsilon$ (i.e., selects the arm with the highest average reward so far).

Another popular algorithm is the Upper Confidence Bound (UCB) algorithm [2]. The UCB algorithm selects each arm once, and then calculates an upper confidence bound on the expected reward for each arm, and the arm with the greatest value is chosen.

There are examples of multi-armed bandit strategies on graphs, but these problem settings differ substantially from ours. See Section 7 for details.

3.2 Predicting Population Size with Random Draws

Suppose that we have probed a node k times, and seen w distinct neighbors and r duplicates ($k = w + r$). What is the estimated degree d of that node?

The maximum likelihood estimate (MLE) of d, given k, w, and r, is approximately $\hat{d} = \frac{w+r}{m(s)}$, where $s = \frac{w}{k}$ and $m(s)$ is the solution to $s = (1 - e^{-m})/m$ [16]. We assume that all edges are equally likely to be observed by a probe. For general distributions, one can use results from Valiant and Valiant [18].

4 PROPOSED METHOD: ϵ-WGX

We view the AEP problem as a version of the general explore-exploit problem: one may probe any node in the incomplete network; and depending on the selection, obtain information of varying value (i.e., reward) for the given goal. For example, if we wish to maximize the number of triangles in the enhanced network $\hat{G}_b$, it would be most valuable to probe nodes in $\hat{G}$ that have high clustering in G. But which nodes are these?

One can imagine many different possible approaches to this problem: for instance, one might use knowledge of graph structure (e.g., degree distribution or community structure) to predict which nodes in $\hat{G}_b$ are most likely to have the structural properties desired. If one knows how $\hat{G}$ was generated, then this information can also be incorporated into the prediction (see, e.g., [17]). However, such heuristic methods may not generalize to different types of graphs and different probing goals.

Alternatively, an explore-exploit approach has the following strengths: (1) It can be used *without background knowledge of the network structure or reward function.* (2) It can *adapt* to the network and reward function. Thus, if probing some node produces low reward, the approach is unlikely to probe that node further. (3) It is *stable* and *robust*, regularly providing the best performance for any given network and reward function (while the outcomes of other strategies vary significantly).

4.1 Overview

We propose ϵ-WGX (Weighted Graph eXplore), an explore-exploit algorithm that takes advantage of the graph structure inherent in the AEP problem. We make the following key observation: *When we probe a node and obtain an edge, we have gained information not just about that node, but also about the observed neighbor.* In a typical explore-exploit problem setting, such as advertising, when one selects an arm, one obtains reward data about only that arm. Although some methods have been developed for cases in which arms have linked rewards (e.g., if a user clicks on an advertisement about cars, we might infer a higher reward for other advertisements about cars), we are not aware of algorithms that operate directly on graphs, in which the graph itself is the structure of interest.

ϵ-WGX requires that the user supply reward functions corresponding to the desired probing goal: for example, if the goal is to add as many new nodes as possible to $\hat{G}$, then the reward function could give a score of 1 for a probe that produces a new node, and a score of 0 to other probes. See Section 4.2 for a discussion of reward functions. As a node is probed, ϵ-WGX keeps track of the rewards observed from those probed, as described in Section 4.3. In Section 4.4, we describe how ϵ-WGX uses these observed rewards to update not only the probed node, but also the observed neighbor. After a node is probed repeatedly, ϵ-WGX must consider not just past rewards obtained from that node, but the probability of obtaining new information if it were to be probed again. This process is discussed in Section 4.5.

ϵ-WGX uses a nested exploration structure. In the outer level, it chooses between the two broad options of graph expansion (i.e., observing a broader area of the underlying network) and graph densification (i.e., obtaining more information about the nodes already observed). Once that choice is made, it must choose which node to probe. See Figure 2 for a pictoral overview of ϵ-WGX.

ϵ-WGX has two important characteristics that differentiate it from existing explore-exploit algorithms:

1. ϵ-WGX uses a two-level nested structure that first chooses between expansion vs. densification, and then selects which node to probe.
2. With each probe, ϵ-WGX is able to update expected rewards for both the probed node as well as the observed neighbor.

ϵ-WGX could be considered to be a multi-armed bandit algorithm; however, we simply refer to it as an explore-exploit algorithm. This is because, unlike in most multi-armed bandit settings, we cannot make any theoretical statements about the underlying distribution of rewards.

4.2 Global and Local Reward Functions

The user must supply two reward functions to ϵ-WGX: global and local. The global reward function is tied to an application goal, such as maximizing the number of nodes observed, and measures

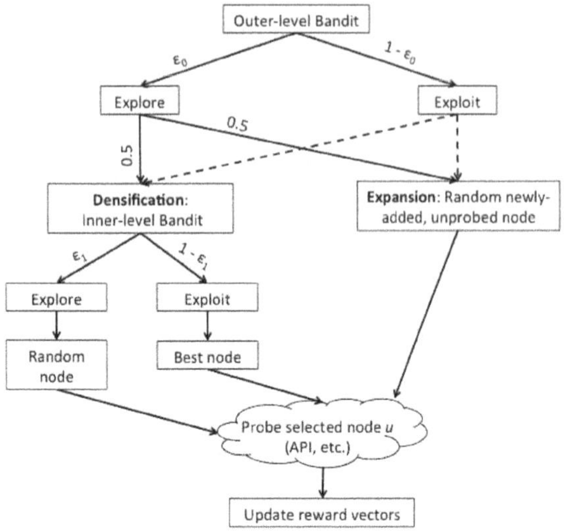

Figure 2: Flowchart depicting the ϵ-WGX node selection process. The outer level chooses between expansion and densification, and then a specific node is selected. Dashed lines indicate that the choice that has been the best in the past is chosen.

the 'quality' of the observed network as a whole. The local reward function is related to the global reward function, and allows ϵ-WGX to evaluate the value of an individual observed edge. In some cases the local reward function may simply be the change in global reward function. However, there are some reasons that this may not necessarily be the case:

1: Graph Complementarities: The local reward function f must take into account complementarities due to graph structure, or interactions between nodes. Consider the case when two observed nodes have the same unobserved neighbor. If we simply define the reward of an edge as the change in the global reward function g after adding that edge, then the mean rewards of probed nodes would be highly dependent on the random order in which the nodes were probed. For example, suppose observed nodes u and v are both adjacent to node w, and ϵ-WGX probes u first and observes (u, w), and then probes v and observes (v, w). If we simply measured the change in total number of observed nodes, the first probe would receive a reward of 1, and the second would receive a reward of 0. But these rewards are dependent entirely on the random order of probes, which is undesirable. Thus, the local reward function should not just measure the change in the global reward function g.

2: Repeated Observations: If a neighbor is observed multiple times, this should not affect the overall mean reward of that node. Instead, as discussed in Section 4.5, as neighbors are observed multiple times, the observed reward is discounted by the probability of observing a new edge if that node is probed again to obtain the expected reward.

We consider three global reward functions and corresponding local reward functions, described below. In each description, let (u, v) be the edge just observed by a probe (i.e., node u was probed and neighbor v observed).

The **Number of Nodes** global reward function g calculates the number of nodes in $\hat{G_b}$. The corresponding local reward function f has a value of 1 if node v was added to $\hat{G}$ after node u was added to the graph, and a value of 0 otherwise. For example, if both u and v were in the original observed network before any probes were made, then ϵ-WGX calculates a reward of 0. If v was added to the graph after u, or the edge (u, v) is observed from multiple probes on u, then each of these probes has a reward of 1.

The **Number of Triangles** global reward function g calculates the number of triangles in $\hat{G_b}$. The corresponding local reward function f has a value of 0 if v had not been observed prior to the probe, or if edge (u, v) was in the original observed network $\hat{G}$. Otherwise, it has a value of c, where c is the number of neighbors that u and v share in $\hat{G_k}$, the current observed network (i.e., the number of triangles in which the edge (u, v) participates). Note that using this reward function does not make the problem equivalent to link prediction, as (1) we are only interested in links to nodes that are two steps away, (2) we must consider the probability of obtaining a new edge upon probing, and (3) we are permitted to add new nodes to the network, as opposed to only adding edges between observed nodes.

The **Number of Targeted Nodes** global reward function is like the Number of Nodes reward, except that only nodes with certain attributes (e.g., nodes representing men over 40) produce a reward of 1.

We refer to the value returned by the local reward function as the reward of a probe.

4.3 Reward Vectors and Node Selection

Recall that ϵ-WGX makes two levels of choices: First, the outer level chooses expansion vs. densification, and if densification is chosen, the inner level makes a decision on which node to probe.

Outer Level: Expansion vs. Densification: In each iteration, with probability ϵ_0, ϵ-WGX explores, and chooses between the choices of expansion and densification with equal probability. With probability $1 - \epsilon_0$, it chooses the best of these two options as described below.

To make this choice, ϵ-WGX maintains two values, r_d and r_e. r_d measures the average reward observed when it chooses densification. r_e is intended to measure the average reward observed from expansion probes. This includes probes conducted when ϵ-WGX chooses expansion, or during a densification probe, when ϵ-WGX selects a node that was not in the original $\hat{G}$ and has not yet been probed.

If expansion is chosen, then ϵ-WGX selects a node from the currently observed network that was not in the original $\hat{G}$ uniformly at random from the set of all such nodes (if no such nodes are available, then ϵ-WGX defaults to densification).

Inner Level: Node Selection: If the outer level chooses densification, then with probability ϵ_1, ϵ-WGX chooses to explore, and chooses a node from the current observed network uniformly at random. With probability $1 - \epsilon_1$, ϵ-WGX chooses the node with the largest R_u^e, which is the mean reward expected for that node (described below).

To track rewards, ϵ-WGX uses three vectors:

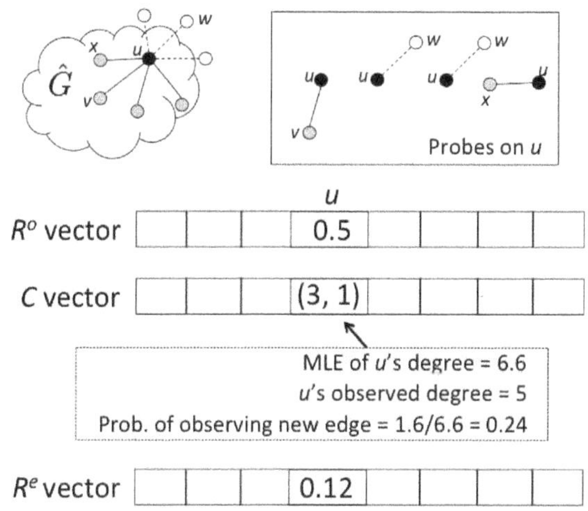

Figure 3: This example depicts rewards for the goal of adding new nodes. Node u is probed four times. The first probe reveals an edge to the known node v, the next two probes produce edges to the new node w, and the fourth probe produces an edge to the known node x. The first and fourth edges produce rewards of 0, and the others produce a reward of 1. R^o_u is thus 0.5. ϵ-WGX estimates u's true degree as 6.6, and the probability of observing a previously-unseen edge upon a probe as $\frac{6.6-5}{6.6} = 0.24$. R^o_u is thus set to $0.5 \times 0.24 = 0.12$.

(1) R^o, a vector of mean observed rewards. R^o_u contains the mean reward observed for each node u that has been observed through probing (that is, either u was directly probed or observed in a probe). Section 4.4 explains how R^o is calculated.
(2) C, a vector of counts. C_u contains the pair (A_u, B_u), where A_u is the number of distinct neighbors of u observed when probing u, and B_u is the number of duplicate neighbors of u observed when probing u. Section 4.5 explains how the probability of observing a new edge when u is probed is calculated from these values.
(3) R^e, a vector of expected rewards. R^e_u contains the reward that we expect to observe if u is probed. R^e_u is equal to $R^o_u \times p_u$, where p_u is calculated as described in Section 4.5.

All reward vectors are updated appropriately after each probe is conducted. Figure 3 contains an example of this process.

4.4 Neighbor Updates

The vector R^o contains the mean of a set of observed rewards for each node. R^o_u captures both rewards observed when directly probing node u, and certain rewards obtained when a neighbor v of u is probed and edge (u, v) is observed. Specifically, R^o_u is the mean of the following values: (1) rewards observed when node u is probed and (2) when a different node v is probed and u is observed as a neighbor of v, if u was already in the network at the time of the probe of v, the reward that *would have been* obtained if u had been probed and (u, v) were observed.

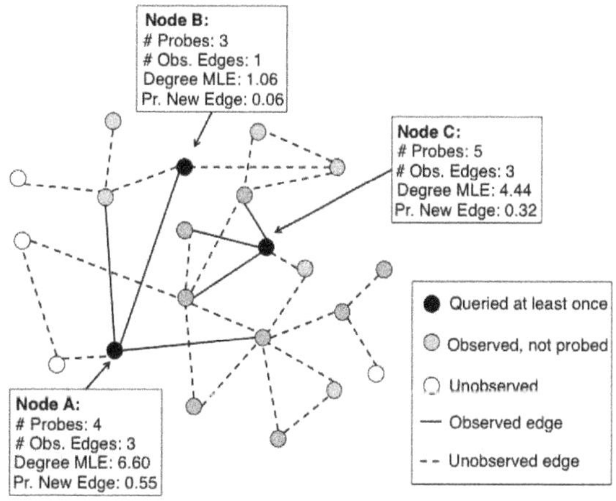

Figure 4: In this example, there are 17 observed nodes (in black and gray). Three have been probed at least once. For each of the black probed nodes, ϵ-WGX calculates the probability of seeing a new edge upon another probing. For the gray unprobed nodes, the probability of seeing a new edge is set to 1. ϵ-WGX expands (select a gray node) or densifies (select from the set of black and gray nodes). If densification is chosen, it may explore, by selecting a random node, or exploit, by selecting the best black node.

4.5 New Edge Probability

For each node u, ϵ-WGX calculates p_u, the probability of seeing a new edge when u is probed. If u has not been probed, or if u has been probed but no duplicate neighbors have been observed, then $p_u = 1$. Otherwise, p_u is calculated as follows: Suppose that for a node u we have conducted C_u probes in total, and have observed A_u distinct neighbors and B_u duplicates. Then ϵ-WGX sets p_u using the MLE method described in Section 3.2.

As an example, consider Figure 4.

4.6 Parameter Settings

The following parameters represent the tradeoff between exploration and exploitation. In general, for the ϵ-Greedy algorithm (which ϵ-WGX is based on), ϵ is set experimentally.

ϵ_0 should be set to a low number, because it governs the choice between only two options (expansion and densification). However, ϵ_0 should not decay to 0 over time, because as the observed graph expands to new regions, the optimal choice may change.

ϵ_1 should be set to a higher number, as it governs the choice between many different nodes. To observe the rewards of such a large number of nodes, frequent exploration is necessary. As before, ϵ_1 should not decay to 0 over time, because new nodes are being added.

Our parameter settings are discussed in Section 5.

4.7 Performance with Respect to Optimal Strategy

Note first that if the underlying network is finite, then ϵ-WGX is trivially a zero-regret strategy. It will eventually fully observe the entire graph, achieving the maximum possible reward.

However, if the total number of probes conducted is small relative to the size of the underlying graph, and if we assume that the reward function is binary- i.e., the reward for a probe can only be 0 or 1, then ϵ-WGX's regret is linear. Here, the regret is measured with respect to the optimal probing strategy, which knows the true expected reward obtained by probing any node. Intuitively, this means that we expect to do some constant factor worse than optimal.

We argue that linear regret is necessary, because as argued above, rapidly changing graph structure leads to rapidly changing rewards, meaning that neither ϵ_0 nor ϵ_1, which control the frequency of exploration, should decay to 0.

THEOREM 4.1. *If the probing budget is small relative to the size of the underlying graph, then for binary reward functions, the expected regret of ϵ-WGX is linear.*

PROOF: To show that ϵ-WGX has linear regret, we will show that it has regret no worse than linear and no better than linear.

First note that after b probes, the optimal strategy achieves a total reward of at most b, because the maximum reward obtained by a single probe is 1.

Consider the worst possible probing strategy, which selects a node whose edges have all already been observed and probes it repeatedly. The per-probe reward achieved by this strategy is always 0, and so its regret with respect to the optimal strategy is clearly linear. ϵ-WGX cannot do worse than this strategy.

Next, observe that ϵ-WGX cannot achieve regret that is better than linear. ϵ-WGX chooses to explore at least e_0 fraction of the time. Let $\bar{r}$ represent the mean reward obtained by probing a random node, and r^* be the expected reward obtained by following the optimal strategy. Then the total regret of ϵ-WGX after T probes is at least $T(r^* - \bar{r})$, which is a linear function of T.

Thus, ϵ-WGX has linear regret.

5 EXPERIMENTAL SETUP

Our experiments aim to support the following claims:

(1) As motivation for a multi-armed bandit strategy, we show that the best baseline strategy varies across tasks, networks, and even probing budgets. Multi-armed bandit algorithms, including ϵ-WGX, are valuable in cases when a user does not know which types of nodes (e.g., high degree) should be probed.
(2) Because ϵ-WGX takes advantage of the graph nature in the AEP problem, it regularly outperforms both the structural baseline strategies as well as other multi-armed bandit strategies.

We assess the performance of our ϵ-WGX algorithm on ten network datasets using incomplete networks generated/observed by the four popular sampling methods, and compare against relevant baseline probing strategies using three reward functions across a variety of budgets. For each incomplete network, we perform 10 trials of each strategy and report averages and standard deviations. For ϵ-WGX, we set $\epsilon_0 = 0.05$ and $\epsilon_1 = 0.3$.

5.1 Datasets

In our experiments, we probe samples of various types from larger network datasets. However, because obtaining complete network data is very challenging, our larger network datasets (from which we sample) may themselves be samples. To address this issue, we made a specific attempt to identify complete network datasets (KDD, ICDM, and SIGMOD, described below). To increase the number of datasets, we also consider incomplete networks.

We use ten network datasets. **FB-Grad** and **FB-UGrad** represent portions of the Facebook network corresponding to, respectively, graduate and undergraduate students at a university. FB-Grad contains 523 nodes and 3,256 edges, and FB-UGrad contains 1,220 nodes and 43,208 edges [13]. **FB-SocCir** represents a portion of the Facebook network collected by the Social Circles application. It contains 4,039 nodes and 88,234 edges.[1] **Amazon** represents book co-purchases from Amazon.com. It contains 270,347 nodes and 741,124 edges.[1] **Pokec** represents the Pokec social network, and contains 1.6 million nodes and 30 million edges. Nodes are annotated with information such as gender, percentage of profile completed, etc.[1] **Retweet** represents retweets from the Twitter network, and contains 39,546 nodes and 45,796 edges.[1] **Enron** contains e-mail networks from the Enron corporation, and contains 84,429 nodes and 325,564 edges.[2] **KDD, ICDM**, and **SIGMOD** represent coauthorship relationships from the named conferences from 2005-2009. They contain 1366, 1654, and 1365 nodes and 2769, 2808, and 3541 edges, respectively. These networks are complete within the specified dates and conferences.[3]

5.2 Incomplete Graphs Obtained by Graph Sampling

We evaluate ϵ-WGX and the baseline algorithms on incomplete networks generated by the following four sampling methods: (1) **Breadth-first search (BFS)** sampling, which is a popular way of exploring portions of the Web [4]. (2) **Random Edge** sampling, which selects a specified number of edges uniformly at random. For example, the Twitter firehose provides a 10% uniform sample over the set of tweets. If retweets constitute edges, then this data produces a sample similar to the Random Edge method. (3) **Random Walk** sampling, which is also a common method for sampling large graphs (see [9]). (4) **Random Walk with Jump** sampling, which is similar to the Random Walk sampling method, except that at each step, there is a specified chance of transitioning to a random node in the graph. In this paper, we used 0.15 as the probability of jumping to a random node.

5.3 Competing Probing Strategies

5.3.1 Structural Baseline Probing Strategies. We considered a variety of simple baseline probing strategies based on structural information, and consistently saw that two baselines performed well: probing high degree nodes and probing low degree nodes. In the `High Degree` and `Low Degree` strategies, we assign each node a value proportional (for `High Degree`) or inversely proportional (for `Low Degree`) to its degree. Additionally, we calculate the probability of seeing a new edge when a node is probed multiple times using the same MLE process as ϵ-WGX uses, and multiply

[1]Obtained from http://snap.stanford.edu.
[2]Obtained from https://www.cs.cmu.edu/~./enron/.
[3]Obtained from http://dblp.uni-trier.de/.

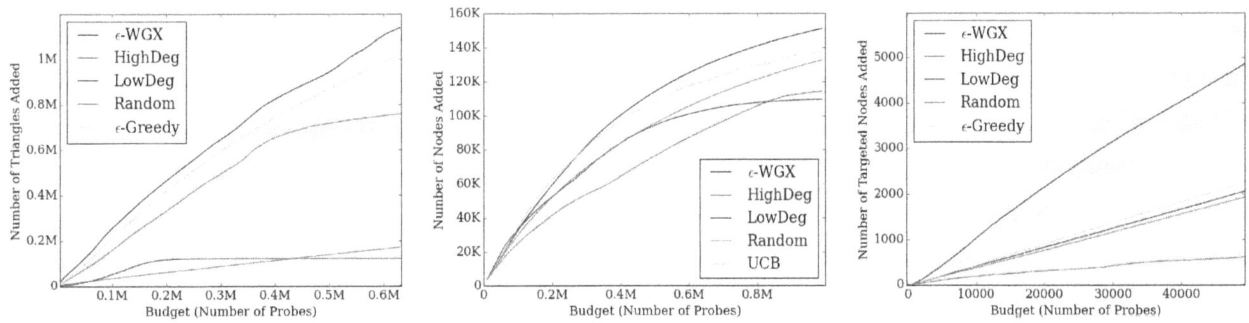

(a) Probing an Enron BFS sample, with the goal of adding triangles. **(b) Probing an Amazon RWJ sample, with the goal of adding nodes.** **(c) Probing a Pokec RW sample, with the goal of adding nodes representing incomplete male profiles.**

Figure 5: Examples of probing results. Shading indicates one standard deviation (not visible when standard deviation is low). Only the better of the two multi-armed bandit algortihms is shown. In all cases shown, ϵ-WGX is the best.

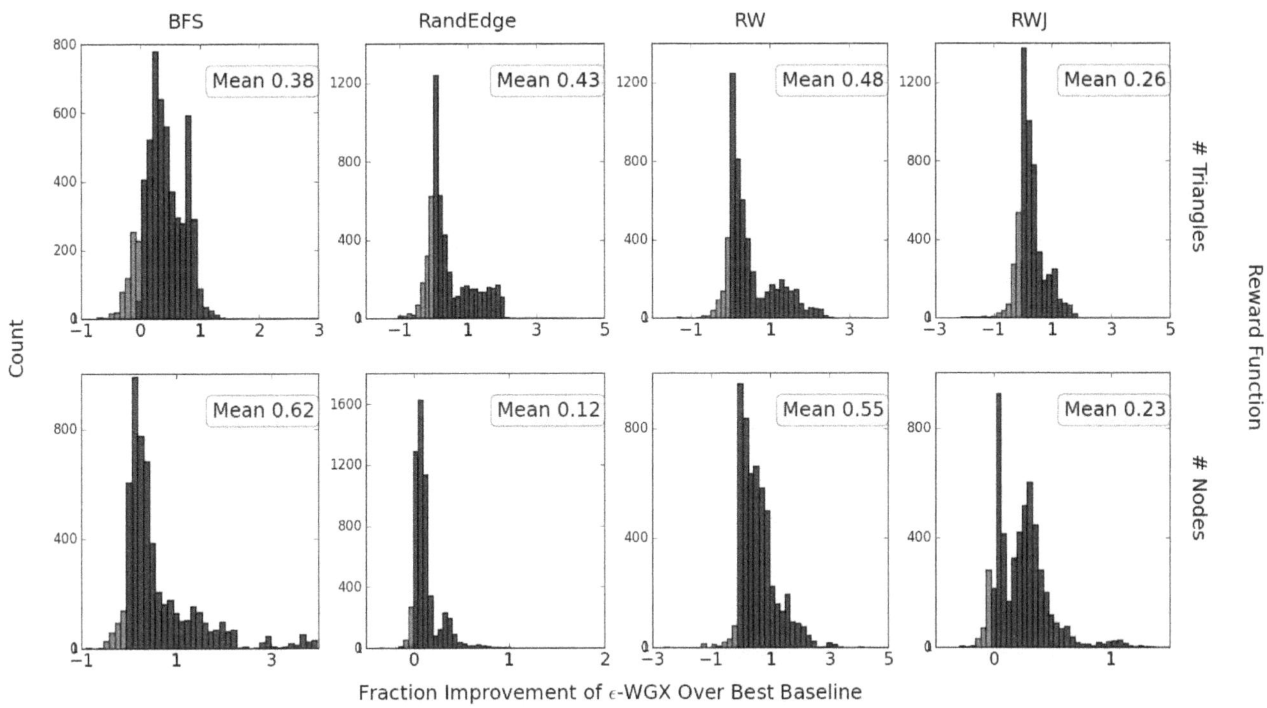

Figure 6: Fraction by which ϵ-WGX outperformed the best degree-based baseline strategy. The top row compares ϵ-WGX to baseline probing strategies with the goal of adding triangles to the observed network, and the bottom row is for the goal of adding new nodes to the observed networks. Results are aggregated over all considered networks. Values are calculated as described in Algorithm 1. The text boxes indicate the means of the distributions. Values in blue are above 0, indicating the fraction by which ϵ-WGX outperformed the baseline method, while values in red are below 0, indicating the fraction by which the baseline method outperformed ϵ-WGX. ϵ-WGX outperforms the best baseline strategy in almost all cases.

the degree-based values by this probability. In each step, the node with the highest value is selected.

In Figure 4, the High Degree strategy selects Node A, which has an observed degree of 3 and a probability of seeing a new edge upon probing of 0.55, and thus a total score of 1.65. The Low Degree strategy selects one of the gray nodes, each of which has an observed degree of 1 and a probability of seeing a new edge upon probing of 1.0.

We also define a random strategy (Random), which randomly selects a node in each step. Random removes from consideration those nodes for which it has observed duplicate edges in more than half of their probes.

5.3.2 Other Explore-Exploit Algorithms. We compare ϵ-WGX to the ϵ-greedy and UCB multi-armed bandit algorithms. As with ϵ-WGX, we multiply the values that these methods assign to each node u by p_u (as described in Section 4.5), to ensure that the nodes are not probed even after their edges are all observed.

5.4 Probing Budgets

For each incomplete network $\hat{G}$, we calculate b_{max}, which is the number of edges adjacent to at least one node in $\hat{G}$ that is not already present in $\hat{G}$. Because one may obtain duplicate edges with multiple probes, it is theoretically possible to probe forever. Thus, we set an upper limit budget at $b^R_{max} = 3 \times b_{max}$, and consider budgets at the 100 quantiles of the interval $(0, b^R_{max})$. Recall that each unit of budget corresponds to probing one node and observing one edge.

6 RESULTS

We present results in 3 sections: First, we observe that performance of the three baseline strategies (`High Degree`, `Low Degree`, and `Random`) is highly variable, and so picking a single strategy is difficult (Section 6.1). Second, we compare ϵ-WGX to the baseline strategies, as well as to the ϵ-Greedy and UCB multi-armed bandit strategies (Section 6.2). Third, we consider the Number of Targeted Nodes global reward function on the Pokec network, and again show that ϵ-WGX outperforms the comparison strategies (Section 6.3).

6.1 Analysis of Baseline Strategies

When evaluating the three baseline strategies described in Section 5.3.1, we observe that the best baseline can vary in surprising ways. For example, we consider incomplete networks generated by random walk and random edge sampling on the ICDM network, for the Number of Nodes reward function. For the random edge sample, probing low degree or random nodes is much better than probing high degree nodes. In contrast, on the network generated by a random walk with jump, `High Degree` probing is best.

As shown in Figure 7, on an incomplete network generated by random edge sampling on the Facebook-SocCir network, the best probing strategy varies: on low budgets, `Random` probing is best, but `High Degree` probing is better for higher budgets. This example illustrates the difficulty in selecting a structural baseline strategy, because the best strategy depends on how the incomplete network was generated (which may not always be known), probing budgets and application. These results motivate the use of explore-exploit strategies, which adapt to the network and reward function.

6.2 Analysis of ϵ-WGX

We show that ϵ-WGX outperforms both the best simple structural baseline strategy and the best multi-armed bandit strategy.

Figure 5a shows results on a BFS sample of the Enron email network, with the Number of Triangles reward function, and Figure 5b illustrates various probing strategies on a random walk sample of the Amazon network, with the Number of Nodes reward function.

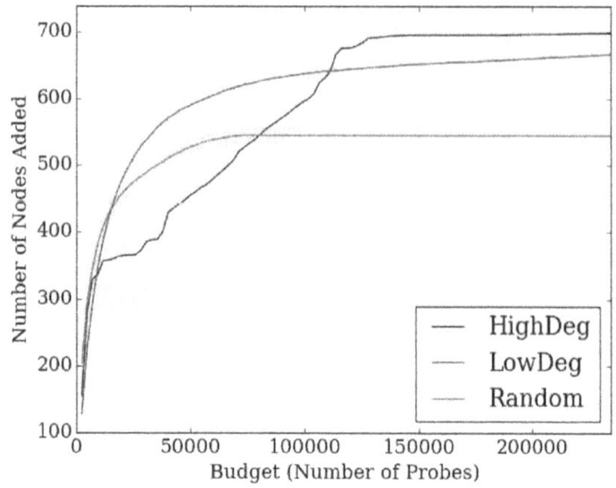

Figure 7: Results of baseline probing strategies on a random edge sample of the FB-SocCir network. Initially, `Random` **is the best, but is soon overtaken by** `High Degree` **probing.**

The x-axis represents the number of probes conducted; and the y-axis represents the number of triangles or nodes, respectively, in the enhanced network $\hat{G}'$. Note that in both cases, ϵ-WGX is clearly the best across all considered probing budgets.

Algorithm 1 Aggregate comparisons of ϵ-WGX to baseline strategies for the # of Nodes reward function (can be trivially modified for other reward functions).

Given sampling method M, baseline strategy C
$Dist \leftarrow []$
for Networks G, budgets b **do**
  $\hat{G} \leftarrow$ sample of G produced by method M
  $N \leftarrow$ number of nodes in $\hat{G}$
  for Trials 1-10 **do**
    $\hat{G}_{WGX} \leftarrow \hat{G}$ after b probes by ϵ-WGX
    $\hat{G}_{comp} \leftarrow \hat{G}$ after b probes by strategy C
    $N_{WGX} \leftarrow$ number of nodes in $\hat{G}_{WGX}$
    $N_{comp} \leftarrow$ number of nodes in $\hat{G}_{comp}$
    if $N_{WGX} > N_{comp} : v \leftarrow \frac{N_{WGX}}{N_{comp}} - 1$
    else: $v \leftarrow 1 - \frac{N_{comp}}{N_{WGX}}$
    $Dist$.append(v)
Plot and calculate mean of $Dist$

We aggregate results as described in Algorithm 1. We calculate the distribution of the fraction improvement of ϵ-WGX over each comparison strategy over networks, budgets, and trials. Fractions above 0 indicate that ϵ-WGX is performing better than the comparison strategies. For symmetry, we use a different calculation depending on which strategy did better. For instance, if ϵ-WGX adds 120 nodes and the comparison strategy adds 100 nodes, this score will be reported as 0.2, and if the values were reversed, it would be reported as −0.2.

For brevity, we only plot ϵ-WGX in comparison to the best structural baseline strategy (chosen from high degree and low degree probing depending on which does better for a given network, sample type, and reward) in Figure 6. The values in boxes indicate the means of the distributions (values above 0 indicate that ϵ-WGX outperformed the comparison strategy).

	Goal: Increase # of Nodes				Goal: Increase # of Triangles			
	BFS	RandEdge	RandWalk	RandWalk/Jump	BFS	RandEdge	RandWalk	RandWalk/Jump
ϵ-Greedy	0.22	0.14	0.54	0.17	0.46	0.68	0.60	0.63
UCB	0.19	0.16	0.23	0.15	2.29	3.47	3.05	3.75
Random	0.63	0.28	0.56	0.32	1.65	1.80	1.42	2.20

Table 1: Fraction by which ϵ-WGX outperformed the comparison strategy, averaged over networks, probing budgets, and trials as described in Pseudocode 1. On average, ϵ-WGX always outperforms the comparison strategy. For example, for the goal of increasing the number of nodes observed, on initial samples produced by a BFS crawl, ϵ-WGX outperforms ϵ-Greedy by 22%.

On average, in every case, ϵ-WGX outperforms all comparison methods. Table 1 contains the means of these distributions for ϵ-WGX vs. ϵ-Greedy, UCB, and random probing. Again, all means are above 0.[4]

6.3 Identifying Certain Types of Nodes

We now consider the Number of Targeted Nodes global reward function on the Pokec network. Here, we wish to find nodes that represent male users who have filled out less than half of their profile.[5] Interestingly, there is little homophily expressed with respect to this characteristic. We conduct 50,000 probes on the Pokec samples, and show results on a random walk sample in Figure 5c. Similar results were observed for other sampling methods. ϵ-WGX is the clear winner.

6.4 Running Time

The running times of the various multi-armed bandit and baseline strategies are similar. For example, on a BFS sample of the FB-SocCir network, `High Degree` probing takes 4.3e-4 seconds per probe, and ϵ-WGX requires approximately 6.5e-5 seconds per probe.

7 RELATED WORK

Our work is related to the literature on graph sampling, network analysis, and multi-armed bandits.

Graph Crawling and Sampling: Leskovec and Faloutsos provide an excellent overview of several popular sampling methods [9]. Maiya and Berger-Wolf [12] and Wu et al. [21], sample graphs for community detection. Maiya and Berger-Wolf [11] estimate centrality measures; and Cho et al. [5] propose a method for determining which URLs to examine in a web-crawl. Unlike these works, we assume that we improve a given incomplete network, as opposed to having control or knowledge of sample creation.

Network Analysis with Limited Information: Another question is how to infer characteristics of a graph from a sample. Hanneke and Xing [7] attempt to predict topology given access to only a few nodes. Kim and Leskovec [8] attempt to infer missing pieces of a network. Avrachenkov et al. [3] propose a method for locating high-degree nodes in a network using a limited number of queries, and Cohen et al. [6] show how one can efficiently immunize a networked population in which the network structure is unobserved. Macskassy and Provost [10] show how one can identify malicious actors in a network by gathering limited information. Soundarajan, et al. consider the problem of adding as many nodes as possible to an incomplete network [17]. Unlike these works, ϵ-WGX considers arbitrary rewards.

Multi-Armed Bandits: The multi-armed bandit problem was introduced by Robbins [15]. The simple ϵ-Greedy approach [20] works well in practice [19]. In graph settings, Reverdy, et al. [14] and Alon, et al. [1] consider a model in which neighbors have similar rewards. In contrast, ϵ-WGX does not assume that the reward for node u is linked to that of its neighbors.

8 CONCLUSIONS

We presented the *Adaptive Edge Probing* (AEP) problem, in which one selects nodes in an incomplete graph for further exploration, without knowledge of or control over how that incomplete network was observed. We presented the ϵ-WGX algorithm: an explore-exploit method, which identifies nodes that, when probed, produce useful information for a specified goal (e.g., making the incomplete graph more whole by increasing the number of observed nodes). Our results illustrated three main points. (1) Explore-exploit strategies are a useful tool for selecting nodes for probing within the context of the AEP problem, as it is difficult to select a simple baseline strategy that will be successful across reward functions, datasets, and sampling/observation methods. (2) ϵ-WGX consistently performs well across various settings. (3) By using neighbor information, ϵ-WGX outperforms both of the competing multi-armed bandit algorithms, as well as the structural baselines.

9 ACKNOWLEDGEMENTS

Tina Eliassi-Rad and Sucheta Soundarajan were supported by NSF CNS-1314603 and by DTRA HDTRA1-10-1-0120. Brian Gallagher's work was performed under the auspices of the U.S. Department of Energy by Lawrence Livermore National Laboratory under Contract DE-AC52-07NA27344. Ali Pinar's work is supported by the Laboratory Directed Research and Development program at Sandia National Laboratories. Sandia National Laboratories is a multimission laboratory managed and operated by National Technology and Engineering Solutions of Sandia, LLC., a wholly owned subsidiary of Honeywell International, Inc., for the U.S. Department of Energy's National Nuclear Security Administration under contract DE-NA-0003525.

REFERENCES

[1] Noga Alon, Nicolo Cesa-Bianchi, Claudio Gentile, Shie Mannor, Yishay Mansour, and Ohad Shamir. 2014. Nonstochastic Multi-armed bandits with graph structured feedback. *CoRR* abs/1409.8428 (2014).

[2] Peter Auer, Nicolo Cesa-Bianchi, and Paul Fischer. 2002. Finite-time analysis of the multiarmed bandit problem. *Machine Learning* 47, 2 (2002), 235–256.

[4] For additional results, please refer to the version of this paper posted at www.soundarajan.org/EpsilonWGX.pdf, which contains an Appendix with more detailed results.

[5] We saw similar results for other targets.

[3] Konstantin Avrachenkov, Nelly Litvak, Liudmila O. Prokhorenkova, and Eugenia Sayargulova. 2014. Quick detection of high-degree entities in large directed networks. In *ICDM*. 54–65.

[4] Andrei Broder, Ravi Kumar, Farzin Maghoul, Prabhakar Raghavan, Sridhar Rajagopalan, Raymie Stata, Andrew Tomkins, and Janet Wiener. 2000. Graph structure in the web. In *WWW*. 309–320.

[5] Junghoo Cho, Hector Garcia-Molina, and Lawrence Page. 1998. Efficient crawling through URL ordering. In *WWW*. 161–172.

[6] Reuven Cohen, Shlomo Havlin, and Daniel Ben-Avraham. 2003. Efficient immunization strategies for computer networks and populations. *Phys. Rev. Lett.* 91, 24 (2003), 247901.

[7] Steve Hanneke and Eric P. Xing. 2009. Network completing and survey sampling. In *AISTATS*. 209–215.

[8] Myunghwan Kim and Jure Leskovec. 2011. The network completion problem: Inferring missing nodes and edges in networks. In *SDM*. 47–58.

[9] Jure Leskovec and Christos Faloutsos. 2006. Sampling from large graphs. In *KDD*. 631–636.

[10] Sofus A. Macskassy and Foster Provost. 2005. Suspicion scoring based on guilt-by-association, collective inference, and focused data access. In *International Conference on Intelligence Analysis*. 6.

[11] Arun S. Maiya and Tanya Berger-Wolf. 2010. Online sampling of high centrality individuals in social networks. In *PAKDD*. 91–98.

[12] Arun S. Maiya and Tanya Berger-Wolf. 2010. Sampling community structure. In *WWW*. 701–710.

[13] Alan Mislove, Bimal Viswanath, Krishna P. Gummadi, and Peter Druschel. 2010. You are who you know: Inferring user profiles in online social networks. In *WSDM*. 251–300.

[14] Paul Reverdy and Naomi Leonard. 2014. Modeling human decision making in generalized Gaussian multiarmed bandits. *Proc. of the IEEE* 102, 4 (2014), 544–571.

[15] Herbert Robbins. 1952. Some aspects of the sequential design of experiments. *Bull. of the AMS* 58 (1952), 527–535.

[16] Ester Samuel. 1968. Sequential maximum likelihood estimation of the size of a population. *Annals of Mathematical Statistics* 39, 3 (1968), 1057–1068.

[17] Sucheta Soundarajan, Tina Eliassi-Rad, Brian Gallagher, and Ali Pinar. 2016. MaxReach: Reducing network incompleteness through node probes. In *ASONAM*. 152–157.

[18] Gregory Valiant and Paul Valiant. 2011. Estimating the unseen: An n/log(n)-sample estimator for entropy and support size, shown optimal via new CLTs. In *STOC*. 685–694.

[19] Joannès Vermorel and Mehryar Mohri. 2005. Multi-armed bandit algorithms and empirical evaluation. In *ECML*. 437–448.

[20] Christopher J. C. H. Watkins. 1989. *Learning from Delayed Rewards*. Ph.D. Dissertation. King's College.

[21] Jianshe Wu, Xiaoxiao Li, Licheng Jiao, Xiaohua Wang, and Bo Sun. 2013. Minimum spanning trees for community detection. *Physica A* 392, 9 (2013), 2265–2277.

Hierarchical Change Point Detection on Dynamic Networks

Yu Wang* Aniket Chakrabarti* David Sivakoff# Srinivasan Parthasarathy*
* Department of Computer Science and Engineering, # Department of Statistics
The Ohio State University, Columbus, Ohio, USA
wang.5205@osu.edu,srini@cse.ohio-state.edu

ABSTRACT

This paper studies change point detection on networks with community structures. It proposes a framework that can detect both local and global changes in networks efficiently. Importantly, it can clearly distinguish the two types of changes. The framework design is generic and as such several state-of-the-art change point detection algorithms can fit in this design. Experiments on both synthetic and real-world networks show that this framework can accurately detect changes while achieving up to 800X speedup.

CCS CONCEPTS

• **Information systems** → **Data mining**; **Social networks**; • **Computing methodologies** → *Modeling methodologies*;

KEYWORDS

Anomaly Detection, Dynamic Social Networks, Community Detection

1 INTRODUCTION

Anomaly detection on networks is a problem arising in various areas: from intrusion detection [10] to fraud detection [6], from email network [17] to fMRI image [13]. One problem of particular interest is change point detection on dynamic social networks [1, 19]. Social networks are known to have the hierarchical structure, where the most well-known one is the community structure [9]. Similar nodes are densely connected and form a community, while dissimilar nodes reside in different communities and are less likely to be connected. The interactions (or edges) among nodes can be classified as inter-community interactions and intra-community interactions. The intra-community interactions are more likely to be present (in unweighted networks) or have more weight (in weighted networks) than the inter-community interactions.

Most state-of-the-art change point detection approaches [6, 10, 13, 14, 21] do not consider the *hierarchical structure* in a network, but treat the network structure as flat. Hence they can hardly distinguish changes in those two kinds of interactions (intra and inter). If there is an event associated with a particular community, the change happens within that community only, and may not affect the global network too much due to its locality and small scale. (Toy example in Figure 1)

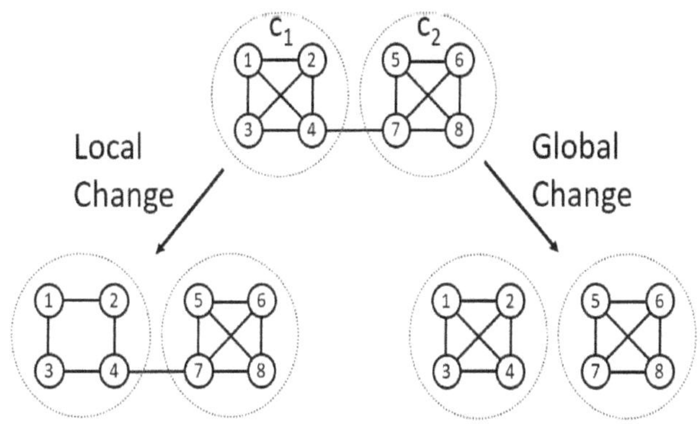

Figure 1: Toy example to distinguish global change and local change on a two-community graph. The edges removal within c_1 has only local impact, and hence is a local change; the edge removal across c_1 and c_2 has global impact (to disconnect the graph), and hence is a global change.

For example, consider the email network of a very big computer science department. If a specific lab is approaching a paper submission deadline, the frequency of email exchange within this lab might outburst. Since the whole department is very big and the daily email throughput of the whole department is high, it is unlikely to detect the change associated with that lab at the global level using the aforementioned algorithms.

On the other hand, if a single community is significantly larger than the others, a significant change in that community will dominate over the other smaller communities. Therefore, regardless of whether there is any change to the rest of the network, the aforementioned algorithms will classify this as a change point. That is, the above algorithms do not answer where the change comes from, neither can they answer if the change comes from within a huge community or from the inter-community interaction.

Continuing with the previous email network example, if a lab consists of half the people in the department (either a big group or a small department), then the outburst of emails within this lab is highly likely to be detected as a global event. Meanwhile, if several groups are jointly working on a funding proposal, it will lead to the email burst between communities, and can also be detected as a global event. The above algorithms can not distinguish between these two global events. Here we see that the existing algorithms either miss minor and local changes, or fail to distinguish between strong local changes and global changes. A recent work ([15]) can answer which pairs of nodes result in change, but it fails to account for the community structure.

WebSci'17, June 25-28, 2017, Troy, NY, USA.

978-1-4503-4896-6/17/06...$15.00
DOI: http://dx.doi.org/10.1145/3091478.3091493

Intuitively, the intra-community interaction captures local information while the inter-community interaction captures global information. Hence, we expect to see the former one evolves differently from the global evolution pattern while the latter one should be similar to the global evolution pattern [2].

In this paper, we show that the network evolution pattern can be decomposed into inter-community evolution and intra-community evolution. We show that running change point detection algorithms at the global level could miss changes associated with a community, and that change can be detected when we run the algorithms within that community. We also show that the inter-community interaction can be approximated by a hyper-network in which each hyper-node is a contracted community [3]. And this contraction also gives us computational benefits.

This paper is organized as follow: we first review the related work, then describe the proposed framework. After that, we introduce the experiments and provide the analysis. Finally, we conclude the paper and discuss future works.

2 RELATED WORK

There are two recent surveys [1, 19] on change point detection. Most state-of-the-art works [13, 21] do not consider the hierarchical structure in a network; Other works [4, 16, 17] mention the hierarchy in their papers, and they all make specific assumption about the underlying generative model: Moreno's work [16] assumes a network is generated from a mixed Kronecker product graph model (mKPGM), which is generated recursively from a seed matrix. The block of the matrix at each level resembles the community. Peel's work [17] assumes a network is generated from a generalized hierarchical random graph model (GHRG), which organizes the network as a tree of which the leaves are nodes in the network and the internal nodes are communities. Bridges's work [4] assumes a network is generated from the generalized block two-level Erdős-Rényi (GBTER) model, which posits the inter-community and intra-community edges are formed in different ways. Although they mention the hierarchical structure, they fail to distinguish between the change associated to a community and the change associated to the whole network. We design a framework that provides a systematic way to detect and distinguish between local and global changes. Our framework is generic and supports several state-of-the-art change point detection algorithms. Another drawback of these network hypothesis test based approaches is their low efficiency due to bootstrapping: Peel's work does not scale very well in our experiments, and its efficiency is improved up to 60 times when superimposed by our framework.

Community detection [9] is also a time-consuming task. The Louvain method [3] alternatively contracts and detects communities on the networks, and has been one of the most efficient community detection algorithm for several years. Its efficiency comes from the network size reduction via contracting. We use the same idea for efficient change point detection.

Another recent work ([15]) considers attributing the global change score to node pairs. It defines change scores at edge level, flags out the top ranked edges and their neighbors as changed regions. That work does not consider the community structure, and its focus is on visualization. Our work distinguishes between inter-community interaction and intra-community interaction, and shows the former one can approximate the global evolution. Moreover, our framework reduces the running time of the state-of-the-art algorithms [13, 17, 21].

3 METHODOLOGY

We follow the Type 4, "Event and Change Detection", in [19], which is to find snapshots from a network snapshot sequence that are "significantly" different from their predecessors. Like [21], we also assume each snapshot is generated from a generative model. Snapshots from the same generative model resemble each other, although they are not identical due to randomness. The change of the generative model leads to "significant change" of the snapshots. This assumption can be illustrated as a Markov network (Figure 2).

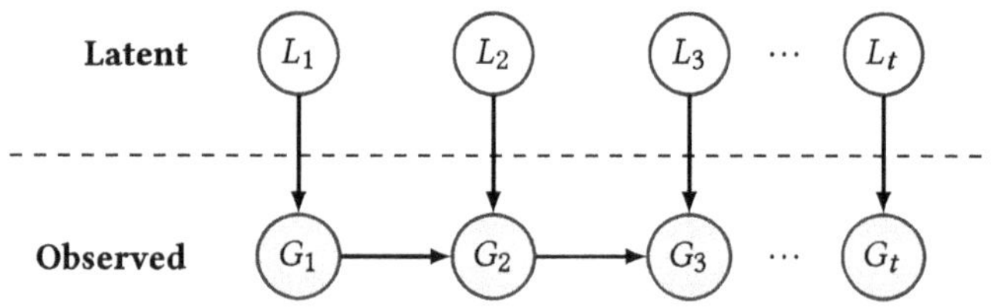

Figure 2: Representation of the underlying generative process. L_ts are latent generative models, and G_ts are observed snapshots. G_t is assumed to be a sample (generated) from L_t. "Significant" change points are $\{t \mid L_t \neq L_{t-1}\}$. Note that graph snapshots and latent models can represent both local structure as well as global structure.

Our work differs from [21] in that we study networks with the community structure, where each snapshot observation consists of multiple components, corresponding to communities and their interactions. In Figure 2, the generative models are latent and we can only observe the generated snapshots. Existing approaches have two directions: to estimate the generative model from multiple snapshots and then compare the estimated model [4, 17, 21]; or to compute the difference of the snapshots directly [13]. Our framework supports both types of approaches. In both cases, the problem and the solution can be generalized as [19]: given a network snapshot sequence $\{G_t\}$ and a dissimilarity function (outlier score) $f : \{G_t\} \times \{G_t\} \rightarrow \mathcal{R}$, a change is defined as a time point t, such that $f(G_t, G_{t-1}) > th_0$, where th_0 is some pre-specified threshold. Change point detection is to find all time stamps ts at which changes occur. All the aforementioned works run on the original network, and hence detect changes at the global level.

We define intra-community change and inter-community change in a similar fashion: let C_{it} be the community i at time t, the intra-community change point is defined as a time point t such that $f_l(C_{it}, C_{i,t-1}) > th_1$. By contracting the community C_{it} in the network G_t into a hyper node n_i, one gets a contracted network G^c_t. The inter-community change point is defined as a time point t such that $f_c(G^c_t, G^c_{t-1}) > th_2$. Our goal is to find both the intra-community change (local change) as well as the inter-community change (global change).

Problem Definition Given a network sequence $\{G_t\}_{t=1}^T$, its community assignment $\{th_i\}_{i=1}^k$, and dissimilarity functions $f_l(\cdot,\cdot)$, $f_c(\cdot,\cdot)$, find all the time points $t \in \{2, \cdots, T\}$ such that either 1) $f_l(C_{it}, C_{i,t-1}) > th_1$, or 2) $f_c(G^c_t, G^c_{t-1}) > th_2$ for some pre-specified threshold th_1, th_2.

3.1 Framework Description

We propose the following framework (Algorithm 1) which reveals both the local change as well as the global change. In Line 1, we first partition communities on the first snapshot. We assume the community assignment does not change over time. If there really is a severe change in community assignment, the event will be detected as a global change. Between global changes, the community assignment will remain constant. Hence one can apply the local change detection part of the framework to the subsequences in which community assignment remains similar. One may argue that it is more robust to partition communities on the aggregated network from the first couple of snapshots. Our reasoning is that if no global change happens during the first couple of snapshots, the community assignment/structure should remain the same; otherwise we flag out that snapshot as abnormal (to be investigated), and redo the community partition on the new snapshot. The for-loop from Line 2 to Line 12 scans over all the snapshots. The original snapshot is contracted in Line 3 into a weighted (hyper-)network in which each hyper-node corresponds to a community in the original snapshot (Figure 3). If the original network is unweighted, the weight of the hyper-edge is the number of actual inter-community edges divided by the number of all possible inter-community edges. Otherwise the weight of the hyper-edge is the summation of the inter-community edge weights divided by the sizes of the two communities. The contraction operation is widely used in hierarchical community partition algorithms [9, 12]. The for-loop from Line 4 to Line 8 iterates over all the communities. The provided change point detection algorithm runs on the community level, and returns the dissimilarity score between two consecutive (sub-)networks. The branch in Line 9 detects the global change by running the detection algorithm on the contracted (hyper-) network.

Algorithm 1 Hierarchical Change Point Detection Framework

Input: network sequence $\{G_t\}_1^t$, any change point detection algorithm *IsChanged*$(\cdot,\cdot)$
Output: global change points $changeSet$, local change points $changeSet_i$ in community i

1: $\{c_i\}_1^k$ = partition(G_1); {community partition}
2: **for** $t = 2$ to T **do**
3: G_t^c =contract($\{c_i\}_1^k$);
{Below: local change detection}
4: **for** $i = 1$ to k **do**
5: **if** *IsChanged*$(c_{it}, c_{i,t-1})$ **then**
6: $changeSet_i = changeSet_i \cup \{t\}$;
7: **end if**
8: **end for**
{Below: global change detection}
9: **if** *IsChanged*(G_t^c, G_{t-1}^c) **then**
10: $changeSet = changeSet \cup \{t\}$;
11: **end if**
12: **end for**

Community partitioning gives us efficacy while network contraction gives us efficiency: each community is a fine-grained subnetwork, and running detection algorithm on each community can avoid fluctuation and noises from neighboring communities, and hence the detected change points are solely associated with this particular community; contraction significantly reduces network size, and in turn, reduces the running time of the algorithms whose complexity is proportional to the network size. On the other hand, network size reduction also implies information loss, and therefore the quality of change points detected on the contracted network is inferior to that on the original network. Fortunately, our experiments show that the ranking of outlier scores on the contracted network is similar to that on the original network, which implies that the inter-community evolution can indeed capture global evolution pattern.

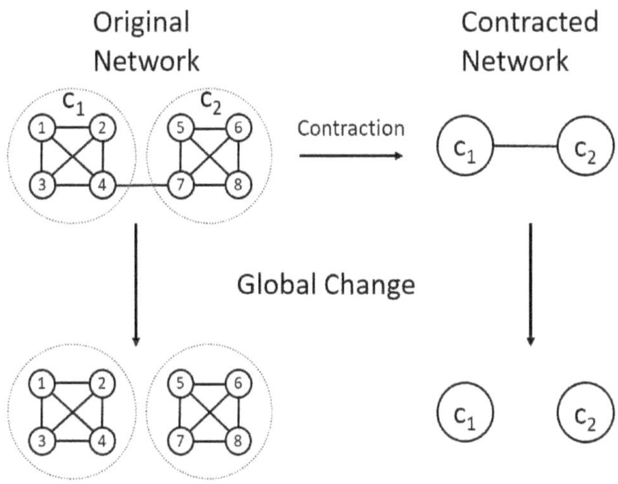

Figure 3: Toy example to illustrate contraction on the previous two-community graph. Communities c_1, c_2 are contracted into hyper-node c_1, c_2 respectively. Global change in the original network (graph disconnection) is captured by the change in the contracted network.

3.2 Algorithms

We superimpose the framework on three state-of-the-art algorithms [13, 17, 21],

3.2.1 DeltaCon. DeltaCon [13] computes the outlier score from the snapshots directly. It extracts a feature vector from each snapshot using personalized PageRank, and computes the rooted Euclidean distance of two consecutive feature vectors.

3.2.2 LetoChange. LetoChange [17] assumes the network is generated from GHRG model in which the network has a tree-like structure: leaves correspond to nodes while internal tree nodes correspond to communities. The network sequence is partitioned into equal sized sliding windows, and the model parameters are estimated within a window. The outlier is flagged out if the model parameters estimated change greater than a threshold. It bootstraps networks from the generative model to calculate a proper threshold. To sample multiple networks from a generative model is time-consuming. We bootstrap outlier scores for threshold determination, which gains much computational benefit (detailed at the end of this section).

3.2.3 EdgeMonitoring. EdgeMonitoring [21] follows LetoChange's fashion: first estimate the model parameters from a window (several snapshots), then detect change points based on model parameters comparison. EdgeMonitoring estimates the edge probability directly from each window (for the unweighted network) and calculates the Kullback-Leibler divergence of the sequences of two consecutive windows. We modify it to account for weighted networks: we normalize the weights at each snapshot, and average over snapshots within a window. This averaged weight is used as the probability estimate in the above KL divergence calculation.

Algorithm 2 Hierarchical Change Point Detection Framework with Threshold Determination

Input: network sequence $\{G_t\}_1^t$, any change point detection algorithm *IsChanged*$(\cdot,\cdot)$
Output: global change points $changeSet$, local change points $changeSet_i$ in community i

$\{c_i\}_1^k$ = partition(G_1); {community partition}
for $t = 2$ to T **do**
  G_t^c =contract($\{c_i\}_1^k$);
  {Below: local change detection}
  for $i = 1$ to k **do**
    $OutlierScore_{i,t}$ = *IsChanged*$(c_{it}, c_{i,t-1})$
  end for
  {Below: global change detection}
  $OutlierScore_t$ = *IsChanged*(G_t^c, G_{t-1}^c)
end for
for $i = 1$ to k **do**
  $Threshold_i$ = Bootstrap($OutlierScore_i$).percentile(0.95)
  $changeSet_i = \{t \mid OutlierScore_{i,t} > Threshold_i\}$
end for
$Threshold$ = Bootstrap($OutlierScore$).percentile(0.95)
$changeSet = \{t \mid OutlierScore_t > Threshold\}$

Although DeltaCon and LetoChange have their own threshold determination strategies, the former one's normality assumption does not hold while the latter one's network bootstrap is too time-consuming. We use an efficient, permutation test based strategy. All the three algorithms use the same way to determine outlier scores: first, run the algorithm on the whole snapshot sequence and obtain an outlier score sequence; then, use bootstrap to compute the 0.95 confidence level of the outlier scores. The rationale of this threshold determination is essentially the same as that of the permutation test [18]. The modified framework is displayed in Algorithm 2, in which the *IsChanged*(,) function again returns the dissimilar score.

4 EXPERIMENTS AND EVALUATION

4.1 Data

We apply the framework to two synthetic networks and one real world network. For the synthetic networks, we test our framework on the Stochastic Block Model (SBM [11]) and the Block Two-Level Erdős-Rényi (BTER [20]) model. SBM assumes edge probability a function of the community membership of the two incident nodes; BTER model assumes the intra-community edges are sampled from Erdős-Rényi model [7], while the inter-community edges are sampled from Chung-Lu model [5]. For both experiments, we do not change community membership (as discussed in Section 3.1), and inject either global or local changes at different time stamps (Table 1).

The SBM experiment has 1k nodes and 8 communities ranging from size 50 to size 300. The edge probability is determined by a

Table 1: Changes Injected to the Synthetic Networks

Event Order	Time Stamp	SBM (1k nodes, 8 communities)	BTER (100 nodes, 5 communities)
①	16	connection rate in the largest community c_0 reduced by 1/3 (Local Change)	connection rate in the largest community c_0 reduced by 1/3 (Local Change)
②	31	inter-community connection rates among c_0, c_1, c_5, c_6 reduced by 1/3 (Global)	Chung-Lu sequence in c_0 change (Global)
③	51	connection rates in two smallest communities c_6, c_7 doubled (Local)	connection rates in two smallest communities c_3, c_4 doubled (Local)
④	76	SBM matrix regenerated (Global)	Chung-Lu sequence of all the nodes regenerated (Global)

symmetric stochastic block matrix whose entries are sampled from $Uniform(0, 1)$ with the restriction that main diagonal entries greater than off-diagonal entries. The BTER experiment has 100 nodes and 5 communities whose sizes are sampled from power a law distribution [23], and range from 15 to 25. ER probability is sampled from a beta distribution [4], while CL sequence is sampled from another power law distribution [8]. Each snapshot is a weighted network where the edge weight is a sample from a binomial distribution and normalized to the range [0,1]. Since LetoChange does not support weighted network, we unweight each network by retaining the edges with probability equal to the edge weight.

For the real world network, we use the international trade network[1] from the year 2001 to the year 2014. We select 90 countries/economies and represent them as nodes. The network is directed and weighted, where the direction specifies import/export and the weight is the trade volume. The network is near a clique since almost every two countries have bilateral trade between them.

There are six ground truth communities in the network, corresponding to free trade zone and/or geopolitics alike nations: Asia-Pacific Economic Cooperation (APEC), black sea economic cooperation (BSEC), fifteen developed western European countries (EU15), Latin American Integration Association (LAIA) and Southern African Development Community (SADC), Organization of Islamic Cooperation (OIC). The Louvain [3] community partition algorithm is also applied to this network and returns consistent partitions.

4.2 Experiments and Results

4.2.1 Synthetic Network. We apply our framework with the three aforementioned detection algorithms on the synthetic networks. The generation process is described in the previous subsection. We present both quality and time efficiency of our framework. We report time efficiency in Table 2, and use both qualitative and quantitative methods to validate the quality.

Figure 4 shows the change points detected on the SBM network. Figure 4a is the result on the global (original) network, and Figure 4b is the result on the contracted network; the curves are

[1] www.worldbank.org

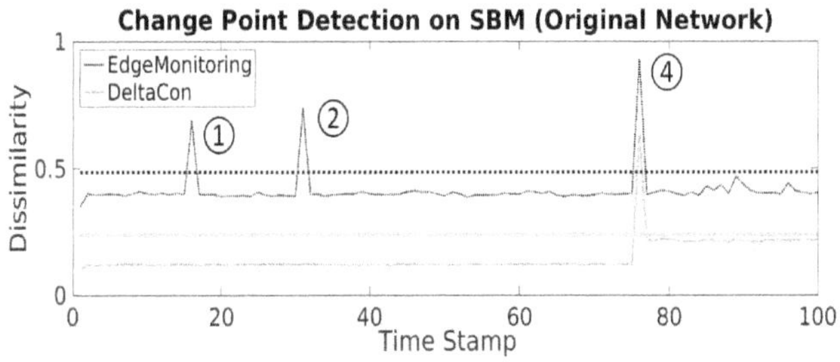

(a) SBM Global (1k nodes, re-scalded and shifted for visualization). Local change ③ in the two smallest communities are insignificant at global level, and hence is ignored by both algorithms.

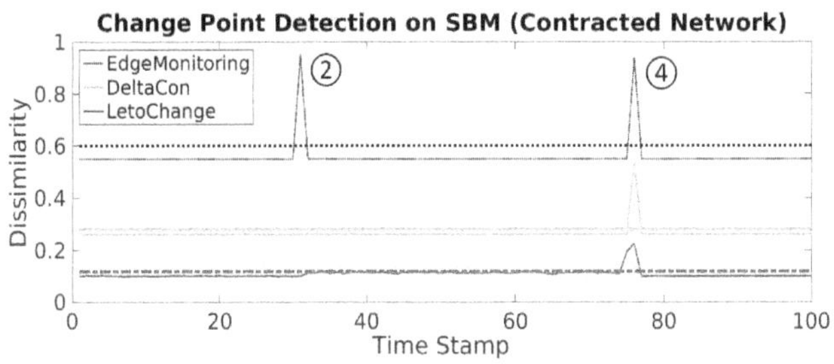

(b) SBM Contract (8 hyper-nodes). EdgeMonitoring (black, top) detects two global events ② and ④, while DeltaCon (green, middle) and LetoChange (red, bottom) detect only one.

Figure 4: Change point detection on SBM at global level.

outlier scores for various change point detection algorithms and the horizontal bars are corresponding thresholds. LetoChange can not finish within 48 hours (Table 2) on the original network, and hence is not displayed in Figure 4a. We can see that EdgeMonitoring correctly captures two global changes and a local change in the largest community of the original network (Figure 4a). After contraction (Figure 4b), EdgeMonitoring only captures the two global changes. This is what we can expect since inter-community interaction reflects the global pattern, and contraction only preserves this global pattern. Although DeltaCon does not capture both the global changes, the quality of DeltaCon on the contracted network is the same as on the original network while achieving 830 times efficiency improvement! Note that the quality of change point detection on the original network is totally determined by the detection algorithm itself. Applying our framework (i.e. to contract the network) does not deteriorate the quality. A similar observation holds for LetoChange.

We note that it is the outlier score ranking (say, top $\alpha_s\%$ as in [21]), rather than the absolute values, that matters in change point determination. Hence we use the Normalized Discounted Cumulative Gain (NDCG [22]) scores to evaluate how good the contracted one approximates the original one. NDCG score quantifies the difference between two rankings, and perfect match results in NDCG = 1.0.

$$\mathrm{NDCG}_T = \frac{\mathrm{DCG}_T}{\mathrm{IDCG}_T}, \quad \text{where}$$

$$\mathrm{DCG}_T = \sum_{i=1}^{T} \frac{2^{r_i} - 1}{\log_2(i+1)}, \quad \mathrm{IDCG}_T = \sum_{i=1}^{T} \frac{2^{i} - 1}{\log_2(i+1)}$$

DCG is calculated on the contracted network, while IDCG (reference) is calculated on the original network. The outlier scores from two networks are sorted in descending order respectively. r_i is the number of matches between the target ranking and the reference ranking within first i scores, and T is the number of snapshots. The NDCG scores for EdgeMonitoring and DeltaCon are 0.832, 0.666 respectively, indicating reasonably good approximation.

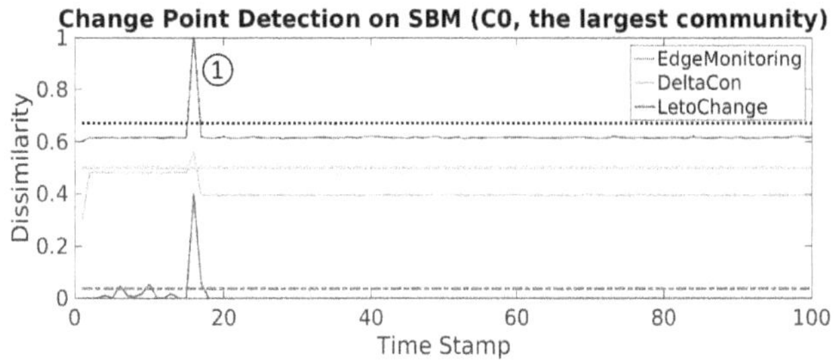

Figure 5: Change point detection on SBM in the largest community (300 nodes). All three algorithms are able to detect the local event ① at T=16.

Figure 5 shows the change points detected on the largest community. All three algorithms detect the local change (① in Table 1) that edge probability reduces at time stamp 16 in C0. It's interesting to note that EdgeMonitoring detects the local change ① on the original network (Figure 4a). This is because the change occurs in the largest community (consisting of 30% of all the nodes), and the node pairs in that community are more likely to be tracked. If we only run the algorithm on the original network, we would not be able to tell if the change corresponds to a global event or a local event. DeltaCon is more conservative in terms of flagging out change points: it not only misses the local event ① in Figure 4a, but also misses the global event ②. Yet it is still able to detect the local change in Figure 5. Similarly, running algorithms within community c_6, c_7 reveals local event ③. This result is not included for brevity.

Figure 6 shows the change points detected on the BTER network. We see that all three algorithms capture the global events ②, ④ on the original network.EdgeMonitoring and LetoChange in addition capture the local event ③, which corresponds to edge probability increase in the two smallest communities (Table 1). Although both ① and ③ are local events, the largest community consists of 23% of all the nodes while the two smallest communities together consist of 35% of all the nodes. Intuitively, the latter should have more impact on the global network than the former. And from the algorithmic perspective, the node pairs of the latter have higher chance to be tracked than the former. Figure 6b shows that after contraction, all three algorithms only capture the global events. Running the algorithms within each community detects the local change and we do not include the result for brevity. The NDCG scores for EdgeMonitoring, DeltaCon and LetoChange are 0.832, 0.666 and 0.832 respectively. The snapshots before and after the global event ④ are visualized in Figures 7 and 8. We can see from Figure 7 that the inter-community interaction between the red community and the others is enhanced after the event, which is also revealed in the contracted network in Figure 8.

Table 2: Time Efficiency Comparison on Different Networks

	EdgeMonitoring[1]				DeltaCon				LetoChange			
Data	Orig.	Contr. (Speedup)	Comm. Avg	Total[2]	Orig.	Contr. (Speedup)	Comm. Avg	Total	Orig.	Contr. (Speedup)	Comm. Avg	Total
SBM	85s	1.5s (60X)	3.7s	31s	500s	0.6s **(830X)**	24s	192s	DNF[3]	2h (>60X)	N/A[4]	N/A
BTER	2.5s	1.5s (2X)	1.7s	10s	5s	0.1s (50X)	1.0s	5.1s	51h	2h (25X)	13h	67h
Trade	22s	0.4s (50X)	0.5s	3.4s	42s	1.3s (30X)	1.2s	8.5s	150m	5m (30X)	9m	60m

[1] EdgeMonitoring and DeltaCon are implemented in MATLAB and run on a commercial desktop, while LetoChange is implemented in Python and runs on a cluster with 28 cores. Each running time averaged over 5 runs.
[2] Total time = community time × number of communities.
[3] The program runs for 120 hours, but still has no sign of finish, so we kill it.
[4] LetoChange takes 110 hours to obtain the result in Figure 5.

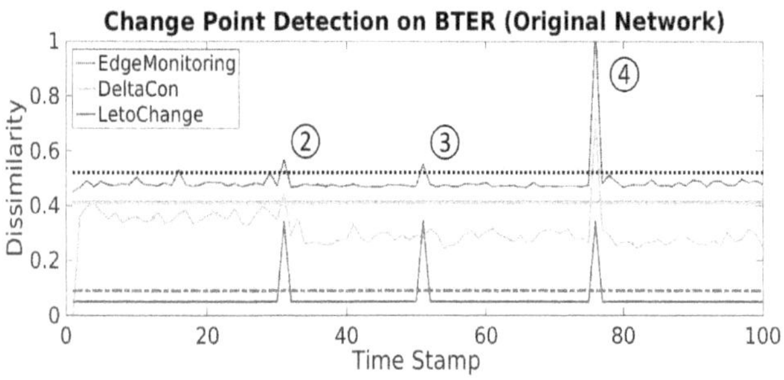

(a) BTER Global (100 nodes, re-scaled and shifted for visualization). Local change ① is ignored by all three algorithms, while ③ is captured by EdgeMonitoring (barely) and LetoChange.

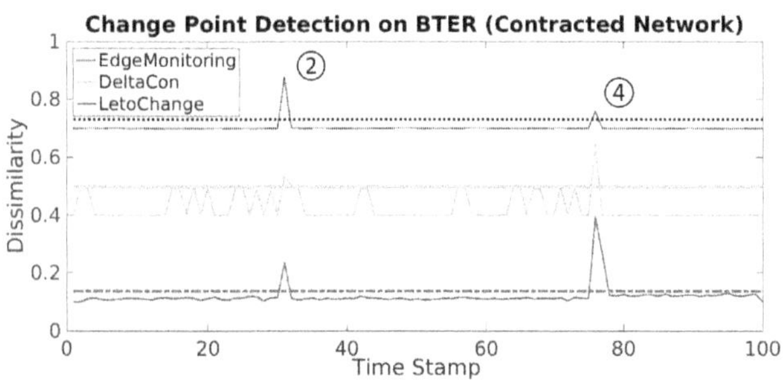

(b) BTER Contract (5 hyper-nodes). EdgeMonitoring (black, top) and LetoChange (red, bottom) detect two global events, while DeltaCon (green, middle) detects only one global event ④.

Figure 6: Change point detection on BTER at global level.

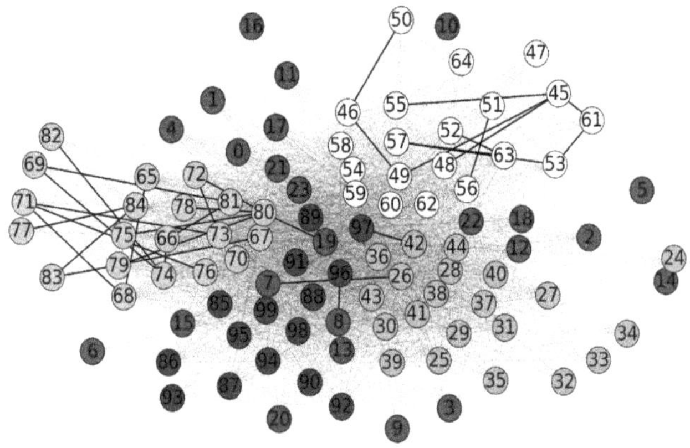

(a) BTER network at T=75, before the global event ④

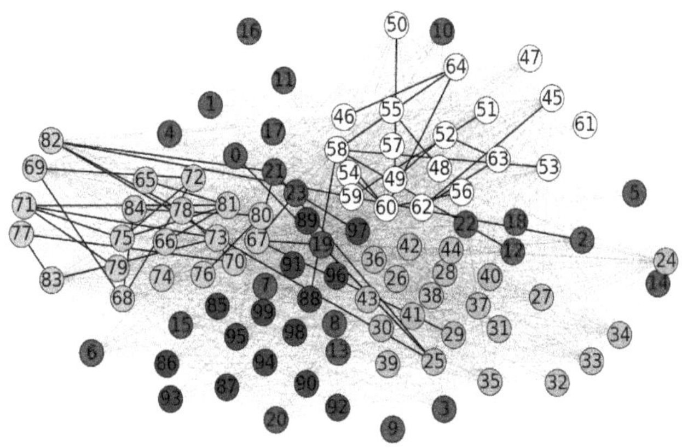

(b) BTER network at T=76, after the global event ④

Figure 7: Visualization of BTER network before and after the global event ④. Edge width and transparency reflect interaction strength, and color represents community membership. Inter-community interaction is enhanced after the global event ④, and the red community in particular has stronger interaction with all other communities after ④.

The two synthetic experiments above show that superimposing our framework on top of the aforementioned change point detection algorithms can indeed distinguish global and local change, and hence gives us finer granularity knowledge of the evolution of a dynamic network.

4.2.2 Real World Network. Figure 9 shows the result of change point detection on the original network and the contracted network using the international trade network. It can be seen that the majority algorithms on both the networks reveal the year 2009 as the most significant outlier. The year 2009 is a year immediately after the global financial crisis, and the term "The Great Recession" is applied to the global recession which started in that year.[2] It is pretty clear that the global trade volume drops significantly during that year. The NDCG scores for EdgeMonitoring, LetoChange and

[2] http://www.cbpp.org/research/economy/chart-book-the-legacy-of-the-great-recession

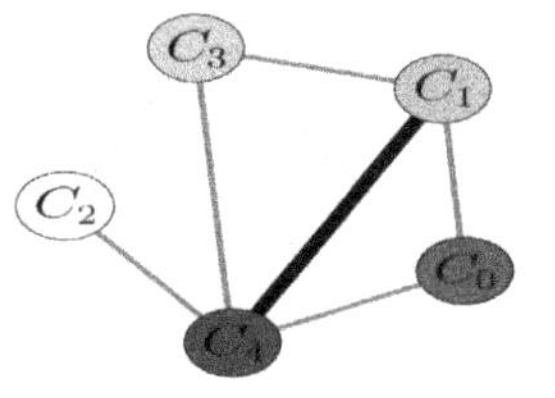

(a) Contracted BTER network at T=75, before the global event ④

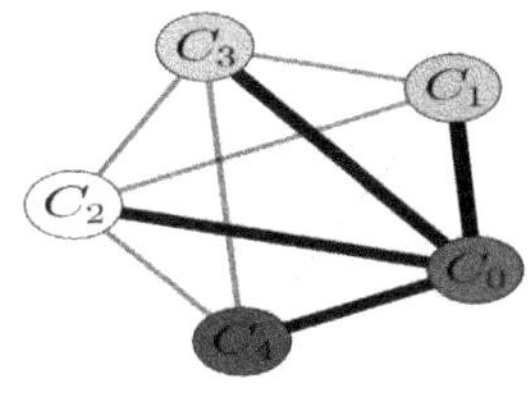

(b) Contracted BTER network at T=76, after the global event ④

Figure 8: Visualization of contracted BTER network before and after the global event ④. The observation that the red community has stronger interaction with others in Figure 7 is nicely captured by the contracted network.

DeltaCon are 0.960, 0.654 and 0.909 respectively, which suggests great approximation for EdgeMonitoring and LetoChange, and good approximation for DeltaCon. The speedup of the framework is reported in Table 2.

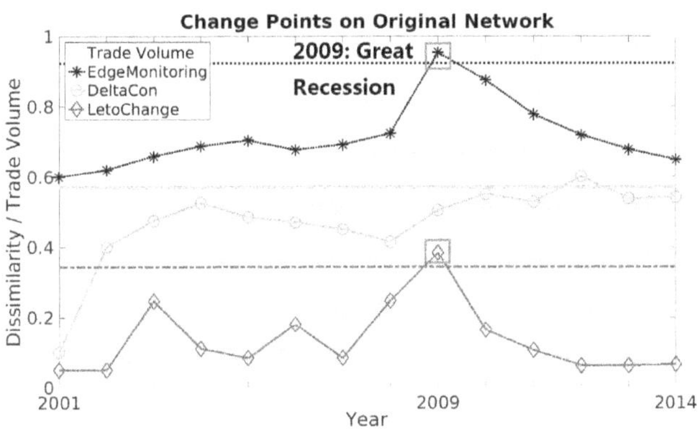

(a) Original Network, both EdgeMonitoring (black star, top) and LetoChange (red diamond, bottom) detect the year 2009 as a change point, at which the international trade volume drops significantly (background bar); DeltaCon detects the year 2012 as abnormal. (re-scaled and shifted for visualization, explainable outliers are blue-boxed)

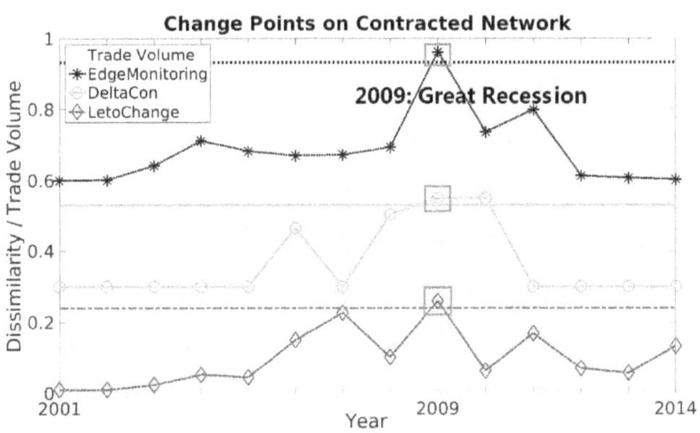

(b) Contracted Network, all three algorithms detect the year 2009 as a change point.

Figure 9: Global change point detected on the international trade network, using both the original network and the contracted network. The Great Recession (global event) in the year 2009 is flagged as abnormal on both the networks. The NDCG scores of the three algorithms on the two networks are 0.960, 0.654, 0.909 respectively, indicating good approximation of the contracted network.

Figure 10 compares global change point detection and local change point detection. Figure 10a is the result of running the detection algorithms on the original network. Figure 10b is the result of running the detection on the APEC community (Asia-Pacific region). We see that the two (sub-)networks have similar outliers: the 2009 recession is detected on both the networks. This is not surprising since this APEC community contributes 44% of the world trade,[3] which can also be observed from the similarity of the two background trade volume bar charts. Here we see the impact of a "big", in terms of edge weight, community to the global network. Two detection algorithms also flag out the year 2010 as a local change point, which could be explained by the GDP growth rebound of the major economies in this region.[4] Figure 11 visualizes the APEC trade network. We can see that the bilateral trade volume drops significantly post crisis, and several economics flip from trade surplus to trade deficit within the region. Comparing Figure 11c and Figure 11b, we see trade volume jumps among several economics, which is a sign of recovery.

Figure 10c shows the result of local change point detection on the Middle East-North Africa community. Its evolution pattern (the trade volume bar chart, as well as the outlier score ranking distribution) is clearly different from that of the global network. This can also be expected given its relatively small scale economy size and relatively homogeneous economic structures. The year 2005 is flagged as an outlier by EdgeMonitoring, which coincides with Iraq's purple revolution. [5] The year 2012 is flagged as an outlier by both EdgeMonitoring and DeltaCon, which coincides with ISIS's rise in Syria.[6] LetoChange flags the years 2013 and 2014 as outliers, we conjecture that might be due to the escalation of the situation with increasing international involvement.

Both change points and outlier ranking distribution reflect network evolution pattern. From Figure 10 we see that while the evolution pattern of a major community might approximate that of the global network, the evolution patterns of other communities differ from that of the global network. We will miss the change points or events associated with a particular community if we only run the detection algorithm on the global network.

5 CONCLUSION

In this paper, we study hierarchical change point detection on dynamic social networks. We distinguish the intra-community evolution and the inter-community evolution. Our framework detects global change points on the inter-community network, and local change points on the intra-community networks. This framework is compatible with several state-of-the-art change point detection algorithms. Extensive empirical evaluation on several networks (both synthetic and real world) show this framework has not only quality advantages but also significant computational benefits.

[3] https://ustr.gov/trade-agreements/other-initiatives/asia-pacific-economic-cooperation-apec/us-apec-trade-facts
[4] http://data.worldbank.org/indicator/NY.GDP.MKTP.KD.ZG
[5] https://en.wikipedia.org/wiki/Colour_revolution
[6] https://en.wikipedia.org/wiki/Islamic_State_of_Iraq_and_the_Levant

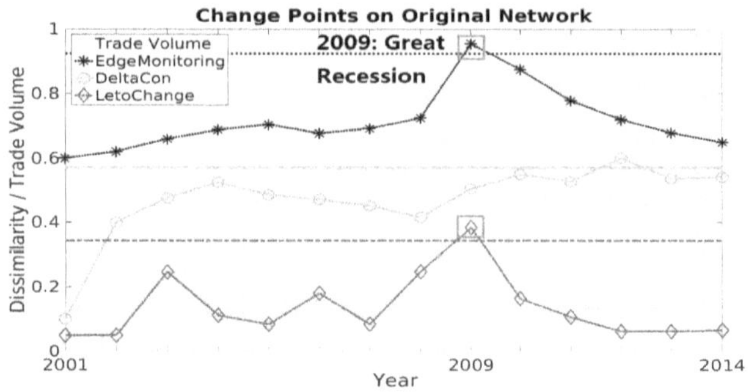

(a) Global network.

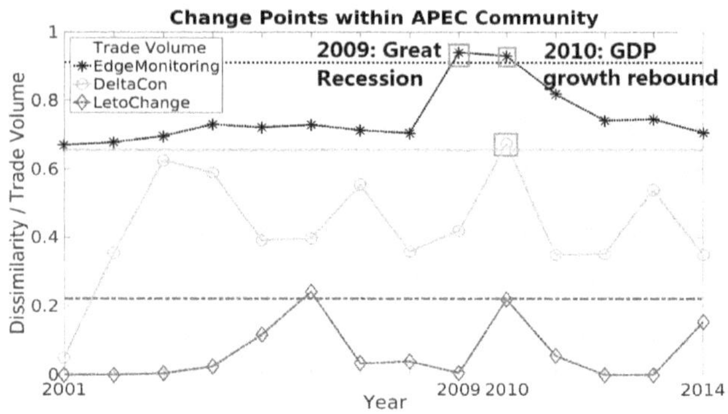

(b) APEC sub-network. Both the years 2009 and 2010 are flagged out as outliers. We did not find a good explanation for LetoChange's outlier at 2006. NDCG scores to the global network are 0.913, 0.827, 0.975 respectively.

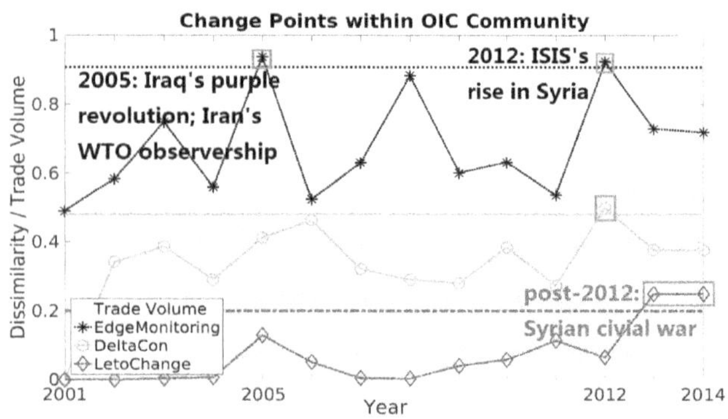

(c) OIC sub-network. The evolution pattern is significantly different from that of the global network in Figure 10a. NDCG scores to the global network are 0.826, 0.714, 0.906 respectively.

Figure 10: Comparison of global vs local. APEC community's evolution resembles that of the global network in both trade volume and outlier ranking due to its major role (heaviest edges) in the global network. OIC community evolves differently from the global network, and changes associated to OIC community is missing in the global network.

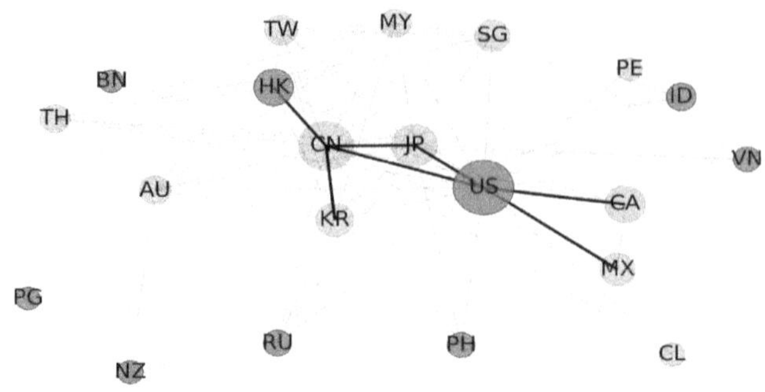

(a) APEC trade network in 2008.

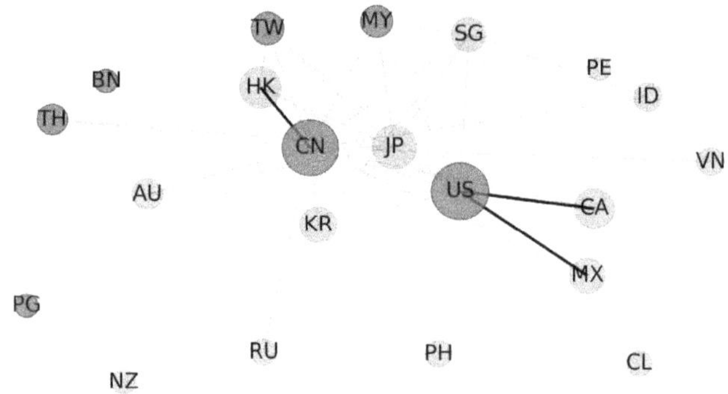

(b) APEC trade network in 2009. International trade volume drops significantly (fewer heavy edges), and several economics flip between surplus and deficit (within the region).

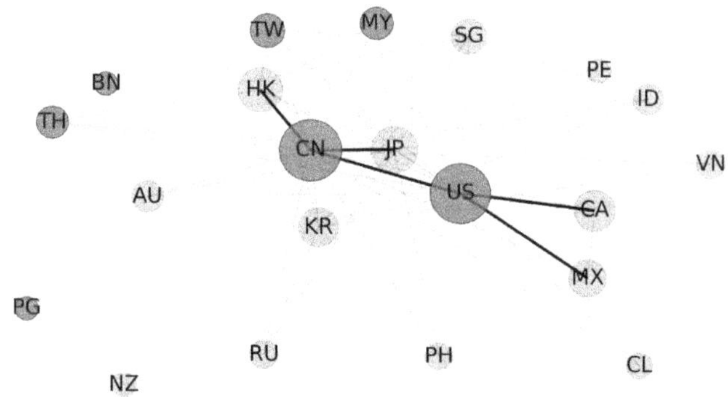

(c) APEC trade network in 2010. More and heavier edges emerge, sign of recovery.

Figure 11: Visualization of APEC trade network (weighted, undirected). Node size is proportional to the economic size, and red nodes have trade deficit while grey nodes have trade surplus. Edge width and transparency reflect bilateral trade volume (export+import).

ACKNOWLEDGMENTS

The authors would like to thank Leto Peel for providing his code base, and Wenlei Bao and and Congrong Guan for helping collect the international trade data. The authors would also like to thank the anonymous referees for their valuable comments. This work is supported in part by NSF grant DMS-1418265, IIS-1550302 and IIS-1629548. Any opinions, findings, and conclusions or recommendations expressed in this material are those of the authors and do not necessarily reflect the views of the National Science Foundation.

REFERENCES

[1] Leman Akoglu, Hanghang Tong, and Danai Koutra. 2014. Graph-based Anomaly Detection and Description: A Survey. *Data Mining and Knowledge Discovery (DAMI)* 28, 4 (2014).

[2] Sitaram Asur, Srinivasan Parthasarathy, and Duygu Ucar. 2009. An event-based framework for characterizing the evolutionary behavior of interaction graphs. *ACM Transactions on Knowledge Discovery from Data (TKDD)* 3, 4 (2009), 16.
[3] Vincent D Blondel, Jean-Loup Guillaume, Renaud Lambiotte, and Etienne Lefebvre. 2008. Fast unfolding of communities in large networks. *Journal of statistical mechanics: theory and experiment* 2008, 10 (2008), P10008.
[4] Robert A Bridges, John P Collins, Erik M Ferragut, Jason A Laska, and Blair D Sullivan. 2015. Multi-Level Anomaly Detection on Time-Varying Graph Data. In *Proceedings of the 2015 IEEE/ACM International Conference on Advances in Social Networks Analysis and Mining 2015.* ACM, 579–583.
[5] Fan Chung and Linyuan Lu. 2002. The average distances in random graphs with given expected degrees. *Proceedings of the National Academy of Sciences* 99, 25 (2002), 15879–15882.
[6] William Eberle and Lawrence Holder. 2016. Identifying Anomalies in Graph Streams Using Change Detection. (2016).
[7] Paul Erdős and A Rényi. 1960. On the evolution of random graphs. *Publ. Math. Inst. Hungar. Acad. Sci* 5 (1960), 17–61.
[8] Michalis Faloutsos, Petros Faloutsos, and Christos Faloutsos. 1999. On power-law relationships of the internet topology. In *ACM SIGCOMM computer communication review*, Vol. 29. ACM, 251–262.
[9] Santo Fortunato. 2010. Community detection in graphs. *Physics reports* 486, 3 (2010), 75–174.
[10] Christopher R Harshaw, Robert A Bridges, Michael D Iannacone, Joel W Reed, and John R Goodall. 2016. GraphPrints: Towards a Graph Analytic Method for Network Anomaly Detection. In *Proceedings of the 11th Annual Cyber and Information Security Research Conference.* ACM, 15.
[11] Brian Karrer and Mark EJ Newman. 2011. Stochastic blockmodels and community structure in networks. *Physical Review E* 83, 1 (2011), 016107.
[12] George Karypis and Vipin Kumar. 1998. Multilevelk-way partitioning scheme for irregular graphs. *Journal of Parallel and Distributed computing* 48, 1 (1998), 96–129.
[13] Danai Koutra, Neil Shah, Joshua T Vogelstein, Brian Gallagher, and Christos Faloutsos. 2016. Deltacon: Principled Massive-Graph Similarity Function with Attribution. *ACM Transactions on Knowledge Discovery from Data (TKDD)* 10, 3 (2016), 28.
[14] Timothy La Fond, Jennifer Neville, and Brian Gallagher. 2014. Anomaly Detection in Networks with Changing Trends. (2014).
[15] Timothy La Fond, Jennifer Neville, and Brian Gallagher. 2016. Generating Local Explanations of Network Anomalies via Score Decomposition. (2016).
[16] Sebastian Moreno and Jennifer Neville. 2013. Network hypothesis testing using mixed Kronecker product graph models. In *Data Mining (ICDM), 2013 IEEE 13th International Conference on.* IEEE, 1163–1168.
[17] Leto Peel and Aaron Clauset. 2014. Detecting change points in the large-scale structure of evolving networks. *arXiv preprint arXiv:1403.0989* (2014).
[18] Edwin JG Pitman. 1937. Significance tests which may be applied to samples from any populations. *Supplement to the Journal of the Royal Statistical Society* 4, 1 (1937), 119–130.
[19] Stephen Ranshous, Shitian Shen, Danai Koutra, Steve Harenberg, Christos Faloutsos, and Nagiza F Samatova. 2015. Anomaly detection in dynamic networks: a survey. *Wiley Interdisciplinary Reviews: Computational Statistics* 7, 3 (2015), 223–247.
[20] C Seshadhri, Tamara G Kolda, and Ali Pinar. 2012. Community structure and scale-free collections of Erdős-Rényi graphs. *Physical Review E* 85, 5 (2012), 056109.
[21] Yu Wang, Aniket Chakrabarti, David Sivakoff, and Srinivasan Parthasarathy. 2017. Fast Change Point Detection on Dynamic Social Networks. *International Joint Conference on Artificial Intelligence (IJCAI)* (2017).
[22] Yining Wang, Liwei Wang, Yuanzhi Li, Di He, Wei Chen, and Tie-Yan Liu. 2013. A theoretical analysis of NDCG ranking measures. In *Proceedings of the 26th Annual Conference on Learning Theory (COLT 2013).*
[23] Jaewon Yang and Jure Leskovec. 2012. Community-affiliation graph model for overlapping network community detection. In *Data Mining (ICDM), 2012 IEEE 12th International Conference on.* IEEE, 1170–1175.

Analyzing the Keystroke Dynamics of Web Identifiers

Andrew G. West
Verisign Labs, Verisign Inc.
Reston, VA, USA
awest@verisign.com

ABSTRACT

Web identifiers such as usernames, hashtags, and domain names serve important roles in online navigation, communication, and community building. Therefore the entities that choose such names must ensure that end-users are able to quickly and accurately enter them in applications. Uniqueness requirements, a desire for short strings, and an absence of delimiters often constrain this name selection process.

To gain perspective on the speed and correctness of name entry, we crowdsource the typing of 51,000+ web identifiers. Surface level analysis reveals, for example, that typing speed is generally a linear function of identifier length. Examining keystroke dynamics at finer granularity proves more interesting. First, we identify features predictive of typing time/accuracy, finding: (1) the commonality of character bi-grams inside a name, and (2) the degree of ambiguity when tokenizing a name – to be most indicative. A machine-learning model built over 10 such features exhibits moderate predictive capability. Second, we evaluate our hypothesis that users subconsciously insert pauses in their typing cadence where text delimiters (*e.g.*, spaces) would exist, if permitted. The data generally supports this claim, suggesting its application alongside algorithmic tokenization methods, and possibly in name suggestion frameworks.

CCS CONCEPTS

• **Human-centered computing** → *Interaction devices*; *Keyboards*; • **Information systems** → *Personalization*; Online advertising; • **Social and professional topics** → Internet governance / domain names;

KEYWORDS

typeability; keystroke dynamics; keyboards; typos; web identifier; domain names; hashtags; usernames

WebSci '17, June 25-28, 2017, Troy, NY, USA

ACM ISBN 978-1-4503-4896-6/17/06...$15.00
https://doi.org/10.1145/3091478.3091482

1 INTRODUCTION

Little needs to be said about the pervasiveness of web identifiers, with 325+ million domain names [29] enabling web navigation/email and billions of social network accounts. The need for careful identifier selection in these naming systems is evidenced both empirically and anecdotally.

For domain names, consider that [16] estimates that *typosquatting* names – registrations intended to capture traffic from misspellings of popular websites – received an estimated 68.2 million clicks/day in 2010. While most such domains are monetized via ad revenue, roughly 4% are leveraged for "hit stealing" and competitive advantage [1]. Proactive name selection could minimize this threat vector. Even in the absence of such threats, consider one registrar's leading tip for domain name selection: "make it easy to type" [22].

Parallel motivations have been seen in other naming systems. For example, "brandjacking" on social networks and less nefariously, the digital land rush when Facebook enabled usernames in 2009 [19]. Mature namespaces demand nuanced identifier selection and evaluation criteria, to include typeability metrics. Our research will reveal a user's ability to "parse" names absent delimiters as an important property, for which Twitter provides an instructive example. Hashtag `#nowthatchersdead`, intended to be parsed as `#now|thatchers|dead` following the death of former UK prime minister Margaret Thatcher, was instead met by grief for the still living American celebrity Cher, being interpreted as `#now|that|chers|dead` [14].

To learn about how end users enter web identifiers we crowdsource 51,002 domain name typings (Sec. 2). We focus on domains in particular because of the: (1) ubiquity of the DNS, (2) availability of related metadata (*e.g.*, popularity), and (3) ability to experiment with a hierarchical namespace. Our experiment masquerades as a CAPTCHA usability study to deflect from our true measurements, wherein the minimally obfuscated CAPTCHA text is generated from domain names. Given the crowdsourced nature of our data, we are attentive to the potential biases of a self selected and pay-per-task workforce.

We then analyze the millisecond-granularity timing data, answering research questions along three themes (Sec. 3):

(1) *Broad measurements*: How does identifier length affect typing time? What is the relationship between backspace usage and typing time?
(2) *Features/models predicting typeability*: Can the keyboard mapping or lexical properties of a name predict input speed and/or correctness? What is the accuracy of a model leveraging all such features?
(3) *Tokenization clues in typing latency*: Do users provide hints about where word boundaries lie with irregularities in their typing cadence?

umclimbing	norwegianblues	monicaandbryce
oaklandbakery	makehomenow	monserrattreviews
loveishypnotic	charliegunn	lokalsportlive
philsmithroofing	laguardiatux	trianglehall
letsbuytickets	killnoise	goldmedalplumbing

Table 1: Example SLDs from the "random" subset

It is from an exploration of these, and related topics, that we identify the key contributions of this work:

- Linear growth in typing times as identifier length increases (at ≈290 ms/char.) reveal no hidden costs in seeking out longer names in mature namespaces
- Familiarity brings increased typeability for both domains and their hierarchical extensions ("random" identifiers are typed 16% slower than "popular" ones)
- Features capturing how an identifier maps onto a physical keyboard (*e.g.,* finger travel distance) are relatively poor predictors of typeability
- Lexical properties are more useful; domains are easier to type when they: (1) can be easily tokenized into component words, and (2) are composed of character bi-grams common in English text
- Models to predict typing times have tepid effectiveness with RMSE=0.31 where the regression target is normalized about 1.0. For a 12-character domain, one standard deviation of confidence spans 2.8 seconds.
- The maximum intra-character latency for an identifier occurs on a word boundary 3× to 4× more often than random chance, yielding helpful tokenization clues

These findings can be integrated into identifier suggestion tools, or serve as guidance to the individuals, corporations, and investors who participate in these naming systems.

To the best of our knowledge, this is the first research to measure the typeability of web identifiers, although it builds on literature about typeability and keystroke dynamics. These related works are reviewed (Sec. 4) before noting future work and concluding (Sec. 5).

2 DATA COLLECTION

To produce keystroke measurements one must first decide what strings will be typed (Sec. 2.1). These are at the core of our experiment design and its crowdsourced distribution (Sec. 2.2). After collecting 51k measurements, we take a cursory look at the data, then scrutinize the workforce and the biases it may introduce (Sec. 2.3).

2.1 Identifier Selection

Domain names are representative of the broader class of web identifiers; sharing their core characteristics, while their name structure and usage data enable additional analysis. This structure is seen in a domain like `example.com`, where "com" is the *top-level domain* (TLD) or *extension* and "example" is the *second-level domain* (SLD). This work does not consider depths beyond the second-level, so we also use the terms *left-of-dot* and *right-of-dot* to refer to the SLD and TLD, respectively. Our primary focus is on SLDs, where the most creative free will is exercised (Sec. 2.1.1). We treat SLDs and TLDs independently, with the ability to comparatively measure TLD typeability a side effect of using domain strings (Sec. 2.1.2).

TLD	P%	GROUPING
COM	20%	
NET	10%	Legacy TLDs (40%)
ORG	10%	
DE	10%	
CN	10%	CC TLDs (30%)
UK	10%	
XYZ	10%	
CLUB	10%	New gTLDs (30%)
ONLINE	10%	

Table 2: TLD selection probabilities (P%)

2.1.1 Second-level Domain Strings. It is our goal to collect typing measurements for SLDs that are: (1) consistent with those typed during ordinary Internet usage, and/or (2) consistent with the class of names an end-user concerned with typeability might consider for registration. To this end, we create two domains sets:

(1) POPULAR: Alexa's top 10,000 domains
(2) RANDOM: Subset of the COM/NET zone where domains that a crawler flagged as "redirecting", "parked", or "pay-per-click advertising" are discarded

Next, we have Amazon Mechanical Turk (MTurk) workers *tokenize* or *segment* a subset of these domains into their component words (*e.g.,* `somedomain.com` → `some|domain`). Workers were told to visit the websites in making this determination, with a 23.6 second average task completion time suggesting these instructions were heeded. Skipping subtleties in the interest of brevity, a minimum of 3 workers and a maximum of 8 workers are asked to tokenize a name until consensus was reached (75%+ of workers agreeing on a tokenization) or the domain was abandoned. These authoritative human tokenizations are critical to Sec. 3.3.

The final dataset contains 14,650 "random" and 7,250 "popular" names. After stripping off the TLD[1] these 21,900 SLDs form the basis of our experimental set. Tab. 1 shows example SLDs drawn from the "random" subset.

2.1.2 Domain Extensions. Retaining the TLDs associated with our ≈22k SLDs would lead to an overwhelming majority of COM and NET names. For purposes of experimenting with TLD typeability, we instead randomly apply extensions to SLD labels per the probabilities of Tab. 2. While this gives rise to some names which are not registered, we assume the "dot" offers a consistent break in typing cadence such that the SLD and TLD may be measured independently. Tab. 2 also shows the selected TLDs draw from three different groupings:

[1] The public suffix list (`http://publicsuffix.org`) is used to determine "effective TLDs". For instance, "co.uk" is the effective TLD for `example.co.uk`.

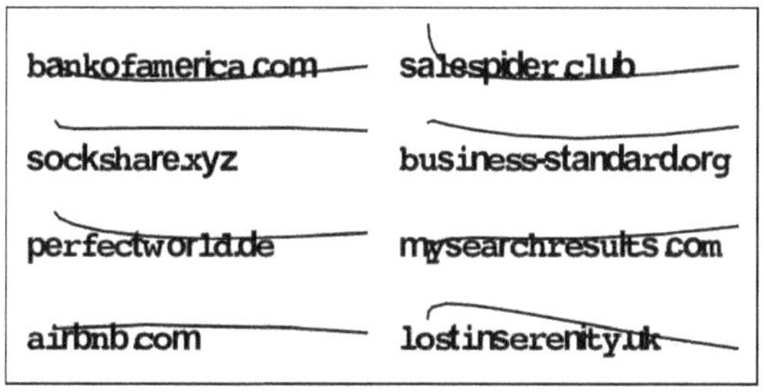

Figure 1: Example domain CAPTCHA images, shown here at reduced size

(1) *Legacy TLDs* were delegated in 1985 and have pervasiveness that could manifest as typing "muscle memory". We test the 3 (COM; NET; ORG) most popular [29].

(2) *Country code extensions* (ccTLDs) are two-letter TLDs that likely have geographically variable familiarity. We have chosen the 3 (CN; DE; UK) most popular per [29], after ommitting the special case of TK.

(3) *New generic TLDs* (new gTLDs) were first deployed in 2013 and have expanded the available extension space. Our selection (XYZ; CLUB; ONLINE) opts for the most popular TLDs marketed towards English-speaking markets at the time of our early 2016 analysis [26].

2.2 Experiment Design

Our 21,900 domains are *what* will be typed. Next is *how* the typing data is collected. We opt to generate domain text as CAPTCHA images (Sec. 2.2.1). Then, we have MTurk workers participate in a purported CAPTCHA usability study, where we instrument the input forms to collect keyboard data (Sec. 2.2.2). In this manner we hope to avoid the Hawthorne effect: telling a participant we are observing typing behaviors potentially modifies such behaviors.

This crowdsourced CAPTCHA strategy does have drawbacks, as discussed subsequently. However, we find it preferable to alternatives such as in-person laboratory experiments that would have high cost and lack scalability. Creating a browser plug-in to monitor native interactions with the URL bar might produce the best data, but would face immense privacy and adoption challenges.

2.2.1 CAPTCHA Generation. For each of our domains (SLDs from Sec. 2.1.1 with TLDs randomly appended per Tab. 2) we generate a CAPTCHA image using the SimpleCaptcha library [24]. Fig. 1 displays some example images. All text is generated in lowercase, and a minimal amount of obfuscation is applied. Our goal is to keep the domain text very legible, adding just enough noise to make our CAPTCHA storyline plausible.

2.2.2 MTurk Instrumentation. These CAPTCHA images are central to the MTurk experiments. Fig. 2 shows the worker interface, coded in HTML, Javascript, PHP, with a MySQL backend. The following points, as annotated in Fig. 2, highlight design decisions:

❶ *Instruction set*: Instructions are straightforward in explaining our CAPTCHA usability study. A bullet makes explicit that all answers are of the form "[text].[text]" after initial trials found frequent dot omissions.

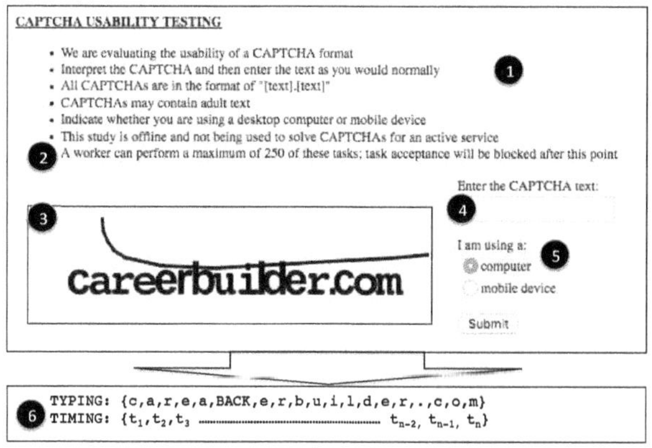

Figure 2: MTurk worker interface

❷ *Participation limit*: No worker can complete more than 250 tasks, limiting one to contributing 0.5% of the dataset. This balances the need to find sufficient workers with the desire to capture typing behaviors of a broad population. The limit is enforced in software.

❸ *CAPTCHA image*: As generated in the previous section, we randomly select from available images (associated with a puzzleID) when the page is generated.

❹ *Solution form*: Where the worker types the CAPTCHA text. The form is instrumented using the JQuery `keydown()` event, which was found to have the most consistent cross-browser behavior. Both the key pressed and the millisecond timing of the event are recorded.

❺ *Device type*: Workers are asked whether they are using a desktop or mobile device. Differing keyboards have obvious ramifications on typing measurements.

❻ *Output*: After "submit" is pressed, we store every key entered and the associated timings. We also have the generated puzzleID, the User Agent string of the worker, and MTurk identifiers/metadata.

The complexity of our interface is such that it cannot be managed via MTurk's web application. We utilize Amazon's command-line tools [3] for task launching and management.

2.3 Data Quality & Workforce

Over two weeks in early 2016, 60,500 typing experiments were launched paying \$0.02 each. Well-formed data came back for 60,135 (99.39%) of these with the few errors assumed to be from atypical browser configurations. We now sanity check this data (Sec. 2.3.1) before examining the workforce that produced it (Sec. 2.3.2).

2.3.1 Data Scrubbing. In a cursory pass of that data, we discard typings that are either (1) incorrect or (2) from a mobile device, a filtering that is visualized in Fig. 6.

A typing is considered *incorrect* if replaying the sequence of characters keyed does not produce a result which matches the generating text of the CAPTCHA displayed. We emphasize that "incorrect" does not preclude the use of [backspace]. The dataset has 51,491 (85.6%) correctly keyed entries and 8,644 (14.4%) incorrect ones, with a number of circumstances giving rise to these faults:

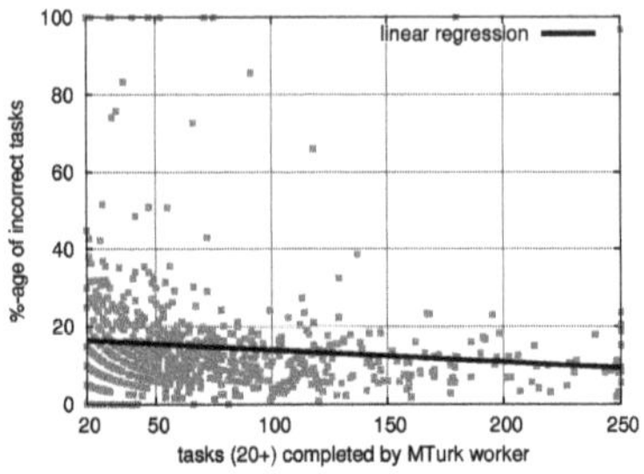

Figure 3: Worker task quantity × incorrect typings[2]

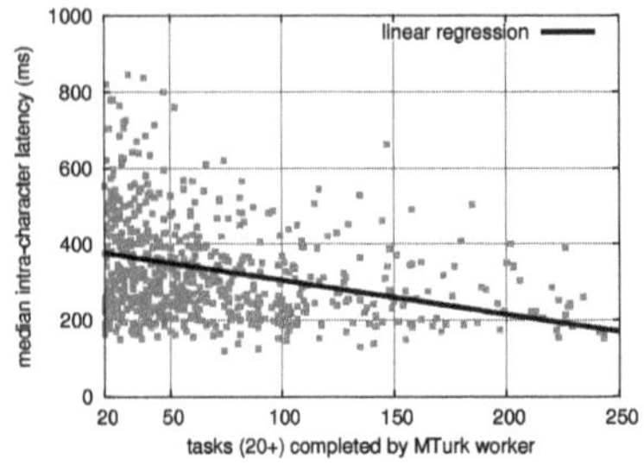

Figure 4: Worker task quantity × typing latency[2]

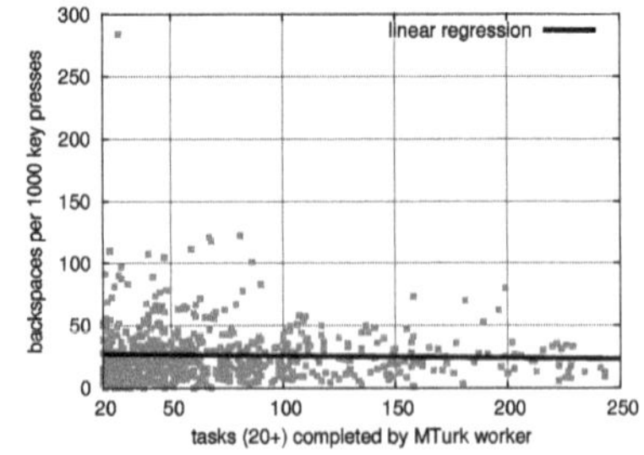

Figure 5: Worker task quantity × backspace usage[2]

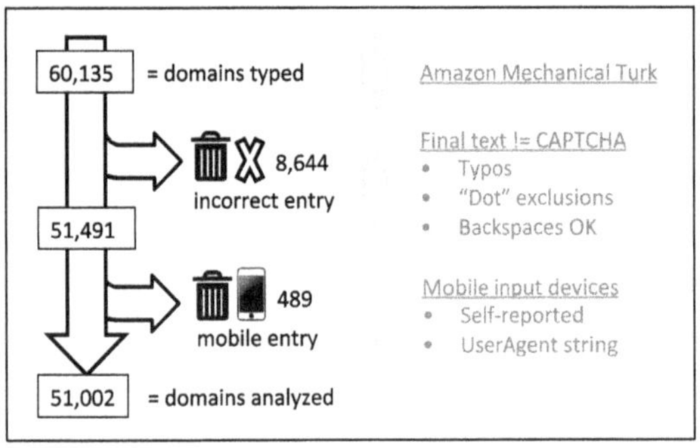

Figure 6: Discarding incorrect and mobile typings

Figure 7: CDF of task distribution over workers

- *Mouse usage*: Mouse actions such as highlighting characters or moving the cursor are manipulations not captured in keyboard data. It is unknown how many "incorrect" typings are the result of such effects.
- *No solution text*: 416 (4.8%) incorrect tasks have blank solution fields. Heavy overlap with mobile device usage suggests these are users with Javascript disabled.
- *Omitted periods*: Despite explicit instructions about generated CAPTCHA structure, 1941 non-blank incorrect typings (22.5%) contained no dot character.
- *Character errors*: The remaining mistakes are typographical or transcription errors. Transpositions, missing characters, duplicate characters, and missing plurality were common.

These 8,644 incorrect typings are discarded. The "character errors" set may be useful in the study of typos but is of less utility in our statistical context here, *i.e.*, if a worker keys more characters than was in the CAPTCHA text, how does one treat the length property?

The second condition for discarding a task is if it was *typed using a mobile device*. There were 1,246 self-reported mobile inputs, only 477 of which were entered correctly, presumbly due to Javascript issues. Analyzing user agent strings confirmed these and found a further 12 cases indicating a mobile browser. Discarding these 489 typings should not be interpreted as irrelevance of mobile typing behaviors. Instead, they demand study with crowdsourcing and instrumentation better tuned for mobile environments.

The 51,002 remaining domain/CAPTCHA typings are the primary basis for analysis in the remainder of this work.

2.3.2 *Workforce & Bias.* We now examine the MTurk workers who contributed to our typing experiments, with a particular eye towards the fact they are a compensated and self selected workforce:

Basic statistics: Over ≈65k tasks there were 1442 unique workers, completing at median 21 tasks each, with the average being 47. The maximum of 250 tasks was reached by 20 workers. Fig. 7 plots the task CDF, showing the top 20% of workers did 50% of all work, and the top 50% of workers accounted for 90% of tasks. Such a distribution is not unexpected, as workers often sample tasks before committing to considerable work. The experiments were popular with batches of 5000 tasks being completed in under an hour, implying our payout was competitive.

Paid workforce: Workers average around 6 seconds/task, which if sustained is $6/hour after Amazon commission. This is non-trivial for workers in developing economies, thus incentivizing them to work quickly through a finite and dissipating task pool. A possible side effect is making "incorrect" typings that we discard, with the portion that are correct being entered at atypically high speeds. Counteracting this is the notion of reputation on MTurk and the ability to halt payouts to underperforming workers. Fig. 3 shows that our most prolific workers commit about 7 less errors per 100 tasks than those who contributed 20 typings.[2] We do not believe this is a severe affect and attribute it primarily to familiarity with interface and CAPTCHA formats.

[2]These figures do not plot workers who performed <20 tasks. They contribute only 10% of tasks and lack a body of work of sufficient size and consistency from which to draw conclusions.

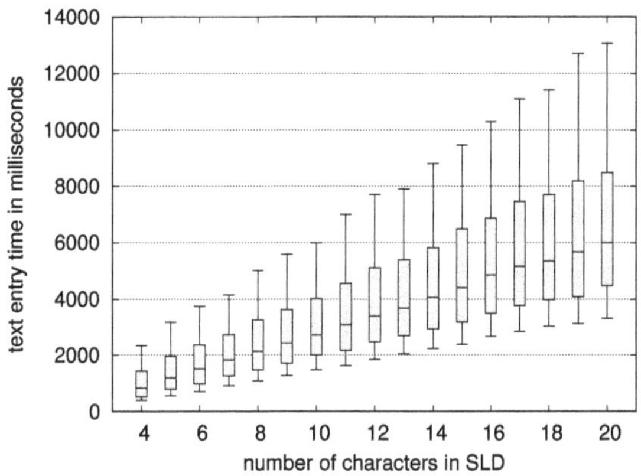

Figure 8: Distribution of SLD typing times, by length[3]

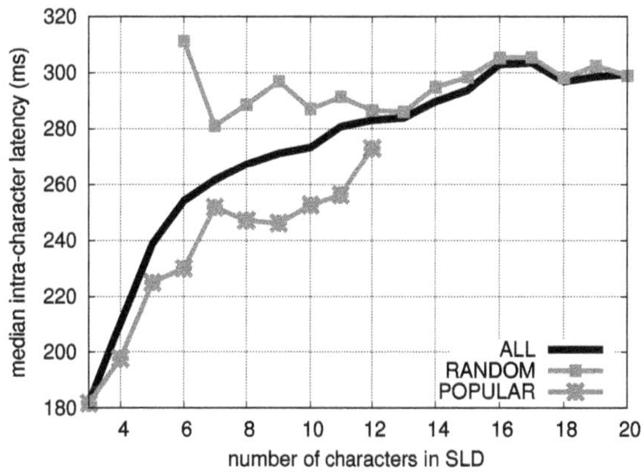

Figure 9: Median intra-char. latency by SLD length. Data points backed by less than 500 typings are not plotted.

Self-selected workers: Workers on the MTurk platform choose the work they perform. Therefore, if one finds a task aligns poorly with their skill set (*e.g.,* typing speed), they might stop performing it to seek more lucrative alternative work. This leaves a non-representative labor pool to perform the bulk of the tasks. Fig. 4 plots the *median intra-character latency* (MICL) by worker, one metric summarizing typing speed. The linear regression shows an MICL of ≈400ms for workers who did 20 tasks, but workers who did 250 tasks were nearly twice as quick at ≈200ms. This is a rather profound difference. It is partially because familiarity breeds speed: For workers who did 150+ tasks, their first 25 tasks were typed at a rate 7.55% slower than subsequent ones. Still, this cannot account for much of the gap. We remain mindful of this bias while noting this work is most concerned with relative, not absolute measures of keystroke dynamics.

It is interesting to note, per Fig. 5, that backspace usage is roughly constant across task quantity. Combined with Fig. 4, this implies that susceptibility to errors/backspace does not correlate strongly with typing speed.

Non-measurable effects: Other biases do not lend themselves to quantification. For example, most MTurk workers are from India or the US [11]. We also make the assumption that typing behaviors when entering CAPTCHA solutions are consistent with those when interacting with web identifiers in a URL bar or email client.

3 DATA ANALYSIS

The dataset of 51k domain typings is now analyzed towards three major goals: First, measuring the speed and correctness of domain typings at both SLD and TLD levels (Sec. 3.1). Second, developing features and producing models predictive of typing times (Sec. 3.2). Third, assessing the feasibility of predicting word boundaries using intra-character latency (Sec. 3.3).

3.1 Broad Measurements

In order to assess SLD and TLD typing speed and correctness, one must determine what keystrokes define these components. When domains are entered without using backspace, this is straightforward. Let's assume correctly typing domain `foo.com` produces a timing vector T of length $|T| = n = 7$: $T = \{t_1, t2, t_3, t_4, t_5, t_6, t_7\}$. We then define a function, $T_{di} = dot\_index(T) = t_4$, that determines where the "dot" character lies in the typing vector. With this we can subset T into $T_{SLD} = \{t_1, t_2 \ldots T_{di-1}\}$ and $T_{TLD} = \{T_{di+1}, T_{di+2} \ldots t_n\}$ with typing times $time(T_{SLD}) = (T_{di-1} - t_1)$ and $time(T_{TLD}) = (t_n - T_{di+1})$, respectively.

Backspace characters introduce complications. For example, take the typing sequence:

| f | o | p | . | c | backspace | backspace | backspace | o | . | c | o | m |

...which is a correct typing of `foo.com`. Now, $dot\_index(\cdot)$ is extended to return only the index of the dot character that persists in the final output (the second dot, in the above example). The dataset has 713 examples of a dot character being erased; 3% of all backspace usages. With this established, we can now do analysis at SLD (Sec. 3.1.1) and TLD granularity (Sec. 3.1.2).

3.1.1 *Second-level Domain Strings.*

Users have the most creative free will in choosing second-level domains. Our analysis emphasizes length ramifications:

Typing speed by length: Fig. 8 shows SLD typing time as broken down by SLD length[3]. The increasing typing times are equal parts insight and sanity check. We find 4 character SLDs are typed in about a second, with 20 character domains taking 6 seconds at median. The 91st percentile of workers types about twice as slow as median typists.

Impact of increasing lengths: Focusing only on the median time growth as length increases, Fig. 9 examines if typing speed is a linear function of SLD length. As namespaces mature, short names become less available, and it is crucial to understand if there is any penalty (beyond linear) of choosing longer, more descriptive names.

The graph shows there are incremental penalties for "popular" names. Indeed, the Alexa top 10k exhibits a positive correlation between popularity and length, *i.e.,* the most trafficked domains

[3]For all box plots, the box markings correspond to the typical 1Q, median, and Q3 of the distribution. The whiskers mark the 9th and 91st percentiles. Workers who pause mid-task sometimes return typing times measured in minutes, one reason we prefer to characterize timing metrics at median.

	COM	NET	DE	ORG	UK	ONLINE	CLUB	XYZ	CN
domains (doms)	10,412	5,248	4,971	5,387	5,171	4,989	5,030	4,783	5,011
length (len)	3	3	2	3	2	6	4	3	2
chars. (c = doms × len)	31,326	15,744	9,942	16,161	10,342	24,945	20,120	14,349	10,022
backspaces typed (bs)	295	254	205	363	291	725	592	752	619
chars. per backspace (c/bs)	105.88	61.98	48.50	44.52	35.54	34.41	33.99	19.08	16.19
TLD per backspace ((c/bs)/len)	35.29	20.66	24.25	14.84	17.77	6.88	8.50	6.36	8.10

Table 3: Backspace statistics broken out by TLD[4]

PROPERTY	RAND	POP	ALL
# SLDs	33,403	17,599	51,002
SLDs w/backspace	6,014	2,215	8,229
minimal keypresses	462,036	148,224	610,260
actual keypresses	489,048	158,380	647,428
backspace (bs) presses	14,018	5,266	19,284
avg. SLD length (chars.)	13.8	8.4	12.0
% SLDs w/bs	18.0%	12.6%	16.1%
actual/min keypresses	105.9%	106.9%	106.1%
bs/actual presses	2.9%	3.3%	3.0%

Table 4: Backspace statistics for SLDs

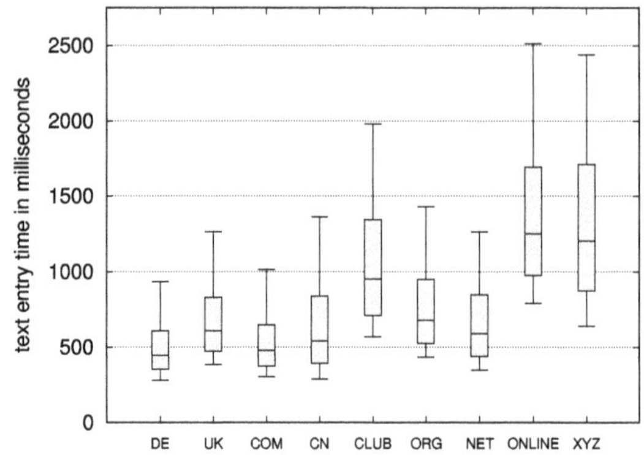

Figure 10: Distribution of TLD typing times[3,4]

tend to be shorter. Consider that popular sites are financially well-positioned to acquire very short names, such as Facebook's $8.5M buy of `fb.com`. Thus, it may be the case that the short names very high in the Alexa rankings are simply being typed atypically fast.

Regardless, popularity is primarily a byproduct of site content, not name selection. All new registrations enter the market as "random" ones so it is more instructive to look at that subset for guidance. There we see a more linear pattern of around 290ms being added for each additional character. We believe for new registrants and the name suggestion task that this is the more salient statistic.

Backspace usage: Tab. 4 displays statistics concerning backspaces in SLD typing. Highlights are that 16% of all domains typed utilized the backspace character, with 3% of all keypresses being backspace. Breaking out the "random" and "popular" sets seemingly reveal gaps with just 12.6% of popular names having a backspace compared to 18% of random ones. However, after the 5 character average length difference is normalized, ratios (*e.g.,* actual/min keypresses) show the error rate per character is quite similar. More informally, because random TLDs are longer they give typists more opportunity to err. The fact that error rate is relatively constant even when a typist is (presumably) familiar with a name hints (see Sec. 3.2) that predictors of typographical errors may tough to identify.

3.1.2 Top-level Domain Strings. Given finite TLD options, we are able to compare relative typeability across a sample of extensions[4]:

Typing speed: Fig. 10 visualizes the typing time distribution by TLD. We see legacy extensions [29] are typed very quickly, even comparably to the two-character ccTLDs. New gTLDs tend to be typed slower than the other classes, perhaps a reflection of the fact only 52% of consumers are aware of any of the new extensions [10]. Once normalized by length the per-character cost of a TLD is ≈250ms, though COM and NET are outliers that tend to be typed much quicker.

[4]Recalling Sec. 2.1.2, this TLD selection compares the most popular extensions of each type per industry statistics [26, 29].

Backspace usage: Tab. 3 presents TLD backspace usage in both raw and length normalized form. Consistent with the timing statistics, COM fares favorably, *e.g.,* only once per 35 typings of "com" do we expect someone to make a mistake; every 106 characters.

3.2 Features/Models Predicting Typeability

While retroactive insights regarding domain text entry are interesting, mining that data enables models which can be applied to unregistered identifiers. Such models could be applied in name suggestion and marketing tools. We first develop features indicative of typeability (Sec. 3.2.1) before evaluating their performance individually and in combination (Sec. 3.2.2). Our primary goal is predicting typing speed for a provided string, although we briefly explain challenges in trying to predict backspace usage (Sec. 3.2.3).

3.2.1 Feature Development. Features are developed in 2 themes: (1) keyboard topology and (2) string properties. We describe each of our 10 features and provide intuition on how they might be predictive. Tab. 5 provides a succinct feature reference.

Keyboard topology: We hypothesize a string's mapping onto the physical keyboard layout offers typeability clues. Though statistics are scarce, we assume universal QWERTY keyboard usage across our primarily Indian and U.S.-based workforce [11]. We repurpose a keyboard measurement library [5] to help calculate these features:

- `distance`: Distance (in meters) traveled by all fingers in typing a string, including moving from, and if necessary, returning to, the home row. Assumes 1.8cm square keys and a standard QWERTY layout; a popular measure in evaluating keyboard efficiency.

FEATURE	RRIf	DESCRIPTION
distance	0.04	finger travel distance (meters)
same_hand_%	0.10	%-age key/trans. on same hand
same_fing_%	0.04	%-age key/trans. on same finger
row1_%	0.16	%-age key/trans. to/from numeric keys
repeat_%	0.04	%-age key/trans. back to same char.
pinky_%	0.10	%-age keys typed with pinky
dom_length	0.05	length of sld in characters
seg_words	0.06	number of words in SLD; per corpus
seg_diff	0.49	ease of tokenizing SLD; per algorithm
2gram_prob	0.16	log-sum of bigram probabilties in SLD

Table 5: Features for typing time prediction. Regressional ReliefF (RRIF) [21] ranks feature efficacy. RRIf*100 is given here.

- same_hand_%: Percentage of key transitions that use the same typing hand. For example, a [q] followed by a [b] might be an awkward stretch.
- same_fing_%: Percentage of key transitions that utilize the same typing finger. Since the finger will not start resting on a home row character, some typists might incur latency in returning home.
- row1_%: Percentage of key transitions that go from the alphabetical keys to the number/hyphen ones and vice-versa. The top row of keys require the longest reach, and we have observed typists abandoning touch typing to find/reach them.
- repeat_%: Percentage of key transitions that repeat the same character, on the presumption these can be typed very quickly since no finger travel is required.
- pinky_%: Percentage of key transitions using the pinky finger. Tangential evidence [7] suggests the little finger is least accurate in striking characters.

String properties: The remaining 4 features are based on lexical characteristics of the string itself:

- dom_length: Domain length is an obvious feature if trying to predict actual typing times, but more subtle if doing regression around length normalized values.
- seg_words: Recall from Sec. 2.1.1 that all SLDs have a consensus tokenization from human workers. Thus it is known how many words compose an SLD, our feature here. Given our hypothesis in Sec. 3.3 that word boundaries cause pauses in typing cadence, word quantity should impact typing time.
- seg_diff: We extend the straightforward algorithmic tokenization method of [13] with numerical and hyphen support. This method considers all 2^{n-1} possible tokenizations of a length n string and sorts them by a relative "fitness" score based on English word commonality [17] with a preference for longer words. The ratio of the highest to the second-highest tokenization score is our feature here, proxying how ambiguous the tokenization appears on the surface (recall workers actually visited the webpages). We imagine quick identification of component keywords makes domain entry more like normal typing, with familiar letter sequences.
- 2gram_prob: Related work suggests that "familiar" sequences are easier to type [31]. Fig. 11 plots the English bi-gram (*i.e.*,

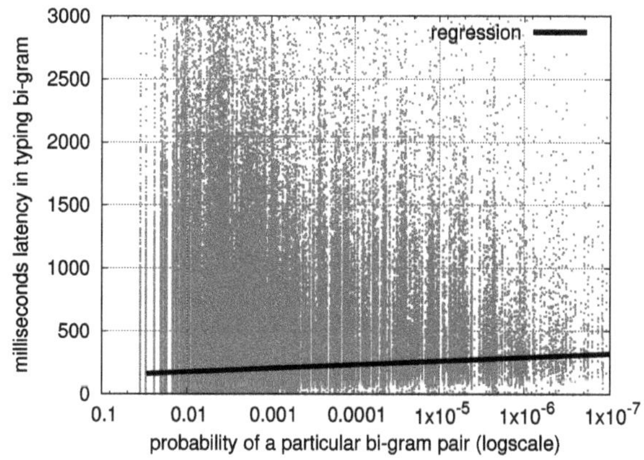

Figure 11: Commonality of bi-gram pairs in English text × typing speed in our experiments

two character) probabilities from a corpus of English text [17] against the intra-character latency for those bigrams per our experiments. Regression reinforces that claim. Accordingly, we encode a feature:

$$\frac{\Sigma\ |log_{10}(bigram\_prob)|\ \forall\ bigrams \in SLD}{length(SLD) - 1}$$

which sums bigram commonality in a string, uses *log* to put very tiny probabilities back in a reasonable number space, and normalizes by string length.

3.2.2 Models & Performance. We next address the prediction target, individual feature performance, model construction, and overall performance:

Predicted values: Given a string, predicting an absolute typing time is difficult. As earlier graphs showed, typing speed between individuals can vary greatly. Instead, we want a dependent variable (*i.e.*, target) that is typist agnostic. This is achieved by first considering only workers with a sufficient body of work: 20+ tasks. The median intra-character latency (MICL) for each worker is calculated. Then, for every SLD he/she has typed[5], one can divide the actual timing time by the expected typing time:

$$\frac{actual\_typing\_time}{(length(SLD) - 1) * MICL_{worker}}$$

to yield a ratio on $(0, \infty)$. These ratios are our regression target, one we believe to be an intuitive representation of typing speed. A ratio < 1.0 indicates a quickly typed string, while ratios greater than 1.0 suggest a slower and more difficult one. While the median ratio is 1.0, the long tail stretches towards slower typing times given their unbounded nature. In practice, few values exist outside of $[0.4, 2.2]$.

Feature performance in isolation: Returning to Tab. 5, rankings show that most keyboard topology features exhibit middling to low performance. Such metrics are often leveraged to assess alternative keyboard layouts, and the 12 character average SLD length

[5]For training, testing, and worker MICL we use exclusively SLDs from the "random" set as these more closely approximate the available names that would be evaluated by potential registrants.

probably provides insufficient opportunity for patterns to emerge. The row1_% feature is the exception. Although only 14.3% of SLDs combine numeric/hypen and alphabetical characters, the penalty is very large where it can be leveraged.

Lexical features show most promise, with features seg_diff and 2gram_prob being highest ranked. Simply put, domains that have straightforward tokenizations and do not contain rare bigrams will be quickly typed. The dominant weight of seg_diff in particular suggests typeability may be improved by choosing longer, keyword-rich strings rather than introducing abbreviations or ambiguity into shorter identifiers.

Model construction & evaluation: To go from features to a predictive model the Weka [8] implementation of support vector regression (SVR) [23] is utilized. Though the actual SVR model is more complex and accurate, we present one built using linear regression over normalized feature values on [0,1] in the interest of human interpretation:

```
+0.7254
+0.6537 * (norm) row1_%
+0.5336 * (norm) 2gram_prob
-0.3262 * (norm) seg_diff
+0.1214 * (norm) distance
+0.0825 * (norm) dom_length
+0.0781 * (norm) pinky_%
+0.0752 * (norm) same_fing_%
+0.0222 * (norm) same_hand_%
```

One thing to notice is that 9 of 10 features are additive in nature. That is, we have identified what a typeable domain should *not* contain if one desires quick entry. For evaluation purposes, 10-fold cross validation is used.

Model performance: The best model parameterization produces a correlation coefficient of 0.2043, mean absolute error of 0.2417, and a root mean squared error (RMSE) of 0.3132. Focusing on RMSE, let's imagine a 12 character string is provided to our model. Suppose the model returns 1.0, predicting the actual typing time will match the expected typing time. Based on Fig. 8, we can estimate that 4 seconds is a reasonable expected typing time for a length 12 SLD. Going ±RMSE in each direction: $(1 - 0.35 = 0.65 * 4 \text{ seconds}) = 2.6$ seconds and $(1 + 0.35 = 1.35 * 4 \text{ seconds}) = 5.4$ seconds, one can state the typing time for the provided string will be between 2.6 and 5.4 seconds with one standard deviation (≈ 70%) of confidence.

In no way do we claim this to be a strong result. Indeed, for the majority of predictions which will cluster about 1.0, this broad confidence interval will encompass typing times ranging from rather quick to moderately slow. Given this, we believe the model has most utility in flagging strings with acute typeability concerns (*e.g.*, scores > 1.5). Because so few features significantly contribute, it would also be easy to communicate corrective actions to a user.

3.2.3 Backspace Prediction. As with typing speed, there are use-cases for algorithms that can predict typing errors. To some extent the prior model already captures this, since backspace usage manifests as additional typing time. However, a purpose built model could better focus on susceptibility to typosquatting and indicate where in a string mistakes might occur. Recall that true typos were

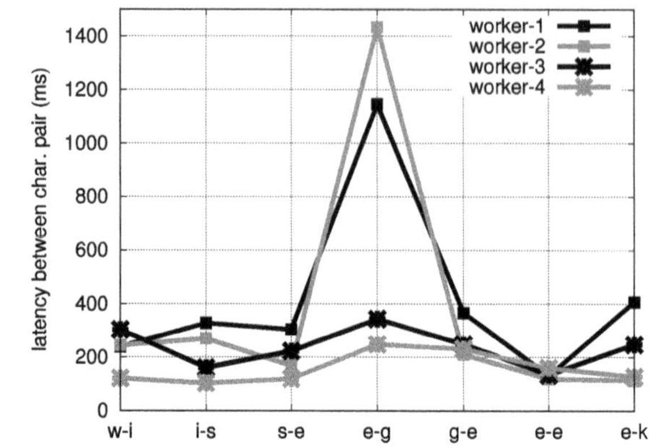

Figure 12: Intra-character latencies for a SLD (wisegeek)

discarded in Sec. 2.3.1, leaving only examples with corrected errors. However, it stands to reason that circumstances giving rise to backspace usage are similar to those of persistent typos.

Preliminary to *where* a backspace will occur is *if* one will occur in a string. This binary formulation lends itself to classification algorithms such as random forests, but unfortunately reusing the feature set of Tab. 5 produces a model that outperforms random chance by only a few percentage points. This begs questions about the ineffectiveness of the model and the tractability of the problem.

Perhaps error patterns are unique to typists and not shared amongst broader populations. Having a maximum of ≈3,000 characters per worker, we are not positioned to explore this hypothesis. Also consider that whereas time elapses *between* keypresses, errors occur *on* keypresses, so they might be less context dependent. Plotting the most mis-keyed characters normalized by occurrence reveals that $\{a, e, i, o\}$ are least error prone and $\{-, c, v, g\}$ are most errror prone. However, all of these differences contribute nominally to the classification accuracy. Gaining little traction, we leave progress on the this task as future work.

3.3 Tokenization Clues in Typing Latency

Statistical methods are the norm when tokenizing web identifiers; recall the word fitness technique based on [13] that was applied in Sec. 3.2.1. When that technique is run over the ≈28k domains for which we have consensus human tokenizations (per Sec. 2.1.1), the accuracy is roughly 75%. Given short lengths and the intersection of many natural languages it is easy to see why the task is a difficult one. Sec. 4 will describe how some tokenization methods use contextual data (*e.g.*, the domain content or associated Twitter message) to improve performance. However, such clues are not available for unregistered identifiers. This motivated a search for alternative tokenization strategies.

Arriving at keystroke dynamics, we hypothesize that users leave small pauses in their typing cadence in locations where they believe word boundaries to exist. Fig. 12 shows a deliberately selected example of how such a pattern might manifest. There, 4 different workers have typed the wisegeek SLD, which is tokenized as wise|geek, as a surface-level parsing would suggest. For each of the 4 workers, albeit to varying degrees, the longest intra-character latency lies on the word boundary. We seek to understand how common this is across the typing dataset. We begin with a proof-of-concept experiment that isolates the hypothesis under very favorable conditions. Then, these constraints are relaxed to learn about potential of the method, before discussing how it might be useful in practice.

Sanity checking: In order to test for typing latency at word boundaries, we identify a set of domain typings which are atypically well-suited for the task. The properties of such a SLD/typing are:

- The name should contain no numbers or hyphens, given "row 1" characters independently incur high latency
- The MTurk workers who came to a consensus tokenization must be in 100% agreement, and that human tokenization should have exactly two words
- Algorithmic tokenization methods should produce the same result as the human workers
- The ratio between the first and second fittest algorithmic tokenizations (our earlier `seg_diff` feature) should not be in the 1Q of that distribution
- Eligible typings should contain no backspaces

These criteria leave 10,034 typings for analysis. If one were to consider domains of more than two words, one would need to identify local maxima as possible word boundaries. Our simpler setup allows us to predict the maximum intra-character latency as the sole tokenization point. The average length amongst these 10k identifiers is 10.97 characters. This implies there are 9.97 possible positions, on average, where the word boundary might lie, giving one a 10.03% chance of randomly guessing the correct boundary.

Results show 41.6% of the time the maximum latency is "correct" in corresponding to the boundary, a 4× lift over random. The average length of correct instances is 10.65 characters, similar enough to the 10.97 overall average to conclude we are not just lucky on short names. Further, 63.7% of the time the word boundary falls on the character pair with the highest or 2nd-highest latency. While not definitive, it is clear these latencies offer tokenization clues.

Practical evaluation & application: The prior experiments were unfairly skewed in favor of our hypothesis. Indeed, the cases where the algorithmic tokenization is confident in its result are precisely those where one does *not* need to rely on keystroke dynamic clues.

There are 2,864 typings that meet the criteria above, except that that segmentation fitness ratio falls in the lowest 1Q; the technique being unsure in its tokenization. In these cases, the maximum latency correctly identifies the word boundary 31.5% of the time (3× lift). Another interesting set are the 3,127 typings where the algorithmic tokenization result and the authoritative one provided by workers disagree. Here, 34.0% of the time the boundary is correctly identified, as per agreement with the human segmentation.

Though not accurate enough for standalone tokenization, these results show latency measurements have utility, particularly where algorithmic methods show ambiguity. It is unclear how well this applies to name suggestion, where the creative process of typing/exploring such names may differ from our straightforward experiments. Still, other applications can be imagined. For instance, latency timings could indicate one intended to type a space character when instead two words were accidentally concatenated, perhaps in/on a mobile device or search engine form field.

4 RELATED WORK

To the best of our knowledge, this is the first research to measure the typeability of web identifiers. Although the potential of such measurements has been proposed [28], we are the first to explore the topic empirically. Indeed, rarely does one get to choose *what* will be typed. Instead, the bulk of typeability research concentrates on the efficacy of different keyboard layouts or devices (*e.g.*, mobile, eye tracking) over longer blocks of text.

However, there is an earlier body of work – some of it predating the mainstream Internet – that examines the relationship between speech, handwriting, and typing behaviors. For example, Zesiger *et al.* [31] contribute that "actual words" are typed quicker than "pseudo words", and that word commonality positively correlates with quicker entry speeds, mirroring findings from the handwriting domain. Priva [18] draws a similar parallel between typing times and the speed/ease of speaking a given word, in addition to surveying many studies showing that "typing is sensitive to language based effects." Gentner's work [9] motivates our feature development and latency hypothesis. First, he shows that typing latency is relatively fixed between sequences of characters, but cannot be determined from characters in isolation. Second, he speaks about the role of word boundaries in resetting typing cadence.

Though "keystroke dynamics" broadly refers to any usage of detailed keyboard timing data, more recently is has become almost synonymous with its application as a biometric marker and authentication mechanism. Proposed in [15], the idea is that individuals have typing signatures that differentiate them from most other typists. Although a miscreant may have stolen your password, they are unlikely to type it in the same manner as you would, raising a security flag. Banerjee and Woodard [4] survey progress in this space, with [12] standardizing a typing corpus and taking a comparative approach. Our work is distinct in that it characterizes the behavior of the entire population of typists rather than trying to identify distinctions between them. As such, our work is similar to [6] which uses keystroke dynamics to develop classifiers for 15 different emotional states. Though they were able to capture native typing behaviors using keylogging, their study recruited just 12 participants, highlighting the challenges of such collections.

This work has utilized existing statistical tokenization algorithms and contributed a novel non-statistical method. Regarding the former, our preference has been the straightforward approach of [13]. Other methods exist, including those espousing multiple dictionary corpora [25], sequential character streams [2], and contextual information from webpage structure [30]. With these, domains and hashtags are the primary strings of interest [20, 25]. Our corpus of 28k crowdsourced domain tokenizations could prove useful to this community, as the 3k expert-sourced segmentations of Srinivasan *et al.* [25] are the only comparable data of which we are aware.

Finally, even our preliminary attempts at predicting typos and where they might occur faltered. While excellent economic [16, 27] and longitudinal [1] studies on typosquatting have been conducted, they answer an easier question: "given a popular domain X and a lexically similar domain Y, is Y typosquatting?". Moore and Edelman [16] introduce "fat finger distance", a metric capturing that mis-struck keys tend to be spatially adjacent to the intended characters. Szurdi *et al.* [27] leverage WHOIS, DNS, Alexa rankings, and HTML content atop lexical clues in making typosquatting determinations. While both well capture the current landscape, we emphasize there are no known techniques to generate the most common mis-typings of a provided string.

5 CONCLUSIONS

The web identifiers – such as domains, hashtags, and usernames – that label our online navigation and communication all tend to share similar naming properties. Particularly in mature namespaces, the name selection process may be complicated by both technical and availability constraints. Backed by the empirical data from this work, we believe that the speed and correctness with which end users can type a name is an important property for consideration. From crowdsourced measurements we collected 51k typing times, of 28k identifiers, via a distributed workforce of 1.4k participants. Domain names were our medium for exploring identifier typeability and keystroke dynamics.

We found that a surprising amount of information can be derived from these short character sequences. Regarding name selection, we learned the shortest names are not necessarily the most typeable ones. Typing times increase linearly as a function of name growth, but it is most important that a name be composed of easily parseable keywords. Familiar character sequences tend to be most quickly typed, a property that also holds for the TLD extensions of domain names. Though our models were only moderately effective at predicting precise typing times, these simple properties proved most indicative. A continued exploration of naming keystroke dynamics led to the finding that high intra-character latencies are often indicative of word boundaries; an important tokenization clue given that many naming systems prohibit traditional delimiters.

Future work remains to understand if mobile typing behaviors mirror their desktop counterparts, and how functionalities such as auto-complete affect identifier usage and entry. However, we believe our measurements herein have applications ranging from simple advice for name-seeking individuals, to the algorithmic foundations for tools implementable by those who distribute and suggest identifiers.

REFERENCES

[1] Pieter Agten, Wouter Joosen, Frank Piessens, and Nick Nikiforakis. 2015. Seven Months' Worth of Mistakes: A Longitudinal Study of Typosquatting Abuse. In *NDSS '15: Proceedings of the ISOC Network and Distributed System Security Symposium.*

[2] Jerry R. Van Aken. 2011. A Statistical Learning Algorithm for Word Segmentation. *arXiv/CoRR* abs/1105.6162 (2011).

[3] Amazon Mechanical Turk Command Line Tools. 2016. https://requester.mturk.com/developer/tools/clt. (2016).

[4] Salil P. Banerjee and Damon L. Woodard. 2012. Biometric Authentication and Identification using Keystroke Dynamics: A Survey. *Journal of Pattern Recognition Research* 7, 1 (2012).

[5] Michael Capewell. 2005. Keyboard Comparison Applet. http://www.michaelcapewell.com/projects/keyboard/compare_applet.htm. (2005).

[6] Clayton Epp, Michael Lippold, and Regan L. Mandryk. 2011. Identifying Emotional States using Keystroke Dynamics. In *CHI '11: Proceedings of the 29th SIGCHI Conference on Human Factors in Computing Systems.*

[7] Leah Findlater, Jacob Wobbrock, and Daniel Wigdor. 2011. Typing on Flat Glass: Examining Ten-finger Expert Typing Patterns on Touch Surfaces. In *SIGCHI '11: Conf. on Human Factors in Comp. Systems.*

[8] Eibe Frank, Mark A. Hall, and Ian H. Witten. 2016. *Data Mining: Practical Machine Learning Tools and Techniques* (4th ed.). Morgan Kaufmann, Chapter The WEKA Workbench.

[9] Donald R. Gentner. 1982. Evidence Against a Central Control Model of Timing in Typing. *Journal of Experimental Psychology: Human Perception and Performance* 8, 6 (1982).

[10] Internet Corporation for Assigned Names and Numbers. 2016. Global Registrant Survey. https://newgtlds.icann.org/en/reviews/cct/global-registrant-survey-15sep16-en.pdf. (2016).

[11] Panagiotis G. Ipeirotis. 2010. Analyzing the Amazon Mechanical Turk Marketplace. *XRDS* 17, 2 (December 2010).

[12] Kevin S. Killourhy and Roy A. Maxion. 2009. Comparing Anamoly-detection Algorithms for Keystroke Dynamics. In *DSN '09: Proc. of the 39th IEEE/IFIP Intl. Conference on Dependable Systems & Networks.*

[13] Jeremy Kun. 2012. Word Segmentation, or Makingsenseofthis. https://jeremykun.com/2012/01/15/word-segmentation/. (2012).

[14] Chris Matyszczyk. 2013. Confusing Twitter Hashtag Leaves Cher Fans in Mourning. https://www.cnet.com/news/confusing-twitter-hashtag-leaves-cher-fans-in-mourning/. (2013).

[15] Fabian Monrose and Aviel Rubin. 1997. Authentication via Keystroke Dynamics. In *CCS '97: Proc. of the Conf. on Comp. and Comm. Security.*

[16] Tyler Moore and Benjamin Edelman. 2010. Measuring the Perpetrators and Funders of Typosquatting. In *FC '10: Proc. of the 14th International Conference on Financial Cryptography and Data Security.*

[17] Peter Norvig. 2009. *Beautiful Data: The Stories Behind Elegant Data Solutions.* O'Reilly Media, Chapter Natural Language Corpus Data.

[18] Uriel Priva. 2010. Constructing Typing-Time Corpora: A New Way to Answer Old Questions. In *CogSci '10: Proceedings of the 32nd Annual Meetings of the Cognitive Science Society.*

[19] Lisa P. Ramsey. 2010. Brandjacking on Social Networks: Trademark Infringement by Impersonation of Markholders. *Buffalo Law R.* (2010).

[20] Jack Reuter, Jhonata Pereira-Martins, and Jugal Kalita. 2016. Segmenting Twitter Hashtags. *Intl. J. on Natural Lang. Computing* 5, 4 (2016).

[21] Marko Robnik-Sikonja and Igor Kononenko. 1997. An Adaptation of Relief for Attribute Estimation in Regression. In *ICML '97: Proc. of the 14th International Conference on Machine Learning.*

[22] Andrea Rowland. 2015. 10 Tips for Choosing the Perfect Domain Name. https://www.godaddy.com/garage/smallbusiness/launch/10-tips-for-choosing-the-perfect-domain-name/. (2015).

[23] Shirish Shevade, S Sathiya Keerthi, Chiranjib Bhattacharyya, and Karaturi Radha Krishna Murthy. 2000. Improvements to the SMO algorithm for SVM regression. *IEEE Transac. on Neural Networks* 11, 5 (2000).

[24] SimpleCaptcha. 2011. http://simplecaptcha.sourceforge.net/. (2011).

[25] Sriram Srinivasan, Sourangshu Bhattacharya, and Rudrasis Chakraborty. 2012. Segmenting Web-domains and Hashtags Using Length Specific Models. In *CIKM '12: Proc. of the 21st ACM International Conference on Information and Knowledge Management.*

[26] New gTLD Statistics. 2017. https://ntldstats.com/. (2017).

[27] Janos Szurdi, Balazs Kocso, Gabor Cseh, Johnathan Spring, Mark Felegyhazi, and Chis Kanich. 2014. The Long Taile of Typosquatting Domain Names. In *SEC '14: Proc. of the 23rd UNIX Security Sym.*

[28] Matthew Thomas and Jasenko Ibrahimbegovic. 2015. Evaluating Typeability of Domain Names. (2015). US Patent 9,195,316.

[29] Verisign, Inc. 2016. The Domain Name Industry Brief. https://www.verisign.com/assets/domain-name-report-july2016.pdf. (2016).

[30] Kuansan Wang, Christopher Thrasher, and Bo-June Paul Hsu. 2011. Web Scale NLP: A Case Study on URL Word Breaking. In *WWW '11: Proc. of the 20th International Conference on World Wide Web.*

[31] Pascal Zesiger, Jean-Pierre Orliaguetand Louis-Jean Boe, and Pierre Mounou. 1994. *Advances in Handwriting and Drawing: A Multidisciplinary Approach.* Europia, Chapter The Influence of Syllabic Structure in Handwriting and Typing Production.

What's Happening and What Happened: Searching the Social Web

Omar Alonso, Vasileios Kandylas, Serge-Eric Tremblay, Jake M. Hofman, Siddhartha Sen
Microsoft
omalonso,vakandyl,sergetr,jmh,sidsen@microsoft.com

ABSTRACT

Every day millions of users share links and post comments on different social networks. At scale, this behavior can be very useful for building a new type of search engine that exploits relevant links and their associated metadata in a temporal fashion. Our goal is to find links that are relevant on social networks as a mechanism to discover what people are talking about at a given point in time and make such information searchable and persistent. In other words, a continually updated archive of relevant content that is currently being shared, beyond the obvious trending news of the day. The techniques we use surface new and interesting content by mining social network posts that contain links, constructing diffusion trees from those links, and extracting related entities and other associated metadata. By looking at the size of the trees and their structure in combination with the conversation around each link and related topics, we designed and implemented a search engine that provides relevant fresh content and features a "wayback machine". We demonstrate the effectiveness of our approach by processing a dataset comprising millions of English language tweets generated over a one year period. Finally, we perform an offline evaluation of our techniques and conduct a use case study using an available data set of fake and real news links.

1 INTRODUCTION

With more than 400 million tweets being generated every day, Twitter has fast grown into one of the largest sources of real time information on the Internet. People tweet about a range of topics varying from personal thoughts to their opinion about ongoing events. The ease with which this information can be published and shared has been one of the primary reasons for the success of such microblogging services. On the flip side, the low barrier for information generation has led to the proliferation of uninteresting content and difficulty in finding relevant information. A lot of the generated data is either noise, duplicates, or information which is of low value for a global audience. In addition, the scale of this data makes it hard to not only index, aggregate and search, but also to efficiently mine it to extract interesting and meaningful insights.

Searching for relevant content in social networks is not a solved problem. The temporal signal is important for real-time search [7] and for re-finding posts [16] but not really exploited as a feature. Twitter and Facebook offer trending features that show a term or phrase that represents a very high activity due to the increased rate of people talking about the topic. By selecting a particular trend, relevant posts are returned, ranked by some engagement metric like number of likes, shares per link, retweets, or similar. Trending features are limited to extremely popular items and fail to surface other relevant, but perhaps less globally popular, content. Also, it is not possible to see what was trending in the past.

Tweets can contain links shared by other users in the form of re-tweets or favorites (likes) producing a cascading effect. That is, collaborative content creation and sharing by users in the platform. We can think of this sharing activity as large-scale human computation that aggregates and filters high-quality information. How can we take advantage of these fresh new links and create a new type of search engine? In contrast to current web search engines that are based on link citation for ranking websites, we propose a different approach that relies on a combination of temporal and sharing behavior making relevant information always fresh, while at the same time providing "wayback machine" functionality.

We present two use case scenarios that involve searching for now and then: 1) a user searches for the latest information on a topic and 2) a user searches for what was said in the past for a given topic. The first scenario may look similar to a popular news or trending scenario. This differs from traditional news in that the content is selected by aggregate user behavior instead of editors and includes more than just the most popular content at any given time. Regarding the second scenario, searching in the past is now limited to using re-finding techniques [16], trying the Internet Archive's wayback machine, or examining the notes and references of a Wikipedia page. We archive what the crowd noted as relevant at a particular point in time and make it easily accessible.

The research questions are: (R1) what are the main characteristics of a search engine that focuses on the social web? and (R2) how feasible would be to search on the past using our techniques?

Our work requires the design and implementation of a working system that indexes Twitter data over a period of time. The engineering effort is driven by our research on a number of specific components. That is, identification of high quality links based on a combination of viral and popular metrics—the quality and appeal of these links has been justified by prior work (see below); the extraction of useful metadata from links and topics; the use of trusted users as an endorsement signal; and the ability to create temporal snapshots that are later used for searching in the past. We also provide a user interface based on social cards (links, people, pivots) as an alternative to the common top-10 links provided by traditional search engines.

WebSci'17, June 25-28, 2017, Troy, NY, USA.

978-1-4503-4896-6/17/06...$15.00
DOI: http://dx.doi.org/10.1145/3091478.3091484

2 RELATED WORK

There is a large body of work that looks at the problem of identifying currently popular content [4, 22]. While the details vary across implementations, the basic idea behind all of this work is to look for items that are experiencing a large and sudden increase in popularity—likes, clicks, retweets, etc.—over a relatively short period of time. This tends to surface the most extremely popular content in any given time window, often revealing celebrity stories, top-line news stories featured across major media outlets, or tweets from popular, real-world events [5]. And while such stories are surely of interest to many users, at the same time, popularity-based trending algorithms miss a good deal of interesting and relevant content.

The work we present here leverages past results in [12] to identify trending content based not just on how popular it is, but by how it spreads throughout the population of a social network. In other words, we seek to identify content that looks "viral" based on how it is being shared. Interestingly, as shown in [12], the most viral content at any given time is often distinct from the most popular content being shared online. As we demonstrate here by identifying and exposing viral stories in near real-time, virality-based rankings tend to surface items that are more niche in nature while still of interest to a large audience.

It is worth noting that since our metric for virality is so different from popularity, even complex analytics or machine learning pipelines based on the latter will tend to yield different stories. This is because the "reward signal" [15] that drives these pipelines is fundamentally different. Algorithms for ranking web pages such as PageRank and HITS are based on the (slowly-varying) linkage of pages on the web. Our research ignores the "web graph" completely, looking instead at how links are shared *over time* through a *social network*. Page-ranking algorithms typically do not incorporate social effects, nor do they vary at the timescales of social sharing.

Augmenting search results with social data, known as social annotations, has been an area of recent product and research work by Google, Microsoft and Yahoo as part of their search engines [19], [18], [10], [14]. It is unclear how effective social annotation is for the social web. Other relevant research includes extracting links from tweets for discovering new information [20], presenting distinct search results compared to Google and Bing [1], and for identifying planned social events [21]. Twitter's Earlybird search engine architecture is presented in [7] but does not expand more on how Twitter uses link sharing information for search.

There is new research that taps into the different motivations and dynamics for link sharing content in social networks. From a non-information retrieval perspective, the study of social buttons and other counters as a metric for user engagement has been coined as the 'Like economy' by [11]. A separate study of the value of tweets as anchor text is presented in [17]. A large analysis on URL sharing behavior on Twitter is described in [8]. Looking at user activity as a human computation image classification task in Pinterest is described in [23].

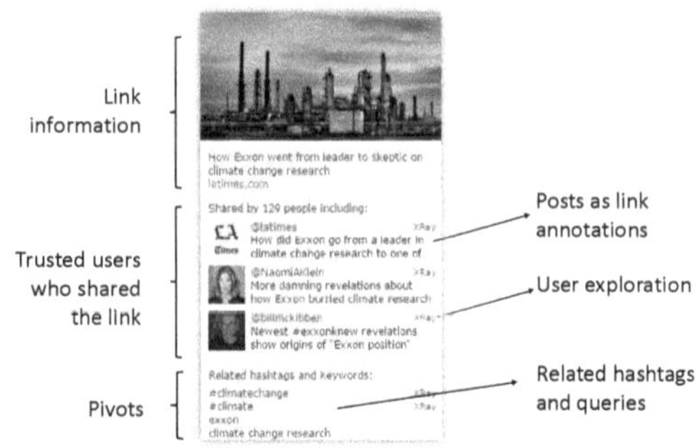

Figure 1: A social card contains three components: link information (e.g., image, title, etc.), a sample of trusted users who have share the link, and a number of pivots.

3 SYSTEM OVERVIEW & PRELIMINARIES

In contrast to traditional web search engines that show the top-10 most relevant links along with query-biased snippets, our system presents search results as social cards (Figure 1). A social card contains an image associated with a link, a page title and short description, the name(s) of high-profile users who have shared the link along with their related posts, "pivots", and the ability to examine user accounts in more detail. Pivots are a subset of the link annotations that allow users to query by related topics or hashtags. We can think of social cards as a variation of social annotations in traditional search engines. However, instead of augmenting links in the search engine result page, the results are more visual and the annotations more prominent, providing context. Related hashtags and queries are selected from a ranked list as explained later.

The functionality works as follows. In the search box, the user can type a query and see a list of social cards that are temporally aware as presented in Figure 2, ranked according to our link relevance technique. By clicking on the calendar and selecting a date, the user can search (or browse) to see what was relevant on that day, thus providing a archival functionality.

Before describing the main techniques, we introduce the following terminology. An *adopter* is a Twitter user who tweeted about a link. A *friend* is someone the Twitter user follows. A *diffusion tree* describes how a link has spread among a set of adopters from one friend to the next. The nodes are the adopters; an edge from user U to user V indicates that V learned about the link from U. A *forest* is the set of all trees for a given link and is used to compute the link popularity and virality as explained below.

4 BACK-END PIPELINE

This section contains a detailed description of our methodology and the back-end pipeline that we use to detect and index relevant links. We discuss the challenges that we faced especially in scaling this pipeline to work on large datasets and provide insights into our design choices. The processing pipeline includes the following basic steps, which are described in detail in the subsequent sections:

(1) Content selection: select tweets that contain links and satisfy simple user, content and time range criteria.

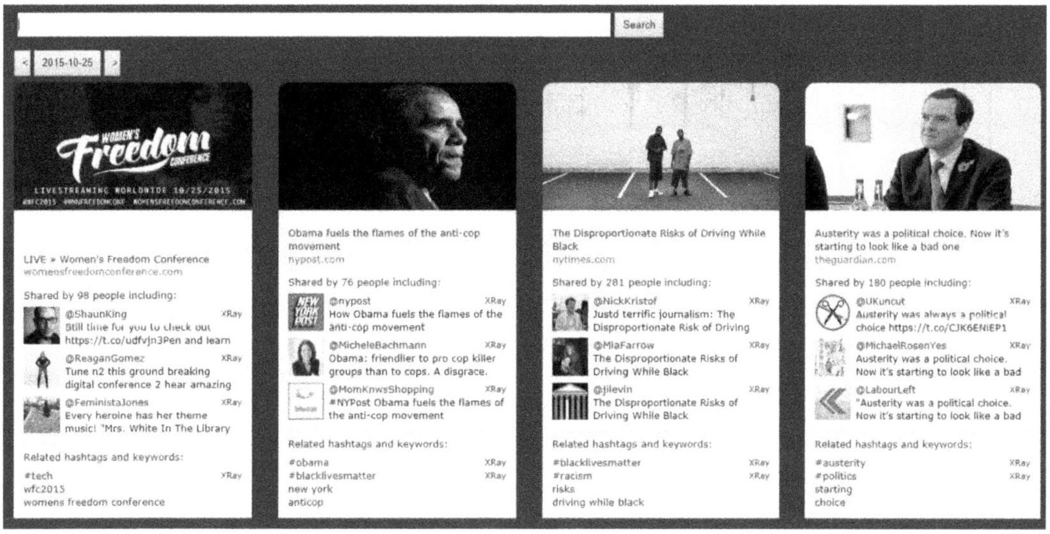

Figure 2: An example of social cards ranked by virality score. Note that user's posts augment the link by providing more context and/or opinions. Using the calendar button on the top left, it is also possible to go back in time and see links that were viral in the past.

(2) User selection: extract and normalize links and select those that have been shared by a minimum number of trusted users.
(3) Link selection: clean-up links, compute link virality and popularity, cluster similar links.
(4) Final cut: apply heuristic criteria to select good quality links.
(5) Annotations: generate metadata for the selected links from the associated tweets.
(6) Indexing and presentation.

4.1 Tweet Selection

As a first step, we select all the tweets that were posted in a chosen time range, including retweets. We have experimented with various ranges from one hour to one month, but for the rest of this paper we use a one day time period. For the tweets in the time range, we keep only those that contain links.

Other simple filters are applied at this stage so that only tweets of good quality are used and spam content is removed. The filtering is done by selecting only tweets whose language is detected as English and have a minimum computed quality score [3].

4.2 Link Pre-Processing and User Filtering

Once an initial set of tweets is selected, the links are extracted and normalized using a set of domain-specific rules to avoid spurious duplicates. For example, query parameters are removed that might make two links appear different when in fact they refer to the same story. Not all query parameters can be removed: the video ID in YouTube links, for example, is critical for distinguishing content. This stage also uses the MinHash clustering algorithm to identify near-duplicate documents at scale [6]. The algorithm works by computing a summary sketch of the content linked to by each URL, specifically the minimum value of a hash function applied to each token on the page. Several of these summary sketches are computed using different hash functions and are combined to form a "shingle print" for the page. As shown in [6], the probability that two pages have the same summary sketch is proportional to the fraction of overlap in their content, and so we can use the shingle print as an identifier for clusters of content later in the pipeline.

Within the time period considered, only one tweet per adopter per link is used; this ensures that the diffusion trees of a link that will be computed later will span disjoint subsets of Twitter users. Associated link information is also extracted from the available metadata (e.g., Twitter cards, Open Graph metadata, etc.), such as the link title, description, image and type. Links are also categorized with an existing system into Open Directory-like categories.

The main filtering that happens in this stage is user-based. First, only links from adopters who have a minimum number of followers are selected. A second filter selects only those links that have been shared by a minimum number of "trusted users". This minimum number depends on the time period under consideration; for a one-day interval, we require at least one trusted user among the set of adopters.

The concept of "trusted users" refers to users who reliably tweet high-quality content and share relevant links [13]. Trusted users are identified by using Twitter's verified users (a manually selected set of users that has been verified by Twitter staff) as a seed set which is expanded by crawling activity on the social network. Starting with the verified users, we detect other users who have had a conversation with them, initiated by the verified user. These users then become trusted and belong to the first "ring" of trusted users.

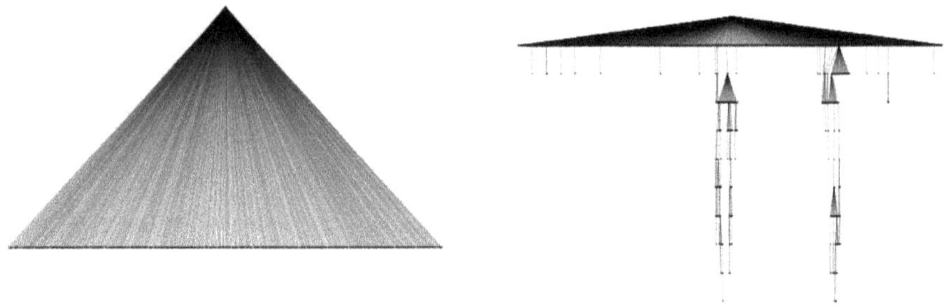

Figure 3: Two diffusion trees for two different links. Each node depicts an account and edges indicate that the child account adopted from its parent. The tree on the left shows "broadcast" diffusion where all adoptions are straight from the source, whereas the tree on the right shows multi-generational diffusion typical of viral content.

This process is repeated several times, gradually increasing the set of trusted users from the thousands of verified to tens of millions of trusted users. This filtering of users is necessary because of the high numbers of fake and spam accounts on Twitter. Because the set of trusted users is in the order of tens of millions, the filtering does not affect the links that are selected later significantly, since a viral link is very likely to have been shared by at least one trusted user. The main result of this filtering is that it limits the influence of fake or spam accounts in the construction of diffusion trees, as explained in the next section.

4.3 Link Selection

This stage focuses on the selection of the links that will be shown in the system. Link selection consists of finding links that are either popular or viral.

To select links we use an algorithm developed by Goel et al. [12]. The algorithm constructs a forest of diffusion trees for each link and computes metrics on this forest to determine the popularity and virality of the links. The algorithm works as follows:

- Aggregate tweets by link.
- For each adopter of a link, crawl his/her friend list to determine the most likely person he/she heard it from. Following Goel et al. [12], we assume this is the friend who most recently tweeted the link unless explicit retweet information is provided. (Other selection rules are possible, e.g. using frequency of communication within a recent time window, but we have yet to explore these alternatives.)
- Use the above to construct the diffusion trees for the link.
- Characterize the size of the trees—a measure of popularity—and the structure of the trees—a measure of virality. Currently, we use the average pairwise distance between nodes of the tree as a measure of virality and the number of nodes as a measure of popularity.

The forest constructed for each link provides a chronological and visual depiction of the diffusion of the story through the Twitter network. Figure 3 shows two example trees for two different links computed by our system, where each node represents an account on Twitter that has posted that link and an edge indicates that the child node adopted from its parent, either through a retweet or repost. The top-most node is the root of the tree, having introduced the story without any of its friends previously doing so. Each generation adopted after its parents, although time is not explicitly shown in the visualization. Both of these trees have approximately the same popularity in that they contain an almost equal number of nodes, but the structure of the two trees differs drastically. In particular, the tree on the left is characteristic of "broadcast" diffusion where a popular outlet with a large direct audience (e.g., the New York Times or CNN) posts content that is adopted by many of its followers but mostly ceases to spread further. The tree on the right, in contrast, depicts "viral" diffusion where the story is continually shared by small audiences over many generations.

In theory there are a number of metrics that can quantify the difference between such diffusion processes. As mentioned above, here we use the Weiner Index proposed by [12], which is simply the average pairwise distance between nodes in the diffusion tree:

$$v(T) = \frac{1}{n(n-1)} \sum_{i=1}^{n} \sum_{\substack{j=1 \\ j \neq i}}^{n} d_{ij}, \tag{1}$$

where d_{ij} indicates the length of the shortest path between nodes i and j. A low score of approximately 2 on this index represents a broadcast event, whereas a higher score represents more viral events.

4.3.1 Crawling the Twitter graph. Constructing the diffusion trees requires knowing the user from whom each adopter heard about a link. We query the Twitter API to obtain the friend list of each adopter, from which we select its parent in the tree (if one exists). Since Twitter imposes a rate limit on their API, issuing these queries on-demand (during the viral link computation) is prohibitively expensive, and thus we run a crawl in the background. The crawl prioritizes both trusted users as well as users with high tweet activity in the preceding month. During viral link detection, queries for the friend list simply return the latest results of the crawl.

4.3.2 Similar link clustering. After the diffusion trees have been computed, similar links are clustered using the link shingle prints computed in a previous stage. Other combinations of features are incorporated, such as a normalized link URL and link title similarity.

ID	Tweet
1	At least 3 dead, 7 injured in #Lafayette shooting, police say gunman 58-year-old 'lone white male' http://t.co/xUcLzsuKgq
2	58-yr-old 'lone white male' killed 2 people & wounded 9 during showing of 'Trainwreck' before turning gun on himself http://t.co/ecBQx9Rbye"
3	Mysterious drifter identified as Louisiana movie theater gunman http://t.co/VtbVW1eZ3J via #Foxnews
4	Police say 'drifter' killed 2, injured 9 in Lafayette, La. movie theater shooting http://t.co/l3DnganpmO http://t.co/YLhj2UP31r

Table 1: The social signature {`movie theater, Lafayette, gunman opens fire`} for the tweets presented in this example.

All normalized links in the same cluster with the same shingle print are deemed to refer to the same story, and so their diffusion trees are merged. Of the links that remain, only those with a minimum number of adopters (across the forest of all trees) are considered for inclusion, and their popularity and virality metrics are computed.

4.3.3 Link selection. At this point the links have already been pre-filtered and the virality and popularity scores have been computed. As found in [12], there is a surprisingly low correlation between popularity and virality, and so we choose links based on both measures. We select popular links that are above a certain threshold, dependent on the time period being used. Separately thresholding by a minimum virality score allows us to identify interesting content that has spread from one person to the next, even if it is not the most popular content being passed around.

Content diversity is often a key requirement of internal customers of our system, and simply presenting the overall most viral (or most popular) links does not guarantee a diverse set of stories. We have found, in general, that the viral structure of stories varies by topic, and thus we leverage the link categories provided during pre-processing to group links by category and select the most viral and popular links across categories.

4.4 Final Filtering

A final filtering stage ensures that the data shown to the user are not only of sufficient quality but are also well-presented to users. To this end we apply a set of empirically derived criteria:

- Links that match their domain are discarded, as these lead to the domain homepage and not to a specific document. Even though they may be popular, such links are not very useful.
- Tweets that are missing important metadata for the shared link (e.g. missing title) are also removed. These tweets are useful when computing the virality and popularity scores of the link, but they are not appropriate for display
- The language of the linked document is detected and non-English links are removed. This could have occurred at an earlier stage, but it is computationally cheaper to reduce the number of links in the previous stages, before scraping and performing language detection for the target page.

The output of this stage is the final set of links used in the system.

4.5 Metadata Generation and Link Annotation

Before any links can be shown to the user, they must be annotated with related information. This information consists of:

- The link title, description and image.
- Selected tweets that mention the link. These are selected after ranking the users by trusted ring number and number of followers. They are also filtered to remove retweets, @user responses, or tweets that contain profanity.
- Hashtags associated with the link, which can be used for re-querying for other links related to the hashtag.
- N-grams associated with the link, computed based on the social signature technique described as follows. Once the high quality links have been identified, we extract the chatter around them in the form of n-grams using a statistical model that identifies salient terms [2]. For computing the signatures, we use the text of the tweets that share the link (after clean-up). Table 1 shows four tweets that link to the same article and the social signature for that link. These can also be used for re-querying for other links related to the n-gram.

4.6 Indexing and Presentation

In the final stage we prepare the data for presentation. The system supports two types of use: (1) show the top viral or top popular links for a given date (overall or per category) as a home page, and (2) allow searching by hashtag or n-gram for relevant viral or popular links.

For the first use case we select the highest quality links relevant to the user's query. We choose links with titles, descriptions and good images (not broken or boilerplate images like the logo of the news site). We also select links that are documents (e.g. no links that are photos, vines, etc.), not redirects, and have "good" file path structure (e.g. file system path depth not too long or too short etc.).

For the second use case we do not apply any of these filters because we assume that a user conducting a search is be looking for an overly complete set of results. In both cases we rank the presented set of links by virality or popularity according to the user's choice. More advanced ranking functions that interleave viral and popular links can also be used.

To support search, we find all the hashtags and n-grams that are mentioned with a link and also the n-grams from the link's social signatures. The top hashtags and n-grams are shown underneath each link as part of the result card and clicking on them conducts a search for related links. We also build an index of links to support searching for any hashtag or n-gram that the user enters in the query box.

5 SYSTEM IMPLEMENTATION

Having presented the logic underlying our pipeline, in this section we provide details of the system that executes it. A distributed cluster is well suited for processing the firehose of tweets and selecting those that match the filtering criteria. We have used the SCOPE [9] language to implement the pipeline. Implementing the viral link detection as a SCOPE job however requires a computationally expensive three-way join between three relations: (adopter, link), (adopter, friend), and (friend, link), in addition to the link processing described above. Therefore, in order to continuously detect viral links over a sliding time window, we need to reuse as much of the computation as possible between runs. We achieve this by decoupling both the link processing and the Twitter graph crawl from the construction of the diffusion trees. Link processing greatly reduces the number of tweets to consider and produces a dataset that can be repeatedly processed by the tree construction algorithm over different (overlapping) time windows. Running the graph crawl in the background avoids the rate-limited, synchronous calls to the Twitter API in the middle of tree construction. Together, this allows us to run the viral link detection every hour over a trailing 24-hour window.

An unfortunate consequence of rate-limited access to the Twitter API is that we cannot pinpoint our view of the Twitter graph to a narrow time interval. Crawling the entire graph takes months, and our current prioritization of users to crawl is not influenced by the tree construction process. Doing the latter is possible, but it would more than double the tree construction time because we first need to determine which trees are viral before we know which user links to refresh, which in turn requires us to reconstruct the trees. Such on-demand refreshing of user links is more viable during real-time construction of the viral trees (discussed below). In general, although we rely on the Twitter firehose, our current processing is not real-time: we wait for a given hour's data to stabilize, e.g. 30 minutes after the hour ends, before including it in a query. This means that our results can be replicated to some degree by relying on the publicly-accessible Twitter Search and Streaming APIs (https://dev.twitter.com/docs). The key difference is that the firehose gives us access to all the Twitter data, not just a sample of the data or the most recent data matching a search criteria.

Providing real-time detection of viral links is the subject of ongoing and future work. In particular, we have built a pipeline that consumes the Twitter firehose directly and incrementally constructs the diffusion trees of each link. This pipeline supports a sliding window similar to that of the SCOPE job, but the window is advanced at a much finer granularity: ancestors of the tree are constantly being phased out while new descendants are being added. The addition of a potential descendant creates an opportunity to refresh the corresponding user's friend list; whether such API calls can be managed at scale remains to be seen. Moreover, incremental processing restricts the amount of link filtering and pre-processing that can be done a priori, thus imposing different resource requirements and scalability challenges outside the scope of this paper.

6 RESULTS AND EVALUATION

Due to confidentiality we cannot disclose the user engagement, query log, or behavioral data we used in evaluating our system. That said, the core of our research is on techniques for manipulating large data sets efficiently and not so much on the end-user perspective so, instead, we present evaluation results as follows. We first report the daily numbers that our system process in every stage of the data processing pipeline. This gives the reader an idea of the computation that is required to run the system on a daily basis and the impact of each step. We then show an offline relevance evaluation task using a standard crowdsourcing approach. For the "wayback machine" feature, we use the US Elections 2016 event as comparison against a well-documented Wikipedia page. Finally, we demonstrate how our techniques help filter fake links using an available data set.

Phase	Tweets	Links	Users	Hashtags	Ngrams
Content selection	227M	54M	25M	-	-
User selection	90M	18M	17M	-	-
Link selection	-	15K	-	-	-
Final cut	-	1K	-	9K	3K

Table 2: Daily numbers produced by the four stages of the data processing pipeline. The "-" indicates that the value is computed at a later stage or because the value is not used in a later stage.

Please help us evaluate the relevance of an article (or link) and associated information (e.g., image, hashtags, and users). You'll be given a recent article that has been shared by a user in a social network like Twitter along with its related hashtag. Your task is to assess the quality of each item in the 4 question below.

Article: [Image] [Link]
Hashtag: "#thehashtag"
Shared by [User]

Q1. Do you think this article would be interesting to at least some users?
[] Yes [] Somewhat [] No
Q2. Do you think the image thumbnail is relevant to the article?
[] Yes [] Somewhat [] No [] Other (broken, too small, low quality)
Q3. Do you think the related hashtag is informative about the article?
[] Yes [] Somewhat [] No
Q4. Do you think the article is shared by a credible user?
[] Yes [] Somewhat [] No

Figure 4: Offline task relevance evaluation template.

6.1 Daily Numbers

For the 24-hour window of tweets that we describe in this paper and after all the filtering we apply, we produce a data set per day consisting of approximately 1,000 links. Table 2 shows more details, including the output of each stage. Some values are missing, either because that value is computed at a later stage (e.g. number of hashtags at the beginning), or because the value is not used in a later stage (e.g. number of tweets in the final stage).

Question	Yes	Somewhat	No
Q1	99%	1%	0%
Q2	80%	10%	8%
Q3	64%	22%	14%
Q4	70%	16%	14%

Table 3: Offline relevance evaluation results.

6.2 Offline Evaluation

We conducted an offline evaluation using an internal crowdsourcing tool[1] for collecting labels. The data set consisted of 100 items selected at random and each item was assessed by 5 human judges with the majority vote treated as final label. Results are presented in Table 3 and the evaluation template is presented in Figure 4. The link relevance results confirm that the link selection works well and the user endorsement numbers are also reliable. The identification of the pivots (i.e., related topics or hashtags) on the other hand is an area that needs improvement. For example, some of the pivots are a bit too generic (e.g., #news) or too brand specific (i.e., #cnn) and they do not seem to provide enough value to the user.

Evaluation results	
R@25	82%
R@25 (filtered)	92%
P@25	86%
R@50	93%
P@50	92%

Table 4: Evaluation metrics for the US Elections. R@25 indicates recall considering the top-25 hashtags comparing to the Wikipedia page. Similarly, P@50 indicates precision considering the top-50 hashtags.

6.3 Wayback Machine

As described earlier, our system contains a wayback machine feature that allows users to go back in time to search and discover. To evaluate the accuracy of this functionality, we extract the top-25 hashtags per day for 2016 (9K in total) and manually annotate the ones that refer to the US elections forming a list of political events in reverse chronological order. We then compare against the Wikipedia US election timeline page that contains an entry per event, used as baseline, and compute precision and recall:

$$\text{Precision (P)} = \frac{\#(\text{relevant entries retrieved})}{\#(\text{retrieved entries})}$$

$$\text{Recall (R)} = \frac{\#(\text{relevant entries retrieved})}{\#(\text{relevant entries})}$$

Overall, our system returns 82% of the entries compared to the baseline. However, if we discount third party events (e.g., Libertarian presidential debate, Libertarian National Convention, Green National Convention, etc.), the recall increases to 92%. If we increase coverage by taking the top-50 hashtags for 2016 (18K in total), the recall is 93%, including the previously discarded third party events. For precision, we use the top-50 hashtags and measure if any of those hashtags match the title of the Wikipedia page entry for the same specific time slot. As example, for 2/18/2016, more than one relevant hashtag are present in top-50 (e.g., SCPrimary, GOPTownHall, DemTownHall) related to the event ("Republican town halls are held in Greenville, South Carolina and Columbia, South Carolina"). The reported precision is 92%. and is computed as the ratio of matched entries over the retrieved entries from Wikipedia page (the ground truth). Table 4 shows a summary of the recall metrics. Due to space constraints, Table 5 presents a condensed version of the US elections timeline along with thc top ranked political hashtag for the same date. In summary, the social tagging in aggregate works pretty well for enumerating the main topics for a given day, thus creating a representative crowd-based temporal annotation.

The wayback machine feature allows the user to zoom into a particular day by searching or browsing. Figure 5 shows an example for the day of the US Elections (November 8) and the day after (November 9). For Election day, the results are mostly about people voting and potential irregularities. The hashtags for that day describe the magnitude of the event with references to the main candidates by name or slogan. The day after the election shows a different picture: celebrities announcing moving to Canada (there is also an associated hashtag) and reactions to the new president. Hashtags like #notmypresident and #calexit (California exit from the US) echo the sentiment from a segment of the population after the election results.

6.4 Fake News Case Study

The proliferation of fake news on social networks has been the technology story of the 2016 US elections. A recent analysis by BuzzFeed[2] examined the engagement on Facebook of top fake and real election news stories from 19 major news outlets. The analysis found that the top fake election news stories generated more total engagement than the top election stories. We used the same set of top fake and top real news to study how our system handled this content. Our study consisted of feeding this data set through our data processing pipeline and reporting how and where each of the many steps contributed in filtering out the fake stories. Even though the dataset from BuzzFeed is limited, it can still indicate to what extent our system is susceptible to fake news.

The set of links under consideration was divided in 3 time buckets (February to April, May to July, and August to Election day). Each bucket has 20 fake and 20 real labeled news articles. Whereas the BuzzFeed study was done on links shared, commented or liked on Facebook, our pipeline operates on links shared on Twitter, so there are differences in engagement. Overall, we found that the total number of shares of the real links was higher than the fake links, with fake link shares exhibiting a big increase in the time bucket just before the election (Figure 6). This differs from the BuzzFeed findings, where the engagement of the fake was higher than the real for the August-Election bucket and where the engagement for the real stories was actually decreasing with time.

[1]http://research.microsoft.com/en-us/um/redmond/events/fs2012/presentations/rajesh_patel.pdf

[2]https://www.buzzfeed.com/craigsilverman/viral-fake-election-news-outperformed-real-news-on-facebook

Date	Hashtag	Entry slot from Wikipedia page
1/14	#GOPDebate	Sixth Republican debate is held in North Charleston, South Carolina
1/17	#DemDebate	Fourth Democratic debate is held in Charleston, South Carolina
1/25	#DemTownHall	A Democratic forum, a Town Hall event, is held in Des Moines, Iowa
1/28	#GOPDebate	Seventh Republican debate is held in Des Moines, Iowa
2/4	#DemDebate	Fifth Democratic debate is held in Durham, New Hampshire
2/6	#GOPDebate	Eighth Republican debate is held in Manchester, New Hampshire
2/11	#DemDebate	Sixth Democratic debate is held in Milwaukee, Wisconsin
2/13	#GOPDebate	Ninth Republican debate is held in Charleston, South Carolina
2/25	#GOPDebate	10th Republican debate is held in Houston, Texas
3/1	#SuperTuesday	Super Tuesday
3/3	#GOPDebate	Eleventh Republican debate is held in Detroit, Michigan
3/5	#SuperSaturday	Democratic and Republican primaries/caucuses
3/6	#DemDebate	Seventh Democratic debate is held in Flint, Michigan
3/8	#MichiganPrimary	Democratic and Republican primaries/caucuses
3/9	#DemDebate	Eighth Democratic debate is held in Miami, Florida
3/10	#GOPDebate	Twelfth Republican debate is held in Miami, Florida
4/14	#DemDebate	Ninth Democratic debate is held in Brooklyn, New York
4/26	#SuperTuesday	Democratic and Republican primaries/caucuses
5/20	#PrimaryDay	Third nationally televised Libertarian presidential debate
6/7	#PrimaryDay	Democratic and Republican primaries/caucuses
6/22	#LibTownHall	Libertarian presidential town hall hosted and aired by CNN
7/18-7/21	#RNCinCLE	Republican National Convention is held in Cleveland, Ohio
7/25-7/28	#DemsInPhilly	Democratic National Convention is held in Philadelphia, Pennsylvania
9/26	#debatenight	First presidential debate was held in Hempstead, New York
10/4	#VPDebate	Only vice presidential debate was held in Farmville, Virginia
10/9	#debate	Second presidential debate was held in St. Louis, Missouri.
10/19	#debatenight	The third presidential debate was held in Las Vegas, Nevada
11/8	#ElectionNight	US Election Day
11/19	#ElectoralCollege	The electors of the Electoral College meet and formally vote.

Table 5: Comparison of the top hashtags detected by our techniques versus slots in the Wikipedia page (https://en.wikipedia.org/wiki/United_States_presidential_election,_2016_timeline#2016) **for the main events in the US Elections 2016. The second column shows the highest ranked political hashtag (other semantically similar hashtags are available).**

To study how our different steps contributed to the filtering of the links, we ran our data pipeline on each temporal bucket and looked for the presence of the labeled data set at each step of the pipeline. Figure 7 shows charts comparing the number of real links and fake links over the four steps of data pipeline. Step 0 in Figure 7 corresponds to the input to the pipeline (i.e. the initial data set of 20 fake and 20 real links).

By looking at the first row, for the first bucket, all the fake links (and 9/20 of real) were filtered out. Step 3 (viral link computation) contributes the most in the reduction of the fake links. Almost all of the fake links are not viral enough to be selected, whereas most of the real news links are viral enough and get selected. The second bucket shows similar behavior. In the last bucket, as we get closer to the election, it becomes harder to filter out fake links based on virality alone, since a lot more people are sharing these types of links. Step 3 contributes but not as much as in the previous two cases; specifically it reduces the fake links to half. However, step 4 further reduces the fake links by applying other filtering on the link metadata and user metadata associated with the link.

Our system was not designed with the goal of identifying and removing fake links. Indeed, even though several fake news links are filtered out, some still remain. As shown in in the first row of figure 7, the bulk of the filtering is happening in step 3, the viral score computation. The removed links all had relatively low viral scores. A few fake links actually had high viral scores and were not removed. This is more prevalent in the last time bucket from August to Election day. In that bucket, a higher proportion of fake links had high viral scores. We cannot say with certainty why this happens and the data set is too small to know if this is a common phenomenon with all fake links. It seems plausible however that as the election day approaches, people become more engaged and share political articles more frequently, thus causing high viral scores for them. We can further improve the fake filtering by fine tuning some parameters. We can imagine many ways of optimizing the pipeline at each step by including additional conditions. For example, we tried adding the following:

- Content selection: > 200 shares per link
- User selection: > 1 verified user and > 50 users from trusted user data set (verified + ring 1 + ring 2)
- Link selection: > 2.2 virality score

By using the above optimizations, the final number of fake and real links that remains does not change much from before. It seems there is some correlation between user/content filters and viral filtering, in that very viral links also tend to get shared by verified users and through high-quality tweets. So, for example, we can filter by either high virality or verified users and both will remove several of the same fake links.

Figure 5: Wayback machine example for the two final days of the 2016 US Election. The screenshot shows search results and top-25 hashtags for both days.

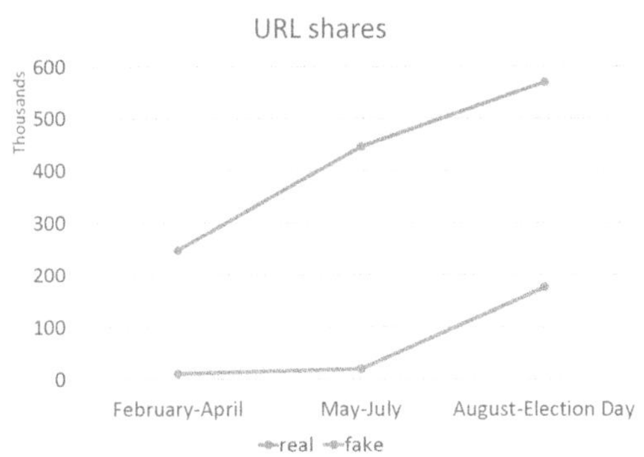

Figure 6: Total shares for the top 20 fake and top 20 real election stories.

The additional filtering conditions however have the effect of moving the filtering of some fake links to earlier steps, so we can improve the filtering and the overall computation cost of the data processing pipeline (there are less links at step 3 for which we need to compute viral scores). Additionally, we can achieve a more gradual change in precision/recall allowing us to stop at an earlier step if needed (so if we stop after step 3 we can get more real links and some fake, but not as many fake as before the optimizations). For example, before the optimizations, most of the fake filtering in the February-April bucket happens in Step 3; before and after that step there is little change on the number of links. After the optimizations (charts in the second row), each step contributes its share of filtering as shown in the figure. For completeness, we also present the charts for the other two time buckets.

Even though our techniques were not designed with the explicit goal of detecting fake links, the filtering, selection and diffusion tree computation are shown to be effective in reducing fake links.

7 CONCLUSION AND FUTURE WORK

Past research in the field of social data mining, especially on the Twitter network, has focused on extracting sentiments, trending topics, communities of similar users and summaries from tweets. Much of this work is based on formulating and evaluating sophisticated algorithms using manually selected datasets that are either small or biased towards noise-free content. Such assumptions about the underlying data makes it hard to deploy these techniques in real-world systems, where efficiency in data processing and scalable implementations are as important as the effectiveness of the system. Our approach consists on techniques that can process large scale data sets and can be implemented in a distributed infrastructure.

Here we emphasized a working system that can ingest and archive data over time, tested with a real-world data set, with the goal of prototyping a new type of search engine. Our findings suggest that mining relevant links shared by trusted users is not only a reliable mechanism for selecting high quality content, but it can also be adopted for ranking content. By applying a number of filters and viral detection techniques, we can identify high quality links discovered within a certain period of time. This temporal aspect helps not only in providing relevant and fresh content, but also with the ability to look back in time.

The content selected by users reflects a collective interest that is very rich when exploring it as an archive. The US 2016 election

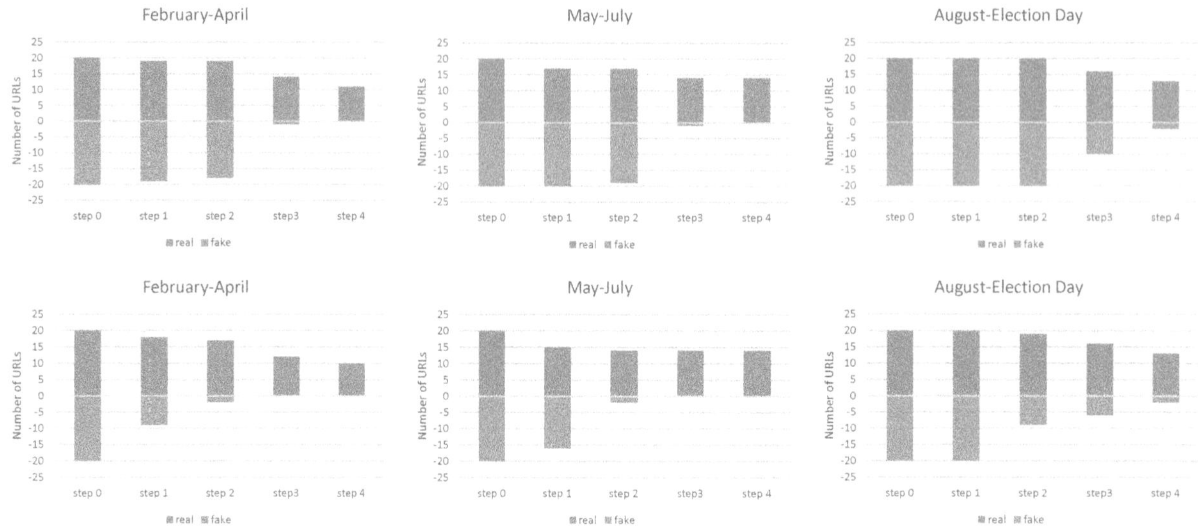

Figure 7: Fake news study on Twitter. The first row shows three charts each comparing the number of real links (colored in blue, positive y-axis) vs. fake links (colored in orange, negative y-axis) over the four steps of the data pipeline (x-axis; step 0 in the the charts means the starting data set). Second row shows the results once we apply optimizations that can help improve the filtering and the computation cost of the processing pipeline.

example shows not only that the system collects the proper data for reconstructing a story, but also that such data mirrors real events. With the wayback machine we can retrieve content and associated chatter that was relevant for a specific period in time.

We provide an extensive description of the techniques and algorithms used along with data points and other data management details so our findings can be replicated by other researchers using Twitter or similar social networks. Unfortunately, business reasons do not allow us to release the source code. As part of our evaluation results, we also demonstrate that the proposed data processing pipeline can be used to identify and filter fake links. While fake link detection was not the goal of our work, the results show that aggressive filtering should be an essential piece of any social web solution that strives for relevant content and not an afterthought like in current systems.

Future work includes personalization of the search results, organization of the links by categories, improving the quality of the pivots, better archiving, and enhancing the diversity of the links.

REFERENCES

[1] Rakesh Agrawal, Behzad Golshan, and Evangelos E. Papalexakis. 2015. Whither Social Networks for Web Search?. In *KDD*. 1661–1670.
[2] Omar Alonso, Sushma Bannur, Kartikay Khandelwal, and Shankar Kalyanaraman. 2015. The World Conversation: Web Page Metadata Generation From Social Sources. In *WWW*. 385–395.
[3] Omar Alonso, Catherine C. Marshall, and Marc Najork. 2013. Are Some Tweets More Interesting Than Others? #HardQuestion. In *HCIR '13*. 2:1–2:10.
[4] Farzindar Atefeh and Wael Khreich. 2015. A survey of techniques for event detection in twitter. *Computational Intelligence* 31, 1 (2015), 132–164.
[5] Hila Becker, Mor Naaman, and Luis Gravano. 2011. Beyond Trending Topics: Real-World Event Identification on Twitter. *ICWSM* 11 (2011), 438–441.
[6] Andrei Z Broder. 1997. On the resemblance and containment of documents. In *Compression and Complexity of Sequences 1997. Proceedings*. IEEE, 21–29.
[7] Michael Busch, Krishna Gade, Brian Larson, Patrick Lok, Samuel Luckenbill, and Jimmy J. Lin. 2012. Earlybird: Real-Time Search at Twitter. In *ICDE*. 1360–1369.
[8] Cheng Cao, James Caverlee, Kyumin Lee, Hancheng Ge, and Jin-Wook Chung. 2015. Organic or Organized?: Exploring URL Sharing Behavior. In *CIKM*. 513–522.
[9] Ronnie Chaiken, Bob Jenkins, Per-Åke Larson, Bill Ramsey, Darren Shakib, Simon Weaver, and Jingren Zhou. 2008. SCOPE: easy and efficient parallel processing of massive data sets. *PVLDB* 1, 2 (2008), 1265–1276.
[10] Jennifer Fernquist and Ed H. Chi. 2013. Perception and understanding of social annotations in web search. In *WWW*. 403–412.
[11] Carolin Gerlitz and Anne Helmond. 2013. The like economy: Social buttons and the data-intensive web. *New Media & Society* 15, 8 (2013), 1348–1365.
[12] Sharad Goel, Ashton Anderson, Jake M. Hofman, and Duncan J. Watts. 2016. The Structural Virality of Online Diffusion. *Management Science* 62, 1 (2016), 180–196.
[13] Martin Hentschel, Omar Alonso, Scott Counts, and Vasileios Kandylas. 2014. Finding Users we Trust: Scaling up Verified Twitter Users Using their Communication Patterns. In *ICWSM*.
[14] Vasileios Kandylas and Ali Dasdan. 2010. The Utility of Tweeted URLs for Web Search. In *WWW*. 1127–1128.
[15] John Langford and Tong Zhang. 2007. The Epoch-Greedy Algorithm for Contextual Multi-armed Bandits. In *NIPS*.
[16] Florian Meier and David Elsweiler. 2016. Going back in Time: An Investigation of Social Media Re-finding. In *SIGIR*. 355–364.
[17] Gilad Mishne and Jimmy J. Lin. 2012. Twanchor text: a preliminary study of the value of tweets as anchor text. In *SIGIR*. 1159–1160.
[18] Aditi S. Muralidharan, Zoltán Gyöngyi, and Ed Chi. 2012. Social annotations in web search. In *CHI*. 1085–1094.
[19] Patrick Pantel, Michael Gamon, Omar Alonso, and Kevin Haas. 2012. Social annotations: utility and prediction modeling. In *SIGIR*. 285–294.
[20] Tom Rowlands, David Hawking, and Ramesh Sankaranarayana. 2010. New-web search with microblog annotations. In *WWW*. 1293–1296.
[21] Yu Wang, David Fink, and Eugene Agichtein. 2015. SEEFT: Planned Social Event Discovery and Attribute Extraction by Fusing Twitter and Web Content. In *ICWSM*. 483–492.
[22] Jianshu Weng and Bu-Sung Lee. 2011. Event Detection in Twitter. *ICWSM* 11 (2011), 401–408.
[23] Changtao Zhong, Dmytro Karamshuk, and Nishanth Sastry. 2015. Predicting Pinterest: Automating a Distributed Human Computation. In *WWW*. 1417–1426.

ASSIST: Automatic Summarization of SIgnificant Structural Changes in Large Temporal Graphs

Charalampos Chelmis*
University at Albany, SUNY
Albany, New York
cchelmis@albany.edu

Reshul Dani
College of Engineering Pune
Pune, Maharashtra, India
reshul.dani@gmail.com

ABSTRACT

Detecting outliers and anomalies in data is vital in numerous applications in areas such as security, finance, health care, and online social media. Such dynamic systems can be modeled as graphs that change over time. Even though considerable work has been performed on finding points in time at which a network notably differs from its past, little work has been done on characterizing or explaining such changes. However, in the era of big data where networked data are getting bigger and bigger, being able to summarize such changes is key for sensemaking and root cause analysis. To address this gap, we present a novel approach to summarize significant structural changes in large temporal graphs. Specifically, we propose an efficient approach to help the user understand sharp changes in the structure of the network by presenting to her only a summary of key subgraphs that contribute most to the change. Extensive evaluation on real-world datasets with ground truth demonstrates both quantitatively and qualitatively the ability of our approach to accurately detect changes and discover "important" structures to succinctly describe the change.

CCS CONCEPTS

•Information systems →Web mining; Summarization; *Data management systems; Data stream mining;* **•Computing methodologies →Anomaly detection;**

KEYWORDS

Anomaly summarization; structural change interpretation; dynamic graph; change attribution

1 INTRODUCTION

Graphs arise in numerous domains [1, 3, 5, 6] including security (e.g., network intrusion), finance (e.g., credit card fraud), health care (e.g., disease outbreaks), and online social media (e.g., fake news spread). A key problem in analyzing both static and dynamic graphs in such settings is spotting suspicious behavior or events [1, 3] before proceeding with post-even analysis. Even though event detection in temporal graphs is a well-studied problem [1, 11], there is currently no way for a practitioner to explain an event. Contrast that with Figure 1, where we highlight the most informative structure that can be used to explain the detected event.

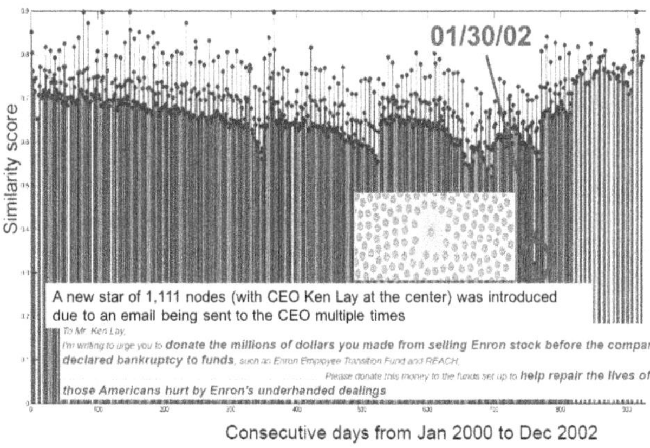

Figure 1: Informative structure identified by *ASSIST* (Section 2.3) to explain a sharp structural change in the Enron communication network (see Section 3 for details). Without *ASSIST* no clear structures stand out.

In this paper, we focus on constructing concise summaries of significant structural changes in large, real-world dynamic graphs in order to better communicate such changes to practitioners. Our hypothesis is that sharp changes in the structure of a graph are not random but instead indicate patterns, which should be discovered and ranked based on their contribution to the change.

We propose *ASSIST* (Section 2.3), a scalable approach to concisely summarize significant structural changes in large, dynamic real-world graphs in terms of a lexicon of subgraph-types. Figure 1 shows an unnaturally large star structure of 1,111 nodes that appears on Jan. 30th of 2002. The finding is the result of applying *ASSIST* to a real-world dataset of 3.6M Enron emails sent between 95.8K email addresses over 4 years. The structure corresponds to a large collection of emails sent to the Enron CEO. Identification of such structures would be labor intensive and time consuming or impossible within reasonable time constraints and with limited available human resources without our proposed approach.

We summarize our contributions as follows:

- We identify the problem of building automatic summaries of significant structural changes in large temporal networks in a fully unsupervised and parameter-free fashion.
- We propose *ASSIST*, a novel approach for summarizing significant structural changes in dynamic graphs.
- We report experiments on real datasets and show that *ASSIST* is *intuitive*, *scalable* and *practical*.

*Corresponding author.

WebSci'17, June 25-28, 2017, Troy, NY, USA.
 978-1-4503-4896-6/17/06...$15.00
DOI: http://dx.doi.org/10.1145/3091478.3091518

2 PROPOSED APPROACH

2.1 Significant Structural Change Detection

Many dynamic systems can be modeled as temporal graphs, which change over time with new nodes and edges arriving or existing nodes and edges disappearing [1]. Event detection in temporal graphs corresponds to finding points in time at which the graph structure notably differs from its past. Formally, given a sequence of graphs $\{G_1, G_2, \ldots, G_t\}$, find time points τ such that G_τ differs significantly from $G_{\tau-1}$.

Several methods have been proposed for the above problem, a survey of which is given in [1]. To date, however, there exists no single method that has been shown to outperform all others, mainly due to the fact that different techniques may identify different classes or types of events depending on their particular formulation.

In this paper, we identify significant changes in structrure by measuring the similarity in connectivity between two graphs $G_1 = (V, E_1)$ and $G_2 = (V, E_2)$. We do so by computing pairwise node affinities in G_1, and comparing them with corersponding affinities in G_2. We use Fast Belief Propagation [8] to compute the affinity, s_{ij}, of any node j with respect to node i in a graph. Other similarity measures (e.g., [17]) can be used, however Fast Belief Propagation has been shown to be linear on the number of edges [8].

We assume that G_1 and G_2 have the same set of nodes V. If the node sets V_1 and V_2 are different, then we assume that $V = V_1 \cup V_2$, and some nodes are disconnected either in G_1 or G_2. Once the pairwise node affinity scores S_1 and S_2 have been computed for each graph G_1 and G_2, we measure the root Euclidean distance of S_1 and S_2, $d(S_1, S_2)$, which has been shown to detect even small changes [8]. We subsequently convert the distance to a similarity measure, i.e., $\sigma(G_1, G_2) = \sigma(S_1, S_2) = \frac{1}{1+d(S_1,S_2)}$, bounding the result to the interval $[0, 1]$. A similarity score of 1 means identical graphs (i.e., the temporal graph has remained unchanged), whereas a similarity score of 0 means totally different graphs.

2.2 Structural Change Summarization

Once a significant structural change between two snapshots G_τ and $G_{\tau-1}$ has been detected (Section 2.1), we need to identify the best collection M of possibly overlapping subgraphs that succinctly describe the main connectivity of the structural change. The rationale is that people can understand more easily a handful of simple structures (ranked by importance) rather than cluttered graphs.

To produce the set of subgraphs that best describes a sharp structural change we rely on a lexicon, Γ, comprising cliques (fc) and near-cliques (nc), stars (st), chains (ch) and (near) bi-partite cores (nb, bc). These structures appear often in real-world networks [1] and have real semantic meaning in practice (e.g., bi-partite cores signify fraudulent activity in transaction networks [12]).

We formulate our task as a **lossless compression problem**. Specifically, we assert that the best summary of a significant structural change is a set of subgraphs M that compresses it best, and, thus, helps a human understand the main characteristics of the change in a simple, intuitive manner. We use Minimum Description Length (MDL) [13], a parameter-free approach to identify M. Given a set of models $\mathcal{M}$, the best model $M \in \mathcal{M}$ by MDL for some observed graph snapshot G_t is that which minimizes $L(M) + L(G_t|M)$, where $L(M)$ is the length in bits used to describe M and $L(G_t|M)$ is the length in bits used to describe G_t encoded using M.

We consider models $M \in \mathcal{M}$ to be composed of ordered lists of graph structures, with possible node (but not edge) overlaps. Each structure $\gamma \in M$ describes the interconnectivity of a subset of nodes in the adjacency matrix $\mathbf{A}$. The family of models $\mathcal{M}$ in our approach consists of all possible permutations of all possible subsets of C, where $C = \cup_x C_x$ denotes the set of possible subgraph-types $x \in \Gamma$ over all possible subsets of V. For example, C_{fc} is the set of all possible full cliques. Given M, we induce the approximation $\mathbf{M}$ of $\mathbf{A}$ as described by each structure $\gamma \in M$, i.e., for each structure γ, we induce the edges of G_t described by γ in $\mathbf{M}$ accordingly. Given that M is a summary to $\mathbf{A}$ it is likely that $\mathbf{M} \neq \mathbf{A}$. Thus, we also compute the error matrix $\mathbf{E} = \mathbf{M} \oplus \mathbf{A}$ so that $\mathbf{A}$ can be reconstructed in a lossless manner from $\mathbf{M}$ and $\mathbf{E}$.

We formalize the problem we tackle as follows:

Given snapshots G_τ and $G_{\tau-1}$ involved in a significant structural change of temporal graph G, and lexicon Γ of sungraph-types;

Find the minimum description model $M' = (M_\tau - M_{\tau-1}) \cup (M_{\tau-1} - M_\tau)$, where M_τ and $M_{\tau-1}$ are the minimum description models that minimize the total encoding lengths $L_{G_\tau}(M_\tau) = L(M_\tau) + L(\mathbf{E}_\tau)$ and $L_{G_{\tau-1}}(M_{\tau-1}) = L(M_{\tau-1}) + L(\mathbf{E}_{\tau-1})$ respectively, where $L(\gamma)$ denotes the number of bits required to describe γ.

Encoding the Model. To encode the length of a model, $L(M)$, we begin by encoding the total number of structures in M. Next, we optimally encode the number of structures of each type $x \in \Gamma$, the type for each structure, and finally the structure itself. We define the encoding for each subgraph-type in our lexicon such that we can compute the encoded length of a model for all structures in the model. For example, we encode a *star* (st), in which a single hub is connected to a set of two or more peripheral nodes as $L(st) = L_N(|st| - 1) + log_2 n + log_2 \binom{n-1}{|st|-1}$, where the first term encodes the number of peripheral nodes (L_N denotes the MDL optimal encoding for integers ≥ 1 [13]), followed by the id of the hub, and the ids of the peripheral nodes. Similarly, we encode a *clique* (fc), in which all nodes are directly connected to all other nodes, by encoding the number of nodes in the clique followed by their ids such that $L(fc) = L_N(|fc|) + log\binom{n}{|fc|}$. We define the encoded length of *near cliques*, *bipartite cores* and *chains* similarly.

Encoding the Error. Next, we discuss how we encode errors made by $\mathbf{M}$ into matrix $\mathbf{E}$. Specifically, we consider two types of connectivity errors, $\mathbf{E}^+$ and $\mathbf{E}^-$, as these two sources of error are likely to have different error distributions. The former corresponds to the areas of $\mathbf{A}$ that M models but for which $\mathbf{M}$ introduces extraneous edges not present in the original graph. The latter consists of the areas of $\mathbf{A}$ which M doesn't model. The encoding for $\mathbf{E}^+$ (similarly $\mathbf{E}^-$) is as follows: $L(\mathbf{E}^+) = log(|\mathbf{E}^+|) + ||\mathbf{E}^+||_{l_1} + ||\mathbf{E}^+||_{l_0}$.

2.3 Automatic Summarization of Significant Structural Changes in Temporal Graphs

We propose *ASSIST* (Alg. 1), an approach for Automatic Summarization of SIgnificant Structural changes in large Temporal graphs. Both components of *ASSIST* are linear on the number of edges. Specifically, Fast Belief Propagation, which we use to detect singificant structural changes has $O(|E|)$ complexity [8]. For summarization, the complexity of calculating the encoding scheme is $O(|E|)$

when there is no overlap between structures in M. In the case of overlapping structures, the complexity of computing the encoding scheme becomes $O(|M|^2 + |E|)$. This is because for any two overlapping structures γ_1 and γ_2, such that γ_1 comes before γ_2, finding how much of **A** γ_2 explains relative to γ_1 requires $O(|M|^2)$ operations. Typically, $|M| \ll |E|$. Thus, *ASSIST* has $O(|E|)$ runtime complexity.

Algorithm 1: ASSIST

Input: A sequence of graphs $\{G_1, G_2, \ldots, G_t\}$ and lexicon Γ
Detection of significant structural changes (Sect. 2.1):
Find time points τ s.t. G_τ differs significantly from $G_{\tau-1}$.
for each pair G_τ and $G_{\tau-1}$
Generate summary $M_{\tau-1}$ **of** $G_{\tau-1}$ **using Alg. 2**
Generate summary M_τ **of** G_τ **using Alg. 2**
Compose structural change summary: Construct model $M'_\tau = (M_\tau - M_{\tau-1}) \cup (M_{\tau-1} - M_\tau)$.
Return the collection of M'_τ, $\forall\tau$ (and their encoding costs).

We begin by identifying time points τ such that G_τ differs significantly from $G_{\tau-1}$ as discussed in Section 2.1. Once graphs $G_{\tau-1}$ and G_τ have been identified, we use the encoding scheme discussed in Section 2.2 on each graph respectively to identify perfect and approximate structures that minimize their corresponding encoding cost. Specifically, given a subgraph in G_τ (similarly $G_{\tau-1}$), we first search for error-free matches with subgraph-types in our lexicon (e.g., perfect clique, or near-clique with missing edges encoded as error). If the subgraph does not belong to Γ, the search continues for the lexicon entry that best approximates the subgraph. Once the structure that has the lowest encoding cost has been identified, we add the structure to the candidate set C. Any combination of clustering or community detection algorithms [10] can be used to decompose G_τ (similarly $G_{\tau-1}$) into subgraphs.

Finally, given a set of candidate structures, C, we induce the model M by associating each candidate structure with the number of bits that are gained by encoding the subgraph as structure x instead of noise, and considering the structures in decreasing order (Section 2.2). Specifically, to reduce the search space of all possible permutations we consider each structure in C sequentially, and include it in M if the graph's encoding cost does not increase. Note that without this heuristic, we would have to consider all possible ordered combinations of the candidate structures; this would lead to a combinatorial problem that would render our solution impractical for any non-trivial candidate set. We compose the summary of the change at time τ by finding the smallest model $M' = M_\tau \cap M_{\tau-1}$ that best summarizes the change from $G_{\tau-1}$ to G_τ.

As new significant structural changes are detected, *ASSIST* tries to link them with detected changes from earlier timeslots. Note that depending on the frequency with which snapshots are acquired a single event may be split across multiple time points. Conversely, multiple events may be mistaken for being one event if the temporal resolution of graph snapshot collection is too coarse. Intuitively, if two graph snapshots of successive timeslots share a significant amount of structures in their summaries, the later snapshot arises from the previous one. To identify that two significant structural changes are referring to the same event we use the structural similarity between the underlying summaries, expressed as the Jaccard coefficient of their structures. If this similarity exceeds a certain threshold, we merge the two changes into a single event.

Algorithm 2: Summary (Sect. 2.2)

Input: Graph G and lexicon Γ
Generate Candidate Structures: Generate candidate subgraphs using graph decomposition methods.
Label Candidate Structures: Label each subgraph as as a perfect or approximate structure $x \in \Gamma$ which minimizes the local encoding cost. Populate the candidate set C.
Summary Composition: Compose a model M of non-redundant structures which summarizes G. Choose M that produces the smallest total encoding cost.

3 EXPERIMENTAL EVALUATION

3.1 Datasets and Experimental Setup

We ran our experiments on a Intel(R) Core(TM) i5-4200U CPU at 1.60GHz with 4GB memory. The significant structure change detection component (Section 2.1) is implemented in Matlab, while the summarization process (Section 2.2) in Python. We use two publicly available real-wolrd dynamic graph datasets [1] for our evaluation.

Large-Scale Twitter Dataset with Ground Truth [1]. We use tweets collected over a period which spans the World Cup 2014 season (Jun 12 - Jul 13), and filtered by popular/official World Cup hashtags, such as #worldcup, #fifa, and #brazil. After named entity extraction and resolution (URLs, hashtags, @ mentions), we created entity-entity co-mention temporal graphs on 5 minute sample rate for a total of 1, 790, 999 time points. Each snapshot contains up to 161, 895 nodes. Compiled ground truth events comprise the goals, penalties, and injuries in all matches that involve at least one of Argentina, Brazil, France, Germany, Netherlands, and Spain teams.

Enron Emails Dataset [1]. We use three years of Enron emails (Jan 01 2000 - Dec 31 2002) which exhibit many periodic structures (e.g., near-cliques that persevere with time) as a reflection of office e-mail correspondence, and one-shot structures (e.g., stars) due to events such as company-wide emails sent out by key players John Lavorato (CEO of Enron America), Sally Beck (COO) and Kenneth Lay (CEO/Chairman). In our temporal graphs, nodes represent email addresses (95, 829 addresses in total) and directed edges depict sent/received relations. We analyze the data with daily sample rate skipping weekends (1, 069 time points in total).

3.2 Significant Structural Change Detection

We begin by evaluating *ASSIST* on detection accuracy as a function of temporal granularity and similarity threshold. Specifically, we experiment with entity-entity co-mention graphs for time windows of 5, 10, and 20 mins and compute the similarity scores between consecutive graphs. We identify graphs G_t that differ "too much" from G_{t-1} if their similarity score $s(G_t, G_{t-1})$ drops below a threshold. To quantify the **threshold impact** on the performance of *ASSIST*, we perform a grid search over threshold values (i.e., threshold is defined as median$\pm 4\sigma$ with step 0.5). High similarities between consecutive graph snapshots (e.g., during weekends in the Enron

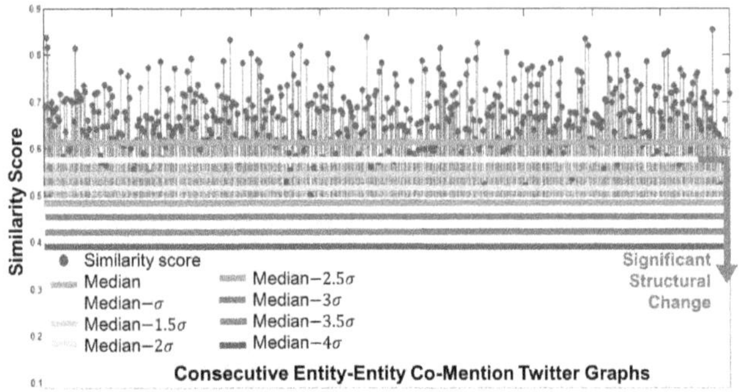

Figure 2: Significant changes identified by *ASSIST* coincide with major World Cup events. Blue points denote similarity scores between consecutive instances of the entity-entity co-mention graphs. Horizontal lines represent lower control limits for median $-k\sigma$, where $k \in [1, 4]$ increases in 0.5 steps.

Emails dataset due to less email communication) do not reflect significant structural changes and hence, we report our findings for median−$k\sigma$, where $k \in [1, 4]$ increases in 0.5 steps.

Figure 2 shows the similarity scores between consecutive entity-entity co-mention Twitter graphs with "anomalous" points laying below the corresponding lower control limits. For threshold set to median−2σ, 20 points relate to actual events that span 13 games in the World Cup. For example, *ASSIST* summarized the goal scored by player Kroos in the infamous match (Game 61) between Brazil and Germany on 8th July 2014 as 2 stars of ~ 200 nodes with hashtags '#tragedy' and '#heartache' as the centers. *ASSIST* also identified stars with '#worldCup', '#worldCup2014' and entities 'brazil' and 'germany' at the time the goals happened during the match.

So far, we used entity-entity co-mention graphs of 5min intervals to evaluate the performance of *ASSIST*. We have also compared its performance for different time windows (5mins, 10mins, 20mins). The performance of *ASSIST* is similar for windows of 10mins and 20mins. This indicates that **temporal granularity** does not impact the performance of *ASSIST*.

ASSIST should not be penalized for an inaccurate detector. This is particularly true when multiple events happen almost **instantaneously** as is the case for our Twitter World Cup dataset. Specifically, the events in this data (e.g., goals and injuries) are quite instantaneous when we use a sample rate of 5 minutes. Moreover, such events are likely to be reflected on Twitter with some **delay** by social media users. As such, it is extremely hard for *ASSIST* to pinpoint the exact time of the events. However, some time delay in detecting an event is often tolerable in practice (e.g., detecting an event that occurred at τ within time window $[\tau - 5; \tau + 5]$ is counted as accurate). For example, during Game 61, 3 goals happened very close to each other (at the 24th, 26th and 29th minutes). Player Kroos scored the 24th and 26th minute goals, whereas player Khedira scored the 29th goal. *ASSIST* could not differentiate between these events using a 5mins window since summaries generated by *ASSIST* comprised mainly stars with centers such as '#worldcup', '#ned', and '#aus' for a match between Australia and Netherlands, making it difficult to identify the exact cause behind such event. To address this issue, we experiment with temporal graphs of 1min sample rate for this match. In this case, the summaries generated by *ASSIST* showed the presence of entity 'Kroos' for the goals in the 24th and 26th minute, whereas entity 'Khedira' was included in the summary for the goal in 29th minute.

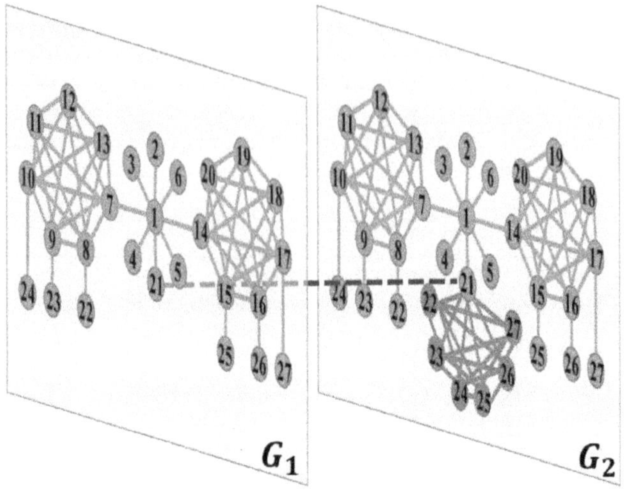

Figure 3: *ASSIST* reports the emergent full clique $\{22, 23, 24, 25, 26, 27\}$ as the cause of the sharp structural change in this toy graph sequence.

3.3 Summarization Quality

To demonstrate that *ASSIST* produces **intuitive** and **informative** summaries of sharp structural changes in temporal graphs, we begin by conducting experiments on small toy networks that include classic topologies (i.e., cliques and stars).

Figures 3 and 4 show two sample graph sequences where *ASSIST* detects the introduction of a clique and the dissolution of a clique into a star. In Figure 3, the intermediate summaries produced by *ASSIST* for G_1 comprises full cliques (fc) $\{14, 15, 16, 17, 18, 19, 20\}$ and $\{7, 8, 9, 10, 11, 12, 13\}$, whereas for G_2 fc $\{14, 15, 16, 17, 18, 19, 20\}$, $\{7, 8, 9, 10, 11, 12, 13\}$, and $\{22, 23, 24, 25, 26, 27\}$. As a result, *ASSIST* reports the emergent fc $\{22, 23, 24, 25, 26, 27\}$ as the cause of the sharp structural change. Similarly, as shown in Figure 4, *ASSIST* generates intermediate summaries consisting of fc $\{15, 16, 17, 18, 19, 20\}$ and $\{8, 9, 10, 11, 12, 13\}$ for G_1 and fc $\{8, 9, 10, 11, 12, 13\}$ for G_2 accordingly. As a consequence, *ASSIST* reports the dissolution of fc $\{15, 16, 17, 18, 19, 20\}$ as the cause of the sharp structural change.

Next, we evaluate *ASSIST* using the Enron communication dataset. The visualization of events identified by *ASSIST* in this dataset (e.g., Figure 1) confirm that sharp topological changes in the Enron communication network correspond to major events in the company's history. For instance, the unnaturally large star structure of 1, 111 nodes that appears on Jan. 30th of 2002 is due to a large collection of emails being sent to the Enron CEO at that time. Such **informative** structures contain (often at their center) high ranking officials.

Finally, we evaluate the ability of *ASSIST* to produce **concise** summaries by measuring the compression ratio, $C_R = \frac{|V_S|}{|V|}$, between the total number of nodes that a practitioner would be required to examine to identify the root cause of a sharp structural change between two graph snapshots $G_\tau = (V, E_\tau)$ and $G_{\tau-1}(V, E_{\tau-1})$, and the number of nodes in the summary $S = (V_S, E_S), V_s \subset V$ produced by *ASSIST*. Thus, smaller compression

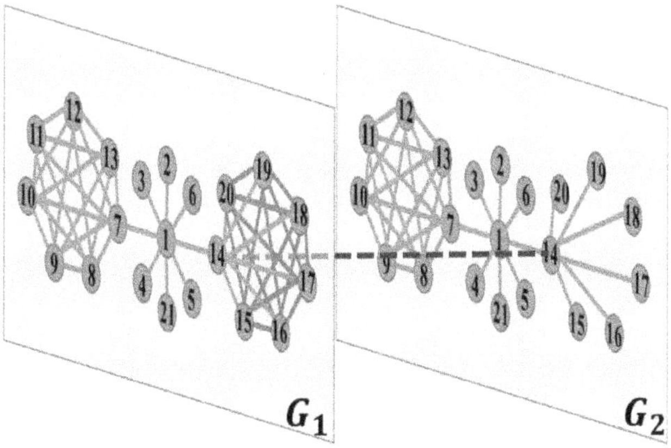

Figure 4: For this sample graph sequence *ASSIST* reports the dissolution of full clique {15, 16, 17, 18, 19, 20} as the cause of the sharp structural change.

ratios indicate better summaries. Note that we use compression ratio not as our end goal but as a principled way for routing the attention of practitioners to significant structures that we believe are associated with the sharp structural changes in the graph.

In our experiments, we found that *ASSIST* produces models with few informative structures (mainly stars and near-bipartite cores) due to its high effectiveness in pruning redundant, overlapping or error-prone structures from the candidate set C, and rewarding structures that explain unexplored parts of the change. For example, *ASSIST* summarizes the event on 30th Jan 2002 in the Enron dataset using just 37% of the total number of nodes; this corresponds to a compression ratio of 63%. Similarly, *ASSIST* achieves a compression ratio of 69% by summarizing the 24th minute goal in Game 61 in the Twitter World Cup dataset.

4 RELATED WORK

Related work comprises three main areas. The advantage of *ASSIST* compared to prior work is that it is scalable, intuitive, extensible, and parameter-free. No existing method has all these properties.

Graph Compression and Summarization. Prior works, such as [2, 4, 7, 9] operate on static graphs. A recently proposed method for dynamic graph summarization [16] uses MDL to discover temporally coherent subgraphs.

Event and Anomaly Detection in Graphs. A comprehensive overview of existing graph-based approaches for event and anomaly detection [11, 15], as well as the open research challenges in developing such algorithms have been presented at [1]. Such approaches focus on anomaly detection rather than the summarization and interpretation of detected abnormalities.

Event Detection and Summarization. Identifying and summarizing events is a fundamental and challenging problem of practical importance in many fields of science [3, 5, 6, 14]. None of these methods focuses on both identifying structural changes in temporal graphs and summarizing these changes at the same time.

5 CONCLUSION AND FUTURE WORK

We identified and studied the problem of building automatic summaries of significant structural changes in large-scale temporal networks in a fully unsupervised and parameter-free fashion. To address this problem, we proposed a *scalable* approach, and we showed that it is producing summaries that agree with common sense and can be easily explained in real-world datasets.

Future work includes incorporating more subgraph-types in our lexicon or conversely tackling the problem with when a lexicon of subgraph-types is unknown, as well as boosting detection performance by exploring other methods for event and anomaly detection in graphs. Another possible direction is in developing a system for the early discovery, warning, prediction, and prevention of disruptive events that cannot be found in historical data. Such "predictive analytics" is of high value and has received significant attention in the last decade mainly due to the Big Data and Data Science revolution.

REFERENCES

[1] Leman Akoglu, Hanghang Tong, and Danai Koutra. 2015. Graph based anomaly detection and description: a survey. *Data Mining and Knowledge Discovery* 29, 3 (2015), 626–688.

[2] Paolo Boldi and Sebastiano Vigna. 2004. The webgraph framework I: compression techniques. In *Proceedings of the 13th international conference on World Wide Web*. ACM, 595–602.

[3] Varun Chandola, Arindam Banerjee, and Vipin Kumar. 2009. Anomaly detection: A survey. *ACM computing surveys (CSUR)* 41, 3 (2009), 15.

[4] Flavio Chierichetti, Ravi Kumar, Silvio Lattanzi, Michael Mitzenmacher, Alessandro Panconesi, and Prabhakar Raghavan. 2009. On compressing social networks. In *Proceedings of the 15th ACM SIGKDD international conference on Knowledge discovery and data mining*. ACM, 219–228.

[5] Victoria J Hodge and Jim Austin. 2004. A survey of outlier detection methodologies. *Artificial intelligence review* 22, 2 (2004), 85–126.

[6] Raymond Kosala and Hendrik Blockeel. 2000. Web mining research: A survey. *ACM Sigkdd Explorations Newsletter* 2, 1 (2000), 1–15.

[7] Danai Koutra, U Kang, Jilles Vreeken, and Christos Faloutsos. 2014. VOG: summarizing and understanding large graphs. In *Proceedings of the 2014 SIAM international conference on data mining*. SIAM, 91–99.

[8] Danai Koutra, Joshua T Vogelstein, and Christos Faloutsos. 2013. Deltacon: A principled massive-graph similarity function. In *Proceedings of the 2013 SIAM International Conference on Data Mining*. SIAM, 162–170.

[9] Saket Navlakha, Rajeev Rastogi, and Nisheeth Shrivastava. 2008. Graph summarization with bounded error. In *Proceedings of the 2008 ACM SIGMOD international conference on Management of data*. ACM, 419–432.

[10] Mark EJ Newman. 2004. Detecting community structure in networks. *The European Physical Journal B-Condensed Matter and Complex Systems* 38, 2 (2004), 321–330.

[11] Caleb C Noble and Diane J Cook. 2003. Graph-based anomaly detection. In *Proceedings of the ninth ACM SIGKDD international conference on Knowledge discovery and data mining*. ACM, 631–636.

[12] Shashank Pandit, Duen Horng Chau, Samuel Wang, and Christos Faloutsos. 2007. Netprobe: a fast and scalable system for fraud detection in online auction networks. In *Proceedings of the 16th international conference on World Wide Web*. ACM, 201–210.

[13] Jorma Rissanen. 1978. Modeling by shortest data description. *Automatica* 14, 5 (1978), 465–471.

[14] Takeshi Sakaki, Makoto Okazaki, and Yutaka Matsuo. 2010. Earthquake shakes Twitter users: real-time event detection by social sensors. In *Proceedings of the 19th international conference on World wide web*. ACM, 851–860.

[15] Hassan Sayyadi, Matthew Hurst, and Alexey Maykov. 2009. Event detection and tracking in social streams. In *In Proceedings of the International Conference on Weblogs and Social Media (ICWSM 2009). AAAI*.

[16] Neil Shah, Danai Koutra, Tianmin Zou, Brian Gallagher, and Christos Faloutsos. 2015. Timecrunch: Interpretable dynamic graph summarization. In *Proceedings of the 21th ACM SIGKDD International Conference on Knowledge Discovery and Data Mining*. ACM, 1055–1064.

[17] Ellen Spertus, Mehran Sahami, and Orkut Buyukkokten. 2005. Evaluating similarity measures: a large-scale study in the orkut social network. In *Proceedings of the eleventh ACM SIGKDD international conference on Knowledge discovery in data mining*. ACM, 678–684.

Automatic Generation of Event Timelines from Social Data

Omar Alonso
Microsoft
omalonso@microsoft.com

Serge-Eric Tremblay
Microsoft
sergetr@microsoft.com

Fernando Diaz
Microsoft
fdiaz@microsoft.com

ABSTRACT

Over the past few years, social media has seen phenomenal growth and has become a very important source for getting real time updates from different parts of the world. While the notion of a trend usually reflects current events, the amount of information accumulated over a period of time can be used to provide another perspective for such events in the form of a timeline. In this paper, we present a technique that uses social information as relevance surrogates to generate an informative timeline. A core component is a variation of pseudo relevance feedback that is automatically generated using social data without external evidence. Finally, we describe the implementation of such technique and present evaluation results using a real-world data set.

KEYWORDS

Timelines, social pseudo relevance feedback, social media, Twitter

1 INTRODUCTION

In corpora with temporal information such as news, email, or social media, timelines provide a convenient interface for information needs that can be decomposed into events (e.g., news topics). Usually timeline generation consists of arranging words [8], document titles [6], extracted sentences [2, 4], or social media posts [7] into a sparse linear order.

The problem of timeline generation can be decomposed into *relevance estimation* and *deduplication*. Relevance estimation refers to determining whether a word, title, sentence, or post is relevant to the user's information need. Deduplication refers to collapsing relevant items that refer to the same topic. For example, for the query `{paris attacks}` over, say, a social media corpus, a system would first have to reason about which posts are relevant to the query (e.g., those posts referring to the attack itself, the government response, and so forth) and then about which relevant posts refer to the same event (e.g., group all of the posts related to attack itself, all of those related to the response, and so forth). If a system has good models for each of these, then a set of relevant, deduplicated posts define a timeline. A timeline for an event is, then, a document that contains relevant entries (e.g., sentences, titles, posts) arranged in a temporal order.

In this work, we focus on the relevance estimation problem in the context of social media. Specifically, we hypothesize that social media signals such as retweets (RTs), links, likes, or shares can be effectively used to better estimate post relevance. We take advantage of all these behavioral data in conjunction with relevant tweets that contain links that point to web pages with good titles from trusted domains as the basis for constructing a timeline. To this end, we present an algorithm, based on pseudo relevance feedback demonstrating that this is possible.

WebSci'17, June 25-28, 2017, Troy, NY, USA.

978-1-4503-4896-6/17/06...$15.00
DOI: http://dx.doi.org/10.1145/3091478.3091519

2 RELATED WORK

Timeline generation is a subarea of multidocument summarization focused on temporal information. The majority of work in the community has studied news articles. Russell and Jensen present a system for generating a timeline with word clusters as items on the timeline [8]. Jones and Diaz use a language modeling approach to detect relevant document titles from an initial retrieval [6]. Qi *et al.* describe a machine learning approach for selecting sentences from a pool of sentence-segmented documents [4]. This work precipitated the TREC Temporal Summarization track [2]. A review of approaches used there is beyond the scope of this paper. Compared to the tweet timeline generation task, our technique outputs link titles extracted from tweets instead of raw tweets.

Our work focuses on the exploitable information in social media corpora and, as a result, prior work, while related conceptually, lacks precisely the signals we are interested in studying. Our research is most related to the generation of social media timelines [9]. Li and Cardie focus on generating timelines for a specific user's Twitter stream [7]. Our work diverges from this work by generating timelines from popular topics as opposed to a collection of user tweets. The timeline techniques that we propose use modifications to relevance feedback, a well-known technique in information retrieval. A detailed description of different strategies for implementing relevance feedback is presented by Harman [5]. Carpineto and Romano published a comprehensive survey of many automatic query expansion techniques [3].

3 TIMELINE GENERATION

The proposed method works as follows. We assume access to a stream of social media (i.e., the Twitter firehose or similar data feed) and the existence of a component that detects trending hashtags or entities over a period of time such as minutes or hours. Along with the trending data, it is possible to extract a contextual vector, that is, a representative set of n-grams for a hashtag for a given timestamp (i.e., date granule). This contextual vector provides a list of keywords as context for the hashtag.

As a first attempt to derive a timeline, we can select the link from the most voted tweet per granule as each link (and tweet) has an associated *counter* expressed by the number of RTs, shares, likes, or any other behavioral signal. However, this approach suffers from selecting non-relevant links as such counters can be exploited and can produce duplicate entries. We introduce a more promising strategy, based on pseudo relevance feedback called *social pseudo relevance feedback* that combines contextual vectors with a voting strategy for identifying relevant link titles extracted from tweets according to the topic. Information extracted from these link titles forms the base for the timeline generation.

3.1 Contextual Vectors

A contextual vector represents a ranked list of n-grams for a set of tweets related to a hashtag or entity. For producing the list of n-grams, we first aggregate all the tweets related to a particular hashtag over the time period of consideration using techniques introduced by Alonso *et al.* [1]. We ingest data from the Twitter firehose and perform the following steps:

- Pre-processing and data cleaning.
- Filtering by tweet quality score, English language, spam, and adult scores.
- Removal of duplicates and near-duplicates tweets using a combination of shingles and Jaccard similarity.
- Clustering short fragments for identifying clusters of tweets.
- Rank the n-grams by relevance.

As an example, based on a single day worth of tweets from January 8, 2015, the Charlie Hebdo terrorist attack was the most important trending topic for that day and `#charliehebdo` one of the most popular hashtags used by people to describe the event on Twitter. By extracting the most relevant n-grams for the hashtag, we construct the associated contextual vectors for that specific granule (8-Jan-2015): `#charliehebdo = (free speech, charlie hebdo, terrorist attack, terror attack, satirical magazine, sad day, paris attack)`.

While not a proper summary, the contextual vector for that specific calendar entry provides enough context for the hashtag. If we compute other contextual vectors per day for the entire duration of the event, we have a data source that contains the many terms and phrases used at specific time granules. This data can be very useful for expanding the original query and re-rank the link titles.

3.2 Social Pseudo Relevance Feedback

Pseudo relevance feedback is an effective mechanism for improving retrieval without any user interaction in contrast to relevance feedback that requires users to mark documents that are relevant or not to a given query.

Our proposed technique, social pseudo relevance feedback (sprf), combines user feedback with query expansion using the contextual vectors presented earlier. The contextual vectors are derived from user generated content (i.e., tweets) and we can think of those n-grams as explicit terms selected by users as votes in aggregate. Similar to pseudo relevance feedback, ranking those document links extracted from tweets by counters (i.e., behavioral data) indicates that the top-k links are relevant to a given hashtag on a specific timestamp. For query expansion, we use the contextual vector to re-rank the links based on how similar the links' titles are to the terms in the contextual vector. Because all these links have been tagged by users with a relevant and frequent hashtag, our hypothesis is that they belong to the same topic.

The technique works as follows. Given a set of tweets that share the same hashtag, we extract a set of document link titles $docs = \{d_1, \ldots, d_n\}$ from those tweets and compute the similarity $sim(q, d)$ between query q (hashtag) and document link title d. For query expansion, we compute the contextual vector $cv = \{t_1, \ldots, t_m\}$ for q (hashtag) and produce a query q' that includes terms t from cv. Given a timestamp, we compute a score that measures the similarity $sim(q', d)$ between the expanded query q' and document link title d multiplied by its counter d_c:

$$\text{score} = sim(q', d) * \log(d_c + 2)$$

where q' contains the original query q and the terms from the contextual vector cv, d is the document link title, d_c is the counter value c for d, and $sim(q', d)$ is implemented as $cos(q', d)$. A counter c here quantifies user engagement via RT, likes, or shares. Each document link title is then ranked by this new score that is computed for a given timestamp as its associated contextual vector and is only valid for that specific timestamp. For each timestamp (i.e., date), which we consider a marker on our timeline, we have a ranked list of link titles to choose from. There are similarities to local context analysis (LCA), a blind relevance feedback technique based on co-occurrence analysis between candidate expansion features and query terms described by Xu and Croft [10]. However, we rely on the contextual vector for candidate expansion terms instead of extracting them from the top-k list.

In summary, sprf takes the following steps to expand a query (hashtag in our case but can be any topic) per time unit on a collection of document links titles and re-ranks them as follows:

- Given a set of tweets, compute contextual vectors for frequent hashtag from tweets per granule. The default granule is date but it can be tuned to any specific time definition. If there is not enough tweet volume, there is no contextual vector for that date.
- Perform an initial retrieval on the set of documents for a given hashtag as query to get a top-ranked set of links extracted from tweets.
- Rewrite the original query with top-t terms from the associated contextual vector.
- Re-rank the retrieval of the link titles using the new score.

3.3 Algorithm

In contrast to other approaches that present a tweet as entry on a timeline, we rely on the link's article title that is included on a tweet as potential candidate for an entry in the timeline. The intuition is that links from trusted news-like domains (e.g., cnn.com, bbc.co.uk, etc.) are likely to be authoritative, contain a title that is well-written in English, and they are easy to read. By relying on a set of world-wide news domains, constructed by mining Twitter accounts and web domains, the timeline has the potential to be diverse.

Both contextual vectors and sprf are local operations because they process the data set given a specific time window (e.g., hours or a single day). The timeline generation is a global operation that needs to ingest data composed of many occurrences of a hashtag and associated contextual vectors over a much large time window (e.g., weeks or months). The main algorithm takes as input a set of timestamped hashtags, each hashtag has a contextual vector and a set of document link titles and outputs a single document that contains a temporal order of link titles that are relevant to a topic

```
Data: Timestamped hashtag ht, docs = {d_1, ..., d_m} and
      contextual vector cv_t = {t_1, ..., t_m}
Result: Timeline in chronological order for ht
timeline[] = ∅ ; q = ht ;
foreach timestamp in ht do
    ds[] = ∅ ;
    q' = q + cv_timestamp ;
    foreach i in docs do
        score = cos(q', d_i) * log(d_i c + 2) ;
        add (i, score) to ds ;
    end
    /* every day there is a ranked list of article titles */
    rank(ds) by score ;
    j = 0;
    / * adds top article from the ranked list to timeline. If
      similar article exists, then pick next article */
    if ds[j] not in timeline then
        add ds[j] to timeline;
    else
        repeat
            j++;
            select ds[j] ;
        until ds[j] is not in timeline;
        add ds[j] to timeline;
    end
end
foreach e in timeline do
    print timeline[e] ;
end
```

Algorithm 1: Timeline generation algorithm.

(i.e., hashtag). Pseudo code is presented in the Algorithm 1 listing. The algorithms for computing contextual vectors, sprf, and the final timeline were implemented in the SCOPE language and runs daily over a large distributed computing cluster.

4 RESULTS AND EVALUATION

We now examine the generated timelines for four different events during 2015. All examples show the timelines verbatim and, due to space limitations, a condensed version is presented. The Paris attack example, `#parisattacks`, presented in Table 1, is very specific as the global event unfolds and condenses the main points. The Republican debate, `#gopdebate`, presented in Table 2, was part of a long series of debates and shows a preview of one of them in time. Table 3 presents `#deflategate`, a niche topic but very popular nevertheless and describes correctly the progress of the NFL football tampering scandal and the actors involved. Finally, Table 4 shows the year-long Formula 1 racing calendar, `#f1`, describing race results as well as intermediate information between grand prixes.

In all cases we can observe gaps in the timelines. In the Paris example, there is no entry for 11/24/2015 which indicates that there was not enough new content discovered by the algorithm, potential removal of duplicate content, or that the associated hashtag did not contain enough data volume to be considered. The NFL example shows more gaps as the topic covers many months and there are days with no activity for such hashtag. Similarly, the F1 example has expected gaps between races. The Republican debate timeline has lesser gaps as many debates were part of the primaries.

As described in Section 2, the TREC TGG data set is a sample (we use the full firehose) and lacks the behavioral signals that we use for our algorithm and therefore is not suitable for comparison. We also note that our timelines are based on link information extracted from tweets and not raw tweets, making it more about informativeness rather than specific data points. In other words, we do not show tweets in the timeline. Instead, our timeline contains the most relevant document link titles extracted from a set of tweets.

We now describe the sprf technique offline evaluation using human judges. We produced timelines for 455 popular hashtags generated over a period of 3 months from October 1 to December 31, 2015. The task consisted on a pair-wise preference selection where each judge has to select which timeline was more informative. We use three timeline generation algorithms: baseline (rank by counter popularity), dedup (rank by counter popularity with no duplicate elimination), and sprf. For the A-B comparison we randomize the order of the algorithms. The task template is presented in Figure 1. We use an internal crowdsourcing platform for gathering labels. Each comparison was assessed by 5 judges and we took majority vote as the final answer.

In this task, you will be presented with a Twitter hashtag representing a specific event or topic. There are two timelines summarizing the sequence of important sub-events related to the hashtag. An effective timeline contains only relevant sub-events and avoids duplicate content. The timelines are not complete and can have missing information. Your task is to select which of the two timelines provides a better summary of the important sub-events.

Hashtag: "`#thehashtag`"
[Timeline A] [Timeline B]

Which of the following timelines is more informative?

[] A is better [] B is better [] They are the same

Figure 1: A-B relevance comparison task template.

We evaluate our method by examining how much the timeline can be reduced in size with duplicate elimination and how good the output is to a wider audience. We present the results of the timeline size reduction in Table 5. As mentioned early on, the popularity voting scheme (baseline) suffers from including duplicate content on the final result because the same link can be popular over more than one day. By adding exact duplicate removal in dedup (baseline vs. dedup), we can reduce the size of the timeline by 8% on average. If we then compare against sprf (baseline vs. sprf), the final size is cut in half. This is expected as baseline has a problem with potential non relevant links which are removed with sprf.

The relevance label distribution is presented in Table 6. In general, regardless of the type of hashtag, sprf has the advantage over

#parisattacks	
11/13/2015	Paris 'shooting': Several casualties after gunman opens fire
11/14/2015	Paris terror attacks: eight attackers dead after killing at least 120 people – live updates
11/15/2015	Why Syrian refugee passport found at Paris attack scene must be treated with caution
11/16/2015	Got a French flag on your Facebook profile picture? Congratulations on your corporate white supremacy
11/17/2015	I was held hostage by Isis. They fear our unity more than our airstrikes
11/18/2015	Diesel named as police dog killed in Saint Denis raids hunting for Paris attackers
11/19/2015	Incredible moment woman survives as Paris gunman tries to shoot
11/20/2015	Paris attacks: 'I will not give you the gift of hating you'
11/21/2015	Sir Richard Branson: Blaming all Muslims for Paris attacks like 'blaming all Americans for past actions of Ku Klux Klan'
11/22/2015	Paris is being used to justify agendas that had nothing to do with the attack
11/23/2015	Frankie Boyle on the fallout from Paris: 'This is the worst time for society to go on psychopathic autopilot'
11/25/2015	Glenn Greenwald: Why the CIA is smearing Edward Snowden after the Paris attacks
11/26/2015	David Cameron to make case for Syria air strikes
11/27/2015	Paris attacks: France holds service two weeks after massacre

Table 1: Unedited output example for #parisattacks, a major global event in November 2015.

#gopdebate	
8/04/2015	Rick Perry and Rick Santorum Left Off the Republican Debate Stage
8/06/2015	Carly Fiorina Knocks Donald Trump: 'I Didn't Get a Phone Call from Bill Clinton'
8/07/2015	Rubio, Bush Differ on Common Core Standards
8/08/2015	Donald Trump criticises Fox debate moderator Megyn Kelly
8/10/2015	Backing Christie Is Good Business for Bridge-and-Tunnel Lawyers
8/11/2015	Trump Leads Iowa GOP Field, Rubio Seen as Debate Winner
8/12/2015	Megyn Kelly not apologising for debate comments
8/13/2015	Roger Ailes to Donald Trump: 'We resolve this now...or go to war'
9/17/2015	Donald Trump bankruptcy: Everything you want to know
9/18/2015	No One Performed Better Than Carly Fiorina in Second Republican Debate
9/19/2015	Fiorina defends citing nonexistent abortion video
9/20/2015	Trump fails to say how he'd make America great again
9/21/2015	U.S. Should Use Offensive Cyber Tactics With China: Bush

Table 2: Unedited output example for #gopdebate, a preview of the many Republican debates during the US elections.

#deflategate	
5/06/2015	Patriots 'probably deflated balls'
5/07/2015	NFL Finds Patriots Employees Likely Deflated Balls
5/08/2015	Cheating Works: NFL tolerates Tom Brady's 'Deflategate'
5/11/2015	Tom Brady suspension seems likely
5/12/2015	Tom Brady set to appeal four-game ban as New England Patriots plot strategy
5/15/2015	NFL ban Super Bowl MVP Tom Brady for first four games
7/28/2015	Deflate-gate: NFL upholds 4-game suspension of Tom Brady
7/29/2015	LIVE VIDEO: Coach Bill Belichick speaks out on the NFL's 'Deflategate' decision
8/12/2015	NFL's Brady and Goodell Squeezed by Judge in Settlement Play
9/03/2015	Patriots' Tom Brady Faces NFL 'Deflategate' Appeal
9/04/2015	Tom Brady case: Judge overturns 'deflategate' suspension

Table 3: Unedited output example for #deflategate, an American football related event that spans several months.

dedup. By manually classifying some of those hashtags as "political", given world events around that time that included unexpected events that have a political connotation, the performance of sprf improves more. This is the kind of scenarios that we believe our timeline method provides the most value: popular events that are heavily discussed in Twitter over longer periods of time. If we look at sports related hashtags, the numbers are very comparable. For games, that usually span a couple of hours, there is not enough differentiation at the day granule. That is, the end result of the game prevails as the most relevant content. A different story is for longer events like a championship where several games are played and a longer timeline is more useful to show the progress of the competition.

For this experiment, we marked a total of 29 unique hashtags under the political category such as #parisattacks, #iran, #isis, #syria, #sanbernardino, #gopdebate, #blacklivesmatter, and

#f1	
7/06/2015	Hamilton & Moss take on Monza
8/19/2015	Nico Hulkenberg partners Sebastian Vettel for 2015 Race of Champions
8/23/2015	Belgian Grand Prix
9/03/2015	Sebastian Vettel and Kimi Raikkonen in harmony over close relationship
9/05/2015	Lewis Hamilton shocked by McLaren's fall from grace
9/06/2015	McLaren reserve Kevin Magnussen says he needs to race in F1 next season
9/07/2015	Red Bull exploring all options for 2016 engine deal
9/16/2015	Renault hint that their engine deal with Red Bull will end this season
9/17/2015	Romain Grosjean reveals he has 'made his decision' on 2016 future
9/18/2015	Volkswagen close to buying Red Bull F1 team
9/19/2015	Red Bull will quit F1 if they don't get a competitive engine in 2016
9/20/2015	Sebastian Vettel starts to dream the 'impossible' after Singapore win
9/21/2015	Daniel Ricciardo believes track invader cost him a shot at winning the Singapore Grand Prix
9/22/2015	Singapore GP track invader charged by authorities
9/23/2015	Force India confirm that Sergio Perez is staying put next season
9/26/2015	Daniil Kvyat crashes in Japanese GP qualifying
9/27/2015	Niki Lauda says Red Bull never came back to confirm engine deal

Table 4: Unedited output example for #f1, a year long racing sports event for 2015.

Timeline comparison	Size reduction %
baseline vs. dedup	8%
baseline vs. sprf	50.5%
dedup vs. sprf	41.5%

Table 5: Timeline size reduction comparison.

Label	All	Political	Sports
baseline	15.5%	10.3%	27%
dedup	35.6%	32.8%	27%
sprf	37.2%	43.1%	27%
same	11.7%	13.8%	19%

Table 6: Relevance evaluation label distribution.

#refugees to name a few. For sports, we marked a total of 22 unique hashtags that describe the name of a club (#barca, #mcfc), the name of a sport (#soccer, #football), or a main competition like the Rugby World Cup (#rwc2015). Finally, timeline evaluation has a number of challenges as well. Judges need to be familiar with the topic and able to recognize a potential sequence of events when assessing. This can be difficult when timelines are longer and somewhat difficult to compare.

5 CONCLUSION AND FUTURE WORK

We presented an algorithm based on social pseudo relevance feedback that constructs a timeline by using only social data as input. The described method has been implemented in a real-world system using the Twitter firehose as input. We provided enough technical information so the technique can be implemented and the experiments and evaluations replicated. We conducted an offline evaluation that shows that our technique produce smaller size timelines with much more relevant content. A data analysis reveals that sprf performs well when the hashtag describes an event that covers multiple days, like political or world events. Sports hashtags have a more specific temporal pattern, mostly due to specific games, so sprf is comparable to other methods.

The overall results are encouraging and we plan to continue improving the techniques. We believe that timeline representations are information rich structures that can be used in many scenarios such as summarization, event descriptions that provide different views or perspectives, event graph annotation, and exploratory search. Future work includes better term ranking for contextual vectors, experimenting with different term weights, and improving the coherence of the timelines.

REFERENCES

[1] Omar Alonso, Sushma Bannur, Kartikay Khandelwal, and Shankar Kalyanaraman. 2015. The World Conversation: Web Page Metadata Generation From Social Sources. In *Proc. of WWW.* 385–395.

[2] Javed Aslam, Fernando Diaz, Matthew Ekstrand-Abueg, Virgi Pavlu, and Tetsuya Sakai. 2013. Overview of the TREC 2013 Temporal Summmarization Track. In *Proc. of TREC.*

[3] Claudio Carpineto and Giovanni Romano. 2012. A Survey of Automatic Query Expansion in Information Retrieval. *ACM Comput. Surv.* 44, 1 (2012), 1:1–1:50.

[4] Qi Guo, Fernando Diaz, and Elad Yom-Tov. 2013. Updating Users about Time Critical Events. In *Proc. of ECIR.* 483–494.

[5] Donna Harman. 1992. Relevance Feedback Revisited. In *Proc. of SIGIR.* 1–10.

[6] Rosie Jones and Fernando Diaz. 2007. Temporal profiles of queries. *ACM Trans. Inf. Syst.* 25, 3 (July 2007), 14.

[7] Jiwei Li and Claire Cardie. 2014. Timeline Generation: Tracking Individuals on Twitter. In *Proc. of WWW.* 643–652.

[8] Russell Swan and David Jensen. 2000. TimeMines: Constructing Timelines with Statistical Models of Word Usage. In *ACM SIGKDD Workshop on Text Mining.*

[9] Yulu Wang, Garrick Sherman, Jimmy Lin, and Miles Efron. 2015. Assessor Differences and User Preferences in Tweet Timeline Generation. In *Proc. of SIGIR.* 615–624.

[10] Jinxi Xu and W. Bruce Croft. 2000. Improving the effectiveness of information retrieval with local context analysis. *ACM Trans. Inf. Syst.* 18, 1 (2000), 79–112.

Cultural Fault Lines and Political Polarization

Yongren Shi
Yale University
New Haven, Connecticut
yongren.shi@yale.edu

Kai Mast
Cornell University
Ithaca, New York
kaimast@cs.cornell.edu

Ingmar Weber
Qatar Computing Research Institute, HBKU
Doha, Qatar
iweber@hbku.edu.qa

Agrippa Kellum
Cornell University
Ithaca, New York
ask252@cornell.edu

Michael Macy
Cornell University
Ithaca, New York
mwmacy@cornell.edu

ABSTRACT

Survey research reveals deep partisan divisions in the U.S. that extend beyond politics to include cultural tastes, lifestyle choices, and consumer preferences. We show how co-following on Twitter can be used to measure the extent to which these divisions are also evident in social media. We measure political alignment (location on the red-blue spectrum), relevance (overlap between cultural and political interests), and polarization (internal division) in music, movies, hobbies, sports, vehicles, food and drink, technology, universities, religions, and business. The results provide compelling evidence that "Tesla liberals" and "bird hunting conservatives" are stereotypes grounded in empirical reality.

CCS CONCEPTS

•Information systems → Online advertising; •Networks → Online social networks; •Applied computing → Sociology;

KEYWORDS

Polarization, Culture, Social Media, Networks

1 INTRODUCTION

Extensive research has revealed deep cultural fault lines in America, not only aligned with politically salient issues, but also geographic regions, class, gender, race, ethnicity, and education [1, 3, 11, 12, 16]. Liberal and conservative ideology has also been shown to align with moral hot buttons, lifestyle choices, and consumer preferences. In his popular book *The Big Sort*, Bishop [5] shows a polarized nation that is divided into red and blue regions not only by voting behavior but also by lifestyle profiles of "Books, Beers, Bikes, and Birkenstocks" (p. 196). A sweeping analysis of opinion items in the General Social Survey cumulative file (1968-2010) shows a consistent pattern of association between political opinions and cultural tastes [10].

WebSci'17, June 25-28, 2017, Troy, NY, USA.

978-1-4503-4896-6/17/06...$15.00
DOI: http://dx.doi.org/10.1145/3091478.3091520

Much of the previous research on cultural polarization has relied on opinion surveys, which measure retrospective responses to items that interest researchers though not necessarily the respondents. More importantly, recent studies reveal a rising rate of non-response in landline-administered surveys, which raises concerns about the external validity of survey methodology. Growing availability of data from social media opens up unprecedented opportunities to use digital traces of human communications to record real-time behavioral indicators of salient preferences [15]. Recent examples include the study of partisan preferences for popular science [21], linguistic usage [17], and TV shows (http://nyti.ms/2ize1lN). People follow, like, comment, reply, purchase, listen to or watch celebrities, organizations, topics, issues, news items, events, books, bands, and videos on myriad social media platforms and in real time. These data capture preferences that may not be detected in survey responses. For example, respondents are less likely to reveal to researchers their "politically incorrect" attitudes that are often criticized by mainstream media. The failure of polls to predict the Brexit vote in Britain or the 2016 Presidential election in the U.S. have been attributed to this "shy voter" problem (http://wapo.st/2ik1EJO), but this explanation has also been challenged (http://53eig.ht/2jbciXC).

This study examines data from one of the largest social media sites, Twitter, to identity lifestyle preferences that reinforce or bridge political divisions in the U.S. Our study proposes a novel method based on co-following graphs to impute political interest in lifestyle accounts using the followers of the U.S. Congress. In contrast to most studies [2, 4, 6, 8] that measured polarization as bi-modality in the distribution of opinion, this study measures polarization as the clustering of the population into opposing camps, each of whose members agree internally across multiple dimensions of the cultural landscape, such that one can predict how someone will vote by knowing their favorite TV show or hot beverage – a pattern also known in political science as "constraint" [3, 9] that creates partisan echo chambers [10]. Co-following graph, measuring alignment between political and cultural issues based on a common set of followers, extends greatly the current research on political polarization in that it allows to measure the political leaning of Twitter accounts that have no direct linkage with politicians. For instance, Pepsi's Twitter account would avoid to be associated with any Congress member, while it doesn't prevent ordinary users from following both Pepsi and members in Congress. Note that a conservative political alignment, e.g. country music, does not mean that the musicians are conservative (although some of them no doubt are). We mean that their social media followers are conservative. We also measure political relevance (overlapping interest in culture and politics) and political alignment (relative interest in the topic by followers of liberal versus conservative Congress members).

2 DATA AND METHODS

The Twitter dataset was created by identifying 553 members of the 111th, 112th, and 113th Congresses who have at least 1000 followers on Twitter. (Below 1000 followers, observations are too sparse for reliable measurements of co-following association between two accounts, as the expected size of co-followers would approach zero). We then collected all the followers of 553 Congress members as well as the Twitter accounts associated with popular culture, personalities and organizations, including pundits, musicians, Fortune 100 companies, restaurants, sports teams, Billboard 100, and religions. The co-follower graph [13, 22] is based on the assumption that each user who follows a popular lifestyle account (e.g. a country music star) and a conservative Congress member is voting with their keyboard for the conservative alignment of a musical genre.

2.1 Political Alignment Index

Political alignment is measured in two steps, which can be illustrated using a Twitter example. First, we calculate the *lift* in the probability that a random member c of the entire set of co-followers in our dataset will follow both a particular politician (a Congress member) j and a particular musician i, compared to the probability that c will follow either j or i. Second, having calculated lift for all the politicians that are co-followed with i, we use lift as a weight to compute the weighted mean of the political scores (S_j) across all the politicians. The mean-centered result is i's political alignment score. Lift can also be interpreted as the ratio between the observed and expected overlap of i and j. The expected value controls for the differences in popularity. For instance, Taylor Swift has many more followers on Twitter than Rodriquez, so she would have a larger overlap with politicians. By adjusting the observed overlap with the expected, we eliminate the bias that is caused by popularity.

$$L_{ij} = \frac{P(i \cap j)}{P(i)P(j)} \tag{1}$$

where $P(i \cap j)$ indicates how likely a randomly chosen user shares interests in both the cultural (i) and political (j) categories. $P(i)P(j)$ indicates the expected probability of intersection between these two categories, given the size of each. In step 2, we use L as a weight when averaging the political scores of all the political categories (Congress members in Twitter data):

$$S_i = \frac{\sum_j L_{ij} \times S_j}{\sum_i L_{ij}} - \bar{S}_J \tag{2}$$

S_i is the mean-centered weighted mean of political scores for all j political categories. We subtract the simple mean ($\bar{S}_J$) to adjust for uneven partisan distribution (which is especially problematic on Twitter where Republican Congress members outnumber Democrats). S_j is derived from Poole and Rosenthal's [18, 19] DW-Nominate (DWN) scores, a standard and reliable measurement of political ideology imputed from the roll call voting records in the U.S. Congress. The DWN scores range from -1 to 1, indicating most liberal and most conservative leaning in the voting behavior in the Congress. For Twitter, we simply assign the DWN score for the Congress member to the political category j for which that Congress member is the unique member.

2.2 Political Relevance Index

Political relevance is measured by the fraction of followers of all accounts in that cultural dimension who also follow members of Congress (whether liberal or conservative). The higher the political relevance, the greater the likelihood that followers of Congress will follow accounts in the cultural topic. Two factors contribute to the political relevance of a Twitter account, the size of politically interested followers and the popularity of the account. Extremely popular cultures, e.g. Billboard 100 musician accounts, are least politically relevant.

2.3 Political Polarization Index

Political polarization of a category, e.g. religion, is the extent to which partisans follow different entities. Polarization measure draws an important distinction from the alignment measure, in that political alignment reports the average ideological leaning of all the users in a category, while political polarization reveals a possible internal divide even when the average alignment is in the middle of the political spectrum. We measure the polarization of a category using kurtosis, the fourth standardized moment of a distribution.

$$k = \frac{E[(X-\mu)^4]}{(E[(X-\mu)^2])^2} - 3 \tag{3}$$

where μ is the mean of the distribution. If the distribution of political alignment scores in one category is peaked (indicating a high level of integration and consensus of ordinary users' choices), kurtosis is positive. If it is flatter than the normal distribution, kurtosis is negative. If the distribution reaches bimodality (roughly half of the accounts are co-followed with Republican Congress members, and the other half co-followed with Democratic Congress Members), kurtosis approaches -2. The kurtosis was used to measure attitude polarization in [11].

3 POLITICAL ALIGNMENT

3.1 Congress

We first impute various culture domains' political alignment and validated our methodology by comparing imputed political alignment with the ground truth obtained from external sources. These included Congress members, pundits, musicians who endorsed candidates, restaurants whose customers were surveyed, and Fortune 100 companies who made political contributions.

For Congress members, we compared the observed DWN score of each member with the imputed score using data from the other 552 members. The results in Figure 1 show a near-perfect correlation (r=0.955). The correlation increases with recency of the Congress, indicating that the following behavior on Twitter may have become more politically salient over time (and slightly less influenced by celebrity), in line with observations in a long-term study [14].

We repeated the procedure for celebrities and companies with known political affiliations. Table 1 shows near-perfect correlations for Congress members and political pundits and highly significant

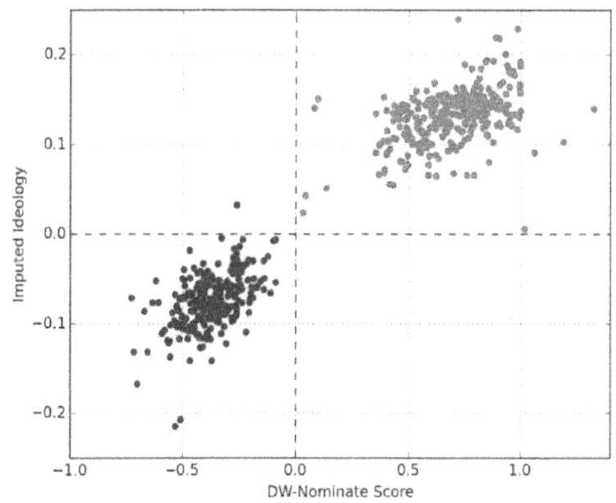

Figure 1: Scatterplot of the imputed ideology and DW-Nominate scores for 553 Congress Members.

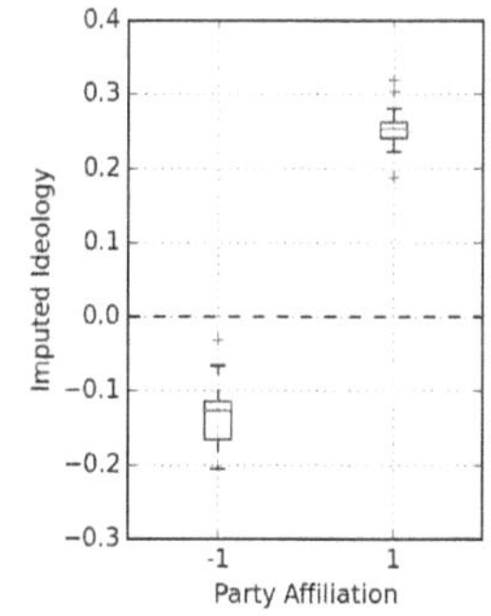

Figure 2: Comparison of the imputed ideology with self-identified party affiliations of 35 political pundits.

but somewhat weaker correlations for the other categories, likely reflecting noise in the ground truth measures. For example, the political alignment of corporations is based on employee contributions, which are often given to both parties in order to hedge the election outcome.

Category	Correlation	p	N
Congress (111th-113th)	0.955	$p < 0.001$	552
111th	0.951	$p < 0.001$	362
112th	0.954	$p < 0.001$	462
113th	0.960	$p < 0.001$	499
Musicians	0.746	$p < 0.001$	66
Fortune 100	0.597	$p < 0.001$	100
Pundits	0.981	$p < 0.001$	35
Chain Restaurants	0.657	$p < 0.01$	24

Table 1: Correlation between imputed ideology and observed political alignments for politicians, pundits, musicians, corporations, and restaurants.

Figure 2 reports imputed ideology for 35 popular liberal and conservative political pundits in the U.S. corresponding to the correlation reported in Table 1 (r=.981, $p < 0.001$).

3.2 Musicians

Similarly, we collected all the musicians who publicly endorsed presidential candidates in the 2008 and 2012 elections. Figure 3 compares imputed alignments of musicians with their political endorsements obtained from Wikipedia pages. Figure 3a plots imputed political alignment by party affiliation (based on candidate endorsements). The results correspond to the correlation reported in Table 1 (r= 0.746, $p < 0.001$). Figure 3 show the bipartite network projections, with node color indicating imputed political alignment (3b) and genre (3c), and node location based on pairwise affiliation. In Figure 3b and all the network projections that follow, nodes are located based on pairwise bipartite affiliations in the projected network [22]. In the network projection, the strength of the affiliation between two pundits increases with the relative overlap of their

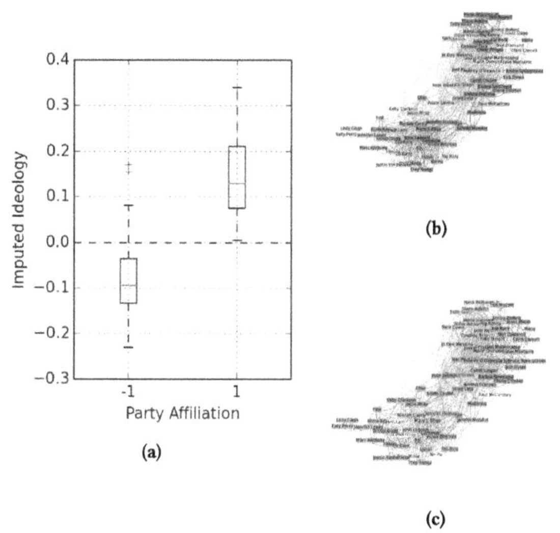

Figure 3: a. Comparison of imputed ideology with party affiliation (based on candidate endorsements) for 66 musicians. b and c are bipartite network projections of musicians, colored by imputed ideology (b) and music genre (c) and located by pairwise affiliations.

co-followers. These affiliations correspond to pairwise proximities in the visualization using the "backbone" procedure introduced in [20] for complex weighted networks. As shown in the figure, country music is the genre most likely to be co-followed with Congressional conservatives, while all the other genres are aligned with moderates or liberals.

Figure 4 extends the analysis to musicians of unknown political affiliation, using data from Musicbrainz.com and allmusics.com. Results are consistent with those in Figure 3b, with country musicians clustered and distinct from other genre whose political alignments are mostly moderate to liberal.

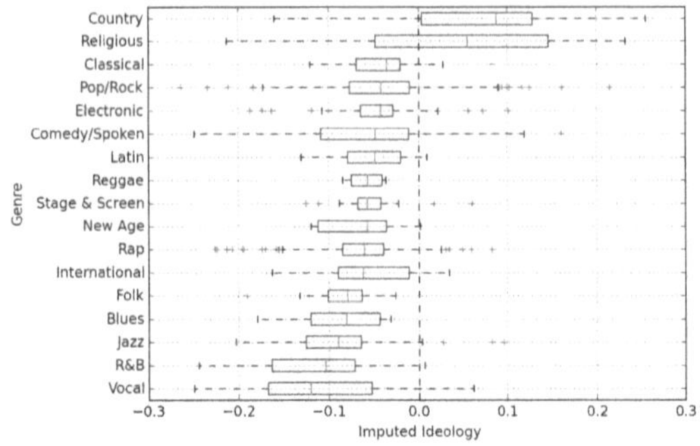

Figure 4: Music genre and political alignment. Ordered political alignment scores for music genres.

3.3 Fortune 100 Companies

We identified political alignments of Fortune 100 companies using employee donations to federal and state political campaigns listed in the Dime database built from the Federal Election Commission data [7]. We constructed two measures of political alignment based on these employee donations, the proportion of the total amount donated that went to the Republican Party (which is heavily biased by the large donations from top executives) and the proportion of the number of unique donations that went to the Republican Party (which indicates the political preference of the majority of employees). We limited the analysis to the top 100 most followed companies that have at least 100 unique donations in the 2008 to 2012 election cycles. Figure 5 visualizes the correlation reported in Table 1 (r = 0.597, $p < 0.001$) between employee campaign donations and the ideology imputed from co-followers of the company and members of Congress, indicating that the larger the proportional contribution made to the Republican Party, the more likely the company is co-followed on Twitter by followers of Congressional conservatives.

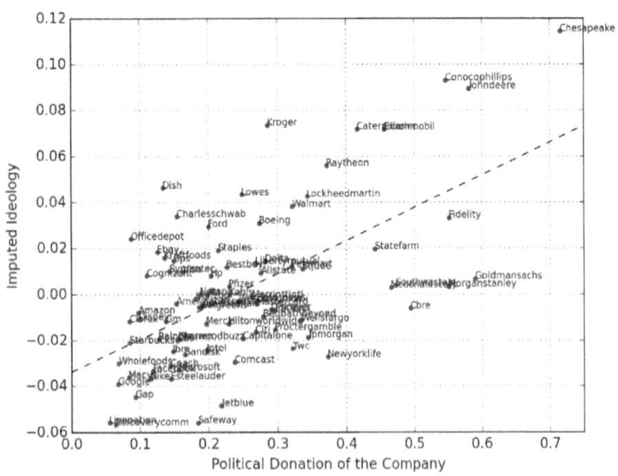

Figure 5: Imputed political alignment of the Fortune 100 and the political donations of employees.

3.4 Restaurants

We measured the political preferences of customers of major restaurants and supermarkets using data from marketing surveys conducted by Experian Marketing Services (http://on.wsj.com/1lGJKzb). Figure 6 visualizes the correlation reported in Table 1 (r=.657, $p < 0.01$) between observed scores and the political alignment imputed from co-followers with Congress. The results indicate general agreement between the restaurants' customers and followers, with the curious exception of the Big Boy restaurant.

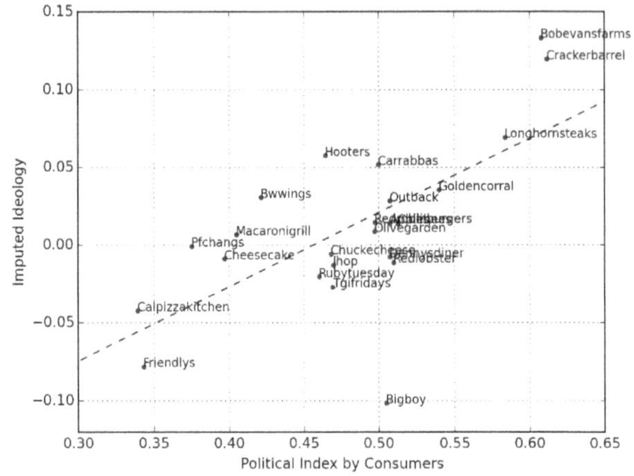

Figure 6: Imputed political alignment of restaurants and the political preferences of customers.

4 POLITICAL RELEVANCE AND POLITICAL POLARIZATION

Figure 7 reports political relevance and polarization of several cultural dimensions, including music and sports, with political alignment indicated by color (ranging from red for conservative followers to blue for liberal). Figure 7 includes Congress members and political pundits to provide a benchmark for assessing the politicization of presumably non-political cultural interests. Results for political relevance show political interest in all the widely followed cultural dimensions is substantially less than for pundits, as might be expected. Nevertheless, these cultural dimensions are not apolitical. Religion attracts the most political interest, followed closely by restaurants. Religious accounts also have the strongest conservative alignment. Religion is also among the most highly polarized, indicating that liberals and conservatives follow different religious accounts. In contrast, music tends to attract more liberals than conservatives, and the Billboard 100 artists are the most polarized, due to the concentration of conservative interest in country western and religious music. Figure 8 graphically shows the polarized following pattern of Billboard 100 musicians. Country Western musicians are highly clustered and separated from other musicians by having much more conservatives followers, in contrast to other musicians whose followers tend to be slightly to the left of center. Figure 7 also shows cultural dimensions that are healing the political divide, including Automobile, News and Media, Fortune 500, and TV programs.

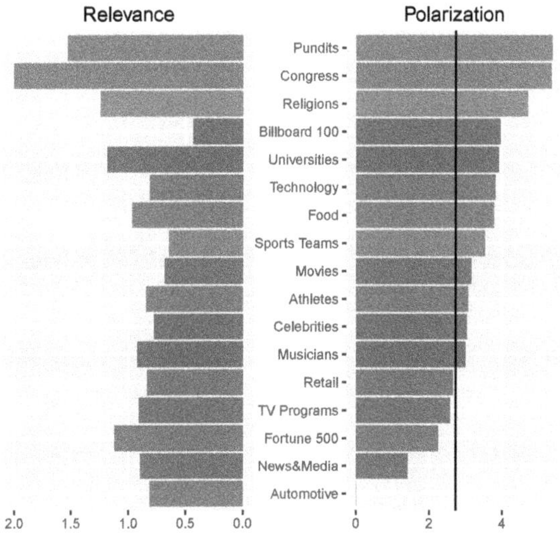

Figure 7: Comparisons of political relevance, polarization and alignment of widely followed cultural dimensions. Color indicates alignment from liberal (blue) to conservative (red), corresponding to the relative interest in the topic by liberals versus conservatives. The widths of the bars (x axis) in the left panel indicate political relevance of cultural topics, and those in the right panel indicate political polarization. Congressmen and pundits are included as a political benchmark for assessing the politicization of cultural dimensions.

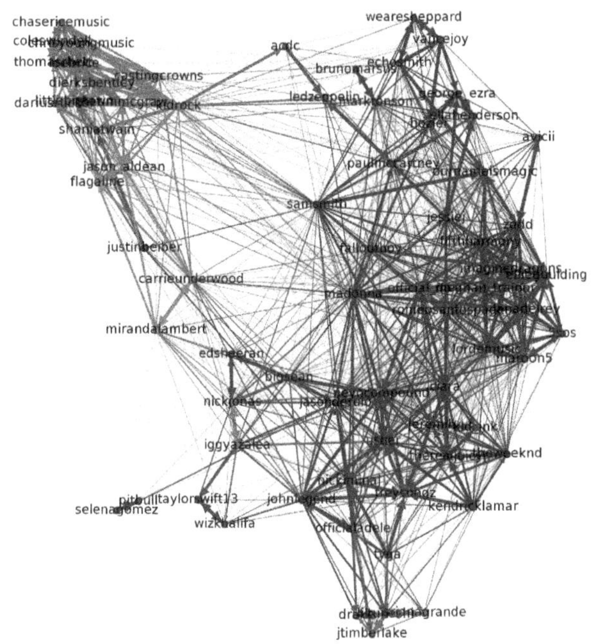

Figure 8: Network Visualization of the Co-following Pattern of the Billboard 100 Music Artists. Nodes are colored according to their imputed political alignment.

5 DISCUSSION AND CONCLUSION

Our analysis of Twitter data suggests that the widely discussed partisan divisions on public policy extend to cultural tastes and lifestyle preferences. Placed in historical context, the cultural fault lines evident on social media have a troubling implication: A long history of assimilating immigrants into a cultural "melting pot" appears to have given way to the formation of politically aligned lifestyle enclaves. Our research also shows how social media data can provide an important window into the polarization of culture that complements traditional survey methods. Opinion surveys are limited to retrospective responses to questions that interest investigators, while social media data provide real time behavioral indicators, significantly expanding the scope and depth of the potential research questions that can be addressed.

REFERENCES

[1] Alan I. Abramowitz. 2011. *The Disappearing Center: Engaged Citizens, Polarization, and American Democracy.* Yale University Press.

[2] Lada A. Adamic and Natalie Glance. 2005. The Political Blogosphere and the 2004 U.S. Election: Divided They Blog. In *LinkKDD*. 36–43.

[3] Delia Baldassarri and Andrew Gelman. 2008. Partisans Without Constraint: Political Polarization and Trends in American Public Opinion. *Amer. J. Sociology* 114, 2 (2008), 408–446.

[4] Pablo Barberá. 2015. Birds of the Same Feather Tweet Together: Bayesian Ideal Point Estimation Using Twitter Data. *Political Analysis* 23, 1 (2015), 76.

[5] Bill Bishop. 2008. *The Big Sort: Why the Clustering of Like-minded America Is Tearing Us Apart.* Houghton Mifflin.

[6] Rorbert Bond and Solomon Messing. 2015. Quantifying Social Media's Political Space: Estimating Ideology from Publicly Revealed Preferences on Facebook. *American Political Science Review* 109, 01 (2015), 62–78.

[7] Adam Bonica. 2013. Database on Ideology, Money in Politics, and Elections: Public version 1.0. (2013). http://data.stanford.edu/dime.

[8] Michael Conover, Jacob Ratkiewicz, Matthew R. Francisco, Bruno Gonçalves, Filippo Menczer, and Alessandro Flammini. 2011. Political Polarization on Twitter. In *ICWSM*.

[9] Philip E. Converse. 2006. The nature of belief systems in mass publics (1964). *Critical Review* 18, 1–3 (2006), 1–74.

[10] Daniel DellaPosta, Yongren Shi, and Michael Macy. 2015. Why Do Liberals Drink Lattes? *Amer. J. Sociology* 120, 5 (2015), 1473–1511.

[11] Paul DiMaggio, John Evans, and Bethany Bryson. 1996. Have American's Social Attitudes Become More Polarized? *Amer. J. Sociology* 102, 3 (1996), 690–755.

[12] Morris P. Fiorina, Samuel J. Abrams, and Jeremy Pope. 2005. *Culture War? The Myth of a Polarized America.* Pearson Longman.

[13] Venkata Rama Kiran Garimella and Ingmar Weber. 2014. Co-following on twitter. In *HyperText*. 249–254.

[14] Venkata Rama Kiran Garimella and Ingmar Weber. 2017. A Long-Term Analysis of Polarisation on Twitter. In *ICWSM*. to appear.

[15] Scott A. Golder and Michael W. Macy. 2014. Digital Footprints: Opportunities and Challenges for Online Social Research. *Annual Review of Sociology* 40, 1 (2014), 129–152.

[16] James Davison Hunter. 1991. *Culture Wars: The Struggle to Define America.* Basic Books.

[17] William Labov. 2010. *Principles of Linguistic Change, Volume III, Cognitive and Cultural Factors.* Wiley-Blackwell.

[18] Keith T. Poole and Howard Rosenthal. 1991. Patterns of congressional voting. *American Journal of Political Science* 35 (1991), 228–278. Issue 1.

[19] Keith T. Poole and Howard Rosenthal. 2001. *Congress: a Political-economic History of Roll Call Voting.* Oxford University Press.

[20] M. Ángeles Serrano, Marián Boguñá, and Alessandro Vespignani. 2009. Extracting the multiscale backbone of complex weighted networks. 106, 16 (2009), 6483–6488.

[21] Feng Shi, Yongren Shi, Fedor Dokshin, Michael W. Macy, and James Evans. 2017. Millions of Online Book Co-purchases Reveal Partisan Differences in the Consumption of Science. *Nature Human Behavior* 3, 0079 (2017). DOI: http://dx.doi.org/10.1145/1219092.1219093

[22] Yongren Shi and Michael W. Macy. 2016. Measuring Structural Similarity in Large Online Networks. *Social Science Research* 59 (2016), 97–106.

EDSV: Emerging Defect Surveillance for Vehicles

Jiejun Xu, Daniel Xie, Tsai-Ching Lu
HRL Laboratories
3011 Malibu Canyon Road
Malibu, CA 90265
{jxu,dkxie,tlu}@hrl.com

John Cafeo
General Motors R&D
30500 Mound Road
Warren, MI 48090
john.cafeo@gm.com

ABSTRACT

We present early findings on building a proof of concept for an automated system to identify emerging trends regarding vehicle defects. The proposed system functions by continuously collecting and monitoring publicly available data from several heterogeneous channels ranging from online social media to vehicle enthusiast forums and consumer reporting sites. By mining the collected data, the system would provide real-time detection of ongoing consumer issues with vehicles. In addition, our system has special emphasis on detecting early signals prior to the widespread knowledge of the general public. One of the system components involves estimating a baseline statistical distribution governing the frequency of observing specific types of vehicle defective complaints from our data sources and subsequently identifying irregular deviations from this distribution. A web interface is made available to visualize descriptive statistics derived from various channels, with the intent to provide timely insights for human analysts.

CCS CONCEPTS

• **Information systems → Data analytics**; *Web mining*;

KEYWORDS

Measurement; Online Social Media; User Generated Content; Business Intelligence; Quality Management

ACM Reference format:
Jiejun Xu, Daniel Xie, Tsai-Ching Lu and John Cafeo. 2017. EDSV: Emerging Defect Surveillance for Vehicles. In *Proceedings of WebSci '17, Troy, NY, USA, June 25-28, 2017,* 4 pages.
https://doi.org/http://dx.doi.org/10.1145/3091478.3091521

1 INTRODUCTION

In recent years, increased public attention has focused on the automotive industry's handling of vehicle recalls due to performance defects. Since the impact of a recall effort is largely proportional to the number of vehicle units sold, the early discovery of defects is critical in maintaining customer goodwill and reducing recall costs for auto manufacturers. Modern automobiles are more complex than ever before, and a minor defect may impact the functionality of a range of other components, making it imperative to identify any potential defects at an early stage.

Traditionally, vehicle manufacturers identify potential vehicle issues through specific inspection and maintenance procedures. These procedures have a long life cycle, but are often slow in anticipating widespread recall events. However, as a result of major advances in web technologies, the general public is now a source for highly accessible information relevant to vehicle performance issues. Researchers have begun exploiting these data sources to tackle ambitious tasks such as predicting potential future vehicle recalls [2, 8], and an eventual goal of preventing future vehicle recalls. Inspired by their works, we developed a novel Emerging Defect Surveillance for Vehicles (EDSV) system which aims to provide high quality topical information and decision support assistance to human analysts monitoring for vehicle defect issues.

In contrast to the aforementioned prior works [2, 8] which focused exclusively on web forum data to analyze and predict vehicle defect-related recalls, EDSV employs data from several heterogeneous sources. Specifically, the proposed system collects information from social media services (e.g., *Twitter*), topical online complaint resources (e.g., *CarComplaints.com*), automotive forums (e.g., *ChevroletForum.com*), and online bulletin boards (e.g., *Reddit*). There are key advantages to utilizing multiple data sources. One immediate advantage is that these sites have different user bases, allowing the system to gather information from diverse segments of the population and to fuse multiple signals into a strong indicator. Another advantage is that some of the new sources utilized by EDSV provide higher data quality. For example, the approach taken in [2, 8] is to identify vehicle defect-related contents based solely on matching of specific keywords from forum text alone, which runs a high risk of generating false positives. By employing information from multiple online sources that are complementary to each other, EDSV obtains a higher level of detail and confidence regarding specific issues. In addition, our system augments prior works by precisely pinpointing potential troublesome issues or recalls to the level of specific vehicle models, years, and general categories of vehicle components (e.g., engine problems or fuel system problems). In the rest of the paper, we expound on the process of building EDSV and provide initial findings. Specifically, we discuss characteristics of our data sources and explain how we use such data for the identification of emerging trends concerning vehicle defects.

2 OPEN SOURCE DATA COLLECTION

A wide range of data sources is collected and integrated into the EDSV system. We briefly describe these sources and their features.

Online Social Media: Social media and microblogging platforms have been widely shown to be useful in the tracking and

ACM ISBN 978-1-4503-4896-6/17/06...$15.00
https://doi.org/http://dx.doi.org/10.1145/3091478.3091521

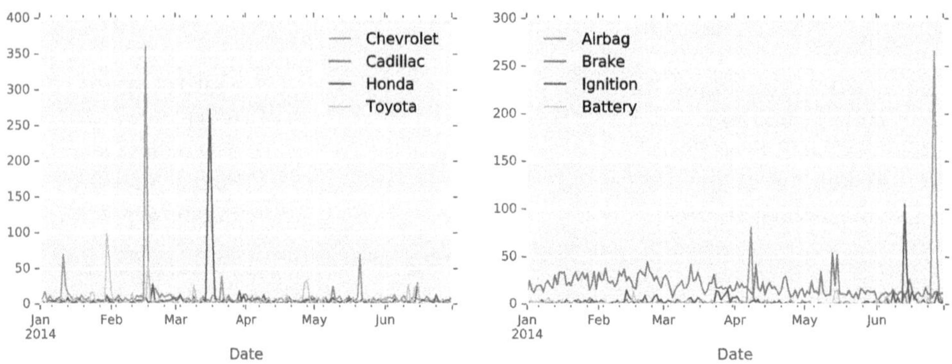

Figure 1: (a) Twitter co-mentions of (a) brands and fire-related key terms; (b) brands (e.g., Chevrolet) and component terms.

monitoring of real-world events. In particular, *Twitter* is considered of particular relevance as the platform has been studied extensively in the literature for emerging event/topic detection [3–5]. We retrieve Twitter data via subscription to the GNIP[1] Twitter Decashose service, which contains a 10% random sample of all public Tweets. The GNIP data is delivered to our system in real-time and stored in an Apache Hadoop cluster with combined memory in the terabyte scale for stream processing.

Consumer Reporting Sites: We collect data from *CarComplaints.com*, a well known consumer reporting web site that serves as a rich source of user-generated vehicle-related complaints. We have developed a specialized web crawler to extract information from this web site on different levels of detail. On one level, for a given vehicle model and year, we extract the number of complaints in a general category grouped by types of component. On another level, we extract a more specific description of those same complaints, with a given numerical score for how many users reported a specific complaint at the sub-component level. We additionally pull aggregate information about NHTSA (National Highway Traffic Safety Administration) complaints for a given model and year using the same source. The web crawler is able to selectively pull information for specific brands and can also be set to automatically ignore models with a number of complaints below some given thresholds. We have successfully utilized this crawler to gather relevant complaint data for eight major automobile brands (see Table 1 and 2).

Forums: We also collect auxiliary data from the specific web forums (e.g., *ChevroletForum.com*) as listed by [1, 2, 8] for automobile enthusiasts. We have constructed another web crawler to recursively download all historical posts from the subforums contained within the targeted forums. Additional information such as post times, user names, and thread titles are also captured and stored in a standardized format for future use to the end users. We have so far successfully gathered all pertinent posts from these forums going back to over a decade. A text-based vehicle tagger was also developed to annotate posts that mention specific vehicle brands, models, and years. In addition, we also collect information on the interaction aspects (e.g., replies) of these forums. We believe that there is additional potential to identify particularly influential users or domain experts to gain insight into vehicle defect and related issues.

Online Bulletin Boards: We have access to years of publicly available complete post data for the online bulletin board Reddit, which has numerous discussion threads ("subreddits") for vehicle maintenance and vehicle enthusiasts. This data is conveniently indexed online and can be publicly accessed through the use of big data processing tools such as Google BigQuery[2]. Currently this data is employed much like the forums as an auxiliary source of information to provide the end user additional detail about vehicle issues.

3 DATA ANALYSIS METHODOLOGY

We have conducted initial analyses for each type of data source, but we focus our discussion on the first two aforementioned data in this paper. These two sources serve in complementary aspects to identify vehicle defect issues.

Real-time Event Detection

We apply a cascade of text-based filters to continually detect and monitor defects and related events from our Twitter data stream. Essentially EDSV searches each Twitter post for (1) vehicle brand mentions (e.g., "Chevrolet", "Toyota"), and (2) keywords that are considered to be highly relevant to defect issues. Posts that pass through both filters are collected and marked for appraisal. The underlying assumption for such an approach is that the selected keywords should show a marked increase in usage during the period an event is unfolding [7]. Therefore an event may be identified by rapid "bursts" in the relevant post counts. In the current implementation, we have compiled two lists of keywords. The first list contains words with fire-related semantics (e.g., fire, flames, melt), which is derived from a subset of SMOKE words described in [2]. The second list contains words harvested from the 2015 NHTSA Defect Investigations Database[3]. This list consists of the most common defective components (e.g., airbags, brakes, steering) mentioned in the database. Note that the first list attempts to identify general fire-related defect events, and the second list focuses on finding potential events related to specific vehicle components.

[1]https://gnip.com/sources/twitter/

[2]https://www.reddit.com/r/bigquery/wiki/datasets

[3]www-odi.nhtsa.dot.gov/downloads/flatfiles.cfm

Figure 1(a) shows the time series of co-mentions of vehicle brands and fire-related keywords from the first half of 2014. Multiple spikes corresponding to various vehicle defect-related events can be observed from the time series. For instance, there is a major fire risk related recall for Honda Odysseys minivan, which corresponds to the spike in March. Several spikes are also observed for Chevrolet that are linked to recalls on a few truck and SUV models due to fire risks. Similarly, there are two major recall events for Toyota identified, which are related to the fire hazard/incidences caused by improper fuel tubes in the FJ cruiser. Figure 1(b) shows the time series of co-mentions of the brand "Chevrolet" and vehicle components. A large spike is seen in June for "airbag", which can be tied to the recall of Chevrolet Cruzes for potential airbag defects. It should be remarked that it is crucial to examine the context of sudden spikes before concluding that a major event is occurring. A large number of small spikes are observed with the co-mention of the term "brakes", but careful inspection reveals that these small spikes are actually due to product promotion rather than a significant event occurring. A key aspect of EDSV that should not be neglected is that we are able to precisely identify the geographic locations where the social media posts are coming from (see Figure 3). This is done by utilizing the large geo-location database of Twitter users identified in prior work [6]. We believe that the spatial-temporal information generated by EDSV is crucial for business operations.

Emerging Trend Detection

In this section, we describe how our system is capable of identifying early indicators for emerging defect-related trends significantly prior to the widespread knowledge of the general public. Our primary method of detecting such emerging events is through analysis of the collected data from the consumer reporting site *CarComplaints.com*. We use the relative frequency of types of car complaints aggregated over a large range of makes, models, and years to generate a baseline distribution for how often we should expect a specific type of complaint relative to other complaints. In Figure 2, we provide a graphic to visualize the relative frequencies of complaints over all years and models compared to a specific model year vehicle. A noticeable deviation from the baseline can be seen for the "steering" category, which corresponds to a known issue with that vehicle [4].

To carry out our analysis, we treat these relative frequencies as density estimates to compute two metrics indicative of whether there is an potential issue with a category of vehicle component for a given model and year. For the first metric, we simply difference the observed relative frequency of a type of complaint aggregated over all years and models from the observed relative frequency of that type of complaint for a specific year and model. We then aggregate these values and use the largest values this metric takes as being indicative of potential issues. For the second metric, we model the number of complaints that occur in a given category as a binomial distribution and conduct one-sided exact binomial tests. We do so by assuming incoming complaints follow independent Bernoulli processes, with success if the complaint falls in the distinguished category and failure if it falls in another category.

[4]http://www.edmunds.com/car-news/2006-2007-chevrolet-malibu-malibu-maxx-recalled-for-loss-of-power-steering-assist.html

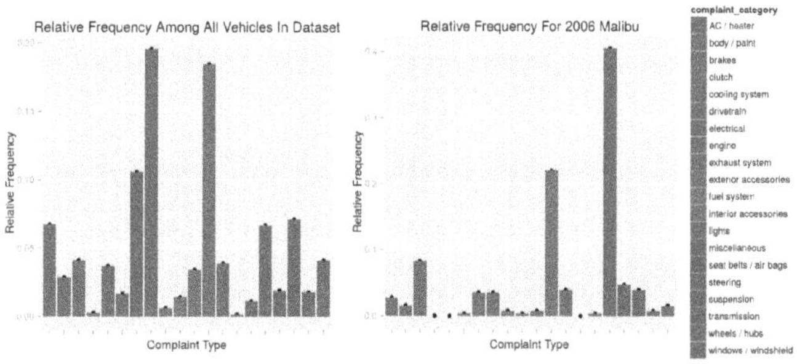

Figure 2: Difference in relative complaint frequencies.

Assume a given model and year has x observed complaints in category c and n complaints across all categories. Let p_c be the relative frequency of complaints for a given category c across all years and models. Let X_c be a random variable representing the number of complaints in category c for the given model and year with n total complaints across all categories, which we will assume follows a binomial distribution with fixed trial number n and probability of success θ unknown. For our metric we look at the probability of the upper tail event $\{X_c \geq x\}$ if $X_c \sim \text{binom}(p_c, n)$. The resulting scores are p-values for one sided binomial tests with the hypotheses

$$H_0 : \theta = p_c$$
$$H_A : \theta > p_c.$$

Instead of using these p-values as criteria to formally test our hypothesis at a given significance level, we use the p-values as a metric to rank categories of vehicle component for different models and years in terms of their potential for having defect and related issues.

To better understand the utility of these metrics in warning for potential vehicle issues, we gather complaint data for eight major car brands totaling 116 models (1883 if model years are considered) and assess whether the top results returned by our metrics have had corresponding NHTSA recalls. We focus on only checking for issues for models with years ranging from 2006 until 2015 based on data availability. We loosely use the term "precision" to denote the percentage of corresponding recalls among the top returned results, and report them at k different levels by pulling the top-k results for each individual brand (see Table 1 and 2).

Table 1: Precision at k using differences in observed relative frequencies.

	k	Chevrolet	Dodge	Ford	GMC	Honda	Hyundai	Nissan	Toyota	Average
1	10	0.30	0.30	0.20	0.10	0.40	0.40	0.10	0.20	0.25
2	15	0.27	0.33	0.13	0.20	0.33	0.33	0.13	0.27	0.25
3	20	0.35	0.25	0.15	0.20	0.30	0.25	0.15	0.35	0.25
4	25	0.32	0.32	0.16	0.24	0.24	0.24	0.16	0.32	0.25
5	30	0.37	0.40	0.20	0.23	0.23	0.27	0.20	0.27	0.27

Table 2: Precision at k using p-values from binomial tests.

	k	Chevrolet	Dodge	Ford	GMC	Honda	Hyundai	Nissan	Toyota	Average
1	10	0.40	0.50	0.10	0.10	0.20	0.40	0.10	0.20	0.25
2	15	0.40	0.40	0.20	0.07	0.13	0.27	0.07	0.13	0.21
3	20	0.40	0.45	0.20	0.10	0.10	0.40	0.15	0.10	0.24
4	25	0.40	0.44	0.20	0.16	0.16	0.40	0.20	0.12	0.26
5	30	0.37	0.43	0.20	0.13	0.17	0.33	0.20	0.20	0.25

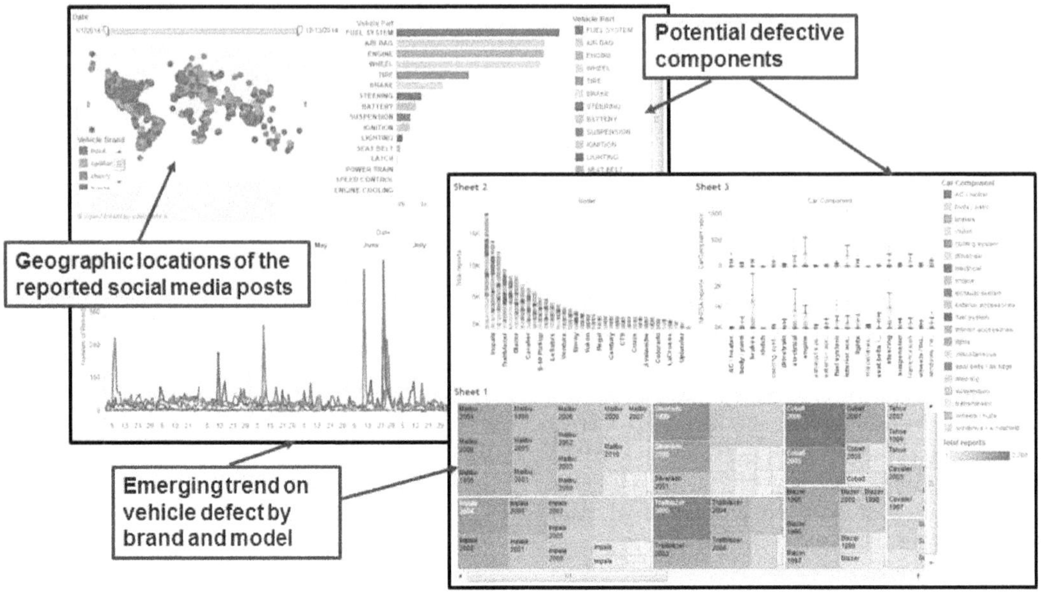

Figure 3: Tableau dashboards showing analyzed results from online social media and consumer reporting sites.

While the majority of the top results returned by our metrics are indicative of vehicle defects or quality control issues, we only mark "true positives" on the issues that have led to actual safety recalls or are currently in an open investigation for a recall. Despite the constraint on evaluation, we find that a sizable number of the top results among several brands (e.g., Hyundai, Dodge, Honda Chevrolet) are highly likely to link to corresponding vehicle recalls. It is important to note that results with lower scores should not be regarded as false signals for the vehicle brands as in traditional classification and prediction settings. This is because our system is designed to identify any potential issues, including the ones that have not caused formal recalls from the automotive manufacturers. Continued generation of such results in conjunction with other aspects of the EDSV system will provide assistance and decision support to human analysts in pinpointing specific emerging threats or other high risk factors.

To facilitate user adaptation, we developed a front end web interface using Tableau[5] to visualize the results and analysis based on the described methods. Figure 3 shows two Tableau dashboards constructed for the Twitter social media platform (back panel) and the *CarComplaint* reporting platform (front panel) respectively. A diverse collection of information is shown in each dashboard. For instance, the social media dashboard displays the aggregated time series of relevant posts on vehicle defect-related issues, geographic distributions of the social media posts, as well as percentage of vehicle components discussed in the extracted posts. Similarly, the consumer report dashboard displays complaints regarding specific model and year of vehicles, distribution of defective components for various brands, and variations in the number of complaints of different components.

4 CONCLUSION

We introduced a system of detecting and assessing problematic vehicle defects and potential future vehicle recalls by capturing data from multiple heterogeneous online sources. These sources range from traditional web forum data to social network services to domain specific consumer reporting sites. We combine together the information from these disparate sources and conduct detailed statistical analysis to provide different levels of information about potential issues on defect relevant to vehicle analyst.

REFERENCES

[1] Alan S. Abrahams, Jian Jiao, Weiguo Fan, G. Alan Wang, and Zhongju Zhang. 2013. What's buzzing in the blizzard of buzz? Automotive component isolation in social media postings. *Decis. Support Syst.* (2013). https://doi.org/10.1016/j.dss.2012.12.023

[2] Alan S. Abrahams, Jian Jiao, G. Alan Wang, and Weiguo Fan. 2012. Vehicle Defect Discovery from Social Media. *Decis. Support Syst.* (2012), 87–97. https://doi.org/10.1016/j.dss.2012.04.005

[3] Luca Maria Aiello, Georgios Petkos, Carlos Martin, David Corney, Symeon Papadopoulos, Ryan Skraba, Ayse Goker, Ioannis Kompatsiaris, and Alejandro Jaimes. 2013. Sensing Trending Topics in Twitter. *Trans. Multi.* 15, 6 (Oct. 2013), 15. https://doi.org/10.1109/TMM.2013.2265080

[4] H. Becker, M. Naaman, and L. Gravano. 2011. Beyond trending topics: Real-world event identification on Twitter. In *International AAAI Conference on Weblogs and Social Media.*

[5] Flavio Chierichetti, Jon M Kleinberg, Ravi Kumar, Mohammad Mahdian, and Sandeep Pandey. 2014. Event Detection via Communication Pattern Analysis.. In *AAAI Conference on Weblogs and Social Media.*

[6] Ryan Compton, David Jurgens, and David Allen. 2014. Geotagging one hundred million twitter accounts with total variation minimization. In *IEEE Big Data.*

[7] Jianshu Weng and Bu-Sung Lee. 2011. Event Detection in Twitter. *AAAI Conference on Weblogs and Social Media* (2011).

[8] Xuan Zhang, Shuo Niu, Da Zhang, G. Alan Wang, and Weiguo Fan. 2015. Predicting Vehicle Recalls with User-Generated Contents: A Text Mining Approach. In *Intelligence and Security Informatics.*

[5] http://www.tableau.com/products/server

Studying Personality through the Content of Posted and Liked Images on Twitter

Sharath Chandra Guntuku
NTU Singapore
sharathc001@e.ntu.edu.sg

Weisi Lin
NTU Singapore
wslin@ntu.edu.sg

Jordan Carpenter
Duke University
jmc51@duke.edu

Wee Keong Ng
NTU Singapore
wkn@pmail.ntu.edu.sg

Lyle H. Ungar
University of Pennsylvania
ungar@cis.upenn.edu

Daniel Preoţiuc-Pietro
University of Pennsylvania
danielpr@sas.upenn.edu

ABSTRACT

Interacting with images through social media has become widespread due to ubiquitous Internet access and multimedia enabled devices. Through images, users generally present their daily activities, preferences or interests. This study aims to identify the way and extent to which personality differences, measured using the Big Five model, are related to online image posting and liking. In two experiments, the larger consisting of ~1.5 million Twitter images both posted and liked by ~4,000 users, we extract interpretable semantic concepts using large-scale image content analysis and analyze differences specific of each personality trait. Predictive results show that image content can predict personality traits, and that there can be significant performance gain by fusing the signal from both posted and liked images.

1 INTRODUCTION

People are increasingly using social media platforms in order to keep records of their daily activities, preferences and interests. This interaction allows researchers to study how people differ in the type of content they post or like. With the ubiquitous nature of camera-enabled mobile devices and Internet in many regions of the world, the complexity of content has increased in the recent years from simple text updates to images focused around platforms such as Twitter or Instagram [2].

In psychology, a key category of individual differences in behaviors is represented by personality, with the Five Factor Model being the most widely used model for representing personality [3, 16]. Under this model, personality consists of five dimensions – extraversion, agreeableness, conscientiousness, openness to experience and neuroticism. Recent studies uncovered the relationship between these traits and users' online behavior, such as language use [26] or ratings on videos [9, 27].

The aim of this paper is to study how personality is related to the content of posted and liked images on social media. For instance, extraversion is in part an orientation toward engaging with the external, social world, which may reflect in posting images of groups by users high in this trait. Users high in openness to experience have an appreciation for art, which could lead them to post or like sketches or images containing musical instruments.

Prior research suggests that personality is strongly expressed on a platform which offers users sufficient self-expression and freedom of control [8]. Previous work in personality analysis through images either have focused on profile images which is a matter of self-presentation [10, 15, 21, 37] or use both small data sets and shallow image features [25, 29, 38], thus limiting the scope and interpretation of results [6, 28, 33, 36].

The main contributions of this work are to:

- Analyze the content of images using interpretable aesthetic and semantic features using a large-scale data set, an order of magnitude larger than previous work;
- Study posted and liked images both separately and jointly;
- Build predictive models of personality traits from image content.

While there has been previous work on predicting personality profiles using images liked on Flickr [11, 28], this is the first attempt, to the best of our knowledge, to analyze and predict personality using content from both posted and liked images on a large-scale social media data set.

Computational models that predict users' personality from their online footprints have several applications. For social science research, these methods offer data-driven insights into human and group behaviors which can be used to generate new hypotheses for testing and can be used to unobtrusively measure large populations over time. Commercial applications include improving targeted online marketing, increasing acceptance of HCI systems and personalized recommendations.

2 DATA

We use two Twitter data sets in our experiments which differ in size and the method of acquiring labels. Both studies received approval from the IRB of our institution.

First, we use a data set ($\mathcal{D}_1$) containing 436 Twitter users whose Big Five personality scores were computed based on the NEO-PI-R inventory [3]. For each user we collected up to 3200 of their most recent tweets and downloaded all images that were embedded in these posts. In total, we downloaded 579,929 tweets which contained 34,875 embedded photos across 232 users. A total of 161 users posted at least 10 photos and we only include these in our experiments.

WebSci'17, June 25-28, 2017, Troy, NY, USA.

978-1-4503-4896-6/17/06...$15.00
DOI: http://dx.doi.org/10.1145/3091478.3091522

A second data set ($\mathcal{D}_2$) is an order of magnitude larger and consists of 4132 Twitter users. Since we do not have personality computed via surveys for this data set, based previous work on personality analysis from profile images [15], we use an automatic text-regression method to assign each user scores for the Big Five personality traits [22]. The model was trained on a sample of over 70,000 Facebook users, using tokens and topics extracted from status updates as features, achieving a validation predictive performance of $r \sim .35$ on average for all five traits [22], which is considered a high correlation in measuring internal states [18]. We downloaded 3200 most recent user tweets, leading to a data set of 5,547,510 tweets, out of which 700,630 contained images across 3498 users. We also downloaded 3,135,764 tweets liked by these users on Twitter (an action previously known as favorite), out of which 909,861 contained an image. We exclude the texts associated with the tweets which contain images when predicting personality to limit any potential confound. Then, for our analysis, we excluded users who posted less than 20 photos, and who had less than 10 images their liked tweets.

3 FEATURES

We extract the following features from each image. To compute user level features, we perform mean feature pooling across all images posted/liked by a user.

Colors. Research has shown that colors can invoke emotions or psychological states [12]. Here, we use the HSV (Hue–Saturation–Value) space to filter grayscale images (4.99%) from subsequent color analysis. We then compute **saturation** and **brightness** followed by Pleasure, Arousal and Dominance [17], along with **hue count**. Hence, we applied the following formulas to extract the three dimensions of color affect: **Pleasure** $= .69 \cdot V + .22 \cdot S$, **Arousal** $= -.31 \cdot V + .60 \cdot S$, **Dominance** $= -.76 \cdot V + .32 \cdot S$ [34]. We also compute the standard deviation of the HSV values, which we will use for prediction only. In addition, we compute a 6-bin histogram which splits pixels into the primary and secondary colors as well as a 12-bin histogram containing also the tertiary colors. Finally, we compute the ratio of pixels with warm colors. The histogram features are used in prediction only. A subset of these features were successfully used in a smaller experiment on social media image content and personality [6, 33].

Image Content. Images can have very diverse content beyond faces, especially in the case of images embedded within tweets on a user's Twitter feed. With the goal of aiding our analysis section, we first use the **Imagga** tagging API[1] as our content analysis engine, which was successfully used by past research [7]. We labeled all images with the Imagga Tagging API and generated for each image a *bag-of-tags* out of the top-10 predicted tags, based on the developers' recommendations. We removed all tags that occurred less than 200 times in our large data set, leaving us with 1,299 distinct tags. With the aim of to increasing interpretability and decreasing sparsity, we learn tag clusters that contain frequently co-occurring tags. We use a procedure that was originally applied to words in a tweet, which produced accurate results for prediction and analysis [14, 24]. The procedure involves first computing the

[1] http://docs.imagga.com/#auto-tagging

Feature	Ope.	Con.	Ext.	Agr.	Neu.
Colors					
Grayscale	.039	-.130	-.128	-.152	.262
Brightness	-.108	.040	.124	.027	-.020
Saturation	-.017	.023	.102	.076	-.077
Pleasure	-.017	.032	-.079	.037	-.024
Arousal	-.007	.005	.119	.048	-.054
Dominance	.005	-.013	.113	.010	-.021
Hue Count	-.094	.040	.118	.085	-.103
Content					
% Posts with People	-.106	.109	.116	.082	-.059
# Posted Images	.068	-.025	.094	-.141	.093

Table 1.A Posted Images

Feature	Ope.	Con.	Ext.	Agr.	Neu.
Colors					
Brightness	-.081	.068	.070	.087	-.093
Saturation	.049	.159	.062	.122	-.142
Pleasure	-.022	-.034	-.029	.018	.042
Arousal	.052	.150	.065	.096	-.139
Dominance	.043	.110	.055	.049	-.107
Hue Count	-.071	.030	.040	.066	-.092
Content					
% Posts with People	-.116	-.054	.117	-.041	.023
# Liked Images	-.049	-.131	.009	-.068	.159

Table 1.B Liked Images

Table 1: $\mathcal{D}_2$: Pearson correlations between color features extracted from posted and liked images on Twitter and user personality, controlled for age and gender. Significant positive correlations are highlighted with green and negative correlations with red ($p < .01$, two-tailed t-test).

Normalised Pointwise Mutual Information (NPMI) between all pairs of tags [1]. This measures the degree to which two tags are likely co-occur in the same context – here, image – and takes a maximum value of 1 if two tags always co-occur and a value of 0 if they occur as according to chance. We can use this metric as a similarity measure and compute a tag × tag similarity matrix. This matrix is fed to the spectral clustering algorithm, a hard-clustering method appropriate for generating non-convex clusters [20, 30, 35], which performs a graph partitioning on the Laplacian of the similarity matrix. The number of clusters needs to be specified in advance, and, after an exploration and analysis of various numbers, we decided to use 400 clusters for the rest of the study. Once these clusters of semantically similar tags are created, we represent each image as a vector containing the normalized number of times a member of each tag cluster is detected. For each user, we derive a feature vector of *image content topics* as the normalized number of times each topic cluster is present in the tweet-embedded images.

Secondly, we use a pre-trained version of the 19-layer **VGG-Net** image classifier based on convolutional neural networks [32], to predict a class probability for 1,000 objects in the ImageNet tagset. However, as this tagset does not contain categories of core interest for our analysis (e.g., faces, building interiors, sports), we use it for personality prediction experiments only.

4 ANALYSIS

To uncover the image features associated with each personality trait, we perform univariate correlation tests between each feature and personality trait. We control for age and gender effects using

r-post	*r*-like	Image Tag Clusters	*r*_post	*r*_like	Image Tag Clusters
Openness (+)			**Openness (–)**		
0.155 (1)	-	senior, old, mature, elderly, husband, grandma, retired, grandfather, retirement	0.207 (1)	0.135 (2)	ball, sports_equipment, game_equipment, basketball, basketball_equipment..
0.148 (2)	0.112 (1)	art, cartoon, clipart	0.195 (2)	0.138 (1)	player, athlete, baseball, contestant, base, baseball_equipment, ballplayer...
0.137 (3)	0.097 (3)	drawing, representation, diagram	0.154 (3)	0.109 (3)	football, helmet, back, football_helmet, crash_helmet
0.120 (4)	-	ancient, palace, castle, historic	0.119 (4)	0.090 (4)	game, puzzle, jigsaw_puzzle
0.119 (5)	0.079 (7)	decoration, sketch, tattoo, graffito	0.117 (5)	-	clothing, garment, shirt, consumer_goods, jersey, sleeve
0.108 (6)	0.090 (4)	office, businessman, professional, corporate, executive, suit, handsome, men	0.109 (6)	-	tennis, racket
0.102 (7)	0.101 (2)	artwork	0.105 (7)	-	runner, diversion, track
-	0.089 (5)	pattern, texture, wallpaper, backdrop, shape, curve	0.099 (8)	0.078 (5)	child, boy, kid, little, childhood, baby, children
Conscientiousness (+)			**Conscientiousness (–)**		
0.153 (1)	0.076 (1)	classroom, whole	0.125 (1)	0.049 (5)	face, pretty, hair, model, fashion, sexy, lady, brunette, glamour
0.132 (2)	0.069 (2)	office, businessman, professional, corporate, executive, suit, handsome, men	0.111 (2)	0.086 (2)	art, cartoon, clipart
0.114 (3)	-	building, architecture, city	0.105 (3)	0.065 (4)	drawing, representation, diagram
0.104 (4)	-	structure, fountain, gas	0.101 (4)	0.084 (3)	expression, looking, beard, head
0.101 (5)	-	business	0.101 (5)	-	cute, eyes
0.099 (6)	0.059 (5)	paper, document, writing, menu, pen, fare, book	0.097 (6)	0.1 (1)	artwork
0.094 (7)	-	furniture, table	0.072 (7)	-	computer, equipment, technology, display,screen, monitor
0.078 (8)	0.062 (4)	home, room, house, interior	0.068 (8)	-	people, person, adult, caucasian, man, male, happy, portrait, attractive, smile...
Extraversion (+)			**Extraversion (–)**		
0.321 (1)	0.128 (1)	people, person, adult, caucasian, man, male, happy, portrait, attractive, smile...	0.253 (1)	0.164 (1)	art, cartoon, clipart
0.243 (2)	0.089 (3)	face, pretty, hair, model, fashion, sexy, lady, brunette, glamour	0.213 (2)	0.122 (2)	drawing, representation, diagram
0.182 (3)	-	women, group, friends, friend, girls, friendship, buddy	0.165 (3)	-	design, sign, icon, graphic, symbol, internet, set, web, button, icons
0.175 (4)	0.080 (4)	lifestyle	0.149 (4)	-	casual, silhouette, sport, laptop, covering, businessperson, element, light...
0.171 (5)	0.075 (5)	happiness, couple, together, love, fun, two, family	0.128 (5)	0.066 (6)	black, african, picture, dark
0.136 (6)	0.093 (2)	disco, cabaret, spot, ballroom	0.127 (6)	0.103 (3)	artwork
0.127 (7)	-	body, swimsuit, slim, bikini, maillot, tights	0.125 (7)	-	text, 3d
0.120 (8)	-	expression, looking, beard, head	0.094 (8)	0.70 (4)	color, motion, futuristic
Agreeableness (+)			**Agreeableness (–)**		
0.144 (1)	0.090 (1)	happiness, couple, together, love, fun, two, family	0.211 (1)	0.096 (1)	office, businessman, professional, corporate, executive, suit, handsome, men
0.108 (2)	0.080 (7)	performance, concert, stage, platform, musician	0.177 (2)	0.076 (3)	press, print_media
0.098 (3)	0.075 (5)	flower, floral, garden, flowers, petal, blossom, flora, bloom	0.132 (3)	0.077 (2)	business
0.094 (4)	-	cat, feline, pet, domestic, fur, kitten, kitty, pets, domestic_cat, whiskers, furry...	0.129 (4)	-	newspaper, money, currency, finance, cash, bank, banking, financial, bill
0.094 (5)	-	trees, season	0.101 (5)	-	work, success, manager, confident, successful
0.093 (6)	-	women, group, friends, friend, girls, friendship, buddy	0.099 (6)	-	signboard, billboard, scoreboard, street_sign
0.089 (7)	-	decoration, sketch, tattoo, graffito	0.092 (7)	-	people, person, adult, caucasian, man, male, happy, portrait, attractive, smile...
0.081 (8)	0.081 (2)	music, guitar, stringed_instrument	0.081 (8)	-	publication, magazine, book_jacket, comic_book, jacket, wrapping
Neuroticism (+)			**Neuroticism (–)**		
0.107 (1)	0.057 (7)	paper, document, writing, menu, pen, fare, book	0.108 (1)	-	casual, silhouette, sport, laptop, covering, businessperson, element, light...
0.104 (2)	0.071 (3)	happiness, couple, together, love, fun, two, family	0.096 (2)	-	computer, equipment, technology, display, screen, monitor
0.104 (3)	0.77 (2)	cute, eyes	0.094 (3)	-	device, machine, slot_machine, slot, vending_machine
0.099 (4)	0.082 (1)	face, pretty, hair, model, fashion, sexy, lady, brunette, glamour	0.064 (4)	-	design, sign, icon, graphic, symbol, internet, set, web...
0.092 (5)	-	animal, dog, domestic_animal, canine	0.063 (5)	-	art, cartoon, clipart
0.082 (6)	0.058 (6)	cat, feline, pet, domestic, fur, kitten, kitty, pets, domestic_cat, whiskers, furry...	0.060 (6)	-	communication, telephone, phone, mobile, call, cellular_telephone
0.079 (7)	0.061 (5)	people, person, adult, caucasian, man, male, happy, portrait, attractive, smile...	0.057 (7)	-	space, digital, fractal, laser, optical_device, glow, render
0.060 (8)	0.062 (4)	sporting_dog, retriever, golden_retriever, labrador_retriever...			

Table 2: $\mathcal{D}_2$: Pearson correlations and feature rank between personality trait and image tag clusters extracted from images embedded in posted tweets (r-post) and liked tweets (r-like) (maximum 8 per personality trait). All correlations are significant at $p < .01$, Simes corrected, two-tailed t-test. Results for every personality trait are controlled for age and gender and other four corresponding personality traits. Tags are sorted by occurrence in our data set within a tag cluster.

partial correlation so that our analysis is not skewed by demographic biases. For robustness, we perform Simes p-correction to account for running multiple significance tests [31]. Additionally, in content analysis, as some personality traits are inter-correlated (e.g. extraversion and agreeableness), we control for all other four traits in order to isolate the peculiarities of each personality dimension.

Results of image color analysis on the $\mathcal{D}_2$ data set are presented for posted and liked images separately in Tables 1.A and 1.B respectively. The content analysis results on posted and liked images are presented in Table 2. In Table 2, the correlations for the top-k topics are shown along with the rank associated with each topic for the trait in brackets. The same set of experiments on personality correlations was conducted on the $\mathcal{D}_1$ data set, but the correlations are not robust to randomness due to the small sample size. This shows the need for this behavior to be studied using larger samples. In Tables 1.A and 1.B we included an additional feature coding the percentage of posts that contained people, identified through the presence of a curated list of Imagga Clusters in the top 10 predicted ones (46.4% of the total number of images). Another feature coded the raw number of images posted or liked by a user.

Openness to Experience. Color analysis shows openness is associated with posting and liking images in grayscale and having low hue count, which indicate artistic and well-composed images specific of this trait. Users high in this trait also prefer and post less bright images and post a greater number of images, while liking fewer. Image content analysis (Table 2) reveals two major themes for users high in openness to experience. First, posting images with drawings (*art, drawing, decoration, artwork* – clusters denoted by their first tag) indicates engagement with aesthetic domains, a known characteristic of openness to experience [4] and especially abstract art [5]. Secondly, these users post fewer images containing people and focus more on objects, but when people are present they represent seniors or businessmen (*senior, office*). Users low in openness prefer posting images of sports or games (*player, football, game, tennis*), which are conventional interests in the US.

Conscientiousness. Conscientiousness is a trait associated with orderliness and preference for planned behaviour. Users high in this trait do not prefer grayscale images and prefer photos of people rather than objects, suggesting a preference for generally normative and conventional posting behavior. Conscientious users are also the most cautious in liking images from other people, perhaps because this action is to a degree impulsive, which is atypical of conscientiousness. Content analysis reveals images containing either landscapes (*building, structure*) or formal, office environments (*classroom, office, paper, home*), the latter related to overall better job performance of users high in conscientiousness [13]. On the other hand, low conscientiousness is portrayed by images of drawings (*art, drawing, artwork*), which again shows a dislike for unconventional posts, as well as a specific type of close-up face images (*face, expression, cute*).

Extraversion. Extraversion is associated with both posting and liking images that are bright, saturated and more chromatically complex as revealed through a high hue-count. This trait is characterized by engagement with other people and, in accordance to theory, users who score high are specifically interested in posting and liking images containing people in general as well as a broad range of types of people (*people, face, women, happiness*). In addition, extraverts are perceived as being energetic and this is reflected by images portraying active interests (*disco*). Introversion is portrayed through drawings (*art, drawing*) or abstract symbols (*design, casual*) and by posting fewer images in general.

Agreeableness. Agreeableness shows similar patterns to extraversion in color associations, which is expected based on their common positive emotion core. Users high in agreeableness are characterized by kindness, generosity and optimism, and their images show a breadth of aspects of the good life: friends (*happiness, women*), pets (*cat*), flowers (*flower*) or music (*performance*). Liked images also reveal similar preferences for music (*music*). On the other hand, low agreeableness is associated with images of office environments (*office, work, business*), text-related content (*press, newspaper, signboard*) and fewer photos of people overall.

Neuroticism. Users high in neuroticism post grayscale images and their images are less saturated and less chromatic diversity by containing fewer hues. Perhaps surprisingly, neuroticism is associated with posting more images, although images of objects rather than people are preferred. Most striking is the preference for liking images from others, which is a more passive way of engagement. Through content analysis, we observe that high neuroticism is disclosed through posting images containing documents (*paper*) or animals (*cat, animal*). Although they are less likely to post pictures of people overall, they favor close-ups of people (*face, cute, people*). Users low in neuroticism are characterized by posting images of art and abstract symbols (*art, design*) and tech items (*casual, device*). Users low in neuroticism had no significant association with liked image content, perhaps caused by the tendency to like more images and, hence, more heterogeneous content. Overall, we highlight that in almost all traits, similar image content tendencies are specific of both posted and liked images.

5 PREDICTION

We study the predictive power of image features in the task of predicting user personality traits. We treat this as a regression problem to which we apply a linear regression with Elastic Net regularization. As personality is text predicted on the $\mathcal{D}_2$ data set, we only perform prediction using text on the $\mathcal{D}_1$ data set where

Feature	# Feat.	Ope	Con	Ext	Agr	Neu
Colors [6, 33]	33	.093	**.147**	.022	**.229**	.085
Imagga Clusters	400	.044	.077	.183	.085	**.404**
VGG-net Classes [32]	1000	.056	.051	.061	.037	.222
Text	100	**.168**	.059	**.223**	.111	.261
All (Image)	3	.081	.177	.187	.229	.416
All (Image+Text)	2	.171	.178	.223	.230	.418

Table 3: $\mathcal{D}_1$: Prediction results for personality traits with all features. Performance is measured using Pearson correlation in 10-fold cross-validation.

Feature	# Feat.	Ope	Con	Ext	Agr	Neu
Colors [6, 33]	33	.284	.352	.293	**.317**	**.398**
Imagga Clusters	400	.275	.364	.317	.221	.383
VGG-net Classes [32]	1000	**.410**	**.383**	**.319**	.198	**.398**
All (Image)	3	.448	.479	.369	.336	.503

Table 4.A Posted Images.

Feature	# Feat.	Ope	Con	Ext	Agr	Neu
Colors [6, 33]	33	.351	.383	.229	.286	.396
Imagga Clusters	400	**.411**	**.492**	**.345**	**.335**	**.412**
VGG-net Classes [32]	1000	.302	.388	.193	.008	.374
All (Image)	3	.468	.530	.366	.378	.467
Posts + Likes (Image)	2	.543	.566	.440	.433	.530

Table 4.B Liked Images.

Table 4: $\mathcal{D}_2$: Prediction results for personality traits with all features on posted and liked images. Performance is measured using Pearson correlation in 10-fold cross-validation.

we have collected survey-based personality scores. We extracted word2vec [19] clusters from the text in $\mathcal{D}_2$ following [23]. Since VGG and Imagga Clusters are high-dimensional features, we employed PCA for dimensionality reduction by setting the explained variance ratio threshold as 95% for $\mathcal{D}_2$, and choosing 51 principal components for $\mathcal{D}_2$ (due to the small size of the data set). We have also experimented with non-linear methods (Support Vector Machines with RBF kernel), but the results did not improve significantly.

To evaluate our results, we split our data into 10 folds and performed cross-validation on one held-out fold at a time. For all our methods, we tune the parameters of all our models on a separate validation fold. The overall performance is assessed using Pearson correlation of the predicted value to the self-reported score. Results are presented in Tables 3 and 4. Feature combination is performed using a linear ensemble over the individual prediction scores of each feature set. The same patterns hold when evaluating the results with Root Mean Squared Error and we omit them for clarity.

On the $\mathcal{D}_1$ data set, features extracted from images perform better than the text-derived features for conscientiousness, agreeableness and neuroticism. For the other traits, the text features perform better. It is to be noted that the small size of the data set might be acting as an artifact. To confirm the contribution of features from text and images, larger data sets with survey-based labels need to be acquired.

On the $\mathcal{D}_2$ data set, for image posts, image content features extracted from either VGG-Net or Imagga performed better than color features in all but one cases. Combining all features using an ensemble works better in predicting all traits, showing colors and content are to some extent complimentary. For image likes, Imagga features outperform VGG-Net classes and color features for all personality traits. Also, colors perform better than VGG-Net classes on all traits except for conscientiousness. By combining the features from the two different groups of images – posted and liked – we obtain significant performance gains (6% for conscientiousness and 10-15% for the remaining traits) over either image posts or likes considered independently. This suggests that both interactions that users have on social media - namely posting images and liking images reveal a more complete picture of users' personality.

Prediction performance using images is overall high, especially for openness and neuroticism – even if excluding from text personality prediction the tweets containing images. Combined with results from the $\mathcal{D}_1$ data set, this indicates that the two modalities disclose both overlapping and complimentary information. However, a larger data set with survey-based personality would further reveal what can be captured through each modality.

6 CONCLUSION

We analyzed image posting and liking preferences using interpretable aesthetic and semantic features using a data set an order of magnitude larger than previous work, with the aim of identifying the way and extent to which they can be related to personality differences measured using the Big Five model. We created tag clusters to analyze the content of images and identified idiosyncrasies of each personality trait, while controlling for all other four traits to isolate the peculiarities of each personality dimension. Finally, predictive models of personality traits show reliable accuracy on held-out data using image features even when text does not. Also, combining the signal from both posted and liked images leads to significant performance gain compared to individual interactions.

ACKNOWLEDGMENTS

The authors acknowledge the support of the Templeton Religion Trust, grant TRT-0048.

REFERENCES

[1] Gerlof Bouma. 2009. Normalized (Pointwise) Mutual Information in Collocation Extraction. In *Biennial GSCL Conference*.

[2] Anne Burdick, Johanna Drucker, Peter Lunenfeld, Todd Presner, and Jeffrey Schnapp. 2012. *Digital Humanities*. The MIT Press.

[3] Paul T Costa and Robert R MacCrae. 1992. *Revised NEO Personality Inventory and NEO Five-factor Inventory: Professional Manual*. Psychological Assessment Resources.

[4] Colin DeYoung, Lena Quilty, and Jordan Peterson. 2007. Between Facets and Domains: 10 aspects of the Big Five. *JPSP* (2007).

[5] Gregory J Feist and Tara R Brady. 2004. Openness to Experience, Non-Conformity, and the Preference for Abstract Art. *Empirical Studies of the Arts* 22, 1 (2004).

[6] Bruce Ferwerda, Markus Schedl, and Marko Tkalčič. 2016. Using Instagram Picture Features to Predict Users' Personality *(MMM)*.

[7] Venkata Rama Kiran Garimella, Abdulrahman Alfayad, and Ingmar Weber. 2016. Social Media Image Analysis for Public Health *(CHI)*.

[8] Samuel D Gosling, Sei Jin Ko, Thomas Mannarelli, and Margaret E Morris. 2002. A Room with a Cue: Personality Judgments based on Offices and Bedrooms. *JPSP* (2002).

[9] Sharath Chandra Guntuku, Weisi Lin, Michael James Scott, and Gheorghita Ghinea. 2015. Modelling the Influence of Personality and Culture on Affect and Enjoyment in Multimedia *(ACII)*.

[10] Sharath Chandra Guntuku, Lin Qiu, Sujoy Roy, Weisi Lin, and Vinit Jakhetiya. 2015. Do others Perceive You as You want them To?: Modeling Personality based on Selfies. In *Workshop on Affect & Sentiment in Multimedia (MM)*.

[11] Sharath Chandra Guntuku, Joey T Zhou, Sujoy Roy, Lin Weisi, and Ivor W Tsang. 2016. Who likes what, and why? Insights into Personality Modeling based on Image 'Likes'. *IEEE Transactions on Affective Computing* (2016).

[12] Kai-Qi Huang, Qiao Wang, and Zhen-Yang Wu. 2006. Natural Color Image Enhancement and Evaluation Algorithm Based on Human Visual System. *CVIU* (2006).

[13] Gregory M Hurtz and John J Donovan. 2000. Personality and Job Performance: The Big Five Revisited. *Journal of Applied Psychology* 85, 6 (2000).

[14] Vasileios Lampos, Nikolaos Aletras, Daniel Preoţiuc-Pietro, and Trevor Cohn. 2014. Predicting and Characterising User Impact on Twitter *(EACL)*.

[15] Leqi Liu, Daniel Preoţiuc-Pietro, Zahra Riahi Samani, Mohsen E. Moghaddam, and Lyle Ungar. 2016. Analyzing Personality through Social Media Profile Picture Choice *(ICWSM)*.

[16] Robert R McCrae and Oliver P John. 1992. An Introduction to the Five-factor Model and its Applications. *Journal of Personality* (1992).

[17] Albert Mehrabian and James A Russell. 1974. *An Approach to Environmental Psychology*. The MIT Press.

[18] GJ Meyer et al. 2001. Psychological Testing and Psychological Assessment: A Review of Evidence and Issues. *American Psychologist* (2001).

[19] T Mikolov and J Dean. 2013. Distributed Representations of Words and Phrases and their Compositionality *(NIPS)*.

[20] Andrew Y. Ng, Michael I. Jordan, and Yair Weiss. 2002. On Spectral Clustering: Analysis and an Algorithm *(NIPS)*.

[21] Jie Nie, Lei Huang, Peng Cui, Zhen Li, Yan Yan, Zhiqiang Wei, and Wenwu Zhu. 2016. Social Media Profiler: Inferring Your Social Media Personality from Visual Attributes in Portrait. In *Pacific Rim Conference on MM*.

[22] Gregory Park, H.Andrew Schwartz, Johannes Eichstaedt, Margaret Kern, Michal Kosinski, David Stillwell, Lyle Ungar, and Martin Seligman. 2015. Automatic Personality Assessment through Social Media Language. *JPSP* (2015).

[23] Daniel Preoţiuc-Pietro, Vasileios Lampos, and Nikolaos Aletras. 2015. An Analysis of the User Occupational Class through Twitter Content *(ACL)*.

[24] Daniel Preoţiuc-Pietro, Svitlana Volkova, Vasileios Lampos, Yoram Bachrach, and Nikolaos Aletras. 2015. Studying User Income through Language, Behaviour and Affect in Social Media. *PLoS ONE* (2015).

[25] Jitao Sang, Huaiwen Zhang, and Changsheng Xu. 2016. Visual BFI: An Exploratory Study for Image-Based Personality Test *(PCM)*.

[26] H Andrew Schwartz, Johannes C Eichstaedt, Margaret L Kern, Lukasz Dziurzynski, Stephanie M Ramones, Megha Agrawal, Achal Shah, Michal Kosinski, David Stillwell, and Martin Seligman. 2013. Personality, Gender, and Age in the Language of Social Media: The Open-vocabulary Approach. *PloS ONE* (2013).

[27] Michael James Scott, Sharath Chandra Guntuku, Weisi Lin, and Gheorghita Ghinea. 2016. Do personality and culture influence perceived video quality and enjoyment? *IEEE Transactions on Multimedia* 18, 9 (2016), 1796–1807.

[28] Cristina Segalin, Dong Seon Cheng, and Marco Cristani. 2016. Social Profiling through Image Understanding: Personality Inference using Convolutional Neural Networks. *Computer Vision and Image Understanding* (2016).

[29] Cristina Segalin, Alessandro Perina, Marco Cristani, and Alessandro Vinciarelli. 2016. The Pictures we like are our Image: Continuous Mapping of Favorite Pictures into Self-Assessed and Attributed Personality Traits. *IEEE Transactions on Affective Computing* (2016).

[30] Jianbo Shi and Jitendra Malik. 2000. Normalized Cuts and Image Segmentation. *Transactions on Pattern Analysis and Machine Intelligence* (2000).

[31] R John Simes. 1986. An Improved Bonferroni Procedure for Multiple Tests of Significance. *Biometrika* (1986).

[32] Karen Simonyan and Andrew Zisserman. 2015. Very Deep Convolutional Networks for Large-Scale Image Recognition *(ICLR)*.

[33] Marcin Skowron, Marko Tkalčič, Bruce Ferwerda, and Markus Schedl. 2016. Fusing Social Media Cues: Personality Prediction from Twitter and Instagram *(WWW Companion)*.

[34] Patricia Valdez and Albert Mehrabian. 1994. Effects of Color on Emotions. *Journal of Experimental Psychology* (1994).

[35] Ulrike von Luxburg. 2007. A Tutorial on Spectral Clustering. *Statistics and Computing* (2007).

[36] Xiaoyu Xiong, Maurizio Filippone, and Alessandro Vinciarelli. 2016. Looking Good With Flickr Faves: Gaussian Processes for Finding Difference Makers in Personality Impressions *(MM)*.

[37] Yan Yan, Jie Nie, Lei Huang, Zhen Li, Qinglei Cao, and Zhiqiang Wei. 2015. Is your First Impression Reliable? Trustworthy Analysis using Facial Traits in portraits *(MMM)*.

[38] Huaiwen Zhang, Jiaming Zhang, Jitao Sang, and Changsheng Xu. 2017. A Demo for Image-Based Personality Test *(MMM)*.

A Large Human-Labeled Corpus for Online Harassment Research

Jennifer Golbeck, Zahra Ashktorab, Rashad O. Banjo, Alexandra Berlinger, Siddharth Bhagwan, Cody Buntain, Paul Cheakalos, Alicia A Geller, Quint Gergory, Rajesh Kumar Gnanasekaran, Raja Rajan Gunasekaran, Kelly M. Hoffman, Jenny Hottle, Vichita Jienjitlert, Shivika Khare, Ryan Lau, Marianna J. Martindale, Shalmali Naik, Heather L, Nixon, Piyush Ramachandran, Kristine M. Rogers, Lisa Rogers, Meghna Sardana Sarin, Gaurav Shahane, Jayanee Thanki, Priyanka Vengataraman, Zijian Wan, Derek Michael Wu
University of Maryland
College Park, MD

ABSTRACT

A fundamental part of conducting cross-disciplinary web science research is having useful, high-quality datasets that provide value to studies across disciplines. In this paper, we introduce a large, hand-coded corpus of online harassment data. A team of researchers collaboratively developed a codebook using grounded theory and labeled 35,000 tweets. Our resulting dataset has roughly 15% positive harassment examples and 85% negative examples. This data is useful for training machine learning models, identifying textual and linguistic features of online harassment, and for studying the nature of harassing comments and the culture of trolling.

KEYWORDS

online harassment; datasets

1 INTRODUCTION

NB: This paper deals with violent online harassment. We include examples of tweets that use violent, including sexually violent, language; threats; vulgarity; hate speech; and degrading racist terms. We do not want readers to be surprised when they come upon this content, hence this note.

Online trolling takes many forms, but at its core are posts that are harassing, offensive, threatening, and intimidating. It is not an isolated problem. The Pew Research Center found that, as of 2013, 73% of people had witnessed harassment online, and a full 40% of people had experienced harassment directly [?]. They reported the following grim statistics:

- 60% of internet users said they had witnessed someone being called offensive names
- 53% had seen efforts to purposefully embarrass someone
- 25% had seen someone being physically threatened
- 24% witnessed someone being harassed for a sustained period of time
- 19% said they witnessed someone being sexually harassed
- 18% said they had seen someone be stalked

ACM 978-1-4503-4896-6/17/06...$15.00.
DOI: http://dx.doi.org/10.1145/3091478.3091509

This behavior can take many forms, but online comments and other social media posts are a major source. Being able to identify the worst of these messages, understanding the motivation of those who post them, and integrating these insights into interfaces that can block or hide the content is a first step that could do a lot to improve people's experiences online.

To do this, we require a large dataset of high-quality data for analysis and model training. In this paper, we present the results of an 18-month project to create such a dataset. Our corpus contains 35,000 tweets labeled by a team of trained researchers.

2 RELATED WORK

Trolling is a term used to describe a very broad range of activities. Because the term is used colloquially, we will opt for "online harassment" as an overarching term in this work. We are specifically interested in the most aggressive, vile forms of online harassment. This includes threats of rape and other violence, intentionally offensive messages (racist, misogynistic, etc.), hate speech, and libelous personal insults. We want to identify messages that most would agree have firmly and completely crossed the line of "freedom of expression" or "encouraging debate". While there is a lot of research to be done in the broader trolling space, we believe that addressing these most egregious abuses will take us a solid step forward toward improving the way people interact online.

This type of trolling / online harassment has been addressed in the CMC and psychological literature. Hardaker [?] offers the following:

> "A troller is a CMC user who constructs the identity of sincerely wishing to be part of the group in question, including professing, or conveying pseudo-sincere intentions, but whose real intention(s) is/are to cause disruption and/or to trigger or exacerbate conflict for the purposes of their own amusement."

Buckels et al. [?] studied the psychological traits of trolls and, in their research, developed a Global Assessment of Internet Trolling (GAIT) scale, which builds on Hardaker's definition. The inventory uses four questions, rated on a 1-5 scale, and the mean is a user's GAIT score. Those questions are:

- I have sent people to shock websites for the lulz

- I like to troll people in forums or the comments section of websites
- I enjoy griefing other players in multiplayer games,
- The more beautiful and pure a thing is, the more satisfying it is to corrupt

They also found that trollers scored extremely high on personality tests for narcissism, sadism, psychopathy, and Machiavellianism. In particularly, attention-seeking was a component of their personality, as was the sadistic impulse to harm others because it brought enjoyment.

Online harassment may extend beyond this, originating from hate groups or others who are not particularly entertained by their offense of others. However, this context of trolling motivation has been particularly helpful to us in this research when developing and applying codes.

3 CORPUS DEVELOPMENT

The lack of a good, large corpus of these kinds of messages has been a hindrance to this type of research in the past. [? ? ?]. Thus, we set out to build one ourselves. We worked with some media organizations to collect and analyze blocked comments, but ultimately could not collect enough content from them to use in applications like machine learning. We turned to Twitter instead to find comments to label.

3.1 Initial Exploration

There is a vast world of trolling and harassment on Twitter. We were hoping to identify a representative sample of these tweets so our final corpus would be fairly representative of the types of harassing content one would find on the platform. We have access to an archive of the Twitter garden hose stream dating back to 2013. We began by randomly selecting tweets from this archive, but the density of harassing tweets was extremely low - only a few dozen tweets even rose to the level of "potentially offensive", and only a handful could have been considered truly harassing. Thus, we decided to move on to content that was more likely to be aggressive.

We considered sources of accounts that had been blocked by others. Block Together [1] is a site where Twitter users can share their block lists and others can subscribe to them. A list of block lists is not provided on the site, so we sought out lists that had been publicly shared. We collected a sample of tweets from each user on these lists and explored this set. Again, there were almost no harassing tweets in our dataset. We suspect this is because people may have been blocked for pestering the user who created the block list or otherwise being annoying without rising to the level of intense harassment or violence.

We then turned to The Block Bot [?], a curated block list. Originally created by an atheist feminist community, the list contains three levels of blocks (1, 2, and 3) with Level 1 blocks being the most severe. These people have made documented threats or harassing tweets to others. Given the community who maintains the list, some issues like misogyny and Gamergate are more prominent while other racially and religious motivated issues are less common. That said, this list gave us our first set of real insights.

[1]https://blocktogether.org/

We took a sample of tweets from Level 1 blocks. As with the other sets, harassing posts were not very common. We identified only about 20 out of thousands we reviewed that rose to the level of harassment that interested us. Below are examples of some of these tweets, with the usernames of the targets anonymized. Please be forewarned that this begins the inclusion of language that may be upsetting.

```
@ANONYMIZED ROT IN HELL BITCH
@ANONYMIZED U FVCKING CVNT. YOU'LL GET URS
SOON ENOUGH
@ANONYMIZED Sorry, Canada. our hollywood
elites & its dumb models are idiots. wish
ISIS would give Chrissy a permanent haircut.
#CyberCaliphate Bloody Valentine's Day #MichelleObama
We're watching you, you girls and your husband
@ANONYMIZED But instead, I'll drink your
blood out of your cunt after i rip it open
@ANONYMIZED i'm going to go to your apartment
and rape you to death. After I'm done, I'll
ram a tire iron up your cunt.
who ever said you could have to many slaves
was definitely one of mine, my sheds crowded
#whitepower
Black people are allowed on tv??? Wtf #fuckniggers
I'm proud to be white! #whitepower #WhitePplRule
#whitepride #whitesupremecy #whitepeoplearesupreme
#fuckniggers #FamousMelaniaTrumpQuotes
@ANONYMIZED teach me your knuckle ball technique
so i can shove my fist in your daughter
Obama is the jews nigger bitch and works
for Israel, not America. Why else would he
give the kikes 38 billion $$$ ?
```

While this set of tweets was not enough to constitute a collection, it gave us clues to begin an exploration of terms and language that could produce a much denser collection of harassing content. We began an exploratory search for terms that would produce a relatively high rate (with a minimum of around 25%) of offensive tweets. Simply searching for offensive words was not effective for this. Some of these have been reappropriated, are used in a relatively non-offensive way within communities, or are used with a much lower level of offense in other cultures. Instead, we turned our attention to hashtags and word structures that would produce a denser set of offensive tweets.

Note that this method abandoned the principle of creating a representative sample of harassing content. Whatever set of terms we defined may produce offensive content, but it would not be a true representation of all the offensive content that was out there. We accept this as a limitation of the work. It was a necessary step to producing a large enough sample.

3.2 Final Collection

To develop our final collection, we did an exploratory search that included derogatory terms for races and religions (e.g. "kike" included above, or "raghead"), hashtags we saw in earlier tweets or discovered in the exploration (e.g. #whitepower, #whitegenocide, #fuckniggers), and phrasing (e.g. "fucking BLANK" where the blank is filled in with a religion or other derogatory term). In the process, we discovered other language that was not offensive by itself, but was used with high density in harassing tweets. For example "The Jews" was used about half the time in religious contexts and half the time in racist tweets at the time of our search. Indeed, simply searching for the word "feminist" produced a very high rate of harassing tweets.

In the end, we settled on the following list of search terms. It will produce a higher rate of tweets from alt-right / white nationalist tweeters, but we were willing to accept a corpus that was not necessarily representative of all harassing content in order to achieve higher density.

- #whitegenocide
- #fuckniggers
- #WhitePower
- #WhiteLivesMatter
- you fucking nigger
- fucking muslim
- fucking faggot
- religion of hate
- the jews
- feminist

We searched our archive of tweets for these terms and pulled all matching tweets. In some cases, if tweets were a response to another tweet, we included the original in the dataset. Some of these responses were harassing the original poster while others were agreeing with another harassing post. We randomly sorted the tweets and selected the first 35,000 from the list as our batch to label.

4 CODE BOOK DEVELOPMENT

4.1 Background and Context

Our team of researchers developed a code book to guide our labeling as we reviewed tweets and developed our final corpus. We made several decisions that are important to the end result in the labels. These were motivated by our desire for this corpus to be a stand-alone, text-based dataset appropriate for automated text analysis and training machine learning algorithms

First, we did not follow any links or look at images included in tweets. Without question, these would provide more context and information about the nature of the tweet. However, much of the media and links were inaccessible (and more have become inaccessible over time). Including such media in our analysis would also mean our results were not purely categorizations of the tweet text, and this is something we wanted to avoid. We believe an analysis of this media, especially images, is an open and important space for future research.

We also did not seek out other contextual elements. For example, a tweet where one user calls another a"fucking faggot" may be used between gay friends as a joke, reappropriating a term used by others as an insult. Determining that context would require a lot of digging into user relationships and guesswork by coders. We decided to ignore this context and analyze the text alone. This means that it is likely that some language which appears offensive without context was labeled as harassment when it was not indented or received that way. However, we believe there is still value in our analysis that says such language is, without special context, likely to be harassing.

We also spent time as a group learning common terms and acronyms likely to occur in this space, including things like Gamer Gate and SJW (social justice warriors), as well as the use of language or notation like white nationalist use of parentheses around Jewish names.

4.2 Coding Guidelines

An important part of our coding guidelines was collectively developing a line between offensive content and trolling / harassing content. We did not want to simply label any tweet that might be offensive. Indeed, we let many many offensive tweets by as "not harassment". This comes back to our main goal of building a corpus that identifies the worst of the worst content.

We broke down harassing tweets into a number of sub-categories. Because there is a lot of overlap amongst these sub-categories, the final corpus does not include these labels. However, they were useful guides for identifying specific types of content to look for. Below, we replicate the code book we developed for our internal use (without the many example tweets included)

4.2.1 *The Very Worst.*

These tweets should be among the worst, most offensive or violent messages you will find. They will include content like:

- Deeply racist, misogynistic or homophobic, or otherwise bigoted. Not a little bit politically incorrect or slightly offensive. Something that would be very upsetting to a general reader.
- The use of shocking language primarily to upset the person who is reading. Words like nigger, cunt, etc. Note that these are used without that shock power by certain groups, so the simple presence of one of these words is not enough to fall into this category.
- Unapologetically or intentionally offensive this could be someone saying something with the intent of upsetting a group, or an extreme account (e.g. Neo nazis) using language that they approve of but they know the general public would disapprove of. Often this will be intended to upset people, but it could be from someone who does not care whether other people are upset and simply chooses to use what he knows will be offensive language.

4.2.2 *Threats.*

These have language intended to make the target or a broader group fearful or to feel unsafe. The threats may be personal ("I saw you hitting on my boyfriend and I'm gonna cut you") or general ("we need to send the Jews back to the gas chambers"). Maybe explicit ("I'm going to a spray your brains all over the wall") or they may generally make the target feel unsafe without a specific threat of direct action (e.g. "someone needs to make you suck his dick" or "you just need the right man to fuck you").

4.2.3 *Hate speech.*

These tweets express hate or extreme bias to a particular group. Could be based on religion, race, gender, sexual orientation, etc. Generally, these groups are defined by their inherent attributes, not by things they do or think.

Do not confuse political disagreement or political speech with hate. "I hate all Democrats" is not hate speech. "I hate all niggers" is. Political hatred is not hate speech because it's based on a political disagreement. The latter example is hate speech because it's based on an inherent trait of a group of people. This is not just hate between two people. "I hate you so much!" would not count. This has to be hate toward a particular group.

4.2.4 Directed Harassment. Language directed at a particular person or group designed to upset them. This language may be milder than in other cases but should be part of the campaign (by one person or a group) to make the target feel threatened or intimidated. This could overlap with any of the above categories, but it does not have to. An @mention that says "you are a loser and I hope you die" would not count as any of the above but would count as directed harassment. There can be a lack of clarity here because sometimes statements are made in jest among friends. For the purposes of this project, imagine the comment coming from an unknown stranger.

Again, do not misconstrue a disagreement with harassment. Someone saying you are an idiot for, say, voting for Candidate X is likely not harassing the other person but disagreeing with them. Think carefully before you call it harassment - is the tweet intended to intimidate or upset the target, or is it intended to express disagreement with an opinion?

The target of Harassment should be a person or a group. People are usually targeted with @mentions ("@jengolbeck you need to die"). Groups may be targeted with a hashtag ("#blacklivesmatter <- no they dont") or by a name (e..g "The Jews").

4.2.5 Potentially Offensive. In our first round of coding, researchers had a hard time letting offensive content, like jokes in poor taste, go by without labeling them as harassment, even though they were relatively mild. To help us psychologically overcome that barrier, we introduced this category of Potentially Offensive content. These tweets will still be labeled as "non-harassing" in the final dataset, but it will help so we dont feel bad about letting offensive content go by unlabeled. For anything that doesnt rise to the level of clearly and unambiguously fitting into the categories above, you can label it Potentially Offensive.

4.2.6 Non-Harassing. This section of coding was for tweets that did not meet the aforementioned criteria. That did not mean these were considered "good" tweets. If a coder was uncomfortable with labeling a tweet with a disapproving label, then the coder could categorize it as potentially offensive. "Potentially Offensive" served as a label to make the coder feel better, though we did not distinguish these tweets from non-harassing tweets in the final dataset. It was critical that we did not apply the labels above too liberally. We made sure the text alone, without seeking extra content, was truly harassing. If the coder was unable to discern the category, then they marked it as 'non-harrasing'.

4.3 Coder Training

The coders on this project underwent extensive training on the codebook. Before labeling our final corpus, we spent three weeks reviewing and refining the codebook above, labeling sample sets of tweets as a group, and discussing the results. We went through four rounds of sample tweet coding, with the chosen examples becoming more ambiguous in each round. We followed each sample coding with extensive discussion to help highlight issues and make sure everyone had a similar calibration for the categories.

5 LABELED CORPUS

We spent 3 months labeling tweets in the corpus. Each tweet was labeled by two coders. If they agreed that it was Harassing or Non-Harassing (including "potentially offensive" labels), it was added to the final corpus. If they disagreed, a third coder was brought in to break the tie.

Of the 35,000 tweets, 2,711 required a third coder. This gives us an inter-rate agreement measured by Cohen's Kappa as 0.84 for the initial codes.

Given the inflammatory terms we used in our data set collection, we expected a high number of harassing tweets. However, only 15.7% of tweets rose to this level. Some were non-harassing because they were relating quotes or news stories, e.g.

`#DrudgeReport 'F*ck the Jews' scrawled at Jewish school in London...: http: / /t.co /ZaUB0piMN4 #News`

Others used the terms in non-offensive ways, such as the following:

`For the record, I see tax havens as the next world war, not fucking Muslims.`

Still others referred to someone else's opinion, so the tweet itself was not harassing:

`He hates all the Jews, he hates all the Jews... Samir Nasri, he hates all the Jews.`

We highlight these issues because they present research challenges for classification. How to differentiate between a tweet asserting a harassing or hateful position and one quoting it or attributing it to another will be a challenge. We hope that this dataset - with 5,495 positive examples and 29,505 negative examples - will be of use in discovering such distinguishing features.

6 DISCUSSION AND CONCLUSIONS

In this paper, we present a hand-coded dataset of 35,000 tweets labeled as Harassing or Non-Harassing. The research team spent months developing, refining, and training on a codebook designed to capture truly harassing content. We believe this dataset significantly contributes to the web science research community, both as a base of ground truth for training algorithms and as a source of data to understand and analyze the online harassment phenomenon.

Beyond its usefulness in machine learning, there is also important web science research to be done on the culture and patterns of online harassment. While this certainly will change as topics of discussion change, our codebook and dataset can provide a launching point for deeper qualitative research. For example, our work has many examples, positive and negative, that use the #WhiteGenocide hashtag. With these thousands of data points, researchers could define a much more detailed set of codes that describe the references and types of use (e.g. to refer to diversity initiatives broadly, as anti-immigration, as white nationalism, as anti-interracial marriage, etc.). Those can be developed, refined, and human coders can be trained on this stable dataset before they may choose to work on live data which presents its own complexities.

Because of Twitter terms of service restrictions and privacy concerns about individuals whose tweets are included, we are not posting the dataset in a public repository. However, this data can be shared with researchers who agree to a Data Terms of Use which includes ethical considerations. Researchers can request access to the data via email to jgolbeck@umd.edu.

7 ACKNOWLEDGMENTS

This work was supported by NSF Award #1546829.

REFERENCES

[1] Uwe Bretschneider, Thomas Wöhner, and Ralf Peters. 2014. Detecting Online Harassment in Social Networks. (2014).

[2] Erin E Buckels, Paul D Trapnell, and Delroy L Paulhus. 2014. Trolls just want to have fun. *Personality and individual Differences* 67 (2014), 97–102.

[3] Maeve Duggan and Aaron Smith. 2013. Social media update 2013. *Pew Internet and American Life Project* (2013).

[4] Claire Hardaker. 2010. Trolling in asynchronous computer-mediated communication: from user discussions to theoretical concepts. *Journal of Politeness Research* 6, 2 (2010), 215–242.

[5] April Kontostathis, Kelly Reynolds, Andy Garron, and Lynne Edwards. 2013. Detecting cyberbullying: query terms and techniques. In *Proceedings of the 5th annual acm web science conference*. ACM, 195–204.

[6] Sara Owsley Sood, Elizabeth F Churchill, and Judd Antin. 2012. Automatic identification of personal insults on social news sites. *Journal of the American Society for Information Science and Technology* 63, 2 (2012), 270–285.

The Fake News Spreading Plague: Was it Preventable?

Eni Mustafaraj
Department of Computer Science
Wellesley College
Wellesley, MA
eni.mustafaraj@wellesley.edu

Panagiotis Takis Metaxas
Department of Computer Science
Wellesley College
Wellesley, MA
pmetaxas@wellesley.edu

ABSTRACT

In 2010, a paper entitled "From Obscurity to Prominence in Minutes: Political Speech and Real-time search" [7] won the Best Paper Prize of the WebSci'10 conference. Among its findings were the discovery and documentation of what was labeled a "Twitter bomb", an organized effort to spread misinformation about the democratic candidate Martha Coakley through anonymous Twitter accounts. In this paper, after summarizing the details of that event, we outline the recipe of how social networks are used to spread misinformation. One of the most important steps in such a recipe is the "infiltration" of a community of users who are already engaged in conversations about a topic, to use them as organic spreaders of misinformation in their extended subnetworks. Then, we take this misinformation spreading recipe and indicate how it was successfully used to spread fake news during the 2016 U.S. Presidential Election. The main differences between the scenarios are the use of Facebook instead of Twitter, and the respective motivations (in 2010: political influence; in 2016: financial benefit through online advertising). After situating these events in the broader context of exploiting the Web, we seize this opportunity to address limitations of the reach of research findings and to start a conversation about how communities of researchers can increase their impact on real-world societal issues.

CCS CONCEPTS

• **Information systems** → **Social networks**; *Spam detection*; • **Human-centered computing** → **Social networking sites**;

KEYWORDS

fake news; misinformation spreading; Facebook; Twitter; Google

ACM Reference format:
Eni Mustafaraj and Panagiotis Takis Metaxas. 2017. The Fake News Spreading Plague: Was it Preventable?. In *Proceedings of ACM Web Science Conference, Troy, NY, USA, June 2017 (WebSci'17),* 5 pages.
https://doi.org/10.1145/3091478.3091523

WebSci'17, June 2017, Troy, NY, USA

ACM ISBN 978-1-4503-4896-6/17/06...$15.00
https://doi.org/10.1145/3091478.3091523

Figure 1: The journalist John Carney (at that time with CNBC), received one of these "reply-tweets", which he retweeted adding a comment expressing his surprise, "<Wow! Political Tweetbots!–JC>", because this was an unknown phenomenon at that time on Twitter. Carney deleted the URL of the original tweet.

1 INTRODUCTION

1.1 The Anatomy of a Political Twitter Bomb

On January 15, 2010, between 18:43 and 18:56, someone created a group of nine Twitter accounts with the names: *CoakleySaidWhat, CoakleyCatholic, CoakleyER, CoakleyAgainstU, CoakleyAG, CoakleyMass, CoakleyAndU, CoakleyWhat,* and *CoakleySaidThat.* The name Coakley refers to Martha Coakley, at that time the Attorney General of Massachusetts and the democratic candidate running in the high-stakes Special Election for the Massachusetts U.S senate seat. After a few hours of inactivity, these nine accounts sent 929 tweets addressed to 573 unique users in the course of 138 minutes. All the tweets contained a URL to the same website `http://coakleysaidit.com`, (also registered on January 15, 2010), that showed video and audio from a speech by Martha Coakley, taken out of context, to advance the false claim that she is against the employment of Catholics in the emergency room.

The nine accounts were sending a tweet per minute and repeating more or less the same content, both reasons to be flagged as a spamming account. Twitter discovered the automated tweets and consequently suspended all nine accounts. Their existence and their misinformation attack would have gone unnoticed had it not been for one fortunate circumstance: we were collecting all tweets containing the names "coakley" and "brown" (respectively for Martha Coakley and Scott Brown, the two candidates for the senate election) in real-time, during the week leading to the election. The tweets sent by these anonymous accounts were no simple tweets, they were so-called "reply tweets", tweets directed to particular users. Why? Because a new account on Twitter doesn't have any followers. Tweets sent by such an account will not be read by anyone. Thus, directing the tweets to a particular user makes it likely that the tweet will be read. But to which users do you reply-tweet, out of the millions that are on Twitter? This is where a common spamming technique on Twitter comes in handy: reply to users who have used certain desired keywords in their tweets, that is, to users already attuned to the topic. Our analysis of the recipients of these "reply tweets" revealed that 96% of them had been tweeting about the MA senate race in the four-hour interval between the time the anonymous accounts were created and when they started to send the "reply tweets". Almost 25% of the users who received a tweet (143 out of 573) retweeted the message. A screenshot from one of the retweets is shown in Figure 1. We chose to show this tweet, because the user is a well known journalist[1] and an experienced Twitter user who joined the site on March 2007. His surprise at the message indicates the novelty of this technique at the time. The retweets had the effect that the followers of the retweeters were likely exposed to the misinformation, which they would have not seen otherwise, given that the messages didn't include hashtags, a common way to group together tweets about a topic, which, when clicked, present with a stream of tweets containing the hashtag. Our estimation of the audience size, based on the followers of the retweeters, amounted to 61,732 Twitter users.

1.2 A Recipe for Spreading Misinformation on Twitter

All the facts presented in the previous subsection were part of the WebSci'10 paper [7]. What we didn't do in that paper was to summarize our findings in an easily memorable recipe, which contains the steps used by the propagandists in spreading their misinformation on Twitter. We're providing this recipe for the first time in this paper.

Step 1	Register a domain name for a new website, for example: `http://coakleysaidit.com`
Step 2	Create anonymous accounts, for example: *CoakleySaidWhat*, etc.
Step 3	Identify a community of users interested in the topic, for example, the MA Senate Election race.
Step 4	Target members of this community with messages, for example, reply to users providing link to website.
Step 5	Wait for members of community to spread message via retweets in their organic subnetworks.

Table 1: A recipe for spreading misinformation on Twitter via a Twitter bomb.

Our discovery attracted the attention of both journalists and other researchers. A team at Indiana University, headed by Fil Menczer, developed Truthy[2], a system that collects Twitter data to analyze discourse in near real-time [12]. In addition, our team at Wellesley developed Twitter Trails[3], a system that can be used to monitor the spreading of rumors on Twitter [6]. This focus on Twitter is justified by the fact that it provides APIs for researchers to collect and analyze its data, as well as the public nature of conversations on Twitter. Both these features are missing on Facebook (not entirely, but they are severely limited), thus, only Facebook employees are able to study them. As evidence, see [1]. Meanwhile, researchers not affiliated with the company have almost no opportunities to study information spreading on Facebook, especially that of rumors, hoaxes, and recently fake news, a topic to which we turn our focus now.

1.3 Spreading Fake News on Facebook

After the surprise results of the 2016 U.S. Presidential Election, the American media directed its ire at Facebook and Google, as in this New York Times piece [19] written by the Editorial Board, on November 19, 2016:

> Most of the fake news stories are produced by scammers looking to make a quick buck. The vast majority of them take far-right positions. But a big part of the responsibility for this scourge rests with internet companies like Facebook and Google, which have made it possible for fake news to be shared nearly instantly with millions of users and have been slow to block it from their sites.

This criticism is only partly well-placed. Facebook had been working toward fixing (or containing) the spread of hoaxes on the site at least since January 2015, almost two years before the election [11]. They defined a hoax as a form of News Feed spam post that includes scams ("Click here to win a lifetime supply of coffee"), or deliberately false or misleading news stories ("Man sees dinosaur on hike in Utah"). As we can notice from this definition, in 2015, the phrase *fake news* wasn't being applied yet to the kind of false stories that flooded Facebook in the weeks before the election.

Step 1	Register many web domains for related websites, with catchy names such as: `http://TrumpVision365.com`, see [16].
Step 2	Create Facebook accounts of fictitious people, e.g, Elena Nikolov or Antonio Markoski, see [17].
Step 3	Identify and join a Facebook group about a political candidate, e.g., "Hispanics for Trump" or "San Diego Bernicrats", see [17].
Step 4	Target members of the Facebook group with posts that link to the fake news website stories, see [17].
Step 5	Wait for members of the group to spread the fake news in their organic subnetworks, by sharing and liking it.

Table 2: The recipe for spreading *fake news* on Facebook ahead of the 2016 U.S. Presidential election. It contains the same steps as the recipe shown in Table 1.

However, since it was difficult for independent researchers to know the extent to which Facebook users were affected by this issue, everything continued more or less as before, and Facebook was alone in its fight. This changed in early 2016, when the online

[1] John Carney, https://twitter.com/carney.
[2] Truthy, now known as OSoMe, http://truthy.indiana.edu
[3] TwitterTrails.com, http://twittertrails.com

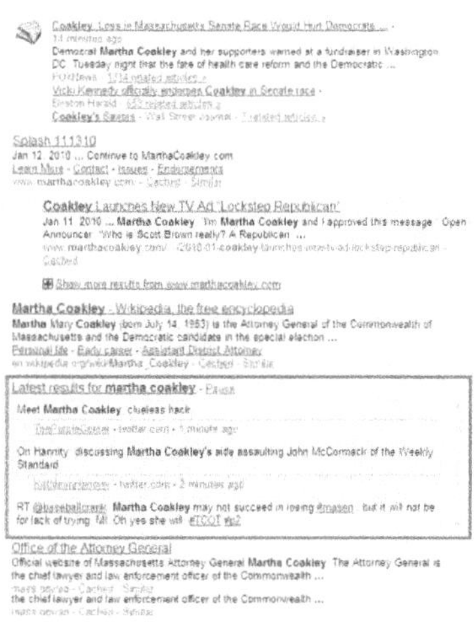

Figure 2: Screenshot from Google search results about Martha Coakley on Jan 12, 2010. Notice in highlighted red, the tweets attacking Coakley. This was a finding from our WebSci'10 paper, on how Google was inadvertently giving premium space to political propagandists, in an effort to have "fresh" and relevant search results.

publication BuzzFeed took an interest on Facebook's unsuccessful efforts to deal with the problem. In an article published in April 2016, BuzzFeed proclaims: "it is the golden age of fake news" [4]. The article reveals that BuzzFeed—using the services of the company *Crowdtangle*, specialized in measuring social engagement—had conducted a study of fake news that was spreading via nine known fake news sites, such as the *National Report*, *Huzlers*, or *Empire News*. The findings emphasized that while traffic for these sites had gone down for a while during 2015, it had started picking up again in early 2016. The article also interviewed Allen Montgomery, a fake identity for Jestin Coler, the creator of a factory of fake news websites, as NPR reporters discovered after the election [18]. Coler's interview sheds light about some of the tricks of the trade of fake news, and points out why he believes he can win over Facebook:

> Coler believes Facebook is fighting a losing battle, doomed to fail no matter what it does. "They can shut down *National Report*. Of course they can do that," he said. "But I could have 100 domains set up in a week, and are they going to stop every one of those? Are they now going to read content from every site and determine which ones are true and which ones are selling you a lie? I don't see that happening. That's not the way that the internet works."

Despite this sounding of alarm bells by BuzzFeed (as early as April 2016), things got only worse with fake news on Facebook. We counted at least 25 articles published on the topic of fake news from April to November 2016 on BuzzFeed, culminating with the story of "How teens in the Balkans are duping Trump supporters with fake news", published on November 3, 2016 and followed up by the related piece on "How Macedonian spammers are using Facebook groups to feed you fake news". These two articles provide details

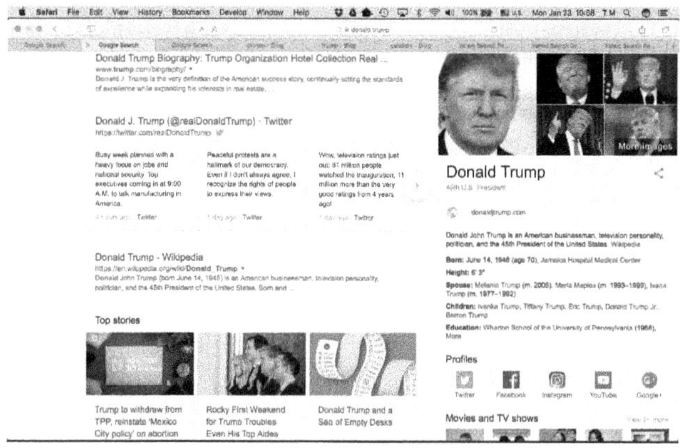

Figure 3: Screenshot from Google search results about Donald Trump on Jan 23, 2017. In addition to the many sections on the page (such as the "featured snippet" on the right column), notice how the tweets shown above the fold belong to Trump himself.

about one of the fake news factories operated by young people in the small town of Ceres, Macedonia, that targeted Facebook users in the United States. After reading these news articles (and others on the same topic), we noticed the clear similarities to the process that lead to the Twitter bomb against Martha Coakley in 2010. In fact, we are able to map the steps in the two recipes one to one, as shown in Table 2. This similarity should not be surprising. Once a spamming technique has been proven successful, it is easily replicated, since the knowledge about its working is also shared on the internet. What should surprise and worry us is the fact that researchers and web platform developers also know about such techniques, but they do little to warn and educate the public of the consequences. It is also unfortunate that tech companies who have been exploited to enable misinformation spreading, do not act proactively or effectively in stopping it. As an example of ineffective action, we discuss in the next section the way Facebook handled the accusation that its news verification was not balanced.

2 FROM PROPAGANDA TO FAKE NEWS

We should not give the reader the impression that **online propaganda** started with Twitter bombs or Facebook fake news. In fact, it is much older than social media, it is as old as the Web itself. However, before the development of search engines it was not easy *for propaganda to find you.* Search engines made it possible for propagandists to spread their message using techniques we now call *Web Spam* [5]. Advertisers, political activists and religious zealots of all kinds have been busy modifying the structure of the Web in an effort to promote their own biased results over organic, unbiased results. The Search Engine Optimization industry has grown out of this effort, sometimes using unethical techniques to promote their messages, and search engines have been continuously evolving to fend off these attacks.

In much of the first decade of the new millennium, search engines tried to defend against Web spam, but the spammers were successful in circumventing their defenses by using first "Link Farms" and later "Mutual Admiration Societies", collections of web sites that would intentionally link to each other in order to increase everyone's PageRank [5]. Even when Google was reportedly using up to 200 different signals to measure quality [13], professional SEOs would manage to get sites like JC Penney's at the top of search results [14]. Google's ingenious solution to the problem of "unfair competition for high placement on a page" was the introduction of the advertising model of AdWords and AdSense that gave spammers an opportunity to make money while following rules. That seemed to work for a while. However, the algorithmically allocated financial benefits of online advertising became so lucrative, they provided a strong reason for *anyone* to have a presence on the Web—especially if they could manage to attract clicks and thus, advertising dollars. This led to "click bait" and to the creation of ads masquerading as outrageous (fake) news stories, as we discussed in the previous section.

But as search engines and social media evolve, so do the propagandistic techniques. Concurrently with the rise of "fake news", we also find the "featured snippets" manipulation [3], and "autocompletion revelations" [2], as the latest chapters in spreading propaganda through search engines and social media so that it will find you. As a community of researchers, we need to embrace the challenge of documenting and understanding these phenomena, as well as finding effective ways to make these issues known to the platform providers. Journalists also need to be informed, as they sometimes give credence to conspiracy theories, confusing the public [20].

3 RESEARCH THAT INFORMS DESIGN

It is important for researchers, journalists and web users to pay attention continuously to the information and misinformation they encounter on the Web, be it on Google, Twitter, or Facebook. In this section, we discuss how research results and their publicizing lead over time to changes in the design features of these systems, addressing the exhibited weaknesses.

3.1 The Evolution of Google Search Results

The central finding that give the title to our WebSci'10 paper [7] was the manipulation of Google real-time search results through repetition of Twitter posts by accounts—real users or bots—supporting a particular candidate. In December 2009, just one month before the Massachusetts special election for the U.S. Senate seat in 2010, Google followed Bing in introducing "real-time search results", placing social media messages near the top of search results for a relevant search query. These messages came mostly from Twitter, since its API makes it easy to pull the tweets. Tweets appearing in the search results were those that had been recently posted. That created the opportunity for political propagandists to exploit the search results, creating a Twitter-enabled Google bomb. As we documented in our paper, the manipulators were repeating the same messages, something also allowed by Twitter, over and over to increase the volume of conversation about a particular topic and keep it fresh for search engines to include in their real-time results. Repetition of a message would be annoying to the propagandist's followers, but the target was not their followers' feed; it was Google and Bing's algorithms.

We can see these highly-placed tweet messages from random Twitter accounts in the screenshot that we took in January 2010 for Martha Coakley's search results, Figure 2. During 2010, Google eventually recognized that giving anonymous social media accounts a premium spot in its search results was not in line with its goals for reliable information and for a few years this feature disappeared. However, it has come back again, but now in a different format: when searching for a person, it will pull up tweets from their timeline, as opposed to tweets about them, as exemplified in Figure 3. This is a great improvement, because it prevents actors—who have an interest in promoting their adversarial messages about an individual or product—to receive an unearned spot at the top of the search results.

3.2 The Evolution of Retweeting

In [7], we had included the following observation at the end of Section 4:

> Our experiments with Google real-time search have shown that, even though Google doesn't display tweets from users that have a spammer signature, it does display tweets from non-suspected users, even when these are retweets coming from spammers. Thus, simply suspending spamming accounts is not sufficient. There should be a mechanism that allows for retroactively deleting retweets of spam and some mechanism that labels some Twitter users as enablers of spam.

At that time (in 2010), Twitter didn't have an easy way to quote a tweet and it allowed users to edit the original tweet text when retweeting, as the tweet shown in Figure 1 indicated. That design feature turned out to be very problematic, among others for the reason mentioned in the quote above: deleted spam tweets lived in the retweets of other Twitter users, but also because users were often purposefully changing the meaning of the text they were retweeting [9]. Most of this was possible via third-party applications that were very popular in the early years of Twitter. These applications were shut down over the years and nowadays Twitter doesn't allow the editing of a tweet that is being retweeted. Additionally, if the original is deleted, the retweet is deleted too, while in a quoted retweet, the text "This tweet is unavailable." will show in place of the deleted tweet.

3.3 The Evolution of Fake News on Facebook

The proliferation of fake news on Facebook achieved new levels once Facebook made a big change in how its algorithm for the Trending News feature worked. Before August 2016 (when this change took effect), the Trending News feature was being curated by human editors, who filtered out unreliable sources and chose neutral or balanced sources for breaking news stories. However, when the online tech blog Gizmodo posted an article (May 2016) [10], in which former employees of the Trending News lamented anti-conservative bias, Facebook—likely worried about potential lawsuits for suppressing freedom of speech—fired its team of human editors and replaced them with algorithms. It didn't take long after that change for fake news to start achieving Trending News status,

Figure 4: Facebook recently moved into implementing a system of warning towards sharing news items that have been disputed.

as BuzzFeed reported on August 30, 2016 [15]. Despite BuzzFeed's relentless reporting on the fake news plague throughout the pre-election season, the rest of the media and the public didn't tune in into this conversation until after the election.

Facebook initially disputed the it had a fake news problem, claiming that it accounts for only 1% of the news stories. However, the company changed course under the increased and sustained public pressure, introducing new features in its interface and algorithms to address the issue [8].

One important feature that has rolled out recently is the labeling of news posts as "Disputed" via fact-checking, third-party providers such as Snopes or PolitiFact. The screenshot in Figure 4 is an example of this feature in action. In addition to adding this label, Facebook warns users with an alert box before they try to share a disputed story, although they are still allowed to share it [8].

It remains to be seen how this new feature will affect fake news spreading. It bears repeating that the lack of access to Facebook data, which could allow independent researchers to evaluate the effectiveness of such interventions, will hinder our understanding of changes in human behavior correlated with or caused by changes in the socio-technical platforms they inhabit. This is a reason for concern for our research communities.

4 DISCUSSION

What is the moral of the story? In the past, researchers were the ones discovering and documenting the misuse and abuse of socio-technical platforms by the hands of dubious actors with dubious agendas. The WebSci'10 [7] paper is only one such example. However, that discovery was possible only because we were collecting data in real-time, after having noticed some evidence of foul play. When one contemplates Twitter's approach to combating spammers, it seems reasonable that tweets created by "spamming" accounts are automatically deleted and retracted from the entire network, once the accounts are suspended. However, the downside of such an approach is that it makes it impossible for researchers and fact-checkers to go back in time and study the origin of misinformation campaigns and the mechanisms for spreading them. That is a severe limitation to research. The problem becomes even more pronounced in the content of fake news spreading on Facebook. Most Facebook groups are private and if they are the source for starting certain cascades of fake news spreading, outside researchers cannot observe them in their early stages, missing crucial information that would lead to their understanding. Thus, it is not surprising that in the current situation created by the fake news plague, researchers didn't play a leading role in their discovery. It were journalists and not researchers in academia or Facebook and Google who raised concerns, but were not heard. This is worrisome. Facebook, by replacing humans with algorithms, might have played a crucial role in fueling the fake news spreading phenomenon. Similarly, the ease with which Google enables earning ad money for page impression provided the financial incentives for the creation of the fake news industry.

In light of what we know so far, here is our open question to the relevant research communities:

> in the current context of the omnipresent, web-based, socio-technical systems such as Facebook, Google, and Twitter, what decisions should be made by humans and what by algorithms?

Our research communities should lead the way in providing answers to this question.

REFERENCES

[1] Adrien Friggeri, Lada Adamic, Dean Eckles, and Justin Cheng. 2014. Rumor Cascades. In *ICWSM*.
[2] Quentin Hardy and Matt Richtel. 2012-11-21. Don't Ask? Internet Still Tells. *http://nyti.ms/2nyWnSx* (2012-11-21).
[3] Adrienne Jeffries. 2017-03-05. Google's Featured Snippets are worse than fake news. *http://bit.ly/2n5vgB2* (2017-03-05).
[4] Alex Kantrowitz. 2015-01-20. Facebook Wanted A Fight Against Fake News. It Got One. *http://bit.ly/2mBUnIF* (2015-01-20).
[5] Panagiotis Metaxas. 2010. Web Spam, Social Propaganda and the Evolution of Search Engine Rankings. *Lecture Notes BIP, Springer-Verlag* (2010). http://bit.ly/ffYsuC
[6] Panagiotis Takis Metaxas, Samantha Finn, and Eni Mustafaraj. 2015. Using TwitterTrails.Com to Investigate Rumor Propagation *(CSCW'15 Companion)*. 69–72. https://doi.org/10.1145/2685553.2702691
[7] Panagiotis T. Metaxas and Eni Mustafaraj. From Obscurity to Prominence in Minutes: Political Speech and Real-Time Search. In *Proc. of the WebSci'10 Conference*.
[8] Adam Mosseri. 2016-12-15. News Feed FYI: Addressing Hoaxes and Fake News. *http://bit.ly/2mzv8pe* (2016-12-15).
[9] Eni Mustafaraj and Panagiotis Takis Metaxas. 2011. What Edited Retweets Reveal about Online Political Discourse.. In *AAAI Workshop on Analyzing Microtext*.
[10] Michael Nunez. 2016-05-09. Former Facebook Workers: We Routinely Suppressed Conservative News. *http://bit.ly/2ngF2k5* (2016-05-09).
[11] Erich Owens and Udi Weinsberg. 2015-01-20. News Feed FYI: Showing Fewer Hoaxes. *http://bit.ly/2mBUnIF* (2015-01-20).
[12] J. Ratkiewicz, M. Conover, M. Meiss, B. Goncalves, S. Patil, A. Flammini, and F. Menczer. 2011. Truthy: Mapping the Spread of Astroturf in Microblog Streams.. In *WWW'11*.
[13] Saul Hansell 2007. Google Keeps Tweaking Its Search Engine. (2007). URL: http://nyti.ms/2n5JjGx [accessed: 2007-06-03].
[14] David Segal. 2012-02-12. The dirty little secrets of search. *New York Times, http://nyti.ms/2nXfSE0* (2012-02-12).
[15] Craig Silverman. 2016-08-30. Facebook Must Either Innovate Or Admit Defeat At The Hands Of Fake News Hoaxsters. *http://bzfd.it/2nMvfia* (2016-08-30).
[16] Craig Silverman and Lawrence Alexander. 2016-11-03. How Teens In The Balkans Are Duping Trump Supporters With Fake News. *http://bzfd.it/2mC6tBm* (2016-11-03).
[17] Craig Silverman and Lawrence Alexander. 2016-11-08. How Macedonian Spammers Are Using Facebook Groups To Feed You Fake News. *http://bzfd.it/2mzvCM0* (2016-11-08).
[18] Laura Sydell. We Tracked Down A Fake-News Creator In The Suburbs. Here's What We Learned. *http://n.pr/2nuHN1T* (????).
[19] The Editorial Board. 2016-11-19. Facebook and the Digital Virus Called Fake News. *New York Times* (2016-11-19).
[20] Craig Timberg. 2017-03-14. Could Google rankings skew an election? New group aims to find out. *Washington Post, http://wapo.st/2mNaOwY* (2017-03-14).

Web Science: Mapping the Curriculum

Elisabeth Coskun
Web and Internet Science
University of Southampton
United Kingdom
eac1g09@ecs.soton.ac.uk

Su White
Web and Internet Science
University of Southampton
United Kingdom
eac1g09@ecs.soton.ac.uk

ABSTRACT

Web Science [1] is an emerging subject, which was formally defined in 2006. Since the inception of Web Science, a number of Web Science taught programs have emerged across the world. Despite the increasing popularity of Web Science, there are still currently very few attempts to provide a formal curriculum definition for Web Science. This paper outlines plans and some initial results of a study which seeks to explore the scope of Web Science in a bottom-up fashion, by examining what is taught as part of Web Science MSc and Undergraduate programs worldwide. This paper presents some early results of the analysis, including the most frequently occurring 'key topics' found from an evaluation of Web Science taught modules. Plans for future work are then outlined; the ultimate aim of the study being to present a view of Web Science as it is taught across the world. A proposed outcome will include a taxonomy of key topics for Web Science, potentially hosted in a wiki, or similar format, which will facilitate both access and contributions from the wider worldwide Web Science community.

KEYWORDS

Web Science, Education, Web Science Curriculum.

1 INTRODUCTION

Web Science was formally outlined as a subject by Berners-Lee et al in 2006. [1] [2] They make the case for a dedicated subject to study and understand the development of the Web, in order to influence and shape its development in ways which benefit society. They describe a science which aims to study the impact of the Web on the world, both from a technological and a social perspective. Recognising the importance of this emerging subject, and the need to study the impact of the Web, a growing number of Universities across the world have begun to teach Web Science programmes. Despite this, there are currently very few definitive subject definitions available for Web Science. Educators and students are then faced with the problem; how do you teach or learn about Web Science or encourage people to study it, when there is no clear definition or easy point of reference for understanding the scope of the subject? This is an issue if Web Science is to continue to gain popularity as a taught subject.

Driven by the rapid growth of the Web as an entity, Web Science exhibits rapid evolution and development. This is challenging for standard top down methods of curriculum development, such as those used by the ACM, [3] which generally take years to produce formal curriculum guidelines. There are currently no formal curriculum guidelines available for Web Science, yet there are a number of Web Science taught curricula in existence. This study conducts a bottom up examination of these current Web Science related curricula and resources, in order to build a picture of Web Science according to what is taught as Web Science worldwide, in a reverse engineering fashion. [4] Instead of the curriculum guidelines shaping the curricula, the curricula will be used to shape and develop a set of Web Science curriculum guidelines in the form of a taxonomy of key topics which are typically taught as part of Web Science programmes. This paper gives a brief overview of the background of the Web Science subject, before explaining the bottom up approach and research methodology used during this study, suggesting why this approach is suited to Web Science. The initial results of a desk survey locating Web Science associated institutions are presented, followed by a further desk survey identifying individual Web Science taught modules. The process of analyzing the modules desk survey is outlined; some early findings are shown and discussed, along with proposals for future work, including a suggested format for the proposed curriculum taxonomy of key topics for Web Science.

2 BACKGROUND

According to Berners-Lee et al. 2006 [1] "We may paraphrase Web Science as the science of the Web." This founding statement is one of the basic definitions which can be used to summarize Web Science. Their publication heralded the introduction of the term Web Science, and argued the need for a science dedicated to the study and understanding of the Web. This lead to the creation of the Web Science Research Initiative. Current Web Science development is promoted by the Web

WebSci '17, June 25-28, 2017, Troy, NY, USA

ACM ISBN 978-1-4503-4896-6/17/06...$15.00
http://dx.doi.org/10.1145/3091478.3091511

Science Trust. Since 2009 there has been an annual conference dedicated to Web Science, and since 2011, this has been sponsored by the ACM.

Despite the increasing number of Web Science taught programmes on offer worldwide, and the fact that the annual Web Science conference has been sponsored by the ACM since 2011, the ACM does not currently provide curriculum guidelines for Web Science programmes, despite doing so other subjects such as Computer Science and Information Science. Hendler et al [5] point out that within the ACM classification system for publications, the best possible classification for Web Science is 'miscellaneous'. White and Vafopoulos [3] argue that Web Science should be included in the ACM family of computing curricula, and therefore that there is a need for curriculum guidelines for Web Science. A key problem when defining curriculum guidelines for Web Science, is the fact that Web Science is a rapidly evolving field. Use of traditional top down methods of formulating curriculum guidelines, such as those used by the ACM for Computer Science, would potentially mean that any similar attempt for Web Science using the top down method would be outdated by the time it were completed. To this end, a bottom up, qualitative Grounded theory based approach is proposed as an alternative method.

3 RESEARCH METHODOLOGY

When using a traditional quantitative research approach, the researcher will typically begin with preconceived ideas or theories, and then set out to prove them. However, when utilizing a qualitative approach, the outcome is influenced by the findings of the research, and the direction of the project is influenced by findings. This study utilizes a Bottom Up approach, which is suited to qualitative Grounded Theory, incorporating mixed methods, as outlined by Strauss and Corbin. According to Strauss and Corbin, [6] theory derived from data is far more likely to resemble reality than a theory drawn only from a series of concepts or speculation. Because Grounded Theory involves deriving theories from the data, it is more likely to offer accurate insight. [7] The Grounded theory approach suggested by Strauss and Corbin [6] is not purely qualitative, it has the benefit of integrating mixed methods. While this study includes largely qualitative data it also includes some qualitative analysis of the data, including keyword analysis. Strauss and Corbin [6] suggest that there is no standard set of methods equally useful for each research step; therefore researchers will typically use a combination of methods, in order to "foster the development of theory". They also propose that there can be interplay between the qualitative and quantitative in an iterative cycle, in which each method contributes and provides insight in ways only it can. When using a Grounded Theory approach, the researcher will typically collect data and then undertake a process of coding the data in order to identify themes in the data [7] [8]. In the case of this study, coding is carried out utilizing the Qualitative data analysis package, Nvivo. This is an iterative cycle, which will be undertaken numerous times, until the data has been thoroughly analyzed and no more insight can be gained from it. The practice of coding as well as some initial findings are outlined in section 5.

4 DATA COLLECTION

Data collection began with the compilation of a simple desk survey of Web Science teaching institutions, shown in Table 1. A list of Web Science education institutions listed on the Web Science Trust website[2] during 2013 was used as a starting point, however upon investigation, it was discovered that a number of the universities identified no longer offered Web Science taught programmes, therefore no website data was available for these.

Table 1:Web Science Institutions

Name	Level	Country
Aristotle University of Thessaloniki	MSc	Greece
British university in Egypt	MSc	Egypt
Cologne University	MSc	Germany
Eindhoven University of Technology	UG	Netherlands
Georgia Tech University		USA
Goldsmiths, University of London	MSc	UK
Johannes Kepler University	MSc	Austria-
Korea Advanced Institute of Science and Technology (KAIST)	MSc/ PhD	South Korea
MIT - Massachusetts Institute of Technology	PhD	USA
Northwestern University School of Communication	PhD	USA
Oxford Internet Institute	MSc/PhD	UK
Rensselaer Polytechnic Institute	UG/MSc/ PhD	USA
RWTH Aachen University		Germany
Saint-Joseph University of Beirut	MSc	Lebanon
The University of Edinburgh	MSc	UK
University of Alcalá	MSc/PhD	Spain
University College London	MSc	UK
University of Erlangen-Nürnberg	MSc	Germany
University of Koblenz-Landau,	MSc	Germany
University of Liverpool	MSc	UK
University of Southampton	UG/MSc/ PhD	UK
VU University Amsterdam	PhD	Netherlands

4.1 Web Science Modules Desk Survey

The list of Web Science institutions was used as the basis for a further desk survey of Web Science taught modules. Out of a total of 21 institutions identified, a total of 15 feature taught modules. The modules desk survey consists of MSc and Undergraduate programmes only, as MSc or undergraduate programmes typically include taught modules, whereas PhD programmes typically do not. Taught modules feature examples of structured Web Science curricula, whereas PhD research groups studying Web Science are more abstract and typically do

[2] http://www.webscience.org/

not feature structured and detailed curriculum information. The modules desk survey was recorded in a spreadsheet, which includes the fields shown in Table 2.

Table 2 Key Fields Used in the Modules Desk Survey

Intuition Location	Resource Title	Topic(s) Taught	Teaching\ Assessment format
Contributors(s)	Materials Used	Level (e.g. Masters)	Module Dates\ Duration

During the survey, a total of 142 modules were identified across the 15 intuitions featuring taught programmes. The survey is populated by information collated from university websites. The website data was recorded in a spreadsheet with the cell headings shown in Table 2. This process was repeated for each of the institutions identified in the study. It was only possible to gather data from institutions which provide public information relating to modules.

5 DATA ANALYSIS AND MANUAL CODING

The process of coding was conducted by a single coder; the main author of this work. The process of coding facilitated the identification of key topics taught within the Web Science programmes identified. Once refined, these key topics will ultimately form the basis of a proposed taxonomy of Web Science key subjects, providing a curriculum outline for Web Science. The coding was conducted by manually analyzing the 'Topic(s) Taught' description field of the Web Science modules desk survey spreadsheet, in order to identify the key subjects covered in each module. Keywords which were identified as being the focus of each module or important to the module were then coded as a key topic. Because key topics were still being identified through the initial iteration of coding, a second iteration enabled a more thorough spread of coding, allowing key topics identified later in the initial sweep to be coded throughout the all institution topic fields on the second iteration. This process will undergo several further iterations in order to refine the key topics; until the data is saturated and no further key topics can be identified. A memo will be compiled for each key topic identified, recording observations and collating resources relating to the key topic, such as URLs linking to modules in which each key topic is taught. Some of the key topics identified are interrelated, and can ultimately be sorted and grouped together. A series of refined memos compiled will ultimately form the basis of the proposed taxonomy of Web Science key subjects; with each memo developing into an associated wiki page for each key topic.

5.1 Nvivo Keyword Analysis

The manual identification of themes was supplemented by a process of keyword analysis, otherwise known as bibliometric mapping. Hooper et al [9] utilize Bibliometric Mapping in their study investigating the coverage of subjects published during the Web Science conference series. The theory behind bibliometric mapping is that any subject can be defined by a set of keywords [10]. While this method alone is not exhaustive, Strauss and Corbin [6] suggest that a mixed method approach incorporating some quantitative methods can be used in combination with the process of manual, coding in order to augment and compare manual results with additional findings. Therefore one of the methods of analysis utilized during this study, is Nvivo's automated keyword analysis feature. This facilitated the automated collation of a list of keywords for the modules identified. The results of this analysis are presented in **Table 3**. The drawback to this method, is the fact that efforts to date suggest that Nvivo is limited to the detection of single keywords, whereas many of the subjects within Web Science consists of key phrases, for example 'social networking' and 'semantic web'. While only able to search for keywords and not key phrases, the Nvivo method of automated keyword analysis will still provide useful data for comparison with the results gained during the manual analysis.

5.2 Current Findings

The manual coding process has currently identified a total of over 70 'Key Topics'. This gives an indication of the subjects being taught as part of Web Science programmes. A simplified list of the top 30 key topics is presented in **Table 3.** In addition to a list of the key topics identified, **Table 3** also shows the frequency at which each of the key topics were coded, across all 15 of the Web Science teaching institutions included in the modules desk survey. Perhaps unsurprisingly, the top three key topics most frequently coded included: 'networks', which was identified on total of 24 occasions, 'web society' 23 and 'semantic web' 21. The resulting key topics identified, would seem indicate that the Socio-technical nature of Web Science [5] [3] is reflected in Web Science taught programmes. Most of the key topics coded are self-explanatory, with the exception of 'General Web Science'. This key topic was used to code modules branded as 'Introduction to Web Science' type modules. Such modules typically aim to provide students with an overview of Web Science, tying together course content and providing context to other subject specific modules.

5.3 Keyword Analysis Results

Table 3 also shows the top 30 results of an automated Nvivo keyword analysis of the 'Topics Taught' field for all 142 modules identified. Although the data analyzed is the same 'topics taught' module data that was used during the manual analysis, the results differ. Aside from the fact that the automated analysis has detected different keywords to those identified during the manual coding process, there is another notable difference which should be considered. As explained previously, Nvivo detects only keywords not key phrases, therefore it is unknown in what context some words appear. For example, the word 'Web' may occur in combination with the word 'science', 'semantic 'or 'society'. If the search were able to detect commonly occurring key phrases, the results might be considerably different. To some extent, there are still similarities between the manually identified key topics and automatically detected keywords. The top 5 keywords are reflected in the top 3 key topics. With the exception of the word 'data', the keywords: 'Web', 'social', 'networks' and 'semantic' reflect the manually identified key topics: 'Networks', 'Web Society' and 'Semantic Web'. Further analysis will be conducted to measure how many of the terms are common to both sets of data, taking into account the fact that key phrases are not represented in the automated keyword search. While it has not been possible to search for key phrases in general within NVivo, it should be possible to conduct a query search for one specific key phrase. Therefore it may be possible to test how many times a specific key phrase occurs; in order to determine for example, how many instances of the word 'social' occur in combination with the word 'networking'. The Nvivo detected keywords will also need to be filtered further, for example, the word 'new' currently has little meaning or context.

Table 3. Frequency of top 30 Manual Key Topics and Automatically Detected Keywords

Manually Identified Key Topics		Automatically Detected Keywords	
Key Topic	Freq.	Keyword	Freq.
Networks	24	web	2257
Web Society	23	social	783
Semantic Web	21	networks	654
Sociology	17	data	524
Network Theory	16	semantic	382
Research Methodology	16	science	359
Web Languages	15	information	348
Social Networking	14	network	333
Web Architecture	12	internet	320
Business	11	design	291
Economics	11	systems	277
Law	10	technologies	276
Big Data	9	research	271
Information and Communications Technology	9	models	252
Privacy and Trust	9	analysis	250
Security	9	computing	232
Statistical Analysis	9	applications	223
Data Mining	8	digital	205
Software Engineering	8	development	197
Web Modelling	8	understandin g	186
Web Technologies	8	technology	184
General Web Science	7	management	181
Linked Data	7	issues	179
Media	7	methods	178
Web Analytics	7	new	172
Web Graph	7	media	171
Web Search	7	society	170
Cloud Computing	6	knowledge	163
Digital Sociology	6	languages	159
Management	6	services	159

6. DISSCUSION AND FUTURE WORK

The data shown within the scope of this paper consists of the available Web Science curriculum data collected from University Websites. However, this will ultimately be combined with coding of more detailed curriculum information where it can be obtained, as well as with publications from Web Science conference series. The conference papers will be coded in order to identify key topics published in the Web Science conferences series. The key topics identified in the conferences series will then be compared with the curriculum key topics, and ultimately a combination of the two groups of key topics will form the basis for the structured taxonomy of Web Science key topics. However, further analysis and sorting of key topics is required, as well as further comparison between the manually identified key topics and the Nvivo keyword analysis. The Nvivo keyword analysis results confirm the prevalence of top few manual results, e.g. 'social networking' and 'semantic web'. However, the Nvivo keywords exhibit less diversity in terms of subjects and less of a socio-technical balance than the manually identified key topics. As explained, this is partly due to the fact that Nvivo software used detects keywords and not key phrases.

6.1 A Taxonomy of Web Science Key Topics

Once the data has been exhaustively coded, it will be necessary to sort and group the key topics according to subject, in order to simplify the list and create the proposed structured taxonomy of key topics for Web Science. This may require further subject related research, in order to determine which of the key topics should be grouped together according to related subjects. The process of sorting the key topics will involve the identification of tiers or levels of key topics. For example, 'Web Society' would most likely class as a higher-level topic, under which other lower level topics such as, for example, 'Privacy and Trust' could be grouped. While the topics which occur most frequently, such as for example, 'Networks', may indicate that it should be a higher level node within the taxonomy, frequency should not be the only criteria by which topics are assigned a node level within the taxonomy. Context will be required in order to assign levels of nodes. For example, 'Economics' occurs less frequently, however it is still a vast subject; therefore, should it have its own root node within the taxonomy and not be grouped under another higher-level node? Questions such as this will need to be considered further, and the final structure will be subject to expert feedback. The sorted and structured key topics should also provide a means of visualizing the data more concisely and in a way in which it can be presented. It should also prove more feasible to produce a visualization for the higher level topics in comparison to the current unsorted list, which includes too much information to visualize concisely in an easily readable printed format. Further work will involve the investigation of ways in which the structured and sorted data can be visualized for effective communication in printed format.

As discussed, the prosed final outcome of this work involves the creation of a taxonomy of Web Science key topics, which would be structured by identifying the higher level key topics, which would form the root nodes of the taxonomy, under which the lower level topics would be grouped. Before it is utilized as a basis for forming the taxonomy for key topics, it is proposed that the list of key topics identified from the modules be refined through expert feedback. This will be achieved by presenting the proposed taxonomy to a group of Web Science PhD students and academics from the University of Southampton Web and Internet Science Research Group, encouraging discussion and feedback in order to refine the structure of the taxonomy and the key topics included. It would also be beneficial to gain feedback from the wider Web Science community beyond Southampton, however, this will be the subject of future work. The proposed taxonomy would incorporate refined memos for each key topic identified, each of which would be hosted online on a wiki type page. Each wiki page would include a brief description of the key topic, as well as a link to related resources, such as related Web Science conference publications and links to taught modules covering the key topic.

The process of qualitative Grounded theory based research defined and used in this work, is by nature a manual process. It may be possible to create an automated process for detecting the subject keywords in Web Science programmes; an initial attempt at this was outlined in one of Coskun and White's previous works. [11] This involved the creation of a simple web crawler to detect a combination of the keywords 'Web' and 'Science' within the .ac.uk domain. While this exercise was useful in detecting and identifying additional Web Science taught programmes, automation on a larger scale would not produce the same level of detail seen in this current manual, and largely qualitative work. Automated keyword detection lacks perspective, and while it is useful in conjunction with the manual method, alone it provides little context to findings. It would therefore be beneficial to foster greater participation and engagement from the wider Web Science community, in order to encourage joint efforts to maintain a collective curriculum taxonomy comprising of continued manual cross-institutional input. The proposed wiki based Web Science curriculum taxonomy is an effort to motivate this collaboration, producing a set of resources accessible for contributions by anyone, subsequent to the lifespan of this study.

7 CONCLUSIONS

This paper has detailed the bottom up, Grounded Theory, mixed method research approach used during this study, explaining why this method is suited to the research of Web Science, due to the subject's rapid evolution. Data sources and analysis methods have been outlined. A series of Web Science teaching institutions and modules have been identified; these were then analyzed and coded, utilizing the qualitative data analysis package Nvivo in order to identify key topics. The key topics were identified from manual coding of the topics taught within Web Science taught modules. The top 30 most common examples of these key topics were presented, and compared with the top 30 keywords identified by employing Nvivo keyword detection tool on the same module topics. In future key topics will also be compared and combined with the results of a second analysis of key topics, charting the most commonly published topics within the Web Science conference series. The final intended outcome of this work is to create a taxonomy of key topics for Web Science, evolved from Web Science as it is taught, and published. This will be presented in a wiki format so that it may be accessed and contributions may be made beyond the initial lifespan of the project. It is hoped that this will encourage further interest and debate within the wider Web Science community, in an attempt to encourage further work towards the development of a formal curriculum for Web Science.

REFERENCES

[1] T. Berners-Lee, D. J. Weitzner, W. Hall, K. O'Hara, N. Shadbolt, and J. a. Hendler, "A Framework for Web Science," Found. Trends® Web Sci., vol. 1, no. 1, pp. 1–130, 2006.

[2] T. Berners-Lee, W. Hall, J. Hendler, N. Shadbolt, and D. J. Weitzner, "Creating a Science of the Web," Science (80-.)., vol. 313, no. 5788, pp. 769–771, 2006.

[3] S. White and M. N. Vafopoulos, "Web Science: expanding the notion of Computer Science," in 43rd ACM Technical Symposium on Computer Science Education, 28th February-3rd March 2012, 2012.

[4] S. White, M. Croitoru, S. S. Bazan, S. Cerri, H. C. Davis, C. Jonquet, G. Prini, F. F. Scharffe, S. S. Staab, T. Tiropanis, M. Vafopoulos, M. Croitoru, S. S. Bazan, R. Folgieri, F. F. Scharffe, S. S. Staab, T. Tiropanis, M. Vafopoulos, S. Cerri, H. C. Davis, C. Jonquet, G. Prini, F. F. Scharffe, S. S. Staab, T. Tiropanis, and M. Vafopoulos, Negotiating the Web Science Curriculum Development through Shared Educational Artefacts. Koblenz, Germany, NY, USA: ACM, 2011, pp. 11:1–11:8.

[5] J. Hendler, N. Shadbolt, W. Hall, T. Berners-Lee, and D. Weitzner, "Web science: An Interdisciplinary Approach to Understanding the Web," Commun. ACM, vol. 51, no. 7, p. 60, 2008.

[6] A. Strauss and J. Corbin, Basics of Qualitative Research: Techniques and Procedures for Developing Grounded Theory, vol. 3. 1998.

[7] K. Bryant, A, & Charmaz, The Sage handbook of grounded theory. Sage Publications, 2007.

[8] L. Bloomberg and M. Volpe, Completing Your Qualitative Dissertation: A Road Map From Beginning to End. Sage Publications, 2012.

[9] C. J. Hooper, G. Bordea, and P. Buitelaar, "Web Science and the two (hundred) cultures: representation of disciplines publishing in Web Science," May 2013.

[10] K. Börner, C. Chen, and K. W. Boyack, "Visualizing knowledge domains," Annu. Rev. Inf. Sci. Technol., vol. 37, no. 1, pp. 179–255, 2003.

[11] E. Coskun, A. Smith, and S. White, "Mapping the Web Science Curriculum(s)," in ACM Web Science 2015, United Kingdom, 2015.

[12] C. J. Hooper, N. Marie, and E. Kalampokis, "Dissecting the butterfly: representation of disciplines publishing at the web science conference series.," WebSci, pp. 137–140, 2012.

Young People's Policy Recommendations on Algorithm Fairness

Elvira Perez Vallejos
Horizon Digital Economy Research Institute, University of Nottingham
Triumph Road Nottingham, UK
NG7 2TU
Elvira.perez@nottingham.ac.uk

Ansgar Koene
Horizon Digital Economy Research Institute, University of Nottingham
Triumph Road Nottingham, UK
NG7 2TU
Ansgar.Koene@nottingham.ac.uk

Virginia Portillo
Horizon Digital Economy Research Institute, University of Nottingham
Triumph Road Nottingham, UK
NG7 2TU
Virginia.Portillo@nottingham.ac.uk

Liz Dowthwaite
Horizon Digital Economy Research Institute, University of Nottingham
Triumph Road Nottingham, UK
NG7 2TU
Liz.Dowthwaite@nottingham.ac.uk

Monica Cano
Horizon Digital Economy Research Institute, University of Nottingham
Triumph Road Nottingham, UK
NG7 2TU
Monica.Cano@nottingham.ac.uk

ABSTRACT

This paper explores the policy recommendations made by young people regarding algorithm fairness. It describes a piece of ongoing research developed to bring children and young people to the front line of the debate regarding children's digital rights. We employed the Youth Juries methodology which was designed to facilitate learning through discussions. The juries capture the deliberation process on a specific digital right, the right to know how algorithms govern and influence the Web and its users. Preliminary results show that young people demand to know more about algorithms, they want more transparency, more options, and more control about the way algorithms use their personal data.

CCS CONCEPTS

• **Social and Behavioral Sciences** → **Psychology** • **Computers and Education** → Computer and Information Science Education; *Literacy* • **Computers and Society** → Public Policy Issues.

KEYWORDS

Youth jury; algorithm fairness; youth opinion; deliberation; digital literacy; digital citizenship, privacy; policy.

WebSci'17, June 25-28, 2017, Troy, NY, USA.

ACM 978-1-4503-4896-6/17/06...$15.00.
DOI: http://dx.doi.org/10.1145/3091478.3091512

1 INTRODUCTION

The UnBias Youth Juries are similar to focus groups designed around the principles of deliberation [1-3]. In this paper we define the deliberation process as a series of steps that allow young people to receive and exchange information, to critically examine an issue, and to come to an agreement which will inform decision making. While there is a considerable amount of literature that documents the efficacy of deliberation within educational settings [4], hardly any systematic research has been conducted on the ways in which children and young people deliberate about their digital rights. Even more scarce are engaging educational interventions which aim to promote digital literacy, aside from the current e-safety programs that have broadly been introduced at primary and secondary schools.

To work in equal partnership with children and young people has been crucial in developing the youth juries. Co-production ensures that the scenarios (i.e., stimuli or prompts) represent real issues and experiences that young people can relate to. As a consequence, scenarios are idiosyncratic and sensitive to cultural differences as they should represent a specific and distinct point in time, avoiding universalistic terms. As smart phone applications, computer games and the lexicon around technologies rapidly evolve with time, the scenarios developed for this first wave of UnBias Youth Juries will differ from those that will be developed in the near future. Working with young people as equal partners is also important to guarantee that the language used to facilitate the juries resonates with their vocabulary and expressions.

The structure and content of these juries is dynamic and changes from jury to jury to accommodate the uniqueness of each group but, as constant variables, the juries usually include an ice-breaking exercise and a group exploration around the definition of algorithms; what are they? (e.g., a series of steps and rules, a predictive mathematical formula), why are they useful? (e.g., to rank or filter large amounts of data), any benefits? (e.g., objectivity) any risks? (e.g., biased inferences). Once the context of the jury has been set up, the facilitator introduces some balanced facts about the way algorithms can affect Web users, for example, by making decisions on the user's behalf (e.g., ranking of newsfeed content) and how personalisation algorithms may influence outcomes from specific search engines (e.g., DuckDuckGo vs. Google). These prompts generate discussions among the jurors, providing opportunities for sharing of personal experiences and learning through conversation [5]. A series of different scenarios are then presented to the jurors as evidence of how algorithms can affect Web users. For example, one of the scenarios illustrates how algorithms are being used in the criminal justice system to predict patterns such as the likelihood of reoffending after release (e.g., Northpointe [6]). The data that feeds this algorithm can include personal data such as postcode, ethnicity, income, and so on. A second scenario describes the role of algorithms linked to Facebook's News Feed and how they track each user's online actions to serve them the posts they are most likely to engage with. These scenarios are packed with dilemmas that trigger discussions and reflections. We are interested in understanding the process of deliberation and opinion formation (e.g., argument and counterargument) and how the jurors may arrive at a consensus.

2 UNBIAS YOUTH JURIES

2.2 Methods

All participants (12 females and 14 males; average age: 16) were self-selected and were recruited via the website of the National Video Game Arcade (i.e., GameCity) in Nottingham, UK, where the juries took place. A large community room in GameCity was hired. The room layout included cabaret style for the first half of the session and circle or round style for the second half with the view to promote participation. In total, two jury sessions were organized, one in the morning and one in the afternoon. Each session had a duration of 2 hours including a break for refreshments. These sessions were part of a feasibility study designed to capture preliminary data to inform a posterior pilot study. Juries were audio recorded and data transcribed for subsequent qualitative analysis. Thematic analysis [7] was carried out by the author VP and transcripts reviewed alongside the analytical frame by all team members to ensure consistency of analysis. Ethical approval was granted by the Ethics Committee at the School of Computer Science at the University of Nottingham, UK. The youth jury methodology is described in detail elsewhere [8, 9].

3 RESULTS AND DISCUSSION

After the ice-breaking exercises, open-ended questions about algorithms were presented to the group to collectively arrive at a consensus about the meaning given to the label 'algorithm'. The qualitative analysis showed that, even though young people had a basic understanding about the conceptual meaning of algorithms:

"[...] a series of steps you take to derive an output from an input"

"a mathematical formula"

"a piece of code"

Jurors were less aware about the constant presence of algorithms controlling the Web and their influence on how search results were displayed. It is also important to highlight that the distinction between 'search engines' and 'browsers' was not clear, often referring to both as 'Google'.

The qualitative analysis generated five themes; online identity, security, privacy, concerns due to lack of transparency and control. In order to protect their online identity many jurors declared the use of pseudonyms, browse in private with incognito mode or carefully design the privacy settings of certain online services to make a distinction between their public vs. private profile.

In general, jurors were aware that likes, clicks and text entered in search engines and social media platforms could influence personalisation algorithms (i.e., recommender systems), however, most of them were unaware of the scale of personal data sharing (e.g., third parties) or the type of other information that could influence recommendation systems (e.g., likes from friends).

"Well, I've noticed with Twitter, like my friends are politically opinionated, and I get recommendations from politicians and stuff they like [...] so probably they [Twitter] see what I follow and [...] I get recommendations based on that"

In general, jurors were aware of their privacy and anonymity options when accessing Web services and, as boyd and Marwick have already pointed out [10], young people care about their online privacy and develop strategies for managing privacy in public spaces in an attempt to assert control over their personal data. Some participants expressed location as being a more sensitive form of personal data that often was not disclosed. In general, jurors were less aware of the extent in which companies owned and traded with their personal data. While some jurors would prefer that there were no tracking systems at all, others felt that exceptions for surveillance would be justified to minimise crime when there are risk indicators:
"I generally don't use my actual name if I do so it would be pretty hard to find me [...] It was kind of a way to stop my friends bugging me."

"I don't really post anything publicly. I would privately do stuff so that not just anybody can see what I've been doing."

"I never really post 'right now I am here'... I wouldn't post where I am all the time"

".... as long as you don't say certain things like: I live in Nottingham...., I am actually at..., you can say things to people and you don't generally need to worry about it being tied up to your name, ...you don't know who each other is"

"[...] I don't want people exploiting my personal enjoyment for the sake of making money."

In general, jurors appreciated the usefulness and need for algorithms:

"I do understand why people do it [use algorithms], because otherwise you have to see thorough lots of information".

"I think they [personalisation algorithms] are useful because it can keep you updated on things you like".

"[...] within the entertainment sector and stuff they [algorithms] are not that bad [...]".

However, sometimes jurors found personalisation "annoying" and tended to ignore outcomes from recommender systems if they were inaccurate or far from their own preferences:

"[...] when I am searching for my music I can't ever find anything I want to find because they [service providers] are trying to tailor it to me but they are getting it wrong, totally wrong, so it's a bit annoying".

"[...] if you watch Netflix a lot for example, and you like certain shows it will give you recommendations of things you should like, but my brother went into my Netflix profile and added a bunch of Anime on to it I didn't watch and ruined my profile... I don't know now I only get Anime recommendations and it would take me ages to undo it so my recommendations don't mean anything anymore."

Most jurors acknowledged not knowing how recommender systems or search engines ranked their results and expressed concerns about the potential for censorship and bias. In general, algorithms were seen as neutral tools but there were concerns about the hidden purpose or intention (i.e., outcome value) and the consequences of 'echo chamber' or 'filter bubble' effects:

"I think that using an algorithm to sort things isn't necessarily a problem. What would be a problem is well, it's what it's actually being selected for."

"It's not just a matter of... what do you think they [industry] are going to do with it [personal info], it's also the information they give back to you. It's probably tailored to your interest. So, you might not see certain things and that could be pretty damaging too."

Jurors demanded plausible solutions to provide users with more options and control over their personal data. In general, jurors expressed a preference for data security over privacy and preferred signing up to Web services that were perceived as more secure and less likely to be hacked (e.g., Google vs. Yahoo) at the cost of their personal data (aware or inadvertently) being shared with third parties. Participants also deliberated on the effects that data protection breaches, from established companies, could have on their corporate reputation and anticipated that large businesses would continue trading with users' personal data without worrying about it or upsetting users.

"Google and Facebook have better infrastructure to handle security than smaller companies"

"Established companies CAN afford to upset users"

When asked about who should regulate fairness policy and ethics guidelines, jurors were unsure of who should take on this important governance work. They argued that a global approach would be ideal, but they were not confident about an international framework due to the need to accommodate so many cultural differences and attitudes to data privacy across countries. They also reasoned that NGOs or independent bodies could lack the resources needed to cope with fast changes, while expressing frustration and lack of trust towards large corporations, which were perceived as powerful entities that could influence countries' economy.
A limitation of the youth jury's methodology is the potential bias that the facilitator inadvertently could introduce either within the examples or facts introduced during the sessions. There are other, more subtle, biases that could also affect the outcome or direction of the discussion including body language and facial expressions that could favor one position or argument more than another. The research team was aware of this limitation and special attention was given to highlighting the neutral nature of algorithms and minimising undesirable effects that could contaminate the juror's arguments and counterarguments illustrating the risks and opportunities embedded in algorithms. How the jury was delivered and implemented was also important to the research team, not only because the juries should be replicable and participants' outputs should not depend on the personal attributes of the facilitator, but because explicit training, guidelines, and processes were in place, and a sense of ownership, responsibility, and care were also part of the training. For example, understanding the current evidence on algorithm fairness and potential sources of biases was important to ensuring that accurate and factual information was discussed during the deliberation process with the view to minimise any potential biases. The same person (lead author EPV) facilitated both juries which resulted in similar outcomes.

4 CONCLUSIONS

Jurors put forward several solutions and recommendations such as plug-ins to add user-friendly interfaces in which users could decide levels of tracking, more control over personal data and ways to influence their outcome (e.g., what exactly is being stored, who is storing it and for how long), or how to combine results from different search engines and compare results depending on users' priorities. There was a consensus that decision-making should not be left entirely to an automated system, especially when the decision had important consequences for the users (e.g., job recruitment). Unanimously, jurors asked for more accessible Terms & Conditions and accessible information about the way algorithms rule the Web. It was agreed that more engaging educational programs and increased knowledge would be beneficial not only for young people but for parents and IT teachers.
The results from this feasibility study have informed a posterior pilot study that, to date, has recruited more than 100 young people. The concerns and recommendations that the jurors of these two preliminary juries have put forward have been very valuable to (1) improve the co-design of scenarios making them more relevant and engaging and (2) identify topics for discussion and reflection (i.e., personalisation through algorithms, autocomplete, search results, fake news and algorithm transparency).

ACKNOWLEDGMENTS

This work was supported by EPSRC Trust, Identity, Privacy and Security grant "UnBias: Emancipating users against algorithmic biases for a trusted digital economy" (EP/N02785X/1)

REFERENCES

[1] Chris Degeling, Lucie Rychetnik, Jackie Street, Rae Thomas, Stacy M Carter 2017. Influencing health policy through public deliberation: Lessons learned from two decades of Citizens'/community juries. *Social Science and Medicine*, 179, 166-171. DOI: http://dx.doi.org/10.1016/j.socscimed.2017.03.003

[2] Stephanie Solomon, Julia Abelson. 2013. Why and when should we use public deliberation? Hastings Cent Rep, 42, 2, 17-20. DOI: 10.1002/hast.27

[3] Julia Abelson, Pierre G. Forest, John Eyles, Patricia Smith, Elisabeth Martin, Francois P. Gauvin. 2003. Deliberations about deliberative methods: issues in the design and evaluation of public participation processes. *Soc. Sci. Med.*, 57, 2, 239–251. DOI http://dx.doi.org/10.1016/S0277-9536(02)00343-X

[4] Timothy J. Shaffer. 2014. Deliberation In and Through Higher Education. *Journal of Public Deliberation*, 10, 1, 10. http://www.publicdeliberation.net/jpd/vol10/iss1/art10

[5] Elvira Perez Vallejos, Deborah Hencker, Dick Churchill. 2016. Video Interactive Guidance (VIG): a reflective pedagogical tool for enhancing learning goals and compassion in the context of Clinical Communication Skills education, 360-362. In Peterkin, A. & Brett-MacLean, P. (Eds.) *Keeping Reflection Fresh*. Kent State Press

[6] Julia Angwin, Jeff Larson, Surya Mattu, Lauren Kirchner, L. 2016. Machine Bias. There's software used across the country to predict

future criminals. And it's biased against balcks. Online article published at Pro Publica. Available https://www.propublica.org/article/machine-bias-risk-assessments-in-criminal-sentencing

[7] Virginia Braun, Victoria Clarke. 2006. Using thematic analysis in psychology. *Qualitative Research in Psychology* 3 (2): 77-101.

[8] Stephen Coleman, Kruake Pothong, Elvira Perez Vallejos, Ansgar Koene. 2017. The Internet on Trial: How children and young people deliberated about their digital rights. Report available at http://casma.wp.horizon.ac.uk/wp-content/uploads/2016/08/Internet-On-Our-Own-Terms.pdf

[9] Elvira Perez Vallejos, Ansgar Koene, Chris J. Carter, Ramona Statache, et al. 2016. Juries: Acting Out Digital Dilemmas to Promote Digital Reflections. *ACM SIGCAS Computers and Society* 45, 3, 84-90. DOI 10.1145/2874239.2874252

[10] boyd, danah and Marwick, Alice E., Social Privacy in Networked Publics: Teens' Attitudes, Practices, and Strategies (September 22, 2011). A Decade in Internet Time: Symposium on the Dynamics of the Internet and Society, September 2011. Available at SSRN: https://ssrn.com/abstract=1925128

Using Facebook Ads Audiences for Global Lifestyle Disease Surveillance: Promises and Limitations

Matheus Araújo♦, Yelena Mejova, Ingmar Weber
Qatar Computing Research Institute
HBKU, Doha, Qatar
maraujo,ymejova,iweber@hbku.edu.qa

Fabrício Benevenuto
Federal University of Minas Gerais ♦
UFMG, Belo Horizonte, Brazil
fabricio@dcc.ufmg.br

ABSTRACT

Every day, millions of users reveal their interests on Facebook, which are then monetized via targeted advertisement marketing campaigns. In this paper, we explore the use of demographically rich Facebook Ads audience estimates for tracking non-communicable diseases around the world. Across 47 countries, we compute the audiences of *marker interests*, and evaluate their potential in tracking health conditions associated with tobacco use, obesity, and diabetes, compared to the performance of *placebo interests*. Despite its huge potential, we find that, for modeling prevalence of health conditions *across* countries, differences in these interest audiences are only weakly indicative of the corresponding prevalence rates. *Within* the countries, however, our approach provides interesting insights on trends of health awareness across demographic groups. Finally, we provide a temporal error analysis to expose the potential pitfalls of using Facebook's Marketing API as a black box.

KEYWORDS

Facebook, Advertising, Epidemiology, Social Media, Health

1 INTRODUCTION

Despite recent media attention on epidemics such as Ebola and Zika, globally, the two most common "killers" are ischemic heart disease and stroke[1] followed by a set of lung health conditions. Though not as photogenic as Ebola or Zika, lifestyle diseases are in fact far bigger burdens on the global health system than AIDS, influenza and malaria combined. Addressing the challenges imposed by *lifestyle diseases* first requires an adequate surveillance system, which not only tracks prevalence rates but also people's awareness of them. Especially for preventable lifestyle diseases, such awareness is required to induce behavior change.

Recently, encouraging studies linked what people like on Facebook to behavioral aspects and interests in various health conditions [2, 4, 5, 7, 9, 18]. These efforts suggest that Facebook data and, particularly, the Facebook advertising system could be a valuable source of behavioral and demographic information, which is key for lifestyle disease surveillance.

[1]http://www.who.int/mediacentre/factsheets/fs310/en/

WebSci'17, June 25-28, 2017, Troy, NY, USA.
 978-1-4503-4896-6/17/06...$15.00
DOI: http://dx.doi.org/10.1145/3091478.3091513

Concretely, Facebook provides its advertisers with access to its users through its targeted advertising platform. Before an ad is launched, and before any cost is incurred, advertisers are provided with an estimate of how many users match the specified criteria, which can include age, gender, sets of interests, specific locations, and much more.

This type of "digital census" opens new avenues for research in public health for several reasons. First, the popularity of Facebook "Likes" makes them a promising data source for tracking awareness. Second, the cost of compiling global health statistics such as the Global Burden of Disease database [14] could be drastically reduced. Third, the latency of compiling statistics would be reduced, which could make it feasible to measure the impact of policy changes, health campaigns or major global events. Lastly, this approach would allow for an international and cross-lingual analysis by piggybacking on Facebook's NLP pipeline. Thus, although Facebook Ads is a proprietary system, it is worth investigating its value as a data source for lifestyle disease surveillance.

In this paper we investigate the feasibility of using Facebook advertising audience estimates for global lifestyle disease surveillance aiming at identifying advantages, disadvantages and limitations of this approach. In particular, we compare these to global disease prevalence across 47 countries, as well as across demographics within the countries. Unlike previous works, we perform quality checks in the form of estimates of "placebo" interests, as well as temporal stability of the results. To the best of our knowledge, Facebook ads audience estimates have not been rigorously tested for data quality and stability across countries. Thus, we illustrate the benefits and dangers of using social media as a "black box", and provide methodological tools for future research of such social media data aggregators.

2 RELATED WORK

In "Social media in public health" Kass-Hout & Alhinnawi assert, "Social media can provide timely, relevant, and transparent information of public health importance" [10], formulating an exciting ongoing research to study health trends via online data. Following this call for action, some researchers focus on information seeking on topics such as abortion [16] and vaccines [19], others use the data to now-cast diseases [8], while others use search logs, most notably using Google Trends, to predict seasonal flu [6].

The large errors in flu prediction from Google Flu Trends offered interesting lessons for the use of this kind of data [12]. While some efforts attempt to fix Google Flu models [15], others have been dedicated to assessing and evaluating the data quality extracted from social media [11]. In this line, we aim at investigating if a new data source can be valuable for health research.

The Facebook advertising API has been studied in terms of determining a relative value of different user demographics and assessing the overall stability of the advertising market [13, 17]. A few studies have attempted to link Facebook audience data to behavioral aspects and interests related to health conditions. Gittelman *et al.* convert 37 Facebook interest categories to nine factors to use in the modeling of life expectancy [7]. Although they show an improvement in the statistical models, their approach avoided determining relationships between each individual category with the real-world data. On the other hand, Chunara *et al.* explore the relationship of two factors – interest in television and outdoor activities – to the obesity rates in metros across the USA and neighborhoods within New York City [4]. Both of these studies are confined to the United States, and are limited to one health topic. In contrast, our study expands the set of real-world health indicators we track, as well as the geographic coverage to global proportions. Crucially, we assess the quality of Facebook data by introducing placebo baselines, normalization alternatives, and performing temporal analysis.

3 FACEBOOK MARKETING API

Facebook, as all large online social networks, relies on advertisement for its revenue. To maximize this revenue it provides advertisers with tools for highly targeted advertising. Before launching the ad, and before any cost is incurred, the advertiser is provided with an audience estimate of the number of monthly active users likely to match the criteria.[2] Facebook provides these so-called "reach estimates" via its marketing API.[3] The available targeting options are truly impressive and, except certain US-specific information related to political leaning or ethnic affinity, are all available in 197 countries worldwide. It is important to highlight that Facebook gathers these estimations based on information from sites other than just facebook.com, as long as those sites have a Facebook Like or share functionality[4].

For our analysis, we make use of basic user-provided demographics such as age and gender, and also a set of inferred *interests*. According to Facebook, "Interest may include things people share on their Timelines, apps they use, ads they click, Pages they like and other activities on and off of Facebook and Instagram [5]. Interests may also factor in demographics such as age, gender and location."[6]. Finally, to automated the data collection, we build a generic python package able to collect data from Facebook Ads [7].

4 EXPERIMENTAL SETUP

Below we describe how we obtain (i) "ground truth" health data, as well as (ii) a set of Facebook-derived features used in our model.

Selection of Health Concerns. To have a well-defined scope, we limit our analysis to three common health concerns: (i) diabetes, (ii) smoking, and (iii) obesity. For all of these, one would expect to find some signal on social media. Furthermore, they cover a mix of one disease (diabetes), one health condition (obesity), and one health-risk behavior (smoking). For each, we obtain the prevalence data from the World Health Organization. For diabetes, we use the *raised fasting blood glucose* statistic for adults (18+)[8]; for smoking, the *adult age-standardized prevalence of smoking of any tobacco product*[9]; and for obesity, the *age-standardized obesity estimates* statistic, where obese is defined as having a body mass index ≥ 30[10].

Selection of Countries. In order to avoid sparsity issues, we perform our analysis for all countries with more than 5 million active Facebook users, as reported by the API. After removing Taiwan due absence of information in the WHO reports, this resulted in 47 countries, including 12 from Europe, 17 from Asia, 7 from South America, 7 from Africa, 3 from North America, and one in Oceania.

Facebook Marker Interests. We define a set of **marker interests** via a bootstrapping approach. We begin with the most obvious interests such as "Obesity awareness" for modeling obesity prevalence, and consider other related interests suggested by Facebook Ads explorer[11]. We then add to the list those interests which have at least hundreds of thousands in potential audience worldwide. Note that it is not our intention in this paper to define an exhaustive list of Facebook interests related to each health concern, but to start with those with the most plausible direct link to the health concern for this study. The final list of interests can be found in Table 1. These interests include both those denoting awareness of an illness (such as *lung cancer awareness*), as well as associated behaviors (*Hookah*), and intervention efforts (*smoking cessation*).

Placebo Interests. As latent factors such as socioeconomic status or demographic variables could affect both national health statistics and Facebook interests, correlations themselves might be spurious and not necessarily indicative of any meaningful relationship. To better weed out spurious correlations, we select a set of **placebo interests**, which are interests on Facebook that should not have an obvious causal link with a given condition, but that might still turn out to be correlated due to latent factors. For this, we use generic interests, including *Facebook*, as well as an OR query of *Reading* OR *Entertainment* OR *Technology*. We also add two health-oriented interests, *Health Care* and *Fitness & Wellness*, to serve as indicators for whether we are picking up (i) interest specific to a health concern, or (ii) generic interest in health topics. Note that providing a "placebo" in such analyses is new, with previous works using Facebook Ads data more as a black box, without determining the merit of using particular marker interests over a baseline [4, 7].

Demographic Variables. Prior work [1] found that the performance for social media based now-casting depends on the subset of users that are being considered. To explore if more fine-grained data could give better models, we also obtained Facebook ad audience estimates for demographic subgroups, in particular for males and females separately, as well as for the age groups 18-24, 25-29, 30-34, 35-39, 40-44, 45-49, 50-54, and 55-59. [12]

User Base Normalization. At a high level, we are interested in finding whether the fraction of Facebook users in a given country with a particular interest is indicative of a health concern's prevalence in that country. Whether or not a given user has a particular

[2]The reader can try out an interactive version of the ads tool at https://goo.gl/GNqgUD.
[3]https://developers.facebook.com/docs/marketing-api/reachestimate/v2.8
[4]http://bit.ly/2dKTJGH
[5]The combined Facebook and Instagram audience were considered for our experiments
[6]https://www.facebook.com/business/help/188888021162119
[7]https://github.com/maraujo/pySocialWatcher

[8]http://apps.who.int/gho/data/node.main.A869
[9]http://apps.who.int/gho/data/node.main.1250
[10]http://apps.who.int/gho/data/node.main.A900A
[11]https://www.facebook.com/ads/manager/creation/creation/
[12]We decided not to include data on minors in our analysis.

Table 1: Facebook marker interests for tracking tobacco use, obesity, and diabetes, along with placebo interests. Also shown is the estimated worldwide Facebook ad audience.

Tobacco Use	
Smoking	30,000,000
Tobacco	20,000,000
Tobacco smoking	11,000,000
Lung cancer awareness	6,200,000
Cigarette	29,000,000
Hookah	10,000,000
Smoking cessation	7,500,000
union of all	77,000,000
Obesity	
Bariatrics	2,400,000
Obesity awareness	58,000,000
Plus-size clothing	29,000,000
Weight loss (Fitness And wellness)	81,000,000
Dieting	218,000,000
union of all	286,000,000
Diabetes	
Gestational diabetes	1,400,000
Insulin index	250,000
Insulin resistance awareness	1,700,000
Diabetes mellitus awareness	55,000,000
Diabetes mellitus type 1 awareness	3,200,000
Diabetes mellitus type 2 awareness	5,300,000
Diabetic diet	4,200,000
Diabetic hypoglycemia	280,000
Managing diabetes	960,000
union of all	60,000,000
Placebos/normalizers	
Facebook	863,000,000
Reading or Entertainment or Technology	1,278,000,000
Health Care	145,000,000
Fitness & Wellness	714,000,000

interest is strongly confounded by the time they spent online in general and on Facebook in particular. A random surfer, randomly clicking and liking pages for hours on end, would end up with more inferred health related interests than a user logging in once a month to receive updates from a diabetes forum. In an effort to correct for this, without being able to access the user-level data, we experimented with different normalizers, including *Health Care* and generic topics of *Reading* OR *Entertainment* OR *Technology*. Subsetting to a more specific user set should, in theory, partially remove the confounding effect of different activity levels. Although we found the results to be somewhat different, there was little cohesive trend between data normalized using these specialized populations and one using the Facebook population. Thus, we leave a more detailed study of this issue for future work.

5 MODELING PREVALENCE

Using the above design, we collected the data on October 19, 2016. Overall, 583,200 requests to the Facebook Marketing API were required, and the collected data is available for the community.

We begin by computing Pearson correlation r of normalized Facebook audience estimates with the corresponding WHO data for each health concern. We find that just two – the interest *Dieting* with ($r = 0.314$) and the OR query *"Obesity awareness OR Plus-size clothing OR Weight loss OR Dieting OR Bariatrics"* ($r = 0.344$) – have a significant correlation to WHO obesity reports. However, we find the placebo interests too often outperform the targeted marker interests. The strongest significant correlations we find are between *Fitness & Wellness* and obesity ($r = 0.590$), and *Health care* and *Facebook* and diabetes ($r = 0.313$ and $r = 0.302$, respectively). Note that with Bonferroni correction for multiple hypothesis testing, even these results may be questioned. The results do not improve when we break down the data by the age and gender group (plots omitted for brevity). Finally, we would like to emphasize the performance of the baseline, generic health interests, often "outperforming" the targeted marker interests. Even the generic placebo interests like *Facebook* and *Read./Tech./Ent.* are often near the top of the list of predictors.

We then turn to comparisons within each country, across gender and age groups. Concretely, we are interested in whether there are certain generalizable age or gender related trends concerning the variation of interest levels in health topics within a country. To obtain such relative trends, we first compute the absolute interest levels for the relevant demographic group. Then we normalize these statistics within each country by computing the z-score (subtracting the mean and dividing by standard deviation across the demographic groups).

Figure 1 shows the average z-scores of (a) placebo interests, and marker interests for (b) tobacco, (c) obesity, and (d) diabetes, broken down by gender. We find the placebo interests to be expressed more by women than men, especially those dealing with fitness and health. One potential explanation for this is that women are generally more active on social media than men, in particular on mobile devices[13]. Yet we also find that women show more interest in topics around obesity and diabetes, though it is expected that, for example, *Gestational diabetes* would be a more popular topic for women than men. We see the opposite for the topics associated with tobacco, with most topics being more favored by men. The only exception is *Lung cancer awareness*, which is, again, a topic associated with health. These findings echo the global statistics of tobacco use, with WHO estimating that "about 40% of men smoke as compared with nearly 9% of women"[14].

Figure 2 shows the similar average z-scores for various age groups. Examining tobacco-related interest, we find the younger users being more interested in *hookah, tobacco,* and *cigarettes,* whereas the older users in *lung cancer awareness* and *smoking cessation.* The users in the age between 30 and 45 do not show preference for one or the other interest. Comparing these figures to the WHO global report on trends in prevalence of tobacco smoking report[15], we observe that the reported evolution of tobacco use by age-groups follows the z-score trend of related interests from Facebook Ads.

Thus, we find that within-country statistics are more statistically separable, which can then be compared to a corresponding "gold standard". Next we focus on error analysis.

6 ERROR ANALYSIS

The greatest advantage of Facebook advertising platform is also its weakness – the extensive natural language processing (NLP) pipeline and an aggregator spanning over a billion of users and many Facebook properties. To us, this black box provides an aggregation on planetary scale, but it also presents a murky opacity.

[13] http://www.ukom.uk.net/news/women-driving-mobile-internet-time
[14] http://www.who.int/gender/documents/10facts_gender_tobacco_en.pdf
[15] http://apps.who.int/iris/bitstream/10665/156262/1/9789241564922_eng.pdf?ua=1

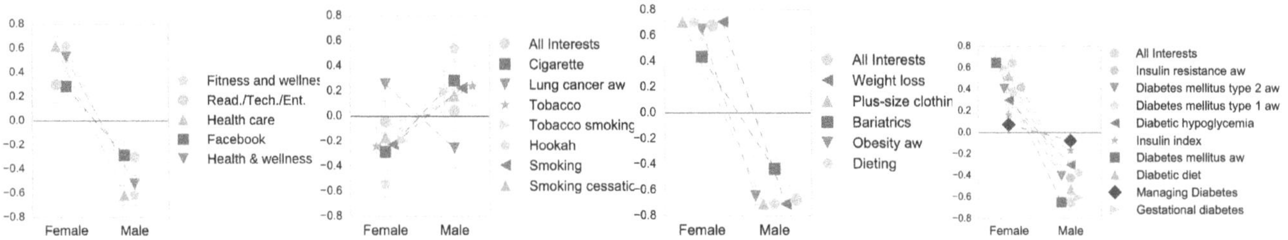

(a) Placebo (b) Tobacco (c) Obesity (d) Diabetes

Figure 1: Average z-scores per gender of (a) placebo interests, and marker interests for (b) tobacco use, (c) obesity, and (d) diabetes with 90% confidence intervals.

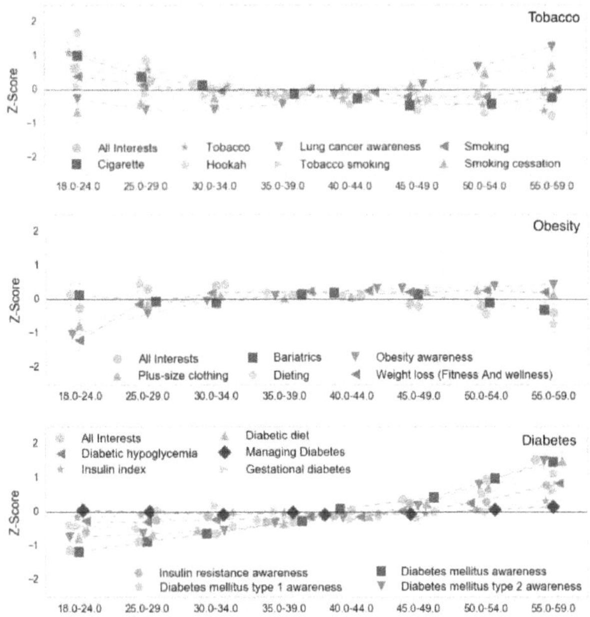

Figure 2: Average z-scores aggregated for age groups of marker interests for tobacco use, obesity, and diabetes with 90% confidence intervals.

As mentioned in Related Work, a similar difficulty faced researchers using Google Trends, which aggregates search volume worldwide, and which potentially can serve as a signal of Google users' interests. A major advantage of Google Trends is its temporal nature, allowing researchers a dimension in which to experiment with various time lags [15]. Similarly, we re-collect the data for the 10 countries with largest Facebook audiences nearly five months later, on 12 March, 2017, to examine its stability. Then, we compute the correlations between the previous and new audience estimates.

When we consider the audience sizes in each country without constraint by interest, sliced across the age (8) or gender (2) demographic groups, we find the data quite stable, with Spearman rank correlation being 1 for most (in two cases 0.99), and Pearson on average at 0.999. Although there were changes, on average the estimates increased by 14% (stdev of 8.9%), which may be due to Facebook's growing usage or increased user tracking reach.

Once we include the distinction by interest (both marker and placebo ones), the correlation between the data from October 2016 and March 2017 degrades. Across each country and interest (N = 10 countries * 29 interests = 290), we run two stability checks, first for both genders combined we compare the relative audiences for different age groups between the two time samples; second, for all combined ages we compare the audiences for the two genders between the two time samples.

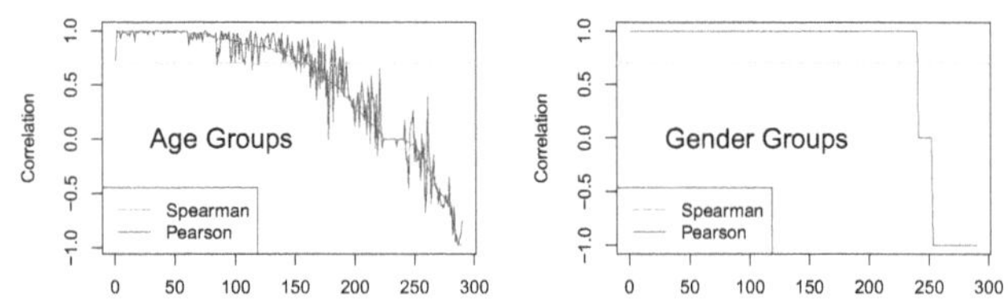

Figure 3: Spearman rank and Pearson correlations of normalized interest-specific audiences between two data samples, differentiating among age groups or genders. Grey line denotes 0.70 Spearman correlation level.

Figure 3 shows the Pearson and Spearman correlations between the (normalized) audience sizes of the two samples, sorted by correlation magnitude. On the left the correlation is computed between the eight age groups, and right the two genders (keeping all other variables constant). In the comparison of the age groups, we find 45% of the comparisons to be below 0.70 mark (point at which p gets under 0.05 level), and 17% even negative, meaning the ordering of the age groups flipped. The gender, being a binary variable, can only be observed to retain or switch their ordering, and for 13% of cases the latter happened.

Moreover, to understand the reasons of such differences between the two samples we asked the following question: Are the interests with lower audiences more volatile? In order to respond this question, we correlated the mean of the Spearman correlations given age group for each mark interest and their average audience among all countries. As result, we came with a negative Pearson correlation of -0.57 (p-value 0.001). Thus, surprisingly, interests with higher audience are more unstable.

Intuitively, if Facebook changes its black box often (for example, redefining the interests), then wild fluctuations may happen. But if the changes reflect the actual changes in user base and their evolving interests, then the changes should be similar in places with similar culture, geography, and language. For example, Google Trends shows dieting spikes at the beginning of each year[16].

Hence, we compare the changes in interest from one sample to another between United States and United Kingdom (two Western countries sharing a language), and between US and India and Brazil. To do this, we calculated the correlation between the audience variation (the deltas) of one country to another country for each interest. For US vs. UK comparison, out of 29 interests, we found 17 to be significantly similar (having Pearson $r > 0$ at $p < 0.05$) and only one interest to be significantly negatively related between the two countries, implying a similarity in the *direction of change* over time. For US vs. India, however, only 5 interests shared a direction (1 negatively), and US vs. Brazil 9 (3 negatively). This suggests that comparisons between more similar countries may be more stable in the same time span.

Thus, upon a closer inspection we find more stability in the data across demographics *without including interests*. This may be due to the definition of such features to be stable in time, and possibly to Facebook's inference algorithms for age and gender being relying on more explicit user-specified information. However once we include interest information, the stability of the audience estimates is much worse, with only 45% of the interest-specific age groups having the same ordering (Spearman's $\rho > 0.7$).

7 CONCLUDING DISCUSSION

This paper explores the use of Facebook ad audience estimates for global lifestyle health concern surveillance. Particularly, we assess the quality of Facebook data by introducing placebo baselines, normalization alternatives, and performing temporal analysis. Among our findings, we show that within-country statistics are more statistically separable than statistics across countries, which is an important observation as previous efforts have showed very promising results, but they focused only on a single country analysis [4, 7]. More important, the high volatility observed between two data snapshots warrants extra caution in the use of Facebook Marketing API as a source of social interest.

We can only speculate about the causes of such instability. It is possible that Facebook is constantly updating and changing its NLP pipeline, unevenly improving its performance over different topics. Further, if the time span implied in the interest estimate is short-term, audience numbers may swing wildly as Facebook usage changes, say, during holiday seasons. Another source of variability could come from the redefinition of what content is included in an interest. For instance, if new brands are included in plus-size clothing interest, its volume will increase. Finally, the advertising market demand may drive Facebook to focus on developing one interest over another.

Still, it may be too early to give up on this potentially rich data source. Our effort is restricted to a specific kind of disease surveillance. Thus, we acknowledge that it is impossible to generalize the limitations we have found without future studies. For example, much as the search volume revealed by Google Trends [3], the sways in Facebook's interests may be seasonal or local. Unfortunately currently neither Facebook's Advertising interface or Marketing API provide historical data, so more work needs to be done to monitor the data – i.e. for over a year if one is to capture seasonal variation. Furthermore, to assess the accuracy of interest assignment, one could use the advertising platform to run a survey assessing the interests of the reached audience directly.

Thus, we hope that this work will encourage future efforts to use our methodology to gather user interest from the Facebook Ads for other applications and scenarios. We also hope that results presented here will encourage future researchers to test the reliability of this potentially rich data source, and inspire more rigor in the future data-driven studies that aim at correlating social media data with offline world data.

[16]https://trends.google.com/trends/explore?q=diet

REFERENCES

[1] Jisun An and Ingmar Weber. 2015. Whom should we sense in "social sensing"-analyzing which users work best for social media now-casting. *EPJ Data Science* 4, 1 (2015), 1.
[2] Matheus Araujo, Yelena Mejova, Michael Aupetit, and Ingmar Weber. 2017. Visualizing Health Awareness in the Middle East. In *ICWSM*. to appear.
[3] Yan Carrière-Swallow and Felipe Labbé. 2013. Nowcasting with Google Trends in an emerging market. *Journal of Forecasting* 32, 4 (2013), 289–298.
[4] Rumi Chunara, Lindsay Bouton, John W. Ayers, and John S. Brownstein. 2013. Assessing the Online Social Environment for Surveillance of Obesity Prevalence. *PLoS ONE* 8, 4 (04 2013), 1–8.
[5] Elia Gabarron, Luis Fernandez-Luque, and others. 2017. Impact of Facebook Ads for Sexual Health Promotion Via an Educational Web App: A Case Study. *IJEHMC* 8, 2 (2017), 18–32.
[6] Jeremy Ginsberg and others. 2009. Detecting influenza epidemics using search engine query data. *Nature* 457, 7232 (2 2009), 1012–4.
[7] Steven Gittelman, Victor Lange, A. Carol Gotway Crawford, A. Catherine Okoro, Eugene Lieb, S. Satvinder Dhingra, and Elaine Trimarchi. 2015. A New Source of Data for Public Health Surveillance: Facebook Likes. *JMIR* 17, 4 (2015), e98.
[8] J. Gomide, A. Veloso, W. Meira Jr., V. Almeida, F. Benevenuto, F. Ferraz, and M. Teixeira. 2011. Dengue surveillance based on a computational model of spatio-temporal locality of Twitter. In *WebSci*.
[9] L. Brianna Haskins and others. 2017. Health Evaluation and Referral Assistant: A Randomized Controlled Trial of a Web-Based Screening, Brief Intervention, and Referral to Treatment System to Reduce Risky Alcohol Use Among Emergency Department Patients. *JMIR* 19, 5 (May 2017), e119.
[10] Taha A. Kass-Hout and Hend Alhinnawi. 2013. Social media in public health. *British Medical Bulletin* 108, 1 (2013), 5–24.
[11] Yoonsang Kim, Jidong Huang, and Sherry Emery. 2016. Garbage in, Garbage Out: Data Collection, Quality Assessment and Reporting Standards for Social Media Data Use in Health Research, Infodemiology and Digital Disease Detection. *JMIR* 18, 2 (26 Feb 2016), e41.
[12] David Lazer, Ryan Kennedy, Gary King, and Alessandro Vespignani. 2014. The parable of Google flu: traps in big data analysis. *Science* 343, 6176 (2014).
[13] Yabing Liu, Chloe Kliman-Silver, Robert Bell, Balachander Krishnamurthy, and Alan Mislove. 2014. Measurement and analysis of osn ad auctions. In *COSN*. 139–150.
[14] Christopher J.L. Murray and Alan D. Lopez. 1997. Alternative projections of mortality and disability by cause 1990–2020: Global Burden of Disease Study. *Lancet* 349 (1997), 1498–1504. Issue 9064.
[15] Tobias Preis and Helen Susannah Moat. 2014. Adaptive nowcasting of influenza outbreaks using Google searches. *Royal Society Open Science* 1, 2 (2014).
[16] Ben Y Reis and John S Brownstein. 2010. Measuring the impact of health policies using Internet search patterns: the case of abortion. *BMC public health* 10 (2010), 514.
[17] Diego Saez-Trumper, Yabing Liu, Ricardo Baeza-Yates, Balachander Krishnamurthy, and Alan Mislove. 2014. Beyond cpm and cpc: Determining the value of users on osns. In *COSN*. 161–168.
[18] Koustuv Saha, Ingmar Weber, Michael L. Birnbaum, and Munmun De Choudhury. 2017. Characterizing Awareness of Schizophrenia Among Facebook Users by Leveraging Facebook Advertisement Estimates. *JMIR* 19, 5 (2017), e156.
[19] Elad Yom-Tov and Luis Fernandez-Luque. 2014. Information is in the eye of the beholder: Seeking information on the MMR vaccine through an Internet search engine. *AMIA Symposium* 2014 (2014), 1238–47.

Ad-blocking: A Study on Performance, Privacy and Counter-measures

Kiran Garimella
Aalto University
Helsinki, Finland
kiran.garimella@aalto.fi

Orestis Kostakis
Aalto University
Helsinki, Finland
orestis.kostakis@aalto.fi

Michael Mathioudakis
Aalto University
Helsinki, Finland
michael.mathioudakis@aalto.fi

ABSTRACT

Many internet ventures rely on advertising for their revenue. However, users feel discontent by the presence of ads on the websites they visit, as the data-size of ads is often comparable to that of the actual content. This has an impact not only on the loading time of webpages, but also on the internet bill of the user in some cases. In absence of a mutually-agreed procedure for opting out of advertisements, many users resort to ad-blocking browser-extensions.

In this work, we study the performance of popular ad-blockers on a large set of news websites. Moreover, we investigate the benefits of ad-blockers on user privacy as well as the mechanisms used by websites to counter them. Finally, we explore the traffic overhead due to the ad-blockers themselves.

INTRODUCTION

Ad-blocking is now a widespread practice among web users. According to current estimates, it is employed by around 200 million desktop and 300 million mobile users, a user base that still grows at 40% annually [7]. The same estimates indicate that ad-blocking translates into significant losses for publishers, reaching 41 billion US dollars for 2016. It is therefore not surprising that there is an arms race between publishers and advertisers, on one hand, and ad-blocking tools (or 'ad-blockers'), on the other[1]. In this context, it is clear that understanding the mechanisms implemented by ad-blockers and their effects is of wide and continuous interest.

In this paper, we study a number of popular ad-blockers and analyze their performance in desktop and mobile settings for a large number of webpages. Specifically, we employ the ad-blockers on two sets of webpages: one consisting of the front pages of popular news websites; and another consisting of around 30,000 web articles.

For each webpage, we collect a number of measures that describe the browser workload with and without the use of an ad-blocker – including, for instance, the amount of data loaded, the load-time of webpages, or the number of data requests. Our results indicate that ad-blockers decrease the data consumption significantly, though the benefits in terms of load times are limited. Moreover, by taking a deeper look into the set of requests incurred by websites and ad-blockers, we identify cases where the websites attempt to counter the ad-blockers, but also requests that the ad-blockers incur on their own. Finally, we investigate the extent to which ad-blockers prevent the transfer of user-tracking information, resulting in privacy benefits for users. When comparing a range of different ad-blockers, we find that uBlock performs the best, in terms of both data savings and user-tracking.

[1]https://techcrunch.com/2016/08/11/facebooks-blocker-blocking-ads-blocked-by-blockers/

WebSci'17, June 25-28, 2017, Troy, NY, USA.

978-1-4503-4896-6/17/06...$15.00
DOI: http://dx.doi.org/10.1145/3091478.3091514

RELATED WORK

Online Advertising Advertising has emerged as one of the main sources of revenue on the web [2]. On one hand, advertisers claim that ads on the web help keep most parts of the web free for consumers [1]. On the other hand, consumers find advertising annoying and obstructive. In one study, the New York Times analyzed the top 50 news websites[2] and found that more than half of all data came from ads.

Moreover, many users perceive web ads as a threat to privacy [3] and tracking is cited as one of the most common reasons for users to install ad-blockers [6]. This is corroborated by many studies that show large scale tracking behavior on the web [3, 9]. For instance, Yu et al. [12] find that 95% of the pages visited contain 3rd party requests to potential trackers and 78% attempt to transfer unsafe data. To counter tracking, ad-blockers also remove tracking buttons (such as Facebook's 'like' button) and protect their users from known malware domains.

Ad blocking In [4], the authors propose methods to detect the users who have installed an ad-blocker and characterize ad-block usage for a large set (2 millions) of users. In addition, they give details on demographics and geographic penetration of ad-blockers on the web. In [8], the authors analyze the use of two ad-blockers, AdblockPlus and Ghostery, on web traffic data from a European ISP. They show that there is a drop in requests to third party services when using ad-block and estimate that around 18% of the traffic is due to ads. There are a few differences between our study and theirs: (i) their study handles only two ad-blockers, (ii) with a constant battle between advertisers and ad-blockers, the ad-blocking and counter ad-blocking scene has been changing over the last few years, and so have some of the related performance measurements. (iii) our study handles in-html ads, which are used by advertisers nowadays to bypass ad-blocking.

In [11], the authors classify third party trackers into various categories including ad trackers, analytics, social, etc and compare the performance of various ad-blocking tools with respect to blocking these third party requests. They find that there is a lot of variance in the type of requests that are blocked by each ad-blocker. They then

[2]http://www.nytimes.com/interactive/2015/10/01/business/cost-of-mobile-ads.html

look deeper into the individual default and possible configurations of these ad-blockers and study the changes in blocking capabilities with the different settings.

There have been privacy concerns with ad-blockers too. Many popular ad-blockers (including AdBlock and AdblockPlus) participate in the *Acceptable Ads* program[3], allowing 'non-intrusive' ads to go through. For an extensive study on the issue see [10].

To counter the effects of increasing ad-blocking, advertisers are relying on counter-ad-blocking tools. In [5], the authors study their use on the most popular five thousand websites and find that at least 6.7% of these sites use them.

DATA

We analyze two datasets, chosen to capture potential differences between content-heavy homepages of large websites and individual webpages.

`Top150` This is a list of the top 150 news websites, as ranked by Alexa[4]. For each of them, we have a URL that points to the website homepage, for both its desktop and mobile version (unless the latter does not exist).

`GDELT` A list of 30,000 URLs pointing to different news articles published on a single day (November 8, 2016). The list was obtained from GDELT[5], a project that collects news stories from all around the world over the years.

We load the webpage of each URL with a clean instance of Chrome browser (no cached content or extensions), using the Selenium Python library[6] on a Macbook pro with 8 cores, with no other major processes running. On each load, we capture the HAR file for the load. The HAR (HTTP Archive File) is a JSON-formatted file that captures the interactions between the browser and the website, including network requests, types and size of objects, and load times.

We load the same URL in six browser modes, all simultaneously: a vanilla mode (no ad-blocker), and one mode for each of five ad-blockers. The ad-blockers are AdBlock[7], AdblockPlus[8], Ghostery[9], uBlock[10] and Privacy Badger[11] – chosen from the most popular ad-blockers on the Chrome Store. For the `Top150` dataset, we also load the mobile version of the page (as loaded on Google Nexus 5) using Selenium's mobile emulation tool[12]. Note that, though we report the data about mobile websites with and without ad-block, the ad-blockers used were for the desktop version. There are no ad-blockers for the mobile version of Chrome and none for any of the Android browsers. Our datasets and code can be accessed here[13].

[3]https://acceptableads.com/
[4]http://www.alexa.com/topsites/category/News/Newspapers. We processed the list manually and removed a few which were not standard news sites (e.g. reddit.com)
[5]http://gdeltproject.org/
[6]http://selenium-python.readthedocs.io/
[7]https://getadblock.com/
[8]https://adblockplus.org
[9]https://www.ghostery.com/
[10]https://www.ublock.org
[11]https://www.eff.org/privacybadger
[12]https://sites.google.com/a/chromium.org/chromedriver/mobile-emulation
[13]https://users.ics.aalto.fi/kiran/adblock/

FINDINGS

This section details our findings on the efficiency of ad-blockers, the ad-blocker benefits on user privacy, the counter-measures used by advertisers, and finally the traffic load that ad-blockers incur on their own.

Ad-blocker Efficiency

For each URL and setting (desktop or mobile, with or without ad-blocker), we collect measures that describe the average performance of the browser in loading the webpages of a dataset. The measures include: the number of distinct domains for all HTTP requests performed during loading; the maximum number of threads that run concurrently at any point; the total number of HTTP requests; the total size of downloaded and uploaded data; the cumulative time for loading the webpage, obtained by summing up the durations of all requests; and, finally, the wall-clock time. We acquire these statistics by parsing the HAR files.

The number of distinct domains indicate the number of different parties that acquire information of the user, such as IP address and the user-agent string (contains device type, name and version of browser and OS, etc). The number of HTTP requests and maximum number of concurrent threads give an indication of the load on the user's machine. The amount of transferred data, and the cumulative and wall-clock time affect the user experience.

Figures 1 and 2 show the results for the desktop and mobile versions of the `Top150` webpages; and Figure 3 for the `GDELT` webpages. Numbers represent the ratio of the measures over the vanilla mode – for example, a value of 0.6 for the number of domains means that using an ad-blocker loads 60% the number of domains compared to using no ad-blocker.

We find that: (i) All ad-blockers except Ghostery give around 25-34% savings in the amount of data transferred (on average). This is a bit higher than the 18% saving reported by [8] and 13-34% reported by [11]. Ghostery is the exception because it is not an ad-blocking tool per se, but gives a choice for a user to track who is tracking them and block those of their choice. So by default Ghostery does not block any content. We still include it in all our measurements, as it still makes sense to study it in other analysis cases that follow in this section. (ii) On average, there is an *increase* in the wall clock time when using an ad-blocker, even as the cumulative time decreases for some of the ad-blockers. This means that ad-blockers incur overhead, but block ad-related threads that were meant to run in parallel while loading content; this overhead is not necessarily experienced by the user, since various scripts can often run in the background, after the important content has loaded. (iii) uBlock gives the best performance, both in terms of data and time saved.

Benefits for User Privacy

By examining the HTTP requests issued by the browser when loading a webpage, we notice that a significant amount of these are intended for tracking the users' behaviour. We attempt to quantify the potential privacy hazard for the user when accessing a webpage by analyzing the parameters passed through these requests. Specifically, to measure the impact of potentially privacy invading requests when using no ad-blocker, we manually examined the tracking parameters from the request headers and found nine frequently used

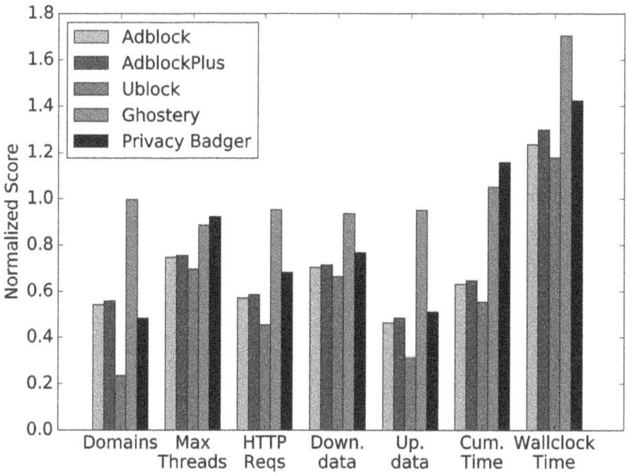

Figure 1: Performance benchmark when using an ad-blocker on the desktop version of `Top150`, normalized over the vanilla mode.

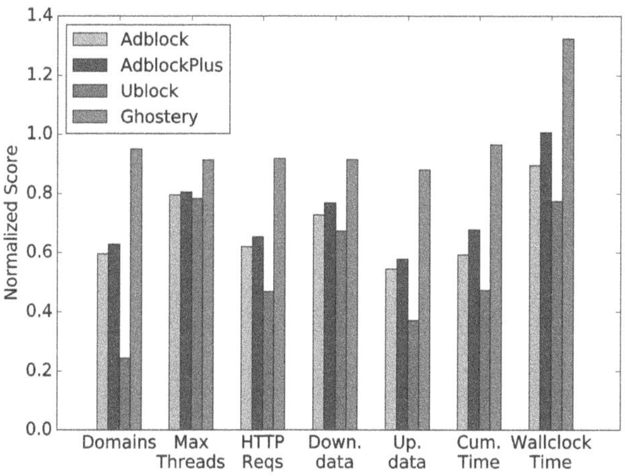

Figure 2: Performance benchmark when using an ad-blocker on the mobile version of `Top150`, normalized over the vanilla mode. Privacy Badger was discarded because of inconsistencies in the data collection.

tracking parameters that accompanied a large set of requests. The parameters were: 'pixel', 'track', 'google_gid', 'user_id', 'partnerid', 'partnerUID', 'partner_device_id', 'uid', 'user_cookie'. The presence of these parameters offers a high-precision method to identify user-tracking, although we currently do not quantify its recall.

Figure 4 shows the fraction of requests containing one, two and three tracking parameters in a request when using an ad-blocker, again normalized over the vanilla mode. We can see from the figure that, again, uBlock achieves near-perfect performance, whereas other ad-blockers (except Ghostery) block about 60-80% of requests with such parameters. The performance remains the same, when considering requests with different numbers of tracking parameters, though the total number of requests goes down exponentially.

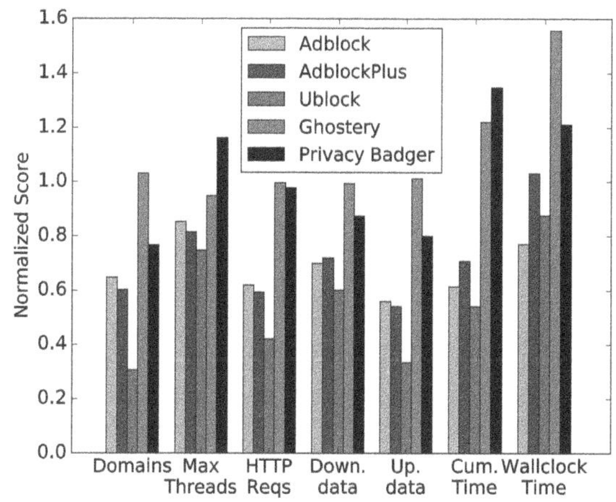

Figure 3: Performance measures when using an ad-blocker on the `GDELT` dataset, normalized over the vanilla mode.

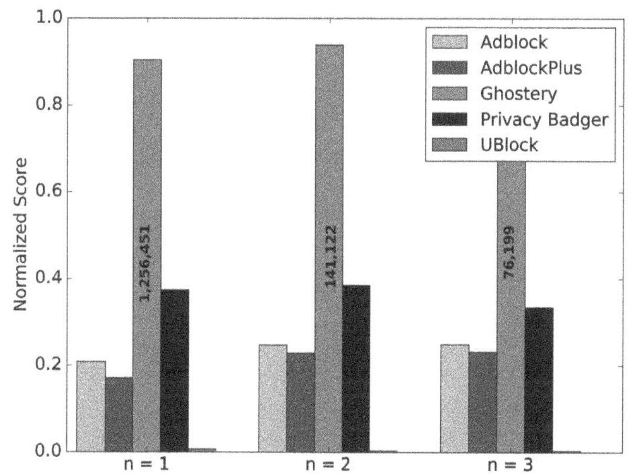

Figure 4: Fraction of distinct requests containing tracking keywords for one, two and three tracking parameters. The black text in the red bar shows the total number of requests containing these tracking parameters in the vanilla mode.

Blocking the Ad-blockers

Online ventures relying on advertising try to counter to the ad-blocking tools [5]. In our analysis, we witness several techniques for countering ad-blockers, with different goals. In certain cases, the goal is simply to detect whether the browser has an active ad-blocking extension. Upon detection, a message is rendered on the webpage and notifies the user about the tool. This message may simply notify the user that the tool interferes with the content and the user-experience. Other times, the message blocks the user from accessing the actual content, until they have turned off the tool. In more extreme cases, the goal is to circumvent the ad-blocking tool altogether.

We examine again the HTTP requests performed when loading a webpage and look for specific Javascript modules designed to counter ad-blocking, such as `blockadblock.js`, `inn-anti- adblock`,

Table 1: Additional Domains loaded by Ad-blockers

Ad-blocker	Extra domains loaded
AdBlock	mixpanel.com, stripe.com
Adblock Plus	quantserve.com,crwdcntrl.net
Ghostery	selectmedia.asia, streamrail.com adlooxtracking.com
Privacy Badger	cdnjs.com
uBlock	Twitter widgets

and adblock html cache buster. When webpages from the GDELT dataset are loaded in the vanilla mode (no ad-blockers), we find more than 3,260 webpages (10.8%) with explicit attempts to determine if any ad-blocking tool is used. When AdBlock or AdblockPlus is activated, the number of webpages rises to 10,097 and 10,226 (33%), respectively, indicating that a large portion of webpages actively track the usage of these ad-blockers. When the other tools are used, the number of webpages with such requests is not as high; 15, 9, 8% of the webpages for Ghostery, Privacy Badger, and uBlock respectively. The variation in numbers between AdBlock and AdblockPlus, on one hand, and the rest of the ad-blockers, on the other, can be explained by the popularity of the former – but also the effectiveness of the ad-blockers in blocking such requests.

Requests due to Ad-blockers

In this section, we try to dissect what *additional* requests are made when using an ad-blocker. Consider the set of HTTP requests required to render a webpage in the vanilla mode, denoted by $\mathcal{V}$. Let $\mathcal{B}$ be the set of requests when using an ad-blocking tool, then we define $\mathcal{A} = \mathcal{V} \setminus \mathcal{B}$ as the identified advertisements, and $C = \mathcal{V} \cap \mathcal{B}$ as the "true" content of the page. Finally, $\mathcal{E} = \mathcal{B} \setminus \mathcal{V}$ is "extra" content loaded due to or by the ad-blocking tool. Unsurprisingly, the most popular domains found in $\mathcal{A}$ are googlesyndication.com and doubleclick.net, in accordance to previous studies, and blocked (characterized as ads) by all tools.

A more interesting question is to identify the "extra" $\mathcal{E}$ requests that incur exclusively at the presence by ad-blockers and to look for potential leakages in information[14]. The domains which most frequently occur only in $\mathcal{E}$ are shown in Table 1. In many cases, we notice that $\mathcal{E}$ contains well-known ad-serving or visitor-tracking domains. This clearly demonstrates that the tools are not perfect and are sometimes bypassed.

For AdBlock, we notice that mixpanel.com appears in 5,125 (17%) of the webpages when using AdBlock, versus 170 (< 1%) of original pages (vanilla mode). This is a Google Analytics-like website that tracks visits by users of AdBlock. Similarly, stripe.com, an online payments platform through which users can donate to AdBlock is added to 2,616 (8%) of the webpages, compared to 40 (< 0.1%) with out ad-blocking.

For Adblockplus, we notice an increase for quantserve .com (an audience-measurement website) from 14% to 21% and for crwdcntrl.net (another audience-measurement website) from 21% to 29% For Ghostery, we notice selectmedia.asia (a video-ad serving company) appears in 1,374 (4.6%) webpages' requests, compared to 47 (< 0.1%) in the vanilla mode, streamrail. com (another video-ad serving company) 1,488 times (5%) versus 63, and adlooxtracking.com (ad tracking company) 2,190 times (7%) versus 240 (< 1%). For PrivacyBadger, cdnjs.com (a repository for open-source web-libraries) stands out with 2,130 webpages (7%). For uBlock we did not witness any significant increase for suspicious domains; but we did notice an increase for Twitter widgets from 11% to 20% of the webpages.

Our preliminary findings indicate that though ad-blockers block external ads and third party trackers to varying degrees, they introduce various tracking services of their own. This is a novel finding and has potential impact on users privacy. We leave a detailed analysis on this for future work.

Conclusions This paper provides a first look at the performance and privacy aspects of popular ad-blocking tools. Based on our analysis, we conclude that (i) uBlock has the best performance, in terms of ad and third party tracker filtering, and least privacy tracking, (ii) The time to load pages is not necessarily faster when using adblockers, and (iii) this is partly the case due to additional trackers and libraries introduced by the adblocking tools. As ad-blockers try to monetise their business by selling ads themselves, our datasets and findings could be used (i) by users, to get an idea on which adblocker to choose, from an increasingly competitive set of providers, and (ii) by researchers, as building blocks for further analysis on privacy and tracking behaviors by ad-blocking tools.

Acknowledgements. This work has been supported by the Academy of Finland project "Nestor" (286211) and the EC H2020 RIA project "SoBigData" (654024).

REFERENCES

[1] Paul Barford, Igor Canadi, Darja Krushevskaja, Qiang Ma, and S Muthukrishnan. 2014. Adscape: Harvesting and analyzing online display ads. In *WWW*. 597–608.

[2] David S Evans. 2008. The economics of the online advertising industry. *Review of network economics* 7, 3 (2008).

[3] Marjan Falahrastegar, Hamed Haddadi, Steve Uhlig, and Richard Mortier. 2014. Anatomy of the third-party web tracking ecosystem. *arXiv preprint arXiv:1409.1066* (2014).

[4] Matthew Malloy, Mark McNamara, Aaron Cahn, and Paul Barford. 2016. Ad Blockers: Global Prevalence and Impact. In *Proceedings of the 2016 ACM on Internet Measurement Conference*. 119–125.

[5] Rishab Nithyanand and others. 2016. Ad-Blocking and Counter Blocking: A Slice of the Arms Race. *arXiv:1605.05077* (2016).

[6] PageFair. 2015. The 2015 Ad Blocking Report. *https://blog.pagefair.com/2015/ad-blocking-report/* (2015).

[7] PageFair. 2016. The 2016 Mobile Ad Blocking Report. *https://pagefair.com/blog/2016/mobile-adblocking-report/* (2016).

[8] Enric Pujol, Oliver Hohlfeld, and Anja Feldmann. 2015. Annoyed Users: Ads and Ad-Block Usage in the Wild. In *IMC*. 93–106.

[9] Sebastian Schelter and Jérôme Kunegis. 2016. On the Ubiquity of Web Tracking: Insights from a Billion-Page Web Crawl. *arXiv preprint arXiv:1607.07403* (2016).

[10] Robert J Walls, Eric D Kilmer, Nathaniel Lageman, and Patrick D McDaniel. 2015. Measuring the Impact and Perception of Acceptable Advertisements. In *IMC*. 107–120.

[11] Craig E Wills and Doruk C Uzunoglu. 2016. What Ad Blockers Are (and Are Not) Doing. In *HotWeb*. 72–77.

[12] Zhonghao Yu, Sam Macbeth, Konark Modi, and Josep M Pujol. 2016. Tracking the Trackers. In *WWW*. 121–132.

[14] e.g. http://thehackernews.com/2016/11/web-of-trust-addon.html

Factors in Recommending Contrarian Content on Social Media

Kiran Garimella
Aalto University
Helsinki, Finland
kiran.garimella@aalto.fi

Gianmarco De Francisci Morales
Qatar Computing Research Institute
Doha, Qatar
gdfm@acm.org

Aristides Gionis
Aalto University
Helsinki, Finland
aristides.gionis@aalto.fi

Michael Mathioudakis
Aalto University
Helsinki, Finland
michael.mathioudakis@aalto.fi

ABSTRACT

Polarization is a troubling phenomenon that can lead to societal divisions and hurt the democratic process. It is therefore important to develop methods to reduce it.

We propose an algorithmic solution to the problem of reducing polarization. The core idea is to expose users to content that challenges their point of view, with the hope broadening their perspective, and thus reduce their polarity. Our method takes into account several aspects of the problem, such as the estimated polarity of the user, the probability of accepting the recommendation, the polarity of the content, and popularity of the content being recommended.

We evaluate our recommendations via a large-scale user study on Twitter users that were actively involved in the discussion of the US elections results. Results shows that, in most cases, the factors taken into account in the recommendation affect the users as expected, and thus capture the essential features of the problem.

1 INTRODUCTION

Polarization around controversial issues is a well-studied phenomenon in the social sciences [11].Social media have arguably amplified polarization, thanks to the scale of discussions and their publicity [7]. This paper studies how to reduce polarization on social media by recommending *contrarian* content, i.e., content that expresses a point-of-view opposing the one held by the target user. In particular, we examine which features might be used to develop such a content recommender system.

We focus on controversial issues that create discussions online. Usually, these discussions involve a fair share of "retweeting" or "sharing" opinions of authoritative figures with whom the user agrees. Therefore, it is natural to model the discussion as an *endorsement graph*: a vertex u represents a user, and a directed edge (u, v) represents the fact that user u endorses the opinion of user v.

Due to phenomena such as homophily, confirmation bias, and selective exposure, social media often create echo chambers [5, 8]. These chambers, in turn, cultivate isolation and misunderstanding in society [18], and deepen its polarization.

A potential solution to this problem is to encourage users to consider points of view different from their own. Thus, in this paper, we study methods to recommend content items (e.g., news articles, opinion pieces, blog posts) that express a contrarian point of view, while at the same time being appealing to the target user.

In particular, given metrics that measure the polarization of users and items (such as those proposed in recent research [3]), our goal is to recommend an item that nudges the user towards the opposite polarity. That is, we seek to propose content produced by a user v to another user u, thus informing u of a different viewpoint, and hoping that u will endorse v.

Clearly, some content is more likely to be endorsed than other. For instance, people in the "center" might be easier to convince than people on the two extreme ends of the political spectrum [13]. We take this issue into account by modeling the *acceptance probability* for a recommendation as a separate component of the model.

We blend these factors, together with other signals such as topic and popularity, to create a ranked list of recommendations. Our solution employs a well-known weighted rank-aggregation algorithm at its core [17].

We evaluate our proposal by running an online user study with Twitter users. We focus on the recent 2016 US presidential elections, and generate recommendations for the thousands of users involved in this highly-polarizing controversial discussion. The results of the study show that the two main factors used in the recommendation, the polarity and the acceptance probability models, are predictive of the responses of the users.

In summary, we make the following contributions:

- We study the problem of bridging echo chambers algorithmically, in a language- and domain-agnostic way. Previous studies that address this problem focus mostly on understanding *how* to recommend content to an ideologically opposite side, while we focus on *which* contrarian content to recommend. We believe that the two approaches complement each other in bringing us closer to bursting filter bubbles.

WebSci'17, June 25-28, 2017, Troy, NY, USA.

978-1-4503-4896-6/17/06...$15.00
DOI: http://dx.doi.org/10.1145/3091478.3091515

- We build on top of results from recent user studies [14, 15, 19] on how users prefer to consume content from opposing views, and formulate the task as a content-recommendation problem based on an endorsement graph, while also taking into account the acceptance probability of a recommendation.
- We evaluate the proposed solution via a user study on Twitter users, and demonstrate the validity of the main factors involved in the recommendation.

2 RELATED WORK

Although the Web was envisioned as a place of open discussions on a wide range of topics, many people tend to restrict themselves to viewing and sharing information that conforms with their beliefs. A wide body of recent studies has explored [1, 2] and quantified [3] the notions of "filter bubble" and "echo chambers".

Munson et al. [15] created a browser widget that measures the bias of users based on the news articles they read. Their study shows that users are willing to slightly change views once they are shown their biases. Graells-Garrido et al. [9] show that mere display of contrarian content has negative emotional effect. To overcome this effect, they propose a visual interface for making recommendations from a diverse pool of users, where diversity is with respect to user stances on a topic. Graells-Garrido et al. [10] propose to find topics that may be of interest to both sides by constructing a topic graph. They define intermediary topics to be those topics that have high betweenness centrality and topic diversity. Park et al. [16] propose methods for presenting multiple aspects of news to reduce bias.

Most relevant to this work is the recent study about the problem of reducing the overall polarization of a controversial topic in a network [6]. The study tries to find the best edges that can be added to an endorsement graph so that the polarization score of the network is reduced. In this paper, we focus on reducing the polarization of an individual user (local objective), instead of the entire network (global objective).

There have also been a number of demos and systems: Wall Street Journal's *Blue feed-Red feed*[1] raises awareness about the extent to which viewpoints on a matter can differ, by showing side-by-side articles expressing very liberal and very conservative viewpoints; *Politecho*[2] displays how polarizing the content on a user's news feed is when compared to their friends'; *Escape your bubble*[3] is a browser extension to add hand-curated content from the opposite side in Facebook; automated bots have been created to respond to posts containing harassment or fake news,[4] with an attempt to de-polarize the discussion and educate users. Moreover, new social media platforms have been proposed that aim to be designed in such a way to encourage discussions and debates, such as the Filterburst project,[5] Rbutr,[6] where users can post rebuttals of other urls, and a wikipedia for debates.[7]

The proposed method differs from existing ones in many ways. First, our approach is completely algorithmic, unlike most demos listed above, which involve manual curation. Second, as discussed above, it builds on top of existing research and incorporates key findings of previous work.

[1] http://graphics.wsj.com/blue-feed-red-feed/
[2] http://politecho.org/
[3] https://www.escapeyourbubble.com/
[4] http://wpo.st/4kVR2, https://goo.gl/Xl6x9t
[5] http://www.filterburst.com/
[6] http://rbutr.com/
[7] http://www.debatepedia.org/en/index.php/Welcome_to_Debatepedia%21

3 PRELIMINARIES

A topic of discussion is identified as the set of tweets that satisfy a text query – e.g., all tweets that contain a specific hashtag. We represent a topic with an *endorsement graph* $G(V, E)$, where vertices V represent users and edges E represent *endorsements*.

It has been shown that an endorsement graph captures well the extent to which a topic is controversial [3]. In particular, the endorsement graph of a controversial topic has a *multimodal clustered structure*, where each cluster of vertices represents one viewpoint on the topic. As we focus on two-sided controversies, we identify the two sides of a controversial topic by employing a *graph-partitioning* algorithm, which partitions the graph into *two* subgraphs. In this work, we specifically focus on recommending content in the form of news items, such as articles, blog posts, and opinion pieces. The item pool for the recommendation comprises all the links shared by the active users during the observation window.

User polarization score. We use a recently-proposed methodology to define the polarization score for each user in the graph [4]. The score is based on the expected hitting time of a random walk that starts from the user under consideration and ends on a high-degree vertex on either side. Typically, in a retweet graph, high-degree vertices on each side are indicators of authoritative content generators. We denote the set of the k highest degree vertices on each side by X^+ and Y^+. Intuitively, a vertex is assigned a score of higher absolute value (closer to $+1$ or -1), if, compared to other vertices in the graph, it takes a very different time to reach a high-degree vertex on either side (X^+ or Y^+) (in terms of information flow). Specifically, for each vertex $u \in V$ in the graph, we consider a random walk that starts at u, and estimate the expected number of steps, l_u^X before the random walk reaches any high-degree vertex in X^+. Considering the distribution of values of l_u^X across all vertices $u \in V$, we define $\rho^X(u)$ as the fraction of vertices $v \in V$ with $l_v^X < l_u^X$. We define $\rho^Y(u)$ similarly. Obviously, we have $\rho^X(u), \rho^Y(u) \in [0, 1)$. The polarization score of a user is then defined as

$$\rho(u) = \rho^X(u) - \rho^Y(u) \quad \in (-1, 1). \tag{1}$$

Following this definition, a vertex that is close to high-degree vertices X^+, compared to most other vertices, will have $\rho^X(u) \approx 1$; on the other hand, if the same vertex is far from high-degree vertices Y^+, it will have $\rho^Y(u) \approx 0$; leading to a polarization score $\rho(u) \approx 1 - 0 = 1$. The opposite is true for vertices that are far from X^+ but close to Y^+; leading to a polarization score $\rho(u) \approx -1$.

Item polarization score. Once we have obtained polarization scores for users in the graph, it is straightforward to derive a similar score for content items shared by these users. Specifically, we define the polarization score of an item i as the average of the polarization scores of the set of users who have shared i, denoted by U_i:

$$\rho(i) = \frac{1}{|U_i|} \sum_{u \in U_i} \rho(u) \quad \in (-1, 1). \tag{2}$$

Acceptance probability. Not all recommendations are agreeable, especially if they do not conform to the user's beliefs. To reduce these effects, we define an acceptance probability, which quantifies the degree to which a user is likely to endorse the recommended content. We use the item and user polarization scores defined above to estimate the likelihood that a target user u endorses (i.e., retweets) the recommended item i. We build an acceptance model by adapting a similar one based on the feature of user polarization [6]. High absolute values of user polarization (close to -1 or $+1$) indicate that the user belongs clearly to one side of the controversy, while middle-range values (close to 0) indicate that the user is in the middle of the two sides. It was shown that users from either side accept content from different sides with different probabilities, and these probabilities can be inferred from the graph structure [6]. For example, a user with polarization close to -1 is more likely to endorse a user with a negative polarization than a user with polarization $+1$. This intuition directly translates to endorsing items, and therefore can be used for our recommendation problem.

Based on this intuition, we define the acceptance probability $p(u,i)$ of a user u endorsing item i as

$$p(u,i) = {N_e(\rho(u),\rho(i))}/{N_x(\rho(u),\rho(i))}, \tag{3}$$

where $N_e(\rho(u),\rho(i))$ and $N_x(\rho(u),\rho(i))$ are the number of times a user with polarity $\rho(u)$ has endorsed or was exposed to (respectively) content of polarity $\rho(i)$. In practice, the polarity scores are bucketed to smooth the probabilities.

4 RECOMMENDATION FACTORS

This section describes the factors used to generate recommendations. Though our main focus is to connect users with content that expresses a contrarian point of view, we also want to maximize the chances of such a recommendation being endorsed by the user. We take into account several factors: reduction in polarization score of the target user; exclusivity of the candidate items (polarity of the items); acceptance probability of recommendation based on polarization scores; topic diversity; popularity/quality of the candidate item. Next, we describe these factors in more detail.

Reduction of user polarization score. The maximum reduction of user polarization score is achieved by putting the user in contact with an authoritative source from the opposing side. Leveraging this idea, we build a list of items L_1 by considering items shared by high degree nodes on the opposite side of the target user, and ranking them by the potential decrease in user polarization score.

Exclusivity on either side. We consider items that are almost exclusively shared by one of the sides. Specifically, we denote by n_i^X and n_i^Y the number of users who shared each item i on side X and Y, respectively. For each side, we generate a list L_2 ranked by the ratio of shares n_i^X/n_i^Y (for side X) and n_i^Y/n_i^X (for side Y).

Acceptance probability. For a given user u, all items sorted in decreasing order of acceptance probability $p(u,i)$ make up list L_3.

Topic diversity. We want to ensure that the recommendations are topically diverse. To achieve this, for each user, we compute a vector t_u that contains the topics extracted from the tweets written and the items shared by the user. Similarly, we extract a vector of topics t_i for each item. Topics are defined as *named entity*, and we extract them using the tool tagme.[8] Given a user vector t_u, we

[8]https://services.d4science.org/web/tagme

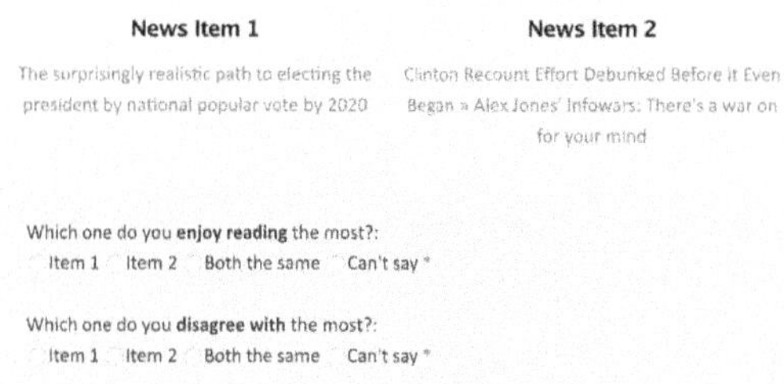

Figure 1: Screenshot of the interface shown for a user with a high polarity on the political left (Democrat).

compute the cosine similarity with all item vectors t_i, and rank items in increasing order of cosine similarity (list L_4).

Popularity on either side. Finally, we take into account the popularity of the recommended items, so that users receive content that is popular and, likely, of good quality. For each item, we compute a popularity score as the maximum number of retweets obtained by a tweet that contains this item. We produce list L_5 of items in decreasing popularity score.

Rank Aggregation. Given the 5 ranked lists discussed above, we use a weighted rank-aggregation scheme to generate the final recommendations. The intuition behind using rank aggregation is that items that are highly ranked in many lists, are also highly ranked in the output list. In particular, we use a weighted rank-aggregation technique proposed by Pihur et al. [17], whose goal is to minimize the objective function

$$\phi(\delta) = \sum_{i=1}^{5} w_i d(\delta, L_i), \tag{4}$$

where δ is the optimal ranked output list, d is any distance function (we use the Spearman footrule distance), and w_i are the importance weights of each list. We can set the weights to generate highly contrarian recommendations (by giving large weights to L_1 and L_2) or recommendations that are likely to be accepted (by giving large weight to L_3).

5 EVALUATION

Dataset. We collect all tweets containing the hashtag `#USelections`, used in discussions about the US presidential elections during Nov 9–12, 2016. From the 6.2 M tweets collected, we build an endorsement graph with 6764 nodes (users) and 9896 edges (retweets). To filter out noise, the graph contains an edge between two users only if at least 5 retweets between the two users occur. We partition the graph to obtain the two sides by using METIS [12]. For recommendation items (urls), we consider items that have been shared at least 5 times in our dataset. The final pool contains 10 210 candidate items, which include news articles, blog posts, opinion pieces, etc.

User study. We run an online user study involving all 6764 users in the dataset with the aim of evaluating how users percieve the two main conflicting factors proposed, i.e. the contrarian features (L_1, L_2) and acceptance features (L_3). For each user in the study, we generate two recommended items that are personalized based on their Twitter activity: one item is highly contrarian, while the other is more likely to be accepted, according to our model. In more

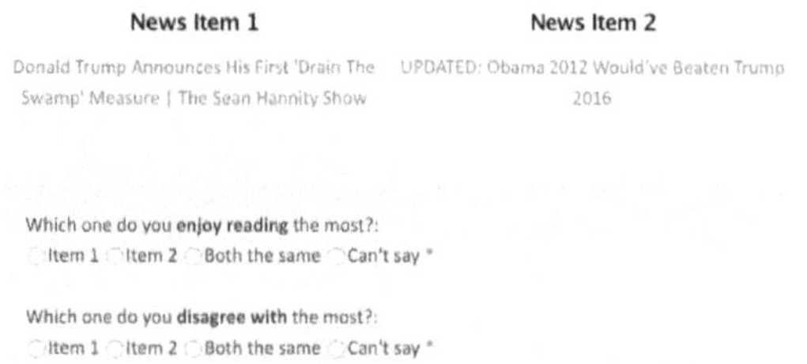

Figure 2: Screenshot of the interface shown for a user with a high polarity on the political right (Republican).

Table 1: Results from the user study.

Main factor	Item1 (Acceptance)	Item2 (Contrarian)	Both the same	Can't say
Enjoy	51	19	8	15
Disagree	22	57	7	7

detail, by using the methodology described above, we compute two recommendations for each user: in the first one we give a high weight (60%) to contrarian features (L_1 and L_2), while in the second one we give high weight (60%) to acceptance probability (L_3). We distribute the remaining 40% equally among other features.

The main research questions we investigate are: (*i*) is a high acceptance probability factor predictive of content with higher acceptance? and (*ii*) are contrarian factors predictive of more disagreement with the user? To simplify the task for the user, we set up the user study as a relative comparison between the two recommendations, rather than asking for absolute judgments. Since the two recommendations are generated completely independently, we assume that they do not influence the users decision making process in choosing one over the other.

We create a web form[9] with two recommended items, customized for each user, with the item weighted by the acceptance features shown on the left and contrarian features on the right. Figures 1 and 2 show two instances of the web form. Looking at Figure 1, given the left-leaning political affiliation of the user, the recommendation on the left side (News item 1) looks more agreeable than the recommendation on the right side (News item 2). The opposite is true for Figure 2, which targets a right-leaning user.

We contacted users on Twitter with the following private message: "@username We are scientists studying social media. Would u like to help science by participating in a survey? http://bit.ly/XXXXX'', and waited for two weeks for them to respond. In total, we sent around 6700 messages and received 93 valid responses after removing duplicates (1.4% response rate).

Our expectation is that users enjoy reading the item with high acceptance probability, and disagree with the contrarian item. The results, summarized in Table 1, confirm our expectations. Indeed, most users enjoy reading the item with high acceptance, and disagree with the contrarian item. Specifically, 44 out of the 93 users (47%) reported that at the same time they enjoy the first item, and disagree with the second. For a few users (n=7), we were able to generate enjoyable recommendations that they disagreed with. While this was not the goal of the specific user study, it is indeed our ultimate goal, and thus these results are highly encouraging.

Acknowledgements. This work has been supported by the Academy of Finland project "Nestor" (286211) and the EC H2020 RIA project "SoBigData" (654024).

[9] http://bit.ly/2jOQBxP

6 REFERENCES

[1] Lada A Adamic and Natalie Glance. 2005. The political blogosphere and the 2004 US election: divided they blog. In *LinkKDD*. 36–43.
[2] Michael Conover, Jacob Ratkiewicz, Matthew R Francisco, Bruno Gonçalves, Filippo Menczer, and Alessandro Flammini. 2011. Political Polarization on Twitter. In *ICWSM*.
[3] Kiran Garimella, Gianmarco De Francisci Morales, Aristides Gionis, and Michael Mathioudakis. 2016. Quantifying Controversy in Social Media. In *WSDM*. 33–42.
[4] Kiran Garimella, Gianmarco De Francisci Morales, Aristides Gionis, and Michael Mathioudakis. 2016. Quantifying Controversy in Social Media. *arXiv preprint arXiv:1507.05224* (2016).
[5] Kiran Garimella, Gianmarco De Francisci Morales, Aristides Gionis, and Michael Mathioudakis. 2017. The Ebb and Flow of Controversial Debates on Social Media. In *ICWSM*.
[6] Kiran Garimella, Gianmarco De Francisci Morales, Aristides Gionis, and Michael Mathioudakis. 2017. Reducing Controversy by Connecting Opposing Views. In *WSDM*. 81–90.
[7] Kiran Garimella and Ingmar Weber. 2017. A Long-Term Analysis of Polarization on Twitter. In *ICWSM*.
[8] R Kelly Garrett. 2009. Echo chambers online?: Politically motivated selective exposure among Internet news users. *Journal of Computer-Mediated Communication* 14, 2 (2009), 265–285.
[9] Eduardo Graells-Garrido, Mounia Lalmas, and Daniele Quercia. 2013. Data portraits: Connecting people of opposing views. *arXiv preprint arXiv:1311.4658* (2013).
[10] Eduardo Graells-Garrido, Mounia Lalmas, and Daniele Quercia. 2014. People of opposing views can share common interests. In *WWW Companion*. 281–282.
[11] Daniel J Isenberg. 1986. Group polarization: A critical review and meta-analysis. *Journal of personality and social psychology* (1986).
[12] George Karypis and Vipin Kumar. 1995. METIS - Unstructured Graph Partitioning and Sparse Matrix Ordering System. (1995).
[13] Q Vera Liao and Wai-Tat Fu. 2014. Can you hear me now?: mitigating the echo chamber effect by source position indicators. In *CSCW*. 184–196.
[14] Q Vera Liao and Wai-Tat Fu. 2014. Expert voices in echo chambers: effects of source expertise indicators on exposure to diverse opinions. In *CHI*. 2745–2754.
[15] Sean A Munson and others. 2013. Encouraging Reading of Diverse Political Viewpoints with a Browser Widget.. In *ICWSM*.
[16] Souneil Park and others. 2009. NewsCube: delivering multiple aspects of news to mitigate media bias. In *CHI*. 443–452.
[17] Vasyl Pihur and others. 2009. RankAggreg, an R package for weighted rank aggregation. *BMC bioinformatics* 10, 1 (2009), 1.
[18] Cass R Sunstein. 2009. *Republic. com 2.0.* Princeton University Press.
[19] VG Vydiswaran, ChengXiang Zhai, Dan Roth, and Peter Pirolli. 2015. Overcoming bias to learn about controversial topics. *JASIST* (2015).

InstaCan: Examining Deleted Content on Instagram

Ramine Tinati
Electronics and Computer Science
University of Southampton
United Kingdom, SO17 1BJ
r.tinati@soton.ac.uk

Aastha Madaan
Electronics and Computer Science
University of Southampton
United Kingdom, SO17 1BJ
a.madaan@soton.ac.uk

Wendy Hall
Electronics and Computer Science
University of Southampton
United Kingdom, SO17 1BJ
wh@soton.ac.uk

ABSTRACT

As the speed, volume, and heterogeneity of data produced on the Web increases, we are faced with developing more intelligent and efficient strategies for storing and archiving data. The archiving of Web data involves many technical, governance, and policy related challenges, however one of the most prominent and timely challenges that archivists face involves the deletion of data which from existing data stores; popularised by the various policy-related movements, such as the 'right to be forgotten'. For social media researchers, organisations, and analysis companies, it is a requirement for them to comply to the removal requests of the streams they consume. However, due to the nature of archiving, this is often difficult to comply to, without becoming a resource intensive exercise. In this paper we investigate deleted content on Instagram, the structure of the Instagram platform, and develop and evaluate a method to identify content which will becomes deleted. Our work contributes to the archiving community, and the Web Science community, interested in understanding the social factors that contribute the use of Social Media.

CCS CONCEPTS

•Information systems →Web and social media search; •Networks → World Wide Web (network structure); Social media networks; Online social networks; •Computing methodologies →Classification and regression trees; Bayesian network models; Feature selection; Support vector machines;

KEYWORDS

Micro-blogging, Social media, Twitter, Instagram, Photo-sharing, Deletion

1 INTRODUCTION

As the volume of data being produced by humans increases, we need ever more intelligent and efficient methods to manage it. This is particularly a problem for social Web platforms which are at the *end* of an increasing stream of heterogeneous human-generated data. Platforms such as Twitter, Facebook, and YouTube have to manage millions (if not billions) of text, images, videos, and links daily, which is both extremely resource intensive and time consuming [14]. Arguably, this has been a the key motivating factor for the development of cheaper and scalable 'Big Data' technology stacks such as Hadoop and *Apache Storm*.

To some extent, the process of archiving Social Web data is similar to existing archiving strategies. given that, for the majority of the time, the data produced ends up being stored and eventually archived for long term storage. However, unlike the archiving of more traditional records, such as newspaper archives, many Web archiving services are now faced with the requirement for users to be able to manage and delete their data when requested [14]. There have been several high profile cases where the concept of *right to be forgotten*[1]' has been exercised by individuals wanting their data to be removed. In order to comply with such requirements, several technical challenges arise, which are made particularly difficult if the data to be removed has already been archived, and no longer available in 'live' storage. Therefore, in practice, removing data after it has been archived is problematic, and in many cases, impractical. As a result, many archives which would provide Web Scientists with rich resources are not accessible due to worries of data privacy, or breaches to the terms and conditions of the service from where the data is being harvested from.

Motivated by the challenges of collecting data on the Web, we wish to address the ongoing challenge of managing data requests for archiving social media content. Our work focuses on the technical aspects involved in this highly socio-technical challenge. To address this, we explore how technical approaches can be used to improve the current, retrospective solutions. We examine the photo-sharing service Instagram, and seek to derive the characteristics of the user-generated content which eventually is deleted. Based on these features, we develop a model to predict the likelihood that user-generated content will be removed, and then consider how this approach can be combined into the archiving data pipeline in order to reduce the computational overheads. To the best of our knowledge, this is the first study to analyse the removal of content on the Instagram platform.

Summary of Contribution.

Our experiment is the first study on the removal of content on the Instagram platform. Using the Instagram API we collected posts during 2015 – 2016 containing a total of 572, 020 Instagram posts, which we subsequently enriched and labelled as posts deleted or present. After conducting an exploratory analysis of the data, we identified a number of features which distinguish deleted posts from those which remain present on the platform. Based on these features we were able to train a classifier in order to predict the likelihood that a post will be deleted, with a 62% accuracy (f1). Based on

WebSci '17, June 25–28, 2017, Troy, NY, USA.
© 2017 ACM. ISBN 978-1-4503-4896-6/17/06...$15.00
DOI: http://dx.doi.org/10.1145/3091478.3091516

[1] http://ec.europa.eu/justice/data-protection/files/factsheets/factsheet_data_protection_en.pdf

this work we consider some of the societal factors which contribute to why individuals delete content on social media platforms, and also describe how our system could be used to improve current archiving strategies in order to deal with the current and future requirements of platform owners and user deletion requests.

2 BACKGROUND

In this section we explore literature related to the Instagram platform, as well studies which have conducted experiments on developing models for predicting the deletion of content on social media platforms.

2.1 Photo-sharing platforms and Instagram

More than 90% of adults now have mobile phones most of which allow them to take photos and instantly share them on online social networks. Half of all Internet users (54%) share original photos and videos online, and an increasing number are using specific photo sharing applications - "apps" - such as Instagram and Snapchat [9].

Instagram, an online photo-sharing platform, has gained increasing popularity. It allows users to take photos, apply digital filters and share them with friends instantaneously by using mobile devices [7]. Instagram's 200 million users have shared over 20 billion photos since the applications creation in 2010 [9]. User studies have started to explore what type of content is being shared, categories of users, and the role of social features within a photo-based social network [5, 6]. Hirsch et al describes "staying connected/maintain relationships", followed by "ease of sharing", "seeing what others are up to", "showing others what I'm doing", and "sharing my events/experiences" as motivations for sharing photos on online social networking websites such as Facebook, Instagram, Twitter and Snapchat. Their study also that people often use photography for social purposes, and increasingly to communicate and build relationships [9]. However, as Jang et al. [2015] shows, the amount of social reciprocity (e.g. likes, comments) a user gains are not necessarily linked to their network size, which is an uncommon feature in large-scale social network.

2.2 Deleted Social Media Content

Whilst there is a growing body of literature that examines the role of Instagram as a social image sharing platform [7], [9], there are few studies which analyse the user deletion behaviour in the Instagram platform. In contrast to this, there are a several studies which have experimented on on-line social networking platforms such as Twitter. In order to determine if it is possible to model and predict what and when content will be deleted. In this section we describe these approaches and summarise their findings w.r.t prediction of deletion of tweets.

A large scale empirical study on characteristics of deleted and non-deleted tweets has been done by Almuhimedi et.al [1]. The analysis determines the reasons for tweet deletion to support users to better manage their content on on-line social networks. It analyses aggregate features of deleted tweets, if they are replies or re-tweets, clients used to produce them, temporal aspects of deletion, and the presence of geo-tagging information area used for predicting deleted tweets. The study is conducted over 1.6M deleted tweets collected from a week long window in March 2012 from a set of 292K Twitter users. Features such as clients used to post these tweets, their conversational aspects, sentiment vocabulary present in them, and the days of the week they were posted are key characteristics of deleted tweets. The temporal analysis by the study exhibit that the majority of the tweets were deleted within an hour of when they were posted, and most of them were either ones labelled as rephrasing or typos. Only 1% of the deleted tweets were Spam according to the Twitter spam categories. The study presents an in-depth understanding of the characteristics of deleted tweets but does not propose a method that can effectively predict tweets which may be deleted based on the identified features.

The work done by Petrovic et.al. is among the first studies for predicting deletion of tweets [11]. Their approach proposes to use feature such as a user's number of friends, followers, statuses, number of lists that include the user, is the user verified, if the tweet is a re-tweet, is the tweet a reply were considered. Along with these number of hashtags, mentions, and links in the tweet IDs and all words in a tweet were also considered [11]. Overall, the selection of featured failed to yield suitable results for predicting if tweets will be deleted. A more recent study by Potash et.al [12] also predicted whether a tweet will be deleted within a month using topic modelling (using LDA) and text embeddings (using word2vec). The study assumes that spam tweets are more likely to be deleted as compared to regrettable content. The main focus of the study is to reduce the feature set size and make the predictive model language independent. they created a feature set with 12 features to determine the spammed tweets, including tweet length, percent of tweet in upper case, percent of tweet in text that is non-alphanumeric, whether it has the 'followers' token or not and number of links specified in the tweet and percentage of the tweet which is links, number of user mentions and hashtags. The paper experiments with several algorithms (SVM, Naive Bayes, Bayes Net, Random Forest, and J48 classifiers), on sample datasets of varying sizes $10,000$ to $255,000$ tweets. Only 3% deleted tweets collected from Twitter stream in May 2015. Overall, Potash et al. managed to obtain a precision of 0.818 by using a hybrid classifier and set of features.

Bagdouri et.al also conducted an experiment to predict deleted tweets within 24 hours on the Arabic Twitter [2]. The experiment uses a mix of system and constructed features such as, and the results of analyses suggest that many of the prolific deleters are automated systems used for advertising, and such accounts maybe important for detecting spam these are important. The study shows that the tweet features are stronger predictors than the user features, with the tweet content having the greatest predictive power. The source of the tweet field indicating how the tweet was published (e.g., through a smart phone, using a third-party application, or from a desktop browser) is the second strongest tweet-based feature as most of the deleted tweets were published from the smartphones.

While the above approaches predicted the deletion of tweets by identifying an optimal feature set (tweet and social features), another recent work relates the prediction of deleted tweets with the user accounts and focuses largely on user account feature. According to Bhattacharya et.al. over 11% of tweets deleted by Twitter or users themselves [3]. The approach analyses the reason for tweet deletion and correlates it with features of tweet publishers. The given study performs data cleaning on a data-stream of about

250, 000 tweets over a duration of four weeks in October 2014 and then in August 2015. The majority of tweets were in English, and the account from which they were published had at least 10 followers and 10 friends. The analyses from the study show that users in the deleter set have significantly higher follower count and the median tweeting rate of users in the deleter set is nearly twice the tweeting rate of users in the non-deleter set. Also, when compared to non-deleted tweets, the percentage of deleted tweets that contain hashtags and URLs is nearly half which indicates that information content in deleted tweets is lower. Moreover, the study explains that conversational tweets are less likely to be deleted and that the deleted tweets contain higher fraction of swear words, and markers that indicate anger, anxiety, and sadness [3].

There has also been a line of work which identifies regrettable tweets from a set of deleted tweets by analysing user preferences (deletion patterns) and tweet content [13]. The study emphasises that correlation between user preferences and content of tweet can predict regrettable tweets more accurately. It considers ten prominent reasons for tweet deletion including negative sentiment, relationship, violence among others [13]. It is interesting to see emergent work on maintaining archives for deleted tweets to envisage transparency in governance and understand candidates contesting an election. This is critical as social media is fast becoming a virtual battlefield for candidates and a peak in their online activities is observed during the election time. One such archive is the Politwoops archive created by the Sunlight Foundation which stores the deleted tweets of candidates during a time-window that they are contesting elections [4]. It proposes to understand phenomena such as impression management, views on particular issues among others [8].

In light of the existing literature on deleted content on alternative social platforms such as Twitter, we draw upon the approaches used for feature selection and the use of specific classifiers in order to examine the production and deletion of content on Instagram.

3 EXPERIMENTAL SETUP

3.1 Data Collection

The data was collected using the Instagram API during December 2015, to March 2016. As the Instagram API does not have a public timeline like many social networking platforms (e.g. Twitter), we collected posts that were part of the 'recent posts' stream. For each post, we collected the posted time, the comment, the post/image URL. Due to limitations in the API, we were not able to capture if the post had comments or not. Also, for privacy and ethical reasons, we did not capture the Instagram username, or the image of the post.

In order to build our gold standard data (labelled), we subsequently performed a HTTP GET against each of the collected post URLs to determine if the post was still accessible; if the content has been deleted or removed, an empty HTML page is returned with a single text element: 'content not available'. This process was conducted during October 2016, which provided a 6-month gap between the original post being published.

Metric	Value
# of posts (total)	572,020
# of non-deleted posts	293,136
# of deleted posts	278,884
# of posts w/o comments	15,241
# of posts w/o hashtags	6,288
# of posts w/o mentions	570,611
Avg/mode/s.d comment length	25/9/52.3
Avg/mode/s.d comment tokens	5/2/9.2
Avg/mode/s.d hashtags	23/26/15.1
Avg/mode/s.d mentions	0.002/0/0.1
Avg/mode/s.d explicit words	0.36/0/0.5
Avg/mode/s.d explicit hashtags	0.35/0/0.6

Table 1: Instagram Dataset Overview

4 RESULTS AND DISCUSSION

4.1 Instagram Dataset Overview

In this section we provide a general descriptive overview of the collected dataset. Table 1 provides a selection of descriptive statistics of the data collected, and Figure 1 provides an temporal overview of the total and deleted posts. As described, nearly 50% of the posts captured during the time period were deleted, which in comparison to other social network platforms, is a significant proportion of the content posted. In Twitter, Potash et al. [12] found that less than 10% of the public timeline is deleted. However, it is not possible to know whether the removal of the posts is through manual (e.g. a user deleting the post), or automate process (e.g. a breach of Instagram's terms of service).

We found that in comparison to other social network platforms such as Twitter, the average length of a message (the comment) added with a post is far shorter, with a fairly wide distribution. With respects to the number of posts with hashtags, posts contained on average more hashtags compared to other social media platforms, yet, which as Hirsch et al. describes [9], may be related to the social practises embedded in posting images, and attracting followers. This is also reflected in the unusually low number of mentions found in comments (less than 1%), rather than functioning as a social network for social communication, the platform facilitates the ability to broadcast and advertise.

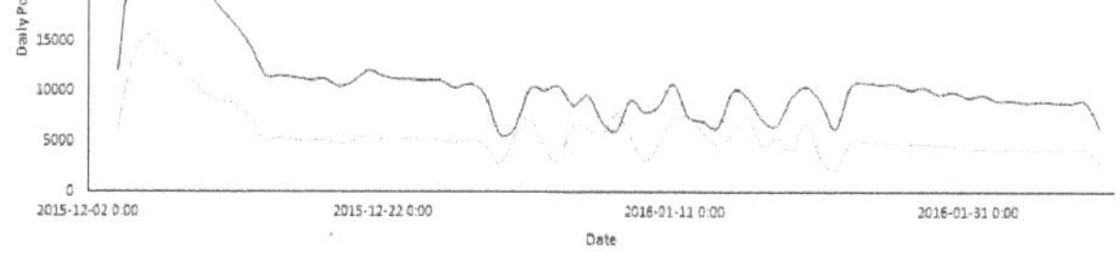

Figure 1: Temporal view of Posts (*solid*) and Deleted Posts (*dashed*) of the 572, 020 **collected Instagram posts.**

4.2 Predicting the deletion of Instagram Posts

Based on our analysis of the Instagram posts, we setup an experiment to determine if it is possible to use a set of features to predict the deletion of Instagram posts. We base our experiment on similar conditions as those used in studies of deleted Twitter posts; we select a range of linear-based classifiers, and experimented with various platform and synthetic features. In all experiments we perform 10-fold cross validation, and use an 80/20 training to validation dataset ratio.

Feature Selection. In order to construct the feature set, we considered the features identified in the related literature as mentioned in the previous section, as well as Instagram's social context and usage. As the related literature has shown, there is a strong tendency to tag a post with several hashtags as a means to attract the greatest audience to a given post, and comments typically convey the mood or feeling of the user, and the image which they are posting [9]. Consequently, our features were primarily based on a combination of properties from the comments, hashtags, and time of the post. Table 2 lists the features which we initially derived, and the final set of features used to train our classifiers. Also, based on existing work, we also calculated the sentiment of the comment, and the number of explicit terms within the comment and hashtags ('#' was removed in order to perform this check).

Feature	Description
Length of Comment	Total characters in comment
Words in Comment	Total words (tokens) in comment, excluding hashtags
Number of Hashtags	Number of unique hashtags in comment
Number of Mentions	Number of '@' mentions in comment
Number of URLs	Number of external URLs in a comment
Comment Sentiment*	Sentiment of Comment
Explicit Hashtags**	Number of explicit hashtags
Explicit Words**	Number of explicit words in comment
Time of Post	Time of post

Table 2: Model Features. *The pre-trained VADAR sentiment classifier was used to compute sentiment scores. **Based on Google's list of explicit search terms

4.3 Results

As shown in Table 3, we examined a number of classifiers across several samples of the total 572,020 posts. In all experiments, a 80/20 training-validation ration was maintained, and the features described in Table 2 we used. All classifiers managed to outperform the random baseline (random prediction if a post is or isn't deleted), and the size of the dataset impacted the ranking of the classifier in terms of overall performance (f1 score). Similar to Petrovic et al. [11], we noted that the use of an SVM is not practical for larger data sizes due to the quadratic complexity of, and on average took 2-orders of magnitude to compute compared to other approaches. We were also interested to see that the Passive Aggressive algorithm, which showed promising results in a similar experiment (including features) yielded less impressive results than expected. Overall, we managed to achieve an accuracy close to 60% for all classifiers used, which demonstrates similar performance to other experiments conducted on Twitter (e.g. Petrovic et al. [11], Potash et al. [12]).

In order to further explore the features used, and determine which are more suitable for predicting the deletion of a post, we performed a feature reduction exercise, and experimented with different combination of features. For this experiment, we used the Logistic Regression algorithm, given that it yielded the most accurate results when applied to the full dataset. The results shown in Table 4 contain the most significant combinations found, against the full feature set. As shown, we found that the length of the comment, or the number of words (tokens) in the post comment had the lowest impact in terms of overall accuracy, whereas features such as the number of explicit words or hashtags, as well as the number of hashtags impacted the accuracy of predicting the deletion of posts. Another feature which was expected to make an impact was the overall sentiment of the post's comment (as identified in Zhou et al.'s study [13]). However, this was not observed in our experiment, which may be due to the large variation in comment length (and purpose), compared to other social networks such as Twitter. We also experimented with constructing a synthetic feature based on the published time of the post (e.g. office hours, non-working hours), however we found that the time of day had very little significance on the accuracy of the results.

Metric	50k	100k	250k	550k	full
Random Baseline	*.48*	*.48*	*0.50*	*0.50*	*0.50*
Logistic Regression	0.57	0.57	**0.60**	**0.61**	**0.62**
Decision Trees	**0.58**	**0.58**	0.58	0.59	0.59
K-Nearest Neighbour	0.57	0.57	0.57	0.57	0.58
Passive Aggressive	0.55	0.55	0.56	0.56	0.58
Naive Bayes	0.52	0.55	0.56	0.56	0.56
Random Forest	0.52	0.52	0.55	0.55	0.55
SVM	0.53	0.54	0.56	0.57	0.58

Table 3: Comparison of classifiers against various dataset sample; f1 scores are shown.

Feature Combination	Precision	Recall	f1
All Features	*0.61*	*0.63*	*0.62*
w/o comment length/tokens	0.58	0.57	0.58
w/o sentiment feature	0.56	0.56	0.56
w/o explicit word/hashtag	0.55	0.53	0.54
w/o hashtags	0.53	0.52	0.53

Table 4: Feature Combinations. All experiments conducted on full dataset, with the LR classifier. All Precision, Recall and f1 scores represent the average score between the two 'deleted' and 'not deleted' classes.

4.4 Limitations

We wish to comment on several limitations in our study which we are aware may impact the results of our analysis. First, as with many social media studies, the sample of data collected is limited by the collection methods available (e.g. the API of the platform). thus without knowing the total population from which the data was sampled from (e.g. the total corpus of posts made during the start and end of the collection period), we are unable to comment on how representative the sample is. Consequently, knowing what demographic representation is contained within the sample is not possible. Second, we are aware that we are not able to determine how long before a post was deleted since its original publish date, or if the post was deleted by the user, or as automatic process (e.g. post not complying to Instagram's terms and conditions).

5 CONCLUDING REMARKS

Through our analysis and experiments, we have identified characteristics of Instagram that differ from other social media platforms, such as Twitter. Namely, we have seen a much higher proportion of posts being removed (automatically or manually), and the use of platform features such as comments, hashtags, and mentions are unlike non photo-based social networks. Comments tended to be much shorter in length, and the number of hashtags per comment tended to be much higher than hashtag/tagging based social networks such as Twitter. We also found the use of social connectivity features such as '@mentions' were used very infrequently, and in our dataset, less than 1% of posts contained mentions.

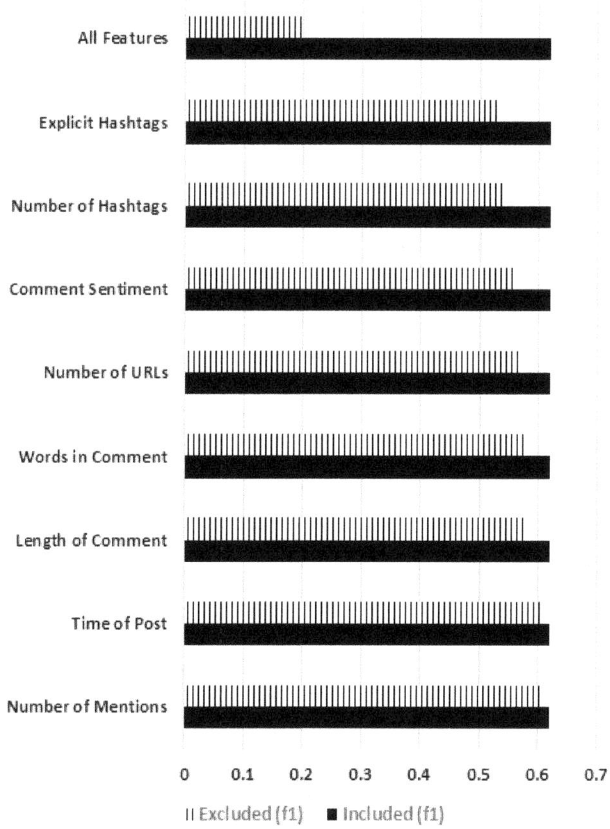

Figure 2: Most important features based on their impact on accuracy on the full Instagram dataset. f1 scores shown, computed using the LR classifier.

With respects to the task of extracting relevant features to help us predict the likeliness that a post would be deleted, we found that in comparison to other social networks such as Twitter textual features such as the length (words and total length) of a comment did not significantly affect the ability to classify deleted posts. This reinforces the initial observations made on the structure of the dataset collected, where comments varied greatly in length. Whilst these findings may seem intuitive given that Instagram is a photo-sharing social media platform, the use of comments and hashtags are the primary way for other users to search and discover content.

Beyond the features used within our experiments, there are several improvements we believe could be made in order to improve the current accuracy achieved. Similar to studies on other social media platforms, including user-specific features, such as friends'/follower counts, post counts, in combination with social features such as comments and likes may improve the accuracy achieved. Another important aspect which we did not cover in our experiment is the use of the actual images for improving the classification and prediction of different user posts. There are a number of ethical and legal issues that need to be considered if the users posted picture itself was to be used a feature, however, we believe that this would yield more accurate results with relation to knowing if a post will be deleted, based on the more recent work conducted on regrettable content on social media platforms [13].

Finally, addressing the original motivation of managing an archive of Web data, we consider how the methods developed in this paper could become part of a complex system where a user's rights and a platforms conditions are upheld. If we were to conceptualise the entire collection-to-archiving process as a pipeline of activity, once content has been transferred from the 'temporary' store and entered the arching stage, it becomes computationally expensive to retrospectively delete a given piece of information. This is because once archived, usually no indexes are made, and retrieving the correct file would require the extraction of a large corpus, re-indexing, and then searching. However, if one was to integrate a prediction mechanism as a component in the system, it would potentially reduce the computational overheads required, by not immediately archiving the posts which could be potentially deleted.

We see several lines of future work from this study, including the development of the features in order to increase the accuracy of the classifiers, and the potential for exploring Pal et al.'s recent work on Localised Topic Authorities [10] as a means to pre-cluster Instagram users. Furthermore, to better understand how and why certain features are more efficient than others, a critical and sociological examination of Instagram's social practises would be essential.

ACKNOWLEDGEMENT

This work is supported under SOCIAM: The Theory and Practice of Social Machines, funded by the UK EPSRC under grant EP/J017728/2.

REFERENCES

[1] Hazim Almuhimedi, Shomir Wilson, Bin Liu, Norman Sadeh, and Alessandro Acquisti. 2013. Tweets Are Forever: A Large-scale Quantitative Analysis of Deleted Tweets. In *Proceedings of the 2013 Conference on Computer Supported Cooperative Work (CSCW '13)*. ACM, New York, NY, USA, 897–908. https://doi.org/10.1145/2441776.2441878

[2] Mossaab Bagdouri and Douglas W. Oard. 2015. On Predicting Deletions of Microblog Posts. In *Proceedings of the 24th ACM International on Conference on Information and Knowledge Management (CIKM '15)*. ACM, New York, NY, USA, 1707–1710. https://doi.org/10.1145/2806416.2806600

[3] Parantapa Bhattacharya and Niloy Ganguly. 2016. Characterizing Deleted Tweets and Their Authors. In *Proceedings of the 10th International AAAI Conference on Web and Social Media*. AAAI Publications, 547–550.

[4] Open State Foundation. 2012. Politwoops. https://politwoops.com/countries. (2012).

[5] Yuheng Hu, Lydia Manikonda, Subbarao Kambhampati, et al. 2014. What We Instagram: A First Analysis of Instagram Photo Content and User Types.. In *ICWSM*. AAAI Publications, 595–598.

[6] Jin Yea Jang, Kyungsik Han, and Dongwon Lee. 2015. No Reciprocity in "Liking" Photos: Analyzing Like Activities in Instagram. In *Proceedings of the 26th ACM Conference on Hypertext & Social Media (HT '15)*. ACM, New York, NY, USA, 273–282. https://doi.org/10.1145/2700171.2791043

[7] Xutao Li, Tuan-Anh Nguyen Pham, Gao Cong, Quan Yuan, Xiao-Li Li, and Shonali Krishnaswamy. 2015. Where You Instagram?: Associating Your Instagram Photos with Points of Interest. In *Proceedings of the 24th ACM International on Conference on Information and Knowledge Management (CIKM '15)*. ACM, New York, NY, USA, 1231–1240. https://doi.org/10.1145/2806416.2806463

[8] Lindsey Meeks. 0. Tweeted, deleted: theoretical, methodological, and ethical considerations for examining politiciansfi deleted tweets. *Information, Communication & Society* 0, 0 (0), 1–13. https://doi.org/10.1080/1369118X.2016.1257041

[9] Anne Oeldorf-Hirsch and S. Shyam Sundar. 2016. Social and Technological Motivations for Online Photo Sharing. *Journal of Broadcasting & Electronic Media* 60, 4 (2016), 624–642. https://doi.org/10.1080/08838151.2016.1234478

[10] Aditya Pal, Amaç Herdagdelen, Sourav Chatterji, Sumit Taank, and Deepayan Chakrabarti. 2016. Discovery of Topical Authorities in Instagram. In *Proceedings of the 25th International Conference on World Wide Web (WWW '16)*. International World Wide Web Conferences Steering Committee, Republic and Canton of Geneva, Switzerland, 1203–1213. https://doi.org/10.1145/2872427.2883078

[11] Sasa Petrovic, Miles Osborne, and Victor Lavrenko. 2013. I Wish I Didn't Say That! Analyzing and Predicting Deleted Messages in Twitter. *CoRR* abs/1305.3107 (2013). http://arxiv.org/abs/1305.3107

[12] Peter J. Potash, Eric B. Bell, and Joshua J. Harrison. 2016. *Using Topic Modeling and Text Embeddings to Predict Deleted Tweets*. Association for the Advancement of Artificial Intelligence, PALO ALTO, CA, United States(US).

[13] Lu Zhou, Wenbo Wang, and Keke Chen. 2016. Tweet Properly: Analyzing Deleted Tweets to Understand and Identify Regrettable Ones. In *Proceedings of the 25th International Conference on World Wide Web (WWW '16)*. International World Wide Web Conferences Steering Committee, Republic and Canton of Geneva, Switzerland, 603–612. https://doi.org/10.1145/2872427.2883052

[14] Michael Zimmer. 2015. The Twitter Archive at the Library of Congress: Challenges for information practice and information policy. *First Monday* 20, 7 (2015). http://journals.uic.edu/ojs/index.php/fm/article/view/5619

Web Science Challenges in Researching Bug Bounties

Huw Fryer
University of Southampton
University Road
Southampton SO17 1BJ
hf1g10@ecs.soton.ac.uk

Elena Simperl
University of Southampton
University Road
Southampton SO17 1BJ
e.simperl@soton.ac.uk

ABSTRACT

The act of searching for security flaws (vulnerabilities) in a piece of software was previously considered to be the preserve of malicious actors, or at least actors who wished to cause chaos. Increasingly, however, companies are recognising the value of running a bug bounty program, where they will pay 'white hat' hackers to locate and disclose security flaws in their applications in order that they can fix it. This is known as a 'bug bounty' or a 'vulnerability reward program', and at present has seen comparatively little research. This paper introduces two existing research on bug bounties in two areas: as a means of regulating the sale of vulnerabilities; and as a form of crowdsourcing. We argue that the nature of bug bounties makes Web science particularly suitable to drive forward research. We identify gaps in the current literature, and propose areas which we consider to be particularly promising for future research.

CCS CONCEPTS

• **Information systems → Crowdsourcing**; • **Security and privacy → Social aspects of security and privacy**;

KEYWORDS

Crowdsourcing; Vulnerability research; Bug bounties

1 INTRODUCTION

A 'bug bounty' or 'vulnerability reward program' (VRP) is the process for rewarding the discovery of a flaw or vulnerability in a piece of software. The concept has been around for a long time, notably Donald Knuth offering rewards for omissions in his *The Art of Programming* books, or flaws in his LaTeXsoftware, and in the 1990s Netscape offered a reward for flaws in its browser. Despite this history, examples of its application have been sparse up until the last few years where its popularity has increased, as this decade high profile programs from companies such as Mozilla and Google[26], and even the US Department of Defense in 2016 have started. There now exist services which act as middlemen in connecting companies with people who are prepared to search their systems for weaknesses.

This paper will provide a brief review of some of the key research into bug bounties. For the most part, this has been tangential, merely acknowledging their existence, as a part of overall Web or application security. Nevertheless, there has been more recent research which has considered bug bounties in their own right, analysing the behaviour of the participants, or the means in which a company operating a bug bounty might seek to optimise the quality of the results of their bug bounty. We will identify the gaps in the literature, and identify areas where crowdsourcing and Web Science research can assist in driving research forward in this area.

In Section 2, we introduce some terminology, and background research, before describing our literature review in Section 3. We then present opportunities for future research in Section 4 based on crowdsourcing literature, and discuss the suitability of this research area for Web Science. We conclude with a summary of our paper, and our recommendations.

WebSci'17, June 25-28, 2017, Troy, NY, USA.
© 2017 ACM. 978-1-4503-4896-6/17/06...$15.00
DOI: http://dx.doi.org/10.1145/3091478.3091517

2 TERMINOLOGY AND BACKGROUND

Within software engineering, a 'bug' can have the meaning of any flaw in the application. However, the term 'bug bounty' as it is generally used is the sort of program where members of a crowd will locate security flaws in a Web application or piece of software. These flaws will be reported responsibly to the vendor of the software or the administrator of the Web application so that they may be fixed. A security flaw is commonly known as a 'vulnerability', a weakness which could be the subject of an 'exploit' - something a malicious actor could use to gain some form of unauthorised access to a system. Usually a seller of a vulnerability will be required to show a potential buyer that an exploit exists [27], otherwise a vulnerability is merely theoretical and of no practical danger to the application in question. Vulnerabilities are distinguished by their level of severity and ease of exploitation, with the most severe allowing total control of a system running the software.

The reason security flaws should arguably be discovered in the first place, is that a black market for these vulnerabilities already exists. A hacker who discovers a flaw may be less inclined to inform the victims, but instead choose to sell it to a criminal who would use it to make a profit[14]. The criminal market has reportedly relied upon specialisation of tasks, including one task being to locate security flaws in popular software or websites and selling them to others who may be better positioned to monetise the information or access gleaned in some other way. There is reportedly a complex, sophisticated black market where different actors specialise in different areas, so the person who makes money out of illicit access to a system will likely be an entirely different person.

Additionally, state actors may wish to acquire vulnerabilities. The ability to exploit a particular system is regarded as valuable to nation states for a variety of reasons - whether to spy on each other; their citizens; or to have a means of retaliation following an attack from another state. A nation state has resources way in advance of almost all other actors and are therefore in a position to offer a considerably higher sum should an individual wish to sell them. A discussion of the government role in vulnerability disclosure is beyond the scope of this paper, but see [34] for more details about this area.

Given that malicious actors are selling vulnerabilities, how should the defenders respond? There is conflicting opinion in the literature about whether searching for vulnerabilities constitutes a social good. On the one hand, Rescorla argues that the probability of a defender finding the same vulnerability before a malicious actor is incredibly small[31], whereas Ozment pointed to a depletion in the amount of reported vulnerabilities in FreeBSD as being an indication that searching for bugs made it more difficult for adversaries to do the same[29]. Miller reported a personal experience in 2007 of an attempt to sell an exploit in Microsoft Powerpoint (before bug bounties were generally used) where the flaw was discovered and patched before an agreement was reached as to the price[27].

Amongst Miller's other points, was the difficulty that a security researcher had in selling a flaw once they had located it [27]. Even were they able to find a buyer, they would have no way of knowing the value which a purchaser would place on it, and being able to prove the effectiveness of the vulnerability without giving away the value of their discovery was also a non-trivial solution. Bug bounties alleviate these difficulties: the price is specified up front, the researcher is aware what kind of vulnerabilities would be in scope, and services which manage bug bounties can act as a trusted third party to ensure they get paid.

This is not to say that bug bounties are the only solution as a means of regulating this. From an economic point of view, the concept of vulnerability markets in general has received some scrutiny in the literature [5, 27, 28, 30]. Böhme identified a typology of different possible means of regulating vulnerability markets, concluding that bug bounties were not the best possible option, having weakness in relation to their efficiency[5]. As an example of an alternative format, there are also competitions related to security flaws, notably 'pwn2own' which occurs at the CanSecWest security conference[1].

3 BUG BOUNTIES

3.1 Methodology

Despite the increasing popularity of bug bounties [6], and their seeming relationship with crowdsourcing, we were unaware of any work which considered bug bounties within the context of crowdsourcing. The one exception to this was Su & Pan, who proposed a system to introduce microtasking to the process, where additional actors would test and verify the vulnerability submitted by another researcher [36].

As a result, we conducted a literature review, based on the methodology of Mao et al's review of the related area of crowdsourced software engineering [24]. The search was for the phrases "bug bount(y|ies)", "vulnerability reward program", "vulnerability disclosure", in any available field in seven online search engines: ACM Digital Library, IEEE Digital Library, Springerlink Online Library, Wiley Online Library, Elsevier ScienceDirect, ProQuest, and Google Scholar. As a fallback, we additionally used snowballing of references where further titles were identified. To identify relevant literature, the title, abstract and introduction sections of each paper were read, which was usually enough to identify it as being outside the criteria for inclusion. Where this was not the case, the whole paper was read.

As an exploratory study, our research question was: what are the gaps in the existing literature related to bug bounties, which can be addressed by crowdsourcing? As a result, the inclusion criteria for the literature review was that the paper in question was about bug bounties specifically, or contained analysis of a bug bounty program, platform, or behaviour of the workers in a program. Literature was excluded where it merely mentioned the existence of bug bounties, or it focused on vulnerability management more generally. In future work, it is intended that this inclusion criteria be widened, because these are all relevant with regards to policy implications, as well as assessing cost-effectiveness for starting a bug bounty.

In conducting this search, a total of 11 papers were discovered which were primarily about bug bounties. This includes a paper which is unpublished[40], and also non-academic work by Bugcrowd[6].

Having established the literature, we make use of established crowdsourcing literature as a means of solving the overall research question. We do not attempt to conduct a survey of crowdsourcing literature, since it is beyond the scope of this research and existing works have conducted surveys of crowdsourcing generally[9], and within software engineering in particular[24]. We contend that according to Estellés-Arolas criteria[12], considering a bug bounty program as crowdsourcing is valid. There is a defined crowd (security researchers) with a clear goal (locate vulnerabilities) and a defined benefit for both the worker and (clearly defined) requester. It is an online process to solve a problem, which uses the Internet, and has some degree of open call. Many calls will have restrictions imposed by the platform based on the reputation of the researcher, particularly in regards to signal to noise ratio yet many will have a completely open call subject only to self-selection by those considering themselves to have enough skill.

Despite this, as a format it is quite different to most crowdsourced programs. The nature of bug bounties is that it accepts all valid unique submissions, provided they are within the scope of the call. Consensus is generally not required, making it differ from many HIT tasks such as image tagging. Competition or innovation crowdsourcing calls will generally accept only one, or a handful of submissions which best solve the problem[8].

3.2 Literature

Whatever reservations there may be about ethics, efficiency or cost effectiveness, and with initial scepticism from major players[13], bug bounties have been embraced by many of the major technology companies as well as gaining support in other industries[6]. Some research about the participants in the programs has started, as well as means of getting around some of the difficulties with running a bug bounty program.

As indicated by [27], prior to the introduction of a formal mechanism for buying and selling bugs through bug bounties, obtaining a seller was challenging. Two reports by Ring illustrated this

[1] See http://blog.trendmicro.com/pwn2own-returns-for-2017-to-celebrate-10-years-of-exploits

in further detail, discussing the competing opinion of whether companies should offer bounties to vulnerability research - and additionally of some companies prosecuting those discovering vulnerabilities[32, 33]. Kuehn & Mueller[16, 17] consider the changing dynamics in information security towards bug bounties being considered a norm. After case studies on Microsoft & Facebook's bug bounty they conclude that bug bounty programs exist as a way of reducing uncertainty when exchanging an information good as a reason for their development.

There are currently two major operators who have had mention made in the literature who facilitate bug bounties: Bugcrowd[2], and Hackerone[3], although other websites offer a list of other Web applications offering a bounty. Bugcrowd now publish an annual report on current trends in the bug bounty area, the most recent being in 2016[6]. Previously, Wooyun offered a forum for researchers to disclose bugs, and had a more coercive model - the Web applications in question were given a certain period of time to fix the flaws, before the flaw was made public. However, the website has been out of action since July 2016 when the founder Fang Xiaodun was reportedly arrested[22]. As of March 2017, the website still displays a message indicating that it is not operational[4].

Two of the older bounty programs, those of Mozilla and Google for their Web browsers Firefox and Chrome respectively were studied in 2013 [26]. Both were found to be better value for the company than hiring a security researcher on a permanent basis when considering the severe security flaws they discovered relative to the cost. They found Google's bug bounty program gleaned more vulnerabilities for a comparable amount of money, which they suggested was due to the tiered reward system they operated compared to Mozilla's flat fee.

In two separate papers, Zhao analysed the behaviour of white hats on the Wooyun[38] and Hackerone[39] platforms. In both platforms they observed the behaviour of white hats in the different systems. In [38], it was observed that the distribution of effort followed a power law, similar to that observed Lotka about academic publication frequency and supporting observations by[26], with a maximum of 291 submissions and an overall average of 4.8. Analysis of both revealed that when divided into categories of productivity each group reported a comparable amount of vulnerabilities, in addition to the severity of the vulnerability and the ranking of the website.

Maillart et al. focus more on the misaligned incentives involved between the companies running a bug bounty program and the researchers themselves[23]. The interest of the company is to exhaust the amount of flaws to a residual level, whereas the interest of the researcher is the cumulative payoff they will gain from discovering bugs. This is best served for the researchers by diversifying their efforts across different programs, since there will be bugs to discover which are easier to locate, and there should be less competition. Analysing 35 programs on Hackerone, they follow [38, 39] and observe a *windfall* effect within a few weeks of the start of the program, after which the amount of reports reduce significantly in quantity. They attribute this to timing effects, where researchers switch to a new program, or possibly stockpile vulnerabilities in advance of the program opening.

These papers regard the interest of a company running a bug bounty that they should seek to encourage as many researchers as possible, in the hope of finding flaws. The diversification meaning that, the higher proportion of white hats, the higher the probability that any flaw discovered is by a white hat rather than an attacker. This is supported by is supported by [10], however they also discovered a positive correlation ($r = 0.3591$, $p = 0.0307$) between the amount of accurate reports, and the amount of false positives. This indicates some tension here in regards to the costs of obtaining too many results of low quality.

Laszka et al use economic modeling to analyse various models employed by Hackerone to mitigate this and hopefully ensure a higher quality of submission[18]. They found that policies such as restricting access to those of high reputation, or rate-limiting submissions could be effective, although care needed to be taken in implementing them otherwise the overall utility would go down. Zhao et al expanded on this, although this work does not yet appear to have been published[40].

4 BUG BOUNTY RESEARCH CHALLENGES

From the existing literature on bug bounties and related research themes in crowdsourcing, we identified four key areas which we argue should drive forward the research agenda in relation to bug bounties. This section takes issues identified in the bug bounty literature, and considers it in the context of the wider crowdsourcing literature.

4.1 Incentives and Budget

Bugcrowd have a set of recommendations for new programs given the 'maturity' of their security processes, and the severity of the flaws to be identified. Based on three years of their data, for a new company they recommend paying between $100 and $1,500, with an average of $300[7]. However, this is still a young industry, and Bugcrowd do not publish their methodology for deciding on their prices. The more general research on incentives can play a role here. In particular, to identify the extent to which bug bounty researchers are motivated by purely financial means. Previous research on open source projects identified a multitude of different motivations amongst participants, and more recent research into crowdsourcing microtasks revealed diverse motivations, such as the owner of the call, and the end result of the research.

Whilst existing work has identified possible models for setting a price, or explaining behaviour researchers, these are theoretical models, and make assumptions such as the fact that the researcher is motivated by ensuring the maximum cumulative payoff [18, 23]. There is evidence to suggest that this may be true for a lot of cases. Algarni conducted attempted to contact top discoverers to identify their motivations finding them to be largely financial (although with a small sample)[2]. Additionally, there has been discussion in the security community prior to the popularity of bug bounties about researchers not reporting vulnerabilities for free [32, 33]. However [39] observed that of the 33 public programs without a monetary reward there were 1201 valid reports from the community.

[2] https://bugcrowd.com/
[3] https://www.hackerone.com/
[4] http://wooyun.org/ Last accessed 15 March 2017

Wooyun also offered no reward for disclosure of vulnerabilities[38], suggesting other motivations at play.

That said, a company with the means to offer higher rewards is at a competitive advantage over others, and more likely to have their tasks completed. With bug bounties in particular, the nature of the task and expertise required, means the highest price could be significant. Increasing the amount of money offered to a worker can lead to an increase in participation[11], although this can also lead to an increase in spammers. More generally, there is some danger that the higher incentives do not necessarily improve the quality of submissions as workers can regard their work as being worth more so do not take correspondingly more care[25].

Whatever value a company sets the incentives at, there is an additional overhead in any crowdsourcing program. Simperl observed that having a large crowd can lead to overhead in terms of processing the submissions, as illustrated by the cases of both Google and Netflix[35]. In the case of bug bounties, a company additionally needs to allocate resources to validate and prioritise the vulnerabilities, as well as implement fixes for valid submissions which an attacker might not even find in any event[31]. The question then arises, how best to optimise a budget for a bug bounty program, or if it is even financially worthwhile at all. The results presented in [26] suggest that bug bounties might be cost effective, at least for two major technology companies, yet the additional overheads and potentially high cost of labour suggest that smaller companies might have different experiences.

4.2 Task Decomposition

The selection of tasks is important in many crowdsourcing applications, in order to ensure that the overall goal is achieved with the minimum of overhead. This is frequently done in a way comparable to the MapReduce programming paradigm, with its advantages for parallelism, and a reduction in the requirements for prior skill of the workers. It is possible to do these in a 'microtask' scenario, but with a 'macrotask' it is not possible to break down the tasks into anything smaller[8, 35], requiring a different set of criteria for consideration. Areas such as validation of reports represent an obvious area where a bug bounty could include additional tasks[36], which are more akin to microtask crowdsourcing where a consensus would be desirable. However, there are obvious security risks with this, so great care would be required before any practical implementation.

Task decomposition is an open problem in software engineering crowdsourcing [24], though there has been some effort in the area. LaToza et al. considered the idea of a software development process where it is possible to introduce microtasking [20, 21], and built a microtasking IDE (integrated development environment) based on that. Though they had some success, they noticed an additional overhead compared to traditional software engineering[19]. Adriano also have a draft proof of concept paper on whether bugs can be discovered in small sections of code, and are planning future work on more complex code[1].

4.3 Quality of Submissions

Obtaining the highest possible amount of submissions, whilst minimising noise and associated costs with running a vulnerability program is also an issue. In particular, for smaller companies this represents a problem. They may not have the resources to pay the high costs for bounties or to manage the high volume of invalid responses, and as such may lose out on the benefits of utilising the crowd. This has already received some attention in researching bug bounties, with Laszka et al providing an economic model [18].

In crowdsourcing research, ensuring quality of submissions has received considerable scrutiny in the literature with many different systems proposed. Bernstein et al. introduced the *Find - Fix - Verify* model, where the task is divided into subtasks in which the location, fixing and verifying are split between different workers[4]. Alternatively, the aggregation of different answers can be used to determine the accuracy based on a different criterion such as a simple majority vote. More refined models include basing the decision on the expertise of the worker, and then iteratively adjusting it based on the continued accuracy of submissions, e.g., Whitehill[37].

The work described earlier by Su & Pan about adding falls into this category specifically relating to bug bounties of adding a microtask for verification[36]. This could additionally be considered as part of task decomposition, but it is better to consider it here, since it is an additional task rather than decomposing the vulnerability discovery.

However, the poor quality of submission for any task can potentially be made up for by the increased diversity. Edmunson et al ran an interesting study where they presented participants with a codebase with known vulnerabilities in, and asked to provide a security review[10]. They discovered that, whatever the experience of the individual researcher, none found all the vulnerabilities, but any randomly selected group of 15 participants had a 95% chance of discovering all seven known vulnerabilities, demonstrating the value of diversification of expertise.

4.4 Relevance to Web Science

As a more general research challenge, we call upon the Web Science community to invest in research in this area since Web Science is particularly suited to it. As an exploratory study, we only scratched the surface of bug bounties as a research area in relation to crowdsourcing, but we additionally consider wider challenges identified in this area. Halford et al. argue that Web Science has never been just about researching wires and protocols, but additionally considers the Web as being a constantly adapting organism which is a product of the people who use it[15]. Web security is a significant cost to society from both preventative and reactive measures[3], and as such is a key element of researching on the Web.

As vulnerability management, disclosure, and mitigation have matured, the effect on the practices of people developing software for the Web, as well as general Web users is something which is worth researching[16]. Much of the work on vulnerability markets has been theoretical, now there is the opportunity to analyse the effect it is having. Similarly, in addition to work carried out by [29, 31] whether these vulnerability markets have caused a depletion of vulnerabilities in Web applications. Beyond the effects of markets, the distortions and ethics of selling to governments is also an important area to consider, in particular where that relates to national security.

5 CONCLUSIONS AND FUTURE WORK

In this paper, we presented an exploratory study into bug bounties as a concept and argued it should be of interest to those working in Web Science in general, and crowdsourcing in particular. It represents an area which has seen comparatively little research, and yet would benefit significantly from a Web science approach. We conducted a literature review, and identified a small corpus of papers, using them to identify promising research areas for the future mapped with crowdsourcing literature. As an extension to this work, we intend to expand the scope of our review into bug bounties, and how they relate to vulnerability markets; ethics; and regulation. In addition, we intend to concentrate more fully on the different dynamics between microtask based crowdsourcing and bug bounty research.

REFERENCES

[1] Christian Medeiros Adriano and Andre van der Hoek. 2016. Exploring Microtask Crowdsourcing as a Means of Fault Localization. *arXiv preprint arXiv:1612.03015* (2016). https://arxiv.org/abs/1612.03015

[2] Abdullah M. Algarni and Yashwant K. Malaiya. 2013. Most Successful Vulnerability Discoverers: Motivation and Methods. In *Proceedings of the International Conference on Security and Management (SAM)*. 1.

[3] Ross Anderson, Chris Barton, Rainer Böhme, Richard Clayton, Michel JG Van Eeten, Michael Levi, Tyler Moore, and Stefan Savage. 2013. Measuring the cost of cybercrime. In *The economics of information security and privacy*. Springer, 265–300.

[4] Michael S. Bernstein, Greg Little, Robert C. Miller, BjÃűrn Hartmann, Mark S. Ackerman, David R. Karger, David Crowell, and Katrina Panovich. 2015. Soylent: A Word Processor with a Crowd Inside. *Commun. ACM* 58, 8 (July 2015), 85–94.

[5] Rainer Böhme. 2006. A comparison of market approaches to software vulnerability disclosure. In *Emerging trends in information and communication security*. Springer, 298–311. http://link.springer.com/chapter/10.1007/11766155_21

[6] Bugcrowd. 2016. The State of Bug Bounty. (June 2016).

[7] Bugcrowd. 2017. Defensive Vulnerability Pricing Model. (2017). https://pages.bugcrowd.com/whats-a-bug-worth

[8] Thierry Burger-Helmchen and Julien Pénin. 2010. The limits of crowdsourcing inventive activities: What do transaction cost theory and the evolutionary theories of the firm teach us. In *Workshop on Open Source Innovation, Strasbourg, France*. 1–26.

[9] A. I. Chittilappilly, L. Chen, and S. Amer-Yahia. 2016. A Survey of General-Purpose Crowdsourcing Techniques. *IEEE Transactions on Knowledge and Data Engineering* 28, 9 (Sept. 2016), 2246–2266.

[10] Anne Edmundson, Brian Holtkamp, Emanuel Rivera, Matthew Finifter, Adrian Mettler, and David Wagner. 2013. An Empirical Study on the Effectiveness of Security Code Review. In *Engineering Secure Software and Systems*. Springer, Berlin, Heidelberg, 197–212.

[11] Carsten Eickhoff and Arjen de Vries. 2011. How crowdsourcable is your task. In *Proceedings of the workshop on crowdsourcing for search and data mining (CSDM)*. 11–14.

[12] Enrique Estellés-Arolas and Fernando González-Ladrón-De-Guevara. 2012. Towards an integrated crowdsourcing definition. *Journal of Information science* 38, 2 (2012), 189–200.

[13] Dennis Fisher. 2010. Microsoft Says No to Paying Bug Bounties. (July 2010). https://threatpost.com/microsoft-says-no-paying-bug-bounties-072210/74249/

[14] Chris Grier, Lucas Ballard, Juan Caballero, Neha Chachra, Christian J Dietrich, Kirill Levchenko, Panayiotis Mavrommatis, Damon McCoy, Antonio Nappa, Andreas Pitsillidis, and others. 2012. Manufacturing compromise: the emergence of exploit-as-a-service. In *Proceedings of the 2012 ACM conference on Computer and communications security*. ACM, 821–832.

[15] Susan Halford, Catherine Pope, and Leslie Carr. 2010. A manifesto for Web Science. *Journal of Web Science* (2010).

[16] Andreas Kuehn and Milton Mueller. 2014. Analyzing bug bounty programs: An institutional perspective on the economics of software vulnerabilities. In *TPRC Research Conference on Communication, Information and Internet Policy*.

[17] Andreas Kuehn and Milton Mueller. 2014. Shifts in the Cybersecurity Paradigm: Zero-Day Exploits, Discourse, and Emerging Institutions. In *Proceedings of the 2014 New Security Paradigms Workshop (NSPW '14)*. ACM, New York, NY, USA, 63–68. DOI:http://dx.doi.org/10.1145/2683467.2683473

[18] Aron Laszka, Mingyi Zhao, and Jens Grossklags. 2016. Banishing misaligned incentives for validating reports in bug-bounty platforms. In *European Symposium on Research in Computer Security*. Springer, 161–178. http://link.springer.com/chapter/10.1007/978-3-319-45741-3_9

[19] Thomas D. LaToza, W. Ben Towne, Christian M. Adriano, and AndrÃľ van der Hoek. 2014. Microtask Programming: Building Software with a Crowd. In *Proceedings of the 27th Annual ACM Symposium on User Interface Software and Technology (UIST '14)*. ACM, New York, NY, USA, 43–54. DOI:http://dx.doi.org/10.1145/2642918.2647349

[20] Thomas D LaToza, W Ben Towne, André Van Der Hoek, and James D Herbsleb. 2013. Crowd development. In *Cooperative and Human Aspects of Software Engineering (CHASE), 2013 6th International Workshop on*. IEEE, 85–88.

[21] Thomas D LaToza and André Van Der Hoek. 2015. A vision of crowd development. In *Software Engineering (ICSE), 2015 IEEE/ACM 37th IEEE International Conference on*, Vol. 2. IEEE, 563–566.

[22] Gene Lin. 2016. Founder of China's largest 'ethical hacking' community arrested. (July 2016). https://www.hongkongfp.com/2016/07/30/founder-chinas-largest-ethical-hacking-community-arrested/

[23] T Maillart, M Zhao, J Grossklags, and J Chuang. 2016. Given enough eyeballs, all bugs are shallow? Revisiting Eric Raymond with bug bounty markets. (2016).

[24] Ke Mao, Licia Capra, Mark Harman, and Yue Jia. 2016. A survey of the use of crowdsourcing in software engineering. *Journal of Systems and Software* (Sept. 2016).

[25] Winter Mason and Duncan J Watts. 2010. Financial incentives and the performance of crowds. *ACM SigKDD Explorations Newsletter* 11, 2 (2010), 100–108.

[26] Matthew Finifter, Devdatta Akhawe, and David Wagner. 2013. An Empirical Study of Vulnerability Rewards Programs. In *Proceedings of the 22nd USENIX Security Symposium*. USENIX Association, Washington DC, 273–288.

[27] Charlie Miller. 2007. The legitimate vulnerability market: Inside the secretive world of 0-day exploit sales. In *In Sixth Workshop on the Economics of Information Security*.

[28] Andy Ozment. 2004. Bug auctions: Vulnerability markets reconsidered. In *Third Workshop on the Economics of Information Security*. 19–26.

[29] Andy Ozment. 2005. The Likelihood of Vulnerability Rediscovery and the Social Utility of Vulnerability Hunting.. In *WEIS*. Citeseer. http://citeseerx.ist.psu.edu/viewdoc/download?doi=10.1.1.479.7888&rep=rep1&type=pdf

[30] Sam Ransbotham, Sabyasachi Mitra, and Jon Ramsey. 2008. Are markets for vulnerabilities effective? *ICIS 2008 Proceedings* (2008), 24.

[31] E. Rescorla. 2005. Is finding security holes a good idea? *IEEE Security Privacy* 3, 1 (Jan. 2005), 14–19. DOI:http://dx.doi.org/10.1109/MSP.2005.17

[32] Tim Ring. 2014. Why bug hunters are coming in from the wild. *Computer Fraud & Security* 2014, 2 (Feb. 2014), 16–20.

[33] Tim Ring. 2015. White hats versus vendors: the fight goes on. *Computer Fraud & Security* 2015, 10 (Oct. 2015), 12–17.

[34] Ari Schwartz and Rob Knake. 2016. *Government's Role in Vulnerability Disclosure: Creating a Permanent and Accountable Vulnerability Equities Process*. Technical Report. Discussion Paper 2016-04, Cyber Security Project, Belfer Center for Science and International Affairs, Harvard Kennedy School.

[35] Elena Simperl. 2015. How to Use Crowdsourcing Effectively: Guidelines and Examples. *LIBER Quarterly* 25, 1 (Aug. 2015).

[36] H. J. Su and J. Y. Pan. 2016. Crowdsourcing platform for collaboration management in vulnerability verification. In *2016 18th Asia-Pacific Network Operations and Management Symposium (APNOMS)*. 1–4.

[37] Jacob Whitehill, Ting-fan Wu, Jacob Bergsma, Javier R. Movellan, and Paul L. Ruvolo. 2009. Whose Vote Should Count More: Optimal Integration of Labels from Labelers of Unknown Expertise. In *Advances in Neural Information Processing Systems 22*, Y. Bengio, D. Schuurmans, J. D. Lafferty, C. K. I. Williams, and A. Culotta (Eds.). Curran Associates, Inc., 2035–2043.

[38] Mingyi Zhao, Jens Grossklags, and Kai Chen. 2014. An Exploratory Study of White Hat Behaviors in a Web Vulnerability Disclosure Program. In *Proceedings of the 2014 ACM Workshop on Security Information Workers (SIW '14)*. ACM, New York, NY, USA, 51–58.

[39] Mingyi Zhao, Jens Grossklags, and Peng Liu. 2015. An Empirical Study of Web Vulnerability Discovery Ecosystems. In *Proceedings of the 22Nd ACM SIGSAC Conference on Computer and Communications Security (CCS '15)*. ACM, New York, NY, USA, 1105–1117. DOI:http://dx.doi.org/10.1145/2810103.2813704

[40] Mingyi Zhao, Aron Laszka, Thomas Maillart, and Jens Grossklags. 2016. Crowdsourced Security Vulnerability Discovery: Modeling and Organizing Bug-Bounty Programs. (2016). http://aronlaszka.com/papers/zhao2016crowdsourced.pdf

Characterizing Regional and Behavioral Device Variations Across the Twitter Timeline: a Longitudinal Study

Laura Cruz-Albrecht*
Stanford University
450 Serra Mall
Stanford, CA 94305
lcruzalb@cs.stanford.edu

Jiejun Xu, Kang-Yu Ni, Tsai-Ching Lu
HRL Laboratories
3011 Malibu Canyon Road
Malibu, CA 90265
{jxu,kni,tlu}@hrl.com

ABSTRACT

Physical devices, such as smartphones and laptops, provide the key interface through which users engage with the social media world. Yet despite the broad range of devices used on social media platforms, relatively little is known about how usage varies on a device to device level. In this work, we use a 10% sample of Twitter data spanning two consecutive years and encompassing 365.98 million users to perform a longitudinal, measurement-driven analysis of five prevalent device types - Android, iPhone-iOS, BlackBerry, other mobile devices, and nonmobile devices - across the time period. We study the global and regional usage patterns, as well as the regional distribution, of devices; investigate differences and similarities in behavioral patterns across devices with respect to tweet sentiment, daytime usage patterns, and feature usage (such as mentions, URLs, hashtags) over time; and quantify the level of "device homophily" (i.e., assortativity) within the Twitter device network. Our results reveal that key variations exist among these device groups, in addition to notable similarities. To the best of our knowledge, this is the first large-scale longitudinal analysis of various distinct Twitter devices.

CCS CONCEPTS

• **Information systems → Web mining**; • **Social and professional topics → User characteristics**;

KEYWORDS

Twitter; Mobile Device; Longitudinal Study; Behavioral Variation; Device Homophily

1 INTRODUCTION

Today, social media has attained astounding ubiquity across the globe. As of the writing of this article, there are 2.34 billion social network users worldwide, and an associated global social network penetration rate of 31% [17]. Twitter alone, a popular social media platform that allows users to send and broadcast short messages, or "tweets", clocks in with 313 million monthly active users, with 500 million tweets sent per day, and 6,000 tweets sent per second [18]. This widespread usage of social media is largely facilitated by the equally widespread means by which users can tap into it. Users can now produce, broadcast, and consume information from smartphones, tablets, laptops and desktop computers alike, making it more accessible than ever to engage in the social media world.

Yet while extensive work has been conducted on different social media platforms, including Twitter [1, 11, 15], Tumblr [20–22], YouTube [7], and Quora [19], among others [3, 23], little research has investigated how usage varies with the specific device used to access the platform. In this paper, we use a 10% sample of Twitter data spanning two consecutive years to conduct an in-depth longitudinal study of device usage across five categories: Android, iPhone-iOS, BlackBerry, other mobile devices and nonmobile devices[1], to uncover both the regional distribution and growth patterns, as well as the usage characteristics, of distinct devices. To the best of our knowledge, this is the first large-scale measurement-driven temporal study of multiple distinct device categories across the Twitter timeline. The main contributions of our work are as follows:

- Temporal analysis of device usage across two years, on both a global and country level.
- Investigation of differences and similarities across devices regarding usage behavior (including temporal sentiment over time, daytime usage patterns, and temporal usage of common tweet features).
- A method for investigating "device homophily", applied to the Twitter device network.

The rest of our paper is organized as follows. In Section 2 we review related works in the literature, and in Section 3 we provide an overview of the dataset used. In Section 4, we analyze device usage growth patterns globally and regionally, and quantify the regional distribution of devices. In Section 5 we investigate device-specific behavior and feature patterns, and in Section 6 we introduce the concept of device homophily and apply it to the Twitter network. Finally, in Section 7 we conclude the paper with a discussion of key findings and directions for future research.

2 RELATED WORK

Most similar to our study is the work by Perreault et al. [14] that investigated differences in tweets produced by mobile versus nonmobile platforms; they categorized Twitter devices into these two

*This research work was done at HRL Laboratories during a summer internship.

[1]The last two categories will be denoted as "Other Mobile" and "Nonmobile" throughout the rest of the paper.

WebSci '17, June 25-28, 2017, Troy, NY, USA

ACM ISBN 978-1-4503-4896-6/17/06...$15.00
https://doi.org/http://dx.doi.org/10.1145/3091478.3091498

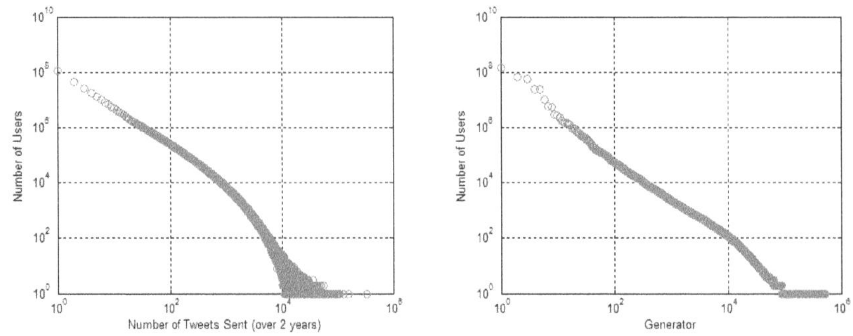

Figure 1: Left: log-log plot of tweets per user over the 2 years time period. Right: log-log plot of users per generator, where we consider a user's most commonly used generator from the time period. Both the distribution of tweets per user and the distribution of users per generator appear to follow a power law distribution.

categories, assessed differences between them, and found that mobile tweets vary considerably from their nonmobile counterparts (e.g., mobile content is more conversational, contains fewer URL links, and its users are more active than nonmobile users). Inspired by the differences found between the two categories considered, we extend this work in part by investigating differences between various mobile devices. In another study, Falaki et al. [6] investigated diversity and similarities among Android and Windows mobile users, and found that some qualities, such as average daily interaction, vary widely among individual users, while other qualities, such as relative application popularity, remain quite similar.

Regarding regional analysis, Poblete et al. [15] studied how Twitter usage varies across the 10 most active countries, studying qualities such as sentiment, activity level, and network structure. Mislove et al. [11] also considered the geography of Twitter users in a demographics-oriented study comparing geographic distribution, gender, and race of Twitter users to the U.S. population, and found that the Twitter community is not proportionally representative of U.S. demographics as a whole. Another work relevant to ours is GNIP (Twitter's enterprise API platform) and Fisher's global visualization of four mobile device categories - Android, iPhone, BlackBerry and Other, using 280 million tweets[2]. Their interactive map visually illustrates the varying distribution of mobile devices across the globe. Motivated by this, we seek to quantify these variations and analyze how these distributions have changed on a country level over time to better understand worldwide device usage.

Finally, much prior work has studied homophily - the tendency for individuals to associate with other similar individuals - across other dimensions, including gender, age, and race [9, 10]. Within Twitter specifically, Zamal et al. [24] studied age, gender, and political orientation homophily, and used this to perform latent attribute inference, and Kang et al. [8] studied Twitter topical lists to demonstrate evidence of topical homophily on Twitter. In this work, we seek to investigate homophily from a novel mobile device perspective.

Our work provides a multi-dimensional synthesis of different previously studied aspects - geography, mobile versus nonmobile devices, homophily - united through novel investigation on a longitudinal, device-oriented level.

[2]https://www.mapbox.com/labs/twitter-gnip/brands/#5/38.000 /-95.000

3 DATASET STATISTICS

For our research, we use a 10% sample of publicly available tweets from May 1, 2012 to April 30, 2014 obtained from GNIP. The dataset consists of 365,976,094 users, 9.9538 TB of compressed JSON data, and spans a two year time period. In order to perform device-driven analysis, we first assign a device to each user. To do so, we look at the "generator" field for each tweet encapsulated in the JSON files, which lists the application or website responsible for producing the tweet in question. The dataset statistics are summarized in Table 1. Upon inspection, we find that there exist thousands of generators capable of producing tweets, and we are able to identify 522,956 distinct generators across the user base. A list of the top generators is shown in Table 2. However, the distribution of users across generators is far from even: the top 100 generators alone already account for 96.39% of users. We observe that the distribution of users per generator, as well as the number of tweets per user, seem to follow a power law distribution (Figure 1).

We next manually map the top 100 generators to one of six device categories: Android, iPhone-iOS, BlackBerry, Nonmobile, Other Mobile, or Unknown. The categories are defined as:

- **Android**: consists of generators used for Android devices, such as "Twitter for Android", "Twitter for Android Tablets", and "Tweetcaster for Android".
- **iPhone-iOS**: consists of generators used by the iPhone, iPad, or simply iOS, such as "Twitter for iPhone", "Twitter for iPad", and "TweetCaster for iOS".
- **BlackBerry**: consists of generators such as "Twitter for BlackBerry" and "UberSocial for BlackBerry".
- **Nonmobile**: includes the "Web" (official Twitter website) generator, the nonmobile-only "Twitterfeed" platform, and generators intended for Macs or PCs.
- **Other Mobile**: generators identifiable as intended for devices such as Windows phone, Nokia, or LG phone.
- **Unknown**: generators which are unidentifiable or ambiguous (ie, could be used by multiple devices without

Table 1: Dataset statistics. Note the number of devices is slightly larger than the number of users; this is due to a small number of users (2.49%) having more than one most commonly used device.

General:			
Time frame	5/1/2012 - 4/30/2014 (2 years)		
Number of users	365,976,094		
Number of devices	375,539,502		
Percentage of devices identified	80.603%		
Types of generators	522,956		
TB JSON data	9.954; compressed		
Device:			
Device type	Count	Percent	Number of Tweets
Android	66,822,701	17.794%	5,520,802,403
iPhone-iOS	66,160,585	17.617%	8,560,164,598
BlackBerry	26,171,384	6.969%	2,850,623,390
Nonmobile	139,566,209	37.164%	5,562,837,645
Other Mobile	3,976,692	1.059%	95,918,241
(unknown)	(72,841,931)	(19.397%)	-

Table 2: Table of the top 15 generators observed from the two-year long Twitter dataset.

Rank	Generator
1	Web (Twitter website)
2	Twitter for Android
3	Twitter for iPhone
4	Twitter for BlackBerry
5	Mobile web
6	Tweet button
7	Twitter for iPad
8	Facebook
9	Instagram
10	iOS
11	Tweetdeck
12	txt
13	Twitter for Windows phone
14	UberSocial for BlackBerry
15	Twitter web client

distinction), such as "Google" and "Echofon". Devices in this category were excluded from the analysis.

Each user is associated with the device that he uses most often, to account for the fact that some users employ more than one device. In the case that devices tie as most prevalent, each device is counted.[3] In total, we are able to categorize 80.603% of devices.

Using this large-scale dataset, our goal is to analyze Twitter in the context of devices, and to uncover what differences, similarities, and patterns exist.

[3]These users in effect appear more than once in the counting. However, this case only affects 2.49% of users, and we felt it was more accurate than excluding them from analysis.

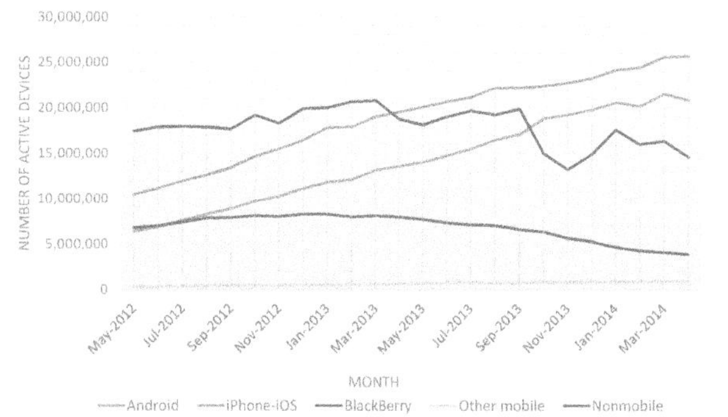

Figure 2: Timeseries of the number of active users over 2 years, measured on monthly intervals.

4 TEMPORAL AND REGIONAL DEVICE CHARACTERIZATION

4.1 Worldwide Temporal Usage Patterns

We begin by investigating perhaps the most immediate temporal question, the worldwide trend of device usage over time. For each month, we counted the number of active devices, where active entailed having sent at least 1 tweet during that month. The results are plotted in Figure 2.

What we find is a temporal stamp on which devices were more actively used during the time frame, as well as growth and decline patterns for each device. Most notable is the dramatic upward growth in the number of iPhone-iOS and Android users over time, as well as the more subtle but observable decline of the BlackBerry. Interestingly, these results prove consistent with general trends in sales of the iPhone, Android, and BlackBerry mobile devices at the time indicating that Twitter usage data effectively shadows larger economic trends [16]. There is a large fluctuation for the Nonmobile category at the end of 2013. We are not sure about the true cause, but we suspect that it is due to internal changes made by GNIP in classifying apps generated from Macs or PCs. Our analysis on the mobile devices remain accurate as we don't observe any unusual deviations from the timeseries, and we are able to see the overall trends spanning across two years for each of the categories.

4.2 Characterizing Regional Device Variations

Twitter's immense popularity lends itself to usage across the globe. We next seek to investigate device usage trends on Twitter on a country by country level. In particular, which devices dominate where? Has this changed in interesting ways over time?

4.2.1 Geotagged Data. In order to perform regional device analysis, we need a way to identify the location of each user's device. To do so, we use a set of 101,846,236 geotagged users identified across 150 countries, pinpointed using total variation minimization from Compton et al. [2]. The idea behind their approach was to turn the task of geotagging users into a convex optimization problem with the goal of minimizing the geographic distance between users identified as socially connected. Social connectivity was determined by the minimum number of mutual mentions between users, where a mention is a particular tweet feature where a user prepends the

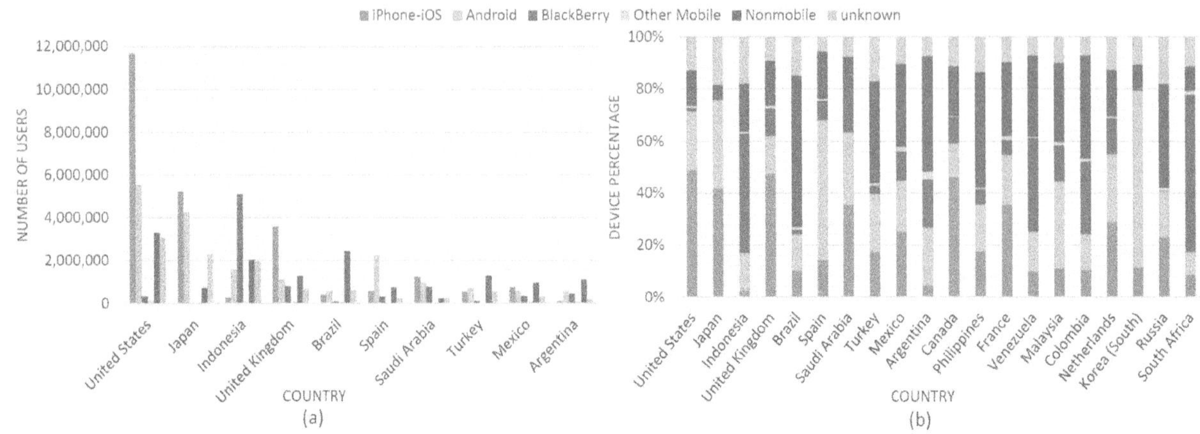

Figure 3: Regional distribution of devices: (a) Devices by count in top 10 countries; (b) device distribution by percentage in top 20 countries.

Table 3: Top countries for each device type. For reference, we also list the top countries with the most total geotagged users (second column).

Rank	Most users	Android	iPhone-iOS	BlackBerry	Nonmobile	Other Mobile
1	U.S.A.	U.S.A.	U.S.A.	Indonesia	U.S.A.	U.S.A.
2	Japan	Japan	Japan	U.K.	Brazil	Indonesia
3	Indonesia	Spain	U.K.	Saudi Arabia	Indonesia	Argentina
4	U.K.	Indonesia	Saudi Arabia	Venezuela	U.K.	U.K.
5	Brazil	U.K.	Canada	Argentina	Turkey	Mexico
6	Spain	Saudi Arabia	Mexico	South Africa	Argentina	Brazil
7	Saudi Arabia	South Korea	France	Colombia	Mexico	Turkey
8	Turkey	Turkey	Spain	Nigeria	Philippines	France
9	Mexico	Brazil	Turkey	Mexico	Spain	Spain
10	Argentina	Mexico	Brazil	U.S.A.	Japan	Malaysia

"@" symbol to another user's username in the tweet, indicating the tweet is intended to directly address the recipient. By merging this user-location data with the previously collected user-device data, we obtain the desired device-location information.

4.2.2 Regional Device Distribution. We first look at the aggregated regional device distribution. For analysis, we consider the top-20 and top-10 countries with the most geotagged users, which should overall correspond to the countries with the most, or at least most active, users.

The results are shown in Figure 3 and Table 3. We observe that notable variations in device distributions exists across different countries. For example, the United States, Japan, and the United Kingdom stand out as possessing an iPhone-iOS majority, whereas Android stands out as the majority phone in Spain and South Korea, and BlackBerry in Indonesia and South Africa. From this, we also find that in most countries, mobile devices taken together dominate over the nonmobile alternatives. However, in countries such as in Brazil, Turkey, and the Philippines, for example, nonmobile devices retain popularity.

4.2.3 Regional and Temporal Device Distribution. Finally, we combine the regional approach with the temporal approach to obtain records of device usage over time, partitioned across countries. Several of these graphs are shown in Figure 4. From these plots, we are able to examine device growth patterns on a country level that the trends vary notably from country to country. Additionally, this partitioning allows us to see which countries are contributing to the worldwide trends previously shown in Figure 2.

For example, we find that globally iPhone-iOS and Android were on the rise, while BlackBerry underwent decline. On a regional level, we see that in the United States, Japan, and the United Kingdom, three of the top-4 countries, iPhone-iOS devices have been seeing ever more users, paralleling the worldwide trend. However, within two of these countries, the U.S. and U.K., we find Android usage has remained relatively static, contrasting with the worldwide trend. Instead, the Android growth observed globally is attributable to countries such as Indonesia, Japan, and Spain, among several others.

Additionally, we obtain further insight regarding regional device distribution: for example, previously we observed Indonesia had the most BlackBerry users, by both magnitude and percentage.

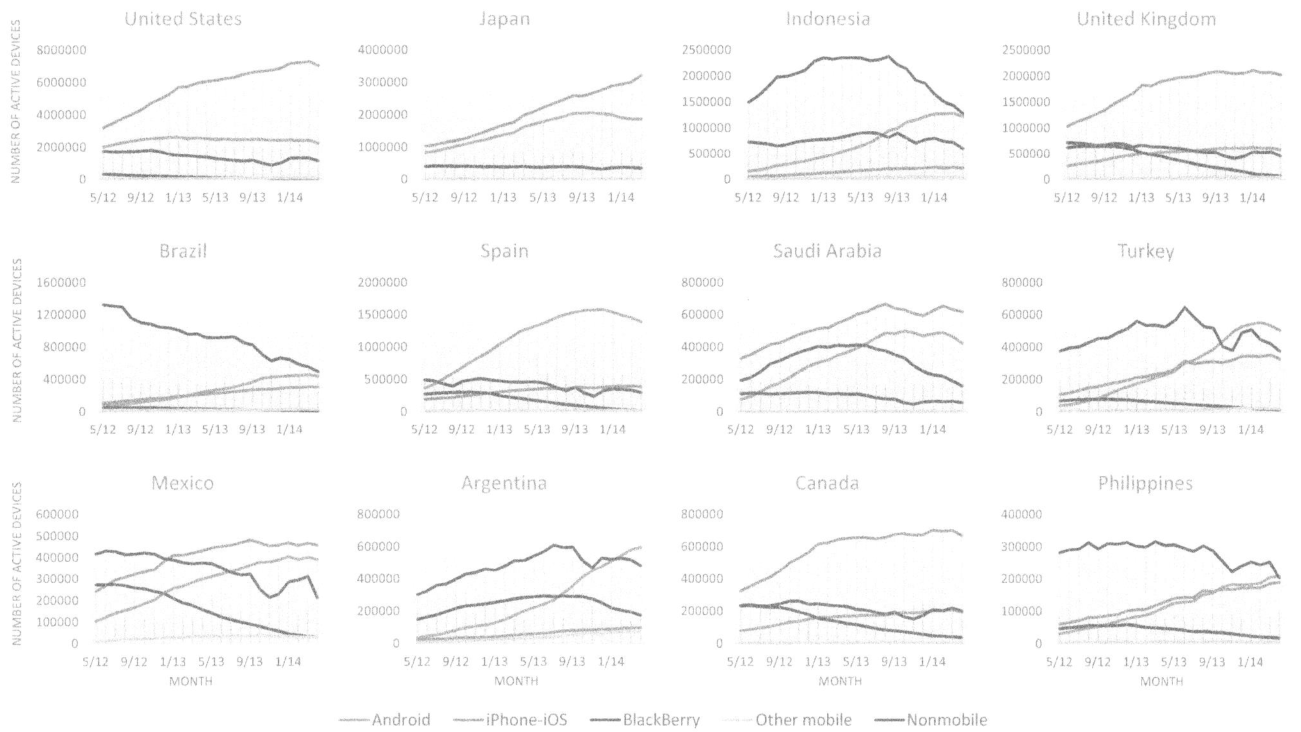

Figure 4: Device usage over time for top-12 countries, in order from upper left to lower right. Number of active devices are measured on monthly intervals.

However, from this longitudinal study, we see precisely how its usage has changed over time: we see that this device is marked by growth in the first year of study, but decline in the second half.

Overall, through performing regional and longitudinal device usage analysis, we successfully gain deeper insight into device adoption and usage across the globe.

5 DEVICE-DRIVEN BEHAVIORAL ANALYSIS

We now move from exploring regional variations among devices to investigating behavioral variations. We focus on three facets: sentiment patterns, daytime usage patterns, and tweet feature patterns. Taken together, these behavioral and usage qualities provide further insight into both differences and similarities that exist across devices.

5.1 Sentiment Patterns

We begin by performing sentiment analysis on Twitter content produced by each device. To do so, we follow the procedure outlined in Dodds et al. [4] and Mitchell et al. [12]. The idea behind sentiment analysis is to quantify the average happiness level (h_{avg}), or sentiment, of a large corpus of words. For our analysis, we use the labMT 1.0 (Language Assessment by Mechanical Turk) word list available in [4]. The corpus is comprised of the 10,222 most common English words obtained from four sources: Google Books, the New York Times, Twitter, and music lyrics. Each word is assigned an average happiness score between 1 and 9, with larger scores indicating higher happiness. To obtain sentiment scores for each device in our set, we leveraged the following calculation:

$$h_{avg}(D_a) = \frac{\sum_{i=1}^{N} h_{avg}(w_i) \cdot f_{i,a}}{\sum_{i=1}^{N} f_{i,a}} \quad (1)$$

where $h_{avg}(D_a)$ is the average happiness of $Device_a$, D_a is the corpus of words derived from tweets by $Device_a$, $h_{avg}(w_i)$ is the average happiness value for word w_i in the labMT word list, and $f_{i,a}$ is the frequency of w_i in D_a.

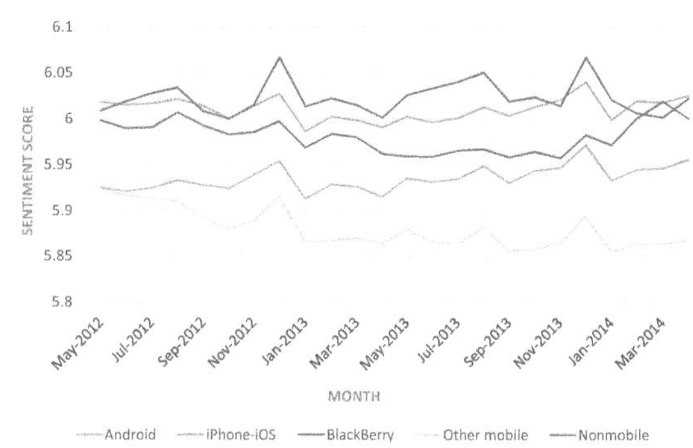

Figure 5: Average sentiment of tweeted content by device type, measured on monthly intervals over 2 years.

To see whether certain devices display higher sentiment than others, as well as whether device-specific sentiment fluctuates over time, we perform a longitudinal sentiment analysis by computing h_{avg} on monthly intervals (see Figure 5). Interestingly enough, across the two years we find that consistent differences in the sentiment of tweet content persist across different devices. For the majority of the year, BlackBerry wins as the device tweeting content with higher sentiment, while Other Mobile (e.g., Windows phone, Nokia, and LG phone) consistently falls below all other devices. The consistent difference in sentiment across devices is surprising, and suggests that perhaps some common quality exists among certain device users which impacts the ambient happiness of the content they choose to tweet and share.

By contrast, we note a similarity that persists across devices; namely, seasonal sentiment peaks. In particular, sentiment across devices tends to peak in December and drop in January. This is consistent with the finding in Dodds et al. [4] that user sentiment increases at the end of the year and drops in the beginning of the new year, and indicates that large phenomenon such as widely observed end-of-the-year holidays has a predictable impact regardless of device.

5.2 Daytime Usage Patterns

We next turn our attention to the time of day during which the different devices are active. To uncover daytime usage patterns, we need to know the local time during which tweets were posted. To do so, we consider devices identified as belonging to users within the United States, Japan, and the United Kingdom. These countries are selected because they are among the countries with the most geotagged Twitter users. Using six evenly spaced months in the two year period[4], we determine the local time of every tweet by these users to the nearest hour, bucketed from time 0 to time 23. The results are shown in Figure 6.

Interestingly, we find no difference in daytime usage patterns across device types: overall all types tend follow the same averaged trend. Similarly, among the different countries examined, the overall daytime trend remains similar, though in Japan, tweeting peaks a bit later (11PM) than in the United States and United Kingdom (10PM), and Japan also features local 8AM and 1PM peaks absent in the other two countries examined. The hours of usage, however, are reasonable: users are inactive in the very early morning, but activity increases as the day progresses, peaks in the late evening, and then drops again as the early morning approaches. However, we do observe that in the United States and Japan, BlackBerry features the lowest tweet percentage relative to other devices in the late evening hours, and has one of the higher tweet percentages relative to other devices in morning hours.

Overall, we find that in the context of Twitter, hourly usage does not vary according to device; rather, it adheres to a fairly consistent device-wide diurnal pattern.

5.3 Tweet Feature Patterns

In this section, we study the patterns of tweet feature usage over time. This style of investigation has been undertaken in prior related works such as [14] and [15]. We extend this work by offering: 1) analysis partitioned across several devices; and 2) a temporal, rather than static, analysis. We examine the following features:

- **Mention**: the body of a tweet contains "@" symbol prepended to another person's username, indicating the tweet is directly addressing him/her.
- **URL**: a tweet contains a link, such as `http://tumblr.com`.
- **Hashtag**: a tweet contains at least one word with "#" prepended to it, indicating the tweet is related to particular topic, such as "#music".
- **Retweet**: a tweet is a re-post of another user's post.

For the mention, URL, and hashtag features, we looked at the fraction of posts by a given device type that contained at least one instance of the feature in question. For the retweet calculation, we looked at the fraction of total tweets (retweets plus posts) that were retweets. In addition, we examined the overall percentage of tweets per device type (see Table 4).

5.3.1 Findings. The results are intriguing - depending on the feature in question, we find evidence of several different cases: distinct usage across all devices, similar usage regardless of device, and an interesting mobile versus nonmobile split.

As shown in Figure 7 we find that mention usage varies mostly depending on the device. BlackBerry, followed by iPhone-iOS and Android, stand out as tweeting with a higher mention rate. Since the use of a mention indicates an active choice to directly address

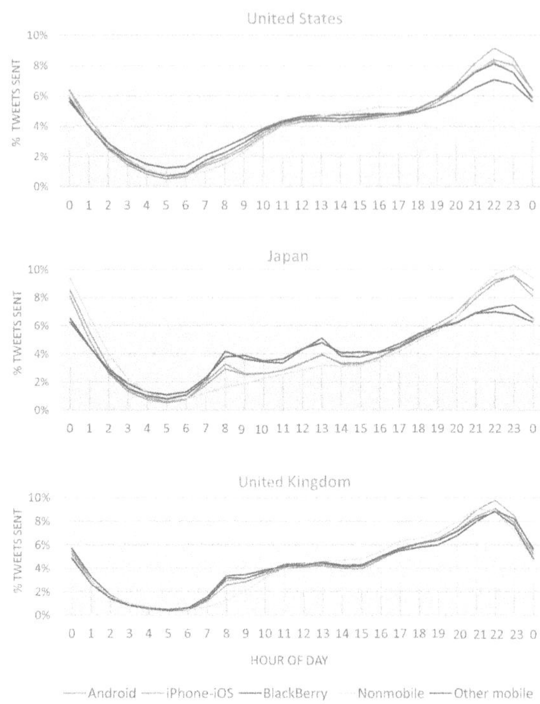

Figure 6: Daytime usage patterns by device type, plotted for 3 different countries. Tweet posted times were converted to local time depending on the device's identified location, and bucketed to the nearest hour.

[4]6/2012, 10/2012, 2/2013, 6/2013, 10/2013, and 2/2014.

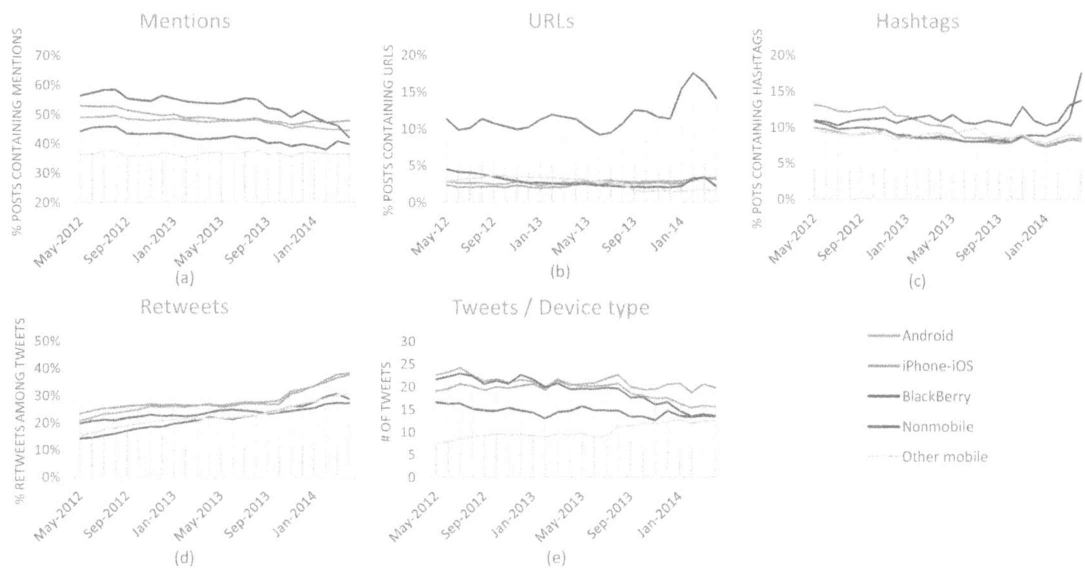

Figure 7: Longitudinal graphs for several tweet features by device type. (a), (b), and (c) display the percentage of posts containing mentions, URLs, or hashtags, respectively. (d) displays the percentage of total tweets (posts + retweets) that were retweets (note: the retweet percentage displayed a dramatic drop in the nonmobile category for the months Oct. 2013, Nov. 2013, Dec. 2013. This drop was highly inconsistent with prior and posterior measured trends; thus, we performed interpolation for those 3 points). (e) displays the average number of tweets sent per device type.

Table 4: Tweet features among devices

Device	@mention %	URL %	Hashtag %	Retweet %
Android	47.2 %	2.8 %	8.5 %	28.6 %
iPhone-iOS	48.8 %	2.5 %	9.8 %	28.7 %
BlackBerry	54.3 %	2.9 %	9.3 %	20.3 %
Nonmobile	42.2 %	11.5 %	11.1 %	21.8 %
Other Mobile	36.6 %	2.4 %	8.9 %	23.8 %

another user, this finding suggests that these devices are more "social".

Moreover, while the three most prevalent mobile devices in the network @mention more than nonmobile devices, Other Mobile devices (e.g., Windows phone, Nokia, and LG phone) consistently display the lowest @mention percentage among all devices, including nonmobile. This indicates that, in the case of mentions, differences do exist between various mobile platforms, differences which could otherwise be lost when not considering these devices separately. It is also interesting to note that among the 4 mobile groups (Android, iPhone-iOS, BlackBerry, Other Mobile), the relative ordering of sentiment scores and @mention percents are the same. Though this does not indicate causation in any way, upon preliminary inspection it does at least appear that devices that @mention others more also tend to post more positively rated content.

By contrast, in the case of URLs, a distinct bipartite split exists among devices - nonmobile tweets consistently contain a significantly higher fraction of URLs, while all mobile devices, regardless of the specific platform, use very few. Our finding is consistent with the findings of Perreault et al. [14] that web links are much more common in nonmobile tweets, and furthers their work by examining the mobile devices separately and demonstrating that, regardless of mobile platform, URL usage remains low.

In the case of hashtags, usage is essentially indistinguishable across devices. This further confirms the findings in [14] by showing that even among different mobile platforms usage remains comparable. Evidently, hashtag usage is inherent to the Twitter platform, and not the device employing it.

In each of these features - mentions, URLs, and hashtags - there is little temporal difference. Retweets, however, pose an exception. Here, we find that overall the percentage of retweets among total tweets has increased with time, showing that users are re-posting content, rather than producing new content, more than before. We additionally note that iPhone-iOS and Android consistently remain above their counterparts with this regard.

Finally, regarding the rate at which different devices produce content, we find that the tweets/device ratio is overall highest for iPhone-iOS, Android, and BlackBerry, but lowest for Other Mobile. This indicates that most mobile devices are more prolific in tweeting than nonmobile devices (which is consistent with [14]'s finding that mobile users are more active than nonmobile users), but curiously, mobile devices in the Other category pose an exception. Additionally, we note that in the most recent months, iPhone-iOS that stands out as the most active device type.

Overall, with regards to the three behavioral and feature facets examined, we find that: 1) sentiment varies consistently across devices, with BlackBerry and iPhone-iOS standing out as the most "positive" devices; 2) daytime usage patterns follow a diurnal pattern that varies little depending on device or country; and 3) some tweet qualities vary across devices (mentions, tweets/device type, and to lesser degree retweets), some vary only between mobile and nomobile (URLs), and some do not vary according to device (hashtags).

6 NETWORK STRUCTURE

We next turn our attention to quantifying the degree of device connectivity in the Twitter network. As Twitter is a social platform, it can be perceived as an immense graph of users connected by social bonds. In previous work, various features have been used as indicators of a social bond, including:

- **Direct followers**: users can opt to follow another user's account and be notified of the followed user's updates. This allows for construction of a directed graph [15].
- **Indirect followers**: Twitter allows for users to create a list with a capped number of member users (direct followers). Users who wish to see tweets from list, without actually following its individual members, can opt to subscribe to this list (indirect followers) [8].
- **Mentions**: users can directly mention another user in their tweet. Since this is an active choice to personally address another user, it indicates social connectivity that can be used to form directed edges, or, in the case of reciprocal mentions, undirected edges [2].

Modeling Twitter as a network enables varied network analysis as well as graph-based algorithm implementation such as label propagation. For the purposes of this paper, we investigate the principle of homophily as applied to devices and apps.

6.1 Homophily Principle

Homophily is, as put by McPherson, "the principle that a contact between similar people occurs at a higher rate than among dissimilar people" [10]. Fundamentally, the homophily principle states that individuals have a tendency to be similar to their friends. This widely studied fundamental organizing principle of social networks has been found across diverse social and demographic attributes, including race, age, religion, gender, occupation, and geographic proximity [5, 9, 10].

While homophily has been widely examined across social and demographic features, little work has been done to investigate this property across other dimensions. In particular, we investigate whether evidence of homophily can be found between distinct devices. For the remainder of this section, we propose a method for analyzing device homophily on social media platforms, and apply the results to the Twitter network.

However, note that though the term "device homophily" is the term we are using to describe the property we are examining (namely, connectivity between similar devices), "device homophily" does not imply that similarity caused connections to form, as in the case of social homophily. Though we are using this term, it can equivalently be conceived of as "device assortativity".

6.2 Device Homophily

6.2.1 Method. In order to investigate device homophily, a network consisting of interconnected devices is needed. To obtain this network, we first look at each user in the Twitter dataset and obtain their associated devices. In the case that a user uses more than one device, the most frequently used device is selected.[5] Each of these devices forms a vertex in our network. To connect the vertices, we use the approach taken by Compton et al. [2] and assign a bidirectional weighted edge between vertices equal to the minimum number of reciprocated @mentions between the user associated with the device. We obtain a graph G containing over 1 billion edges and 110 million vertices.

We next quantify the level of device homophily within the network. To do so, we use the procedure proposed by Newman [13]. First, we create a matrix C consisting of all the weighted counts of device-device edges in the network, where C_{ij} is equal to the sum of the weights of the edges between a device of type i and a device of type j. We then normalize C to create the mixing matrix M, where $\sum_{ij} M_{ij} = 1$. Thus, M_{ij} represents the fraction of edges between device i and device j, and, as G is undirected, M is symmetric.

Using M, we next compute the level of assortativity in the network using the following assortativity coefficient equation derived from [13]:

$$h = \frac{\sum_i M_{ii} - \sum_i a_i^2}{1 - \sum_i a_i^2}, \quad (2)$$

where $a_i = \sum_i M_{ij} = \sum_i M_{ji}$. This equation is selected for two reasons: 1) since assortativity is the propensity for connections to exist between similar vertices, we can leverage such computations to measure the "device homophily" we seek to quantify; and 2) this equation, as compared to alternatives, remains effective even when certain vertex types are much more common than others.

The idea behind this calculation is to quantify the dominance of the diagonal, as compared to the off-diagonal, values. If the network is truly homophilous, or assortative, we would expect the diagonal values to be larger, and thus h to have a larger value. Thus, in the case of a network with high homophily, $h = 1$; in a network absent of homophily (often, random mixing), $h = 0$; and in a network that possesses perfect heterophily (nodes tend to be connected to dissimilar nodes), $-1 \leq h < 0$.[6]

6.2.2 Device and Generator Homophily Results. Using the above method, we compute the value h to determine the device homophily level in the Twitter network. In Figure 8 (left), we show the device-device mixing matrix and corresponding heatmap. Overall, we obtain a network device homophily score of $h = 0.094$. This overall suggests that the distribution of devices across the Twitter network is close to a randomly mixed network; it seems that when it comes to Tweeting, it is not significantly more likely for users of a certain device to be connected to other users of the same device compared to a different device. However, it is interesting to note that among

[5]In the case that multiple devices tied as most prevalent, each one is considered. Conceptually, we create a hybrid "device" for that user consisting of respective fractions of each device, i.e., half Android, half nonmobile. However, as mentioned previously, this affects only a small percentage of users (2.49%).

[6]See [13] for a more detailed explanation on why a perfectly dissortative network is not just $h = -1$.

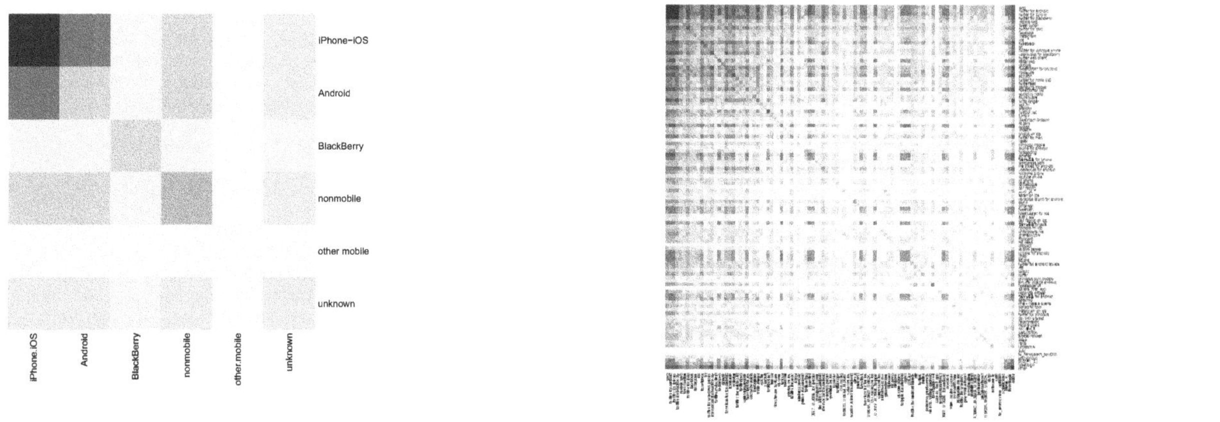

Figure 8: Heatmap of device-device mixing matrix (left); heatmap of generator-generator mixing matrix (right). Darker values correspond to a higher count of edges of that type in the network.

iPhone-iOS, BlackBerry, and Nonmobile devices, there are more homophilous edges than heterophilous edges, suggesting that among certain device types, "device homophily" is stronger than others.

We also apply the above procedure on the generator level (recall that the generator is the app or website responsible for producing tweets, such as "Twitter for iPhone" and "Ubersocial for BlackBerry"); we consider the 100 most common generators in the Twitter dataset (accounts for 96.386 % of users), with remaining generators grouped into "other". From this, we obtain $h = 0.089$, a result comparable to the device homophily value. However, from the heatmap in Figure 8 (right), we observe a diagonal line indicating the homophily relations exist among certain generators. In addition, we observe a darker vertical strip on the left boundary of the heatmap, indicating that any given generator is likely to be connected to one of the four most common generators. Intuitively, this makes sense - since these generators account for 75.278 % of users in our dataset, their abundance in the network makes their dominance understandable. Table 5 summarizes the overall homophily results for both devices and generators at different threshold levels.

Table 5: Device and generator homophily results. Used threshold on minimum edge weight required between devices for edge to be included in calculation (i.e., edge weight ≥ threshold. As all edges have a minimum weight of 1, threshold of 1 is equivalent to no threshold). We observe a slight increase in h as threshold is increased.

threshold	Device	Generator
1	$h = 0.094$	0.089
3	0.102	0.095
5	0.105	0.098

Although the overall Twitter network exhibits low levels of homophily on both the device and generator levels, it is interesting to observe that certain "apps" exhibit higher levels of connectivity with similar "apps" than others. A more in-depth analysis among these "apps" and applying the device homophily concept to alternate device networks, are potential areas for further research.

7 CONCLUSION

In this paper, we have presented a multi-dimensional quantitative analysis of multiple prevalent devices across the Twitter timeline. Using a large-scale dataset, we examined distinctions and similarities among different devices with regards to: 1) global as well as regional growth patterns; 2) regional distribution among the top-20 countries; and 3) temporal behavioral and feature patterns. Additionally, we proposed a method for measuring device homophily within online microblogging platforms and applied it to the Twitter network.

Overall, we found that, on a global level, iPhone-iOS and Android device usage is on the rise, while BlackBerry usage is declining. We further investigated growth patterns on the country level, where we found that both device distribution and device growth patterns vary widely. On a behavioral and feature level, we found consistent, quantifiable differences in both sentiment levels and @mention usage across all device types, suggesting that some differences do exist among distinct device type user groups; exploring potential factors contributing to this phenomenon is a potential area for further research. In contrast, we found that other qualities, such as hashtag and daytime usage patterns are virtually identical regardless of devices. Additionally, through our analysis of homophily on the device and app level, we found that overall devices and apps appear to be faintly homophilous, but overall tend to be connected in a fashion akin to that of a randomly mixed network.

In future research, it would be interesting to explore: 1) how regional and global device growth patterns harvested from social media data can be employed to forecast future growth trends; and 2) how properties that vary across devices can potentially be leveraged to infer the identities of currently unidentifiable devices in the network.

REFERENCES

[1] Jisun An and Ingmar Weber. 2016. #greysanatomy vs. #yankees: Demographics and Hashtag Use on Twitter. *CoRR* abs/1603.01973 (2016). http://arxiv.org/abs/1603.01973

[2] Ryan Compton, David Jurgens, and David Allen. 2014. Geotagging One Hundred Million Twitter Accounts with Total Variation Minimization. *CoRR* abs/1404.7152 (2014). http://arxiv.org/abs/1404.7152

[3] Cristian Danescu-Niculescu-Mizil, Robert West, Dan Jurafsky, Jure Leskovec, and Christopher Potts. 2013. No Country for Old Members: User Lifecycle and Linguistic Change in Online Communities. In *Proceedings of the 22Nd International Conference on World Wide Web (WWW '13)*. ACM, New York, NY, USA, 307–318. https://doi.org/10.1145/2488388.2488416

[4] Peter Sheridan Dodds, Kameron Decker Harris, Isabel M. Kloumann, Catherine A. Bliss, and Christopher M. Danforth. 2011. Temporal Patterns of Happiness and Information in a Global Social Network: Hedonometrics and Twitter. *CoRR* abs/1101.5120 (2011). http://dblp.uni-trier.de/db/journals/corr/corr1101.html#abs-1101-5120

[5] David Easley and Jon Kleinberg. 2010. *Networks, Crowds, and Markets: Reasoning About a Highly Connected World.* Cambridge University Press, New York, USA.

[6] Hossein Falaki, Ratul Mahajan, Srikanth Kandula, Dimitrios Lymberopoulos, Ramesh Govindan, and Deborah Estrin. 2010. Diversity in Smartphone Usage. In *Proceedings of the 8th International Conference on Mobile Systems, Applications, and Services (MobiSys '10)*. New York, NY, USA, 179–194. https://doi.org/10.1145/1814433.1814453

[7] Flavio Figueiredo, Fabrício Benevenuto, and Jussara M. Almeida. 2011. The Tube over Time: Characterizing Popularity Growth of Youtube Videos. In *Proceedings of the Fourth ACM International Conference on Web Search and Data Mining (WSDM '11)*. New York, NY, USA, 745–754. https://doi.org/10.1145/1935826.1935925

[8] Jeon Hyung Kang and Kristina Lerman. 2012. Using Lists to Measure Homophily on Twitter. In *AAAI Technical Report WS-12-09*. Association for the Advancement of Artificial Intelligence, 26–32.

[9] Peter Li, Jiejun Xu, and Tsai-Ching Lu. 2015. Leveraging Homophily to Infer Demographic Attributes: Inferring the Age of Twitter Users Using Label Propagation. In *In Proceedings of Workshop on Information In Networks (WIN15)*.

[10] Miller McPherson, Lynn Smith-Lovin, and James M Cook. 2001. Birds of a Feather: Homophily in Social Networks. *Annual Review of Sociology* 27, 1 (2001), 415–444. https://doi.org/10.1146/annurev.soc.27.1.415 arXiv:http://arjournals.annualreviews.org/doi/pdf/10.1146/annurev.soc.27.1.415

[11] Alan Mislove, Sune Lehmann, Yong-Yeol Ahn, Jukka-Pekka Onnela, and J. Niels Rosenquist. 2011. Understanding the Demographics of Twitter Users. In *Proceedings of the 5th International AAAI Conference on Weblogs and Social Media (ICWSM'11)*. Barcelona, Spain.

[12] Lewis Mitchell, Kameron Decker Harris, Morgan R. Frank, Peter Sheridan Dodds, and Christopher M. Danforth. 2013. The Geography of Happiness: Connecting Twitter sentiment and expression, demographics, and objective characteristics of place. *CoRR* abs/1302.3299 (2013). http://dblp.uni-trier.de/db/journals/corr/corr1302.html#abs-1302-3299

[13] M. E. J. Newman. 2003. Mixing patterns in networks. *Phys. Rev. E* 67, 2 (Feb. 2003), 026126. https://doi.org/10.1103/PhysRevE.67.026126

[14] Mathieu Perreault and Derek Ruths. 2011. The Effect of Mobile Platforms on Twitter Content Generation. In *International AAAI Conference on Web and Social Media*. http://www.aaai.org/ocs/index.php/ICWSM/ICWSM11/paper/view/2798

[15] Barbara Poblete, Ruth Garcia, Marcelo Mendoza, and Alejandro Jaimes. 2011. Do All Birds Tweet the Same?: Characterizing Twitter Around the World. In *Proceedings of the 20th ACM International Conference on Information and Knowledge Management (CIKM '11)*. New York, NY, USA, 1025–1030. https://doi.org/10.1145/2063576.2063724

[16] Statista-The Statistics Portal. 2016. Statistics and facts about Smartphones. https://www.statista.com/topics/840/. (2016). Accessed: 2016-10-1.

[17] Statista-The Statistics Portal. 2016. Statistics and facts about Social Networks. http://www.statista.com/topics/1164/. (2016). Accessed: 2016-10-1.

[18] David Sayce. 2016. Number of tweets per day? http://www.dsayce.com/social-media/10-billions-tweets/. (2016). Accessed: 2016-10-1.

[19] Gang Wang, Konark Gill, Manish Mohanlal, Haitao Zheng, and Ben Y. Zhao. 2013. Wisdom in the Social Crowd: An Analysis of Quora. In *Proceedings of the 22Nd International Conference on World Wide Web (WWW '13)*. ACM, New York, NY, USA, 1341–1352. https://doi.org/10.1145/2488388.2488506

[20] Jiejun Xu, Ryan Compton, Tsai-Ching Lu, and David Allen. 2014. Rolling Through Tumblr: Characterizing Behavioral Patterns of the Microblogging Platform. In *Proceedings of the 2014 ACM Conference on Web Science (WebSci '14)*. ACM, New York, NY, USA, 13–22. https://doi.org/10.1145/2615569.2615694

[21] Jiejun Xu and Tsai-Ching Lu. 2015. Toward precise user-topic alignment in online social media. In *Big Data (Big Data), 2015 IEEE International Conference on*. IEEE, 767–775.

[22] Jiejun Xu, Tsai-Ching Lu, Ryan Compton, and David Allen. 2014. Civil unrest prediction: A tumblr-based exploration. In *International Conference on Social Computing, Behavioral-Cultural Modeling, and Prediction*. Springer, 403–411.

[23] Jiejun Xu, Tsai-Ching Lu, Ryan Compton, and David Allen. 2014. Quantifying cross-platform engagement through large-scale user alignment. In *Proceedings of the 2014 ACM conference on Web science*. ACM, 281–282.

[24] Faiyaz Al Zamal, Wendy Liu, and Derek Ruths. 2012. Homophily and Latent Attribute Inference: Inferring Latent Attributes of Twitter Users from Neighbors.. In *ICWSM*, John G. Breslin, Nicole B. Ellison, James G. Shanahan, and Zeynep Tufekci (Eds.). The AAAI Press. http://dblp.uni-trier.de/db/conf/icwsm/icwsm2012.html#ZamalLR12

Exploring Web Archives Through Temporal Anchor Texts*

Helge Holzmann, Wolfgang Nejdl, Avishek Anand
L3S Research Center
Appelstr. 9a
30167 Hannover, Germany
{holzmann,nejdl,anand}@L3S.de

ABSTRACT

Web archives have been instrumental in digital preservation of the Web and provide great opportunity for the study of the societal past and evolution. These Web archives are massive collections, typically in the order of terabytes and petabytes. Due to this, search and exploration of archives has been limited as full-text indexing is both resource and computationally expensive. We identify that for typical access methods to archives, which are navigational and temporal in nature, we do not always require indexing full-text. Instead, meaningful text surrogates like *anchor texts* already go a long way in providing meaningful solutions and can act as reasonable entry points to exploring Web archives.

In this paper, we present a new approach to searching Web archives based on temporal link graphs and corresponding anchor texts. Departing from traditional informational intents, we show how temporal anchor texts can be effective in answering queries beyond purely navigational intents, like finding the most central webpages of an entity in a given time period. We propose indexing methods and a temporal retrieval model based on anchor texts. Further, we discuss several interesting search results as well as one experiment in which we demonstrate how such results can be integrated in a data processing workflow to scale up to thousands of pages. In this analysis we were able to replicate results reported by an offline study, showing that restaurant prices indeed increased in Germany when the Euro was introduced as Europe's currency.

CCS CONCEPTS

• **Information systems → Retrieval models and ranking**; • **Applied computing → Digital libraries and archives**;

KEYWORDS

Web Archives; Temporal Information Retrieval; Big Data Analysis

1 INTRODUCTION

Web Science is the interdisciplinary endeavor of studying the Web to derive insights into our world [13]. While Web archives constitute extremely valuable datasets for this task by providing access to the Web in a temporal manner, methods and tools as well as best practices to work with these archives have widely been neglected. We address both in this paper: first, we present a live system that provides retrieval models useful for downstream historical analysis, and second, we outline an example use case that exemplifies how historical phenomena on the Web can be investigated using our temporal retrieval approach with Web archives.

Web Archives have been continually archiving the Web in an attempt to document the digital history of human society. In the process, they have been amassing Web content in the order of terabytes and sometimes up to petabytes. What makes such archives attractive is that they are repositories of past contents that encode evolution. Consider the example of German's chancellor *Angela Merkel*, who developed from the leader of a political party to the leader of a country, playing an important role in Europe. This evolution is reflected by the websites representing her on the Web, which used to be a subpage under her party's site and is now her official website and social media profiles (cp. Sec. 5.2). For users of Web archives, such changes make it difficult to lookup past records on the Web.

Supporting keyword search with temporal predicates on these massive datasets typically requires full-text indexing infrastructures. However, due to the large sizes of archives, creating those indexes can be both computationally expensive as well as resource intensive, even with distributed architectures in place. We note that whereas full-text search is beneficial for a wide variety of informational intents, there are specialized intents on archives for which we might not always require indexing full-text. Specifically, most of the intents for information in Web archives is navigational and temporal in nature. Users are often interested in specific URLs or subjects and their evolution over time: versions of people's webpages and social media pages, movements, societies and organizations, or entities in general. In this work, we explore the possibility of identifying surrogate information units that is accurate enough for such information needs.

Towards this, we identify such surrogate information units as anchor texts with their accompanying link structure and propose lean index organization methods to support such temporal, navigational needs. Anchor texts are short, concise, important and non-noisy descriptors of information content typically desired by navigational queries. Another immediate benefit of indexing anchor texts as surrogates of the actual webpages is that they are many orders smaller than the original full text. The accompanying index is leaner, computationally less intensive for construction and storage as well as faster to query.

We introduce a temporal Web model that represents a Web archive as an edge-labeled, temporal, directed graph. Further, we

*This work is partly funded by the European Research Council under ALEXANDRIA (ERC 339233)

WebSci'17, June 25-28, 2017, Troy, NY, USA.
© 2017 ACM. 978-1-4503-4896-6/17/06...$15.00
DOI: http://dx.doi.org/10.1145/3091478.3091500

propose a retrieval model based on the semantics of anchor texts towards ranking webpages not only by overall relevance but under consideration of their decisive times and versions. While this retrieval method does not cover pure informational needs, it successfully identifies results beyond navigational needs including representative pages for entities that vary over time. With this retrieval model we present a fully functional indexing and retrieval system based on anchor texts, called Tempas (*Temporal archive search*), that can be accessed live at :

http://tempas.L3S.de

Further, we discuss several interesting search results as well as one experiment in which we demonstrate how such results can be integrated into a data processing workflow to scale up to thousands of pages, showing how restaurant prices increased in Germany when the Euro as a new currency was introduced, as reported by an offline study [11].

2 TEMPORAL WEB ARCHIVE SEARCH

Information needs of users are different on Web archives than on the current Web. The goal of our Tempas system is to satisfy those needs, which are primarily navigational with a temporal aspect, as we discuss in Section 2.1. In Tempas users can formulate their information need by specifying a textual query with the option of selecting a time interval of interest. The screenshot in Figure 1 shows the user interface. Tempas (v2) is based on anchor texts, which feature some specific characteristics that make them well-suited for this our purpose, as listed in Section 2.2. Ultimately, in Section 2.3, we summarize the problem that we address with our system by following the approach presented in Section 4.

2.1 User Intent in Web Archives

User intents formulated as queries and issued to a Web search engine are commonly classified by their information needs into *informational*, *navigational* and *transactional*. Broder [6] analyzed query logs and found that around a half of the queries are informational. The other half is roughly split into 40% navigational and 60% transactional queries.

These proportions are different for Web archives. There is seldom the need to issue an informational query to a Web archive, partly because most informational facts and intents can be served on the current Web as well. Also, transactional queries, which refer to an action that a user wants to perform, e.g., chat or shop online, are typically not applicable in an archive. Therefore, the majority of queries to a Web archive are navigational.

Costa and Silva [9] confirmed this assumption by analyzing query logs of their full-text search engine for the *Portugese Web Archive*. They report more than a half of the queries to be navigational. From the other half a large majority was informational with only 5-10% being transactional. However, what they consider transactional is much more specific than the original definition, such as downloading an old file or recovering a specific website. Similarly, their informational need refers to collecting information about a subject in the past and can often be interpreted as navigational.

Indeed, all information needs of Web archives could be considered navigational in a broad sense. That is, instead of navigating to a specific resource, we want to navigate to a specific information or subject, e.g., an entity. Some of these entities are represented on the Web by their personal or official websites, others by profiles on social networks or sub-pages on related websites, as well as Wikipedia or similar knowledge bases. We refer to these *central* resources as *authority pages* for a subject / an entity. These are dynamic though, and may change over time by some disappearing or moving to a different domain as well as new ones emerging.

2.2 Searching Anchor Texts

Links between pages are typically anchored by a text segment, i.e., the text in the source page that can be clicked on, called *anchor text*. Anchor texts are a special type of text and should not be treated as running text, like articles or similar content. Although those snippets have some disadvantages in being potentially less descriptive than the text surrounding a link or the content of a linked page, they have great advantages for our primary use case of finding *authority pages* as described above:

- Anchor texts describe with a high confidence the linked webpage with **little distracting or unrelated content**. This prevents pages from showing up for unrelated query terms and gives a higher relative relevance to page actually related to a query term.
- Often, anchor texts contain the name of the linked page or a **concise label of the linked content**. Hence, these terms are frequently used to link to authority pages of entities. For instance, the name of a person is outstandingly often used to link to the person's website, which is therefore likely to be ranked high for this query.
- As probably intended by the original reason for hyperlinks on the Web, anchor texts frequently point to pages containing a more detailed description of the contained terms. This way, instead of repeating **descriptions or definitions**, pages link to the most meaningful explanation of the linked text, which often is a social profile, the official website, or an encyclopedic article, e.g., *Wikipedia*.
- Within a website, anchor texts are used as **navigational elements** to refer to certain parts of the site, e.g., the menu on a restaurant site (s. Sec 6). The same term is then commonly used in connection with the site's name to deep link into that part of the website from external pages.

2.3 Problem Statement

The main objective of Tempas is to meet the information need of a user exploring a Web archive and fulfill the user's intent as defined in Section 2.1: Given a textual keyword query together with a time interval we want to identify those webpages that are central for the subject addressed by the query in the specified time period. For instance, before the *European Union* received its own `.eu` top-level domain in 2005, the official website resided under `.eu.int` (cp. Sec. 5.2). Another kind of pages that are of interest when working with Web archives are those in a certain category or with a certain type of contents, such as online shops or restaurant menus. In contrast to queries for *authority pages*, which are rather precision oriented, here recall matters, for instance in data mining tasks (cp. Sec. 6).

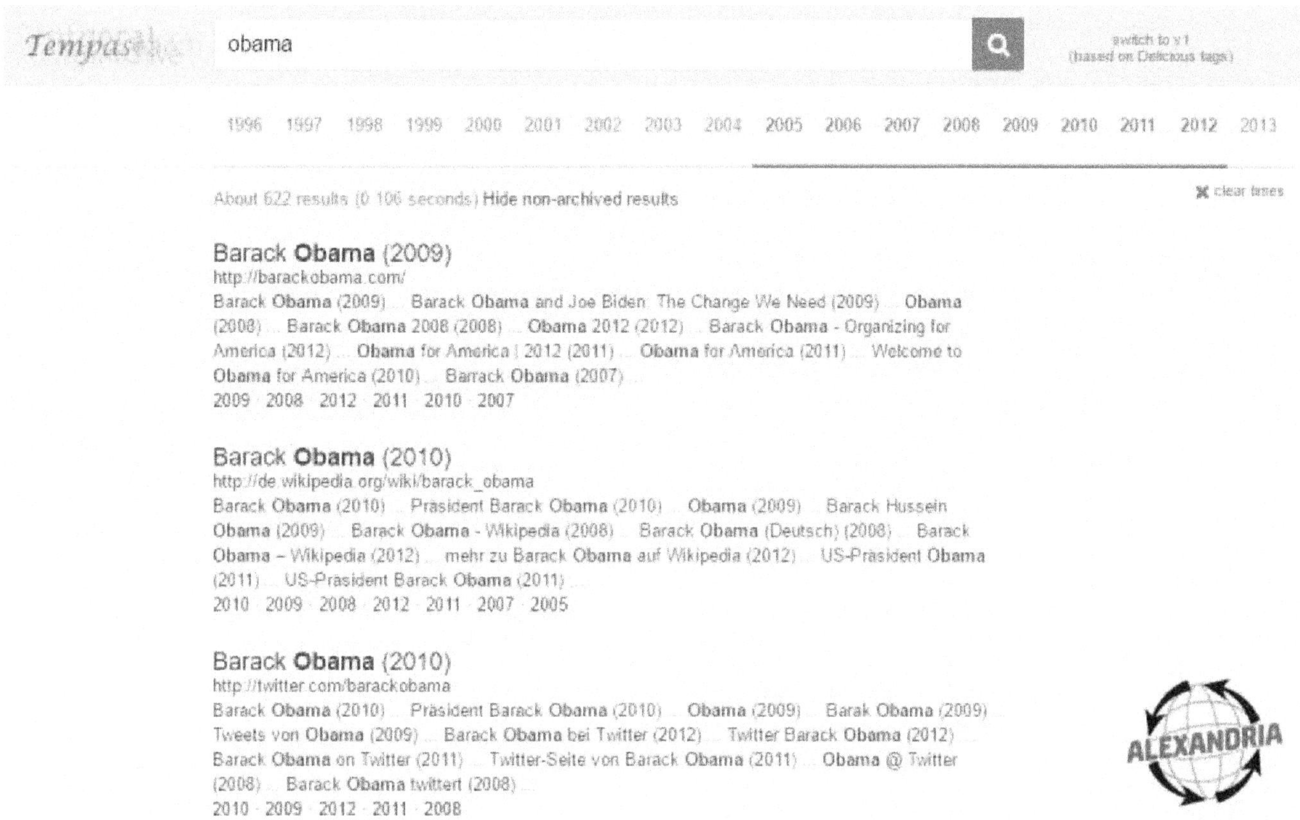

Figure 1: Tempas v2 screenshot for query '*obama*' in period 2005 to 2012.

In summary, both types of navigational queries serve as important entry points into huge Web archives, which is what we are aiming for. Even though users commonly have a subjective understanding of this problem, a quantitative evaluation is not trivial due to the lack of a crisp definition of an authority page or appropriate entry point. Moreover, we found that existing relevance judgments used in Web information retrieval are not suitable for evaluating this task. For instance, in the *TREC 2012 Web Track* adhoc judgements[1], `phoenix.edu` was considered irrelevant for the query *university of phoenix*, which we consider a perfect hit. Therefore, we conduct a qualitative evaluation based on example queries in Section 5 and a data analysis scenario in Section 6.

3 RELATED WORK

The predecessor of the system presented in this work, i.e., the first version of Tempas (v1), was built with the same goals in mind: *temporal Web archive search* for *authority pages* given a keyword query together with a time interval [14]. However, instead of using anchor texts, we incorporated tags attached to URLs on the social bookmarking platform *Delicious*. Without evaluating the precision of the ranking, which was based on the frequency of a tag used with a URL, we showed that this approach results in a good recall with respect to URLs clicked on available query logs from AOL and MSN [16]. Switching to anchor texts was the natural consequence, since Delicious is a closed system and available data is limited, with our dataset ranging only from 2003 to 2011. We also showed that it is very biased towards a certain group of users and the shift to anchor texts can deliver better results, for more diverse queries.

Navigational intent in Web archive search: Web archive search can be considered a special case of temporal information retrieval (IR). While information needs in IR are traditionally classified according to the taxonomy introduced by Broder [6], user intents are different for Web archives as studied by Costa and Silva [9]. In contrast to the majority of queries being informational, where users search for information, in Web archives queries are predominantly navigational, because users often look for specific resources in a Web archive under a temporal aspect (cp. Sec. 2.1). The Internet Archive's *Wayback Machine*[2] recently got a *site search* feature based on anchor texts [12], using an approach similar to ours. However, in contrast to our Tempas system, the *Wayback Site Search* has no explicit temporal search support. Users cannot specify a time interval for their queries, and results are limited to homepages, i.e., the hostname of a URL without a path. Thus, it can find *Barack*

[1] http://trec.nist.gov/data/web2012.html

[2] http://archive.org/web

Obama's official website, but not his Wikipedia article or social media profiles.

Temporal indexing and retrieval models: Temporal information retrieval has emerged as an important subfield in information retrieval with the goal to improve search effectiveness by exploiting temporal information in documents and queries [7]. The value of the temporal dimension was clearly identified in [1] and has led to a plethora of work which utilizes temporal features in query understanding [17], retrieval models [5, 22] and temporal indexing [2, 3]. A survey by Campos et al. [7] gives an elaborate overview of the field. Most of the temporal retrieval models either focus on temporal informational intents [5] or are concerned with increasing recall with diversification [4, 22]. Temporal indexing approaches [2, 3] over Web archives assume documents to be versions of full-text content. A survey of existing Web archive search architectures was presented by Costa et al. [8]. We posit that building a suitable temporal full-text index for Web archive data is challenging and expensive though, and has never been shown to be very effective. Contrary to previous approaches that concern themselves with full-text indexes and ad-hoc retrieval tasks we focus on building minimalistic indexes for temporal navigational intents.

Effectiveness of anchor texts: The effectiveness of anchor texts for the task of *site finding* was already shown by Craswell et al. [10], though not in the context of Web archives or a temporal setting. They are reported to be twice as effective as searching the contents of pages. The authors in Kraaij et al. [20] combined anchor texts with content features for the task of *entry page search* and also found that search just based on anchor texts outperforms basic content features. In a similar experiment, Ogilvie and Callan [21] showed that anchor texts are the most effective features among others, such as full text and title, for the task of finding homepages and are only slightly behind full-text search for finding so-called *named pages*. Koolen and Kamps [19] re-evaluated the effectiveness of anchor texts in ad-hoc retrieval and showed that propagated anchor text outperforms full-text retrieval in terms of early precision on the TREC 2009 Web track. The authors in Kanhabua and Nejdl [18] studied anchor texts in a temporal context and analyzed their value in Wikipedia. Similar to our findings presented in Section 5.2, they were able to observe evolutions of entities through anchor texts, such as the transition of *Barack Obama* from senator to president. They also proposed a temporal anchor text model for their study, though specific to Wikipedia.

4 APPROACH

Our approach to temporal Web archive search is based on indexing anchor texts extracted from time-varying Web corpora. We build our work on the observation that anchor texts are crucial text segments, which in many cases succeed well to describe succinctly the target webpage, and hence are a natural choice for navigational queries. In Section 4.1 we first detail the temporal Web model with hyperlinks and anchor texts used as node descriptors. We then describe our retrieval model based on the indexed anchor text statistics in Section 4.2, before we outline the index layout, construction and query processing for efficient retrieval in Section 4.3.

4.1 Temporal Web Model

Web archive model: A Web archive is a collection of pages $p \in \mathcal{P}$, each with one or multiple versions / captures $p = \{c_{p,t_1} \dots c_{p,t_n}\}$ representing the page at different points in time $(t_1 \dots t_n)$, that is when the page was crawled and archived. Each capture c_t represents a response of the web server returned to the crawler at time t for a requested page p. This can be a successful response including the contents of the page or it could be a different status reply hinting at the page being offline or moved. As we are only interested in the hyperlinks on a page, we model a capture as the set of contained links if successful or the empty set otherwise: A capture $c_i \subseteq L$ of page p_i is a set of links where each link $l_{ijm} \in L$ points from p_i to another page p_j, anchored by a text segment $a_m \in A$ (on p_i), i.e., the text that can be clicked on, typically called *anchor text*. In essence each link l_{ijm} connects a source page p_i with the anchor text a_m to a destination page p_j.

Since the **Web is dynamic** and pages change over time, **links can change** as well. While this can happen multiple times between two captures, we only consider those changes than can be observed through one of the captures in the archive. Link changes are constituted by either:

- a link is removed from a page,
- a new link is added to a page,
- the anchor text of a link changes,
- the target page of a link changes.

A change of the source would be considered the link to be removed from its original page and added to a new one. As we identify a link by its properties, i.e., an edge consisting of a source and a target page as well as its anchor text, the result of any of the four types of changes applied to a link would be considered a different link. However, a link l_{ijm} being removed from page p_i and added back later to it with the same target page p_j and the exact same anchor text a_m is treated as the same link again.

Graph model: Let $G = (V, E)$ be a graph with a set of nodes / vertices $v_i \in V$ and a set of directed edges $e_{jk} = (v_j, v_k) \in E \subseteq V \times V$ pointing from node v_j to v_k. For the Web or a Web archive, such a graph represents the links connecting webpages: each node $v_i \in V$ represents a webpage and an edge $e_{jk} \in E$ corresponds to a link from webpage v_j to page v_k. Two or more links on the same page with the same destination and anchor text are considered to be equal and only counted as one. However, it is possible that multiple links $l_{jkm} \in L$ exist for the same edge e_{jk}. Hence, the Web $\mathcal{W}$ can be modeled as a edge-labeled, directed graph, with the labels being the set of anchor texts accompanied by a set of links: $\mathcal{W} = (G, A, L)$.

In Web archives, which have a temporal dimension, there are multiple ways to **extract a representation of the Web** W as defined above **for a time interval** $[t_a, t_b]$. As the graph G as well as the set of anchor texts A in $\mathcal{W}$ can be derived from the set of links L, the temporal representation depends on how we extract the links from the captures during the given interval: $L \subseteq \bigcup_{p \in \mathcal{P}} c \in \{c_t \in p | t \geq t_a \wedge t \leq t_b\}$. While there exist various ways to define this set, we identified the following three:

1. **Merge**. The most straight-forward way is to merge all links that existed in some capture during the time interval under consideration. Hence, the resulting graph also includes links that existed

in some capture but were deleted later in another capture of the same page during the interval. Two or more links corresponding to the same edge but labeled with different anchor texts at different time points during the interval are all included:

$$L_{\texttt{merge}} = \bigcup_{p \in \mathcal{P}} c \in \{c_t \in p | t_a \leq t \leq t_b\}$$

This is the most complete representation as it merges all links, regardless of whether they still exist at the end of the interval or not.

2. **Temporal Snapshot**. A temporal snapshot or simply *snapshot* refers to a single point in time as opposed to a period. For a given time interval $[t_a, t_b]$, the snapshot representation at time t_b contains only links from the latest captures c_t for each page from that interval with $t \leq t_b$, i.e., links that actually exist at time t_b:

$$L_{\texttt{snapshot}} = \bigcup_{p \in \mathcal{P}} \underset{c_t \in \{c_t \in p | t_a \leq t \leq t_b\}}{\arg\max} t$$

This model resembles the actual Web at time t_b most closely and is best suited for analyzing the Web or its structure. However, it is not ideal for information retrieval as we miss the intermediate states in the considered time period corresponding to the granularity of our index.

3. **Emergence**. *Emergence* refer to the links posted / created in a given time interval $[t_a, t_b]$. In that respect it is as complete as a *merged* representation if all consecutive intervals are considered. However, it is more space efficient as it does not contain the captures already present before the considered interval:

$$L_{\texttt{emergence}} = \bigcup_{p \in \mathcal{P}} c \in \{c_t \in p | t_a \leq t \leq t_b\} \setminus \bigcup_{p \in \mathcal{P}} c \in \{c_t \in p | t < t_a\}$$

This representation has two major advantages for temporal search, which is the reason why we chose $L_{\texttt{emergence}}$ to build our indexes: 1) only pages that are actively being linked in the queried time period are considered, while pages that got frequently linked earlier but are not relevant anymore are ignored even if the old links still exist on the Web, 2) the index size is significantly reduced as each link is only included in one interval.

4.2 Temporal Retrieval Model

Based on a given granularity (we use one year), we split the duration of a provided Web archive collection into equally sized time intervals $\{[t_0, t_1], [t_2, t_3], \ldots, [t_{n-1}, t_n]\}$. For each of these time intervals we create a temporal Web representation, derived from the set of links $L_{[t_a, t_b]}$, which is defined as described above (here: $L_{\texttt{emergence}}$):

$$\mathcal{W}_{[t_a,t_b]} = (G_{[t_a,t_b]}, A_{[t_a,t_b]}, L_{[t_a,t_b]})$$

In the following we omit the interval and treat the Web model $\mathcal{W} = (G, A, L)$ for every interval independently. From the graph $G = (V, E)$ of W, each node $v \in V$ represents a page that is either part of the Web archive in the current interval or is linked to from such a page but not necessarily contained itself. Let $freq(v, a)$ be a scoring function used to compute the relevance of the page represented by node v for a given anchor text $a \in A$. We define this function based on the edges $e = (u, v) \in E$ with source $u \in V$ and destination v for which a link $l \in L$ exists with anchor text a (l_{uva}). Instead of counting these edges directly, we count the number of different hosts $host(u)$ of the source nodes u of the edges, i.e., the hostname in the URL of the page corresponding to node u, e.g., `en.wikipedia.org` in `https://en.wikipedia.org/wiki/World_Wide_Web`:

$$freq(v, a) = |\{host(u) | e = (u, v) \in E \wedge (e, a) \in L\}|$$

Host frequencies have turned out to be more resistant against link spam in our experimentation. While many pages linking to a single URL may all belong to the same website and hence, created by the same domain owner, these are counted only once in our system.

To compute the **relevance score** $rel(v, a)$ this frequency score is normalized based on the maximum among all $v \in V$ and all $a \in A$, which results in numbers between 0 and 1. Finally, we introduce a multiplicative factor γ to get positive scores along with a logarithmic function to dampen the differences:

$$rel(v, a) = log(\frac{freq(v, a)}{\max_{v \in V, a \in A} freq(v, a)} \cdot \gamma)$$

This score is used to **boost the textual relevance** of the query, i.e., a double boost means a match is twice as important. The textual relevance is computed among all anchor texts for a page that fall into the same relevance class $\varphi = relc(v, a)$, which we consider the floor of the relevance score, i.e., the greatest integer less than or equal to this score:

$$relc(v, a) = \lfloor rel(v, a) \rfloor$$

For the boosting we multiply the relevance class score with the logarithm of the maximum score to account for time intervals with low overall frequencies. Since it is *easier* for a page to receive a high relevance score if only very few pages are archived in that time period and potentially link to a page, we want to reward those hits for a query that receive a high relevance score in a time period with a larger number of pages in the archive:

$$boost(\varphi) = \varphi \cdot log(\max_{v \in V, a \in A} freq(v, a))$$

The **result ranking** is then computed based on the textual relevance scores retrieved from our index (s. Sec 4.3) for all relevance classes φ and boosted according to the boosting score as defined above. The final score is the linear combination of all boosted scores.

4.3 Index Construction and Retrieval

The indexes for our Tempas (v2) system have been computed according to the models described above on the German Web archive from 1996 to 2013, which was collected and generously provided to us by the *Internet Archive*[3]. It comprises of more than 2 billion distinct archived webpages under the German `.de` top-level domain. These link to a total of 26, 443, 384, 902 URLs, not only under `.de`. After filtering malformed / invalid URLs as well as those that are very infrequently linked, i.e., $rel(v, a)$ is smaller than 1 for any anchor text a that links to the page represented by node v, we are left with 319,574,156 URLs that go into our index. The maximum frequencies of links from distinct hosts to distinct destinations with

[3]http://archive.org

distinct anchor texts, that are used for normalizing the relevance scores as well as for boosting, are listed in Table 1.

Table 1: Maximum frequencies per year

Year	Count	Year	Count	Year	Count
1996	17	2002	3109	2008	28764
1997	166	2003	16222	2009	30132
1998	92	2004	225066	2010	49658
1999	120	2005	42378	2011	64692
2000	128	2006	85691	2012	87444
2001	955	2007	111561	2013	48871

Tempas (v2) is implemented using *Elastic Search*[4] (ES). ES creates a separate **full-text index** for each indexed field in its **schema**. We defined this schema such that a field of a document, i.e., a page / URL, represents a relevance class φ in one time interval. We used a yearly granularity for building our indexes, so one time interval represents a year $y \in \{1996, 1997, \ldots, 2013\}$: $[t_a, t_b]$ = [y/01/01 - 00:00:00, y/12/31 - 12:59:59]. For each of these time intervals we extracted the link list $L_{\texttt{emergence}}$ and corresponding temporal model (s. Sec. 4.1). To compute the relevance scores (s. Sec. 4.2) we set the parameter $\gamma = 10,000$, i.e., we consider four decimal places of the normalized frequencies, and used basis 3 for the logarithm. This results in relevance classes between 0 and 8. Finally, the anchor texts $a \in A$ that describe any of the links to a URL represented by a node $v \in V$ form the document of the corresponding webpage, with a indexed in the field of its relevance class $relc(v, a)$, e.g.:

```
{
  "url": "http://.../wiki/World_Wide_Web",
  "years": {
    "2013": {
      "8": ["World Wide Web", "WWW", ...],
      "7": ["internet", ...]
      ...
    },
    "2012": {
      ...
    },
    ...
  }
}
```

Depending on the selected time period the corresponding fields are queried. Textual relevance is computed by ES among all anchor texts in these field based on a vector space model using a variant of `tf-idf`, i.e., a combination of the *term frequency, inverse document frequency* and *field-length norm*[5]. This is boosted and averaged as defined above and the results are ranked accordingly. The title and snippets shown in Figure 1 are generated from matching anchor texts sorted by the boost values of the fields that the anchor text appears in as returned by ES's *highlight* feature. The same order is used for the years listed below each search result, with the first year being selected as the main year linked by the title.

[4]http://www.elastic.co

[5]https://www.elastic.co/guide/en/elasticsearch/guide/current/scoring-theory.html

5 EMPIRICAL EVALUATION

In the following we give a qualitative evaluation of the Tempas (v2) system. Before we will look at some example queries and analyze the results returned by Tempas for these queries in more detail, we discuss our general observations of the system in Section 5.1.

5.1 General Discussion

In our current Tempas version not all of the returned search results are available in the underlying Web archive, as that is not checked when the indices are built. Instead, we provide a feature to check search results for presence in the Internet Archive's *Wayback Machine* at the displayed years after they have been returned to the user and hide them in case they are not archived. In the following we will ignore this and discuss all results returned by Tempas, regardless of whether they are archived or not.

Anchor text search: Anchor texts have special characteristics and should not be treated as running texts as we discussed in Section 2.2. We found our result rankings often to be highly satisfactory for queries taking those characteristics into account, but less useful when formulated differently. For instance, the name of a website typically yields what is expected, while the topic does not. E.g., the query *google* results in `google.com` and `google.de` at the top ranks, however, the query *search engine* does not even return these URLs on the first page. A reason for this is that famous websites are usually linked by their name instead of a description, while the descriptive terms may be part of another site's name, which is then ranked higher, such as `searchenginewatch.com`.

This meets our objective of finding suitable entry points into a Web archive, such as a specific page even if the **URL changes over time**. However, we do not cover the opposite case where the name of a website has changed, and possibly the URL too. For such renamings one would like to find the former URL under the current name, which would require a deeper evolution analysis of the Web graph, which is out of the scope of this work.

Another assumption is that pages are sufficiently frequently linked to. This is not always the case especially in the earlier periods of our Web archive due to the limited number of available pages (cp. Table 1). As a result, the performance of `Tempas` is better for queries at query intervals starting from around the mid 2000s.

German Web dataset: Although the index of Tempas was build from a German Web archive (s. Sec 4.3), it is not limited to webpages from the German Web but can also find pages under different top-level domains that are linked from a page under `.de`. For multi-lingual websites, such as *Wikipedia*, the German versions are typically preferred, as these are more frequently linked from other German websites and therefore receive higher frequency scores (s. Sec 4.2).

We observed that English query terms or non-German entities work quite well in many cases and return the expected results, but overall result in less hits, e.g., *obama* has only 724 results, while *merkel* has 11,913. This is usually not critical, as similar to what happens with popular search engines like Google or Bing, often only the very first hits in Tempas are relevant for a query. While

Table 2: Selected temporal hits for query '*obama*'

***obama* @ [2005, 2006]**
1. http://obama.senate.gov
2. http://de.wikipedia.org/wiki/barack_obama
***obama* @ [2005, 2007]**
1. http://myspace.com/barackobama
4. http://obama.senate.gov
5. http://youtube.com/profile?user=barackobamadotcom
***obama* @ [2008, 2013]**
1. http://barackobama.com
2. http://de.wikipedia.org/wiki/barack_obama
3. http://twitter.com/barackobama

that is typically the first page, i.e., first ten hits, in Tempas we found that very often only the first one to five results are subjectively very relevant to the query. This can be partially explained by the diversification features of the big, multi-purpose search engines, as well as their goal to meet various kinds of information needs as opposed to the more focused navigational needs we are adressing. Thus, a general query issued to search engines is often multi-faceted and the sought information is scattered among multiple pages, while navigational queries on Google or Bing are usually answered by only a few hits.

Temporal granularity: By temporally searching Tempas, i.e. entering both a textual query and a time interval, we found that the quality of results is much lower when only single years are selected as opposed to selecting a range of consecutive years. Even though our indices are build on a yearly basis (with separate fields for each relevance class), it appears that only combining multiple indices leads to the expected results. By further analyzing this issue, we found that more famous pages are permanently linked over time but often do not show peaks for single years like less popular pages sometimes do. Averaging over multiple years results in a smoothing of these peaks and drops the subjectively less relevant results below these temporally highly frequent hits. For that reason, all example queries shown in Section 5.2 are issues for periods of multiple years instead of single years.

5.2 Example Queries

Let us now discuss a few example queries that we consider to be potentially interesting for the problem of temporally navigational queries in Web archives (s. Sec. 2): *Barack Obama*, *Angela Merkel*, *European Union*, *Creative Common License* and *Wikipedia*. All of them feature temporal characteristics, stressing different aspects.

Barack Obama. One of those entities popular all around the world is the US president. During the later times of our dataset this was *Barack Obama*. Therefore, he will serve as our first example query. Figure 1 shows the results for the time from when he became Senator of Illinois in 2005 until 2012 when he was re-elected as president. Although in this case the query is only his last name *obama*, we receive hits solely for *Barack Obama* as he is more prominently linked on the German Web than for example his wife *Michelle Obama* and search result diversification features are not implemented in our retrieval model.

Table 3: Selected temporal hits for query '*merkel*' and '*angela merkel*'

***merkel* @ [2000, 2004]**
1. http://merkel.de *(university bookstore Merkel)*
2. http://angela-merkel.de
***angela merkel* @ [2000, 2004]**
1. http://angela-merkel.de
2. http://cdu.de/idx-merkel.htm
3. http://cdu.de/ueber-uns/buvo/pv/pv.htm
***merkel* @ [2005, 2010]**
1. http://angela-merkel.de
2. http://de.wikipedia.org/wiki/angela_merkel
***merkel* @ [2010, 2013]**
1. http://angela-merkel.de
2. http://facebook.com/angelamerkel?...
3. http://de.wikipedia.org/wiki/angela_merkel
4. http://twitter.com/search?q=%23merkel

When searching this long time frame of eight years, Tempas finds the overall most prominent authority websites of Barack Obama in these years, as expected: 1. his official website, 2. his Wikipedia article, 3. his Twitter account. More temporally sensitive results are retrieved when meaningful time frames of Barack Obama are queried, as shown in Table 2. For instance, in 2005 / 2006, i.e., Obama's first two years as senator of Illinois, his senate page is the top hit, followed by his Wikipedia article. By extending the time interval to 2007, that page gets pushed to rank 4, caused by the rise of social media with his *Myspace* page taking the lead and his *YouTube* profile on rank 5. In between are German news articles reporting about his run for president (not shown in Table 2). Starting from when Obama was elected president in 2008 we get the same results as discussed above, including his official website and Twitter replacing Myspace as his main social media profile. Before 2005 there are no hits for Barack Obama at all, because he was very famous in Germany and therefore, not sufficiently linked.

Angela Merkel. An equally famous politician, especially in Germany, is the German chancellor *Angela Merkel*. However, it is interesting to search only her last name before 2005. In contrast to *Obama*, which always referred to Barack Obama and was not relevant at all before, *Merkel* was the name of a university bookstore, which received even more links from 2000 to 2004 than the later chancellor, as shown in Table 3. Unfortunately, this website is not present in the archive and the domain is used differently today.

Therefore, to query for the person Angela Merkel, her full name should be used in earlier years. After 2004 this does not make a difference anymore. Angela Merkel exhibits a similar evolution as the US president, which can be observed through Tempas as well. Before she was elected chancellor in 2005 she became the leader of her party *CDU* in 2000. Therefore, next to her official website, pages on the party's site are among the top hits. From 2005, with her election, also her Wikipedia page become more popular. Later, in 2010, her social media profiles on Facebook and Twitter began to gain popularity.

Table 4: Selected temporal hits for query '*european union*'

european union @ [1996, 2005]
1. http://europa.eu.int
***european union* @ [2005, 2013]**
1. http://en.wikipedia.org/wiki/european_union
2. http://europa.eu
3. http://europa.eu.int

European Union. Like many international organizations, the European Union's official website was located under the top-level domain `.int`: `http://europa.eu.int`. In 2005 they received their own top-level domain `.eu`: `http://europa.eu`. Today the `.int` URL does not exist anymore and the `.eu` one replaced it completely. This evolution is reflected by the queries shown in Table 4. In addition, as for most famous entities, their Wikipedia article has become one the most important resources about the EU.

This is a classical example where looking up a website in a Web archive is difficult as we need to be aware of the former URL that was active at the time of interest. Without a system like Tempas the best bet would be the current URL of the EU, which did not exist prior to 2005.

Creative Commons License. *Creative Commons* (CC) is one the most popular copyright and open content licenses. Since the inception of the CC organization in 2001 and the release of the first version in 2002, there have been three updates until its current version 4.0 was released in 2013[6].

The different variants of the CC license, e.g., *BY-NC-SA*, *BY-NC-ND*, ..., are used by many projects on the Web. As they are commonly linked under the name *Creative Commons License*, their version history can be traced through the Tempas search results, shown in Table 5. At any time the query leads to the current version of the license. Even though the URLs change over time, the query together with a timespan can be considered a temporal reference.

Wikipedia. Today Wikipedia is widely known under its domain `wikipedia.org` or corresponding language versions, e.g., `de.wikipedia.org` for the German version of Wikipedia. However, when it was launched in 2001, its domain was under `.com`

[6]https://wiki.creativecommons.org/wiki/License_Versions

Table 5: Selected temporal hits for query '*creative commons license*'

creative commons license @ [2002, 2003]
1. http://creativecommons.org/licenses/by-nc-sa/1.0
2. http://creativecommons.org/licenses/by-nd-nc/1.0
***creative commons license* @ [2004, 2006]**
1. http://creativecommons.org/licenses/by-nc-sa/2.0
2. http://creativecommons.org/licenses/by-nc-nd/2.0
***creative commons license* @ [2007, 2013]**
1. http://creativecommons.org/licenses/by/2.5
2. http://creativecommons.org/licenses/by/3.0
3. http://creativecommons.org/licenses/by-nc-sa/3.0

Table 6: Selected temporal hits for query '*wikipedia*'

wikipedia @ [2001, 2002]
1. http://de.wikipedia.com/wiki.cgi?wikipedia_willkommen
2. http://wikipedia.com
3. http://de.wikipedia.com
***wikipedia* @ [2003, 2013]**
1. http://de.wikipedia.org
2. http://de.wikipedia.org/wiki/hauptseite
3. http://wikipedia.de
3. http://wikipedia.org

and moved to `.org` one year later. Today, the `.com` domain and subdomains forward to their `.org` counterparts and no one is aware of the old URLs anymore. Without this information, it is impossible to look up the early website of Wikipedia in a Web archive. Again, this is revealed by the search results in Tempas, shown in Table 6, which make such a lookup very easy.

6 DATA ANALYSIS

Besides manual exploration of Web archives in order to look at webpages from previous times, finding the right entry points into such an archive is crucial for data analysis tasks. Due to the vast sizes of Web archives in the order of hundreds of terabytes or even petabytes, scanning all pages is impossible. Temporal Web search capabilities such as provided by Tempas help to find the right entry points over time, which allows for temporal analyses. From these pages the archive can be scanned further. Although this does not guarantee a full coverage of all interesting contents, it is likely that we find relevant pages and thus, constituting an efficient way to create a representative sample supporting significant analysis results. As an example, we studied the evolution of restaurant prices in Germany during the time when the Euro was introduced as Europe's new currency.

6.1 ArchiveSpark

ArchiveSpark was presented in Holzmann et al. [15] and is available open source[7]. This distributed data computing framework for efficient Web archive processing and analysis exploits the fact that archive data is commonly organized with corresponding metadata in order to randomly access archived resources. The *Wayback Machine* uses these metadata records to locate a archived webpages for a given URL and timestamp as well as its embedded resources, such as images and scripts, in the Web archive. In ArchiveSpark these metadata records are incorporated as surrogate of an actual Web archive collection. Because of their small size and easily parsable structure this enables much more efficient loading and processing compared to the full records. After performing the necessary operations on the available metadata, like filtering, sorting and grouping based on URLs, status codes and mime types, the actual content is seamlessly integrated in a so-called *enrichment* step. During this phase, third-party libraries can be applied to extract or derive additional information.

[7]https://github.com/helgeho/ArchiveSpark

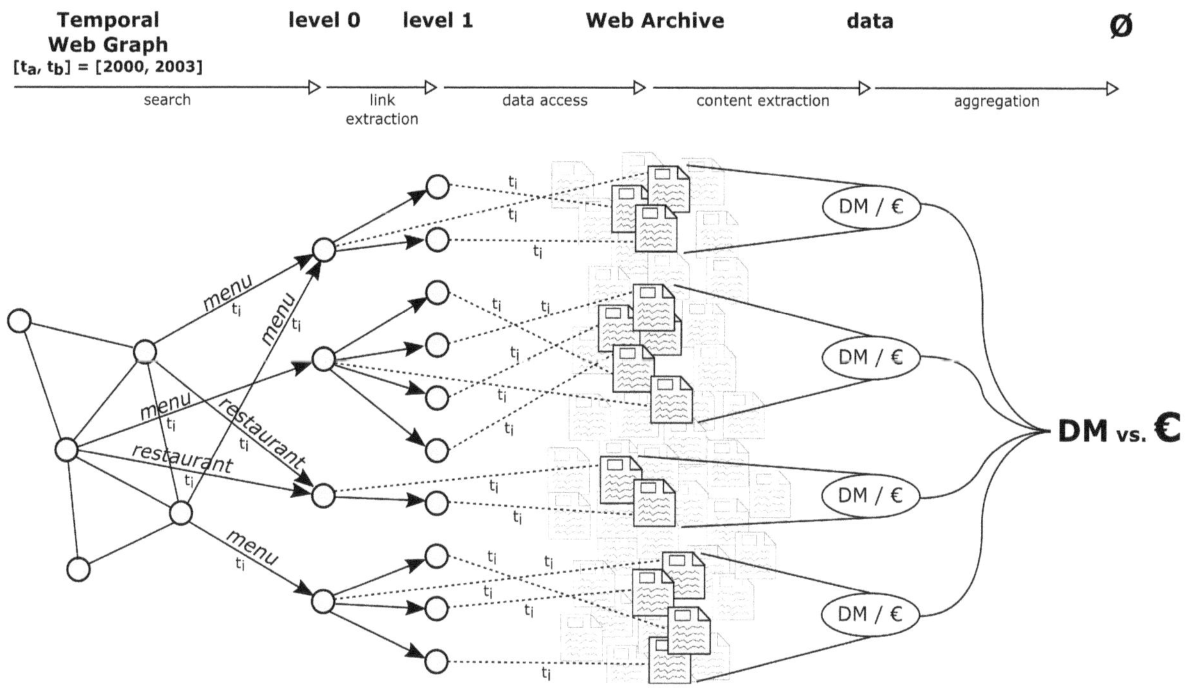

Figure 2: Data analysis pipeline from Web archive search on temporal anchor texts over selective Web archive data access and extraction to the result as shown in Section 6.2: Restaurant prices increased when the Euro replaced the DM as the currency in Germany.

We later generalized this approach to work with any kind of metadata as well as various data sources. For instance, metadata can be loaded from a database system or search engine now, and the data records can be integrated from remote services through HTTP instead of a local file store, for example directly from the *Wayback Machine.* In addition to that, we also added support for arbitrary new data types other than Web archives. This allows for very flexible data analysis and *distant reading* workflows. In contrast to *close reading,* which refers to looking at every record individually in a manual fashion, *distant reading* refers to the analysis of larger collections of documents through aggregations and statistical methods.

For the work described in this paper, we integrate Tempas as an alternative metadata provider, while the archived webpages corresponding to the search results are loaded from the *Wayback Machine.* Hence, a pre-filtering of the Internet Archive's Web archive is performed by keyword as well as time through the Tempas index, before content is loaded for returned hits. The logic for this data loading and integration step is defined in separate modules for ArchiveSpark, called data specifications (dataspecs). The dataspec used in this experiment has been published under *Tempas2ArchiveSpark*[8] together with the code that describes the pipeline for this particular analysis as illustrated in Figure 2. As metadata and data records are loaded remotely, the study can be repeated or similar studies can be conducted by anyone even without having a suitable dataset available.

[8]https://github.com/helgeho/Tempas2ArchiveSpark

6.2 Example Study

In this small example study we utilize ArchiveSpark to analyze menus of German restaurants at the time when the Euro was introduced as the new currency in Europe and replaced the former German currency *Deutsche Mark (DM)* in 2001/2002. According to many voices in Germany this resulted in increased prices particularly in restaurants. In 2011 the German federal office of statistics published a report in which they studied the effect of the Euro in various areas and categories [11]. According to that study, restaurant prices increased around the time of currency reform by about 4% on average based on more than 700 examined restaurants. However, while some restaurants even reduced their prices, others increased them by up to 20% to 40%.

To get entry points into the archive for our analysis, we queried Tempas for the keywords *'speisekarte'*, which is the German word for menu, as well as *'restaurant'* to find menus after one additional hop, in case it is not linked with this anchor text. Both queries were issued for the time period from 2000 to 2003 and we considered the first 10 pages with 100 results per page, hence 1,000 hits each. As some of the returned URLs were found in multiple years, we started off with 3,567 hits of URL / timestamp pairs for which we integrated contents from the *Wayback Machine.* By manually investigating a few of the result pages on Tempas, we found that they often do not show the prices directly, but link to subpages, such as for starters or main courses. Therefore, we extracted all links under the same hostname and fetched the contents for those URLs as well, which resulted in additional 6,028 pages. From each of these pages we extracted the amounts of money mentioned on the pages as floating point numbers prefixed or suffixed with either *DM*, *Euro*, *EUR* or the Euro symbol €. To verify that we were actually dealing with restaurant menus, we required the pages to mention the term *speise*, which is the German word for meal / dish, and to contain at least three prices. This filtering left us with menus for 49 entry point URLs.

After converting DM to Euro amounts with an exchange rate of 1 EUR = 1.95583 DM, we averaged the amount per currency and URL as well as among URLs. Finally, we ended up with an average of 9.58 Euros and 15.24 DM = 7.79 Euros. That is an increase of 23%. Although this is higher than the average 4% as reported by the study mentioned above, it is in the range between 20% and 40% that was found in the statistics report. We can therefore consider it a reasonable result, although not significant due to the limited number of analyzed menus. The experiment does show, however, how Web archives can be used for studying social issues with temporal anchor texts serving as entry points to access and analyze these extremely big collection, which are otherwise almost impossible to process. With 49 menus out of the initially 3,567 hits and 6,083 analyzed URLs, studying Web archives often is like finding a needle in a haystack. This shows the need of effective ways to identify entry points for both manual search / *close reading* as well as *distant reading* tasks such as the study presented here. Anchor texts have been proven suitable as starting points for exploring Web archives. Thus, given a better domain knowledge of the studied subject and by investing some additional effort, we should be able to produce interesting and significant results with this approach.

7 CONCLUSION AND OUTLOOK

In this paper we propose an alternative to full-text indexing for navigational query intents on Web archives. Full-text indexing over Web archives, which are massive collections (typically in the order of TB and PB), is computationally intensive. To lower the entry barrier for search and recognizing that most interesting query intents are navigational in nature, we can to a large extent satisfy them using surrogates such as anchor texts. The results of such navigational queries can then be used as hooks into more detailed temporal exploration of the Web archive.

Our Tempas system supports these queries and provides a fully functional indexing and retrieval infrastructure for Web Archives. It is based on anchor texts and the underlying Web graph structure. Tempas makes it easy to search for entities in a Web archive and through its results provides useful hooks for further exploration of these entities and aspects related to them.

We also note that *TREC* (Text REtrieval Conference) style empirical evaluations of such temporal navigational tasks are difficult to accomplish, even in a controlled user setup. One promising direction for future work is to improve the effectiveness and soundness of Tempas by building on query logs. We will evaluate our retrieval models on our logs by characterizing specific navigational intents in Web archive search. Further, we plan to outline other informational intents and adapt our retrieval models accordingly.

REFERENCES

[1] Omar Alonso, Michael Gertz, and Ricardo Baeza-Yates. 2007. On the Value of Temporal Information in Information Retrieval. *SIGIR Forum* 41, 2 (Dec. 2007), 35–41. DOI: https://doi.org/10.1145/1328964.1328968
[2] Avishek Anand, Srikanta Bedathur, Klaus Berberich, and Ralf Schenkel. 2011. Temporal index sharding for space-time efficiency in archive search. In *Proceedings of the 34th international ACM SIGIR conference on Research and development in Information Retrieval.*
[3] Avishek Anand, Srikanta Bedathur, Klaus Berberich, and Ralf Schenkel. 2012. Index maintenance for time-travel text search. In *Proceedings of the 35th international ACM SIGIR conference on Research and development in Information Retrieval.*
[4] Klaus Berberich and Srikanta Bedathur. 2013. Temporal diversification of search results. In *SIGIR 2013 Workshop on Time-aware Information Access (TAIA 2013).*
[5] Klaus Berberich, Srikanta Bedathur, Omar Alonso, and Gerhard Weikum. 2010. A Language Modeling Approach for Temporal Information Needs. In *Proceedings of the 32Nd European Conference on Advances in Information Retrieval (ECIR'2010).* Springer-Verlag, Berlin, Heidelberg, 13–25. DOI: https://doi.org/10.1007/978-3-642-12275-0_5
[6] Andrei Broder. 2002. A taxonomy of web search. In *ACM Sigir forum*, Vol. 36. ACM, 3–10.
[7] Ricardo Campos, GaĂćËĘÅąĂĈÅťl Dias, AlĂćËĘÅąĂćâĂřÅăpio M. Jorge, and Adam Jatowt. 2014. Survey of Temporal Information Retrieval and Related Applications. *ACM Comput. Surv.* 47, 2 (Aug. 2014), 15:1–15:41. DOI: https://doi.org/10.1145/2619088
[8] Miguel Costa, Daniel Gomes, Francisco Couto, and Mário Silva. 2013. A Survey of Web Archive Search Architectures. In *Proceedings of the 22nd International Conference on World Wide Web (Companion).*
[9] Miguel Costa and Mário J Silva. 2010. Understanding the Information Needs of Web Archive Users . In *Proceedings of the 10th International Web Archiving Workshop.*
[10] Nick Craswell, David Hawking, and Stephen Robertson. 2001. Effective Site Finding using Link Anchor Information. In *Proceedings of the 24th annual international ACM SIGIR conference on Research and development in information retrieval.* ACM.
[11] German Federal Statistical Office (Statistisches Bundesamt, Destatis). 2011. Fast zehn Jahre Euro - Preisentwicklung vor und nach der BargeldeinfĂČÂijhrung. Article number: 5611105119004 (Decenber 2011). https://www.destatis.de/DE/Publikationen/Thematisch/Preise/Verbraucherpreise/Fast10JahreEuro5611105119004.html [Accessed: 16/03/2017].
[12] Vinay Goel. 2016. Beta Wayback Machine - Now with Site Search! (October 2016). https://blog.archive.org/2016/10/24/beta-wayback-machine-now-with-site-search [Accessed: 16/03/2017].
[13] Wendy Hall, Jim Hendler, and Steffen Staab. 2017. A Manifesto for Web Science @10. *arXiv:1702.08291* (2017).
[14] Helge Holzmann and Avishek Anand. 2016. Tempas: Temporal Archive Search Based on Tags. In *Proceedings of the 25th International Conference Companion on World Wide Web.*
[15] Helge Holzmann, Vinay Goel, and Avishek Anand. 2016. ArchiveSpark: Efficient Web Archive Access, Extraction and Derivation. In *Proceedings of the 16th ACM/IEEE-CS on Joint Conference on Digital Libraries.*
[16] Helge Holzmann, Wolfgang Nejdl, and Avishek Anand. 2016. On the Applicability of Delicious for Temporal Search on Web Archives. In *Proceedings of the 39th International ACM SIGIR conference on Research and Development in Information Retrieval.*
[17] Rosie Jones and Fernando Diaz. 2007. Temporal Profiles of Queries. *ACM Trans. Inf. Syst.* 25, 3 (July 2007). DOI: https://doi.org/10.1145/1247715.1247720
[18] Nattiya Kanhabua and Wolfgang Nejdl. 2014. On the Value of Temporal Anchor Texts in Wikipedia. In *SIGIR 2014 Workshop on Temporal, Social and Spatiallyaware Information Access (TAIA).*
[19] Marijn Koolen and Jaap Kamps. 2010. The importance of anchor text for ad hoc search revisited. In *Proceedings of the 33rd international ACM SIGIR conference on Research and development in information retrieval.* ACM, 122–129.
[20] Wessel Kraaij, Thijs Westerveld, and Djoerd Hiemstra. 2002. The Importance of Prior Probabilities for Entry Page Search. In *Proceedings of the 25th annual international ACM SIGIR conference on Research and development in information retrieval.* ACM.
[21] Paul Ogilvie and Jamie Callan. 2003. Combining Document Representations for Known-Item Search. In *Proceedings of the 26th annual international ACM SIGIR conference on Research and development in informaion retrieval.* ACM.
[22] Jaspreet Singh, Wolfgang Nejdl, and Avishek Anand. 2016. History by Diversity: Helping Historians Search News Archives. In *Proceedings of the 2016 ACM on Conference on Human Information Interaction and Retrieval (CHIIR '16).* ACM, New York, NY, USA, 183–192. DOI: https://doi.org/10.1145/2854946.2854959

Observing Web Archives

The Case for an Ethnographic Study of Web Archiving

Jessica Ogden
University of Southampton
Southampton, UK
jessica.ogden@soton.ac.uk

Susan Halford
University of Southampton
Southampton, UK
susan.halford@soton.ac.uk

Leslie Carr
University of Southampton
Southampton, UK
lac@ecs.soton.ac.uk

ABSTRACT

This paper makes the case for studying the work of web archivists, in an effort to explore the ways in which practitioners shape the preservation and maintenance of the archived Web in its various forms. An ethnographic approach is taken through the use of observation, interviews and documentary sources over the course of several weeks in collaboration with web archivists, engineers and managers at the Internet Archive - a private, non-profit digital library that has been archiving the Web since 1996. The concept of *web archival labour* is proposed to encompass and highlight the ways in which web archivists (as both networked human and non-human agents) shape and maintain the preserved Web through work that is often embedded in and obscured by the complex technical arrangements of collection and access. As a result, this engagement positions web archives as places of knowledge and cultural production in their own right, revealing new insights into the performative nature of web archiving that have implications for how these data are used and understood.[1]

KEYWORDS

web archiving, knowledge production, STS, materiality, information labour

ACM Reference format:
Jessica Ogden, Susan Halford, and Leslie Carr. 2017. Observing Web Archives. In *Proceedings of WebSci '17, Troy, NY, USA., June 25–28, 2017,* 10 pages.
https://doi.org/10.1145/3091478.3091506

1 INTRODUCTION

The World Wide Web has emerged as the preeminent mechanism for global communication, political, economic and cultural exchange and more. Yet, at the same time, the Web is ephemeral. For a medium that has become pre-eminent, its dynamism and transience has become increasingly worrisome. These concerns have been illustrated in various longitudinal studies of link rot [55] and investigations which found that during a period between 2009 and 2012, on average 11% of online resources shared on social media failed to resolve one year later [60]. In this context, it is increasingly claimed that the ephemerality of the Web demands intervention to preserve web content - in web archives - that reconstruct sites and the 'web experience' for posterity [2]. However, there has been rather less attention to the nature of this intervention: how it is done and why this matters. This paper explores the critical decisions being made now that will shape future generations' ability to understand the history of the Web.

[1]This paper is based on data collected and fieldwork undertaken by the first author as part of their PhD research.

ACM ISBN 978-1-4503-4896-6/17/06.
https://doi.org/10.1145/3091478.3091506

1.1 Web Archiving

Web archiving has roots in a wider digital preservation movement which emerged in the 1980s-1990s, led by memory institutions to develop strategies for addressing the rise of personal computing and the impact of digital artefacts on their abilities to capture and preserve 'records of social phenomena' [61]. This was particularly fuelled by fears over the so-called 'digital dark ages,' a term first used by Kuny [41] to describe a scenario where the development pace of technologies (used to produce digital objects) outweighs that of the investment in technologies, infrastructures and policies to preserve them long-term. As the world's information and communication platforms are increasingly born-digital and online, a diverse community of practitioners have positioned web archives as key to capturing and preserving digital cultural heritage, ensuring stability and access to pre-existing web resources and facilitating new knowledge via scholarly research. Web archives in their various forms - including social media archives - have thus become a sort of 'prosthesis' for the Web and a necessary pre-condition for any research into the Web(s) of the past and near-present.[2]

The history of web archiving has been documented to varying degrees in existing overviews [9, 13, 77] which chart the emergence of a field of practice around web archiving. Each have used a series of factors to characterise the domain over time, including: the tools and technologies used, the frequency and scale of selection/collection methods (e.g. broad versus targeted) and the various motivations behind the creation of web archives. These motivations may reinforce and represent, at least in part, a continuation of classical interpretations and analogue conceptions of the value and role of libraries and archives as institutions that provide access to cultural heritage, information and knowledge resources; facilitate evidence-based accountability and promote community memory and identity, amongst others [18, 26].

Web archiving projects have spanned from the large-scale collection of web resources by organisations such as the Internet Archive

[2]Inspiration for this analogy is taken from Derrida's [20] treatment of 'technological devices for archiving' as prostheses for memory formation and storage.

and national libraries and archives, to networked 'rogue' collectives such as Archive Team[3] and DataRefuge,[4] and the individual efforts of activists and scholars creating web archives for their own purposes. Surveys of the field reveal a growing number of organisations that are web archiving, albeit with limited staff-time resources and with the majority of respondents using some form of external service to collect or manage their web archives [3, 52].

Much of the focus of the web archiving community has been on the continued development of technologies and practices for web collection development [35], with an increased attention in recent years on facilitating the scholarly use of web archives [21]. Web archiving has thus become representative of an interdisciplinary space where practitioners and scholars from a range of backgrounds (e.g. libraries, archives, information science, engineering and computer science) come together with scholars from a variety of disciplines (humanities, social sciences and computer science) to study the Web, its application and the users who derive value from its use.

This research examines this space from the perspective of web archival practitioners with the aim of documenting the practices that determine and create the archived Web within the context of the Internet Archive. From the point of view of Web Science, web archiving should not be seen as merely a series of technical solutions to the short-comings of the Web's infrastructure, but rather as an assemblage of contingent sociotechnical practices that shape what is known about the Web. These practices - and the entanglement of both human and non-human actors - are important for understanding the affordances of web archives and their implications for interpreting an increasingly dynamic Web. This type of engagement raises wide-ranging epistemological questions concerning the role of the web archive (and the archivist) in shaping knowledge about the Web. From this perspective, the mechanisms and circumstances surrounding the production of web archives are therefore fundamental to understanding them as 'new forms of social data' [45, p.31].

1.2 Problematising Web Archival Practices

The field of web archiving, the practices and technologies used to facilitate the creation, maintenance and use of web archives are all continually evolving, but not without their issues. The different legal, economic, technical and ethical challenges to preservation and access presented by both 'web documents' and social media have led to a mix of overlapping and divergent collection and access strategies. Existing overviews of the field [9, 48], literature reviews [54] and best practice documents [8, 56] provide models for mapping the general components of web archiving. However, some of this documentation has failed to keep up to date with the pace of web/archiving technology development, and is often limited to specific software, tools and professional contexts (e.g. library or bibliographic approaches to web archiving). Surveys of the field have yielded insights into the types and number of organisations participating in web archiving, the tools and services used, the types of content being archived, and the availability of institutional policy documents and staff-time resources [3, 29, 52]. These surveys provide useful information for understanding the broader landscape of web archiving. However, by virtue of the methods used, they do not provide in-depth information about the day-to-day decisions, activities and processes that facilitate web archiving in practice.

Web technologies are evolving at a faster pace than that of web preservation technologies and practice [21], presenting challenges for preserving an 'infinite stream with finite resources' [42]. The limitations of web harvesters in the face of new markup languages (e.g. HTML5), executable content (e.g. JavaScript and Flash) and other dynamic content (e.g. streamed multimedia, database-driven or password-protected) all often lead to missing elements in the representation of web resources in archives [56]. Problems for use are often presented as issues with the 'quality' of web archives, as measured by the relative 'likeness' between archived web objects and the 'live web.' As Brügger [14, p.108] has described, a combination of both collection decisions and 'technical problems' leads to archived web objects that are not *copies* of the live web, but rather *contingent constructions* where 'the process of archiving itself may change what is archived, thus creating something that is not necessarily identical to what was once online.'

There is an abundance of research within the field pertaining to improving the efficiency and quality of web crawlers, detecting change in web resources and automating frequency decisions associated with captures [64], as well as technical overviews of crawling technologies at the time of production [51]. Yet, little research exists around the interactive nature and structuring effects of algorithmic and automated agents in decisions around what and when to archive. Recent calls for the study of 'archival algorithmic systems' [70, p.11] point towards the need to further consider the performative nature of crawlers and other web archiving technologies, as well as the ways in which different environmental contexts shape the technological development [40] driving collection and access tools. Here web crawlers (non-human, automated agents, bots, algorithms, code) are conceived as not merely passive or objective participants in the collection of web resources [47], but are intricately implicated in the active shaping of the 'doing' of web archiving.

At the heart of conflicts over the collection and use of web archives are often problems with defining the boundaries of the web object to be captured and studied. Whilst recognising that web archives are by nature, inherently and necessarily incomplete [28], they are also highly 'subjective reconstructions' [11, 12] of what exists on the live Web at any given time. As argued by Dougherty and Meyer [21], often the specific ontological and epistemological assumptions made during the collection and curation of web archives are either not made explicit to potential users or are seen as an impediment to their use and/or re-use [21]. Collection decisions, whether thematic or broad, domain-based harvesting [57], the temporal dimensions of when to capture and for how long [46] and issues over geographic [72] and language [1] coverage and representation of the global Web(s), have all highlighted methodological concerns over provenance, the subjectivity of records, the lack of transparency and metadata for harvester algorithms and problems with the generalisability of potential research findings based on web archives.

[3]http://archiveteam.org
[4]https://www.datarefuge.org

Issues of provenance in web archives - the why, when, and how web archives are collected - have inspired calls for greater documentation around intent, particularly around what to preserve and why [76]. Others have focused on calling for greater transparency in how web archives are built, some with a particular focus on the Internet Archive [43]. However, practices that surround the capture and maintenance of web archives remain relatively understudied, and for initiatives that sit outside of mainstream memory institutions, continue to exist almost wholly unexamined. Investigations into how curation strategies and collection tools structure the nature of collections - for example, the timing, frequency and length of collection - have the potential to yield insights into the contingencies that lead to the archived Web(s). Recent qualitative research on web archival appraisal practices by Summers and Punzalan [70] underlines the value of such an approach for both situating web archiving within wider institutional/archival paradigms, as well as exposing undocumented practices largely missing from the archival record. Taking a different approach, Milligan et al. [50] contribute to a discussion of curatorial practices by reverse engineering selection through a comparison of algorithmic, manual and social media-generated web archives associated with the 2015 Canadian Elections. These studies, plus the previously mentioned work of Dougherty and Meyer [21], can be seen as complementary to this research both in methodology and in their aims to address how collection practices structure the nature of web archival engagement. The following sections outline the ways in which this paper aims to extend current knowledge of web archival practice.

1.3 Aims and Outline

This paper aims to examine the ways in which web archives and associated practices - as sociotechnical phenomena - are structured and organised by an array of actors and environmental factors that actively shape the practice of archiving. This research contends that these (often) undocumented activities and processes are critical for interpreting the affordances of web archives as contingent reconstructions of the previously live Web.

The argument for a practice-based approach to web archiving is further examined through a theoretical framework. This framework draws on aspects of archival theory and Science and Technology Studies (STS) investigations into the *materiality* of information mediation practices. Here, examining web archiving from the perspective of the materiality of practice enables two paths of inquiry. The first acknowledges the ways in which new knowledge is embedded and produced as part of the creation of web archives; the second addresses how practice transforms knowledge through the maintenance of web archival systems.[5]

A case for the chosen methodology is then made along with a description of the data collection, in an effort to highlight the ways in which this research may have implications for a Web Science approach to examining sociotechnical practices. The theoretical approach is then worked through empirical examples and discussion drawn from vignettes of ethnographic fieldwork at the Internet Archive. A brief summary discussion is provided that highlights some of the broad findings at this stage of the empirical research.

[5]For further inspiration into the types of inquiries enabled by a focus on the materiality of media technologies, see Gillespie et al. [25].

2 FRAMING PRACTICE ENGAGEMENT

Postmodernism and its application in archival and social theory lays the groundwork for critically engaging with web archiving as knowledge production. From this perspective, there has been a longstanding interest in knowledge production activities where the record is often positioned as 'evidence of process, of activity, [and] of transaction' [34, p.12].

First coined by Stoler [68], 'the archival turn' denotes a shift from 'archive as source' to 'archive as subject', signalling wide-ranging epistemological questions concerning the role of the archive (and the archivist) in shaping and legitimising knowledge and particular ways of knowing. Cook [16, p.4-5] argues that postmodern archival theory represents a fundamental paradigm shift within a community of practice that hitherto had been largely grounded in scientific rationalism, 'archival science,' the merits of record stability and the objective role of archivists; towards one which recognises the incompleteness of records and attends to context and the interpretive role of archivists in the construction of social memory. This signified a theoretical move away from the framing of archives as 'sites of knowledge retrieval' towards a recognition that archives are deeply reflective of and implicated in the production of knowledge [68, p.90]. The conditions of historical narrative-making are intrinsically tied to the processes of archival construction, where certain narratives are privileged and others marginalised through the active reshaping by the archivist [62, 71, 74]. These usually invisible practices involved in the maintenance of archives, have ramifications for the ways in which archival holdings are then (re)presented as being a view from nowhere or of 'all possible statements' rather than 'the law of what can be said' [6].

In contrast, Brown and Davis-Brown [10] focus on the 'technical-rational work' of archivists - or the everyday decisions and practices related to the collection and maintenance of archives. They characterise a profession where the 'explicitly political *who* is often reduced to the technically instrumented *how*' - a sentiment also echoed by critical information studies [7], as well as practitioners from within the web archiving field [76]. In light of this, an engagement with the political nature of web archival practice would then include an examination of what comes to count as the 'professional decision-making' [10] involved in a host of activities that mark the everyday tasks of (organisational) archivists.

The turn also ascribes the importance of unpicking digital information technologies and not falling into the trappings of either equating them to analogue technologies, nor essentialising their capabilities or potentialities for capturing the cultural record. Cook [17], describes the impact of the transition to electronic archival records and the role of postmodern critique in strengthening the role of the archivist in the digital age:

> We will move from databases to knowledge bases. We will move, in the language of the post-modernists, to re-contextualize our activities: we will reorient ourselves from the content to the context, and from the end result to the original empowering intent, that is, from the artifact (the actual record) to the creating processes behind it, and thus to the actions, programmes, and functions behind those processes [17, p.410-411].

As such, archives can be further considered in light of the digital technologies that are intimately tied to both the production and preservation of web resources. Waterton [75, p.653-654] and others make the case for examining digital archives and the 'generative capabilities' of technologically-enabled data, information, and knowledge which are in an 'eternal process of becoming' [33]. Questions are therefore raised regarding how prior conceptualisations of significance and potential use are manifested in the ways in which digital 'objects' are collected and preserved. Pinch and Henry [58]'s notion of the 'materiality of knowledge' is useful here for considering the ways in which knowledge is also 'embedded in physical artefacts, technologies, and ways of doing things'. This is manifested in how practice produces 'material bodies' [4, p.808-809] but also how materiality is bound to and embedded in practice. In this instance Barad [4] is referring to how the body (e.g. the anatomy and physiology) actively contributes to the processes of 'materialisation,' but in the case of web archives it warrants an examination of how the materiality of technologies (platforms, tools, interfaces, code, algorithms) is both implicated in the production of archives but also potentially produced through practice.

In this theoretical context, we extend the focus on materiality and practice, to include the role that labour plays in the production and maintenance of web archives. Whereas practice embodies the action, artefacts and tacit knowledge that gives meaning to both [15]; labour is conceptualised here to encompass the work it takes to produce and transform web archives into information sources. To frame our analysis, we draw on Downey's [23] concept of '*information labor*', or the human and algorithmic labour that '[enables] and [constrains] the constant circulation of information.' Downey argues that a focus on information labour, particularly in the context of media literacy, reveals the contingent 'social relations' that exist between information producers and consumers, through the process of acknowledging the work of agents that are often obscured by the technical arrangements of access. Here, by acknowledging and exploring the interconnected collection and maintenance work of both human agents (web archivists, engineers, users) and non-human agents (algorithms, bots, code) in web archiving, we open the doors for new enquiry into the value and role of the work of web archivists in the production of knowledge.

3 METHODOLOGY

Ethnographic methods were chosen to document the routine activities of archival practices and the 'typical patterns of work' [32, p.169] through the use of observation, interviews and documentary sources for understanding the day-to-day activities of web archivists.

3.1 The Case for an Ethnographic Approach

An 'upward trend' has been observed in the use of ethnographic methods in library and information science research [38]. Although there are comparatively fewer examples of ethnographic methods being used within the context of archives, ethnography has been identified as a means for conducting in-depth, comparative and cross-cultural studies of archival practice [49]. Gracy's [31] ethnographic work of archives provides the stimulus and methodological framework for an 'archival ethnography', or rather, the study of archival practice *in situ*:

> Archival ethnography is a form of inquiry which positions the researcher within an archival environment to gain the cultural perspective of those responsible for the creation, collection, care and use of records [30].

Specifically focused on record creation, other studies have used ethnographic observation to understand archives as a form of knowledge production in scientific laboratories [63]; to investigate communication and organisational accountability in record-keeping [79]; and to understand both the technical and the social apparatuses that facilitate record creation and maintenance within organisational contexts [73]. The motivations for these studies, as well as their findings, have all emphasised the importance and effect of context on the production and management of the archival record and reinforce the value of ethnographic methods for documenting situated practices and the wider interactions between archivists, archival institutions and users of archives.

Ethnographic methods have been argued to enable a more 'complex' appreciation of the development, use and role of technologies in society - beyond a view of technologies as simply 'functional instruments' [59, p.110]. One key assumption of this research design is that the direct observation of technologies and their use in web archiving is central to understanding and documenting practices. Suchman [69] provides relevant assistance here, defining *technology* as 'the assemblage of skilled practices and associated logics characteristic of modern industrial societies' and *artefacts* as the 'material production of skilled practice'. This approach allows for an exploration of the materiality of web archiving through a discussion of the relationship between practice and the production of digital artefacts, as well as the role of the environment (the policies, activities, infrastructure, and communities) that actively inform them.

Our aim, clearly, is not to fetishise web archives as either technological objects or sociomaterial culture, a point mirrored in STS debates which attend to the pitfalls of determinism and advocate for the avoidance of reductionist conceptualisations of either social or technical agents as essentially defined by the other [69, p.165]. Rather, we understand web archives as produced by an assemblage that require attention be paid to both the structure and agency of technical actors, as well as the sociocultural elements of technical practices - as evidence for the ways in which 'cultural values are enacted, produced, shared, reified, represented and reaffirmed' [22].

3.2 Data Collection and Analysis

A combination of interviews, observation records and documentary sources were collected over a four week period in collaboration with web archivists, engineers and managers at the Internet Archive. Both organisational (for observations) and individual consent (for interviews) were sought and received prior to data collection. In accordance with this consent all individual participant names reported here are pseudonyms.

Ethnographic interviews are a form of research interview that are distinguished by not only the types of questions that are asked, but also the ways in which the interviews are broken down into 'ethnographic elements' or 'speech acts' designed to elicit specific types of cultural responses from informants [65]. They were used in combination with observation as a mechanism for developing rapport with informants, as well as to clarify existing observation records and focus subsequent observation activities. In an effort to not to predetermine what practices were discussed, the interviews took a largely unstructured approach using a combination of descriptive, structural and contrasting questions in direct response to the answers provided by informants within the context of the interview. A number of participant-led 'walkthroughs' were undertaken as part of the interviews in order to allow practitioners to narrate their daily activities in real-time. In total, 16 interviews were conducted with 11 staff members at the Archive. The length of each interview varied, ranging from 20 minutes to over 2 hours, all of which were audio recorded. Most interviews took place in person, barring two which took place on Skype as the informants worked remotely. All interview data were fully transcribed.

The purpose of ethnographic observations is to provide access to 'practices and actions as they unfold' [5, p.55], in the form of 'non-elicited data' that can allow insights into the implicit and embodied activities that form everyday life. This is predicated on the notion that some actions cannot be articulated by participants/or 'insiders' through other research methods such as interviews. Boellstorff [5] and others [53] have long argued that 'elicitation methods' (such as interviews) cannot be a substitute for observation as there are inherent differences and disconnects between *what people do* and *what they say they do*. Furthermore, people do not always have the perspective or ability to report on all aspects of the processes (particularly cognitive processes) that underly the decisions and activities that make up practice [53]. Observation therefore, offers another window into understanding the relationship between meaning and action in everyday practice.

Ethnographic records were made documenting participation activities - including all-staff and tool development meetings, staff and application training seminars, troubleshooting and quality assurance tasks with participants - all with the aim of providing the basis for 'thick descriptions' [24] of practices. Observation pro-forma were not used, however ethnographic records were created for observations describing: *what was done* - action, activities, *what was made and used* - 'cultural artefacts' and *what was said* - speech acts, discursive activities [66, p.10-12]. Varying degrees of researcher participation was undertaken as part of the observations (as deemed appropriate by the host), where 'passive' participant observation was used during staff meetings, more 'active' participant observation took place during workshop and community events held at the Internet Archive.[6]

Documentary sources in various forms were collected to supplement the observations and interviews. 'Documents' are used here to refer to various types of materials (not just textual) produced by organisations, communities and individuals to describe procedures, policies and preferred ways of practicing web archiving. The use of documentary sources here offers insights into aspects of (otherwise) implicit knowledge that underlies practices [15, p.401].

[6]For a further breakdown of the types of participation levels common to participant observation, see Spradley [66, p.58].

Strategies for synthesising ethnographic data advocated by Spradley [65] were used to develop the analytical themes. This involved the identification of 'things informants know' in an effort to elicit everyday practices through the various kinds of participant knowledge (e.g. knowledge about crawl behaviours, scoping rules, reporting tools) and their connections to ways of doing things (e.g. maintenance and quality assurance tasks, de-duplication techniques). All data were analysed together in order to identify common themes present across the dataset. Lists and groupings were compiled by repeatedly listening to the audio recordings, reading the transcripts and observation records, and comparing the subject matter across the data. The methods used provided the opportunity for mapping heterogenous data and highlighted particular groupings of practitioner knowledge and activities for further analysis. The themes presented here are not exhaustive but rather, subjective and reflective of both the aims and current state of this research.

4 FINDINGS AND DISCUSSION

In what follows we explore the theoretical framework described above through an initial analysis of data collected from fieldwork carried out at the Internet Archive ('The Archive'). This is the result of four weeks spent at the Archive in October-November 2016 and February-March 2017. Before addressing the findings, some background is provided to set the scene. Through the presentation of findings that follows, the concept of *web archival labour* is examined and explored through the *knowledge work*, *breakdown* and *repair* activities that shape web archiving at the Archive.

4.1 Site Background and Setting

In 1996, Brewster Kahle and Bruce Gilliat established the Internet Archive as a nonprofit organisation alongside *Alexa Internet*, a commercial web indexing service [39]. The Internet Archive headquarters are based in San Francisco, California, a state which officially designated them a library in 2007 [37]. Since 1999, the Internet Archive has expanded their holdings beyond archived web content to provide web-based access to both digitised and born-digital resources, including but not limited to: books, audio, film/video, images, documents, software and video games [78]. According to web traffic statistics provided by Alexa Internet (now a subsidiary of Amazon), the Internet Archive regularly ranks between the 250-350th most visited website globally, with roughly 30% of search engine results driven by users looking for the Wayback Machine.[7]

The Archive forms a central component of the web archiving landscape through their provision of both large-scale web indexing and preservation services, as well as steering the direction of standards and practice through the development of tools and technologies that support web archiving at scale. The Archive is widely considered the largest web archive in the world, containing in excess of 15 petabytes of 270+ billion captures of web content [27]. They are one of the few institutions to employ 'exhaustive' global web crawling, which harvests web resources both within and beyond national domain boundaries or thematically-driven captures for the primary purpose of preservation (rather than indexing for other search or commercially-driven purposes). The collection of web archives at the Archive was originally (solely) facilitated

[7]http://www.alexa.com/siteinfo/archive.org [Accessed: 3 February 2017]

by the Alexa Internet 'toolbar', a browser-based plugin developed for the purposes of improving early-web navigation and analytics [44, p.274]. Based on user navigation, the toolbar captures and preserves each web page as it is visited, subsequently donating it to the Archive with a six month access embargo (a practice that continues to this day).

The Archive released the Heritrix web crawler as open source in 2002 alongside leading the development of the Wayback Machine software which currently forms the predominant mechanism by which users collect and access web archives. In 2006, the Archive began supporting *Archive-It*, the widely used subscription-based web archiving service. The Archive-It team work as part of the 'web group' at the Archive, providing technical and storage support for service subscribers and partner organisations. As such, this case study offered the opportunity to observe some of the ways the Archive-It team supports the development of tools and practice for web archiving.

4.2 Mapping Practice Roles and Activities

The web archival activities of the Archive can be broken down into three broad areas: *crawling*, *access* and *tool development*. The Archive is engaged in crawling at many different levels and thus this area includes the crawl activities that are self-directed, those that are fully undertaken at the direction of other organisations and those crawls that are initiated and directed by other organisations using their subscription service Archive-It. The Archive facilitates access and hosting for crawls undertaken by themselves and others through the Wayback Machine, including the provision of tools that allow others to deposit and donate their own WARCs to the collection. And lastly they facilitate web archiving through their ongoing tool and technology development for crawling and replay. In practice, these three areas do not sit in isolation of one another and represent a working environment of overlapping roles, tasks and activities at the Archive. The work that makes up *web archival labour* permeates each of these activity areas, explored further in the following sections.

4.3 Knowledge Work: Crawling and Curating

Elsewhere, others have acknowledged a certain pre-occupation with abundance and 'plenitude' at 'universal archives' such as the Internet Archive, an observation which De Kosnik [19, p.95] argues implicitly denies, or at least distracts from, attention to any selectivity in archiving. Although it is clear that the Archive is overtly concerned with abundance and scale in their endeavours to capture more, our observations point strongly towards efforts on their part to increasingly shape and prioritise the web resources that they capture. This point was made clear at the Archive's 20th Anniversary Party (2016) when Kahle announced that the Archive had (at that point) archived '273 billion webpages from over 361 million websites' with the help of robots and '1000 librarians.' Here and in an interview with Kahle, the Archive signals the creation of the Archive-It subscription service as a significant step towards archiving more selectively, by providing librarians with the tools to save web resources. However, the selection narrative is more complex than this, or as an informant indicated when I enquired about the Archive's appraisal practices: 'the process is strategically mish-mashed.' Collectively, these strategies (some of which are discussed below) can be seen as one component of what Downey [23] calls the '*knowledge work*', or the 'high value labour' that goes into the production of information that is obscured, or marketed as either automated or infinite. The notion of knowledge work is explored below as it relates to the curation of seed lists and what one informant called the 'hybrid' crawling activities of the Archive.

One informant relayed that a common misconception about the Archive's crawling activities is that they employ 'one giant crawler' to archive the global Web.'[8] This is repeated in research literature and popular media articles around the perceived automation of the Archive's crawling activities. At any given moment, in fact, the Archive has an (unknown) number of crawlers engaged in selective archival activities. A key priority was to begin to map these crawling events during fieldwork, in an effort to understand each as a contingent, sociotechnical assemblage. These crawl events or '*crawl modalities*' [70] define what is collected in the Archive. Each is shaped by different motivations, priorities and approaches to web archiving.[9]

Looking further back in history to 2010, a moment of significance can be observed when the Wayback team started engaging in and directing their own global crawls. Several informants described the motivations that led to this shift in direction, which was driven (at least in part) by the perceived inadequacies of the crawl data that were seeded, crawled and donated by Alexa Internet to the Archive. The Alexa crawling approach[10] is raised here as it is representative of a historical focus on the *popularity* of sites as a factor in the selection of seeds, one which (until recently) continued to influence the ways in which crawls were prioritised - even in those crawls directed by the Archive itself. The use of Alexa's 'top million' sites as the starting seeds for the 'wide crawls' (see below) was discussed as a common place practice but often resulted in the over-prioritising of popularity as an indicator of the value in capturing certain web resources - with Gregory claiming that: 'over 50% of our wide crawl was from 2,000 websites.' Further complaints were relayed about the quality of Alexa crawls as they do not capture images or embedded dynamic resources, often leading to web archives with extensive missing elements.

Various crawl events have subsequently become associated with the Archive's global crawling efforts, including for example, the 'survey crawls' and 'wide crawls.' Survey crawls are being used to supplement wide crawls by taking a snap shot of the home page of every domain/host ever identified by the Archive. Wide crawls are run twice a year over 4-6 months, though as Arthur described they had originally envisaged the crawl cycle to run 4-6 times a year. Wide crawls start from a seed list (initially the Alexa top million, as described above) and are then allowed to run autonomously, the bot

[8]personal communication

[9]The term 'crawl modality' is borrowed from Summers and Punzalan [70] who in a study of web archival appraisal practices describes the different ways in which crawling activities were broadly conceptualised and implemented. Although different (but overlapping) crawling modalities were identified at the Archive, the focus is similarly on determining how these modalities come to pass and how they shape what is collected.

[10]The mechanisms behind Alexa's crawlers were presented by informants as not fully understood, and based on a historical understanding of 'how they used to work.' The proprietary nature of their crawlers and the resulting crawl data were flagged as an impediment to ever fully understanding the provenance of how resources are prioritised over others within this data.

following each outlink until 'it doesn't produce any interesting data any more.' When asked how wide crawls were stopped, Arthur said they have to regularly check on each Heritrix instance by manually go into the machine in question and looking at the logs to see what is actually being captured, a process they described as 'daunting.' Alex described what they were looking for when they examine the logs, which largely involves a visual inspection of the domain names contained within the capture URLs, watching out for strings that resemble 'calendar traps,' pornography and endless Facebook sites. In direct result of some of the manual labour required to shape and monitor the large-scale crawls at the Archive, engineers began developing various ad-hoc tools to mitigate the need for interacting with the harvester logs and other shell scripts. One such tool is something Arthur calls the 'Domain Browser tool' used in conjunction with *Hericrawler*, a crawl queue management system the Archive developed for orchestrating large-scale crawls:

> The domain browser manual tool is for identifying undesirable domains. It's used to establish and prioritise 'shades of gray,' for example only crawl this site if there are no other sites to crawl. It's used as a ranking mechanism for prioritising domains based on time, resources and place in the queue, as certain important URLs can get blocked by many instances of unimportant URLs. For example people linking to Facebook pictures can create an infinite loop of queued Facebook links because of the nature of the graph. These types of sites are really slow to crawl as they are hosted on a single site, which must be crawled in succession because of the nature of the Heritrix crawler. Each domain/host is assigned a budget and the crawler is paused if it reaches its budget.

The Domain Browser tool is thus used to (manually) curate undesired domains based on a visual inspection of a gallery of home page thumbnails of each domain/host. The tool is set up to facilitate users tagging the site as pornography, a domain squatter or 'link farm' in order to remove it from subsequent crawls. Alex describes the process:

> What we did was hired half a dozen people - they would just go through it and get the top 30,000 hosts [...] and they go through 4-5,000, that's what one person can do in a month or so. And then we get actual human interaction to say yes, this is a good website. And then we would delete or modify or prioritise based on that input. So having humans actually spend a little bit of time at the top really helped. We'd love to do it further of course.

In addition, Arthur described another similar manual tool called 'Live Update' that they use to curate new domains that are discovered through their Wordpress crawls (crawls that are triggered by edits to sites hosted on Wordpress.com). Different to the Domain Browser tool, the Live Update tool dynamically displays the domain/host thumbnail of new domains in realtime allowing users to choose between overlay buttons tagged 'P' for pornography, and 'F' for link farms, or visit the site for further investigation. Arthur said it was developed in an effort to 'gamify' the process of curation and described using the tool whenever he had downtime. When asked how to spot a link farm, Arthur responded that 'it's obvious, there's usually a giant box [iframe] with keywords and a list of domains on the home page, easy to spot.' The use of manual curation tools reveals both the role of human intervention in the process of curating millions of links and the tensions and trade-offs that exist between the use of bots and a desire to capture 'high quality' sites.

In response to the restrictive number of URLs collected by the wide crawls seeded with the Alexa 'top million' sites, several informants described some of the Archive's more recent efforts to study the wide crawls through a grant they received to improve the Wayback Machine in various respects. One such study of wide crawl 12 is captured in a grant milestone report (that was made available) which describes the various techniques used and makes recommendations for improving future crawls. Here Gregory describes the process of studying the hyperlink structure of existing archives to seed crawls:

> I do a lot of link analysis where I study the hyperlink structure of our crawls and try to figure out in certain pockets, use some rank methodologies to figure out 'oh these are important resources,' for instance they have a lot of links to them or traffic is really high - let's seed the crawl with those. The most recent wide crawl I took the most linked to pages from every single website, so 230 million websites [...] and instead of crawling the Alexa top million, let's crawl this bit. Sort of like a hybrid survey and wide model [...]. And we found resources that we had never crawled before. I'm not saying one is better than the other, I'm saying that hybridising this process might be one way of balancing the scales a little bit.

This type of link analysis thus assists in finding the edge nodes of websites that the crawlers have identified - sometimes upwards of 60 million sites - but do not get around to crawling before the crawl is stopped. These are then used as seeds for the survey crawl (to crawl the home pages of the sites) and to iteratively expand the net and number of websites captured by the Archive. Gregory indicates that through these types of studies, they estimate that at any given time they are only crawling around 20% of the Web. Gregory structures the issues surrounding balance in selection priorities as a problem of *resources* (a theme which repeatedly arises), but outlines three considerations for determining 'better crawls' and ensuring they are crawling the right 20%:

> The way I think of it [...] there's three branches, there's *popularity*, there's *novelty* and there's the *risk of going away*. How do you achieve that balance? You want to get stuff that people are using - not just junk that is on the Web that you're just filling up the servers with that won't ever be found useful, like calendar pages, things like that, crap [...] - there's no novelty. It's new? We want to make sure it's preserved because it just came out, it's a new article, it's a new website. And then there's the risk of going away [...] - if you're going to shut down this service - Vine is going away - we jump

> in and crawl. So as we're crawling the Web can we do a good job of sort of achieving that balance? We don't quite know what the solution is to achieving that balance.

If we expand the picture to look at some of the other crawl modalities of the Archive, the multi-faceted approach to selection becomes even more apparent. A number of techniques for selecting domain/hosts were described by participants associated with the Archive's contract crawling, or the custom and domain-level crawling undertaken on behalf of partner institutions. A manager, Elaine described the use of zone files, partner-submitted seed lists (via Google spreadsheets or forms), links embedded in particular social media streams, and using geographical look-ups of existing content held by the Archive to extract relevant domains for crawling. Other sources for selection include 'listening in' on Twitter to determine which YouTube videos get linked to, as well as what outlinks get added to Wikipedia - both of which trigger crawl events. Increasingly, the Archive has also been developing a variety of tools that use their longstanding 'Save Page Now' feature to promote the saving of web resources to the Wayback Machine by anyone with access to the archive.org home page, or a Firefox plugin.

These methods highlight some of the ways the Archive is leveraging the power and labour of 'the crowds' - through the users of Twitter, Wikipedia and Save Page Now - to not only diversify and 'balance' the domains/types of resources that are archived, but also (implicitly) co-opt and transform these users into potential stakeholders. Furthermore, the Archive is in multiple ways, leveraging the web archives amassed in the Wayback Machine project over the last 20 years to continuously increase their net resources.

4.4 Breakdown and Repair: Maintaining Archives

Many informants described scenarios where human mediation was required in either otherwise (seemingly) automated processes. Examples that require manual intervention include: running *patch crawls* when bots failed to crawl designated seeds, or in the event of a *crawler trap* where bots are trapped in an infinite loop of seed requests (discussed above), or when *missing* or *altered* elements are observed in the playback of archived web pages. Fundamentally, each of these boil down to issues surrounding either the capture or replay of web resources. Borrowing from Star and Ruhleder [67], these moments could be considered a form of *breakdown* which in turn reveals the contingent assemblage of processes that for example, enable the capture of intended web resources or provide 'high fidelity' access to the archived collections.

The issues around the *quality assurance* of collection capture and playback is not an unknown dimension of web archival practice, however, the processes that are undergone to mitigate these issues are not well documented. Here we draw on the work of Jackson [36] who advocates for an examination of the moments of *breakdown, repair* and *maintenance* of technologies, in that they redirect attention to the act and 'ethics of care' and embody the creation of value by their maintainers. In other words, the practice and processes involved in fixing and maintaining technologies can be used as evidence for their worth by those who sustain these practices over time. These moments of repair in web archiving are present throughout the study, including the repair and maintenance of crawl data and crawling technologies, Wayback and access tools, as well as the repair of broken links on the live Web by the Archive. Some of these practices are discussed further below, as they highlight some of the factors that influence the decision-making and technical processes that enable the repair of web archives (and the technologies that enable access).

A few training sessions for a web archivist on the Archive-It team, Karen were observed. Through listening to Karen's Q&A with other team members, certain junctures were highlighted where support staff are regularly required to prioritise activities, particularly in response to the 'quality' or 'completeness' of web archives (and as raised by partner organisations). To set the scene a bit, we draw on interpretive notes following an observation session:

> *In the second session we all sat on the couch in the pit. Lydia asked Karen if she wanted to continue the training they began in the morning, which was aimed at addressing a recent support request that came in from a partner. When the conversation got a bit technical - as a result of Karen asking increasingly detailed questions about how certain seeds and test crawls are rendered in playback - Mike (a support engineer) was called over by Lydia. Mike walked over and leaned on the couch and began to explain some common differences between capture and playback issues. The consensus from Lydia and Mike seems to be that the first task in the support role is to determine whether the issue is related to capture or playback. Karen is concerned about waiting to solve issues based on partner requests, advocating for the team to be more actively QA'ing collections in case they are at risk of disappearing. Mike responds that there are different issues at play (including time and resources) and that it's key to understand that capture issues will always take precedent over playback issues - for exactly that reason.*

From this vignette several points can be interpreted. First, we can see that Karen is getting to grips with a key aspect of the role of the web archivist at Archive-It, which (in conjunction with support engineers) is to determine the difference between playback and collection issues and respond accordingly. Second, the comment that capture problems will always trump replay problems is insightful. It emphasises the goal of capture and reflects the underlying motivation driving activities - the fear of disappearance. This observation also emphasises the active role of the web archivist and support engineer in the processes that shape the 'fidelity' of web archives. They are implicitly driven by time and resource constraints but they are also active participants in the practice of choosing which support issues are prioritised. Mike indicated that specific repair tasks are prioritised in each daily 'stand-up' where team members report on upcoming development goals. Web archivists and programme managers will mark tasks as high priority either because the content is at risk of changing or going way or because the request comes from a high priority partner (as both were the case for the whitehouse.gov and End of Term archives that were being captured at the time).

5 SUMMARY AND FUTURE WORK

The aims of the paper were to examine how web archives are structured by the practices associated with collecting and maintaining archives. The use of an ethnographic approach, with a focus on observing practice as web archival labour at the Internet Archive has revealed a number of insights. The data points towards a complex system of knowledge and maintenance work for prioritising which web assets to collect and repair. The Archive is leveraging their extensive existing archives for understanding networked linking behaviour in an effort to balance the breadth and depth of crawling activities, while discovering new sources for identifying websites to crawl based on measures of popularity, 'novelty' and sites that are endanger of going offline. The team has devised multiple mechanisms for identifying different types of 'undesirable domains,' including rule-based link pattern-matching and the development of 'gamified' tools for the manual curation of sites.

Collectively, the efforts of the Archive can be seen as knowledge work, and these activities, seen in combination with other practices around the prioritisation, repair and maintenance of tools and archives all have ramifications for how web resources are transformed for use. It is the labour of non/human agents that enables the preservation and ingestion of information from the Web into the Archive, and then once again back to the Web where archives are reassembled via the Wayback Machine. Although imperfect, this labour is increasingly recognised as an essential element of the web architecture. The information labour and knowledge work of potential web archival users is therefore intimately tied to the web archival labour of the Internet Archive. As the global Wayback Machine currently provides access to billions of webpages - often inaccessible elsewhere - editorial decisions have implications for not only the fidelity of archived captures, but indeed whether or not certain parts of the Web are preserved at all. Future work will aim to address any shortcomings in the ethnographic methods presented by further examining the labour of algorithmic and other non-human actors (e.g. hyperlinks, software) implicated in these processes. By continuing to make these practices visible, both the contingencies and value of this labour are revealed and open a new window on this increasingly vital activity.

ACKNOWLEDGMENTS

This work was supported by the UK Engineering and Physical Sciences Research Council and the Web Science Centre for Doctoral Training, Grant No. EP/G036926/1. The authors would also like to thank the Internet Archive and staff for opening their doors and being so generous with their time and feedback.

REFERENCES

[1] Ahmed AlSum, Michele C. Weigle, Michael L. Nelson, and Herbert Sompel. 2014. Profiling web archive coverage for top-level domain and content language. *International Journal on Digital Libraries* 14, 3 (2014), 149–166. DOI:https://doi.org/10.1007/s00799-014-0118-y

[2] William Y. Arms, Roger Adkins, Casey Ammen, and Allene Hayes. 2001. Collecting and Preserving the Web: the MINERVA Prototype. *RLG DigiNews* 5, 2 (April 2001). http://worldcat.org/arcviewer/2/OCC/2009/08/11/H1250005040496/viewer/file2.html

[3] Jefferson Bailey, Abigail Grotke, Kristine Hanna, Cathy Hartman, Edward McCain, Christie Moffatt, and Nicholas Taylor. 2014. *Web Archiving in the United States: A 2013 Survey.* Technical Report. The National Digital Stewardship Alliance. 1–24 pages. http://www.digitalpreservation.gov/documents/NDSA_USWebArchivingSurvey_2013.pdf

[4] Karen Barad. 2003. Posthumanist Performativity: Toward an Understanding of How Matter Comes to Matter. *Signs* 28, 3 (2003), 801–831. http://www.jstor.org/stable/10.1086/345321

[5] Tom Boellstorff. 2012. Rethinking Digital Anthropology. In *Digital Anthropology*, Heather A. Horst and Daniel Miller (Eds.). Bloomsbury Publishing, London, 39–60.

[6] Geoffrey C. Bowker. 2005. *Memory Practices in the Sciences.* MIT Press, Cambridge, MA.

[7] Geoffrey C. Bowker and Susan Leigh Star. 1999. *Sorting Things Out: Classification and Its Consequences* (paperback ed.). MIT Press, Boston, MA.

[8] Molly Bragg and Kristine Hanna. 2013. *The Web Archiving Life Cycle Model.* Technical Report. The Archive-It Team and Internet Archive. http://ait.blog.archive.org/files/2014/04/archiveit_life_cycle_model.pdf

[9] Adrian Brown. 2006. *Archiving Websites: A Practical Guide for Information Management Professionals.* Facet, London.

[10] Richard Harvey Brown and Beth Davis-Brown. 1998. The making of memory: the politics of archives, libraries and museums in the construction of national consciousness. *History of the Human Sciences* 11, 4 (1998), 17–32.

[11] Niels Brügger. 2008. The Archived Website and Website Philology. *Nordicom Review* 29, 2 (2008), 155–175.

[12] Niels Brügger. 2009. Website history and the website as an object of study. *New Media & Society* 11, 1-2 (2009), 115–132. DOI:https://doi.org/10.1177/1461444808099574

[13] Niels Brügger. 2011. Web Archiving - Between Past, Present, and Future. In *The Handbook of Internet Studies*, Mia Consalvo and Charles Ess (Eds.). Wiley-Blackwell, Oxford, 24–42.

[14] Niels Brügger. 2012. When the Present Web is Later the Past: Web Historiography, Digital History, and Internet Studies. *Historical Social Research* 37, 4 (2012), 102 – 117.

[15] Christian Bueger. 2014. Pathways to practice: praxiography and international politics. *European Political Science Review* 6, 3 (Aug. 2014), 383–406. DOI:https://doi.org/10.1017/S1755773913000167

[16] Terry Cook. 2001. Archival science and postmodernism: new formulations for old concepts. *Archival Science* 1, 1 (2001), 3–24. DOI:https://doi.org/10.1007/BF02435636

[17] Terry Cook. 2007. Electronic Records, Paper Minds: The Revolution in Information Management and Archives in the Post-Custodial and Post-Modernist Era. *Archives & Social Studies: A Journal of Interdisciplinary Research* 1, 0 (March 2007), 399–443.

[18] Terry Cook. 2013. Evidence, memory, identity, and community: four shifting archival paradigms. *Archival Science* 13, 2 (2013), 95–120. DOI:https://doi.org/10.1007/s10502-012-9180-7

[19] Abigail De Kosnik. 2016. *Rogue Archives: Digital Cultural Memory and Media Fandom.* MIT Press, Cambridge, Massachusetts; London, England.

[20] Jacques Derrida. 1995. *Archive Fever: A Freudian Impression.* University of Chicago Press, Chicago and London.

[21] Meghan Dougherty and Eric T. Meyer. 2014. Community, Tools, and Practices in Web Archiving: The State-of-the-Art in Relation to Social Science and Humanities Research Needs. *Journal of the Association for Information Science and Technology* 65, 11 (2014), 2195–2209.

[22] Paul Dourish and Genevieve Bell. 2011. *Divining a Digital Future: Mess and Mythology in Ubiquitous Computing.* MIT Press, Cambridge, MA.

[23] Gregory J. Downey. 2014. Making Media Work: Time, Space, Identity, and Labor in the Analysis of Information and Communication Infrastructures. In *Media Technologies: Essays on Communication, Materiality, and Society*, Tarleton Gillespie, Pablo J. Boczkowski, and Kirsten A. Foot (Eds.). MIT Press, Cambridge, Massachusetts; London, England, 141–165.

[24] Clifford Geertz. 1973. *The Interpretation of Cultures.* Basic Books, New York.

[25] Tarleton Gillespie, Pablo J. Boczkowski, and Kirsten A. Foot. 2014. Introduction. In *Media Technologies: Essays on Communication, Materiality, and Society*, Tarleton Gillespie, Pablo J. Boczkowski, and Kirsten A. Foot (Eds.). MIT Press, Cambridge, Massachusetts; London, England.

[26] Anne J. Gilliland-Swetland. 2000. *Enduring Paradigm, New Opportunities: The Value of the Archival Perspective in the Digital Environment.* Technical Report 89. Council on Library and Information Resources, Washington, D.C. https://www.clir.org/pubs/reports/pub89/pub89.pdf

[27] Vinay Goel. 2016. Defining Web pages, Web sites and Web captures. (Oct. 2016). http://blog.archive.org/2016/10/23/defining-web-pages-web-sites-and-web-captures/

[28] Daniel Gomes, Sérgio Freitas, and Mário J. Silva. 2006. Design and Selection Criteria for a National Web Archive. In *Research and Advanced Technology for Digital Libraries*, Julio Gonzalo, Costantino Thanos, M. Felisa Verdejo, and Rafael C. Carrasco (Eds.). Lecture Notes in Computer Science, Vol. 4172. Springer Berlin Heidelberg, 196–207. http://dx.doi.org/10.1007/11863878_17

[29] Daniel Gomes, João Miranda, and Miguel Costa. 2011. A Survey on Web Archiving Initiatives. In *Research and Advanced Technology for Digital Libraries*, Stefan

Gradmann, Francesca Borri, Carlo Meghini, and Heiko Schuldt (Eds.). Lecture Notes in Computer Science, Vol. 6966. Springer Berlin Heidelberg, 408–420. http://dx.doi.org/10.1007/978-3-642-24469-8_41
[30] Karen F. Gracy. 2001. *The Imperative to Preserve: Competing Definitions of Value in the World of Film Preservation.* PhD. University of California, Los Angeles.
[31] Karen F. Gracy. 2004. Documenting Communities of Practice: Making the Case for Archival Ethnography. *Archival Science* 4, 3 (2004), 335–365. DOI:https://doi.org/10.1007/s10502-005-2599-3
[32] Martyn Hammersley and Paul Atkinson. 2007. *Ethnography: Principles and Practice* (third ed.). Routledge, London and New York.
[33] Donna Haraway. 1988. Situated Knowledges: The Science Question in Feminism and the Privilege of Partial Perspective. *Feminist Studies* 14, 3 (1988), 575–599.
[34] Verne Harris. 2000. Law, Evidence and Electronic Records: Strategic Perspective from the Global Periphery. *S. A. Archives Journal* 41 (2000), 3–19.
[35] Helen Hockx-Yu. 2014. Access and Scholarly Use of Web Archives. *Alexandria: The Journal of National and International Library and Information Issues* 25, 1-2 (2014), 113–127. DOI:https://doi.org/10.7227/ALX.0023
[36] Steven J. Jackson. 2014. Rethinking Repair. In *Media Technologies: Essays on Communication, Materiality, and Society*, Tarleton Gillespie, Pablo J. Boczkowski, and Kirsten A. Foot (Eds.). MIT Press, Cambridge, Massachusetts; London, England, 221–239.
[37] Brewster Kahle. 2007. Internet Archive officially a library. (June 2007). https://archive.org/post/121377/internet-archive-officially-a-library
[38] Michael Khoo, Lily Rozaklis, and Catherine Hall. 2012. A survey of the use of ethnographic methods in the study of libraries and library users. *Library & Information Science Research* 34, 2 (2012), 82 – 91. DOI:https://doi.org/10.1016/j.lisr.2011.07.010
[39] Michele Kimpton and Jeff Ubois. 2006. Year-by-Year: From an Archive of the Internet to an Archive on the Internet. In *Web Archiving* (first ed.), Julien Masanès (Ed.). Springer, Berlin, Heidelberg, 201–212.
[40] Rob Kitchin. 2016. Thinking critically about and researching algorithms. *Information, Communication & Society* 20, 1 (2016), 14–29. DOI:https://doi.org/10.1080/1369118X.2016.1154087
[41] Terry Kuny. 1997. A Digital Dark Ages? Challenges in the Preservation of Electronic Information. In *Proceedings of the 63rd International Federation of Library Associations and Institutions.* Copenhagen, Denmark.
[42] Kalev Leetaru. 2015. Why It's So Important To Understand What's In Our Web Archives. (Nov. 2015). http://onforb.es/1VDPHPH
[43] Kalev Leetaru. 2016. The Internet Archive Turns 20: A Behind The Scenes Look At Archiving The Web. (Jan. 2016). http://www.forbes.com/sites/kalevleetaru/2016/01/18/the-internet-archive-turns-20-a-behind-the-scenes-look-at-archiving-the-web/#747db6257800
[44] Jessica Livingston. 2007. *Founders at Work: Stories of Startups' Early Days.* Apress, United States of America.
[45] Deborah Lupton. 2015. *Digital Sociology.* Routledge, London.
[46] Peter Lyman. 2002. Archiving the World Wide Web. In *Building a National Strategy for Preservation: Issues in Digital Media Archiving.* Council on Library and Information Resources and the Library of Congress, 38–51. http://www.clir.org/pubs/reports/pub106/web.html
[47] Noortje Marres and Esther Weltevrede. 2013. Scraping the Social? *Journal of Cultural Economy* 6, 3 (2013), 313–335. DOI:https://doi.org/10.1080/17530350.2013.772070
[48] Julien Masanès (Ed.). 2006. *Web Archiving* (first ed.). Springer-Verlag Berlin Heidelberg.
[49] Sue Mckemmish and Anne Gilliland. 2013. Archival and recordkeeping research: Past, present and future. In *Research Methods: Information, Systems and Contexts*, K. Williamson and G. Johanson (Eds.). Tilde Publishing, Prahran, Victoria, 79–112.
[50] Ian Milligan, Nick Ruest, and Jimmy Lin. 2016. Content Selection and Curation for Web Archiving: The Gatekeepers vs. the Masses. In *JCDL âĂŹ16, June 19 - 23, 2016, Newark, NJ, USA.* ACM, Newark, NJ. DOI:https://doi.org/DOI:http://dx.doi.org/10.1145/2910896.2910913
[51] Gordon Mohr, Michael Stack, Igor Ranitovic, Dan Avery, and Michele Kimpton. 2004. An Introduction to Heritrix: An open source archival quality web crawler. In *Proceedings of the 4th International Web Archiving Workshop.* Bath, UK. https://webarchive.jira.com/wiki/download/attachments/5441/Mohr-et-al-2004.pdf
[52] National Digital Stewardship Alliance. 2012. *Web Archiving Survey Report.* Technical Report. NDSA Content Working Group. http://www.digitalpreservation.gov/documents/ndsa_web_archiving_survey_report_2012.pdf
[53] Richard E. Nisbett and Timothy DeCamp Wilson. 1977. Telling More Than We Can Know: Verbal Reports on Mental Processes. *Psychological Review* 84, 3 (May 1977), 231–259.
[54] Jinfang Niu. 2012. An Overview of Web Archiving. *D-Lib Magazine* 18, 3/4 (April 2012). http://www.dlib.org/dlib/march12/niu/03niu1.html
[55] Fatih Oguz and Wallace Koehler. 2015. URL decay at year 20: A research note. *Journal of the Association for Information Science and Technology* 67, 2 (2015), 477–479. DOI:https://doi.org/10.1002/asi.23561
[56] Maureen Pennock. 2013. *Web-Archiving.* Technical Report Technology Watch Report 13:01. Digital Preservation Coalition, Great Britain. 1–50 pages. http://dx.doi.org/10.7207/twr13-01
[57] Margaret E. Phillips. 2005. What Should We Preserve? The Question for Heritage Libraries in a Digital World. *Library Trends* 54, 1 (2005), 57–71. http://muse.jhu.edu/journals/library_trends/v054/54.1phillips.html
[58] Steven Pinch and N Henry. 1999. Discursive Aspects of Technological Innovation: The Case of the British Motor-Sport Industry. *Environment and Planning A* 31, 4 (1999), 665–682. DOI:https://doi.org/10.1068/a310665
[59] P. Prasad. 1997. Systems of Meaning: Ethnography as a Methodology for the Study of Information Technologies. In *Information Systems and Qualitative Research: Proceedings of the IFIP TC8 WG 8.2 International Conference on Information Systems and Qualitative Research, 31st May - 3rd June 1997, Philadelphia, Pennsylvania, USA*, Allen S. Lee, Jonathan Liebenau, and Janice I. DeGross (Eds.). Springer US, Boston, MA, 101–118. http://dx.doi.org/10.1007/978-0-387-35309-8_7
[60] Hany M. SalahEldeen and Michael L. Nelson. 2012. Losing My Revolution: How Many Resources Shared on Social Media Have Been Lost? In *Theory and Practice of Digital Libraries: Second International Conference, TPDL 2012, Paphos, Cyprus, September 23-27, 2012. Proceedings*, Panayiotis Zaphiris, George Buchanan, Edie Rasmussen, and Fernando Loizides (Eds.). Springer Berlin Heidelberg, Berlin, Heidelberg, 125–137. http://dx.doi.org/10.1007/978-3-642-33290-6_14
[61] Steve Schneider and Kirsten Foot. 2008. Archiving of Internet Content. In *The International Encyclopedia of Communication*, Wolfgang Donsbach (Ed.). Wiley Publishing.
[62] Joan M. Schwartz and Terry Cook. 2002. Archives, Records, and Power: The Making of Modern Memory. *Archival Science* 2 (2002), 1–19.
[63] Kalpana Shankar. 2004. Recordkeeping in the Production of Scientific Knowledge: An Ethnographic Study. *Archival Science* 4 (2004), 367–382.
[64] Marc Spaniol, Dimitar Denev, Arturas Mazeika, Gerhard Weikum, and Pierre Senellart. 2009. Data Quality in Web Archiving. In *Proceedings of the 3rd Workshop on Information Credibility on the Web.* ACM, New York, NY, USA, 19–26. DOI:https://doi.org/10.1145/1526993.1526999
[65] James P. Spradley. 1979. *The Ethnographic Interview.* Holt, Rinehart and Winston, United States.
[66] James P. Spradley. 1980. *Participant Observation.* Wadsworth/Thomson Learning, United States.
[67] Susan Leigh Star and Karen Ruhleder. 1996. Steps Toward an Ecology of Infrastructure: Design and Access for Large Information Spaces. *Information Systems Research* 7, 1 (March 1996).
[68] Ann Laura Stoler. 2002. Colonial archives and the arts of governance. *Archival Science* 2, 1-2 (2002), 87–109. http://rd.springer.com/article/10.1007%2FBF02435632
[69] Lucy A. Suchman. 2001. Building Bridges: Practice-based Ethnographies of Contemporary Technology. In *Anthropological Perspectives on Technology*, Michael Schiffer (Ed.). University of New Mexico Press, Albuquerque, 163–177.
[70] Ed Summers and Ricardo Punzalan. 2016. Bots, Seeds and People: Web Archives as Infrastructure. *The Computing Research Repository* abs/1611.02493 (2016). http://arxiv.org/abs/1611.02493
[71] Diana Taylor. 2003. *The Archive and the Repertoire: Performing Cultural Memory in the Americas.* Duke University Press, London.
[72] Mike Thelwall and Liwen Vaughan. 2004. A fair history of the Web? Examining country balance in the Internet Archive. *Library & Information Science Research* 26 (2004), 162–176.
[73] Ciaran B. Trace. 2002. What is recorded is never simply 'what happened': Record keeping in modern organizational culture. *Archival Science* 2, 1 (2002), 137–159. DOI:https://doi.org/10.1007/BF02435634
[74] Michel-Rolph Trouillot. 1995. *Silencing the Past: Power and the Production of History.* Beacon Press, Boston.
[75] Claire Waterton. 2010. Experimenting with the Archive: STS-ers As Analysts and Co-constructors of Databases and Other Archival Forms. *Science, Technology, & Human Values* 35, 5 (2010), 645–676.
[76] Collin Webb, David Pearson, and Paul Koerbin. 2013. 'Oh, you wanted us to preserve that?!' Statements of Preservation Intent for the National Library of Australia's Digital Collections. *D-Lib Magazine* 19, 1/2 (Feb. 2013). http://www.dlib.org/dlib/january13/webb/01webb.print.html
[77] Peter Webster. 2017 (forthcoming). Users, technologies, organisations: towards a cultural history of world web archiving. In *Web 25: histories from the first 25 years of the World Wide Web*, Niels Brügger (Ed.). Peter Lang.
[78] Aaron Ximm. 2014. Active Personal Archiving and the Internet Archive. In *Personal Archiving: Preserving Our Digital Heritage.* Information Today, Medford, US, 187–213.
[79] Elizabeth Yakel. 2001. The Social Construction of Accountability: Radiologists and Their Record-Keeping Practices. *The Information Society* 17, 4 (2001), 233–245. DOI:https://doi.org/10.1080/019722401753330832

Generating Stories From Archived Collections

Yasmin AlNoamany
University of California, Berkeley
Berkeley, California 94720, USA
yasminal@berkeley.edu

Michele C. Weigle and Michael L. Nelson
Old Dominion University
Norfolk, Virginia 23529, USA
{mweigle,mln}@cs.odu.edu

ABSTRACT

With the extensive growth of the Web, multiple Web archiving initiatives have been started to archive different aspects of the Web. Services such as Archive-It exist to allow institutions to develop, curate, and preserve collections of Web resources. Understanding the contents and boundaries of these archived collections is a challenge, resulting in the paradox of the larger the collection, the harder it is to understand. Meanwhile, as the sheer volume of data grows on the Web, "storytelling" is becoming a popular technique in social media for selecting Web resources to support a particular narrative or "story".

We address the problem of understanding archived collections by proposing the Dark and Stormy Archive (DSA) framework, in which we integrate "storytelling" social media and Web archives. In the DSA framework, we identify, evaluate, and select candidate Web pages from archived collections that summarize the holdings of these collections, arrange them in chronological order, and then visualize these pages using tools that users already are familiar with, such as Storify. Inspired by the Turing Test, we evaluate the stories automatically generated by the DSA framework against a ground truth dataset of hand-crafted stories, generated by expert archivists from Archive-It collections. Using Amazon's Mechanical Turk, we found that the stories automatically generated by DSA are indistinguishable from those created by human subject domain experts, while at the same time both kinds of stories (automatic and human) are easily distinguished from randomly generated stories.

CCS CONCEPTS

•Information systems →Information retrieval;

KEYWORDS

Web Archiving, Storytelling, Information Retrieval, Document Similarity, Archived Collections, Web Content mining, Internet Archive

1 INTRODUCTION

Today's ordinary information will be tomorrow's resources for historical research. The content captured and published on the Web narrating the incidents and giving unfiltered insights for future generations and historians is important to clarify the exact turning points in history. Therefore, archiving Web pages into themed collections is an important method for ensuring these resources are available for posterity. Many initiatives exist to allow users to perform this task [28]. Many initiatives exist to allow people to archive Web resources into themed collections for ensuring these resources are available for posterity [7]. For example, Archive-It[1], a subscription service from the Internet Archive (IA)[2], allows institutions to develop, curate, and preserve topic-oriented collections of Web resources by specifying a set of seeds, Uniform Resource Identifiers (URIs), that should be crawled periodically. Archive-It provides users a listing of all seeds in the collection along with the number of times and dates over which each page was archived, as well as a full-text search of archived pages.

An archived collection can include hundreds of seed URIs. Over time, each of these URIs can be crawled hundreds or thousands of times, resulting in a collection having thousands to millions of archived Web pages. Understanding the contents and boundaries of a collection can be difficult [10], resulting in the paradox of the larger the collection, the harder it is to use. For example, a user of Archive-It interested in understanding the key events of the Jan. 25 Egypt Revolution will find multiple collections about this topic, and each of these collections may have a different focus. Aside from the brief metadata about the collection (Figure 1(a)), the interface mainly consists of a list of seed URIs in alphabetical order (Figure 1(b)), and for each of these URIs a list of the times when the page was archived (Figure 1(c)). It is not feasible for a user to figure out what is inside the collection without going through all the URIs in the collection and their relative archived copies. Understanding the essence of the collection from the current interface of Archive-It is not easy.

Providing a summary of the content of archived collections is a challenge because there are two dimensions that should be summarized: the URIs that comprise the collection (e.g., cnn.com) and the archived copies (called "mementos") of those URIs at different times (e.g., cnn.com@t_1, cnn.com@t_2,.., cnn.com@t_n). Either dimension by itself is difficult, but combined they present a number of challenges, and are hard to adapt to most conventional visualization techniques.

We developed the Dark and Stormy Archives[3] (DSA) framework [2], which automatically extracts summary stories[4] from Archive-It collections to help the user to understand the collections. Events in these stories are summarized by sampling Web pages from the Archive-It collections, arranged in a narrative structure ordered by time, and replayed through storytelling social media interfaces

WebSci'17, June 25-28, 2017, Troy, NY, USA.

DOI: http://dx.doi.org/10.1145/3091478.3091508

[1] http://www.archive-it.org/
[2] http://archive.org/
[3] Inspired by "It was a dark and stormy night", a well-known storytelling trope: https://en.wikipedia.org/wiki/It_was_a_dark_and_stormy_night/
[4] We use "story" in its current, loose context of social media, which is sometimes missing elements from the more formal literary tradition of dramatic structure, morality, humor, improvisation, etc.

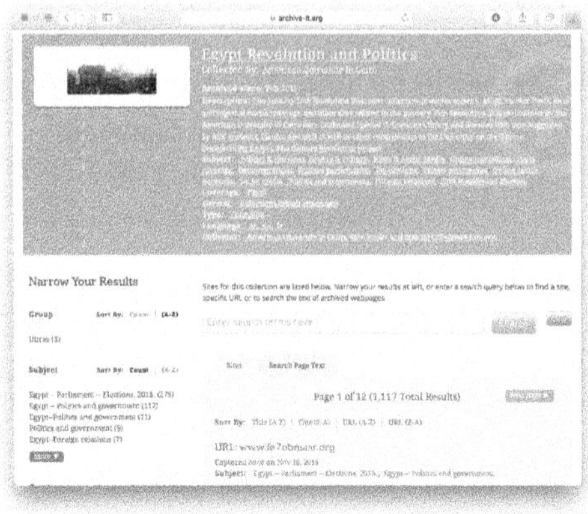

(a) Archival metadata for the collection.

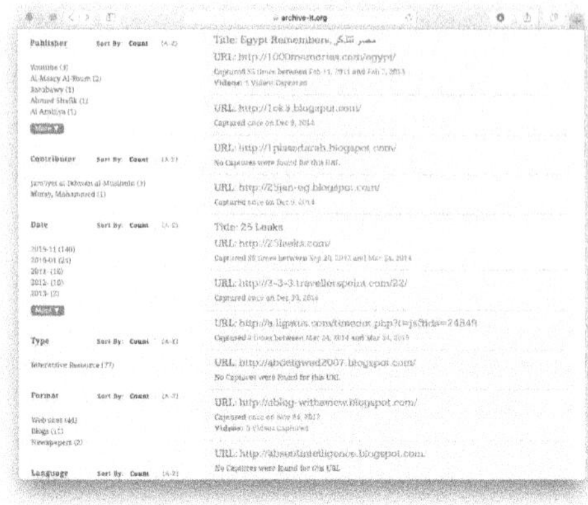

(b) Alphabetical list of URIs in the collection.

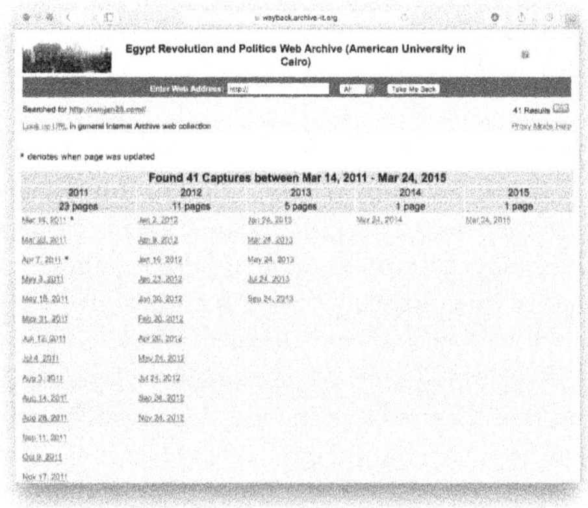

(c) Archived copies of a URI in the collection.

(d) A copy of "Iam25Jan"

Figure 1: Current browsing and searching services for the "Egypt Revolution and Politics" collection in Archive-It.

such as Storify. By studying existing human-generated stories in Storify [3], we were able to profile different kinds of stories by examining the typical length (in terms of the number of resources included), time frames covered, structural metadata (e.g., page rank, images and video, social media vs. news) and other features. We used the structural characteristics of human-generated stories, with particular emphasis on "popular" stories (i.e., the top 25% of views, normalized by time available on the Web), that are applicable to the resources in Archive-It collections. For example, we generate stories automatically from archived collections with a typical length close to 28 (more or less based on the collection size).

What makes a good story is a matter of human judgment and is difficult to evaluate. We consider a story to be "good" if a person considers it to be indistinguishable from a human-generated story. Inspired by the Turing Test [27], we used ground truth dataset of hand-crafted stories from Archive-It collections and let humans select between the human-generated stories and the automatically generated stories. We consider our method to be a success if humans are as likely to choose the automatically generated story as they do the human-generated story. From this composite, we asked expert archivists to generate hand-crafted stories from Archive-It collection, then used Amazon's Mechanical Turk[5] to evaluate the automatically generated stories against the stories that were created by experts. Based on 332 comparisons by 30 unique Mechanical Turk workers (or "turkers") between human-generated stories and automatic stories, the results showed that at confidence level 95%, , turkers could not distinguish between the human-generated stories and the automatically generated stories ($p > 0.5$).

2 RELATED WORK

Since the digitization process has started, most institutions, e.g., libraries and archives, have focused on storing digital collections and making them accessible online [12]. Most of the current digital collection interfaces are text-based search with very limited browsing features. Much research has been dedicated to developing visualizations for viewing and querying documents, and towards graphical browsing of the results [1, 16, 17, 29]. While Web archives are solutions for preserving the Web, they lack tools that allow users to understand the archived collections.

[5] https://www.mturk.com/

Our initial attempt to browse Archive-It collections and highlight the collections' underlying characteristics was applying four alternate visualizations (Bubble chart, Image plot with histogram, Timeline, Wordle) for the Archive-It interface [24]. The results are sufficient for those already with an understanding of what is in the collection, but they do not facilitate an understanding to those who are unfamiliar with collection.

Karmer-Smyth [20] developed ArchivesZ, an information visualization for archived collections inspired by the availability of structured data in the Encoded Archival Description [10] standard for encoding finding aids. The ArchivesZ prototype interface helps users explore the metadata that describes archival collections through searching for content by year and subject in a tightly coupled dual histogram interface. ArchivesZ gives users a visual representation of the total amount of content available in an archive on a given topic. It also visualizes the overlapping assignment of subjects terms to archival collections.

The UK Web Archive[6] provides a visualization for the collections through a 3D wall of sites allowing interaction through zooming.

One problem with the above approaches is that there is often an implicit assumption that everything in a collection is equally valuable and should be visualized. Some of the Web pages change frequently, some are near-duplicates, and some go off-topic and no longer contribute to the collection. Visualization techniques with an emphasis on recall (i.e., "here's everything in the collection") do not scale. Instead, we are informed by emerging trends in social media storytelling, which focus on a small number of exemplary pages (i.e., high precision) as chosen by a human, to sample from the collection by choosing representative pages that best exemplify the topic of the collection. Our work in selecting candidate Web pages leverages previous work in image collection summarization and video abstraction. Many image collection summarization techniques [6, 10, 11] divide the image collection by time, then cluster the images by content, and finally select a representative image from each cluster. In our framework, we take a similar approach to selecting representative mementos. Some video abstraction techniques [18, 22, 30] select keyframes that differ from each other in terms of their features, such as color, shape, motion, etc. In our work, we use text similarity to eliminate near duplicate mementos.

3 TYPES OF STORIES GENERATED FROM ARCHIVED COLLECTIONS

In the DSA framework, we apply IR and machine learning techniques to identify and select different sets of k mementos that compose stories, in which each story (S) provides an overview about the collection. So, we extract stories from a collection, $C \rightarrow S$, where $C \subset S$.

An archived collection has two dimensions. As we mentioned before, the collection is composed of a set of seed URIs and each seed has many copies through time. There may be multiple stories that convey different perspectives of the collection [5]. In Table 1, we list four possible kinds of stories and name each story according to the change that happens to the URI and time:

- Fixed Page, Fixed Time (FPFT) is a different representation for the same Web site because of GeoIP, mobile, and other environmental factors [19]. It is generated using the same URI at a specific point of time with differences in the representation.
- Sliding Page, Sliding Time (SPST) is the broadest possible coverage of a collection. It is generated using different URIs at different times.
- Fixed Page, Sliding Time (FPST) is the evolution of a single page (or domain) through time. The possible scenario of this story is when a user wants to see how the story evolved over time from a specific Web site, e.g., cnn.com.
- Sliding Page, Fixed Time (SPFT) is different perspectives at a point in time. It is generated using different original URIs at nearly the same datetime.

[6] https://www.webarchive.org.uk/ukwa/

Note that the FPFT story can not be supported by the current capabilities of Web archives because currently they do not provide users the ability to navigate representations by their environmental influences [19].

Table 1: Four basic story types (others may be possible).

		Time: fixed	Time: sliding
URIs:	fixed	differences in GeoIP, mobile, etc.	evolution of a single page (or domain) through time
	sliding	different perspectives at a point in time	broadest possible coverage of a collection

It is also possible that there are additional types of stories beyond those in Table 1, and we plan to investigate this in future work.

4 THE DARK AND STORMY ARCHIVES (DSA) FRAMEWORK

In this section, we present the Dark and Stormy Archives (DSA) Framework to select k archived pages that comprise a "story" that summarizes an Archive-It collection, arrange them in a narrative structure ordered by time (or any other type of story), then import them into existing storytelling tools or other visualizations.

4.1 Establish a Baseline

To support automatic story creation, we needed to better understand as a baseline the structural characteristics of human-generated stories. In our previous work [3], we investigated the structural characteristics of human-generated stories on Storify, with particular emphasis on "popular" stories. Upon analyzing 14,568 stories comprising 1,251,160 elements, we modeled the structural characteristics of the popular stories. We found that the popular stories have a median value of 28 elements. This informs our framework for generating stories from archived collections that will be composed of a number of resources that is close to 28.

4.2 Reduce the Candidate Pool

Archive-It provides their partners with tools that allow them to build themed collections of archived Web pages hosted on Archive-It's machines. This is done by the user manually specifying a set of seed URIs that should be crawled periodically based on a predefined frequency set by the collection curator. This frequency may be daily,

Figure 2: Snapshots of an Egyptian news Web site (http://news.egypt.com/en/) from the "Egypt Revolution and Politics" collection in Archive-It. Each group of similar mementos are grouped and annotated with the same color.

weekly, or even yearly. Due to the nature of Web evolution, some of these snapshots may change little or not at all. Some of the pages go off-topic and some other pages just become duplicates to other pages. We define off-topic pages as the Web pages that have changed through time to move away from the initial scope of the page. Currently, there are no content-based tools that allow curators to detect when seed URIs are off-topic. We apply the following steps on an archived collection to reduce the candidate pool of mementos:

(1) Exclude the off-topic pages from the collection.
(2) Exclude the (near-)duplicate mementos of each TimeMap, a list of mementos.
(3) Exclude the non-English language mementos.

In a previous work [4], we investigated and evaluated different approaches for detecting off-topic pages in individual TimeMaps on multiple Archive-It collections. In the DSA framework, we adopted the best performing method on Archive-It collections to eliminate the off-topic pages.

After excluding the off-topic pages, we eliminate (near-)duplicates. An example of duplicates in a TimeMap is illustrated in Figure 2. We select the first memento of the TimeMap and compare it to other subsequent mementos using Hamming Distance d. If the most recent memento exceeds a specific threshold α, which was determined empirically, it is selected to be the current memento that we compared to the subsequent mementos. We used 64-bit SimHash fingerprints with $k = 4$ to calculate the (near-)duplicates between Web pages in individual TimeMaps because of its time efficiency [15]. The goal is to generate a reduced TimeMap that contains only unique mementos of the URI.

Finally, we selected the English language mementos and excluded other languages. We detected the language of the content using the language detection library created by Shuyo [25] with precision $\geq 99\%$ [8, 25]. The DSA framework can be applied on pages with other languages, but currently, we evaluate English language pages only.

4.3 Select Good Representative Pages for Each Story

The previous step produces a set of reduced TimeMaps that have unique, relevant mementos to the topic of the collection. The following step is to evaluate and select the "best" representative k mementos, where k is much smaller than the number of mementos in the collection. As mentioned earlier, suggested values of k are determined by the results of previous work [3], and other tunable parameters will include the timeline of the desired story (which may exclude some portions of the collection), the percentage of damage of the memento (incomplete pages are not desirable candidates), the story type (cf. Table 1), etc. We combine all of mementos of all the TimeMaps into one set (the filtered mementos from all of the seeds) and then the following steps to select representative mementos for the story:

(1) Slice the collection dynamically and distribute the mementos equally on the slices.
(2) Cluster the pages in each slice.
(3) Evaluate and select the best representative page from each cluster based on multiple quality metrics.
(4) Put the selected pages in chronological order.
(5) Extract the metadata of the selected pages.
(6) Visualize the pages by leveraging storytelling tools, such as Storify.

We started by slicing the collection into a predefined number of slices Sc that is specified based on the number of mementos N in the collection after excluding the off-topic pages, non-English language pages, and the (near-)duplicates [2], so that:

If $|N| > 28$

$$Sc = \lceil 28 + log_{10}|N| \rceil \tag{1}$$

Else

$$Sc = |N| \tag{2}$$

We then distribute the mementos equally on the slices and then cluster the mementos in each slice using the Density-Based Spatial Clustering of Applications with Noise (DBSCAN) algorithm [13] based on their textual contents. DBSCAN does not require the specification of the number of clusters a priori, as opposed to k-means clustering [14]. The output of this step is a set of Cs clusters, where $Cs \geq Sc$.

From each of the resulting clusters, we evaluate and select the best representative page based on multiple quality metrics. We specified the memento quality based on the amount of damage for the memento and if the memento generates a visually attractive link preview when inserting into a tool like Storify. We adopted Brunelle's algorithm for assessing memento damage [9]. The quality of the visual link preview will tremendously affect the quality of the created story. When a user posts a link on social media networks, e.g., Facebook and Storify, a visual *snippet* with a title, a summary of the content, and an image is extracted from that link. These visual snippets are created from the HTML tags of the Web page. Based on experimenting the the generation of visual snippets for many different kinds of URIs [2], we discovered that social media sites

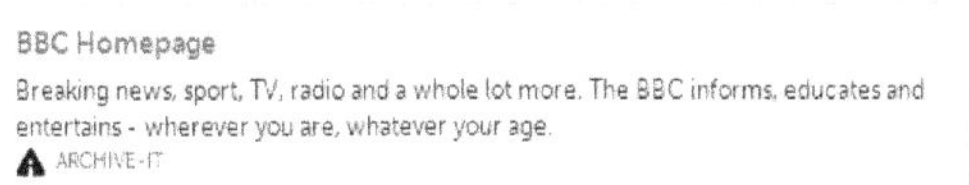

(a) Feb. 11, 2011: a memento of the homepage of BBC on Storify

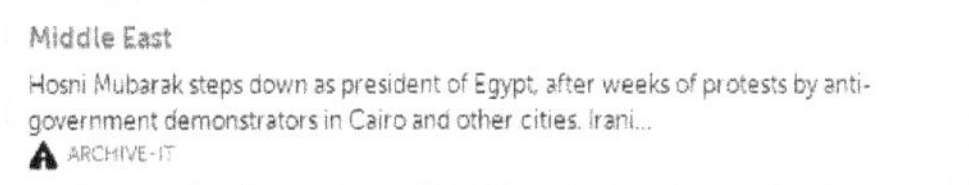

(b) Feb. 11, 2011: a memento of the homepage of BBC Middle East section on Storify

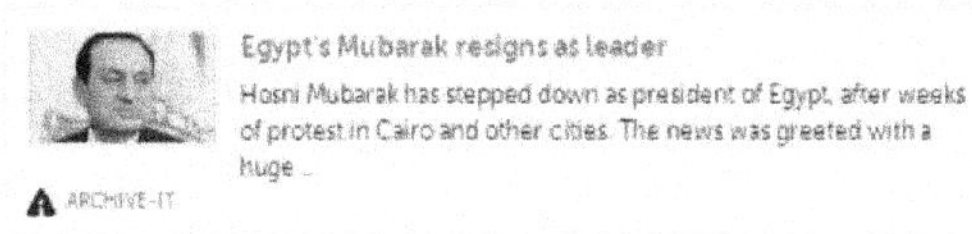

(c) Feb. 11, 2011: a memento of the BBC article page on Storify

Figure 3: Storify creates better snippets from a specific article (i.e., deep links) than a homepage about the same event.

can generate better snippets from articles that focus on only one topic (these articles also often have a long URI path length, e.g., cnn.com/a/b/c/2011/4/2), while they do not extract nice snippets from homepages that have an overview of multiple topics (these pages often have a short URI path length, e.g., cnn.com), as illustrated in Figure 3. Furthermore, the page category may affect the quality of the extracted snippets. For example, there are different kinds of URIs in which the extraction fails to capture information related to the topic of the collection such as URIs for pages on Facebook, Facebook accounts, Twitter accounts, Google groups, etc. When these pages are posted on Storify, the text of the snippet is extracted from the description of the profiles or pages.

Therefore, for specifying the quality of the memento, we weight each memento with quality measure M_q, which calculated as follows:

$$M_q = (1 - w_d \times D_m) + w_l \times M_l + w_c \times M_c \quad (3)$$

where D_m is the value of memento damage, M_l is URI level, and M_c is the URI category. We set level weight ($w_l = 0.45$), memento damage weight ($w_d = 0.40$), and category weight ($w_c = 0.15$). Setting these weights needs further testing with multiple collections. In the DSA framework, the value of M_l is normalized in the range of [0, 1]. For example, the M_l of cnn.com/a/b/c/2011/4/2 will be assigned 0.6 and $M_l = 0.1$ for cnn.com/. For calculating M_c, we adopted our previously proposed heuristic-based categorization [24], which classifies the URI based on its domain component, then assigns each category a weight $0 \leq M_c \leq 1$ based on how the category affects the snippet quality [2]. We give higher weights to news Web sites, video, social media posts, then blogs come next, and the lowest weight goes to Facebook pages, Twitter accounts, Google groups, etc.

After specifying the the best representative pages, extract the publish date of the page using the "Newspaper: Article scraping and curation" Python library [23]. It applies multiple strategies such as extracting the date from a URI or from the Web page metadata. If neither of these strategies succeed to estimate publishing date, we use the Memento-Datetime (the datetime the resource was crawled).

Finally, we order the mementos chronologically based on their dates and visualize the pages by leveraging storytelling tools. In our implementation, we used Storify, a popular platform for storytelling, to visualize the set of $k \approx 28$ mementos that represent the extracted story from the collection. Storify provides an API[7] that allows users to create and publish stories by sending objects of the elements of the stories in JSON format. Once a story is created and pushed to Storify, it can be edited and shared. For each story, we generate a JSON object that contains the metadata of the story, such as the story name and description, and the details of each element such as the hyperlink, the extracted title, etc. We override the favicon of the resource that is created by Storify because Storify uses the Archive-It favicon for all the pages regardless of the original source (see Figure 3).

5 EVALUATING THE DSA FRAMEWORK

In this section, we evaluate the automatically generated stories from archived collections.

5.1 Hand-crafted Stories from Archived Collections

We group Archive-It's collections into three main categories [4]. First, there are collections that are devoted to archiving governmental pages (e.g., all Web pages published by the State of South Dakota[8]). Second, there are collections that are event-based (e.g., Occupy Movement collection[9]). Third, there are theme-based collections (e.g., the Columbia Human Rights collection[10]).

We tested the DSA framework against event-based collections. We asked expert archivists, with the help of the Archive-It team and Archive-It partners, to generate hand-crafted stories from Archive-It collections. We provided them with guideline documents that contained instructions for generating stories from Archive-It collections by selecting 28 representative mementos (more or less based on the collection size) that best represent each collection. We showed them the type of stories that can be generated. We also provided them the criteria for selecting the mementos. They suggested 10 different collections to generate stories from (see Table 2).

The following is the list of the guidelines that we provided to the expert archivists for generating the stories:

- The representative mementos should be selected from within the collection. There should not be any memento from outside the collection.
- The default value for the number of selected mementos is $k \approx 28$. This value can be more or less based on the nature and size of each collection.
- We expect to have three generated stories out of each collection. Depending on the nature of the collection, some kind of stories may not be applicable. For those collections, please specify if any of the previous kinds of stories cannot be created.

---

[7] http://dev.storify.com/api/
[8] https://archive-it.org/collections/192/
[9] https://archive-it.org/collections/2950/
[10] https://archive-it.org/collections/1068/

Table 2: The characteristics of the collections used for the evaluation.

Collection	ID	Timespan	URIs	Mementos
2013 Boston Marathon Bombing	3649	2013/04/19 - 2015/03/03	318	1,907
Occupy Movement 2011/2012	2950	2011/12/03 - 2012/10/09	955	30,581
Egypt Revolution and Politics	2358	2011/02/01 - 2013/04/18	1,112	42,740
April 16 Archive	694	2007/05/23 - 2008/04/28	88	362
2013 Government Shutdown	3936	2013/10/22 - 2013/10/22	186	246
Russia Plane Crash Sept 2011	2823	2011/09/08 - 2011/09/15	104	558
Wikileaks 2010 Document Release Collection	2017	2010/07/27 - 2013/08/26	41	1,126
Earthquake in Haiti	1784	2010/01/20 - 2011/02/27	132	967
Brazilian School Shooting	2535	2011/04/09 - 2011/04/14	650	1,492
Global Health Events	4887	2014/10/01 - 2015/12/21	169	3,026

Table 3: The number of resources in the 23 stories (10 SPST, 6 SPFT, 7 FPST) generated by domain experts and from the DSA framework.

		SPST		SPFT		FPST	
Collection	ID	Human	Automatic	Human	Automatic	Human	Automatic
2013 Boston Marathon Bombing	3649	28	29	28	25	7	5
Occupy Movement 2011/2012	2950	16	45	9	20	9	7
Egypt Revolution and Politics	2358	16	20	11	17	12	7
April 16 Archive	694	17	32	14	19	5	4
2013 Government Shutdown	3936	17	27	14	15	-	-
Russia Plane Crash Sept 2011	2823	28	25	27	23	-	-
Wikileaks 2010 Document Release Collection	2017	25	32	-	-	7	10
Earthquake in Haiti	1784	28	34	-	-	11	14
Brazilian School Shooting	2535	26	24	-	-	23	20
Global Health Events	4887	36	34	-	-	-	-

- You can choose a specific time period for generating the story. If the collection spans many years, you can choose a subset of the timespan of the collection.

We also put criteria for selecting the mementos: the language of the memento should be in English; the memento should be on-topic (the content is related to the topic of the collection); the memento should produce a visually attractive snippet on Storify, an article (cnn.com/a/b/12/2015) is more preferred than a homepage (cnn.com); the memento should not be a (near-)duplicate of another memento in the list; a memento with no missing resources is a better choice than a memento that is missing resources.

Along with the criteria of the stories and the selected mementos within each story, we illustrated to the Archive-It team the suggested possible types of stories that can be generated from each collection.

The domain experts provided us with lists of mementos for 23 different stories from the 10 different collections (see Table 3). Table 3 also shows the number of resources per story that were generated by experts and by the DSA framework. An example of a manually generated story by archivists from the Boston Marathon Bombing collection is shown in Figure 4(a).

There were some collections that spanned a short period of time, so the archivists did not provide the FPST stories for these collections (for example, the "Brazilian School Shooting", which spans over three days only). Another reason for not generating the FPST story is that none of the seeds of the collection change over time (e.g., news articles). For example, the seed URIs of "Russia Plane Crash Sept 2011" collection are all news articles which do not evolve over time.

5.2 Automatically Generated Stories from Archived Collections

We then applied the steps of the DSA framework (Section 4) on the set of suggested collections in Table 2. We automatically generated 23 stories[11] from the collections (see Table 3). The FPST stories and the SPFT stories require input parameters such as the TimeMap for FPST stories and time frame for SPFT stories. In these stories, we use the same parameters that were used in the human-generated stories and input them to the DSA (Table 2). The SPST stories do not require any parameters because they represent a broad summary for the whole collection from all the seed URIs at different times. An example of an automatically generated story by the DSA framework is illustrated in Figure 4(b).

The number of the resources in the generated stories are presented in Table 3. Note that although the Egypt Revolution and Politics collection is the largest collection in the dataset, the resulting number of the resources for the SPST story from this collection is just 20 mementos. That is because we selected the pages from within the same time frame (2011/02/01-2011/02/14) that was used for the human-generated story.

[11] Links to these stories are available at https://github.com/yasmina85/DSA-stories

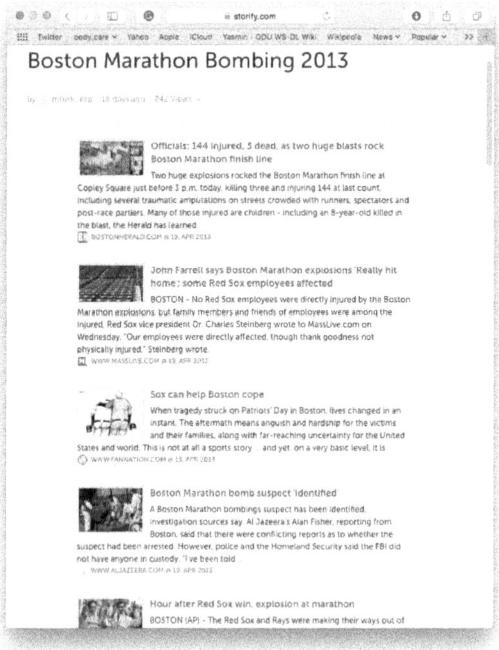

(a) Human-generated story[12].

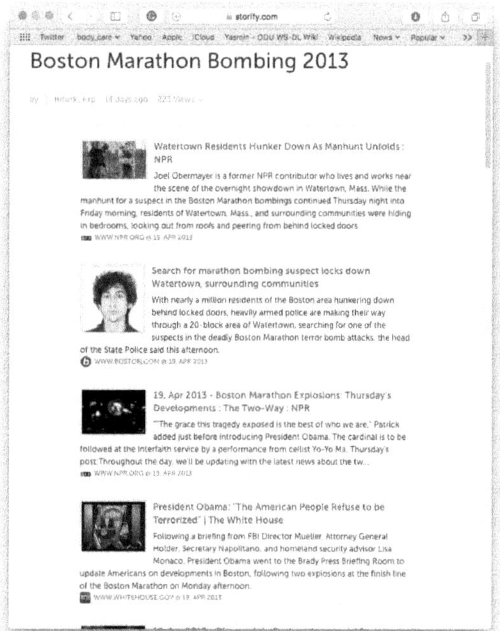

(b) Automatically-generated story[13].

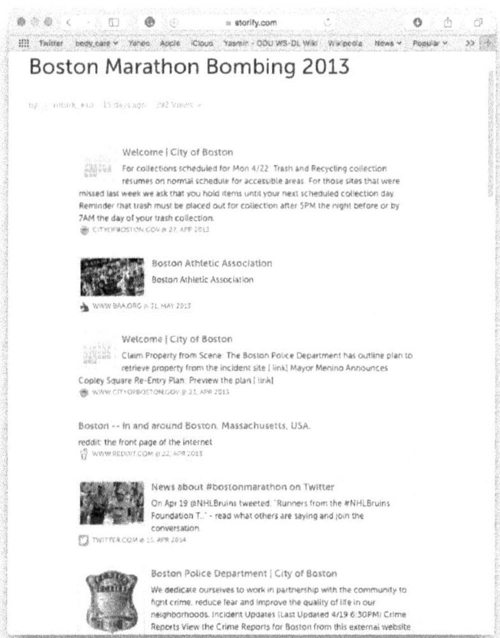

(c) Randomly-generated story[14].

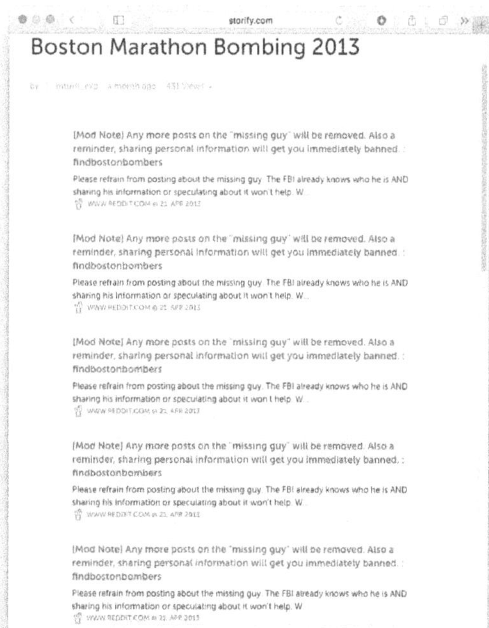

(d) Poorly-generated story[15].

Figure 4: Example for SPST stories from the Boston Marathon Bombing collection.

Figure 5: A sample HIT that shows two stories that turkers evaluate and select their preferred story. Each HIT contains two comparisons.

Table 4: The results of comparing human-generated stories versus automatically generated stories.

	Selections	Human	Automatic
SPST	142	50.7%	49.3%
SPFT	87	46.0%	54.0%
FPST	103	51.5%	48.5%

5.3 Random and Poor Stories

We use randomly generated stories to be compared against the human-generated stories and the automatically generated stories as a baseline. In other words, we expect that both the automatically generated stories and human generated stories will perform better than random stories. We selected $k \approx 28$ mementos randomly (see Figure 4(c)) from the set of mementos in each collection as a baseline for evaluating the automatically generated stories. The selection was done on the mementos in the collection before excluding the off-topic or the duplicates. The selected mementos were not sorted chronologically in the generated stories.

We generated poor stories by randomly selecting a memento from collection's TimeMap and repeating this memento 28 times. This story represents a control to ensure that the turkers do not choose randomly between the stories.

We used the same extraction methods for visualizing the human-generated stories, automatically generated stories, randomly generated stories, and poorly generated stories on Storify.

[12]https://storify.com/mturk_exp/3649b1s-57218803f5db94d11030f90b
[13]https://storify.com/mturk_exp/3649b0s
[14]https://storify.com/mturk_exp/3649b2s-57227227bb79048c2d0388dc
[15]https://storify.com/mturk_exp/3649bads

5.4 Experiment Setup

We use Mechanical Turk to compare four types of stories (human-generated, automatically generated, randomly generated, poorly generated), asking turkers to choose between two stories at a time.

Our goal is to assess if the automatically generated stories by the DSA framework are indistinguishable from the human-generated stories. We provided turkers a description of a simple task to perform (a Human Intelligence Task, or HIT), choosing their preferred story (see Figure 5). We provided a simple generic description for the task as follows:

> *Storify is a service that allows users to organize news stories, tweets, etc. to tell a story about a particular topic. We show two different stories for the same topic below. The goal of the stories is to provide an overview of the topic. This HIT contains two sets of comparisons to complete. Of the two stories shown in each comparison,* ***choose*** *the one you prefer.*

Each HIT consists of two comparisons, in which one of the two comparisons was a control, a comparison between one of the stories and a poorly generated story. We reject the HITs where users selected a poorly generated story (i.e., a false positive selection).

To reduce the cognitive load of the task, we assigned one comparison for each HIT along with the comparison that includes the poor story. Therefore, for evaluating one story, we have three HITs as follows:

HIT_1 : human vs. automatic, human vs. poor

HIT_2 : human vs. random, human vs. poor

HIT_3 : random vs. automatic, automatic vs. poor

We ensured that the position of each pair of composites was reversed among different stories to ensure there was not a bias in the HIT layout. We posted 69 HITs to evaluate 23 different stories. For each HIT, we required 15 turkers with "master" qualification requirements[16]. Based on many studies for deciding the number of participants in user studies, group sizes between eight and 25 are typically good numbers for conducting comparative studies [21, 26]. We chose to use 15 participants for each HIT in our experiment. We rejected the HITs in which the submissions contained poorly generated stories and the HITs that were completed in less than 10 seconds. TWe rejected a total of 46 HITs. In total, we had 989 out of 1,035 (69×15) valid HITs. These HITs were performed by 30 unique Master level turkers. We awarded the turker \$0.50 per HIT. The turkers took seven minutes on average to complete the selections of the two comparisons.

5.5 Results

Figure 6(a) shows a summary of the results of the turkers selections for the three comparisons: human vs. automatic, random vs. automatic, and human vs. random. The results in Figure 6(a) show that both the automatically generated stories and the human-generated stories were selected $\approx$ 50% of the time. The figure also shows that the automatic stories are better than the randomly generated

[16]https://www.mturk.com/mturk/help?helpPage=worker#what_is_master_worker

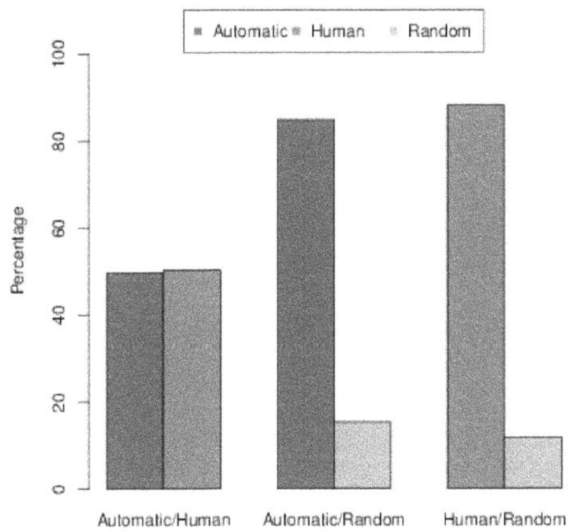

(a) A summary of the results.

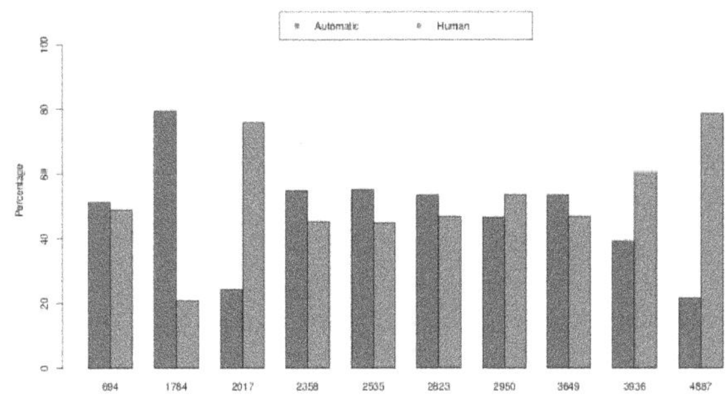

(b) Automatic versus Human per collection.

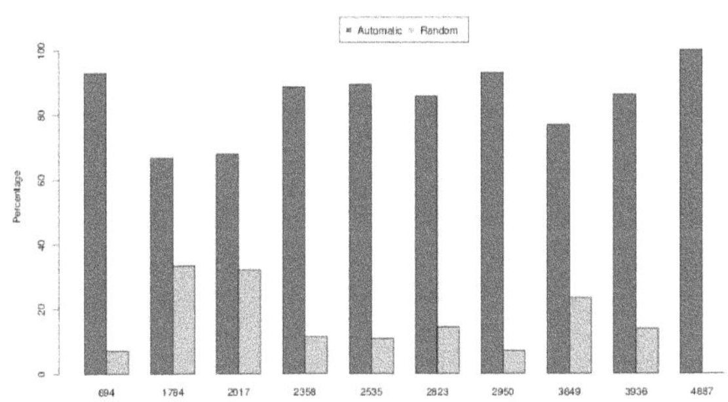

(c) Automatic versus Random per collection.

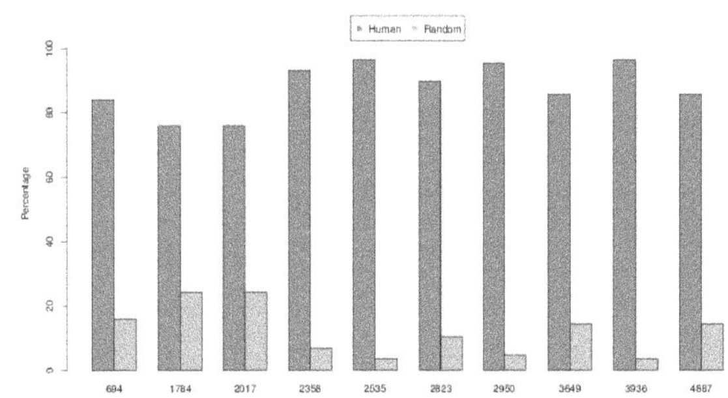

(d) Random versus Human per collection.

Figure 6: DSA-generated stories are indistinguishable from human-generated stories, and both are distinguishable from random stories.

stories. Based on the results of the two-tailed t-test on the number of votes received, we found that at confidence level 95% the automatically generated stories with $mean = 7.17$ are indistinguishable from the human-generated stories with $mean = 7.26$ ($p = 0.9134$, $t = 0.1094$, $df = 43.9$). However, at confidence level 95%, the automatically generated stories with $mean = 12.04$ and the human-generated stories with $mean = 12.65$ are significantly different from the randomly-generated stories with $mean \approx 2$ ($p < 2.2e{-}16$).

We zoom in on the results of the human-generated sto ries versus the automatically generated stories to interpret the results based on the different types of stories (SPST, SPFT, FPST). Table 4 shows that for all types of stories, the percentages of the turkers preferences to human and automatic stories are close. We applied a two-sided paired t-test on the samples based on the story type. We found that at confidence level 95% there is no significant difference ($p > 0.5$) between the human-generated stories and the automatically generated stories for all the types of the stories. However, the difference between the automatically generated stories and the randomly-generated story is statistically significant ($p < 0.001$) for all the types of stories at 95% confidence level. There is also a significance difference between the randomly generated stories and the human-generated stories ($p < 0.001$) at 95% confidence level

We show the results of the turkers' preferences for the three selections for each collection in Figure 6. Figure 6(b) shows that for most of the collections, the automatically generated stories are indistinguishable from the human-generated stories. There are two collections that human-generated stories were selected more than the automatically generated stories: the "Wikileaks 2010 Document Release" (2017) and "Global Health Events" (4887). The automatically generated stories for the "Earthquake in Haiti" (1784) were preferred by turkers. Further investigation with more collections is required to test if the type of collections affects a human's selection.

6 CONCLUSIONS AND FUTURE WORK

In this paper, we presented the DSA framework, in which we identify, evaluate, and select candidate mementos to support the events of the stories. Our goal is to allow users to get many perspectives about the collection and also about how the story of the collection has evolved over time. We leverage narrative visualizations and storytelling tools, such as Storify, to visualize the created stories and demonstrate how they have evolved over time. We evaluated the stories generated by the DSA framework. We obtained a ground truth dataset of 23 stories that were generated manually from 10 Archive-It collections by expert archivists. We used Amazon's Mechanical Turk to compare the automatically generated stories with the human-generated stories. Based on 332 comparisons by 30 unique turkers between human-generated stories and automatic stories, the results showed that at confidence level 95%, the automatically generated stories are indistinguishable from the human-generated stories ($p > 0.5$). We also created random stories as a baseline for the automatic stories. The results show that the turkers were able to distinguish the random stories from the automatic and the human stories ($p < 0.001$). The code and gold standard dataset are available at https://github.com/yasmina85/DSA-stories.

We provided preliminary evaluation for the stories generated by the DSA framework. Although the humans were not able to distinguish the automatically generated stories from the human-generated stories, future research should investigate the usefulness of the generated stories and evaluate the discovery tasks for people given the summarized stories. Furthermore, we plan to collaborate with humanities researchers to conduct user studies on important events, e.g., the Arab Spring, and check if a specific kind of story provides the best insight into the events and the corresponding collections. For example, how do the Sliding Page, Fixed Time stories help humanities researchers to get different perspectives about news coverage and how much time is saved from manual search by providing them this kind of story.

7 ACKNOWLEDGMENTS

This work supported in part by the Institute Museum and Library Services (LG-71-15-0077-15). We thank the Archive-It team and partners for creating the gold standard data set.

REFERENCES

[1] Christopher Ahlberg, Ben Shneiderman, and Ben Shneidennan. 1994. Visual information seeking: tight coupling of dynamic query filters with starfield displays. In *Proceedings of the SIGCHI Conference on Human Factors in Computing Systems (CHI '94)*. 313–317. DOI: https://doi.org/10.1145/191666.191775
[2] Yasmin AlNoamany. 2016. *Using Web Archives to Enrich the Live Web Experience Through Storytelling*. Dissertation. Old Dominion University.
[3] Yasmin AlNoamany, Michele C Weigle, and Michael L Nelson. 2016. Characteristics of Social Media Stories. What makes a good story? *International Journal on Digital Libraries* 17 (2016), 239–256. DOI: https://doi.org/10.1007/s00799-016-0185-3
[4] Yasmin AlNoamany, Michele C Weigle, and Michael L Nelson. 2016. Detecting Off-Topic Pages Within TimeMaps in Web Archives. *International Journal on Digital Libraries* 17 (2016), 203–221. DOI: https://doi.org/10.1007/s00799-016-0183-5
[5] Yasmin AlNoamany, Michele C Weigle, and Michael L Nelson. 2017. *Stories from the Past Web*. Technical Report arXiv:1705.06218.
[6] Ahmed AlSum and Michael L Nelson. 2014. Thumbnail Summarization Techniques for Web Archives. In *Proceedings of the 36th European Conference on Information Retrieval (ECIR '14)*. 299–310. DOI: https://doi.org/10.1007/978-3-319-06028-6_25
[7] Jefferson Bailey, Abigail Grotke, Kristine Hanna, Cathy Hartman, and Nicholas Taylor. 2004. Web Archiving in the United States: A 2013 Survey. http://www.digitalpreservation.gov/documents/NDSA_USWebArchivingSurvey_2013.pdf. (2004).
[8] Ralf D. Brown. 2013. Selecting and Weighting N-Grams to Identify 1100 Languages. In *Text, Speech, and Dialogue (Lecture Notes in Computer Science)*, Vol. 8082. 475–483.
[9] Justin F. Brunelle, Mat Kelly, Hany SalahEldeen, Michele C. Weigle, and Michael L. Nelson. 2015. Not All Mementos Are Created Equal: Measuring The Impact Of Missing Resources. *International Journal of Digital Libraries* 16, 3 (2015), 283–301. DOI: https://doi.org/10.1007/s00799-015-0150-6
[10] Michelle Chang, John J. Leggett, Richard Furuta, Andruid Kerne, J. Patrick Williams, Samuel A. Burns, and Randolph G. Bias. 2004. Collection Understanding. In *Proceedings of the 4th ACM/IEEE-CS Joint Conference on Digital Libraries (JCDL '04)*. 334–342. DOI: https://doi.org/10.1145/996350.996426
[11] Wei-Ta Chu and Chia-Hung Lin. 2008. Automatic Selection of Representative Photo and Smart Thumbnailing Using Near-duplicate Detection. In *Proceedings of the 16th ACM International Conference on Multimedia (MM '08)*. ACM Press, 829–832. DOI: https://doi.org/10.1145/1459359.1459498
[12] Laura Deal. 2015. Visualizing Digital Collections. *Technical Services Quarterly* 32, 1 (2015), 14–34. DOI: https://doi.org/10.1080/07317131.2015.972871
[13] Martin Ester, Hans-Peter Kriegel, Jörg Sander, and Xiaowei Xu. 1996. A density-based algorithm for discovering clusters in large spatial databases with noise. In *Proceedings of 2nd International Conference on Knowledge Discovery and Data Mining (KDD-96)*. AAAI Press, 226–231.
[14] John A Hartigan and Manchek A Wong. 1979. Algorithm AS 136: A k-means clustering algorithm. *Journal of the Royal Statistical Society. Series C (Applied Statistics)* 28, 1 (1979), 100–108.
[15] Monika Henzinger. 2006. Finding near-duplicate web pages: a large-scale evaluation of algorithms. In *Proceedings of the 29th Annual International ACM SIGIR Conference on Research and Development in Information Retrieval*. ACM Press, 284–291. DOI: https://doi.org/10.1145/1148170.1148222
[16] Keyun Hu. 2014. *VisArchive: A Time and Relevance Based Visual Interface for Searching, Browsing, and Exploring Project Archives (with Timeline and Relevance Visualization)*. Dissertation. University of Victoria.
[17] Keyun Hu, Melanie Tory, Sheryl Staub-French, and Madhav Prasad Nepal. 2016. VisArchive: a time and relevance based visual interface for searching, browsing and exploring project archives. *Visualization in Engineering* 4 (2016). DOI: https://doi.org/10.1186/s40327-016-0036-8
[18] Hang-Bong Kang. 2002. *Video Abstraction Techniques for a Digital Library*. IGI Global. 120–132 pages.
[19] M Kelly, JF Brunelle, MC Weigle, and ML Nelson. 2013. A Method for Identifying Personalized Representations in Web Archives. *D-Lib Magazine* 19 (2013), 2. DOI: https://doi.org/10.1045/november2013-kelly
[20] J Kramer-Smyth, M Nishigaki, and T Anglade. 2007. ArchivesZ: Visualizing Archival Collections. http://archivesz.com/ArchivesZ.pdf. (2007).
[21] Ritch Macefield. 2009. How to specify the participant group size for usability studies: a practitioner's guide. *Journal of Usability Studies* 5, 1 (2009), 34–45.
[22] Jung Oh, Quan Wen, Sae Hwang, and Jeongkyu Lee. 2004. Video abstraction. *Video data management and information retrieval* (2004), 321–346.
[23] Lucas Ou-Yang. 2013. Newspaper: Article scraping & curation. http://newspaper.readthedocs.io/. (2013).
[24] Kalpesh Padia, Yasmin AlNoamany, and Michele C. Weigle. 2012. Visualizing Digital Collections at Archive-It. In *Proceeding of the 12th Annual International ACM/IEEE Joint Conference on Digital Libraries (JCDL '12)*. 437–438. DOI: https://doi.org/10.1145/2232817.2232821
[25] Nakatani Shuyo. 2012. Language Detection Library for Java. http://code.google.com/p/language-detection/. (2012).
[26] Janet M Six and Ritch Macefield. 2016. How to Determine the Right Number of Participants for Usability Studies. UXmatters, http://www.uxmatters.com/mt/archives/2016/01/how-to-determine-the-right-number-of-participants-for-usability-studies.php. (2016).
[27] Alan M Turing. 1950. Computing machinery and intelligence. *Mind* 59, 236 (1950), 433–460.
[28] Khoi Duy Vo, Tuan Tran, Tu Ngoc Nguyen, Xiaofei Zhu, and Wolfgang Nejdl. 2016. Can We Find Documents in Web Archives Without Knowing Their Contents?. In *Proceedings of the 8th ACM Conference on Web Science (WebSci '16)*. 173–182. DOI: https://doi.org/10.1145/2908131.2908165
[29] M Whitelaw. 2009. Exploring Archival Collections with Interactive Visualisation. http://www.eresearch.edu.au/docs/2009/era09_submission_74.pdf. In *Proceedings of E-Research Australasia Conference*.
[30] HongJiang Zhang, Jianhua Wu, Di Zhong, and Stephen W Smoliar. 1997. An integrated system for content-based video retrieval and browsing. *Pattern recognition* 30, 4 (1997), 643–658.

Deconstructing Diffusion on Tumblr: Structural and Temporal Aspects

Nora Alrajebah
University of Southampton
N.Alrajebah@soton.ac.uk

Leslie Carr
University of Southampton
lac@soton.ac.uk

Markus Luczak-Roesch
Victoria University of Wellington
mail@markus-luczak.de

Thanassis Tiropanis
University of Southampton
t.tiropanis@soton.ac.uk

ABSTRACT

Online social networks enable collectives of users to create and share content at scale. The diffusion of content through the network, and the resulting information cascades, are phenomena that have been widely investigated on various platforms, which facilitate information diffusion using diverse technical mechanisms, user interfaces and incentives. This paper focuses on Tumblr, an online microblogging social network with a core 'reblogging' functionality that allows information to diffuse across its network by appearing on multiple user blogs. The formation of any cascade network is visible as a list of reblogging events attached as notes to each appearance of the post in the cascade. In this paper, we examine cascade networks on Tumblr, recreated from the series of diffusion events, and analyse them from structural and temporal perspectives. To achieve this, we utilise a cascade construction model that create cascade networks, overcoming problems of a lack of contextual information and missing/degraded data. Finally, we compare cascades in Tumblr with those appearing on other social network platforms. Our analysis shows that popular content on Tumblr creates 'large' cascades that are deep, branching into a large number of separate and long paths, having a consistent number of reblogs at each depth and at each given time.

CCS CONCEPTS

• Information systems → Social networks; • Networks → Online social networks;

KEYWORDS

Social Network Analysis, Information Diffusion, Cascades, Tumblr

1 INTRODUCTION

The evolution of the World Wide Web brought out online social networks (OSNs) as one of the most important and dynamic facility for information sharing. The availability of data about the digital traces of humans in OSNs made these an extensively studied artifact with reference to information sharing. Over the years, OSN platforms grew to acquire functionalities that allow users to share content posted by others conveniently with a click on a button. This allows content to travel through the network from one user to another in a 'cascading' fashion, a phenomenon named information cascades or information diffusion. This phenomenon has been extensively studied in Economics and Social Sciences [7, 17]. They are attempts to model behavioural traces "when it is optimal for an individual [...] to follow the behaviour of the preceding individual without regard to his own information" [7]. A diffusion event in an OSN occurs when a distinct piece of information (a post, a quotation, a hashtag, or a url) [16] posted by a user is shared by other users creating a cascade that can be observed [19, 22, 28]. The availability of rich context about the users and the diffusion events was used to predict the future growth of cascades [10, 20, 31]. While great progress has been made in quantitative research on online information diffusion, we also see critical reflections about the "simple epidemiological view" [14]; a critique, which is amplified by studies investigating biases and inequalities in social media systems and data [26, 32]. Here we seek to contribute to this line of research that does not just investigate prospects of diffusion models for online advertising or political campaigning, but uncovers epistemological issues arising from the multiplex of features that are used to derive such models. We make a distinction between *diffusion* and *cascade*. The term *diffusion* is used to refer to the phenomenon of content spread in social networks, while the term *cascade* refers to the outcome of the diffusion, this means that *cascades* are the structural representation of diffusion on social network.

In this paper, we are interested in analysing the cascades of popular content on the OSN *Tumblr* from two perspectives: structural and temporal. For this purpose, we use the acclaimed *Year in Review* blog which is, in Tumblr's staff words, "a showcase of the best stuff on the Internet" each year. This blog contains a mixture of popular posts and trendy topics in different categories curated by Tumblr's staff. Hence, we attempt to 'deconstruct' the most popular posts from the *Year in Review* blog structurally and temporally. Our quest is to move beyond reporting aggregate numbers such as the total number of reblogs or views to provide a detailed analysis of the 'life story' of the popular content on Tumblr. The data harvested from the *Year in Review* blog is biased towards popular content. Nonetheless, this dataset allows us to unravel the diffusion dynamics in popular content on Tumblr over a long time scale. To the best of our knowledge, this work is thefi rst that investigates the

WebSci '17, June 25–28, 2017, Troy, NY, USA.

ACM ISBN 978-1-4503-4896-6/17/06...$15.00.
https://doi.org/10.1145/3091478.3091491

structural and temporal aspects of popular content's cascades on Tumblr in such depth.

This paper aims to establish an understanding of the diffusion dynamics on Tumblr in light of some well-defined measures that has been used to analyse cascades on other platforms (mainly Twitter and Facebook). The data we gathered has twofolds: structural and temporal. The structural allows us to construct cascade networks representing the causal relationships of reblogging between users, i.e., who influenced whom to reblog a post. While the temporal, facilitates studying the 'rise and fall' of cascades popularity. However, cascade networks must be constructed as a prerequisite for the structural analysis. Thus, we introduce a cascade construction model that provides an accurate representation of cascades on Tumblr taking into account the challenges arising from not having a privileged access to the data in addition to the challenges of Tumblr's affordances as a platform that include reblogging reoccurrences and reblogging deletion. Therefore, our objective is not only to analyse cascades using the existing models and measures but also to understand information diffusion in a platform that exhibits different information discovery and reblogging mechanisms. Whilst most of the analysis done in previous work is heavily dependent on rich contextual data (often obtained with privileged access); we show that it is possible to provide an in depth overview of the structural and temporal aspects of cascades on Tumblr with minimal contextual data.

The structural analysis focuses on two aspects, the first estimates users' impact on the overall cascade size, i.e., estimates how influential the users are. The second aspect aims to examine the topology of cascades' networks, i.e., their shape in terms of the number of paths, path lengths and the number of reblogs at each depth. The temporal analysis, on the other hand, aims to provide some insights about cascades' growth i.e., how quickly posts get reblogged, the different growth patterns of cascades and the branching factors per day and hour. The mainfi ndings of our analysis shows that, cascades on Tumblr are deep reaching 32.78 steps away from the author on average, the maximum depth in one cascade is 145. These numbers are in fact high compared to the depths reported in previous work [1, 12, 24, 28]. Also, we show that Tumblr's cascades branch out to long and separate paths, meaning that the cascades of popular content on Tumblr are wide and deep. On the other hand, Posts on Tumblr are reblogged quickly after being published, 95.84% offi rst reblogs occur within one day which is consistent with Chang et al. [9] remark about the tendency towards recency on Tumblr. Andfi nally, by investigating the patterns of growth in relation to the time, we found that cascades of different sizes grow in different ways accumulating reblogs at different rates at any given time.

This paper is organised as follows, Section 2 discusses related work. In Section 3 we present the methods used for the analysis. Sections 4 and 5 describes the results we obtained from analysing Tumblr's cascades structurally and temporally. Section 6 discusses the results reflecting on some of the aspects of the cascades. Finally, Section 7 concludes and outlines future work.

2 RELATED WORK

This paper builds on a relatively long history of cascades analysis studies on OSNs and the Web in general, e.g., in internet chain-letters [24] and blogosphere [2, 18, 22]. As new platforms emerge, cascades on these platforms have been analysed to understand the diffusion phenomenon [6, 10, 12, 31]. Research about information diffusion and cascades varies according to the purpose of the study. Some investigated the type of content that spreads [25, 27], others looked at the possible roles that users play to spread the content [4, 8], while others analysed the aftermaths after a content spreads i.e., the characteristics of cascades, either the structural or temporal characteristics [10–12, 15, 22, 24].

Cascade construction

Watts [29] defines a cascade as a diffusion event of any size that is triggered by an initial seed (a user). To be precise, we consider the diffusion of each post as an individual cascade. In most of the early research, cascade networks were often inferred, because the mechanisms of diffusion were not implemented as functionalities in the platform [13]. On Tumblr the reblogging history is explicitly shown as a list of notes, but sometimes has some missing information which present certain challenges during the cascade construction phase. Thus, we utilise some of the models in [5, 28] to handle these situations.

Aspects of cascades

As mentioned earlier there are two aspects of cascades, the structural and the temporal. We use the structural measures used by [3, 12, 13, 16, 24] to analyse the structure of cascade's networks. We apply these measures on the cascades obtained from Tumblr and compared Tumblr's cascades to those observed in different platforms. The work of [12] is one of closest works to ours, they analysed cascades on Facebook, focusing on two large memes. In this paper, we analyse Tumblr's most popular content which contains a number of large cascades in comparison to those in other platforms. For the temporal features we compare Tumblr's cascades to cascades obtained in [3, 12, 21].

Cascades analysis on Tumblr

There are two recent related studies about cascades on Tumblr [9, 30]. Chang et al. [9] noted that users sometimes appear more than once as they utilise reblogging as a form of communication. We expand on this and include it in our proposed cascade construction model that preserves the order of reblogging. The cascades they analyse in their paper are small, hence, we aimed to analyse larger cascades on Tumblr. Xu et al. [30] analysed the reblogging mechanism by constructing one large weighted network of reblogs. Here, we analyse individual cascade networks to reflect on each post's reblogging dynamics separately rather than the dynamics of the reblogging network on Tumblr as a whole.

3 METHODS

3.1 Tumblr

Tumblr is a hybrid social network platform [9] that allows users to create blogs and publish posts in any multimedia form, yet, like any social network platform, it provides various social interaction

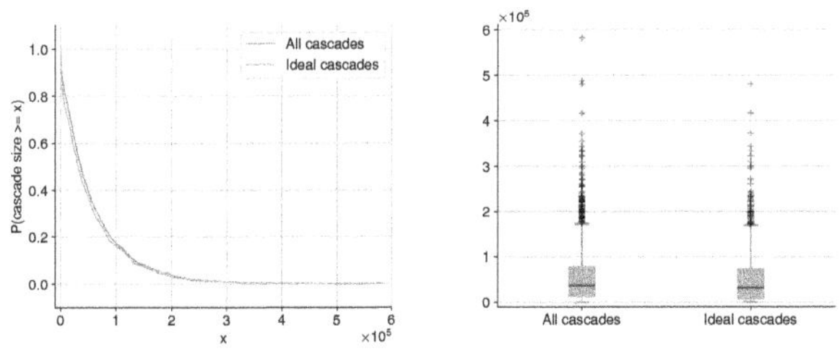

Figure 1: Cascade size distribution (CCDF) and cascade sizes boxplots for all cascades and ideal cascades show that most of popular posts has a cascade size below 100000

functionalities, such as following, reblogging and liking [30]. Reblogging is the main functionality that facilitates the diffusion of information on Tumblr. It allows users to reblog posts to their own blogs. Once a post is reblogged, it will appear in the reblogger's blog with a new ID. However, it will still link to the original post and the original author. As they reblog a post, users can add a comment and they can, in fact, reblog either original or reblogged posts. Reblogs appear as a list of notes attached to each post in the format: *X reblogged this from Y* or *X reblogged this from Y and added a comment.* Explicitly showing the source of a reblog allows us to construct the cascade network of a particular post, following the paths at which the post spreads. In addition to its basic role, reblogging on Tumblr is implemented in a unique way that allow users to reblog the same post more than once using the same conventional mechanism. This means that users might appear in different parts in one cascade. Chang et al. [9] reported this behaviour; they stated that users use reblogging to communicate with each other by adding comments to their reblogs.

3.2 Data Sampling and Collection

Our dataset was harvested from Tumblr's 2014 "Year in Review" blog, which is a blog curated by Tumblr's staff at the end of each year to highlight the most popular posts and tags in that year. The details of the methodology Tumblr follows to create this blog is not published. However, it is stated that it takes into account many factors such as the web traffic, the growth in the number of followers, and the size of both the original and reblogged post. This blog is useful to study cascades because it is not possible to catalogue all of Tumblr's cascades, and select the "successful" ones that have large number of reblogs. Hence, this blog allows us to analyse the characteristics of large cascades. Thus, we take advantage of Tumblr's staffeff ort to harvest the dataset, leveraging their privileged access. The harvesting process started by getting the URLs of the most reblogged posts from the Tumblr's 2014 year in review blog, where each post belongs to one category that Tumblr's staff chose. For each post we obtained the following information: the URL, the author (blog-name), publishing timestamp, type and category. Initially, we used a web scraper to fetch the notes list for each post, starting from the most recent activities going down to the earliest ones. We gathered both reblogging and liking activities. For each reblog we obtained: the username (blog-name) of the user who reblogged (reblogger), the username of the user from whom the post was reblogged (reblogee), the URL of the reblogged post, whether it has a comment and the comment's text. We then used Tumblr's API for each reblog to get its timestamp i.e., the time at which a reblog was made. Hence, the harvested data has two aspects; thefirst allows us to construct cascades networks using the information about users reblogging from other users. The second, allows us to create a time series dataset, where we record the number of reblogging activities at a given time (day or hour) after publishing. Figure 2 illustrates these two data representations that were used for the analysis. As a result, the harvested dataset contains the top posts in 57 different categories. The number of the harvested posts in each category ranges from 10 to 115 posts, and the total number of the harvested posts is 1292. In the whole dataset there are 73,048,903 independent reblogging events across all the posts, see table 1.

Table 1: Dataset description

No. of posts	1292
No. of posts (Ideal cascade)	796
No. of reblogs (rebloggers)	73,048,903
No. of reblogees	3,541,110

3.3 Data Pre-processing

Data harvesting with non-privileged access comes with its own set of challenges that must be taken into account during the harvesting process and before the data analysis phase. As explained above, for each post we crawled the list of notes that carries details about the reblogging history of each post. This list is ordered chronologically, with the most recent reblogs at the top of the list. Hence, during the harvesting process, the crawler started by getting the most recent reblogs and it kept fetching the next page of notes until it reached the veryfi rst reblog. However, because the harvesting process started long after the posts' publishing dates, we were faced by two challenges. Thefi rst challenge is the missing reblogs. Missing reblogs occur as a result of reblog deletion, or due to the deactivation of the whole blog (i.e., account). The direct implication in this case is that there will be disjoint parts in the cascade network. We will explain in detail how we addressed this challenge. The second challenge is related to the reblogs timestamps. In some cases, Tumblr's API does not provide a timestamp, or when it does, it provides an invalid one. For instance, sometimes it provides an invalid timestamp from the year 2000 or even 1970. In other cases it provides a timestamp before the posting timestamp. Hence, all of the invalid timestamps were excluded. For the missing timestamps, we used a simple interpolating algorithm. The algorithmfi lls in the timestamps using the time delta between two existing, consecutive and valid timestamps. In case there are no available timestamps to calculate the delta the reblogs are excluded from the analysis. On average, posts have 0.02% invalid timestamps, 15.6% interpolated timestamps and 84.38% valid timestamps.

In this paper, we carried out two types of analyses; the structural and the temporal. For the structural aspect, we are mainly concerned with the relationship between users. This was achieved

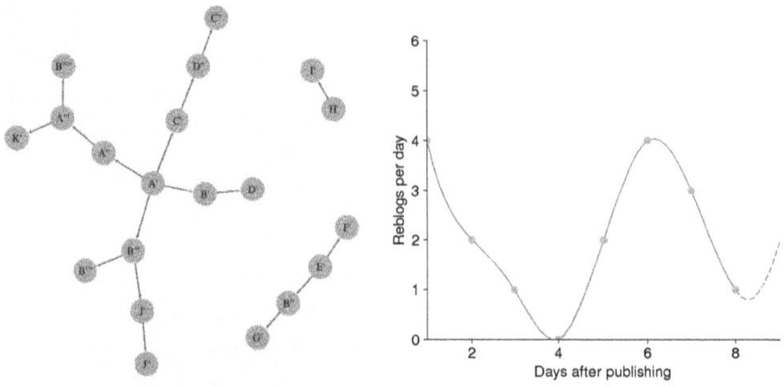

(a) Cascade network (b) Time-series

Figure 2: Two data representation obtained from table 2. Left: shows the relation between the users, right: reflects the number of reblogs recorded per day

by analysing the topology of the cascade network, taking into account the reblogging causality between the users. The temporal aspect, however, is concerned with analysing the relationship between the reblogging rates and the time. Thus, accurate timestamps are essential for the temporal analysis but are not always needed for the structural analysis. Therefore, two conditions were used to accept posts for some parts of the structural analysis and all of the temporal ones. The conditions are: 1) thefi rst reblog must be from the post's author; hence, appropriate linkage to the source is preserved, 2) the timestamps of thefi rst reblog must be after the posting timestamp. In fact, as explained earlier, we checked all the reblogging timestamps and excluded all of the outliers that have invalid timestamps. Thefi rst constraint yields 806 posts. The second constraint excluded 10 posts, leaving us with 796 posts: 'ideal' cascades.

The average cascade size in our dataset is 56539.4, while the median is 36771.5 (51876.23 and 31493.0 respectively for the ideal cascades). The maximum cascade size is 581895 while the minimum is 3 (Figure 1). The distributions in Figure 1 shows that about 78% of the cascades were reblogged at least 10000 times, but only 18% were reblogged more than 100000 times. Heavy-tailed distributions of cascade sizes are widely observed in previous studies. In our case, these posts were selected as the top ones in 57 categories curated by Tumblr's staff, yet they exhibit similar characteristic, highly diverse cascade sizes, with larger cascades being a minority. We will discuss the notion of large cascades further in Section 6.

3.4 Constructing Cascades Networks

Here we will explain the cascade construction model that we used to construct cascade networks. We construct a separate cascade network for each post. In these networks, the nodes are the users and the edges represent thefl ow of information between them. This model represents the causal relationship between users i.e., who reblogged from whom. It preserves the causal relationships between the users according to the timestamps when the reblogging occurs. Hence, thefl ow of information and the order of reblogging are preserved. The direction of the edges shows the direction of informationfl ow. Thus, node's in-degree in the these network will either be one or zero because there will always be one source

Table 2: An example of the reblogging history for one post

Notes	Day	Notes	Day
A posted	1	B Reblogged from A	5
B Reblogged from A	1	C Reblogged from D	6
C Reblogged from A	1	J Reblogged from B	6
D Reblogged from B	1	A Reblogged from A	6
F Reblogged from E	1	J Reblogged from J	6
B Reblogged from E	2	B Reblogged from B	7
G Reblogged from B	2	A Reblogged from A	7
I Reblogged from H	3	K Reblogged from A	7
D Reblogged from C	5	B Reblogged from A	8

(parent node/rebloggee) or this information might be missing so the in-degree will be zero.

The Process: We define a cascade network $C\{V,E\}$ where $\{V\}$ is the set of nodes (users) and $\{E\}$ is the set of edges in the network. In this network a node $v \in V$ will be connected to its parent node $u \in V$, and an edge $(v,u,t) \in E$ will be drawn to indicates that user v reblogged from user u at time t. The direction of the edge will be from u to v and it will indicate the direction of informationfl ow. Ideally, cascade networks' topology will be a tree where the root is the post's author. Unfortunately, due to missing/deleted reblogs not all networks are ideal. There are a number of cases that we observed during the construction process. These cases are listed below:

- Case 1: On Tumblr users can reblog the same post more than once, hence, appear in different places in the cascade network. Thisfl exibility sets a challenge when another user reblogged from a user who appeared in many places in the network as we need to decide to which parent node we are going to link the newly added child node.
- Case 2: Sometimes reblogs are deleted and the direct consequence when this happen is that we encounter cases where we don't know the parent user. Thus, we will have an isolated pair of two connected users.

To handle thefi rst case, there are many approaches in previous work [5, 28] that were suggested to infer which node to choose from if there are a number of possibilities, we adopted two approaches: the most-recent and the least-recent, which add new children nodes to the most recent parent or least recent parent respectively. In other words, we link rebloggers to either their parents'fi rst appearance (least-recent) or their parent's last appearance (most-recent). However, due to the limited space we have in this paper we only present the results from the most-recent approach. The difference between the two is subtle and it is beyond the scope of this paper. As for the second case (the isolated components) there are three approaches: first, we can ignore them and only analyse the largest component (large connected component). Second, analyse the whole network (forest) including the isolated components. The third approach is inferring the missing links to connect the isolated fragments to the main component [28]. Thefi rst approach has a major disadvantage, because if we ignore these bits we will be missing important information about the reblogging dynamics, also the size of the cascade will be affected as a result. To be able to reconnect the graph

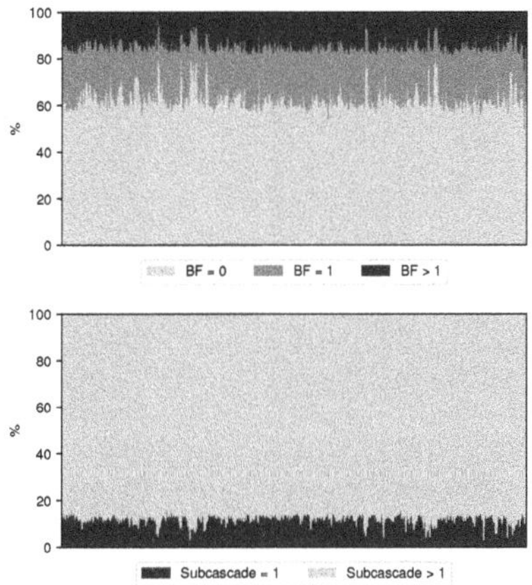

Figure 3: Top: the percentages of nodes' branching factors, Bottom: the percentages of nodes' subcascade size, most node's have zero branching factor while the majority have more than one subcascade size

by inferring missing links we need to have access to Tumblr's social network and possibly some historic reblogging information to make a better judgement about the accuracy of the inferred links. In our case, we do not have such information, thus, we are left with the second option which is to analyse the forest as whole taking into consideration the isolated fragments as a disconnected bits of the cascade network. Figure 2a illustrates a cascade network constructed from the reblogging information in table 2.

4 STRUCTURAL FEATURES

To analyse the structure of the constructed cascade networks we used a number of measures, the branching factor (the out-degree), the subcascade size, the depth, number of paths and path lengths. We apply these measures to the individual cascades we constructed. Thefi rst two measures are related to the influence of individual users, while the rest act as an estimators of the cascade overall structure. Because the cascades of the top posts on Tumblr contain a large number of nodes, it is difficult to model their complex structures, thus, we use these measures so we can quantify and assess their characteristics.

4.1 Branching Factors and Subcascade Sizes

How many users a user influences?

Using the loose definition of influence in social networks [8, 21], the branching factor is simply the number of children a node has (its out-degree); i.e., in Tumblr's context, the number of users who were influenced by a particular user to reblog the post. This means that the branching factor is useful to estimate the contributions of a particular node in the network (a user) to the cascade overall size; the higher the branching factor of a user the higher the user's influence. One way to analyse branching factors is to differentiate between three classes of users, those who have no impact (Branching factor = 0), those who at least influenced one user (Branching factor = 1), and the others who have an impact on more that one user (Branching factor > 1). Figure 3 illustrates the percentages of nodes with zero, one or more branching factors respectively in each cascade. Figure 3 shows that most of the nodes have zero children (the mean equals 67.44%), meaning that in most cases the cascade stops when it reaches these users. While about 20.21% of the nodes have one child at most, and only few nodes contributed to the growth of the cascade by having more than one child (12.33% on average). The average percentage for the nodes with one child is close to the percentage found in [24] (equals: 19.04%), where a 10-fold simulation were run to model informationfl ow on Internet chain-letters. These percentages show that in most cases, cascades die-out soon after reaching a large number of users who have zero reblogging children. The average branching factor across all the posts equals to 1.02 which reflects the percentages shown in Figure 3. Most nodes have zero branching factors, but there are about 32.54% of nodes whose branching factors are one or above. A similar average (1.02) was obtained when we aggregated the branching factors for all of the different user occurrences in the cascade network.

Scale: The impact of the post's author

The scale is the branching factor of the author, i.e., the number of users who reblogged directly from the root. Obviously, the whole cascade is initially generated by the root, but, the overall cascade size cannot be attributed to the author alone, as it is the result of the cumulative contributions of everyone who reblogged it. However, the scale can be used to estimate the direct influence of the author and the direct impact the author has on the cascade. We calculate the author's contribution to the cascade as a function of its branching factor in relation to the cascade size. On average, the post's author contributes about 8.94%, the median equals 0.5%. Figure 4(a), plots the CDF (cumulative distribution function) for the percentages of author's contributions to the total cascade size, we can see that there are some cases where the author contributed more than 20%, but for the majority of cascades, author's contributions are below 10%. These percentages must be taken into their appropriate context, as we are trying to measure the direct impact of the author. The author's contribution to the cascade decreases for large cascades, however, we noted that, for some cascades up to size 40000, the author contributed up to 80% of the overall cascade size, i.e., a large number of reblogs follow from the root directly. Which means that, cascades with such characteristics are shallow, as most of the nodes reside one step away from the root. But for the majority of cascades (75%) author's contributions are lower than 2.89%. Thus, most cascades' networks are deep, branching out beyond one step away from the author. We will investigate the depth of cascades in the subsequent section.

Subcascades sizes

The subcascade size extends the notion of influence measured by the branching factor to include the whole subcascade that follows from one user. Only nodes with branching factors equal to one or more are considered in the analysis in this part. Because the nodes with zero branching factors will consequently have no subcascades. We compute the size of the subcascade generated from each node excluding the post author and all the users who have zero branching factors. The average subcascade size across all the posts equals 10.8.

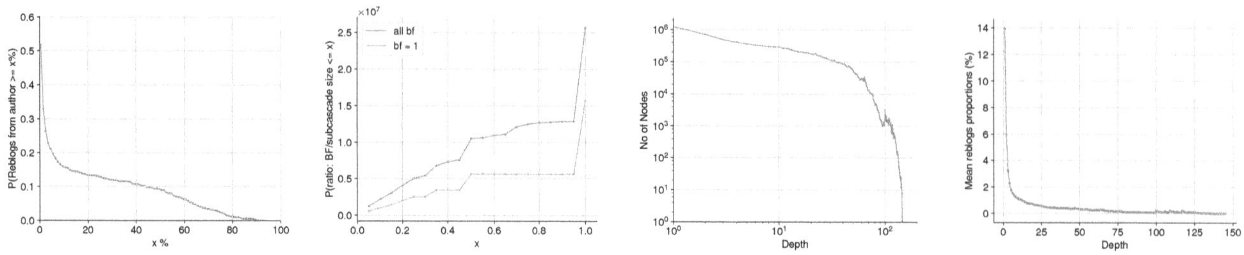

(a) (b) (c) (d)

Figure 4: (a) CCDF distribution of the percentages of author's contributions to the cascade (scale), (b) CDF distribution of the branching factor to the subcascade size ratios, (c) Aggregate number of reblogs at each depth, (d) The percentages of the mean reblogs proportions per depth

The maximum subcascade size is 183157. Which means that for that particular post, a user contribution to the cascade is about 98%. On average, users with high subcascade sizes contribute about 29% to the overall size of a cascade. This percentage means that in some cases the size of the cascade might be highly dependent on one user only. Figure 3 shows the percentages of nodes with subcascade sizes that equals one or above across all cascades. We can see that most nodes have subcascade sizes that are above one, meaning that they branch out beyond their direct children. On average, about 13.33% of the nodes have cascade sizes that equal one, hence, their branching factors are one as well.

Small branching factor but high impact?

Considering the branching factor only as an estimator of the user's influence, can sometimes lead to underestimations. In some cases, the subcascade generated from a user with a branching factor that equals one is larger than the initial anticipation. We noticed that the average subcascade size for these nodes equals to 13, while the maximum subcascade size equals 182986. These numbers are computed by excluding the root, to avoid including cascades where the author's branching factor equals one. To be able to assess the relation between the branching factors and the subcascade sizes, we divide the branching factor by the subcascade size to compute the ratio that will allow us to assess this relation. Small ratios (close to zero) means that the branching factor is small but the subcascade size is large. Which also means that this particular user has created a subcascade that goes beyond one step away from the user. As the ratio increases, it means that the user's does not create a large subcascade, meaning that the generated subcascade looks like broadcasting where it does not branch away from that node. If the ratio equals one then the branching factor equals the subcascade size, meaning that it does not go beyond one step away. Figure 4(b) shows the CDF distribution for the ratios generated for nodes with one branching factor or more. It shows that for about half the nodes their generated subcascades are larger than their branching factors, meaning that their impact is actually higher than their branching factors. Also, thefi gure shows that, nodes with branching factors above one generate slightly larger subcascades than the ones generated from the nodes with branching factors that equal one.

4.2 Cascades' Depth and Paths

Here we utilise another set of measures for the structural aspects of cascades: the number of paths, paths lengths and depth. Each of these measures shed some light on a different aspect of the structure of a cascade. Nodes' depth in a cascade network is simply their distances from the root, i.e., how far are they from the root (the post's author). While the path lengths and the number of paths in a cascade networks are respectively measures of how far content travels away from the root until they reach a user whom no one reblogs from (leaf nodes, branching factor = 0). The total number of paths indicates the number of different paths a post travels thorough as it spreads. Because these measures are highly dependent on the distances from the root, we only consider ideal cascades, i.e., the ones that have the author as a source of thefi rst reblog.

Depths

Figure 4(c), plots the aggregate number of nodes at each depth across all cascades, which corresponds to the number of reblogs at each depth. Thefi gure shows that the majority of nodes are at depth one. The number of nodes per depth decreases after that until depth 10, where the number of nodes starts to decrease sharply after that. This means that most of the time, rebloggers are not far away from the author. Nonetheless, some cascade networks grow far away from the root reaching 32.78 steps on average. Also, the maximum depth found across all cascades equals 145. In fact, the maximum depth is below 46 for about 75% of the cascades, the rest have a maximum depth larger than 46. The maximum depth across all cascades is 145. Overall, the depths recorded for Tumblr cascades are considered non-trivial depth as [12] describes. Adamic et al. [1] reported a maximum depth that equals to 40, while [24] reported a median node depth that equals to 288. On the other hand, in their analysis on Twitter [28] noted that the average diameter is four. Thus, Tumblr cascades' depth is relatively higher than the depths observed in other platforms. We compute the average proportion of reblogs per depth for all cascades, (figure 4(d)). We can see that, on average, reblogs at depth one comprise about 14% of the overall cascade size. The mean reblogs proportions decreases after that, remaining slightly above zero. The mean reblogs proportions drops below 2 from depth 5 onwards. Thus, even though posts got reblogged after depth 5, the majority of reblogging users are only few steps away from the post's author. It is important to note that in this section, our concern is the structure of cascades, thus, all of the measures are taken without taking the time into consideration. Meaning that, nodes that appear at depth one are not necessary caused by reblogs in the cascade's early stages. We will revisit the changes in branching factors in relation to time in the next section.

Number of path and path lengths

We compute the total number of paths the post spread through to reach different users and the length of these paths. We took into consideration the leaf nodes (nodes that have BF = 0) to mark the termination of cascade paths. On average, cascades consist of 9167 different paths (the median = 3768.5). Half of the cascades consist of about 923 to 12531 different paths, with some outliers above and below these numbers. For instance, in one cascade there are 104061 different paths from the root (author). The correlation coefficient between the cascade size and the number of paths in the cascade network is 0.54, which means that it is more likely that as the cascade grow it will have more paths, but that is not always the case, for there are some moderate sized cascades that have large number of paths ($R^2 = 0.29$). The average path length across all cascades is 11.07, and the longest path across all cascades is 145, which is the furthest depth too.

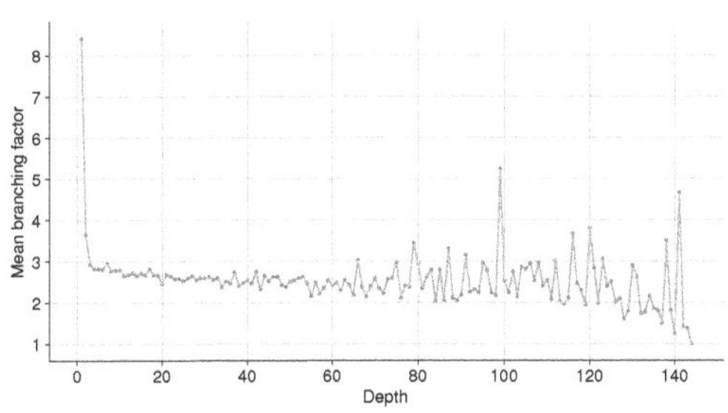

Figure 5: Mean branching factor per depth

Mean branching factor per depth

Looking at branching factor as a function of depth allow us to understand how cascades grow in relation to rebloggers distances from the root (their depths). Figure 5 shows that the average branching factor at depth one equals to 8.4, then it decreases to 3.6 at depth two. After that, it remains just above two and below three up to depth 79. For depths from 100 and deeper, the average branching factorfl uctuates between 2 and 5, sometimes it is close to one, but overall it does not go below 1 at any given depth. A possible explanation for thefl uctuating part is that there might be some users who reside away from the author. These users were not exposed to the post directly from the author or one of the author's closest users. Nonetheless, when these users reblog that post, a surge in the post's popularity emerged as many users reblogged after them. It is worth noting that the average branching factor on Tumblr is higher than the average branching factor on two of Facebook's large cascade memes [12], where the average branching factors per depth are between 0.5 and 1 for depths from 1 until 20. Therefore, it appears that popular content's cascades on Tumblr exhibit higher numbers of branching factors at each depth in comparison to Facebook's popular content.

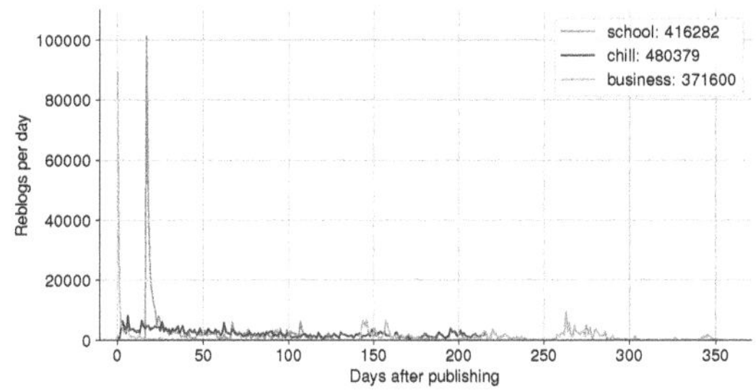

Figure 6: The timelines of three large cascades

5 TEMPORAL FEATURES

In the previous section we looked at cascades' structure, here, we will analyse the temporal features of cascades. As we explained in section 3.3, to provide an accurate analysis, only ideal cascade will be considered. These have cascade networks with the author as the root and all the timestamps of the reblogging activities are valid. The temporal analysis is split into two main divisions, cascades' growth and branching factors per time. Simply put, analysing cascade growth looks into the cumulative increase in the number of reblogs in relation to the time after publishing the post. While branching factors per depth gives us an idea of how cascades grow as a function of their average branching factors at a given time after publishing.

Posts' Age

Before we present our analysis of the temporal aspect of cascades, there are a couple of points that need to be clarified. The posts we analyse in the dataset, were published sometime before Dec 2014, and Tumblr's Year in Review blog is published before the New Year's Eve. Our harvesting process took place for about a month from 29 Dec 2014 to 2 Feb 2015. Thus, we record all the reblogging activities that were available before 2 Feb 2015. We calculate posts' active age, which is the difference in days between the post's publishing timestamp and the last day in which any reblogging activity was recorded. On average, the recorded posts' active age is 237 days which is slightly below a year. The oldest post in our dataset was active for 617 days (more than one year) it was posted on May 2013. Which means that there are some posts published before 2014 and remained active during 2014. Surprisingly, this old post, has a very small cascade size of 131 reblogs, but still managed to survive for 617 days. The youngest post was posted on 9 Mar 2014 and was active for 28 days only, and it was tiny as well with 68 reblogs over the period of 28 days, where about 61% of its reblogs occur on the first day after publishing. However, it is important to note that we refer to the cascade age, as active-age because it is not definite and many of these posts will remain active after the data collection. Nonetheless, we are not estimating or predicting cascade lifetime, we are merely interested to understand cascades' growth patterns.

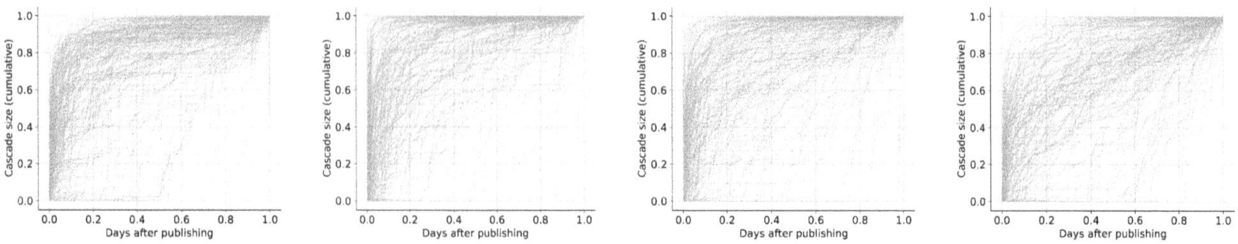

(a) Below 25th%   (b) 25th-50th%   (c) 50th-75th%   (d) above 75th%

Figure 7: Normalised cascade cumulative growth against days after publishing for four cascade size categories shows that there is no uniform pattern for cascades' growth

5.1 Cascade Growth

As they attract more reblogging users, posts' cascades size increases, here we estimate cascade growth looking at the relation between the cumulative cascade size and the time after publishing.

How long it takes for a post to be reblogged?

Before delving into cascade growth analysis, we will look into the time lag between posting and reblogging. Around 87% of first reblogs occur on the first hour after publishing, and 97.11% of first reblogs occur within 24 hours after publishing. These figures are similar to the ones reported by [9], who also analysed cascades on Tumblr. Their results show that 75.03% of reblogs occur on the first hour and 95.84% occur within one day. Kwak et al. [21] famous study on Twitter shows that 50% of retweets occur within an hour while 75% occur in a day. Our results, confirms the tendency towards 'recency' in Tumblr as Chang et al. described it [9]. However, there is a minority (2.6%) that did not get their first reblogs on the first 24 hours and only 1.13% that actually were idle for more than 100 days before the first reblog occurs. Nonetheless, being late at getting their first reblog did not affect their active-age or cascade size. In fact, some of these posts managed to survive for more than 600 days. There is one post that got its first reblog on its 105 day but has 43660 reblogs cumulatively.

Growth Patterns

In this part of the analysis, we will look into the patterns of the cumulative cascades' size advancements during their lifetime. The question we attempt to answer is: Is there a pattern of cascade growth on Tumblr that we can detect? I.e., does popular content follow the same growth pattern as time goes by? To answer this question let's first take a look at the timelines the largest cascades (416282, 416282, and 371600) as shown in figure 6. We can recognise three different patterns, the first one (in blue), starts off with few reblogs (27 on its first day) but picks up the pace on its 17th day with 101351 reblog on one day, then it maintains its popularity with moderate number of reblogs until its last recorded reblogging activity. The second one (in dark red), in contrast, maintains a moderate number of reblogs each day, it has no high spikes in its lifetime. The third one (in light red) starts off with high volume of reblogging on its first day, then it declines having a moderate number reblogs each day. Again, our focus here is not about how long it lasts, but rather how it accumulates its popularity. Motivated by this observation, we want to examine whether cascades of similar sizes follow the same growth pattern or not. We categorise ideal cascade according to the distribution of their cascade sizes (See figure 2). Precisely, we use four categories, the first category has cascades that reside below the 25th%, these are cascades of relatively small sizes (below 7697). The second category for cascade between 25th% and 50th%, roughly these are moderate cascades below the median (31493), the third category for the slightly large cascade between the 50th% and the 75th% (above the median 31493 and below 72475). The last category for large cascades beyond the 75th%. Figure 7 illustrates the normalised cumulative growth in cascade sizes for all cascades in the four cascade categories. Each line in the figure corresponds to one cascade, and the normalised cumulative growth is computed using the total number of reblogs a cascade has at a given day. As the figure shows, there are no particular patterns that cascades in different category follow, which simply mean that cascades reach their maximum recorded sizes in various ways. Across all categories, the increase in cascade sizes does not occur at a constant rate. In contrast, the diffusion of Linked-in invitation [3] has a liner growth pattern for both large and medium cascades (over 4000 and 500 respectively). The lack of uniform pattern might be related to the cascade size itself, or probably platform specific i.e., the different mechanisms in which the users become exposed to a particular content.

5.2 Branching Factors Across Time

The last temporal measure that will be used is actually a measure that combines the structure of the cascade in relation to the time. The average branching factors each day or hour after publishing will expand our understanding of the way popular content gains its popularity. Figure 8 shows the average branching factor per day and hour. We can see that, during the first 100 days, the average branching factor starts below 2.8 and drops after that, it fluctuate between 2.1 and 2.4 for the rest of the period. If we consider the first 3 days (i.e., 72 hours), we can see that in this period, the branching factor starts slightly above 4, then it loses almost half of its value in the next hour as it becomes slightly above 2.5. After that it drops remaining above 1.5.In comparison to the average branching factors per hour in [12], the average branching factors for popular content on Tumblr is higher than their counterpart on Facebook (branching

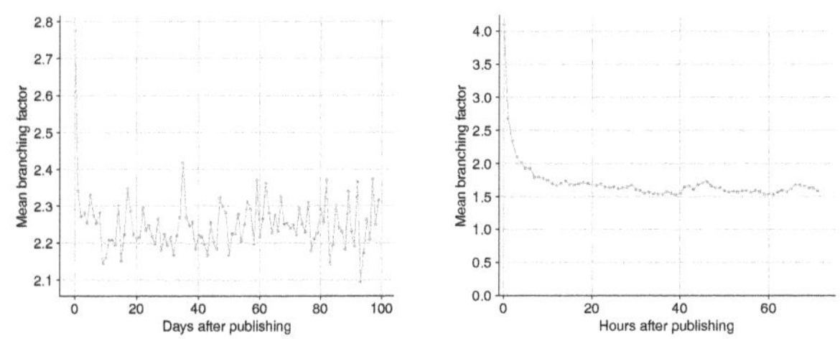

(a) (b)

Figure 8: (a) Mean branching factor per day for thefi rst 100 days, (b) mean branching factor per hour for 72 hours

factors per hour are between 0.5 and 1). Thus, it seems that Tumblr's content attract higher number of users at each point in its lifetime.

6 DISCUSSION

In the previous sections we shed some lights on the structural and temporal aspects of cascades on Tumblr. The results of the analysis show that:

- The majority of users have zero branching factors; some users have small branching factors but they have higher impact.
- Tumblr's cascades are deep reaching 32.78 steps away from the author on average which is higher compared to the depths reported in previous work [1, 12, 24, 28].
- Tumblr's cascades branch out to 9167 separate paths on average. Coupled with the previous remark, it means that cascades of popular content on Tumblr are wide and deep.
- Posts on Tumblr are reblogged quickly after being published, 95.84% offi rst reblogs occur within one day, which is quicker than those of Twitter [21], and consistent with [9] remark about the tendency towards recency on Tumblr.
- There is no single pattern at which a cascade grow in relation to its lifetime, regardless of its size.

Since the analysis we carried out in this paper was done on content that was promoted as the most popular content. We would like to make some remarks about large cascade, estimating influence and some of data harvesting considerations to study cascades.

How 'big' are large cascades?

This seems an easy question to answer, and a possible response might be, "well, large enough!". In fact, many studies in thefield, especially these with privileged access to the data, use the term 'large' loosely in their analysis and, in most cases, large cascades are the largest ones in the dataset. For instance, in the dataset used in this work, the mean cascade size is 56,539, while the median is 36,771, and about 18% of the cascades are larger than 100,000 (about 227 cascades). To put these numbers into perspective, in their study on Twitter [15] studied cascades of up to 10,000 nodes in their trees. Analysis by [10] of cascades on Facebook, states that the maximum cascade size is around 10,000 shares per post. Another study of Facebook analysed the diffusion of two photos that were shared 618,015 and 150,759 times respectively [12]. Thus, in light of the reported large cascade sizes on other platforms, it is noted that some of Tumblr's most reblogged posts exhibit high numbers of reblogging. However, there is much debate when it comes to the existence of large cascades. Goel et al. [16] state that large cascades are rare while 99% of cascades are shallow and die in one step. Earlier work also claims that most cascades are shallow and fragmented [22] while a few of them are relatively large [23]. Thefi rst step is to achieve some level of agreement on an acceptable lower-bound at which a cascade can be considered large. Secondly, it might be true that most content posted does not end up 'large', but there is some evidence for their existence, when content spreads in high volume creating a cascade with complex structures. These need special consideration in the construction and analysis phases. Such content is a serious source for marketeers, who want to replicate its success. For a scientist wishing to reveal this phenomenon, however, the question is where tofi nd them? In this work, they were deliberately harvested from posts that were promoted as popular, but it is unlikely that such content would be stumbled upon accidentally without prior planning and much speculation.

Estimating influence

A user with a high branching factor means that this user plays a major role in spreading the content which might be related to its position in the social network (the number of followers the user has). If a user with high number of follower is exposed to a post, the probability that the post will continue to spread will increase. Whilst if a user has few followers most likely the user will have a small branching factor (or zero), hence, the cascade will eventually stop after reaching this particular user (a sink in graph theory terminology). It is widely acceptable to use the number of reblogs (or retweets) that results from a user as a proxy to estimate influence [8, 21]. It is reasonable because it helps estimating the user's direct impact, since most of the users who will reblog a post from another user have most likely done so after being exposed to the user's feed. Our analysis shows the difference between using the branching factor and the subcascade size as influence estimators. Because in some cases branching factors can underestimate the overall impact of a user. However, branching factors are useful to assess the direct impact, while the subcascade sizes are useful to assess the overall impact whether it is caused by the same user or possibly some other users in the network.

Data Harvesting Considerations

To be able to analyse cascade wefi rst need to differentiate between two types of content that spreads: viral content (such as memes) and non-viral content (ordinary content). This has an effect on the data harvesting stage, i.e., if our interest is to study viral content, more deliberate efforts must take place to make sure that we harvest a representable dataset as appose to the harvesting methods that involvefi rehose access that harvest everything being shared within a timeframe then analyses different types of cascades which might or might not be viral. I.e., getting a sample of what users share within that specific timeframe. Due to the harvesting method we used in this paper, our dataset has some missing information.

These include missing reblogs that make the cascade network disjoint with many isolated parts that are difficult to link to the main cascade network because have access to the social graph via the API. Thus, to be able to predict the missing links correctly we need to take into account the previous reblogging history between users, which can help to predict, and rate possible links that is beyond the scope of this paper. In addition, our observation shows that it is common that users revisit their reblogging decisions and they either delete reblogs or deactivate their accounts. The rate of deletions we encountered tells us that the status on Tumblr (and presumably any other social network) can rapidly change.

7 CONCLUSION AND FUTURE WORK

Analysing cascades provides us with many insights about the diffusion mechanism and the role of users involved in the process. This paper provided a thorough investigation of the structural and temporal aspects of cascades on Tumblr. Our analysis shows that cascades on Tumblr can reach remarkable sizes in comparison to the sizes reported in previous works. As for the structural aspects, Tumblr's cascades can sometimes branch out deeply beyond one step away from the author reaching 145 in depth. In addition the branching factors by depth show that a considerable number of rebloggers were recorded at each level. The temporal analysis shows that, regardless of the cascade size, there is no pattern for cascades growth, they expand in size and each individual cascade has different proportions of the number of reblogs at a given time. In the future, we aim to investigate the diffusion on Tumblr taking into account other factors, such as the characteristics of the content and the people who are engaged with it (i.e., the people who found it interesting and contributed to spreading it). In addition, deconstructing a cascade, as presented in this paper, can be seen a first step towards two fundamental data-driven tasks that can be carried out in the future i.e., modelling cascades that exhibit the features of the cascades of popular content and using these features for predicting the future growth of them.

REFERENCES

[1] Lada A Adamic, Thomas M Lento, and Andrew T Fiore. 2012. How You Met Me.. In *The 6th International AAAI Conference on Weblogs and Social Media (ICWSM)*.

[2] Eytan Adar and Lada A. Adamic. 2005. Tracking Information Epidemics in Blogspace. In *Proceedings of the 2005 IEEE/WIC/ACM International Conference on Web Intelligence (WI '05)*. IEEE, Washington, DC, USA, 207–214.

[3] Ashton Anderson, Daniel Huttenlocher, Jon Kleinberg, Jure Leskovec, and Mitul Tiwari. 2015. Global diffusion via cascading invitations: Structure, growth, and homophily. In *Proceedings of the 24th International Conference on World Wide Web*. ACM, 66–76.

[4] Isabel Anger and Christian Kittl. 2011. Measuring Influence on Twitter. In *Proceedings of the 11th International Conference on Knowledge Management and Knowledge Technologies (i-KNOW '11)*. ACM, New York, NY, USA, Article 31, 4 pages.

[5] Eytan Bakshy, Jake M. Hofman, Winter A. Mason, and Duncan J. Watts. 2011. Everyone's an Influencer: Quantifying Influence on Twitter. In *Proceedings of the Fourth ACM International Conference on Web Search and Data Mining (WSDM '11)*. ACM, 65–74.

[6] Eytan Bakshy, Itamar Rosenn, Cameron Marlow, and Lada Adamic. 2012. The Role of Social Networks in Information Diffusion. In *Proceedings of the 21st International Conference on World Wide Web (WWW '12)*. ACM, New York, NY, USA, 519–528.

[7] Sushil Bikhchandani, David Hirshleifer, and Ivo Welch. 1992. A theory of fads, fashion, custom, and cultural change as informational cascades. *Journal of political Economy* (1992), 992–1026.

[8] Meeyoung Cha, H Haddadi, F Benevenuto, and PK Gummadi. 2010. Measuring User Influence in Twitter: The Million Follower Fallacy. In *Proceedings of 4th International AAAI Conference on Weblogs and Social Media (ICWSM)*. 10–17.

[9] Yi Chang, Lei Tang, Yoshiyuki Inagaki, and Yan Liu. 2014. What is Tumblr: A Statistical Overview and Comparison. *ACM SIGKDD Explorations Newsletter* 16, 1 (2014), 21–29.

[10] Justin Cheng, Lada Adamic, P. Alex Dow, Jon Michael Kleinberg, and Jure Leskovec. 2014. Can Cascades Be Predicted?. In *Proceedings of the 23rd International Conference on World Wide Web (WWW '14)*. ACM, 925–936.

[11] Justin Cheng, Lada A. Adamic, Jon M. Kleinberg, and Jure Leskovec. 2016. Do Cascades Recur?. In *Proceedings of the 25th International Conference on World Wide Web (WWW '16)*. International World Wide Web Conferences Steering Committee, Republic and Canton of Geneva, Switzerland, 671–681.

[12] P. Alex Dow, Lada A. Adamic, and Adrien Friggeri. 2013. The Anatomy of Large Facebook Cascades. In *Proceedings of the Seventh International Conference on Weblogs and Social Media, ICWSM*.

[13] Wojciech Galuba, Karl Aberer, Dipanjan Chakraborty, Zoran Despotovic, and Wolfgang Kellerer. 2010. Outtweeting the Twitterers - Predicting Information Cascades in Microblogs. In *Proceedings of the 3rd Wonference on Online Social Networks (WOSN'10)*. USENIX Association, Berkeley, CA, USA, 3–3.

[14] Ashish Goel, Kamesh Munagala, Aneesh Sharma, and Hongyang Zhang. 2015. A Note on Modeling Retweet Cascades on Twitter. In *Algorithms and Models for the Web Graph*. Springer, 119–131.

[15] Sharad Goel, Ashton Anderson, Jake Hofman, and Duncan Watts. 2013. The structural virality of online diffusion. *Preprint* 22 (2013), 26.

[16] Sharad Goel, Duncan J. Watts, and Daniel G. Goldstein. 2012. The Structure of Online Diffusion Networks. In *Proceedings of the 13th ACM Conference on Electronic Commerce (EC '12)*. 623–638.

[17] Mark Granovetter. 1978. Threshold models of collective behavior. *American journal of sociology* (1978), 1420–1443.

[18] Daniel Gruhl, R. Guha, David Liben-Nowell, and Andrew Tomkins. 2004. Information Diffusion Through Blogspace. In *Proceedings of the 13th International Conference on World Wide Web (WWW '04)*. ACM, 491–501.

[19] Adrien Guille, Hakim Hacid, Cecile Favre, and Djamel A. Zighed. 2013. Information Diffusion in Online Social Networks: A Survey. *SIGMOD Rec.* 42, 2 (July 2013), 17–28.

[20] Andrey Kupavskii, Liudmila Ostroumova, Alexey Umnov, Svyatoslav Usachev, Pavel Serdyukov, Gleb Gusev, and Andrey Kustarev. 2012. Prediction of Retweet Cascade Size over Time. In *Proceedings of the 21st ACM International Conference on Information and Knowledge Management (CIKM '12)*. ACM, New York, NY, USA, 2335–2338.

[21] Haewoon Kwak, Changhyun Lee, Hosung Park, and Sue Moon. 2010. What is Twitter, a Social Network or a News Media?. In *Proceedings of the 19th International Conference on World Wide Web (WWW '10)*. ACM, New York, NY, USA, 591–600.

[22] Jure Leskovec, Mary McGlohon, Christos Faloutsos, Natalie Glance, and Matthew Hurst. 2007. Cascading Behavior in Large Blog Graphs. In *7th SIAM International Conference on Data Mining (SDM)*. 1–21.

[23] Jure Leskovec, Ajit Singh, and Jon Kleinberg. 2006. Patterns of Influence in a Recommendation Network. In *Proceedings of the 10th Pacific-Asia Conference on Advances in Knowledge Discovery and Data Mining (PAKDD'06)*. Springer-Verlag, Berlin, Heidelberg, 380–389.

[24] David Liben-Nowell and Jon Kleinberg. 2008. Tracing informationfl ow on a global scale using Internet chain-letter data. *Proceedings of the National Academy of Sciences* 105, 12 (2008), 4633–4638.

[25] Zongyang Ma, Aixin Sun, and Gao Cong. 2013. On predicting the popularity of newly emerging hashtags in Twitter. *JASIST* 64, 7 (2013), 1399–1410.

[26] Fred Morstatter, Jürgen Pfeffer, and Huan Liu. 2014. When is it biased?: assessing the representativeness of twitter's streaming API. In *Proceedings of the companion publication of the 23rd international conference on World wide web companion*. International World Wide Web Conferences Steering Committee, 555–556.

[27] Sasa Petrovic, Miles Osborne, and Victor Lavrenko. 2011. RT to Win! Predicting Message Propagation in Twitter. In *Proceedings of the Fifth International Conference on Weblogs and Social Media*. 586–589.

[28] Io Taxidou and Peter M. Fischer. 2014. Online Analysis of Information Diffusion in Twitter. In *Proceedings of the Companion Publication of the 23rd International Conference on World Wide Web Companion (WWW Companion '14)*. ACM, 1313–1318.

[29] Duncan J Watts. 2002. A simple model of global cascades on random networks. *Proceedings of the National Academy of Sciences* 99, 9 (2002), 5766–5771.

[30] Jiejun Xu, Ryan Compton, Tsai-Ching Lu, and David Allen. 2014. Rolling Through Tumblr: Characterizing Behavioral Patterns of the Microblogging Platform. In *Proceedings of the 2014 ACM Conference on Web Science (WebSci '14)*. ACM, 13–22.

[31] Jiang Yang and Scott Counts. 2010. Predicting the Speed, Scale, and Range of Information Diffusion in Twitter. In *Fourth International AAAI Conference on Weblogs and Social Media ICWSM*. 355–358.

[32] Linhong Zhu and Kristina Lerman. 2016. Attention Inequality in Social Media. *arXiv preprint arXiv:1601.07200* (2016).

A Deep Study into the History of Web Design

Bardia Doosti
School of Informatics and Computing
Indiana University Bloomington
bdoosti@indiana.edu

David J. Crandall
School of Informatics and Computing
Indiana University Bloomington
djcran@indiana.edu

Norman Makoto Su
School of Informatics and Computing
Indiana University Bloomington
normsu@indiana.edu

ABSTRACT

Since its ambitious beginnings to create a hyperlinked information system, the web has evolved over 25 years to become our primary means of expression and communication. No longer limited to text, the evolving visual features of websites are important signals of larger societal shifts in humanity's technologies, aesthetics, cultures, and industries. Just as paintings can be analyzed to study an era's social norms and culture, techniques for systematically analyzing large-scale archives of the web could help unpack global changes in the visual appearance of websites and of modern society itself. In this paper, we propose automated techniques for characterizing the visual "style" of websites and use this analysis to discover and visualize shifts over time and across website domains. In particular, we use deep Convolutional Neural Networks to classify websites into 26 subject areas (e.g., technology, news media websites) and 4 design eras. The features produced by this process then allow us to quantitatively characterize the appearance of any given website. We demonstrate how to track changes in these features over time and introduce a technique using Hidden Markov Models (HMMs) to discover sudden, significant changes in these appearances. Finally, we visualize the features learned by our network to help reveal the distinctive visual elements that were discovered by the network.

CCS CONCEPTS

• **Information systems** → **Surfacing**; • **Human-centered computing** → **Web-based interaction**; • **Computing methodologies** → **Interest point and salient region detections**; *Supervised learning by classification*; *Neural networks*; • **Mathematics of computing** → Kalman filters and hidden Markov models;

KEYWORDS

Web Design, Deep Learning, Convolutional Neural Networks, Cultural Analytics

1 INTRODUCTION

The advent of digital technologies has brought about a revolution in analyzing and unpacking "culture." Cultural Analytics is a relatively new field that aims to study the humanities and other disciplines through computational analysis of large-scale cultural data [16]. For example, work in cultural analytics has automatically analyzed patterns in large historical and contemporary samples of art [25], pop music [6], comic books [17], Vogue magazine covers [24], and architecture [14]. Ironically, however, perhaps the most important and best reflection of today's "new media" [16] – the world wide web itself – has had little examination through the lens of cultural analytics. There is growing recognition that such new media should be preserved. For instance, The Internet Archive [4] attempts to store a comprehensive history of the web, while the University of Michigan Library houses the Computer and Video Game Archive [2]. The web is now a first-class cultural artifact with at least one quarter of a trillion archived pages across nearly 30 years [4].

Recent work has argued that analyzing the *visual designs* of websites could provide a window into the evolution of the web, and specifically how visual design reflects changes in visual aesthetics, role of technology, cultural preferences, and technical innovations [8, 22]. Reinecke *et al.* [22, 23] defined specific low-level metrics for quantifying visual properties of websites, such as color distribution, amount of white space, and structure of page layout, and developed a model of perceived visual complexity based on these low-level measures. They used this technique to reveal cultural preferences for particular aesthetic styles, for example. Chen *et al.* [8] asked web designers, developers, and artists to view historical collections of web pages and reflect on the changes they observed across time, and specifically to speculate on the web's design "periods" including the key changes and causes of changes that have occurred over time. While limited in scope, these papers represent a first step in understanding cultural patterns via analysis of the visual designs of websites.

Although similar in many respects, the web has a number of key differences from more traditional cultural artifacts. Automated studies of art and music tend to be limited by the quantity of available data, while the number of web artifacts is essentially boundless, with millions of new pages coming online each day. On one hand, this may make it easier to find statistically-significant general patterns among all of the "noise" of individual web pages; on the other hand, it makes manual study and organization of web design impractical. Moreover, unlike art and music, the web lacks well-developed theories to compare and contrast visual design styles. We thus need to develop automated techniques that can be used to characterize, compare, and contrast visual design styles in a meaningful way.

In this paper, we take initial steps towards this goal and make four key contributions, using recent progress in computer vision and machine learning. We first ask how much "signal" can be derived from the visual designs of websites – how much information about cultural patterns are encoded solely in the visual appearance of sites? We describe an approach in which we train state-of-the-art classifiers borrowed from computer vision, specifically deep Convolutional Neural Networks (CNNs), to recognize the eras and

WebSci'17, June 25-28, 2017, Troy, NY, USA.

978-1-4503-4896-6/17/06...$15.00
DOI: http://dx.doi.org/10.1145/3091478.3091503

genres of web pages. Our results show that classifiers are able to classify websites by their genre by more than 4 times the baseline and recognize website design era by 2.5 times the random baseline, which indicates that modern computer vision can indeed discern particular patterns from large scale datasets of website designs. The results are accurate enough to suggest that visual appearance could be an important signal for societal change as reflected by the web.

Second, we show that the key features identified by the classifier during this supervised learning task can be used to characterize *new web pages* in an unsupervised way, without predefining hand-crafted visual attributes. Intuitively, these features generate a new visual similarity space that is automatic, objective, and potentially more meaningful than metrics defined by human intuition. With this framework, we can, for instance:

(1) Measure the visual design similarity between two pages. How similar is a website to a prominent, trend-setting website – how "Apple-like" is `cnn.com`?
(2) Measure the similarity of a given page to a particular genre of website. How "news-site-like" or "entertainment-site-like" is the visual design of `cnn.com`?
(3) Measure the similarity between a given page and a particular website era. How "modern" is the design of `cnn.com`?

Third, we present techniques for using these measures to perform cultural analytics over time at a large scale. We take historical snapshots of a single website, as captured by the Internet Archive, and characterize each individual snapshot using our objective metrics to give a (noisy) time series quantifying how the design has changed over time. We then develop a Hidden Markov Model to robustly identify sudden changes in the time series corresponding to actual changes in visual design (and ignoring the day-to-day changes caused by updates to content). This historical perspective gives us a glimpse on how websites have evolved over time, which could lead to broader, more fundamental insights on the relation of visual design and society and culture. For instance, we could measure how a particular company's website has become influential on other websites' designs (e.g., to what extent have companies sought to emulate Apple's aesthetics or vice versa?).

Lastly, we show that with our trained CNN, we can randomly generate *novel* website designs by inverting the process, by using the CNN to sample a design for a given point in the similarity space. Such tools not only shed light on the most basic question of "what does it mean to be a website design?" but also could serve to inspire current website designers on the future of web design.

2 RELATED WORK

While we are aware of very little work that tries to characterize website design automatically across time and genres, the basic idea of applying machine learning and data mining algorithms to analyze websites is not new. Kumar *et al.* [12] introduced a data mining platform called Webzeitgeist which used WebKit [1] to generate features such as ratio, dominant colors, and number of words. Webzeitgeist can extract useful information about a website, but is based on HTML code and thus captures only a rough sense of a page's visual design. Many other papers classify the genre and other properties of web pages from text (HTML) analysis (see Qi *et al.* [20] for an overview). In contrast, our goal is to analyze websites based on the way that people experience them: viewing the visual appearance of a website and making inferences based only on it, without examining the underlying HTML code.

Perhaps the closest line of work to ours is that of Reinecke *et al.* [23] and Reinecke and Gajos [22], who design visual features to measure properties of websites like color distribution, page layout, amount of whitespace, etc. They proposed a model to predict higher-level perceived visual properties of websites such as visual complexity from these low-level features, and used them to characterize cross-cultural differences and similarities in web design. Similar to our study, their features are based on rendered images as opposed to HTML. However, they rely on hand-engineered features that may be subjective and not necessarily representative. In contrast, we learn visual features in a data-driven way, and use these to track changes in web design across genres and eras. The two approaches are complementary: our automatic approach might discover visual features that are hard to describe or would not otherwise be apparent, whereas their features are explicitly tied to a human perceptual model, which may make their results easier to describe and interpret.

We also draw inspiration from the work of Chen *et al.* [8], who interviewed experts and asked them to critique and group together the design of prominent websites over time. Their study identified certain design elements or "markers" (such as search and navigation bar placement, color scheme, relative proportion of text and imagery, etc.) that distinguished various "eras" of web design. The study also suggested that web design evolution is driven by multiple factors including technological developments (e.g., new HTML capabilities and features), changing roles and functions of the web over time, impression management of companies and individuals (e.g., companies wishing to project confidence, friendliness, etc.), as well as changing aesthetic preferences. We use this non-technical exploration of web design as the inspiration for our paper, which seeks to study visual design automatically and objectively, at a large scale.

Our work uses computer vision to define visual features and similarity metrics for comparing and characterizing web design. Quantifying the similarity of images is a classic and well-studied problem in computer vision. A traditional approach is for an expert to engineer visual features, by hand, that they think are relevant to the specific comparison task at hand, and then apply machine learning to calculate the similarity of two images. Often these features are specialized versions of more general features, such as Scale Invariant Feature Transforms (SIFT) [15] which tries to capture local image features in a way that is invariant to illumination, scale, and rotation. A disadvantage of these approaches is that they are fundamentally limited by the programmer's ability to identify salient visual properties and to design techniques for quantifying them.

More recently, deep learning using Convolutional Neural Networks (CNNs) has become the de facto standard technique for many problems in computer vision. An advantage of this approach is that it does not require features to be designed by hand; the CNNs instead learn their own optimal features for a particular task from raw image pixel data. These networks, introduced by LeCun *et al.* [13] in the 1990's for digit recognition, are very similar to traditional feed-forward neural networks. However, in CNNs some layers have special structures to implement image convolution or sub-sampling operations. These deep networks with many alternating convolution and downsampling layers help make the classifiers insensitive to spatial structure of the image and recognize both global and detailed image features. In 2012 Krizhevsky *et al.* [11] succeeded in adapting LeCun *et al.*'s CNN idea for a more general class of images using many more layers, very large training datasets with millions of images [9], huge amounts of computational power with Graphics Processing Units (GPUs), and innovations in network architecture. Since then, CNNs have been successfully applied to a large range of applications.

Here we show how to apply CNNs to the specific domain of web design. Contemporaneous with our work, Jahanian *et al.* [10] have also applied deep learning to website design, although they focus on the classification task of identifying a website's era based on its visual appearance. We take this idea a step further: we create CNNs to classify particular genres and eras of websites, and then use the trained features as data mining tools to characterize the visual features of websites and how they change through time.

3 METHODOLOGY

Our overall goal is to analyze the archive of a website, consisting of a time series of HTML pages, and characterize the changes in its visual appearance over time, including finding key transition points where the design changed. While we could analyze the HTML source code directly to detect design changes, this is difficult in practice since the HTML itself may reveal little about the physical appearance of a page: a page may be rewritten using a new technology (e.g. CSS and JavaScript) such that the source code is completely different but the visual appearance is the same, or a small change in the HTML (e.g. new background image) may create a dramatically different appearance. We thus chose to analyze the visual characteristics of rendered pages, emulating how a human user would see the page. The main challenge is that many pages (e.g., news sites) are highly dynamic, so that nearly every piece of content and most pixels in the rendered image change on a day-to-day basis. We wish to ignore these minor variations and instead find the major changes that correspond to evolutions in web site design.

We use two techniques for addressing this challenge. First, we extract high-level visual features that have been shown to correspond with semantically-meaningful properties using deep learning with Convolutional Neural Networks [13]. These features abstract away the detailed appearance of a page, and instead cue on more general properties that may reflect design, such as text density, color distribution, symmetry, busyness or complexity, etc. However, even these abstract properties vary considerably on a highly dynamic website, where content like prominent photos might change on a daily basis. We thus also introduce an approach for smoothing out these variations over time, in effect looking for major changes in the "signal" as opposed to minor variations caused by "noise." We apply Hidden Markov Models, a well-principled statistical framework for analyzing temporal and sequential data in domains like natural language processing, audio analysis, etc.

3.1 Dataset

We began by assembling a suitably large-scale dataset of visual snapshots (images) of webpages. Our dataset consists of (1) a large number of *current* snapshots of a wide variety of websites organized by *genre* (news, sports, business, etc.), and (2) a longitudinal collection of a large number of *historical* snapshots of a handful of pages over time.

For the genre dataset, we used CrowdFlower's URL categorization dataset, which consists of more than 31,000 URL domains, each hand-labeled with one of 26 genres [3]. We downloaded the HTML code for each URL and then rendered the page into an image using PhantomJS [5], a headless Webkit API [1], at a resolution of 1200 × 1200 pixels. (We chose this resolution because it works well with both the wide-screen format that many websites today support and earlier, less technologically-advanced designs). For websites that must be rendered at greater than 1200 pixels on either dimension (as is frequently the case along the vertical dimension), we cropped the snapshot.

For our second, longitudinal dataset, we collected snapshots for a set of prominent websites with a long history (from the early 1990s through the present) from the Internet Archive [4]. Unfortunately, this set of websites is sparse since most well-known websites did not exist or were not well-known before the 1990s (and thus were not archived by the Internet Archive until more recently). Many websites from the 1990s also disappeared after 2000. We chose the same 9 websites studied by Chen *et al.* [8] as well as 26 additional websites which were present in the 1990s (covering most of the genres mentioned in the CrowdFlower dataset). In total, we captured 7,303 screenshots from our 35 chosen websites from *archive.org*, spanning 1996 through 2013. We used the same process described above for rendering these websites to images.

We acknowledge that our relatively small dataset introduces limitations: a small dataset makes it difficult to pinpoint the accuracy and generalizability of a classifier. Our intent, however, is not to provide a robust, production-ready classifier. Instead, our results provide evidence that such classifiers can indeed reflect how information valuable to cultural informatics are signaled purely by a website's aesthetics. We hope future work will build validated CNNs or other models from which we can glean cultural signals.

3.2 Visual Features

For automatically and objectively measuring visual properties of large-scale collections of web pages, we need to develop quantitative measures of the visual appearance of a page. To do this, we first develop a technique for measuring the visual similarity between two rendered web page images, but in a way that attempts to ignore minor differences between pages and instead focuses on overall design.

In the Computer Vision community, deep learning with Convolutional Neural Networks (CNNs) has recently emerged as the *de facto* standard image classification technique, yielding state-of-the-art results on almost all vision tasks [11]. The basic idea is that unlike traditional approaches which use hand-designed visual features and whose performance is thus limited by human skill and intuition, CNNs learn the (hopefully) optimal low-level visual features for a given classification task automatically, directly from

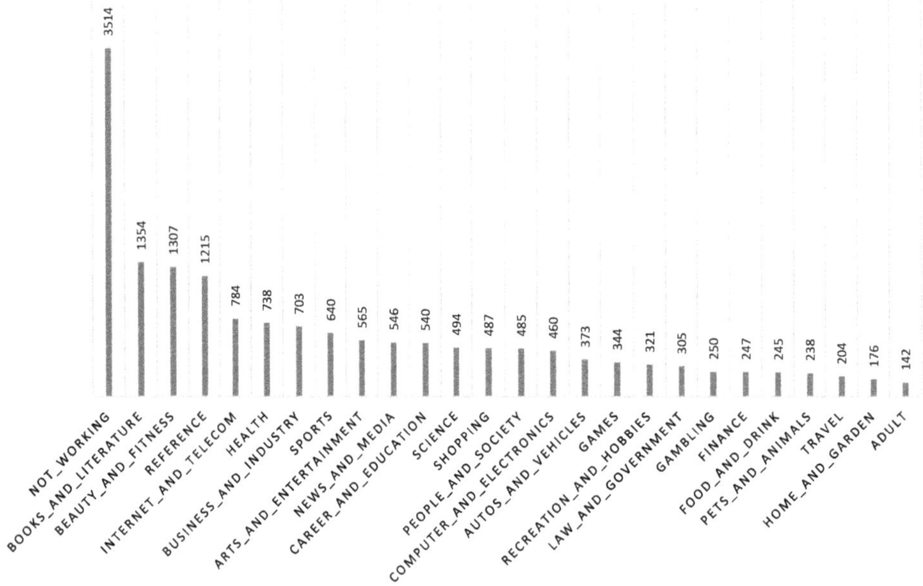

Figure 1: Frequency of website genres in our dataset

the raw image pixel data itself. Learning a CNN classifier can thus be thought of as simultaneously solving two tasks: (1) finding the right low-level features that are most distinctive and meaningful for a particular domain, and (2) learning a classifier to map these features to a high-level semantic class or category.

We use this property of CNNs in the following way. We train a classifier to estimate properties of web pages, including their genre and their "era" (when they were created), using visual features of the page itself. We can measure performance of the classifiers on these tasks, but producing accurate classifications is *not* our goal. (If it were our goal, we would just analyze the HTML source code itself instead of using the rendered image.) Instead, our goal is to train a classifier so that the CNN learns the important low-level features corresponding to visual style; we can then discard the classifier itself, and simply use these "optimal" features to compare websites directly.

3.2.1 Network Details. More specifically, we train CNNs for both genre and era classification tasks using the dataset described above. We use the popular AlexNet [11] CNN architecture, which consists of 5 convolutional layers that can be thought of as feature extractors, and 3 fully connected layers that classify the image based on those features. Each convolutional layer applies a series of filters (which are learned in the training phase) of different sizes to the input image and then finally pushes a 4096-d vector to the fully connected layers for classification. Since our dataset is not large enough to learn a deep network from scratch (which has tens of millions of parameters), we follow recent work [19] and initialize our network parameters with those pre-trained on the ImageNet dataset [9], and then "fine-tune" the parameters on our dataset.

3.2.2 Classification Results. For website genre categorization, the specific task was to classify each website into one of 26 different genre categories. We partitioned the dataset into training and test subsets, using half of the websites for training and half for testing. Since the frequency of classes was non-uniform (Figure 1), we also balanced the classes in both training and testing, so that the probability of randomly guessing the correct class is about 3.8%. Our classifier achieved about 16% correct classification rate on this task, i.e., four times the random baseline. These results may seem low, but we stress the difficulty of the task: the classifier only sees the visual rendering of the website (no textual or other features), and there is substantial noise in the dataset because many sites could be labeled in multiple ways (e.g. is Sports Illustrated a sports website or a news website?).

For website era categorization, we discretized time into four eras, 1996-2000, 2001-2004, 2005-2008, and 2009-2013, and again balanced classes. We split the test and training sets by *website*, i.e. all of the historical snapshots of `cnn.com` were in either the training set or test set, since the task could be very easy if very similar snapshots for the same site were in training and test sets. Here our CNN-based classifier achieved about 63% accuracy relative to a baseline of 25%, or about 2.5 times baseline. This is again a relatively difficult task because pages near the end of one era can be easily misclassified as belonging to the beginning of the next era, for example. Table 1 shows a confusion matrix on this task, which confirms that many misclassifications occur in adjacent bins.

These results show that while the visual classifiers are not perfect, the fact that the recognition rates are significantly higher than baseline shows that they are learning meaningful visual features. This suggests that our hypothesis of defining a similarity measure for website visual design using these features may succeed.

3.2.3 Visualization. The above results suggest that features extracted by deeply-trained networks carry meaningful information about visual style, but reveal little about what exactly this information is. Of course, this is one of the major disadvantages of deep

Table 1: Confusion matrix for recognizing website era.

	Predicted class			
	1996-2000	2001-2004	2005-2008	2009-2013
1996-2000	41	18	14	5
2001-2004	15	18	33	12
2005-2008	5	8	37	28
2009-2013	0	2	13	63

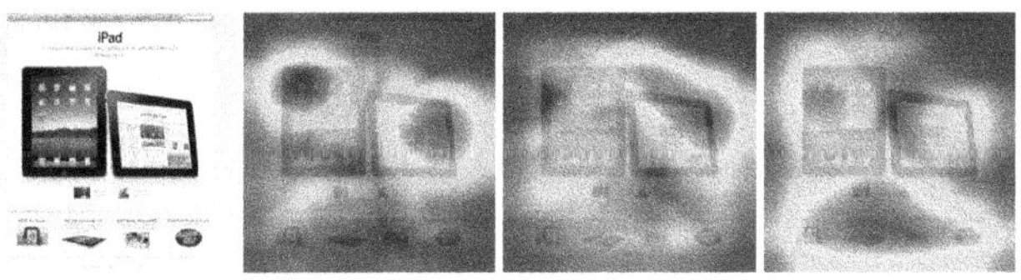

Figure 2: Heat maps showing which parts of a website support each of three different class hypotheses, according to the classifier.

machine learning: it is very difficult to interpret or "debug" the parameters of a learned classifier. One potential way of gaining some insight is to create visualizations that try to reveal which image features the network is actually cueing on.

We use a modification of the technique of Zhou *et al.* [26] to do this. Very briefly, this technique inserts a general average pooling layer into the network, which allows us to visualize the importance of each pixel as a heat map for each class. Although this method successfully generates an attention map of the network, it decreases the accuracy of the network by a few percentage points. Our compromise solution to preserve accurate results is to train both networks separately and substitute the convolutional layer weights learned by the classic AlexNet in the attention map network. This network has good results with both the classification and visualization of the attention maps. Figure 2 shows a sample input website snapshot and the attention map of three different classes for this image. In these visualizations, red regions are the most influential cues used by the network to conclude that the image belongs to a specific class, and blue corresponds to less important regions. These generated heat maps help us find the most important parts of each image for each class.

3.2.4 Website Generation. Although we trained our deep networks to extract features from websites and classify them into categories, an interesting property of these networks is that they can actually be run "in reverse" to generate novel exemplars. The intuitive idea here is that the networks learn a mapping from visual features into mathematical vectors in some high-dimensional space and it is possible to reverse the process by generating a random high-dimensional vector and then producing an image that has that feature representation.

To do this, we use Generative Adversarial Networks (GANs) [21]. Figure 3 shows some examples. These images are, at least in theory, novel website designs that do not appear in the training set but have similar features to websites that are in the training set. We believe that many of these designs seem quite plausibly "real," although it can be subjective. The network's architecture also limits the resolution of these generated images, so they appear blurry. Nevertheless, such a technique could provide a means of inspiring web developers, helping suggest new directions of visual design to pursue.

3.3 Temporal Smoothing

Given a time series of a visual feature over time, like that shown in Fig 8, our goal now is to segment into periods of generally homogeneous design. The challenge is to ignore spurious variations due to day-to-day changes in site content (e.g. different photos or text), and instead identify more major, longer-term changes that reflect shifts in the underlying visual design. This problem is reminiscent of filtering problems in signal processing, where the goal is to reconstruct an underlying low-frequency signal in the presence of added high-frequency noise.

Using this signal processing view, we initially tried applying a low-pass filter (e.g. a mean filter or a Gaussian filter) to the time series of visual feature values. While this succeeded in smoothing out the time series, it has the unfortunate effect of also smoothing out the sharp changes in the signal that are the transitions we are looking for. As shown, the problem is that a low-pass filter imposes the (implicit) assumption that the visual feature's value on one day should be almost the same as the value on the next, and does not permit the occasional discontinuities caused by major design changes.

We thus explored an alternative model that explicitly permits discontinuities. Suppose that we wish to analyze a website over a period of N days. For each day i, let f_i denote the value of the visual feature computed on the rendered image for that day, or the special value $\emptyset$ if the value is bad or missing. We assume that the value of this visual feature is a result of two different forces: the inherent design of the page, and the content on that day. We model this as an additive process, i.e. $f_i = d_i + c_i$, where d_i represents the value related to the design and c_i is the "noise" caused by changes in day-to-day content.

Our goal is to infer d_i, which we cannot observe, from the observations f_i which can be observed. From a probabilistic perspective, we want to find the values for $d_1, d_2, ..., d_N$ so as to maximize their probability given the observations,

$$\arg \max_{d_1,...,d_N} P(d_1, ..., d_N | f_1, ..., f_N). \tag{1}$$

To do this, we build a model that makes several assumptions; although these assumptions are not likely to hold perfectly in practice, we have found that they work well enough for our purposes in analyzing the noisy visual feature time series. We first assume that the design in effect on any given day depends only on the design of the day before it, i.e. d_i is independent from earlier days, conditioned on d_{i-1}. This reflects the assumption that a site's design tends to stay consistent over time and not, for example, flip back and forth between two designs on alternating days of the week. Second, we assume that c_i is independent from c_j for any $j \neq i$, conditioned on d_i. This means that content changes from one day to the next are independent from one another. Taken together, and using Bayes'

Figure 3: Novel website designs generated automatically by our network. (Images are blurry because the network architecture limits the resolution of generated images.)

law, these assumptions let us rewrite equation (1) as,

$$\arg \max_{d_1,\ldots,d_N} \frac{P(f_1,\ldots,f_N|d_1,\ldots,d_N)P(d_1,\ldots,d_N)}{P(f_1,\ldots,f_N)} \quad (2)$$

$$= \arg \max_{d_1,\ldots,d_N} P(f_1,\ldots,f_N|d_1,\ldots,d_N)P(d_1,\ldots,d_N) \quad (3)$$

$$= \arg \max_{d_1,\ldots,d_N} \prod_{i=1}^{N} P(f_i|d_i) \prod_{i=2}^{N} P(d_i|d_{i-1}) \quad (4)$$

where the denominator can be ignored since it depends only on observations, which do not depend on the values of d_i.

Equation (4) is a Hidden Markov Model, which are widely used to analyze sequences in areas such as natural language processing, speech recognition, robotics, computer vision, etc., and can be solved efficiently using the Viterbi algorithm. All that remains is for us to define the emission and transition probability distributions (i.e. first and second terms of equation (4), respectively). For the emission probability, we model c_i as a zero-mean Gaussian distribution, which assumes that day-to-day content changes modify the visual feature of the page in a similar way to white noise in signal processing (sometimes adding a bit, sometimes subtracting a bit),

$$P(f_i|d_i) = \mathcal{N}(f_i - d_i; \mu = 0, \sigma_1),$$

with some constant variance σ_1. For the transition probability distribution, we assume that on any given day, there is some small probability p_1 that the design changes, which causes an arbitrary change in the visual feature d_i, while with probability $1 - p_1$, the feature of the underlying design remains nearly the same (with the change modeled by a Gaussian distribution with a small sigma),

$$P(d_i|d_{i-1}) = p_1 + \mathcal{N}(d_i; \mu = d_{i-1}, \sigma_2).$$

We stress that our intention is not to create an accurate model of the process by which design changes happen, but instead to propose a reasonable enough model that it can be used to identify potential design changes automatically. The constants p_1, σ_1, and σ_2 are parameters of our analysis technique, and can be used to adjust the type of results that are found. For instance, increasing p_1 permits the technique to find more frequent design changes, but is also more likely to respond to random noise patterns. Increasing σ_1 or σ_2 allows greater flexibility in the observed visual feature relative to the underlying design feature, but again is likely to cause more noise. Unless otherwise specified, for our analyses in this paper, we set $p_1 = 0.1$, $\sigma_1 = 1.0$, and $\sigma_2 = 0.01$.

4 RESULTS

We now present results of our analysis techniques on our corpus of webpages. Since CNNs hide the "logic" behind their reasoning in a "black box," we first present visualizations that elucidate the features of the trained deep network itself. Next, we demonstrate application of our deep learning with website designs to cultural analytics. In this set of analyses, we examine the degree that visual designs of websites resemble other websites over time. We show how this can be applied to individual websites and a group of websites. Lastly, we propose that our deep network can also serve to inspire the future by generating new website designs that encapsulate the visual aesthetics of a specific era or category.

4.1 Visualizing Features of the Network

We visualized the output of the neurons to understand *how* the deep network recognizes the era and genre of the website. We found that in most cases, these features at least resemble what humans might look for when performing the same task.

4.1.1 Features for Era. Figure 4(a) depicts the attention map of the "1990s website" class. The visualizations suggest that the margins (the white areas) on the right side and the bottom of the image are the most important parts for this class. By "most important," we mean the part of the image that is most influential for the classifier in reaching a conclusion that the design is from the 1990s. Thus, one possible interpretation is that the network believes margins are a key marker for 1990's-era websites.

In contrast, Figure 4(b) shows that the attention map of the "2009-2013" class has multiple areas of visual importance. Many websites in this class encompass the entire browser frame; we surmise that an image that fills up the frame is important for the network. Interestingly, the visualization also points to a growing importance in designs that prominently feature computer technologies (e.g., laptops, tablets, and smartphones). For instance, in `apple.com`we see that their products increasingly take up a larger proportion of a website's space over time (Figure 5).

4.1.2 Features for Genre. In recognizing a website's genre, it appears that specific objects get the attention of the network. For example, our sports website classifier seems to focus on sports objects such as basketballs, baseballs, bicycles, and so on. This same observation follows for the food and drink, automotive, home and

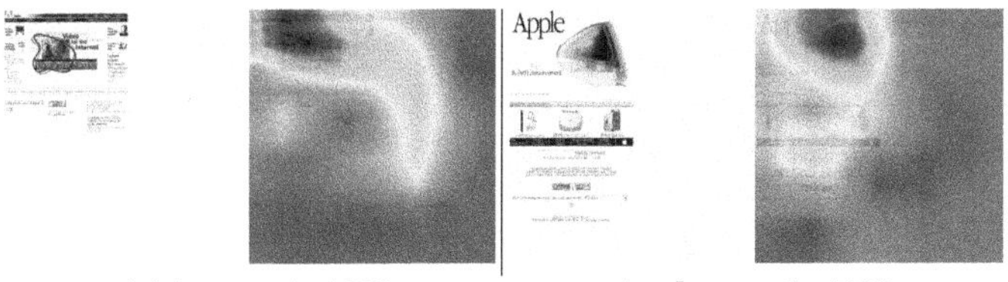

Adobe.com in 1997 Apple.com in 1999

(a) 1990's class

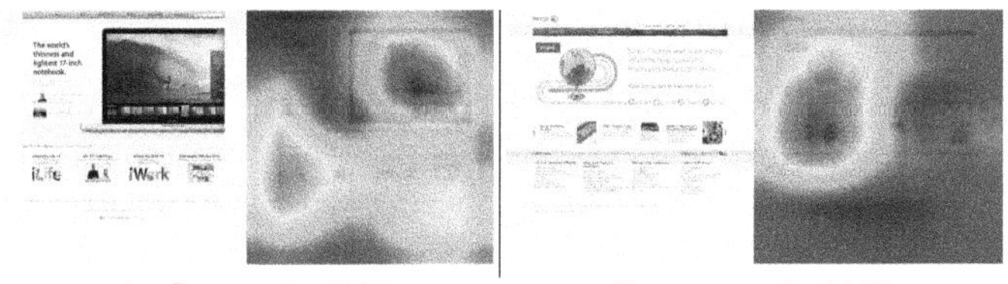

Apple.com in 2009 Xerox.com in 2013

(b) 2003-2013 class

Figure 4: Heat maps showing the importance of various image features in reaching the conclusion that the websites are from (a) the 1990's and (b) 2009-2013.

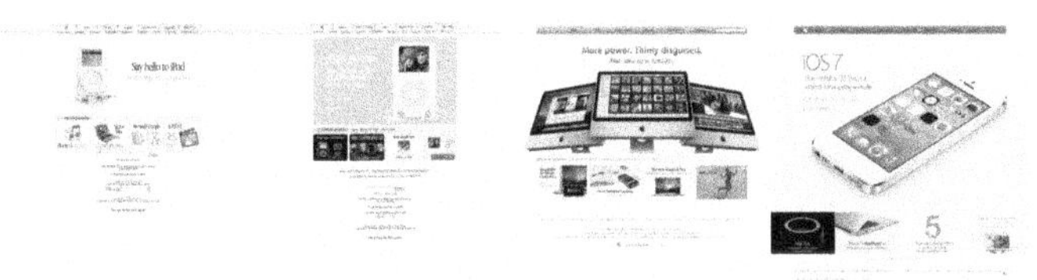

2001 2004 2008 2013

Figure 5: Changing product sizes in `Apple.com`'s design through time.

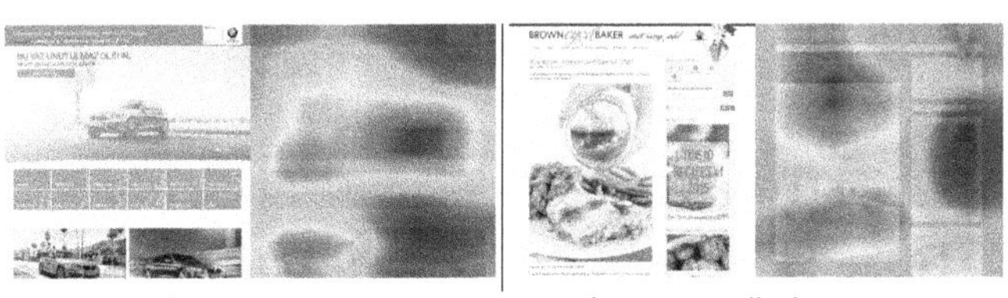

bmw.com.tr browneyedbaker.com

Figure 6: A website from `automotive` class (left) and a website from `food and drink` class (right), and the network's attention for recognizing the classes.

garden, pets and animals, and adult genres. Figure 6 shows some examples.

4.2 Web Designs Across Eras

We characterize the changing appearance of a website over time by comparing its appearance to a small number of exemplar sites. We chose five websites as our exemplars: `apple.com`, `msn.com`, `cnn.com`, `slac.stanford.edu`, and `whitehouse.gov`. We chose these as "canonical" pages because they are regarded as leaders in the technology and design industry. For instance, `apple.com` and

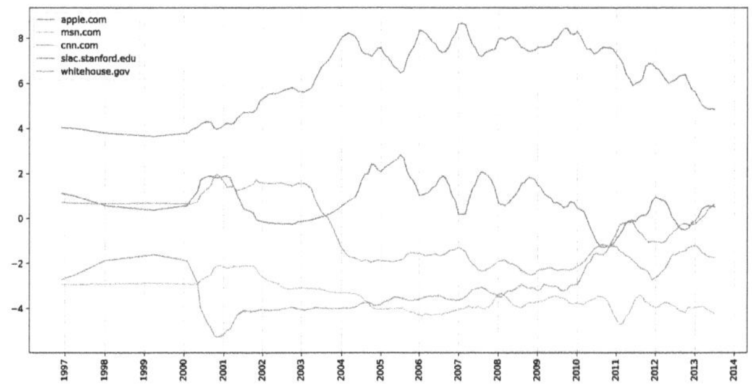

(a) Raw similarity scores

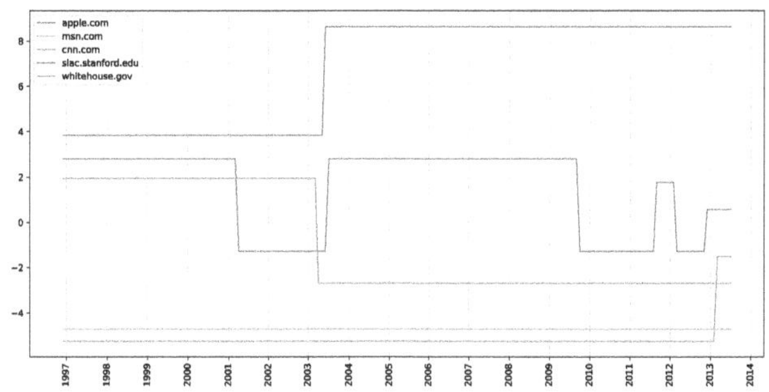

(b) Sudden moves of similarity, as identified by an HMM

Figure 7: Similarity of `indiana.edu` to each canonical site.

`msn.com` are regarded by some as interaction design pioneers. One hypothesis is that, just as their products have been influential, their website designs may have influenced other organizations' websites.

For example, Figure 7 shows the similarity of one particular academic website, `indiana.edu`, to these fives sites over time. We see that `slac.stanford.edu` (another academic website) is the most similar website among our five exemplars. This is intuitive since a university's web design should most resemble another university's website versus websites of companies in the technology and design industry. (Note that in all of our plots, the *absolute* y-axis units are not really meaningful for either the raw similarity scores or the HMM outputs, so we focus on examining the relative values and trends over time.)

The web portal `yahoo.com`, founded in 1994, has a particularly long history. Since `yahoo.com` and `msn.com` are both portal websites, we might expect the two to be alike across eras, and Figure 8(a) verifies this similarity for nearly six years, until 2010 when it became more similar to `apple.com`. This behavior is even more apparent in the results smoothed by the Hidden Markov Model in Figure 8(b). Note that our dataset is missing snapshots from `yahoo.com` between 2006 and 2010. This explains why the lines have no fluctuation during this period on both graphs in Figure 8. Yahoo is also judged to be similar to `whitehouse.gov` initially, but loses that similarity over time. This is consistent with the observation that websites of some genres initially looked like each other but became more diverse as the web evolved.

Figure 9(a) repeats this analysis for `amazon.com`. We observe that similarity to `apple.com` has increased while it has become less

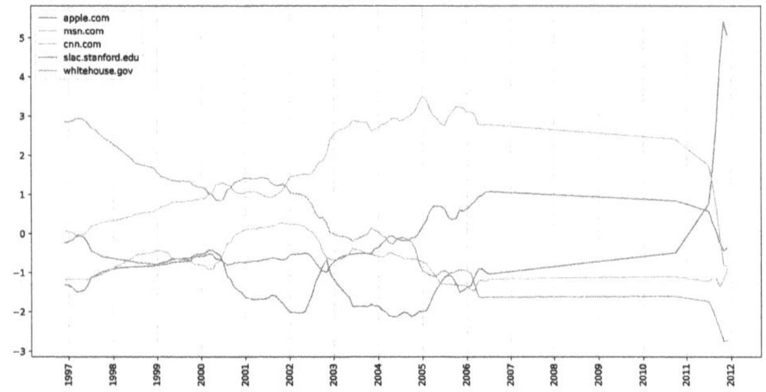

(a) Raw similarity scores

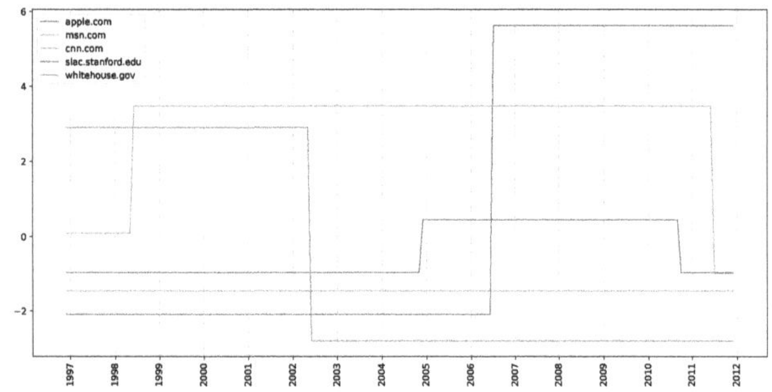

(b) Sudden moves of similarity, as identified by an HMM

Figure 8: Similarity of `yahoo.com` to each canonical site.

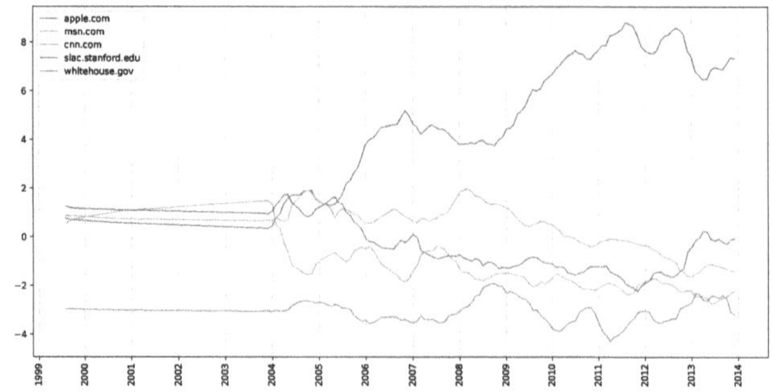

(a) Raw similarity scores

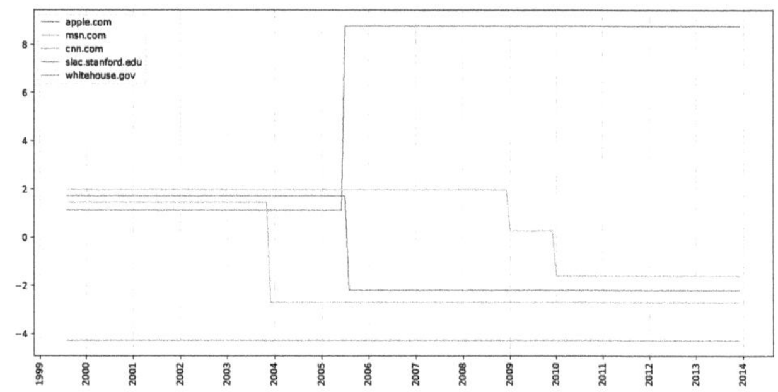

(b) Sudden moves of similarity, as identified by an HMM

Figure 9: Similarity of `amazon.com` to each canonical site.

similar to the other websites. Figure 9(b) starkly shows that this move began shortly before 2004. This phenomenon may be because both websites have followed the design trend of featuring large product images, which caused the network to recognize them as very similar to each other.

Lastly, to give a sense for how design on the web has changed in general, we took the "basket" of 35 pages in our dataset and compared all of them (aggregated together) to the five canonical pages. Figure 10 shows that websites were similar to Microsoft for nearly eight years but Apple gradually became dominant after 2005. We may speculate that the visual designs of Microsoft's website was globally representative or influential of the web, but after some time the designs of Apple better represented the state of visual design on the web.

4.3 Multi-Genre Classification

Categorization of websites into particular genres is not an exact science. Many websites (especially contemporary ones) now serve a number of different purposes: `bloomberg.com` could be easily categorized as, for example, a financial, news, or media website. Thus instead of requiring the classifier to produce a single genre estimate for each page, we ask it for five hypotheses along with the confidence of each class. These confidences reflect the extent to which the network believes a given site belongs to a given genre. For example, confidences of the network for seven categories and seven classes are shown in Figure 11. If we were to take the highest confidence genre, our classifier yields some good results: shopping for `amazon.com`, computer for `apple.com`, adult for `pornhub.com`, and finance for `bloomberg.com`. More importantly, however, we also observe some intuitive confidence values for multiple genres: `espn.com` has high scores for both sports and news, for example.

Thus, a strength of our techniques is in showing a more nuanced view on which *multiple* genres are signaled by the visual designs of websites. That is, we may speculate that there is probably something inherent in visual designs that suggests certain genres and that, more intriguingly, these designs can also suggest a mixture of genres.

4.4 Generating New Website Designs

The utility of a deep network lies in its ability to uncover patterns to classify images. Yet one innovative function of a trained network is its power to use its learned features to "hallucinate" an entirely new image based on the snapshots in the training data. Figure 12 shows images generated by the network trained on snapshots of about 17,000 contemporary websites. Each image is generated by a random point in the similarity space. We observe that the new images "look" a lot like real designs. This is a highly subjective observation; nevertheless, the method could potentially give designers not only a tool to analyze which features are important for each genre or each design era, but also a framework to find inspirations for new designs. For example, such a network can generate multiple images as templates for designing a news or shopping website, which in turn could serve as a basis for designers to creatively build their own website.

(a) Raw similarity scores

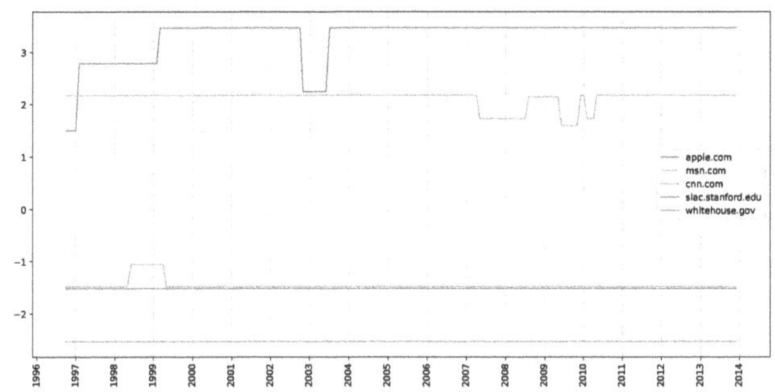

(b) Sudden moves of similarity, as identified by an HMM

Figure 10: Similarity of all 35 websites in our corpus, aggregated together, to each of our 5 canonical sites.

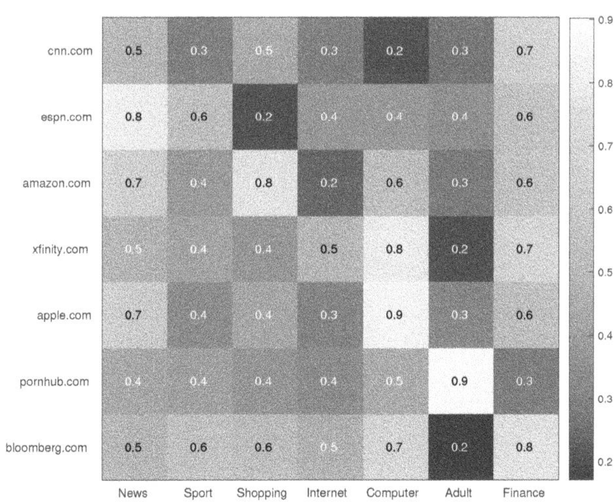

Figure 11: Confidence of the network for seven websites on seven genres.

5 CONCLUSION AND FUTURE WORK

In recent years, deep learning and large-scale datasets have helped artificial intelligence meet or surpass human abilities in some narrow tasks [18]. It remains a question to what degree artificial intelligence can support and complement the arts and humanities. In

Figure 12: Websites generated by our GAN network.

this paper, we take first steps towards answering, computationally, a question we often ask ourselves when viewing any visual object created by people: irrespective of its context (e.g., creator, history, circumstances) can we find real meaning in the image itself? In some respects, we might claim that our algorithm adheres to the philosophy behind formalism [7], that what matters in art is contained purely in the art piece itself. Thus, we believe our work represents an application of computer vision and machine learning that takes notions of art and design seriously. The techniques we introduce in this paper could complement and add to extant theories in the humanities.

We have begun to develop techniques that researchers can use to study large-scale collections of web pages, from a design perspective, without analyzing all pages manually. In particular, we have shown how CNNs could provide quantitative measures of website design styles, how to compare these designs, chart their evolution over time, and find transition points among these noisy signals. We have also showed how novel designs could be sampled from the CNN. Future work can include a more detailed analysis of the feature(s) being cued on by the CNN, as well as application to larger and broader datasets. We hope that our work can be a step towards developing practical tools for Cultural Analytics and some day lead to finding patterns and insights into the study of culture that would not be possible to find through human analysis alone.

ACKNOWLEDGMENTS

We thank Wen Chen and Mingze Xu for early development of our HMM for temporal smoothing. This work was supported in part by the National Science Foundation through CAREER grant IIS-1253549 and Nvidia, and used the compute facilities of the FutureSystems Romeo cluster which is supported by Indiana University and NSF RaPyDLI grant 1439007.

REFERENCES

[1] 2017. Apple Inc. WebKit. http://www.webkit.org. (2017).
[2] 2017. Computer & Video Game Archive | U-M Library. https://www.lib.umich.edu/computer-video-game-archive. (2017).
[3] 2017. Data For Everyone Library. https://www.crowdflower.com/wp-content/uploads/2016/03/URL-categorization-DFE.csv. (2017).
[4] 2017. The Internet Archive. http://www.archive.org. (2017).
[5] 2017. PhantomJS. http://www.phantomjs.org. (2017).
[6] Arram Bae, Doheum Park, Juyong Park, and Yong-Yeol Ahn. 2016. Network Landscape of Western Classical Music. *Leonardo* 49, 5 (March 2016), 448–448.
[7] Clive Bell. 1914. *Art.* Frederick A. Stokes Company, New York.
[8] Wen Chen, David J. Crandall, and Norman Makoto Su. 2017. Understanding the Aesthetic Evolution of Websites: Towards a Notion of Design Periods. In *Proceedings of the 2017 CHI Conference on Human Factors in Computing Systems (CHI '17).* ACM, New York, NY, USA, 5976–5987. DOI: http://dx.doi.org/10.1145/3025453.3025607
[9] Jia Deng, Wei Dong, Richard Socher, Li-Jia Li, Kai Li, and Li Fei-Fei. 2009. Imagenet: A large-scale hierarchical image database. In *IEEE Conference on Computer Vision and Pattern Recognition (CVPR).* IEEE, 248–255.
[10] Ali Jahanian, Phillip Isola, and Donglai Wei. 2017. Mining Visual Evolution in 21 Years of Web Design. In *Proceedings of the 2017 CHI Conference Extended Abstracts on Human Factors in Computing Systems (CHI EA '17).* ACM, New York, NY, USA, 2676–2682. DOI: http://dx.doi.org/10.1145/3027063.3053238
[11] Alex Krizhevsky, Ilya Sutskever, and Geoffrey E Hinton. 2012. ImageNet Classification with Deep Convolutional Neural Networks. In *Advances in Neural Information Processing Systems.* 1097–1105.
[12] Ranjitha Kumar, Arvind Satyanarayan, Cesar Torres, Maxine Lim, Salman Ahmad, Scott R. Klemmer, and Jerry O. Talton. 2013. Webzeitgeist: Design Mining the Web. In *Proceedings of the SIGCHI Conference on Human Factors in Computing Systems (CHI '13).* ACM, New York, NY, USA, 3083–3092. DOI: http://dx.doi.org/10.1145/2470654.2466420
[13] Yann LeCun, Leon Bottou, Yoshua Bengio, and Patrick Haffner. 1998. Gradient-based learning applied to document recognition. *Proc. IEEE* 86, 11 (Nov 1998), 2278–2324. DOI: http://dx.doi.org/10.1109/5.726791
[14] Stefan Lee, Nicolas Maisonneuve, David Crandall, Alexei Efros, and Josef Sivic. 2015. Linking past to present: Discovering style in two centuries of architecture. In *IEEE International Conference on Computational Photography (ICCP).* 1–10.
[15] David G Lowe. 1999. Object recognition from local scale-invariant features. In *IEEE International Conference on Computer Vision (ICCV)*, Vol. 2. IEEE, 1150–1157.
[16] Lev Manovich. 2016. The science of culture? Social computing, digital humanities and cultural analytics. *The Datafied society: social research in the age of big data.* (2016).
[17] Lev Manovich, Jeremy Douglass, and William Huber. 2011. Understanding Scanlation: How to Read One Million Fan-Translated Manga Pages. *Image & Narrative* 12, 1 (2011), 206–228.
[18] John Markoff. 2015. A Learning Advance in Artificial Intelligence Rivals Human Abilities. https://www.nytimes.com/2015/12/11/science/an-advance-in-artificial-intelligence-rivals-human-vision-abilities.html. (Dec. 2015).
[19] Maxime Oquab, Leon Bottou, Ivan Laptev, and Josef Sivic. 2014. Learning and transferring mid-level image representations using convolutional neural networks. In *IEEE Conference on Computer Vision and Pattern Recognition (CVPR).* 1717–1724.
[20] Xiaoguang Qi and Brian D. Davison. 2009. Web Page Classification: Features and Algorithms. *ACM Comput. Surv.* 41, 2, Article 12 (Feb. 2009), 31 pages. DOI: http://dx.doi.org/10.1145/1459352.1459357
[21] Alec Radford, Luke Metz, and Soumith Chintala. 2015. Unsupervised Representation Learning with Deep Convolutional Generative Adversarial Networks. *CoRR* abs/1511.06434 (2015). http://arxiv.org/abs/1511.06434
[22] Katharina Reinecke and Krzysztof Z. Gajos. 2014. Quantifying Visual Preferences Around the World. In *Proceedings of the SIGCHI Conference on Human Factors in Computing Systems (CHI '14).* ACM, New York, NY, USA, 11–20. DOI: http://dx.doi.org/10.1145/2556288.2557052
[23] Katharina Reinecke, Tom Yeh, Luke Miratrix, Rahmatri Mardiko, Yuechen Zhao, Jenny Liu, and Krzysztof Z. Gajos. 2013. Predicting Users' First Impressions of Website Aesthetics with a Quantification of Perceived Visual Complexity and Colorfulness. In *Proceedings of the SIGCHI Conference on Human Factors in Computing Systems (CHI '13).* ACM, New York, NY, USA, 2049–2058. DOI: http://dx.doi.org/10.1145/2470654.2481281
[24] Holly Rushmeier, Ruggero Pintus, Ying Yang, Christiana Wong, and David Li. 2015. Examples of challenges and opportunities in visual analysis in the digital humanities. In *SPIE/IS&T Electronic Imaging.* International Society for Optics and Photonics, 939414–939414.
[25] Maximilian Schich, Sune Lehmann, and Juyong Park. 2008. Dissecting the Canon: Visual subject co-popularity networks in art research. In *European Conference on Complex Systems.*
[26] Bolei Zhou, Aditya Khosla, Agata Lapedriza, Aude Oliva, and Antonio Torralba. 2016. Learning Deep Features for Discriminative Localization. In *IEEE Conference on Computer Vision and Pattern Recognition (CVPR).* 2921–2929.

The Ethical Challenges of Publishing Twitter Data for Research Dissemination

Helena Webb
Marina Jirotka
University of Oxford,
Department of Computer Science
Oxford, United Kingdom
helena.webb@cs.ox.ac.uk
marina.jirotka.cs.ox.ac.uk

Rob Procter*
University of Warwick,
Department of Computer Science
Coventry, United Kingdom
rob.procter@warwick.ac.uk
*Corresponding author

Bernd Carsten Stahl
De Montfort University,
Department of Informatics
Leicester, United Kingdom
bstahl@dmu.ac.uk

Omer Rana
Pete Burnap
Cardiff University, School
of Computer Science and Informatics
Cardiff, United Kingdom
ranaof@cardiff.ac.uk
p.burnap@cs.cardiff.ac.uk

William Housley
Adam Edwards
Matthew Williams
Cardiff University,
School of Social Sciences
Cardiff, United Kingdom
housleyw@cardiff.ac.uk
edwardsa2@cardiff.ac.uk
williamsm7@cardiff.ac.uk

ABSTRACT
Empirical research involving the analysis of Internet-based data raises a number of ethical challenges. One instance of this is the analysis of Twitter data, in particular when specific tweets are reproduced for the purposes of dissemination. Although Twitter is an open platform it is possible to question whether this provides a sufficient ethical justification to collect, analyse and reproduce tweets for the purposes of research or whether it is necessary to also undertake specific informed consent procedures. This paper reports on an ethics consultation that formed part of a wider research study and that aimed to identify best practice procedures for the publication of Twitter data in research findings. We focus largely on the UK context and draw on the outcomes of the consultation to highlight the range and depth of ethical issues that arise in this area. We can see Twitter as a case study for a wide number of data sources used in Web Science. This is a highly complex landscape in which questions crystallise around fundamental principles such as informed consent, anonymisation and the minimisation of harm. Furthermore, tensions exist between commercial, regulatory and academic practices, and there are also circumstances in which good ethical practice might compromise academic integrity. There is an absence of consensus in Web science and related fields over how to resolve these issues and we argue that constructive debate is necessary in order to take a proactive approach towards good practice.

WebSci '17, June 25-28, 2017, Troy, NY, USA

ACM ISBN 978-1-4503-4896-6/17/06.
http://dx.doi.org/10.1145/3091478.3091489

Keywords
Research ethics, Twitter, social media, informed consent

1. INTRODUCTION
Twitter provides a highly popular data source in Web science research. It is easy to understand why this is the case. Twitter is a widely used social media platform across the world and it is relatively easy for researchers to collect data from it. As an open platform the majority of posts are available to public view and researchers can collect large numbers of tweets in a very short period of time via the platform's Application Programming Interface (API). Much existing work draws upon large scale quantitative approaches which present aggregated findings to discuss, for instance, voting intentions [1], the propagation of content [2], and the expression of sentiment and tension in particular social contexts [3]. Twitter data have also been used for smaller scale qualitative analyses [4], which often use linguistic or discourse analytic approaches to examine how posts are constructed and how the messages within them are conveyed.

Research in the field has already highlighted some of the ethical issues involved in this kind of research – much of it in terms of social media data as an instance of Big Data [5]. These important discussions focus on concerns arising from the use of automated processes to collect large volumes of data and what implications this has for participant recruitment, privacy and identification etc. Discussions have also focused on the appropriate handling and archiving of such data [6]. Suggestions for what might constitute good ethical practice in these areas vary, often in relation to the different levels of risk associated with different data sources (e.g. private vs public internet platforms) but also as a reflection of different ethical positions [7].

In our own research project, we encountered a number of challenges relating to the responsible handling of Twitter data. Due to the specific nature of our project focus and methodological approach we identified questions that had not yet been addressed in full in the existing literature. These related specifically to questions over the publication of individual tweets in research dissemination and whether, in order to publish them (in an anonymised or non-anonymised form), it was first necessary to contact the original users who posted them to solicit their informed consent. We conducted a consultation to overview current guidance and expert opinion on these matters. In this paper we report and discuss the findings of that consultation. We show that the publication of Twitter data in research raises significant questions for research ethics and that as yet there is an absence of consensus in the field over how to resolve them. We argue that the challenges posed relate to fundamental ethical principles such as the minimisation of harm and the value of informed consent. These challenges also create tensions between commercial (relating in particular to the Twitter platform and the use of tweets by media organisations), regulatory and academic practice. Finally, there are also occasions where suggestions for good practice might be seen to compromise academic integrity. We argue that these tensions identified in our consultation are relevant not only to the publication of Twitter data but also to a range of other ongoing research activities in Web science. It is therefore necessary for open and constructive debate to take place so that researchers can discuss these issues in full and the field of Web science can take a proactive approach towards ethical practice.

2. BACKGROUND: THE DIGITAL WILDFIRE PROJECT

The recently completed 'Digital Wildfire' project[1] was an interdisciplinary research study that sought to identify opportunities for the responsible governance of digital social spaces. The project was funded by the UK's Economic and Social Research Council (ESRC) and was a collaboration between social scientists, computer scientists and computer ethicists. The background to the project lies in the contemporary popularity of social media platforms and the capacity for digital content to spread on a broad and rapid scale [8]. Where rapidly spreading content is in some way inflammatory, antagonistic or provocative – for instance in the form of rumour, hate speech, malicious campaigns etc. – it can risk causing serious harms to individuals, groups and entire communities. The Digital Wildfire project team undertook a range of research activities designed to further understand how these kinds of content propagate across social media, the consequences they have, and how responsible governance strategies might limit the spread of content without impeding freedom of speech [9]. As part of this work we used Twitter data as a case study to investigate the posting and spread of cyber hate on social media.

[1] www.digitalwildfire.org

We collected tweets via the Twitter API and collated conversational 'threads'. Each thread began with a post that might be considered as an instance of cyber hate – that is, an antagonistic post targeted at an individual or group based on personal attributes. These were identified through the accounts of well-known inflammatory posters in the public eye and via sentinel sites such as #YesYou'reRacist and #YesYou'reSexist that serve to collate and expose inappropriate content posted by others. Subsequent posts responding to the opening tweet were also collected and arranged in posting order. This enabled us to observe and analyse how Twitter users respond to each other's posts.

In our analysis we were interested in 1) how users on Twitter construct posts that are treated by others as hateful and 2) how users construct responses to an opening post to perform interactional actions such as expressing agreement or disagreement with it. To give a brief example, Figure 1 shows an opening post tweeted by Katie Hopkins – a public figure in the UK well-known for the expression of inflammatory opinions[2], often targeted towards certain groups of people– and two responses that followed it[3].

Figure 1. Opening tweet and two responses

We can observe that the opening post draws on specific rhetorical devices such as short sentences, the use of emotive categories – e.g. babies – and the presentation of (extreme)

[2] https://www.theguardian.com/media/katie-hopkins

[3] For the purposes of this paper, we have used the following criteria to determine whether consent is needed in order to reproduce Twitter posts: posts made by figures in the public eye who tweet as part of their public role, are reproduced in full without consent being sought. Other users – such as those who posted tweets 2 and 3 were contacted via Twitter and their opt in consent was sought to include their posts in our project publications.

opinion as fact – to construct a message that can be seen as inflammatory and likely to provoke responses from others. We can further observe how subsequent posts draw on interactional resources and the functionality of the Twitter platform to produce disagreeing replies that both address Katie Hopkins directly – e.g. through the use of the @handle and terms such as 'what gives you the right' - whilst also producing negative assessments and directives that are designed to be viewable to other users – e.g. #blockKT. This kind of granular, qualitative analysis of individual posts helped us to understand in detail how cyber hate is posted and responded to on the Twitter platform, and subsequently to conceptualise what forms counter speech – posts serving to push back against the spread of hateful content – might take. This analysis informed statistical modelling work that examined the impact of the occurrence of counter speech on the length of threads that were started after an initial cyber hate post. It also produced valuable insights in its own right that we wanted to disseminate via written publications and conference presentations.

The preference amongst some members of the project team was that this dissemination of our qualitative findings should include the reproduction of certain Twitter posts in order to illustrate the wider patterns found across the dataset. The use of data in this way is standard in the methodological approaches drawn on in the conduct of the analysis – ethnomethodology and conversation analysis (EMCA), membership categorisation analysis (MCA) and interaction analysis [10]. These approaches all emphasise the collection of naturally occurring data for analysis and the (anonymised) reproduction of data to enable audiences to assess for themselves the validity of that analysis. Much work conducted using these approaches is based on the examination of audio or video recorded face-to-face interactions. Anonymisation of this data can be relatively easy to achieve, through the removal of real names in transcripts and the blurring of faces etc., and the capacity for individual participants to be identified is arguably low – particularly in comparison to social media data gathered from a 'public' platform such as Twitter.

As we made plans to disseminate our qualitative analysis, debate arose amongst the team over whether it would be ethically appropriate to reproduce tweets in publications, even if anonymised, and whether we should perhaps contact individual users to seek their informed consent before doing so. Concerns that publication might go against good practice were crystallised into three areas:

1. Covering up usernames and @handles does not create meaningful anonymisation as it is sometimes possible to enter the main text of a tweet into Twitter's search function, recover the tweet and its associated meta-data, including the username and @handle of the user who posted it. Though Twitter allows users to post under a pseudonym, the meta-data (including picture, location etc.) may enable the poster's identity to be discovered.
2. Given that the Digital Wildfire project includes the examination of hate speech, there is concern that users may come to harm if it is possible to identify them and they have been posting content considered to be hateful, inflammatory etc.
3. Twitter's User Development policy requires any reproduction of tweets to be done in full, so anonymisation procedures are in breach of that.

To help us examine these areas more fully, and ideally to find ways to resolve the challenges we faced, we decided to run a consultation exercise to scope existing guidance and practice in this area.

3. ETHICS CONSULTATION

Our project team agreed to undertake a consultation to review the three issues listed above and also to seek answers to a more global question:

In order to publish (anonymised) individual social media posts is it first ethically necessary to contact the user and solicit their informed consent?

In the conduct of the consultation we carried out three strands of activity:

1) *Scoping of current relevant guidance.* We surveyed current regulatory guidance on the use of social media data in research. This included guidance arising from individual academic institutions, research funding bodies and other research and regulatory organisations.
2) *Survey of expert opinion.* We made contact with a number of experts working in the fields of research ethics and computer ethics. We asked them for their thoughts on the questions and challenges covered in the consultation. We also reviewed available relevant literature on the ethics of social media/internet research.
3) *Survey of current practice and opinion* We surveyed the opinion of various individuals working in the field to identify their views on the consultation questions and their current practices regarding the use of social media data. This survey was conducted in a number of ways including – reviews of the content of relevant journals; email conversations with the editors of a number of research journals; email and face-to-face conversations with researchers; and group discussions with researchers at relevant events, such as the Social Media and Society conference in London 2016.

The findings of the consultation were compiled into a dossier which was then used at the basis for further discussion. In this paper we draw on the outcomes of the consultation to discuss the challenges faced by researchers when trying to determine what equates to best practice when working with Twitter data. We found an absence of consensus across the field that reflected the disagreements occurring in our own research team. Perspectives vary amongst individuals but also across institutions. Furthermore, research using Twitter data creates a complex landscape in which various ethical challenges arise. These relate in particular to key ethical criteria such as informed consent, minimising harm and anonymisation. Challenges also arise through tensions between academic, commercial and regulatory practice as well as in contradictory criteria for behaving ethically and upholding academic integrity.

4. THE ETHICAL CHALLENGES OF PUBLISHING TWITTER DATA

4.1 Absence of academic consensus

As noted above it is standard practice in Web science that tweets are collected for analysis via the platform's API. This can be done without users being aware at all that their tweets are being collected. Users are typically not approached directly to solicit their informed consent to take part in research, instead consent is often assumed to have been given by the user's acceptance of Twitter's Terms of Service. These state[4]:

"By submitting, posting or displaying Content on or through the Services, you grant us a worldwide, non-exclusive, royalty-free license (with the right to sublicense) to use, copy, reproduce, process, adapt, modify, publish, transmit, display and distribute such Content in any and all media or distribution methods (now known or later developed). This license authorizes us to make your Content available to the rest of the world and to let others do the same".

Regarding the further handling of this data, including the publication of specific posts, there is an absence of consensus. In the US a 2015 amendment to the 'Common Rule' Federal Policy[5] for the Protection of Human Subjects suggests that certain forms of online behaviours can be classed as public behaviour and therefore do not require further ethical review.

"Any research involving standardized testing, surveys, interviews, or observations, including audio and video recording, of public behavior, including behavior online, will be able to proceed without further review".

This amendment is a significant development as the 'Common Rule' tends to determine the decision-making conducted by Institutional Review Boards (IRBs). By contrast in the UK, the ESRC, which funds the Digital Wildfire project, recommends the full ethics review of projects intending to collect social media data, noting potential tensions regarding traceability and what might or might not considered public.

"The potential for identifiabilty of online sources, as well as ethical debates about how privacy is constituted in digital contexts, means that full ethics review may be appropriate for research involving these communities".

Similarly, other ethics guidelines, such as those published by the British Psychological Association [11] and the Association of Internet Researchers [12] – recommend careful consideration of ethical issues when using social media data with particular regard to privacy. These guidelines do not take an overt stance on the matter of consent for publication. On the other hand, a 2016 output produced by the University of Aberdeen [13] and based on project work funded by the ESRC advocates that in the case of sensitive social media content, researchers should either consider the use of paraphrased/composite data instead of reproducing actual posts or use an informed consent approach. Similarly, in 2016 the University of Oxford produced updated guidance[6] on internet-based research. This advises that in the case of Twitter (as a public platform) researchers do not need to solicit consent to collect data but should seek consent to publish individual posts. Alternatively, they can create composite data for the purpose of publication.

"Researchers who wish to display direct quotes and the username and picture of the person in their work (especially if it is published in any way) should normally seek informed consent to do this, especially in cases of very sensitive data (e.g. hate speech). They should contact the participants directly having decided which consent procedure should be followed (e.g. online information sheet, online consent form, click boxes, etc.). If gaining informed consent is not possible, quotes should normally be paraphrased and usernames/pictures de-identified in order to protect the 'participants'".

The lack of consensus in research guidance is mirrored by an absence of consensus in the research community. In our scoping of existing literature and survey of individual researchers we identified a range of opinion based on alternative ethical positions and underlying assumptions about the status of the Twitter platform. This includes different positions regarding whether any consent to publish should be opt-in or opt-out, whether published posts should be anonymised and whether composite data is an acceptable alternative to publishing real posts. We also came across a high number of researchers working in this field and determined to follow good practice who were genuinely uncertain what form that good practice should take. We can see this current absence of consensus as a genuine barrier to the conduct of work in this area with particular obstacles occurring when research collaborations involve team members from institutions whose guidance is not compatible.

4.2 Informed consent

The principle of informed consent is a cornerstone of ethical guidance in contemporary research involving human participants. In its classic form, derived from research in bio-medicine [14], it requires informed consent to be given by participants at the point of data collection. In the case of research involving the collection of Twitter data, informed consent for data collection is typically based on user acceptance of its Terms of Service. Given the large volume of tweets typically collected in a Twitter-based study, it would certainly be time consuming and challenging to attempt to contact all users

[4] https://twitter.com/tos?lang=en#us

[5] http://www.hhs.gov/ohrp/regulations-and-policy/regulations/nprm-home/index.html

[6] http://www.admin.ox.ac.uk/media/global/wwwadminoxacuk/localsites/curec/documents/BPG_06_Internet-Based_Research.pdf

in a more direct way. However, survey research[7] suggests that social media users are unlikely to read or remember the full Terms and Conditions (T&Cs) of the platforms they sign up to – undermining the assumption that informed consent for data collection has been given. Furthermore, research on public opinion suggests individuals are wary of research that collects and publishes social media data without more overt user consent. For instance, research reported by the UK think tank Demos [15] found a low level of awareness amongst members of the public that their posts might be used for research purposes and a general concern over the implications of research for privacy and the risk of harm. However, in comparison to other platforms, respondents were less worried about the collection of Twitter data for research due to public nature of the platform.

We have found some instances of small scale studies involving Twitter data that overtly seek informed consent from users at the point of data collection. For instance, as part of a study on the responsible collection of social media data Moffat and Koene (2016) [16] made use of a prototype web tool. This tool allowed users to monitor and manage their Twitter interactions whilst also enabling them to determine when their posts were being collected as research data. In order to assess for ourselves how practical a 'full' informed consent procedure might be, the project team agreed to attempt to contact a number of Twitter users and seek their opt-in consent to publish specific tweets. Having identified a data thread of interest we contacted individual users over Twitter via a reply to the specific tweet we wanted to publish. Due to Twitter's character limit, the contact request was split over two tweets and a link was provided to access further information:

Hi we are researchers studying social media communications. We are looking at 'heated' discussions on Twitter (1 of 2)
We would like to use this tweet in our publications. Please see https://sites.google.com/site/digitalwildfireesrc/home/consent-for-publication and reply if this is OK. (2 of 2)

Over 20 requests to different users were sent out and two responses were received – both giving consent for publication. The process of sending out requests was very quick and it was possible to send many messages in a short period of time. As none of the users involved followed our Twitter account we were unable to send direct (private) messages. This meant our requests were visible to other users on the platform, arguably drawing attention to the post being referred to. When we did not hear a response from users we had contacted, we sent them the same request again around a week later in case they had missed it the first time. We did not feel comfortable sending more than two requests as we did not want our contact to appear intrusive[8].

[7] https://www.theguardian.com/commentisfree/2014/apr/24/terms-and-conditions-online-small-print-information

[8] One of the anonymous reviewers of this paper also made the helpful suggestion that we could have deleted our tweets sent to users after a certain period of time to further limit their potential obtrusiveness.

Our trial with informed consent was based on an opt-in model. An alternative format is an opt-out model, in which users need to specifically state that they do not want to be involved in the research. This model relieves some of the time burden involved in securing consent but could arguably provide a means to ensure good practice – particularly for instance where the social media posts involved are not sensitive or very personal in content. However, many Twitter uses receive a high volume of messages in their feed, or perhaps go for long periods of time without logging on to the platform. So opt-out consent does not provide a guarantee that a request to publish (if sent via a Twitter message) has been seen or understood.

More fundamentally, the often anonymous nature of social media challenges the informed consent model. Twitter does not have a real name policy and users are easily able to set up profiles that do not include their name or any 'real' facts about them. Even with opt-in consent we cannot be totally sure of the identity of the users involved if the only access we have to them is via their public user profiles. In the case of the users we contacted in our own trial, we checked their profiles to identify available details about their age, job etc. We wanted to ensure that they met the criteria of adults capable of giving informed consent. Even though their user profiles indicated that they were, we cannot be totally certain that these details are accurate. As in the case of any informed consent procedure reliant on public profiles and conversations over a social media platform, we cannot necessarily rule out the possibility that a user is under the age of 16 or in some way vulnerable and therefore someone who might typically be regarded as unable to give consent.

4.3 Minimising harm

One of the main causes for concern we identified over the use of individual tweets in research dissemination is that publication of posts might cause harm. Even though Twitter is an open platform, users do not necessarily expect that their tweets will be collected and published to other audiences elsewhere. Publishing tweets can bring users to new or larger forms of attention and if their identities are revealed, they might be at risk from their (potentially unknowing) participation in research.

The minimisation of harm is another key ethical principle in research involving human participants. This was highly relevant to the Digital Wildfire project as our focus was on inflammatory posts such as messages containing cyber hate. It is possible that the victims of a cyber hate post might be identifiable (to themselves and others) when an individual post is reproduced in a publication; this might cause them further harm in addition to the harm they experienced when the content was originally posted. Furthermore, if publication makes identifiable a user who has posted cyber hate messages, this also risks harm. Readers of the publication might seek to retaliate by sending accusatory or 'shaming' messages over social media or even identifying the user offline and seeking to report him/her to the police, contacting his/her employer etc. Although we have not come across any instances in which this kind of harm has occurred as a direct result of research involving social media data, practices of online shaming or 'digilantism' [17] are frequent across contemporary society and there have been numerous cases in which users have been excessively punished for tweets that were perhaps poorly worded or published in the heat of the moment and quickly regretted.

Whilst minimising harm is a central component of good research practice, almost all forms of research carry at least some risk of causing harm. It is therefore necessary to attempt to assess the level of risk involved in individual projects. As part of our consultation exercise we conducted a risk assessment of the Digital Wildfire project's work involving the analysis of social media posts. Whilst noting the inflammatory nature of many of the posts we were analysing we also identified that large numbers of the posts we had collected were non-contentious or mundane in content. We also noted that some users do not include any kind of identifying detail (name, image, place of work etc.) in their profile or tweets. Subsequently we devised an assessment matrix in which risk to users was calculated according to two dimensions. These were: 1) the extent to which the user is identifiable and 2) the extent to which the content of the tweet is antagonistic, provocative etc. This matrix is shown in Figure 2.

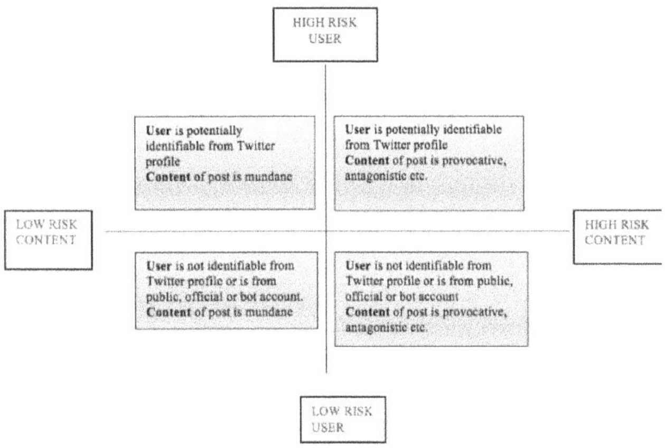

Figure 2. Proposed risk assessment matrix for tweets

At first our risk matrix appeared to provide a useful means to assess the likelihood of harm arising from the publication of individual twitter posts and we considered adopting alternative consent strategies consent (no consent, opt-out, opt-in) in relation to the different levels of risk identified. However, on further reflection, this model became problematic in some ways. It was noted that even if a user's offline identity is unknown, their online one is likely to be identifiable and this leaves open the possibility that publication can cause them some kind of harm through online messages or 'shaming' etc. Furthermore, it was observed that if readers look up a user's tweets when published, they will also have access to that user's entire profile and (public) posting history – including posts made after publication. Even if a publication quotes only mundane posts from a user, it is possible that readers might find more provocative ones that were not identified in the study or posted after the publication of the study. Similarly, users with non-identifying profiles at the point of publication may change this at some point in future so that their personal details can be seen by readers.

The dynamic nature of Twitter means that it is very difficult to use a static model to assess the extent to which publishing an individual user's posts risks causing them harm. As researchers in this area we are challenged to ask where our responsibilities towards participants begin and end: do we have to protect them from harm both in the present and in the possible future? As discussed next, the principle of minimsing harm is further complicated by the extreme difficulty of ensuring the meaningful anonymisation of individual Twitter posts.

4.4 Anonymisation

It is often standard practice in research to anonymise data for publication. Participants' identities are protected to ensure that they cannot be identified by dissemination audiences and this therefore helps to protect them from harm. Research outputs including individual tweets sometimes attempt to anonymise them by covering or altering the username and @handle of the poster. However, due to the open status of the Twitter platform it can often possible to identify the user with relative ease.

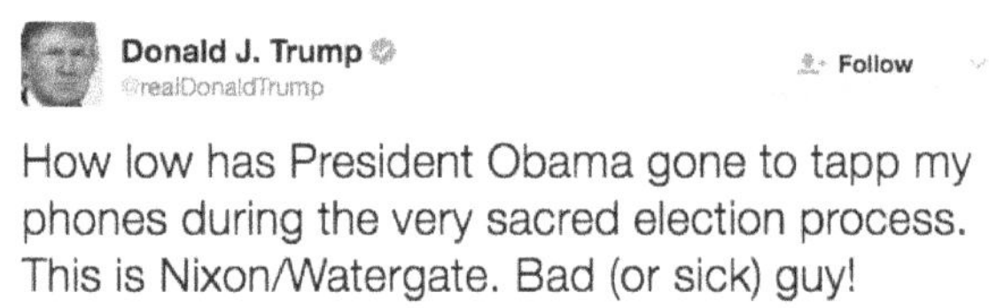

Figure 3: recent tweet posted by Donald Trump

We can take as an example a recent tweet posted by Donald Trump – see Figure 3. Even if we do not know the user name or @handle of the poster, we can put the content of the post into Twitter's search function and it will show us the original post as a result – revealing the user's online identity. To overcome this, we might try to make small amendments to the content of the post. Correcting spelling errors or removing or substituting words might (arguably) not affect the integrity of the analysis but provide a means to shroud the identity of the poster. So, we might amend the post in question to:

How low has Obama gone to tap my phones during the very special election process. This is Nixon/Watergate. Bad or sick guy!

However, putting this content into Twitter's Advanced Search produces a small number of results, including the original tweet and tweets that quote it. This also occurs when entire sentences are removed from the original post. Once again the identity of the user can be easily deduced. Although we have used a high profile user as demonstration, we have carried out this exercise with some of the content posted by unknown users in our datasets and achieved similar results. Twitter's Advanced Search function can consistently identify the profile of a user or narrow it down to a very small subset and further investigation can quickly reveal the relevant user.

4.5 Commercial vs regulatory vs academic practice

Incompatibilities between commercial, regulatory and academic practices present a further challenge to determining best practice in the use of Twitter data. As has already been mentioned, Twitter's own Terms of Service are often relied on in academic work as providing informed consent for the collection and analysis of tweets. For researchers working within the European Union this reliance is clouded by Data Protection[9] legislation which states, broadly, that *data should not be used for purposes other than which it was created.* Posting content to communicate on a platform is an objectively different purpose to providing data to be included in research. The notion that users provide informed consent for their tweets to be used in research is further undermined by evidence suggesting that users do not read the Terms and Conditions of a platform in full or understand their implications. If we accept that informed consent occurs at the point of data collection, then we are required to question even standard, apparently non-controversial, practices of collecting tweets via the platform's API. A more fundamental question is to what extent should our own research obligations to ensure good ethical practice be passed over to, and rely on, the actions of commercial agents such as Twitter?

A further form of incompatibility lies in the requirement of Twitter's User Development Policy[10] that tweets are reproduced in full in publications. Any alternations – such as to remove or change a username – would be considered a breach. This requirement challenges standard academic practices of anonymisation (although as already noted, this is hard to achieve with tweets in any case) and also conflicts with European Union[11] and (in the UK) Information Commissioner's Office[12] regulations regarding the handling of data.

On account of Twitter's policy, it is standard to see tweets reproduced in full in media articles. This creates an interesting scenario in research dissemination in which we can link to a news item showing tweets in full but cannot be assured that showing those same tweets that we have perhaps collected via the API would be an acceptable practice. Twitter's policy regarding the reproduction of tweets without alteration is in fact often breached in academic publications. We have seen various instances of published journal articles that cover up usernames and @handles [18] and have heard that journals will sometimes insist on this practice where the content of the tweets is in some way sensitive. To the best of our knowledge, Twitter have not taken any action in response to these breaches.

[9] http://ec.europa.eu/justice/data-protection/

[10] https://dev.twitter.com/overview/terms/agreement-and-policy

[11] http://eur-lex.europa.eu/legal-content/en/TXT/?uri=CELEX:31995L0046

[12] https://ico.org.uk/for-organisations/guide-to-data-protection/

4.6 Research integrity

Although ethical practice should always take priority over academic findings, our consultation highlighted a number of questions over the importance of academic integrity in research using social media data and the ways in which this can be challenged by procedures designed to minimise harm. One key example is in the suggestion that qualitative analysis should present composite or paraphrased data rather than publish actual tweets. This has been suggested in academic publications (in relation to various data contexts) [19] as well as some of the guidance we discussed earlier. It can be seen to present an ideal solution as findings are represented in a global way without any threat to individual identities being revealed, providing a qualitative equivalent of aggregated data.

However, whilst this approach appears acceptable to some it is very problematic to others, in particular to those in research communities where analysis and publication emphasises the value of naturally occurring data. As noted earlier in the paper, the interactional approach followed in our project is one form of analysis that emphasises this approach. It is typically necessary to illustrate findings using data fragments and these fragments are routinely based on naturally occurring data. We contacted the editors of journals we would typically seek to publish in and asked if composite data would be accepted in their publication. We included the suggestion that the actual data could be made available to reviewers to help them evaluate the robustness of the analysis. Their response was that they would reject any articles that used this approach. One editor told us:

Most journals would be reluctant to contemplate fabricated data. There are two reasons for this. The first is that it is not a good proxy for the real thing... The second is that it runs across all the current concerns about research integrity and the potential for falsifying findings. Making data available to reviewers but not publishing it would also run into problems with the open data movement... We accept that qualitative materials may be minimally edited for anonymity - see above- but we cannot contemplate publishing papers that offer no opportunity for readers independently to evaluate the interpretations and analyses offered by their authors.

As this respondent indicates, the reasons to be wary of composite data on the basis of academic integrity are both specific to the type of analysis being undertaken and broadly applicable to research in general. In specific terms the interactional analysis of tweets depends on the detailed and precise analysis of content. To return to the Katie Hopkins post in Figure 1, we consider that it is the particular combination of descriptive terms, use of grammar, sentence construction etc. that makes this post inflammatory and likely to provoke others. The precise content of the responses following this post is also dependent on these particular features. Due to the highly detailed focus of our analysis we are dependent on showing the exact posts to convey our argument. It is virtually impossible for us to accurately illustrate our argument with anything other than the original data as the different wording of a composite post would suggest a different analytic reading of it.

In broader terms we need to ask whether it is ever acceptable to fabricate data in the publication of research. Even if done with genuine intentions this practice contradicts standard understandings of academic integrity. For instance, the Universities UK Concordat to Support Research Integrity[13] states on page 17 that:

"Research misconduct can take many forms, including:
• fabrication: making up results or other outputs (eg, artefacts) and presenting them as if they were real
• falsification: manipulating research processes or changing or omitting data without good cause"

The creation of composite data therefore creates a risk of being seen as research misconduct. We might counter this by stating that the fabrication of posts would be done in a robust and systematic way – but how would we be able to judge this and who would evaluate it?

In our consultation other arguments have been raised around research integrity. As researchers we have a duty to examine difficult topics and social problems. The spread of hate speech on social media can be seen as an instance of this. The prevalence and impact of hateful content is frequently reported in the news and the major platforms are often criticised for not doing enough to stop it[14]. We might therefore argue that it is a priority for us to conduct research into these matters and share our results in a suitable way. This can help to identify solutions to the social problem and perhaps hold platforms to account for their lack of action. However, it might be reasonable to assume that users posting extreme forms of hate speech would not give their consent to be involved in research – for purposes of data collection and publication. Does this mean we cannot carry out the research? It is possible that requirements for informed consent might form a barrier to research being undertaken and lead to researchers shying away from these important issues in favour of topics that are 'easier' to deal with in ethical terms. Another point is that justice for participants is also an ethical principle. It can be argued that those who have been made victims of abuse on a public social media platform have a right for that abuse to be exposed in its original form. If we attempt to paraphrase the content of the abuse or hide the identity of the user who posted it, could it be argued that we are doing a dis-service to the victim of that abuse? Academic integrity is itself an ethical issue and poses significant questions for work in this area.

[13] http://www.universitiesuk.ac.uk/policy-and-analysis/reports/Documents/2012/the-concordat-to-support-research-integrity.pdf

[14] https://www.theguardian.com/media/2017/mar/14/face-off-mps-and-social-media-giants-online-hate-speech-facebook-twitter

5. DISCUSSION

This paper has drawn on the outcomes of an ethics consultation to illustrate the challenges that arise when trying to determine what constitutes good practice in research involving the collection, analysis and publication of Twitter data. We have used our own project research as a starting point to investigate the ethical issues that require consideration when working in this area, particularly in the case of publishing specific tweets when disseminating research findings. As illustrated in the sections above, scoping the field has revealed a highly complex landscape that presents major challenges for ongoing research.

We have identified a lack of consensus in the field over the appropriate ways to collect and handle social media data and procedures through which to disseminate it. These differences exist across institutions, academic publishers and individuals. Reliance on Twitter's Terms of Service to assume informed consent to collect data is standard in many studies but is problematic. Direct approaches to users to seek consent (for instance to publish specific posts) can be achieved but are time consuming and, more fundamentally, do not necessarily guarantee that a user is capable of giving consent. Research using Twitter data – in particular when the content of posts is in some way sensitive – carries a risk of harm to participants. It is therefore necessary to assess this risk when determining procedures for data handling and publication. Challenges arise when we consider that Twitter is a dynamic platform: users will continue to post after we have collected the posts that particularly interest us. If publishing drives audiences towards a particular user, their risk of harm relates to all their posts rather than just the posts we have published. Does that mean our risk assessment needs to attend to previous posts and possible future ones? As an open platform, standard practices of anonymisation do not map well onto Twitter posts as it can be very easy to identify users by putting the content of their posts into the platform's search function. Furthermore, attempts at anonymisation are a breach of Twitter's User Development policy. Twitter's requirements for data handing are also potentially incompatible with regulatory requirements and media practices for publishing posts frequently differ from academic ones. Finally, the use of composite data in place of publishing actual tweets is incompatible with certain analytic approaches and genuine questions arise over how ethical practice can be balanced with the demands of academic integrity. In particular, it could be argued that as researchers we have a duty to study difficult social problems such as the spread of hate speech on social media and that the creation of barriers to accessing and publishing data might lead us to neglect this duty in favour of 'easier' topics.

Our ethics consultation was not able to draw firm conclusions about best practice with regard to publishing tweets and in relation to the use of Twitter data more generally. Instead it highlighted division of opinion across the field that reflected differences of perspective within our own project team. These divisions are frequently founded in different conceptions of what it means to collect data from an open platform and to what extent the status of data as publicly available does or does not alter standard ethical obligations relating to informed consent, anonymisation and the minimisation of harm. They can also be seen to reflect a more fundamental stalemate between two ethical positions. On the one hand a universalist approach might state that if consent cannot be gained and anonymity cannot be assured, then in any and every case research cannot be published. On the other hand, a situated approach might operate on a case-by-case basis, taking into account factors such as the nature of the content being studied and the status of the users involved (as in the public eye or easy to identify etc.). Without taking a stance on either side of this debate, we note that researchers working in the fields of Web science and social science are subject to different and constantly negotiated ethical positions and interpretations of what constitutes harm etc. The implementation of general rules does not map well onto these negotiations and interpretations, and carries a real risk of leading to the censorship of academic work.

The current complexities surrounding good practice and Twitter research create significant challenges for ongoing work in the field. How can researchers collaborate successfully if they are following different guidelines and competing ethical standpoints? How can the results of qualitative research be published if informed consent is necessary but impossible to achieve and if composite data is regarded as unacceptable fabrication? These issues are not specific to Twitter data alone and apply to other forms of Web science research such as those using blogs and forums as data sources in addition to other social media platforms. Furthermore, the challenges we have highlighted have also been discussed in relation to other uses of digital data [20]. The fact that they remain unresolved demonstrates how intractable they are. Our discussions over the ethical handling of Twitter data serve as a case study for a broader range of data sources in Web science and highlight the challenges that the field needs to address.

It is our position that having identified these various tensions around the ethical use of Twitter data in research, it is our obligation to attend to them and reflect seriously on how we can pursue genuine good practice in our work. Furthermore, we also argue that these tensions create real dilemmas for Web science and that it is crucial that attempts are made to address them to enable the field to move forwards. We suggest that open and constructive debate should take place in relation to all of the issues we have highlighted here. Whilst it is unlikely that full consensus could ever be reached, it is possible - and vital - to find a shared pathway that researchers can follow. This debate should include the broad examination of key ethical criteria. For instance, fields such as ubiquitous computing [21] have made attempts to move beyond traditional concepts of informed consent and we can ask whether alternative strategies could acceptably be applied to social media research. Similarly, we need to pose questions such as: in the age of Big Data, to what extent is it possible for informed consent to occur at the point of data collection? To what extent are existing (often static) models of anonymity and risk compatible with public and dynamic sources of data? Where do our responsibilities to minimise harm begin and end in relation to these kinds of data and how can we assess them? How can we balance the risks of conducting and publishing research against the potential risks of not conducting research? Whilst these questions are undoubtedly challenging and the route towards a shared pathway for good practice might be a rocky one, these issues create an exciting opportunity for genuine debate to occur and to effect meaningful change.

6. ACKNOWLEDGMENTS

Our thanks to all those who participated in the ethics consultation reported on in this paper. Plus, thanks to the anonymous reviewers for their comments on the submission. We are also grateful to the Economic and Social Research Council (ESRC) for funding the project: 'Digital Wildfire: (Mis)information flows, propagation and responsible governance' ref ES/L0133981.

7. REFERENCES

[1] For overview see: Gayo-Avello, D. 2013. A meta-analysis of state of the art electoral prediction from Twitter data. *Social Science Computer Review* 31, 6 (Aug. 2013) 649-679. DOI=10.1177/0894439313493979

[2] For overview see: Webb, H., Burnap, P., Procter, R. Rana, O., Stahl, B., Williams, A., Housley, W., Edwards, A., and Jirotka, M. 2016 Digital Wildfires? Propagation, Verification, Regulation and Responsible Innovation *ACM Transactions on Information Systems*.34, 3 (April 2016). DOI= 10.1145/2893478

[3] For example see: Burnap, P. and Williams, M.L. 2016 Us and them.: indentifying cyberhate on Twitter across multiple protected characteristics. *EJP Data Science* 5, 11. Available online at http://orca.cf.ac.uk/88072/. And: Pak, A., and Paroubek, P. 2010 Twitter as a Corpus for Sentiment Analysis and Opinion Mining. *LREc*. Vol. 10. No. 2010.

[4] For overview see: Marwick, A. 2013 Ethnographic and Qualitative Research on Twitter. In Weller, K., Bruns, A., Puschmann, C., Burgess, J. and Mahrt, M. (eds.) *Twitter and Society* New York: Peter Lang, 109-122.

[5] For example, see: Stahl, B. C. Heersmink, R. Goujon, P. Flick, C. van den Hoven, J. Wakunuma, K. Veikko Ikonen, V.T.T. and Rader, M. 2010. Identifying the ethics of Emerging Information and Communication Technologies. *International Journal of Technoethics* 1,4,20-38; boyd, d and Crawford, K. 2012 Critical questions for big data *Information, Communication and Society* 15,6. 662-679 DOI= 10.1080/1369118X.2012.678878; Zimmer, M. 2010. "But the data is already public" on the ethics of research in Facebook. *Ethics and Information Technology* 12,4, 313-325; Zwitter, A.J. 2014. Big Data Ethics *Big Data and Society* 1,2 Nov 2014 doi/10.1177/2053951714559253; Schroeder, R. 2014. Big Data and the brave new world of social media research *Big Data and Society* 1,2 Dec 2014. DOI=10.1177/2053951714563194.

[6] For example see: Neuhas, F. and Webmoor, 2012. Agile ethics for massified research and visualization. *Information, Communication and Society* 15,1, 43-65 DOI= 10.1080/1369118X.2011.616519. And: McNeily, M Hutton, L. and Henderson, T. 2013. Understanding ethical concerns in social media privacy studies. In *Proceedings of the ACM CSCW Workshop on measuring networked social privacy: Qualitative and Quantitative approaches.*

[7] For overview see: Zimmer, M. and Proferes, N.J. 2014. A topology of Twitter research: disciplines, methods and ethics. *Aslib Journal of*

Information Management 66,3, 250-261. , 1-10. DOI= 10.1108/AJIM-09-2013-0083.

[8] World Economic Forum, 2013 *Digital Wildfires in a hyperconnected world.* Global Risks Report. World Economic Forum (Feb. 2013). Available online at: .http://reports.weforum.org/global-risks-2013/risk-case-1/digital-wildfires-in-a-hyperconnected-world/

[9] Webb, H., Jirotka, M., Carsten Stahl, B., Housley, W., Edwards, A., Williams, M., Procter, R., Rana, O. and Burnap, P. (2015). Digital wildfires: hyper-connectivity, havoc and a global ethos to govern social media. *Computers and Society 45(3), 193-201.* DOI=10.1145/2874239.2874267

[10] For further details of these approaches see: Housley, W., Webb, H., Williams, M. et. al. (forthcoming) Social Media, Interaction and Categorisation: The Case of Twitter Campaigns. *Social Media and Society* special issue on Social Movements and Social Media. And: Tolmie, P., Procter, R., Rouncefield, M., Liakata, M. and Zubiaga, A. Microblog Analysis as a programme of work. Submitted to *ACM Transactions on Social Computing.*

[11] British Psychological Society, 2013. *Ethics Guidelines for Internet-mediated Research.* INF206/1.2013. Leicester: British Psychological Society. Available online at: www.bps.org.uk/publications/policy-andguidelines/research-guidelines-policydocuments/research-guidelines-poli

[12] Markham, A. and Buchanan, E, 2012. *Ethical Decision-Making and Internet Research: Recommendations from the AoIR Ethics Working Committee (Version 2.0).* AoIR. Available online at: https://aoir.org/reports/ethics2.pdf

[13] Townsend, L. and Wallace, C. *Social Media Research: A guide to ethics.* Available online at: http://www.dotrural.ac.uk/socialmediaresearchethics.pdf

[14] Dingwall, R. and Murphy, E. 2003. *Qualitative Methods and Health Policy Research.* New York: Aldine de Gruyter.

[15] Evans, H., Ginnis, S. and Bartlett, J 2015. *#social Ethics: a guide to embedding ethics in social media research.* Demos. Available online at https://www.ipsos-mori.com/Assets/Docs/Publications/im-demos-social-ethics-in-social-media-research-summary.pdf

[16] Moffat, A. and Koene, A. 2016. Public Outreach Evaluation Tool (TOOL). Poster presented at the *Social Media and Society Conference* July 2016.

[17] For example, see: Ronson, J. *2015 So You've been publicly shamed.* London: Penguin Publishing group. And see also: http://www2.warwick.ac.uk/fac/soc/pais/people/sorell/tom_sorrell_-_digilantism.mp4

[18] For example, Awan, I. 2014. Islamophobia on Twitter: A Typology of Online Hate Against Muslims on Social Media *Policy & Internet* 6, 2, 133-150.

[19] Markham, A. 2005. "Go ugly early": Fragmented narrative and bricolage as interpretive method. *Qualitative Inquiry 11,16, 813-819* DOI=10.1177/1077800405280662.

[20] Carus, A., and Jirotka, M. 2009 From Data Archive to Ethical Labyrinth *Qualitative Research* 9, 3, 285- 299

[21] See for example: Moran, S., Luger, E. and Rodden, T. 2014. An emerging toolkit for attaining informed consent in UbiComp. *UbiComp '14 Adjunct* Sep 2014 Available online at: http://ubicomp.org/ubicomp2014/proceedings/ubicomp_adjunct/workshops/Consent/p635-moran.pdf

Broad, Interdisciplinary Science *In Tela*: An Exposure and Child Health Ontology

James P. McCusker
Sabbir M. Rashid
Zhicheng Liang
Yue Liu
Katherine Chastain
Paulo Pinheiro
Rensselaer Polytechnic Institute
Troy, NY, USA

Jeanette A. Stingone
Icahn School of Medicine at Mount Sinai
New York, NY, USA

Deborah L. McGuinness
Rensselaer Polytechnic Institute

ABSTRACT

Data curation for interdisciplinary collaborative science requires a new online web-based approach that integrates domain knowledge from multiple resources and enables *in tela* (in the web) interactive collaboration between data providers, domain specialists, and data analysts. The Children's Health Exposure Analysis Resource (CHEAR) is a resource for child development and environmental exposure data. The CHEAR Data Center has developed an ontology that integrates study and exposure data in a way that is consistent across the program, and integrates with many best practice relevant vocabularies and repository schemas. This includes the World Wide Web Consortium's recommended Provenance Ontology (PROV), Semanticscience Integrated Ontology (SIO), the Chemical Entities of Biological Interest (CheBI) ontology, the Uberon multi-species anatomy ontology, and the Units Ontology as the starting point for our domain modeling. We mapped terms where they overlapped and extended these ontologies with classes that were required to support modeling and integrating data from epidemiology and chemical exposure measurements that comprise the majority of the data recorded by the CHEAR data center. In response to this challenge, we used an on-demand approach to develop the ontology based on a set of representative pilot projects in CHEAR. After initial development, we evaluated the ontology for completeness in representing an additional pilot study. An epidemiologist was able to produce a mapping of the project to the ontology with only minor corrections needed by an ontology expert. In the large dataset that was tested, one third of the classes needed to represent the dataset needed to be added to the ontology, all of them in areas where we expected to see more ontology expansion. Our overall approach is to drive towards completion of coverage while being relatively easy to use for domain experts. Ultimately we aim to have domain experts handle the majority of extensions and evolution with small interactions with ontology experts. In this paper, we report on our on-demand approach for web-based collaborative interdisciplinary ontology development and maintenance and also introduce the resulting extensible and interoperable exposure and child health ontology.

WebSci'17, June 25-28, 2017, Troy, NY, USA.

978-1-4503-4896-6/17/06...$15.00
DOI: http://dx.doi.org/10.1145/3091478.3091497

1 INTRODUCTION

Interdisciplinary science typically requires collaboration across multiple laboratories, often involving people with a wide variety of expertise areas, and it is critical to align data across multiple organizations typically in multiple domains. When these efforts evolve into large scale collaborations, as in the case of the National Institute of Environmental Health Sciences (NIEHS)-funded Children's Health Exposure Analysis Resource (CHEAR), the challenges also increase. In order to support the alignment, we are developing an interdisciplinary ontology addressing issues related to exposure and health at a variety of levels of granularity and from a wide range of perspectives. Challenges arise when developing such an interdisciplinary ontology relating to determining what should be modeled, at what level of detail, what vocabularies, schemas, and ontologies should be used as starting points, what alignments are needed, and what gaps need to be addressed. To manage the representational load and great diversity in content, we have attempted to apply the YAGNI (You Aren't Gonna Need It) principle from software engineering [11], only adding something on demand when we are sure we will need it. One question is how does YAGNI mesh with managing appropriate modeling of diverse data collections resulting from epidemiologically motivated studies? The data that the CHEAR program needs to manage covers several domains, and the data gathered by epidemiologists, while containing some commonalities, is diverse in its consideration of social, environmental, developmental, educational, and other factors, making the potential space of data representation large. These studies are themselves a combination of medical, social, behavioral, and economic data with environmental exposure data, that in turn, covers a broad set of chemical analysis, proteomic, genomic, and epigenomic data.

CHEAR supplements existing epidemiological studies with exposure data in an effort to provide a more holistic setting for data analysis over individual and pooled data. One goal is to provide a resource that includes an integrated representation of many independently-funded studies across the public health domain. In this broad interdisciplinary setting, as in most situations, it was essential to pick a core set of ontologies to provide a starting point. We looked for well used, well designed ontologies that were extensible, that covered key areas, and that were maintained by appropriate groups on which to base our work. In this paper, we report on the very positive experience we had using on-demand approach to ontology generation and maintenance in combination with web standards and enhanced web-based semantic infrastructure. We found that we can facilitate efficient collaboration by supporting and integrating to a common view of data from epidemiology, materials analysis labs, and -omics (proteomics, genomics, and others) specialists to provide a coherent view for data analysts. This paper provides insight into our approach, describes some of the benefits, and also introduces the resulting interdisciplinary and extensible exposure and health ontology.

2 RELATED WORK

While there is a range of related work on which to build, no single ontology and in fact, no set of ontologies adequately covers the breadth and depth needed for exposure science, health, and development as a foundation for integrative data repositories. Only one ontology that we know of provides explicit support for environmental exposures, the Environmental Exposures Ontology (ExO) [18]. It focuses on modeling exposure events, but does not itself support data representation. Other ontologies and knowledge graphs, such as ChEBI [4], PubChem [29], and UniProt [13] provide identifiers for specific chemicals and changes to blood chemistry, but do not model how they relate to outcomes or to conventional epidemiological variables.

2.1 Ontology Development

Much of the current literature on ontology development involves the application of either top-down or bottom-up approaches, specifically the ones reviewed in [14] and [3]. Our approach, called the "Semantic eScience Methodology" [8], initially developed for virtual observatories, proposed a middle out approach, which was use case driven and iterative, and grows the representations into specificity without focusing initially on alignment with an upper level ontology. We extend this approach through two main directions. First, we have developed additional tools to more tightly integrate domain experts into the ongoing ontology development team through use of tabular editing tools. Second, we focus on coverage of data representation for a growing set of studies. We use these studies as use cases to determine requirements and priorities for expansion. Third, we start with a core set of ontologies that provide a common upper- and mid-level ontology representation in appropriate areas. These provide a lens through which to organize our data representation efforts.

2.2 Foundational Ontologies

In order to leverage the existing best practices work from the ontology and relevant domain communities, the CHEAR Ontology builds on several foundational ontologies. The ontologies discussed here are all integrated and organized in the Human-Aware Science Ontology (HAScO) [24], which the CHEAR Ontology in turn imports. The Semanticscience Integrated Ontology (SIO) [5] defines types and relations for objects, processes and attributes, and therefore provides the integrated framework from which the ontology is rooted. SIO is a self-contained ontology that provides support for information resources; as well as hypothetical, fictional, and imaginary entities, and it has seen increasing usage, particularly in biomedical settings. It is not integrated with other ontologies, but we were able to easily integrate it with other ontologies in HAScO. In order to capture the provenance of concepts included in the ontology, such as the source or how a term was generated, we use the World Wide Web Consortium's (W3C)'s [16] recommended language for provenance on the web - the PROV-O ontology. In order to maintain details about data acquisition measurements, such as instruments or analytical methods used, the Virtual Solar Terrestrial Observatory Instruments (VSTOi) Ontology [8] and the Human-Aware Sensor Network Ontology (HASNetO) are leveraged [24]. The Units Ontology (UO) is used to incorporate a taxonomy of both English and Metric units into the ontology [9]. While UO does not cover every possible unit of measure, we have not yet had a need to represent units that go beyond the ones in UO. As with all ontology integration efforts, there were some mismatches in modeling perspectives. For example, while SIO treats units as OWL individuals, UO treats them as classes. We solved this mismatch using punning (in OWL 2) the UO classes to individuals as they are used. For terms related to chemical entities and anatomy, we turn to the Chemical Entities of Biological Interest (CheBI) [4] and Uberon multi-species anatomy [23] ontologies, respectively. CHeBI contains a large fraction of the chemicals analyzed in CHEAR, but not yet all of them. CHeBI's entities are well-defined with useful data about chemical structure, biological roles, and other details. We replicated the CHeBI style for the entities that we needed to add and also submitted extension requests to the CHeBI team for future integration, but in the meantime, those terms are in our CHEAR ontology. We also use PubChem [15] as a source of additional chemical entities that aren't yet in CheBI. Uberon contains all of the biospecimen types that we expect to be processing in CHEAR, except for buccal cells. The disease ontology (DO) [27] and ExO provide good starting points for capturing disease and exposure terms. While DO is not as comprehensive as ICD, it is focused on a more scientific treatment of diseases, instead of classifying diseases for medical administrative purposes, which has been the primary use case of ICD. Our statistical classes, especially variable types (like z-score) and methods are borrowed on demand from the Statistics Ontology (STATO).[1] Finally, we use properties from the Simple Knowledge Organization System (SKOS) [22] and The Dublin Core Terms (DC-Terms) [12] vocabularies to annotate classes in our ontology.

3 DEVELOPMENT METHODS

We developed the CHEAR ontology by extending the Human-Aware Science Ontology (HAScO)[2] (which in turn integrates the PROV-O and SIO ontologies). HAScO provides a standardized base for many of our scientific data-oriented projects, and serves as the integration point for our core science ontologies. HAScO contains concepts for representing various studies, as well as the data acquisition process,

[1] http://stato-ontology.org/
[2] http://hadatac.org/ont/hasco/

Table 1: Table of ontologies used in the CHEAR Ontology organized by role. Imported ontologies are adopted wholesale into CHEAR, while Annotation ontologies are used for concept metadata. MIREOT (Minimum Information to Reference and External Ontology Term) ontologies have been identified as on-demand sources for ontology extension. These ontologies are compatible with CHEAR-O, and some of their classes have been included in CHEAR-O using MIREOT principles [2].

Role	Ontology	Prefix	URI
Imported	SIO [5]	sio	http://semanticscience.org/resource/
	PROV-O [16]	prov	http://www.w3.org/ns/prov#
	Units Ontology [9]	uo	http://purl.obolibrary.org/obo/UO_
	HAScO [24]	hasco	http://hadatac.org/ont/hasco#
	HASNetO [24]	hasneto	http://hadatac.org/ont/hasneto#
	VSTO-I [8]	vstoi	http://hadatac.org/ont/vstoi#
Annotation	SKOS [22]	skos	http://www.w3.org/2004/02/skos/core#
	DC Terms [12]	dc	http://purl.org/dc/terms/
MIREOT	CheBI [4]	chebi	http://purl.obolibrary.org/obo/CHEBI_
	STATO	stato	http://purl.obolibrary.org/obo/STATO_
	PubChem [15]	pubchem	http://rdf.ncbi.nlm.nih.gov/pubchem/compound/
	Uberon [23]	uberon	http://purl.obolibrary.org/obo/UBERON_
	Disease Ontology	do	http://purl.obolibrary.org/obo/DOID_

including instruments, deployments and platforms involved. From a web semantics standpoint, HAScO provides a schema for modeling the acquisition process and attributes, which in turn allows for mapping of study variables to ontology concepts. This gives us our foundation on which we base our ontology work. We then map terms to each other as needed and identify ontology term gaps that must be filled by reviewing the CHEAR data specifications and the CHEAR study data dictionaries, codebook terms and laboratory information. We use LabKey [3], a web-based Laboratory Information Management System (LIMS), to gather and curate class definitions, annotations, and hierarchies. LabKey is also used to manage identifiers for subjects and samples across CHEAR studies. LabKey supports creation of "lists", essentially spreadsheets, that we use to generate the ontology from a Semantic Extract, Transform, and Load (SETL) process that is described for SETLr.[4] Both domain experts and ontology engineers have been using the web-based LabKey lists as the means to collaborate on ontology development by contributing and reviewing ontology definitions. SETLr is a tool for transforming data from tabular, Extensible Markup Language (XML), and JavaScript Object Notation (JSON) data sources into Resource Description Framework (RDF). This approach of building the ontology from class definitions curated in a LIMS allows domain experts to provide content for and review the ontology within a tabular format, organized through tables of things like analyte types, sample types, roles, and epidemiological attributes. It does this by using ETL-like workflows and templating based on existing web and semantic standards, like JSON-Linked Data (JSON-LD) [1], PROV-O [16], and python libraries like Pandas [21], Jinja2[5], and RDFlib.[6]

The overall process is detailed in Figure 1. For CHEAR, we primarily focus on the representational needs of the Pilot Study data dictionaries and codebooks, as well as the data reporting templates created by the CHEAR program. For each potential class we identify, we first check the ontology and foundational ontologies to see if there is an adequate class. If there is an exact match, we note it in a mapping table. If there is a partial match, we subclass that match with the needed specialization. New classes are added to one of several LabKey lists, depending on the subtree it is part of. We have lists in LabKey for subtypes of object, attribute, role, sample, analyte, and process. More complex class definitions that are not yet supported by the SETLr conversion process are included as ontology fragments in Turtle. The SETL script enumerates the fragments and LabKey lists and processes them all into a single RDF graph. The classes and their definitions, labels, and alternate labels are reviewed by domain experts, and the lists are processed by SETLr to create a generated ontology. This ontology is imported into HADatAC, where curators and reviewers can further comment on it. That feedback is incorporated into LabKey as well.

The resulting ontology is published to the web. [7] This initial ontology was developed using five pilot studies that were determined to be representative of the studies that are anticipated to be submitted to the CHEAR program. The five pilot studies consisted of four prospective birth cohorts and a clinical study of pediatric allergic disease. In order to represent the expected future studies that would enroll in CHEAR, the pilot studies were selected to cover multiple health outcomes and multiple critical windows of exposure and development including pregnancy, early infancy and childhood. The birth cohorts included questionnaire and biological data on mother-child pairs while the clinical study also included treatment data extracted from the child's medical record. One of the birth cohorts was conducted within an international study population. While all pilot studies had stored biospecimens that would be analyzed within the CHEAR laboratories, the biological matrices (sample types) varied by study and included serum, urine and placenta.

With each study, we added classes that were determined to be necessary to represent the data as presented in those studies. As

[3] http://www.labkey.com/
[4] https://github.com/tetherless-world/setlr/
[5] http://jinja.pocoo.org
[6] http://rdflib.readthedocs.io

[7] http://hadatatac.org/ont/chear/

we accept more studies, the CHEAR ontology will be expanded to support those studies. We anticipate a long-tail function in the need to create additional classes, once we have covered the most common classes. This long tail is consistent with the YAGNI principle - the most commonly needed capabilities are introduced at first, and as new capabilities are needed, that are added to the system (or ontology, in our case).

We have initial evidence that this approach is working well. We used one of the initial pilot studies to evaluate coverage for the required terms. We had excellent coverage except in two areas (fertility methods and BMI rating categories), where we had not attempted to provide any modeling primitives, so this gap was anticipated. Based on the evaluation, we had 74% coverage of demographics, 100% coverage of environmental exposures, and 57% of health/disease outcomes. Given the small number of initial pilot studies and the anticipated gap filling requirements for diseases as related content emerges, we were impressed with these statistics. As we reviewed one additional birth-cohort pilot we found similar results. We had approximately 67% total coverage.The primary gaps were in investigator-defined categorizations of existing concepts, like education.

We found the ontology useful to anyone who needs to model data in epidemiology, especially with studies that perform significant sample analysis. It is ready to be used as a public health data interchange standard, and we expect that studies that use the ontology will find most of the classes they need in it. We are actively recruiting users of the ontology and are encouraging requests if the ontology is missing terminology needed to cover study data in the general areas of exposure and child health.

We did not need to add any new properties to the CHEAR ontology, as the approach of SIO is to create new attributes as objects rather than statements. This also allows us to add information about when the attribute was determined (*sio:measuredAt*), if the attribute was measured in relation to something else (*sio:inRelationTo*), what the unit of measure is (*sio:hasUnit*), (for instance, concentration of a substance in relation to the sample the substance is from), as well as provenance information, like what other measurements (or other objects) an attribute is derived from (*prov:wasDerivedFrom*) and what methods were used (*prov:wasGeneratedBy*).

In Figures 2, 3, 4, and 5 we show how fundamental types of data are represented. Figure 2 shows how child, mother, study, and household relate in a set of core social/familial relationships, using subclasses of *sio:Role* and the *sio:hasRole*. Figure 3 shows how basic measurements are expressed via subclasses of *sio:TimeInterval*. Anthropometry attributes, like head circumference, are expressed on objects that are a type of head (from the UBERON Ontology) that have an attribute of *sio:Circumference*. The head objects are then stated to be *sio:isPartOf* the subject the measurement was taken from. Figure 4 shows how laboratory analysis can be expressed, by deriving a sample from the subject, and expressing the sio:Concentration (*sio:inRelationTo* the sample) of a particular molecular entity. Most of these entities are identified in either ChEBI or in PubChem. Figure 5 shows how the most common genomic, transcriptomic, and epigenomic data can be represented. The figure covers Single Nucleotide Polymorphisms (SNPs) and Variations (SNVs), genomic region Copy Number Variations (CNVs), gene expression, and regulatory site methylation fraction.

The ontology was developed initially using the CMap Ontology Edition (COE) tool to model coverage of the initial four pilot studies in the CHEAR program with a data scientist/ontologist and an epidemiologist. This was aggregated into a set of lists stored in LabKey, broken out by subtrees in the ontology. These lists continue to be curated by data scientists, epidemiologists, and ontologists to extend and improve the ontology as needed. The official ontology is generated using the Semantic Extract, Transform, and Load-r (SETLr) by writing an ontological interpretation of the lists and their columns. A number of classes, like Z-Fenton Birth Weight [7], BMI, and others have been enriched with extended OWL restrictions that are difficult to express in a tabular format. We include those definitions in OWL/RDF fragments that are combined during the SETL process. The resulting ontology is published (with incremented versioning) at http://hadatac.org/ont/chear/, and is used by the HADatAc (Human Aware Data Acquisition Framework) system as a basis for ingesting data from the CHEAR program for search, discovery, and curation.

While our approach does not attempt a one to one mapping of ontology concepts to datasets, we attempt to provide the ability to compose descriptions of specific measurements, like "Mother's Pre-Pregnancy BMI" from concepts contained in the ontology. A dataset could be annotated with a formal definition that uses OWL property restrictions that *compose* into the attribute of interest. For example, the OWL Manchester notation [10] for "Mother's Pre-Pregnancy BMI" (here encoded as a column called "MPPBMI") would be:

```
Class: MPPBMI
SubClassOf: chear:BMI,
  sio:measuredAt only chear:PrePregnancy,
  sio:isAttributeOf only (
    sio:hasRole some (
     chear:Mother and sio:inRelationTo only chear:Child
    )
  )
```

Similarly, *chear:BMI* is defined in terms of the attributes it uses, and records the required unit of measure:

```
class: chear:BMI
SubClassOf: sio:Quantity,
  prov:wasDerivedFrom some sio:Height,
  prov:wasDerivedFrom some sio:Mass,
  sio:hasUnit value uo:000086 # kg/m^2
```

This allows us to be much more flexible in how we map data from a given study into the CHEAR Ontology. Concentrating on mapping many data sets to one single conceptual structure serves the semantic web goal of interoperability: any dataset for which the mapping is completed has a mapping to the SIO conceptualization, and can be compared to any other dataset that has also been mapped.

4 EVALUATION

We attempted to annotate a new pilot study with the CHEAR ontology as a way to determine what the coverage of the current version of the ontology was. Our epidemiologist created an initial semantic version of a data dictionary with our lead ontology expert.

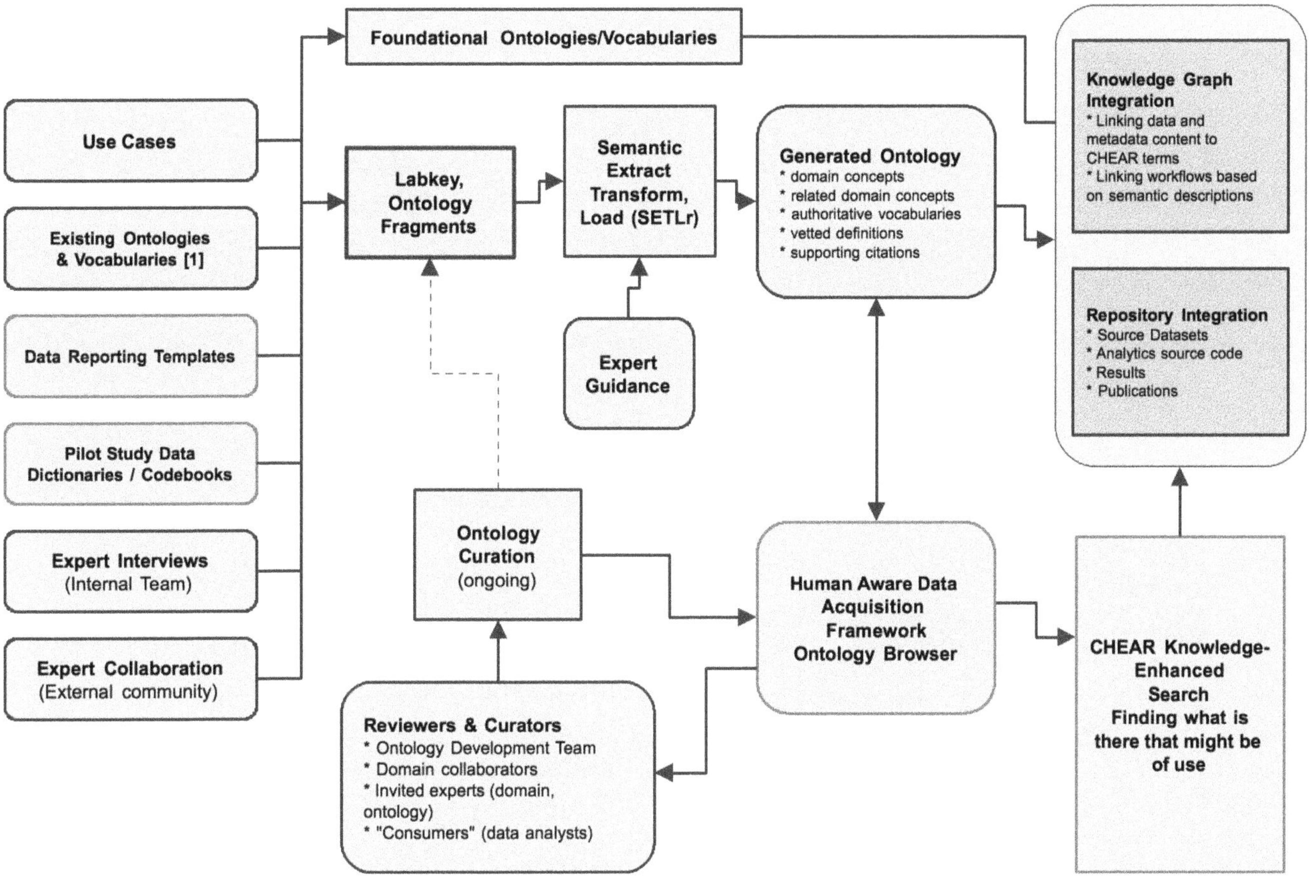

Figure 1: Ontology Development process for the CHEAR Ontology.

The epidemiologist indicated where classes were missing from the ontology and wrote suggested concepts and definitions.

The annotated data dictionary was then curated by an ontology expert to correct any mistakes, which were minimal, and to find existing terms in our adopted ontologies only minor corrections needed by an ontology expert. Of the 96 classes used to represent the data, we needed to introduce 32 new classes, 16 of which were in the study codebook, mapping enumerated values to attributes. Additionally, of the 32 new classes, 11 of them mapped into existing classes in the set of MIREOT ontologies.

We find this level of class introduction is acceptable for early stage ontology development. The new classes will be released in the CHEAR Ontology version 0.9,[8] while the version of the ontology used for analysis is version 0.8.[9]

5 DISCUSSION

The YAGNI principle has been a guiding force for prioritizing capabilities in software. As the name "You aren't gonna need it" implies, this principle recommends incorporation of only essential functionality. While sometimes it can result in technical debt due to a lack of foresight, when properly managed and paired with a long term vision of how a work will grow, can result in powerful and relevant software. YAGNI can sometimes result in technical debt. However, vision does not need to immediately lead to implementation. Maintaining a long-term vision of how the software or ontology will grow while only implementing what is immediately needed helps keep scope and, as the vision's elements become relevant, also validates that vision.

Similarly, we found that when it was applied to ontology development, YAGNI can quickly find the most relevant classes to model, and when paired with a useful set of core ontologies, can create a monotonic development process, minimizing the need to change existing classes. This approach of on-demand ontology extension has proven to us to be a scalable approach, since, as new data comes in, fewer and fewer classes are needed. New classes have fit easily within existing ones. One component with significant variability is the mention and encoding of education level as granuarlity varies rather significantly and education paths also vary in different countries, so not surprisingly, education level has been encoded quite differently in some datasets. We did find that we could leverage the general monotonicity of education - one generally completes previous grade levels before proceeding to more advanced grades. There were some challenges around aligning education levels and terminologies across countries. We found the

[8] http://hadatac.org/ont/chear/0.9/
[9] http://hadatac.org/ont/chear/0.8/

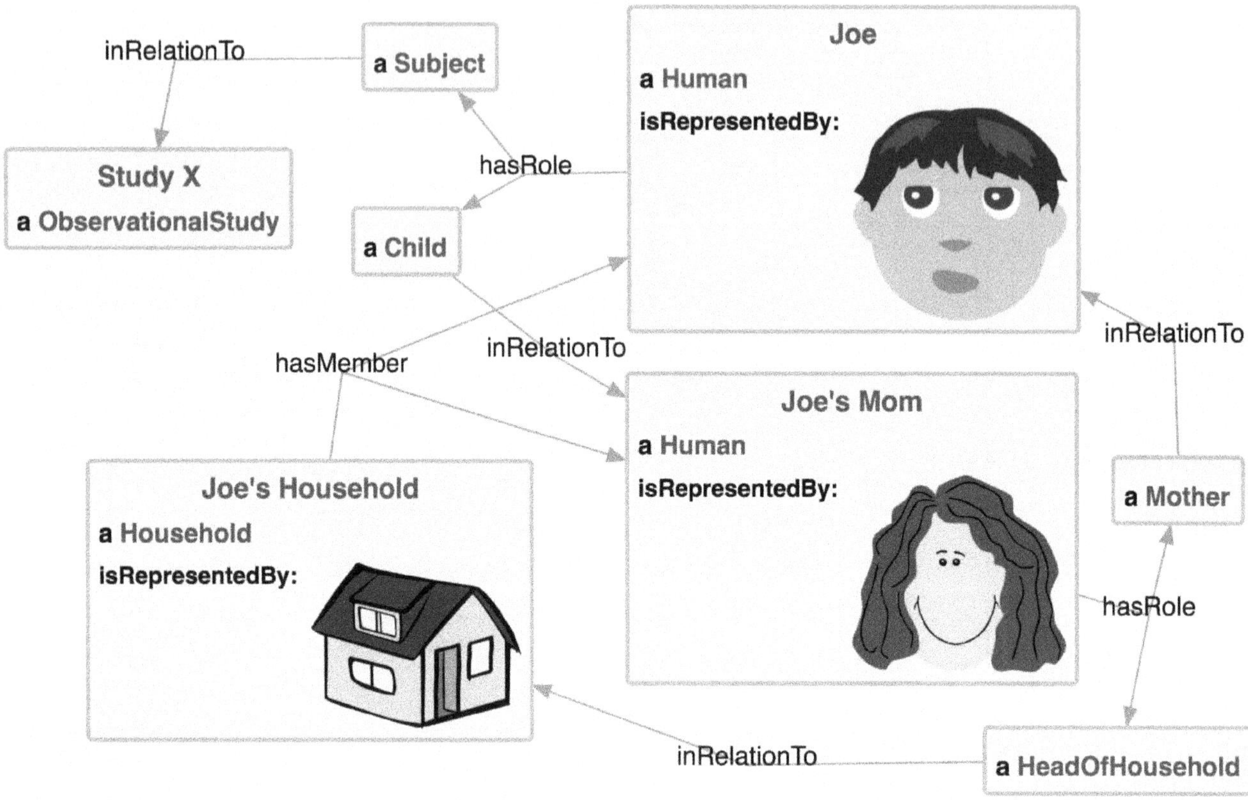

Figure 2: Representation of Familial Roles and Relations. Roles (Child, Subject, Mother, Head of Household) link entities (Joe, Joe's Mom, Joe's Household) together via *sio:hasRole* and *sio:inRelationTo*. Household membership is indicated via *sio:hasMember*.

combination of PROV-O, SIO, HAScO, and HASNetO to be a very useful core ontology set for describing scientific data. In fact, we found it to provide almost surprisingly good coverage for the types of studies we have seen so far. Coverage of entities, roles, attributes, samples, lab analysis variables, instruments, methods, and even -omics data was straightforward to model.

5.1 Representation Considerations

There are a number of representations that might be common to some data representation-driven ontologies, but are not used in the CHEAR Ontology. The term "observation" has been used with a range of meanings and it can be ambiguous and sometimes misleading. Because we record attributes as reified objects, they mostly serve in the role that observation objects might, including time of measurement, provenance of the attribute, unit of measure, and other attributes. This approach is consistent with the use of ontologies that attempt to model the world as described, as opposed to language-oriented ontologies, that attempt to model the description of the world.

We subscribe, for the purposes of this ontology, to Platonic realism, where classes are allowed to be made that predict unobserved, hypothetical instances in the world, or fictional instances that are marked as such. This form of scientific realism, which SIO was designed for, was laid out in [6]. We therefore borrow, at times from ontologies that, in their details, align well with SIO, even if their upper level ontologies do not follow quite the same philosophical underpinnings.

One important consideration to make when using this approach is to carefully pick the foundational ontologies that are used. When dealing with ontologies that may have different approaches to representation, it may be necessary to select subtrees from an ontology to use. If the ontology outright prohibits that approach by including statements that lead to reasoning contradictions, it may be necessary to take relevant subtrees, and, where allowed by license, duplicate them with references to the source. For instance, if a conceptual ontology, like SNOMED-CT [28], LOINC [20], or MeSH [17] has a useful, consistent subtree that can be used in a realist ontology, a 1:1 mapping can be made using SPARQL queries into an ontology module. Each class can be related back to the originating URI using a property from the Conceptual Model Ontology (CMO) called *hasPrimaryConcept* [19]. CMO provides a generalized framework for associating realist ontologies that focus on data models with conceptual ontologies that are often used for coding or similar applications. Attribution can also be used by stating that the copy *prov:wasDerivedFrom* the original version.

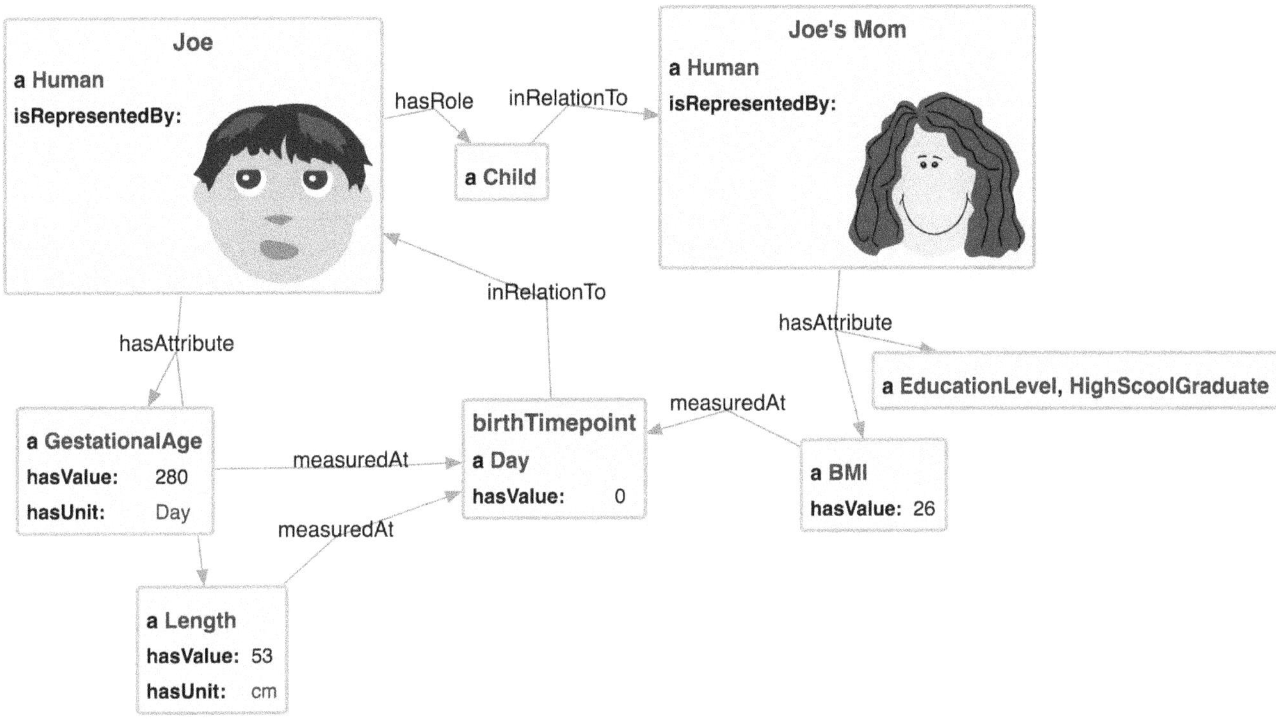

Figure 3: Time Interval Representation of Measurements. Most epidemiological attributes are measurements, here we show Gestational Age at birth, length at birth, and mother's BMI at birth. They are all related to the birth timepoint, measured in days. The mother's attribute of education level, being a High School graduate, is shown without a timepoint.

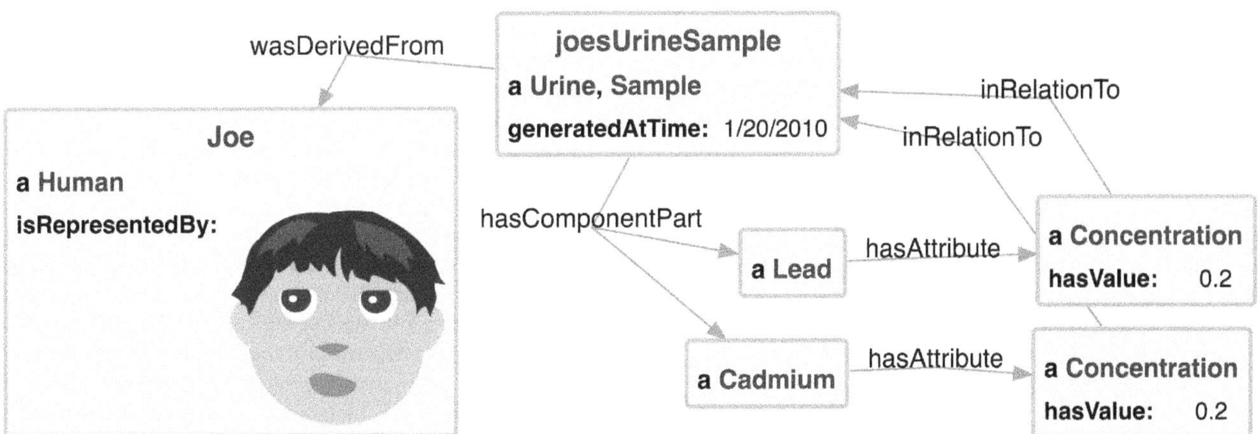

Figure 4: Representation of Analyte Concentrations in relation to a Human Derived Urine Sample. Most of the biomarker data in CHEAR is in the form of chemical analysis of elements and other analytes in blood, urine, and other sample types. We identify the component parts of the sample (Lead, Cadmium), and give them concentrations in relation to the sample itself, which was *prov:wasDerivedFrom* Joe.

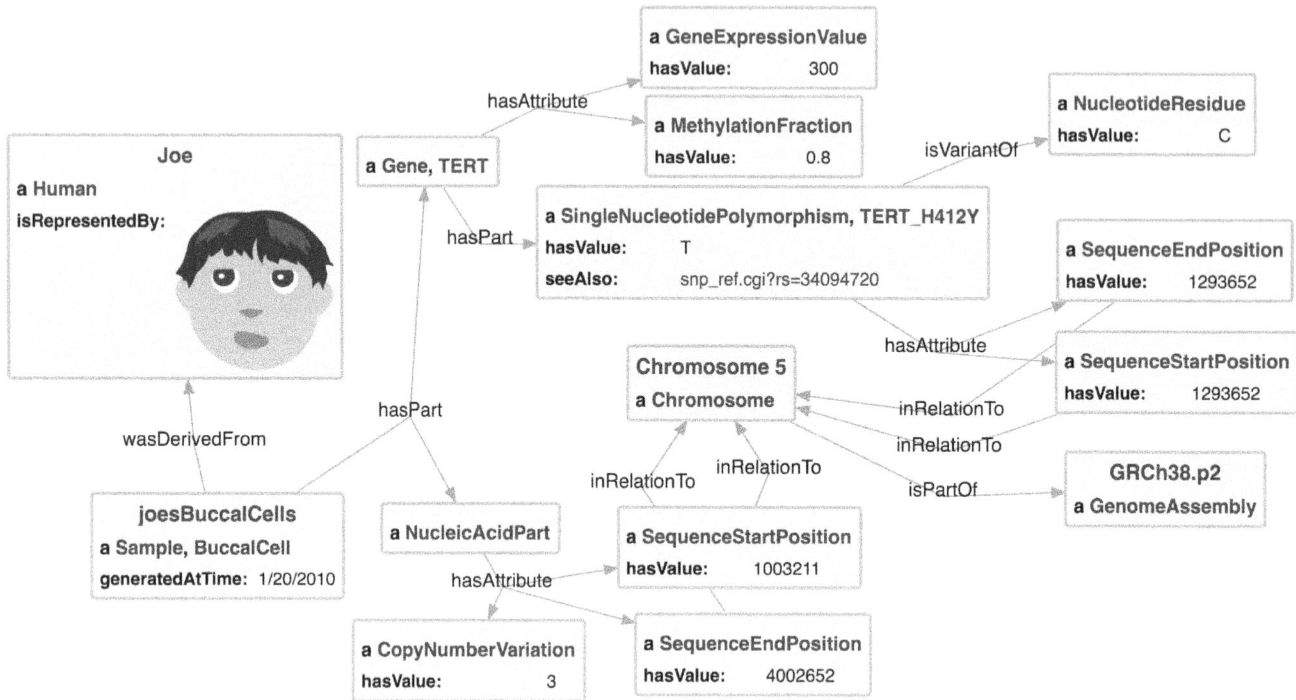

Figure 5: Representation of Genomic, Transcriptomic and Epigenomic Data. Finally, we are able to represent a wide array of genomic data using SIO's genomics modeling capabilities. Joe has a mutation on his TERT gene at on chromosome 5 at position 12993652, and that gene is part of a DNA region that has an extra copy on one chromosome. The data was against a Buccal Cell sample (often used for genomics analysis), derived from Joe.

We were also able to resolve differences in perspective between domains. For instance, in epidemiology, the term "metals" refers to any element that reacts biologically in the way that metals do. This therefore includes metalloids. We introduced a "metals an metalloids" class, into the CHEAR ontology, and since it is familiar to epidemiologists as "metals", we gave it the URI *chear:Metal*. It is not equivalent to *CHEBI:33521* (metal atom), but instead has metals and metalloids as subclasses. Additionally, we found it necessary to provide high-level classes for attributes, entities, and processes that relate to specific areas of interest within epidemiology. These classes are parallel to, but have no bearing on, the subsumption hierarchies of the domain-specific ontologies.

6 FUTURE WORK

We plan to build a much larger expansion of the CHEAR Ontology by attempting to model many key National Health and Nutrition Examination Survey (NHANES) [25] data dictionaries, which cover a number of epidemiological domains over many decades. NHANES includes datasets pertaining to other categories that are of interest to CHEAR research, including concepts related to dietary, laboratory and examination measures. We also plan to incorporate metabolite classes into the analyte hierarchy from the Reference Metabolite (RefMet) database from Metabolomics workbench.[10]

[10]http://www.metabolomicsworkbench.org/data/refmet.php

Additional near term expansion areas for analytes include inflammation and oxidative stress.

One future goal is to create Semantic Data Dictionaries for the variables described in these datasets, in order to expand the range of concepts included in the CHEAR Ontology. A Semantic Data Dictionary will provide a formal means to map dataset columns into a compositional structure like the ones used in our examples. It will do so in a way that allows us to produce 1) OWL-based metadata for those datasets, creating explicitly defined classes that dataset columns map to, and 2) RDF data, or formal mappings of data to RDF, for the actual data that is described by the data dictionary that conforms to the OWL metadata we create. These Semantic Data Dictionaries are an expansion of the mapping process we used on the pilot data, and currently require human curation. For some studies, like NHANES, tools for web scraping can be used, such as the Python library Beautiful Soup [26], allowing for automatic population of variable names, labels, and definitions. Nevertheless, automating the population of entities, roles or relations that correspond to the variable cannot be accomplished simply by using web scraping techniques. Thus, an additional research direction is to leverage Natural Language Processing (NLP) methods to extract potential semantic qualities of variables from their label and description. Further, in preliminary discussions, we have found that it may be helpful to provide pre-populated starting points for the most commonly used data. Domain experts could then customize the mapping to their own studies. Further, we plan to produce a number of Semantic Data Dictionaries to describe the data specifications that the CHEAR program is already developing for different kinds of laboratory analysis results, where appropriate.

7 CONCLUSIONS

We presented a new ontology for *in tela* integration of knowledge and data in global health and exposure research, called the CHEAR Ontology. We showed that it is possible and efficient to apply on-demand development approaches from agile software development (You Aren't Going to Need It) to developing broad, interdisciplinary ontologies. This process was facilitated through web-based collaboration of researchers from multiple domains. We were able to converge on a common data representation standard that covers the most commonly used data within the CHEAR program, with clear room for expansion to cover other types as they are needed. Using this approach, we generated an ontology that is ready for reuse that provides coverage in the areas of exposure and child health and that is compatible with many of the most widely used best practice ontologies and/or vocabularies in relevant areas. We are actively seeking partners and users for the ontology and welcome collaborators on the web-based semantic framework for on-demand ontology evolution and maintenance environments.

8 ACKNOWLEDGEMENTS

This work was funded by the National Institute of Environmental Health Sciences (NIEHS) Award 0255-0236-4609 / 1U2CES026555-01. We would like to thank Susan Teitelbaum at the Icahn School of Medicine at Mount Sinai for her leadership on the overall CHEAR data resource project, guidance in exposure and health domains, and feedback on the paper and ontology.

REFERENCES

[1] Consortium, W. W. W., et al. Json-ld 1.0: a json-based serialization for linked data.
[2] Courtot, M., Gibson, F., Lister, A. L., Malone, J., Schober, D., Brinkman, R. R., and Ruttenberg, A. Mireot: The minimum information to reference an external ontology term. *Applied Ontology 6*, 1 (2011), 23–33.
[3] Cristani, M., and Cuel, R. A survey on ontology creation methodologies. *International Journal on Semantic Web and Information Systems (IJSWIS) 1*, 2 (2005), 49–69.
[4] Degtyarenko, K., De Matos, P., Ennis, M., Hastings, J., Zbinden, M., McNaught, A., Alcántara, R., Darsow, M., Guedj, M., and Ashburner, M. Chebi: a database and ontology for chemical entities of biological interest. *Nucleic acids research 36*, suppl 1 (2008), D344–D350.
[5] Dumontier, M., Baker, C. J., Baran, J., Callahan, A., Chepelev, L., Cruz-Toledo, J., Del Rio, N. R., Duck, G., Furlong, L. I., Keath, N., Klassen, D., McCusker, J. P., Queralt-Rosinach, N., Samwald, M., Villanueva-Rosales, N., Wilkinson, M. D., and Hoehndorf, R. The semanticscience integrated ontology (sio) for biomedical research and knowledge discovery. *Journal of Biomedical Semantics 5*, 1 (2014), 14.
[6] Dumontier, M., and Hoehndorf, R. Realism for scientific ontologies. In *FOIS* (2010), pp. 387-399.
[7] Fenton, T., and Sauve, R. Using the lms method to calculate z-scores for the fenton preterm infant growth chart. *European journal of clinical nutrition 61*, 12 (2007), 1380–1385.
[8] Fox, P., McGuinness, D. L., Cinquini, L., West, P., Garcia, J., Benedict, J. L., and Middleton, D. Ontology-supported scientific data frameworks: The virtual solar-terrestrial observatory experience. *Computers & Geosciences 35*, 4 (2009), 724–738.
[9] Gkoutos, G. V., Schofield, P. N., and Hoehndorf, R. The units ontology: a tool for integrating units of measurement in science. *Database 2012* (2012), bas033.
[10] Horridge, M., and Patel-Schneider, P. F. Owl 2 web ontology language manchester syntax. *W3C Working Group Note* (2009).
[11] Hunt, A., and Thomas, D. The trip-packing dilemma [agile software development]. *IEEE Software 20*, 3 (May 2003), 106–107.
[12] Initiative, D. C. M., et al. DCMI metadata terms. *http://purl.org/dc/terms/* (2012).
[13] Jain, E., Bairoch, A., Duvaud, S., Phan, I., Redaschi, N., Suzek, B. E., Martin, M. J., McGarvey, P., and Gasteiger, E. Infrastructure for the life sciences: design and implementation of the uniprot website. *BMC bioinformatics 10*, 1 (2009), 136.
[14] JONES, D., BENCH-CAPON, T., and VISSER, P. Methodologies for ontology development. In *IFIP world computer congress* (1998), pp. 62–75.
[15] Kim, S., Thiessen, P. A., Bolton, E. E., Chen, J., Fu, G., Gindulyte, A., Han, L., He, J., He, S., Shoemaker, B. A., et al. Pubchem substance and compound databases. *Nucleic acids research* (2015), gkv951.
[16] Lebo, T., Sahoo, S., and McGuinness, D. PROV-O: The PROV Ontology. http://www.w3.org/TR/prov-o/, 2013.
[17] Lipscomb, C. E. Medical subject headings (mesh). *Bulletin of the Medical Library Association 88*, 3 (2000), 265.
[18] Mattingly, C. J., McKone, T. E., Callahan, M. A., Blake, J. A., and Hubal, E. A. C. Providing the missing link: the exposure science ontology exo, 2012.
[19] McCusker, J. P., Luciano, J. S., and McGuinness, D. L. Towards an ontology for conceptual modeling. In *ICBO* (2011).
[20] McDonald, C. J., Huff, S. M., Suico, J. G., Hill, G., Leavelle, D., Aller, R., Forrey, A., Mercer, K., DeMoor, G., Hook, J., et al. Loinc, a universal standard for identifying laboratory observations: a 5-year update. *Clinical chemistry 49*, 4 (2003), 624–633.
[21] McKinney, W., et al. Data structures for statistical computing in python. In *Proceedings of the 9th Python in Science Conference* (2010), vol. 445, van der Voort S, Millman J, pp. 51–56.
[22] Miles, A., and Bechhofer, S. SKOS Simple Knowledge Organization System Reference, 2009.
[23] Mungall, C. J., Torniai, C., Gkoutos, G. V., Lewis, S. E., and Haendel, M. A. Uberon, an integrative multi-species anatomy ontology. *Genome biology 13*, 1 (2012), R5.
[24] Pinheiro, P., McGuinness, D. L., and Santos, H. Human-aware sensor network ontology: semantic support for empirical data collection. In *Proceedings of the 5th Workshop on Linked Science. Bethlehem, PA, USA* (2015).
[25] Pirkle, J. L., Brody, D. J., Gunter, E. W., Kramer, R. A., Paschal, D. C., Flegal, K. M., and Matte, T. D. The decline in blood lead levels in the united states: the national health and nutrition examination surveys (nhanes). *Jama 272*, 4 (1994), 284–291.
[26] Richardson, L. Beautiful soup documentation, 2007.
[27] Schriml, L. M., Arze, C., Nadendla, S., Chang, Y.-W. W., Mazaitis, M., Felix, V., Feng, G., and Kibbe, W. A. Disease ontology: a backbone for disease semantic integration. *Nucleic Acids Research 40*, D1 (2012), D940.
[28] Snomed, C. Systematized nomenclature of medicine-clinical terms. *International Health Terminology Standards Development Organisation* (2011).
[29] Wang, Y., Xiao, J., Suzek, T. O., Zhang, J., Wang, J., and Bryant, S. H. Pubchem: a public information system for analyzing bioactivities of small molecules. *Nucleic acids research 37*, suppl 2 (2009), W623–W633.

A Turn for the Scruffy: An Ethnographic Study of Semantic Web Architecture

Lindsay Poirier
Rensselaer Polytechnic Institute
110 8th St.
Troy, New York 12180
poiril@rpi.edu

ABSTRACT

This paper examines how legacies of thinking about ontology, logic, and how best to approach knowledge representation have become interwoven in the architecture of the technologies that enable a Semantic Web. As a cultural anthropologist, I approach this study with qualitative historical and ethnographic methodologies, positioning the community of researchers that have been involved in the design and implementation of Semantic Web protocols and technologies as my primary field site. Two concepts from Science and Technology Studies are introduced - thought styles and design logics. The paper demonstrates how diverse thinking about how to approach knowledge representation on the Web is rooted in debates that emerged in artificial intelligence in the 1970s and 1980s. It then goes on to discuss how the diverse approaches to Web semantics that emerged from these legacies have cultural and political implications. The paper concludes with a call for further research that positions Web architectures as objects of social and cultural study.

CCS CONCEPTS

• **Social and professional topics → History of computing theory**; **Cultural characteristics**; *Historical people*; • **Information systems →** *Resource Description Framework (RDF)*; *Web Ontology Language (OWL)*; • **Theory of computation →** *Description logics*;

KEYWORDS

Semantic Web, Logic, Science and Technology Studies, Thought Styles, Design Logics

1 INTRODUCTION

This paper examines how legacies of thinking about how best to represent knowledge to a machine have become interwoven in the architecture of the World Wide Web and the technologies that support and extend it. In particular, it demonstrates how different styles of thinking about ontology, logic, and how best to approach knowledge representation - styles of thinking that are rooted in debates that emerged in the artificial intelligence community in the 1970s and 1980s - have shaped the design of protocols and technologies that enable machines to integrate and interpret meaning from Web data. These protocols and technologies, which include the Resource Description Framework (RDF), the Web Ontology Language (OWL), as well as a variety of schemas, controlled vocabularies, and knowledge bases, constitute the "Semantic Web." [2] The paper concludes that, in moving knowledge representation onto the Web, the field has taken a turn for the "scruffy" and that this has important implications for how Web users access, integrate, and make sense of Web knowledge.

This study is guided in part by recent literature emerging at the intersection of Information Studies and Science and Technology Studies (STS). This literature argues that, in order to understand the technological, political, and social implications of information infrastructures, we need to first understand the assumptions, values, and knowledge work that have oriented their design. [5, 15] In this literature, information infrastructures are defined as fundamentally relational; they represent a series of relationships that emerge as a result of organized practice. [48] Much like the Web, information infrastructures are more than the sum of their parts; instead, they "emerge" from complex socio-technical processes. [43]

Two concepts from STS can be used to examine how legacies of thinking impacted the design of the Semantic Web as an information infrastructure. First, drawing on the work of Ludwig Fleck, it is possible to show how designers of protocols and technologies for the World Wide Web bring different "thought styles" - or perceptions and dispositions - to their work. [17] Second, these thought styles are eventually codified into various "design logics" - or design directives oriented by the assumptions and commitments that a design community brings to their work. [21, 44]

Today Semantic Web technologies are having a significant impact on how Web search engines query the Web and display Web information to users. At a time when there is considerable debate about how information should be curated and filtered, particularly in light of concerns about "fake news," theorizing how the design of Web information infrastructure impacts how computers interpret, integrate, and move information is a significant undertaking for Web Science. Further, a great deal of research in Web Science relies on Web data classified and structured according to these architectures; in order to characterize how diverse users interact with and build out the Web using this data, Web Scientists need to understand how legacies of thinking have shaped particular architectural designs and how this implicates whose knowledge gets represented on the Web and how it gets represented. This research is currently being taken up in different ways by researchers in STS, information studies, the digital humanities [24], and emerging interdisciplinary

WebSci'17, , June 25-28, 2017, Troy, NY, USA.

ACM ISBN 978-1-4503-4896-6/17/06...$15.00
https://doi.org/10.1145/3091478.3091505

subfields (such as information infrastructure studies [5, 15], software studies [23], critical code studies [37], platform studies [41], and Internet studies [33]) but has been cited only sparsely in the field of Web Science. Drawing on arguments that have emerged in this literature, the paper concludes with a call for further research in Web Science that aims to put the design of Web architecture into historical, cultural, and political context.

2 METHODOLOGY

As a cultural anthropologist, I approached this study with qualitative historical and ethnographic methodologies, positioning the community of researchers that have been involved in the design and implementation of Semantic Web protocols and technologies as my primary field site. Trained in experimental ethnography, STS, and information technology and Web Science, I aimed to examine the cultural, historical, and infrastructural conditions that have shaped the design of the Semantic Web's infrastructure, as well as how the designers of the Semantic Web have engaged the ontological, epistemological, and technical limits of data integration.

The analysis conducted in this paper is based on two years of fieldwork with the Semantic Web community. First, I conducted 15 interviews with researchers and practitioners that have been closely involved in standardizing protocols for the Semantic Web. Some of these interviews were conducted at Web-related academic conferences and other interviews were conducted virtually. In the first half of each interview, interviewees were asked oral history questions and went on to recount how they became involved in the Semantic Web community, which individuals had most influenced their thinking about the structure and function of the Semantic Web, and how they recalled their experience working on W3C committees for standardizing Semantic Web protocols. In the second half of each interview, I asked interviewees to reflect on the Semantic Web's enduring challenges, recalling which lines of research they perceived to have been the most productive in advancing the Semantic Web and which had been distracting. I asked researchers to describe how they dealt with semantic disagreement and how much structure they deemed necessary for making the Semantic Web productive.

From interview responses, I learned that many Semantic Web researchers had been trained in the field of knowledge representation and had been influenced by many of the founders of this field. A common theme that emerged from interviews was that the Semantic Web community has been divided into different camps - each with different aims and ideas for how to make the Semantic Web useful and different understandings of how semantics should be formalized. In order to further examine the genealogies of these divisions, I went on to review a number of primary materials - journal articles, conference proceedings, and magazine articles from the 1970s through the early 1990s - in which knowledge representation researchers discussed the debates cited by those individuals I had interviewed. I also traversed the archives of several years of W3C public forums that documented the development of RDF, OWL, and other linked data technologies, aiming to examine how different legacies of thinking influenced specific arguments that emerged in the design of these standards. Throughout this archival work, I focused primarily on examining the conversations around technical disagreements that interviewees had referenced during our interviews. The research presented in this paper is thus based interview data, primary materials documenting historical rifts in the field of knowledge representation, and archival data documenting the development of Semantic Web standards. In analyzing these materials, I found two concepts from the field of STS - *thought styles* and *design logics* - to be useful in characterizing how cultural, historical, and infrastructural conditions shaped the design of the infrastructure.

3 THOUGHT STYLES AND DESIGN LOGICS

In their seminal article "A Manifesto for Web Science?" Halford, Pope, and Carr outline several concepts from social scientific theory that can be leveraged to advance understanding of the Web. [27] Notably, many of these concepts come from the field of Science and Technology Studies (STS). The concept that society and technology are "co-constituted" is rooted in conversations in STS concerned with challenging the extent to which social factors *determine* the design of technology, as well as the extent to which technological factors *determine* social organization. Halford, Pope, and Carr argue, "The point of co-constitution, then, is to look at how technology and society shape each other. In web science this means we must examine how the web impacts on what people do and how people impact on what the web becomes" (2). They also introduce the STS concept of "heterogeneous networks" to the Web Science community. Drawing on Bruno Latour's work outlining Actor-Network Theory, they argue that the Web must be understood as relations between both material and non-material actors in a network. [36]

Halford, Pope, and Carr's article has had a notable impact on the direction of Web Science since 2010. For instance, much of the literature in Web Science on social machines has examined how emergent phenomena are co-constituted through the interactions between humans and machines. [14] Further, there has been growing recognition that studying the Web will require mixed methods analyses to understand the "co-constitutive nature of humans and technologies in the emergent Web" (1). [48]

In this paper, I introduce two additional concepts from Science and Technology Studies that can help advance understanding of how the Web and society are co-constituted. These concepts serve as a framework for my analysis of ethnographic interviews with the Semantic Web community.

3.1 Thought Styles

Ludwig Fleck's book *The Genesis and Development of a Scientific Fact* has served as foundational work for the field of Science and Technology Studies, helping STS scholars examine how knowledge gets produced, evolves, and disseminates. [17] Fleck interrogated the presuppositions that scientists bring to their research. His concept "thought styles" represents how scientists' discourses and material practices are shaped by their cognitive dispositions. According to Fleck's theory, scientists that share particular thought styles come together in "thought collectives."

Several similar concepts in STS describe the values, assumptions, commitments, and biases that scientists bring to their research. For instance, Thomas Kuhn's (1970) *paradigms* offers a temporal perspective; paradigms serve as the body of work that guides researchers following epochal moments of discovery when scientists reject theories that are no longer compatible with the new theory, shifting the focus of standards and scientific work. [35] Kleinman and Suryanarayanan's (2013) *epistemic forms* refer to the institutionalized standards, approaches, and methods, ingrained in disciplinary histories, which shape the design of systems for supporting work. [34] The concept of a "thought style" is distinct from these other concepts in that it deals with how scientists *perceive* their research, not merely how they do it or talk about it. As Barbara Herrnstein Smith argues:

> These perceptual-conceptual dispositions are not 'biases', a term that suggests disabling distortions of otherwise clear of direct perceptions. Rather, and precisely because of how they *constrain* cognition, such dispositions *enable* what we call facts to be known, what we call reality to be brought forth and experienced. (58-58) [47]

Web engineers, knowledge representation experts, graph theorists, and network engineers all bring certain perceptual-conceptual dispositions to their work, which constrains their thinking and shape their discourse and practice in ways that enable the Web to be designed. For instance, Vannevar Bush brought a particular perception about how humans think to the ideas that eventually became the basis for hypertext. [10] For Bush, human minds do not work by indexing concepts into pre-established classes, but instead according to an association of thoughts. This thought style enabled Bush to imagine an information system that could mechanize associative thinking. Enabling associative selection could be characterized as one of hypertext's 'design logics' - a concept that I will turn to next.

3.2 Design Logics

Design logics refer to the design directives that orient how researchers in a particular thought collective structure the architecture of the systems they produce. [21, 44] Notably, different styles of thinking provoke different understandings of how architectures should be designed and ordered. Consider, for instance, the difference between object-oriented databases, relational databases, and graph databases. While there are considerable differences in computational efficiency in each of these data infrastructures, there are also more tacit differences in understanding about the way data should be ordered and related to other content. Some argue, for instance, that object-oriented databases better reflect how ideas are organized in the 'real world,' an argument based on a particular perception of what constitutes the 'real world.'[25]

According to Tim Berners-Lee, one design logic for the World Wide Web was based in a recognition that no one schema would serve everyone, or in other words, that scientists in different communities organized their work according to diverse thought styles.[1] As he writes of his time at CERN:

> I had seen numerous developers arrive at CERN to tout systems that "helped" people organize information. They'd say, "To use this system all you have to do is divide all your documents into four categories" or "You just have to save your data as a WordWonderful document" or whatever. I saw one protagonist after the next shot down in flames by indignant researchers because the developers were forcing them to reorganize their work to fit the system. I would have to create a system with common rules that would be acceptable to everyone. This meant as close as possible to no rules at all. (15)

Notably, no infrastructure emerges out of nothing. The design of any infrastructure relies on leveraging existing infrastructure, also designed according to certain design logics. While design logics do not dictate how a user will leverage an infrastructure, they do place constraints on user interactions with it. For instance, while the Web's design does not inhibit Web users from linking their content according to tree-like structures, it does constrain users from positioning any node as more central than another.

4 LEGACIES OF THINKING ABOUT KNOWLEDGE REPRESENTATION

In an October 2016 interview I conducted with Pat Hayes, he recounted his time participating in the first W3C working group to formalize the Web Ontology Language (OWL) into a recommendation. He characterized how different styles created friction on committees to standardize the language:

> The thing is it used to be considered sort of almost an intellectual war in AI. And now I think it's settled down into...we all agree it's a matter of *style*... almost a personality rather than a content. But certainly both styles are clearly visible in the way things happen. And released a friction on committees of course. (emphasis mine)

The *styles* that Hayes referred to were articulated in many of the interviews that I conducted with members of the Semantic Web community. Describing his time on the OWL working group, Ora Lassila told me, "Knowledge representation as a research community has different schools of thought. They have these cliques of people that believe that things should be done in a certain way."

The W3C working group for the Web Ontology Language was unique in that it comprised mostly of individuals from academic communities (as opposed to industry or other applied domains). Indeed, many individuals were trained in diverse traditions of knowledge representation - traditions that have been divided over how best to conduct knowledge representation for several decades. In what follows, drawing on data from interviews, archival research on W3C web forums, and quotes from primary materials that depicted early debates in artificial intelligence, I outline historical divisions in the field of knowledge representation that have gone on to influence the design of OWL. I argue that these divisions marked diverse *thought communities* whose knowledge representation work was oriented according to diverse *thought styles*. Researchers in different thought communities thus approached the design of knowledge representation systems with different design directives, or *design logics*, which had a considerable impact on how such systems were architected.

4.1 Divisions in Knowledge Representation: 1970s to 1990s

Artificial intelligence research on how to imbue machines with everyday knowledge was coming of age in the early 1970s. In 1969, John McCarthy and Pat Hayes introduced "situation calculus" - a form of formal logic adapted for AI systems. [38] A few years later, at MIT, Marvin Minsky began theorizing how to design knowledge representation frameworks that model the way that humans think; his concept of *frames*, which would go on to play a significant role in many knowledge representation languages including OWL, emerged in the mid-1970s. [39] While many of the ideas that cut across this early work are still referenced in knowledge representation communities today, at the time many researchers tended to flock around particular frameworks. This created considerable schisms in the artificial intelligence community about how best to approach knowledge representation. [40]

One division, which was hotly debated in publications throughout the 1970s, was that between the declarativists and the proceduralists. Declarativists tended to apply first order predicate calculus to knowledge representation, aiming to precisely, completely, and consistently formalize semantics, whereas proceduralists tended to focus on modeling data structures, often using Marvin Minsky's notion of frames, and then applying programming techniques to these structures. According to some, the distinction marked different world-views about how knowledge worked. Terry Winograd, for instance, argued:

> The proceduralists assert that our knowledge is primarily a "knowing how". The human information processor is a stored-program device, with its knowledge of the world embedded in the programs. What a person (or robot) knows about the English language, the game of chess, or the physical properties of his world is coextensive with his set of programs for operating with it. The declarativists, on the other hand, do not believe that knowledge of a subject is intimately bound with the procedures for its use. They see intelligence as resting on two bases: a quite general set of procedures for manipulating facts of all sorts, and a set of specific facts describing particular knowledge domains. In thinking, the general procedures are applied to the domain-specific data to make deductions. Often this process has been based on the model of axiomatic mathematics. (1) [50]

A second division was between what Roger Schank referred to as the 'neats' vs. the 'scruffies.' [13] Neats aimed to implement 'neat' systems for knowledge representation, whereas scruffies tended to cobble solutions together, prioritizing getting a system to work over modeling the system correctly. In an interview with Pat Hayes, he characterized the distinction:

> ...the way Roger characterized it is between the neats and the scruffies - people wanted to sort of use well-defined systems with nice clean semantics (like logic) and other people that just want to sort of get in there and make something that works and then throw it away and make something else that works, and they're very pragmatic and kind of loosey-goosey about anything fundamental, and they don't want to bother with proving theorems or anything.

Both of sets of divisions characterize *thought styles* that guided knowledge representation work in the early 1970s; cognitive dispositions about how knowledge worked constrained the way that researchers approached their work and designed their knowledge representation systems. The thought styles also shaped a variety of design directives, or *design logics*, for knowledge representation systems. Systems deriving from different thought styles were structured differently and produced different results. For instance, systems like Daniel Bobrow and Terry Winograd's Knowledge Representation Language (KRL) were organized around objects (structured according to Minsky's frame concept) with associated descriptions and procedures.[4] This differed from systems like LISP, PROLOG, and 'situational calculus,' which aimed to formalize rules for manipulating data independent of the data itself. [38]

Throughout the 1980s, there had been concerted efforts to merge declarativist and proceduralist tendencies. Systems like FRAIL applied first order predicate calculus to frame-based knowledge representation systems. [11] The description logic community, which would go on to play a major role in the design of OWL, also aimed to add more precise semantics and enable logical reasoning on frame based systems. [9] Description logics introduced the idea of subsumption, or categorization, to knowledge representation systems; guided by a thought style that posits knowledge to be structured into discrete data units and ordered hierarchically, a design logic for the DL community was that knowledge representation systems should enable data to inherit properties from encompassing classes. (See for example [7]).

During this time, while the lines between declarativist and proceduralist approaches were blurring, calls for greater "neatness" began dominating knowledge representation discourse. Ronald J Brachman, often considered the father of description logics, writes in a 1987 article titled "The Myth of One True Logic" that the field had "taken a turn for the 'neat'":

> Back in the early days of the Shift, the impetus was (I think) to eliminate sloppy, inconsistent, and meaningless informal work by encouraging analysis in terms of a precise formal system. First-order logic (FOL) was thought to be a reasonable tool, but not crucial per se to the enterprise. Yet, despite Hayes' strong statement that the important thing was *knowing what a solution meant* and not FOL itself, the formal side of the field has gradually come to be dominated by a standard, first-order predicate logic point of view. Evidence of the centrality of FOL is rampant; one merely need look at some of the most representative Logicist papers for a good dose of it. Merely gentle suggestions that the tools of mathematical logic could be of use in AI (with the requisite protests that FOL was not of itself important) have given way to dogmatic

> proclamations from the heart of the new Logicist camp: "There is only one language suitable for representing information - whether declarativist or procedural - and that is first-order predicate logic" (Kowalski 1980). (169) [8]

In turning towards a "neat" thought style, the design logics that dominated AI at this time involved formalizing precision in knowledge systems, or in other words, getting the system to "know what a solution meant" versus just knowing how to make a solution work. Others went on to characterize a "victory of the neats" in the 1990s and early 2000s.[46] However, moving knowledge representation on to the Web would pose several new challenges to this type of formalism.

4.2 Knowledge Representation Moves onto the Web: 1990s to early 2000s

By the time work had begun to formalize the DARPA Agent Markup Language (DAML) as a standard ontology language for the Web in 2000, many research groups across the United States and Europe (composed of many researchers that had been students of those that had been in the thick of aforementioned debates in AI) had already been thinking about how to make knowledge representation work on the Web. The Resource Description Framework (RDF) had already been formalized into a W3C-recommended Web standard. Jeff Heflin, Jim Hendler, and Sean Luke had been developing SHOE at the University of Maryland.[31] Several researchers trained in description logics had been designing the Ontology Interface Layer in Europe.[16] Eventually, efforts to produce DAML and OIL merged and became the foundation for formalizing the Web Ontology Language (OWL) into a W3C-recommended Web standard. With over 40 members, the working group for OWL was abnormally large and brought together many individuals that had been trained in diverse genealogies of knowledge representation.

In even the earliest discussions about how to formalize a mark-up language for the Web, there was recognition that applying a "neat" semantics to data on the World Wide Web posed new challenges - that the Web's messiness would get in the way of precision and consistency. For instance, in public W3C forums where planning for DAML was being conducted, Ian Johnson responded to a thread about "cleaning up" semantics:

> Maybe we should get everyone to drive on the same side of the road while we're at it? :-) Seriously, while I can see the point you're making, isn't it the case that the web is always going to be messy? It seems to me that the web is unlikely ever to reach a state of rectitude according to clean theoretical principles, so tying success to that state could hold a lot of good work up.[1]

Historic debates about how knowledge representation should be structured and what it should enable resurfaced. The mathematical principles of "soundness," "completeness," and "decidability" served as design logics that shaped how researchers from the description logic community oriented their work. This group of researchers held a firm commitment to the idea that OWL should enable a reasoner to correctly make inferences about the relationships between data in a realistic amount of time. This group approached their work with thought styles that rejected infinity and paradox - concepts that could make reasoning impossible. In doing so, they advocated for a system that offered a restricted set of primitives that could guarantee tractable results. This would considerably limit the expressivity of the language.

On the other hand, for others on the working group, producing decidable results was not the most important aspect of the ontology language. Instead, this group was committed to a design logic that prioritized being able to express any set of statements - to "say anything about anything" - even if it may break some inferential properties of the language. The thought style that guided this community was much scruffier; it posited messiness and paradox as inevitable. As Jim Hendler wrote in one commentary:

> ... on the Web there is no way to guarantee consistency. It also contains information that is inconsistent, incorrect, lacking reliable sources, combined with other information without author approval, and much more. Even worse, if I point at terms in your ontology, and then you change it (or move it), my representation becomes ungrounded. KR has never before had to deal with the AI equivalent of an Error 404! (74) [30]

The distinctions between these *thought communities* were referenced often throughout the development of OWL. In one publication, Guus Schreiber noted, "The debate about what a Web ontology language should look like is reminiscent of past neatâĂŞscruffy struggles. Knowledge modelers want expressiveness, logicians stress decidability. The main difference is that the Semantic Web actually forces us to make some choices: there is a strong need for real-world knowledge representation" (78). [30] Jim Hendler noted in one email to the group:

> In fact, if one goes back to a famous talk given by Roger Schank somewhere in the late 1970s (sorry. my memory fails me as to what meeting it was - I know I was there and remember it was in California), he referred to the neats and the scruffies and at that time, this particular debate we're still having today was one of the examples used as a differentiator! For thos[e] who still haven't figured it out, Peter is the quintessential neat and I'm the archetype for a scruffy.[2]

Bringing these diverse thought styles to their work, the process of formalizing the ontology into a standard was quite contentious. Ultimately, three versions of OWL were produced - OWL DL, based on the description logic design logic, OWL Full, based on the "say anything about anything" design logic, and OWL Lite, which prioritized usability. In one email chain, Frank van Harmelen referred to these flavors of OWL as "neat," "scruffy," and "wimpy," respectively.[3] OWL was thus interlaced with competing perceptions how best to

[1] https://lists.w3.org/Archives/Public/www-rdf-logic/2001Jan/0019.html

[2] https://lists.w3.org/Archives/Public/www-webont-wg/2002Jan/0170.html

[3] https://lists.w3.org/Archives/Public/www-webont-wg/2002Oct/0130.html

represent knowledge. Users who wanted to perform reasoning on data and ensure tractable results would use OWL DL or OWL Lite - a "neat" semantics that emphasized decidability. Users who wanted to describe data and its relationships in a more expressive way would use OWL Full, accepting a bit more scruffiness in exchange for expressivity.

4.3 "Swimming in Troubled Waters": Mid-2000s to present

During the WWW 2016 conference, Peter Norvig, Director of Research at Google, presented a keynote entitled "The Semantic Web and the Web of Semantics: Where Does Meaning Come From?" [42] He put a slide up on the screen that presented two books - the first Ronald J. Brachman and Hector Levesque's *Knowledge Representation and Reasoning*, the second Vinit Nayak's *Copying and Pasting From Stack Overflow*. With a click of the mouse, a large red prohibition symbol displayed over Brachman and Levesque's book. Norvig's talk presented an optimistic outlook for "scruffy" approaches to Web semantics. Reflecting on 15 years of Semantic Web research, he argued that, while systems like DAML and OWL, championed by "highly trained logicians," produced excellent expressiveness, in practice, they also produced a more than 40 percent page error rate. He also noted that very few sites had adopted these technologies. However, new knowledge representation systems like Schema.org, which emphasized simplicity over consistency, were growing at an exponentially faster rate. Norvig discussed how such approaches were guiding the design of knowledge graphs at Google.

Christian Bizer reiterated Norvig's comments in an interview with me later that day:

> If you ask Tim, kind of everybody is shifting. But basically there's strong deployment on the distributed data provision side, which is an integral part of the Semantic Web. There's strong deployment on the ontology side because basically people agree on the global ontology, which is schema.org, which is not as formal. You can't do reasoning with it ... but you do some other kind of reasoning. You do more statistical reasoning, not so much based on ontology constructs. It's more based on the data...

For Wendy Hall, the problem with the strategies put forth by "highly trained logicians" was that they tried to settle the ontologies before there was any data to model. She described in an interview with me, "...a lot of theory was talked about - a lot of upside down As and backward Es to try and prove things about ontologies and try and work out the theory of a Semantic Web before there was any data to experiment with."

With the emergence of discourse around "linked data," a new thought community has emerged within the Semantic Web domain. [3] A "linked data" *thought style* tends to put empiricism before theory, believing that ontologies will evolve organically as everyday webmasters figure out what schemas they need to describe and link their data. In this sense, the ontologies are much more "scruffy." Different assumptions also guide the way reasoning gets applied to data. Rather than designing ontologies that provide data with an internal coherence so that reasoners can later infer the relationships between data points, many in the linked data community propose applying statistical reasoning to the data after it has been described and linked, making inferences based on trends that emerge rather than based on modeling rules formalized ahead of time. The creators of Schema.org describe:

> Schema.org also shares the linked-data community's skepticism toward the premature formalism (rule systems, description logics, and so on) found in much of the academic work that is carried out under the Semantic Web banner. While Schema.org also avoids assuming that such rule-based processing will be commonplace, it differs from typical linked-data guidelines in its assumption that various other kinds of cleanup, reconciliation, and postprocessing will usually be needed before structured data from the Web can be exploited in applications. (50) [26]

Thus, the linked data community approaches the design of Semantic Web protocols with different *design logics* - emphasizing pragmatism and simplicity over formalism and consistency. These design logics come with recognition that the system will not always produce one correct answer. In a Schema.org public forum post, Bernard Vatant characterized this recognition in a response to Peter Patel-Schneider, a prominent figure in the description logic community:

> ...problems you point at (lack of documentation, semantic glitches etc) will always be present in this scruffy-work-in-progress called "Web semantics" (read : fuzzy, plural, inconsistent etc). I'm sure you will ever ever fight it with all your will and strength given where you come from, but I'm afraid this battle has been lost for quite a while now. As Pat Hayes told me a while ago "My ivory tower has been seriously shaken those days, waters of real world are slowly rising around us." Time to learn swimming in troubled waters ...[4]

Thus, much like the knowledge representation community had been taking a "turn of the neat" in the late 1980s, knowledge representation on the Web can be said to have taken a "turn for the scruffy" in the late 2000s and early 2010s. Next, I will show why this turn matters for how knowledge gets represented on the Web.

5 THE SOCIOLOGY OF SCRUFFY WEB SEMANTICS

Situating a sociological lens on the design of the Semantic Web, Halford, Pope, and Weal have argued that it is important that researchers studying the Web recognize the "social construction" of Semantic Web infrastructure - "to ensure that the micro-politics of its artefacts are understood as *politics*, representing choices and interpretations, rather than as neutral fact or engineering design" (185). [28] This is important because the design of information

[4] https://lists.w3.org/Archives/Public/public-vocabs/2013Nov/0033.html

architectures can go on to shape what becomes knowable in an information system. [45]

For instance, Heather Ford and Mark Graham have demonstrated how, when drawing on linked data techniques to integrate and display data in Google's knowledge graph, often political nuances in the data are lost as data moves from claims on a Wikipedia page into structured databases. [18] Examining how Google's knowledge graph displays information following a search for 'Jerusalem', they show how political struggles over the city's status in relation to Israel and Palestine are lost as the data moves into the knowledge graph. Similarly, using an ontology language like OWL to specify that two classes are disjoint can eclipse anomalies in the data. As Christian Bizer described to me in an interview "Civic Structures" and "Places of Residence" had long been considered disjoint classes in dbpedia. This posed a problem when they came across a Wikipedia page for a tunnel that also served as a slum. Keeping these classes disjoint can prevent the tunnel from becoming known *as a place of residence.* Thus, the ontology could potentially be encoded to ignore the lived experience of a certain group of people.

Further critiques examining the political implications of the Semantic Web posit that its design has been founded in assumptions of objectivity, neutrality, and credibility. [49] However, in this paper, I have aimed to show how there has been a great deal of conflicting choices and interpretations involved in the engineering of Semantic Web technologies, each producing layers of the infrastructure with diverse socio-political implications for how we access and interpret Web information.[5] In the design of OWL, many individuals from the description logic community aimed to build knowledge representation infrastructure based on precision and consistency; they aimed to build stable ontologies that could guarantee tractable results. Literature in Science and Technology Studies, however, has argued that stabilizing information systems can serve to ignore the uncertainties that are always already present in data. [20] Further, feminist literature - in particular literature that focuses on how different ways of being and knowing are represented in society - has argued that no information architecture can be designed to encapsulate all knowledge. [12] There are always different ways of being in the world and knowing the world that information systems will ignore. [29] Thus, any attempt to stabilize an ontology will inevitably be exclusionary and will always represent a set of political decisions.[6]

Others in the community conceded that, with the messiness of the Web, ontologies may not be so stable - that the rules designed into the Semantic Web may not produce correct results 100 percent of the time. Instead this group has focused on proposing schemas for linking data. However, literature in Science and Technology Studies and Information Studies has also shown that all classification systems are embedded with cultural values. [6] Currently, in the Person schema in schema.org, there is a classifier for Gender but no classifier for Race. This represents a political decision about how knowledge about demographics can be represented on the Web.

While such critiques point to important considerations about the politics of imposing structure, they often do not consider the social implications of "structurelessness." [22] Semantic Web infrastructure enables users to find information that may otherwise get lost on the Web. Linked data technologies enable data practitioners to draw together information that produce meaningful narratives for advancing social justice âĂŞ for instance that there are links between where toxic pollutants tend to be released and where minority populations live. Without some structure, such data integration would not be possible.

Thus, echoing Halford, Pope, and Weal's assertion, all engineering choices on the Semantic Web - whether rooted in declarative, procedural, neat, or scruffy styles of thinking - should be understood as politics; they represent non-neutral interpretations about how knowledge should be represented to a machine and produce political implications for whose knowledge gets represented on the Web and how it gets represented. [28] In turning towards the "scruffy" - towards more "lightweight ontologies" [32] and statistical reasoning over formal reasoning, the sociology of the architecture turns towards more inclusivity in whose knowledge gets represented on the Web and how it gets represented.

With scruffy ontologies, it becomes possible to classify information that does not fit "neatly" into rules codified ahead of time. In particular, it becomes possible to codify anomalies and differences in world-views without breaking the knowledge representation system. The way that data can come together is not imposed on the information system ahead of time, but instead emerges from how diverse Web users link their data. Thus, in opposition to what anthropologist Diana Forsythe has referred to as "I am the world" reasoning that had characterized knowledge engineering work in the field of AI in the 1990s (a conception of knowledge engineering in which the engineer assumed that her own perceptions of the world also applied to all other human beings) [19], knowledge representation on the Web is crowd-sourced; linked data has made it possible to represent different ways of being in and knowing the world on the Web.

Linked data technologies have had an exponentially faster adoption rate than Semantic Web technologies aimed at enabling formal reasoning. While often this uptake is attributed to linked data technologies being simpler to understand and use than formal ontologies, it is also notable that the design logics that are often attributed to enabling the viral uptake of the Web are similar to the design logics that appear to be enabling the viral uptake of linked data. As quoted earlier in this paper, Tim Berners-Lee brought to the design of the Web a design logic that had been averse to prematurely codifying how information could come together:

> I saw one protagonist after the next shot down in flames by indignant researchers because the developers were forcing them to reorganize their work to fit the system. I would have to

[5]Notably, many critiques of the semantic Web from STS and adjacent fields refer to "the logic of the semantic Web."[18, 49] In this paper, I aim to show that the Semantic Web has been designed according to more than one conception of "logic."

[6]In this sense, moving towards justice in information systems is not so much about attempting to remove biases from information architectures. Since exclusions will always be a part of an information system, claiming a system to be "objective" or "neutral" denies the existence of other ways of being in the world and knowing the world. Instead, moving towards justice in information systems requires acknowledging the politics always already present in information systems and then designing systems in such a way that they can transform as new ways of being and knowing manifest. [12]

> create a system with common rules that would be acceptable to everyone. This meant as close as possible to no rules at all. (15) [1]

With linked data, Web users too have had an opportunity to semantify their data without being forced to reorganize their work to fit the system. Thus, a "turn for the scruffy" has enabled more diverse thought styles to be represented in Web semantics.

6 CONCLUSION

Today, there are a variety of options for Web masters that wish to "semantify" their Web data. For instance, some Web masters may decide to use simple microformats like schema.org to mark up their Web pages, while others may decide to leverage ontology languages such as OWL. Each option offers different degrees of expressivity, inferential decidability, and computational tractability, and each is interwoven with legacies of thinking about how to represent knowledge to a machine. Representing data with neat information infrastructures makes it much easier to do things, decide things, and build things with data.

"Scruffier" information infrastructures, on the other had, make it possible for different concepts and ideas to be represented on the Web than "neater" information infrastructures. Scruffy information infrastructures are more conducive to representing inconsistencies and anomalies - to the things that may not fit "neatly" into decidable logic. Notably, emerging scalable computing paradigms, such as statistical reasoning, are making it possible to advance knowledge representation in the face of scruffiness, in turn allowing more diverse ways of being in and knowing the world to get acknowledged through Web semantics.

The way that data gets represented through Web information infrastructures in turn shapes how users access, extract, and integrate Web data. Examining the styles of thought that have shaped the logics of information architecture design enables us to understand how politics emerge, reminds us that there are alternative approaches to ordering knowledge, and provides insight on how to adapt the infrastructure to be more inclusive of alternative ways of being in and knowing the world. This is important to a study of the Web.

In this paper, I have shown how qualitative ethnographic and historical methodologies can be used to characterize the cultural and political import of various Web architectures. Web Scientists often rely on data that has been structured with various Semantic Web tools to examine social phenomena on the Web. If Web Scientists are to take seriously the argument that the Web is co-constituted through interactions between society and technology then it will be important to draw greater attention to how assumptions and commitments that Web engineers bring to their work, along with the sociologies of various architectures, go on to shape Web tools and protocols. It will also be important to examine how the resulting configurations impact how information is interpreted, integrated, and moved on the Web. This will likely require an expansion to the understanding of what it means to be a social scientist in the field of Web Science. Social scientists can bring more to Web Science than examining society and culture through the lens of the Web. Repositioning the architecture of the Web as an object of societal and cultural study can advance our understanding, not only of how the Web works, but also how and why certain Web trends emerge and how Web engineers can intervene to build a "Web We Want."

ACKNOWLEDGMENTS

Thanks are due to Jim Hendler, Deborah McGuinness, and John Erickson, who read and offered feedback on various versions of this paper.

REFERENCES

[1] Tim Berners-Lee. 1999. *Weaving the Web: The Original Design and Ultimate Destiny of the World Wide Web by Its Inventor.* Harper Business.
[2] Tim Berners-Lee, James Hendler, and Ora Lassila. 2001. The Semantic Web. *Scientific American* (May 2001), 29–37.
[3] Christian Bizer, Tom Heath, and Tim Berners-Lee. 2009. Linked Data: The Story So Far. *International Journal on Semantic Web and Information Systems* 5, 3 (2009), 1–22.
[4] Daniel G. Bobrow and Terry Winograd. 1977. An Overview of KRL, a Knowledge Representation Language. *Cognitive Science* 1, 1 (Jan. 1977), 3–46. https://doi.org/10.1207/s15516709cog0101_2
[5] Geoffrey Bowker, Karen Baker, Florence Millerand, and David Ribes. 2009. Toward Information Infrastructure Studies: Ways of Knowing in a Networked Environment. In *International Handbook of Internet Research*, Jeremy Hunsinger, Lisbeth Klastrup, and Matthew Allen (Eds.). Springer Netherlands, 97–117. http://link.springer.com/chapter/10.1007/978-1-4020-9789-8_5 DOI: 10.1007/978-1-4020-9789-8_5.
[6] Geoffrey C. Bowker and Susan Leigh Star. 1999. *Sorting Things Out: Classification and Its Consequences.* MIT Press.
[7] Ronald J. Brachman. 1978. *A Structural Paradigm for Representing Knowledge.* Technical Report.
[8] Ronald J. Brachman. 1987. The myth of the one true logic. *Computational Intelligence* 3, 1 (Feb. 1987), 168–172. https://doi.org/10.1111/j.1467-8640.1987.tb00187.x
[9] Ronald J. Brachman and James G. Schmolze. 1985. An Overview of the KL-ONE Knowledge Representation System*. *Cognitive Science* 9, 2 (April 1985), 171–216. https://doi.org/10.1207/s15516709cog0902_1
[10] Vannevar Bush. 1945. As We May Think. *Atlantic Monthly* 176 (1945), 101–108.
[11] Eugene Charniak. 1981. A common representation for problem-solving and language-comprehension information. *Artificial Intelligence* 16, 3 (July 1981), 225–255. https://doi.org/10.1016/0004-3702(81)90001-1
[12] Drucilla Cornell. 1992. *The Philosophy of the Limit.* Routledge, Chapman & Hall, Incorporated.
[13] Daniel Crevier. 1994. *AI: The Tumultuous History of the Search for Artificial Intelligence.* BasicBooks.
[14] David De Roure, Clare Hooper, Kevin Page, SÃĺgolÃĺne Tarte, and Pip Willcox. 2015. Observing Social Machines Part 2: How to Observe?. In *Proceedings of the ACM Web Science Conference (WebSci '15).* ACM, New York, NY, USA, 13:1–13:5. https://doi.org/10.1145/2786451.2786475
[15] Paul N. Edwards, Steven J. Jackson, Melissa K. Chalmers, Geoffrey C. Bowker, Christine L. Borgman, David Ribes, Matt Burton, and Scout Calvert. 2013. *Knowledge Infrastructures: Intellectual Frameworks and Research Challenges.* Working Paper. http://deepblue.lib.umich.edu/handle/2027.42/97552
[16] D. Fensel, F. van Harmelen, I. Horrocks, D. L. McGuinness, and P. F. Patel-Schneider. 2001. OIL: an ontology infrastructure for the Semantic Web. *IEEE Intelligent Systems* 16, 2 (March 2001), 38–45. https://doi.org/10.1109/5254.920598
[17] Ludwik Fleck. 1981. *Genesis and Development of a Scientific Fact.* University of Chicago Press.
[18] Heather Ford and Mark Graham. 2016. Semantic Cities: Coded Geopolitics and the Rise of the Semantic Web. In *Code and the City*, Rob Kitchin and Sung-Yueh Perng (Eds.). Routledge, 200–214.
[19] Diana E. Forsythe. 1993. Engineering Knowledge: The Construction of Knowledge in Artificial Intelligence. *Social Studies of Science* 23, 3 (Aug. 1993), 445–477. https://doi.org/10.1177/0306312793023003002
[20] Kim Fortun. 2004. From Bhopal to the Informating of Environmentalism: Risk Communication in Historical Perspective. *Osiris* 19 (2004), 283–296.
[21] Kim Fortun, Mike Fortun, Erik Bigras, Tahereh Saheb, Brandon Costelloe-Kuehn, Jerome Crowder, Daniel Price, and Alison Kenner. 2014. Experimental Ethnography Online. *Cultural Studies* 28, 4 (2014), 632–642. https://doi.org/10.1080/09502386.2014.888923
[22] Jo Freeman. 1972. The Tyranny of Structurelessness. *Berkeley Journal of Sociology* 17 (1972), 151–164. http://www.jstor.org/stable/41035187
[23] Matthew Fuller. 2008. *Software Studies: A Lexicon.* MIT Press. Google-Books-ID: LFJ3ashVBuIC.
[24] Matthew K. Gold. 2012. *Debates in the Digital Humanities.* University of Minnesota Press, Minneapolis, MN.

[25] David Golumbia. 2009. *The Cultural Logic of Computation.* Harvard University Press.
[26] R. V. Guha, Dan Brickley, and Steve Macbeth. 2016. Schema.Org: Evolution of Structured Data on the Web. *Commun. ACM* 59, 2 (Jan. 2016), 44–51. https://doi.org/10.1145/2844544
[27] Susan Halford, Catherine Pope, and Leslie Carr. 2010. A manifesto for Web Science, John Erickson and Stefan Gradmann (Eds.). 1–6. http://journal.webscience.org/297/
[28] Susan Halford, Catherine Pope, and Mark Weal. 2013. Digital Futures? Sociological Challenges and Opportunities in the Emergent Semantic Web. *Sociology* 47, 1 (Feb. 2013), 173–189. https://doi.org/10.1177/0038038512453798
[29] Donna Haraway. 1988. Situated Knowledges: The Science Question in Feminism and the Privilege of Partial Perspective. *Feminist Studies* 14, 3 (1988), 575. https://doi.org/10.2307/3178066
[30] Frank van Harmelen, Ian Horrocks, Peter Clark, Peter F. Patel-Schneider, Michael Uschold, Marie-Christine Rousset, James Hendler, and Guus Schreiber. 2002. Ontologies' KISSES in standardization. *IEEE Intelligent Systems* 17, 2 (March 2002), 70–79. https://doi.org/10.1109/MIS.2002.999223
[31] Jeff Heflin, James Hendler, and Sean Luke. 1999. SHOE: A Knowledge Representation Language for Internet Applications. (Oct. 1999). http://drum.lib.umd.edu/handle/1903/1044
[32] James Hendler. 2012. Increasing Access to the Web of "Broad Data". In *Proceedings of the International Cross-Disciplinary Conference on Web Accessibility (W4A '12).* ACM, New York, NY, USA, 31:1–31:2. https://doi.org/10.1145/2207016.2207041
[33] Christopher M. Kelty. 2008. *Two Bits: The Cultural Significance of Free Software.* Duke University Press Books, Durham.
[34] Daniel Lee Kleinman and Sainath Suryanarayanan. 2013. Dying Bees and the Social Production of Ignorance. *Science, Technology & Human Values* 38, 4 (July 2013), 492–517. https://doi.org/10.1177/0162243912442575
[35] Thomas S Kuhn. 1970. *The structure of scientific revolutions.* University of Chicago Press, Chicago.
[36] Bruno Latour. 2005. *Reassembling the Social: An Introduction to Actor-Network-Theory.* OUP Oxford.
[37] Mark Marino. 2006. Critical Code Studies. *electronic book review* (2006). http://www.electronicbookreview.com/thread/electropoetics/codology
[38] John McCarthy and Patrick J. Hayes. 1969. Some Philosophical Problems from the Standpoint of Artificial Intelligence. In *Machine Intelligence.* Edinburgh University Press, 463–502.
[39] Marvin Minsky. 1974. A Framework for Representing Knowledge. (June 1974). http://dspace.mit.edu/handle/1721.1/6089
[40] Marvin Minsky. 1991. Logical Versus Analogical or Symbolic Versus Connectionist or Neat Versus Scruffy. *AI Magazine* 12, 2 (June 1991), 34–51. https://doi.org/10.1609/aimag.v12i2.894
[41] Nick Montfort and Ian Bogost. 2009. *Racing the Beam: The Atari Video Computer System* (2nd ptg edition ed.). The MIT Press, Cambridge, Mass.
[42] Peter Norvig. 2016. The Semantic Web and the Semantics of the Web: Where Does Meaning Come From? (April 2016).
[43] Kieron O'Hara, Noshir S. Contractor, Wendy Hall, James Hendler, and Nigel Shadbolt. 2013. Web Science: Understanding the Emergence of Macro-Level Features on the World Wide Web. *Foundations and TrendsÂő in Web Science* 4, 2âĂŞ3 (2013), 103–267. https://doi.org/10.1561/1800000017
[44] L. Poirier. 2017. Devious Design: Digital Infrastructure Challenges for Experimental Ethnography. *Design Issues* 33, 2 (April 2017), 70–83. https://doi.org/10.1162/DESI_a_00440
[45] David Ribes and Geoffrey C. Bowker. 2009. Between meaning and machine: Learning to represent the knowledge of communities. *Information and Organization* 19, 4 (Oct. 2009), 199–217. https://doi.org/10.1016/j.infoandorg.2009.04.001
[46] Stuart Russell and Peter Norvig. 1995. *Artificial Intelligence: A Modern Approach* (1st edition ed.). Prentice Hall.
[47] Barbara Herrnstein Smith. 2006. *Scandalous Knowledge: Science, Truth and the Human.* Duke University Press.
[48] Ramine Tinati, Susan Halford, Leslie Carr, and Catherine Pope. 2014. Big Data: Methodological Challenges and Approaches for Sociological Analysis. *Sociology* (Feb. 2014), 0038038513511561. https://doi.org/10.1177/0038038513511561
[49] Vivienne Waller. 2016. Making knowledge machine-processable: some implications of general semantic search. *Behaviour & Information Technology* 0, 0 (May 2016), 1–12. https://doi.org/10.1080/0144929X.2016.1183710
[50] Terry Winograd. 1975. Frame Representations and the Declarative/Procedural Controversy. In *Representation and Understanding: Studies in Cognitive Science,* Daniel Bobrow and Allan Collins (Eds.). Academic Press, Inc., New York, 185–210. Google-Books-ID: JImLBQAAQBAJ.

Understanding Temporal Backing Patterns in Online Crowdfunding Communities

Yiming Liao
Penn State University
yiming@psu.edu

Thanh Tran
Utah State University
thanh.tran@aggiemail.usu.edu

Dongwon Lee
Penn State University
dongwon@psu.edu

Kyumin Lee
Utah State University
kyumin.lee@usu.edu

ABSTRACT

Online crowdfunding platforms such as Kickstarter and Indiegogo make it possible for users to pledge funds to help creators bring their favorite projects into life. With an increasing number of users participating in crowdfunding, researchers are progressively motivated to investigate on improving user experiences by recommending projects and predicting project outcomes. To prompt the sustainable development of these platforms, understanding backers' behaviors becomes also important, as it helps platforms provide better services and improve backer retention. In particular, studying backers' *temporal* behaviors allows them to monitor the dynamics of backers' actions and develop appropriate strategies in time. Therefore, in this paper, we analyze a large amount of backer data from Kickstarter and Indiegogo, and do a comprehensive quantitative analysis on users' temporal backing patterns. Employing time series clustering methods, we discover four distinct temporal backing patterns on both platforms. In addition, we explore various characteristics of these backing patterns and possible factors affecting backers' behaviors. Finally, we leverage these insights to build a prediction model and show promising results to identify users' backing patterns at a very early stage. The datasets used in this paper are available at: https://goo.gl/ozgLvP.

CCS CONCEPTS

• **Social and Behavior Sciences → Sociology**; • **Probability and Statistics → Time series analysis**; • **Database Applications → Data mining**;

KEYWORDS

Crowdfunding; User Behavior Analysis; Temporal Pattern

1 INTRODUCTION

Online crowdfunding platforms such as Kickstarter and Indiegogo have opened up a new avenue for entrepreneurs to raise funding, overcoming the barriers of small start-up companies [15]. In such platforms, users, known as *backers*, are given the opportunity to pledge funds to join entrepreneurs, known as *creators*, to bring their favorite projects into life. Taking Oculus Rift for example, the virtual-reality gaming headset had reportedly raised $2.4 million dollars via crowdfunding, which clearly displays the power of crowdfunding [26]. According to Kickstarter's report[1], around March 2017, 12 million backers have pledged approximately $2.9 billion dollars for more than 120k projects. Among these 12 million backers, however, only less than 4 million of backers have backed two or more projects. Similarly, less than 30% of user retention rate has been reported on other two crowdfunding platforms, DonorsChoose.org [1] and Indiegogo (Section 3).

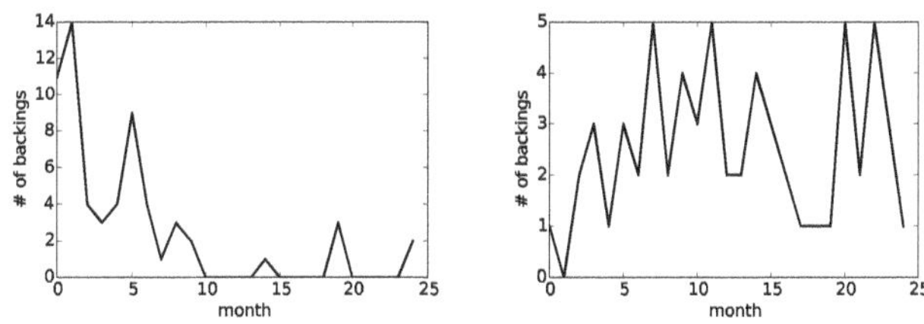

(a) From Apr. 2012 to May 2014 (b) From Aug. 2014 to Sep. 2016

Figure 1: Kickstarter user example

As a motivating example, see Figure 1, where actual backing numbers of two backers on the Kickstarter platform are plotted. Note that two users show radically different backing behavior for the same duration of 24 months over different years. The user in (a) shows active backings in the early stage but gradually backs less, while the user in (b) more or less remains active throughout. Clearly, identifying such users as (a) early and encourage them to remain active is beneficial to crowdfunding platforms. To increase such backer retention rate, therefore, we argue that monitoring and understanding backers' behaviors is indispensable.

Previous studies have pointed it out that there are distinguished differences between: (1) occasional backers, who back only a small number of projects and mostly join to support their friends' projects, and (2) frequent backers, who invest on many projects and show clear backing interests [2, 22]. In addition, users' first backing behaviors are shown to be closely correlated with user retention and

[1] https://www.kickstarter.com/help/stats

WebSci'17, June 25–28, 2017, Troy, NY, USA.

ACM ISBN 978-1-4503-4896-6/17/06...$15.00.
DOI: http://dx.doi.org/10.1145/3091478.3091480

even can be used to predict which backers will return [1]. Nevertheless, none of the previous crowdfunding studies has investigated on the "temporal dynamics" of users' backing behaviors over multiple years. Users' temporal backing behaviors could reflect users' dynamic relationships with platforms, which is quite valuable information for platforms to improve backer retention. For example, if a platform observes a backer gradually becomes less active, platforms may take timely actions, such as special promotion, to restore their interests. Furthermore, knowing backers' temporal behaviors enables platforms to be able to provide better personalized services, for instance, adjusting recommendation strategies at times.

Therefore, in this paper, we propose to analyze users' temporal backing behaviors on online crowdfunding platforms. In particular, we intend to investigate the following three research questions:

- **RQ1:** Do users have any temporal backing patterns?
- **RQ2:** If so, what are the characteristics of those backing patterns and possible factors impacting those patterns?
- **RQ3:** Can we identify users' backing patterns at early stages?

In answering these research questions, we make the following main contributions:

- To our best knowledge, we are the first to analyze users' temporal backing behaviors on crowdfunding platforms.
- We discover four distinct temporal backing patterns on two most popular crowdfunding platforms with hundreds of thousands frequent backers.
- We analyze the characteristics of each pattern from various aspects, including success rate and pledged money, and explore possible factors impacting users' backing patterns.
- We validate our analysis by showing the possibilities to build early prediction models in inferring all four temporal backing patterns.
- Based on the analysis, we achieve encouraging results in identifying those who will progressively become inactive at very early stages.

The rest of the paper is organized as follows. In Section 2, we review related works on crowdfunding platforms. Section 3 introduces our data collection strategy and the experimental dataset. The approach to uncover users' temporal backing behaviors and its results are given in Section 4. In Section 5, we analyze characteristics of backing patterns and explore possible factors impacting users' behaviors. Early prediction models are discussed in Section 6 and we conclude the paper with a discussion on limitations and future work in Section 7.

2 RELATED WORK

In this section, we review crowdfunding research work in three categories: (i) analysis of crowdfunding platforms, (ii) project success prediction and recommendation, and (iii) crowdfunding backer behaviors.

There are a rich set of studies on analyzing crowdfunding platforms [4, 7, 10, 11, 14, 25]. For example, studies have examined the dynamics of crowdfunding projects [19], revealed motivations of both creators and backers [11], and made comparisons of different crowdfunding platforms [12]. With the rise of social media, researchers noticed the close relationship between crowdfunding platforms and social networks, and started leveraging social media activities to study crowdfunding [2, 17, 22]. For example, social media have been found to be quite helpful in project promotion and strongly correlated with project outcomes [17]. In addition, other factors, such as geography, project updates and rewards, have also been proved to be closely connected with crowdfunding projects [16, 20, 28].

Aimed at helping creators get funded and backers find favorable projects, research has focused on using machine learning algorithms to do project success prediction [6, 9, 13, 18] and project recommendation [2, 22, 23]. Besides static and dynamic features on crowdfunding platforms, both Chung and Lee [6] and Rakesh et al. [24] leveraged social network features to achieve state-of-the-art performance in project success rate prediction and project recommendation respectively.

Although various studies have been conducted on crowdfunding platforms, few works have investigated on backers' behaviors. Previous studies have shown different backing strategies or behaviors between occasional and frequent backers. For example, frequent backers are found to be more likely to invest fast-growing projects [2]. [15] classified backers into three categories, immediate backers, delayed backers and serial backers. In addition, only based on one's first backing, researchers showed the possibility to predict whether that user will come back or not [1].

In our paper, instead of uncovering different backing behaviors between occasional and frequent backers, we intend to focus on frequent backers, who carry out more activities and are more valuable for platforms, and dig into their temporal backing behaviors, which has rarely been explored before.

3 DATASET DESCRIPTION

Aimed at understanding user behaviors in online crowdfunding communities, we collect a large amount of user data from two of the most popular crowdfunding platforms, Kickstarter and Indiegogo. To make our analysis more reliable, we have collected all projects that are available and thereby, to our best knowledge, obtain the largest datasets on both platforms (comparison of raw datasets is given in Table 1). In this section, we introduce data collection strategy, data cleaning process and overview of our dataset.

3.1 Dataset Collection

Due to the disparate strategies of Indiegogo and Kickstarter for displaying user backing histories, we adopt two different collection methods for these two platforms.

3.1.1 *Kickstarter Dataset.*

Kickstarter prevents users from obtaining backer list of certain project by only displaying limited backers' avatars without profile URLs. Fortunately, however, we can find backers' profile URLs in project comments page, and with one's profile URL, we are able to collect the complete project backing history of that user. At the end, we have gathered 233,534 ended projects, spanning from April 2009 to December 2016, and corresponding comments. Then we collected users' full backing histories through user profile URLs from comments, which resulted in more than 500,000 backers.

Table 1: Raw Dataset Comparison

Data source	Platform	# of unique users	# of projects
Ours	Kickstarter	**508,850**	**233,534**
Ours	Indiegogo	**2,314,199**	**124,292**
[6]	Kickstarter	146,721	168,851
[19]	Kickstarter	N/A	59,115
[26]	Kickstarter	239,000	N/A
[7]	Indiegogo	N/A	47,139

Table 2: Our frequent Backer Dataset

Platform	# of users	# of projects	# of backings per user
Kickstarter	150,122	174,938	38.0
Indiegogo	12,528	41,450	15.4

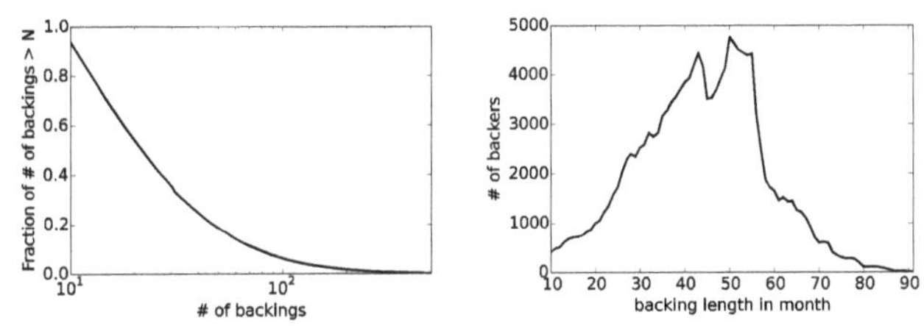

(a) CCDF of users' backing numbers (b) Backing Length Distribution

Figure 2: Kickstarter Frequent Backer Distribution

3.1.2 Indiegogo Dataset.
Different from Kickstarter, Indiegogo displays projects' backer lists with some anonymous backers but only shows recent backings of each user on their profile URLs. Hence, we directly collected Indiegogo's project backer lists after gathering all available ended 124,292 projects, which spans from January 2008 to January 2017. Identifying users by profile URLs, there are around 2,300,000 unique backers. Although we cannot guarantee to obtain full backing history of each backer and each user's backing history in our dataset ought to be viewed as a sample of the true history, the influence of sampling should be negligible as we have a large number of projects.

3.2 Frequent Backers

Despite a large number of unique backers identified on both platforms, the majority of them only back very limited projects. Taking Indiegogo backers for example, only 536,727 backers (23%) back more than twice, which is consistent with the previous study (26%) on another crowdfunding platform [1]. In order to reduce the impact of occasional backers and better understand users' backing behaviors, we filter out those infrequent backers and only keep those frequent backers who have backed more than 10 times. As a result, we have 150,122 Kickstarter and 12,528 Indiegogo frequent backers. Table 2 shows overall statistics of our frequent backer dataset and Figure 2(a) illustrates the complementary cumulative distribution function (CCDF) of Kickstarter users' backing numbers. For each

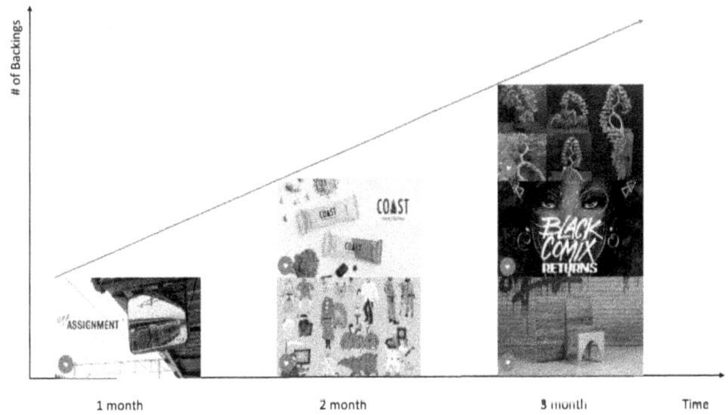

Figure 3: Example of backing behavior

backing number N, CCDF of users' backing numbers shows the proportion of backers who invest more than N projects, for example, there are more than 20% of Kickstarter backers supporting at least 40 projects.

In our paper, we analyze users' backing behaviors during their lifetime, which is defined as the observed backing history in our dataset. As shown in Figure 2(b), the majority of backers have lifetimes lying between 2 and 5 years, which means users' baking histories in our dataset are reasonably long enough for temporal backing behavior analysis.

4 TEMPORAL BACKING PATTERNS

In this section, we intend to answer *RQ1: do users have any temporal backing patterns?* We start by introducing our definition of users' temporal backing behaviors, then describe our approach to cluster those temporal behaviors and finally discuss about the clustering results.

4.1 Temporal Backing behavior

With the purpose of uncovering users' possible backing strategies, we monitor users' backing numbers over time and define a user's temporal backing behavior as a backing number function of time, $N(t)$. Although the exact timestamp when one user back a certain project is not available in our dataset, we propose to use the middle time between each project's start and end time as its backers' joining time. Since projects' average duration is around 1 month and most of our backers have more than 2 years lifetimes, it should be reasonable to ignore the several days' shifting. Knowing the timestamps of all backings, each user's backing behavior can be viewed as a time series, $N(t) = \{n_1, n_2, ...\}$, which models users' backing numbers through time. For example, Figure 3 shows one possible temporal backing behavior, where the user tends to back an increasing number of projects over time.

4.2 Dynamic Time Warping Clustering

Having converted users' temporal backing behaviors into time series, we investigate whether there exist any backing patterns. Because different backing behaviors correspond to different shapes in time series, we propose to use time series clustering to find distinct patterns. Since only the shape of time series matters, we

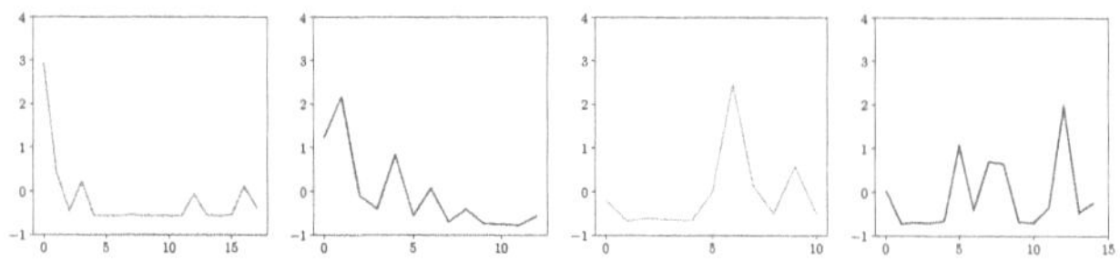

(a) 10-20 months

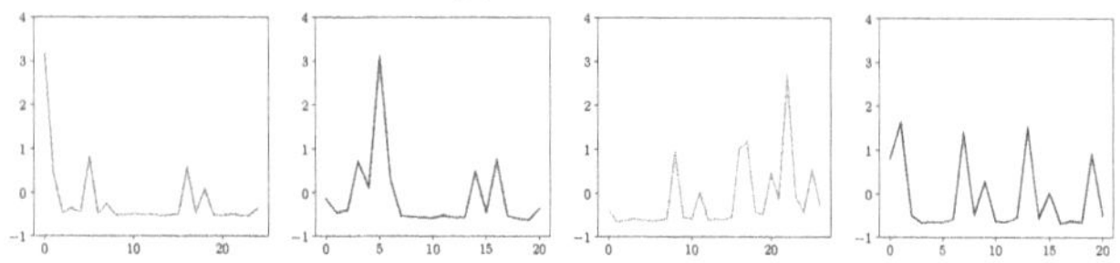

(b) 20-30 months

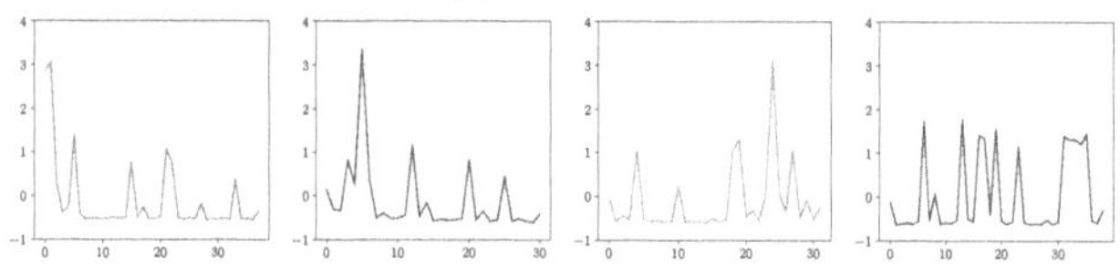

(c) 30-40 months

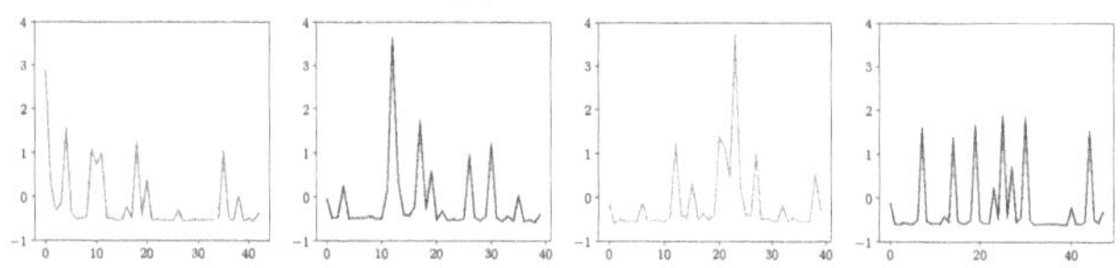

(d) 40-50 months

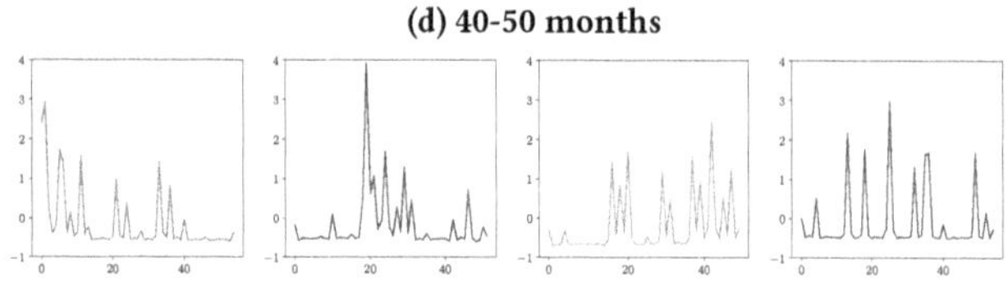

(e) 50-60 months

Figure 4: Patterns in various backing length groups. X-axis stands for months. Y-axis stands for Z-normalized backing number.

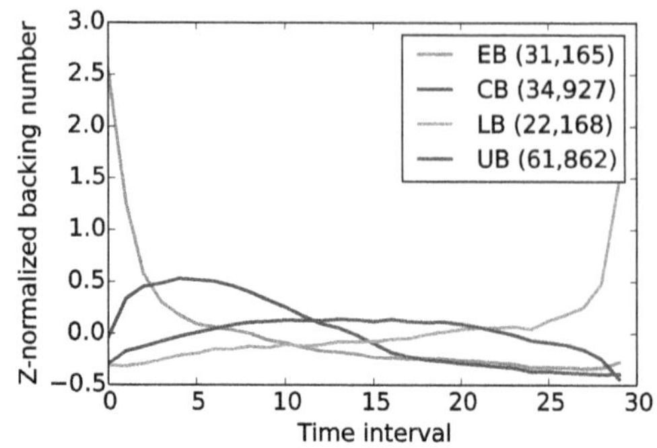

(a) Kickstarter

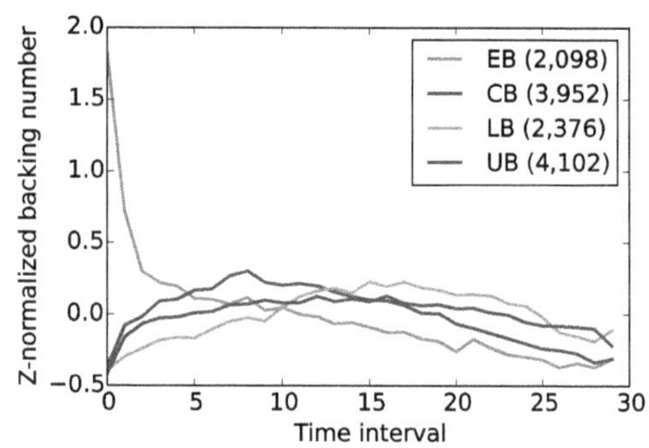

(b) Indiegogo

Figure 5: Clustering results (with # of backers in parentheses)

do Z-normalization on all time series at first to make comparisons between two time series meaningful [24]. Then, in order to allow slight shifting in time and warping in shape, we take advantage of Dynamic Time Warping (DTW) [5] clustering to find discriminative patterns.

More specifically, we adopt Dynamic Time Warping with Dtw Barycenter Averaging (DBA) [21], a state of the art time series averaging method, to do the clustering. As for parameter settings, we try various time window sizes and cluster numbers, and run DBA-based DTW 100 times with different kmeans++ initialization [3] for each set of parameters and keep the clusters with minimum inertia. Finally, we find the most discriminative patterns when DTW window size is $\frac{1}{3}$ of time series length and the cluster number is 4.

4.2.1 Effect of backing length.
Due to the fact that backing history length varies with users, it is difficult to compare two time series that differ too much in length (e.g. one user with 2-year backing history while another with 5-year backing history). Thus, we intend to study the effect of users' backing length by running clustering on different backing length groups and the results are shown in Figure 4. Apparently, similar backing patterns are discovered in all groups, and there is no distinct pattern that is exclusively found in some groups. As a result, it should be reasonable to normalize each user's backing history into the same length (*Binning*): 1) we regard each user's first and last project backing time as one's lifetime start and end time respectively; 2) evenly split one's lifetime into 30 intervals and count the number of backings in each interval; 3) apply Z-normalization on the time series.

4.3 Clustering Results

After binning and clustering, we do pairwise averaging on the 30-interval time series per group to obtain smoothed clusters. As shown in Figure 5, similar backing patterns have emerged on both crowdfunding platforms, which are also consistent with clustering results on different backing length groups in Figure 4. We name the 4 distinct backing patterns as follows:

(1) **Early backer (EB)**: those backers back a lot at the very beginning of their lifetime but gradually lose interest and seldom back later.

(2) **Cautious backer (CB)**: although the majority of their backings still happen at the beginning, they are more cautious than early backers, as they try a few projects before conducting massive investments.
(3) **Late backer (LB)**: contrary to early backers, they back limited projects at first, but gradually back more.
(4) **Uniform backer (UB)**: they actively back all the time with their backings almost evenly distributed through their lifetime.

Two matters should be noted here: 1) Kickstarter clusters look much more smooth than Indiegogo clusters; 2) there is a slight difference between LB on both platforms, i.e., LB on Kickstarter shows a more sharp increase at later months than LB on Indiegogo does. The first issue results from the fact that Indiegogo dataset is smaller (with respect to # of backers) and sparser (with respect to # of backings per user) than Kickstarter dataset. As for the second issue, it may be because our Indiegogo dataset does not guarantee containing users' full backing histories and lacks some projects. However, we can still see an obvious increase in the backing pattern of LB on Indiegogo, which is matched with Kickstarter's.

5 UNDERSTANDING BACKING PATTERNS

Figure 5 indicates an interesting phenomenon that both EB and CB invest a lot at the beginning, but gradually lose interest and become less active, while UB is active in backing all the time and LB even supports an increasing number of projects over time. As EB and CB account for a large proportion (more than 40%) of frequent backers, figuring out why they have become inactive will not only help those backers out of the possible problems they are trapped in, but also contribute to the development of crowdfunding platforms. Therefore, we intend to do a quantitative analysis on the characteristics of these 4 groups of backers and propose some empirical answers to *RQ2: what are the characteristics of those backing patterns and possible factors impacting those patterns?* Note that here, we only show results on Kickstarter dataset but similar results are found on Indiegogo dataset as well, except for the success rate[2].

This section starts with analyzing characteristics of backing patterns, and based on these characteristics, we propose some possible factors explaining users' behaviors or backing patterns.

5.1 Characteristics of Patterns

When analyzing characteristics of backing patterns, cumulative distribution functions (CDF) are frequently adopted for displaying the distribution differences among those four groups in various aspects. For a certain value X, CDFs show the fraction of backers who have values less than or equal to X. To quantitatively measure the differences between distributions of two backing patterns' samples, we conduct *Kolmogorov-Smirnov* test [27], a wildly used significance test for checking whether two samples are drawn from the same distribution. Accordingly, for any pair of backing patterns in any situation, KS tests reject their samples being drawn from the same distribution with p-value less than 0.01.

[2]Besides *All-or-Nothing*, Indiegogo gives one more choice, *Take-it-All*, to creators, which means backers are still able to get their rewards even if the goal amount is not reached. With more than 90% of Indiegogo projects starting with flexible funding, we cannot determine whether projects are successful or not on Indiegogo dataset.

5.1.1 *Backing length and backing number.*

Figure 6(a) presents the CDF of backers' lifetime backing length. As expected, EB has obvious shorter lifetime backing length than other three groups, both in general and on average, in that it gradually loses interest in backing from the beginning. Despite the fact that CB has similar backing length distribution as UB, its backing number is apparently larger than UB's as indicated in Figure 6(b), which suggests that CB is as valuable as UB. CB could even contribute more to the platforms if it remained active during the second half backing history. In addition, we examine the change of each group's backing number over time and find some inflection points. As shown in Figure 6(c)[3], on average, EB is actively backing during the first 12 months, while the passion of CB lasts 24 months, two times longer than EB's, after cautiously investing 3 months at the beginning.

5.1.2 *Project Cost.*

Besides participation duration and backing numbers, the amount of pledged funds is another important measurement for the contribution of users to the platforms. We compare different groups' spending behaviors and make several observations. First, as shown in Figure 7(a), on average, EB spends the least, whereas LB contributes the most. Considering the proportion of each group on the platform, UB, even if ranked 3rd on average spending, invests 151 million dollars in total, which is almost 1.5 times more than the second CB does. Because of the small number of LB, it only pledges 62 million dollars, which is slightly more than EB does. The fact that EB and CB pledge around 30% of funds among frequent backers implies that they are indispensable for the platforms. Second, Figure 7(b) demonstrates that EB and CB prefer offering smaller pledging fund per project, while LB and UB are willing to spend a little bit more on each project. Interestingly, both Figures 7(b) and 7(c) suggest EB and CB have similar average offering per project. Last but not least, Figure 7(c) shows that EB offers less money for each project when starting investments but gradually increases its offerings. We can see a similar pattern in CB's average offerings over projects as well. Taking together with their temporal backing patterns, this phenomenon may occur due to their limited budget. At the beginning, in order to support multiple projects, EB and CB have to lower down their offering per project, but with their backing numbers gradually decreasing, they are able to afford more offering per project.

5.1.3 *Success Rate.*

Next, we investigate on the success rate of each backing group. Surprisingly, 22.4% of the 150K frequent backers (with at least 10 backings) in Kickstarter dataset have never failed in backing, even though their average backing number is 18. As for each backing group, 25.1% of UB, 24.4% of LB, 21.2% of EB and 17.6% of CB achieve the perfect backing histories. Although we analyze frequent backers, who have up to 90.5% success rate on average, there are still some differences among these four groups. Figure 8(a) shows that LB and UB are better at backing and have higher success rate than other two groups, which is consistent with the ratios of perfect backers in each group to some extent. Moreover, looking at each group's

[3]Note that it is the overall trend that matters not the absolute values, which are relatively small due to the data sparsity (not all users invest projects in every month).

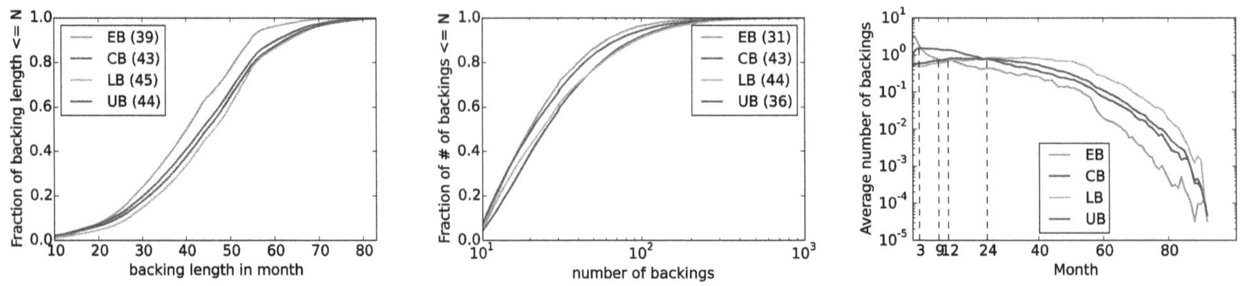

(a) CDF of backing history length

(b) CDF of total backing number

(c) Average backings per month.

Figure 6: Backing length and backing number of each pattern (with average value in parentheses)

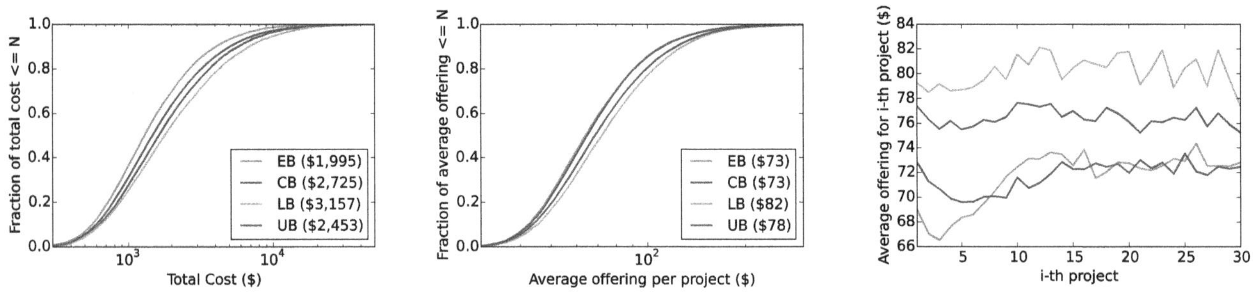

(a) CDF of total cost

(b) CDF of average offering

(c) Average offering for each backer's i-th project

Figure 7: Backing cost (with average value in parentheses). Cost refers to the money spent on successful projects, while offering just indicates the prices that users are willing to offer for the projects, which may or may not be successful.

average success rate at i-th project from Figure 8(b), we can see a clear gap between success rates of EB and CB and those of LB and UB. In addition, we note the slopes of CB and EB's curves are relatively smaller, indicating a faster drop in their success rates. Considering temporal backing patterns of EB, the low success rate may result from the fact that EB invests very frequently at the beginning without caring much about its backings' outcomes, while other three groups, especially LB, gain more experience before conducting massive investments and certainly reach much higher success rate in backings.

5.1.4 *Categories and Creators.*

Previous studies have shown that topical preference and connections with creator play an important role in users' backing behaviors [11, 22]. Category entropy is applied to measure users' topical preference and defined as follows:

$$CatEntropy(u) = -\sum_{i=1}^{C} \frac{n_i}{N} log_2 \frac{n_i}{N} \tag{1}$$

In the equation, C is the number of categories, N is the total number of projects backed by user u and n_i is the number of backed projects under category i. Compared with uniformly backing all 15 project categories on Kickstarter, where category entropy is around 4, Figure 9(a) indicates that all four groups have strong preferences in backing categories, which is consistent with previous studies. We also notice that EB and CB have larger entropies than other two groups in general, which means they have broader interests in backing projects. As expected, Figure 9(b) shows that there are big chances that frequent backers will support creators whom they have supported before. In addition, the probability of LB and UB funding a past supported creator is at least 40% higher than that of EB and CB during the first 20 backings. Although EB and CB's lower probability at the first a few backings may result from their more frequent backings in a short time at the beginning, they are still less likely to fund a past supported creator than LB and UB after a longer time, say after 20 backings.

5.2 Causes of Patterns

Having observed various characteristics of users' temporal backing patterns, we seek potential factors impacting users' behaviors. Since users' backing behaviors can rely on diverse factors, including personal backing strategies, we just provide some general empirical analysis here and leave user studies for future investigation. Specifically, we focus on the impact of project outcomes and creators in this section.

5.2.1 *Project Success.*

In Section 5.1.3, we have identified the huge differences among each group's backing success rate that success rates of EB and CB are not only much lower than those of LB and UB, but also drop faster than other two groups at the early stage. Considering EB and CB gradually lose interests in backing from the beginning, the

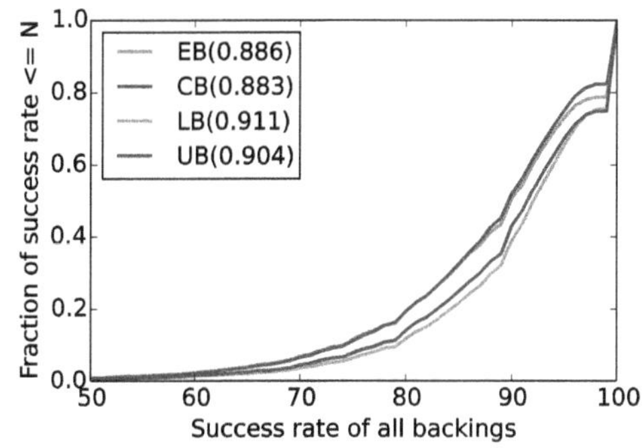

(a) CDF of success rate

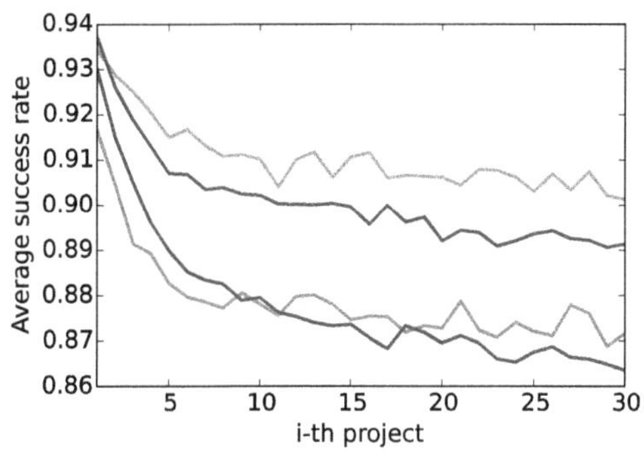

(b) Average success rate for each backer's i-th project

Figure 8: Success rate (with average value in parentheses)

relatively low success rate should play an important role in their later inactivity. Thus we argue that EB and CB may be discouraged by experiencing relatively low backing success rates and failing several projects initially, and thereby progressively become less active in backing. Based on this finding, in order to encourage users to be active, platforms may recommend some easily successful projects to those who have a bad start initially in backing.

5.2.2 Connections with Creators.
Another interesting observation comes from Section 5.1.4. Note that both LB and UB are more likely to fund their past supported creators, indicating stronger connections between them and their creators. During the first 20 backings, after which EB and CB gradually become inactive, LB and UB show at least 40% higher probability to support a recognized creator. Because of LB and UB's willingness to return to fund past supported creators, there could be some long-term connections being established between them and their creators. Accordingly, favorable relationship between users and creators may increase the probabilities of users being a returned backer, and encourage users to continue backing on the platforms. Hence, both platforms and creators should pay more attention to building up mutual trust between backers and creators.

6 EARLY PREDICTION

In addition to the differences in the dynamics of backing numbers, we have shown clear distinctions among these 4 groups in various

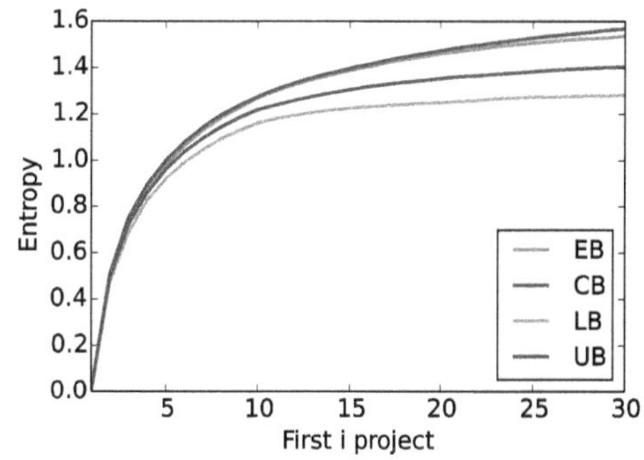

(a) Average entropy of each backer's first i projects

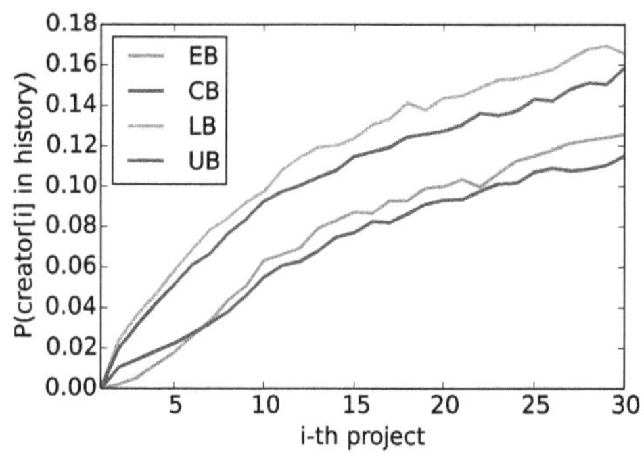

(b) Probability of each backer's i-th project being created by his/her past supported creator

Figure 9: Categories and creators

Table 3: Duration in days at i-th finished project

at i-th finished project	1	2	3	4	5	6
Kickstarter	18	104	166	220	271	320
Indiegogo	26	162	252	327	396	465

aspects, including project cost and success rate, in the previous section. To validate the insights from the previous section, we build up models on users' early backing features to see whether we are able to predict users' later backing patterns. Apparently, the earlier we can detect the loss of users' interests, the better we may help them stay active by taking actions such as promotion. Therefore, we turn to *RQ3: can we identify users' backing patterns at early stages?* and investigate on building early prediction models in this section.

6.1 Set-up

To validate our analysis, we build 4-class classifiers to predict users' backing patterns at first. Then, based on the observation in section 5.1.2 that EB and CB pledge around 30% of funds among frequent backers and had the potential to contribute even more if they stayed active, we propose to build binary classifiers to distinguish EB and CB from UB and LB as well.

6.1.1 Prediction Time.

Section 5.2.1 points out the influence of project outcomes on users' future behaviors. As such, it should be reasonable to make inferences after observing a few project outcomes. Table 3 displays Kickstarter and Indiegogo users' duration in days[4] when their i-th project is finished. As shown in Figure 6(c), since 9th month, EB has already been less active than all other three groups, which might be too late for user retention. Consequently, we propose to predict users' backing patterns at the end of their 1st to 4th project on Kickstarter and correspondingly, at the end of 1st to 3rd project on Indiegogo.

6.1.2 Features.

After setting up the prediction time, we extract the following features from users' behavior data during the time period to build classifiers. Note that, when clustering users' backing patterns, we only used Z-normalized time series of users' backing numbers in their entire lifetimes. However, here we only utilize users' first a few months data to extract features.

(1) **Temporal (4 features)**: As indicated in Figure 6(c), even when just joining the platforms, different groups of users behave differently in backing. Therefore, dynamics of users' backing numbers should be valuable features. In addition, we include the number of backed projects[5], duration in days, mean and standard deviation of the time difference between two adjacent backings.
(2) **Backer (3 features)**: In sections 5.1.2 and 5.1.3, we observe that averaging offering per project and success rate vary with different groups in the first a few backings. Therefore, we formulate backer features, including backing success rate, mean and standard deviation of backed money per project.
(3) **Creator (4 features)**: Sections 5.1.4 and 5.2.2 discuss about the potential encouragement of favorable connections between backers and creators. Thus, based on the assumption that experienced creators may be good at establishing favorable relationship with backers, we also extract features from creators, involving their past backing numbers, backing success rate, creating numbers, and creating success rate.

6.1.3 Criteria.

Because of the imbalance of our data, we evaluate the multi-class classification results using two popular measures–i.e., macro-F1 score and G-means, to be defined as follows:

$$Macro\text{-}F1 = \frac{1}{N_c} * \sum_{i=1}^{N_c} F1_i \qquad (2)$$

$$G\text{-}means = \sqrt[N_c]{\prod_{i=1}^{N_c} recall_i} \qquad (3)$$

with

$$F1_i = \frac{2 * precision_i * recall_i}{precision_i + recall_i}$$

[4]By the end of i-th project, how long have that user been on the platform?
[5]At the end of i-th project, users may back more than i projects, though their outcomes are not available then.

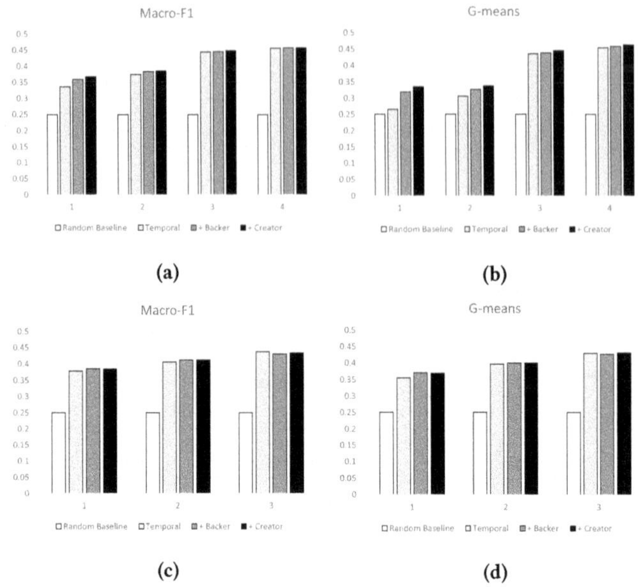

Figure 10: Predictive performance for inferring users' future behavior patterns at the end of first few projects. (a) and (b) show results on Kickstarter dataset, while (c) and (d) display Indiegogo's.

$$precision_i = \frac{\sum TP_i}{\sum TP_i + \sum FP_i}$$

$$recall_i = \frac{\sum TP_i}{\sum TP_i + \sum FN_i}$$

In the equations, N_c stands for the number of classes, TP for True Positive, FP for False Positive, and FN for False Negative. For 4-class classification, random baselines will score 0.25 on both metrics.

As for binary classification, Area Under the ROC Curve (AUC) is employed to measure the possibility that the classifier will rank a randomly chosen positive instance higher than a randomly chosen negative one. Thus, a random baseline will have 0.50 of AUC score.

To handle our imbalanced data, via preliminary testing, we chose the AdaBoost algorithm [29] with a decision tree classifier and under-sampling [8], which has given the best performance on 10-fold cross validation.

6.2 Results

6.2.1 Predicting backing patterns.

The results are given in Figure 10. Generally, based on our proposed features, we can achieve promising performance on inferring users' future backing patterns when they just complete first 3 to 4 projects. As expected, backer and creator features contribute to the prediction, especially at the end of their first or second project, which validates our analysis in the previous section. With more user backings being observed, although overall performance is improved significantly, temporal features play a more essential role in the prediction and other two features only lead to smaller increments. Consistent with the fact that success rate is indeterminable on Indiegogo dataset as mentioned in section 5, backer and creator features show very limited improvement in the prediction.

Table 4: Binary classification results (ROC AUC)

at i-th finished project	1	2	3	4
Random Baseline	0.50	0.50	0.50	0.50
Kickstarter	0.71	0.78	0.81	0.82
Indiegogo	0.63	0.70	0.73	0.75

6.2.2 Identifying early backers and cautious backers.
Having validated our analysis and corresponding features, we build a binary classifier to identify EB and CB from all frequent backers for user retention. As shown in Table 4, at the end of each user's 1st project, we are able to tell whether that user will be EB and CB with 0.71 AUC on Kickstarter and 0.63 AUC on Indiegogo. When one's finished project number reaches 4, AUC increases to 0.82 and 0.75 respectively. Additionally, when joining the platforms for just 5 months, which corresponds to the time of 3rd project finished on Kickstarter and second project finished on Indiegogo, EB and CB can be identified very well by the built classifier, with 0.81 AUC and 0.70 AUC, correspondingly.

6.2.3 Discussion.
Although 4-class classification models do not achieve superior performance in backing pattern inference, we show the possibility of building predictive models, which confirms the relationship between users' early activities and their future behaviors. Based on the assumption that platforms may do some user retention to help potential EB and CB stay active, we formulate the identification of EB and CB as a binary classification problem and obtain very promising results. At the end of users' 3rd project, we are able to identify EB and CB with 0.81 AUC on Kickstarter and 0.73 AUC on Indiegogo. Certainly, there is still much room for improvement in EB and CB identification. For example, we can incorporate more user behavioral features, such as users' view and clicking histories. We leave this for future study. Throughout these preliminary studies, we emphasize that there are four distinct backing patterns, which are proved to be strongly related with users' very early behaviors, and show encouraging results in identifying those who tend to progressively become inactive at early stages.

7 CONCLUSION

7.1 Concluding Remarks

Having a better understanding of the backers' dynamic and temporal behaviors allows crowdfunding platforms to provide better services and improve customer retention. In spite of such an importance, however, prior studies lack the exploration of the temporal dynamics of backer behaviors. As such, this paper aimed to take a step to investigate on backers' temporal behaviors.

To analyze backers' temporal behaviors, we have collected large-scale datasets from two of the most popular crowdfunding platforms, Kickstarter and Indiegogo. Employing time series clustering methods, we discovered four distinct temporal backing patterns on both platforms (**RQ1**), including Early Backer (EB), Cautious Backer (CB), Uniform Backer (UB), and Late Backer (LB). Among these patterns, both EB and CB show decreasing interests in backing, whereas UB constantly invests on projects and LB even progressively supports an increasing number of projects. Driven by the research question why backers have such temporal backing patterns (**RQ2**), we conducted a quantitative analysis, explored the characteristics of these patterns in various aspects, and proposed possible factors affecting users' backing behaviors.

In our findings, we noted that the outcomes of backers' first a few projects are closely correlated with their future backing behaviors. For instance, initial low success rate may discourage users from investing further. In addition, we found that the connections with project creators could be an another factor impacting users' backing behaviors–that is, favorable relationship between backers and creators seems to encourage backers to keep supporting the same creators and/or invest on more projects. In order to validate our analysis, we extracted related features from users' first few backings, and showed promising results in early predicting all four temporal backing patterns (**RQ3**). Moreover, aimed at helping platforms with respect to user retention, we proposed to build binary classification models to identify two types of backers–EB and CB–at a very early stage and achieved encouraging performance.

7.2 Limitations and Future Work

Despite encouraging results, our work is not without limitations.

First, as usual for data-driven study using social media data, our study is based on a small fraction of real-life datasets sampled from two crowdfunding platforms. Due to the limitation of programming APIs, we had to adopt two different data collection strategies that may have introduced two types of sampling bias: (1) For Kickstarter dataset, as we obtained users' profile URLs from projects' comments, backing histories of those backers who seldom leave comments are missing. However, we hypothesized that frequent backers care more about their backings than occasional backers and therefore should be more active in leaving comments. (2) On Indiegogo, in each project's backer list, there are lots of anonymous users that we could not identify. Therefore, our dataset might be from those users who are less concerned about their privacy. In addition, we could not obtain users' full backing histories, which may affect some users' temporal backing patterns and make them act as noises in our dataset. As to these potential issues in our datasets, we attempted to mitigate the effect by obtaining relatively large-scale datasets and verified that there were consistent results on both platforms. Nevertheless, to be able to generalize our findings further, we plan to collect less-biased datasets and repeat our study on other types of crowdfunding platforms (e.g., Change.org) as well.

Second, in this paper, we mainly focused on the relationship between users' temporal backing behaviors and project features. However, it is worth noting that user features, including users' demographics and logging histories, could be equally informative. Therefore, we intend to explore connections between users' temporal backing behaviors and user features.

Third, although our investigation was based on quantitative analysis, some unforeseen factors affecting users' backing behaviors may not be reflected by the collected data. For example, users' backing behaviors might be influenced by their friends'. Accordingly, conducting user studies can be a good complement to fully understand users' temporal behaviors. Such a study will not only validate our findings in this paper but also provide potential causes of backers' actions.

ACKNOWLEDGMENTS

The authors would like to thank the anonymous referees for their valuable comments and helpful suggestions. This work was supported in part by NSF CNS-1553035, NSF CNS-1422215, NSF IUSE-1525601, and Samsung GRO 2015 awards. Any opinions, findings and conclusions or recommendations expressed in this material are the author(s) and do not necessarily reflect those of the sponsors.

REFERENCES

[1] Tim Althoff and Jure Leskovec. 2015. Donor retention in online crowdfunding communities: A case study of donorschoose. org. In *Proceedings of the 24th International Conference on World Wide Web*. ACM, 34–44.

[2] Jisun An, Daniele Quercia, and Jon Crowcroft. 2014. Recommending investors for crowdfunding projects. In *Proceedings of the 23rd international conference on World wide web*. ACM, 261–270.

[3] David Arthur and Sergei Vassilvitskii. 2007. k-means++: The advantages of careful seeding. In *Proceedings of the eighteenth annual ACM-SIAM symposium on Discrete algorithms*. Society for Industrial and Applied Mathematics, 1027–1035.

[4] Paul Belleflamme, Thomas Lambert, and Armin Schwienbacher. 2014. Crowdfunding: Tapping the right crowd. *Journal of business venturing* 29, 5 (2014), 585–609.

[5] Donald J Berndt and James Clifford. 1994. Using dynamic time warping to find patterns in time series.. In *KDD workshop*, Vol. 10. Seattle, WA, 359–370.

[6] Jinwook Chung and Kyumin Lee. 2015. A Long-Term Study of a Crowdfunding Platform: Predicting Project Success and Fundraising Amount. In *Proceedings of the 26th ACM Conference on Hypertext & Social Media*. ACM, 211–220.

[7] Douglas J Cumming, Gaël Leboeuf, and Armin Schwienbacher. 2014. Crowdfunding models: Keep-it-all vs. all-or-nothing. In *Paris December 2014 finance meeting EUROFIDAI-AFFI paper*, Vol. 10.

[8] Chris Drummond, Robert C Holte, et al. 2003. C4. 5, class imbalance, and cost sensitivity: why under-sampling beats over-sampling. In *Workshop on learning from imbalanced datasets II*, Vol. 11. Citeseer.

[9] Vincent Etter, Matthias Grossglauser, and Patrick Thiran. 2013. Launch hard or go home!: predicting the success of kickstarter campaigns. In *Proceedings of the first ACM conference on Online social networks*. ACM, 177–182.

[10] Elizabeth M Gerber and Julie Hui. 2013. Crowdfunding: Motivations and deterrents for participation. *ACM Transactions on Computer-Human Interaction (TOCHI)* 20, 6 (2013), 34.

[11] Elizabeth M Gerber, Julie S Hui, and Pei-Yi Kuo. 2012. Crowdfunding: Why people are motivated to post and fund projects on crowdfunding platforms. In *Proceedings of the International Workshop on Design, Influence, and Social Technologies: Techniques, Impacts and Ethics*, Vol. 2. 11.

[12] Michael D Greenberg, Julie Hui, and Elizabeth Gerber. 2013. Crowdfunding: a resource exchange perspective. In *CHI'13 Extended Abstracts on Human Factors in Computing Systems*. ACM, 883–888.

[13] Michael D Greenberg, Bryan Pardo, Karthic Hariharan, and Elizabeth Gerber. 2013. Crowdfunding support tools: predicting success & failure. In *CHI'13 Extended Abstracts on Human Factors in Computing Systems*. ACM, 1815–1820.

[14] Julie S Hui, Michael D Greenberg, and Elizabeth M Gerber. 2014. Understanding the role of community in crowdfunding work. In *Proceedings of the 17th ACM conference on Computer supported cooperative work & social computing*. ACM, 62–74.

[15] Venkat Kuppuswamy and Barry L Bayus. 2015. Crowdfunding creative ideas: The dynamics of project backers in Kickstarter. (2015).

[16] Yusan Lin, Wang-Chien Lee, and Chung-Chou H Chang. 2016. Analysis of rewards on reward-based crowdfunding platforms. In *Advances in Social Networks Analysis and Mining (ASONAM), 2016 IEEE/ACM International Conference on*. IEEE, 501–504.

[17] Chun-Ta Lu, Sihong Xie, Xiangnan Kong, and Philip S Yu. 2014. Inferring the impacts of social media on crowdfunding. In *Proceedings of the 7th ACM international conference on Web search and data mining*. ACM, 573–582.

[18] Tanushree Mitra and Eric Gilbert. 2014. The language that gets people to give: Phrases that predict success on kickstarter. In *Proceedings of the 17th ACM conference on Computer supported cooperative work & social computing*. ACM, 49–61.

[19] Ethan Mollick. 2014. The dynamics of crowdfunding: An exploratory study. *Journal of business venturing* 29, 1 (2014), 1–16.

[20] Michael Muller, Werner Geyer, Todd Soule, and John Wafer. 2014. Geographical and organizational distances in enterprise crowdfunding. In *Proceedings of the 17th ACM conference on Computer supported cooperative work & social computing*. ACM, 778–789.

[21] François Petitjean, Alain Ketterlin, and Pierre Gançarski. 2011. A global averaging method for dynamic time warping, with applications to clustering. *Pattern Recognition* 44, 3 (2011), 678–693.

[22] Vineeth Rakesh, Jaegul Choo, and Chandan K Reddy. 2015. Project Recommendation Using Heterogeneous Traits in Crowdfunding.. In *ICWSM*. 337–346.

[23] Vineeth Rakesh, Wang-Chien Lee, and Chandan K Reddy. 2016. Probabilistic Group Recommendation Model for Crowdfunding Domains. In *Proceedings of the Ninth ACM International Conference on Web Search and Data Mining*. ACM, 257–266.

[24] Thanawin Rakthanmanon, Bilson Campana, Abdullah Mueen, Gustavo Batista, Brandon Westover, Qiang Zhu, Jesin Zakaria, and Eamonn Keogh. 2012. Searching and mining trillions of time series subsequences under dynamic time warping. In *Proceedings of the 18th ACM SIGKDD international conference on Knowledge discovery and data mining*. ACM, 262–270.

[25] Michael Siering, Jascha-Alexander Koch, and Amit V Deokar. 2016. Detecting Fraudulent Behavior on Crowdfunding Platforms: The Role of Linguistic and Content-Based Cues in Static and Dynamic Contexts. *Journal of Management Information Systems* 33, 2 (2016), 421–455.

[26] Michael A Stanko and David H Henard. 2016. How Crowdfunding Influences Innovation. *MIT Sloan Management Review* 57, 3 (2016), 15.

[27] R Wilcox. 2005. Kolmogorov–smirnov test. *Encyclopedia of biostatistics* (2005).

[28] Anbang Xu, Xiao Yang, Huaming Rao, Wai-Tat Fu, Shih-Wen Huang, and Brian P Bailey. 2014. Show me the money!: An analysis of project updates during crowdfunding campaigns. In *Proceedings of the SIGCHI conference on human factors in computing systems*. ACM, 591–600.

[29] Ji Zhu, Hui Zou, Saharon Rosset, and Trevor Hastie. 2009. Multi-class adaboost. *Statistics and its Interface* 2, 3 (2009), 349–360.

A Keyword-Based Method for Measuring Sentence Similarity

Yuanjun Bi, Kai Deng and JinXing Cheng
Suning R&D center, Palo Alto, CA, USA
{sophia.bi, kai.deng, jim.cheng}@ussuning.com

ABSTRACT

In this paper, a sentence similarity computing approach based on keywords is presented. First, it extracts the keywords from a sentence. Then the approach computes ranking scores for the keywords. Finally it applies these ranking scores into the sentence similarity computation using the Jaccard similarity coefficient. Experiments on a real word chatterbot system dataset demonstrate that this proposed approach significantly improves the relevance of sentence similarity method up to 30%.

1 INTRODUCTION

In recent years, chatterbot becomes a hot research area, which also has wide industrial applications. One important application is online customer services, which saves significant time and human resource by simply texting or asking a chatterbot. One common approach in a chatterbot system is to pull a response with the most matching sentence from a database, in which conversations are stored as question-answer pairs. Then answering a query can be reduced to the problem of similarity identification between the query and candidates in a database. Next, the chatterbot replies with the answer towards the most similar question. Most research work for detecting similarity between two documents focus on shared words [3]. But when it comes to a short term sentence, the similarity computation may be occupied with shared less informative words. Here we found that by using keywords to represent a sentence, we can avoid the confusion of noisy words. In this paper, we explored a novel method of computing ranking score for keywords and applying them to the similarity computation. We conducted the experiments on the Suning chatterbot system *Sunny* that provides online customer service for transactions on Suning.com. The task is to find the most similar question at the semantic level for a query.

2 KEYWORDS EXTRACTION AND RANKING

For computing the ranking score of keywords, we worked from three heuristic aspects. Firstly, we generated possible key terms from our database by their frequency. Secondly, we considered the parts of speech of the words. Last but not least, we took into account the position of the words. **(1) Keywords Extraction**. To generate the key terms from the database, we classified the database sentences by intents, such as greeting, shipping and returning. For each intent, we extracted top N frequent words. The reason for extracting top N frequent words from each class instead of from all documents is that, it is possible some classes have much less instances than other classes. Extracting keywords independently can avoid keywords in minor classes replaced by non keywords in major classes. For example, in our database, the greeting class has more queries than the shipping class. The word *"hello"* appears only two times, but it should be considered as a keyword in the greeting class. The word *"tomorrow"* appears five times, but it should not be considered as a keyword in the shipping class. Also, classification guarantees words that present the same intent will appear together [4]. After stop-words removal, we obtain the keywords list. **(2) Keywords Ranking**. For our database, we observed that verbs normally play an important role in a sentence. So in the ranking progress, we assign weight to words that are verbs. We also found that in our database, the intent of a query relies on the position of verb. Statically, the verb closer to the end of a sentence is more important than the verb in the front of a sentence. Therefore, we take into account the position for keywords ranking. The keywords ranking algorithm is shown in Algorithm 1.

Algorithm 1: KEYWORDS RANKING ALGORITHM

Input: $Sentence \leftarrow \{w_1, w_2, \ldots, w_n\}$
$K \leftarrow$ generated keywords set
$decay_v \leftarrow$ verb decay weight
$decay_k \leftarrow$ non-verb decay weight
$score_v \leftarrow$ initialized verb score
$score_k \leftarrow$ initialized non-verb keywords score
$score_{min} \leftarrow$ bottom value of score
Output: keywords score s_i for each $w_i \in Sentence$;
1 $S \leftarrow \varnothing$
2 **foreach** w_i *in Sentence in reverse order* **do**
3 $\quad POS_i \leftarrow$ part-of-speech of w_i
4 $\quad$ **if** POS_i *is verb* **then**
5 $\quad\quad s_i \leftarrow score_v$
6 $\quad\quad score_v \leftarrow max\{score_{min}, score_v - decay_v\}$
7 $\quad$ **else if** $w_i \in K$ **then**
8 $\quad\quad s_i \leftarrow score_k$
9 $\quad\quad score_k \leftarrow max\{score_{min}, score_k - decay_k\}$
10 $\quad$ **else**
11 $\quad\quad s_i \leftarrow score_{min}$
12 $\quad S \leftarrow S \cup \{(w_i, s_i)\}$
13 return S

The keywords set K in the input of Algorithm 1 is pre-generated from our database. This offline input may not work for words not in the database. To address this, line 4 assigns weights to verbs even though they are not shown in K. Besides the part-of-speech, we found that the words closer to the end of a sentence are more informative to represent its intent. To utilize this observation, we parsed words a sentence segments in reverse order. And decay weights in lines 6 and 9 guarantee scores become smaller as words approach the beginning of the sentence. Also, all the scores have a lower bound $score_{min}$ to avoid negative value.

WebSci '17, June 25-28, 2017, Troy, NY, USA
 978-1-4503-4896-6/17/06.
DOI: http://dx.doi.org/10.1145/3091478.3098878

Table 1: Differences evaluation compared to General

Category change	Keywords	Keywords&POS
0→ [1, 2]	54(28%)	75(31%)
2→ [1, 0]	44(23%)	53(22%)
0→0	93(49%)	113(47%)
Total	191	241

3 SENTENCE SIMILARITY

There is a large portion of work focused on the sentence similarity. Achananuparp [1] evaluate fourteen existing similarity score between two sentences. In this work, we choose Jaccard similarity coefficient to compute the similarity between two sentences. Jaccard similarity coefficient is defined as the size of intersection set divided by the size of the union set. i.e., Function 1 Here, Q is our query sentence words set. C is the candidate sentence words set. It is high efficient and easy to implement for industry application.

$$J(A, B) = \frac{|A \cap B|}{|A \cup B|} \tag{1}$$

To apply keywords acquired from Algorithm 1 into Function 1, we generated Function 2. In this function, the similarity score between query Q and candidate C equals the division of their intersection set score and union set score. Let $f(S, w_i)$ be the ranking score of the word w_i by applying Algorithm 1 on sentence S, where w_i is one word from sentence S. Then the intersection set score is the sum of $f(Q, w_i)$ for all words w_i both in Q and C. In the union set, if a word w_i only comes from query Q, then its ranking score is $f(Q, w_i)$. While a word w_i that only belongs to candidate C's gets the ranking score $f(C, w_i)$. Since the union score adds keywords score not in query Q, candidates whose keywords are different from keywords in query get a smaller similarity score. For example, *"Please ship my order."* has three intersection words with *"Please cancel my order."*. But since these two sentences' keywords(*"ship"* vs *"cancel"*) are different, it gets a smaller score from Function 2. This makes finding the matching candidate more reasonable. Function 2 reduces to Function 1 if all keywords scores are the same value.

$$J_{keywords}(Q, C) = \frac{\sum_{w_i \in Q \cap C} f(Q, w_i)}{\sum_{w_i \in Q} f(Q, w_i) + \sum_{w_j \in C \setminus Q} f(C, w_j)} \tag{2}$$

4 EXPERIMENTS

Experiment Setup: Our experiments are conducted on the database of Suning Chatbot system. There are 12,816 question-answer pairs in our database. They can be classified into 22 different intents. By using top N frequent method, we generate 1,827 keywords. We generated two kinds of testing data set. (1) **Raw Test** 2,069 testing queries which are extracted from real-world human customer service online chatting logs. We use this dataset to evaluate our methods to questions that may not appear in the given database. (2) **Standard Test** 1,724 testing queries which are all relevant to questions in our databases. For each query in testing cases, we used three methods to get the matching question. (1) **General** Jaccard similarity computation in Function 1; (2) **Keywords** method only considers words in the keywords file. That means line 4 to line 6 in Algorithm 1 will be ignored when computing the ranking score. Then use the score in Jaccard similarity computation of Function 2.

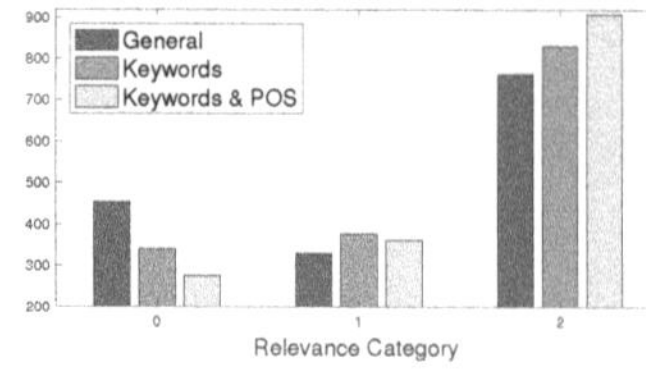

Figure 1: Distribution of relevance category on Raw Test

(3) **Keywords&POS** method applies ranking score from Algorithm 1 to the Jaccard similarity computation of Function 2.
Performance: We evaluated the effectiveness of three methods mentioned above at different levels of similarity. Define category 2 as *Exact Match*, 1 as *Relevant* and 0 as *Unrelated*. We first run three methods on Raw Test. Figure 1 shows the relevance category distribution, which clearly shows Keywords and Keywords&POS methods outperform the baseline General method. They have more cases in category 1 and 2, and less cases in category 0. In addition, Keywords&POS method performs much better than the Keywords method in category 2, which means Keywords&POS method has better similarity judgement when met with sentences with different representations. Then we run three methods on Standard Test. To compare the performance of Keywords and Keywords&POS methods in detail, we focused on cases where these three methods have different results. Table 1 shows that Keyword&POS method has more different cases than the Keywords method. This is because Keyword&POS method considers verbs that don't belong to key terms list. It changed the baseline results more aggressively. But Keyword&POS has a greater ratio change from Unrelated to more relevant(1 or 2), and has less ratio change from 2 or 1 to Unrelated. Both experiments indicate our keywords approach is more effective than original Jaccard similarity in measuring sentences' similarity.

5 CONCLUSIONS AND FUTURE WORK

We present a novel sentence similarity measurement which computes each words' ranking score utilizing words' frequency, part-of-speech and their position in the sentence. It applies theses scores on a modified Jaccard similarity coefficient method, to get the most matching candidate sentence. Experiments on a Suning Chatbot dataset validated the effectiveness of the proposed methods, and showed that the extracted keywords and words' part-of-speech significantly improved the overall effectiveness of finding the most similar sentence. For the future direction, instead of simply assigning larger weight to later position, we plan to study advanced utility of words' position [2] to further improve the performance.

REFERENCES

[1] Palakorn Achananuparp, Xiaohua Hu, and Xiajiong Shen. 2008. The evaluation of sentence similarity measures. In *International Conference on Data Warehousing and Knowledge Discovery*. Springer, 305–316.
[2] Yuhua Li, Zuhair Bandar, David McLean, and James O'shea. 2004. A Method for Measuring Sentence Similarity and ilts Application to Conversational Agents.. In *FLAIRS Conference*. 820–825.
[3] Donald Metzler, Yaniv Bernstein, W Bruce Croft, Alistair Moffat, and Justin Zobel. 2005. Similarity measures for tracking information flow. In *Proceedings of the 14th ACM international conference on Information and knowledge management*. ACM, 517–524.
[4] Rada Mihalcea, Courtney Corley, Carlo Strapparava, and others. 2006. Corpus-based and knowledge-based measures of text semantic similarity.

Paving the WAI: Defining Web-Augmented Interactions.

Fabien Gandon
UCA, Inria, CNRS, I3S
2004 rt Lucioles
Sophia Antipolis, France 06992
Fabien.Gandon@inria.fr

Alain.Giboin
UCA, Inria, CNRS, I3S
2004 rt Lucioles
Sophia Antipolis, France 06992
Alain.Giboin@inria.fr

ABSTRACT

We define and provide real cases of "Web-Augmented Interactions" (WAI) with the world, a new family of interactions designed to exploit resources from the Web to improve the users' experience with the devices surrounding them.

CCS CONCEPTS

• **Human-centered computing** → **Web-based interaction**; *Interaction design theory, concepts and paradigms*; • **Information systems** → *World Wide Web*; *Web interfaces*;

KEYWORDS

Web, Interaction, Augmentation

1 WEB-AUGMENTED INTERACTIONS (W.A.I.) A NEW CLASS OF INTERACTIONS

As the access to the Web spreads through the world, it also becomes a ubiquitous resource available for almost any application i.e. the Web is a part of the commons on which we can build new systems. In particular, by providing a growing number of services and data sources in almost any domain it has an impact on how we perceive our world (e.g. augmented reality), on how we move into it (e.g. enriched GPS) or how we act on it (e.g. Web APIs). The Web is deeply modifying our interaction means with the world to the point it creates new classes of interactions. Our experience in designing and implementing Social Semantic Web applications [10] led us to see the emerging of a new class of interactions we call Web-Augmented Interactions (WAI).

Definition 1.1. A Web-Augmented Interaction (WAI) is a user's interaction with a system that is improved by allowing the system to access Web resources in the background in order to analyze, specify or enrich the user's requests or the system's responses, for the benefit of the user (matching her goals, tasks and interaction context).

For instance the access to the Web for a robot can improve the interactions it can offer by providing it with additional knowledge about its environment to take decisions and initiatives. In a WAI, systems are using resources from the Web to simplify the interaction or enrich the user experience in a variety of ways: contextualizing the interaction, improving natural language processing, accessing pragmatic aspects, acquiring and using background knowledge, fueling dialogues with new material, proposing more hypermedia links and paths, etc. In this short paper, (1) we provide real cases of WAI from our research projects [10], and (2) we compare WAIs with related notions. So doing we complement the characterization of what is a WAI. Characterizing the WAI class of interactions is for us a first step in the elaboration of an approach to designing WAIs that will include guidelines and standards.

WebSci '17, June 25-28, 2017, Troy, NY, USA

ACM ISBN 978-1-4503-4896-6/17/06.
https://doi.org/10.1145/3091478.3098876

2 REAL CASES OF WEB-AUGMENTED INTERACTIONS

The idea of defining a new family of interactions emerged from a number of very different projects conducted in our team [10]. We selected a sample of these projects stressing the way they use the Web to improve interactions. This shows at the same time the diversity of cases and the transverse nature of WAIs. For each case we identify the kind of interaction, the provided augmentation, the Web resources allowing the augmentation, and the user's interaction goal.

- In the ALOOF project the goal is to interact with a robot more naturally by allowing it to learn missing knowledge about objects [15]. In order to better answer the request of the users, the robot accesses data on Web and even reads texts from the Web for instance to guess which room in the house is the most likely to have an object it was asked to fetch.
- In AZKAR [4] a robot supports remote visits of museums. To go beyond joystick-based navigation, the system combines cultural knowledge about the collections with data about the museum setup and from the Web to support abstract goals such as a topic based visit (e.g. all clothes in display). By accessing to Semantic Web resources such as ontology-based descriptions of museum objects and scenes, the AZKAR robot helps a remote visitor improve her interaction with the objects and scenes as she moves in the museum.
- The QAKIS search engines performs question-answering over linked data [6]. To improve its robustness to linguistic variations of questions it learns these variations from Web pages by looking at the different ways the same data is expressed across the pages.
- The OCKTOPUS project focused on analyzing on-line epistemic communities to detect them, their experts and the topics which bind them [11]. To interact with the results and in particular to label the detected communities in meaningful ways the system relied on Web resources (StackOverflow

tags and DBpedia) to find labels that made the results understandable.
- The WASABI project is interested in improving the analysis and access means to music collections. The project uses resources from the Web to augment the interactions of the users with a piece of music he is listening or creating. Adding information, suggestions and links by using the Web (natural language analysis of lyrics sites, linked data, APIs) it provides new routes and interaction means with the musics [3, 5].
- The SeaLife Browser [14] was an early experiment to automatically link Web resources (data, references) to the Web content a user was browsing and augment its experience with additional content and links.
- The myCampus project [9] relied on a Web based e-Wallet to represent personal knowledge about the user that was then used to simplify the interactions with on-line services in a context-aware way.

This non exhaustive list serves the purpose of showing diverse and real cases of WAIs. It also shows that this idea is transverse to application domains being used in robotics, connected objects (e.g. Amazon echo), augmented reality (e.g. Google glasses), tourism applications, e-book reader (e.g. translations), building automation, etc. But in every case we have a system that accesses Web resources (data, texts, services, etc.) to augment its knowledge about the users and the context of the interaction or to improve its analysis of the requests (disambiguate, variations, expand, narrow, etc.) and the quality of its reactions (additional knowledge, representations, suggestions, etc.).

3 WAI V.S. RELATED NOTIONS

Other kinds of augmented interactions have been identified. In *Instrumental interaction* [1], interactions between users and domain objects are mediated by software instruments. In a WAI the Web is used to provide domain objects or additional resources to the instruments of the interactions. *Knowledge-based augmented reality* (e.g. [8]) concentrates on the special case of local knowledge bases used to support a specific type of interaction namely augmented reality. *Ontology-driven document enrichment* (e.g. [12]) focuses on improving information retrieval and document access services using ontologies i.e. a very specific kind of resource and not necessarily on the Web. *Augmented browsing* (e.g. [13, 14]) targets the specific task of browsing and uses specific sources to automatically add definitions, links and additional resources. Finally, *Web Augmentation* [2] focuses on augmenting the functionality of the Web itself.

What distinguishes WAIs from other kinds of augmented interactions? (a) the interaction is augmented through the access or analysis of Web resources related to the user, the context or the task; (b) the augmentation is mainly performed by the system during the interaction although it can benefit from preprocessing; (c) this processing is intended to be transparent to the user, the goal being to simplify the user's task and support a partnership between the user and the system [7]; (c) the resulting interaction is improved in terms of user experience compared to the same interaction without using Web resources.

4 CONCLUSIONS

We proposed a definition of Web-Augmented Interaction (WAI) in what could be called a Web-Wide World. We provided real cases of this new type of interactions in very different contexts. We believe this domain requires the extension of current interaction design methodologies and places additional constraints on the Web architecture in terms of security, quality and real-time access.

REFERENCES

[1] Michel Beaudouin-Lafon. 2000. Instrumental interaction: an interaction model for designing post-WIMP user interfaces. In *SIGCHI*. ACM, 446–453.
[2] Niels Olof Bouvin. 1999. Unifying strategies for Web augmentation. In *Proc. Hypertext and hypermedia*. ACM, 91–100.
[3] Michel Buffa, Maxime Demetrio, and Nouriel Azria. 2016. Guitar pedal board using WebAudio. In *Web Audio Conference*. https://hal.inria.fr/hal-01400910
[4] Michel Buffa, Catherine Faron Zucker, Thierry Bergeron, and Hatim Aouzal. 2016. Semantic Web Technologies for improving remote visits of museums, using a mobile robot. ISWC Posters & Demonstrations. (Oct. 2016). https://hal.inria.fr/hal-01400924 Poster.
[5] Michel Buffa, Amine Hallili, and Philippe Renevier. 2015. MT5: a HTML5 multitrack player for musicians. In *WAC Web Audio Conference*. https://hal.inria.fr/hal-01150455
[6] Elena Cabrio, Julien Cojan, Alessio Palmero Aprosio, and Fabien Gandon. 2012. Natural Language Interaction with the Web of Data by Mining its Textual Side. *Intelligenza Artificiale* Special Issue on Natural Language Processing in the Web Era (2012), 137–154. https://hal.inria.fr/hal-01171879
[7] Marianela Ciolfi Felice, Sarah Fdili Alaoui, and Wendy Mackay. 2016. How Do Choreographers Craft Dance? Designing for a Choreographer-Technology Partnership. In *Proceedings of the 3rd International Symposium on Movement and Computing*, ACM (Ed.). Thessaloniki, Greece. https://doi.org/10.1145/2948910.2948941
[8] Steven Feiner, Blair Macintyre, and Dorée Seligmann. 1993. Knowledge-based augmented reality. *Commun. ACM* 36, 7 (1993), 53–62.
[10] Fabien Gandon, Michel Buffa, Elena Cabrio, Olivier Corby, Catherine Faron-Zucker, Alain Giboin, Nhan Le Thanh, Isabelle Mirbel, Peter Sander, Andrea G. B. Tettamanzi, and Serena Villata. 2013. Challenges in Bridging Social Semantics and Formal Semantics on the Web. In *Proc. ICEIS 2013 (LNBIP)*, Vol. 190. Springer, 3–15. https://hal.inria.fr/hal-01059273
[9] Fabien Gandon and Norman Sadeh. 2004. Semantic web technologies to reconcile privacy and context awareness. *Journal of Web Semantics* 1, 3 (2004), 20. https://doi.org/10.1016/j.websem.2003.07.008
[11] Zide Meng. 2016. *Temporal and semantic analysis of richly typed social networks from user-generated content sites on the web*. Theses. Université Côte d'Azur. https://hal.inria.fr/tel-01402612
[12] Enrico Motta, Simon Buckingham Shum, and John Domingue. 2000. Ontology-driven document enrichment: principles, tools and applications. *International Journal of Human-Computer Studies* 52, 6 (2000), 1071–1109.
[13] Evangelos Pafilis, Seán I O'Donoghue, Lars J Jensen, Heiko Horn, Michael Kuhn, Nigel P Brown, and Reinhard Schneider. 2009. Reflect: augmented browsing for the life scientist. *Nature biotechnology* 27, 6 (2009), 508–510.
[14] Michael Schroeder, Albert Burger, Patty Kostkova, Robert Stevens, Bianca Habermann, and Rose Dieng-Kuntz. 2006. Sealife: A Semantic Grid Browser for the Life Sciences Applied to the Study of Infectious Diseases. In *Proceedings of Healthgrid*. 167–178. http://www.booksonline.iospress.nl/Content/View.aspx?piid=4734
[15] Jay Young, Valerio Basile, Lars Kunze, Elena Cabrio, and Nick Hawes. 2016. Towards Lifelong Object Learning by Integrating Situated Robot Perception and Semantic Web Mining. In *Proceedings ECAI*. https://doi.org/10.3233/978-1-61499-672-9-1458

Understanding Para Social Breakups on Twitter

Kiran Garimella
Aalto University
Helsinki, Finland
kiran.garimella@aalto.fi

Jonathan Cohen
University of Haifa
Haifa, Israel
jcohen@com.haifa.ac.il

Ingmar Weber
Qatar Computing Research Institute
Doha, Qatar
ingmarweber@acm.org

ABSTRACT

Celebrity and fandom have been studied extensively in real life. Perceived virtual relationships, commonly known as para-social relationships (PSR) have been shown to exist between celebrities and fans [3]. The end of such relationships, para-social breakups (PSB), have also been studied [1]. However, with more and more celebrities using social media, the dynamics of PSR and PSB have changed. Using data from 57,000 fans for the top followed celebrities on Twitter, we try to understand how para-social breakups manifest on Twitter. We hypothesize that a PSB on Twitter happens as an act of unfollowing the celebrity and study the differences in engaging in a PSB between various types of fans. We find that, surprisingly, the most devoted fans are more likely to be involved in a para-social breakup. Given our scale and dependence on non-reactive data, our paper opens new avenues for research in para-social interactions.

INTRODUCTION

Since the advent of electronic media, para-social relationships (PSR) or para-social interactions (PSI) have been a widespread feature of advanced societies [3]. Horton and Wohl [3] define PSR as a one-way relationship that is imagined as a mutual relationship. Eyal et al. [1] introduce the idea of a para-social breakup, the end of a PSR. They find that a para-social breakup is like a regular romantic relationship breakup but not as intense.

Traditionally, the celebrity-fan relationship was very lop-sided, with one way interaction between the celebrity and the fan (typically through the television). With the advent of social media, PSR have become more reciprocal and 'social', or at least intensified the illusion of sociability by creating seemingly more personal and frequent communication between a celebrity and their fans. This has lead to the creation of a special type of fan behavior with fans expecting personal intimacy with celebs, leading to a para-social breakup, in cases where the fans don't get what they expected. This para-social breakup is manifested on social media by an act of unfollowing the celebrity.

In this paper, we perform the first large scale analysis of para-social breakups of fans with celebrities on Twitter. We define various fan types, based on their intimacy of interaction with the celebrity and study how fans belonging to the various types involve themselves in para-social breakups with celebrities.

WebSci'17, June 25-28, 2017, Troy, NY, USA.

DOI: 10.1145/3091478.3098877

Though para-social interactions [6] and breakups [2] on social media have been studied in the past, para-social breakups have special characteristics and understanding them at a large scale would be of great interest, with applications in brand loyalty, advertising and societal good, in general. Work has also been done on reasons for unfollowing on Twitter [4]. Kwak et al. conclude that most users unfollow 'those who left many tweets within a short time, created tweets about uninteresting topics, or tweeted about the mundane details of their lives.'. In the case of a para-social breakup, we find that most unfollowing happens as an act of defiance against the celeb and despair of not receiving the personal attention that fans perceive they deserve.

DATASET

We started with a set of the 15 most followed celebrities from popular culture on Twitter (in May 2015), from http://followerwonk.com/bio. The selected celebrities were: @justinbieber, @katyperry, @taylorswift13, @ladygaga, @rihanna, @jtimberlake, @theellenshow, @kimkardashian, @cristiano, @britneyspears, @jlo, @shakira, @selenagomez, @arianagrande, and @ddlovato. Note that we did not include politician @barackobama, as we assume political fandom to have very different characteristics.

Each of these celebrities has tens of millions of Twitter followers (fans). Since it is not feasible to analyze all their followers, we sampled a subset of fans for each celebrity. We used stratified sampling to sample fans of three types, defined based on their level of interaction with the celebrity.

The three types of fans we defined were: (i) Involved – This is the set of fans who regularly interact with the celebrity in an intimate manner. To get this set, we first obtained all users replying to the tweets from celebrities and obtained users who replied to tweets from celebrities at least on five tweets with messages containing 'i love you' (or similar variations, like, ILY).[1] (ii) Casual – This is a set of fans who interacted with (replied/mentioned/retweeted) the celebrity at least once in the previous year (May 2014 – May 2015). (iii) Random – Random sample of followers of the celebrity, sampled randomly from the millions of followers the celebrity has. These fans need not have interacted with the celebrity beyond the act of following.

The choice for these three sets was made in order to obtain the complete spectrum of fans, from the highly invested fans, who engage with the celebrity all the time, to people who just follow the celebrity out of curiosity. We first sampled approximately 2,000 users from each set for each celebrity. We then applied simple heuristics to remove bots and inactive accounts (at least 10 tweets/followers/friends, been on Twitter for at least one year, etc.).

[1] This is common for many celebrities on Twitter. As an example, see any tweet from Justin Bieber https://twitter.com/justinbieber/status/809785232186478592

We then up and down sampled each group for each celeb to be approximately of the same size. This left us with a set of 57,609 fans.

For all the users, we used Face++ Api[2] on their profile pictures to obtain estimates of their age and gender. Face++ uses computer vision and data mining techniques applied to a large database of celebrities to generate estimates of age and sex of individuals from their pictures. We were able to obtain confident age and gender predictions for around 50% of the users (27,889 users).

PARA-SOCIAL BREAKUPS

In this section, we try to understand how different types of fans engage in para-social breakups. We assume that a para-social breakup on Twitter manifests itself as an act of unfollowing the celebrity. We tracked all the 57k fans for a period of 26 weeks (between 21 May 2015 – 21 Nov 2015), and got data on whether they still follow the celebrity every week. At the end of the data collection period, we recorded 2,369 fans unfollowing a celebrity during this period. We also estimate when the fans started following the celebrity using the method proposed by Meeder et al [5].

We model unfollowing behavior using Survival analysis. Survival analysis is a statistical tool for analyzing the expected time to an event (unfollowing, in this case). It can be used to answer questions such as: whether a group of fans is more likely to unfollow than others. We set up survival analysis as follows: (i) *Event*: The act of unfollowing a celeb, (ii) *Survival time/event time*: Months since following the celebrity to unfollow. e.g. if a fan follows a celeb in Jan 2015 and unfollows in Oct 2015, this variable is 10. We have data going back to the last 4 years (48 months). (iii) *Censoring event*: All users who haven't unfollowed yet. For example, if a user followed the celebrity in Jan 2015 and is still following, we censor the user after 27 months (Jan 2015 to Apr 2017) (iv) *Survival function*: Probability of unfollowing after x months.

Given this set up, our first task is to see if there is any difference in para-social breakups between the three fan types (involved, casual and random). Figure 1 shows the survival probability for the various fan types using a Kaplan Meier non-parametric analysis. Compared across groups, involved users have a statistically significantly higher probability of unfollowing. We can also see that the chance of unfollowing for random users is almost non-existent.

This finding might be counter intuitive, given we expect involved fans to feel "closer" to the celebrity. We can interpret this behavior in terms of a cost/benefit analysis. The more a fan engages the celeb, the more likely it is for the relationship to end. The more involved a fan is the more the emotional cost they invest in the relationship and thus the more likely they are to end it when it does not reward them.

We also looked at a para-social breakup using the demographics of the fans, inferred from Face++. We found that young and female fans tend to be high investors in engaging with the celebrity, whereas as older fans are less invested and less prone to disappointment and breakup (details omitted due to lack of space).

We manually looked at the profile descriptions of users who unfollowed, before and after unfollowing, and found interesting examples. (i) Before: '@arianagrande followed and faved (30.11.14)', After: 'dreams dont work unless you do. good vibesss!!' (ii) Before: 'thank you justin my life', After: 'find your purpose' (iii) Before: 'queen faved x2. pls follow 2, ma queen', After: 'im loving the pain, i never wana live without it'. These examples show cases of despair and a sense of defiance after not getting the personal attention they desired.

[2]http://www.faceplusplus.com/

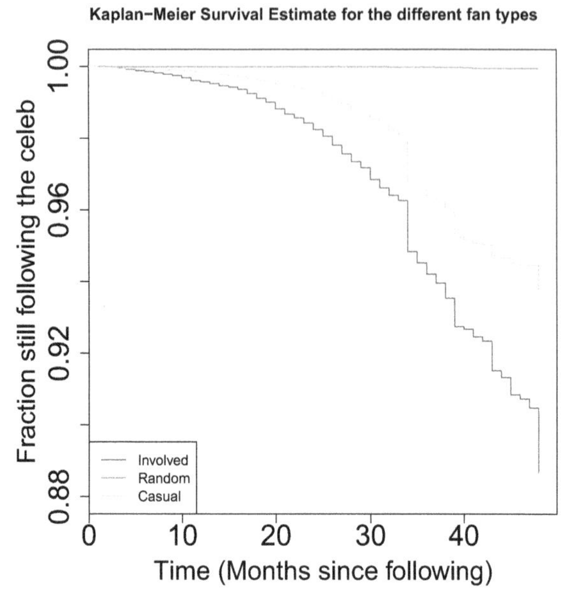

Figure 1: Survival probability for the three fan types

In summary, our analyses point to the complexity that social media use adds to fandom behavior and the various ways different fans engage in para-social breakups. As celebrities - and now presidents - continue to use social media as a central avenue to cultivate their following, engage their fans and influence society, it is worthwhile to study the ways such relationships are developed, maintained and dissolved.

ACKNOWLEDGEMENTS.

This work has been partly supported by the Academy of Finland project "Nestor" (286211) and the EC H2020 RIA project "SoBigData" (654024).

REFERENCES

[1] Keren Eyal and Jonathan Cohen. 2006. When good friends say goodbye: A parasocial breakup study. *Journal of Broadcasting & Electronic Media* 50, 3 (2006), 502–523.
[2] Venkata Rama Kiran Garimella, Ingmar Weber, and Sonya Dal Cin. 2014. From 'I love you babe' to 'leave me alone' - Romantic Relationship Breakups on Twitter. In *SocInfo*. Springer, 199–215.
[3] Donald Horton and R Richard Wohl. 1956. Mass communication and para-social interaction: Observations on intimacy at a distance. *Psychiatry* 19, 3 (1956), 215–229.
[4] Haewoon Kwak and others. 2011. Fragile online relationship: a first look at unfollow dynamics in twitter. In *CHI*. 1091–1100.
[5] Brendan Meeder, Brian Karrer, Amin Sayedi, R Ravi, Christian Borgs, and Jennifer Chayes. 2011. We know who you followed last summer: inferring social link creation times in twitter. In *WWW*. ACM, 517–526.
[6] Jimmy Sanderson and Carrie Truax. 2014. 'I hate you man!': Exploring maladaptive parasocial interaction expressions to college athletes via Twitter. *Journal of Issues in Intercollegiate Athletics* 7 (2014), 333–351.

Consolidating identities of authors through egonet structure

Janaína Gomide
Federal University of Rio de Janeiro
Brazil
janainagomide@macae.ufrj.br

Hugo Kling
Federal University of Rio de Janeiro
Brazil
hugo@land.ufrj.br

Daniel Ratton Figueiredo
Federal University of Rio de Janeiro
Brazil
daniel@land.ufrj.br

ACM Reference format:
Janaína Gomide, Hugo Kling, and Daniel Ratton Figueiredo. 2017. Consolidating identities of authors through egonet structure. In *Proceedings of WebSci'17, Troy, NY, USA, June 25-28, 2017,* 2 pages.
DOI: 10.1145/3091478.3098862

1 INTRODUCTION

Individuals often appear with multiple names when considering large datasets collected from different sources, giving rise to the name ambiguities. Name ambiguity comes in two flavors: a single individual appearing with more than one name (synonym problem); a single name being used to refer to more than one individual (homonym problem). This works focuses on the synonym problem and explores structural patterns of the collaboration network. We consider a scenario where the individual has a specific profile page that lists its bibliographic records. Despite more restrictive, this scenario has become quite common among digital libraries such as DBLP[1] and Google Scholar[2]. Such profiles often have name ambiguities as the profile owner appears with different names within the bibliographic records (e.g., different name spellings, typos, etc). This paper tackle these name ambiguities without resorting to any content information!

The methodology proposed first builds a weighted collaboration network with all the names and co-authorships appearing in a given profile. We call this the *egonet* of the individual, even if the individual may be represented by more than one node in the network, due to name ambiguities. We then remove all label information (i.e., node names become random ids). We propose an algorithm that takes this network, and no other information, and outputs the set of nodes that (might) correspond to the profile owner. We call the algorithm EgoIds since it aims at identifying the nodes (ids) of the profile owner taking as input an ambiguous *egonet*. The key insight behind this approach is that the individual has a structural signature that is independent from content and is different from its collaborators, even when considering the multiple nodes representing the individual.

Note that by ignoring the content (i.e., the name string, paper title, etc) we focus solely on the co-authorship *structure*. In a sense, our goal is to determine the power of the collaboration structure in resolving name ambiguities in social networks. Can *structure* alone help? As we will soon show, the answer to this question is surprisingly positive.

[1]http://dblp.uni-trier.de
[2]https://scholar.google.com

WebSci'17, June 25-28, 2017, *Troy, NY, USA*
 978-1-4503-4896-6/17/06...$15.00
DOI: 10.1145/3091478.3098862

2 RELATED WORKS

A natural approach to tackle name disambiguation is to use content information. This approach has been explored over the past decades to build successful name disambiguation algorithms, based on a variety of techniques [1, 6]. Another kind of context more recently explored is relational, available in different networks. For example, considering the ambiguous collaboration network (i.e., names and collaborations between them), a node corresponding to two individuals with the same name is likely to have two very different neighborhoods [5]. Recent techniques leverages both kinds of context in building more effective name disambiguation algorithms [2, 7], and even so the problem is still considered challenging [4]. In this work, the synonym name ambiguity problem is studied solely from the perspective the structure of collaboration networks using real data and egonets.

3 EGOIDS

EgoIds starts by constructing an *egonet* for every profile owner. Let $\mathcal{P}$ denote the set of publications in a profile and $\mathcal{L}_k$ denote the set of labels corresponding to the co-author names of publication $p_k \in \mathcal{P}$. Let $\mathcal{L}$ denote the set of labels that appear across all publications. Let $G = (V, E)$ be an undirected weighted graph with vertex set $V = \{1, 2, \ldots, n\}$ where vertex $i \in V$ corresponds to label $l_i \in \mathcal{L}$. Every set $\mathcal{L}_k$ creates a clique in G with the nodes corresponding to the labels that appear in publication p_k. Thus, $(i, j) \in E$ iff $l_i, l_j \in \mathcal{L}_k$ for some $p_k \in \mathcal{P}$. Three weights are associated with each edge $(i, j) \in E$:

$$w1_{i,j} = \sum_{k=1}^{|\mathcal{P}|} \mathbb{1}(l_i, l_j \in \mathcal{L}_k) \tag{1}$$

$$w2_{i,j} = \sum_{k=1}^{|\mathcal{P}|} \frac{\mathbb{1}(l_i, l_j \in \mathcal{L}_k)}{|\mathcal{L}_k| - 1} \tag{2}$$

$$w3_{i,j} = \sum_{k=1}^{|\mathcal{P}|} \frac{\mathbb{1}(l_i, l_j \in \mathcal{L}_k)}{\binom{|\mathcal{L}_k|}{2}} \tag{3}$$

where $\mathbb{1}(\cdot)$ is the indicator function. Intuitively, $w1_{i,j}$ denotes the number of publications where labels l_i and l_j appear as co-authors; $w2_{i,j}$ and $w3_{i,j}$ denote the normalized collaboration strength between labels l_i and l_j with the former penalizing more large sets of co-authors. Moreover, $w2$ and $w3$ can be used to recover other aspects concerning the labels and publications.

The problem we address is to determine the set of nodes in G that correspond to the profile owner. Moreover, we assume the node labels have no information about the profile owner or the co-authors, and can thus be viewed as a random number.

3.1 The Algorithm

Consider an egonet and assume that node i corresponds to the profile owner. Assume node i has one or more nodes at distance two. These nodes must have appeared in a publication with at least one common neighbor of i (necessary condition to be as distance two). Since the profile owner is in every publication, one of these nodes at distance two from i must correspond to the profile owner. Thus, we can use this observation to determine the set of nodes that could correspond to the profile owner.

Let $\mathcal{S}$ denote a set of nodes that could correspond to the profile owner of an *egonet* defined by $G = (V, E)$. Then the following must be true:

(1) For every $i \in V$, either $i \in \mathcal{S}$ or there exists an edge $(i,j) \in E$ such that $j \in \mathcal{S}$.
(2) For every $i,j \in \mathcal{S}$, edge $(i,j) \notin E$.
(3) If $|\mathcal{S}| > 1$, then for every $i \in \mathcal{S}$, there exists $j \in \mathcal{S}$ such that $d(i,j) = 2$, where $d(i,j)$ is the hop distance between nodes i and j.

Note that statement 1 is identical to the definition of a dominating set in a graph. Statement 2 is identical to the definition of an independent set in a graph. Thus, $\mathcal{S}$ is an independent and dominating set of G. However, statement 3 adds an additional constraint to nodes in the independent and dominating set. In fact, we would like to find the set $\mathcal{S}$ that *most likely* corresponds to the exact set of labels of the profile owner.

We propose the following greedy algorithm to construct the set $\mathcal{S}$. For each connected component, let S_c be the current set of candidate nodes for $\mathcal{S}$ and initially, let $S_c = V$ and the set of nodes corresponding to the owner $\mathcal{S} = \emptyset$.

(1) Choose the node with highest degree in S_c and include it in the set $\mathcal{S}$, remove all its neighbors from the set S_c;
(2) Choose a node from S_c that is at distance two from at least one of the nodes in $\mathcal{S}$. If there is more than one option:
   (a) Select the nodes with the largest degree;
   (b) From that set, select the nodes with more common neighbors with nodes already in $\mathcal{S}$;
   (c) From that set, select the nodes that the edges have a higher sum of weight $w2$;
   (d) From that set, select the nodes with lowest sum of weight $w3$ (across all edges incident to the node).
(3) If more than one node remains after step 2, stop the algorithm returning the (incomplete) set $\mathcal{S}$.
(4) Repeat 2 and 3 until S_c is empty and return $\mathcal{S}$.

4 EMPIRICAL EVALUATION

We used two bibliographic records to build collaboration networks and are readily available online: the DBLP and a small subset of Google Scholar that we collected. We considered three different collections from DBLP database. The first is the entire DBLP, version of May 2014, with 14,290 individuals. A collection derived from DBLP with 477 individuals collected and used in [6] and a collection derived from DBLP referred by KISTI with 6,908 individuals used in [3]. The Google Scholar dataset has 7,624 individuals. For all these datasets we have the set of names for each individual that appears with more than one name (e.g., ground truth).

Table 1: The average and the standard deviation for the precision, recall and F1 scores of the individuals in all datasets.

Dataset	Precision	Recall	F1	F1 (in [6])
DBLP-GT	0.77(0.42)	0.68(0.41)	0.71(0.41)	n/a
DBLP-UFMG	0.83(0.37)	0.74(0.38)	0.77(0.37)	0.92(0.02)
KISTI	0.95(0.21)	0.89(0.25)	0.92(0.23)	0.82(0.01)
Google Scholar	0.97(0.15)	0.66(0.28)	0.76(0.22)	n/a

The `EgoIds` algorithm outputs a set of vertices that might represent the nodes of a *egonet* that correspond to the profile owner. We evaluate the performance of `EgoIds` considering precision, recall and F1 measure. We also compare `EgoIds` results on DBLP-UFMG and KIST datasets with the results in [6].

Table 1 shows the precision, recall and F1 score across all individuals in all datasets. The precision is more than 77% for all datasets and for KIST and Google Scholar precision is above 95%. The KISTI dataset has the highest recall. For the DBLP-GT and Google Scholar datasets the recall is around 66% and that is because these two datasets have the more names per individual and thus, recall decreases when the algorithm does not find all the identities or if it starts with the wrong node. The F1 is more than 71% for all datasets and 92% for KIST. In comparison with [6], `EgoId` performs better for KIST dataset but not for DBLP-UFMG, probably because of the reduced dataset size and use of content information.

The results indicate that structural information with respect to collaborations has a strong signal that can be effectively leveraged to identify synonyms in an individual's egonet. Work in progress is modifying `EgoIds` to better select the first candidate node in order to improve its robustness.

ACKNOWLEDGMENTS

This work has received financial support from CNPq and FAPERJ through different research grants.

REFERENCES

[1] Anderson A Ferreira, Marcos André Gonçalves, and Alberto HF Laender. 2012. A brief survey of automatic methods for author name disambiguation. *Acm Sigmod Record* 41, 2 (2012), 15–26.
[2] Janana Gomide, Hugo Kling, and Daniel Figueiredo. 2015. A Model for Ambiguation and an Algorithm for Disambiguation in Social Networks. In *Complex Networks VI*. Springer, 37–44.
[3] In-Su Kang, Pyung Kim, Seungwoo Lee, Hanmin Jung, and Beom-Jong You. 2011. Construction of a large-scale test set for author disambiguation. *Information Processing & Management* 47, 3 (2011), 452 – 465.
[4] Jinseok Kim and Jana Diesner. 2015. Distortive effects of initial-based name disambiguation on measurements of large-scale coauthorship networks. *J. of the Assoc. for Inform. Science and Tech.* (2015).
[5] Jinseok Kim, Heejun Kim, and Jana Diesner. 2014. The impact of name ambiguity on properties of coauthorship networks. *Journal of Information Science Theory and Practice* 2, 2 (2014), 6–15.
[6] Alan Santana, Marcos Gonçalves, Alberto Laender, and Anderson Ferreira. 2015. On the comb. of domain-specific heuristics for author name disambiguation: the nearest cluster method. *Int. Journal on Dig. Libraries* 16, 3 (2015), 229–246.
[7] Dongwook Shin, Taehwan Kim, Joongmin Choi, and Jungsun Kim. 2014. Author name disambiguation using a graph model with node splitting and merging based on bibliographic information. *Scientometrics* 100, 1 (2014), 15–50.

Ongoing Events in Wikipedia: A Cross-lingual Case Study

Simon Gottschalk*, Elena Demidova*, Viola Bernacchi**, Richard Rogers***
*L3S Research Center, Hannover, Germany
**DensityDesign Research Lab, Milano, Italy
***University of Amsterdam, Amsterdam, The Netherlands
demidova@L3S.de,gottschalk@L3S.de,viola.bernacchi@live.it,R.A.Rogers@uva.nl

ABSTRACT

In order to effectively analyze information regarding ongoing events that impact local communities across language and country borders, researchers often need to perform multilingual data analysis. This analysis can be particularly challenging due to the rapidly evolving event-centric data and the language barrier. In this abstract we present preliminary results of a case study with the goal to better understand how researchers interact with multilingual event-centric information in the context of cross-cultural studies and which methods and features they use.

1 INTRODUCTION

In case of events concerning several communities, event-centric information available in different languages can reflect community-specific bias [5]. As events unfold, it therefore becomes particularly important to analyze language-specific differences across the local event representations to better understand the community-specific perception of the events, the propagation of event-centric information across languages and communities as well as its impact.

Wikipedia with its large multicultural user community and editions in over 290 languages is a rich source of multilingual information with respect to ongoing and past events. Information about ongoing events of global importance can evolve quickly in different language editions as the event unfolds [2], making Wikipedia an important and up-to-date source for cross-cultural studies.

The potentially large amount of multilingual information to be analyzed, event dynamics and the language barrier limit the analysis methods, in particular with respect to the features accessible for the analysis, making cross-cultural studies of ongoing events particularly challenging. Although existing tools facilitate automatic cross-lingual article comparisons in Wikipedia with respect to selected features, including for example a cross-lingual text alignment for articles pairs by MultiWiki [3], a comparison of the topics covered by the articles by Omnipedia [1] and a computation of the article similarity in Manypedia [4], there is still a significant room for further developments in this area.

In this abstract we present preliminary results of a case study concerning an analysis of cross-lingual event-centric information in Wikipedia exemplified through the Brexit referendum in June 2016. In this study, we observed an interdisciplinary, multicultural group of information professionals (communication design and sociology researchers) who performed the task of cross-cultural analysis of the Brexit representation in the multilingual Wikipedia in June 2016. In the study, six participants worked for 14 hours together as a team, resulting in a total of 84 person-hours spent.

WebSci '17, June 25-28, 2017, Troy, NY, USA
 978-1-4503-4896-6/17/06.
DOI: 10.1145/3091478.3098879

2 OBJECTIVES & METHODOLOGY

The key study objective was to *observe which methods and features can be efficiently used to perform cross-lingual analytics on multilingual Wikipedia*. As a first step, we introduced the participants to the topic of Brexit in Wikipedia and presented them with several example tools that can assist Wikipedia analytics in general. We asked the participants to: 1) define their own research questions and analysis methods related to Brexit and its international perception from the social and cultural perspectives; and 2) conduct an analysis of the Brexit-related articles across different Wikipedia language editions with respect to these questions. We focus the discussion on two Brexit-related articles selected by the participants: the "United Kingdom European Union membership referendum, 2016" (*referendum*) article and the "United Kingdom withdrawal from the European Union" (*withdrawal*) article.

3 OBSERVATIONS

3.1 Content Analysis

Due to the language barrier, the participants focused on the content features involving less text, e.g. the tables of contents and images.

Textual features: Most Wikipedia articles contain a table of contents (TOC) that is arranged individually in each language edition. As the effort to read through whole Wikipedia articles – especially when the reader is not proficient in the particular language – was estimated too high, the participants decided to focus on the TOCs as an approximation of textual analysis. The participants arranged the TOC entries from the English, German, French and Italian article revisions by their frequency across languages. This TOC comparison has shown that the articles differed in many aspects: While the German article focused on the referendum results in the different regions, the English Wikipedia covered much more aspects, especially on economical and societal implications of the withdrawal.

Multimedia features: Wikipedia articles can contain images that can be shared across different language editions. It became evident that images containing the map of the UK and the referendum ballot paper were shared most frequently across languages. Smaller deviations were observed for several languages, e.g. the German article contained many photos of the politicians.

3.2 Temporal Analysis

The description of ongoing events may vary substantially over time.

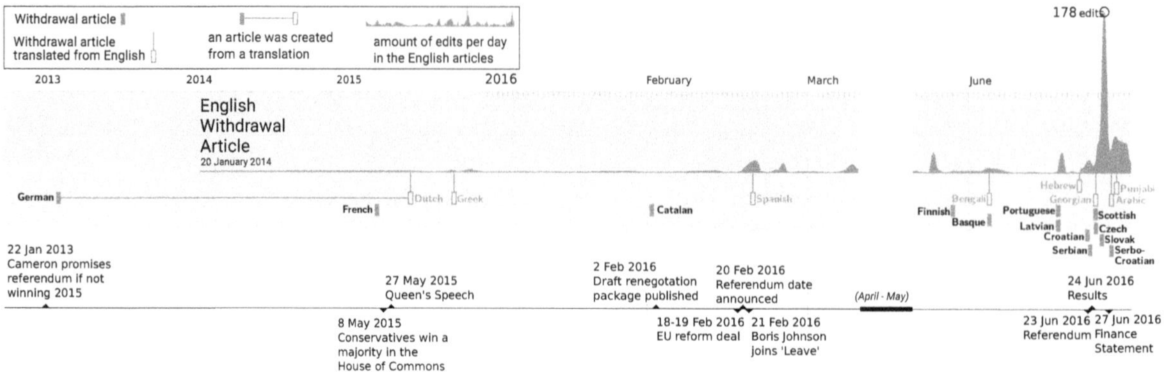

Figure 1: Timeline of the withdrawal article showing the edit frequency of the English withdrawal article over time and the creation of the article editions in other languages.

Textual features: The TOC of a Wikipedia article is subject of change over time. To observe this behavior, the participants extracted the TOC three times per day, in the time from the 22nd to the 24th of June 2016 (with the 23rd of June being the referendum date). The TOCs of two of these points in time made visible that the French version did not have the referendum results on the 23rd of June as opposed to other language versions under consideration. Within the following day, the English TOC stayed nearly unchanged in contrast to the other languages where especially the German article showed a major increase of new sections. The analysis on the withdrawal article revealed that the German version contained detailed historical and legislative entries while the French version focused on the referendum's impact and the public opinion.

Edit-based features: A valuable temporal aspect with respect to the cross-lingual information propagation comes from the editing process by the Wikipedia editors and the origin of the first revision per language. To explore this feature, the lists of all language editions for the referendum (48 language editions) and the withdrawal articles (59 language editions) have been analyzed using the Wikipedia Edits Scraper and IP Localizer tool. This way, the participants gained the edit histories of 107 article language editions. They manually created two annotations for the initial revision of each article: "Creation date", i.e. the date of the first edit, and "Origin", i.e. the reference to other language editions that were utilized to create the respective edition.

A visualization presented in Figure 1 has been created by the participants and illustrates the English articles' development including the number of edits and the creation of the other language editions. Article editions directly translated from other languages are marked and important events related to Brexit are added to the timeline. Edit peaks correlate with the sub-events in particular during the referendum held on the 23rd of June 2016.

3.3 Network & Controversy Analysis

The interlinking between Wikipedia articles across languages can provide useful insights into the coherence of the language editions.

Category-based features: In Wikipedia, editors can assign categories like "Politics" or "EU-skepticism in the UK" to the articles. To gain more insights into the perception of Brexit within the network of Wikipedia articles, the participants analyzed this categorization in all available language editions.The majority of the categories was related to basic concepts like "Referendum". The Scottish and the English Wikipedia were rather disconnected from the network. In the withdrawal articles, "Eurocentrism" was identified as a main category connecting languages.

Links-based features: Each Wikipedia article can contain links to external sources that the participants extracted and compared using the MultiWiki tool. For most of the language editions, the overlap of the linked web pages was rather low , and just in some cases it reached higher values: the English and German withdrawal articles shared 17.32% of links, mainly related to news pages like the BBC or The Guardian.

Edit-based features: To observe controversies, the participants reviewed the English discussion pages on the articles using their TOCs. A major finding facilitated by this feature was a discussion among the Wikipedia editors on the question to which article the search term "Brexit" should link to. Having initially redirected to the referendum article, the term lead to the withdrawal article a few days after the actual referendum.

4 CONCLUSION

As our case study illustrates, certain types of cross-lingual analysis on Wikipedia mostly relying on non-textual features (e.g. links, images and category structures) can be performed efficiently, manually or by using existing tools, and can already provide interesting insights. In contrast, analysis of textual content and discussion pages appears to be limited through the language barrier.

5 ACKNOWLEDGMENT

Partially funded by ALEXANDRIA (ERC 339233) and Data4UrbanMobility (German Federal Ministry of Education and Research (BMBF) 02K15A040).

REFERENCES

[1] Patti Bao, Brent Hecht, Samuel Carton, Mahmood Quaderi, Michael Horn, and Darren Gergle. Omnipedia: Bridging the Wikipedia Language Gap. In *CHI 2012*.
[2] Besnik Fetahu, Abhijit Anand, and Avishek Anand. 2015. How much is Wikipedia Lagging Behind News?. In *Proceedings of the ACM Web Science*. ACM, 28.
[3] Simon Gottschalk and Elena Demidova. 2017. MultiWiki: Interlingual Text Passage Alignment in Wikipedia. *ACM Trans. Web* 11, 1 (April 2017).
[4] Paolo Massa and Federico Scrinzi. 2012. Manypedia: Comparing Language Points of View of Wikipedia Communities. In *WikiSym 2012*. 21.
[5] Richard Rogers. 2013. *Digital Methods*. MIT Press.

Predicting Research that will be Cited in Policy Documents

Bharat Kale
Northern Illinois University
bkale@niu.edu

Harish Varma Siravuri
Northern Illinois University
hsiravuri@niu.edu

Hamed Alhoori
Northern Illinois University
alhoori@niu.edu

Michael E. Papka
Argonne National Laboratory
Northern Illinois University
papka@niu.edu

ABSTRACT

Scientific publications and other genres of research output are increasingly being cited in policy documents. Citations in documents of this nature could be considered a critical indicator of the significance and societal impact of the research output. In this study, we built classification models that predict whether a particular research work is likely to be cited in a public policy document based on the attention it received online, primarily on social media platforms. We evaluated the classifiers based on their accuracy, precision, and recall values. We found that Random Forest and Multinomial Naive Bayes classifiers performed better overall.

KEYWORDS

Public Policy, Policy documents, Altmetrics, Social Media

1 INTRODUCTION

Policy documents influence large sections of society [4]. Because of the unique importance of policy documents across diverse organizations, citations included in this type of material support both the credibility of the author cited and the credibility of the policy document itself [6]. Likewise, in this context, it may be appropriate to assign a policy document citation more weight than a regular citation included in a literature review in a scholarly paper, for example.

Haunschild and Bornmann [7] studied the percentage of papers in Web of Science that are mentioned in policy-related documents and found that less than 0.5% of the papers on a range of subjects had been mentioned at least once in policy-related documents. Lauren [5] analyzed patterns in the types of altmetric attention received by papers that make it into policy documents and found that papers are often being referenced quickly, i.e., within 2 years of publication, such that they are having a real-world impact sooner than expected

Winterfeldt [12] presented a framework to bridge the gap between science and decision making in the policy sphere. Orduna-Malea, Thelwall, and Kousha [7] explored the relationship between citations in patents and technological impact and found that the number of patents citing a resource indicates the technological capacity or relevance of that resource. According to Black [3], although evidence-based policy-making is being encouraged in all areas of public service, research is currently under-used in policy-making and there is a need for a better mutual understanding between research and policy communities.

Citation analysis is self-limiting because it does not account for many other signals through which research receives attention. An increasing amount of scholarly content is being shared and discussed daily on social media platforms [1]. Whereas citations measure research impact within scholarly boundaries, non-traditional web-based metrics or altmetrics [8][2] make it possible to measure different influences, including readers who read an article or share, and/or discuss it with others, but do not formally cite it in traditionally published articles.

Thelwall et al. [11] studied the potential value of altmetrics for evaluating funding criteria and found that some metrics can be helpful in this sphere. Sarewitz and Pielke [10] proposed a method to strengthen the connection between science policy decisions, scientific research, and social outcomes using the example of climate change research. Pawson [9] discussed various ways to incorporate research results into the policy-making process. To date, most studies focus on understanding and using altmetrics in reference to only a few measures. The present study is the first to explore modeling altmetrics in order to predict citations in policy documents.

2 DATA COLLECTION

The dataset in this study is a database dump that we obtained from altmetric.com, which consists of 5.2 million articles. Our initial analysis showed that of these articles, 89,350 had been cited in at least one policy document whereas 5,097,207 had not been included in a document of this kind. To create a balanced dataset for further analysis, along with the 89,350 articles that had been cited in a policy document, we randomly chose another 89,350 articles that had not been cited in a policy document. The result was a balanced dataset with approximately 180,000 records, half of which had been cited in policy documents.

3 FEATURE SELECTION

The dataset has a very rich set of features for each article. However, in our analysis, we considered only features related to online attention. The dataset consists of mention counts on various online sources including reference managers, mainstream news outlets,

WebSci '17, June 25-28, 2017, Troy, NY, USA

ACM ISBN 978-1-4503-4896-6/17/06.
https://doi.org/10.1145/3091478.3098865

blogs, peer-review platforms (e.g., PubPeer and Publons), social media, public policy documents, and Wikipedia.

We used mention counts on Twitter, Facebook, Reddit, Mendeley, Google+, Wikipedia, Weibo, mainstream news outlets, blogs, videos, and peer review sites as features to build the classifiers. Yet, we left a few sources out of our account, including Connotea, which was discontinued in 2013, and Pinterest and Stackoverflow, which together contributed to less than 1% of the articles in the sample. We replaced the policy citation count with a binary class label denoting whether a given article had been cited in a policy document.

4 METHODS AND RESULTS

4.1 Classification

To predict the likelihood of a research article being cited in a policy document, we implemented three classifiers: the Multinomial Naive Bayes classifier, the Random Forest classifier with the number of trees set at 100, and a C-Support Vector Machine with the Radial Basis Function (RBF) kernel. We then divided the entire dataset into training and test sets comprising 80% and 20% of the entire dataset, respectively. We trained the models using a 10-fold cross-validation technique and evaluated them based on accuracy, precision, recall, and F1-measure metrics, as shown in Table 1.

Table 1: Accuracy, Precision, Recall, and F1-Measure for different models

	Multinomial Naive Bayes	Random Forest	SVM
Accuracy	0.842	0.870	0.868
Precision	0.802	0.826	0.820
Recall	0.905	0.870	0.868
F1-Measure	0.850	0.844	0.824

4.2 Feature Ranking

With the classification models built, we calculated the weight for each feature to determine the significance of each in making the final prediction. Given that feature weights in the case of a Support Vector Machine can be determined only for linear kernels, we ranked the features based on their relevance for only the Random Forest and Multinomial Naive Bayes classifiers. We ranked the features in regard to their importance to the Random Forest classifier from most to least important, as shown in Table 2.

5 CONCLUSIONS AND FUTURE WORK

In this study, we used a specific set of features that track online attention received by scholarly articles to build classifiers to predict the likelihood of an article being cited in public policy. The Random Forest classifier showed better results in making predictions. We found mention counts on peer-review platforms to be the most influential feature, whereas news rated as the least influential feature. The promising results obtained in this work show that a relationship exists between the online attention that a scholarly work receives and the policy citations it generates, which we were able to exploit. We intend to extend our work in this area by building regression models to predict the number of policy citations a given work is likely to receive. We also plan to build more classifiers with different feature sets and to compare our results.

Table 2: Feature ranking for different models

Platform	Random Forest	Multinomial Naive Bayes
peer-review	0.273595	4.4267
Google+	0.197488	3.4210
Reddit	0.151016	4.4087
video	0.098035	4.9458
Twitter	0.068745	2.2421
Weibo	0.088242	3.7988
Mendeley	0.030116	0.3210
Wikipedia	0.026027	4.9668
blogs	0.018631	4.4571
Facebook	0.016189	3.2314
news	0.008926	3.7307

ACKNOWLEDGMENTS

MEP was supported in part by the Office of Advanced Scientific Computing Research, Office of Science, U.S. Department of Energy, under Contract DE-AC02-06CH11357.

REFERENCES

[1] Euan Adie and William Roe. 2013. Altmetric: enriching scholarly content with article-level discussion and metrics. *Learned Publishing* 26, 1 (2013), 11–17. https://doi.org/10.1087/20130103

[2] Hamed Alhoori and Richard Furuta. 2014. Do altmetrics follow the crowd or does the crowd follow altmetrics?. In *Proceedings of the 14th ACM/IEEE-CS Joint Conference on Digital Libraries.* 375–378. https://doi.org/10.1109/JCDL.2014.6970193

[3] Nick Black and Anna Donald. 2001. Evidence based policy: proceed with careCommentary: research must be taken seriously. *BMJ* 323, 7307 (2001), 275–279. https://doi.org/10.1136/bmj.323.7307.275

[4] Lutz Bornmann, Robin Haunschild, and Werner Marx. 2016. Policy documents as sources for measuring societal impact: how often is climate change research mentioned in policy-related documents? *Scientometrics* 109, 3 (2016), 1477–1495. https://doi.org/10.1007/s11192-016-2115-y

[5] Lauren Cadwallader. 2016. Papers, policy documents and patterns of attention. In *3:AM The Altmetrics Conference.* https://doi.org/10.17863/CAM.4844

[6] Richard Freeman and Jo Maybin. 2011. Documents, practices and policy. *Evidence & Policy: A Journal of Research, Debate and Practice* 7, 2 (2011), 155–170.

[7] Robin Haunschild and Lutz Bornmann. 2017. How many scientific papers are mentioned in policy-related documents? An empirical investigation using Web of Science and Altmetric data. *Scientometrics* 110, 3 (2017), 1209–1216. https://doi.org/10.1007/s11192-016-2237-2

[8] Kim Johan Holmberg. 2015. *Altmetrics for information professionals: Past, present and future.* Elsevier. https://books.google.com/books?id=GhdiBQAAQBAJ

[9] Ray Pawson. 2002. Evidence-based Policy: In Search of a Method. *Evaluation* 8, 2 (2002), 157–181. https://doi.org/10.1177/1358902002008002512

[10] Daniel Sarewitz and Roger A Pielke. 2007. The neglected heart of science policy: reconciling supply of and demand for science. *Environmental Science & Policy* 10, 1 (2007), 5–16. https://doi.org/10.1016/j.envsci.2006.10.001

[11] Mike Thelwall, Kayvan Kousha, Adam Dinsmore, and Kevin Dolby. 2016. Alternative metric indicators for funding scheme evaluations. *Aslib Journal of Information Management* 68, 1 (2016), 2–18. https://doi.org/10.1108/AJIM-09-2015-0146

[12] Detlof von Winterfeldt. 2013. Bridging the gap between science and decision making. *Proceedings of the National Academy of Sciences* 110, Supplement 3 (2013), 14055–14061. https://doi.org/10.1073/pnas.1213532110

Algorithmic Fairness in Online Information Mediating Systems

Ansgar Koene, Elvira Perez
University of Nottingham
{ansgar.koene,elvira.perez}@nottingham.ac.uk

Sofia Ceppi, Michael Rovatsos
University of Edinburgh
{sceppi,mrovatso}@inf.ed.ac.uk

Helena Webb, Menisha Patel, Marina Jirotka
University of Oxford
{helena.webb,menisha.patel,marina.jirotka}@cs.ox.ac.uk

Giles Lane
Proboscis
giles@proboscis.org.uk

ABSTRACT

This paper explores the challenges around fair information access when the limits of human attention require algorithmic assistance for 'finding the diamond in the coal mountain'. While often demanded by users, the seemingly intuitive concept of fairness has proven to be very difficult to operationalise for implementation in algorithms. Here we present two pilot studies aimed at getting a better understanding of the conceptualisation of algorithmic fairness by users. The first was a multi-stakeholder focus-group discussion, the second a user experiment/questionnaire. Based on our data we arrive at a picture of fairness that is highly dependent on context and informedness of users, and possibly inherently misleading due to the implied projecting of human intentions onto an algorithmic process.

1 INTRODUCTION

Driven by competition for greater efficiency, online services are increasingly optimizing the user experience (as measured by attention capture) using Big Data algorithms that process massive-scale multi-dimensional data sets. The complexity of these algorithms is prompting concerns among service users, professional organizations and regulators [2, 5] regarding the breakdown of people's ability to (intuitively) grasp the general principles – let alone the more detailed elements – of these algorithms. In recognition of the potential for (inadvertent) abuse by means of algorithmic manipulation, computer scientists (e.g. [4]) are exploring how to design fair algorithms or verify the fairness of existing algorithms. From a computational perspective, there are many competing ways to operationalise the algorithm fairness. One might, for instance, prioritizes individual fairness [1] over group fairness [3] , "equality of outcomes" over "equality of treatment", etc. As confirmed by our results, this ambiguity reflects the more general problem that the concept of fairness, which initially appears to be very intuitive based on people's experience of human-human interactions, quickly reveals itself to be highly context-dependent when applied as a system design guideline. Even when referring to the same algorithmic system, two people discussing its fairness may be referring to different criteria depending on perspectives such as the ones mentioned above. In order to gain a better understanding of the multi-faceted experiences of algorithmic system fairness/unfairness by a range of user groups, the UnBias project (http://unbias.wp.horizon.ac.uk/) is running a series of studies comprising of "Youth Juries" deliberations with young digital natives, user observation studies and stakeholder engagement workshops. In this paper we present results from our first stakeholder engagement workshop and a questionnaire/discussion with computer science students.

WebSci '17, June 25-28, 2017, Troy, NY, USA

ACM ISBN 978-1-4503-4896-6/17/06.
DOI: http://dx.doi.org/10.1145/3091478.3098864

2 MULTI-STAKEHOLDER ENGAGEMENT

The 1st UnBias stakeholder workshop on "bias considerations of information mediating algorithms" took place on February 3rd 2017. The 26 participants represented four Small-Medium-Enterprises, three innovation incubators, two consultants, ten academics, five not-for-profit civil-society organizations, and two teachers. Prior to the workshop, participants were sent a questionnaire eliciting their experiences as a user and/or developer of algorithm-driven information systems. Included in the questions was a 'working definition' of fairness and questions regarding the usefulness of this definition and how they would propose to change it.

The 'working definition' defined fairness as "a context-dependent evaluation of the algorithm processes and/or outcomes against socio-cultural values. Typical examples might include evaluating: the disparity between best and worst outcomes; the sum-total of outcomes; worst-case scenarios; everyone is treated/processed equally without prejudice or advantage due to task-irrelevant factors".

Most of the stakeholders rated this definition as "good" or a "reasonable starting point". When asked how to change and improve the definition, the following points were highlighted:

Criteria relating to social norms and values: *(i)* Sometimes disparate outcome are acceptable if based on individual lifestyle choices over which people have control; *(ii)* Ethical precautions are more important than higher accuracy. *(iii)* There needs to be a balancing of individual values and socio-cultural values. Problem: How to weigh relevant social-cultural value?

Criteria relating to system reliability *(i)* Results must be balanced with due regard for trustworthiness. *(ii)* There needs to be independent system evaluation and system monitoring over time.

Criteria relating to (non-)interference with user control/ agency: *(i)* Subjective experience of fairness depends on the user's objectives at the time of use and therefore requires an ability to tune the data and algorithm. *(ii)* Individuals should be able to limit the data collection about them and its use. Inferred personal data are still personal data. Any meaning that is assigned to the data must be clearly justified towards the user. *(iii)* It must be possible to demonstrate and explain the reasoning and behaviour of the algorithm in a way that can be understood by the data subject. *(iv)* If the algorithm is not indispensable to the task, it should be possible to opt-out of the algorithm but still use the other components of the service. *(v)* Users must have freedom to explore algorithm effects, even if this would increase the ability to figame the systemfi. *(vi)* There need to be clear means of appeal/redress for impact of the algorithmic system that the user cannot control.

In a dissenting opinion one participant rated the original working definition of fairness as "way off", stating that:

I struggle with the underlying antrhopomorphisation of algorithms when one speaks of fialgorithm fairnessfi. In my view, the concept of fairness is as you rightly noted deeply enshrined in the specific socio-cultural codes of the respective group of actors. Since algorithms as such constitute only the tools that actors in the social context use to achieve (some of) their objectives , one should also judge fairness probably more along the behaviour of these actors, their objectives, and methods. This implies that both the process of the algorithm and its outcomes need to be taken into account.

The 'working definition' of fairness and the suggestions provided by the stakeholders focused on scenarios like search engines and news recommendation systems, in which algorithms can optimize the outcome for each user independently. In the next section/study we considered cases where such independently optimized outcomes are not possible.

3 COLLECTIVE DEFINITION OF FAIRNESS

Many multi-user scenarios have a combinatorial nature, i.e., decisions applied to one user also affect other users such that decision optimization must consider the requirements and preferences of all users at the same time. Examples of such scenarios are sharing economy applications, where users seek peers to form teams, and situations in which resources are limited and/or variable in type, e.g. hotel rooms. Consider for example ride-sharing. Assume there are four users, *A*, *B*, *C*, and *D*, each car can transport at most two users, and users have preferences for peers. In particular, assume *A* prefers to travel with *B* over *D* over *C*, *B* prefers to travel with *C*, *C* with *B*, and *D* is indifferent. If an algorithm tries to solve this problem by considering each user individually, it would suggest to *A* to travel with *B*, violating the wish of *B* to travel with *C*. By considering the collective of users at once, the algorithm could propose a feasible solution in which *A* travels with *D* and *B* with *C*.

Generally, such scenarios are characterized by collectives of users with conflicting preferences and constraints (due to the combinatorial nature of the problem) that limits feasible solutions. Note that users may have conflicting ideas also about the fairness concept to use. To explore this fairness selection problem we conducted a pilot-experiment aimed to (i) explore problems related to identifying a collectively approved definition of fairness, and thus the most appropriate algorithm to use in a constrained collective scenario, and (ii) observe how transparency of the values embedded in an algorithm affects users' judgment.

We considered the problem of allocating coursework topics to students when each student must have exactly one topic and each topic can be assigned to at most one student. Each student expressed his/her preferences over each topic by assigning them a score from 1 to 7 representing the desirability of that topic to the student.

To identify possible student-topic assignments we used five algorithms differing in the adopted fairness concept as defined by the trade-off between maximizing the aggregated level of preference-matching summed over all students vs minimizing the preference-match differences between students.

We gave a two part questionnaire to students with graphs showing the preference score each student gave to their assigned topic and the difference between the level of preference-matching reached for every student. In the first part of the questionnaire, students had chose the most and least preferred algorithms only on the basis of above mentioned graphs, while in the second part, they were also given the description of the algorithms. The two parts of the questionnaire were sequentially presented in order to observe how transparency of the algorithms' values affected the outcomes.

The results are summarized by three observations. First, the outcome confirms the importance of transparency; indeed there was a drastic change in algorithm selections between the first and the second part of the questionnaire. Second, since students' preferences of least and most preferred algorithms were spread across several options, we conclude that users judge algorithms using different criteria even when experiencing exactly the same scenario. Finally, this pilot experiment proves that for constrained collective scenarios it is impossible to guarantee that, independently and without the support of a mediating agent, users can agree on an algorithm to use. The different fairness criteria users adopt can conflict with each other making it impossible for an algorithm to guarantee them simultaneously.

4 CONCLUSION

Combining the results from both our studies we conclude that there is no unique, globally approved, definition of fairness. Several crucial characteristics of fair algorithms can be highlighted that are, however, not always simultaneously achievable.

Our findings show the need to extend the study on (i) fairness concepts, in order to coherently integrate the stakeholders' suggestions on defining fairness and highlight their conflicts, and (ii) the design of techniques that can be adopted to (partially) coordinate the heterogeneous fairness preferences of groups of users.

5 ACKNOWLEDGEMENT

This work forms part of the UnBias project supported by EPSRC grant EP/N02785X/1.

REFERENCES

[1] Toniann Pitassi Omer Reingold Cynthia Dwork, Moritz Hardt and Richard Zemel. 2012. Fairness through awareness. In *ITCS '12 Proceedings of the 3rd Innovations in Theoretical Computer Science Conference*. ITCS, 214–226. https://www.cs.toronto.edu/~Etoni/Papers/awareness.pdf.
[2] IEEE 2016. *Ethically Aligned Design. A Vision for Prioritizing Human Wellbeing with Artificial Intelligence and Autonomous Systems. Version 1.* IEEE. http://standards.ieee.org/develop/indconn/ec/autonomous_systems.html.
[3] J. Moeller C. Scheidegger M. Feldman, S. A. Friedler and S. Venkatasubramanian. 2015. Certifying and removing disparate impact. In *21th ACM SIGKDD International Conference on Knowledge Discovery and Data Mining*. 259fi?!268.
[4] Suresh Venkatasubramanian Sorelle A. Friedler, Carlos Scheidegger. On the (im)possibility of fairness. In *arXiv:1609.07236*.
[5] U.S. Executive Office of the President 2016. *Big Data: A Report on Algorithmic Systems, Opportunities, and Civil Rights*. U.S. Executive Office of the President. https://obamawhitehouse.archives.gov/sites/default/files/microsites/ostp/2016_0504_data_discrimination.pdf.

Pokémon Go: Impact on Yelp Restaurant Reviews

Pavan Ravikanth Kondamudi
Northern Illinois University
DeKalb, IL 60115
pkondamudi1@niu.edu

Bradley Protano
Northern Illinois University
DeKalb, IL 60115
bprotano1@niu.edu

Hamed Alhoori
Northern Illinois University
DeKalb, IL 60115
alhoori@niu.edu

ABSTRACT

Pokémon Go, the popular Augmented Reality based mobile application, launched in July of 2016. The game's meteoric rise in usage since that time has had an impact on not just the mobile gaming industry, but also the physical activity of players, where they travel, where they spend their money, and possibly how they interact with other social media applications. In this paper, we studied the impact of Pokémon Go on Yelp reviews. For restaurants near PokéStops, we found a slight drop in the number of online reviews.

KEYWORDS

Pokemon Go; PokéStops; Augmented Reality Games; Yelp; Local Businesses; Restaurants; Reviews; Social Media.

1 INTRODUCTION AND RELATED WORK

Augmented reality games allow users to play in a mediated reality produced by imposing the graphics from the game onto a real-world environment. This technology is having an impact on the world in social, cultural, and economic ways. Pokémon Go is one such popular augmented reality game that was built around the famous Pokémon, or "Pocket Monsters", series in which a player catches the titular creatures using PokeBalls. Yelp a popular website that provides crowdsourced reviews of local businesses in various countries, added an option whereby its users can identify whether a business has a PokéStop nearby, which allows users to filter the search results of businesses, including restaurants. We studied the impact of PokéStops on local restaurant reviews that have a PokéStop nearby. We compared the most recent three years of review trends for these restaurants to analyze the impact of common factors during the period following Pokémon Go's release date.

As the augmented reality industry matures, researchers have studied its socioeconomic impact as well as its impact on users' physical and mental health. Studies to date on Pokémon Go have tried to quantify the socioeconomic effect of the game using survey information. Zach and Tussyadiah [17] analyzed the results from players responding to their survey on likelihood to travel, spend money, and visit restaurants while playing. Overall, the results indicated playing the game encouraged traveling. However, they found players that spent one hour or more playing were less likely to spend money on traveling for the game. Colley et al. [3] combined national field surveys with a geo-statistical analysis of the distribution of PokéStops throughout the U.S. They found that urban areas and areas with large (non-hispanic) white populations were heavily favored in Pokémon Go. Further, they found that 46% of players had purchased goods at places near where they traveled to play Pokémon Go.

A study done at Microsoft Research by Althoff et al. [1] focused on determining the physical activity involved in playing Pokémon Go by combining signals from large-scale corpora of wearable sensor data and search engine logs for 32,000 users over a period of three months. Pokémon Go players, identified through search engine queries and with activity measured by accelerometry, were found to have a significant increase in physical activity. Based on data collected from the iOS Health app, Howe et al. [5] observed a similar increase in physical activity among both children and adults. Nigg et al. [10] conducted a pre-post study and found among survey recipients that Pokémon Go increased physical activity of various intensity levels by 50 minutes per week and reduced sedentary activity by 30 minutes each day.

Williamson [16] provided anecdotal evidence that suggests numerous users are logging many kilometers in an effort to catch and hatch elusive Pokémon. In addition to referencing claims that Pokémon Go helps its users to fight depression, McCartney [9] reported that the game is playing a positive role in fighting obesity in the U.S. Quinn [13] described how, by remembering the monsters' names and capabilities, children improved their memory capabilities through playing Pokémon Go.

Wang [15] looked at Pokémon Go as an opportunity to examine the effect of crowdsourced information on the real world. Mansilla and Perkis [8] suggested that augmented reality games such as Pokémon Go can contribute to setting up multi-use public spaces called "Adressaparken," that are designed to increase social interaction between community members. Dzodom and Shipman [4] studied how fantasy games play an important role in increasing the social interaction. Some studies have found Pokémon Go to be a dangerous distraction for drivers, passengers, and pedestrians in some instances [6][7]. Pourmand et al. [11] found, by reviewing the PubMed, Medline, and PsycInfo databases, that there was an increase in fractures and dislocations compared to previous video game related injuries. In a study focused on addressing the safety of players engaged in augmented reality games, Pyae and Potter [12] presented four engagement models designed to capture engagement in the games. The researchers discussed each model based on the individual user scenario and used Pokémon Go as their focal case study. Although there are some reports that Pokémon Go has increased the number of visits made to museums and national parks and also increased sales [2], it is not clear whether the game has had an effect on online reviews of local businesses and restaurants, which is the focus of our analysis.

WebSci '17, June 25-28, 2017, Troy, NY, USA

ACM ISBN 978-1-4503-4896-6/17/06.
https://doi.org/10.1145/3091478.3098861

2 METHODS AND RESULTS

For the present study, all the data pertaining to restaurant reviews were collected from Yelp, which has provided a search filter so that its users can search for restaurants with a PokéStop nearby. We used the Selenium [14] browser automation framework to navigate the Yelp website and to collect restaurant reviews. We collected 592,120 reviews from 3,719 distinct local restaurants in 26 U.S. and U.K. cities. We collected the data by running four individual threads: two collected the data for restaurants with a PokéStop nearby, and two for restaurants without a PokéStop in the vicinity.

From our two sets of restaurants, those with PokéStops and those without, we narrowed our initial selection by excluding any restaurant that did not have at least five reviews in each month since 2014. From this selection, we took 50 restaurants with the most reviews for each category as our final sample. Thus, we ended with 50 restaurants that were known to have PokéStops nearby and 50 restaurants without, for a total sample of 100 restaurants across both categories. To determine whether the proximity of a PokéStop had any impact on the restaurant reviews, we used the Pearson correlation and Paired T-Test. We split our data points, i.e., the number of reviews year-wise for our two 50 restaurant samples.

We applied the Paired T-Test over another random data samples with 95% confidence. We selected 20 random sample sets (10 samples for restaurants with a PokéStop and 10 samples for those without). Each set consists of 10 randomly selected restaurants from each of the 26 cities, where each city has at least 25 restaurants and each of the restaurants has at least 10 reviews. By applying the previous approach, we eliminated effects of other factors such as weather, special events, etc. We compared the reviews in the months of August to November to see if Pokémon Go affected reviews during that period. August to November were chosen because Yelp added the PokéStop filter in mid-July and our final dataset was collected in the second week of December. As seen in Table 1, we applied tests to compare the previous year, 'Before' period, to the subsequent years 'After' period to measure the change in restaurant reviews.

Table 1: Data division for the analysis.

Test #	Before	After
1	August-November 2015	August-November 2016
2	August-November 2014	August-November 2015

We studied the impact of Pokémon Go on the restaurants with and without PokéStops for the years 2014 to 2016. We analyzed the reviews from the same period for the previous years, i.e., 2014 and 2015, and found an increase in the number of reviews from 2014 to 2015. To verify these results, we applied the Pearson correlation on data within the stated periods. Table 2 shows the results of the Pearson correlation coefficients after performing the correlation analysis. Restaurants with PokéStops nearby had lower correlation compared to that of the restaurants without PokéStops nearby.

We then applied the Paired T-Test for test period #1, as indicated in Table 3, which shows that there is no significant difference between the Before and After periods in the case of restaurants with a PokéStop, indicating no statistically significant difference in the number of restaurant reviews. However, the test on restaurants without a PokéStop for the same period indicate a significant difference in restaurant reviews for that group. We applied the Paired T-Test for test period #2. The tests show significant differences between the two data sets for the periods of test #2, indicating an increase in the number of reviews from 2014 to 2015.

Table 2: Pearson correlation coefficients for restaurants with and without PokéStops compared to previous years.

August-November	With PokeStops	Without PokeStops
2016-2015	**0.746**	0.934
2015-2014	0.967	0.921

Table 3: P-values for tests #1 and #2.

Test #	Without PokéStops	With PokéStops
1	0.0067	**0.3282**
2	0.0154	0.0031

From the previous results, it can be concluded that restaurants with a PokéStop nearby have experienced a slight decrease in the number of reviews on Yelp after the release of Pokémon Go in July 2016, especially in October and November.

REFERENCES

[1] Tim Althoff, Ryen W. White, and Eric Horvitz. 2016. Influence of Pokémon Go on Physical Activity: Study and Implications. *JMIR* 18, 12 (dec 2016), e315.

[2] Walter Chen. 2016. How Pokemon Go Is Driving Insane Amounts of Sales at Small, Local Businesses. (2016). https://goo.gl/M5j9BY

[3] Ashley Colley, Jacob Thebault-Spieker, Allen Yilun Lin, Donald Degraen, Benjamin Fischman, Jonna Häkkilä, Kate Kuehl, Valentina Nisi, Nuno Jardim Nunes, Nina Wenig, and Others. 2017. The Geography of Pokémon GO: Beneficial and Problematic Effects on Places and Movement. In *Proceedings of CHI 2017.*

[4] Gabriel S Dzodom and Frank M Shipman. 2014. Data-driven Web Entertainment: The Data Collection and Analysis Practices of Fantasy Sports Players. In *Proceedings of the 2014 ACM Conference on Web Science.* 293–294.

[5] Katherine B Howe, Christian Suharlim, Peter Ueda, Daniel Howe, Ichiro Kawachi, and Eric B Rimm. 2016. Gotta catch'em all! Pokémon GO and physical activity among young adults: difference in differences study. *BMJ* 355 (2016).

[6] John W. Ayers, Eric C Leas, Mark Dredze, Jon-Patrick Allem, Jurek G Grabowski, and Linda Hill. 2016. Pokémon GO—A New Distraction for Drivers and Pedestrians. *JAMA Internal Medicine* 176, 12 (2016), 1865–1866.

[7] Bellal Joseph and David G Armstrong. 2016. Potential perils of peri-Pokémon perambulation: the dark reality of augmented reality? *Oxford Medical Case Reports* 2016, 10 (2016), 255–256.

[8] Wendy Ann Mansilla and Andrew Perkis. 2016. Technology & Art in Stimulating Creative Placemaking in Public-Use Spaces. In *Proceedings of MM 2016.*

[9] Margaret McCartney. 2016. Margaret McCartney: Game on for Pokémon Go. *BMJ* 354 (2016). https://doi.org/10.1136/bmj.i4306

[10] Claudio R Nigg, Desiree Joi Mateo, and Jiyoung An. 2017. Pokémon GO May Increase Physical Activity and Decrease Sedentary Behaviors. *American Journal of Public Health* 107, 1 (jan 2017), 37–38. https://doi.org/10.2105/AJPH.2016.303532

[11] Ali Pourmand, Kevin Lombardi, Evan Kuhl, and Francis O'Connell. 2017. Videogame-Related Illness and Injury: A Review of the Literature and Predictions for Pokémon GO! *Games for Health Journal* 6, 1 (feb 2017), 9–18.

[12] Aung Pyae and Leigh Ellen Potter. 2016. A Player Engagement Model for an Augmented Reality Game: A Case of Pokémon Go. In *Proceedings of the 28th Australian Conference on Computer-Human Interaction (OzCHI '16).* 11–15.

[13] Jasmine Quinn. 2016. Identity of Pokemon Go Players: How Social Gaming Affects Behavior. *Advanced Writing: Pop Culture Intersections* 19 (2016).

[14] Selenium. 2017. Selenium. (2017). http://www.seleniumhq.org/

[15] Mingzhong Wang. 2017. FollowMe if you can: a study of mobile crowd sensing with Pokémon go. In *Proceedings of ACSW 2017.*

[16] Jon W Williamson. 2016. Will the 'Pokémon' be Heroes in the Battle Against Physical Inactivity? *Sports and Exercise Medicine* 2, 1 (2016), 13–14.

[17] Florian J. Zach and Iis P Tussyadiah. 2017. To Catch Them All—The (Un)intended Consequences of Pokémon GO on Mobility, Consumption, and Wellbeing. *Information and Communication Technologies in Tourism* (2017), 217–227.

Developing Ontologies and Web-based Data Management System for Additive Manufacturing Processes

Congrui Li
Tetherless World Constellation
Rensselaer Polytechnic Institute
110 8th St
Troy, NY 12180
lic10@rpi.edu

Bryan Chu*
Department of MANE
Rensselaer Polytechnic Institute
110 8th St
Troy, NY 12180
bchu@sandia.gov

Charles Parslow
Department of MANE
Rensselaer Polytechnic Institute
110 8th St
Troy, NY 12180
parslc@rpi.edu

Johnson Samuel
Department of MANE
Rensselaer Polytechnic Institute
110 8th St
Troy, NY 12180
samuej2@rpi.edu

Peter Fox
Tetherless World Constellation
Rensselaer Polytechnic Institute
110 8th St
Troy, NY 12180
pfox@cs.rpi.edu

ABSTRACT

This article introduces a project in which researchers from across different disciplines including semantic web, materials science, manufacturing engineering, and software engineering collaborate to develop ontologies and a data management system for additive manufacturing processes.

KEYWORDS

ontology, additive manufacturing, information modeling, data management

1 INTRODUCTION

The field of additive manufacturing (AM), also known as 3D printing, is growing at an incredible pace. One issue that is slowing its progress is the difficulty in finding data for using new equipment and materials as well as the design of new processes. This often necessitates lengthy and expensive periods of trial and error. Worse yet, intellectual property constraints often lead to these parameters being kept proprietary to prevent competition, adding to the difficulties.

The creation of an ontology modeling AM processes will help solve both the issue of finding useful data and using the data to develop and improve AM processes. Creating a unified ontological framework will reduce the fragmentation caused by the multitude of proprietary formats, making searching for useful data easier. Leveraging the power of semantic web and web-based software applications will aid in validating hypothesized relations, as well as potentially revealing hidden ones.

*Currently at Sandia National Laboratories.

WebSci '17, June 25–28, 2017, Troy, NY, USA
 ISBN 978-1-4503-4896-6/17/06.
DOI: http://dx.doi.org/10.1145/3091478.3098863

2 ONTOLOGY DESIGN

A number of existing ontologies were used in the creation of the Additive Manufacturing Processing Ontology (AMPO):

- PROV Ontology (PROV-O). This provides a set of classes, properties, and restrictions that can be used to represent and interchange provenance information generated in different systems and under different contexts. It can be specialized to create new classes and properties to model provenance information for different applications and domains.[1]
- Semanticscience Integrated Ontology (SIO). This ontology is used to facilitate biomedical knowledge discovery. SIO features a simple upper level comprised of essential types and relations for the rich description of arbitrary objects, processes, and their attributes.[2]
- Quantities, Units, Dimensions and Data Types Ontologies (QUDT). This provides semantic specifications for units of measure, quantity kind, dimensions, and data types.[3]

Figure 1 shows a schematic representation of major classes in AMPO. Each line connecting two boxes represents an object property. This is just an oversimplified representation of a conceptual map (Cmap) to give readers a brief idea.[1]

Here are some key points we would like to mention about AMPO:

(a) The class hierarchies of AMPO are connected with the upper level ontology, SIO. Each class in AMPO is a subclass of one of these three SIO classes: sio:Attribute, sio:Object, or sio:Process.

(b) Both ampo:Step and ampo:Process are subclasses of sio:Process. They are disjoint classes. Their definitions are used to differentiate them. ampo:Process must contain more than one step. ampo:Step is atomic and indivisible. Additionally, ampo:Process may be a component of a higher level ampo:Process. ampo:happensDirectlyBefore defines the sequential relationship between two processes, or two steps, or a process and a step.

(c) We define ampo:Process and ampo:Step as subclasses of prov:Activity. In order to record the timestamps of ampo:Process and ampo:Step instances, we use the properties prov:startedAtTime

[1]Due to space limit, the full AMPO Cmaps could not be included. Readers can access them at: https://goo.gl/WvgZwa

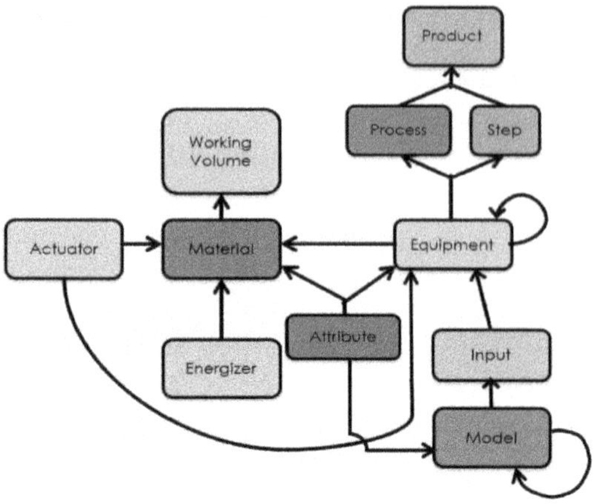

Figure 1: Simplified graph representation of AMPO.

and prov:endedAtTime from PROV-O. The above assertion also allows AMPO to connect ampo:Process and ampo:Step with prov:Person and prov:Role.

(d) ampo:QuantitativeInput and ampo:QuantitativeAttribute are subclasses of qudt:Quantity since an instance of these two classes is a quantitative measurement along with a unit.

(e) ampo:Process is defined as a subclass of both prov:Activity and sio:Entity. This makes ampo:Process a subclass of two classes which belong to two different ontologies. This is valid and no conflict would occur.

(f) ampo:QuantitativeInput and ampo:DynamicQuantitativeAttribute have a datatype property ampo:downloadURL. Instances of these two classes are usually time series data which contain different values at multiple timestamps. Our best practice is to access each time series as a .csv file through a cloud storage application such as Dropbox or Google Drive, while only providing the access URL, i.e. the metadata, in the use case RDF data.

3 SYSTEM ARCHITECTURE

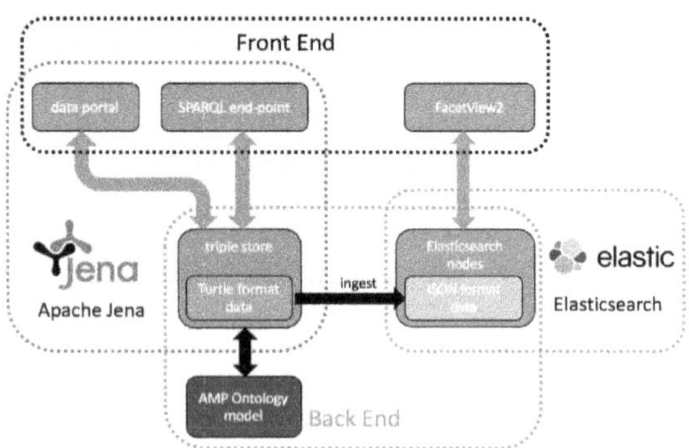

Figure 2: Data management system architecture.

Figure 2 shows the detailed architecture of our data management system with data storage, search, and browsing features for AMPO use cases.

Apache Jena Fuseki is a SPARQL server, which contains a built-in data portal user interface (UI), a SPARQL end-point, as well as triple stores. Fuseki provides REST-style interaction with the RDF data which allows the triples it contains to be exposed as a SPARQL end-point accessible over HTTP.[4] Both the AMPO ontology and use cases are coded in machine readable RDF Turtle (.ttl) format. We could load all the RDF data through the frontend UI. The ontology Turtle file needs to be loaded first since it serves as the fundamental framework for all the use cases, similar to the schema in a relational database. Elasticsearch is a distributed, RESTful search and analytics engine which uses standard RESTful APIs and JSON.[5]

Python scripts were written to automatically extract, transform, and load (ETL) the relevant data from Fuseki into an Elasticsearch instance, which serves as the backend of the faceted data browsers. The extracting functions in the scripts send GET query requests to the SPARQL end-point of Fuseki. The transforming functions convert the query results into semi-structured JSON format data. The loading functions load the JSON data into our Elasticsearch instance by sending PUT or POST requests. We give the whole ETL process another name — ingest.

FacetView2[6] offers a decent faceted-browsing frontend for the JSON data in ElasticSearch. For AMPO use cases, extensive modifications to the code of FacetView2 are made to customize the browsers.

Readers can access a toy demo of the faceted browsers through the following URLs[2]:

- equipment browser: https://dofamp.tw.rpi.edu/equipment.html
- material browser: https://dofamp.tw.rpi.edu/material.html

Users can select different facets on the left side of the webpage. Users can also search and rerank the data using the toolbar on top.

4 FURTHER WORK

The design process of AMPO is use case driven. Although the use case data is often sparse and non-structured, the AMPO framework can easily be modified or extended to accommodate additional use cases due to its flexibility.

Our innovative work, initially sponsored by the Rensselaer Institute for Data Exploration and Applications, has drawn tremendous attention from the Defense Advanced Research Projects Agency (DARPA). We were given additional funding supports to build another management system on a much larger scale for the materials processing data provided by DARPA (grant number DARPA: A12746.1102). AMPO has also been reused as part of a bigger ontology named DARPA Materials Ontology (DMOnto). Due to the confidential nature of the data owned by DARPA, no further details can be revealed here.

REFERENCES

[1] Timothy Lebo, Satya Sahoo, and Deborah McGuinness. PROV-O: The PROV Ontology, 2013.
[2] Michel Dumontier, Christopher JO Baker, Joachim Baran, Alison Callahan, Leonid Chepelev, José Cruz-Toledo, Nicholas R Del Rio, Geraint Duck, Laura I Furlong, Nichealla Keath, et al. The semanticscience integrated ontology (sio) for biomedical research and knowledge discovery. *Journal of biomedical semantics*, 5(1):14, 2014.
[3] http://www.qudt.org/, 2017.
[4] https://jena.apache.org/, 2017.
[5] https://www.elastic.co/products/elasticsearch, 2017.
[6] https://github.com/cottagelabs/facetview2, 2014.

[2] This toy demo might not be very interesting since only the data of one toy use case (fused deposition modeling) is used. In real situations, the faceted browsers could easily handle huge amount of instances and many more faceted categories.

The Tragedy of the Identity Assurance Commons

Vincent Marmion, David E. Millard, Enrico H. Gerding, and Sarah V. Stevenage*
University Of Southampton
Highfield Campus
UK SO171BJ
V.Marmion@soton.co.uk

ABSTRACT

Identity assurance is the processing of personal identifying information (PII) to reach a desired confidence that an individual is who they claim to be. However, identity assurance is beyond a process; it is a commons, a natural resource accessible to all whereby individual actions can affect the group. Because each time we copy an item of PII we inadvertently expose it to misuse, which reduces the identifying utility of PII, and therefore reduces the confidence of identity assurance. Akin to the prisoner's dilemma, there is a usage dilemma in sustaining PII. A dilemma heightened by the Web as PII is being digitally exchanged, processed, and stored, with ever-increasing volume, variety and veracity.

To explore identity assurance as a commons, we develop an agent-based simulation of a simple resource strategy game. Building on work regarding the persistence of PII exploitation, our initial findings suggest that there is a potentially unsustainable dynamic in identity assurance. Therefore suggesting that in the long-term our current regulatory attempts are inapt.

CCS CONCEPTS

• **Security and privacy → Social aspects of security and privacy;**

KEYWORDS

Identity Assurance; Personal Identifying Information; Commons

1 INTRODUCTION

Identity assurance of a person is the processing of personally identifying information (PII) to reach a desired confidence that the person is who they claim [1]. This process is integral to high-stakes activities such as the police matching fingerprints. It is also an integral part of activities on the Web, and therefore is an unavoidable and increasingly frequent part of daily life. Despite this broad and often significant application, a persistence of individual misjudgements, imposter innovations, and organisation exploitations, makes obtaining 100% confidence an unachievable goal [6]. Yet, using ever-innovative methods of extraction, i.e., biometric scanners, or a combination of methods, it is possible to get ever-closer to a person's true idenity [2].

However, each process innovation has potential for negative consequences. For instance, switching from passwords to biometrics may increase assurance, but it also provokes legal, social, and ethical considerations as it enables individuals to be covertly tracked across many systems. This is because identity assurance is beyond a process; it is also a socio-technical system comprised of competing security and privacy desires, amidst commercial and social incentives, each governed by national and global regulations [5]. Moreover, identity assurance might be best considered as a commons, as the fuel of identity assurance, PII, share the same qualities as other common pool resources (CPR) [4]. Meaning, over-using PII can deplete its identifying utility in future uses, as usage involves making a copy, and each copy adds doubt as to its legitimate user. Therefore, the dilemma is in sustaining the utility of PII.

In this regard we learn from other *'tragedy of the commons'* usage dilemmas, wherein regulation is essential [3]. Insufficient regulation can allow for the accumulation of seemingly innocuous yet self-interested decisions towards the depletion of a CPR. On the other hand, simply increasing regulation can be too blunt, as over-cautious protections can frustrate and waste a valuable resource. Therefore, regulation must fit.

As PII is being digitally exchanged, processed, and stored, with ever-increasing volume, variety and veracity, using ever-innovative methods of extraction, our belief is that regulation is insufficient. However, to get regulation right, first we must better understand the system. Therefore, this work builds on an existing game theoretic model to develop an agent-based simulation to study the stability and sustainability of PII within the identity assurance commons.

2 STABILITY IN THE SYSTEM

Within a game theoretical model Vila et al. [7] explores privacy akin to a second-hand car market where users pay to check for faulty cars. Likewise, the current consent model for PII disclosure costs the user in *time, effort or money* to discover whether an organisation is faulty, which in this context could be whether they extract more PII than required and/or sell it for profit. These 'faulty' organisations can capitalise on the asymmetric information between user and organisation if it is deemed that users are unwilling to pay to discover any faults. Classifying their results as a free-riding problem, they describe an oscillation between users depending on others to discover a fault, yet many individuals with this same conclusion can tempt organisations to exploit the free-riding, this in turn eventually leads to more users paying to discover while discovery exists

*Vincent Marmion; PhD Candidate of the Institute of Complex Systems Simulation.
Dr. Millard; Associate Professor of Computer and Web Science.
Dr. Gerding; Associate Professor in the Agents, Interaction and Complexity group.
Prof. Stevenage; Institute of Criminal Justice Research

WebSci '17, June 25-28, 2017, Troy, NY, USA
 978-1-4503-4896-6/17/06
DOI: 10.1145/3091478.3098882

(Figure 1). Their results suggest the possibility of a long-term, albeit sensitive, mixed-point equilibrium comprising some attending users, others not, and some respecting organisations, others not. Therefore, exploitation persists.

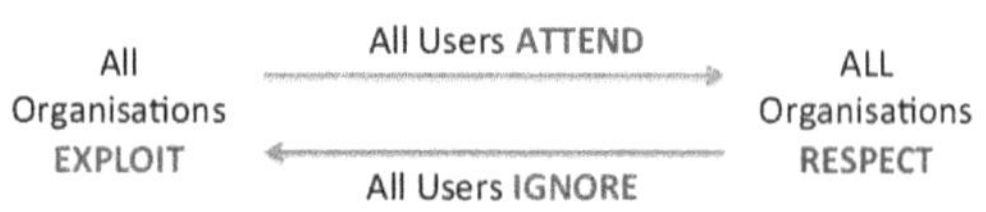

Figure 1: A Privacy Free Riding Problem [7].

3 SUSTAINABILITY IN THE SYSTEM

Whilst the game-model described in [7] provides an insight into the persistence of data exploitation, the implication of the long-term sustainability of a privacy market is misleading. Because, the equilibrium is sensitive to oscillation due to environmental changes such as innovative extraction technologies. During these oscillations the asymmetry of information is heightened, leading to a higher potential of exploiting organisations, contributing to an accumulating exposure of PII over time, necessitating further innovation in the extraction of higher veracity PII. Only then, as a commons with escalating extraction and a depleting CPR, does a sustainability concern emerge.

Additional complexity is needed in order to go beyond the assumption of identical users engaging with identical organisations, and beyond a catch all of treating PII as one homogeneous entity. Repurposing [7] into an agent-based model provides the flexibility to add these elements, and also add realism to the insights gained.

4 A NEW AGENT-BASED MODEL

The following simple outline of an agent-based version of [7] describes two service agents competing for the engagement of a population [P] of user agents. The service perspective amounts to a 2-player, iterated, pure strategy game. Each service selects either a respect [R] or an exploit [E] strategy. They have knowledge of their opponents current strategy, and a basic calculation of predicted market change. Profit is calculated per number of users (u) as $eu = ru + u\epsilon$. The user perspective equates to a simple decision problem, whereby in each turn [T] a random set of users (1-4%) evaluate their position; ignoring users join, or remain engaged with, any service, attending users join or remain with a respecting service, and leave or remain disengaged from an exploiting service.

Figure 2 illustrates the results of this, *in essence*, agent-based simulation of [7]. The top and middle panels indicate the oscillations as described in Figure 1 with exploitation coinciding with cycles in market latency, i.e. disengaged users. The middle panel showing user reaction to exploitation reflects what Westin [8, p. 24] describes as a 'shift in public mood', during 1999 and 2002 as 'privacy fundamentalists' rose from 24% to 34%. Not shown here, is the model sensitivity to changes in ϵ, as slight decreases reduce the oscillations in favour of stable respect strategies, whereas slight increases causes exploitation strategies to dominate.

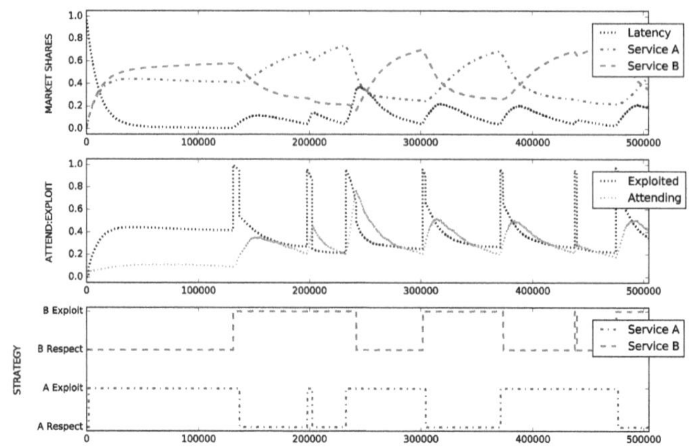

Figure 2: *Top:* Market shares, and latency. *Middle:* Periods of exploitation and the reactive user attend strategies. *Bottom:* Oscillation of dominant strategies as size changes reach tipping points. *Parameters:* $r = 1, \epsilon = 0.005, P = 15000, T = 3000$

5 CONCLUSION AND FUTURE WORK

This abstract sets out an argument for examining identity assurance as a commons. Building on this premise could have significant implications for the regulation of identity assurance, and specifically, for how we regulate for the sustainable use of PII in a digital age. It also illustrates the first development steps of an agent-based simulation of the identity assurance commons. This approach provides a flexible base from which to explore different aspects of the Identity assurance commons, including what drives or tempers usage escalations in identity assurance. To this end, two sets of empirical studies are underway to enrich this model. The first exploring the different ways users make disclosure decisions, i.e., calculative vs heuristic, and a second examining how users personally value individual items of PII.

REFERENCES

[1] Yolanta Beres, Adrian Baldwin, Marco Casassa Mont, and Simon Shiu. 2007. On identity assurance in the presence of federated identity management systems. In *Proceedings of the 2007 ACM workshop on Digital identity management - DIM '07*. ACM Press, New York, New York, USA, 27.

[2] Sue M Black, Sadie Creese, Richard M Guest, Bill Pike, Steve J Saxby, Danaë Stanton Fraser, Sarah V Stevenage, Monica T Whitty, Danae Stanton Fraser, Sarah V Stevenage, and M T Whittty. 2012. Superidentity: Fusion of identity across real and cyber domains. *ID360: Global Identity* (2012).

[3] Garrett Hardin. 2009. The Tragedy of the Commons. *Journal of Natural Resources Policy Research* 1, 3 (2009), 243–253.

[4] Charlotte Hess and Elinor Ostrom. 2003. Ideas, artifacts, and facilities: information as a common-pool resource. *Law and contemporary problems* 66, 1/2 (2003), 111–145.

[5] Daniel J. Solove. 2007. 'I've Got Nothing to Hide' and Other Misunderstandings of Privacy. *San Diego Law Review* 44, May (2007), 1–23. DOI: https://doi.org/10.2139/ssrn.998565

[6] Umut Uludag, Sharath Pankanti, Salil Prabhakar, and Anil K. Jain. 2004. Biometric cryptosystems: Issues and challenges. *Proc. IEEE* 92, 6 (2004), 948–959. DOI: https://doi.org/10.1109/JPROC.2004.827372

[7] Tony Vila, Rachel Greenstadt, and David Molnar. 2003. Why we can't be bothered to read privacy policies models of privacy economics as a lemons market. In *Proceeding ICEC '03 Proceedings of the 5th International Conference on Electronic Commerce*. ACM, 403–407. DOI: https://doi.org/10.1145/948005.948057

[8] Alan F Westin. 2003. Social and political dimensions of privacy. *Journal of social issues* 59, 2 (2003), 431–453.

A Typology of Socialbots (Abbrev.)

Gregory Maus
School of Informatics and Computing
Bloomington, Indiana
gmaus@iu.edu

KEYWORDS

socialbots, social bots, online automation, digital propaganda, twitterbot, social botnet, social spam, spam 2.0

1 INTRODUCTION

As a new organism in the human social ecosystem, socialbots (defined here as automated or largely automated programs that interface with online platforms in largely the same way that a typical human would be expected to: they hold normal accounts, make connections, and post content) are rapidly rising to prominence as influencers. They've been used by governments and political worldwide to influence public narratives[1], spread misinformation[2][3][4], commit advertising fraud on reviews for mobile apps[5], ad-clicks[6], video views [7], conduct phishing campaigns [8][9] [10][11], and mass defrauding of infidelity-seeking men[12]. On the other hand, they've also demonstrated positive potential, however, performing administrative tasks on Wikipedia [13], are useful for curating information [14] [15], and can provide a number of other unique services such as algorithmically created music on demand [16], reporting the arrival of dictators in Geneva[17], etc.
Unfortunately, most of the work on socialbots thus far has been in isolated case studies. Thus, the purpose of this work is to provide a unified typological framework for the discussion of the different species of socialbot in both known and hypothetical instances. The typology has already proven fruitful in clarifying discussion and prompting new lines of inquiry on socialbots for our research team and we believe that it could provide similar clarity elsewhere. Further elaboration on the classifications, their traits and implications will be presented in future publications.

2 RELATED WORK

Previous work in bot classification schema has been relatively sparse.
Oentaryo et al. (2016) propose a broad behavioral categorization of bots into broadcasters (which share benign content with general audiences), consumers (which aggregate content from multiple sources and/or provide updates), and spammers (which post malicious or irrelevant content).[14]
Mitter et al. (2013) offer a multi-level categorization of malicious social bot campaigns based on the campaignfis targets, vulnerabilities exploited, bot account type, attack method, and result .[18] While thorough and detailed in analyzing malicious bot attacks, it spares little analysis for the bots themselves and none for benign bots.
Woolley (2016) divides the use of political bot campaigns by governments into the three categories of demobilizing opposition, fostering pro-government messages, and padding follower numbers for government and/or candidate accounts.[1]
Ji et al (2016) provides an overview of mechanisms used by bots to evade detection.[19]

WebSci '17, June 25-28, 2017, Troy, NY, USA
 978-1-4503-4896-6/17/06
DOI: 10.1145/3091478.3098860

3 CATEGORIZATION CAVEATS

Attempting to categorize socialbots runs into similar issues as categorizing biological organisms in that new discoveries may complicate or invalidate existing classification systems. New discoveries of socialbots are likely to occur in two ways.
Firstly, new types of bots can be developed with novel applications and features that defy or expand known categories.
Secondly, existing covert socialbots are discovered with some regularity.[1, 2, 7, 8, 12, 20–31] Thus we know that many bots trying to evade detection exist, but we can't know how many exist that successfully avoid detection. Therefore there could already be unknown legions of socialbots, some of which might defy current categorization.
More broadly, the categories are in some cases fuzzy, especially in terms of Objectives as bots may have multiple objectives and the distinctions between them can be somewhat blurry.

4 CATEGORIZATION FRAMEWORK

Most of the categories and examples are outlined in the table below. However, there are three exceptions unlisted because they exist more along the lines of a spectrum than as discrete categories: Content Creation Autonomy (the degree to which an automated program produces the content to be broadcast), Content Broadcast Autonomy (the selection of which content to broadcast as well as when and where to share it), and Network Graph Autonomy (how much freedom the bot has to choose how it engages with the network whether that be other users directly or established content.)
A table displaying the derived typology is available on Figshare here: https://figshare.com/s/1bb45cfbd2dc5dd6958a

5 ACKNOWLEDGEMENTS

Thank you to Onur Varol, Fil Menczer, John Paolillo for their advice and feedback.

Classification of the Syrian Social Botnet and the Star Wars Botnet would also not have been possible without the helpful correspondences of Norah Abokhodair and Juan Echeverria Guzman respectively.

REFERENCES

[1] Samuel Woolley. Automating power: Social bot interference in global politics. *First Monday*, 21(4), 2016.

[2] Alessandro Bessi and Emilio Ferrara. Social bots distort the 2016 u.s. presidential election online discussion. *First Monday*, 21(11), 2016.

[3] Dan Misener. Political bots spread misinformation during u.s. campaign. November 2016.

[4] Jacob Ratkiewicz, Michael Conover, Mark Meiss, Bruno Goncalves, Alessandro Flammini, and Filippo Menczer. Detecting and tracking political abuse in social media, 2011.

[5] Zhen Xie and Sencun Zhu. Appwatcher: Unveiling the underground market of trading mobile app reviews. In *Proceedings of the 8th ACM Conference on Security & Privacy in Wireless and Mobile Networks*, WiSec '15, pages 10:1–10:11, New York, NY, USA, 2015. ACM.

[6] Adrian Neal, Sander Kouwenhoven, and OB SA. Quantifying online advertising fraud: Ad-click bots vs humans. Technical report, 2015.

[7] Miriam Marciel, Rubén Cuevas, Albert Banchs, Roberto Gonzalez, Stefano Traverso, Mohamed Ahmed, and Arturo Azcorra. Understanding the detection of fake view fraud in video content portals. *CoRR*, abs/1507.08874, 2015.

[8] Hongyu Gao, Jun Hu, Christo Wilson, Zhichun Li, Yan Chen, and Ben Y. Zhao. Detecting and characterizing social spam campaigns. In *Proceedings of the 10th ACM SIGCOMM Conference on Internet Measurement*, IMC '10, pages 35–47, New York, NY, USA, 2010. ACM.

[9] Sidharth Chhabra, Anupama Aggarwal, Fabricio Benevenuto, and Ponnurangam Kumaraguru. Phi.sh/$ocial: The phishing landscape through short urls. In *Proceedings of the 8th Annual Collaboration, Electronic Messaging, Anti-Abuse and Spam Conference*, CEAS '11, pages 92–101, New York, NY, USA, 2011. ACM.

[10] George Khourey. How to spot bot-generated craigslist scams. November 2016.

[11] Better Business Bureau. Scam alert – how to spot spam profiles on tinder, July 2015.

[12] Annalee Newitz. How ashley madison hid its fembot con from users and investigators. September 2015.

[13] Maxime Clment and Matthieu J. Guitton. Interacting with bots online: Usersfi reactions to actions of automated programs in wikipedia. *Computers in Human Behavior*, 50:66 – 75, 2015.

[14] Richard J. Oentaryo, Arinto Murdopo, Philips K. Prasetyo, and Ee-Peng Lim. *On Profiling Bots in Social Media*, pages 92–109. Springer International Publishing, Cham, 2016.

[15] A marvellous incomplete compendium of reddit automatons bots, author=Lock, Duncan, year=2013, month=June, day=19, url=http://duncanlock.net/blog/2013/06/19/a-marvellous-incomplete-compendium-of-reddit-automatons-bots/.

[16] Ngai Zhang. The musical twitter bot: Who has the copyright for ai-facilitated works?, October 2016.

[17] Amar Toor. This twitter bot is tracking dictators' flights in and out of geneva. October 2016.

[18] Silvia Mitter, Claudia Wagner, and Markus Strohmaier. A categorization scheme for socialbot attacks in online social networks. *CoRR*, abs/1402.6288, 2014.

[19] Yuede Ji, Yukun He, Xinyang Jiang, Jian Cao, and Qiang Li. Combating the evasion mechanisms of social bots. *Computers Security*, 58:230 – 249, 2016.

[20] Norah Abokhodair, Daisy Yoo, and David W McDonald. Dissecting a social botnet: Growth, content and influence in twitter. In *Proceedings of the 18th ACM Conference on Computer Supported Cooperative Work & Social Computing*, pages 839–851. ACM, 2015.

[21] Lawrence Alexander. Social network analysis reveals full scale of kremlin's twitter bot campaign. April 2015.

[22] Natalie Andrews. Pro-trump twitter bots at center of nevada mystery. February 2016.

[23] Yazan Boshmaf, Ildar Muslukhov, Konstantin Beznosov, and Matei Ripeanu. The socialbot network: When bots socialize for fame and money. In *Proceedings of the 27th Annual Computer Security Applications Conference*, ACSAC '11, pages 93–102, New York, NY, USA, 2011. ACM.

[24] Klint Finley. Pro-government twitter bots try to hush mexican activists. August 2016.

[25] Michelle Forelle, Phil Howard, Andrés Monroy-Hernández, and Saiph Savage. Political bots and the manipulation of public opinion in venezuela. *CoRR*, abs/1507.07109, 2015.

[26] Oana Goga, Giridhari Venkatadri, and Krishna P. Gummadi. The doppelgänger bot attack: Exploring identity impersonation in online social networks. In *Proceedings of the 2015 ACM Conference on Internet Measurement Conference*, IMC '15, pages 141–153, New York, NY, USA, 2015. ACM.

[27] Adrianne Jeffries. It's your face. it's your photos. meet the creepiest kind of instagram spambot. September 2014.

[28] Derek O'Callaghan, Martin Harrigan, Joe Carthy, and Pádraig Cunningham. Network analysis of recurring youtube spam campaigns. *CoRR*, abs/1201.3783, 2012.

[29] Sergey Sanovich, Denis Stukal, Duncan Penfold-Brown, and Joshua Tucker. Turning the virtual tables: Government strategies for addressing online opposition with an application to russia. June 2015.

[30] Ernie Smith, Seth Millstein, Chris Tognotti, Patrick deHahn, Scott Craft, and Matthew Keys. Why you might get tons of tumblr likespam (and what to do about it), October 2011.

[31] Pablo Suárez-Serrato, Margaret E. Roberts, Clayton A. Davis, and Filippo Menczer. On the influence of social bots in online protests. preliminary findings of a mexican case study. *CoRR*, abs/1609.08239, 2016.

Public Perception of a Country: Exploring Tweets About Qatar

Shahan Ali Memon
Rohith Krishnan Pillai
Carnegie Mellon University
Doha, Qatar
samemon,rohithkp@andrew.cmu.edu

Susan Dun
Northwestern University Qatar
Doha, Qatar
s-dun@northwestern.edu

Yelena Mejova
Ingmar Weber
Qatar Computing Research Institute, HBKU
Doha, Qatar
ymejova,iweber@hbku.edu.qa

ABSTRACT

Is it possible to "hack" an image of an international entity by driving international and domestic media? Here, we present an image/brand monitoring tool for a country, Qatar, which presents an overview of the contexts and references to media in which it is mentioned on social media. Tracking dozens of languages, this tool allows a global understanding of the perceptions and concerns Twitter users associate with Qatar, and which mainstream media may be driving these sentiments.

CCS CONCEPTS

• **Human-centered computing** → **Empirical studies in HCI**; **Social networking sites**; • **Applied computing** → *Sociology*; • **Information systems** → *Web mining*;

KEYWORDS

Nation Branding, Public Opinion, Twitter

1 INTRODUCTION

Since winning the bid for the FIFA World Cup 2022 in December 2010, beating a bid from the United States, Qatar has received a lot of international attention. For example, a blog article[1] from May 2015 was shared more than 32k times on social media. Qatar's official response[2] also posted by the Guardian only received 540 social shares. Similarly, an article in the Washington Post[3] which contained factually inaccurate claims "went viral", whereas Qatar's official response[4] received little attention.

Here we present a simple tool that aims to visualize the public discussion surrounding Qatar on Twitter in different countries. Our tool is publicly accessible at http://scdev5.qcri.org/TweetsAboutQatar/.

Related to our work is research on how often Twitter users in different countries mention a Twitter user in another country [1] or how often Twitter users have international follow links [5]. Furthermore, work on news coverage in one country on disasters in another country also relates to country-specific media attention [3]. However, as far as we know, no prior work has looked at in which contexts a target country is being mentioned on social media around the globe. Work on "nation branding" on social media is also different but related. For example, [2] studies the active use of Twitter of the Obama administration as a means of diplomacy. Our tool, by contrast, is only for monitoring, not for engaging.

2 DATA COLLECTION AND PROCESSING

As a first step, we compiled a list of translations of the name "Qatar" to 35 distinct languages, including English, Arabic, Portuguese, and German. Tweets containing one of these references were then collected through the Twitter Streaming API. This was done for a period from 3rd of May to 15th of November, 2015, with one two week period inadvertently omitted, resulting in a total of 4,458,914 tweets. Metadata including the posting date and time, the user-disclosed location (location from their bio page), and, most importantly, the tweet text, were parsed out. Tweets were geo-coded to countries by passing user-disclosed location to Nominatim, which provides geo-coding for the OpenStreetMap project[5], resulting in 1,837,280 geo-coded tweets. For each country, terms as well as bi-grams (two-word phrases) were extracted, and for each of them the distinct users using them were counted. Finally, frequently used terms were then visualized by using wordclouds for each country with more than 30 distinct users. Thus, our tools using Carto map[6] shows data for 660,006 distinct users, covering 173 countries.

3 THE INTERFACE

The main element of the visualization is a world map (as shown in Figure 1). Countries are color-coded by the number of tweets captured – from many (dark blue) to few (light yellow/green). Countries that are marked as white did not have the required minimum number of tweets to be included in the analysis. Clicking on a country brings up an info box with a summary of the tweets originating from this location. The main element of this info box is a tag cloud that shows the most frequent uni- and bi-grams after the removal of stop words. The tag cloud provides an intuitive summary of the topics that dominate the discussion of Qatar originating from this country. The second most important element in the info box is the list of domains that are referenced in tweets mentioning Qatar, providing insights into whether the discussion is influenced more by domestic media or by international media. Finally, the info box also provides the raw tweet count.

[1] https://goo.gl/4RlMTu
[2] https://goo.gl/JfWmGa
[3] https://goo.gl/wmyCUW
[4] https://goo.gl/2vebuz

[5] https://wiki.openstreetmap.org/wiki/Nominatim
[6] https://carto.com/

WebSci '17, June 25-28, 2017, Troy, NY, USA
 978-1-4503-4896-6/17/06
DOI: 10.1145/3091478.3098872

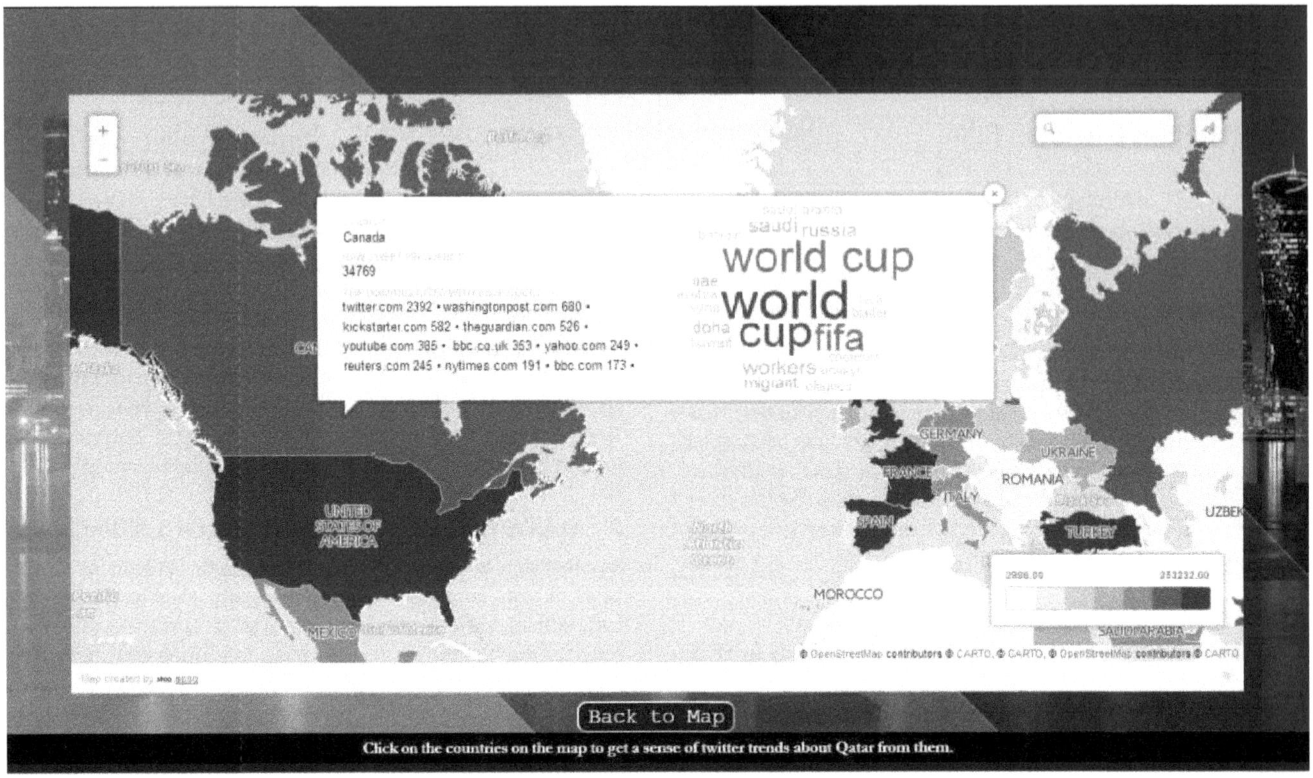

Figure 1: Screenshot of the exploration tool showing the data for Canada.

4 EXAMPLE USE CASES

The tool allows discovery of both commonalities and distinctiveness in topics across countries. In most countries, the World Cup is mentioned quite frequently. However, what aspects of the World Cup are tweeted about can be quite different. In the United States, migrant workers are a common topic, but there is very little mention of the FIFA bribery allegations. However, in France and Australia, the corruption issue is prominent. Yet, users in Australia also Tweet about the migrant worker issue. In Spain, migrant workers are mentioned although corruption is not, while in India the topic is dominated by different issues such as fans and Qatar Airways. There are also topics popular in one country that are barely mentioned in others. For example, Xavi's move to play for a local side in Qatar is frequently mentioned in Spain whereas elsewhere it is almost non-existent. Our tool allows the comparison of the common themes within and across countries, making discovery and analysis of social media content easy for analysts. Similar analysis can be done by utilizing the tool to examine what domains are tweeted most often – both within and across countries– enabling the discovery of opinion influencers in regional and global social media content.

5 CONCLUSIONS

The tool in its current form is simple but attempts to address an important task: summarizing the global social chatter on Twitter involving an entity –Qatar in this case– and giving hints at who "drives" this discussion. Through this tool one can easily discover that the topics are generally similar and that part of the reason for this convergence could lie in similar sources being referenced around the globe. It may also assist in addressing the growing concern over foreign influence on domestic politics, such as the alleged Russian "hacking" of US elections[7], where information may be strategically released by international players. Going forward, it could be interesting to attempt to detect "global astro-turfing" or trolling using approaches such as Truthy [4].

REFERENCES

[1] Ruth García-Gavilanes, Yelena Mejova, and Daniele Quercia. 2014. Twitter ain't without frontiers: Economic, Social, and Cultural Boundaries in International Communication. In *CSCW*. 1511–1522.
[2] Britney Harris. 2013. Diplomacy 2.0: The Future of Social Media in Nation Branding. *Exchange: The Journal of Public Diplomacy* 4 (2013), 3. Issue 1.
[3] Haewoon Kwak and Jisun An. 2014. A First Look at Global News Coverage of Disasters by Using the GDELT Dataset. In *SocInfo*. 300–308.
[4] Jacob Ratkiewicz, Michael Conover, Mark Meiss, Bruno Goncalves, Snehal Patil, Alessandro Flammini, and Filippo Menczer. 2011. Truthy: mapping the spread of astroturf in microblog streams. In *WWW*. 249–252.
[5] Bogdan State, Patrick Park, Ingmar Weber, and Michael Macy. 2015. The Mesh of Civilizations in the Global Network of Digital Communication. *PLOS ONE* 10 (05 2015), 1–9.

[7] https://goo.gl/e6ZIVn

A Semantic Workflow Approach to Web Science Analytics

Extended Abstract

Spencer C. Norris
Rensselaer Polytechnic Institute
Troy, New York 12180
norris@rpi.edu

John S. Erickson
Rensselaer Polytechnic Institute
Troy, New York 12180
erickj4@rpi.edu

Deborah L. McGuinness
Rensselaer Polytechnic Institute
Troy, New York
dlm@cs.rpi.edu

ABSTRACT

Reproducibility and reuse are rapidly becoming guiding principles in publishing and sharing scientific results[1, 10]. In order to enhance researchers' ability to leverage existing results, many are moving in the direction of semantic workflow systems, which enable users to define and share experimental procedures as linked data on the Web. These workflows provide a powerful mechanism for reproducing *in silico* experiments and thus are well-suited for Web Science tasks. In order to aid users in the process of experiment design and reproduction, we are integrating the Workflow INstance Generation and Specialization (WINGS) system [7] with our existing Semantic Numeric Exploration Technology (SemNExT) framework [9]. This will provide a completely open-source stack for designing *in silico* experiments using a combination of semantic and numeric analyses.

We will explore how this system may be configured to create reproducible Web Science workflows, especially as it pertains to data federation across the Web. We are leveraging our existing tooling as we develop new approaches for automatically generating provenance for interacting with remote endpoints of heterogeneous data sources. This will support not only the aggregation of diverse and geographically-disparate data sources across the Web, but also collaborative science by allowing other users to reproduce and expand on the same results using shared workflows.

CCS CONCEPTS

•**Information Systems** → *Semantic web description languages;* •**Computer Systems Organization** → **Architectures - Other Architectures - Heterogeneous (hybrid) systems;** *Architectures - Distributed architectures;* •**Web interfaces** → Mashups;

KEYWORDS

Semantic Workflows, Reproducibility, Data Federation

1 BACKGROUND

Semantic workflows can be viewed as descriptions of computational procedures encoded using the Resource Description Framework (RDF) [8], the Web Ontology Language (OWL) [3] and other open Web standards. Semantic workflows have been shown to provide a robust approach for reproducing *in silico* experiments, especially in systems biology and bioinformatics domains. Because of this, there is a strong motivation for using them to coordinate and publish reproducible experiments in the domain of Web Science, such as data collection and aggregation methods that rely on the federation of heterogeneous, geographically-separated data sources.

WebSci '17, June 25–28, 2017, Troy, NY, USA
 978-1-4503-4896-6/17/06..
DOI: http://dx.doi.org/10.1145/3091478.3098875

2 RELATED WORK

Semantic workflows have seen early successes concerning reproducibility, e.g., in recreating the Tuberculosis drugome [4], demonstrating their applicability to *in silico* experiments for -omics and systems biology. However, there have not been many examples of semantic workflows being used to explicitly support tasks pertinent to Web Science. The closest analogues have been standalone software solutions, such as BioMart, and experiments designed using the Galaxy workflow system. The BioMart data federation system has been used to support aggregation across geographically-dispersed data stores [11]. While BioMart is a powerful, highly scalable system, it suffers the usual drawbacks of a non-generic interface, as it requires that the databases it wraps to expose their data as BioMart datasets. Additionally, BioMart is only an aggregation tool; it does nothing in terms of experimental workflow design.

The Galaxy workflow system has done similar work with workflows for data aggregation using SADI services [2]. However, a key drawback of Galaxy's approach to workflows is the lack of provenance capture as RDF. Galaxy workflows are encoded as unintuitive JSON representations, notably lacking URIs for output results, module names and other important features. Retrospective provenance is captured as a history log which can be exported and reused in other experiments. However, these encodings only support other instances of Galaxy and fail to capture the semantics of the workflow using either an ontology or controlled vocabulary. This limits Galaxy's usefulness in workflow discovery and recombination, and thus its applicability to collaborative Web Science.

3 WEB SCIENCE AS SEMANTIC WORKFLOWS

The Semantic Numeric Exploration Technology (SemNExT) project [9] aims to address the issue of workflow reproducibility for Web Science by integrating with the WINGS semantic workflow system [7]. Building on top of WINGS confers a number of benefits, most notably automated prospective and retrospective provenance capture for workflows as linked data. This allows workflows not only to be reproduced, but also to be readily discovered and recombined to generate larger experiments. Additionally, WINGS has developed a recommendation system for dataset discovery, assisting users in selecting datasets based on their semantic qualities [5] [6]. These factors make WINGS an attractive candidate for supporting workflow reuse and publication on the Web.

SemNExT introduces the components necessary to interface with WINGS and hook it into data repositories across the Web. Specifically, it provides the Python object model required to wrap data sources and expose their results in semantically consistent ways. Datasource objects expose a given service through a collection of developer-defined methods. Datasources are then plugged into Annotator objects, which interface with Datasources and narrowly define how they will be used to annotate an input RDF graph. These components all have analogues in the SemNExT ontology, allowing the different elements to be recombined using semantic reasoning.

Using this approach, we can recombine Web resources while preserving the consistency of assumptions about the processing steps performed on the input data, the types of different entities, and much more. This approach is inspired by SADI services but is generalizable as a method of wrapping any remote data source in reusable objects capable of mapping query results into RDF. Using the associated ontological concepts, WINGS is able to reason about their behavior and use in a given workflow, as well as recommend them to experimenters during the design process.

4 REPRODUCIBILITY AND REUSE

Combining WINGS and SemNExT will drive the creation of reproducible workflows for Web Science tasks in a way that supports discovery, reuse and collaboration. Because all WINGS workflows are encoded using W3C standards, they can be discovered and reasoned over as semantically-enriched linked data. This is an important next step for workflow technology, as defining workflows with open standards supports interoperability, recombination, and future research inquiries, as well as potentially improving the representation of workflows in online data observatories.

Additionally, the segmentation of programmatic interfaces into unique components and the association of those components with ontological concepts allows the discovery and reuse of the code itself supporting the workflow. Because the code would be structured atomically and have minimal external dependencies, it would allow code segments with well-defined interfaces to be dynamically loaded according to the requirements of a given workflow. This has the effect of treating code as data on the Web and allowing it to be used in contexts outside of monolithic software paradigms. Furthermore, embracing Annotator and Datasource entities as atomic operational units means that both transformative and generative procedures can be directly invoked based only on the semantics of their associated concepts rather than relying on human inference. This means that the programmatic components would no longer require coding expertise to invoke.

Lastly, the use of ontologies as organizing utilities in workflow design, generation and execution means that the interactions between these atomized components are also subject to logical constraints; thus, they can be recombined using lightweight reasoning methods making data mash-ups that invoke Web-based data repositories trivial to implement (provided the desired components already exist). This could lead to fully-automated service composition in future work, provided that the semantics are rigorous enough and the code requirements properly encapsulated.

The ability to create semantic workflow descriptions that rely on openly accessible data resources and reusable components for automating transactions with endpoints has the potential to create a new approach to composing services over the Web. By allowing code components to be directly referenced in workflow descriptions and exposing that code as linked data, it may be possible to create fully atomized workflow descriptions in support of Web Science.

5 CONCLUSION

As the amount and diversity of data on the Web continues to grow, it is increasingly important to develop experimentation methods that allow Web Science analyses to be recreated and recombined. By fusing programmatic interfaces for Web resources with semantic workflows, researchers will be able to consistently reproduce results and aggregate information across the Web, as well as redistribute their experiments and recombine them with others in a semantically consistent way. Because of their suitability for this task, we will likely start by ingesting SADI service descriptions and wrapping them in Datasource and Annotator objects to support the SemNExT project with robust annotation methods for open genetics data. Beyond this, we will likely attempt a similar configuration using remote SPARQL endpoints and relational databases.

REFERENCES

[1] On data availability, reproducibility and reuse. 19 (????), 259. Issue 4. https://doi.org/10.1038/ncb3506

[2] Mikel Egaña Aranguren and Mark D Wilkinson. 2015. Enhanced reproducibility of SADI web service workflows with Galaxy and Docker. *GigaScience* 4 (2015), 59. https://doi.org/10.1186/s13742-015-0092-3

[3] Frank van Harmelen Deborah L. McGuinness. 2004. Owl web ontology language overview. *W3C recommendation 10.2004-03* 2004, February (2004), 1–12. https://doi.org/10.1145/1295289.1295290

[4] Daniel Garijo, Sarah Kinnings, Li Xie, Lei Xie, Yinliang Zhang, Philip E. Bourne, and Yolanda Gil. 2013. Quantifying reproducibility in computational biology: The case of the tuberculosis drugome. *PLoS ONE* 8, 11 (2013). https://doi.org/10.1371/journal.pone.0080278

[5] Yolanda Gil, Pedro A Gonzalez-Calero, Jihie Kim, Joshua Moody, and Varun Ratnakar. 2011. A semantic framework for automatic generation of computational workflows using distributed data and component catalogues. *Journal of Experimental & Theoretical Artificial Intelligence* 23, 4 (2011), 389–467.

[6] Yolanda Gil, Varun Ratnakar, and Christian Fritz. 2010. Assisting Scientists with Complex Data Analysis Tasks through Semantic Workflows.. In *AAAI Fall Symposium: Proactive Assistant Agents.* Citeseer.

[7] Yolanda Gil, Varun Ratnakar, Jihie Kim, Pedro González-Calero, Paul Groth, Joshua Moody, and Ewa Deelman. 2011. Wings: Intelligent workflow-based design of computational experiments. *IEEE Intelligent Systems* 26, 1 (2011), 62–72. https://doi.org/10.1109/MIS.2010.9

[8] Graham Klyne and Jeremy J Carroll. 2004. Resource Description Framework (RDF): Concepts and Abstract Syntax. *W3C Recommendation* 10, October (2004), 1—20. http://www.w3.org/TR/2004/REC-rdf-concepts-20040210/

[9] D.L. McGuinness and K. Bennett. 2015. Integrating Semantics and Numerics: Case Study on Enhancing Genomic and Disease Data Using Linked Data Technologies. In *Proceedings of SmartData 2015 (August 18-20 2015, San Jose, CA).*

[10] Gaël Varoquaux. 2015. Of software and Science. Reproducible science: what, why, and how. (2015).

[11] Junjun Zhang, Syed Haider, Joachim Baran, Anthony Cros, Jonathan M. Guberman, Jack Hsu, Yong Liang, Long Yao, and Arek Kasprzyk. 2011. BioMart: A data federation framework for large collaborative projects. *Database* 2011 (2011). https://doi.org/10.1093/database/bar038

The Limits of Abstract Evaluation Metrics: The Case of Hate Speech Detection

Alexandra Olteanu
IBM Research

Kartik Talamadupula
IBM Research

Kush R. Varshney
IBM Research

ABSTRACT

Wagstaff (2012) draws attention to the pervasiveness of abstract evaluation metrics that explicitly ignore or remove problem specifics. While such metrics allow practitioners to compare numbers across application domains, they offer limited insight into the impact of algorithmic decisions on humans and their perception of the algorithm's correctness. Even for problems that are mathematically the *same*, both the *real-cost* of (mathematically) identical errors, as well as their *perceived-cost* by users, may significantly vary according to the specifics of each problem domain, as well as of the user perceiving the result. While the real-cost of errors has been considered previously, little attention has been paid to the perceived-cost issue. We advocate for the inclusion of *human-centered metrics* that elicit error costs from humans from two perspectives: the nature of the error, and the user context. Focusing on hate speech detection on social media, we demonstrate that even when fixing the performance as measured by an abstract metric such as *precision*, user perception of correctness varies greatly depending on the nature of errors and user characteristics.

KEYWORDS

Evaluation metrics; hate speech; human-centered metrics

1 ON THE USE OF ABSTRACT METRICS

In computing research the goal is often to develop methods that improve on some well-established and well-understood metrics. Such metrics are typically abstract and domain-agnostic to allow comparisons across different settings and domains [6], such as the precision of a classification method. As a result, their real-world impact–"*dollars saved, lives preserved, time conserved*" [6]—is often unknown and may diverge depending on the specifics of each domain [3]. The same point can be made about how well such metrics estimate users' *perception* of performance, which may further vary according to their idiosyncrasies and context. For instance, White [7] reports that when searching for medical information, users often settle on wrong answers that confirm their personal beliefs. This is concerning, suggesting that evaluations that optimize for domain-agnostic metrics may also need to correct and account for what users may *perceive* as the correct or wrong answer.

We build on the argument of Wagstaff that *abstract metrics* are insufficiently grounded in the application domain to offer meaningful insights about the effects of the performance numbers that they output for a given domain. However, focusing on the cost of different types of errors, we distinguish between *real costs* that are directly measurable—such as response time or monetary gains—and *perceived-costs* that attempt to capture what the cost of an error *appears to be* for the users of a system. While these costs are often contingent on each other or may even overlap, there may also be important differences in the signals they capture.

Error Costs Vary Across & Within Domains. For discussion purposes, let us consider the task of classifying content from social platforms. Even in this limited setting, achieving a certain accuracy, e.g., 65%, might be adequate for some applications (e.g., identify cat pictures for image search), but not for others (e.g., identify online hate speech for content moderation) [4, 6]. Thus, given a task to be algorithmically performed and a fixed performance threshold, there may be wide variations in how the same performance on a given metric translates in terms of both real-costs, and *how adequate users perceive the performance of the system to be.* Even with an overall high performance for a classification task and application domain, it is hard to know what that implies, as it might also vary widely across the feature space [2]. We may see a high performance for one category of users or data, and a low one for a different category that may represent a minority; or we may even see high cost variations for errors associated with different classes of users.

On the Inclusion of "Human-in-the-loop" Metrics. On social platforms, algorithmic decisions are typically made *for* people (e.g., search results) and/or *about* people (e.g., friend recommendations) [5]; and user participation is important for both of these tasks. This should have made the use of a standard set of *human-centered metrics* across semantically different domains commonplace; alas, this is rare. Such *human-centered metrics* should account, among others, for how the *perceived-cost* of erroneous decisions varies depending on (1) the specific problem (e.g., hate speech detection); (2) the type of the mistakes; and (3) user characteristics and context.

In this abstract, we advocate for research into characterizing how the perceived and the real costs of different kinds of errors—and the utility of popular metrics—depend on the problem domain specifics, and on the peculiarities of users that evaluate and are affected by those errors. Through a brief case study on hate speech detection on social media we provide initial evidence into how the perception of performance is influenced by users' context and the type of errors an automated system makes.

2 CASE STUDY: HATE SPEECH DETECTION

To quantify the relation between abstract metrics and user perception of correctness, in our experiment we set the performance of a classification system and vary the nature of the mistakes it makes

WebSci '17, June 25-28, 2017, Troy, NY, USA

ACM ISBN 978-1-4503-4896-6/17/06.
https://doi.org/10.1145/3091478.3098871

to measure their impact on the users' overall perception of quality. We also measure how user traits appear to affect their evaluations. We present preliminary results from our experiments, where the application domain is *hate speech detection on social media.*

Dataset & Experimental Setup. We use the initial dataset released by [1], which contains over 14*K* tweets annotated as *contains hate speech* (2399 tweets), *uses offensive language but not hate speech* (4836 tweets), and *is not offensive* (7274 tweets); allowing us to distinguish between different kinds of *false positive* errors that an automated hate speech detection system for social media may make: classifying as hate speech messages containing offensive language but not hate speech, versus classifying as hate speech messages that neither contain hate speech nor are offensive. For our evaluation, to avoid borderline cases, we filter out those tweets whose labels were established with a low confidence (< 70%).

Using this dataset, we design a crowdsourcing task that asks annotators on the GetHybrid.io platform to evaluate an (hypothetical) automated system that outputs social media messages it classifies as *hate speech.* We generate random samples of 8 messages each, containing from 0 to 7 misclassified instances (corresponding to precision scores varying from 100% to 12.5%); instances sampled either from messages containing offensive language but not hate speech (*low cost errors*), or from messages that are not offensive (*high cost errors*; as the distinction between these messages and hate speech message should be clearer). For each precision score and type of error, we generate 6 different samples (to ensure results are not an artifact of a given sample), and for each of them we collect annotations from 5 different annotators. This resulted in 30 annotations for each precision score. Finally, to understand how user traits may affect their evaluation, we also ask the annotators if they have been the target of hate speech, and if they believe hate speech should be moderated on social media—see Table 1 for the exact questions and the distribution of answers.

Does the nature of errors influence users' perception of quality? Figure 1 (left plot) shows how users' perception of quality varies as the system makes more errors (the precision decreases) when the "misclassifications" are sampled from messages that are offensive but not hate speech (*low cost errors*), versus when the sampling is done from messages that are not offensive (*high cost errors*). We see that the perception gap between the two cases increases with the error rate—showing that classifying too many non-offensive messages as hate speech leads to a more rapid drop in quality perception, while for misclassification of other types of offensive language it flattens. This pattern holds even if we condition on the users experience with *hate speech*, or their stance on online moderation.

Do user attributes play a role in how they evaluate quality? Figure 1 (right plot) shows a consistent gap in evaluations between annotators that self-identify as targets of hate speech vs. those that report never having been a target of online harassment. Noting first that annotators who never experienced online harassment make more accurate evaluations w.r.t. the original annotations (figure omitted), we observe that the evaluation gap among the two groups tends to widen mainly for *low cost errors.* It appears that those that were the target of hate speech apply a broader definition of what constitutes hate speech. We noticed similar patterns between those

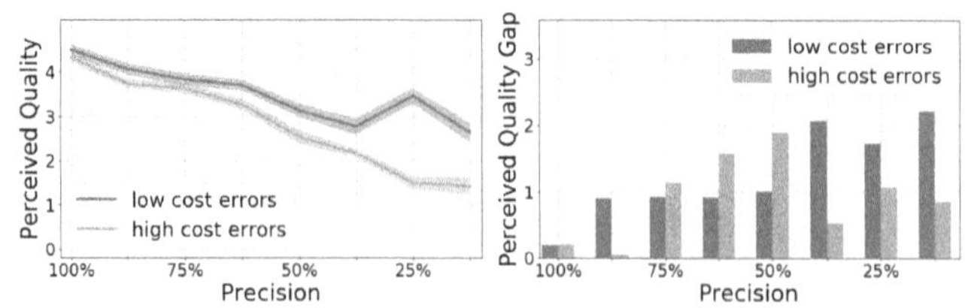

Figure 1: Quality perception variation as a function of precision. Low-cost errors refer to offensive tweets classified as *hate speech,* while high-cost errors to non-offensive tweets classified as *hate speech.* Left plot: quality perception for errors of different kinds. Right plot: differences in quality perception between annotators targeted by hate speech vs. those that never experienced online harassment.

Total	480
Were you ever the direct target of hate speech?	
Yes, unfortunately	213
No, but I've experienced other forms of online harassment	176
No, never	91
How important it is to moderate hate speech content on social media?	
I think this is increasingly necessary.	104
Some form of moderation is needed, but I also worry about free speech rights.	373
It is not necessary. If you don't like what folks say, do not engage with them.	3

Table 1: Answers distribution according to annotators experience with "hate speech" and their stance on moderation

that think there is an increasing need to moderate hate speech online versus those that take a more moderate stance on this, with the latter again making more accurate evaluations. Untangling the relation between the two self-declared traits and its impact on user evaluations is left to future work.

3 CONCLUSIONS

Our results are preliminary and larger scale experiments across multiple application domains are needed. However, we believe they provide initial evidence that (1) the nature of errors made by automated systems affects users' overall perception of quality, and (2) user traits also play a role (e.g., being a victim of hate speech or not, or their stance on online moderation). This supports our main point of wanting to elicit quality metrics based on the semantics of the problem rather than allowing them to be domain-agnostic.

REFERENCES

[1] Thomas Davidson, Dana Warmsley, Michael Macy, and Ingmar Weber. 2017. Automated Hate Speech Detection and the Problem of Offensive Language. In *Proc. of ICWSM.*
[2] Moritz Hardt. 2014. How big data is unfair: Understanding sources of unfairness in data driven decision making. *Medium. Available at: https://medium.com/@mrtz/how-big-data-is-unfair-9aa544d739de* (2014).
[3] Pat Langley. 2011. The changing science of machine learning. *Machine Learning* 82, 3 (2011).
[4] Alexandra Olteanu, Carlos Castillo, Fernando Diaz, and Emre Kiciman. 2016. Social Data: Biases, Methodological Pitfalls, and Ethical Boundaries. *SSRN Preprint* (2016).
[5] Kush R Varshney. 2015. Data science of the people, for the people, by the people: A viewpoint on an emerging dichotomy. In *Bloomberg Data for Good Exch. Conf.*
[6] Kiri Wagstaff. 2012. Machine learning that matters. In *Proc. of ICML.*
[7] Ryen White. 2013. Beliefs and biases in web search. In *Proc. of SIGIR.*

The Effect of Accelerating Migration of Services to Digital Channels on the Elderly

Ann Masterton Perry
Australian National University
ann.mastertonperry@anu.edu.au

Terhi Nurmikko-Fuller
Australian National University
terhi.nurmikko-fuller@anu.edu.au

ABSTRACT

In this paper, the effect of the ongoing migration of government and commercial services to the Web is examined. We report on preliminary results from the qualitative analysis of the experiences of a representative focus group of Australian citizens age 65 and over, who reside in the Australian Capital Territory (ACT).

CCS CONCEPTS

•Human-centered computing → Accessibility; •Social and professional topics → Seniors;

KEYWORDS

Accessibility; seniors; aging populations; qualitative analysis

1 INTRODUCTION

As the online environment continues to develop and grow, new digital models for service provision become available. The affordances of these platforms have prompted both public and private sector organisations to increasingly migrate their services to the Web. The benefits for the organisations are clear: lowering costs in a range of areas including staffing and infrastructure (physical shopfronts) as well as improving customer analytics based on user-provided data (a revenue generator in its own right). Although the convenience of digital channels with the most up-to-date content perpetually available has been noted as a positive [2, 15], the full impact of this shift in service provision for all user groups is far from clear.

As life expectancy continues to increase, the growing need for services that adequately address the access requirements of older demographics becomes apparent. What is less clear, is whether the needs of the elderly have been adequately taken into consideration in the push to adopt the digital as the medium for service provision: to date, there has been little systematic research.

We report on an on-going study that uses mixed methods to record and examine the attitudes and experiences of a focus group of senior citizens residing in the Australian Capital Territory (ACT) to a defined and finite set of online service provisions including banking, bill paying, accessing information on government services, and undertaking other financial transactions (such as booking travel, or buying legally mandated insurance). The surveyed focus group consists of individuals of 65 years of age or more.

WebSci '17, June 25-28, 2017, Troy, NY, USA
 978-1-4503-4896-6/17/06
DOI: 10.1145/3091478.3098867

We begin with a view on existent literature, outline our methodology, and report on preliminary findings and an initial analysis. We conclude with a view to future work.

2 BACKGROUND AND MOTIVATIONS

The Australian Federal Government's stated policy agenda resulted in the creation of the Digital Transformation Agency in 2015 "to make it easy for people to deal with government, by helping government transform services to be simple, clear and fast" [4]. The Australian Capital Territory (ACT) released their Digital Strategy in late 2016, with the purpose of "clearly [expressing our] intentions and create the impetus and architecture for fully digitized services" [7]. Neither document explicitly addresses the provision of online services that meet the requirements of elderly users. The research outlined here is primarily a response to these omissions, and takes the first steps to systematically document and analyse the experiences and opinions of this older demographic.

An important distinction exists between services that are *pulled* by users (voluntarily sought out), and those that are *pushed* towards them [13]. The former tend to aid communication with family and friends [16], while the latter are typically those which result from a public agency or corporate entity either seeking efficiencies in their service provision (often cost-driven) or in the case of government agencies, a policy requirement to implement a published digital agenda. Pushed services typically replace a traditional method of service delivery (e.g. electronic bank statements replacing paper equivalents), either immediately or as part of a phasing-out strategy.

3 EXISTING RESEARCH

Existing research into the ways the elderly engage with the digital and online media falls into five main categories: the use of technology as a whole, including the use of mobile phones and other communication devices [5, 8]; the rates of Internet uptake [1, 9, 16]; accessibility requirement assessment [3, 6]; improvements to health care provision [10, 11]; and the impacts of the shift of government services onto the Web [2, 14]. In most cases, little attention has been awarded to the qualitative assessment of the *user experience*, although the importance of control and agency have been high-lighted as a key finding by [13].

4 METHODOLOGY

This mixed methods research project ran over four months. Data collection was completed over four weeks, using a combination of web-based and paper surveys, as well as one-to-one interviews. Preliminary qualitative analyses examined the response rates of different survey mediums. A statistical analysis comparing the survey participants to the region's overall demographics was completed.

The survey captures qualitative information regarding participants' self-efficacy, preferences regarding the mode of service provision (face-to-face, online), benefits of that chosen mode (perceived or otherwise), and self-reported experiences (positive and negative). The survey consists of 50 questions, with multiple choice answers. Participants also had the opportunity to decline to answer any given question. Initial concerns over the length of the questionnaire were found to be of little concern to the participants, who instead suggested additional questions to be included in the survey.

5 INITIAL FINDINGS

Preliminary findings show a negative reaction to *pushed* services:

> "They just put things [online] whenever they like. They don't care about whether I can use them or not. And there's no-one you can ask for help."

There was significant resistance when participants felt forced to use an online channel, in the case of bank statements, for example:

> "[Getting the preferred paper version is] too expensive, but I don't seem to have a choice."

Two factor authentication (used by government agencies and most Australian banks) was found to be problematic. Those focus group members who have mobile phones reported a preference for using them exclusively for calls, making this method for authentication largely unsuitable. There was also an observable lack of confidence regarding participants' ability to successfully carry out online transactions, and find the right keywords for search engines.

Where available, training opportunities (and the type of training provided) improved responses to services. Informal training (by friends or relatives) resulted in a greater degree of confidence than those provided in a more formal setting (e.g. a community centre).

The participants acknowledged two clear benefits of service provision through the online medium: convenience, which cannot be understated for those who have transport or mobility issues; and immediacy, with online transactions seen as superior to lengthy wait times either at a physical location (a branch) or on the phone.

6 EVALUATION

Setting aside the notable gender-bias among the responders (predominantly women), the participants are only representative of the demographics of the ACT. The region is highly educated, affluent, and culturally diverse, with over 28% of the population being born outside of Australia [12]. The focus group is thus not a representative sample of the entire Australian over 65 population. For a more complete perspective, future research must draw participants from a wider geographic base including urban, regional, and remote areas, as well as gathering data to show how education and cultural background may effect attitudes to online provision of services.

The Australian Government's digital transformation agenda, the ACT Government strategy, and these preliminary findings highlight the need for a considered approach to the online shift of additional services. The long-term effects this change can have on the ability of this demographic to access essential services (e.g. the Australian Medicare scheme, or pension payments), remains unclear.

7 CONCLUSIONS AND FUTURE WORK

This research represents an initial investigation towards the bridging of an identified gap in the assessment of the use of online services by the elderly. Preliminary findings show that, whilst online services can improve the the experience of the elderly demographic when engaging with public and government services, training and agency (the ability to choose) are fundamentally important.

Further research is required to address not only specific niches such as health care, but broader topics including the development of methods for increasing self-efficacy, and the long-term effect of the provision of exclusively online services can have on this group.

Future work will include a longer, multidisciplinary study to examine this topic more closely across a wider population, as well as qualitative user experience observations and participant responses.

REFERENCES

[1] Leopoldo Abad. 2014. Media Literacy for Older People facing the Digital Divide: The e-Inclusion Programmes Design/Diseño de programas de e-inclusión para alfabetización mediática de personas mayores. *Comunicar* 21, 42 (2014), 173.

[2] Lemuria Carter, Vishanth Weerakkody, Brandis Phillips, and Yogesh K. Dwivedi. 2016. Citizen Adoption of E-Government Services: Exploring Citizen Perceptions of Online Services in the United States and United Kingdom. *Information Systems Management* 33, 2 (2016), 124–140.

[3] Diana Castilla, Azucena Garcia-Palacios, Ignacio Miralles, Juana Breton-Lopez, Elena Parra, Sergio Rodriguez-Berges, and Cristina Botella. 2016. Effect of Web navigation style in elderly users. *Computers in Human Behavior* 55 (2016), 909–920.

[4] Australian Government Commonwealth of Australia. 2016. Digital Transformation Agency. (2016). https://www.dta.gov.au/

[5] Mario Conci, Fabio Pianesi, and Massimo Zancanaro. 2009. Useful, social and enjoyable: Mobile phone adoption by older people. *Human-computer interaction–INTERACT 2009* (2009), 63–76.

[6] World Wide Web Consortium. 2010. Web Accessibility and Older People: Meeting the Needs of Ageing Web Users. (2010). https://www.w3.org/WAI/older-users/

[7] Jon Cumming. 2016. ACT Government Digital Strategy 2016-2019. (2016).

[8] Susan L Gatto and Sunghee H Tak. 2008. Computer, Internet, and e-mail use among older adults: Benefits and barriers. *Educational Gerontology* 34, 9 (2008), 800–811.

[9] Päivi Hakkarainen. 2012. "No good for shovelling snow and carrying firewood": Social representations of computers and the internet by elderly Finnish non-users. *New Media & Society* 14, 7 (2012), 1198–1215.

[10] Tsipi Heart and Efrat Kalderon. 2013. Older adults: are they ready to adopt health-related ICT? *International journal of medical informatics* 82, 11 (2013), e209–e231.

[11] Stephanie Medlock, Saeid Eslami, Marjan Askari, Derk L Arts, Danielle Sent, Sophia E de Rooij, and Ameen Abu-Hanna. 2015. Health information–seeking behavior of seniors who use the internet: a survey. *Journal of medical Internet research* 17, 1 (2015), e10.

[12] Australian Bureau of Statistics. 2016. Migration, Australia, 2015-16. (2016).

[13] Anabel Quan-Haase, Kim Martin, and Kathleen Schreurs. 2016. Interviews with digital seniors: ICT use in the context of everyday life. *Information, Communication & Society* 19, 5 (2016), 691–707.

[14] Anu Siren and Sine Grnborg Knudsen. 2017. Older Adults and Emerging Digital Service Delivery: A Mixed Methods Study on Information and Communications Technology Use, Skills, and Attitudes. *Journal of Aging & Social Policy* 29, 1 (2017), 35–50.

[15] Godwin J. Udo, Kallol K. Bagchi, and Peeter J. Kirs. 2010. An assessment of customersfi e-service quality perception, satisfaction and intention. *"International Journal of Information Management* 30, 6 (2010), 481 – 492.

[16] Nicole Wagner, Khaled Hassanein, and Milena Head. 2010. Computer use by older adults: A multi-disciplinary review. *Computers in human behavior* 26, 5 (2010), 870–882.

Community Photo Tagging: Engagement and Quality Study

Andrew Ponomarev
St.Petersburg Institute for Informatics and Automation of the Russian Academy of Sciences
39, 14th Line, 199178
St. Petersburg, Russian Federation
ponomarev@iias.spb.su

ABSTRACT

With today's dissemination of digital cameras, running events are usually well-presented in various photo sharing platforms. The number of photos from one medium-sized race can easily exceed a thousand or two, therefore, it is a tedious task for a participant to find photos where he/she is depicted. Bibtaggers is a crowd-based service allowing volunteers (usually, race participants) to collectively tag photos with race bib numbers, therefore enabling fast photo search. The paper presents results obtained using the service, specifically, the quality of tags collected and the user engagement data. These results are also compared to bib tags collected with a help of Amazon Mechanical Turk using similar procedure but different (monetary) incentive.

KEYWORDS

Image tagging; image labeling; crowdsourcing; non-monetary; incentives; microtask; collaborative work

1 INTRODUCTION

Non-professional long distance running races are a very popular pastime activity [1, 2]. Most of these events are shot by many photographers, both professional and amateur. After the race, participants usually want to find photos they are in, however, it is not easy, taking into account the number of photos from medium and big events (there may be thousands of them).

Among different ways of simplifying the task of finding relevant phots, one of the most universal ways is to tag the photos with bib numbers of runners visible on them. It does not require special equipment (like RFID tags and gates) and can be applied at any race, as bib numbers are used in all of them.

There are, of course, automated solutions for bib number recognition leveraging computer vision and OCR technologies [3, 4], but as bib numbers are soft (and thus, can be distorted) and can be partially obscured by runners' hands, fully automated solutions often do not allow to achieve perfect results.

WebSci '17, June 25-28, 2017, Troy, NY, USA

ACM ISBN 978-1-4503-4896-6/17/06.
http://dx.doi.org/10.1145/3091478.3098874

2 APPROACH

This paper explores the possibility to use voluntary crowdsourcing to tag race photos with bib numbers of runners visible on them. Although image labeling is probably one of the most used and studied applications of crowdsourcing, both in commercial (using Amazon Mechanical Turk (AMT) or other platform) and non-commercial [5-7] contexts, there are special traits that distinguish the explored process from the existing ones. First, the crowd is formed (mostly) from the runners that took part in the event, and they may be more interested in watching event photos than random AMT workers (thus, emotional involvement). Second, as a reward, tagging contributor is granted a privilege of searching photos by bib numbers (instead of doing it manually looking through large collection). To the best of our knowledge, there are no such systems and no published papers exploring this context.

To explore the possibility of using runners crowd a web application was implemented (available online at bibtaggers.ru), and several experiments were performed (a) to verify if this specific incentive is adequate to attract contributors and provide the required level of participation; (b) to estimate the expected quality of tags and compare it to the quality of bib number tags obtained with a help of monetary incentivized AMT workers.

2.1 Quality Control Procedure

To increase the reliability of the results, implemented application assigns a photo to up to three random contributors until two of them provide similar (according to a preset threshold on a Jaccard index) sets of bib numbers. If it happens, the photo is tagged by the union of similar sets. If all the contributions are pairwise different, the photo is assigned to a trusted user (administrator) who individually decides on the set of relevant bib numbers.

In addition, the application uses a number of gold standard photos shown in the beginning of the session and later during the session (with some probability).

3 USAGE EXPERIENCE

3.1 Participation and engagement

By this time, the web application was used in nine running races with the number of photos ranging from 563 to 7126 (average number of photos per race – 2931). Only photos from four races were tagged completely. The completely tagged races had active communities in social networks where link to the web application

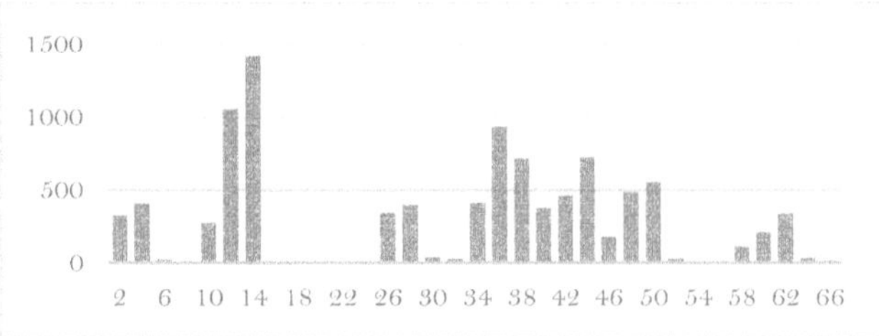

Figure 1: Number of contributions and the time from the start of the tagging project (in hours).

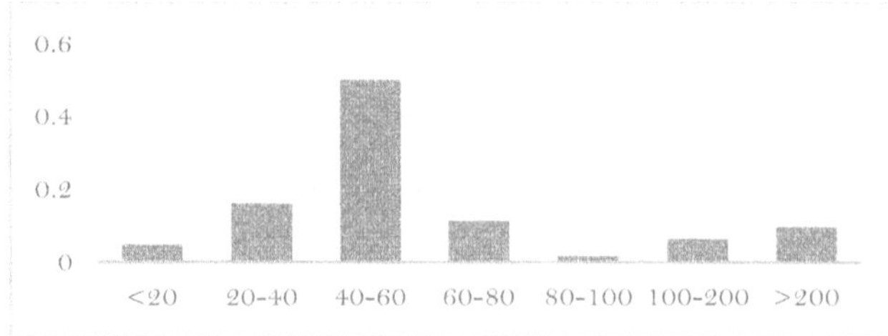

Figure 2: Distribution of tagging participants by the number of contributions.

was placed. Among the completely tagged events, the biggest had about 7300 participants (runners), and approximately 380 of them took part in tagging of 7126 event photos (only 5.2%). However, there were search queries for about 3200 bib numbers (about 44% of the race participants). While near 40% ratio was also typical for other races (setting the approximate ratio of people who are interested in photos), the huge gap between taggers and the numbers searched can be explained by the fact that all photos were tagged relatively fast (in 34 hours), and most of the visitors didn't have to contribute.

Figure 1 demonstrates typical time perspective of the number of contributions. It can be seen, that users are most active during 48 hours after the start of the tagging project (which happens a few hours after the event, typically in the evening of the event day) and then the activity gradually decreases.

Figure 2 shows a typical distribution of participants by the number of contributions (from one of the events). Noticeable peak at 40-60 is due to the fact that to reach the search privilege one had to tag at least 40 photos. So, half of the contributors did just enough to obtain needed privilege or slightly more. However, about 17% of contributors did significantly (more than two times) more than it was required. Overall, these overperforming contributors completed about half (50.6%) of all tagging assignments. Online survey among them revealed three main reasons of overperforming: (a) gratitude to the photographers sharing the result of their labour for free; (b) feeling that the result of their work is useful to others; (c) addictive nature of the tasks.

3.2 Quality

Two etalon datasets (based on the same 100 photos) were prepared to evaluate the collected tags[1]: DS0 – is a bib number tagged dataset, where all information available to a tagger is the photo itself; DS1 – (a superset of DS0) is a bib number tagged dataset, where a tagger can also explore two adjacent photos (taken immediately before and immediately after the one being tagged) to disambiguate partially obscured numbers. To measure quality F1 score of the collected number of tags against DS0 and DS1 were used.

The same 100 photos were tagged by Bibtaggers' users and also by AMT workers with two different rewards ($0.02 and $0.05 per photo) and the same quality control procedure.

The F1 score (against DS0) of Bibtaggers' and two AMT tag sets are 0.919, 0.914, and 0.905 respectively. First, it confirms that the size of the reward in microtask markets doesn't influence quality [8], second, it shows that non-monetary incentivized crowd produces results with nearly the same quality. However, very few contributors explored the adjacent photos, and that resulted in a significantly lower quality measured against DS1 (0.849, 0.836, and 0.835 respectively).

4 CONCLUSION

A web application for running event photo tagging using non-monetary incentive (save time of searching photos) was implemented. Usage analysis has shown, that this incentive is sufficient to attract enough taggers, however, its effectiveness gradually decreases with time from the event. The quality of obtained tags is similar to the quality of tags obtained from monetarily incentivized AMT workers.

To increase the quality it is important to incentivize contributors to use the additional information (e.g. adjacent photos).

ACKNOWLEDGEMENTS

This work is financially supported by Russian Foundation for Basic Research (projects 16-37-60107 and 16-07-00466).

REFERENCES

[1] Running USA. 2015. Running USA's State of the Sport Series. [Online]. Available: http://www.runningusa.org/statistics
[2] Jeroen Scheerder, Koen Breedveld, and Julie Borgers (eds). 2015. *Running Across Europe: The Rise and Size of One of the Largest Sport Markets.* Palgrave Macmillan. DOI: http://dx.doi.org/10.1057/9781137446374
[3] Sangheeta Roy et al. 2015. A New Multi-modal Technique for Bib Number/Text Detection in Natural Images, *Advances in Multimedia Information Processing - PCM 2015*, LNCS 9314, 483–494. DOI: http://dx.doi.org/10.1007/978-3-319-24075-6_47
[4] Idan Ben-Ami, Tali Basha, and Shai Avidan. 2012. Racing Bib Numbers Recognition, *British Machine Vision Conference (BMVC)*
[5] Luis von Ahn, Manuel Blum, and John Langford. 2004. Telling Humans and Computers Apart Automatically. *Communications of the ACM*, 47, 2 (2004), 57–60. DOI: http://dx.doi.org/ 10.1145/966389.966390
[6] Jafar Muhammadi, Hamid R. Rabiee, and Abbas Hosseini. 2013. Crowd labeling: a survey. Available at: http://arxiv.org/abs/1301.2774
[7] Yunus E. Kara et al. 2015. Modeling annotator behaviors for crowd labeling. *Neurocomputing*, 160, 141–156. DOI: http://dx.doi.org/10.1016/j.neucom.2014.10.082
[8] Winter Mason and Duncan J Watts. 2009. Financial incentives and the performance of crowds. In *Proceedings of the ACM SIGKDD Workshop on Human Computation.* New York: ACM. 77–85. DOI: http://dx.doi.org/10.1145/1600150.1600175

[1] The sets are available at http://bibtaggers.ru/static/datasets.html

An Ontology for a Polymer Nanocomposite Community Data Resource

Vipula Rawte
Department of Computer Science
Rensselaer Polytechnic Institute
Troy, New York 12180
rawtev@rpi.edu

James McCusker
Department of Computer Science
Rensselaer Polytechnic Institute
Troy, New York 12180
mccusj2@rpi.edu

He Zhao
Department of Mechanical Engineering
Northwestern University
Evanston, Illinois 60201
hezhao2012@u.northwestern.edu

L. Catherine Brinson
Department of Materials Science and Engineering
Northwestern University
Evanston, Illinois 60201
cbrinson@northwestern.edu

Wei Chen
Department of Mechanical Engineering
Northwestern University
Evanston, Illinois 60201
weichen@northwestern.edu

Linda Schadler
Department of Materials Science and Engineering
Rensselaer Polytechnic Institute
Troy, New York 12180
schadl@rpi.edu

Deborah L. McGuinness
Departments of Computer, Cognitive, and Web Sciences
Rensselaer Polytechnic Institute
Troy, New York 12180
dlm@cs.rpi.edu

ABSTRACT

Interest in polymer nanocomposites has been increasing because of their unique properties. Since the field draws on a wide range of disciplines, a data resource aimed at adequately supporting the field needs to include vocabulary from many disciplines. We are building an ontology that aims to connect to relevant vocabularies and include well-specified interconnections between those vocabularies. Coverage is determined by a set of use cases. We will describe our ontology along with the growing data resource that it supports and introduce how our ontology-based approach can enable collaborative community research in polymer nanocomposites. Further, we mention how this approach can be leveraged more broadly in material science.

CCS CONCEPTS

•**Information systems → Web Ontology Language (OWL);** *Extensible Markup Language (XML);* **Ontologies; Semantic web description languages;**

KEYWORDS

knowledge graph; ontology; semantic data resource; microstructure; polymer nanocomposite; visualization; nanofiller dispersion; interfacial area

WebSci '17, June 25-28 2017 Troy, NY, USA,
 978-1-4503-4896-6/17/06.
DOI: 10.1145/3091478.3098866

1 INTRODUCTION

We are building an open access, user-friendly, living, growing, data resource for the polymer nanocomposites community called NanoMine. We aim for it to be scalable and enable improved understanding of key processing - structure - property (p-s-p) relationships. We aim for it to be used by domain scientists to facilitate faster nanocomposite design and insertion into advanced applications [7]. By bringing together data that is scattered throughout public literature and private files and by creating a protocol for recording and tagging data, this resource has the potential to be an unprecedented compilation of accessible information.. We will introduce our ontology along with the provenance annotation strategy and briefly describe the ontology and provenance usage in building and accessing a knowledge graph aimed at helping domain scientists explore information relevant to designing new polymer nanocomposite materials.

Members of the materials science community along with the National Institute of Standards and Technology have produced NIST's Materials Data Curation System (MDCS) that captures, shares, and transforms materials data into an XML-based structured format. This supports data organization using user-selected XML Schema encoded templates that are used to build data entry forms. The MDCS approach is web based using the full web stack of tools including Python, Django, MongoDB, REST API, XML, and SPARQL queries but lacks visualization of the collected data for better analysis and understanding [1].

The initial version of NanoMine used only an XML schema to address the problem of identifying relationships between processing, structure, and properties [8]. Our version of NanoMine leverages deeper semantic relationships encoded in an OWL ontology and supports enhanced semantic queries.

2 RESULTS AND DISCUSSION

Our NanoMine ontology is created using the XML Schema and also domain knowledge about polymer nanocomposites. We are using other vocabularies like Semanticscience Integrated Ontology (SIO) [2], Nanopublications Vocabulary [5], and also planning for PubChem [3] and Units Ontology [4]. The data is collected, represented and stored in the form of nanopublications.

The ontology currently includes the basic concepts of characterization methods, materials, microstructure, processing methods, properties and publications and is being expanded based on use cases.

The ontology supports structured queries that go well beyond the traditional keyword search approach. Our community wanted to ask questions such as "What is the highest reported T_g change in a polymer nanocomposite? Or in a PMMA-based nanocomposite?" Prior to the XML-based Nanomine effort, the community could leverage web searches such as "polymer nanocomposite" and possibly refine those using "glass transition" or by "thermal property" but the answers to these queries may miss many relevant papers and the process was very slow and painful [6].

The previous XML-based NanoMine was able to encode some relatively straightforward simple relationships for nanomaterials but had very limited search capabilities and no visualization options.

We can now support queries using any parameter in the ontology and display answers textually or graphically and support improved exploration concerning different factors related to elements in the query (e.g. T_g) and their sources. We support this search using the Nanomaterials Knowledge Graph, built using our RPI Tetherless World Satoru Knowledge Graph Project. The ontology is used to connect related terms together, to provide support in hierarchically-based faceted browsing and ontology-enabled visualizations.

Currently, NanoMine is hosted on Northwestern University's server at http://nanomine.northwestern.edu:8001/.

Provenance is encoded using nanopublications. Figure 1 displays an assertion and Figure 2 shows the related publication from which it was obtained.

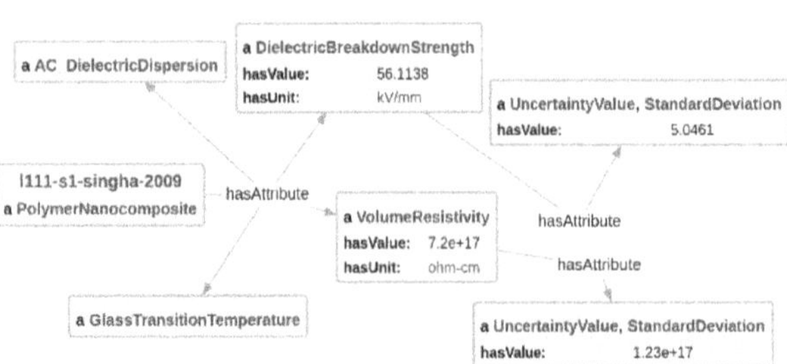

Figure 1: Assertion.

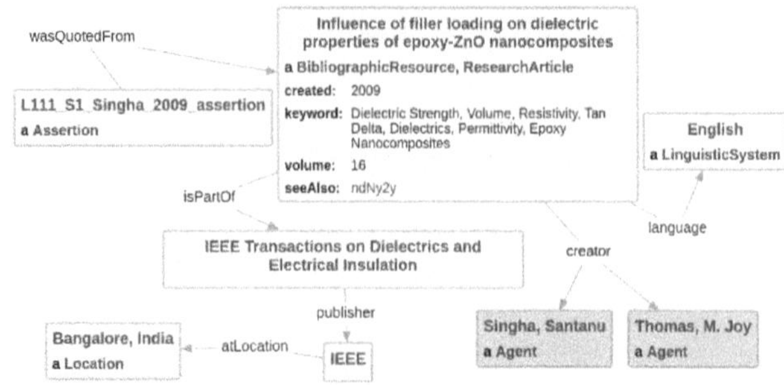

Figure 2: Publication Information.

The foundational infrastructure supports provenance encoding and the domain curation is handled by our materials collaborators at Northwestern and RPI.

3 CONCLUSIONS AND FUTURE WORK

Our provenance-aware semantic data resource is currently supporting a range of material scientists in encoding content related initially to processing-structure-property relationships. Our goal is to enhance computer and human understanding of polymer nanocomposites, thus enabling next generation collaborative research. The ontology and the knowledge graph that uses it are used to support visualizations including a customizable dashboard aimed at nanomaterials researchers. The work is in early stages, however, is currently available for collaboration and reuse.

ACKNOWLEDGMENTS

This work is a collaboration between Rensselaer Polytechnic Institute and Northwestern University and is funded through NSF ACI-1640840.

REFERENCES

[1] Alden Dima, Sunil Bhaskarla, Chandler Becker, Mary Brady, Carelyn Campbell, Philippe Dessauw, Robert Hanisch, Ursula Kattner, Kenneth Kroenlein, Marcus Newrock, et al. 2016. Informatics Infrastructure for the Materials Genome Initiative. *JOM* 68, 8 (2016), 2053–2064.
[2] Michel Dumontier, Christopher JO Baker, Joachim Baran, Alison Callahan, Leonid Chepelev, José Cruz-Toledo, Nicholas R Del Rio, Geraint Duck, Laura I Furlong, Nichealla Keath, et al. 2014. The Semanticscience Integrated Ontology (SIO) for biomedical research and knowledge discovery. *Journal of biomedical semantics* 5, 1 (2014), 14.
[3] Gang Fu, Colin Batchelor, Michel Dumontier, Janna Hastings, Egon Willighagen, and Evan Bolton. 2015. PubChemRDF: towards the semantic annotation of PubChem compound and substance databases. *Journal of cheminformatics* 7, 1 (2015), 34.
[4] Georgios V Gkoutos, Paul N Schofield, and Robert Hoehndorf. 2012. The Units Ontology: a tool for integrating units of measurement in science. *Database* 2012 (2012), bas033.
[5] Paul Groth, Andrew Gibson, and Jan Velterop. 2010. The anatomy of a nanopublication. *Information Services & Use* 30, 1-2 (2010), 51–56.
[6] Bharath Natarajan, Yang Li, Hua Deng, L Catherine Brinson, and Linda S Schadler. 2013. Effect of interfacial energetics on dispersion and glass transition temperature in polymer nanocomposites. *Macromolecules* 46, 7 (2013), 2833–2841.
[7] Richard A Vaia and John F Maguire. 2007. Polymer nanocomposites with prescribed morphology: going beyond nanoparticle-filled polymers. *Chemistry of Materials* 19, 11 (2007), 2736–2751.
[8] He Zhao, Xiaolin Li, Yichi Zhang, Linda S Schadler, Wei Chen, and L Catherine Brinson. 2016. Perspective: NanoMine: A material genome approach for polymer nanocomposites analysis and design. *APL Materials* 4, 5 (2016), 053204.

Open Governance as a Service

Andrei Sambra
Massachusetts Institute of Technology
77 Massachusetts Ave, Cambridge MA, USA
Cambridge, Massachusetts 02139
asambra@mit.edu

Lalana Kagal
Massachusetts Institute of Technology
77 Massachusetts Ave, Cambridge MA, USA
Cambridge, Massachusetts 02139
lkagal@csail.mit.edu

ABSTRACT

This extended abstract discusses how public services can become more open and engage citizens more actively, by providing the local, public administration with the right tools. It calls for public services to think more creatively about how they can collaborate with the public to make better use of the energy and enthusiasm, as well as missing skills that people have and want to offer. It explores the challenges, both in terms of policy and technology, that public services face in mobilizing resources that are by nature voluntary. We intend to provide the governance tools that enable public services to leverage skills coming from the local community, and improve their autonomy, transparency and analytical tools required for true open governance.

KEYWORDS

Open governance, public service, decentralization, transparency, web platform, citizen engagement

ACM Reference format:
Andrei Sambra and Lalana Kagal. 2017. Open Governance as a Service. In *Proceedings of ACM Web Science Conference 2017, Troy, NY, USA, June 25-28 (WebSci '17)*, 2 pages.
https://doi.org/10.1145/3091478.3098873

INTRODUCTION

Open governance is the governing philosophy that gives citizens the right to access documents and proceedings of the government, to engage in an open discussion with legislators and to hold them accountable when possible. It has high levels of transparency and mechanisms for public scrutiny and oversight, with an emphasis on government accountability. Traditionally transparency was the most important aspect in an open government implying that citizens should have access to information, documents and proceedings of the government. However, recently the definition has been expanded to include increased citizen participation and collaboration in government processes through the use of open technologies. It can now be thought of as governance through a collaboration between citizens and their government.

The way in which people want to engage with public services has changed, and the demands being placed upon public services are growing. The need for public services to change presents many challenges, both in terms of policy and technology. The idea of the *participatory public administration* can be useful for rethinking the relationship between people and public services, as well as the way in which public services need to be redesigned and reshaped.

Social action can become a key tool in reshaping the public services that a participatory administration would demand. It would bring in new kinds of expertise, capacity and resources that can help tackle the complex problems society confronts - such as chronic health conditions, the consequences of an ageing population and long-term unemployment - as well as enable the creation of more personalised services.

Becoming closely involved with the way services are delivered may also help users to get a better understanding of how services work and develop more empathy for staff, changing how they feel about services. At the same time, they can have more influence and improve the way that services operate. When this happens, user experience is improved not only because services work better but because they feel more ownership over them.

POLICY CHALLENGES

By its nature, social action is voluntary. Much of it takes place informally and it is often not publicised. It is often not connected to public services, and people have a wide range of motivations for getting involved. When applied to public administrations, mobilizing volunteers means managing resources outside of its direct control, thus placing a burden on staff to take a different approach to planning and designing services, managing quality and risk, and also ensuring accountability.

A good example comes from Baltimore's *Power in Dirt* initiative, which since 2011 aimes to tackle the blight caused by large numbers of vacant lots, by making it possible for residents to adapt these for a range of uses. The initiative involved working with the housing department to identify and map vacant lots and create a method to allow citizens legal right of entry, and working with utility providers to come up with a way of providing water to the lots at a reasonable cost. The city has created an online portal that citizens can use to search for lots, apply to 'adopt' them and request a water supply. So far, more than 1,100 lots have been adopted, 79% of which have been revitalised and maintained[1]

TECHNOLOGY CHALLENGES

Increased use of technology brings both opportunities and challenges to citizen engagement processes, including opportunities for collecting, analyzing and evaluating data about these processes. We have seen recent efforts from companies to provide tools that can

[1] www.powerindirt.com

WebSci '17, June 25-28, Troy, NY, USA

ACM ISBN 978-1-4503-4896-6/17/06.
https://doi.org/10.1145/3091478.3098873

be used to facilitate collaboration with residents in an accessible, participatory, and enjoyable way.

Neighborland[2] collects insights from workshops and public installations, SMS, Twitter, etc. Then it maps insights to specific places and all participant data is uploaded to specific project websites.

On the other hand, services like mySidewalk[3] believe data should be easy to access, understand, and share. To that regard they offer visualization tools that when applied to specific locations, help answer questions based on a very long list of predefined templates such as high density of children, cost of commuting, impact of air quality, uninsured seniors, and many more.

However, when a single company is responsible for storing all the data, it may become a target for attacks, or even data manipulation (i.e. changing the records to reflect a specific view on a subject). This is where a decentralized architecture, like the one offered by the Solid project [3] can add more transparency by removing the single point of failure, but also adding several key features, such as data *imutability* - storing data without destroying previous versions, *accountability* - the cornerstone of a transparent public service [5, 6], and also *open data visualization* similar to LOGD [2].

VISION

Based on all the above, putting everything into practice requires iteration and experimentation, rather than top down policy or passing new legislation. Below we provide a list of changes that can help shape the new social norm.

Cultural change is required to make social action a central design principle for public services. This needs to be led from the top, championed by local and national politicians and senior leaders in public services.

Mobilising citizens needs to become a part of staff roles at all levels. Creating senior roles with the capacity to design and implement a strategy for change might be useful in some cases.

Social action needs to be factored into service planning. Public services should map community assets and resources that they don't directly control, identifying how they could open up and enable people to get involved.

Staff will need to acquire different skills. Future public services will require a different set of workforce roles from the past and these roles will be more *relational* [1], with a greater emphasis on communication, empathy, facilitation and the ability to mobilise [4].

Public services need to think creatively about the opportunities they offer for people to get involved. Opportunities should reflect the range of motivations people have for taking part and the different ways they might want to engage.

CONCLUSION

While citizen engagement programs are not new phenomena, the major role that digital technology plays in these programs is relatively recent. We intend to build a decentralized, Web-based platform that fosters collaboration between public servants and citizens through social tools in a transparent way, while at the same time offering a high level of privacy and security.

[2]https://neighborland.com/
[3]http://app.mysidewalk.com/

REFERENCES

[1] Helen Dickinson and Helen Sullivan. 2014. Imagining the 21st century public service workforce. *Melbourne: School of Government, University of Melbourne* (2014).

[2] Li Ding, Timothy Lebo, John S Erickson, Dominic Difranzo, Gregory Todd Williams, Xian Li, James Michaelis, Alvaro Graves, Jin Guang Zheng, Zhenning Shangguan, et al. 2011. TWC LOGD: A portal for linked open government data ecosystems. *Web Semantics: Science, Services and Agents on the World Wide Web* 9, 3 (2011), 325–333.

[3] Essam Mansour, Andrei Vlad Sambra, Sandro Hawke, Maged Zereba, Sarven Capadisli, Abdurrahman Ghanem, Ashraf Aboulnaga, and Tim Berners-Lee. 2016. A demonstration of the solid platform for social web applications. In *Proceedings of the 25th International Conference Companion on World Wide Web*. International World Wide Web Conferences Steering Committee, 223–226.

[4] Geoff Mulgan. 2012. Government with the people: the outlines of a relational state. *G. Cooke and R. Muir, The relational state: How recognising the importance of human relationships could revolutionise the role of the state, IPPR, London* (2012).

[5] Oshani Seneviratne and Lalana Kagal. 2010. HTTPa: accountable HTTP. In *IAB/w3C internet privacy workshop*, Vol. 42.

[6] Oshani Wasana Seneviratne. 2012. Augmenting the web with accountability. In *Proceedings of the 21st International Conference on World Wide Web*. ACM, 185–190.

'Dark Germany': Temporal Characteristics and Connectivity Patterns in Online Far-Right Protests Against Refugee Housing

Sebastian Schelter
Technische Universität Berlin, Germany
sebastian.schelter@tu-berlin.de

Jérôme Kunegis
University of Namur, Belgium
jerome.kunegis@unamur.be

ABSTRACT

We present a quantitative study of the social media activities of a contemporary nationwide protest movement against local refugee housing in Germany, which organizes itself via dedicated city-level Facebook pages. We analyse data from 2015, containing more than one million interactions by more than 200,000 users. We investigate the temporal characteristics of the social media activities of this protest movement, as well as the connectedness of the interactions of its participants. We find several activity metrics such as the number of posts issued, negative polarity in comments, and user engagement to peak in late 2015, coinciding with chancellor Angela Merkel's much criticized decision of September 2015 to temporarily admit the entry of Syrian refugees to Germany. Furthermore, our evidence suggests a low degree of direct connectedness of participants in this movement, (i.a., indicated by a lack of geographical collaboration patterns), yet we encounter a strong affiliation of the pages' user base with far-right political parties.

1 INTRODUCTION

In recent years, Europe has experienced a massive influx of refugees from Middle Eastern and African regions, mainly due to civil wars and economic stagnation in these areas. In Germany, this influx peaked in 2015 with 890,000 people seeking asylum; in early September of that year, chancellor Angela Merkel decided to admit the entry of Syrian refugees stuck in South-East European countries. These developments have been accompanied by a steep rise in popularity of German right-wing organizations, especially in the form of the political party *AfD – Alternative für Deutschland*, ("Alternative for Germany") [2], which managed to enter the European parliament as well as multiple German state parliaments since its inception in 2012. The AfD and other right-wing organizations successfully leverage social media to communicate with their followers; recent research shows that their gains in popularity are highly correlated with growing interaction rates and user engagement on Facebook [3].

The refugees in Germany have been registered and temporarily placed in hastily implemented shelters distributed all over Germany. As a reaction to these refugee shelters, a large number of local protest movements have formed against their placement in the corresponding cities. Also, refugee shelters and refugees have become targets of a series of more than a thousand crimes in 2015 (including arsony of buildings and attacks with explosives against inhabitated shelters) [1]. Communication within anti-refugee housing movements often happens via dedicated Facebook pages, a large proportion of which promote racist, xenophobic and islamophobic views. We present a limited quantitative study on the scale of 136 such protest pages in 2015, including more than one million interactions of more than 200,000 users with these pages. Given this data, we focus our efforts on two research questions (i) *What are the temporal characteristics of the social media activities of this protest movement?* (ii) *What is the degree of connectedness and cooperation in this protest movement?* The goal of the first question is to obtain insights into general activity patterns of this protest movement, the general keynote of the content posted on these pages, and to find hints on how these activities relate to external events. For the second question, we focus on the connectedness of users of these pages in order to investigate the nature of cooperation between the participants in this protest movement. We focus on direct interactions as well as on interactions with the Facebook pages of political parties, which serve as an indicator for indirect connections between the users.

Data Acquisition. In order to find a large number of protest pages, we consulted online articles listing pages and conducted several exhaustive searches on Facebook using the queries *"Nein zum Heim"* and *"wehrt sich"*, where we manually inspected all search results. For the found protest pages, we crawled all publicly available posts with their corresponding likes and comments, restricted to the year 2015. Furthermore, we manually added geographical information to each protest page. Thereby, we obtained 136 such pages, as depicted in Figure 1. Our dataset comprises more than 46,000 posts and more than one million interactions (comments and likes) by more than 200,000 users.

2 ANALYSIS

Time course of page posts. We analyze the time course of the number of published posts to gain insight into a general activity pattern of the pages. We observe a peak at the end of the third quarter of 2015, which coincides with the aforementioned admission of Syrian refugees into Germany in September [4]. The same phenomenon has also been recognized in previous studies of far-right engagement on social media [3].

Polarity in user comments. Next, we place our focus on the users interacting with the pages and investigate the time course of overall sentiment in the user comments. For that, we employ a dictionary denoting the negative sentiment $\phi^-(t)$ and positive sentiment $\phi^+(t)$ of a German term t when used in certain parts of speech [5]. We apply part-of-speech tagging to all comments

WebSci '17, June 25-28, 2017, Troy, NY, USA
 978-1-4503-4896-6/17/06.
DOI: 10.1145/3091478.3098880

Figure 1: Geolocation of the pages.

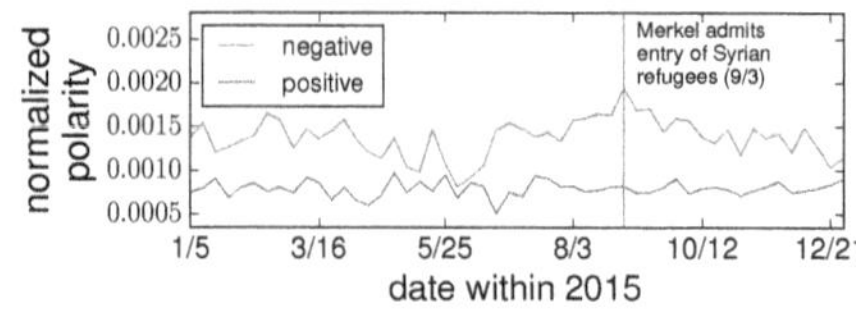

Figure 2: Time course of normalized polarity in user comments.

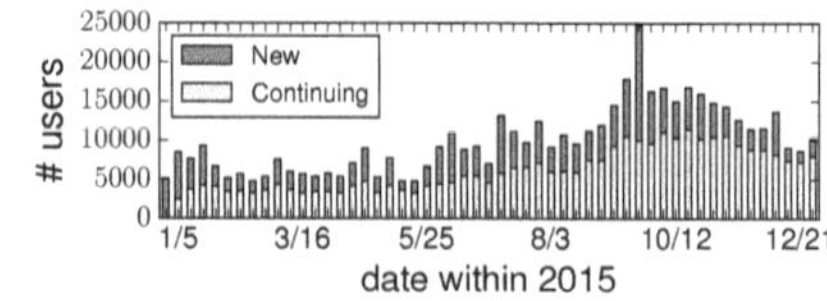

Figure 3: Weekly active users on the protest pages in 2015.

in a given week w, which gives us all contained terms T_w. Next, we compute the normalized negative polarity per week $p_{w^-} = \frac{1}{|T_w|} \sum_{t \in T_w} \phi^-(t)$ (and analogously, the normalized positive polarity). In Figure 2, we observe that negative speech dominates the comments throughout the whole year. Furthermore, we encounter a peak in negative polarity in early September, which confirms that Merkel's decison provoked widespread anger in the far-right political spectrum.

User attraction. Subsequently, we analyze the pages' ability to attract users over time. For that, we compute the set of active users U_w for every week w, (users who interact with at least one of the protest pages during that week). For every week w, we split these active users into two groups: *new* users, which we encounter for the first time and *continuing* users, whom we have already seen previously. The corresponding sizes of these users sets for all weeks in 2015 are shown in Figure 3. We see a slight increase in both new and continuing users in the late second half of 2015. However, this increase starts to diminish again towards the end of the year. We note that the number of mean weekly active users (9,935) is very small compared to the overall number of users. We encounter a strong and significant correlation of the number of continuing users with time index i, but cannot determine a similar significant correlation for new users. These findings suggest that the protest pages maintain a low constant growth of users, but fail at its acceleration.

Low correlation between geographical distance and amount of shared users. In order to investigate geographical aspects of the data, we compute the geographical distance between the corresponding cities for each pair of pages, and compare this to the Jaccard similarity between their sets of users. We expect to see a strong negative correlation if geographical closeness implicates co-operating user bases. However, the maximum Jaccard similarity is only 0.1428, and 4,727 pairs exhibit non-zero similarity, leaving 3,916 pairs with zero shared users. Even for pairs of pages with non-zero similarity, the correlation is rather low (−0.19), which suggests against a geographical collaboration pattern.

Absence of a giant connected component in the user co-like network. Next, we construct the *user co-like network* as follows: users form the vertices of this network, and for every post, we introduce edges between all users that liked this post. The resulting network has 95,639,173 edges (co-likes among users). We study the connectivity of this network by computing the size of its largest connected component. This size amounts to 89,094 users, which account for only 57.5% of the overall user base. This gives a hint that the social media activities of the users might be highly separated, as real-world social networks typically exhibit a giant component containing nearly all users.

Strong affiliation with far-right organizations. Finally, we analyse the affiliations of the users on the protest pages to political parties in Germany, to see whether these users are connected in that way. For that, we employ additional data about likes of posts on the parties' Facebook pages from previous work [3]. We compute the *affiliation* $\text{aff}_{p,o}$ between a page p and a political party o as the ratio of users interacting with the page that also liked posts on the party's page. In the resulting distributions, we observe that the median affiliation with the right-wing parties *AfD* (0.45) and *NPD* (0.41) is about one order of magnitude higher than the affiliation with parties from the remaining spectrum, such as the Christian conservative *CDU* (0.04), the social democratic *SPD* (0.04), the green party *Die Grünen* (0.03) and the socialist left party *Die Linke* (0.02). While it is expected to see a strong affiliation with the *NPD* (which is commonly considered to be the voice of the extreme right and has repeatedly been the target of party ban trials by the German state), it is suprising to see an even stronger affiliation with the *AfD*, as the latter party claims to locate itself in the conservative spectrum rather than the extremist-right spectrum.

3 CONCLUSION

We encountered peaks in several activity metrics that coincide with chancellor Merkel's decision to temporarily admit the entry of Syrian refugees to Germany, which suggests that this political move caused anger and outrage in far-right circles. However, despite the presumed mobilization effects stemming from Merkel's policies in 2015, our evidence suggests a low degree of user growth, connectedness and cooperation in this protest movement. From all German political parties, the *AfD* exhibited the strongest affiliation among the user base of the studied protest pages, which contradicts previous classifications of the *AfD* as not belonging to the far-right political spectrum [2]. *This work has been supported by the German Federal Ministry of Education and Research (BBDC 01IS14013A).*

REFERENCES

[1] Amadeu Antonio Stiftung. 2015. Chronik flüchtlingsfeindlicher Vorfälle. (2015). https://www.mut-gegen-rechte-gewalt.de/service/chronik-vorfaelle?field_date_value[value][year]=2015
[2] Kai Arzheimer. 2015. The AfD: Finally a Successful Right-Wing Populist Eurosceptic Party for Germany? *West European Politics* (2015).
[3] Sebastian Schelter, Felix Biessmann, Malisa Zobel, and Nedelina Teneva. 2016. Structural Patterns in the Rise of Germany's New Right on Facebook. *Data Mining in Politics Workshop at ICDM* (2016).
[4] Marcus Walker and Anton Troianovski. 2015. Behind Angela Merkel's Open Door for Migrants, Wall Street Journal. (2015). http://www.wsj.com/articles/behind-angela-merkels-open-door-for-migrants-1449712113
[5] Ulli Waltinger. 2010. GermanPolarityClues: A Lexical Resource for German Sentiment Analysis. In *LREC*.

On Social Synchrony in Online Social Networks

Nirmal Kumar Sivaraman
Sakthi Balan Muthiah
Pushkal Agarwal
Lokesh Todwal
nirmal.sivaraman@lnmiit.ac.in
sakthi.balan@lnmiit.ac.in
pushkalagarwal@gmail.com
lokeshtodwal005@gmail.com
Department of Computer Science and Engineering
The LNM Institute of Information Technology
Jaipur, Rajasthan, India 302031

ABSTRACT

In this work, we characterize a phenomenon called social synchrony that occurs in the online social networks. Social synchrony is a kind of collective social activity associated with some event where the number of people who participate in the activity first increases exponentially and then decreases exponentially. Also, some users continually participate in the activity for a considerable period of time. We define this phenomenon and propose a method to detect it.

CCS CONCEPTS

• **Human-centered computing** → **Social network analysis**; • **Applied computing** → *Sociology*;

KEYWORDS

Social Network Analysis, Social Synchrony, Online Social Synchrony, Twitter Analysis, Event Analysis

ACM Reference format:

Nirmal Kumar Sivaraman, Sakthi Balan Muthiah, Pushkal Agarwal, and Lokesh Todwal. 2017. On Social Synchrony in Online Social Networks. In *Proceedings of WebSci '17, Troy, NY,USA, June 25-28, 2017, 2 pages.*
DOI: 10.1145/3091478.3098881

1 INTRODUCTION

In this work, we look at a particular social phenomenon called *social synchrony* with respect to online communication in the online social media. Social synchrony is a social phenomenon where many people do a similar action in unison over a brief period of time. This can be observed at a very large scale in the online space as well – especially in the online social media. *Twitter*[1] is a good example for this. When popular events take place, a lot of *tweets* get posted on that topic in a short span of time. In this short span of time, the number of people who tweet regarding the event increases exponentially and then decreases exponentially. We consider this phenomenon as a kind of online social synchrony at a very large scale where the action is defined as *communicating over Twitter on that particular topic.*

The increase and decrease of activity around an event is called burst. However, synchrony requires sustained activity from the users unlike burst [2]. A method to predict the occurrence of synchrony can be found in [1], but detection of synchrony is done manually. In this work, we propose a definition for social synchrony and a method to detect it.

In Section 2, we present our definition of social synchrony. In Section 3, we propose a method to detect synchrony.

[1]www.twitter.com

WebSci '17, June 25-28, 2017, Troy, NY, USA
 978-1-4503-4896-6/17/06...$15.00
DOI: 10.1145/3091478.3098881

2 DEFINITION OF SOCIAL SYNCHRONY

Social synchrony is a social phenomenon that satisfies the following criteria.

(1) *Many users perform an action at the same time.*
(2) *The number of users who perform the action first increases exponentially and then decreases exponentially.*
(3) *There is at least one user who performs the action from the starting of the phenomenon till the peak of the phenomenon consecutively.*
(4) *There is at least one user who performs the action from the peak of the phenomenon till the end of the phenomenon consecutively.*

In the next section, we define a method to detect whether an observation of activities in Twitter is a synchrony or not according to this definition.

3 DETECTION OF SOCIAL SYNCHRONY

In order to detect the synchrony, first we fix the length of the time slice T according to the nature of the activity and the event associated with it.

We denote the topic of interest as t. The set of all users who participate in the topic of discussion d is represented as

$$U = \{u_1, u_2, \ldots, u_n\}$$

We assume that our period of focus for the topic of discussion d, is P units of time. The length of each time slice is denoted as l in terms of the same unit as P. This gives the number of time slices for our study of social synchrony for the topic of discussion d,

$$N_d = \frac{P}{l}$$

Let us denote the set of time slices as S.

$$S = \{s_1, s_2, \ldots, s_{N_d}$$

where P and l are measured in the same unit.

Let the count of unique users at time slice t be x_t.

The following are three steps in detecting synchrony from an observation.

(1) Detect the surge in the number of users performing an action.
(2) Detect the starting and ending points of the possible synchrony by looking at the .
(3) Detect the synchrony based on the scale of the phenomenon.

Steps 1, 2 and 3 are explained in the algorithm 1, 2 and 3 respectively.

Algorithm 1 Algorithm to detect the surge in the number of users performing an action

1: Observe the social activity in a continuous time period.
2: Divide observation into equal time slices.
3: Count the number of unique users who participated in the activity in each time slice and plot it.
4: Detect the global maximum (peak) of the observation and label the time slice at which it occurs as p. Let the count of unique users at time slice p be x_p.
5: Fix a threshold value L (as a % of x_p). If the activity does not go below $L\%$ of x_p, the observation will not be considered as a synchrony.
6: Detect points before and after the peak that are below the threshold, i.e., $L\%$ of x_p. Let us denote them as x and y respectively.

$$x_x \leq x_p \frac{L}{100}$$

$$x_y \leq x_p \frac{L}{100}$$

7: **If** such a points do not exist
then stop with the conclusion that there is no synchrony in the observation.
else go to algorithm 2.

Algorithm 2 Algorithm to detect the starting and ending points of the possible synchrony

1: Calculate backward user retention $B\alpha_t^n$ for $n = 0, 1, 2, \ldots$

$$B\alpha_t^n = \frac{\bigcap_{i=0}^n U_{t-i}}{U_t}$$

where, U_t is the number of users who participated in the time slice t. $B\alpha_t^n$ will give the fraction of the number of users who had participated in the activity from time slice $t-n$ to time slice t with respect to the total number of users at time slice t.
2: Find a time slice a such that
$B\alpha_t^n = 0$ for $n = a$ and
$B\alpha_t^n \neq 0$ for $n \leq a$
3: **If** such a point does not exist
then consider the first time slice as a.
4: Calculate forward user retention $F\alpha_t^n$ for $n = 0, 1, 2, \ldots$

$$F\alpha_t^n = \frac{\bigcap_{i=0}^n U_{t+i}}{U_t}$$

where, U_t is the number of users who participated in the time slice t. $F\alpha_t^n$ will give the fraction of the number of users who had participated in the activity from time slice t to time slice $t+n$ with respect to the total number of users at time slice t.
5: Find a time slice b such that
$F\alpha_t^n = 0$ for $n = b$ and
$F\alpha_t^n \neq 0$ for $n \leq b$
6: **If** such a point does not exist
then consider the last time slice as b.
7: Denote the activity between time slices a and b as possible synchrony S_{ab}.
8: Go to algorithm 3.

Algorithm 3 Algorithm to detect the synchrony based on the scale of the phenomenon

1: Fix the upper threshold and lower threshold of the total number of participants in the synchrony. This will allow us to detect only those synchronies that are of a particular scale.
2: **If** $|U| \geq$ lower threshold and $|U| \leq$ upper threshold
then stop with the conclusion that S_{ab} is a synchrony.
3: **else** stop with the conclusion that S_{ab} is not a synchrony.

4 CONCLUSION

In this work, we proposed a definition of synchrony and a method to determine whether the phenomena that a dataset represents is a synchrony or not. We analyzed examples of synchronies and non-synchronies and observed that there is a relevant event present whenever there is a synchrony in the dataset and the time when the event occurs correlates with the peak of the synchrony. Hence, synchrony can be seen as a marker of an event relevant to the hashtag. More details of this work can be found in [3].

REFERENCES

[1] Munmun De Choudhury, Hari Sundaram, Ajita John, and Dorée Duncan Seligmann. 2009. Social synchrony: Predicting mimicry of user actions in online social media. In *Computational Science and Engineering, 2009. CSE'09. International Conference on*, Vol. 4. IEEE, 151–158.
[2] Jon Kleinberg. 2002. Bursty and hierarchical structure in streams. In *Proceedings of the eighth ACM SIGKDD international conference on Knowledge discovery and data mining*. ACM, 91–101.
[3] Nirmal Kumar S, Sakthi Balan M, Pushkal Agarwal, and Lokesh Todwal. 2017. Social Synchrony in Online Social Networks. Manuscript. (2017).

Analysis of Temporal and Web Site References in History-related Tweets

Yasunobu Sumikawa
Dept. of Information Sciences,
Tokyo University of Science
ysumikawa@acm.org

Adam Jatowt
Dept. of Social Informatics,
Kyoto University
adam@dl.kuis.kyoto-u.ac.jp

Marten Düring
Institute for Contemporary History,
University of Luxembourg
marten.during@uni.lu

ABSTRACT

Having good knowledge and comprehension of history is believed to be important for a variety of reasons. In this paper we report the initial results of an exploratory analysis of history-focused references in microblogs based on 11-months' long snapshot of Twitter data. In particular we focus on the time periods referred in history-related tweets and on web sites shared in such tweets.

CCS CONCEPTS

•**Information systems** →**Specialized information retrieval;**

KEYWORDS

social media analysis; history; collective memory; Twitter

ACM Reference format:
Yasunobu Sumikawa, Adam Jatowt, and Marten Düring. 2017. Analysis of Temporal and Web Site References
in History-related Tweets. In *Proceedings of WebSci '17, June 25-28, 2017, Troy, NY, USA*, , 2 pages.
DOI: 10.1145/3091478.3098868

1 INTRODUCTION

Social media has been commonly utilized to study public attitudes towards current events such as the US American elections [7]. Yet, similarly to other media, microblogs are also used for sharing information related to the past, sometimes to the distant past. This offers unique opportunities for computational studies on explicit references to past events and opens up novel perspectives for the analysis of collective memories as well as for the pursuit of public history.

While computational studies of collective memory have already been conducted on news articles [1] and Wikipedia [3–5], with regard to microblogging, still little investigation has been done. For example, the authors of [2] analyzed tweets related to the First World War and compared commemorative cultures across different countries. We then try to fill in this gap by focusing on Twitter as a common social media platform that is also frequently used in the computational social science. Our analysis has exploratory character and aims to provide initial investigation of selected aspects about history-related content sharing in social networks.

WebSci '17, June 25-28, 2017, Troy, NY, USA

DOI: 10.1145/3091478.3098868

2 DATA COLLECTION

To collect tweets that refer to the past or are related to collective memory of historical events/entities, we performed hashtag based crawl together with bootstrapping procedure. At the beginning, we gathered several historical hashtags selected by experts (e.g. `#history`, `#HistoryTeacher`, `#WmnHist`) [1]. In addition, we prepared several hashtags that are commonly used when referring to the past: `#throwbackthursday`, `#historicalevent`, `#onthisday`, `#otd`, `#thisdayinhistory`. We then collected tweets that contain these hashtags by using Twitter's official API[2].

The collected tweets were issued from 8 March 2016 to 24 February 2017. To increase the coverage, during this period, we searched for other hashtags that are frequently used with the seed hashtags by applying bootstrapping. These were iteratively included into the seed set after manual inspection as for their relation to the past and the history. In total, we gathered 147 history-related hashtags which allowed us to collect 888,251 tweets.

3 ANALYSIS

Temporal Reference Analysis. We first analyze which time periods users are interested in. For this we extract *time-references* from tweet content. We use both absolute and relative temporal references. To extract both types of time references, we use Heideltime [6], which is a temporal tagger with a specialized option for tweet processing. We then convert all relative temporal expressions to the absolute ones. In total, we have found over 357k tweets with temporal expressions.

We next map all the extracted temporal expressions on timeline as shown in Fig. 1 to reflect the strength of the collective attention of users towards different time periods of history. To plot the remembering curve, we convert the extracted temporal references to probability distributions over their corresponding timespans using year level granularity. We then combine all the probability distributions for every year.

Looking at Fig. 1 (especially, at the zoomed out plot in the inner graph), we can observe that the number of time references is rapidly increasing towards the present time. In general, the recent past matters more than the distant one and the memory decay is fastest in the recent years. This is intuitive and correlates with the corresponding study conducted on news articles about several countries [1]. When comparing the tweet line (blue color) and retweet line (green color) we also notice relatively strong difference between the two over the course of the recent years. For the distant past however the two lines have more similar values.

[1] http://blog.historians.org/2013/08/history-hashtags-exploring-a-visual-network-of-twitterstorians/
[2] https://dev.twitter.com/rest/public

There are also *several significant peaks visible in Fig. 1 which represent two key events in the last century: WWI and WWII*, and the last year (2016). Two dates common for WWII are: 1941 denoting the Pearl Harbor attack and the subsequent participation of USA in the war, and 1945 which is related to the Normandy landing and the end of the war. Fig. 2 shows the most common hashtags used with content containing the peak years found in Fig. 1. We can notice that 1916 and 1941, 1945 have strong connection with hashtags `#ww1` and `#wwii` as the two events were held during these respective years. Interestingly, Fig. 2 shows there are many mentions of 2016 with `#ww1`. This is because 2016 marked the 100th anniversary of the Battle of Verdun which is well-remembered due to the estimated 1 million casualties.

Finally, `#otd` and `#onthisday` as shown in Fig. 2 are commonly used labels for indicating historical content that occurred on the same calendar day in the past. Past-to-present connection by the calendar day is in fact a popular way of recalling past events and is typically used in newspapers (e.g., "Events reported in our newspaper on this day in the past"). `#otd` and `#onthisday` are hashtag-based mechanisms for indicating this type of connection in Twitter.

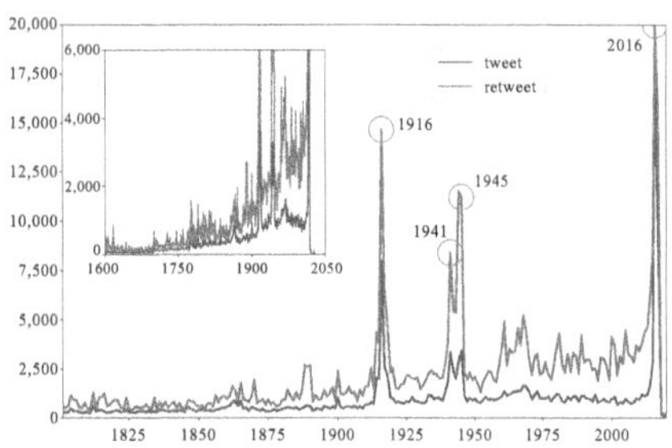

Figure 1: Distribution of time references in tweets. The peaks are in years 1916, 1941, 1945 and 2016.

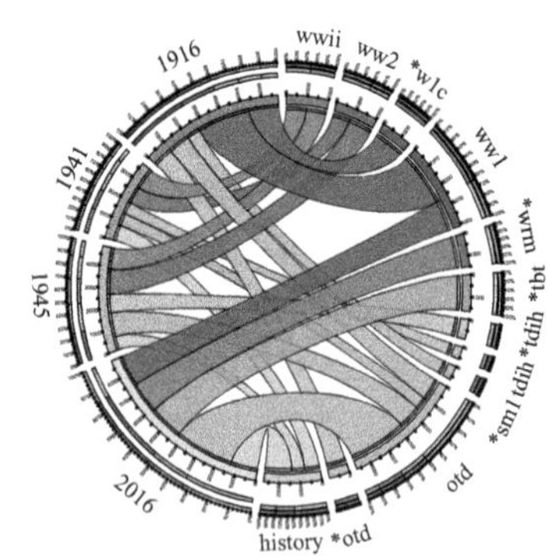

Figure 2: Top hashtags associated with the four peaks of Fig. 1. "*" is used to indicate abbreviations made for saving space (*w1c: `#ww1centenary`, *wrm: `#weremember`, *tbt: `#throwbackthursday`, *tdih: `#thisdayinhistory`, *sm1: `#somme100`, *otd: `#onthisday`).

URL Analysis. The past is commonly remembered by making use of diverse artifacts such as images, videos, or historical documents. Indeed, many web services offer such kinds of data, and *approximately half of tweets in our dataset include links to some kind of web services.* We analyze then what kind of external data users refer to when they post history-related tweets. Fig. 3 lists the top 20 websites mentioned in the tweets in our dataset[3]. For obtaining the original URLs, we used twitter-text-python library[4]. As expected, *users often enrich tweets with images (Instagram) or videos (YouTube and vine).* In addition, users tend to sometimes link to shopping sites (e.g., Amazon, eBay) using past-related hashtags. Closer manual investigation of such tweets revealed that the posted links refer to history related items such as movies about historical events or entities.

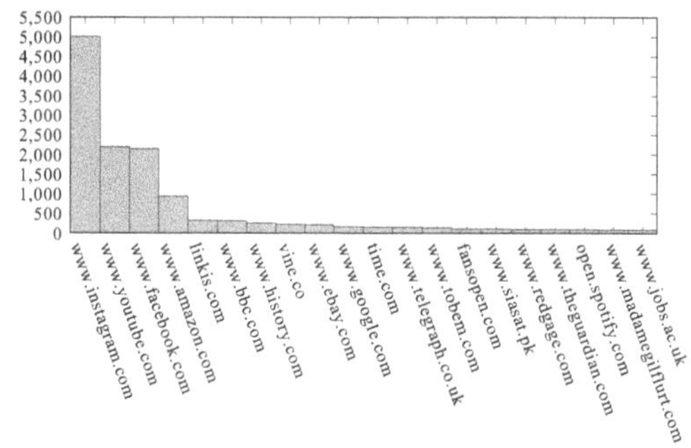

Figure 3: Top 20 web sites referred in tweets.

4 CONCLUSIONS

In this paper we have performed initial analysis of collective memory in Twitter focusing on temporal expressions mentioned in tweets which are related to the past and on associated URLs. Future work will shed more light on the way in which history-related content is used and shared in microblogging to encourage research and development of systems aiming at educating history.

Acknowledgments This work was supported in part by MEXT Grant-in-Aid (#17H01828).

REFERENCES

[1] Ching-man Au Yeung and Adam Jatowt. 2011. Studying How the Past is Remembered: Towards Computational History Through Large Scale Text Mining. In *Proceedings of CIKM2011*. ACM, 1231–1240.

[2] Frdric Clavert, Benot Majerus, and Nicolas Beaupr. #ww1. Twitter, the Centenary of the First World War and the Historian. https://halshs.archives-ouvertes.fr/halshs-01148548/document

[3] Michela Ferron and Paolo Massa. 2011. Collective Memory Building in Wikipedia: The Case of North African Uprisings. In *Proceedings of WikiSym2011 (WikiSym '11)*. ACM, 114–123.

[4] Adam Jatowt, Daisuke Kawai, and Katsumi Tanaka. 2016. Digital History Meets Wikipedia: Analyzing Historical Persons in Wikipedia. In *Proceedings JCDL2016 (JCDL '16)*. 17–26.

[5] Nattiya Kanhabua, Tu Ngoc Nguyen, and Claudia Niederée. 2014. What Triggers Human Remembering of Events?: A Large-scale Analysis of Catalysts for Collective Memory in Wikipedia. In *Proceedings of JCDL2014 (JCDL '14)*. IEEE Press, 341–350.

[6] Erdal Kuzey, Jannik Strötgen, Vinay Setty, and Gerhard Weikum. 2016. Temponym Tagging: Temporal Scopes for Textual Phrases. In *Proceedings of WWW2016 (WWW '16 Companion)*. 841–842.

[7] Andranik Tumasjan, Timm Oliver Sprenger, Philipp G. Sandner, and Isabell M. Welpe. 2010. Predicting Elections with Twitter: What 140 Characters Reveal about Political Sentiment.. In *Proceedings of ICWSM 2010*.

[3] We have removed twitter.com focusing on external websites.

[4] https://github.com/edburnett/twitter-text-python

When Friend Becomes Abuser: Evidence of Friend Abuse in Facebook

Sajedul Talukder
Florida Int'l University
stalu001@fiu.edu

Bogdan Carbunar
Florida Int'l University
carbunar@gmail.com

ABSTRACT

We show through 2 user studies (n = 80), that a high number of participants have at least 1 Facebook friend whom they believe is likely to abuse their posted photos or status updates, or post offensive, false or malicious content, or with whom they never interact in Facebook and in real life. Our results reveal the importance of developing tools that automatically detect and defend against friend abuse in social networks.

ACM Reference format:
Sajedul Talukder and Bogdan Carbunar. 2017. When Friend Becomes Abuser: Evidence of Friend Abuse in Facebook. In *Proceedings of WebSci '17, June 25-28, 2017, Troy, NY, USA*, , 2 pages.
DOI: 10.1145/3091478.3098869

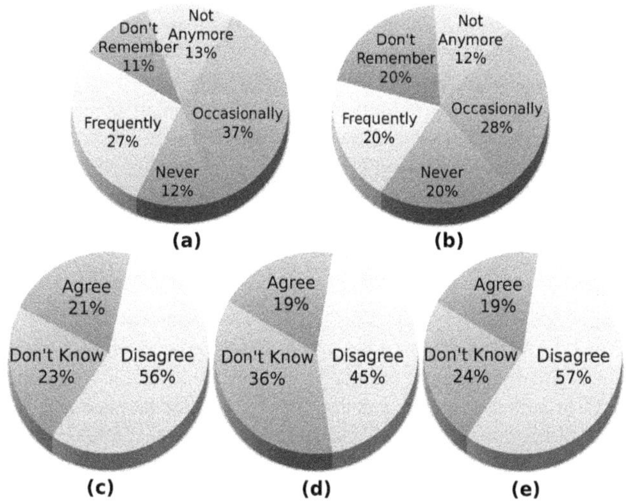

Figure 1: Distribution of responses for questionnaire over 1,600 Facebook friend relationships, from 80 participants. (a) Q1: frequency of Facebook interaction, (b) Q2: frequency of real world interaction, (c) Q3: friend would abuse posted sensitive picture, (d) Q4: friend would abuse status update post, and (e) Q5: friend would post offensive, misleading, false or potentially malicious content. The red sections correspond to potential strangers or abusive friends.

1 INTRODUCTION

Social network abuse includes not only the passive collection of sensitive user information, but also active attacks, such as cyberbullying [4, 5, 7], trolling and distribution of fake news, malware and propaganda [1, 3, 6]. For instance, Singh et al. [7] showed that emerging online features, including the prevalence of images and videos, anonymity and hyperlocal communications influence cyberbullying, and generate negative socio-psychological effects. Yang et al. [8] have introduced techniques to translate surveys into surveillance strategies on social media. i.e., that find a the posts of a user that can be interpreted as valid survey responses. Brown et al. [2] found that in Facebook, attackers could send sophisticated context-aware email to approximately 85% of users, including to people with private profiles.

We study abusive friend behaviors in Facebook, the most popular social network. We briefly describe Facebook's most relevant features: the friends, timeline and news feed. Facebook users form *friend* relationships through friend invites. Each user has a global *friend list* of other users with whom she has formed friend relationships.The *timeline* (a.k.a wall, or profile) is Facebook's central feature, the place where the user can share her updates, photos, check-ins, and other activities (e.g., posting comments on a status or picture of a friend, confirming a new friend, etc). Users can control with whom they share each story, i.e., through the *audience selector.* A user's *news feed* shows, stories created by her friends, groups, and subscribed events.

WebSci '17, June 25-28, 2017, Troy, NY, USA

DOI: 10.1145/3091478.3098869

Despite the progress made by Facebook in raising user awareness to the dangers of making information public and to the importance of deciding who can access it, many users still allow all their friends to access their information. Friends can then leverage social networking features such as walls and news feeds to easily collect sensitive information from users and to actively abuse them.

2 CONTRIBUTIONS

In this work we have explored the perception of Facebook users on their exposure to abusive behaviors perpetrated by friends. To evaluate the user perceived exposure to such friend abuse, we have developed a mobile friend abuse questionnaire whose responses can help pinpoint Facebook friends who (1) form unverified relationships with the user, (2) publish abusive responses to pictures and status updates posted by the user, and (3) publish and distribute fake, malicious or abusive posts.

Specifically, our questionnaire consists of 5 questions for each friend of the user. The first question seeks to capture the user's frequency of interaction with the friend on Facebook with possible responses being "Frequently", "Occasionally", "Not Anymore", "Never" and "Don't Remember". The second question asks the user about her frequency of interaction with the friend in real life, and has the same response options as the first question. For both questions, we are particularly interested in the "Never" responses: a friend with whom the user has never interacted in real life and in Facebook may be a fake, "trojan" friend who secretly monitors the user. We note that the "Not Anymore" option covers the case of friends with whom the user no longer interacts, e.g., due to moving away.

The third and fourth questions seek to identify friends that are perceived by the user as capable to abuse or misuse photos or status updates posted by the user. Such friends could be cyberbullies. The fifth question seeks to identify trolls, as friends that are perceived by the user to post offensive, misleading, false or potentially malicious content on their timelines. This content can later propagate to the user through her newsfeed. The possible responses for questions 3-5 are "Agree", "Disagree" and "Don't Know". A choice of "Agree" signals abuse.

3 RESULTS

We performed two user studies (n = 20 and 60 respectively) to collect questionnaire responses for 1,600 friend relationships (20 from each participant). Figure 1 shows the distribution of the responses for each of the 5 questions.

Figure 1(a) shows that in 12% of the 1,600 friend relationships, the participants stated that they have never interacted with that friend in Facebook. However, 64 (80%) of the 80 participants have at least one such friend. Figure 1(b) shows that in 20% of the 1,600 friend relationships, the participants stated that they have never interacted with the corresponding friend in real life. 73 (91%) of the participants had at least one such friend.

In 21% of the 1,600 friend relationships, participants stated that the queried friend would abuse a photo they post (Figure 1(c)), in 19% of the cases they admit the friend would abuse their status updates (Figure 1(d)), while in 19% of the cases, they admit that the friend would post offensive, misleading, false or potentially malicious content (Figure 1(e)).

However, 68 (85%) of the participants have at least 1 friend who would abuse their photos, 62 (77%) of the participants have at least 1 friend who would abuse their status updates, and 62 (77%) of the participants have at least 1 friend who would post offensive, misleading, false or potentially malicious content.

Furthermore, 55 (68.75%) of the 80 participants have at least 1 friend with whom they have never interacted in real life and in Facebook. 71 participants (88.75%) have a friend whom they believe is either a potential trojan, a cyberbully or troll.

In addition, 55 (68.75%) of the 80 participants have at least 1 friend with whom they have never interacted in real life and in Facebook. 71 participants (88.75%) have a friend whom they believe is either a potential trojan, or a cyberbully or troll.

4 LIMITATIONS

In our user studies we have only recruited remote participants. Further user studies would need to be performed to validate our findings with local participants. Further studies are also needed to investigate the impact of the number of friends that participants are required to evaluate (20-30 in our studies), on the accuracy of the responses. Relevant dimensions to investigate include the impact of fatigue and the scalability of the findings to the entire friend population.

5 CONCLUSIONS

The high number of Facebook users who are exposed to friend abuse reveals the importance of developing tools to automatically identify potentially abusive friends, and take defensive actions against them. Example of defensive actions include unfriending, unfollowing, restricting the access and blocking the friend. This problem is made complex by the conflicting requirements of seeking user approval when taking such defensive actions, while minimizing user involvement.

REFERENCES

[1] Jessikka Aro. 2016. The cyberspace war: propaganda and trolling as warfare tools. *European View* 15, 1 (2016), 121–132.

[2] Garrett Brown, Travis Howe, Micheal Ihbe, Atul Prakash, and Kevin Borders. 2008. Social networks and context-aware spam. In *Proceedings of the ACM CSCW.*

[3] Justin Cheng, Michael S. Bernstein, Cristian Danescu-Niculescu-Mizil, and Jure Leskovec. 2017. Anyone Can Become a Troll: Causes of Trolling Behavior in Online Discussions. In *Proceedings of the ACM CSCW.*

[4] Robin M Kowalski, Susan P Limber, Sue Limber, and Patricia W Agatston. 2012. *Cyberbullying: Bullying in the digital age.* John Wiley & Sons.

[5] Grace Chi En Kwan and Marko M Skoric. 2013. Facebook bullying: An extension of battles in school. *Computers in Human Behavior* 29, 1 (2013), 16–25.

[6] Daisy Sindelar. 2014. The Kremlin's Troll Army. *The Atlantic* 12 (2014).

[7] Vivek K. Singh, Marie L. Radford, Qianjia Huang, and Susan Furrer. 2017. "They basically like destroyed the school one day": On Newer App Features and Cyberbullying in Schools. In *Proceedings of the ACM CSCW.*

[8] Chao Yang and Padmini Srinivasan. 2014. Translating surveys to surveillance on social media: methodological challenges & solutions. In *Proceedings of the ACM WebSci.*

Author Index

www.ingramcontent.com/pod-product-compliance
Ingram Content Group UK Ltd.
Pitfield, Milton Keynes, MK11 3LW, UK
UKHW051412290926
15471UKWH00009B/1560

9 781450 356046